All In One

Computer Concepts and Applications

Shelley Gaskin, Nancy Graviett, and Cathy LaBerta

PEARSON

Boston Columbus Indianapolis New York San Francisco Upper Saddle River
Amsterdam Cape Town Dubai London Madrid Milan Munich Paris Montreal Toronto
Delhi Mexico City São Paulo Sydney Hong Kong Seoul Singapore Taipei Tokyo

Editor in Chief: Michael Payne
Executive Editor: Jenifer Niles
Product Development Manager: Laura Burgess
Development Editor: Nancy Lamm
Editorial Assistant: Carly Prakapas
Director of Digital Development: Zara Wanlass
VP, Director of Digital Strategy & Assessment: Paul Gentile
Director, Media Development: Cathi Profitko
Senior Editorial Media Project Manager: Alana Coles
Production Media Project Manager: John Cassar
Director of Marketing for Business & Technology: Patrice Lumumba Jones
Marketing Coordinator: Susan Osterlitz
Marketing Assistant: Darshika Vyas
Associate Managing Editor: Camille Trentacoste
Operations Director: Nick Sklitsis
Operations Specialist: Maura Zaldivar-Garcia
Senior Art Director: Jonathan Boylan
Cover Photo: © Ben Durrant
Text and Cover Designer: Blair Brown
Manager, Cover Visual Research & Permissions: Karen Sanatar
Full-Service Project Management: PreMediaGlobal
Composition: PreMediaGlobal
Printer/Binder: Quad Graphics
Cover Printer: Lehigh-Phoenix Color
Text Font: MinionPro

Credits and acknowledgments borrowed from other sources and reproduced, with permission, in this textbook appear on appropriate page within text.

Library of Congress Cataloging-in-Publication Data

Gaskin, Shelley.
GO! All in one : computer concepts and applications / Shelley Gaskin, Nancy Graviett, and Cathy Laberta.
p. cm.
Includes index.
ISBN 978-0-13-284412-3 (alk. paper)
1. Computers—Textbooks. 2. Application software—Textbooks. I. Graviett, Nancy. II. LaBerta, Catherine. III. Title.
QA76.27.G37 2012
004—dc23

2011045721

2 3 4 5 6 7 8 9 10 V064 16 15 14 13 12

ISBN-10: 0-13-284412-5
ISBN-13: 978-0-13-284412-3

Brief Contents

Contents

GO! All In One Reviewers

We thank the following people for their hard work and support in making the *GO!* System all that it is!

James Anthos	South University
Sue Bajt	Harper College
Clay Bandy	Metropolitan State College of Denver
Bob Benavides	Collin College
Jill Canine	Ivy Tech Community College, Columbus
Gene Carbonaro	Long Beach City College
Frank Clements	State College of Florida, Manatee-Sarasota
Stephanie Cook	State College of Florida, Manatee-Sarasota
Becky Curtin	Harper College
Jeanette Dix	Ivy Tech Community College, Bloomington
Cathy Dutton	John Abbott College
Laszlo Eosze	Central Texas College
Biswadip Ghosh	Metropolitan State College of Denver
Martha Gibson	Central Texas College
Kim Gil	California State University, Fullerton
Natalia Grigorants	Pierce College
Christie Hovey	Lincoln Land Community College
Jon Jasperson	Texas A&M University
Chris Johnson	South Piedmont Community College
Jeff Kimball	Southwest Baptist University
Mike LoSacco	College of DuPage
Miriam Lynch	Long Beach City College
Nicole Lytle	California State University, San Bernadino
Susan Mahon	Collin College
Pat Miller	Bluegrass Community and Technical College
Tim Moriarty	Waubonsee Community College
Erika Nadas	Wilbur Wright College
Eloise Newsome	Northern Virginia Community College
Michael Nguyen	Santa Ana College
Robert Nichols	College of DuPage
James Perry	University of San Diego
Mary Rasley	Lehigh Carbon Community College
Pat Riola	Lehigh Carbon Community College
Zoila Rosillo	Long Beach City College
Patty Roy	State College of Florida, Manatee-Sarasota
Vicky Seehusen	Metropolitan State College of Denver
Sheila Sicilia	Onondaga Community College
Steve Siedschlag	Chaffey College
Mary Jo Slater	Community College of Beaver County
Karen Smith	Technical College of the Lowcountry
Zenaida Spradlin	California State University, Northridge
Jason Stevens	Long Beach City College
Gladys Swindler	Fort Hays State University
Joyce Thompson	Lehigh Carbon Community College
Craig Watson	Bristol Community College
Dave Wilson	Parkland College
Floyd Winters	State College of Florida, Manatee-Sarasota
Wanda Wong	Chabot College
Margaret Yau	Crafton Hills College
Mary Ann	Zlotow College of DuPage

Technical Editors

Julie Boyles
Lisa Bucki
Lori Damanti
Janet Pickard
Mara Zebest

About the Authors

Shelley Gaskin, Series Editor, is a professor in the Business and Computer Technology Division at Pasadena City College in Pasadena, California. She holds a bachelor's degree in Business Administration from Robert Morris College (Pennsylvania), a master's degree in Business from Northern Illinois University, and a doctorate in Adult and Community Education from Ball State University. Before joining Pasadena City College, she spent 12 years in the computer industry where she was a systems analyst, sales representative, and Director of Customer Education with Unisys Corporation. She also worked for Ernst & Young on the development of large systems applications for their clients. She has written and developed training materials for custom systems applications in both the public and private sector, and has written and edited numerous computer application textbooks.

This book is dedicated to my students, who inspire me every day.

Nancy Graviett is a professor in the Business and Computer Science department at St. Charles Community College in Cottleville, Missouri, where she is the program coordinator for the business Administrative Systems program and teaches within the program. Nancy is also very active with distance learning and teaches in face-to-face, hybrid, and online formats. She holds a master's degree from the Unviersity of Missouri. Nancy holds Microsoft® Certified Application Specialist certification in multiple applications and provides training both on and off campus. In her free time, Nancy enjoys quilting and spending time with family and friends.

I dedicate this book to my husband, David, my children (Matthew and Andrea), and my parents, whose love and support I cherish more than they could ever know.

Cathy LaBerta is an adjunct professor with SUNY at Buffalo and Canisius College, an independent contractor who provides application and technical training for the Western New York Work Force Development Institute, and a former Professor of Computer Science/Mathematics at Erie Community College in Buffalo, New York. She teaches courses that range from an introduction to computers to programming in C++ and Web development. Originally a math major, Cathy took additional courses in computers and programming and found another field that clicked for her. She enjoys the constant changes in the computer and related fields because they force her to keep up and constantly learn. Not a total bookworm, Cathy loves skiing (with Purgatory, Colorado, being a favorite spot) and boating (especially schooner trips off the coast of Maine) and will be always be working on that golf game.

I dedicate this book with love to my parents, Eleanore and Chester, for constant encouragement and my son, Michael, for continual challenges and inspiration.

GO! All In One: Computer Concepts and Applications is the right choice!

Teach Computer Concepts and Applications together—the way it is in the real world! Engage your students right away by focusing on jobs and incorporating Web 2.0 apps in a logical way. With this book, you can put concepts into action using a unique, integrated, jobs-focused approach.

- **Practical –** Focuses on real-world jobs and the skills and knowledge they require. Each Unit opens with a career focus and a video interview of a person working in that field.
- **Engaging –** Computer Concepts and Applications are integrated together logically to focus on the needs of students in the current economic reality.
- **Affordable –** Covers the core Computer Concepts and Applications needed all in one book.
- **Current –** Shows students how to create and collaborate—using all the latest Web 2.0 tools, including cloud applications, social media, and video communications such as Skype.
- **Enhanced –** Not only does it come in an enhanced eText form that provides video, simulation, and quick-check quizzes built in, it also includes MyITLab grading of both hands-on Microsoft Office projects and objective tests.

Retains the hallmarks of the *GO! Series* Microsoft® Office textbook designed for student success!

- **Project-Based –** Students learn by creating projects that they will use in the real world.
- **Microsoft Procedural Syntax –** Steps are written to put students in the right place at the right time.
- **Teachable Moment –** Expository text is woven into the steps—at the moment students need to know it—not chunked together in a block of text that will go unread.
- **Sequential Pagination –** Students have actual page numbers instead of confusing letters and abbreviations.

Student Outcomes and Learning Objectives – Objectives are clustered around projects that result in student outcomes.

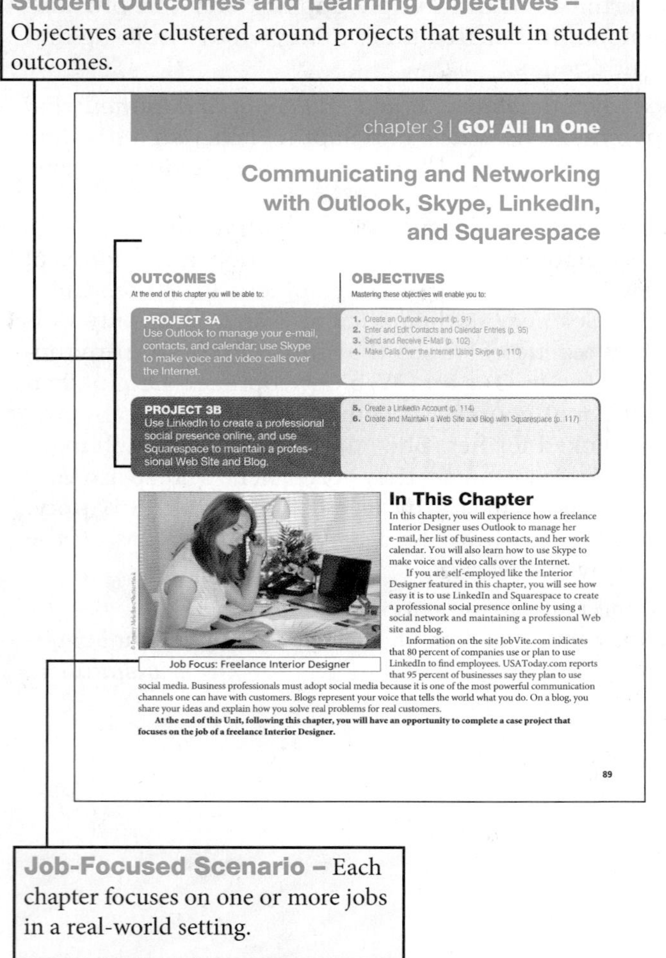

chapter 3 | **GO! All In One**

Communicating and Networking with Outlook, Skype, LinkedIn, and Squarespace

OUTCOMES At the end of this chapter you will be able to:	OBJECTIVES Mastering these objectives will enable you to:
PROJECT 3A Use Outlook to manage your e-mail, contacts, and calendar; use Skype to make voice and video calls over the Internet.	1. Create an Outlook Account (p. 91) 2. Enter and Edit Contacts and Calendar Entries (p. 95) 3. Send and Receive E-Mail (p. 102) 4. Make Calls Over the Internet Using Skype (p. 110)
PROJECT 3B Use LinkedIn to create a professional social presence online, and use Squarespace to maintain a professional Web Site and Blog.	5. Create a LinkedIn Account (p. 114) 6. Create and Maintain a Web Site and Blog with Squarespace (p. 117)

In This Chapter

In this chapter, you will experience how a freelance Interior Designer uses Outlook to manage her e-mail, her list of business contacts, and her work calendar. You will also learn how to use Skype to make voice and video calls over the Internet.

If you are self-employed like the Interior Designer featured in this chapter, you will see how easy it is to use LinkedIn and Squarespace to create a professional social presence online by using a social network and maintaining a professional Web site and blog.

Information on the site JobVite.com indicates that 80 percent of companies use or plan to use LinkedIn to find employees. USAToday.com reports that 95 percent of businesses say they plan to use social media. Business professionals must adopt social media because it is one of the most powerful communication channels one can have with customers. Blogs represent your voice that tells the world what you do. On a blog, you share your ideas and explain how you solve real problems for real customers.

At the end of this Unit, following this chapter, you will have an opportunity to complete a case project that focuses on the job of a freelance Interior Designer.

Job Focus: Freelance Interior Designer

89

Job-Focused Scenario – Each chapter focuses on one or more jobs in a real-world setting.

Project Activities – A project summary stated clearly and quickly.

Project Files – Clearly shows students which files are needed for the project and the names they will use to save their documents.

Project 8A Sales Report with Embedded Column Chart and Sparklines

myitlab Project 8A Training

Project Activities

In Activities 8.01 through 8.16, you will create an Excel worksheet for Roslyn Thomas, the President of Texas Spectrum Wireless. The worksheet displays the first quarter sales of wireless accessories for the current year, and includes a chart to visually represent the data. Your completed worksheet will look similar to Figure 8.1.

Project Files

For Project 8A, you will need the following file:

New blank Excel workbook

You will save your workbook as:

Lastname_Firstname_8A_Quarterly_Sales

Project Results

Texas Spectrum Wireless
First Quarter Accessory Sales

1st Quarter Sales

Figure 8.1
Project 8A Quarterly Sales

340 GO! All In One | Chapter 8: Excel Worksheets, Charts, Formulas, Functions, and Tables

Project Results – Shows students how their final outcome will appear.

GO! All In One Key Features

Key Feature

Microsoft Procedural Syntax – Steps are written to put the student in the right place at the right time.

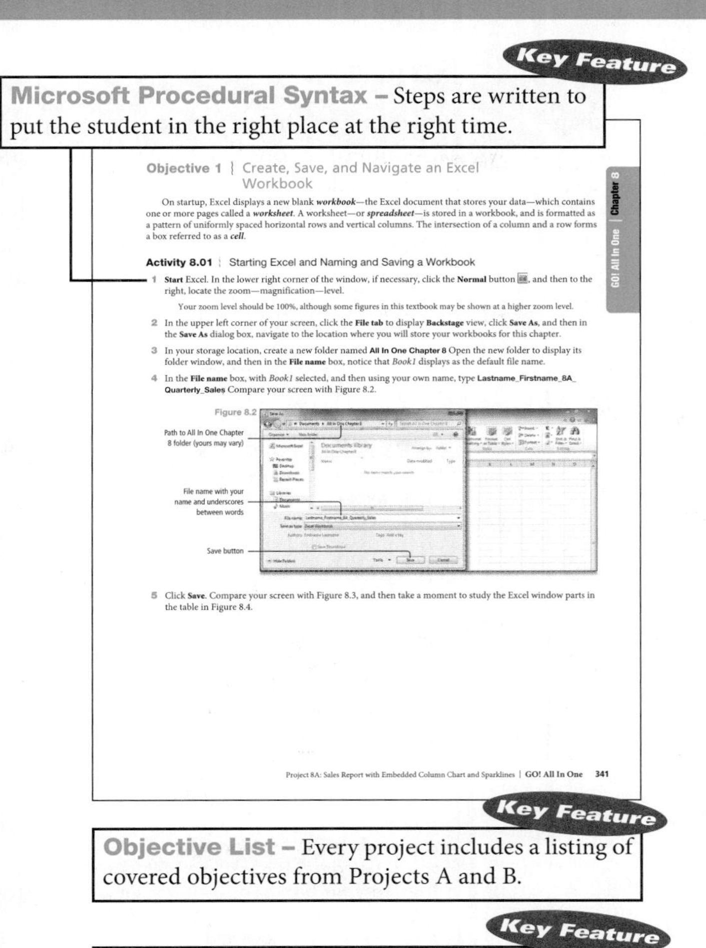

Objective 1 | Create, Save, and Navigate an Excel Workbook

On startup, Excel displays a new blank *workbook*—the Excel document that stores your data—which contains one or more pages called a *worksheet*. A worksheet—or *spreadsheet*—is stored in a workbook, and is formatted as a pattern of uniformly spaced horizontal rows and vertical columns. The intersection of a column and a row forms a box referred to as a *cell*.

Activity 8.01 | Starting Excel and Naming and Saving a Workbook

1. **Start** Excel. In the lower right corner of the window, if necessary, click the **Normal** button, and then to the right, locate the zoom—magnification—level.

   Your zoom level should be 100%, although some figures in this textbook may be shown at a higher zoom level.

2. In the upper left corner of your screen, click the **File tab** to display **Backstage** view, click **Save As**, and then in the **Save As** dialog box, navigate to the location where you will store your workbooks for this chapter.
3. In your storage location, create a new folder named **All In One Chapter 8** Open the new folder to display its folder window, and then in the **File name** box, notice that *Book1* displays as the default file name.
4. In the **File name** box, with *Book1* selected, and then using your own name, type **Lastname_Firstname_8A_Quarterly_Sales** Compare your screen with Figure 8.2.

Figure 8.2

5. Click **Save**. Compare your screen with Figure 8.3, and then take a moment to study the Excel window parts in the table in Figure 8.4.

GO! All In One | Chapter 8

Project 8A: Sales Report with Embedded Column Chart and Sparklines | GO! All In One 341

Key Feature

Color Coding – Color variations among the projects in each chapter make it easy to identify which project students are working on.

Key Feature

Manageable Length – Every chapter contains small projects that are designed to be concise and not overly long.

3. With the selected range still active, from the following table, beginning in cell **C4** and pressing Enter after each entry, enter the data for the **Average Cost** column and then the **Retail Price** column.

Average Cost	Retail Price
9.75	19.99
9.25	19.49
16.90	39.99
9.55	16.90
4.20	12.99
10.45	20.99

Recall that the default number format for cells is the *General* number format, in which numbers display exactly as you type them and trailing zeros do not display, even if you type them.

4. Click any blank cell. Correct any errors you may have made while entering data, and then click **Save**.

Objective 9 | Construct Formulas for Mathematical Operations

Operators are symbols with which you can specify the type of calculation you want to perform in a formula.

Activity 8.19 | Using Arithmetic Operators

1. Click cell **E4**, type **=b4*d4** and notice that the two cells are outlined as part of an active formula. Then press Enter.

   The *Total Retail Value* of all *Antenna Signal Booster* items in inventory—*22508.74*—equals the *Quantity* (1,126) times the *Retail Price* (selling price) of 19.99. In Excel, the asterisk (*) indicates multiplication.

2. Take a moment to study the symbols you will use to perform basic mathematical operations in Excel, as shown in the table in Figure 8.39, which are referred to as *arithmetic operators*.

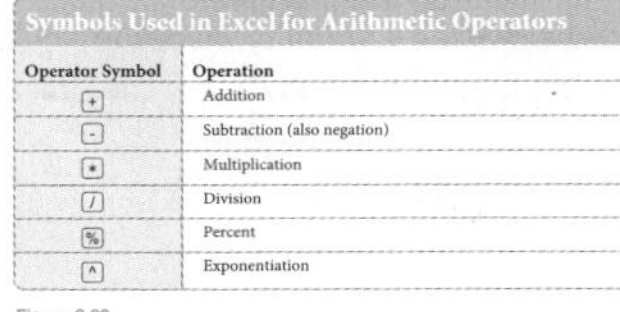

Symbols Used in Excel for Arithmetic Operators

Operator Symbol	Operation
+	Addition
-	Subtraction (also negation)
*	Multiplication
/	Division
%	Percent
^	Exponentiation

Figure 8.39

3. Click cell **E4**.

   You can see that in cells E5:E9, you need a formula similar to the one in E4, but one that refers to the cells in row 5, row 6, and so forth. Recall that you can copy formulas and the cell references will change *relative to* the row number.

4. With cell **E4** selected, position your pointer over the fill handle in the lower right corner of the cell until the + pointer displays. Then, drag down through cell **E9** to copy the formula.

GO! All In One | Chapter 8

Project 8B: Inventory Valuation | GO! All In One 365

Key Feature

Objective List – Every project includes a listing of covered objectives from Projects A and B.

Key Feature

Job-Focused Approach – puts Concepts and Application projects in the context of a real-world job.

End-of-Chapter

A variety of both content-based and outcomes-based assessments accompany the chapter, and additional skills-based and critical thinking projects are available in the Instructor Resources.

Mastery-level Projects – A variety can be found in each Application chapter.

Summary and Key Terms

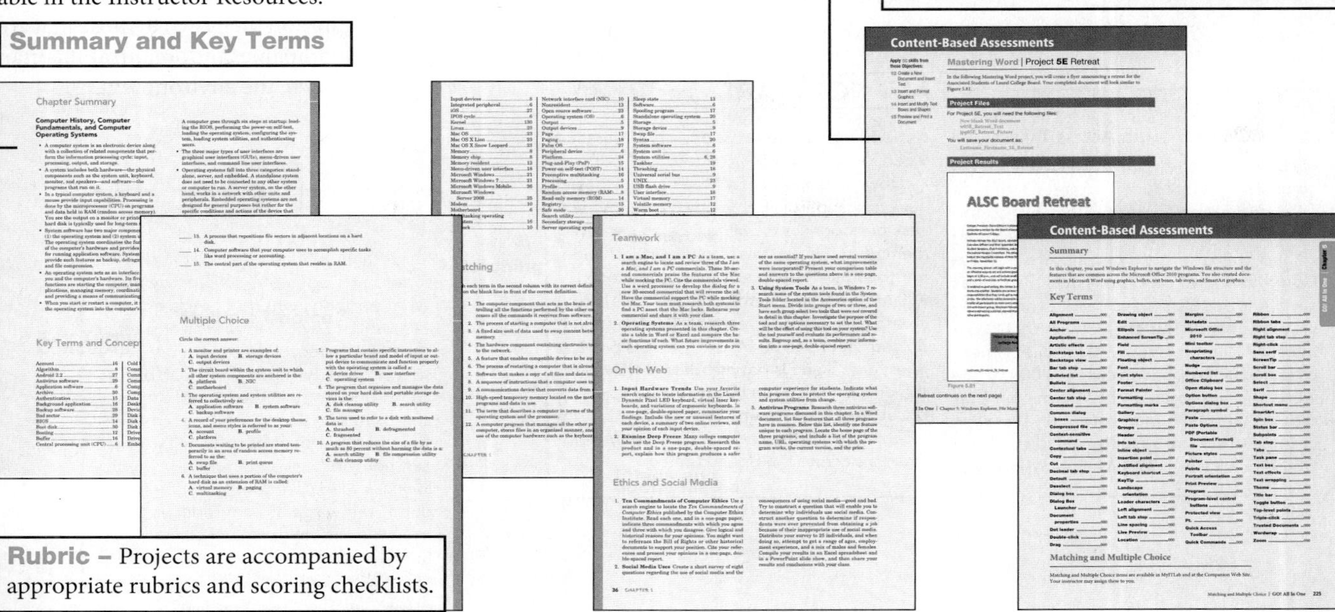

Rubric – Projects are accompanied by appropriate rubrics and scoring checklists.

Technology on the Job

Informs students about how the technologies they are studying in the chapter relate to jobs—and specifically to the job that is the focus of the chapter. Students see how important it is to have specific computer skills to succeed in a variety of jobs.

TECHNOLOGY ON THE JOB

As a Marketing Assistant in the field of entertainment, you need both marketing skills and technology skills. Because companies are striving to understand their customers and respond to customer needs quickly, you also need Internet skills and social networking skills. Review the list of technology skills recently posted for a position of Marketing Assistant. Are you surprised at the level of technology required? Do you already possess any of these skills? Individuals in this type of position often travel, so knowledge of portable devices, backup procedures, and network attached storage (NAS) or Internet storage is critical in order to maintain communication with team members and guarantee the availability of data. Try to gain as much experience in these areas as possible.

Technology skills recently posted for a Marketing Assistant position include:

- Developing media packs and organizing conferences and trade shows.
- Serving as liaison between advertising agencies and the company, print suppliers, freelance talent, and various marketing services.
- Preparing press releases, company newsletters, and event announcements.
- Updating company headlines and news in the corporate Web site.
- Assisting in promotional strategies.

Fast Forward

Addresses emerging technologies related to the chapter content. Current research findings and companies that are working on these technologies are spotlighted so students can see the practical applications of these new technologies.

FAST FORWARD

FCC's Broadband Access Target

Networking and using the Internet for communication, education, and commerce will continue to increase. In a bid to ensure broadband access to all people in the United States within a decade, the Federal Communications Commission (FCC) has set a 4 Mbps download target for universal broadband. This project will cost $23.5 billion. Although nearly 200 million Americans had broadband access in 2009, there were still approximately 100 million that did not. The FCC plan is to plug the gaps in the current infrastructure and establish DSL, 4G wireless, or satellite coverage—depending on the location—in underserviced areas.

Download speed of 4 Mbps is not fast by current standards, but for those with no access or poor access, this will be an improvement. Additionally, this plan seeks to provide improved service over the next decade to 100 million homes in the United States by increasing download speeds to 100 Mbps and upload speeds to 50 Mbps. The FCC project is just a goal and is not mandated. However, the plan should get a boost toward its goal, because Google plans to release its own 1Gbps fiber-to-the-home (FTTH) network in locations across the United States.

Ethics

Provides an ethical perspective on decisions and situations that involve computers and technology. The student is challenged to consider "what if" type questions by asking what he or she would do in certain situations. This feature prompts thoughtful discussion and debate.

USB flash drives are very popular, but many experts worry that they pose a great security risk. Some companies are so concerned about corporate espionage that they disable USB ports to prevent the unauthorized copying of data. Even so, many people carry a lot of critical or personal data on their USB flash drives. What are the implications if the device is lost? Should USB drive manufacturers be required to provide a means of securing these devices or some type of registration process? With such processes in place, a lost device could be returned to the manufacturer and matched to the owner. What actions should individuals take to safeguard their data? Is hooking a USB flash drive to your backpack or keychain a very good idea? If you found a USB flash drive and did not know who it belonged to, what would you do? What should you do?

Green Technology

Suggests eco-friendly solutions to living and working with technology, from actions students can apply on their own to those that are initiated by companies and organizations in an effort to preserve the environment.

More than 700 million inkjet and laser toner cartridges are sold every year. What happens when they are empty? Although many organizations and retail stores have recycling programs, every second nearly eight used cartridges are thrown away in the United States—approximately 875 million pounds of environmental waste each year! So what can you do? Take advantage of your local recycling program. Keeping them out of the waste stream reduces toxicity levels and saves landfill space. Additionally, a half-gallon of oil is saved for every toner cartridge you recycle!

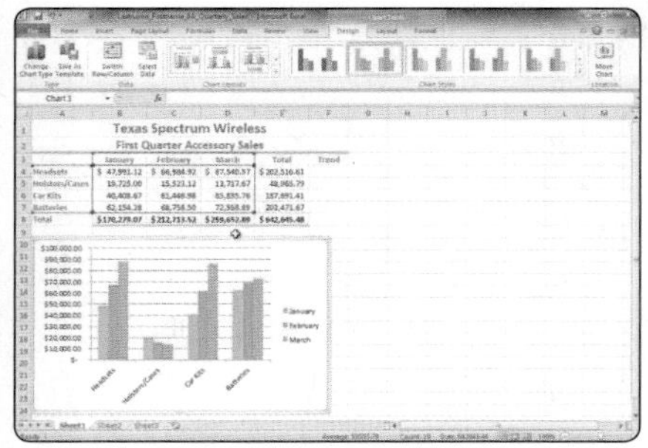

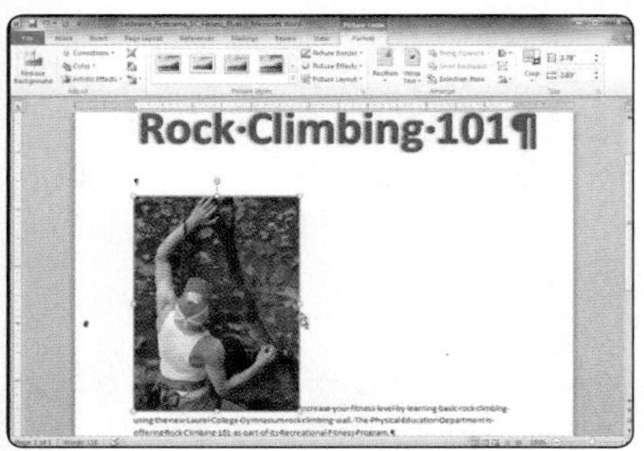

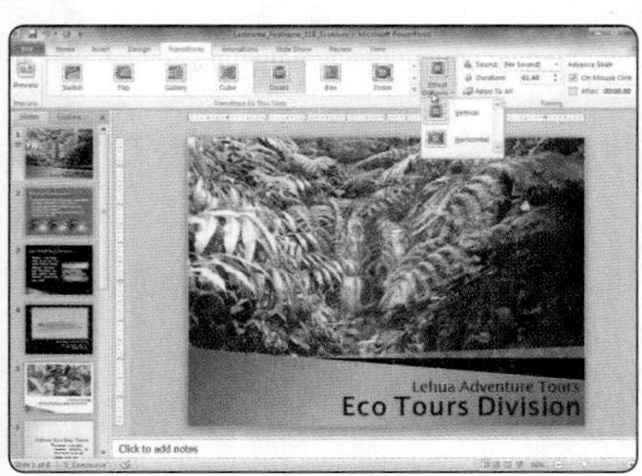

Student Resources

Student Companion Web Site (pearsonhighered.com/go) – Includes all student data files referenced in the book, Glossary, Objectives, an interactive study guide, and Check Your Knowledge quizzes. Also provides all of the supporting media, such as videos and simulations.

Student Videos – 3 Types

- **Instructor-Led Videos –** The authors, who are instructors, guide students through the Objectives of each project, just as they do in their own classrooms, providing a visual and audio walk-through of project Objectives in the Office Application chapters.
- **Interviews with Real-World Job Holders –** Each unit begins with a video of a person in a real job talking about how they use Office applications in their occupation.
- **Video Simulations –** Short animations of interesting or difficult topics are provided in the Concepts chapters.

Interactive Simulations – Each Concepts chapter is supported by an interactive simulation of a key computer concept that allows students to learn by doing.

Check Your Knowledge Quizzes – At key points in the Concepts chapters, students can take the Check Your Knowledge quiz, which is an online quiz to assess knowledge of and maintain engagement with the content.

Enhanced E-Text – This fully hyperlinked book allows students to jump right to videos, simulations, and Check Your Knowledge quizzes as they read through the book.

Instructor Resources

Additional Project Exams by Application, Chapter, and Project – A cumulative exam for each application, chapter, and project.

Additional Skill and Critical Thinking Projects – Bonus projects for Application chapters available online.

Annotated Solution Files – Solution files with annotations and callouts that indicate each skill the student should demonstrate in the project.

Answer Key – Answers to the end-of-chapter questions that assess student understanding of the concepts.

Assignment Sheet – Lists all the assignments for the chapter. Just add in the course information, due dates, and points. Providing these to students ensures they will know what is due and when. Can be uploaded to Blackboard, MyItLab, or other course management systems.

Image Library – A library of all the figures from the book.

Instructor Manual – An instructor tool that contains Teaching Tips, Discussion Topics, and Ethics Topics.

PowerPoint Lectures – PowerPoint presentations for each chapter.

Scorecards and Scoring Rubrics – Can be used by students to check their work or by instructors as a quick check-off for the items that need to be corrected.

Scripted Lectures – Classroom lectures.

Solution Files, Solution PDFs, and Solution Files with Formulas – For Applications projects, solutions are provided as native files, as PDFs of the native files, and for Excel files as PDFs showing the formulas.

Student Data Files – Files needed to complete each project.

Syllabus Template – For 8-week, 12-week, and 16-week courses.

Test Bank – Includes 100–150 questions per chapter, in a variety of formats.

Videos – Instructor-Led, Job Interviews, and Video Simulations.

Computer History, Windows 7, Internet, and Social Media

Chapters in Unit 1:

Job Focus: Freelance Interior Designer

View Unit 1 Video to meet a Freelance Interior Designer

At the end of this unit, you will have the opportunity to complete a case project that focuses on the job of a Freelance Interior Designer. If you had a position like this, some of the things you might do are: partner with architectural firms to complete interior designs for homes, offices, and retail stores; maintain electronic files of projects; search the Internet for furnishings and materials to show to clients; build professional relationships in the community to market yourself; and create a Web site and blog to promote your business.

Computer History, Fundamentals, and Operating Systems

OUTCOMES

At the end of this chapter you will be able to:

Identify current and future computer trends and associate the steps of the information processing cycle with common computer activities.

Recognize and describe the features of computer operating systems and system utilities.

OBJECTIVES

Mastering these objectives will enable you to:

Job Focus:
Interior Designer

In This Chapter

In your job as a freelance Interior Designer, your success depends not only on your interior design skills, but also on your ability to communicate. You must use good computer skills to market yourself to get new opportunities. After you have a new project, you must use well developed computing techniques and communication methods to connect with the contractors you hire, the architectural firms with whom you often partner, and with your client.

In this chapter, you will learn about the basic functions of your computer system and the features and utilities of your operating system. Understanding the capability and power of your computer system and its installed programs will enhance your skills as a designer and enable you to market yourself effectively.

Objective 1 | Understand Computers: Yesterday, Today, and Tomorrow

As a freelance Interior Designer, you have just accepted a project to work with an architectural firm that has a combination of old and new computer equipment. You are working specifically with three individuals who use both desktop units and mobile devices. You need to be sure that all of the programs that the project requires are compatible with all systems. Where do you start?

Computers are an integral part of daily life; depending on your age, you may not even remember a time without them. Think about it, how many technology-based applications or devices do you use in a day? Do you know how many of these applications or devices did not exist 10 years ago? How many do you think will be in use 10 years from now? From the following list of computer applications and devices, how many have you used?

- Word processor: A popular application that you use to create documents and to automatically check spelling and grammar in a document.
- Internet: A connected system of computers with which you search for information and which enables activities such as social networking.
- Online banking: An Internet application provided by a bank that enables you to open an account, transfer money from one account to another, or pay a mortgage—all from the comfort of your own computer or mobile device.
- Online classes: Instruction offered, over the Internet, using learning management software such as Blackboard, Moodle, or Pearson's MyITLab, and which enables you to communicate with your instructor and other students in the class.
- GPS systems: Computing devices that provide driving directions from your current location to a destination that you enter, and can provide information about local restaurants, gas stations, fast-food chains, and even the phone number for your favorite pizza place.
- ATMs: An automated teller machine that connects to the database of banking institutions with which you can perform financial transactions from public places.
- Mobile phones: Your favorite telecommunication device that, in addition to communication, also provides conveniences such as a calculator, a calendar, and Internet connectivity.

You use computers at home, at work, and in school; they are embedded in your car, your phone, and your camera. The real power of a computer is when you use technology to collect information and then share that information with others locally and globally, and use the information to make decisions. It is useful to look back at the events that led up to the current state of technology and then look forward to future technological advancements to see how they relate to your education and your future employment.

Concept 1.01 | Taking a Brief Look Back

Looking at the past clarifies the present and directs your future. Think about changes that have occurred in your life as a result of technological innovations in the past decade. Then think of your parents and how the changes in technology over the past three decades have affected them.

In the 1980s, only the U.S. government and large universities were able to access the Internet—including e-mail. Cell phones were just coming into use. Fax machines were the fastest way for most businesses to share documents across distances. The World Wide Web would not become viable until 1993. Today millions of people around the world use the Internet in both their professional and personal lives. Cell phones, laptop computers, and the need for instant connectivity are a vital component of daily mobile life. GPS units guide travelers to their destinations. Retail e-commerce, which did not begin until 1995, had sales of $32 billion in the third quarter of 2009, and is projected to grow to $203 billion by 2013.

For a more detailed look back, examine Figure 1.1, which shows a compressed computer history timeline. Or, go to **www.computerhope.com/history** for a year-by-year breakdown of computer developments and advances. If you are interested in the development of the Apple computer, you can

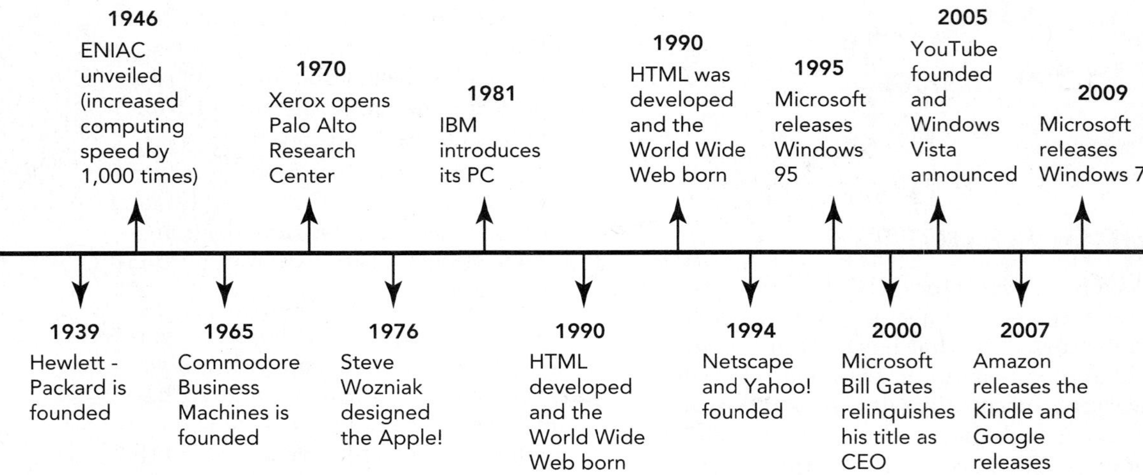
1946
ENIAC unveiled (increased computing speed by 1,000 times)
1970
Xerox opens Palo Alto Research Center
1981
IBM introduces its PC
1990
HTML was developed and the World Wide Web born
1995
Microsoft releases Windows 95
2005
YouTube founded and Windows Vista announced
2009
Microsoft releases Windows 7
1939
Hewlett - Packard is founded
1965
Commodore Business Machines is founded
1976
Steve Wozniak designed the Apple!
1990
HTML developed and the World Wide Web born
1994
Netscape and Yahoo! founded
2000
Microsoft Bill Gates relinquishes his title as CEO
2007
Amazon releases the Kindle and Google releases Android

FIGURE 1.1 This timeline focuses on significant events in the computer development lifecycle.

SOURCE: www.computerhope.com/history

visit **http://www.theapplemuseum.com** and study the advances made over the years.

Concept 1.02 | Looking at the Present

Today it is difficult to find an activity or job that does *not* involve computers, technology, and sharing of information (Figure 1.2). You will need computer and Internet skills to succeed in almost any job. Studies consistently show that workers with good computer and Internet skills are in demand and earn salaries significantly above the median personal income level of approximately $35,000 (Figure 1.3). At **www.cis.udel.edu/jobs/market** you can get information about the future of the computer science job market and links to related sites. At **www.salary.com** a free salary wizard displays a chart of salary ranges based on the job and location entered.

© StockLite/Shutterstock

FIGURE 1.2 Once considered tools only for the technically savvy, now computers, and the devices they are embedded within, are part of most jobs and daily life.

Average Salaries of Workers in Computer and Computer-Related Jobs

Categories	High ($/yr.)	Low ($/yr.)	Average ($/yr.)
Computer operations	$220,000	$23,000	$59,000
Database systems	$120,000	$30,000	$67,000
E-commerce/Internet	$175,000	$37,000	$79,000
Hardware	$100,000	$30,000	$56,000
Help desk	$110,000	$23,000	$44,000
Networking	$333,000	$22,000	$69,000
Project management	$130,000	$34,000	$83,000
Technical writing	$77,000	$45,000	$59,000
UNIX	$108,000	$50,000	$79,000
Windows development	$101,000	$40,000	$69,000
Wireless systems	$95,000	$46,000	$66,000

Figure 1.3

Note: This is a selection of common job types reflecting salary ranges affected by geographical location and level of responsibilities.
SOURCE: www.salary.com.

Concept 1.03 | Gaining an Insight into the Future

Isolated skills will not be enough to keep you connected or job-ready in the future. You will need to understand the concepts that underlie computer and Internet technologies. Additionally as computers and the Internet play a more direct and

FIGURE 1.4 Becoming familiar with the latest technology will help you select the correct device for a task based on need and usability, not based on advertising hype.

noticeable role in your life it is harder to understand the difference between the appropriate and inappropriate use of these technologies. Even trying to decide on the type of computer to purchase for your daily life can be an overwhelming task (Figure 1.4). But the more you understand and learn about computers the less mysterious and confusing they will seem and the better prepared you will be to make technology-related decisions.

Objective 2 | Identify Computer Fundamentals

In your job as a freelance Interior Designer, you want to develop a list of the programs, the operating systems they are compatible with, and the hardware specifications each requires for both yourself and your clients. This will determine if any programs need to be eliminated or any hardware updated before the project begins. Where do you start?

Concept 1.04 | Understanding the Computer: Basic Definitions

A ***computer*** is an electronic device that performs the four basic operations that comprise the ***information processing cycle*** (Figure 1.5). The four basic operations are:

- ***Input***: The action of entering data into a computer; for example, typing your login ID.
- ***Processing***: The manipulation of the input—data—by a sequence of instructions that converts the input into ***information***. Information is data converted into a meaningful format. Examples of processing would be aligning the return address in a letter that you are typing in Microsoft Word, using a function to average a column of numbers in a Microsoft Excel worksheet, or searching a database to confirm a login ID number.
- ***Output***: The display of the information; for example, the realigned return address in your letter, the computed average of the numbers in your worksheet, or the confirmation of the entry of a valid login ID.
- ***Storage***: The action of saving information for later use.

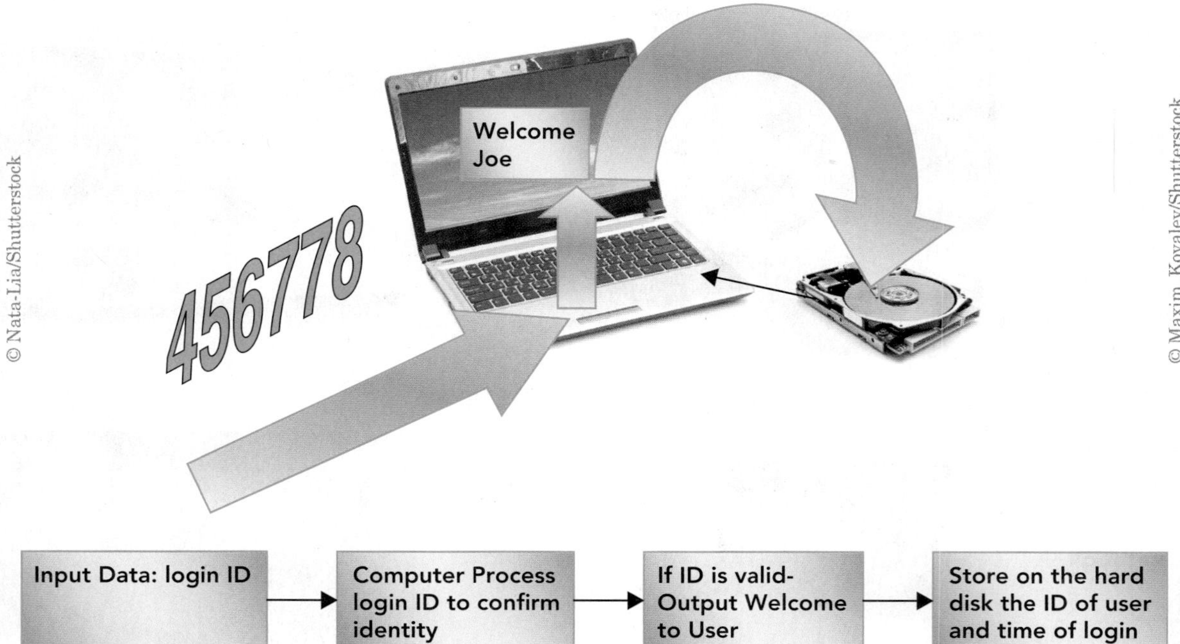

Welcome
Joe
456778
© Nata-Lia/Shutterstock
© Maxim_Kovalev/Shutterstock
Input Data: login ID
Computer Process login ID to confirm identity
If ID is valid- Output Welcome to User
Store on the hard disk the ID of user and time of login

FIGURE 1.5 The information processing cycle is the sequential path that data travels from input through output.

Because these operations depend on one another, the information processing cycle, commonly abbreviated as the ***IPOS cycle***, is always performed in this sequence.

A ***computer system***, also referred to as a system, is a collection of related components that work together to accomplish a task. A computer system has two categories of components—***hardware*** and ***software***. A computer system's hardware includes all the physical components of the computer and its related devices. The ***system unit*** is the base unit of the computer and is made up of the plastic or metal enclosure. The system unit houses the ***motherboard*** and the ***integrated peripherals***. The motherboard is a circuit board that connects the ***central processing unit***, which is anchored to the board along with other system components. The central processing unit, also referred to as the ***CPU***, acts as the brain of the computer by controlling all the functions performed by the other components, and processing all the commands it receives from software. Integrated peripherals are the devices embedded within the system unit case and generally include the power supply, cooling fans, memory, CD or DVD drive, and internal hard drive. Hardware also includes the ***peripheral devices***—components *outside* the system unit that are connected physically or wirelessly to the system unit and motherboard. Peripheral devices include such things as keyboards, mice, monitors, printers, speakers, external webcams, external modems, and external storage devices (Figure 1.6).

A computer system's hardware must have software—also referred to as programs—to function. Software is a set of instructions that tells the hardware how to perform a certain task. The two primary types of software are:

Application software includes all the programs that direct the computer to carry out specific tasks; for example, doing word processing, playing a game, or computing numbers on a worksheet. Often, multiple programs are integrated to create an application; for example the programs to check spelling, check grammar, locate synonyms, and insert a header or footer are combined with many other such programs to create a word processing application.

System software includes the programs that enable the computer's hardware to work with and run the application software, which is computer software that your computer uses to accomplish specific tasks like word processing or accounting. System software is the interface between you and the other programs and the computer's hardware. There are two categories of system software—***operating systems*** and ***system utilities***. The operating system, also referred to as the ***OS***, is a computer program that

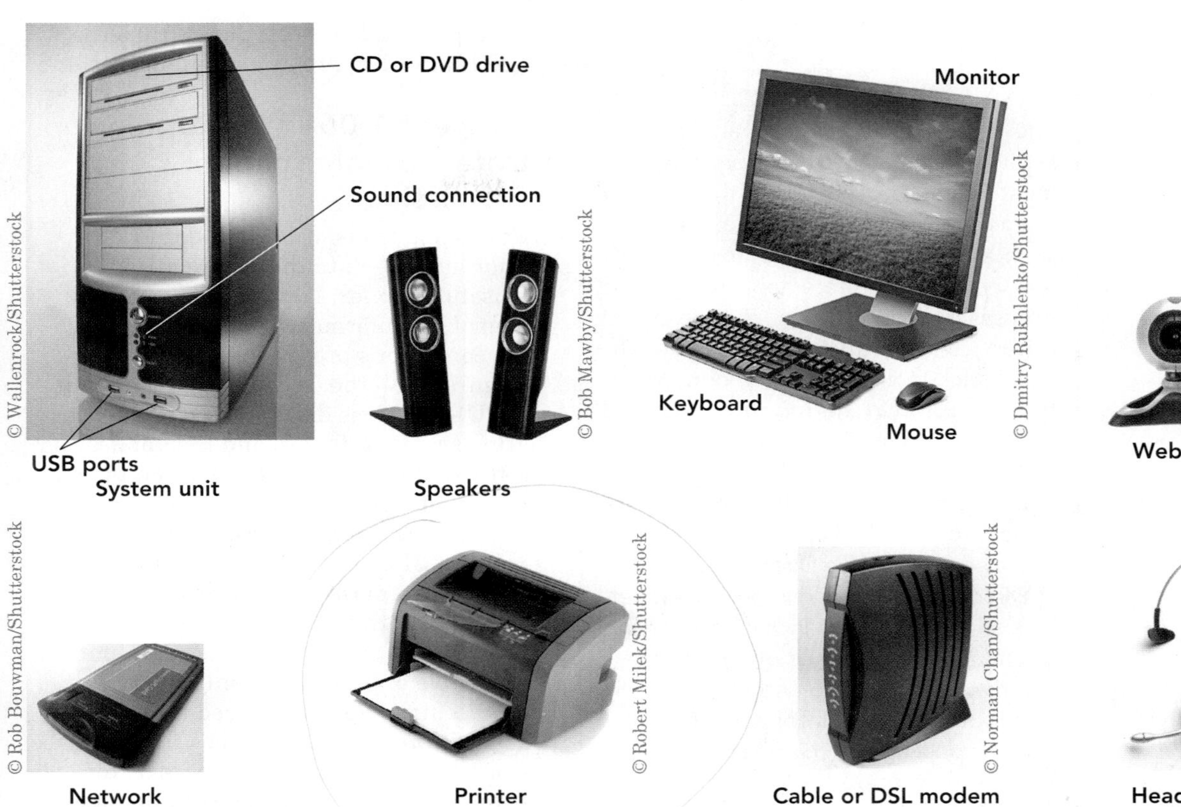

FIGURE 1.6 Can you identify these hardware components on your system?

manages all the other programs on your computer, stores files in an organized manner, and coordinates the use of the computer hardware such as the keyboard and mouse. Because of the operating system, you do not have to interact directly with the hardware—other than clicking the mouse button or pressing keys on the keyboard—to complete tasks. Common operating systems include Microsoft Windows 7, Microsoft Vista, Microsoft Windows XP, Linux, Mac OS X Snow Leopard, and Mac OS X Lion. Due to advances in both hardware and software, new versions of operating systems are released frequently; for example, the next version of Microsoft Windows will be available in 2012, and Mac OS X Lion was released in 2011. New releases of operating systems typically improve performance and accommodate new hardware devices. System utility programs differ from operating systems in that they aid in the *maintenance* of your system, your individual devices, or your installed programs. Examples of system utilities include backup programs, hard disk cleanup tools, and antivirus software. You could compare a computer system to an aquarium. The computer hardware is the fish tank, the operating system is the water, and the software applications are the fish (Figure 1.7). Fish

FIGURE 1.7 To be useful, a computer system must have an operating system and applications.

TECHNOLOGY ON THE JOB

The job responsibilities of an Administrative Assistant might surprise you. In most positions of this type, the requirements to create and modify documents such as invoices, reports, memos, letters, and financial statements using word processing, spreadsheet, database and other software such as Microsoft Office, QuickBooks, or other programs are typically listed in the *top three* required skills. Additional skills required include: the ability to conduct efficient research and searches; compile data and prepare papers for consideration and presentation to the Executive Director and Board of Directors; set up and coordinate meetings and conferences including verifying attendance via e-mail or other electronic means; and preparing and electronically distributing agendas for meetings. Recent job postings for this position indicate experience with both Windows and Mac OS operating systems as a requirement. Are you surprised at the level of familiarity with technology that is expected from a candidate for an Administrative Assistant position? Evaluate your own credentials. Could you apply for such a position? If not, what courses should you take to prepare yourself for jobs that require computer skills?

cannot survive without water, just as software applications cannot function without an operating system. Without the water and fish, an aquarium is an empty box—without an operating system and application software, a computer is also an empty box.

FIGURE 1.8 The keyboard and mouse are the most common input devices for nonportable systems.

© Chiyacat/Shutterstock

Concept 1.05 | Getting Data into the Computer: Input

You input ***data***—numbers, words, pictures, or sounds that represent facts about people, events, things, or ideas—into a computer for processing by using ***input devices***. The most common input devices are the keyboard and mouse (Figure 1.8). Microphones, scanners, digital cameras, and camcorders are also input devices.

Concept 1.06 | Transforming Data into Information: Processing

Processing transforms your data into information—data that is organized in a useful manner. During the processing step of the information processing cycle, the computer's processing circuitry (Figure 1.9)—the central processing unit (CPU)—receives directions from the operating system software and the application software to perform operations on the data you input. The CPU is sometimes referred to as the microprocessor or just processor.

The CPU—a single chip located on the motherboard—is often referred to as the brain of the computer; however, computers do not actually think. A computer is capable of performing only repetitive processing actions organized into an ***algorithm***—a series of steps that describe what a computer program must do to solve a logical or mathematical problem or to perform a task. After an algorithm is developed and approved, it is coded into a language that the computer hardware understands, tested for accuracy, and becomes the program or software that the system uses to solve that problem.

Because the CPU must juggle multiple input and output requests at the same time, it uses ***memory***—a device where information can be stored and retrieved—in the form of high-speed ***memory chips*** to store program instructions and data so it can move between requests quickly. A memory chip is an integrated circuit devoted to memory storage. A typical

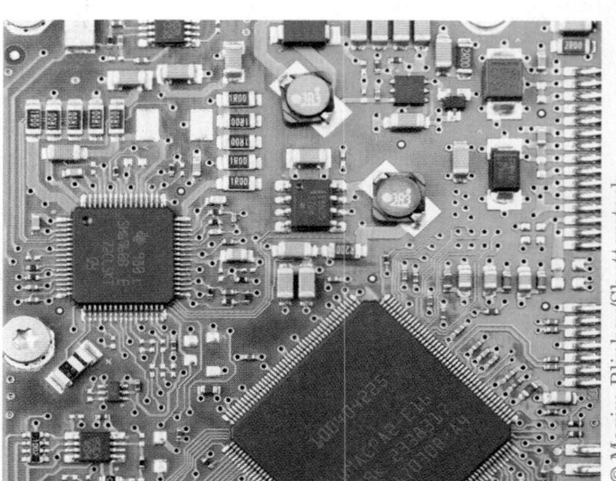

© Maxim Blinkov/Shutterstock

FIGURE 1.9 The CPU performs operations on the data to convert it to information.

computer contains several types of memory on the motherboard, the most important of which is ***random access memory*** abbreviated as ***RAM***. RAM temporarily stores the programs and data with which the CPU is interacting. RAM is also referred to as primary memory or temporary memory. RAM is temporary because it does not retain any content when power is interrupted or turned off.

Concept 1.07 | Displaying Information: Output

You experience output through ***output devices*** such as a monitor, printer, or speakers that enable you to view, see, and hear the results of processing operations (Figure 1.10).

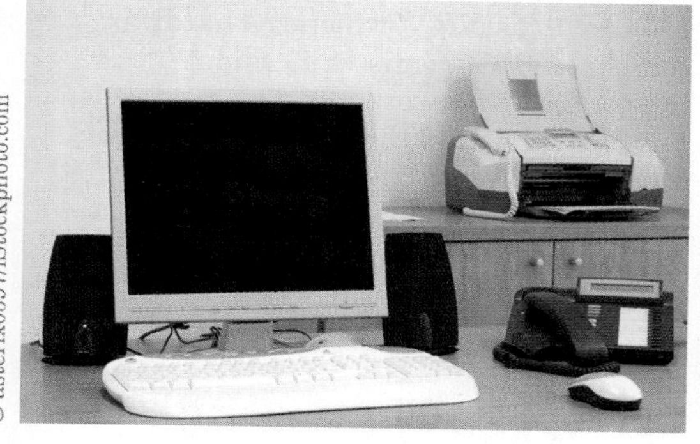

© asterix0597/iStockphoto.com

FIGURE 1.10 The display on a monitor or a paper printout is the most common output.

Concept 1.08 | Holding Programs and Data for Future Use: Storage

Think of the task of typing data in a word processing program such as Microsoft Word. While you are typing, your data—input—is held in RAM until you save and name your document. When you save your work, your computer uses a ***storage device***—hardware that retains your programs and data even when power is disrupted or turned off. Storage devices, also referred to as ***secondary storage***, can be both integrated and external peripherals (Figure 1.11), depending on whether you want the information you are storing to remain on the computer at which you are working or needs to be portable and transferable to another computing device. The internal hard disk on your system holds all the programs—both system and application software—and data that are intended to remain within your computer system. This storage device is usually an integrated peripheral, which means it is mounted inside your system unit's enclosure. It is not visible and most often never replaced. If you have a lot of data that you want to be portable, or if you want to back up critical data, you can use a nonintegrated hard disk connected to the system unit by a USB cable. These external storage devices are often colorful, fit into an average sized eyeglass case, and are economical. If your file sizes are smaller, but you still want your data to be portable, use a CD, DVD, media card, or ***USB flash drive***—a small data storage device that plugs into a computer's USB port—instead of an external hard drive (Figure 1.12). USB is an acronym for ***universal serial bus***, which is a standard for data transfer when connecting peripherals to a computer.

The USB flash drive is very popular. It is small and often referred to as a *thumb drive* because it is about the size of an adult's thumb. Additionally, a USB flash drive can store up to 256 GB of data—the equivalent of approximately 365 CDs or 51,000 images—uses solid-state technology, conveniently plugs into a computer's USB port, is easy to use, is rewritable, and is inexpensive.

© Maxim_Kovalev/Shutterstock

© Mastio1/Shutterstock

FIGURE 1.11 Hard drives can store very large quantities of data, making them the media of choice for activities that generate large files like movies, pictures, and backups.

© Mastio1/Shutterstock

© dundanim/Shutterstock
Card Reader/Writer
Compact Flash

© upthebanner/Shutterstock

FIGURE 1.12 Popular and inexpensive external storage devices include CD and DVD drives, media card readers that are used with flash memory cards, and flash drives that connect through a USB port.

Concept 1.09 | Moving Data: Communications

Communications, in the digital sense, is the high-speed exchange of information within and between computers or other communication devices. Communication is vital to our increasingly global and mobile society. You depend on the easy transfer of information from your computer or smartphone to the server that hosts your Web site, from a school computer to the one at your home, or from your iPad to a company server. To communicate, computers must be connected to a network by a ***communications device***, which is a hardware component that moves data into and out of a computer. These include modems, cables, ports, and devices like smartphones, tablets, and notebooks. Two or more connected computers are called a ***network***. You create a network so that you can share information and also share computer resources such as printers and other input/output devices.

Most computers are equipped with a ***modem***, which is short for modulator/demodulator. A modem is a communications device that converts data from one form into another. A modem enables the computer, which is a *digital* device, to access data through *non-digital* media such as telephone lines, cable, satellite, and cellular connections. Many computers have internal modems for dial-up Internet access over a standard telephone line. External modems provide high-speed access to the Internet via cable, DSL (digital subscriber line), or satellite.

Another important communication device is the ***network interface card***—also referred to as ***NIC***—which is a hardware component that connects a computer to a network. The network interface card is usually located within the system unit. Many computers already have the NIC integrated into the motherboard, but external NICs can be plugged into a USB port or inserted into a specially designed slot. NICs can connect to wired or wireless networks.

Concept 1.10 | Examining the Information Processing Cycle in Action

The following example illustrates your role and the computer's role in each step of the information processing cycle (Figure 1.13):

- *Input*: You are writing a research paper for a class. You know it has misspellings and grammatical errors, but you keep typing because you can run

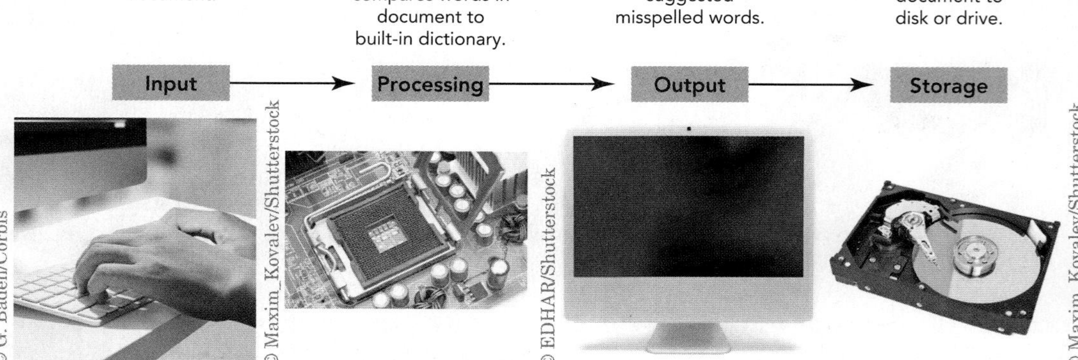
Your role:
Enter word-processed document.
Computer's role:
Receive document.
Your role:
Start spell-checker program.
Computer's role:
Spell-checker program compares words in document to built-in dictionary.
Computer's role:
Display list of misspelled words.
Your role:
Accept or reject suggested misspelled words.
Your role:
Save corrected document.
Computer's role:
Store final document to disk or drive.
Input
Processing
Output
Storage
© G. Baden/Corbis
© Maxim_Kovalev/Shutterstock
© EDHAR/Shutterstock
© Maxim_Kovalev/Shutterstock

FIGURE 1.13 The information processing cycle in action.

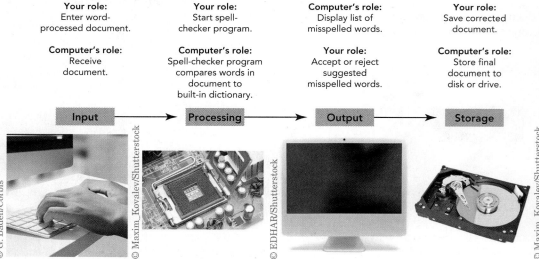

your word processing program's spelling checker at any time to help correct the errors. The document that you are typing is the input.

- *Processing*: A spelling checker program uses the computer's ability to perform processing operations to construct a list of all of the words in your document. The program compares your words against its own dictionary of correctly spelled words. If you use a word that is not in the computer's dictionary, the program flags the word as a misspelling.

The computer's spelling checker program does not have the intelligence to check your spelling. Rather, it simply flags words that do not match any of the words in its dictionary. Such a program will not flag the word *sign* as misspelled even though you intended to type *sing a song* rather than *sign a song*, because both words are contained in the program's dictionary. Your own knowledge and proofreading skills are still required.

- *Output*: The result—the output—of the spelling checker processing operation is a document containing words that are flagged as being possibly misspelled. Word processing programs typically flag possible misspellings with a red wavy line under the word. Many words that are flagged as misspelled are actually spelled correctly; they are simply not in the program's dictionary.
- *Storage*: After you correct any misspellings in your document, you save or store the revised document to the integrated hard disk or an external portable storage device.

Check Your Knowledge: From either the Companion Web Site or MyITLab, take the quiz covering Objectives 1 and 2

Objective 3 | Recognize Operating Systems and Their Functions

In your job as a freelance Interior Designer, you realize you have an older version of an operating system than members of the architectural firm with whom you are working on this project. You want to upgrade your system but are hesitant because your other projects are still in progress and clients associated with them are still using the older systems. You need to know how an update to your system will affect the files associated with your other projects. Where do you start?

Recall that system software includes all the programs that provide the infrastructure and hardware control necessary for the computer and its peripheral devices. System software tells the computer how to *be* a computer. Some system software works without any action on your part, and some requires your guidance and control.

Recall also that system software has two major components—the operating system and the system utilities.

The operating system manages the resources of a computer; its primary functions include:

- Starting the computer and transferring files from the storage device to RAM memory
- Managing programs that are active or running in the background
- Managing random access memory (RAM) to optimize its use
- Coordinating tasks including the communication between input and output devices and programs
- Providing a user interface to allow for easy and seamless communication between you and your computer

Thus, a computer must have an operating system to coordinate the interactions of its hardware components and to coordinate the interaction of the hardware with the application software. The operating system software is typically stored on the computer's hard disk, although it can be stored and transferred from a USB drive, CD, or DVD. On some small handheld computers and smartphones, the operating system is held on a memory chip within the system unit.

You can think of the operating system as a traffic officer standing at a busy intersection (Figure 1.14). Imagine the traffic at a downtown intersection at rush hour, and you will have a good idea of what it is like inside a computer. Bits of information travel around at incredible speeds, sent in different directions by the operating system, the electronic equivalent of a busy traffic officer. Impatient peripherals and programs are honking their horns trying to get the officer's attention. Then

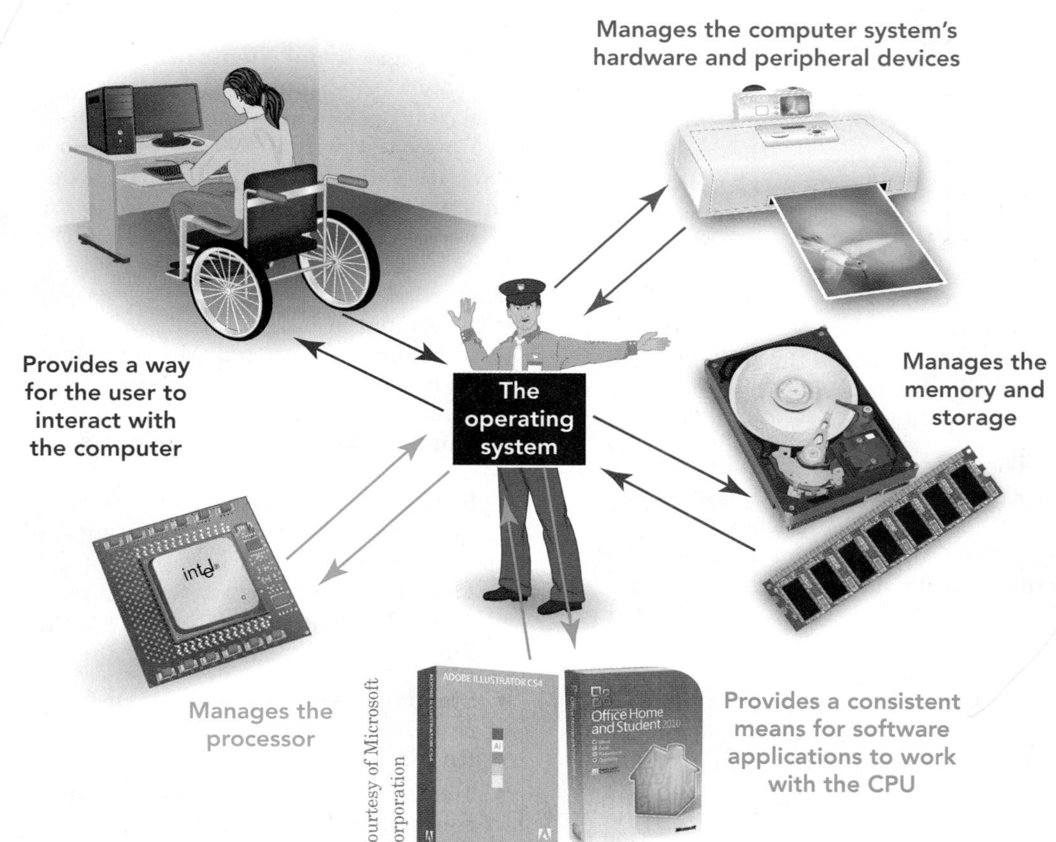
Manages the computer system's hardware and peripheral devices
Provides a way for the user to interact with the computer
The operating system
Manages the memory and storage
Manages the processor
Provides a consistent means for software applications to work with the CPU
Courtesy of Microsoft Corporation

FIGURE 1.14 The operating system works at the intersection of application software, the computer's hardware, and you.

the city's mayor—you—wants to come through right now. Just like a traffic officer, the computer's operating system—standing at the intersection of the computer's hardware, application programs, and you—keeps traffic running smoothly.

Concept 1.11 | Starting the Computer

When you start a computer, the operating system is transferred from a storage device, such as the hard disk, into the computer's RAM (random access memory). RAM is a form of ***volatile memory***, which is storage that is very fast, located on the motherboard, and whose content is erased when the power goes off. RAM stores the programs you are using and computer files on which you are working, for example, a Microsoft Word document. The process of loading the operating system into memory is called ***booting***. A ***cold boot*** refers to starting a computer that has not yet been turned on. A ***warm boot*** refers to restarting a computer that is already on. A warm boot, also called a restart, is typically required after installing new software, after an application stops working, or when your system becomes unresponsive. On a computer running the Microsoft Windows 7 operating system, you can perform a restart by following these steps (Figure 1.15):

1. Click the Start button.
2. Click on the right arrow located to the right of the Shut down button.
3. Click Restart.

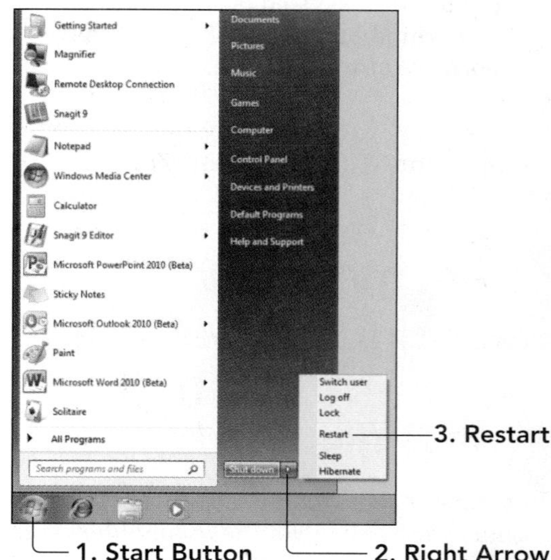
3. Restart
1. Start Button
2. Right Arrow

FIGURE 1.15 Using the Restart option from the Start button is the preferred way of reactivating a nonresponsive system.

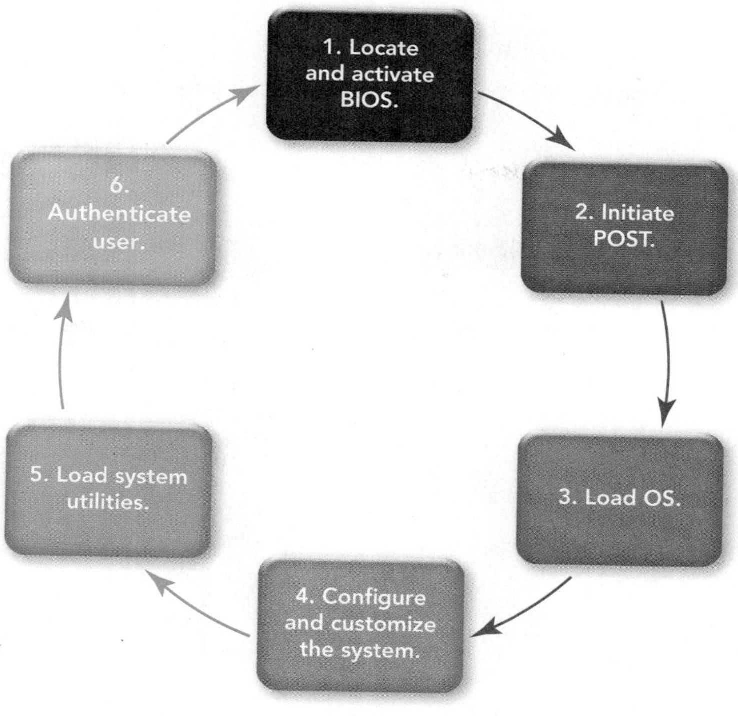

FIGURE 1.16 The six sequential steps involved in starting a computer.

With both types of booting, the computer copies the ***kernel***—the central part of the operating system that manages memory, files, and devices; launches applications; and allocates system resources—from the hard disk into the computer's RAM memory. Because the kernel remains in RAM during the time a computer is powered on, it is referred to as being ***memory resident***. Less frequently used portions of the operating system are stored on the hard disk and retrieved as needed, and thus are referred to as ***nonresident*** because they do not reside in memory.

The booting of a system, whether it is a cold or warm boot, is a step-by-step process (Figure 1.16):

1. Activate the basic input/output system (BIOS)
2. Perform the power-on self-test (POST)
3. Load the operating system into RAM
4. Configure and customize settings
5. Load needed system utilities
6. Authenticate the user

The following sections discuss each of these boot steps in detail.

Leaving a computer running when it is not in use is wasteful. By default, a computer running Windows 7 and Windows Vista will go into sleep mode after a period of inactivity, saving its owner $70 or more in annual energy costs. There are three energy states you can adjust in Windows 7 to help conserve energy.

- Use the ***sleep state*** to transfer the current state of your computer to RAM, turn off all unneeded functions, and place the system in a low power state. Returning from the sleep state is faster than returning from hibernate state because the computer's settings are held in RAM memory.
- Use the ***hibernate state*** to save battery power. Primarily for use in laptops, this state saves your open documents and programs on your hard disk and then turns off your computer. When you restart your system, all windows and programs that were open restore automatically.
- On a desktop computer, use the ***hybrid sleep state***. This state combines sleep and hibernate. It places open documents and programs in both RAM *and* on your hard disk, and then places the system in a low power state so you can resume your work quickly. If power is suddenly terminated, your work can be restored. The hybrid sleep state is usually turned on by default on most desktop computers.

To access the settings for sleep and hibernate states in Windows 7, click the Start button, click Control Panel, click System and Security, and then click Power

Change settings for the plan: Balanced

Choose the sleep and display settings that you want your computer to use.

	On battery	Plugged in
Turn off the display:	5 minutes	10 minutes
Put the computer to sleep:	15 minutes	30 minutes

Change advanced power settings

Restore default settings for this plan

Save changes Cancel

FIGURE 1.17 The On battery options should be 5 minutes or less to conserve battery life on a laptop computer.

Options. Select the Balanced option and click the link to the right—*Change plan settings* (Figure 1.17).

In Windows 7, to place your system in the sleep or hibernate state, click the Start button, and then from the arrow to the right of the Shut down button, click either Sleep or Hibernate (Figure 1.18). To wake your system, press the Power button on your system unit.

Step 1: Activate the BIOS and Setup Program

When you first turn on or reset a PC, electricity flows from the power supply through the system. When the CPU receives the signal that the power level is sufficient, it is directed to the BIOS ROM for the start of the system's BIOS boot program. The ***BIOS*** (basic input/output system) information is permanently written in the computer's ROM. ***ROM***, or ***read-only memory***, is nonvolatile memory located on the motherboard that is not easily edited and keeps its content even when the system powers off. BIOS data consists of descriptions of the equipment that your system contains, typically the CPU, hard disk, RAM, and video component—equipment you do not usually replace. The operating system then uses the BIOS data to control those devices. Other external devices that you change frequently, such as jump drives and speakers, are not run by BIOS, but are controlled and accessed by the operating system directly. After the BIOS is located, you may briefly see the BIOS screen, a text-only screen that provides information about BIOS-controlled devices (Figure 1.19). BIOS information should not be changed by an amateur; making an incorrect change will cause your system not to boot.

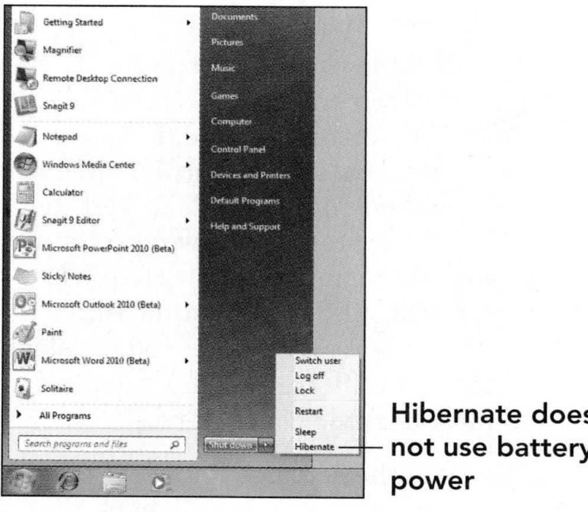
Hibernate does not use battery power

FIGURE 1.18 In Windows 7, hibernate and sleep states are activated from the Start menu.

Step 2: Initiate the Power-On Self-Test

After the BIOS instructions are loaded into RAM memory, a series of tests are conducted to make sure that the computer and associated peripherals are operating correctly. Collectively, these tests are known as the ***power-on self-test (POST)***. Among the components tested are the computer's main memory (RAM), the keyboard, mouse, disk drives, and the hard

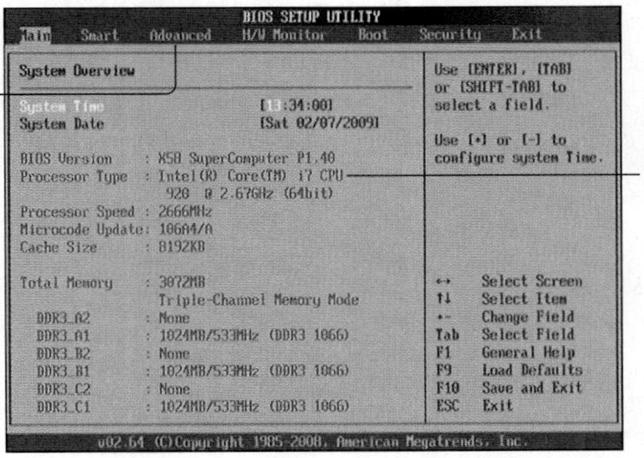

Advanced settings include the sequence of devices on which the OS might be located

CPU manufacturer, type, and speed

FIGURE 1.19 This BIOS screen is for a system with an Intel Core i7 CPU running at 2666 MHz.

disk. If any of the power-on self-tests fail, you will hear a beep, see an error message, and the computer will stop. You can often correct such problems by making sure that components, such as keyboards, are plugged in securely. If you cannot correct the error, count the number of beeps, call technical support, and convey the number of beeps and the error message.

Step 3: Load the Operating System

After the power-on self-test is successfully completed, the BIOS initiates a search for the operating system. On most PCs, the operating system is on the computer's hard disk. If other possible locations for the operating system exist such as an optical drive, a floppy drive, or a hard disk, BIOS will specify these options and the order in which they are to be searched.

When BIOS locates the operating system, it loads the operating system's kernel into RAM memory. At that point, the operating system takes control of the computer from BIOS and begins loading system configuration information.

Step 4: Configure the System

In Microsoft Windows, configuration information about installed peripheral devices and software is stored in a database called the ***registry***. The registry also contains information about your personalized choices, such as background graphics and mouse settings.

After the operating system's kernel is loaded, it checks the system's configuration to determine which drivers and other utility programs are needed. A ***driver*** is a program containing instructions that make a peripheral device, like an external hard drive, printer, or DVD player, usable by an operating system.

Windows and Mac operating systems are equipped with ***plug-and-play (PnP)*** capabilities, which automatically detect new PnP-compatible peripheral devices that you might have installed while the power was switched off, load the necessary drivers, and check for conflicts with other devices. Peripheral devices equipped with PnP features identify themselves to the operating system and require no action by you.

Step 5: Load System Utilities

After the operating system detects and configures all of the system's hardware, it loads system utilities such as speaker volume control, antivirus software, and power management options. In Microsoft Windows, you can view available custom configuration choices by right-clicking the icon of the feature you want to reconfigure. The icons are located in the notification area on the right side of the Windows taskbar and also on the Control Panel that you can access from the Start menu (Figure 1.20).

Step 6: Authenticate a User

When the operating system finishes loading, you may see a request for a user name and password. Through this process, called ***authentication*** or login, you verify that you are the person who is authorized to use the computer.

Most consumer-oriented operating systems, such as Microsoft Windows and the Mac operating system, require or highly recommend that you supply a user name and password to use the computer. A ***profile***, a record of a specific user's preferences for the desktop theme, icons, and menu styles, is associated with a user name. If you set up a profile for yourself, your preferences will display on the screen after you log in.

On multiuser computer systems such as your college lab or office, you must have

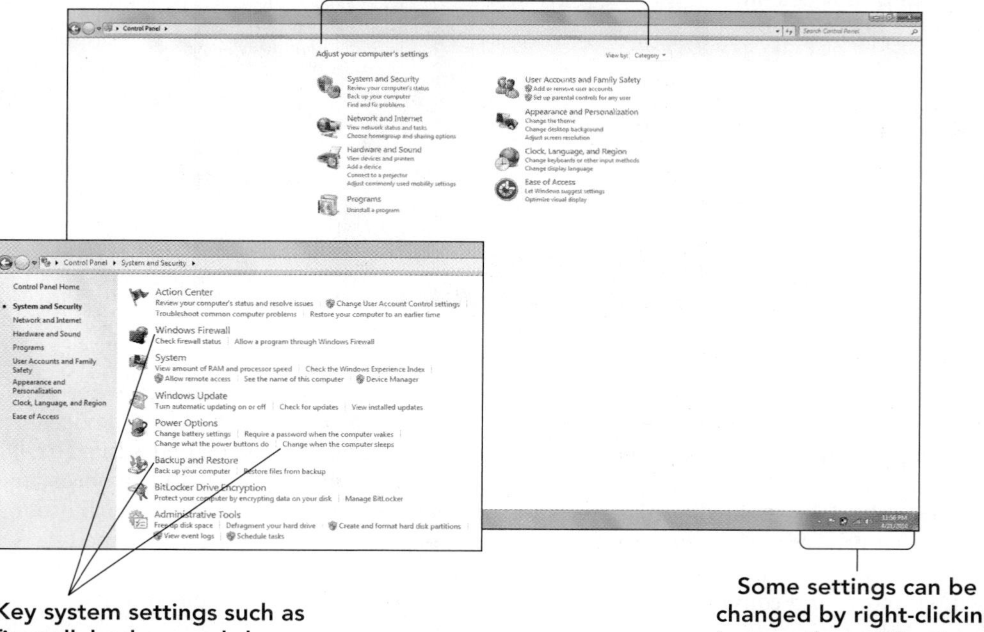
The control panel uses categories to group related features
Key system settings such as firewall, backup, and sleep can be set from the System and Security category
Some settings can be changed by right-clicking an icon on the notification area

FIGURE 1.20 Many options for managing and customizing your computer system are in the Control Panel under one of the main categories.

an account created by a computer administrator to access a computer. Your ***account*** consists of your user name, password, and allotted storage space. This information is stored in a user folder or user directory.

After the operating system is loaded and running, the next task that the operating system must perform is to manage applications.

Concept 1.12 | Managing Applications

Running and managing applications is an important task of the operating system.

Operating systems are referred to as ***multitasking operating systems*** because they permit more than one application to run at the same time and can manage multiple applications running simultaneously. The operating system is able to switch between applications as needed. For example, you can run Microsoft Word and Excel at the same time. When you are using Word, it is active and is referred to as the ***foreground application***. Excel is inactive, although it is running, and is referred to as the ***background application***, as indicated by its appearance on the desktop (Figure 1.21).

A clear measure of an operating system's stability is the technique it uses to handle multitasking and thus avoid conflicts among open programs. Modern operating systems use ***preemptive multitasking***—an environment in which programs do not run from start to finish but are interrupted or suspended in order to start or continue to run another task. Each task receives a recurring slice of time from the CPU. The time slice may or may not be the same for all programs. When one task uses its time slice or is interrupted by a task of higher priority, the task is suspended and the other task starts. This method of multitasking ensures that all applications have fair access to the CPU.

Concept 1.13 | Managing Memory

Your computer programs would run very slowly if the operating system had to constantly access the program instructions from their storage location on the hard disk. To ensure that programs run quickly, operating systems use the computer's RAM as a ***buffer***—an area that temporarily holds data and instructions. Because the computer's operating system is responsible for managing this memory area, it gives each running program, and some devices, a portion of RAM, and then keeps

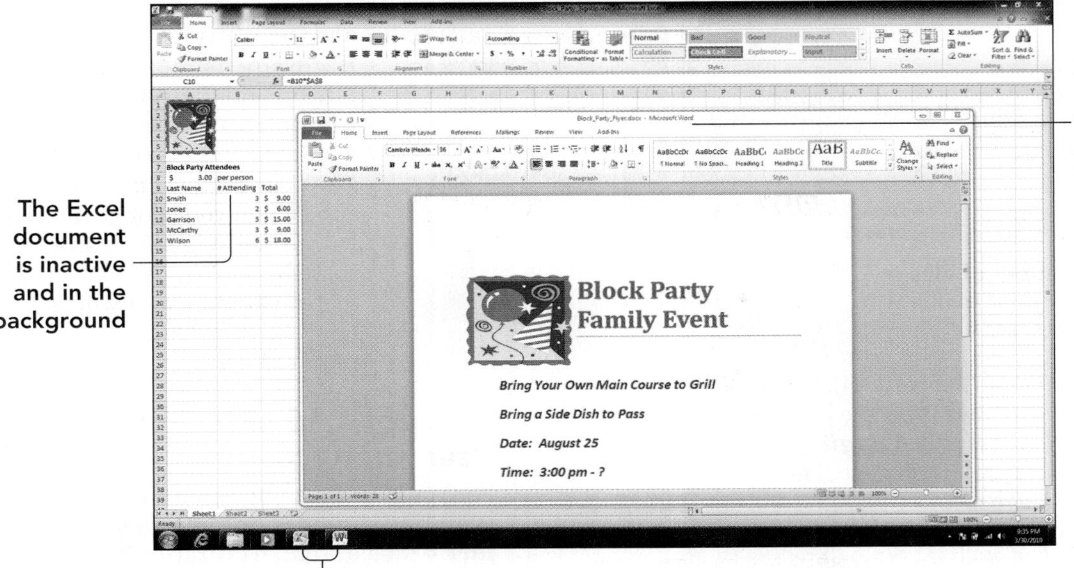
The Word document is active and in the foreground
The Excel document is inactive and in the background
An icon appears on the taskbar for each open application
Block Party Family Event
Bring Your Own Main Course to Grill
Bring a Side Dish to Pass
Date: August 25
Time: 3:00 pm - ?

FIGURE 1.21 Multi-tasking operating systems typically display all open programs on a taskbar at the bottom of the screen.

the programs from interfering with each other's use of memory (Figure 1.22).

For example, if you give a command to print three documents one right after another, while the printer is printing the first document, the second and third documents are held in the print buffer. The documents wait in the buffer until the ***spooling program***—a program that monitors the print requests in the buffer and the busy state of the printer—indicates that the printer is available. Then the second document moves from the buffer to the printer. This process continues until the print buffer is empty. For this reason, turning off the printer to stop the printing of a document will not work, because turning off the printer does not empty the computer's print buffer. When you turn the printer on again, the documents in the print buffer continue to print. To stop documents in the print buffer from printing, follow the steps in Figure 1.23.

Modern operating systems can artificially extend the computer's RAM by using ***virtual memory***—a technique that uses a portion of the computer's hard disk as an extension of RAM. Program instructions and data are divided into fixed size units called ***pages***. If memory is full, the operating system starts storing copies of pages in a hard disk file called the ***swap file***, thereby creating a temporary storage space for instructions that the operating system can access as you do your work. When the pages are needed, they are copied back into

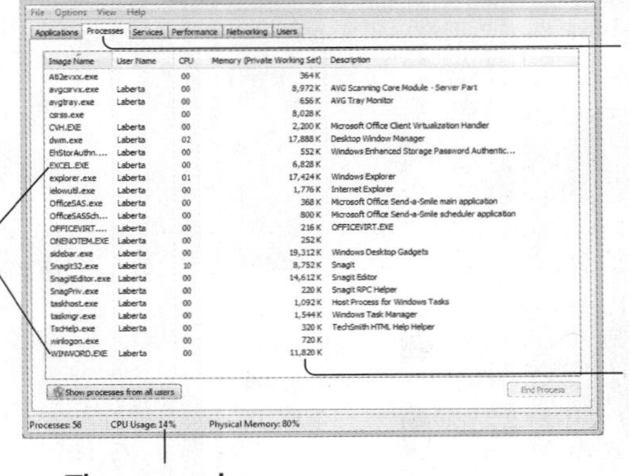
Select the Processes tab to view a list of processes running
You might recognize the Excel and Word application in the first column
In the memory column, the current amount of RAM each process is using is displayed
The status bar provides details on CPU and memory usage

FIGURE 1.22 Access Windows Task Manager by pressing Ctrl + Alt + Del, select the Start Task Manager option, and then click the Processes tab. All running programs display, along with total CPU and RAM memory usage for each program.

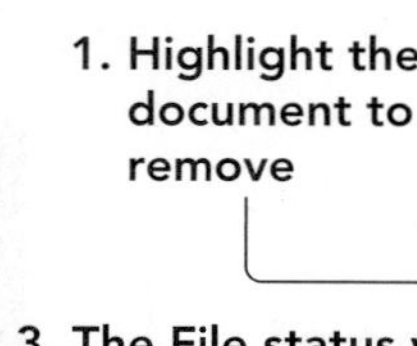

FIGURE 1.23 The print icon, located near the system clock, provides fast access to the print buffer dialog box. On a network, you might need administrator rights to delete documents in the buffer.

RAM (Figure 1.24). The process of transferring files from the hard disk to RAM and back is called ***paging***.

Although virtual memory gives you more memory than the amount of RAM installed on your computer, excessive paging—referred to as ***thrashing***—can slow down your system over time.

Concept 1.14 | Coordinating Tasks

Your operating system coordinates tasks involving input and output devices, and also enables communication with these devices and the programs in use.

Most operating systems come with ***device drivers*** for popular input and output devices. Device drivers are programs containing specific instructions to allow a particular brand and model of input or output device to communicate and function properly with the operating system. Printers, scanners, monitors, speakers, and the mouse all have drivers. Hardware manufacturers usually update their drivers when new operating systems become available and make the upgrades available on their Web site. When you change devices within the Windows operating system, the Windows Update feature automatically detects new hardware and installs the required driver.

FIGURE 1.24 Only a portion of a hard drive is allocated to virtual memory. It is possible to increase this amount; however, a better solution would be to purchase more RAM.

Concept 1.15 | Providing the User Interface

For you, the most important function of an operating system is providing a ***user interface***—the part of the operating system that lets you interact with the computer and the programs—that is efficient and easy to use. Three types of user interfaces include the ***graphical user interface***, the ***menu-driven user interface***, and the ***command line user interface*** (Figure 1.25).

By far the most popular user interface is the graphical user interface, which is commonly abbreviated ***GUI*** and pronounced GOO-ee. You are probably familiar with this interface, which uses graphics and the point-and-click technology of the mouse to give commands to the operating system and your application programs. By using this interface, you work with ***icons***, small images that represent computer resources such as programs, data files, and network

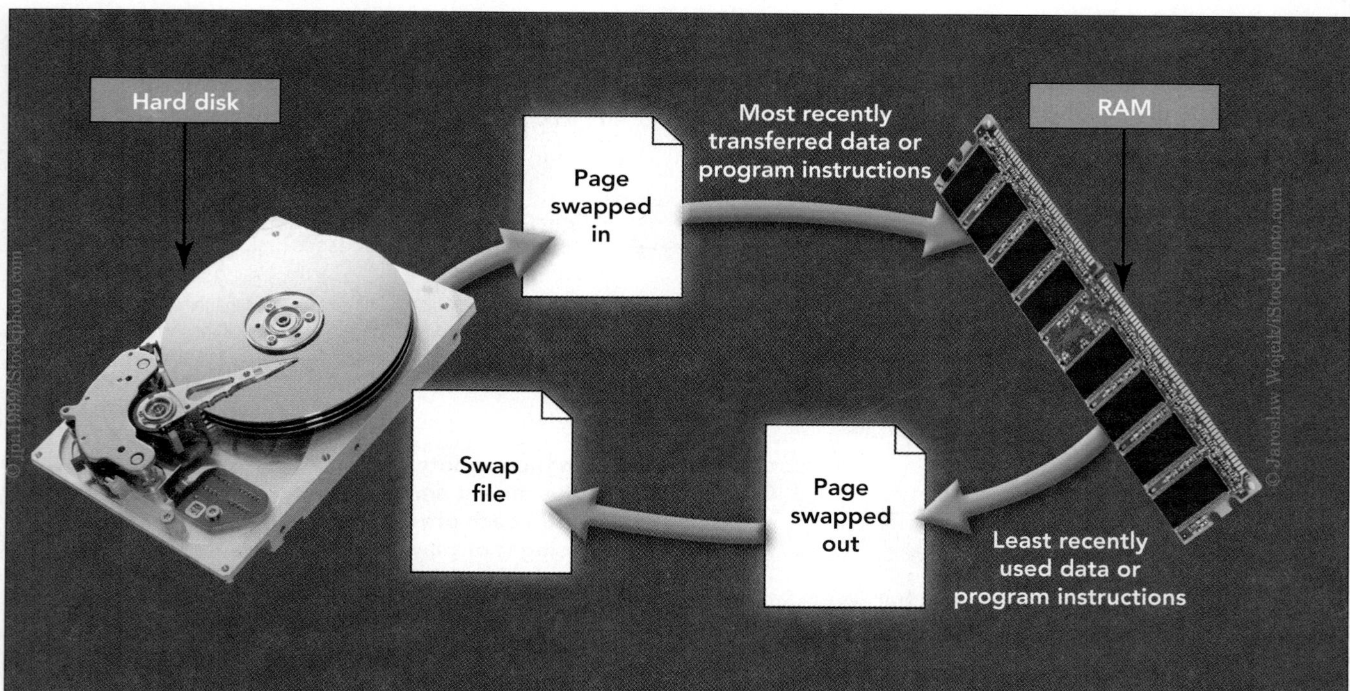

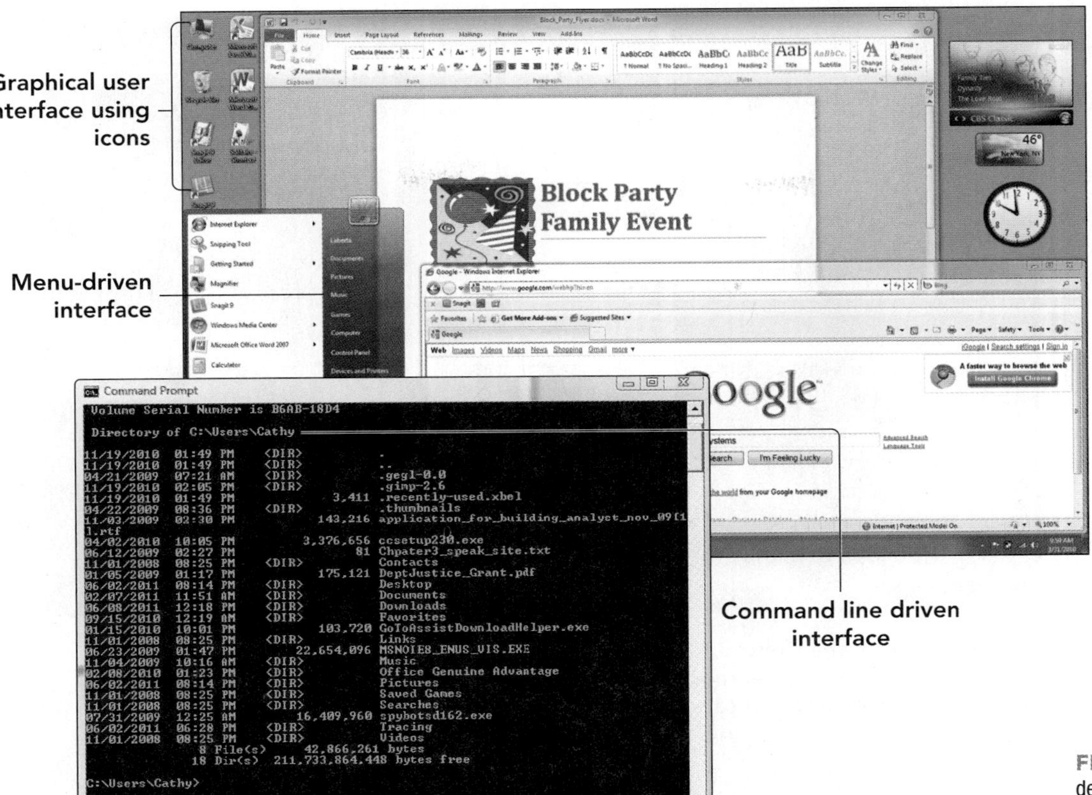

FIGURE 1.25 Most devices combine a graphical interface with some menus.

connections. Icons are positioned on the ***desktop***, the opening screen that displays after the operating system loads and simulates your work area. The lower edge of the desktop displays the ***taskbar***—the area that contains the Start button, optional program buttons, and buttons for all open programs (Figure 1.26).

In Microsoft Windows, you can use the Appearance and Personalization option

FIGURE 1.26 The desktop and taskbar.

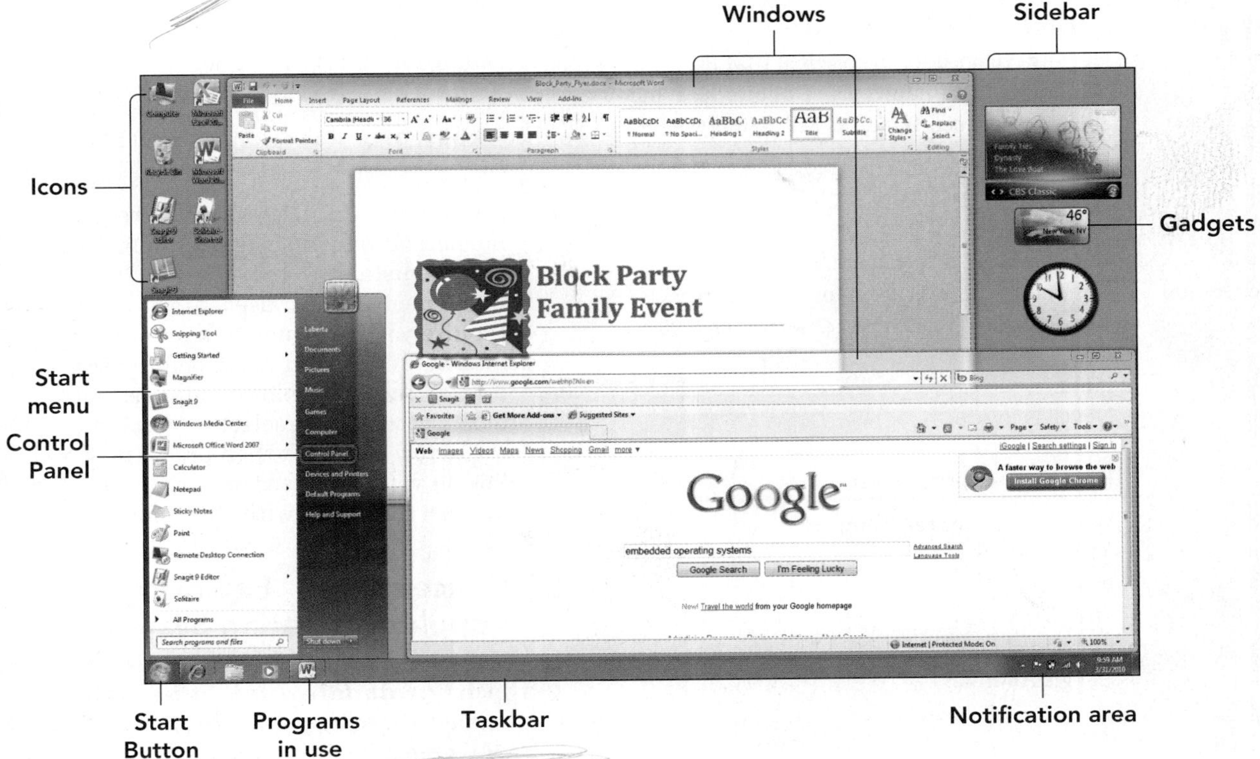

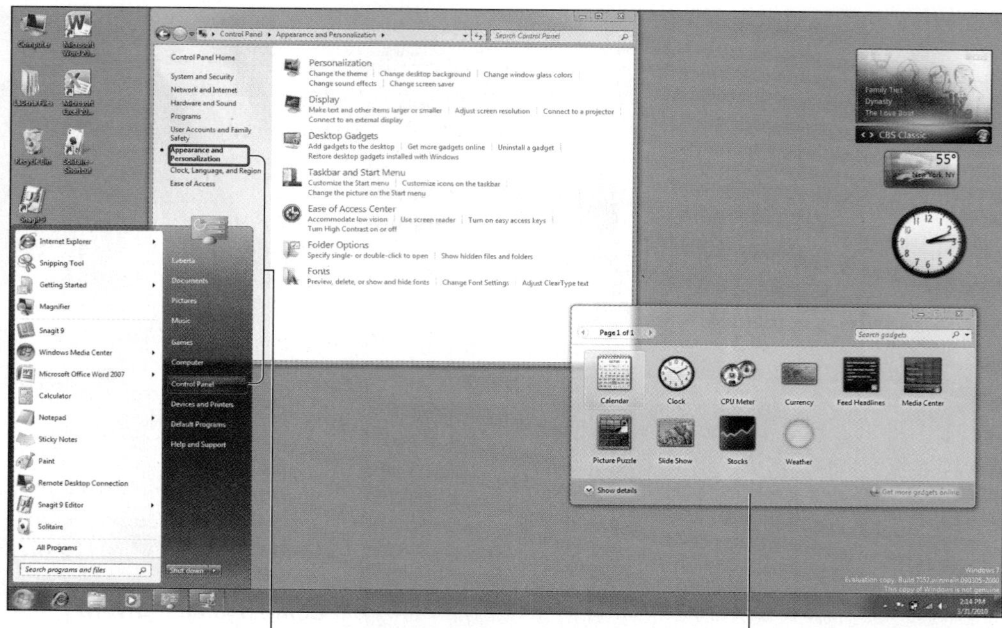
From the Control Panel, select the Appearance and Personalization category
Right-clicking in the sidebar will allow you to quickly add or delete gadgets without using the Control Panel

FIGURE 1.27 You can set desktop preferences from the Control Panel.

located in the Control Panel to make changes to the desktop appearance (Figure 1.27).

A command line user interface requires you to type commands using keywords that tell the operating system what to do—such as *Format* or *Copy*—one line at a time. You must observe complex rules of ***syntax***—a set of rules for entering commands—that specify exactly how and where you can type the commands. For example, the following command copies a file from the hard disk drive, which is designated as C, to a removable USB drive identified as F:

```
copy C:\myfile.txt F:\myfile.txt
```

A command line user interface requires memorization, and it is easy to make a typing mistake.

A menu-driven user interface does not require you to memorize keywords and syntax. Text-based menus on the screen display the available commands. With most systems, you select a command with the arrow keys and then press the ENTER key on your keyboard or simply click the desired command with the mouse.

Concept 1.16 | Exploring Popular Operating Systems

Three categories of operating systems include ***standalone operating systems***, ***server operating systems***, and ***embedded operating systems*** (Figure 1.28).

Operating Systems by Category	
Standalone operating systems	DOS—developed for the original IBM PC Windows 3.X, Windows 95, Windows 98, Windows 2000 Professional, Windows ME, Windows XP, Windows Vista, Windows 7 MAC OS X UNIX Linux
Server operating systems	Windows NT Server, Windows 2000 Server, Windows Server 2003, Windows Server 2008 UNIX Linux Novell Netware Solaris Red Hat Enterprise Server
Embedded operating systems	Windows Embedded Compact 7 iOS Palm OS BlackBerry OS Embedded Linux Google Android

Figure 1.28

Objective 4 | Utilize Standalone Operating Systems

In your job as a freelance Interior Designer, you frequently visit the office of your clients and those with whom you partner on some projects. You need a new portable computer system, because your current laptop computer is outdated. Although an iPad or netbook is appealing, you are unsure of the compatibility of the operating systems on these devices with the operating system on the desktop in your office. Where do you start?

A standalone operating system works on a desktop computer, laptop, notebook, or any portable computing device. The term *standalone* indicates that it does not need to be connected to any other system or computer to run. Almost all of the operating systems in the standalone category are enhanced with enough networking capabilities and connectivity options to allow them to manage a home or small business network; these options are usually installed when the system is purchased. The key word here is *small*.

Concept 1.17 | Using Microsoft Windows

Microsoft Windows is by far the most popular group of operating systems in this category. Since its introduction in 1985, this operating system, known simply as *Windows*, has gone through a number of iterations and is the most widely used operating system in the world. The first quarter of 2011, however, saw Window's usage drop below 90 percent of the market. The reason associated with this statistic was the increase in use of mobile devices and operating systems like iOS and Android. To view a compressed timeline highlighting some key developments in the Windows operating system, see Figure 1.29. A more detailed timeline is available at **www.computerhope.com/history/windows.htm**.

Microsoft Windows 7 was released in late 2009 and is available in six different versions: Starter, Home Basic, Home Premium, Professional, Enterprise, and Ultimate (Figure 1.30). All versions of Windows 7 claim to be more efficient than its predecessor, Windows Vista, performing equally or better on the same hardware, and resolving the compatibility issues that existed between applications. The next version of Windows will release in 2012.

FIGURE 1.29 Windows operating systems timeline.

SOURCE: http://www.computerhope.com/history/windows.htm

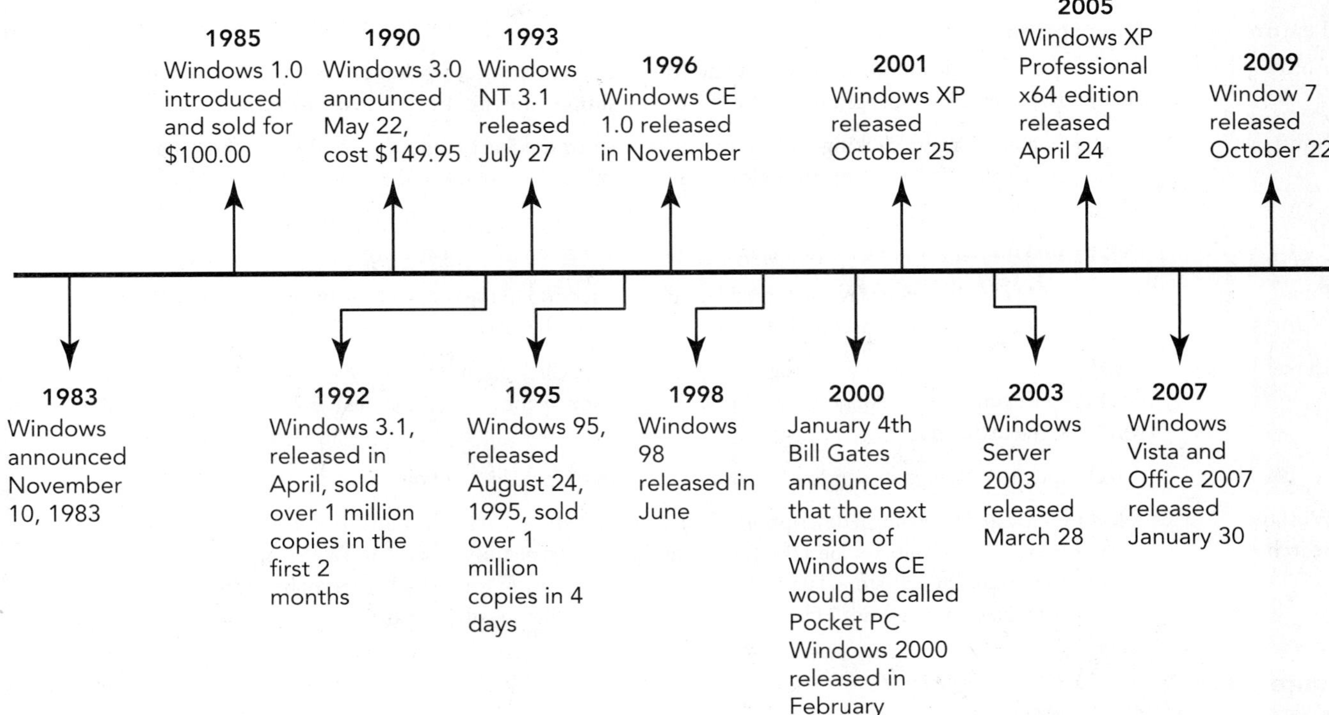
1985
Windows 1.0 introduced and sold for $100.00
1990
Windows 3.0 announced May 22, cost $149.95
1993
Windows NT 3.1 released July 27
1996
Windows CE 1.0 released in November
2001
Windows XP released October 25
2005
Windows XP Professional x64 edition released April 24
2009
Window 7 released October 22
1983
Windows announced November 10, 1983
1992
Windows 3.1, released in April, sold over 1 million copies in the first 2 months
1995
Windows 95, released August 24, 1995, sold over 1 million copies in 4 days
1998
Windows 98 released in June
2000
January 4th Bill Gates announced that the next version of Windows CE would be called Pocket PC Windows 2000 released in February
2003
Windows Server 2003 released March 28
2007
Windows Vista and Office 2007 released January 30

Windows 7 Editions

Edition	Features
Windows 7 Starter	Designed for small laptop computers. This edition must be preinstalled on systems and is not available for individual purchase.
Windows 7 Home Basic	This is the other *non-premium* edition and is available only in emerging markets, not in the United States, Canada, Europe, and other developed nations. It is more graphically interesting than Starter but lacks premium features like Windows Media Center.
Windows 7 Home Premium	This is the entry-level edition for most consumer PCs. It has the full Aero interface—translucent design, subtle animation, and additional colors—and includes Windows Media Center.
Windows 7 Professional	This is the preferred edition for businesses and advanced home users. It builds on Home Premium and runs a remote desktop server, encrypts files, and makes network folders available offline.
Windows 7 Enterprise	Enterprise and Ultimate editions have most of the same features, but the Enterprise edition is geared to companies and organizations that have users and systems to manage. It is available through volume licensing.
Windows 7 Ultimate	The Ultimate edition is for the high-end user, gamer, and multimedia professionals. It includes BitLocker disk encryption, which also works on USB flash drives.

Figure 1.30
SOURCE: http://www.winsupersite.com/article/windows-7/windows-7-product-editions-a-comparison

Windows 7 includes features to make using your system and its components simpler. See Figure 1.31 for an overview of some of these features.

The next version of Windows will include file download verification, a built-in PDF reader, a history vault that will take a snapshot of your entire hard drive and let you restore your system easily to a prior state, and multi-touch screen capability. Additionally, rather than requiring multiple versions for different devices, this next version of Windows will have a single version to run on all devices—laptops, tablets, and desktops.

Windows 7 Features That Make Using Your System Simpler

Feature	Description
Aero	A feature that enables subtle animations and translucent glass windows that can be custom colored. It also enables live previews of programs on the taskbar by simply moving the mouse over them.
Jump List	A list activated by right-clicking an icon on the taskbar or the Start menu. The options in the list are specific to the icon clicked. By selecting an option in the jump list, you are taken directly to that location.
Peek	A feature that makes all open windows transparent enabling you to see through them and view all icons and gadgets on your desktop. Point to the end of the taskbar to enable this feature.
Pin	The action of dragging your favorite program from the desktop to the taskbar or Start menu. Removing it from the taskbar or Start menu is accomplished by dragging it off the taskbar.
Shake	A way to focus on only one window on a cluttered desktop. Click on the title bar of the window you want to focus on and shake your mouse. All other windows, except the one your mouse is on, will disappear. To restore all windows, shake the mouse again.
Snap	A technique to resize open windows by dragging them to the edges of your screen.
Windows Search	A feature activated by typing a description of what you want to locate in the search box located at the bottom of the Start menu. The results will be a list of relevant documents, pictures, music, and e-mail that match your search term. Because most people store data on several devices, Windows 7 can search external hard drives, networked PCs, and libraries—a Windows 7 feature that groups related files together regardless of their storage location.

Figure 1.31
SOURCE: http://windows.microsoft.com/en-US/windows7/products/features

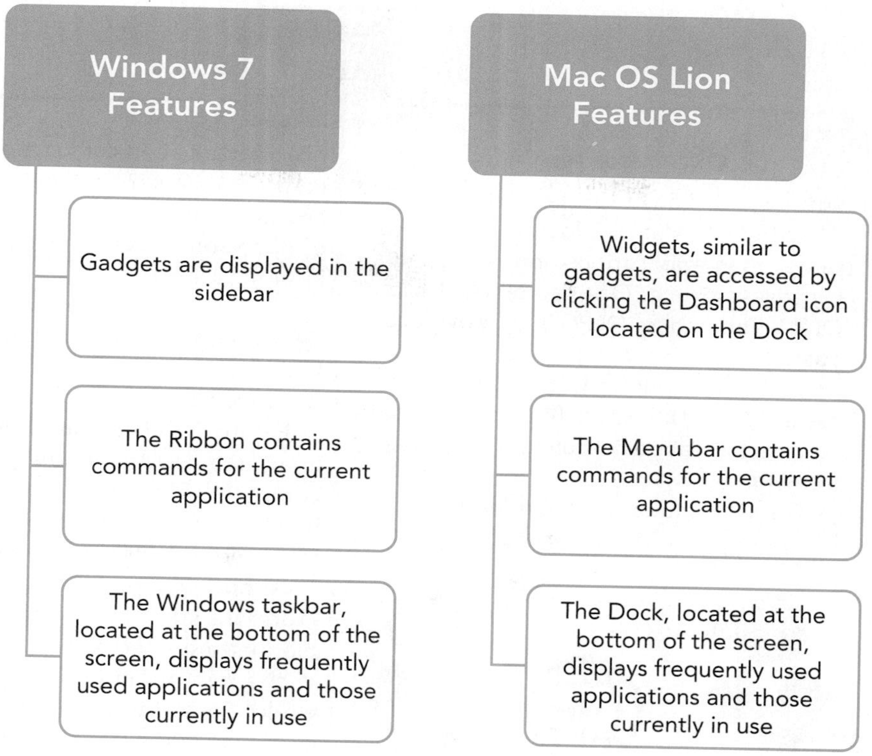

Windows 7 Features

- Gadgets are displayed in the sidebar
- The Ribbon contains commands for the current application
- The Windows taskbar, located at the bottom of the screen, displays frequently used applications and those currently in use

Mac OS Lion Features

- Widgets, similar to gadgets, are accessed by clicking the Dashboard icon located on the Dock
- The Menu bar contains commands for the current application
- The Dock, located at the bottom of the screen, displays frequently used applications and those currently in use

FIGURE 1.32 The Mac OS X interface and Windows 7 interface are very similar.

Concept 1.18 | Using MAC OS

The original Macintosh operating system, called ***Mac OS*** and released in 1984, was the first operating system to popularize the graphical user interface. Although Apple eventually lost market share to Microsoft, the Apple Macintosh has a large user base and they are avid fans of the system. Many people prefer the Mac OS for its stability and ease of use, although the interfaces of Macs and PCs are very similar (Figure 1.32). Operating systems for the Macintosh were numbered as Mac OS 8, Mac OS 9, and Mac OS X (X for the Roman numeral 10). Newer versions of Mac OS X have, in addition to their numeric identification, names associated with large cats. Mac OS v10.0 is Cheetah and Mac OS v10.6 is Snow Leopard. For a detailed explanation of Mac OS X, go to **www.apple.com/macosx/what-is/**.

Mac OS X Snow Leopard, released in 2009, occupies up to 50 percent less RAM than the previous version. It includes a more responsive Finder, a Put Back option to return deleted items to their original location, more reliable ejection of external drives, faster shut down and wake up, four new fonts, 80 percent faster Time Machine backup, increased Airport signal strength for wireless networks, and built-in support for Microsoft Exchange Server 2007.

Mac OS X Lion, Apple's newest operating system released in 2011, claims to have over 250 new features. Go to **http://www.apple.com/macosx/whats-new/features.html** to view details on this new and more intuitive operating system.

Concept 1.19 | Using Unix

UNIX is a pioneering operating system that was developed at AT&T's Bell Laboratories in 1969 and continues to define what an operating system should do and how it should work. Pronounced YOU-nix, it is a free operating system, defaults to a command line interface, features preemptive multitasking, and is installed primarily on workstations. An online tutorial on UNIX is available at **www.ee.surrey.ac.uk/Teaching/Unix**.

Concept 1.20 | Using Linux

In 1991, Finnish university student Linus Torvalds introduced ***Linux***, a freeware operating system for personal computers. Linux is ***open source software***, meaning that its source code—the code of the program itself—is available for you to see and use. Users of open source software are invited to scrutinize the source code for errors and to share their discoveries with the software's publisher.

One Laptop per Child

Sugar is a version of Linux developed by the company Red Hat that focuses on activities rather than applications and is used in an initiative known as One Laptop per Child or OLPC. The goal of OLPC is to provide low-cost, low-power, rugged and connected notebook computers to the world's poorest children. The aim is to encourage self-discovery, collaboration, and self-empowered learning.

The OLPC idea was founded by Nicholas Negroponte and others associated with MIT Media Lab in conjunction with several corporate partners including Google, AMD, and Red Hat—one of the largest providers of open source solutions. There is inequity in computer equipment and computer-related knowledge between developed, developing, and underdeveloped nations. Initiatives such as OLPC attempt to close this gap.

FIGURE 1.33 Simple images make navigation easy and language neutral.

Figure 1.33 illustrates some of the first images a child will see using an OLPC computer. The letter X with an O on top is symbolic of a man; other symbols stand for home, friends, and community.

Although support for OLPC is strong, there are still some obstacles, for example, getting Internet connectivity to some of the remote and poorer regions of the world. Some say that without Internet accessibility in the poorest regions, the computers given to the children will not close the knowledge gap. Instead, they say the project will increase toxic waste due to discarded computers that either do not work or are in need of repair. What do you think?

Three things make Linux desirable: It is powerful, runs on all computers, and is free. Linux brings to the PC many features similar to those found in commercial versions of UNIX, including multitasking, virtual memory, Internet support, and a GUI. Although Linux is powerful and free, some versions are proprietary or are available for a fee. Because Linux is not a commercial product with a single stable company behind it, many corporate chief information officers do not want to adopt it to manage their systems and users. For the latest in Linux news and developments, visit Linux Today at **www.linuxtoday.com**. Linux beginners can get assistance at **www.justlinux.com**.

Concept 1.21 | Comparing Windows, MAC OS, and Linux

Traditionally, computer users have had two major platforms to choose from—a Mac or a PC. Your system's ***platform*** is determined by the combination of microprocessor chip and installed operating system. Depending on which operating system is loaded, your system is simply referred to as a Mac or a PC.

As the Linux operating system becomes more popular, some people may want to consider this third alternative.

Linux can be installed on a Mac or a PC, and because it is open source software, cost is not an issue. Additionally, because very few types of malware are targeted at Linux systems, they are more secure. Casual computer users are unlikely to use a Linux system because it lacks a structured computer support system and because setting up and maintaining a Linux system requires a higher level of computer knowledge.

PCs still dominate in both consumer and business use, have the largest portion of the market, are the choice of corporate America, and tend to be cheaper in terms of both hardware and software. There is also a much larger selection of software products to choose from for PCs than there is for Mac or Linux systems. In recent years, Apple, through its humorous *I am a Mac, I am a PC* commercials, has tried to move PC users to Macs by promoting the idea that Macs are easier to use. Figure 1.34 illustrates differences in the use of the three main operating systems as of May 2011.

Concept 1.22 | Understanding Server Operating Systems

Server operating systems are operating systems installed on the server computer of a network and designed with specific instructions for delivering programs and data over the network. Normally they are complete operating systems with a file and task manager. Additional features like a Web server, directory services, and a messaging system are often included.

Microsoft Windows Server 2008 is an upgrade to Microsoft Windows Server 2003 and is the most current version of a sophisticated operating system specifically designed to support client/server computing systems in an enterprise environment. Servers are special computers used to manage resources on a network, including printers, file storage, and Web sites.

Other server operating systems include:

- UNIX and Linux, which are also categorized in the standalone section. They are referred to as multipurpose operating systems because they fall into both categories.
- Netware by Novell, which is a client/server system that manages concurrent requests from clients and provides the security needed in a multiuser environment.
- Solaris, a version of UNIX developed by Sun Microsystems and designed for networks using e-commerce applications. Solaris is known for its scalability—the ability to expand.
- Mac OS X Server, by Apple, supports an unlimited number of users and is suitable for big companies and IT departments as well as small businesses and retail stores.

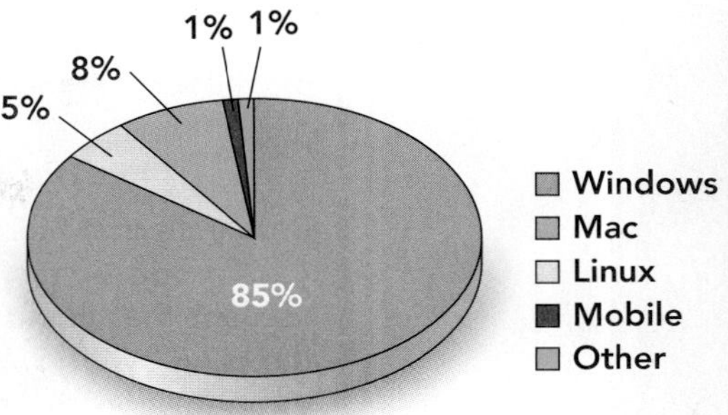

FIGURE 1.34 Windows operating systems dominate the market, with Mac OS X and Linux quite a distance behind.

SOURCE: http://www.w3schools.com/browsers/browsers_os.asp

Concept 1.23 | Understanding Embedded Operating Systems

Embedded operating systems are specialized operating systems designed for specific applications. They are usually very compact and efficient. They also eliminate many features that non-embedded computer operating systems provide because the specialized application has no need for them. PDAs, cell phones, point-of-sale devices, DVDs, industrial robot controls, and even modern toasters that control the temperature based on bread type are examples of devices that contain embedded systems (Figure 1.35). Some of the more common embedded operating systems installed on handheld devices are Microsoft Windows Mobile, Windows CE, Palm OS, Android, and iPhone OS.

From either the Companion Web Site or MyITLab, try the Chapter 1 System Software Simulation

FIGURE 1.35 Embedded operating systems are found in devices that you use every day. How many more devices can you identify?

FAST FORWARD

The Bionic Eye

Researchers at Bionic Vision Australia (BVA) have produced a prototype of a bionic eye implant that could bring limited vision to the blind by 2013. With the Australian government contributing $40 million to the research, the timeframe and continual improvements on the prototype look promising. Here is how the system works:

- A camera is mounted on top of a pair of glasses.
- The images are sent to a small processor housed in a unit about the size of a cell phone and carried by the individual.
- The processor, with the help of an embedded operating system, sends a condensed image to the chip directly implanted onto the retina.
- The chip stimulates the visual neurons that, in turn, send rough images to the brain for processing.

The challenge in the bionic eye is not to get the signals to the brain—that has been accomplished—but to improve the resolution and detail of that signal (Figure 1.36). The implication for visually impaired individuals is beyond anything ever hoped for. What are some of the possible applications for those of us with sight? Think about having text magnified without a magnifying glass, shading your eyes from bright light without having to wear sunglasses, and Mom actually having eyes in the back of her head. Although the immediate excitement is sight for the blind, who cannot help but take that glimpse into the future?

© Dmitriy Kiryushchenkov/Shutterstock

FIGURE 1.36 There are several variations of a bionic eye implant currently under development.

Designed for smartphones and PDAs, ***Microsoft Windows Mobile*** provides a user interface for simplified versions of Windows programs, such as Microsoft's own Office applications. You can create documents on the go and then transfer them to a desktop computer for further processing and printing. Personal information management tools, such as a calendar and address book, along with an e-mail client and a Web browser are included along with support for handwriting recognition and voice recording. Windows Mobile version 6.x will not be upgraded. Rather, it

FIGURE 1.37 Users of the iPhone like the iOS for its quick response and multi-tasking capability.

has been superseded by ***Windows Phone 7***, a mobile operating system designed for both the consumer and the business market. It has the ability to combine calendars into one color-coded image, run Microsoft Office and Xbox Live, and use a single stroke to send an e-mail.

Windows Embedded Compact, one of the early embedded operating systems, was introduced in 1996 as Windows CE. Used by consumer electronic devices like handheld PCs, video game players, digital cameras, and industrial products like barcode readers, it is characterized by low overhead device drivers and a built-in power manager.

The ***Palm OS*** was initially developed by Palm Inc. for personal digital assistants (PDAs) in 1996. It was designed to use with a touch screen running a graphical user interface and comes with a suite of personal information management applications. The most current versions power smartphones like the Palm Pixi that runs on the Palm webOS platform and responds to a multi-touch screen and natural gestures.

Google released an operating system for mobile devices, ***Android 2.2***, in 2011. The operating system supports CDMA—Code Division Multiple Access—and provides a higher screen resolution. Supporting CDMA enables carriers such as Verizon to sell Android phones. Android phones use a touch-screen scroll system with which you can scroll to the left and right, creating the same three divisions—left, center, and right—on your portable device that you have on a computer monitor.

Apple's iPhone uses ***iOS*** (Figure 1.37). A new version of this popular operating system, iOS 5.0, was released in 2011. Some features of the current version include:

- Genius Mixes: Automatically generated music mixes based on what types of music are already in your library
- Genius Recommendations: Suggestions for applications—referred to as apps—based on those you have already downloaded
- Saving video from mail and MMS: Multimedia message service—directly into Camera Roll
- Save as New Clip option: Enables you to keep your original video and save the new version when trimming a video on the iPhone 4Gs

Objective 5 | Use System Utilities

In your job as a freelance Interior Designer, you have noticed that your desktop computer system seems slow while performing tasks like saving a document and multitasking. You have been too busy to perform a backup and virus check like a friend recommended. As the lead designer on this project, you have the final version of many of the developed designs. You must back up, check for viruses, and defragment your hard disk. Where do you start?

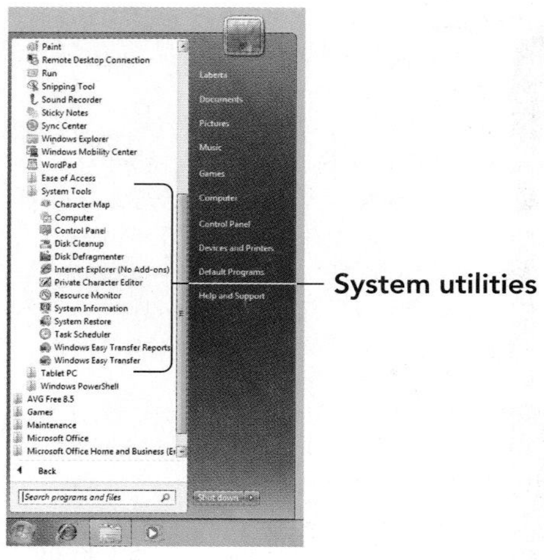

FIGURE 1.38 Some utilities run only when selected; others can be programmed to run on a regular schedule.

System utilities—also called utility programs—are programs that work in tandem with the operating system and perform services that keep the computer system running smoothly. Sometimes these programs are included in the operating system; sometimes you must purchase them from other software vendors. They include programs that perform such tasks as:

- Backing up system and application files
- Providing antivirus protection
- Searching for and managing files
- Scanning and defragmenting disks and files
- Compressing files so that they take up less space on storage media
- Providing additional accessibility utilities to meet the needs of individuals with special needs

You can access these utilities by opening the Start menu, selecting All Programs, selecting Accessories, and then from the Accessories submenu, selecting System Tools (Figure 1.38). Or, on the Start menu, click Control Panel, and then click System and Security.

Concept 1.24 | Using Backup Software

Backup software copies data from the computer's hard disk to backup devices such as flash drives, CDs, DVDs, an external hard drive, or an online storage location. Using backup software is an essential part of safe, efficient computer use. If your hard disk fails, you can recover your data from the backup disk you create with this utility (Figure 1.39).

FIGURE 1.39 Backing up applications and data is an important part of maintaining a viable computer system. You can guarantee that backups are performed on a regular schedule if you use the automatic backup feature in Windows 7.

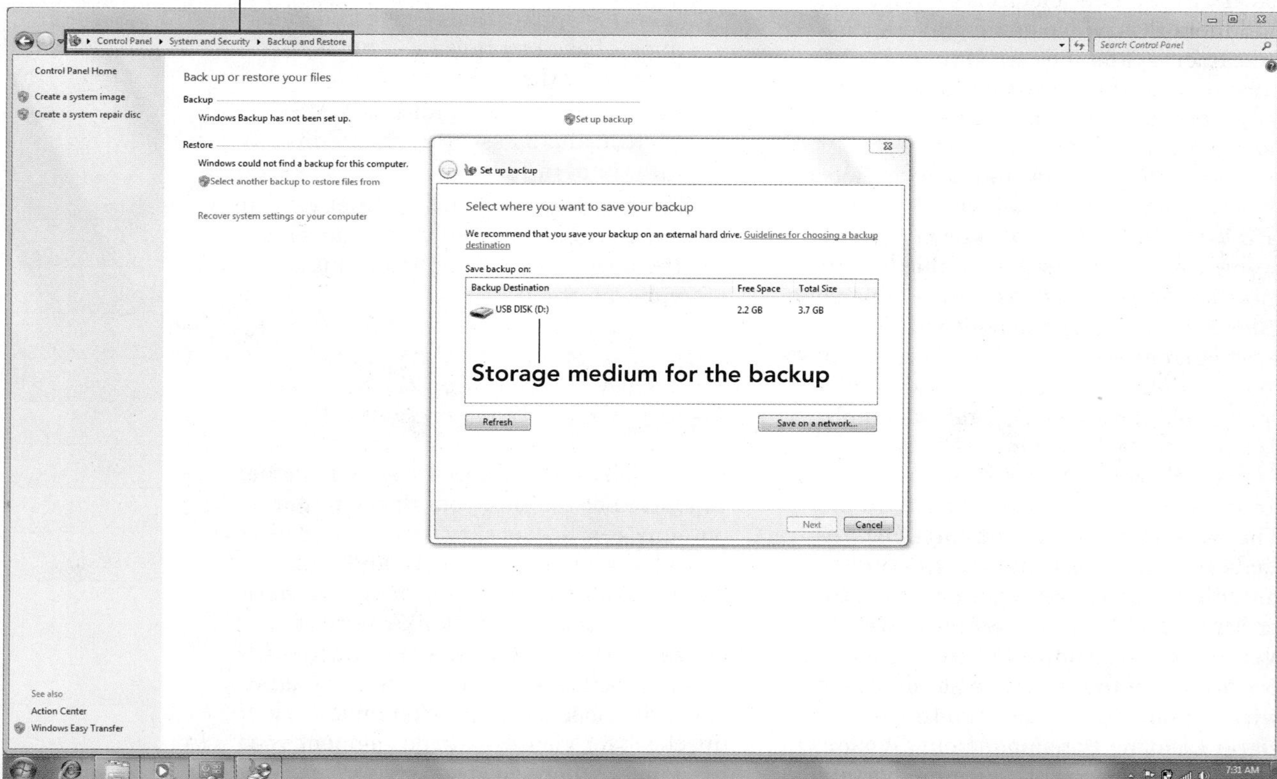

Backup software can run a ***full backup***, which includes all files and data on the entire hard disk, or an ***incremental backup***. In an incremental backup, the backup software copies only those files that have been created or changed since the last backup occurred.

Drive imaging software goes beyond backups and creates a mirror image of the entire hard disk—including the operating system and applications, as well as all files and data. In the event of a hard disk or computer system failure, you can use the drive image to restore the entire system. Windows 7 provides a solid and simple drive imaging solution but lacks some features of other independent programs. You will be asked to set the destination storage device—a hard drive, DVD, or a network drive. A brief wizard walks you through the necessary steps.

Concept 1.25 | Using Antivirus Software

Antivirus software protects a computer from computer viruses. Such software uses a pattern-matching technique that examines all of the files on a disk looking for virus code *signatures*. One limitation of such programs is that they can detect only those viruses whose signatures are in their databases. If your system becomes infected by a virus that is not in the system's database, the virus may not be detected. Because of this shortcoming, many antivirus programs now include programs that monitor system functions to detect abnormal behavior and stop the destructive activities of unknown viruses before they start. Microsoft Security Essentials is a free antivirus program that provides real-time protection against viruses, spyware, and other malicious software without slowing down your system.

Concept 1.26 | Searching for and Managing Files

Another important system utility is the ***file manager***, a program that helps you organize and manage the data stored on your disk. The file manager enables you to perform operations on the files and folders created on your computer's storage devices. For example, you can use a file manager to make copies of your files, manage how and where they are stored, and delete unwanted files. Operating systems usually come with a file manager program. Windows 7 and Vista use Windows Explorer and Mac OS X uses Finder.

On a large hard disk with thousands of files, the task of finding a needed file can be time consuming and frustrating if you try to do it manually. For this reason, most operating systems include a ***search utility***, with which you can search an entire hard disk or any indexed network storage device for a file. In Microsoft Windows, search is integrated into every Windows Explorer window. Here you can query for files in a number of ways, including by name, date, and size. The Spotlight utility in the Mac OS performs similar tasks.

Concept 1.27 | Scanning and Defragmenting Disks

A ***disk scanning program***, also known as an error checking program, can detect and resolve physical and logical problems that can occur when your computer stores files on a disk. The Mac OS X scanning utility is called Disk Utility. One physical problem that a scanning program might detect involves an irregularity on the disk's surface that results in a ***bad sector***—a portion of the disk that is unable to store data reliably. The scanning program marks and locks out the bad sector so that it is no longer usable.

A ***disk cleanup utility*** differs from a disk scanning program in that it does not correct any problems. Instead, it improves system performance and increases storage space by removing files that you no longer need. Without your knowledge, some programs create temporary files on the hard drive to perform actions that improve the performance of the program. These files are automatically removed when the program is properly closed. A power outage can cause these files to remain on your hard drive and waste valuable storage space. A disk cleanup utility will search for and delete these unusable files along with any files in the Recycle Bin.

As you use your computer, it creates and erases files on the hard disk. The result is that the disk soon becomes a patchwork of files, with portions of files stored in different places. This slows disk access because the system must look in several locations to find all of a file's segments. A disk with data scattered around in this way is referred to

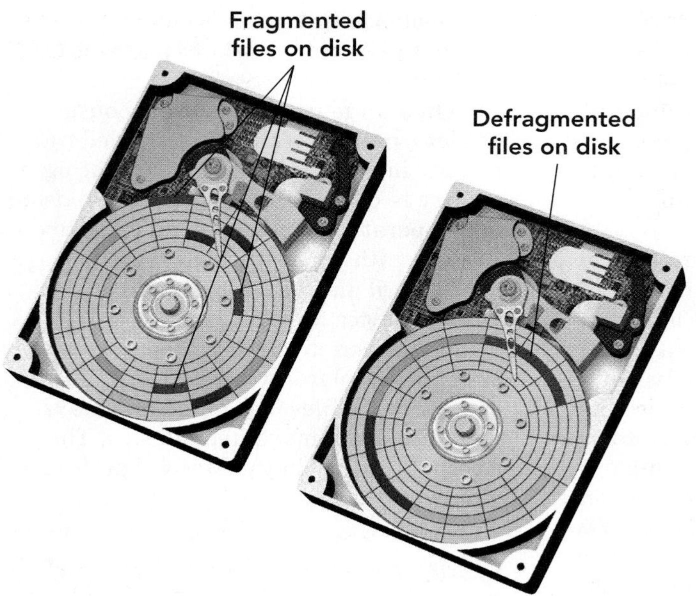

FIGURE 1.40 The defragmentation process repositions the sectors of a file into adjacent locations.

as being ***fragmented. Disk defragmentation programs*** are utility programs that reorganize data on the disk so that file pieces are reassembled as one chunk of disk space, which decreases disk search time (Figure 1.40).

From either the Companion Web Site or MyITLab, watch Chapter 1 Video 1

Concept 1.28 | Using File Compression Utilities

Most downloadable software is compressed. A ***file compression utility*** enables the exchange of programs and data efficiently by reducing the size of a file by as much as 80 percent without harming the data. Most file compression utilities work by searching the file for frequently repeated but lengthy data patterns and then substituting short codes for these patterns. Compression enables faster downloads, but you must decompress a file after downloading it. When the file is decompressed, the utility restores the lengthier pattern where each short code is encountered. Both compressed and decompressed files can be saved and opened on a computer system, but a file must be decompressed prior to use if changes that are made to that file are to be saved.

Most compression utilities also can create archives. An ***archive*** is a single file that contains two or more files stored in a compressed format along with additional information about each file—like the name and file lengths—so that proper reconstruction is possible. Archives are convenient for storage as well as file-exchange purposes because as many as several hundred separate files can be stored in a single archive unit. To edit and save the changes to any file in the archived packet, you must first restore the packet to its original format.

To compress—also known as zip—a file or folder in Windows 7 or Vista, right-click it and choose Send to Compressed, also called zipped, folder. This action creates a new zipped file with the same file name. There are several ways to decompress, or unzip, a zipped file. One way is to double-click the file and use the Extract all files button. Another way is to right-click the zipped file and click Extract All.

Concept 1.29 | Using Accessibility Utilities

Accessibility utilities make computing easier for individuals with special needs. Windows 7 includes the following utilities, which are accessible from the Control Panel in the Ease of Access category:

- Magnifier: Increases the size of a portion of the screen to make reading easier for the visually impaired
- On-Screen Keyboard: A keyboard that displays on the screen that you can then use by clicking the mouse on desired keys

- Speech Recognition: A program with which you can use your voice to control your computer and dictate documents
- Narrator: A basic speech program that reads aloud everything on the screen

Concept 1.30 | Performing a System Update

Microsoft provides an operating system update service called ***Windows Update*** that keeps your operating system up to date with fixes—also called service packs—and protections against external environment changes. If you are using Windows 7, you can ensure that your operating system is current by opening the Control Panel's System and Security category, clicking Windows Update, and setting Windows Update to automatically download and install updates at a time of your choosing. You can also get more information at Microsoft's Security at Home page at **www.microsoft.com/protect**.

Besides system utilities, there are additional ways to safeguard your data or take care of operating problems.

Concept 1.31 | Troubleshooting a Computer

Everyone experiences computer problems once in a while. Review the following problems and possible causes that can help you solve many common problems:

- If your computer fails to start normally, you may be able to get it running by inserting a ***boot disk***—also called an emergency disk. The boot disk is a storage device, like a USB drive, CD, DVD, or network device, which in case of an emergency or boot failure, can load a reduced version of the operating system for troubleshooting purposes. Consult the documentation that came with your computer on how to create a boot disk.
- When you have finished using the computer, be sure to shut it down properly. Do not just switch off the power.
- In Microsoft Windows, you might encounter a configuration problem that typically arises after you add a new peripheral device such as an external hard drive or new printer to your system. Such additions might cause conflicts that could interfere in the boot cycle. Conflicts can often be resolved by starting the computer in Windows ***safe mode***, an operating mode in which Windows loads a minimal set of drivers that are known to function correctly. Within safe mode, you can use the Control Panel to determine which devices are causing the problem. You access safe mode by pressing the F8 key repeatedly during the startup process—before the Windows screen with the logo displays. Safe mode will reset or report any conflicting programs or device drivers. After the reset is complete, shut down the system, boot up normally, and then correct any conflicts that were not reset in safe mode (Figure 1.41).

It is exciting to purchase a new computer. Understanding the processing cycle, the installed operating system, and utility programs will help you to keep it running smoothly. You will be able to maximize your systems capabilities, eliminate down time, and overall be more productive.

Check Your Knowledge: From either the Companion Web Site or MyITLab, take the quiz covering Objectives 3, 4, and 5

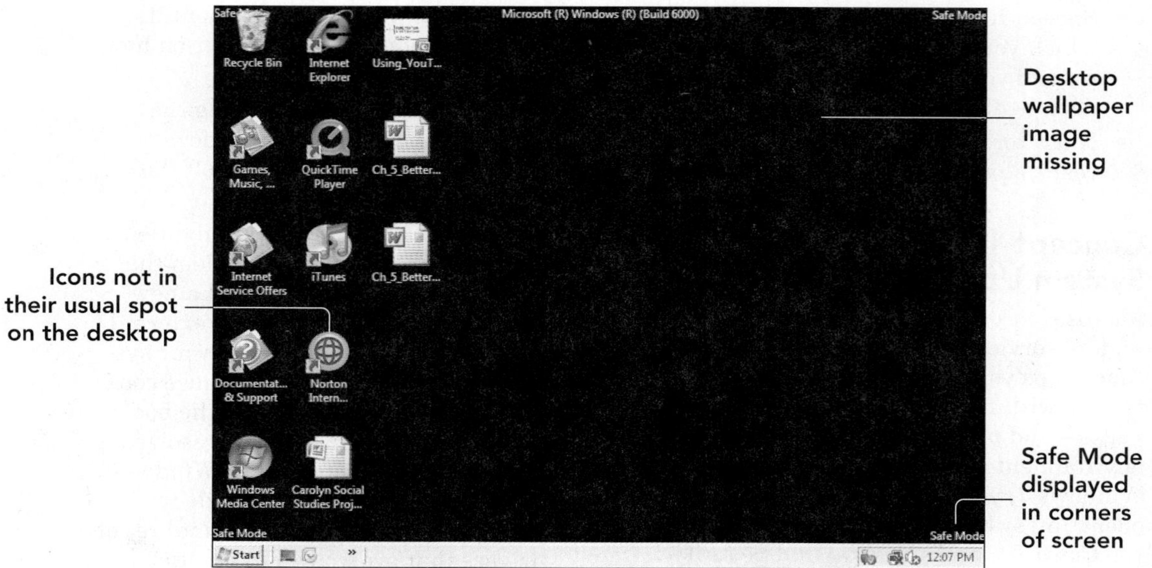

FIGURE 1.41 An error during the boot process may cause your system to open in safe mode, where some settings may be adjusted. To exit safe mode, shut down your computer and then restart the system.

Chapter Summary

Computer History, Fundamentals, and Operating Systems

- A computer system is an electronic device along with a collection of related components that perform the information processing cycle: input, processing, output, and storage.
- A system includes both hardware—the physical components such as the system unit, keyboard, monitor, and speakers—and software—the programs that run on it.
- In a typical computer system, a keyboard and a mouse provide input capabilities. Processing is done by the microprocessor (CPU) on programs and data held in RAM (random access memory). You see the output on a monitor or printer, and a hard disk is typically used for long-term storage.
- System software has two major components: (1) the operating system and (2) system utilities. The operating system coordinates the functions of the computer's hardware and provides support for running application software. System utilities provide such features as backup, defragmentation, and file compression.
- An operating system acts as an interface between you and the computer's hardware. Its five basic functions are starting the computer, managing applications, managing memory, coordinating tasks, and providing a means of communicating with you.
- When you start or restart a computer, it reloads the operating system into the computer's memory. A computer goes through six steps at startup: loading the BIOS, performing the power-on self-test, loading the operating system, configuring the system, loading system utilities, and authenticating users.
- The three major types of user interfaces are graphical user interfaces (GUIs), menu-driven user interfaces, and command line user interfaces.
- Operating systems fall into three categories: standalone, server, and embedded. A standalone system does not need to be connected to any other system or computer to run. A server system, on the other hand, works in a network with other units and peripherals. Embedded operating systems are not designed for general purposes but rather for the specific conditions and actions of the device that they are embedded within.
- The major strength of Microsoft's Windows operating system is that it has dominated the market for more than 15 years and is installed and maintained on approximately 90 percent of the personal computers in the world.
- Essential system utilities include backup software, antivirus software, a file manager, search tools, file compression utilities, disk scanning programs, disk defragmentation programs, and ease of access utilities for those with special needs. Additionally, features like Windows Update keep your operating system up to date with fixes—service packs—or protections against external environment changes. These features are also available for a Mac in the Mac OS X Toolbox or the Utilities folder.

Key Terms and Concepts

Matching

Match each term in the second column with its correct definition in the first column by writing the letter of the term on the blank line in front of the correct definition.

_____ 1. The computer component that acts as the brain of the computer by controlling all the functions performed by the other components, and processes all the commands it receives from software.

_____ 2. The process of starting a computer that is not already on.

_____ 3. Fixed size units of data used to swap content between RAM and virtual memory.

_____ 4. The hardware component containing electronics to connect the computer to the network.

_____ 5. A feature that enables compatible devices to be automatically detected.

_____ 6. The process of restarting a computer that is already on.

_____ 7. Software that makes a copy of all files and data on an entire hard disk.

_____ 8. A sequence of instructions that a computer uses to perform a task.

_____ 9. A communications device that converts data from one form into another.

_____ 10. High-speed temporary memory located on the motherboard that holds programs and data in use.

_____ 11. The term that describes a computer as the combination of the operating system and the processor.

_____ 12. A computer program that manages all the other programs on your computer, stores files in an organized manner, and coordinates the use of the computer hardware such as the keyboard and mouse.

_____ 13. A process to reposition file sectors in adjacent locations on a hard disk.

_____ 14. Computer software that your computer uses to accomplish specific tasks like word processing or accounting.

_____ 15. The central part of the operating system that resides in RAM.

A Application software
B Backup software
C Cold boot
D CPU
E Disk defragmentation
F Kernel
G Modem
H Network interface card
I Operating system
J Pages
K Platform
L Plug-and-play (PnP)
M Random access memory (RAM)
N Software
O Warm boot

Multiple Choice

Circle the correct answer:

1. A monitor and printer are examples of:
   A. input devices **B**. storage devices
   C. output devices
2. The circuit board within the system unit to which all other system components are anchored is the:
   A. platform **B**. NIC
   C. motherboard
3. The operating system and system utilities are referred to collectively as:
   A. application software **B**. system software
   C. backup software
4. A record of your preferences for the desktop theme, icons, and menu styles is referred to as your:
   A. account **B**. profile
   C. platform
5. Documents waiting to be printed are stored temporarily in an area of random access memory referred to as the:
   A. swap file **B**. print queue
   C. buffer
6. A technique that uses a portion of the computer's hard disk as an extension of RAM is called:
   A. virtual memory **B**. paging
   C. multitasking
7. Programs that contain specific instructions to allow a particular brand and model of input or output device to communicate and function properly with the operating system is called a:
   A. device driver **B**. user interface
   C. operating system
8. The program that organizes and manages the data stored on your hard disk and portable storage devices is the:
   A. disk cleanup utility **B**. search utility
   C. file manager
9. The term used to refer to a disk with scattered data is:
   A. thrashed **B**. defragmented
   C. fragmented
10. A program that reduces the size of a file by as much as 80 percent without harming the data is a:
    A. search utility **B**. file compression utility
    C. disk cleanup utility

Teamwork

1. **I am a Mac, and I am a PC** As a team, use a search engine to locate and review three of the *I am a Mac, and I am a PC* commercials. These 30-second commercials praise the features of the Mac while mocking the PC. Cite the commercials viewed. Use a word processor to develop the dialog for a new 30-second commercial that will reverse the ad: Have the commercial support the PC while mocking the Mac. Your team must research both systems to find a PC asset that the Mac lacks. Rehearse your commercial and share it with your class.
2. **Operating Systems** As a team, research three operating systems presented in this chapter. Create a table in Word or Excel and compare the basic functions of each. What future improvements in each operating system can you envision or do you see as essential? If you have used several versions of the same operating system, what improvements were incorporated? Present your comparison table and answers to the questions above in a one-page, double-spaced report.
3. **Using System Tools** As a team, in Windows 7 research three of the system tools found in the System Tools folder located in the Accessories option of the Start menu. Divide into groups of two or three, and have each group select a tool that was *not* covered in detail in this chapter. Investigate the purpose of the tool and any options necessary to set the tool. What will be the effect of using this tool on your system? Use the tool yourself and evaluate its performance and results. Regroup and, as a team, combine your information on the three system tools into a one-page, double-spaced report.

On the Web

1. **Input Hardware Trends** Use your favorite search engine to locate information on the Luxeed Dynamic Pixel LED keyboard, virtual laser keyboards, and variations of ergonomic keyboards. In a one-page, double-spaced paper, summarize your findings. Include the new or unusual features of each device, a summary of two online reviews, and your opinion of each input device.
2. **Examine Deep Freeze** Many college computer labs use the Deep Freeze program. Research this product and in a one-page, double-spaced report, explain how this program produces a safer computer experience for students. Indicate what this program does to protect the operating system and system utilities from change.
3. **Antivirus Programs** Research three antivirus software programs discussed in this chapter. In a Word document, list four features that all three programs have in common. Below this list, identify one feature unique to each program. Locate the home page of the three programs, and include a list of the program name, URL, operating systems with which the program works, the current version, and the price.

Ethics and Social Media

1. **Ten Commandments of Computer Ethics** Use a search engine to locate the *Ten Commandments of Computer Ethics* published by the Computer Ethics Institute. Read each one, and in a one-page paper, indicate three commandments with which you agree and three with which you disagree. Give logical and historical reasons for your opinions. You might want to reference the Bill of Rights or other historical documents to support your position. Cite your references and present your opinions in a one-page, double-spaced report.
2. **Social Media Uses** Create a short survey of eight questions regarding the use of social media and the consequences of using social media—good and bad. Try to construct a question that will enable you to determine why individuals use social media. Construct another question to determine if respondents were ever prevented from obtaining a job because of their inappropriate use of social media. Distribute your survey to 25 individuals, and when doing so, attempt to get a range of ages, employment experience, and a mix of males and females. Compile your results in an Excel spreadsheet and share your results and conclusions with your class.

Sources

http://www.businessandleadership.com/marketing/item/12650-us-ecommerce-sales-growth-f

www.computerhope.com/history

www.salary.com

http://www1.salary.com/Help-Desk-Support-salary.htmltml

http://swz.salary.com/SalaryWizard/Project-Manager-II-Salary-Details.aspx

http://www.physorg.com/news186046477.html

http://windows.microsoft.com/en-US/windows7/products/compare

http://www.winsupersite.com/article/windows-7/windows-7-product-editions-a-comparison

http://windows.microsoft.com/en-US/windows7/products/features

http://health.howstuffworks.com/medicine/modern-technology/bionic-eye.htm

Use Windows 7 to Manage Files and Programs and to Browse the Internet

OUTCOMES

At the end of this chapter you will be able to:

OBJECTIVES

Mastering these objectives will enable you to:

PROJECT 2A
Create folders, create and save files, download and save files from the Web, and manage your programs using Windows 7.

1. Create a New Folder and Save a File on a Removable Storage Device (p. 39)
2. Download and Save Files from the Web (p. 48)
3. Display Libraries, Folders, and Files in a Window (p. 49)
4. Start Programs and Open Data Files (p. 53)
5. Manage the Display of Individual and Multiple Windows (p. 55)

PROJECT 2B
Copy, move, and manage your computer files using Windows Explorer.

6. Copy Files from a Removable Storage Device to the Hard Disk Drive (p. 61)
7. Navigate by Using Windows Explorer (p. 62)
8. Create, Name, and Save Files (p. 64)
9. Create Folders and Rename Folders and Files (p. 66)
10. Select, Copy, and Move Files and Folders (p. 67)

PROJECT 2C
Browse and search the Internet efficiently, print and save Web information, and manage your browsing history.

11. Search the Internet (p. 72)
12. Use Tabbed Browsing (p. 72)
13. Organize Favorites (p. 77)
14. Print Web Pages (p. 79)

Job Focus: Freelance Interior Designer

In This Chapter

In this chapter, you will experience how a freelance Interior Designer uses Windows 7 to organize and manage her computer files and to use the programs on her computer. You will also learn how to search the Internet efficiently to find information necessary for serving clients.

At the end of this Unit, following Chapter 3, you will have an opportunity to complete a case project that focuses on the job of a freelance Interior Designer.

Project 2A Using Windows 7

Project Activities

In Activities 2.01 through 2.11, you will participate in training along with Barbara Ramos, a freelance Interior Designer, who is working on a project at the Boston headquarters office of the Bell Orchid Hotels. After completing these activities, you will be able to create folders and save files on a removable storage device, open and use application programs, open data files, manage multiple windows on your desktop, and locate files and folders on your computer system. Your screen snips will look similar to Figure 2.1.

Project Files

For Project 2A, you will need the following files:

A flash drive containing the student data files for this textbook, which you will download from the Pearson Web site in Activity 2.04 or that you will obtain from your instructor

You will save your files as:

Lastname_Firstname_2A_USB_Snip
Lastname_Firstname_2A_Grouped_Snip
Lastname_Firstname_2A_WordPad_Snip
Lastname_Firstname_2A_SideBySide_Snip

Project Results

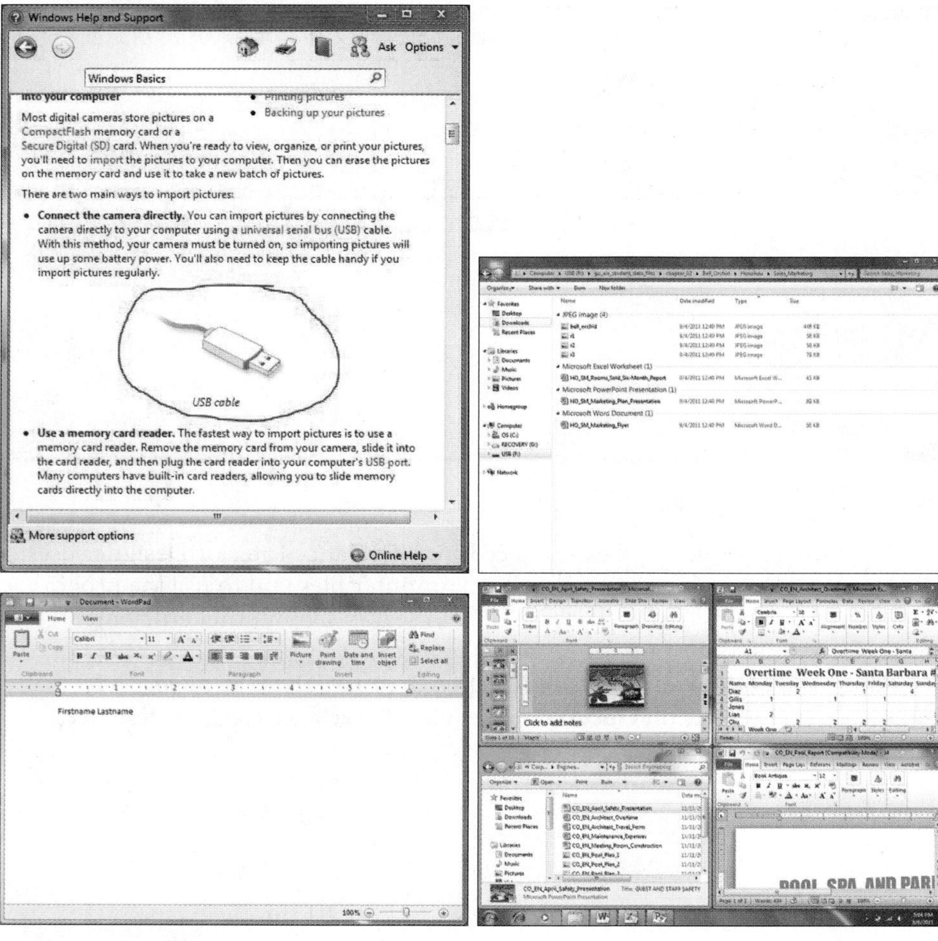

Figure 2.1
Project 2A Using Windows 7

Objective 1 | Create a New Folder and Save a File on a Removable Storage Device

A ***program*** is a set of instructions that a computer uses to accomplish a task, such as word processing, accounting, or data management. A program is also referred to as an ***application***.

Windows 7 is an ***operating system*** developed by Microsoft Corporation. An operating system is a computer program that manages all the other programs on your computer, stores files in an organized manner, allows you to use software programs, and coordinates the use of computer hardware such as the keyboard and mouse.

A ***file*** is a collection of information that is stored on a computer under a single name, for example, a text document, a picture, or a program. Every file is stored in a ***folder***—a container in which you store files—or a ***subfolder***, which is a folder within a folder. Windows 7 stores and organizes your files and folders, which is the primary task of an operating system.

> **Alert! | Variations in Screen Organization, Colors, and Functionality Are Common in Windows 7**
>
> Individuals and organizations can determine how Windows 7 displays; thus, the colors and the organization of various elements on the screen can vary. The basic functions and structure of Windows 7 are not changed by such variations. You can be confident that the skills you will practice in this textbook apply to Windows 7 regardless of available functionality or differences between the pictures in the book and your screen.

Activity 2.01 | Turning On Your Computer, Logging On to a Windows 7 User Account, and Exploring the Windows 7 Environment

In this activity, you will turn on your computer and log on to Windows 7. If you are the only user of your own computer, you can disable the logon process if you want to do so. In most organizations, you will be required to log on in some manner.

> **Note | Comparing Your Screen with the Figures in This Textbook**
>
> Your screen will more closely match the figures shown in this textbook if you set your screen resolution to 1024 × 768—this is optional. At other resolutions, your screen will closely resemble, but not match, the figures shown. To view your screen's resolution, on the desktop, right-click in a blank area, click Screen resolution, and then click the Resolution arrow. To adjust the resolution, move the slider to the desired setting, and then click OK.

1 If necessary, turn on your computer and monitor.

The Windows 7 screen displays and indicates the names and pictures associated with all active user accounts.

There are several editions of Windows 7. The editions you might see commonly in the United States are Home Premium, Professional, Ultimate, and Enterprise. For the tasks you complete day to day, all of the functionality exists in all of these editions.

2 If there are two or more users on the computer you are using, point to your user account name to display a glow effect, and then click your user account name or its associated picture. If necessary, type your password in the Password box, and then click the circled arrow to the right of the Password box—or press Enter.

> **Note | Differing Logon Procedures and Passwords**
>
> Depending on whether you are working on your own computer, in a college lab, or in an organization, your logon process may differ. If you have a different logon screen, log on as directed and move to Step 3 of this activity. On your own computer, use your own user account name and password. If no passwords are set on your computer and you do not need to log on, you are ready to begin Step 3.

3 Take a moment to compare your screen with Figure 2.2 and study the table in Figure 2.3.

Figure 2.2

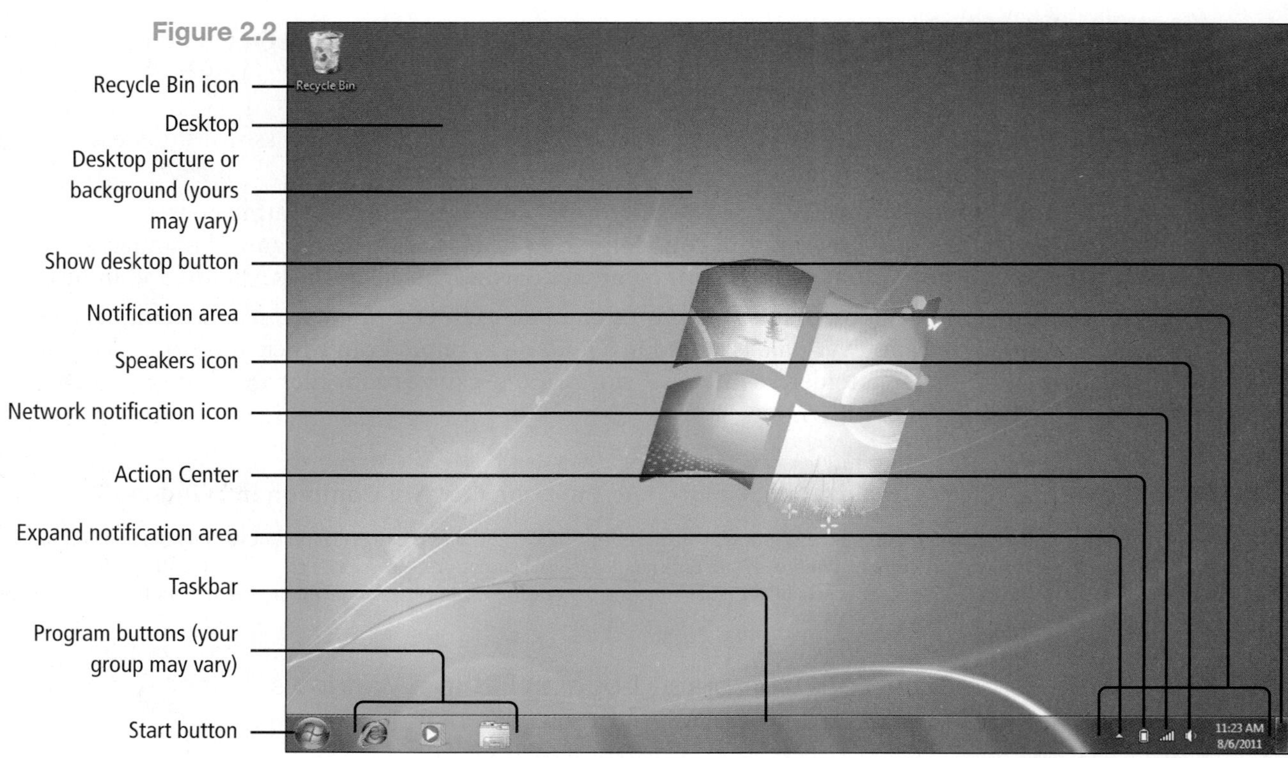

Parts of the Windows 7 Desktop	
Action Center icon in the notification area	Displays the Action Center, which is a central place to view alerts and take actions related to things that need your attention.
Desktop	Serves as a surface for your work, like the top of an actual desk, and is the main screen area that you see after you turn on your computer; here you can arrange ***icons***—small pictures that represent a file, folder, program, or other object—on the desktop such as shortcuts to programs, files, folders, and various types of documents.
Desktop background	Displays the colors and graphics of your desktop; you can change the desktop background to look the way you want it such as using a picture or a solid color. Also called ***wallpaper***.
Network notification icon	Displays the status of your network.
Notification area	Displays notification icons and the system clock and calendar; sometimes referred to as the ***system tray***.
Program buttons	Launch Internet Explorer, the Web browser included with Windows 7; Windows Explorer, the program that displays the files and folders on your computer; and Windows Media Player, the program that plays and organizes your digital media files.
Recycle Bin	Contains files and folders that you delete. When you delete a file or folder, it is not actually deleted; it stays in the Recycle Bin if you want it back, until you take action to empty the Recycle Bin.
Show desktop button	Displays the desktop by making any open windows transparent (when pointed to) or minimized (when clicked).
Speakers icon	Displays the status of your speakers (if any).
Start button	Displays the ***Start menu***—a list of choices that provides access to your computer's programs, folders, and settings.
Taskbar	Contains the Start button, optional program buttons, and buttons for all open programs; by default, it is located at the bottom of the desktop, but you can move it.

Figure 2.3

4 In the lower left corner of your screen, move the mouse pointer over—***point*** to—the **Start** button, and then ***click***—press the left button on your mouse pointing device—to display the **Start** menu.

The ***mouse pointer*** is any symbol that displays on your screen in response to moving your mouse.

The Start menu has three parts: The large left pane displays a list of some installed programs, which might be customized by your computer manufacturer, and the All Programs button. The Search box enables you to look for programs and files on your computer by typing search words in the box. The right pane provides access to commonly used folders, files, settings, and features, and an area where you can log off from Windows or shut down (turn off) your computer.

5 Compare your screen with Figure 2.4 and take a moment to study the parts of the **Start** menu described in the table in Figure 2.5.

In Figure 2.4, portions of the Start menu are transparent; for example, you can see parts of the desktop design behind the right pane of the Start menu. If your version of Windows 7 has this capability and it is enabled, and if your computer system's graphics hardware supports transparency, you might also notice this transparent effect.

Figure 2.4

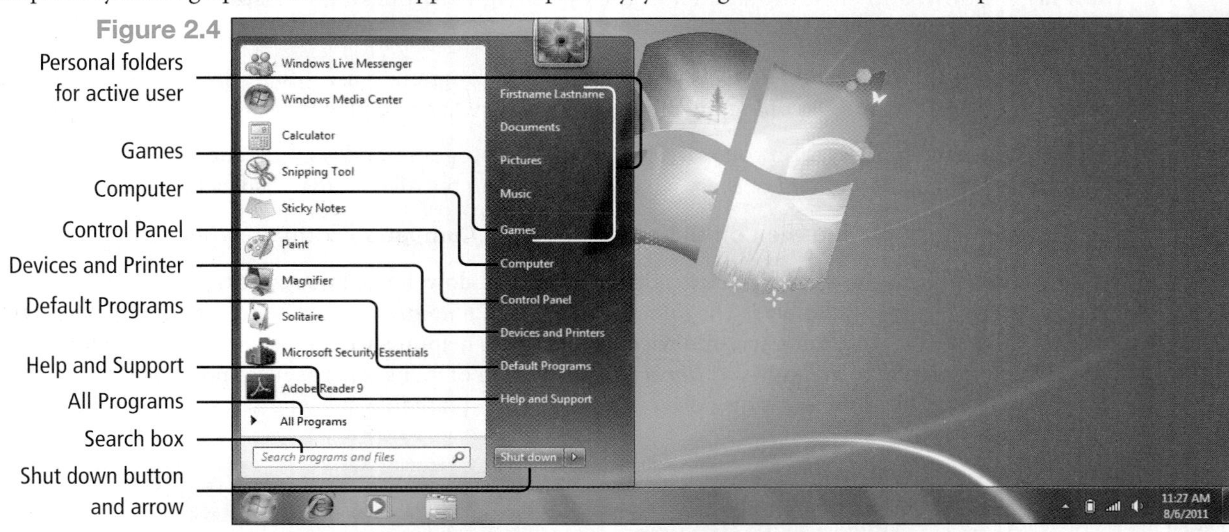

Parts of the Start Menu

All Programs	Displays all the programs on your computer system that are available to you; some groups of programs display in a folder.
Computer	Opens a window from which you can access disk drives, cameras, printers, scanners, and other hardware connected to your computer.
Control Panel	Opens the Control Panel, where you can customize the appearance and functionality of your computer, install or uninstall programs, set up network connections, and manage user accounts.
Default Programs	Opens a window where you can choose which program you want Windows 7 to use for activities such as Web browsing or photo viewing.
Devices and Printers	Displays a window where you can view information about the printer, mouse, and other devices installed on your computer.
Games	Opens the Games folder, from which you can access all of the games on your computer.
Help and Support	Opens Windows Help and Support, where you can browse and search Help topics about how to use Windows and your computer.
Personal folders	Displays, for the user currently logged on, the user account picture, personal folder, and the user's Documents, Music, Pictures, and Videos folders, the locations in which the user logged on would most likely store files.
Pinned programs	Displays programs, at the top above the menu separator, that you have ***pinned***—placed in a manner that remains until you remove it—to the Start menu because they are programs you use frequently (no pinned programs shown in this figure). Below the menu separator, Windows displays recently used programs or programs that Windows detects as those that you use frequently.
Search box	Searches your programs, personal folder, e-mail messages, saved instant messages, appointments, and contacts by typing search terms.
Shut down button and arrow	Turns off the computer; clicking the arrow displays a menu with additional options for switching users, logging off, restarting, or shutting down.

Figure 2.5

Activity 2.02 | Creating a New Folder on a Removable Storage Device

In this activity, you will create a new folder on a ***removable storage device***. Removable storage devices, such as a USB flash drive or a flash memory card, are commonly used to transfer information from one computer to another or when you want to work with your files on different computers. A ***drive*** is an area of storage that is formatted with a file system compatible with your operating system and is identified by a drive letter.

> **Alert! | Locate Your USB Flash Drive**
>
> You will need a USB flash drive to complete this activity.

1 Insert a USB flash drive into your computer. In the upper right corner of the **AutoPlay** window, **Close** the **AutoPlay** window, and click the small x in the upper right corner of any displayed message in the notification area.

AutoPlay is a Windows 7 feature that lets you choose which program to use to start different kinds of media, such as music CDs, or CDs and DVDs containing photos. It displays when you plug in or insert media or storage devices.

A ***window*** is a rectangular area on your screen that displays programs and content, and which can be moved, resized, minimized, or closed; the content of every window is different, but all windows display on the desktop.

2 Display the **Start** menu, and then on the right side, click **Computer**. Compare your screen with Figure 2.6.

The ***navigation pane*** is the area on the left side of a folder window; it displays Favorites, Libraries, and an expandable list of drives and folders. The ***folder window*** for *Computer* displays. A folder window displays the contents of the current folder, library, or device, and contains helpful parts so that you can ***navigate***—explore within the organizing structure of Windows. A ***library*** is a collection of items, such as files and folders, assembled from various locations. A ***location*** is any disk drive, folder, or other place in which you can store files and folders.

Figure 2.6

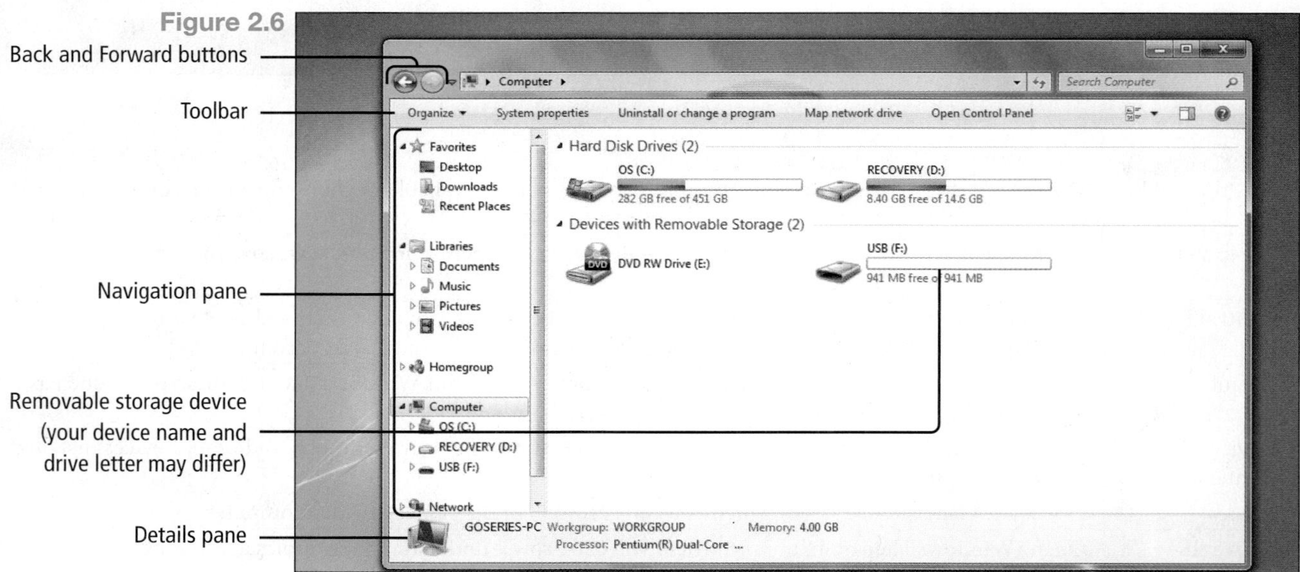

3 Under **Devices with Removable Storage**, locate the removable storage device you inserted in Step 1, move your mouse over—point to—the device name to display the pointer, and then click the *right* mouse button one time—referred to as ***right-click***—to display a ***shortcut menu***.

A shortcut menu is a context-sensitive menu that displays commands and options relevant to the selected object.

4 On the displayed shortcut menu, click **Open** to display the file list for this device. Notice that in the **navigation pane**, *Computer* expands to display all of the drives that you can access, and the commands on the **toolbar** change. Compare your screen with Figure 2.7.

A ***toolbar*** is a row, column, or block of buttons or icons, usually displayed across the top of a window, which contains commands for tasks you can perform with a single click or buttons that display a menu of commands. The toolbar contains commands for common tasks that are relevant to the displayed folder window.

Figure 2.7

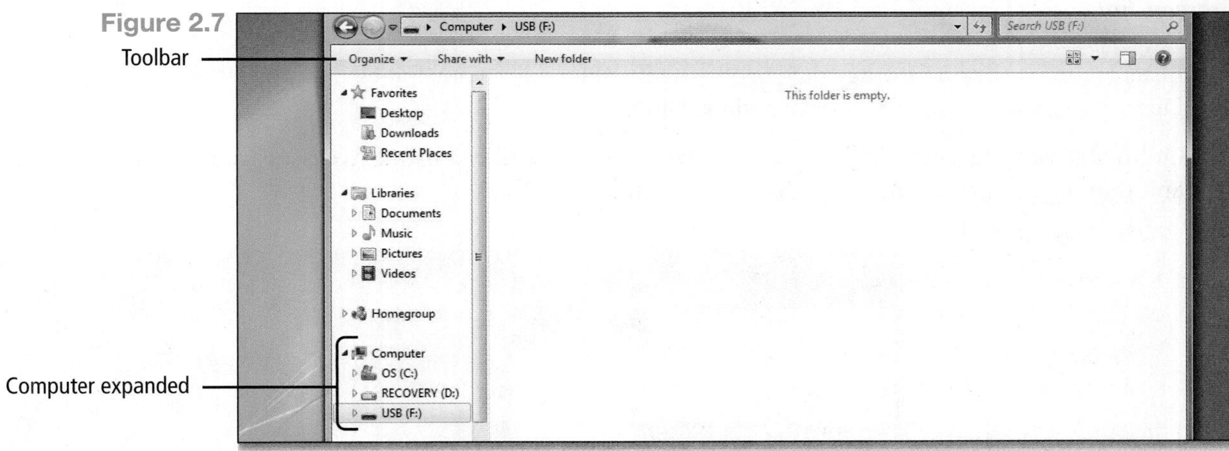

5 On the toolbar, click **New folder**, and notice in the file list, a folder icon displays with *New folder* highlighted in blue, as shown in Figure 2.8.

Figure 2.8

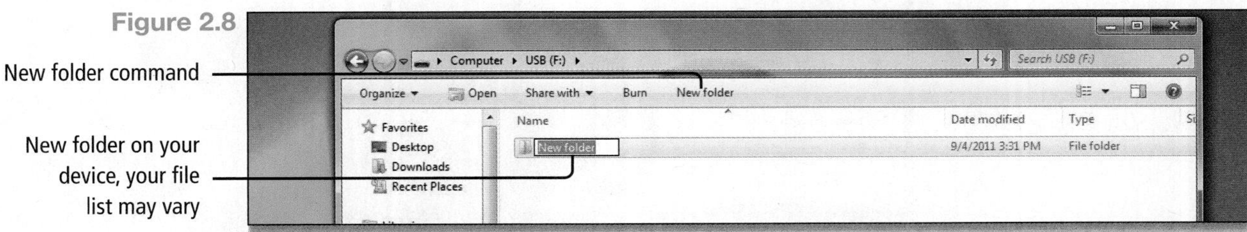

6 With the text *New folder* highlighted, type **All In One Chapter 2** and press Enter to confirm the folder name. With the folder selected, press Enter again to open the folder window. Compare your screen with Figure 2.9.

A new folder is created on your removable storage device. In the ***address bar***, the ***path*** from Computer to your device to your folder is indicated. The address bar displays your current location in the folder structure as a series of links separated by arrows. A path is a sequence of folders (directories) that leads to a specific file or folder.

Figure 2.9

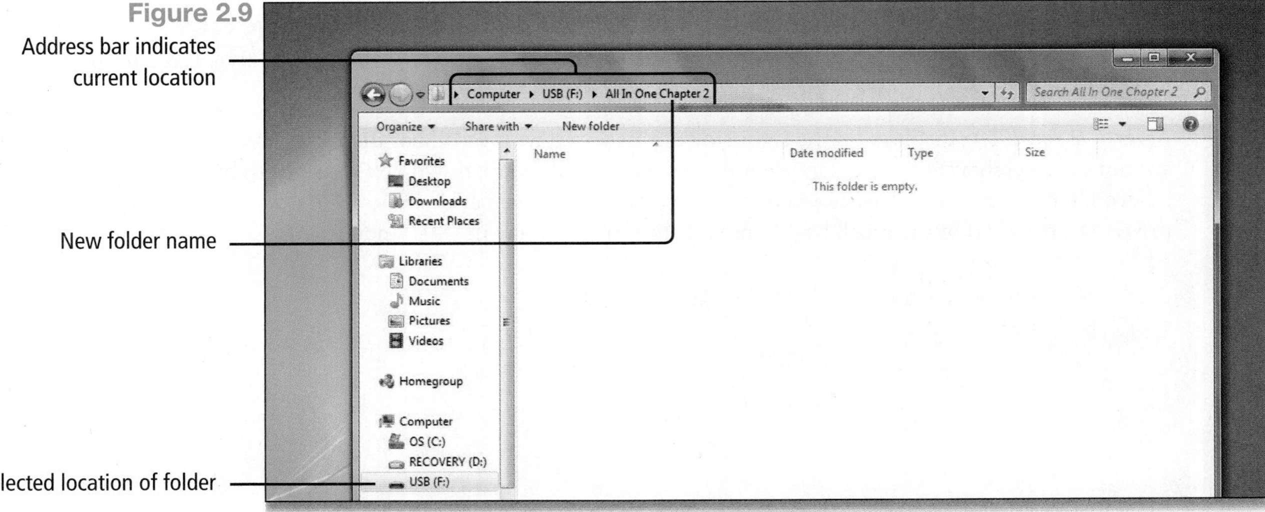

7 In the upper right corner of the window, click the Close button to close the window.

Activity 2.03 | Using Snipping Tool to Create a File

Snipping Tool is a program that captures an image of all or part of a computer screen. A ***snip***, as the captured image is called, can be annotated, saved, copied, or shared via e-mail. This is also referred to as a ***screen capture*** or a ***screenshot***.

1 Be sure the removable storage device on which you created your folder is still inserted in the computer. Display the **Start** menu, and then click **All Programs**.

2 On the list of programs, click the **Accessories** folder to display a list of Accessories. *Point* to Snipping Tool, and then right-click. Compare your screen with Figure 2.10.

Figure 2.10

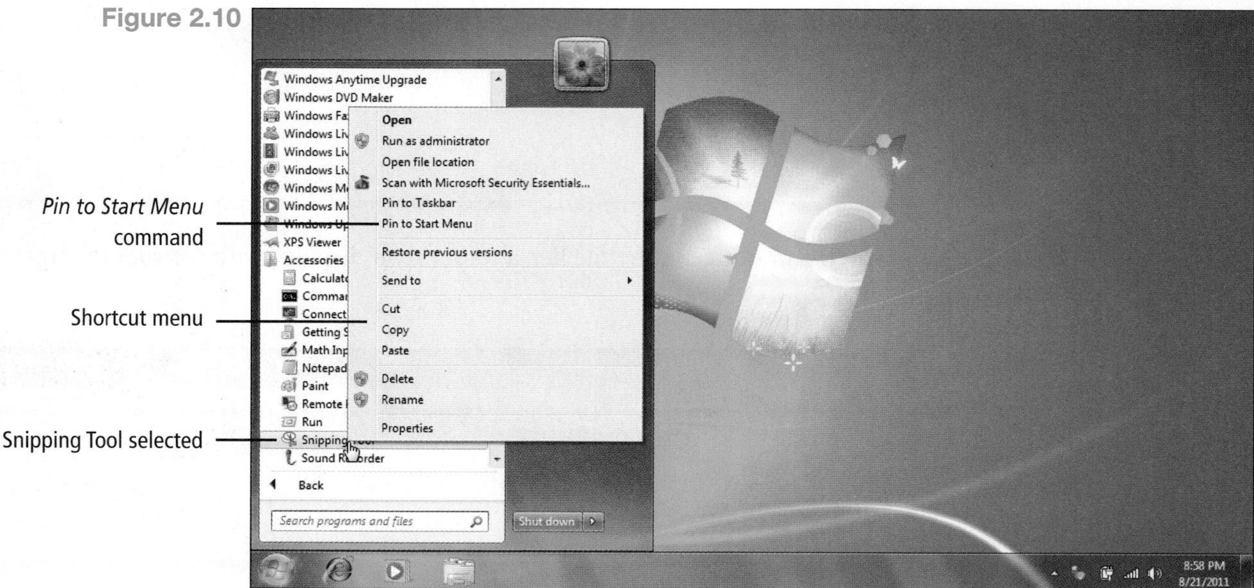

3 On the shortcut menu, click **Pin to Start Menu** (if *Unpin from Start Menu* displays instead, skip this step) and then click in an empty area of your desktop. Display the **Start** menu again. Notice that **Snipping Tool** displays in the pinned (upper) portion of the left pane of your **Start** menu.

Because you will use Snipping Tool frequently while completing the projects in this textbook, it is recommended that you leave Snipping Tool pinned to your Start menu.

4 From the displayed **Start** menu, at the bottom of the right pane, click **Help and Support**. In the **Windows Help and Support** window, in the **Search Help** box, type **Windows Basics** and then press Enter. On the displayed list, click **Windows Basics: all topics**. Compare your screen with Figure 2.11.

A vertical ***scroll bar*** displays on the right side of this window. A scroll bar displays when the contents of a window are not completely visible; you can use it to move the window up, down, left, or right to bring the contents into view. A scroll bar can be vertical as shown or horizontal and displayed at the bottom of a window. You can click the ***scroll arrow*** at either end of the scroll bar to move within the window in small increments.

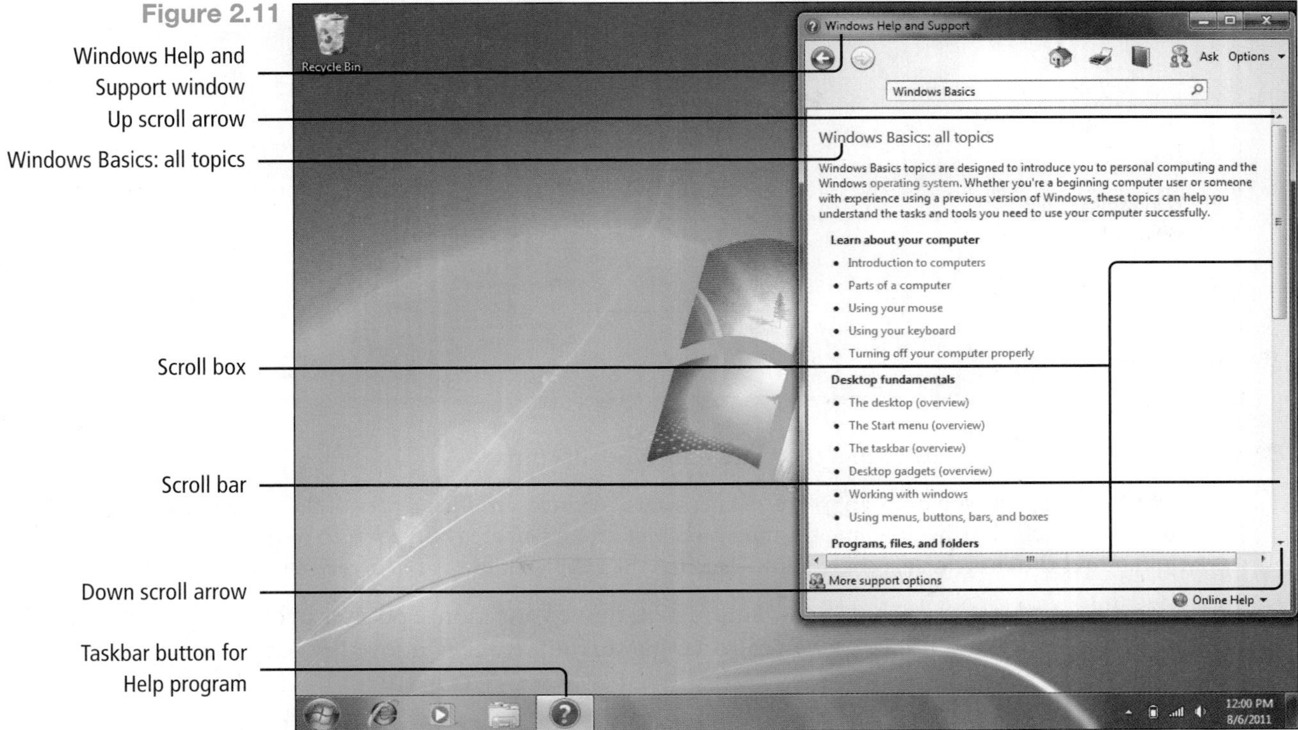

Figure 2.11

5 Click the down scroll arrow as necessary to bring the heading **Pictures and games** into view—or move the wheel on your mouse if you have one—and then click **Working with digital pictures**. Scroll down, if necessary, until you can see the illustration of a **USB cable**, as shown in Figure 2.12.

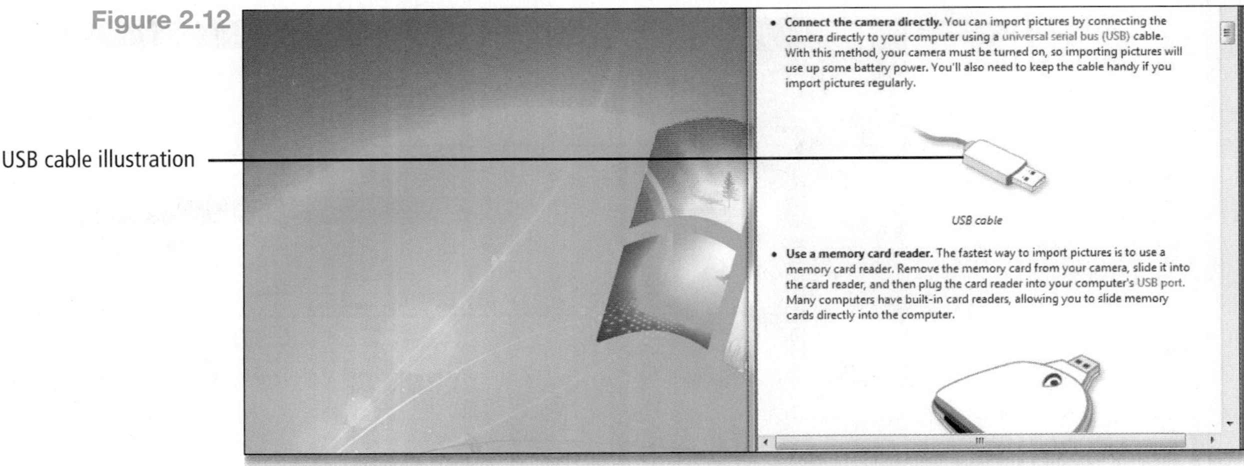

Figure 2.12

6 Display the **Start** menu, and then from the pinned area, click **Snipping Tool** to display the small **Snipping Tool** window.

7 On the **menu bar** of the **Snipping Tool**, click the **arrow** to the right of *New*—referred to as the **New arrow**—and then compare your screen with Figure 2.13.

The Windows Help and Support window dims. An arrow attached to a button will display a menu when clicked. Such a button is referred to as a ***split button***—clicking the main part of the button performs a command and clicking the arrow opens a menu with choices. A ***menu*** is a list of commands within a category, and a group of menus at the top of a program window is referred to as the ***menu bar***.

Figure 2.13

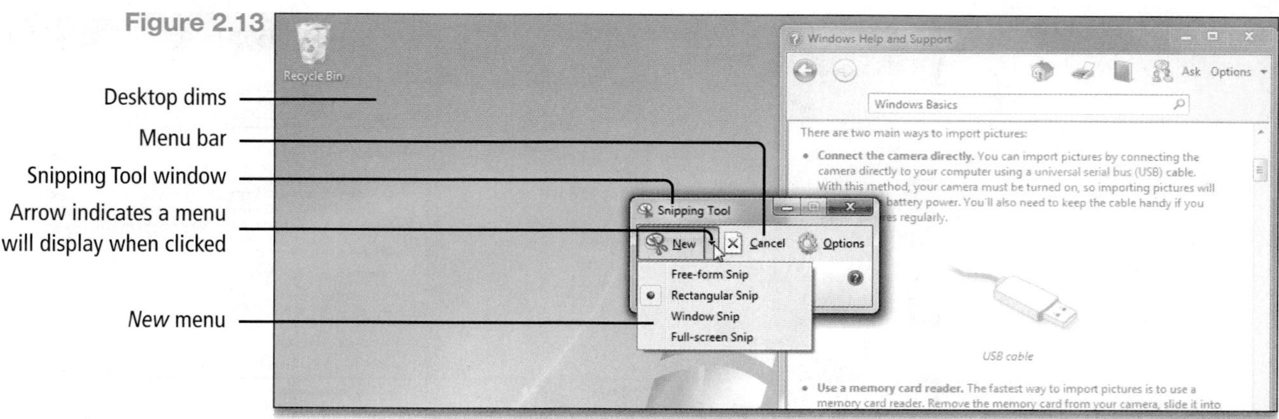

8 On the displayed menu, notice that there are four types of snips.

A ***free-form snip*** lets you draw an irregular line, such as a circle, around an area of the screen. A ***rectangular snip*** lets you draw a precise box by dragging the mouse pointer around an area of the screen to form a rectangle. A ***window snip*** captures the entire displayed window—such as the Help window. A ***full-screen snip*** captures the entire screen.

9 From the displayed menu, click **Window Snip**. Then, move your mouse pointer over the open **Windows Help and Support** window, and notice that a red rectangle surrounds the window; the remainder of your screen dims.

10 With the pointer positioned anywhere over the surrounded window, click the left mouse button one time. Drag the scroll box to position the snip near the top of the window, and then compare your screen with Figure 2.14.

Your snip is copied to the Snipping Tool mark-up window. Here you can annotate—mark or make notes on—save, copy, or share the snip.

Figure 2.14

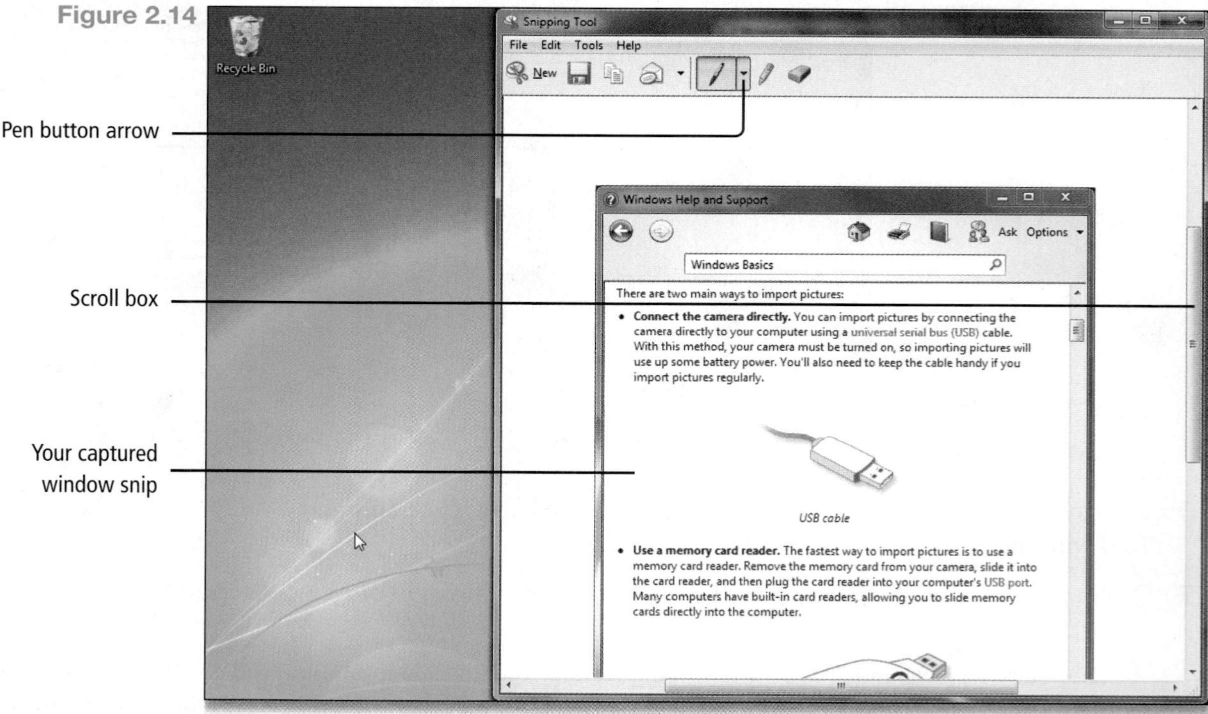

11 On the toolbar of the **Snipping Tool** mark-up window, click the **Pen button arrow**, and then click **Red Pen**. Notice that your mouse pointer displays as a red dot.

12 In the illustration of the USB cable, point to the end of the cable in the upper left portion of the picture, and then while holding down the left mouse button, draw a red free-form circle around the illustration of the USB cable as shown in Figure 2.15. If you are not satisfied with your circle, on the toolbar, click the Eraser button, point anywhere on the red circle, click to erase, and then begin again.

Figure 2.15

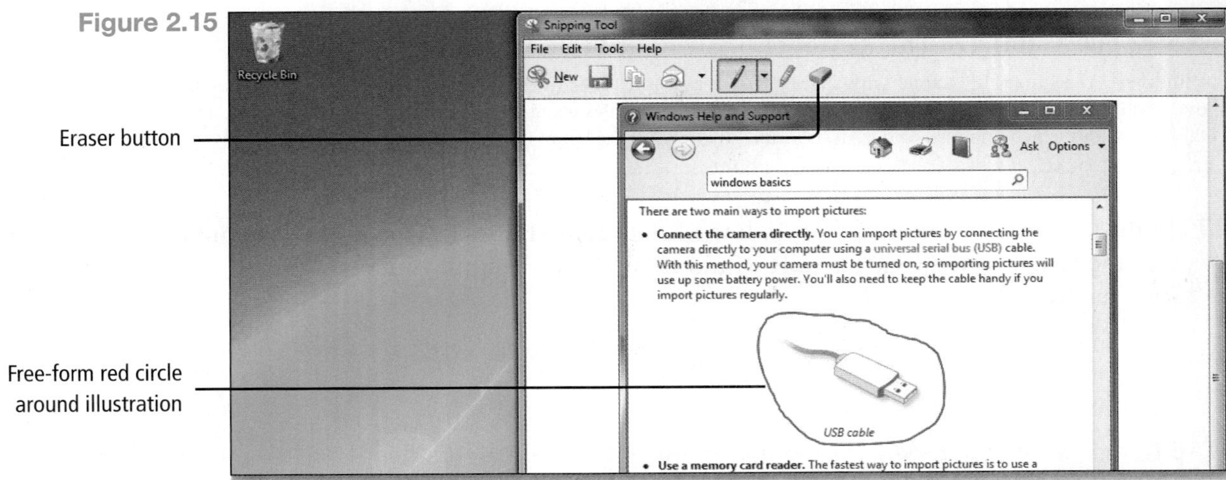

13 On the **Snipping Tool** mark-up window's toolbar, click the **Save Snip** button to display the **Save As** dialog box.

14 In the **Save As** dialog box, in the **navigation pane** on the left, drag the scroll box down as necessary to view **Computer**. Under **Computer**, click the name of your USB flash drive. In the **file list**, scroll as necessary, locate and ***double-click***—press the left mouse button two times in rapid succession while holding the mouse still—your **All In One Chapter 2** folder. Compare your screen with Figure 2.16.

Figure 2.16

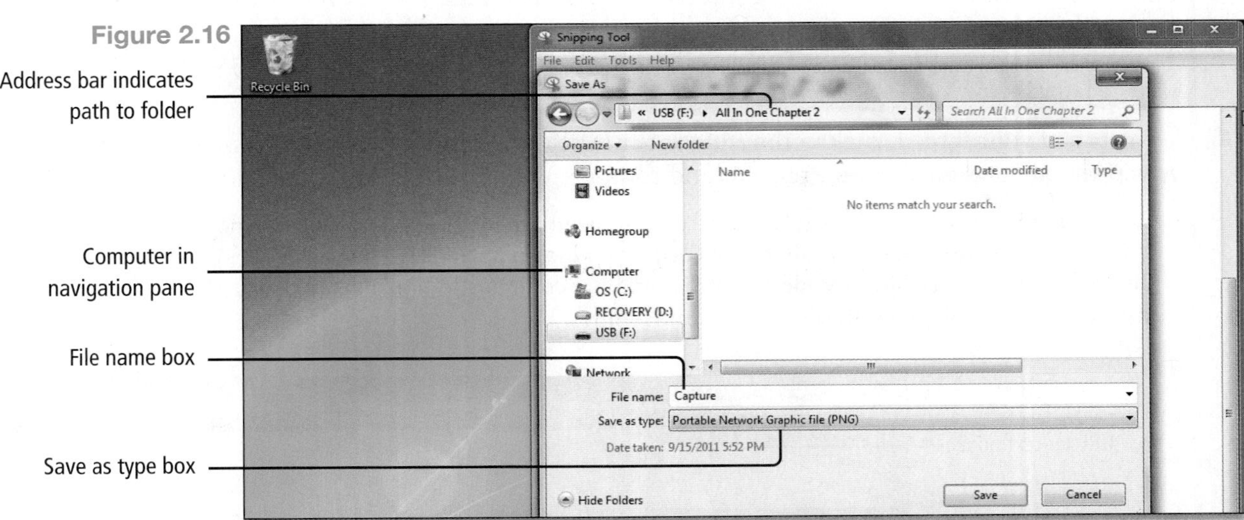

Note | Successful Double-Clicking Requires a Steady Hand

Double-clicking needs a steady hand. The speed of the two clicks is not so important as holding the mouse still between the two clicks. If you are not satisfied with your result, try again.

15 At the bottom of the **Save As** dialog box, locate the **Save as type** box, click anywhere in the box to display a list, and then from the displayed list click **JPEG file**.

JPEG, which is commonly pronounced *JAY-peg*, and stands for Joint Photographic Experts Group, is a common file type used by digital cameras and computers to store digital pictures. JPEG is popular because it can store a high-quality picture in a relatively small file.

16 At the bottom of the **Save As** dialog box, click in the **File name** box to select the text *Capture*, and then using your own name, type **Lastname_Firstname_2A_USB_Snip**

Within any Windows-based program, text highlighted in blue—selected—in this manner will be replaced by your typing.

> **Note | File Naming in This Textbook**
>
> Windows 7 recognizes file names with spaces. However, some older Internet file transfer programs do not. To facilitate sending your files over the Internet, in this textbook you will be instructed to save files using an underscore instead of a space. The underscore key is the shift of the [-] key, and which on most keyboards, is located two keys to the left of [Backspace].

17 In the lower right corner of the window, click the **Save** button. **Close** [X] the **Snipping Tool** mark-up window and the **Windows Help and Support** window. Hold this file until you finish Project 2A, and then submit as directed by your instructor.

You have successfully created a folder on a removable storage device and saved a file within that folder.

Objective 2 | Download and Save Files from the Web

The projects in this textbook begin with a new blank file or from a student data file that has been started for you. In this chapter, student data files provide you with a folder and file structure to explore and navigate. These data files are available online for you to download from the Pearson Web site. Alternatively, your instructor might provide these to you.

Activity 2.04 | Downloading Data Files and Saving Them on Your USB Drive

In this activity, you will download the student data files from the Web to your USB flash drive.

1 On the taskbar, click the **Internet Explorer** button. If a Welcome screen displays, in the lower right, click Ask me later.

2 At the top of your screen, click in the **address bar** to select the current Web address, and type **www.pearsonhighered.com/go** Press [Enter] and compare your screen with Figure 2.17.

In Internet Explorer, the ***address bar*** is the area at the top of the Internet Explorer window that displays, and where you can type, a ***URL—Uniform Resource Locator***—which is an address that uniquely identifies a location on the Internet. A URL is usually preceded by http:// and can contain additional details, such as the name of a page of hypertext, which often has the extension .html or .htm.

Figure 2.17

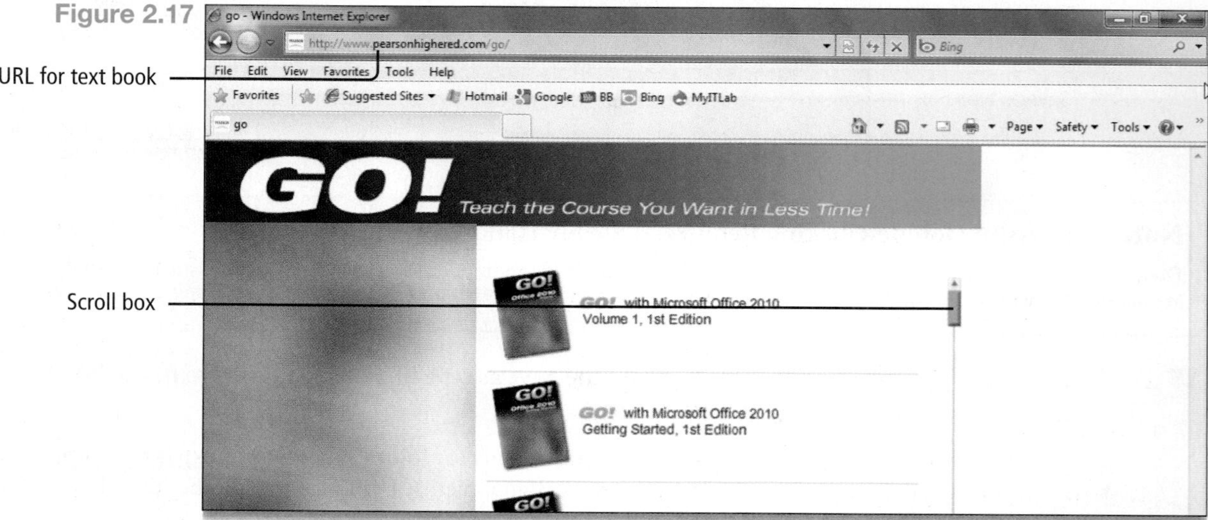

3 On the right side of the textbook list, drag the green scroll box down until you see the link for the **GO! All In One** text. Click the link to display the companion Web site in a new window.

4 Next to the textbook image, click **Student Data Files**. If the File Download box displays, click Save and if the Windows Internet Explorer dialog box displays, click Save as.

5 In the **Save As** dialog box, notice the file type you are saving is *Compressed (zipped) Folder*.

A ***ZIP file*** identifies a folder that contains one or more files that have been compressed to reduce file size. When downloading files from the Internet, a zipped file will download a group of files at one time, and it will be faster than downloading each file individually.

6 In the **Save As** dialog box, on the left under **Computer**, click your **USB drive** one time to display its contents in the **file list**. Then click **Save**.

A green progress bar displays the download progress; it may take a few minutes for the files to download to your USB drive.

7 When the download is complete, in the **Download complete** dialog box, click **Open Folder** to display the **file list** on your USB flash drive.

The icon next to *go_aio_student_data_files* indicates it is a zipped folder

8 Right-click **go_aio_student_data_files**, and then from the shortcut menu, click **Extract All**. Compare your screen with Figure 2.18.

Because the files are zipped together in a folder, they must be ***extracted***—the folder must be decompressed and the files must be pulled out—before they can be used.

Figure 2.18

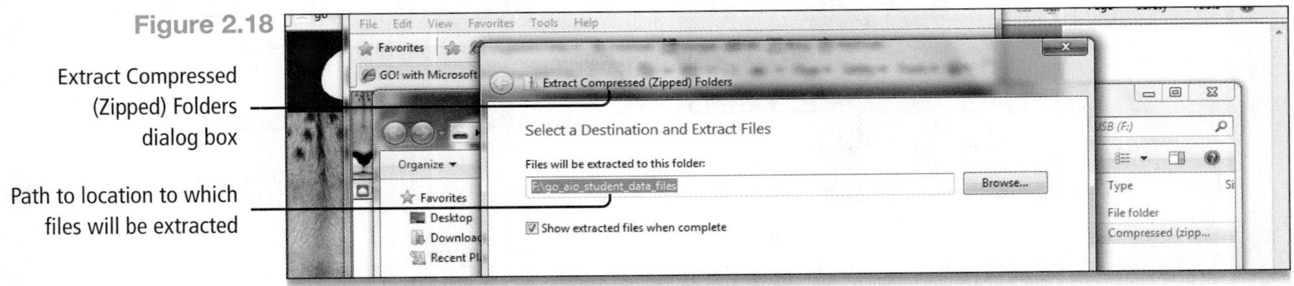

9 Be sure the **Show extracted files when complete** box is checked. In the **Extract Compressed (Zipped) Folders** dialog box, in the lower right corner, click **Extract**. After the files are extracted, double-click the **go_aio_student_data_files** folder to display your data files for this textbook.

The data files are organized by chapter.

10 **Close** all open windows.

Objective 3 | Display Libraries, Folders, and Files in a Window

A file is the fundamental unit of storage that enables Windows 7 to distinguish one set of information from another.

A folder is the basic organizing tool for files. In a folder, you can store files that are related to one another. You can also put a folder inside of another folder, which is referred to as a subfolder. You can create any number of subfolders, and each can hold any number of files and additional subfolders. Windows 7 arranges folders in a structure that resembles a ***hierarchy***—an arrangement where items are ranked and where each level is lower in rank than the item above it. In this manner, a hierarchy gives a visual representation of related files and folders. The hierarchy of folders is referred to as the ***folder structure***. A sequence of folders in the folder structure that leads to a specific file or folder is a path.

A library is a collection of items, such as files and folders, assembled from various locations; the locations might be on your computer, on an external hard drive connected to your computer, or on another computer in your network. A library provides a single access point from which you can open folders and files from different locations.

Activity 2.05 | Displaying Libraries, Folders, and Files in a Folder Window

When you open a folder or library, a folder window displays. The folder window is the one feature you will use most often in Windows 7. A folder window shows you the contents of a folder or library. The design of the folder window helps you navigate—explore within the folder structure for the purpose of finding files and folders—Windows 7 so that you can save and locate your files and folders efficiently. In this activity, you will open a folder window and examine its parts.

1 On the taskbar, click the **Windows Explorer** button to display the **Libraries** window.

   Windows Explorer is the program within Windows 7 that displays the contents of libraries, folders, and files on your computer, and also enables you to perform tasks related to your files and folders such as copying, moving, and renaming.

2 In the right portion of the window, under the text *Open a library to see your files and arrange them by folder, date, and other properties*, double-click **Documents**. Compare your screen with Figure 2.19, and then take a moment to study the parts of the window as described in the table in Figure 2.20.

   The window for the Documents library displays.

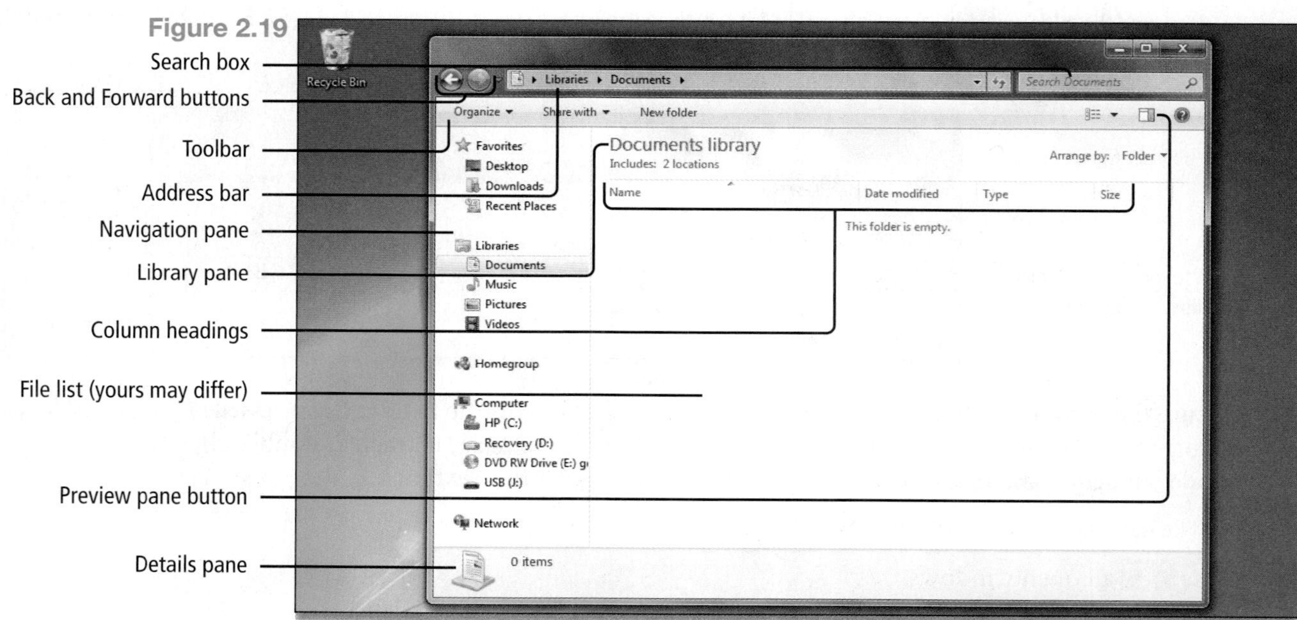

Figure 2.19

Parts of the Documents Library Window

Window Part	Function
Address bar	Displays your current location in the file structure as a series of links separated by arrows.
Back and Forward buttons	Provide the ability to navigate to other folders you have already opened without closing the current folder window. These buttons work with the address bar; that is, after you use the address bar to change folders, you can use the Back button to return to the previous folder.
Column headings	Identify the columns. By clicking on the column heading, you can change how the files in the file list are organized; by clicking on the arrow on the right, you can sort items in the file list.
File list	Displays the contents of the current folder or library. If you type text into the Search box, only the folders and files that match your search will display here—including files in subfolders.
Library pane	Enables you to customize the library or arrange files by different ***file properties***—information about the files, such as the author, the date the file was last changed, and any descriptive ***tags*** (a property that you create to help you find and organize your files) you might have added to the file. This pane displays only when you are in a library, such as the Documents library.
Navigation pane	Displays Favorites, Libraries, a Homegroup if you have one, and an expandable list of drives and folders in an area on the left side of a folder window. Use Favorites to open your most commonly used folders and searches; use Libraries to access your libraries. If you have a folder that you use frequently, you can drag it to the Favorites area so that it is always available.
Preview pane button	Opens an additional pane on the right side of the file list to display a preview of a file (not a folder) that you select in the file list.
Search box	Enables you to type a word or phrase and then searches for a file or subfolder stored in the current folder that contains matching text. The search begins as soon as you begin typing, so for example, if you type *G*, all the files that start with the letter *G* will display in the file list.
Toolbar	Provides buttons with which you can perform common tasks, such as changing the appearance of your files and folders, copying files to a CD, or starting a digital picture slide show. The buttons change in context with the type of file selected; for example, if a picture file is selected, different buttons display than if a music file is selected.

Figure 2.20

3 Move your pointer anywhere into the **navigation pane**, and notice that a **black arrow** displays to the left of *Favorites, Libraries, and Computer*, to indicate that these items are expanded, and a **white arrow** displays to the right of items that are collapsed (hidden).

You can click these arrows to collapse and expand areas in the navigation pane.

4 In the **navigation pane**, under **Computer**, click your **USB device** one time to display its contents in the **file list**. Double-click the **go_aio_student_data_files** folder, and then compare your screen with Figure 2.21.

In the navigation pane, *Computer* displays all of the drive letter locations attached to your computer, including the internal hard drives, CD or DVD drives, and any connected devices such as USB flash drive.

Figure 2.21

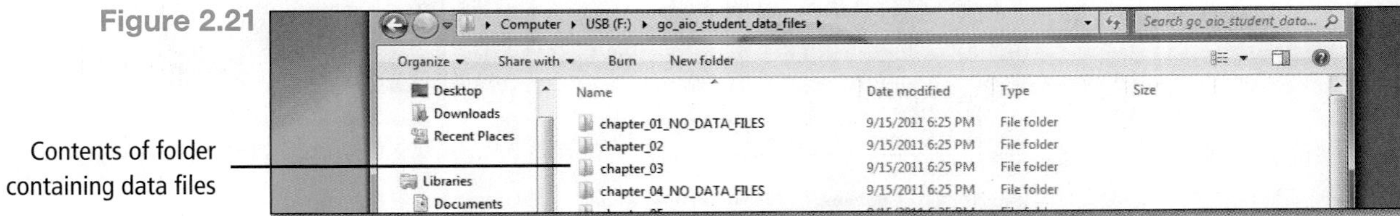

5 In the **file list**, double-click **chapter_02**, and then double-click **Bell_Orchid** to display the subfolders.

Recall that the corporate office is in Boston. The corporate office maintains subfolders labeled for each of its large hotels in Honolulu, Orlando, and San Diego.

6 In the **address bar**, to the right of **Bell_Orchid**, click the arrow to display the subfolders in the **Bell_Orchid** folder.

7 On the list of subfolders, click **Honolulu**. In the **file list**, double-click **Sales_Marketing** to display its contents in the file list. Compare your screen with Figure 2.22.

The files in the Sales_Marketing folder for Honolulu display. To the left of each file name, an icon indicates the program used to create each file. Here, there is one PowerPoint file, one Excel file, one Word file, and four JPEG images.

Figure 2.22

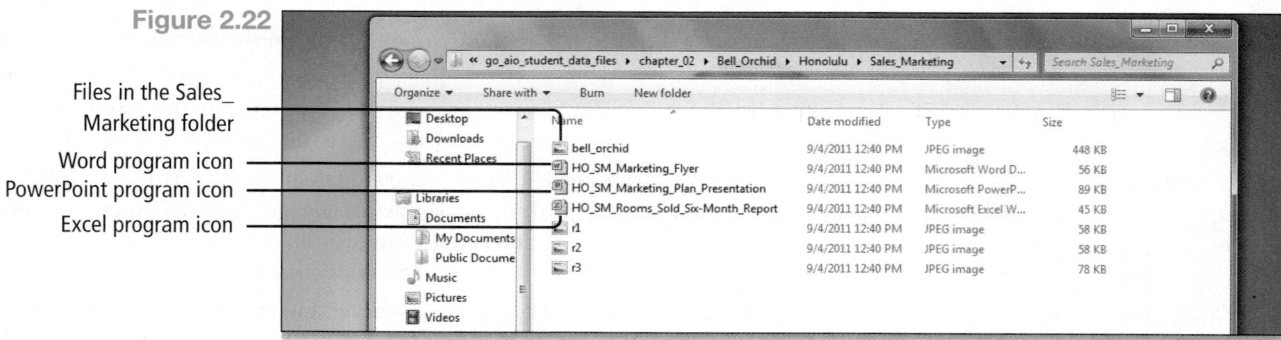

8 In the upper left corner of the folder window, click the **Back** button.

The Back button retraces each of your clicks in the same manner as clicking the Back button when you are browsing the Internet.

9 In the upper right corner of the folder window, click the **Close** button.

Activity 2.06 | Changing Views, Sorting, Grouping, and Filtering in a Folder Window

When looking at a list of files and folders in a folder window, there are a variety of useful arrangements in which you can view your data.

1 On the taskbar, click the **Windows Explorer** button. In the **navigation pane**, click **Computer** to display in the **file list** all the disk drives and removable devices attached to your computer.

2 In the upper right corner of the **Computer** window, on the toolbar, click the **View button arrow**. Compare your screen with Figure 2.23.

By default, the Computer window displays in Tiles view—small icons arranged in two columns. Seeing the icons helps you distinguish what type of devices are attached. The Computer window is divided into the Hard Disk Drives section and the Devices with Removable Storage section.

Figure 2.23

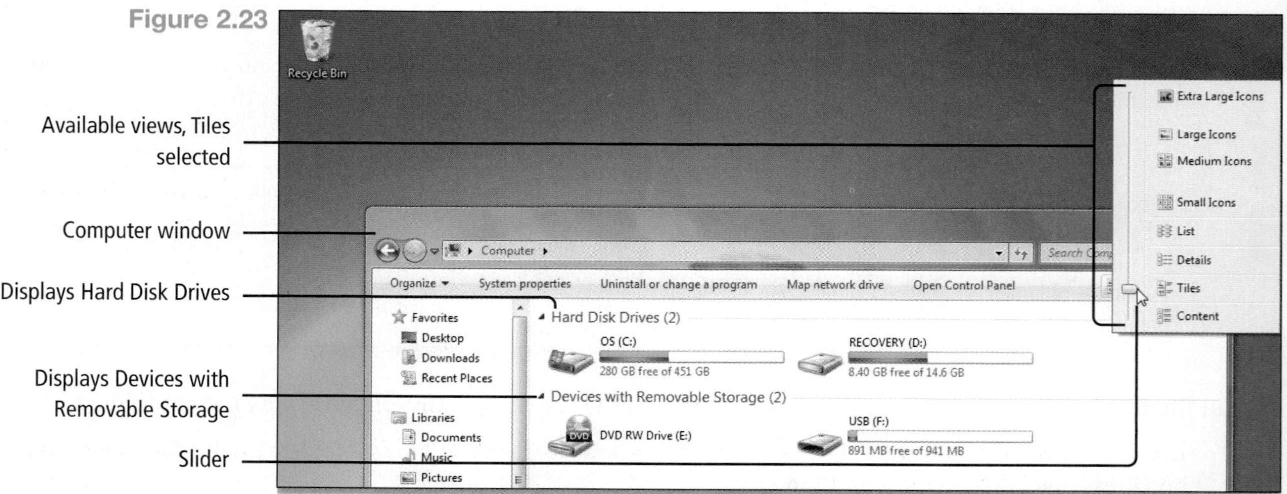

3 In the list of available views, drag the slider up and down slowly, but do not release the left mouse button—instead, pause at each view and notice how the view in the **file list** changes as you move from one to the next. Return the view to the Computer window's default **Tiles** view.

4 In the **file list**, double-click your **USB drive** to display its contents. In the **file list**, double-click the **go_aio_student_data_files** folder to open it. Double-click the **chapter_02** folder to open it. Open the **Bell_Orchid** folder, and then open the **Honolulu** folder to display its subfolders. In the list of **Honolulu** subfolders, open the **Sales_Marketing** folder.

5 Click the **View button arrow**, and then set the view to **Details**. In the upper right corner of the folder window, click the **Maximize** button, and then notice that the folder window fills the screen.

When you are working with folder windows, enlarge or maximize windows as necessary to make it easier to view your work. The Maximize command optimizes your workspace for a single window.

6 Click anywhere in a blank area of the file list, and then right-click. On the shortcut menu, point to **Group by**, and then on the submenu, click **Type**. If necessary, click the **Type** column heading to sort it in ascending order. Compare your screen with Figure 2.24.

The files are grouped by type, and the types are in alphabetical order. That is, JPEG is first, followed by Microsoft Excel, and so on. When you group files by a file property such as Type, a separate group will display for each file type, and a heading identifies each group and indicates the number of files in the group.

Figure 2.24

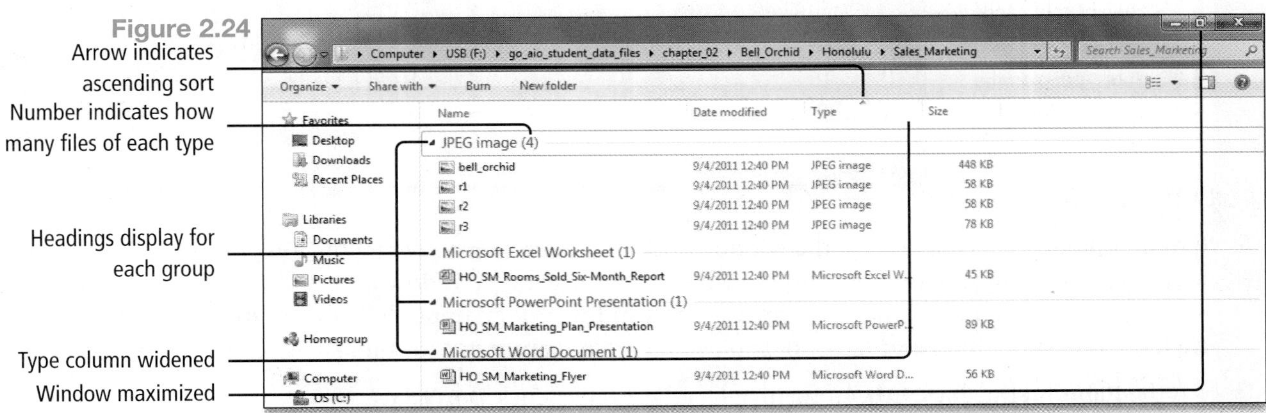

7 Display the **Start** menu, and then either from the pinned programs area, or by clicking All Programs, Accessories, and then Snipping Tool, display the **Snipping Tool window**.

8 Click the **New arrow**, click **Window Snip**, click anywhere in the **Sales_Marketing** folder window to select the window, and then on the **Snipping Tool** mark-up window's toolbar, click the **Save Snip** button. In the **Save As** dialog box, navigate to your USB flash drive. In the **file list**, scroll as necessary, locate and double-click your **All In One Chapter 2** folder.

9 In the **File name** box and using your own name, type **Lastname_Firstname_2A_Grouped_Snip** Be sure the file type is **JPEG**. Click the **Save** button, and then **Close** the **Snipping Tool** window. Hold this file until you finish Project 2A, and then submit this file as directed by your instructor.

10 Right-click in a blank area of the **file list**, point to **Group by**, and then click **(None)** to ungroup the files. In the upper right corner, click the **Restore Down** button and then **Close** all open windows.

Restore Down returns the window to the size it was before you maximized it.

Objective 4 | Start Programs and Open Data Files

When you use the software programs installed on your computer, you create and save files—the documents, worksheets, databases, songs, pictures, and so on that you need for your job or personal use. Thus, most of your work with Windows 7 is concerned with locating and starting your programs and locating and opening your files.

You can open your data files from within the program in which they were created, or you can open a data file from a folder window, which will simultaneously start the program and open your file.

Activity 2.07 | Starting Programs and Opening Data Files

One way to start a program is from one of the three areas of the Start menu: the upper left, which displays the programs you have pinned there for easy access; the bottom left, which displays programs that you have recently used; or the All Programs list.

1 Be sure the flash drive containing the student data files is inserted in your computer. From the **Start** menu, point to **All Programs**, locate and click the **Accessories** folder, and then on the displayed list, click **Paint**. Compare your screen with Figure 2.25.

Paint is a program that comes with Windows 7 with which you can create and edit drawings and display and edit stored photos. Recall that *All Programs* lists all of the programs available on your computer. If your list of programs is larger than the window, a scroll bar displays so that you can scroll the list. Names that display a file folder icon to the left will open to display the programs within the folder.

Figure 2.25

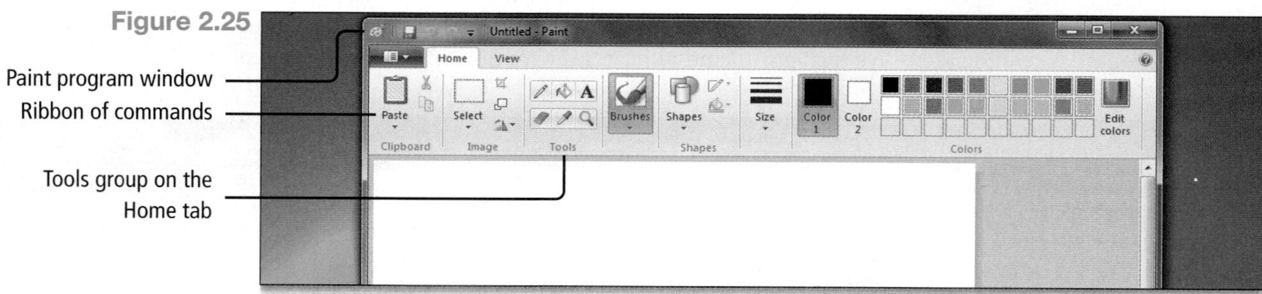

2 On the **Ribbon** across the top of the window, with the **Home tab** active, in the **Tools group**, click the **Pencil** icon. Move your mouse pointer into the white drawing area, hold down the left mouse button, and then try writing your first name in the white area of the window. In the upper left corner, to the left of the **Home tab**, click the blue tab—the **Paint** tab—to display a menu of commands of things you can do with your picture.

3 On the **Paint** menu, click **Exit**. In the displayed message, click **Don't Save**.

Messages like this display in most programs to prevent you from forgetting to save your work. A file saved in the Paint program creates a graphic file that can be saved in various file formats.

4 Display the **Start** menu, and then at the bottom of the menu, notice that your insertion point is blinking in the box labeled *Search programs and files*. Type **wordpad** When the program name displays in the list above, click the name to open the program.

If you do not immediately see a program on the All Programs list, type all or part of the name in the Search box in this manner. WordPad is another program included with Windows 7; it is a convenient program for simple word processing tasks.

5 With the insertion point blinking in the document window, type your first and last name.

6 From the **Start** menu, start **Snipping Tool** and create a **Window Snip**. Click anywhere in the WordPad window to display the **Snipping Tool** mark-up window. Save the snip in the chapter folder you created on your flash drive as **Lastname_Firstname_2A_WordPad_Snip** Hold this file until you finish Project 2A, and then submit this file as directed by your instructor.

7 **Close** the **Snipping Tool** window. In the upper right corner of the **WordPad** window, click the **Close** button and then click **Don't Save**.

8 On the taskbar at the bottom of your screen, click the **Windows Explorer** button. In the **navigation pane**, under **Computer**, click your **USB Drive** to display its contents in the file list. Double-click the **go_aio_student_data_files** folder to open it, and then double-click the **chapter_02** folder to open it.

9 In the **file** list, open the **Bell_Orchid** folder, open the **Corporate** folder, and then open the **Accounting** folder. In the **file list**, double-click the **CO_AC_Loan_Presentation** file to open the presentation.

The PowerPoint program window has features that are common to other programs you have opened. When you create and save data in PowerPoint, you create a PowerPoint presentation file.

10 **Close** the PowerPoint program window. **Close** the Windows Explorer window.

Objective 5 | Manage the Display of Individual and Multiple Windows

Activity 2.08 | Moving, Sizing, Hiding, Closing, and Switching Between Windows

When you start a program or open a folder, it displays in a window. You can move, resize, maximize, minimize (hide from view), and close windows. You can also freely arrange and overlap multiple open windows on your screen, with the window currently in use on top.

1 From the **Start** menu, open the **WordPad** program—either from the recently used programs area on the left side, or by opening the Accessories folder from the All Programs menu.

Notice that in the taskbar, a button displays representing the open program, and the button displays a glass frame, indicating the program is open.

2 Point to the **WordPad** window's ***title bar***—the bar across the top of the window that displays the program name—to display the pointer, and then if necessary, drag the window until its position is approximately in the center of the desktop. Point to the window's lower right corner until the pointer displays, and then drag up and to the left about 1 inch—the measurement need not be precise. Compare your screen with Figure 2.26.

When you drag the corner of a window in this manner, the window resizes both vertically and horizontally. You can resize a window by pointing to any of the window's borders or corners to display a two-headed arrow, and then drag the border or corner to shrink or enlarge the window.

Figure 2.26

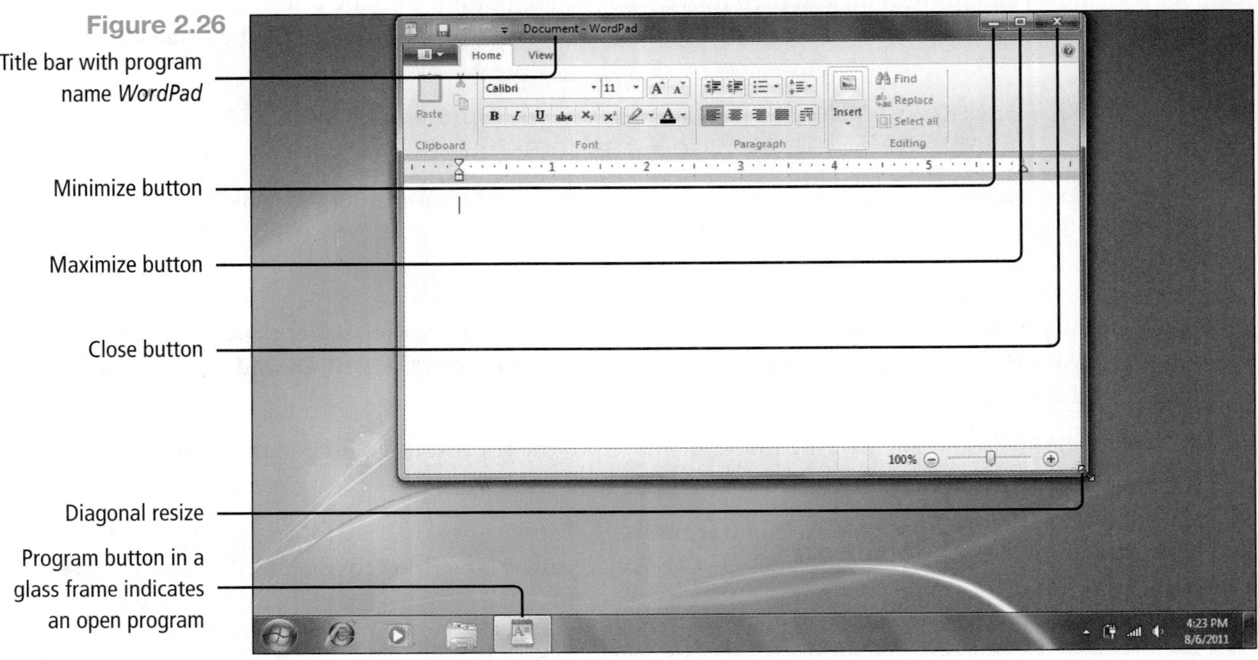

3 From the **Start** menu, point to **All Programs**, click the **Accessories** folder, and then click **Calculator**. If necessary, drag the title bar of the **Calculator** window so that it overlaps an area of the **WordPad** window.

4 Click anywhere in the **WordPad** window, and notice that it becomes the active window and moves in front of the **Calculator** window, as shown in Figure 2.27.

Additionally, the WordPad button on the taskbar becomes the brighter of the two open programs.

Figure 2.27

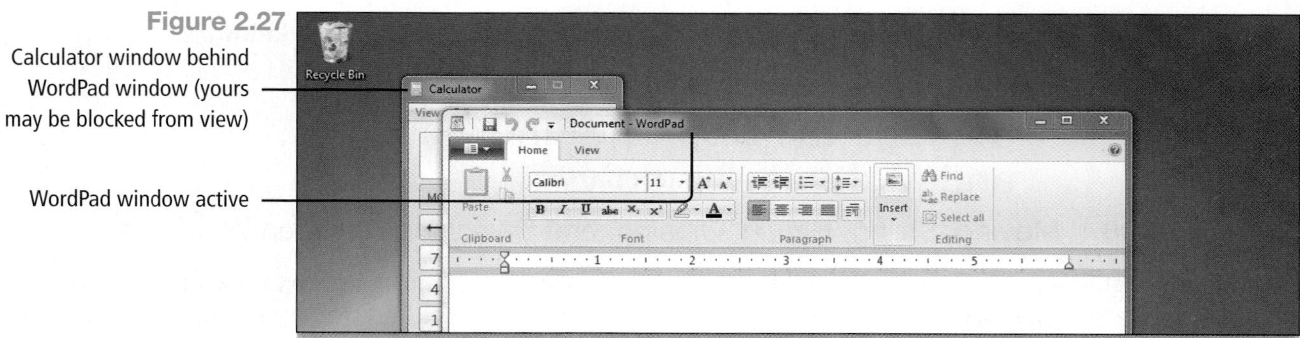

5 In the upper right corner of the **WordPad** window, click the **Minimize** button. Then, in the taskbar, click the **Calculator** button to minimize the window.

You can use either of these techniques to minimize a window without closing it. Minimizing a window hides the window, but it remains open—visible only as a button on the taskbar. The taskbar is your tool to switch between open windows. To open or switch to another window, just click its taskbar button.

6 Move your mouse pointer into the desktop area, and then on the taskbar, point to the **Calculator** button to display a thumbnail representation of the program window.

A ***thumbnail*** is a reduced image of a graphic.

7 On the taskbar, point to the **WordPad** button, right-click, and then on the displayed **Jump List**, click **Close window**. Notice that the button is removed from the taskbar, because the window is closed.

A ***Jump List*** displays destinations and tasks from a program's taskbar button.

8 Point to the **Calculator** button, and then move your mouse pointer into the thumbnail. Notice that the window opens and in the thumbnail, a **Close** button displays. In the thumbnail, click the small **Close** button.

Activity 2.09 | Using Aero Peek and Displaying Multiple Windows in the Cascade, Stack, and Side by Side Arrangements

You have seen that you can have multiple windows open and move among them by clicking the buttons on the taskbar. There are several different arrangements by which you can *display* multiple open windows on the desktop.

1 On the taskbar, click the **Windows Explorer** button. In the **navigation pane**, click your **USB Drive**, and then from your student files, open the **chapter_02** folder, and then open the **Bell_Orchid** folder. Open the **Corporate** folder, and then open **Engineering** to display the files.

2 With the files from the **Engineering** folder displayed in the **file list**, double-click the Word document **CO_EN_Pool_Report**. If necessary, **Maximize** the Word window.

3 On the taskbar, click the **Windows Explorer** button and notice that the folder window for the **Engineering** folder displays. Double-click the Excel file **CO_EN_Architect_Overtime** to open it. If necessary, **Maximize** the Excel window.

4 On the taskbar, click the **Windows Explorer** button again to redisplay the **Engineering** folder window, and then open the PowerPoint file **CO_EN_April_Safety_Presentation**. If necessary, **Maximize** the PowerPoint window. Compare your screen with Figure 2.28.

On the taskbar, icons display for all of the open programs.

Figure 2.28

5 In the taskbar, point to the **Word** icon, and then move your mouse pointer into the thumbnail that displays. Notice that the Word document fills the screen. Then, move your pointer back into the taskbar, and notice that the Word document no longer fills the screen.

This full-screen window preview is provided by ***Aero Peek***, a technology that assists you when you have multiple windows open by allowing you to peek at either the desktop that is behind open windows (***Preview Desktop***) or at a window that is hidden from view by other windows (***Full-Screen Window Preview***). Then, you can move the mouse pointer back into the taskbar to close the peek.

6 On the taskbar, point to an open area—an area where no buttons display—and right-click. On the displayed shortcut menu, click **Cascade windows**. Compare your screen with Figure 2.29.

In the ***cascade*** arrangement, the open windows display in a single stack, fanned out so that each title bar is visible. From the cascaded arrangement, you can click the title bar of any of the windows to make it the active window.

Figure 2.29

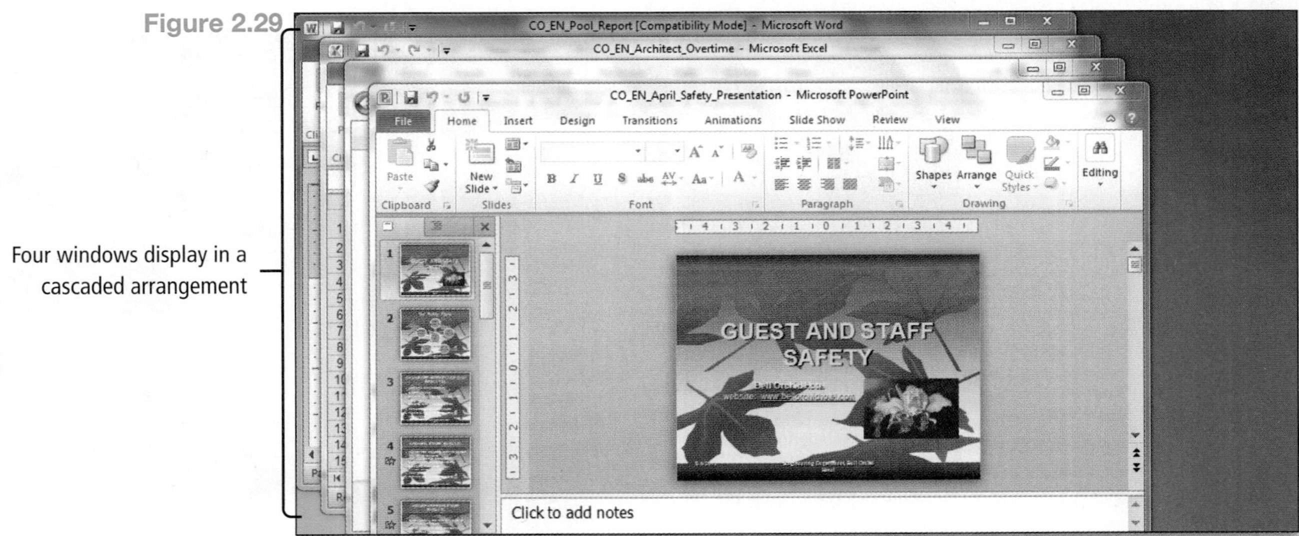

7 Display the taskbar menu again, and then click **Show windows side by side**.

In the ***side by side*** arrangement, the open windows display side by side. You can work in any of the files. Clicking in a window makes it the active window until you click in another window.

8 Create a **Full-screen Snip**, and then on your USB flash drive, save the snip file in **JPEG** format in your **All In One Chapter 2** folder as **Lastname_Firstname_2A_SideBySide_Snip** Hold this file until you finish Project 2A, and then submit this file as directed by your instructor.

9 Right-click in an open area of the taskbar to display the taskbar menu again, and then click **Undo Show side by side**.

10 When the display returns to the stacked arrangement, in the upper right corner of each window, first click the **Maximize** button so that the program fills the entire screen, and then click the **Minimize** button to leave the window open but not displayed. **Close** the **Windows Explorer** window. Leave the three document windows open on the taskbar for the next activity.

Maximizing the windows assures that the next time the program is opened, it will be maximized; otherwise, the program may display in its most recently used size.

Activity 2.10 | Switching Windows by Using Aero Flip 3D

Aero Flip 3D arranges your open windows in a three-dimensional stack that you can flip through quickly without having to click buttons on the taskbar.

> **Alert! | Versions of Windows 7 with Aero Flip 3D**
>
> Aero Flip 3D is available in Windows 7 Home Premium, Professional, Ultimate, and Enterprise editions.

1 Be sure the three files from the previous activity are open and minimized to display only as glass-framed buttons on the taskbar. On your keyboard, locate the [Windows] key, which is typically in the lower left corner of your keyboard between Ctrl and Alt.

2 Hold down [Windows] and then press the Tab key repeatedly to flip through the open windows as shown in Figure 2.30, and then release both keys to display the document at the top of the stack.

Your desktop is considered to be one of the open windows.

Figure 2.30

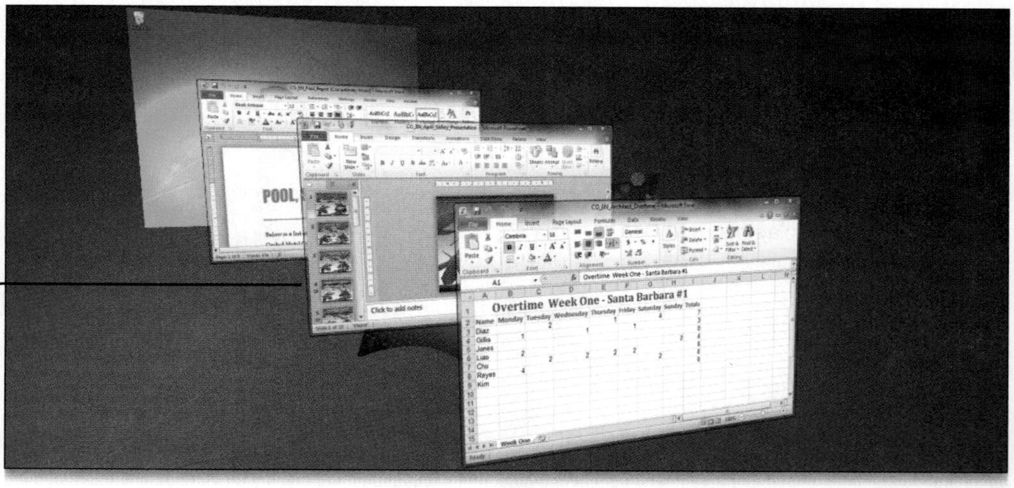

Open documents and the desktop display in a stack (your order may differ)

3 Repeat the technique you just practiced, and then flip through the stack until the PowerPoint presentation with the maple leaves is on top. Release the keys to maximize and make the PowerPoint document the active window.

4 **Close** the PowerPoint window. In the taskbar, point to the **Excel** icon, right-click, and then on the displayed **Jump List**, click **Close window**. Leave the Word window open on the taskbar for the next activity.

> **More Knowledge | Aero Shake**
>
> If you have several unmaximized windows open, for example your Documents library window and your Music library window, you can point to the title bar of the active window, hold down the left mouse button, and then move your mouse back and forth vigorously in a shaking motion; all other windows will minimize. This feature is ***Aero Shake***. Shake the window again, and all the minimized windows will be visible again. Use Aero Shake when you want to focus on a single window without minimizing all your other open windows one by one.

Activity 2.11 | Using Snap to Display Windows

Snap is a Windows 7 feature that automatically resizes windows when you move—*snap*—them to the edge of the screen. You can use Snap to arrange windows side by side, expand windows vertically, or maximize a window. You will find Snap useful to compare two documents, copy or move files between two windows, maximize a window by dragging instead of clicking the Maximize button, and to expand long documents to reduce the amount of scrolling.

1. If necessary, on the task bar, click the Word icon to display the Word document **CO_EN_Pool_Report**. If necessary, **Restore Down** the Word window.
2. Point to the **title bar**, and then drag to the left until your pointer reaches the edge of the screen and an outline of the window displays, as shown in Figure 2.31.

Figure 2.31

3. Release the mouse button, and notice that the window expands to half of the left side of the screen and extends fully from top to bottom.
4. Drag the title bar into the center of the screen, and notice that the window reverts to its former size.
5. **Close** all open windows.

> **More Knowledge | Snap to Display Two Windows Side by Side**
>
> If you have two unmaximized windows or files open, for example your Documents library window and a Word document window, you can point to the title bar of the active window, drag to the left until your pointer reaches the left edge of the screen, and then release the mouse button to snap it to the left side of the screen. Then, point anywhere in the visible title bar of the other window or file, and then drag the pointer to the right side of the screen and release the mouse button to snap it to the right side of the screen.

End You have completed Project 2A

Project 2B Managing Files and Folders

Project Activities

In Activities 2.12 through 2.21, you will assist Barbara Ramos, a freelance Interior Designer working at the Boston headquarters office of the Bell Orchid Hotels. Your screen snips will look similar to Figure 2.32.

Project Files

For Project 2B, you will need the following files:

A flash drive containing the student data files

You will save your files as:

Lastname_Firstname_2B_NewFolders_Snip
Lastname_Firstname_2B_FutureHotels_Snip
Lastname_Firstname_2B_CompressedFolder_Snip

Project Results

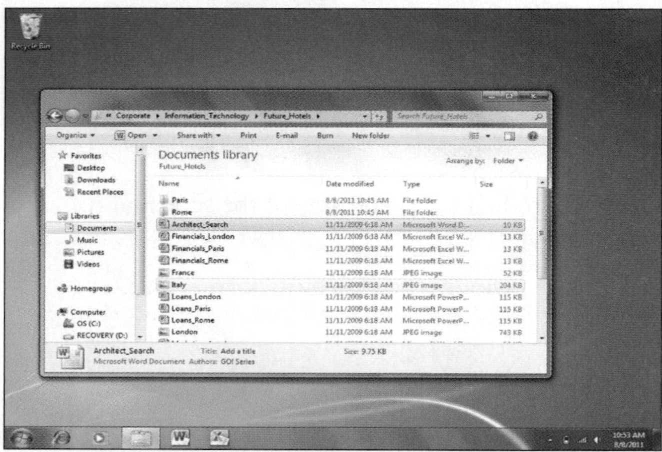

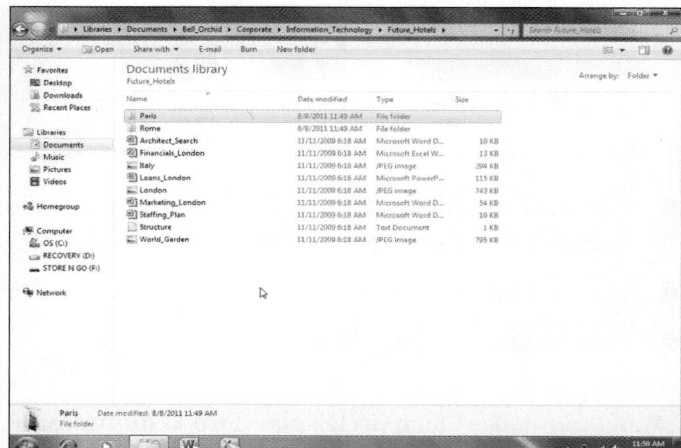

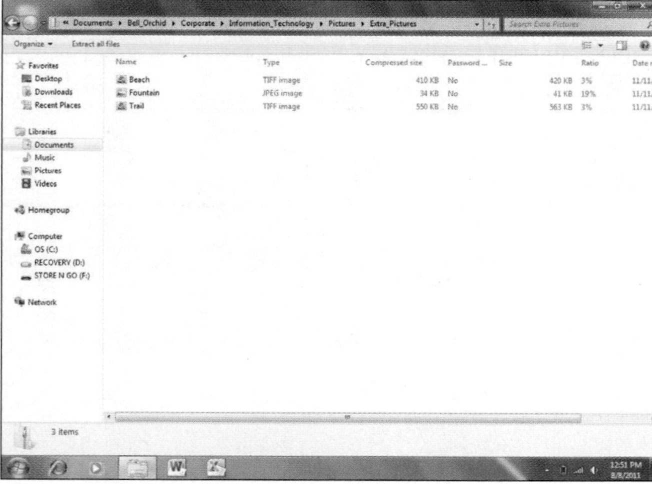

Figure 2.32
Project 2B Managing Files and Folders

Alert! | If you are working on a computer that is not your own, for example in a college lab, plan your time to complete Project 2B in one working session.

Because you will need to store and then delete files on the hard disk drive of the computer at which you are working, it is recommended that you complete this project in one working session—*unless you are working on your own computer or you know that the files will be retained.* In your college lab, it is possible that files you store will not be retained after you log off. Allow approximately 45 to 60 minutes to complete Project 2B.

Objective 6 | Copy Files from a Removable Storage Device to the Hard Disk Drive

Data on a computer network can be accessed by employees at any of the hotel locations through the use of sharing technologies. For example, ***SharePoint*** is a Microsoft technology that enables employees in an organization to access information across organizational and geographic boundaries.

Activity 2.12 | Copying Files from a Removable Storage Device to the Documents Library on the Hard Disk Drive

In this activity, you will copy the data files from your USB drive to the Documents library.

1 Be sure the USB drive where you have stored your student data files is inserted. On the taskbar, click the **Windows Explorer** button to display the **Libraries** window.

Windows Explorer is at work any time you are viewing the contents of a library, a folder, or a file.

2 In the **navigation pane**, under **Computer**, click your **USB** drive to display the contents in the **file list**. Navigate to your student files for **chapter_02**.

3 In the **file list**, point to the **Bell_Orchid** folder and right-click. On the displayed shortcut menu, point to **Send to**. Compare your screen with Figure 2.33.

From the Send to submenu, you can copy the selected file or folder to a variety of places. From this menu you can also create a desktop shortcut to the selected file or folder.

Figure 2.33

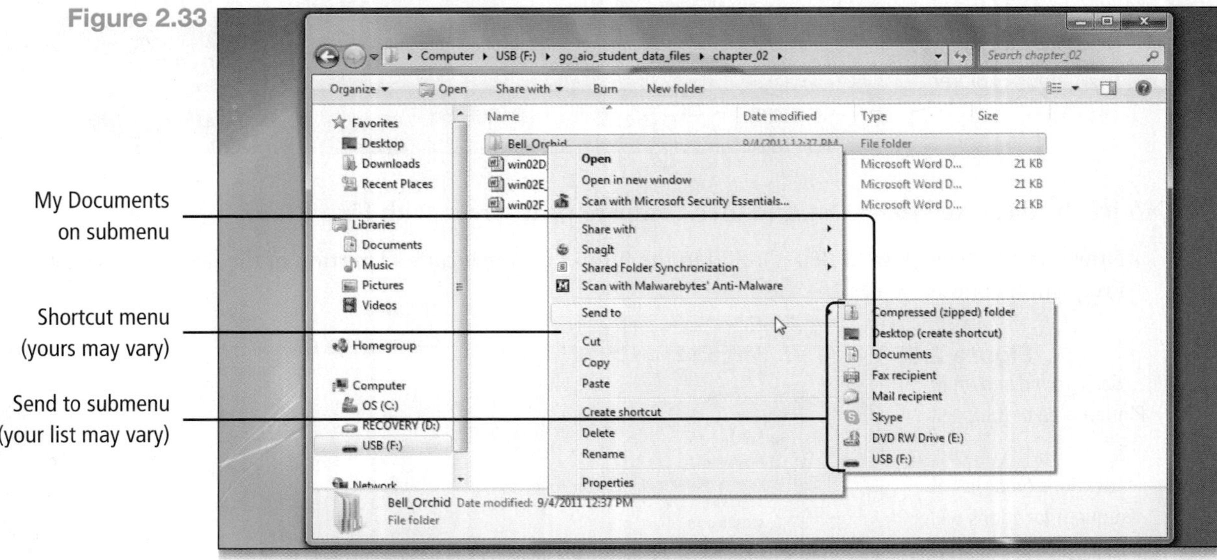

4 On the **Send to** submenu, click **Documents**, and then wait a few moments while Windows 7 copies the Bell_Orchid folder from your device to your Documents library on the hard disk drive.

A ***progress bar*** displays in a dialog box, and also displays on the Windows Explorer taskbar button with green shading. A progress bar indicates visually the progress of a task such as a download or file transfer.

5 When the copy is complete, **Close** the window.

Objective 7 | Navigate by Using Windows Explorer

Managing your data—the files and the folders that contain your files—is the single most useful computing skill you can acquire. Become familiar with two important features in Windows 7 if you want to manage your data easily and efficiently—the Windows Explorer program and the folder window. Recall that a folder window shows you the contents of a folder.

Activity 2.13 | Pinning a Location to a Jump List

Navigation refers to the actions you perform when you display a window to locate a command, or when you display the folder window for a folder whose contents you want to view. In this activity, you will practice various ways in which you can navigate by using Windows Explorer.

1. On the taskbar, click the **Windows Explorer** button. In the **file list**, double-click **Documents** to display the contents of the Documents library in the file list.
2. In the **file list**, point to the **Bell_Orchid** folder, hold down the left mouse button, and then as shown in Figure 2.34, drag the selected folder down to the **Windows Explorer** button until the ScreenTip *Pin to Windows Explorer* displays. Release the mouse button.

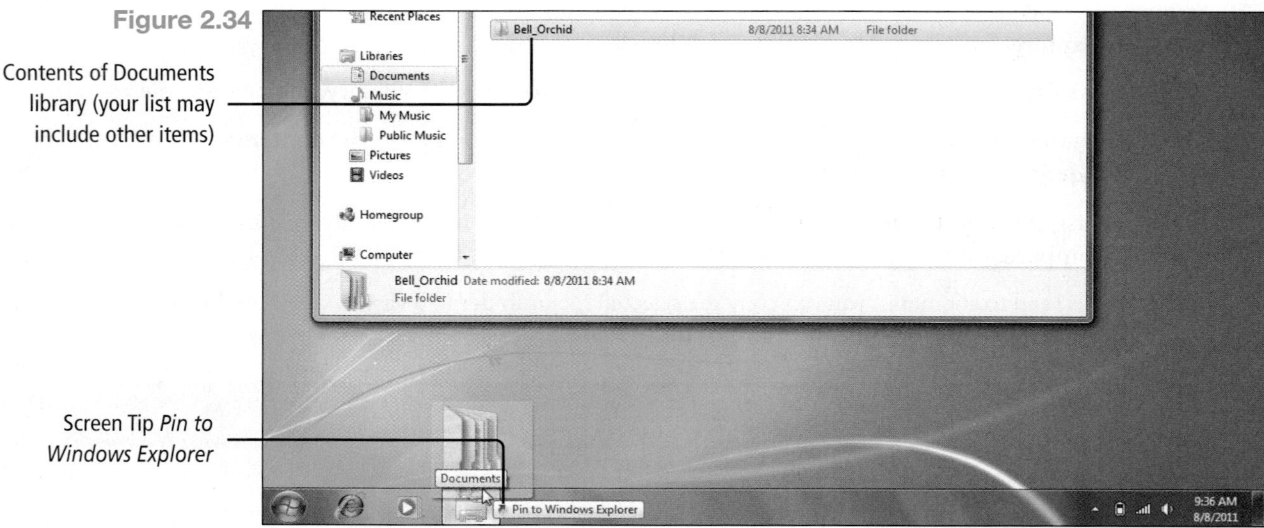

Figure 2.34

3. Notice the displayed **Jump List**, and then compare your screen with Figure 2.35.

   Now that you have pinned Bell_Orchid to the Jump List, the locations portion of the list displays both Pinned and Frequent locations.

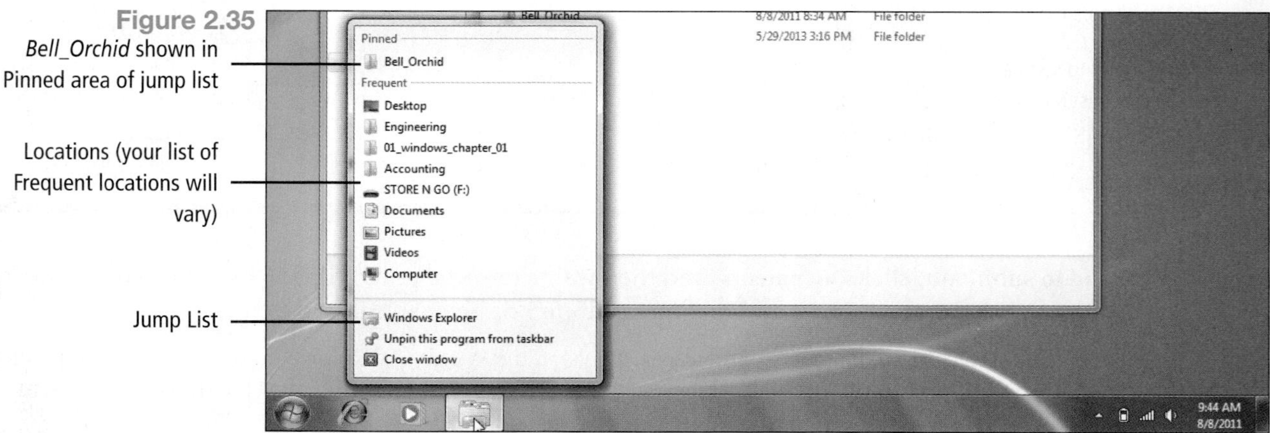

Figure 2.35

4 Click anywhere on the desktop to close the **Jump List**, and then **Close** the **Documents** window.

5 On the taskbar, right-click the **Windows Explorer** button to display the **Jump List**. From the **Pinned** area, click **Bell_Orchid**.

Use the taskbar—rather than the Start menu—as often as you can to start programs and navigate to specific files and folders. Doing so will increase your efficiency, because it eliminates extra clicks that are necessary to display the Start menu.

Activity 2.14 | Navigating by Using the Address Bar

A primary function of your operating system is to store and keep track of your files. A file folder on a disk in which you store files is referred to as a ***directory***. The location of any file can be described by its path. Recall that a path is a sequence of folders—*directories*—that leads to a specific file or folder.

1 In the **address bar**, click the **location icon** one time, and then compare your screen with Figure 2.36.

The path that describes the folder's location displays and is highlighted. The path begins with the disk, which is indicated by *C:*—the main hard disk drive of your computer.

Following the disk is the sequence of subfolders, each separated by a backslash (\). On the C: hard disk drive, the folder *Users* contains your personal folder. Your personal folder contains the *Documents* library, which contains the *Bell_Orchid* folder that you copied there.

Figure 2.36

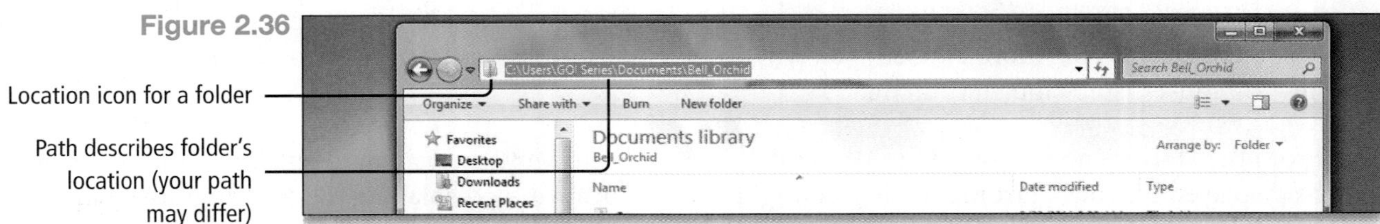

2 Click in a blank area of the **file list** to cancel the display of the path.

3 In the **navigation pane**, under **Computer**, click your **C:** hard disk drive. In the **address bar**, notice the hard disk drive icon that displays as the **location icon**—a small Windows logo may display there. In the **navigation pane**, click your **USB flash drive**, and notice the **location icon**.

The location icon changes to depict the location being accessed.

4 On the **address bar**, click the **Back** button two times or as many times as necessary to redisplay the **Bell_Orchid** folder window.

Recall that the Forward and Back buttons enable you to navigate to locations you have already visited. In a manner similar to when you are browsing the Web, the locations you have visited are stored in a location history, and you can browse that location history by clicking the Back and Forward buttons.

5 To the immediate right of the **Forward** button, locate and click the **Recent Pages** button. Compare your screen with Figure 2.37.

The ***Recent Pages*** button displays a list of recently accessed locations, and the current location is indicated by a check mark. By clicking an item on this list, you can move to a recently accessed location quickly. The list is limited to the current session; thus, only locations you have accessed since starting Windows Explorer display on the list.

Figure 2.37

6 **Close** Windows Explorer.

> **Note | Different Ways to Navigate Your Computer**
>
> There is no *correct* way to navigate your computer. You can use any combination of techniques in the navigation pane, the address bar, and in the file list of a folder window to display the location you want.

Objective 8 | Create, Name, and Save Files

In many programs, for example in Paint and the programs in Microsoft Office, the program opens and displays a new unnamed and unsaved file. As you begin creating your file in the program, your work is temporarily stored in the computer's memory until you initiate a Save command, at which time you must choose a file name and a location that is reachable from your computer in which to save your file.

For saving files or opening existing files, Windows-based programs use a set of ***common dialog boxes***. These are dialog boxes provided by the Windows programming interface that enable programs to have a consistent appearance and behavior. This means that in such dialog boxes, you will find navigation tools that are essentially the same as those in a Windows 7 folder window.

Activity 2.15 | Pinning a Program to the Taskbar

For programs that you use frequently, it is useful to pin the program to the taskbar. The more you perform tasks from the taskbar, the more efficient you will become. Performing tasks from the taskbar reduces the number of times you must display the Start menu.

1 From the **Start** menu, locate the **Microsoft Word** program on your system; the program might already be displayed on your Start menu, or you might need to locate it by displaying the All Programs menu and opening the Microsoft Office folder.

2 Point to the program name, and then as shown in Figure 2.38, drag the program to the taskbar. Release the mouse button when the ScreenTip *Pin to Taskbar* displays. (If the Word program is already pinned to the taskbar on your system, skip this step.)

For programs you use frequently, pin them to the taskbar in this manner.

Figure 2.38

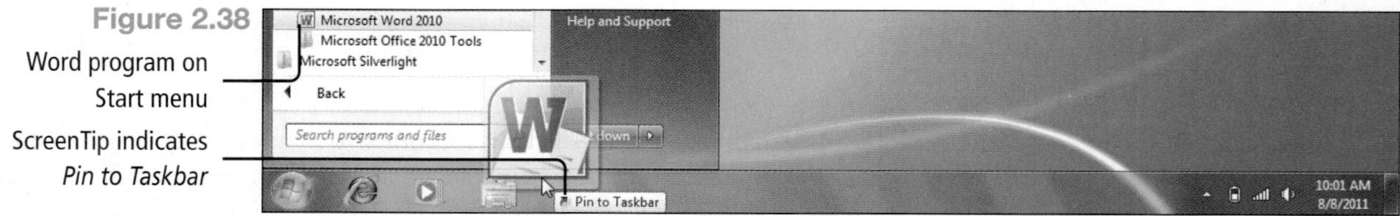

3 Using the technique you just practiced, pin the **Excel** program to the taskbar, and then click anywhere on the desktop to close the Start menu. Compare your screen with Figure 2.39

Figure 2.39

Activity 2.16 | Naming and Saving Files in Word

In this activity, you will create a Word file to be stored in an existing folder.

1 On the taskbar, click the **Word** icon to start the program. If necessary, on the **Home tab**, in the **Paragraph group**, click the **Show/Hide** button ¶ to display formatting marks. Then, on the **View tab**, in the **Show group**, be sure the **Ruler** check box is selected. Compare your screen with Figure 2.40.

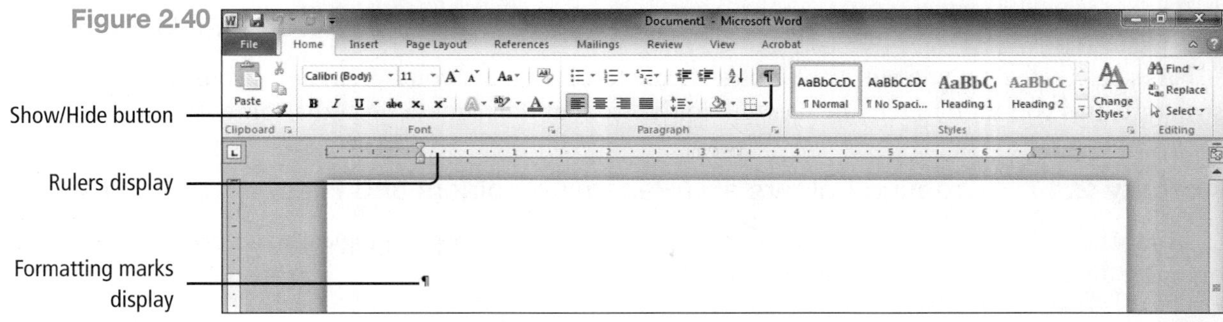

Figure 2.40

2 In the Word window, at the insertion point, type **The data for this overview of the Europe project will be provided at a later date by the Chief Operations Manager**.

3 Across the top of your keyboard, locate the function keys numbered F1 to F12, and then press F12 to display the **Save As** dialog box. Compare your screen with Figure 2.41.

In the Microsoft Office programs, F12 displays the Save As dialog box. The Save As dialog box is an example of a common dialog box; that is, this dialog box looks the same in Excel and in PowerPoint and in most other Windows-based programs. In the Save As dialog box, you must indicate the name you want for the file and the location where you want to save the file.

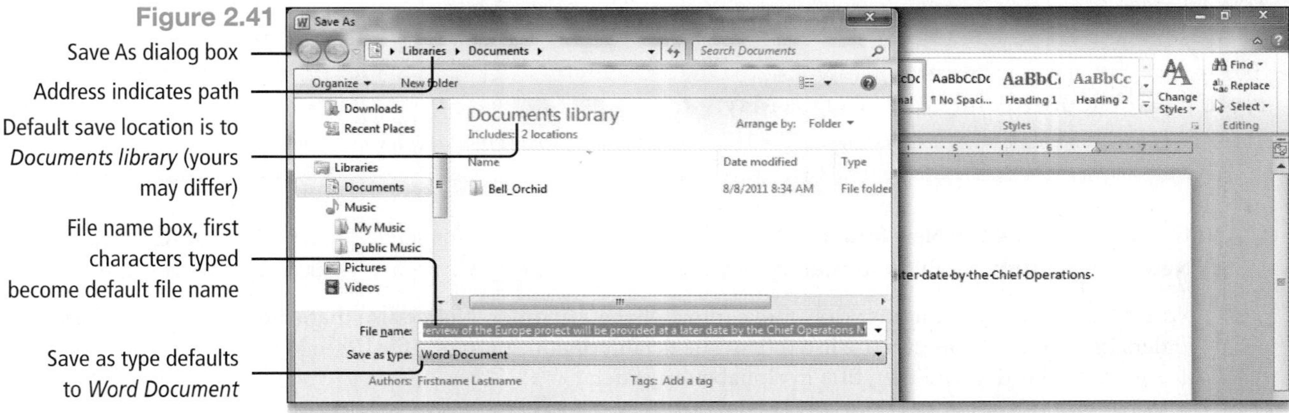

Figure 2.41

4 In the **Save as type box**, notice that the default file type is a **Word Document**. In the **File name** box, notice that Word selects the first characters of the document as the default name.

Recall that many programs use the Documents library as the default storage location; however, you can navigate to other storage locations from this dialog box.

5 Be sure the text in the **File name** box is selected—highlighted in blue; if it is not, click one time with your mouse to select it. Type **Europe_Project** as the **File name**. Then in the lower right corner of the dialog box, click **Save** to save the file in the **Documents** folder.

The Word document is saved and the file name displays in the title bar of the Word window.

6 **Close** the Word window.

More Knowledge | Rules for Naming Files

Consider these rules when naming files:

- File names usually cannot be longer than 255 characters.
- You cannot use any of the following characters in a file name: \ / ? : * " > < |
- File names must be unique in a folder; that is, two files of the same type—for example two Excel files—cannot have the exact same name. Likewise, two subfolders within a folder cannot have the exact same name.

Objective 9 | Create Folders and Rename Folders and Files

As you create files, you will also want to create folders so that you can organize your files into a logical folder structure. It is common to rename files and folders so that the names reflect the content.

Activity 2.17 | Creating Folders and Renaming Folders and Files

In this activity, you will create, name, and rename folders to begin a logical structure of folders in which to organize the files related to the European hotels project.

1 On the taskbar, right-click the **Windows Explorer** button to display the **Jump List**, and then under **Pinned**, click **Bell_Orchid**.

2 In the **address bar**, to the right of **Bell_Orchid**, click ▶, and then on the list click **Corporate**. To the right of **Corporate**, click ▶, and then click **Information_Technology**. To the right of **Information_Technology**, click ▶, and then click **Future_Hotels**.

   Some computer users prefer to navigate a folder structure using the address bar in this manner. Use whichever method you prefer.

3 Be sure the items are in alphabetical order by **Name**. At the right end of the toolbar, click the **View button arrow**, and if necessary, set the view to **Details**.

   This view is useful when you are organizing files and folders.

> **Note | Date Modified and Other Details May Vary**
> The Date modified and some other details shown in the figures may differ from what displays on your screen.

4 On the toolbar, click the **New folder** button. With the text *New folder* selected, type **Paris** and press Enter. Click the **New folder** button again, and then type **Venice** and press Enter. Compare your screen with Figure 2.42.

   Notice how the folders automatically move into alphabetical order. Notice also that when you have both files and folders in a folder, the folders are listed first.The default organization of a file list in Windows 7 is to list folders first, in alphabetical order, and then files in alphabetical order.

Figure 2.42

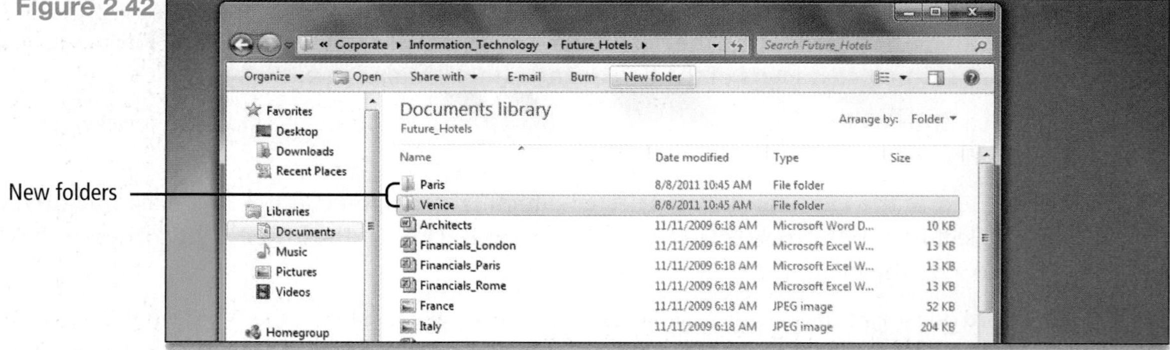

5 Point to the **Venice** folder and right-click. From the displayed menu, click **Rename**, and then notice that the text *Venice* is selected. Type **Rome** and press Enter.

6 Point to the file **Architects** and click one time to select it. Click the file one time again to select the text. Position your mouse pointer anywhere over the selected text and notice that the I pointer displays.

7 Position the I pointer to the left of the s in the word *Architects* and click one time to position the insertion point within the file name. Press Delete one time. Type **_Search** and then press Enter.

8 Create a **Full-screen Snip**, click in the folder window to capture the window, and then on your USB flash drive, save the snip file in **JPEG** format in your **All In One Chapter 2** folder as **Lastname_Firstname_2B_NewFolders_Snip** Hold this file until you finish Project 2B, and then submit this file as directed by your instructor.

9 Leave the window open for the next activity.

Objective 10 | Select, Copy, and Move Files and Folders

To ***select*** is to highlight, by clicking or dragging with the mouse, one or more file or folder names in the file list. Selecting in this manner is commonly done for the purpose of copying, moving, renaming, or deleting the selected files or folders.

Activity 2.18 | Selecting Groups of Files or Folders in the File List

The techniques you will practice in this activity apply not only to Windows 7, but also to lists of files that display in other applications.

1 With the **Future_Hotels** folder open, in the **file list**, click the Word file **Architect_Search** one time to select it. With the file name selected, hold down Shift, and then click the Excel file **Financials_Rome**. Compare your screen with Figure 2.43.

This technique, commonly referred to as ***Shift Click***, selects a consecutive group of files or folders. To select all the items in a consecutive group, you need only to click the first item, hold down Shift, and then click the last item in the group.

Figure 2.43

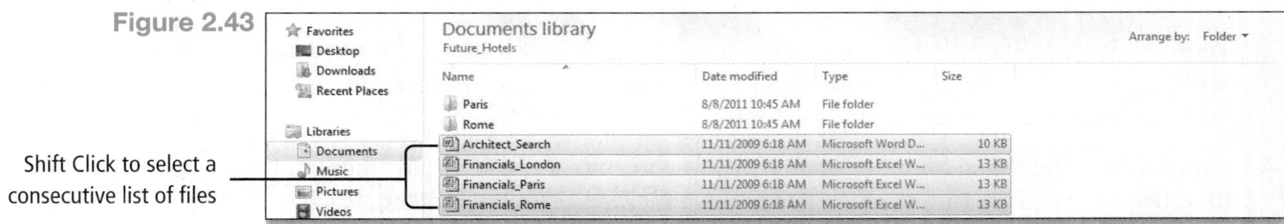

2 Click in a blank area of the **file list** to cancel the selection—also referred to as ***deselect***.

3 Select the file **Financials_Paris**, hold down Ctrl, and then click **Loans_Paris**. Notice that only the two files are selected. With the two files selected, hold down Ctrl, click **Italy**, and then click **France**. Release Ctrl.

Three files are selected. Use this Ctrl key technique when you want to select a group of *nonconsecutive* items.

4 With the four files still selected, hold down Ctrl, and then click the selected file **Italy**. Release the key. Compare your screen with Figure 2.44.

To cancel the selection of individual items within a selected group, hold down Ctrl, and then click the items you do not want to include.

Figure 2.44

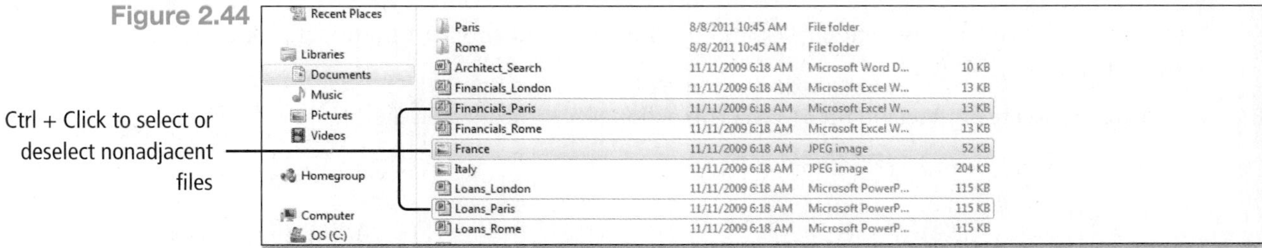

5 Click anywhere in the file list to deselect. Leave the window open for the next activity.

Activity 2.19 | Copying Files

When you *copy* a file or a folder, you make a duplicate of the original item and then store the duplicate in another location. In this activity, you make copies of the Staffing_Plan file, and then placing a copy in each of the two folders you created—Paris and Rome.

1 With the **Future_Hotels** folder open, in the **file list**, point to the file **Staffing_Plan** and right-click. On the displayed menu, click **Copy**.

The Copy command places a copy of your selected file or folder on the ***Clipboard*** where it will be stored until you replace it with another Copy command. The Clipboard is a temporary storage area for information that you have copied or moved from one place and plan to use somewhere else. In Windows 7, the Clipboard can hold only one piece of information at a time. Whenever something is copied to the Clipboard, it replaces whatever was there before.

2 At the top of the **file list**, point to the **Paris folder**, right-click, and then click **Paste**. Then double-click the **Paris** folder to open it. Notice that the copy of the **Staffing_Plan** file displays. Compare your screen with Figure 2.45.

Figure 2.45

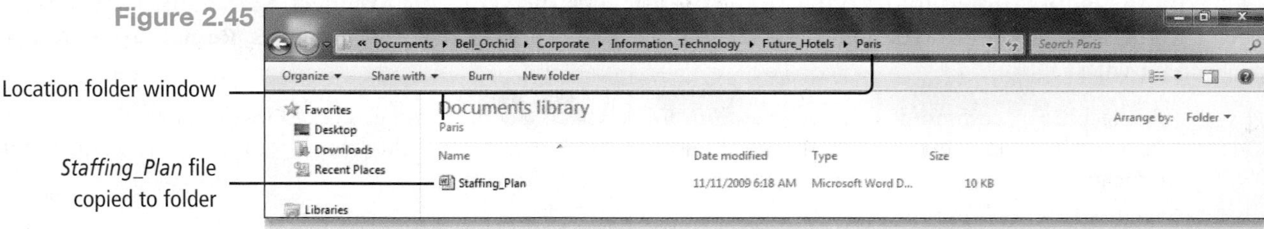

3 With the **Paris** folder open, by using any of the techniques you have practiced, rename this copy of the **Staffing_Plan** file to **Paris_Staffing_Plan** In the address bar, click **Future_Hotels** to redisplay this folder window and move up one level in the folder structure.

4 Double-click the **Rome** folder to open it. With your mouse pointer anywhere in the file list, right-click, and then from the shortcut menu click **Paste**. Rename the file **Rome_Staffing_Plan**

A copy of the Staffing_Plan file is copied to the folder. Because a copy of the Staffing_Plan file is still on the Clipboard, you can continue to paste the item until you copy another item on the Clipboard to replace it.

5 On the **address bar**, click **Future_Hotels** to move up one level and open the **Future_Hotels** folder window. Leave this folder open for the next activity.

Activity 2.20 | Moving Files

When you *move* a file or folder, you remove it from the original location and store it in a new location. In this activity, you will move items from the Future_Hotels folder into their appropriate folders.

1 With the **Future_Hotels** folder open, in the **file list**, click the Excel file **Financials_Rome** to select it. Hold down Ctrl, and then in the file list, click **Loans_Rome**, **Rome**, and **Marketing_Rome** to select the three additional files. Right-click on one of the selected files, and on the displayed shortcut menu, click **Cut**. Compare your screen with Figure 2.46

The file icons are dimmed on the screen. This action places the item on the Clipboard.

Figure 2.46

Cut file icons display dim

Navigation	Name	Date modified	Type	Size
Pictures	Financials_Paris	11/11/2009 6:18 AM	Microsoft Excel W...	13 KB
Videos	Financials_Rome	11/11/2009 6:18 AM	Microsoft Excel W...	13 KB
	France	11/11/2009 6:18 AM	JPEG image	52 KB
Homegroup	Italy	11/11/2009 6:18 AM	JPEG image	204 KB
	Loans_London	11/11/2009 6:18 AM	Microsoft PowerP...	115 KB
Computer	Loans_Paris	11/11/2009 6:18 AM	Microsoft PowerP...	115 KB
OS (C:)	Loans_Rome	11/11/2009 6:18 AM	Microsoft PowerP...	115 KB
RECOVERY (D:)	London	11/11/2009 6:18 AM	JPEG image	743 KB
STORE N GO (F:)	Marketing_London	11/11/2009 6:18 AM	Microsoft Word D...	54 KB
	Marketing_Paris	11/11/2009 6:18 AM	Microsoft Word D...	54 KB
Network	Marketing_Rome	11/11/2009 6:18 AM	Microsoft Word D...	53 KB
	Paris	11/11/2009 6:18 AM	JPEG image	56 KB
	Rome	11/11/2009 6:18 AM	JPEG image	161 KB
	Staffing_Plan	11/11/2009 6:18 AM	Microsoft Word D...	10 KB

2 Point to the **Rome** folder, right-click, and then click **Paste**. Notice that the files are removed from the file list. Then open the **Rome** folder, and notice that the files were pasted into the folder.

3 On the **address bar**, click **Future_Hotels** to move up a level. In the **file list**, click **Financials_Paris**, press Ctrl and click **France**, **Loans_Paris**, **Marketing_Paris**, and **Paris**. Point to **Paris**, hold down the left mouse button, and then drag the files upward over the **Paris** folder until the ScreenTip →*Move to Paris* displays. Release the mouse button.

4 Create a **Window Snip**, click in the folder window to capture the window, and then on your USB flash drive, save the snip file in **JPEG** format in your **All In One Chapter 2** folder as **Lastname_Firstname_2B_FutureHotels_Snip** Hold this file until you finish Project 2B, and then submit this file as directed by your instructor.

5 Leave the window open for the next activity.

> **More Knowledge | Copy and Move Files by Using Two Windows**
>
> To copy or move files using two windows, open two instances of Windows Explorer, and then use the Snap feature to display both instances on your screen. Then use drag and drop; use copy (or cut) and paste commands to copy or move files or folders into a different level of a folder structure, or to a different drive location.

Activity 2.21 | Copying Files to a Compressed Folder

To ***compress*** is to reduce the size of a file. Compressed files take up less storage space and can be transferred to other computers, for example in an e-mail message, more quickly than uncompressed files. Because pictures are typically large files, it is common to compress graphic files like pictures. When the picture is expanded, there will be no loss of visual quality.

1 On the **address bar**, click **Information_Technology** to move up a level, and then double-click the **Pictures** folder.

2 If necessary, in the upper right corner, click the **Maximize** button so that the folder window fills the screen. On the toolbar, click the **View button arrow**, and then set the view to **Tiles**. Compare your screen with Figure 2.47.

Figure 2.47

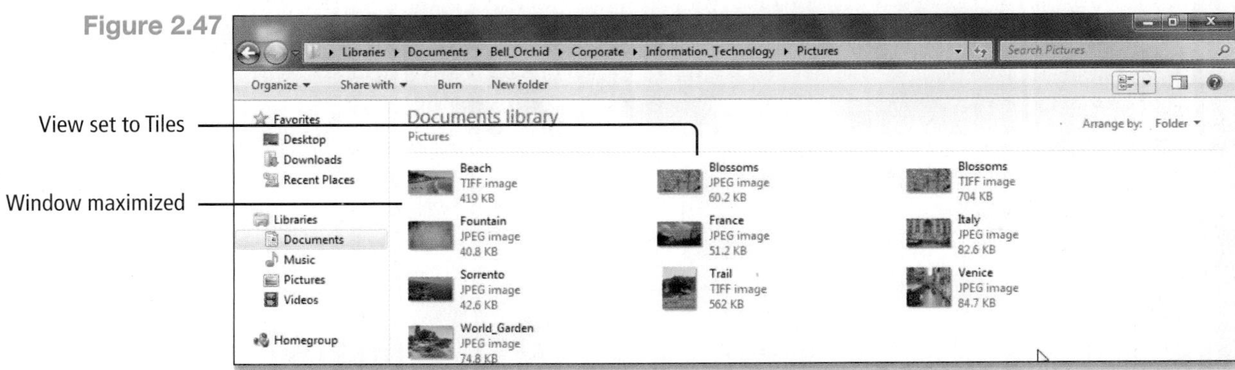

3 Hold down Ctrl, and then select the files **Beach**, **Fountain**, and **Trail**. Release Ctrl, point to *any* of the selected files, right-click, point to **Send to**, and then click **Compressed (zipped) folder**.

A compressed folder is created containing the three files and is stored in the existing folder—the Pictures folder.

4 With the current folder name highlighted, type **Extra_Pictures** and press Enter two times to accept the name and open the folder.

The new compressed folder will display the name of the file to which you were pointing when you right-clicked. You can change the name if you want to do so by using any renaming technique.

5 Create a **Window Snip**, click in the folder window to capture the window, and then on your USB flash drive, save the snip file in **JPEG** format in your **All In One Chapter 2** folder as **Lastname_Firstname_2B_CompressedFolder_Snip** Hold this file until you finish Project 2B, and then submit this file as directed by your instructor.

6 In the upper right corner of the folder window, click the **Restore Down** button to restore the window to its smaller size, and then **Close** the folder window. Submit your three snip files from this project as directed by your instructor.

End **You have completed Project 2B**

Project 2C Browsing the Web with Internet Explorer 8

Project Activities

In Activities 2.22 through 2.27, you will work with Barbara Ramos, a freelance Interior Designer working at the headquarters office of Bell Orchid Hotels, as she explores how to browse and navigate the World Wide Web by using Internet Explorer 8. Barbara will review research on the Web related to operating her small business and selecting materials for her clients. Your completed screens will look similar to Figure 2.48.

Project Files

You will save your files as:

Lastname_Firstname_2C_Searches_Snip
Lastname_Firstname_2C_Favorites_Snip
Lastname_Firstname_2C_Print_Snip

Project Results

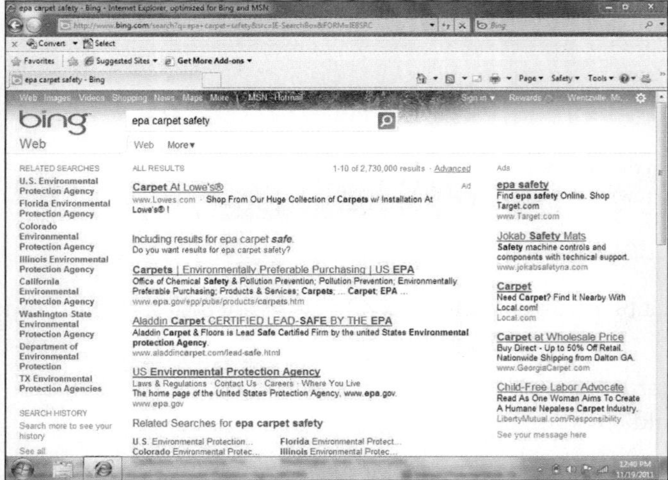

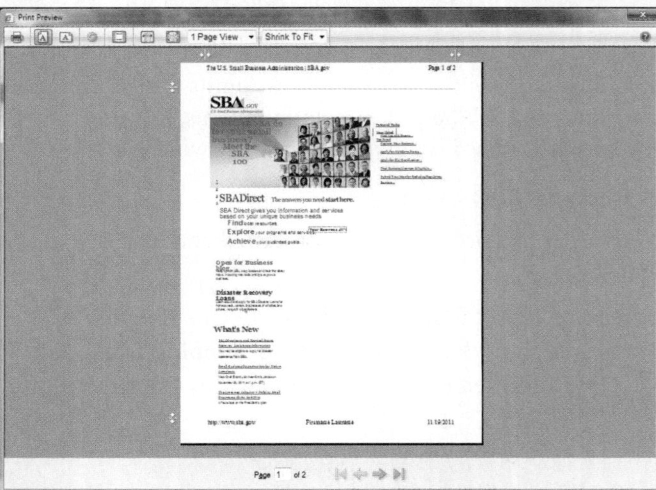

Figure 2.48
Project 2C Internet Explorer

Objective 11 | Search the Internet

The Internet can connect you to a vast amount of information, but first you have to find the information that you need. From within Internet Explorer, there are two ways in which you can search for information on the Internet without navigating to a specific Web site. The easiest method is to type a ***search term*** in the Search box in the upper right corner of the Internet Explorer screen. A search term is a word or phrase that describes the topic about which you want to find information. You can also type a search term directly in the Address bar.

Activity 2.22 | Searching the Internet

A ***search provider*** is a Web site that provides search capabilities on the web. The default search provider in Internet Explorer is Microsoft's Bing.

1 On the taskbar, click the **Internet Explorer** button. If a Welcome screen displays, close it. In the upper right corner, locate the **Search** box, and then at the right end of the box, click the **Search arrow ▼**. Compare your screen with Figure 2.49.

Figure 2.49

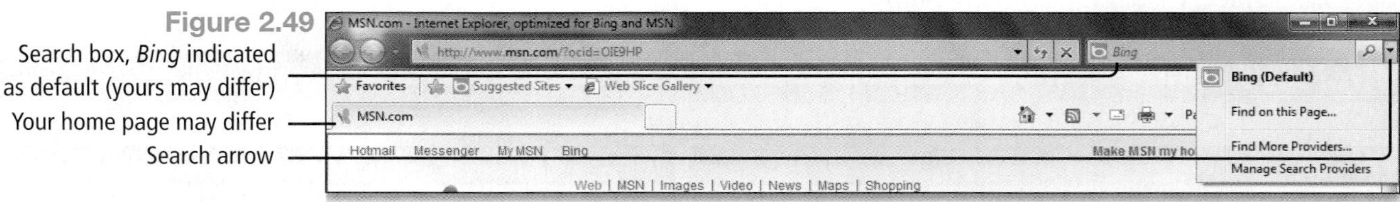

> **Note | If Bing Is Not Your Default**
>
> If Bing is not the default, set it as the default for this project as follows: On the displayed menu, click Find More Providers, and then click Bing Search. Click Click to Install, and then click Add. Then, click the search arrow, click Manage Search Providers, click Bing, and then in the lower right corner, click Set as default. Click the Close button.

2 With **Bing** set as your default search provider, click in a blank area of the screen to close the Search menu, and then click in the Search box.

3 Type the following, including the quotation marks: **"carpet safety"** and then press Enter. In the list of results, notice that your exact term *carpet safety* displays in bold.

Bing displays the search results, and on the right, displays ***sponsored links***—paid advertisements shown as a links, typically for products and services related to your search term. Sponsored links are the way that search sites like Bing, Google, and others earn revenue. On the left, related searches are suggested.

Use quotation marks to search for specific phrases. Surrounding terms with quotation marks limits the search results to only those Web pages that contain the exact phrase that you typed. Without the quotation marks, the search results will include any page that contains the terms that you typed, regardless of the order of the words.

4 Open a **New Tab**, in the **Address bar** type **epa carpet safety** and then press Enter.

When you type a search term directly in the Address bar, Internet Explorer tries to find a URL that matches; if it cannot do so, the default search provider conducts the search.

5 **Start** the **Snipping Tool** program and create a **Full-screen Snip**. **Save** the snip in your **All In One Chapter 2** folder as a **JPEG** file with the name **Lastname_Firstname_2C_Searches_Snip Close** the **Snipping Tool** mark-up window. Hold this file until you complete Project 2C, and then submit it as directed by your instructor.

6 **Close** Internet Explorer.

Objective 12 | Use Tabbed Browsing

A ***Web browser*** is a software program that you use to display Web pages and navigate the Internet. Internet Explorer 8 is the Web browser software developed by Microsoft Corporation and that is included with Windows 7. ***Browsing*** is the term used to describe the process of using your computer to view Web pages. ***Surfing*** refers to the process of navigating the Internet either for a particular item or for anything that is of interest, and quickly moving from one item to another.

Activity 2.23 | Using Tabbed Browsing

Tabbed browsing is a feature in Internet Explorer that enables you to open multiple Web sites in a single browser window. You open each new Web page in a new tab, and then switch among your open Web pages by clicking the tab that displays in the upper portion of the screen. The advantage to using tabbed browsing is that you have fewer items open on the taskbar. In this activity, you will conduct research on the new hotel in Miami.

1. On the taskbar, click the **Internet Explorer** button.

   The ***home page*** that is set on your computer displays. On your computer, home page refers to whatever Web page you have selected—or is set by default—to display on your computer when you start Internet Explorer. When visiting a Web site, home page refers to the starting point for the remainder of the pages on that site.

2. At the top of your screen, click in the **address bar** to select (highlight) the current Web address, and then, type **www.usa.gov** and then press Enter. Notice the URL in the **address bar**, and then compare your screen with Figure 2.50.

   The Web site for the United States Government displays. By typing in the address bar, the new URL opens and the original URL—whatever your home page site was—closes.

   A URL contains the ***protocol prefix***—in this instance ***http***—which stands for ***HyperText Transfer Protocol***. HTTP represents the set of communication rules used by your computer to connect to servers on the Web. Internet Explorer defaults to the http prefix, so it is not necessary to type it, even though it is part of the URL for this site.The protocol prefix is followed by a colon and the separators //. A URL also contains the ***domain name***—in this instance www.usa.gov. A domain name is an organization's unique name on the Internet, and consists of a chosen name combined with a ***top level domain*** such as .com or .org or .gov.

Figure 2.50

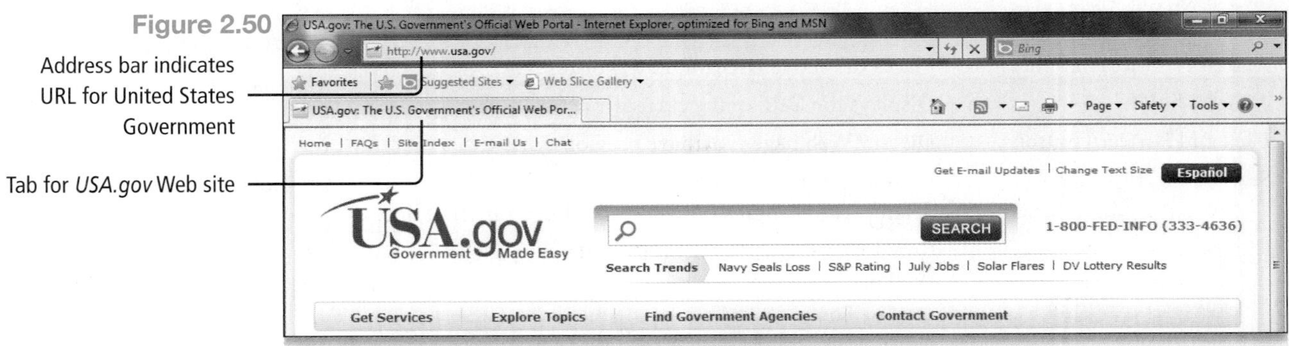

> **Alert! | Web Sites Update Content Frequently**
>
> As you progress through the projects in this chapter, the pictures of various Web sites in this textbook may not match your screens exactly, because Web site administrators frequently update content. This will not affect your ability to complete the projects successfully.

3. Click in the address bar to select the URL text, and then type **osha.gov/SLTC/lead** and press Enter.

   The acronym *www*, which stands for *World Wide Web*, is used for uniformity on the Web. You can usually omit typing www and its following dot, because most Web servers are configured to handle a URL with or without it. If a Web page does not display without typing www, retype the URL and include www.

4. Click the New Tab button one time. Compare your screen with Figure 2.51, and then take a moment to study the parts of the Internet Explorer window in the table in Figure 2.52.

   The screen for a new tab displays, and in the address bar, *about:Tabs* is selected. This *What do you want to do next?* page will display a list of sites that you have opened and then closed during this session, which is useful if you have closed a browser window by mistake and want to go back to it.

Figure 2.51

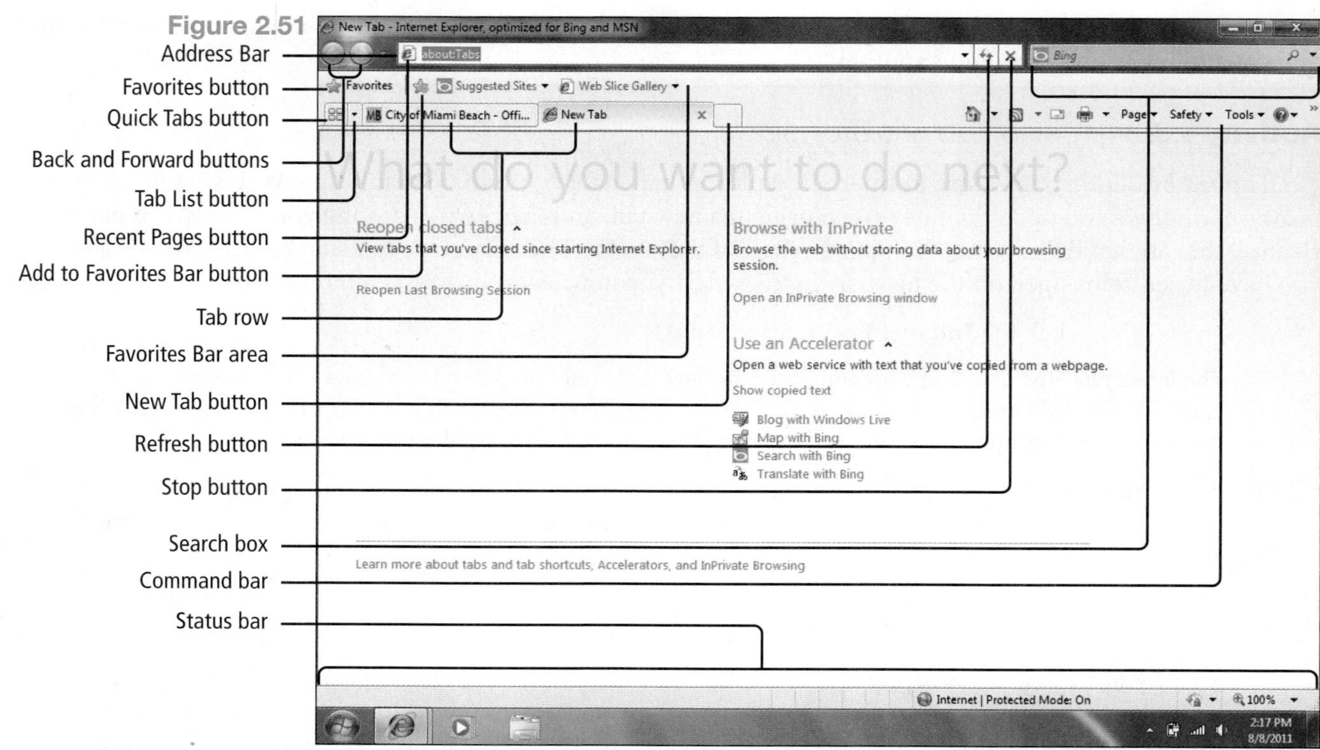

Window Elements and Functions

Window Element	Function
Add to Favorites Bar button	Places the active URL on the Favorites Bar.
Address bar	Displays the URL of the currently active Web page.
Back and Forward buttons	Display Web pages you have previously visited.
Search box	Provides an area in which you type a search term to conduct an Internet search; Bing is the default search engine but you can select a different one.
Command bar	Contains, by default, the buttons to view your Home page; view your Feeds; view mail; print Web pages; manipulate Web pages, for example by saving; select safety settings; and to display a list of Tools.
Favorites Bar	Displays links to favorite Web sites that you have placed there.
Favorites button	Opens the Favorites Center pane, which is an area to manage your Favorites, browser history, and subscribed RSS feeds.
New Tab button	Opens a new tab.
Quick Tabs button	Displays a thumbnail of each Web site that is currently open on a single tab.
Recent Pages button	Displays a list of recently visited Web sites.
Refresh button	Updates the content of the displayed Web page; for example, to update temperatures on a weather site or update stock prices on a financial site.
Status bar	Displays, on the left, the URL for a link to which your mouse is pointing; on the right, displays information about the download process of a Web site and also icons to change your security settings and Zoom level.
Stop button	Stops the download of a Web page that you requested.
Tab List button	Lists the names of all Web sites currently open on a tab.
Tab row	Displays a tab for each open Web page.

Figure 2.52

5 With the text in the **address bar** selected, type **epa.gov/lead** and then press Enter to display the Web site for the **EPA regarding lead**. Click the New Tab button, type **hud.gov/content/releases** and then press Enter. Compare your screen with Figure 2.53.

A Web site for the US Department of Housing and Urban Development opens in the new tab.

Figure 2.53

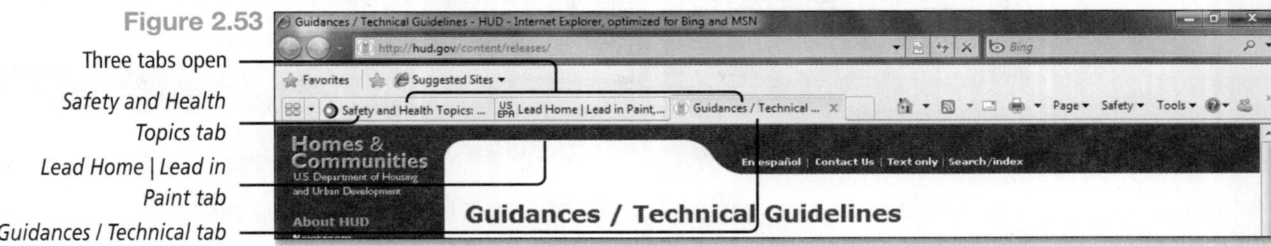

6 On the **tab row**, click the first open tab—the **Safety and Health Topics tab**.

The Web site for OSHA redisplays. Recall that by opening multiple sites on tabs, you can switch between Web sites easily by clicking a tab.

7 On the taskbar, *point* to the **Internet Explorer** icon to display a thumbnail for each open tab.

Here you can see the Web sites that you have open in Internet Explorer, and can navigate to a site by clicking its thumbnail.

8 Click the New Tab button, and then type **cdc.gov** and press Enter. Click the New Tab button, and then type **sba.gov** and press Enter.

Five Web sites are open and five tabs display in your tab row. As you open more tabs, the width of each tab decreases slightly and you can no longer read all the text on the tab.

> **More Knowledge | Using the Address Bar Efficiently**
>
> The address bar, based on the first few characters that you type, will search across your History, Favorites, and RSS Feeds, displaying matches from the address or any part of the URL. When you see a match, click it to avoid retyping the entire URL of a site you have previously visited.

Activity 2.24 | Using the Tab List, Quick Tabs, and Shortcuts to Navigate Among Open Tabs

When you have multiple Web pages open at once, each one is displayed on a separate tab. When many Web pages are open and the width of each tab is decreased, it may become difficult to determine which tab represents a specific site. In this activity, you will practice various ways to navigate the open tabs to find the one you want easily.

1 On the left end of the tab row, click the **Tab List** button, and then compare your screen with Figure 2.54.

The Tab List displays. When multiple tabs are open, the Web site name on each tab is truncated—cut short. By clicking the Tab List button, you can see a list of all open Web sites, in the order they were opened, and you can see the complete name of each Web site that is open on a tab. Additionally, the highlighted section indicates tabs that are visible on the tab row—tabs outside of the highlighted area. From this list, you can click a site to move to another tab, regardless of whether the tab is visible on the tab row.

Figure 2.54

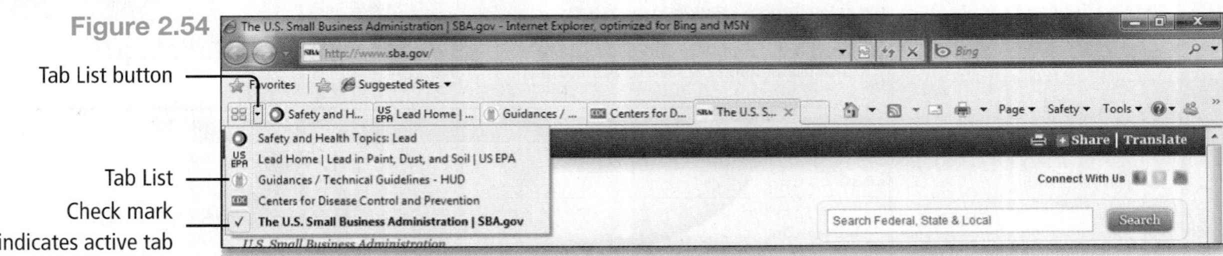

2 On the displayed **Tab List** menu, click **Guidances/Technical Guidelines - HUD**. Point to the **Guidances/Technical Guidelines - HUD** tab, and then notice that a ScreenTip displays the site name and the site's URL. Notice also that because this is the active tab, the **Close Tab** button [x] displays, as shown in Figure 2.55.

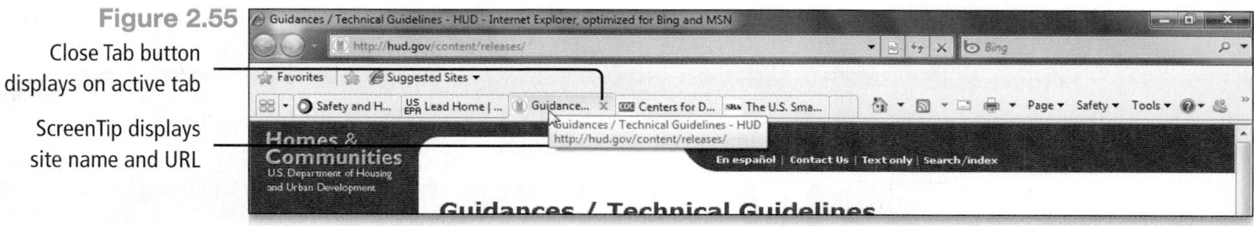

Figure 2.55

3 On the **Guidances/Technical Guidelines - HUD**, click the **Close Tab** button [x] to close the **HUD** Web site and to make the next tab in the row the active tab and display the **CDC** Web site.

4 On the left end of the **tab row**, click the **Quick Tabs** button [88], and then compare your screen with Figure 2.56.

When you have multiple Web pages open and the tab names are truncated, you can use the Quick Tabs display. The Quick Tabs feature provides a thumbnail view of all open tabs. From this view, you can click any thumbnail to open a Web page or click the Close Tab button to close a Web page. The Quick Tabs button displays only when you have more than one Web page open.

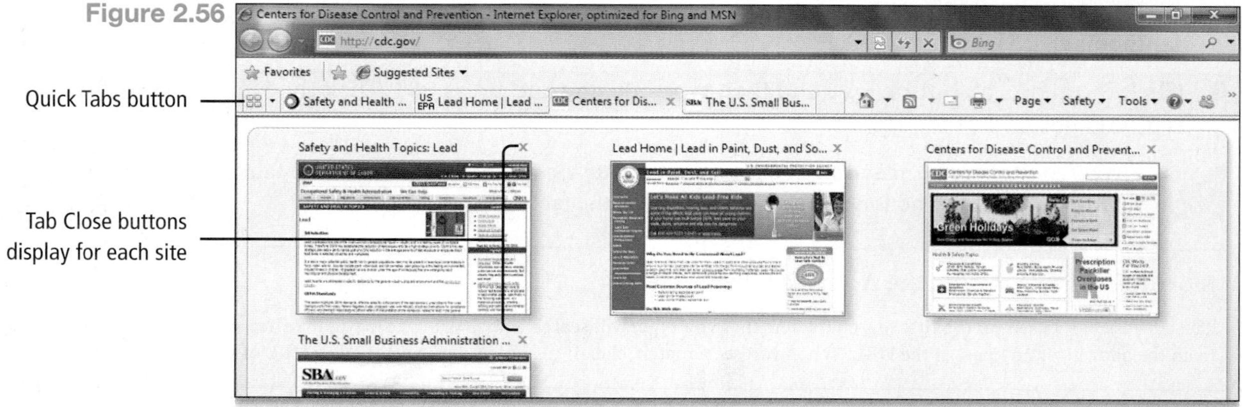

Figure 2.56

5 In the **Quick Tabs** display, click the **Close Tab** button [x] for the **Centers for Disease Control and Prevention** and notice that in the display, the thumbnails rearrange to fill the blank space. *Except* for the **Safety and Health Topics: Lead** site (do not close it), use the same technique to close all other sites. Then click the thumbnail image for the **Safety and Health Topics: Lead** to display the site. Compare your screen with Figure 2.57.

Although the content of this Web page may differ from what you currently have displayed, you can see that this Web page contains various links—other pages in this Web site that you can display. Groups of links are sometimes referred to as a ***navigation bar***.

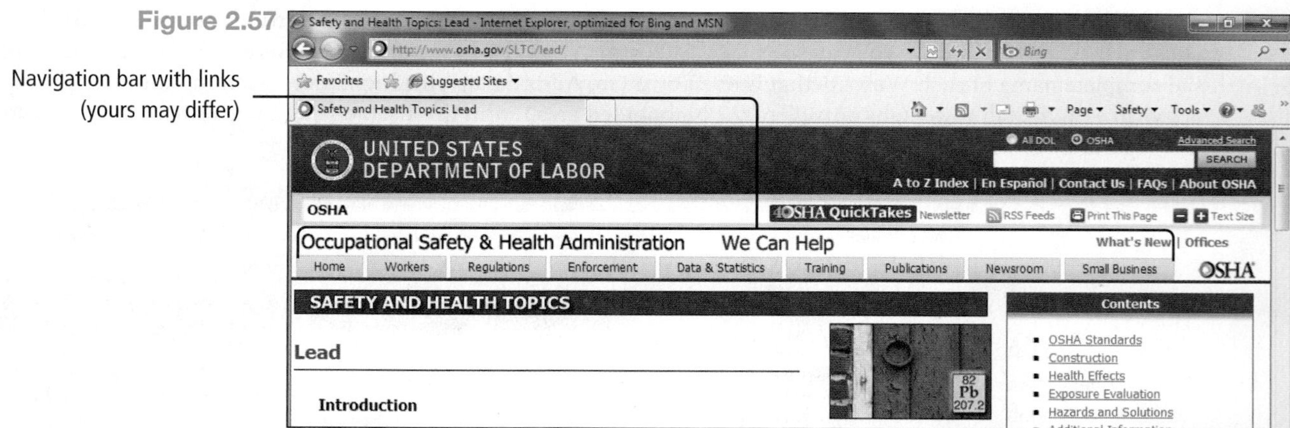

Figure 2.57

6 On the second row of the navigation bar, click **Small Business**; or, click any link on the page. Compare your screen with Figure 2.58.

When you click a link on a Web page, the new page opens on the same tab.

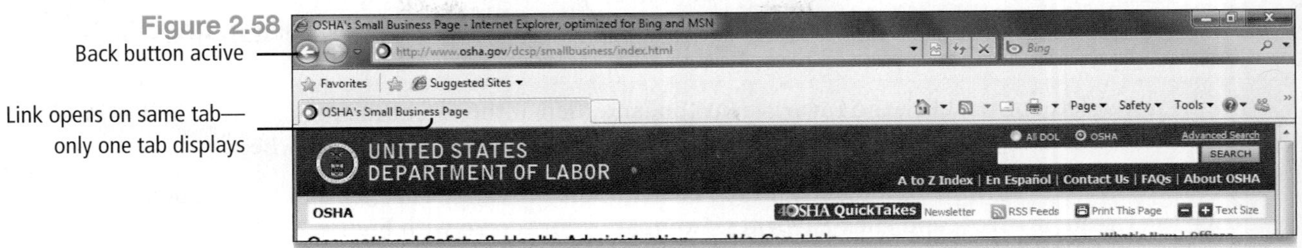

Figure 2.58

7 In the upper left corner, click the **Back** button one time to return to the previous page. Then, click the **Forward** button to redisplay the page regarding Small Business information from OSHA.

In this manner, you can click the Back and Forward buttons as necessary to redisplay pages you have visited.

8 Hold down Ctrl, and then in the navigation bar in the upper portion of the page, click **Publications**. Notice that a new tab opens for the **OSHA Publications** page but the page itself does not display. Notice also that the two tabs display in the same color.

In this manner, you can open links in separate tabs without actually displaying them. When you are finished viewing the active page, you can investigate the other links you opened. Additionally, the tabs are colored to match so that you know they are related.

9 Hold down Ctrl and press T to open a new tab. Type **usa.gov** and press Enter. In the **tab row**, point to the **OSHA Publications tab**. If you have a mouse wheel, also referred to as the *middle mouse button*, click it and notice the tab is closed. Point to the **Safety and Health Topics: Lead tab**, right-click, and then click **Close Tab**.

Use either of these techniques to close a tab without first making it the active tab. This is useful when you have some tabs open that you no longer need and want to close them quickly.

10 Press Ctrl + T to open a new tab, and then compare your screen with Figure 2.59.

After you have opened and closed sites, you can view a list of all the sites you have visited in this session by opening a new tab. Then, if you want to do so, you can click a site name to open it on this tab.

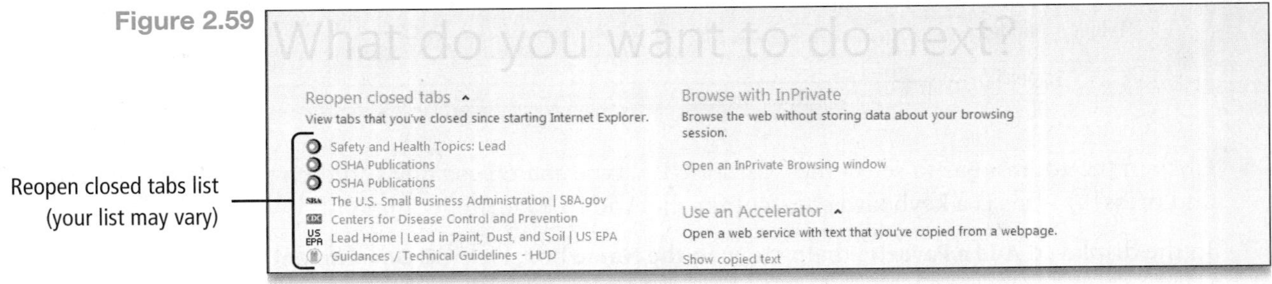

Figure 2.59

11 **Close** Internet Explorer. In the **Internet Explorer** dialog box, click **Close all tabs**.

Objective 13 | Organize Favorites

The Favorites Center is a list of links to Web sites that is saved in your Web browser. Saving a Web site as a favorite allows you to return to it quickly. Returning to the site requires only one or two clicks instead of typing a complete URL. You can create a folder to organize your favorite links into groups that are meaningful to you. Then, you can either open one site from the folder, or open all the sites in the folder with a single click.

Activity 2.25 | Organizing Favorites

In this activity, you will help Barbara save Web sites as favorites for easy access in the future.

1 **Close** [Close button] any open windows and display your Windows 7 desktop. On the taskbar, click the **Internet Explorer** button [Internet Explorer button], click in the **address bar**, and then type **pasadena.edu** and press Enter. Click the New Tab button [New Tab button] type **florida.edu** and then press Enter.

2 In the upper left corner, click the **Favorites** button, and then at the top of the pane, to the right of Add to Favorites, click the [arrow button] **arrow**. On the displayed list, click **Add Current Tabs to Favorites**.

3 In the **Add Tabs to Favorites** dialog box, in the **Folder Name** box, type **Colleges and Universities** If necessary, click the Create in arrow and click Favorites. Compare your screen with Figure 2.60.

Figure 2.60

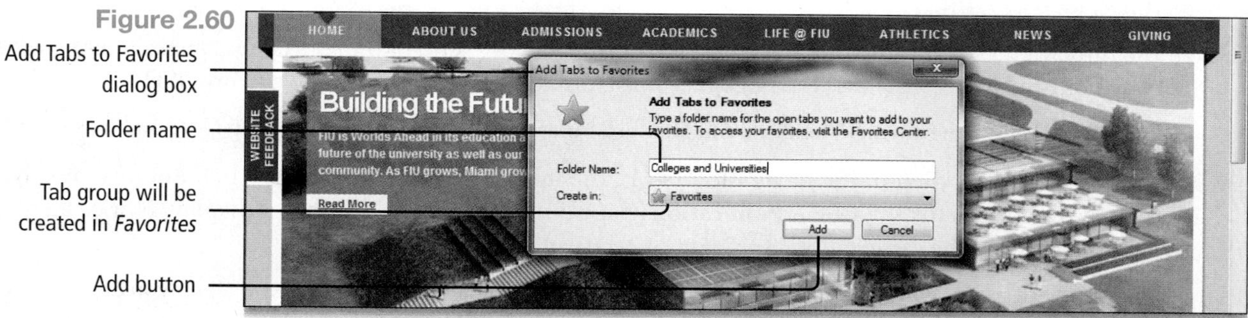

4 In the dialog box, click the **Add** button. **Close** [Close button] Internet Explorer and all tabs.

5 Open **Internet Explorer** [Internet Explorer button] again, and then in the upper left corner, click the **Favorites** button. If necessary, at the top of the displayed list, click the Favorites tab. Scroll down as necessary, click **Colleges and Universities** to expand the list, and then point to the arrow to the right of **Colleges and Universities** to display the ScreenTip. Compare your screen with Figure 2.61, and then click the **Favorites** button to collapse the list.

Figure 2.61

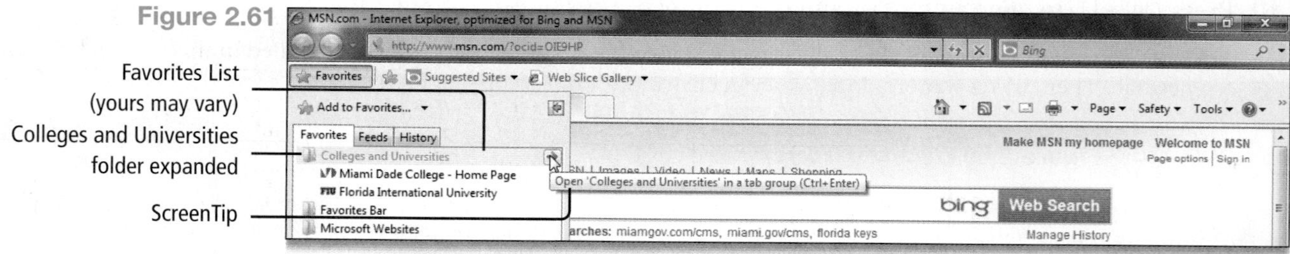

6 Click in the **address bar** to select the existing URL, type **search.usa.gov** and then press Enter. Hold down Ctrl and press D—this is a keyboard shortcut for the Add to Favorites command.

7 In the displayed **Add a Favorite** dialog box, in the **Name** box, type **US Government Search Engine** to replace the selected text. Compare your screen with Figure 2.62.

You need not accept the default name of a Web site stored in your Favorites list. Change the name as necessary so that you can easily identify the site.

Figure 2.62

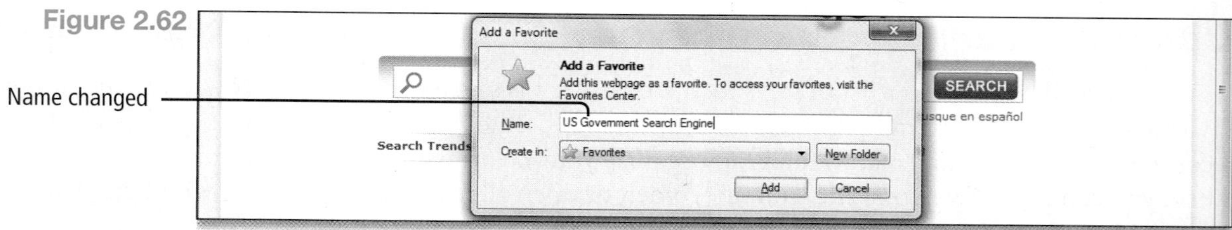

8 In the **Add a Favorite** dialog box, click the **Add** button.

In this manner, you can create folders for your favorite sites at the time you save the site as a Favorite. Be sure to notice where the folder is being stored, and place it either at the Favorites level or within other folders if you want to do so.

9 **Close** [X] Internet Explorer.

Activity 2.26 | Using the Favorites Bar

The Favorites bar is a toolbar that displays directly below the address bar and to which you can add or drag Web addresses you use frequently.

1 On the taskbar, click the **Internet Explorer** button. Click in the **address bar** to select the existing URL, type **weather.gov** and then press Enter.

2 Directly below the **address bar**, click the **Add to Favorites Bar** button. Compare your screen with Figure 2.63.

Figure 2.63

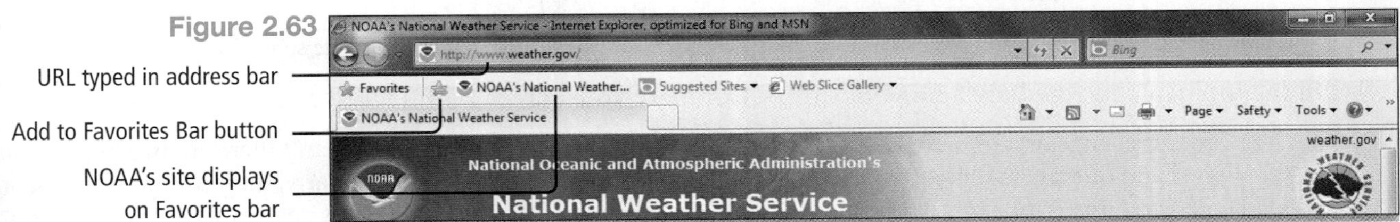

3 Click in the **address bar**, type **fsu.edu** and press Enter. At the left end of the **address bar**, point to the **Florida State University logo**, hold down the left mouse button, and then drag the logo onto the **Favorites bar** until a black line displays to the right of the NOAA's site, as shown in Figure 2.64. Then release the mouse button.

Figure 2.64

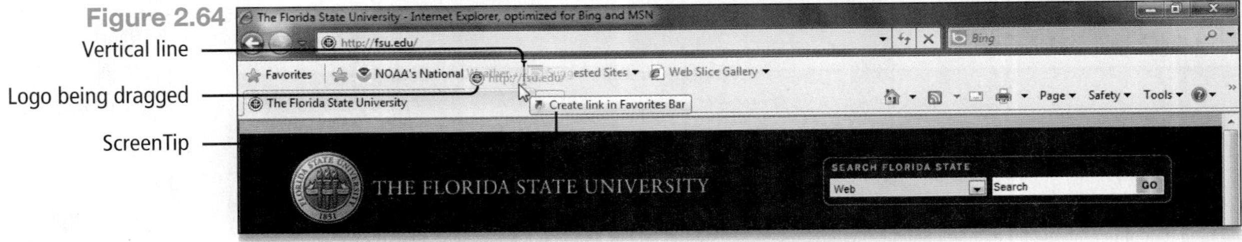

4 Create a **Full-screen Snip**, and then on your USB flash drive, save the snip file in **JPEG** format in your **All In One Chapter 2** folder as **Lastname_Firstname_2C_Favorites_Snip** Hold this file until you finish Project 2C, and then submit this file as directed by your instructor.

5 Point to the FSU link on the Favorites bar, right-click, click Delete, and then click Yes. By using the same technique, delete the link for NOAA. Close [X] Internet Explorer.

On your own computer, place links to the sites you use most frequently on the Favorites bar, and for other favorite sites, add them to the Favorites Center.

Objective 14 | Print Web Pages

By default, Internet Explorer 8 will shrink a Web page's text just enough to ensure that the entire page prints properly.

Activity 2.27 | Printing Web Pages

Internet Explorer 8 provides useful options for formatting and then printing a Web page. In the following activity, you will print a Web page.

1 **Close** any open windows. On the taskbar, click the **Internet Explorer** button, click in the **address bar**, type **sba.gov** and then press Enter.

The home page for the U.S. Small Business Administration displays.

2 On the **Command bar**, locate and click the **Print button arrow** to display a menu. Compare your screen with Figure 2.65.

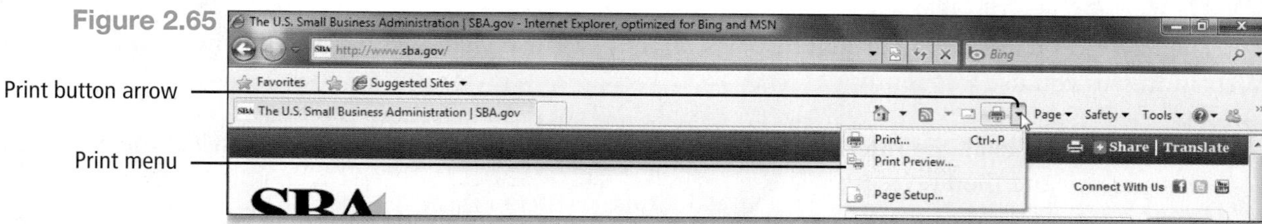

Figure 2.65

3 On the menu, click **Print Preview** to display the Web page as it will look when you print it.

Recall that Internet Explorer will shrink the page as necessary to fit horizontally on the selected paper size.

4 On the toolbar, click the **Page Setup** button. Compare your screen with Figure 2.66.

Here you can change or add to the headers and footers on a printed Web page. By default there are two headers, one left aligned and one right aligned, which will display the page title and the URL. Similarly, there are two footers, one left aligned and one right aligned, which will display the page number with total pages and the date in short format.

The default setting for the centered header and footer is Empty. You can change any of the headers and footers by clicking the arrow and selecting an item or by selecting Custom and creating a new entry. You can also change the font of the headers and footers.

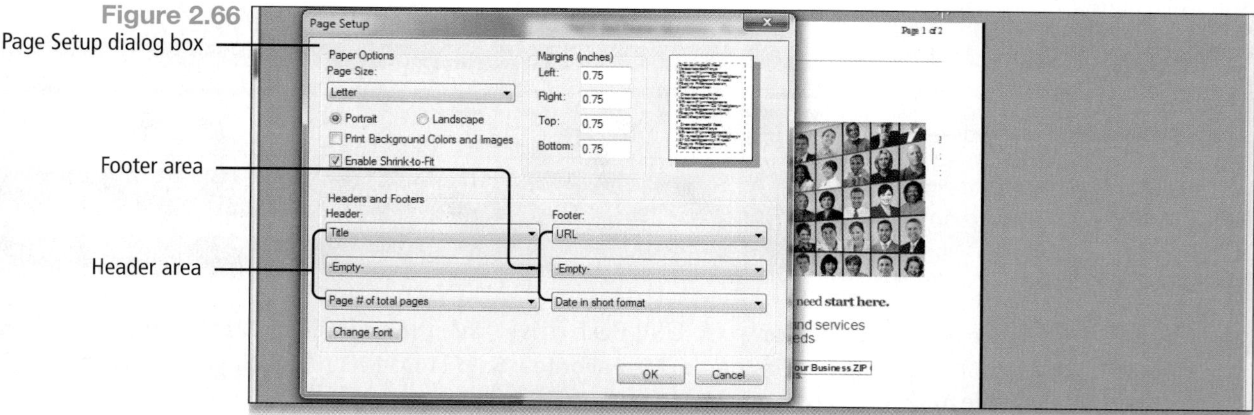

Figure 2.66

5 Under **Footer**, click the second arrow, click **Custom**. In the Custom dialog box, using your own name, type **Firstname Lastname** Click **OK**, and then, in the **Page Setup** dialog box, click **OK**.

In the Print Preview screen, your name displays as a centered heading.

6 Create a **Full-screen Snip**, and then on your USB flash drive, save the snip file in **JPEG** format in your **All In One Chapter 2** folder as **Lastname_Firstname_2C_Print_Snip**

7 **Close** [X] the Print Preview screen, and then **Close** [X] Internet Explorer. Submit your three snip files from this project as directed by your instructor.

More Knowledge | Printing Specific Parts of a Web Page

To print only a specific part of a Web page, use your mouse to select the content that you want to print. Then, click the Print button arrow, click Print, and then in the Print dialog box, click the Selection option button. Click Print.

End **You have completed Project 2C**

Content-Based Assessments

Summary

Windows 7 is an operating system program that manages your hardware, manages your software programs, and stores and manages your data. In this chapter, you used Snipping Tool to capture screen shots, created a folder on a removable device and saved files, used Windows 7 Help and Support, searched for files, and used Internet Explorer.

Key Terms

Check Your Knowledge

Matching and Multiple Choice items are available in MyITLab and on the Companion Web Site.

Skills Review | Project 2D Exploring Windows

Project Files

For Project 2D, you will need the following files:

A USB flash drive containing the student data files
win02D_Answer_Sheet (Word document)

You will save your file as:

Lastname_Firstname_2D_Answer_Sheet

1 **Close** [X] all open windows. On the taskbar, click the **Windows Explorer** button. In the **navigation pane**, click the drive that contains the student files for this textbook, and then double-click the Word file **win02D_Answer_Sheet** to open Word and display the document. Press F12 to display the **Save As** dialog box in Word, navigate to your **All In One Chapter 2** folder, and then using your own name, save the document as **Lastname_Firstname_2D_Answer_Sheet** Click OK if you see a message regarding file formats.

On the taskbar, click the **Word** button to minimize the window and leave your Word document accessible from the taskbar. **Close** the **Windows Explorer** window. As you complete each step in this project, click the Word button on the taskbar to open the document, type your one-letter answer in the appropriate cell of the Word table, and then on the taskbar, click the button again to minimize the window for the next step.

From the **Start menu**, click **Control Panel**, and then with the insertion point blinking in the search box, type **get** In the list that displays, click **Getting Started**. Which of the following is true?

a. From this screen, you can create a new folder.

b. Several links on this screen will take you to sources of information.

c. From this screen, you can shut down your computer.

2 Close [X] the Getting Started window. **Close** [X] the **Control Panel** window. Display the **Start menu**, and then at the top of the right side of the menu, under the picture, click your user name. In the displayed window, where does your user name display?

a. In the address bar

b. In the details pane

c. In the file list

3 In the **navigation pane**, click **Computer**. What is your result?

a. The storage devices attached to your computer display in the file list.

b. All of the files on the hard drive display in the file list.

c. Your computer restarts.

4 According to the toolbar in this window, which of the following is true?

a. From this window you can restart your computer.

b. From this window you can open the PowerPoint application.

c. From this window you can uninstall or change a program.

5 **Close** [X] the **Computer** window. From the **Start** menu, click **Help and Support**. In the **Search** box, type **shortcuts** and then press Enter. Click **Keyboard shortcuts**, scroll down as necessary, and then click **Windows logo key keyboard shortcuts**. Scroll as necessary to view the table. According to this information, to open the **Start** menu using the keyboard, you can press:

a. [Windows logo]

b. [Windows logo] + 1

c. Alt + F4

6 **Close** [X] **Help and Support**. Display the **Start** menu, click **Control Panel**, click **Hardware and Sound**, and then click **Power Options**. In the introduction, click **Tell me more about power plans**. Based on the information in the Windows Help and Support window, which of the following is *not* true?

a. Power plans can reduce the amount of power your computer uses.

b. Power plans can maximize your system's performance.

c. A power plan is a collection of software settings.

(Project 2D Exploring Windows continues on the next page)

Skills Review | Project 2D Exploring Windows (continued)

7 **Close** [Close button] **Help and Support**. **Close** [Close button] the **Control Panel**. On the taskbar, click the **Windows Explorer** button. In the **navigation pane**, click the flash drive that contains the student files. Open the data files for Chapter 2. In the file list on the right, how many *folders* display?

- **a.** None
- **b.** One
- **c.** Two

8 In the file list on the right, double-click the **Bell_Orchid** folder to open it, and then double-click the **Corporate** folder to open it. Which of the following best describes the contents of the Corporate folder?

- **a.** Only individual files display.
- **b.** Only folders display.
- **c.** Both individual files and folders display.

9 In the **file list**, double-click the **Engineering** folder to open it. In an open area, right-click. On the displayed shortcut menu, point to **Group by**, and then on the displayed submenu, click **Type**. How many different groups of file types display?

- **a.** Three
- **b.** Four
- **c.** Five

10 Right-click anywhere in the file list, point to **Group by**, and then click **(None)**. **Close** [Close button] Windows Explorer. On the **Start** menu, click **All Programs**, click **Accessories**, and then click **Notepad** to start the program. Using the same technique, start the **Paint** program, and then the **Calculator** program. On the taskbar, which program button is shown as active—the glass frame is brighter and less translucent than the other two?

- **a.** Notepad
- **b.** Paint
- **c.** Calculator

Be sure you have typed all of your answers in your Word document. Save and close your Word document, and submit as directed by your instructor. **Close** [Close button] all open windows.

End **You have completed Project 2D**

Skills Review | Project 2E Managing Files and Folders

Project Files

For Project 2E, you will need the following files:

A flash drive containing the student data files
win02E_Answer_Sheet (Word document)

You will save your file as:

Lastname_Firstname_2E_Answer_Sheet

1 **Close** all open windows. On the taskbar, click the **Windows Explorer** button. In the **navigation pane**, click the drive that contains the student files for this textbook, and thendouble-click the Word file **win02E_Answer_Sheet** to open Word and display the document. Press F12 to display the **Save As** dialog box in Word, navigate to your **All In One Chapter 2** folder, and then using your own name, save the document as **Lastname_Firstname_2E_Answer_Sheet** If necessary, click OK regarding new formats.

On the taskbar, click the **Word** button to minimize the window and leave your Word document accessible from the taskbar. **Close** the **Windows Explorer** window. As you complete each step in this project, click the Word button on the taskbar to open the document, type your one-letter answer in the appropriate cell of the Word table, and then on the taskbar, click the button again to minimize the window for the next step.

If necessary, from your USB drive with the student data files, using the **Send to** command, copy the **Bell_Orchid** folder to your **Documents** library—you will need a new copy of the files for this project. On your USB flash drive, create a folder named **Europe** By which of the following methods can you create a new folder:

a. In the file list, right-click, point to New, and then click Folder.

b. On the toolbar, click the New folder button.

c. Either A. or B.

2 Display your **Documents** folder, and then navigate to **Bell_Orchid ▶ Corporate**. In the **address bar**, click **Corporate** to display this folder window. In the **address bar**, to the immediate right of the **location icon**, click **▶**. What is your result?

a. A list of available base locations displays below the separator line.

b. A list of the subfolders within the Corporate folder displays.

c. The path that describes the folder's location displays and is highlighted.

3 Display the **Bell_Orchid** folder window. On the toolbar, click **New folder**, and then create a new folder named **Florida_Keys** Drag the **Florida_Keys** folder to become the first item under Favorites. Which of the following is true?

a. The Florida_Keys folder no longer displays in the file list.

b. The Florida_Keys folder window opens.

c. The Florida_Keys folder displays in the Favorites area with a buff-colored folder.

4 Display the **Documents** file list, and then navigate to **Bell_Orchid ➢ Corporate ➢ Food_Beverage ➢ Restaurants**. The *quickest* way to select the **Breakfast_Continental, Breakfast_Form, Breakfast_Menus**, and **Brunch_Menus** files is:

a. Hold down Ctrl and click each file.

b. Hold down Ctrl and press A.

c. Draw a selection area around the four contiguous files.

5 Be sure the **Restaurants** window displays. In the **file list**, the quickest way to select the noncontiguous files **Grill_Menu** and **Refreshments** is to:

a. Hold down Ctrl and then click each file name.

b. Hold down Tab and then click each file name.

c. Hold down Shift and then click each file name.

6 Select **Grill_Menu** and **Refreshments** and send them to your USB flash drive. Then display your USB flash drive window. Rename the folder **Europe** to **Menus** Rename the file **Refreshments** to **Pool_Menu** Which of the following is true:

a. Your USB flash drive now contains a folder named Europe and a folder named Menus.

(Project 2E Managing Files and Folders continues on the next page)

Content-Based Assessments

Skills Review | Project 2E Managing Files and Folders (continued)

b. You can use the same technique to rename a file and to rename a folder.

c. You must have permission to rename a folder or a file.

7 In your USB flash drive folder window, in the **file list**, select the files **Grill_Menu** and **Pool_Menu** and then drag them into the **Menus** folder. The result of this action is:

a. The files were copied to the Menus folder.

b. The files were moved to the Menus folder.

c. The files were deleted.

8 Open the **Menus** folder on your USB flash drive. Right-click the **Pool_Menu** file, and then from the displayed menu, click **Copy**. Right-click in an empty area of the **file list**, and then click **Paste**. Your result is:

a. A file named *Pool_Menu- Copy* displays in the file list.

b. A file named *Second_Pool_Menu* displays in the file list.

c. An error message indicates *Duplicate File Name, Cannot Copy.*

9 In the **navigation pane**, click to select your USB flash drive. Delete the **Menus** folder. In the **Delete Folder** dialog box, the following message displays:

a. Are you sure you want to permanently delete this folder?

b. Are you sure you want to copy this folder to the Recycle Bin?

c. Are you sure you want to move this folder to the Recycle Bin?

10 In the **Delete Folder** dialog box, click **Yes**. In the navigation pane, click **Documents**, and then delete the **Bell_Orchid** folder. In the **Delete Folder** dialog box, the following message displays:

a. Are you sure you want to permanently delete this folder?

b. Are you sure you want to copy this folder to the Recycle Bin?

c. Are you sure you want to move this folder to the Recycle Bin?

Click **Yes**. In the upper right corner of the folder window, be sure you have typed all of your answers in your Word document. **Save** and **Close** your Word document, and submit as directed by your instructor. **Close** [X] all open windows.

End **You have completed Project 2E**

Skills Review | Project 2F Browsing the Web with Internet Explorer 8

Project Files

For Project 2F, you will need the following file:

win02_2F_Answer_Sheet (Word document)

You will save your file as:

Lastname_Firstname_2F_Answer_Sheet

1 **Close** [X] all open windows. On the taskbar, click the **Windows Explorer** button. In the **navigation pane**, click the drive that contains the student files for this textbook, and then double-click the Word file **win02_2F_Answer_Sheet** to open Word and display the document. Press F12 to display the **Save As** dialog box in Word, navigate to your **All In One Chapter 2** folder, and then using your own name, save the document as **Lastname_Firstname_2F_Answer_Sheet** If necessary, click OK regarding new formats.

On the taskbar, click the **Word** button to minimize the window and leave your Word document accessible from the taskbar. **Close** the **Windows Explorer** window. As you complete each step in this project, click the Word button on the taskbar to open the document, type your one-letter answer in the appropriate cell of the Word table, and then on the taskbar, click the button again to minimize the window for the next step.

Start Internet Explorer again. In the **Search** box, click the **Search** arrow ▼, and then click **Manage Search Providers**. If necessary, set **Bing** as the default and close the Manage Add-ons dialog box. What is your result?

a. *Bing* displays in the Search box.

b. *Default Search* displays in the Search box.

c. *Start your search here* displays in the Search box.

2 In the **Search** box, type **"florida university"** and press Enter. What heading displays above the left column of links?

a. All Results

b. Related Searches

c. Suggested Sites

3 Click in the **address bar** and navigate to **doh.state.fl.us** Open a **New Tab**, and then go to the site **miamigov.com** On a **New Tab**, go to the site **hsmv.state.fl.us** On the **tab row**, click the **Quick Tabs** button. What is your result?

a. Thumbnails for each open site display.

b. A list of recently visited Web sites displays.

c. The tabs in the tab row are rearranged in alphabetical order.

4 On the **tab row**, click the **Tab List** button. How many sites display on the list?

a. one

b. two

c. three

5 On a **New Tab**, go to the site **florida.edu** and then click the Favorites button. Click **Add to Favorites**. What is your result?

a. The Favorites Center pane displays on the left side of the screen.

b. The Create Favorites Folder dialog box displays.

c. The Add a Favorite dialog box displays.

6 Click **Cancel**. On the displayed home page for **Florida International University**, on the **navigation bar**, point to the link for **Athletics** and right-click. From the displayed shortcut menu, which of the following actions are possible?

a. You can open the Athletics link in a new tab.

b. You can send the Athletics link to your Documents folder.

c. You can create a tab group.

7 Click in a blank area of the screen to close the shortcut menu. Click the **Favorites** button to open the **Favorites Center** pane. Across the top, which tabs display?

a. Favorites, Tab Groups, Feeds

b. Favorites, Feeds, History

c. Favorites, History, Recent Pages

(Project 2F Browsing the Web with Internet Explorer 8 continues on the next page)

Content-Based Assessments

Skills Review | Project 2F Browsing the Web with Internet Explorer 8 (continued)

8 Click the **History tab**, and then click the **arrow**. Which of the following is not a viewing arrangement?

a. By Date

b. By Favorites

c. By Most Visited

9 Click in a blank area of the screen to close the **Favorites Center** pane. On the **Command bar**, click the **Safety** button, and then click **Delete Browsing History**. According to this information, cookies consist of:

a. Saved information that you have typed into forms.

b. Buttons added to the tab row.

c. Files stored on your computer by Web sites to save preferences.

10 With the **FIU** site displayed, click the **Print button arrow**, and then click **Print Preview**. Click the **Page Setup** button to display the **Page Setup** dialog box. From this dialog box, which of the following can be changed?

a. Left and right margins

b. Headers and footers

c. Both A and B

Be sure you have typed all of your answers in your Word document. **Save** and **Close** your Word document, and submit as directed by your instructor. **Close** all open windows.

End **You have completed Project 2F**

Communicating and Networking with Outlook, Skype, LinkedIn, and Squarespace

OUTCOMES

At the end of this chapter you will be able to:

OBJECTIVES

Mastering these objectives will enable you to:

PROJECT 3A
Use Outlook to manage your e-mail, contacts, and calendar; use Skype to make voice and video calls over the Internet.

1. Create an Outlook Account (p. 91)
2. Enter and Edit Contacts and Calendar Entries (p. 95)
3. Send and Receive E-Mail (p. 102)
4. Make Calls Over the Internet Using Skype (p. 110)

PROJECT 3B
Use LinkedIn to create a professional social presence online, and use Squarespace to maintain a professional Web Site and Blog.

5. Create a LinkedIn Account (p. 114)
6. Create and Maintain a Web Site and Blog with Squarespace (p. 117)

© Dmitry Melnikov/Shutterstock

Job Focus: Freelance Interior Designer

In This Chapter

In this chapter, you will experience how a freelance Interior Designer uses Outlook to manage her e-mail, her list of business contacts, and her work calendar. You will also learn how to use Skype to make voice and video calls over the Internet.

If you are self-employed like the Interior Designer featured in this chapter, you will see how easy it is to use LinkedIn and Squarespace to create a professional social presence online by using a social network and maintaining a professional Web site and blog.

Information on the site JobVite.com indicates that 80 percent of companies use or plan to use LinkedIn to find employees. USAToday.com reports that 95 percent of businesses say they plan to use social media. Business professionals must adopt social media because it is one of the most powerful communication channels one can have with customers. Blogs represent your voice that tells the world what you do. On a blog, you share your ideas and explain how you solve real problems for real customers.

At the end of this Unit, following this chapter, you will have an opportunity to complete a case project that focuses on the job of a freelance Interior Designer.

Project 3A Client Communication

Project Activities

In Activities 3.01 through 3.10, you will communicate with your clients using Outlook and Skype. You will maintain a contact list, create calendar entries, and communicate via e-mail using Microsoft Outlook 2010. You will use Skype for making phone calls over the Internet. Upon completion, your printed message, calendar, and screen snips will look similar to Figure 3.1.

Project Files

For Project 3A, you will need the following file:

ou03A_Burrows_Design

You will save your files as:

Lastname_Firstname_3A_Contact_Cards
Lastname_Firstname_3A_Burrows_Week
Lastname_Firstname_3A_Burrows_Outbox
Lastname_Firstname_3A_Skype_Contact
Lastname_Firstname_3A_Reply_Message

Project Results

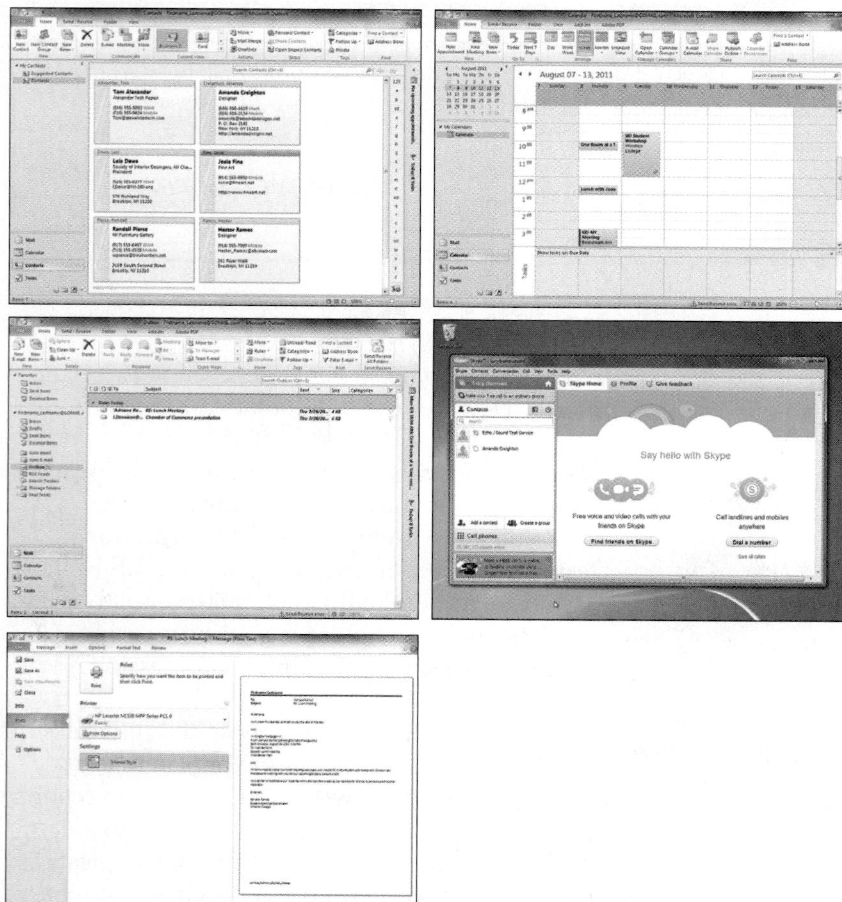

Figure 3.1
Project 3A Client Communication

Objective 1 | Create an Outlook Account

View the video on the Companion Web Site or in MyITLab

Microsoft Outlook 2010 has two functions: it is an e-mail program, and it is a ***personal information manager*** that enables you to store information about your contacts, your daily schedule, your tasks to complete, and other information that you need to access.

> **Alert! | Starting Project 3A**
>
> Because Outlook stores information on the hard drive of the computer at which you are working, it is recommended that you schedule enough time to complete Activities 3.01–3.09 in one working session, unless you are working on a computer that is used only by you. Allow approximately one hour for these activities.

Activity 3.01 | Creating a User Account in Windows 7

A ***user account*** is a collection of information that tells Windows 7 what files and folders the account holder can access, what changes the account holder can make to the computer system, and what the account holder's personal preferences are. Each person accesses his or her user account with a user name and, if desired, a password, to access his or her own desktop, files, and folders.

> **Alert! | To Protect Your Existing Outlook Information, Create a New Windows 7 Account.**
>
> It is recommended that you create your own Windows 7 user account so that your screens will match the figures in the textbook and so that you do not delete personal Outlook information that you already have on your own computer.
>
> Some Windows 7 features are available only to users who are logged on with an administrator account; for example, only an administrator can add new user accounts or delete user accounts. If you are logged on with administrator rights, you can complete the steps in this activity. If you are in a classroom or computer lab, check with your instructor for permission to create an account.

1. From the **Start** menu, display **Control Panel**, and then under **User Accounts and Family Safety** (or User Accounts), click **Add or remove user accounts**—enter the password if prompted.

2. In the lower portion of the screen, click **Create a new account**.

   The Create New Account window displays. The default user account type is a Standard user, as indicated by the selected option button. Once created, the new user account name will display on the Windows 7 welcome screen and in the Start menu when this account holder is logged on.

3. In the **New account name** box, using your own first and last names, type **Firstname Lastname** (or a variation of your name if this is your own computer and you have already used your own name as the primary user) and then compare your screen with Figure 3.2.

Figure 3.2

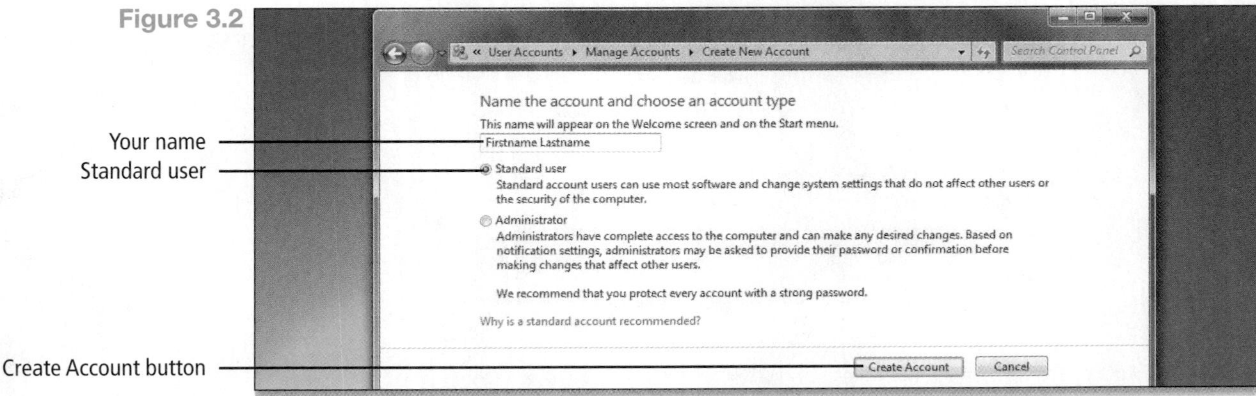

4 Click the **Create Account** button, and then **Close** the **Manage Accounts** window to create the new account.

5 On the **Start** menu, *point* to the **Shut down arrow**, and then compare your screen with Figure 3.3.

Figure 3.3

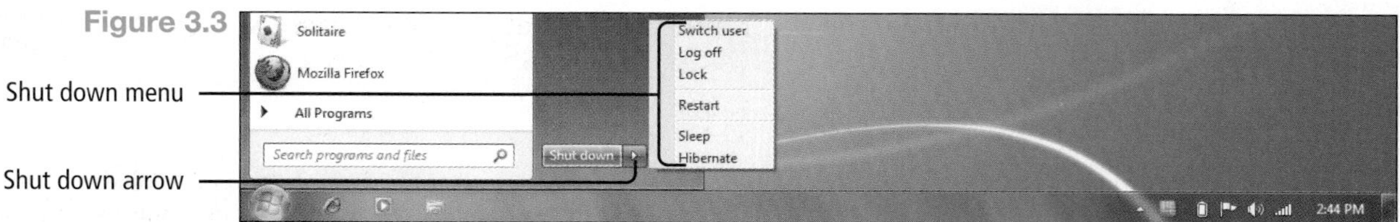

6 Click **Switch user**. When the Welcome screen displays, click the new account that you just created, and then wait a few moments until Windows 7 prepares your new desktop.

Activity 3.02 | Creating an Outlook Account and Exploring the Outlook Window

Outlook uses an e-mail ***profile*** to identify which e-mail account you use and where the related data is stored. When initially configured, Outlook creates a single profile. You might choose to create separate profiles to keep your work data and personal information separate.

1 On the **Windows taskbar**, click the **Start** button to display the **Start** menu. Locate and open the program **Microsoft Outlook 2010.**

The Microsoft Outlook 2010 Startup Wizard displays to configure Outlook 2010 in your new user name account.

> **Alert! | Did Microsoft Outlook Open without Displaying the Startup Wizard?**
>
> If Microsoft Outlook was previously configured on your system or if you were unable to create the user account in Activity 3.01, Outlook will open without displaying the Startup Wizard. To create the user account, click the File tab to display Backstage view, and then on the Info tab, under Account Information, click Add Account to open the Add New Account dialog box. Then, continue with Steps 3 through 9.

2 In the **Microsoft Outlook 2010 Startup** dialog box, click **Next** two times.

The Add New Account dialog box displays for you to create an e-mail account to complete the activities in this chapter.

3 In the **Add New Account** dialog box, in the **Your Name** box, using your own name, type **Firstname Lastname.** In the **E-mail Address** box, type **Firstname_Lastname@GOMAIL.com**

4 In the lower left corner, click the **Manually configure server settings or additional server types** option button, and then compare your screen with Figure 3.4.

Figure 3.4

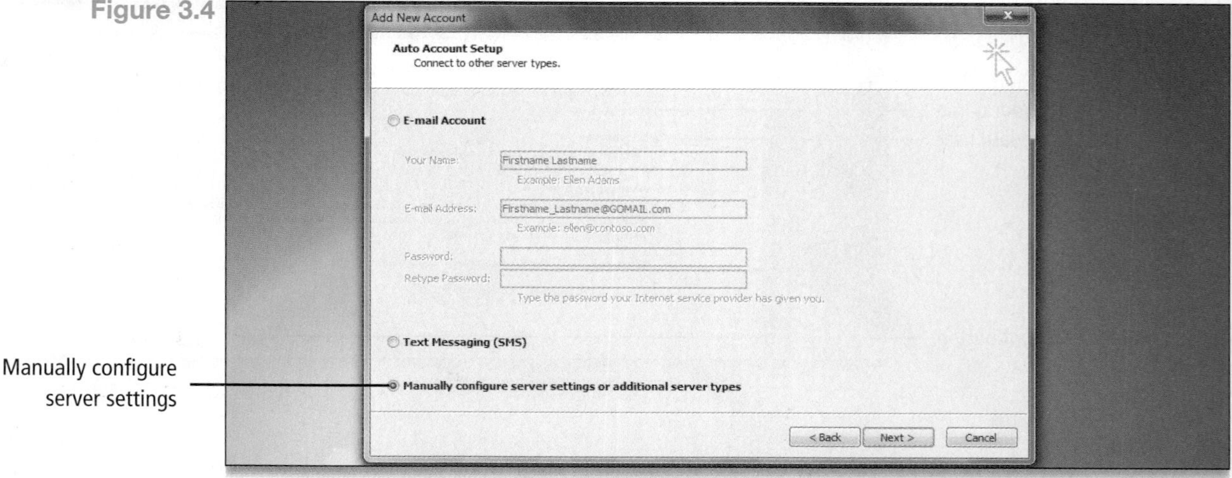

5 Click **Next** two times. If necessary, set the **Account Type** to **POP3**. In the **Incoming mail server** box, type **GOMAIL.com** and in the **Outgoing mail server (SMTP)** box, type **PHMAIL.com** Under **Logon Information**, in the **User Name** box, type your **Firstname_Lastname** and in the **Password** box, type **123456**

> **Note | GOMAIL.com and PHMAIL.com Are Fictitious Domains.**
> GOMAIL.com and PHMAIL.com are fictitious domains used only for this activity.

6 In the right column, click to *clear* the check box to the left of **Test Account Settings by clicking the Next button.** Click **Next**. In the screen indicating *Congratulations!* click **Finish** to return to **Outlook**.

7 Click **OK** to close the **User Name** dialog box. If a Microsoft Hotmail Connector dialog box displays, click No. If the Welcome to Microsoft Office 2010 dialog box displays, click Use Recommended Settings, and then click OK. If a User Account Control dialog box displays, click Yes—or type your admin password and click Yes.

Outlook configures your account, and the Outlook window displays.

8 Compare your screen with Figure 3.5, and then take a moment to study the description of the screen elements in the table in Figure 3.6.

Your Outlook screen might differ from the one shown in Figure 3.5. The appearance of the opening screen depends on settings that were established when Outlook was installed on the computer you are using. A Send/Receive error may display at the bottom of your Outlook window as a result of the fictitious e-mail address used.

Figure 3.5

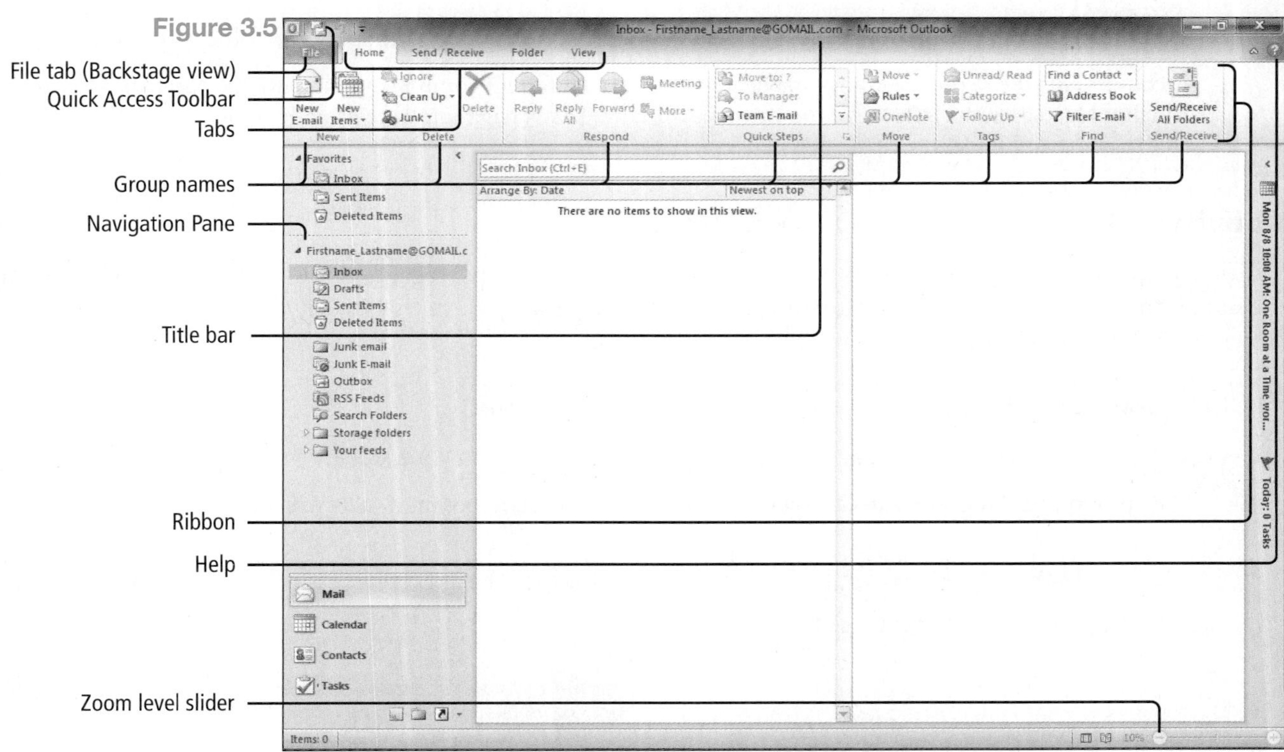

Microsoft Outlook Screen Elements

Screen Element	Description
Navigation Pane	Displays a list of shortcuts to Outlook's components and folders.
Title bar	Displays the name of the program and the program window control buttons—Minimize, Maximize/Restore Down, and Close.
File tab	Displays Microsoft Office Backstage view, a centralized space for all of your file management tasks such as opening, saving, or printing—all the things you can do *with* a file.
Ribbon	Displays a group of task-oriented tabs that contain the commands, styles, and resources you need to work in Outlook. The look of your Ribbon depends on your screen resolution. A high resolution will display more individual items and button names on the Ribbon.
Tabs	These task-oriented tabs found on the Ribbon display the names of tasks relevant to the open program.
Group names	Indicate the names of the groups of related commands on the displayed tab.
Help button	Displays the Microsoft Office Help system for Outlook.
Quick Access Toolbar	Displays buttons to perform frequently used commands with a single click. You can add and delete buttons to customize the Quick Access Toolbar.
Zoom level	Displays the Zoom levels on a slider.

Figure 3.6

9 At the bottom of the **Navigation Pane**, click the **Folder List** button to display the folders in your account.

A convenient way to move among—navigate—Outlook's different components is to use the ***Navigation Pane***, which is located on the left side of the Outlook window. The Navigation Pane provides quick access to Outlook's components and folders.

Activity 3.03 | Importing an Outlook Data File

Importing data into your Outlook account involves the same steps, regardless of whether you are importing the data into the Personal Folders or into an Exchange Server mailbox. In this activity, you will import the contacts and messages for Lucy Burrows into your account.

1 In the **Navigation Pane**, under your **GOMAIL account**, click **Inbox**.

2 From **Backstage** view, click **Open**, and then click **Import**. Compare your screen with Figure 3.7.

The Import and Export Wizard dialog box displays. A ***wizard*** is a tool that walks you step by step through a process.

Figure 3.7

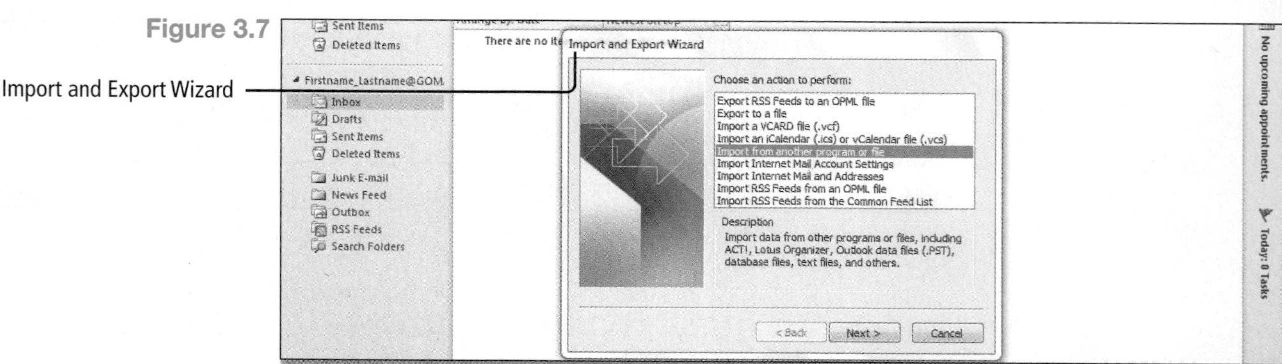

3 In the **Import and Export Wizard** dialog box, under **Choose an action to perform**, click **Import from another program or file**, and then click **Next**.

4 In the **Import a File** dialog box, under **Select file type to import from**, click **Outlook Data File (.pst)**, and then click **Next**. In the **Import Outlook Data File** dialog box, click **Browse**. In the **Open Outlook Data Files** dialog box, navigate to the location where the student files that accompany this textbook are stored. Locate **ou03A_Burrows_Design**, and click one time to select it. Then, in the lower right corner, click **Open**.

The Open Outlook Data Files dialog box closes, and the path and file name display in the File to import box.

5 Click **Next** and compare your screen with Figure 3.8.

The Import Outlook Data File dialog box displays the folder structure for the file you are going to import.

Figure 3.8

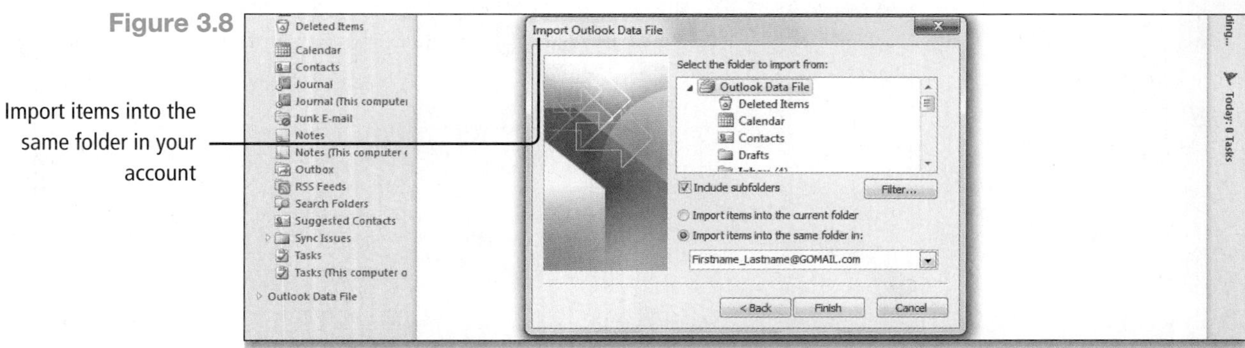

6 If necessary, under **Select the folder to import from**, click **Outlook Data File**, and then click the **Import items into the same folder in** option button. Click **Finish**, and then compare your screen with Figure 3.9.

The data file is imported, and the Inbox displays your e-mail messages.

Figure 3.9

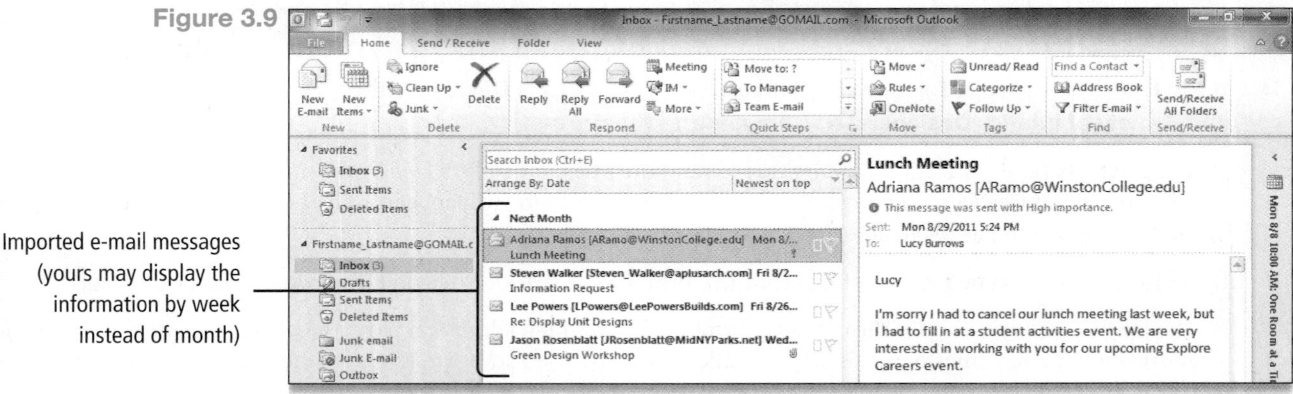

Objective 2 | Enter and Edit Contacts and Calendar Entries

View the video on the Companion Web Site or in MyITLab

The ***Contacts*** component of Outlook is your e-mail address book for storing information about people, organizations, and businesses with whom you communicate. A ***contact*** is a person or organization about whom you can save information such as street and e-mail addresses, telephone and fax numbers, birthdays, and pictures. The default location for Outlook's Contacts information is the ***Contacts folder***. To create, edit, or display the contents of your Contacts list, you must display this folder. The ***Calendar*** component of Outlook stores your schedule and calendar-related information. The default location for Outlook's calendar information is the ***Calendar folder***.

Activity 3.04 | Creating and Editing Contacts

In this activity, you will add Lois Dawe to the Contacts list and edit contact information for Josie Fine.

1. At the bottom of the **Navigation Pane**, click **Contacts** to display the Contacts folder, and notice that six contacts display; these were imported as part of the Outlook data file.
2. On the **Home tab**, in the **New group**, click **New Contact** to display the **Untitled – Contact** form, and then compare your screen with Figure 3.10.

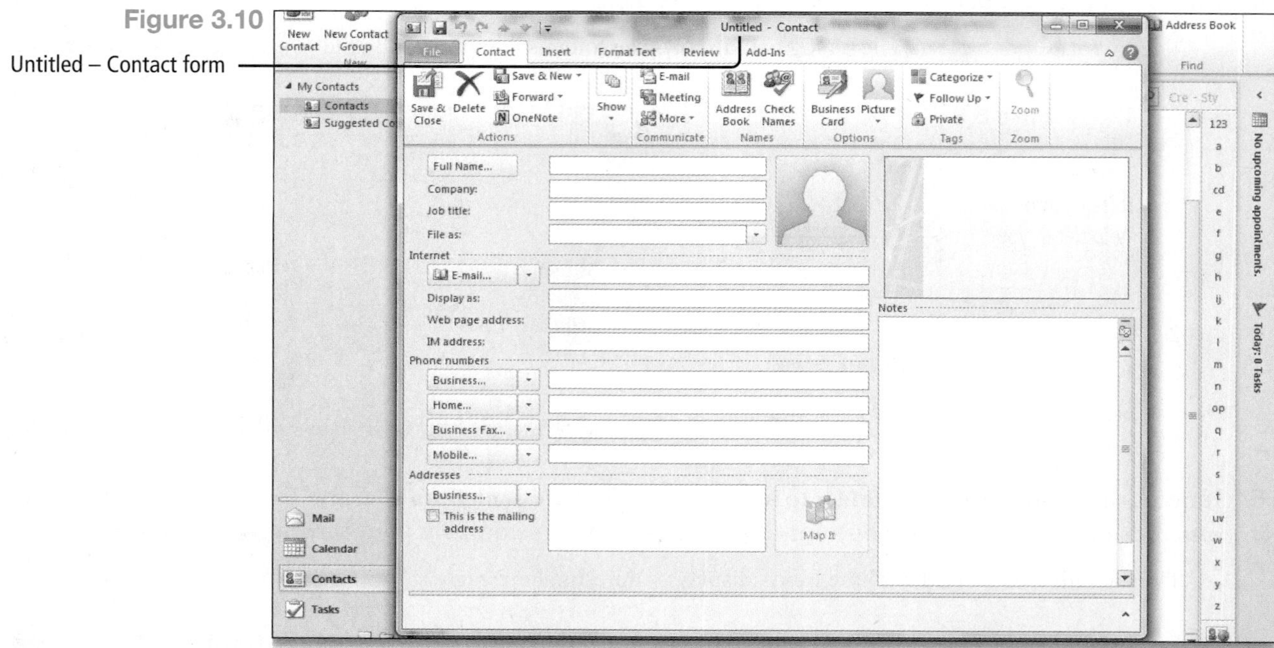

Figure 3.10

3. In the **Untitled – Contact** form, in the **Full Name** box, type **Lois Dawe** and then press Tab. In the **Company** box, type **Society of Interior Designers, NY Chapter** and then press Tab.

   The insertion point moves to the Job title box, and the title bar displays *Lois Dawe - Contact*. The *File as* box displays the contact name as *Dawe, Lois*, which is how this person's name will appear in the Contacts list. Outlook displays names in the Contacts list in alphabetical order by last names.

4. In the **Job title** box, type **President** Click in the **E-mail** box, and then type **LDawe@NY-SID.org** Press Tab.

   The Display as box indicates the contact's name with the e-mail address in parentheses. When you use the contact's address in an e-mail message, this is how Outlook displays the address to associate the person and the e-mail address.

5. Under **Phone numbers**, click in the **Business** box, type **516-555-0277** and then press Tab. If a Location Information dialog box displays, select your country or region, type your area code, and click OK two times. Compare your screen with Figure 3.11.

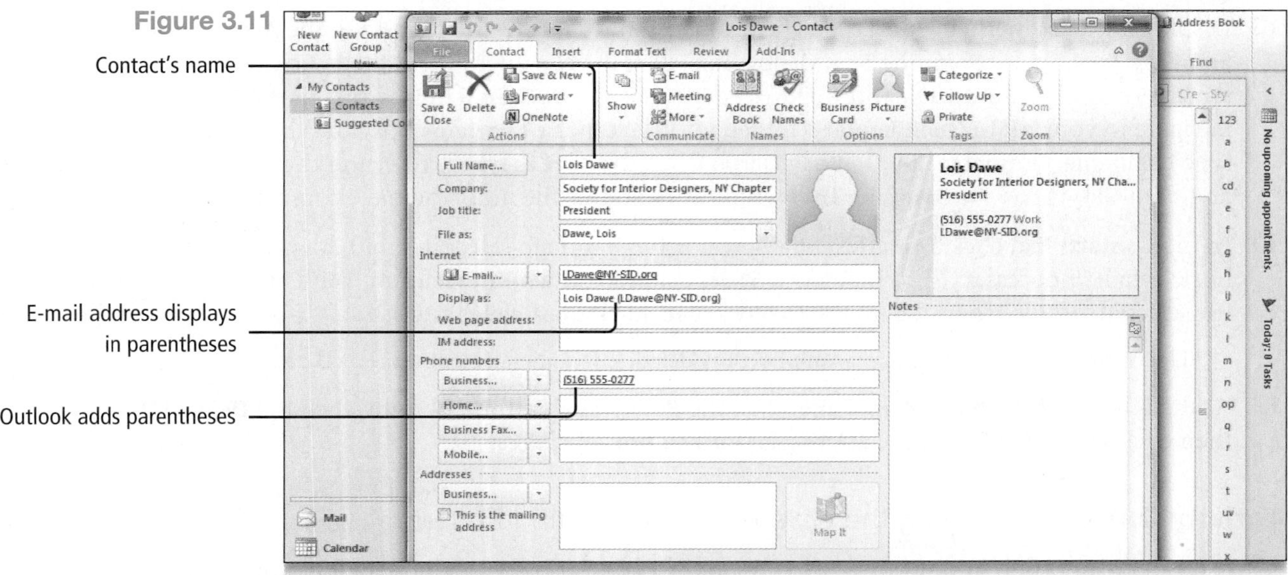

Figure 3.11

6 Under **Addresses**, click in the **Business** box, and then type **570 Richland Way** Press Enter, and then type **Brooklyn, NY 11210**

7 On the **Contact tab**, in the **Actions group**, click **Save & Close**. If necessary, scroll up to see the new contact, and then compare your screen with Figure 3.12.

Outlook saves the new contact and the Contacts folder displays in Business Card view.

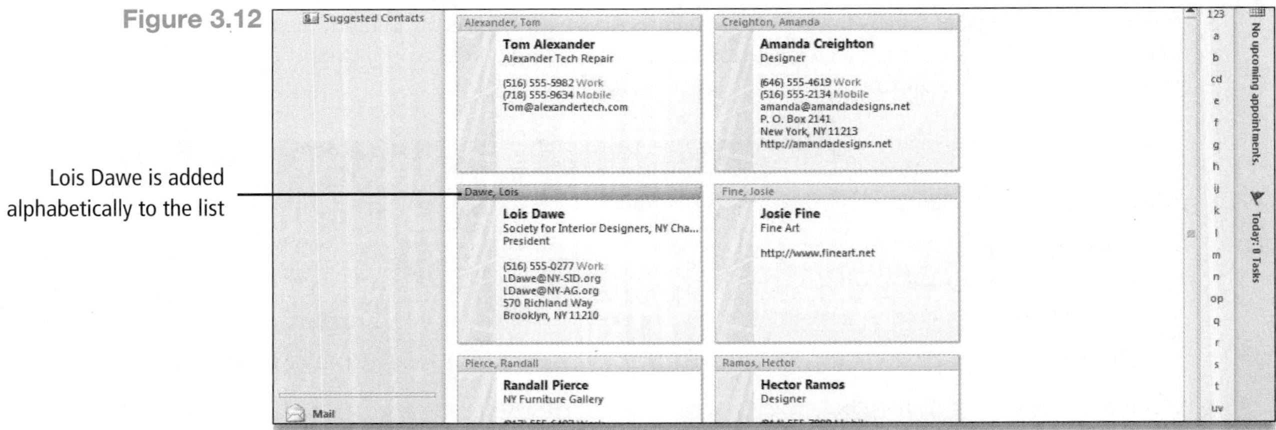

Figure 3.12

8 Double-click the **Business Card** for **Josie Fine** to open it.

9 In the **Josie Fine – Contact** form, click in the **E-mail** box, and then type **Josie@fineart.net** Under Phone numbers, click in the **Mobile** box and type **914-555-9950** On the Ribbon, in the **Actions** group, click the **Save & Close** button.

Outlook saves the changes to the existing contact and displays the updated information in Business Card view. Use this technique to update information about your contacts.

10 Navigate to the location where you are saving your files for this chapter, and then create a folder named **All In One Chapter 3**

11 Display the **Start** menu, and then click **All Programs**. Locate and then click the **Accessories** folder. Click **Snipping Tool**. In the **Snipping Tool** dialog box, click the **New arrow**, and then click **Window Snip**. Click anywhere in the window to capture it, and then click the **Save Snip** button. In the **Save As** dialog box, navigate to your **All In One Chapter 3** folder, and click in **the File name** box, and then, using your own name, type **Lastname_Firstname_3A_Contact_Cards** Click the **Save as type** arrow, and then click **JPEG file**. Click **Save**, and then **Close** the **Snipping Tool** window. Hold this file until you have completed this project.

12 In the **Contacts list**, click **Tom Alexander's** contact one time to select it. Hold down Shift, scroll vertically or horizontally if necessary, and then click **Styles Salon's** contact information. With all the items in your **Contacts list** selected, on the **Home tab**, in the **Delete group**, click the **Delete** button.

The Contacts list is deleted. You can undo any deletion if you make a mistake or change your mind.

13 At the bottom of the **Navigation Pane**, click the **Folder List** button, right-click the **Deleted Items** folder, and then click **Empty Folder**. In the **Microsoft Outlook** box, click **Yes**.

Activity 3.05 | Navigating the Calendar and Creating Entries

You can create a new appointment directly in the calendar by typing it in a blank time slot in the appointment area or by using the ***Appointment form***. By using an Appointment form, you can enter more detailed information about an appointment. In this activity, you will schedule appointments in Lucy's Calendar.

1 At the bottom of the **Navigation Pane**, click the **Calendar** button. Compare your screen with Figure 3.13.

The ***appointment area*** displays on the right side of the screen, which is a one-day view of the current day's calendar entries. An ***appointment*** is a calendar activity occurring at a specific time and day that does not require inviting people or reservations. The ***Time Bar*** displays one-hour time increments. The ***Date Navigator*** displays above the Navigation Pane; use this to display specific days in a month. The highlighted date in the Date Navigator and at the top of the appointment area is the date that you are viewing, which is, by default, the current date. On either side of the appointment area, buttons for Previous Appointment and Next Appointment enable you to move quickly through your day's appointments.

Figure 3.13

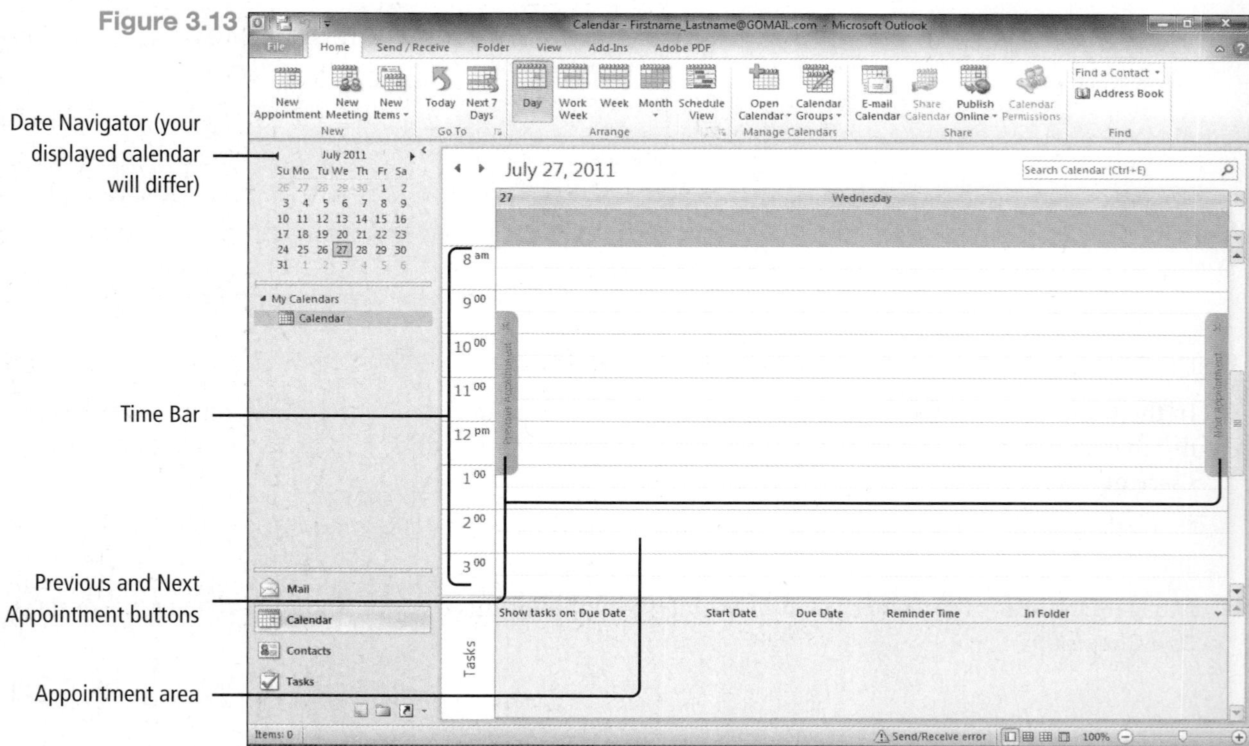

Alert! | Does Your Screen Differ?

The time range for your appointment area may differ from Figure 3.13. Larger computer screens and screens with a higher resolution may display a much larger time span. Your Date Navigator may also display two or three months instead of one. Clicking the arrows to move forward and backward in the Date Navigator displays different months based on what you click.

2 On the **Home tab**, in the **Arrange group**, click **Week**, and then click the **Work Week** button.

The ***Work Week view*** option shows only the weekdays, Monday through Friday, instead of a full seven-day week, which is displayed in the ***Week view***.

3 On the **Home tab**, in the **Go To group**, click **Today** to return to the current day, and then in the **Arrange group**, click the **Day** button to return to Day view. In the **Date Navigator**, click the **right arrow** one time, advancing the calendar to the next month. In the calendar, click the second **Monday** of the displayed month, and notice that it displays at the top of the appointment area.

4 In the **appointment area**, click the **10:00 am** time slot, type **One Room at a Time workshop** and notice that as you type, the time slot displays blue shading surrounded by a black border. Compare your screen with Figure 3.14.

Figure 3.14

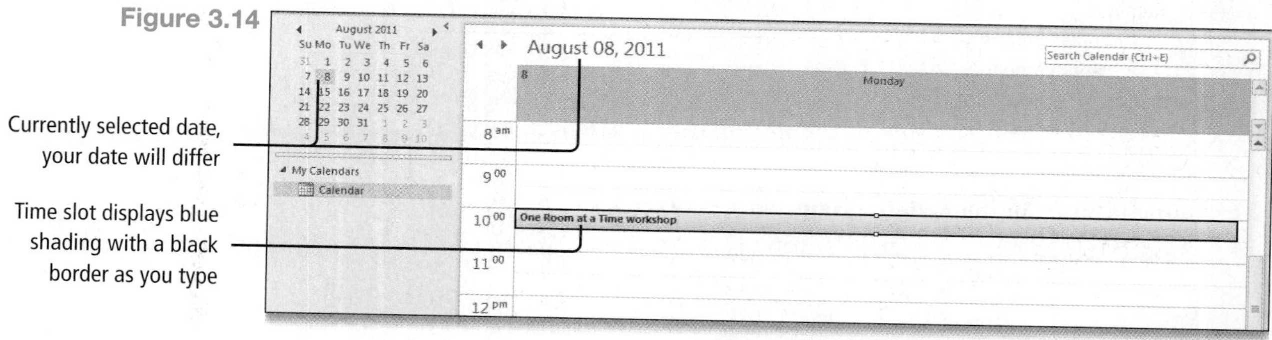

5 Click any other time slot in the appointment area.

The appointment is scheduled from 10:00 to 10:30 am. When you use this method to enter an appointment, the default appointment time frame is 30 minutes. The day number of a date in the Date Navigator changes to bold when an appointment is scheduled on that day.

6 In the **appointment area**, click the **12:30 pm** time slot—the lower half of the 12:00 pm time slot—to enter an appointment on the half hour. Type **Lunch with Josie** Click any other time slot in the appointment area.

7 On the **Home tab**, in the **New group**, click **New Appointment**, and then compare your screen with Figure 3.15.

The Untitled - Appointment form displays. The starting and ending times for the new appointment default to the time you clicked in the appointment area. A ***comments area*** in the lower half of the form enables you to enter information about the appointment not otherwise specified in the form.

Figure 3.15

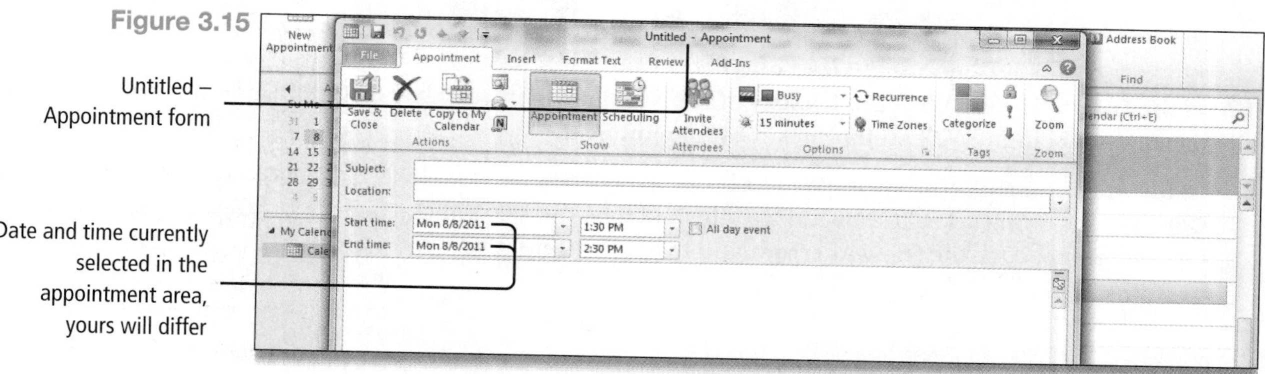

8 As the **Subject** of the appointment, type **SID-NY Meeting** In the **Location** box, type **Boardwalk Inn**

9 In the right **Start time** box, click the **time arrow**, and then locate and click **3:00 PM**. In the right **End time** box, click the **time arrow**, and then locate and click **4:00 PM (1 hour)**.

10 On the **Appointment tab**, in the **Options group**, click the **Reminder arrow**, and then click **30 minutes**.

Outlook will remind you 30 minutes before the appointment with a ScreenTip and chime. A reminder can be set up to two weeks before the scheduled appointment.

11 On the **Appointment tab**, in the **Options group**, click the **Show As arrow**, and then click **Out of Office**. Compare your screen with Figure 3.16.

There are four Show As options you can apply to appointments. ***Busy*** is the default setting for appointments you set and is used when you are in the building but are unavailable. Other options include ***Free*** for appointments that can be interrupted or do not make you unavailable. Use ***Out of Office*** when you are out of the building and possibly some distance away and ***Tentative*** for appointments that have not yet been confirmed.

Figure 3.16

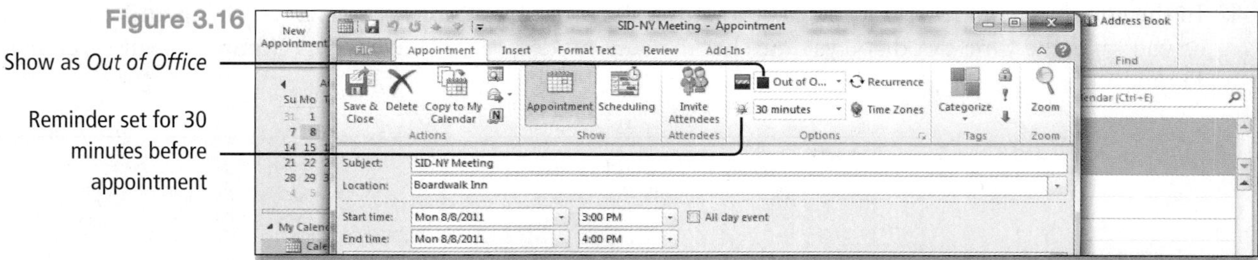

12 On the Ribbon, in the **Actions group**, click **Save & Close**, and then compare your screen with Figure 3.17.

The new appointment displays on the calendar, and the appointment's location displays below the subject. The purple border identifies the appointment as *Out of Office*.

Figure 3.17

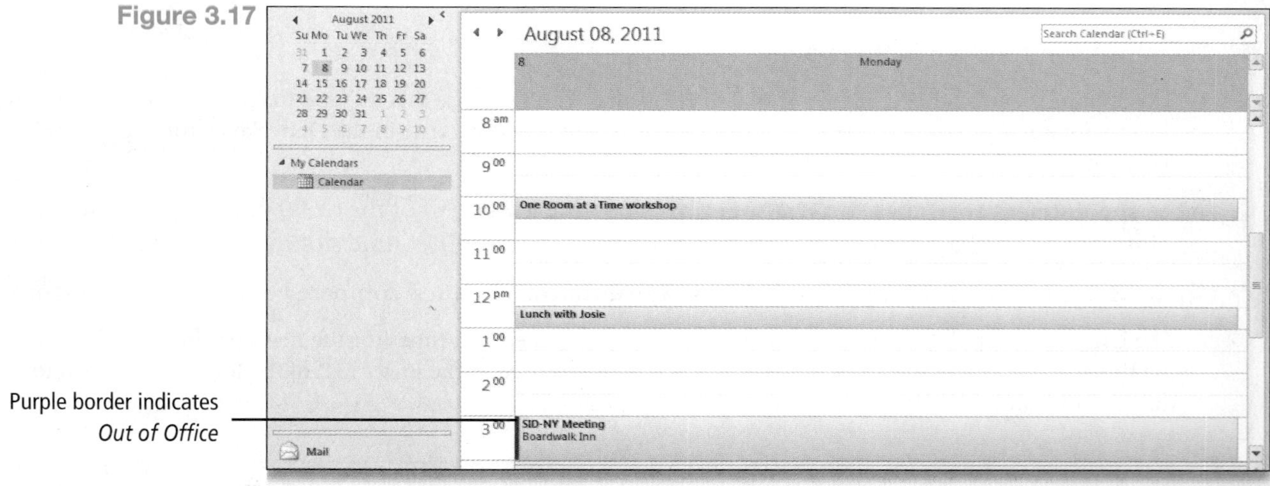

13 In the **Date Navigator**, click the **Tuesday** of the week in which you are scheduling appointments, and then, on the **Home tab**, in the **New group**, click **New Appointment**.

14 In the **Appointment** form, in the **Subject** box, type **SID Student Workshop** In the **Location** box, type **Winston College** Set the **Start time** to **9:30 AM** and the **End time** to **12:00 PM (2.5 hours)**. On the **Appointment tab**, in the **Options group**, click the **Show As arrow**, and then click **Tentative**.

15 On the **Appointment tab**, in the **Options group**, click **Recurrence**.

In the Appointment Recurrence dialog box, you can set the ***recurrence pattern***—the frequency—of an appointment, which may be daily, weekly, monthly, or yearly. You can also set the ***range of recurrence***, which is the date of the final occurrence of the appointment based on its end date or the number of times an appointment occurs.

16 In the **Appointment Recurrence** dialog box, under **Recurrence pattern**, select **Weekly**. Next to **Recur every**, type **2** and then select the **Tuesday** check box if it is not already selected. Under **Range of recurrence**, click the **End after** option button, and then press Tab so that the number in the **occurrences** box is selected. Type **3** and then compare your screen with Figure 3.18.

The recurrence is set for every two weeks, for three occurrences.

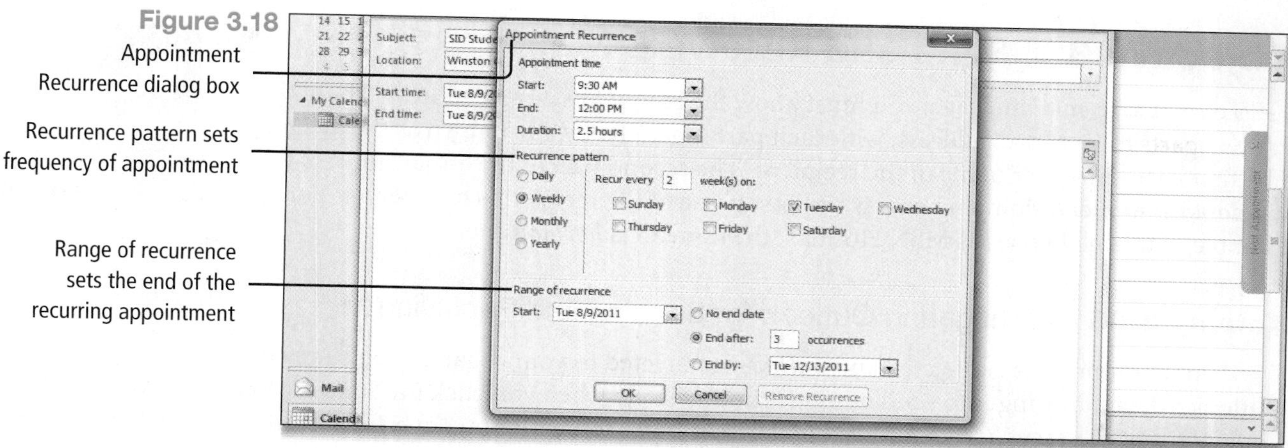

Figure 3.18

17 Click **OK** to redisplay the Appointment form.

The Start time and End time boxes are replaced by Recurrence information. The appointment is set to repeat every two weeks.

18 **Save & Close** the appointment, and then compare your screen with Figure 3.19.

The new appointment displays on the calendar. The recurrence icon in the lower right corner of the appointment indicates that this is a recurring appointment. The Date Navigator for the day displays in bold, indicating that this date has an appointment scheduled. The days on which the appointment repeats also display in bold.

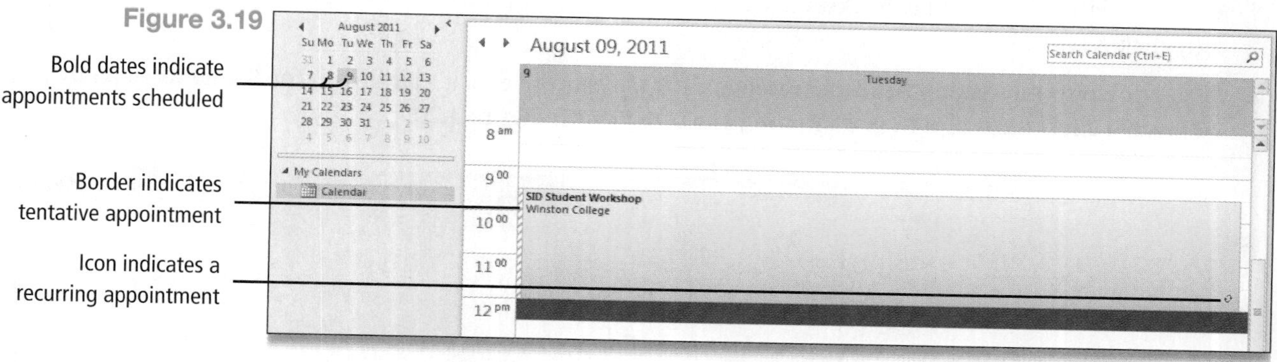

Figure 3.19

More Knowledge | Removing or Changing Appointment Recurrence

To change or remove an appointment's recurrence information, open the appointment by double-clicking one of its occurrences in the appointment area. Select *Open the series* and then click OK. In the Appointment form, click the Recurrence button to display the Appointment Recurrence dialog box. Change the recurrence pattern or the range of recurrence. Click Remove Recurrence to remove all the recurrence information.

19 On the **Home tab**, in the **Arrange group**, click **Week**. Display the **Start** menu and open the **Snipping Tool**. Click the **New arrow**, and then click **Window Snip**. Click in the window to capture it, and then click the **Save Snip** button. Navigate to your **All In One Chapter 3** folder. As the **File name** type, using your own name, **Lastname_Firstname_3A_Burrows_Week** Set **Save as type** to **JPEG file**, and then click **Save**. **Close** the **Snipping Tool**. Hold this file until the end of this Project.

20 Click the **View tab**. In the **Current View group**, click **Change View**, and then click **Active**. Press Ctrl + A, right-click on any of the selected appointments, and then click **Delete**. On the **View tab**, in the **Current View group**, click **Change View**, and then click **Calendar**. At the bottom of the **Navigation Pane**, click the **Folder List** button. Right-click the **Deleted Items** folder, click **Empty Folder**, and then click **Yes**.

Objective 3 | Send and Receive E-Mail

View the video on the Companion Web Site or in MyITLab

To send an e-mail message, you must know the recipient's e-mail address. There are two parts to an e-mail address, with each part separated by @—known as the ***at sign***. The first part is the user name of the recipient. The second part of the e-mail address is the ***domain name***. A domain name is the host name of the recipient's mail server. For example, if the mail server is MSN Hotmail, the domain is *hotmail.com*.

Activity 3.06 | Configuring Outlook for Sending and Receiving Messages

If your computer is connected and ***online***—connected to your organization's network or to the Internet—Outlook's default setting is to send messages immediately when you click the Send button in the Message form. Copies of sent messages are then stored in the Sent Items folder. If you are ***offline***—not connected to a network or to the Internet—messages are stored in the Outbox.

Alert! | In This Activity, You Will Configure Outlook to Store Sent Messages in the Outbox Instead of Actually Sending the Messages.

In this activity, you will configure Outlook to store all your sent messages in the Outbox instead of actually sending the messages from your GOMAIL account. You will be handling the e-mail activities of Lucy Burrows. You can create and send her messages even if your computer is not actually connected and online.

1 Click the **File tab** to display **Backstage** view, and then click **Options**. In the **Outlook Options** dialog box, on the left, click **Advanced**.

2 Scroll down to the section **Send and receive**, click to *clear* the check mark from the **Send immediately when connected** check box, and then compare your screen with Figure 3.20.

Figure 3.20

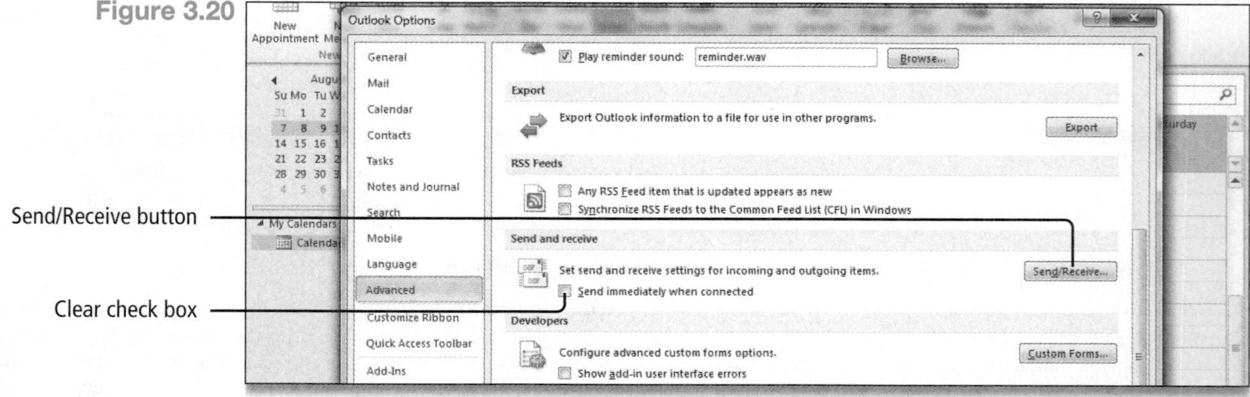

3 To the right, click the **Send/Receive** button. In the **Send/Receive Groups** dialog box, under **Setting for group "All Accounts"**, click to *clear* the **Include this group in send/receive (F9)** check box, and then click to *clear* the **Schedule an automatic send/receive every** check box.

4 Under **When Outlook is Offline**, click to *clear* the **Include this group in send/receive (F9)** check box. In the lower right corner, click **Close**, and then in the **Outlook Options** dialog box, click **OK**.

Activity 3.07 | Creating and Sending a New E-mail Message

In this activity, you will create a message for Lucy Burrows using the Word editor and then send it to one of her associates.

1 At the bottom of the **Navigation Pane**, click **Mail**. In the **Navigation Pane**, under your GOMAIL account name, click **Inbox**.

The Inbox folder displays. The middle pane of the Outlook window displays any e-mail messages you have received. The ***Reading Pane*** displays on the right, in which you can preview an e-mail message without actually opening it. If your Inbox contains no messages, the Reading Pane is blank. If you have messages, the contents of the first message display in the Reading Pane.

2 On the **Home tab**, in the **New group**, click **New E-mail**, and then compare your screen with Figure 3.21.

The top of the form displays a ***Ribbon*** with commands organized by groups and tabs based on particular activities, such as setting message options or formatting text.

Figure 3.21

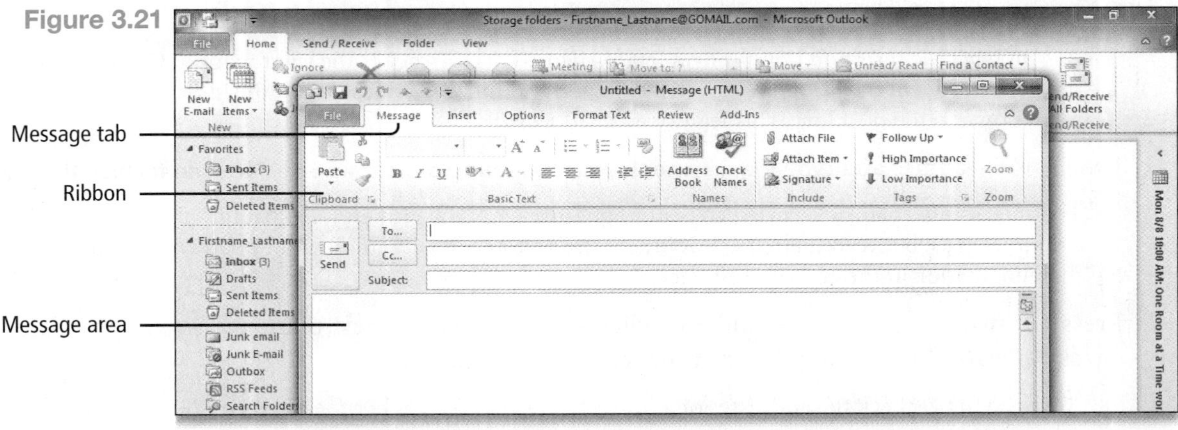

Alert! | Does your Ribbon look different?

The size of the Outlook window determines how much information displays with each command on the Ribbon. Depending on your screen size and resolution, you might notice both icons and words for all commands or only the icons for certain commands.

3 In the **To** box, type **LDennison@LanceConst.com**

This is the e-mail address of the recipient. Notice the ***syntax***—the way in which the parts of the e-mail address are put together. The user name is to the left of the @ symbol, and the domain name is on the right. If another student has used this computer, you may see Mr. Dennison's e-mail address display in blue.

4 In the **Cc** box, click to place the insertion point, and then type **STarasov@MidNYChamber.org**

This sends a ***courtesy copy***, or ***carbon copy***, of the message to the address specified in the Cc box. In both the To and the Cc boxes, you can enter multiple addresses, separating each address with a semicolon. Send a courtesy copy to others who need to see the message.

> **More Knowledge | Carbon Copies**
>
> Old-fashioned carbon paper is rarely used anymore, but the term carbon copy has remained. Sometimes Cc is referred to as a courtesy copy. Sometimes people will just say "I cc'd (pronounced see-seed) you on an e-mail."

5 Press Tab one time to position the insertion point in the **Subject box**, type **Chamber of Commerce presentation** and then press Tab.

You can move the insertion point from one box to another either by clicking in the box or by pressing Tab.

> **Note | Underlined E-mail Addresses**
>
> Outlook may display an underlined e-mail address after you type it in the box. Outlook remembers previously typed addresses, and this change in its appearance shows that this address has been used before, either by you or a previous user. Your system may also be set to automatically underline all e-mail addresses that use correct syntax.

6 With the insertion point in the message area of the Message form, type **Lance,** and then press Enter two times.

This is the beginning of your message. It is considered good etiquette to address the recipient(s) by name. Keep your messages short and to the point. It is usually helpful to the recipient if you restrict your message to only one topic.

7 Type **I just received confirmation from the Chamber of Commerce; they would like to have us speak at one of their upcoming meetings. Let's arrange a time for you, Sandra, and me to meet and discuss which meeting is best and select a topic.**

As you type, the insertion point moves left to right. When it reaches the right margin, Outlook determines whether the next word will fit within the established margin. If the word does not fit, the insertion point moves the whole word down to the next line. This feature is called ***wordwrap***.

8 Press Enter two times and type **Please check your schedule for next week so we can finalize the plans quickly.**

To leave a single blank line between paragraphs, press Enter two times. Keep paragraphs short and single-spaced with a double-space between them. Do not indent the first line of paragraphs, and press Spacebar only one time following the punctuation at the end of a sentence.

9 Press Enter two times, type **Lucy** and then click somewhere in the text of the message. Review the message to check for errors, and then compare your screen with Figure 3.22.

Always double-check the addresses of your recipients to avoid either the return of the message or delivery to the wrong person. Edit and proofread your messages carefully. Messages containing errors reflect poorly on you, the sender.

Figure 3.22

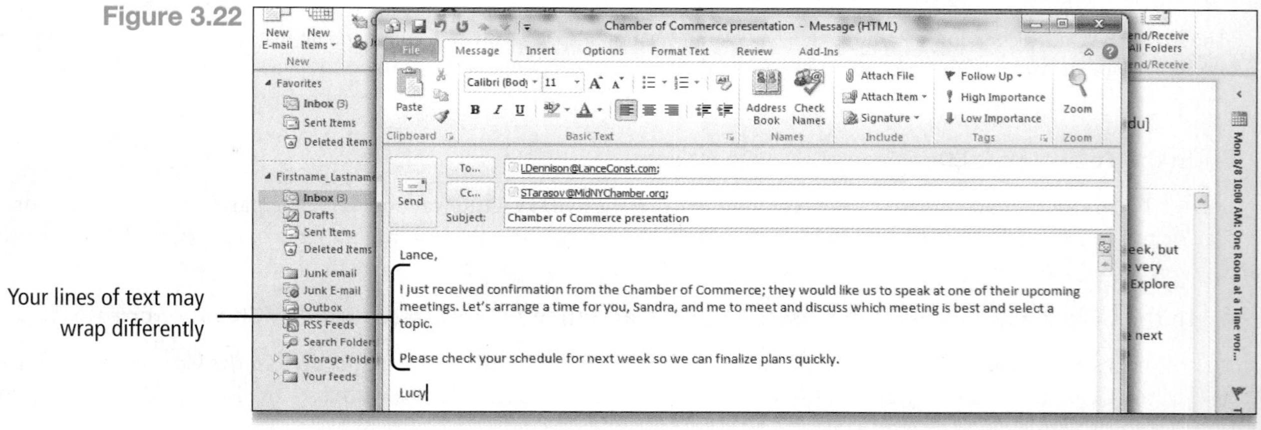

10 In the message header, to the left of **To**, click the **Send** button.

> **More Knowledge | Sending a Message without a Subject**
>
> Outlook displays a message box if you do not enter a Subject for an e-mail message before clicking Send. The message box allows you to go back to the e-mail form and enter a subject or send the messages without one. A subject makes it easier for people who receive your messages to quickly know the contents. It is a good idea to include a brief, meaningful subject for your messages.

11 In the **Navigation Pane** under your account, locate and then click the **Outbox** folder. Compare your screen with Figure 3.23.

The contents of the Outbox folder display. When the Outbox folder contains unsent messages, the folder name is displayed in bold followed by the number of items in brackets.

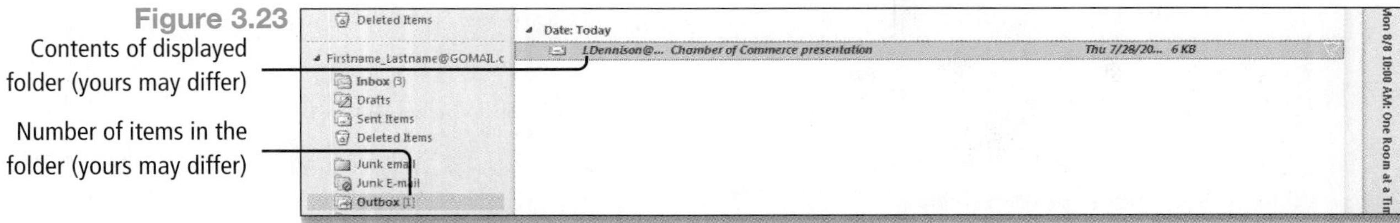

Figure 3.23

Activity 3.08 | Opening and Responding to an E-mail Message

Messages you receive are stored in Outlook's Inbox folder. Each message displays the name of the message sender, the subject, and the date and time sent. You can respond to a received message by either replying to the message or forwarding the message to another individual. In this activity, you will work with messages that are in your Inbox. You will also work with different types of received messages.

1 In the **Navigation Pane**, under your account, click **Inbox**, and take a moment to study the messages shown in Figure 3.24.

In the Navigation Pane, the number in parentheses to the right of Inbox displays the number of unread messages. The Inbox pane lists the ***message header*** for each message. Message headers include basic information about an e-mail message such as the sender's name, the date sent, and the subject. The message header for an e-mail that has not yet been read or opened displays in bold, and the icon at the left shows a closed envelope. After a message has been read, the bold is removed, and the icon changes to an open envelope.

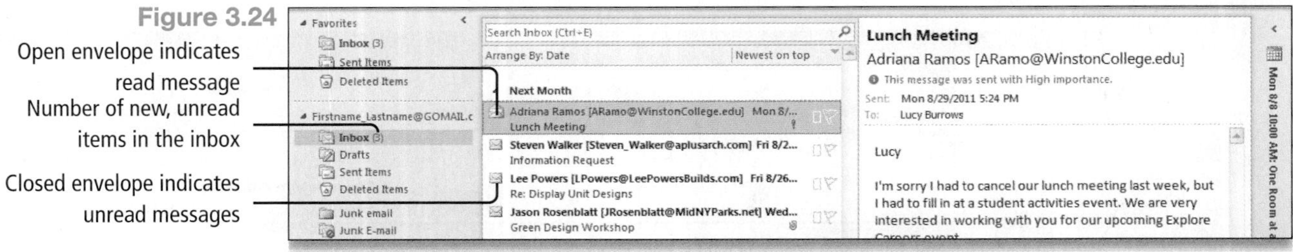

Figure 3.24

2 Notice that the first message in the **Inbox**, which is from *Adriana Ramos* and has as its subject *Lunch Meeting*, displays in the Reading Pane.

In Inbox, next to the subject, a red exclamation point indicates a message that is sent with *High Importance*. In the Reading Pane, under the sender's name, the *This message was sent with High importance* displays.

3 In the center Inbox pane, double-click the **Lunch Meeting** message to open it. Compare your screen with Figure 3.25.

The Message form displays the message. The area above the text of the message contains the message header information, which includes the sender's name and the date of the message. On the left side of the Message form title bar, the Quick Access Toolbar displays. Here you can perform frequently used commands such as saving an item, viewing a previous item, or viewing the next item. In the center of the Message form title bar, the subject of the message displays.

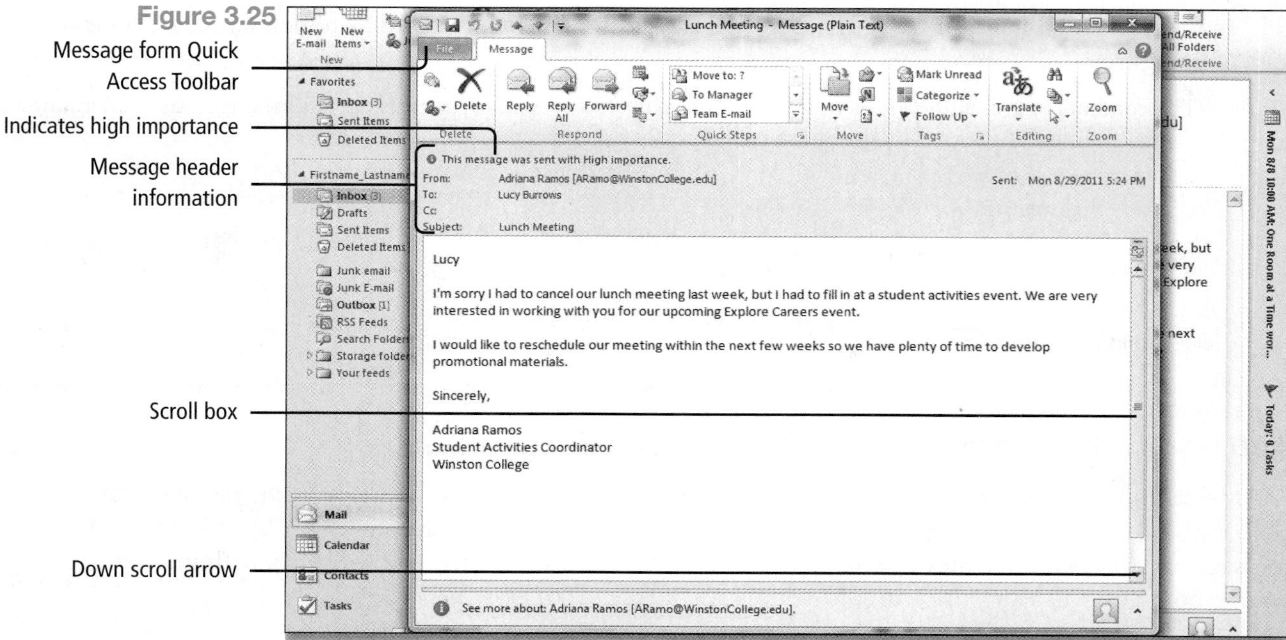

Figure 3.25

4 On the Message form title bar, click the **Close** button.

5 In the **Inbox**, locate the message from *Jason Rosenblatt* with the subject heading **Green Design Workshop** and click it one time to display it in the Reading Pane. Compare your screen with Figure 3.26.

In the Inbox, a small paper clip icon displays under the date of the message. This indicates that the message has an attachment. In the Reading Pane, the name of the attachment file displays. The icon representing the Word program indicates that the attachment is a Word document.

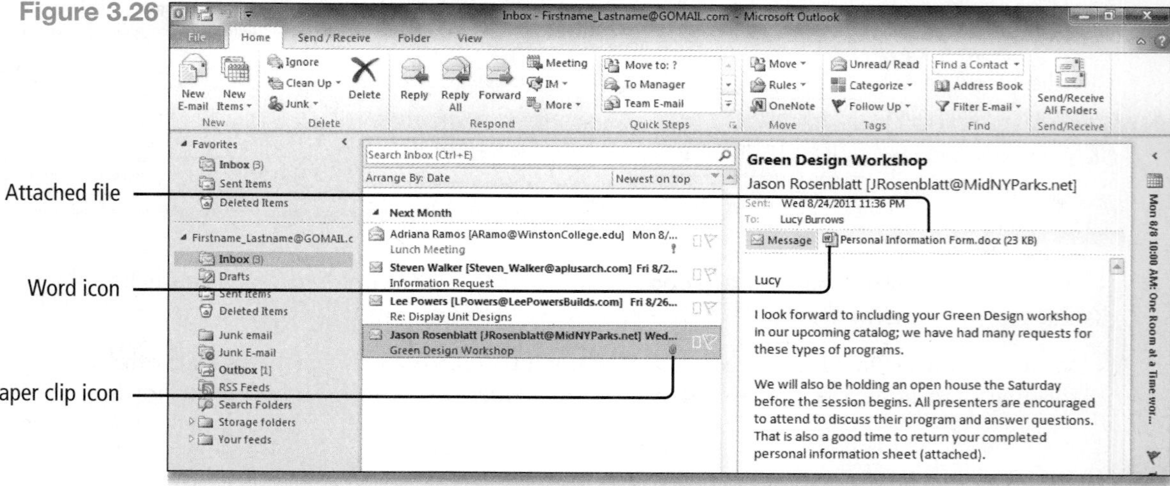

Figure 3.26

6 In the center pane, double-click the **Green Design Workshop** message to open it in its Message form and to display the attachment file name in the header.

7 Double-click the **Word icon** in the attachment file name to open the attachment. Alternatively, right-click the attachment, and then click Open. If the Opening Mail Attachment dialog box appears, click Open.

The Opening Mail Attachment dialog box may display. Outlook displays this dialog box to remind you that attachments might contain viruses. You should not open an attachment unless it is from a known source. Your system may include an antivirus program that scans attachments, but unless you are certain that this is the case, it is safer to save the attachment as a file and scan it with an antivirus program before opening it.

8 If Microsoft Word displays the document in Protected View, click **Enable Editing**.

Microsoft Word starts the Word program and displays the attached file, which is a Word document. An attachment is part of an e-mail message unless you save it separately. You can save an attachment by right-clicking the Word icon in the attachment file name and then clicking Save As.

9 In the **Microsoft Word** title bar, click the **Close** button to close the attachment. **Close** the message.

10 Locate the second message in the **Inbox**, which is the message from *Steven Walker* with the subject heading *Information Request*, and then double-click the message to open it.

After you view a message in the Reading Pane, Outlook considers its status as read after you move to another message.

11 In the **Message form**, on the Quick Access Toolbar, click the **Next Item** button.

The message closes, and the Message form displays the next message in your Inbox, which is the message from *Lee Powers* with the subject *Display Unit Designs*.

12 **Close** the Message form, and notice that no unread items remain in the Inbox.

13 In the **Inbox**, select the first message to display it in the Reading Pane. Then, on the **Home tab**, in the **Respond group**, click **Reply**. Compare your screen with Figure 3.27.

It is not necessary to open a message to reply to it—selecting and displaying it in the Reading Pane is sufficient to create a reply. A Message form displays. Outlook adds the prefix *RE:* to the subject and title of the message. ***RE:*** is commonly used to mean *in regard to* or *regarding*. The text of the original message is included in the message area of the form, and Outlook places the sender's e-mail address in the To box.

Figure 3.27

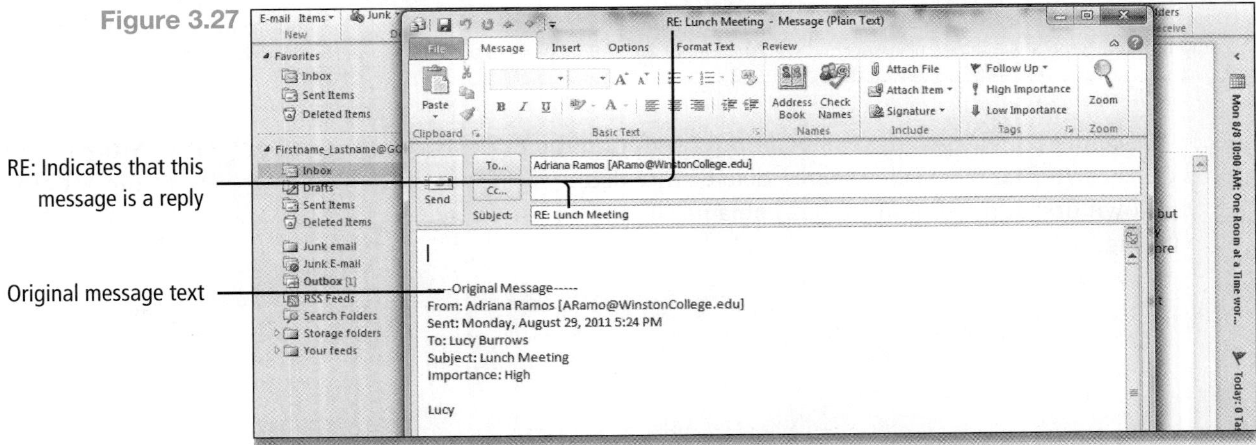

14 With the insertion point at the top of the message area, type **Hi Adriana,** and press Enter two times. Type **I will check my calendar and call you by the end of the day.** Press Enter two times, and type **Lucy**

15 On the Message form, click the **Send** button. In the **Navigation Pane** under your account, locate and then click the **Outbox** folder.

The message is sent to the Outbox, and the Message form closes.

16 Display the **Start** menu, open the **Snipping Tool**, click the **New arrow**, and then click **Window Snip**. Click in the window to capture it, and then click the **Save Snip** button. Navigate to your **All In One Chapter 3** folder, click in the **File name** box, and then using your own name, type **Lastname_Firstname_3A_Burrows_Outbox** Set **Save as type** to **JPEG file**, click **Save**, and then **Close** the **Snipping Tool**. Hold this file until you have completed this Project.

More Knowledge | Forwarding E-Mail Messages

You can forward an e-mail message you receive to someone else—commonly referred to as a third party. This is called forwarding. However, do not forward messages to others unless you are sure the sender of the original message would approve of forwarding the message. On the Home tab, in the Respond group, click the Forward button. You do not have to open a message to forward it. A Message form displays. Outlook adds the prefix FW: to the subject and title of the message. The text of the original message is included in the message area of the form.

Activity 3.09 | Printing and Deleting Messages

Recall that Outlook organizes its information in folders. To print information in Outlook, each folder type has one or more predefined print styles associated with it. A ***print style*** is a combination of paper and page settings that determines the way items print.

After you read and reply to a message, it is good practice to either delete it or store it in another folder for future reference. When you delete a message in your Inbox folder, Outbox folder, or any other mail folder, it is placed in the Deleted Items folder. Items remain in this folder until you empty them from this folder, at which time they are permanently deleted. This is helpful in case you delete a message by mistake; you can still retrieve it from the Deleted Items folder until that folder is emptied. In this activity, you will print Lucy's Outbox and one of her sent messages before deleting the Inbox messages.

1 If necessary, in the **Navigation Pane**, click **Outbox** to display the Outbox folder. Click the first message in the Outbox one time to select it.

2 From **Backstage** view, click **Print** and notice that *Memo Style* is selected.

Memo style is the default print setting; it prints the text of the selected items one at a time. Use Memo Style to print individual items, such as an entire e-mail message.

Note | Account Names in Printouts

Depending on the print style you use, your printout may include the name associated with the e-mail account that you are using on your computer. In Memo Style, the name associated with the e-mail account displays in bold just above the header.

3 In the center panel, click the **Print Options** button. In the **Print style** section, click the **Page Setup** button. On the **Header/Footer tab**. under **Footer**, delete any existing information in the three boxes. In the left box, using your own first and last name, type **Lastname_Firstname_3A_Reply_Message** and then compare your screen with Figure 3.28.

Figure 3.28

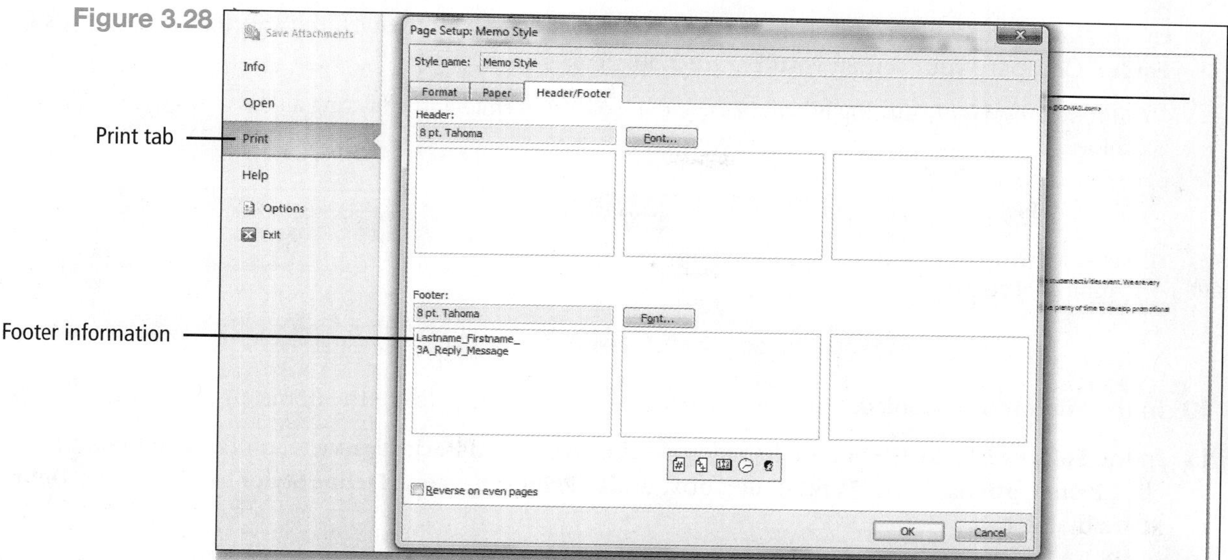

4 Click **OK**. Click **Cancel**, start the **Snipping Tool**, and then create a **Window Snip**. Save the snip as a **JPEG file** in your **All In One Chapter 3** folder as **Lastname_Firstname_3A_Reply_Message Close** the **Snipping Tool** window. With the print preview still displayed, on the left of **Backstage** view, click **Close** to close the message and return to **Inbox** folder.

5 In your **Outbox** folder, click the first message, press Shift, and then click the last message to select both messages.

6 On the **Home tab**, in the **Delete group**, click **Delete** to move the messages to the **Deleted Items** folder.

7 Display the **Inbox** folder. Select the messages, right-click any of the selected messages, and then on the shortcut menu, click **Delete**.

8 Display the **Deleted Items** folder. To the left of each item, notice the icons, which indicate the type of Outlook item, such as a received message or a message to which you replied. Compare your screen with Figure 3.29.

Figure 3.29

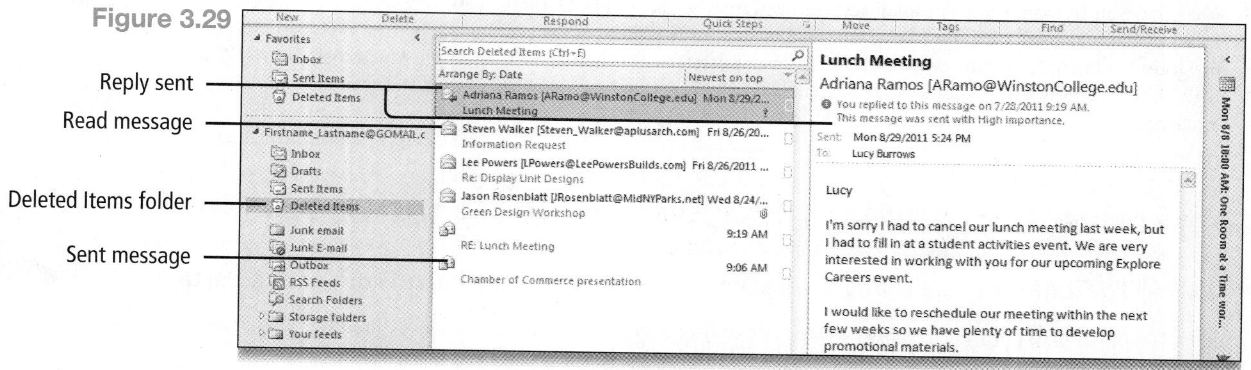

9 In the **Navigation Pane**, right-click the **Deleted Items** folder, and then on the shortcut menu, click **Empty Folder**. Compare your screen with Figure 3.30.

Outlook displays a warning box indicating that you are permanently deleting all the items in the Deleted Items folder.

Figure 3.30

Message warning of permanent deletion

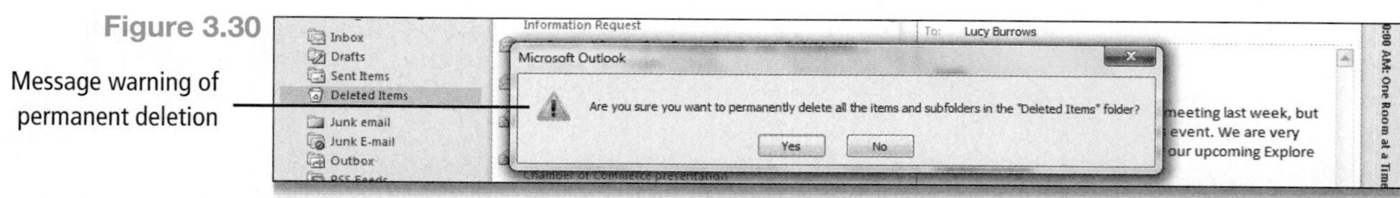

10 In the **Microsoft Outlook** dialog box, click **Yes** to permanently delete the items and empty the folder.

11 In the **Folder List**, click **Inbox** to display the Inbox folder. In **Backstage** view, on the **Print tab**, under **Printer**, click **Print Options**. In the **Print** dialog box, under **Print style**, click **Define Styles** to display the **Define Print Styles** dialog box.

12 In the **Define Print Styles** dialog box, click **Memo Style**, click **Reset**, and then click **OK**. **Close** the dialog box. In the **Print** dialog box, click **Cancel**.

13 In **Backstage** view, click **Options**. In the **Outlook Options** dialog box, on the left, click **Advanced**. Under **Send and receive**, click to select the **Send immediately when connected** check box. Then, to the right of the check box, click the **Send/Receive** button.

14 In the **Send/Receive Groups** dialog box, under **Setting for group "All Accounts"**, select both the **Include this group in send/receive (F9)** and if necessary, the **Schedule an automatic send/receive every** check box if this is a default setting on your computer. Under **When Outlook is Offline**, if necessary, select the check box for **Include this group in send/receive (F9)** if this is a default setting on your computer. Click **Close** and then click **OK**. **Close** [X] Outlook.

Outlook's default setting is restored.

More Knowledge | Using Outlook Web Access

If you have an Exchange Server e-mail account, you may be able to use Outlook Web Access. This feature enables you to access your Microsoft Exchange Server mailbox from any computer that has an Internet connection by using your Web browser. Outlook Web Access is a useful program for individuals who work in different computer environments, such as Apple Macintosh or UNIX. It is also useful for individuals who require remote access. Outlook Web Access is usually set up by a network administrator or Internet service provider. You must have an Exchange Server e-mail account to use Outlook Web Access.

Objective 4 | Make Calls Over the Internet Using Skype

Alert! | To Communicate Using Skype, You Must Identify and Then Work with a Partner.

When completing Activity 3.10, identify a classmate or friend who has or can set up a Skype account. Then, partner with this individual to complete the project. You will both need to be online at the same time, but you do not have to be in the same location.

View the video on th Companion Web Si or in MyITLab

Skype is a software application with which you can make voice calls, make video calls, transfer files, or send messages—including instant messages and text messages—over the Internet. It is free to set up a basic account, and you can pay for more sophisticated services such as those you might need in a business. Skype functions through a peer-to-peer network. In a peer-to-peer network, individuals communicate directly with each other rather than through a central server. Free services include calls to other users within the Skype service, one-to-one video calls, instant messaging, and screen sharing. Other services, for example calls to landline and mobile phones, can be made for a fee.

Activity 3.10 | Participating in a Skype Call

In this activity, you will work with your partner to conduct a Skype call.

Alert! | Downloading Skype and Using Web-Based Applications and Services

You must have or download Skype on your computer to complete this activity. To install, go to **www.skype.com** and download the free version; follow the directions to create an account. Keep in mind that computer programs on the Web receive continuous updates and improvements. Thus, your screen may differ from the ones shown. You can often look at the screens and the information presented to determine how to complete the activity.

1 Display the **Start** menu. With your insertion point blinking in the **Search** box, type **Skype** and then on the menu above, click **Skype**.

2 In the **Skype** dialog box, click in the **Skype Name** box, and then type your Skype name. Click in the **Password** box, and then type your password exactly as you did when you set up the account. Click **Sign me in** and then compare your screen with Figure 3.31; you might be asked to update or select a profile picture.

The Skype window displays two panes. Use the Contacts pane to add contacts, create groups, or search your contacts. The pane on the right displays two tabs. The first tab, *Skype Home*, can find friends or make calls to a landline or mobile phone number for a fee. On the *Profile* tab, you can edit your Skype profile and view information about you that is available to the public or limited to contacts.

Figure 3.31

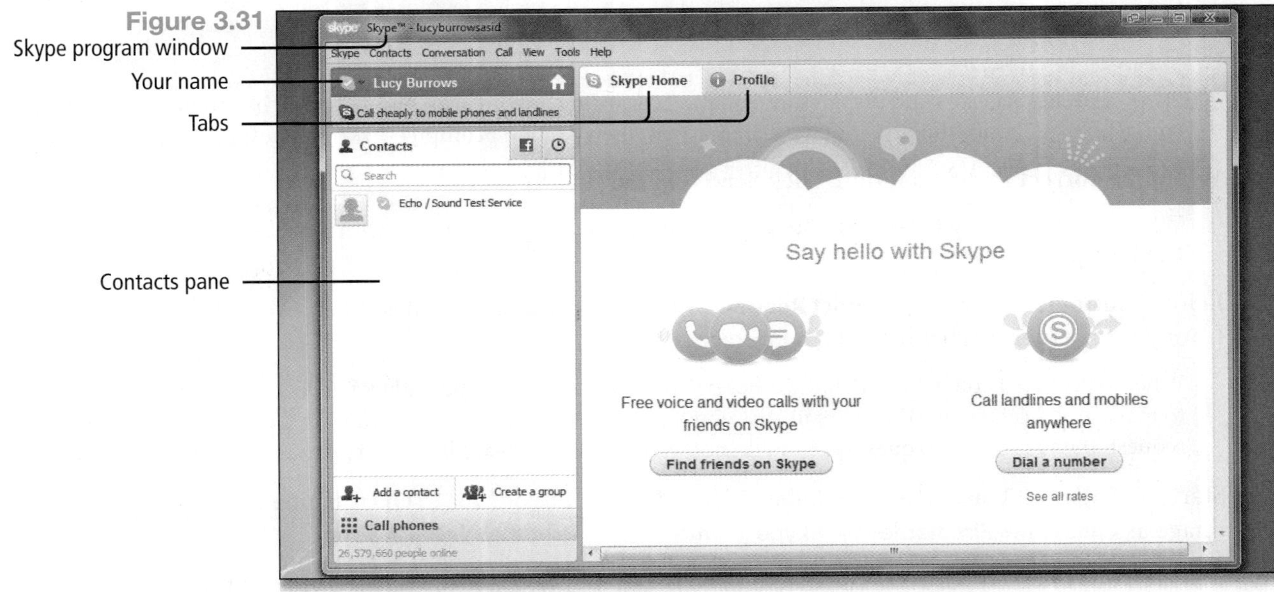

3 In the upper left portion of the window, to the left of your name, click the **status arrow**. Compare your screen with Figure 3.32, and then review the options described in the table in Figure 3.33.

A green indicator next to your name shows that you are Online; thus, you cannot select the Online option on the status menu.

Figure 3.32

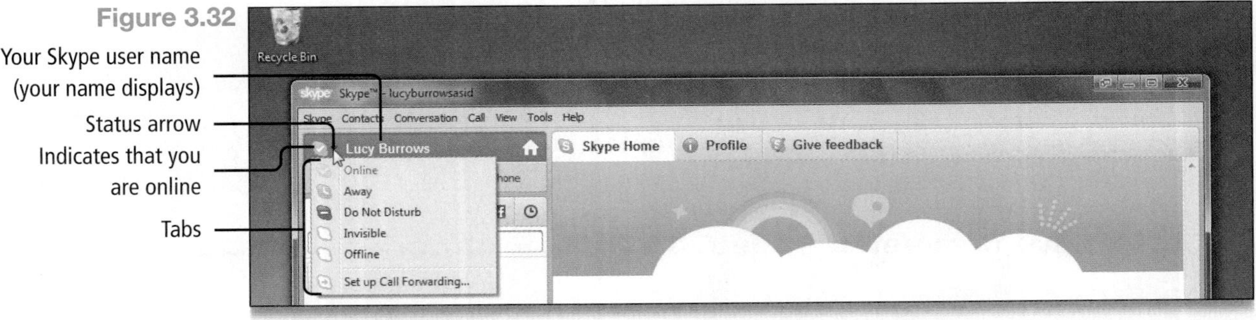

Skype Status Options

Status option	If you select this option, your status is:
Online	Default setting when you sign in. Your contacts can see that you are signed in, and they can call you and you can receive instant messages.
Away	Your contacts can see that you are signed in, but you may be away from your computer. Contacts can try calling you, and you can receive instant messages.
Do Not Disturb	Your contacts can see that you are signed in but you do not want to be disturbed. You can receive instant messages, but you will not hear any sounds.
Invisible	Your contacts cannot see that you are signed in, but you may use Skype. You will not receive instant messages or calls from others.
Offline	Automatic setting when you are not signed in to Skype. You cannot send or receive instant messages or calls.
Set up Call Forwarding	Option used to set up call forwarding so that you can receive Skype calls at another number.

Figure 3.33

4 On the list, be sure **Online** is selected. At the bottom of the **Contacts** pane, click the **Add a contact** button, type all the details you know about your partner for this activity, and then click the **Add** button. You can also use the Find friends on Skype button to find contacts you already communicate with through other e-mail or other social media sites.

Skype searches its users and displays information regarding anyone who has matching information. If you are contacting someone who does not have an account, then you are prompted to send an e-mail invitation to join Skype.

5 When the correct match is found, click **Send request**.

While you are waiting for someone to accept your contact request, an icon with a question mark displays in the Contacts pane.

6 Below your name, click the **Contact Request** button to display the request form. Accept the request you receive from your partner by clicking **Add to Contacts**.

When accepting a contact request, the other person does not need to be online. However, both parties must be online to make and receive calls. If you are unsure about a request you receive, you can view the person's profile or ignore their request. If you receive a request that you do not want to accept, click Block to prevent future contact with that person.

7 Start the **Snipping Tool**, create a **Window Snip**, and then in your **All In One Chapter 3** folder, save the **JPEG** image as **Lastname_Firstname_3A_Skype_Contact** **Close** the **Snipping Tool**.

8 Be sure your selected partner is available to call, and then in the Contacts pane, click the name of the person you want to call. On the menu bar at the top of the window, click **Call**, and then click **Call** if you want to participate in an audio only call; click **Video Call** if you and the person you are calling have a Web cam and want to include video in the phone call.

9 When the call is complete, click **End Call**, sign out of Skype and **Close** Skype.

10 As directed by your instructor, submit the five Snip files that you created in the this project:
Lastname_Firstname_3A_Contact_Cards
Lastname_Firstname_3A_Burrows_Week
Lastname_Firstname_3A_Burrows_Outbox
Lastname_Firstname_3A_Skype_Contact
Lastname_Firstname_3A_Reply_Message

End **You have completed Project 3A**

Project 3B Online Presence

Project Activities

In Activities 3.11 through 3.13, you will create a professional online presence by using LinkedIn and Squarespace for a professional Web site and blog. Upon completion, your screen snips will look similar to Figure 3.34.

Project Files

For Project 3B, you will not need any files.

You will save your files as:

Lastname_Firstname_3B_LinkedIn_Profile
Lastname_Firstname_3B_LinkedIn_Update
Lastname_Firstname_3B_Squarespace_Post

Project Results

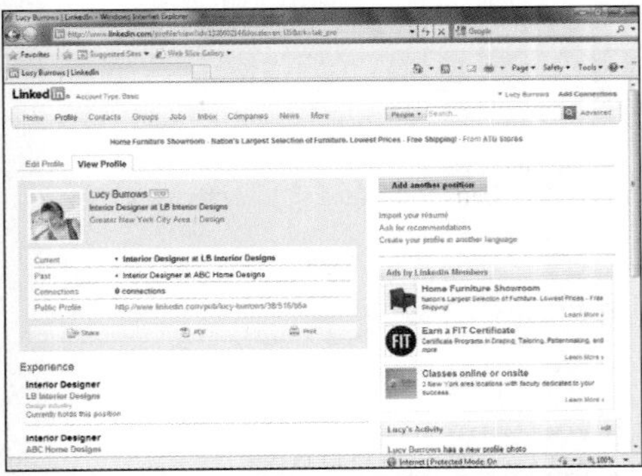

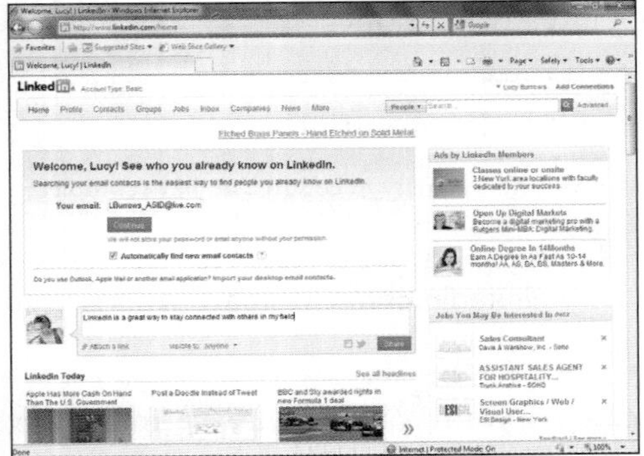

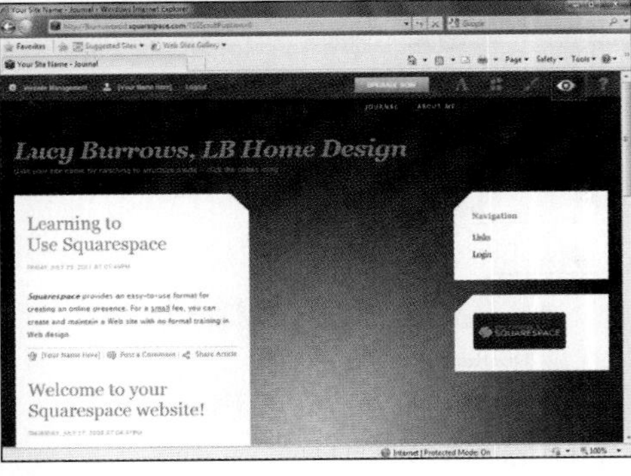

Figure 3.34
Project 3B Online Presence

Objective 5 | Create a LinkedIn Account

View the video on the Companion Web Site or in MyITLab

LinkedIn is a professional social networking site where you can find past and present colleagues and classmates, connect with appropriate people when seeking a new job or business opportunity, or get answers from industry experts. LinkedIn is widely accepted as the best place to become more active in your industry or search for a new career. LinkedIn communication occurs within your list of ***Connections***. Connections are the people with whom you have some level of online relationship using LinkedIn. To use LinkedIn, you develop a profile that includes information such as your recent work experience, education, photo, and specific skills that you have.

> **Alert! | Working with Web-Based Applications and Services**
>
> Computer programs and services on the Web receive continuous updates and improvements. Thus, the steps to complete this Web-based activity may differ from the ones shown. You can often look at the screens and the information presented to determine how to complete the activity.

Activity 3.11 | Creating a LinkedIn Account and Profile

Creating a LinkedIn account and completing a profile will provide your connections—the people with whom you have formed LinkedIn relationships—with information about you. In this activity, you will create a LinkedIn account and profile if you do not already have one.

> **Alert! | Do You Already Have a LinkedIn Account?**
>
> If you already have a LinkedIn account, review this activity to be sure you have completed your profile. Then, you can skip to Activity 3.12.

1 In Internet Explorer, go to **www.linkedin.com** Compare your screen with Figure 3.35.

> **Note | For this activity, you can use your Windows Live e-mail address if you want to do so.**

Figure 3.35

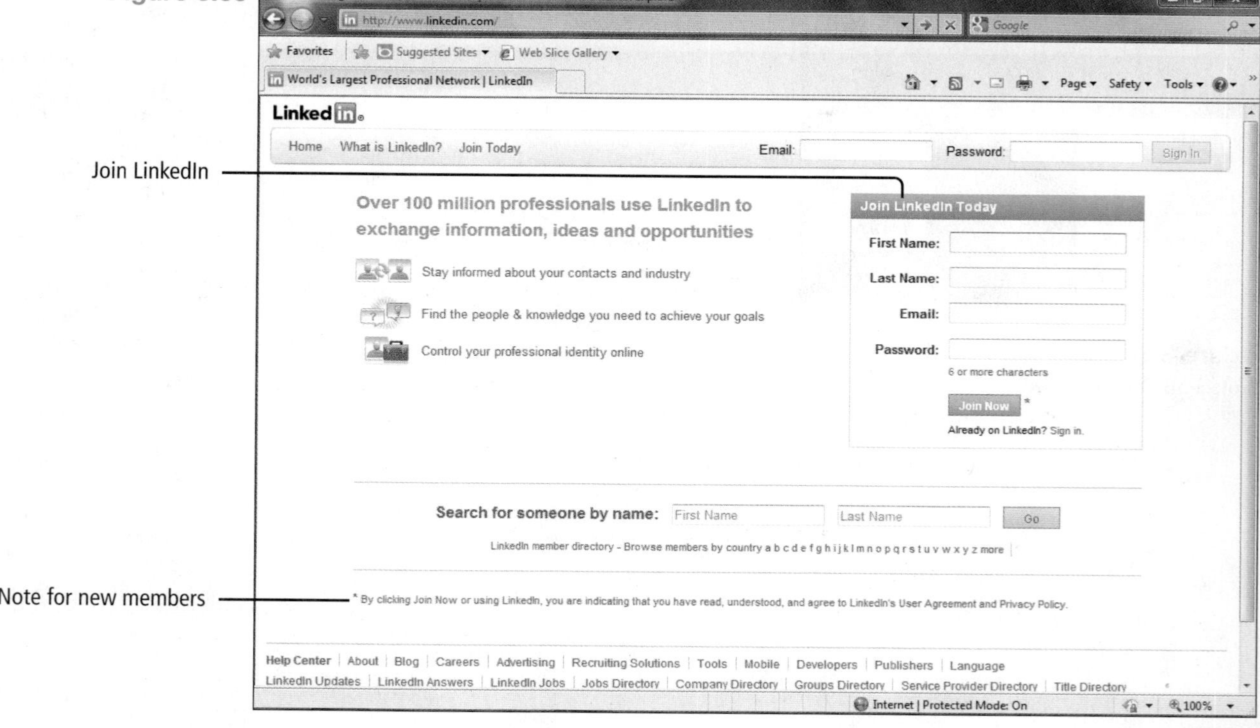

2 Be sure you know your Windows Live e-mail address to use for this step—or use another e-mail address that you have. If you do not have a LinkedIn account, in the **Join LinkedIn Today** box, type your first and last name, your e-mail address, and a password of six or more characters, and then click the **Join Now** button.

3 Fill out the professional profile information page—the fields with asterisks are required. If you are not currently employed, use your school as the Company, select Higher Education as the Industry, and then type Student as your Job Title. Click **Create my profile.**

4 In the **See Who You Already Know** on LinkedIn, unless you want to use the LinkedIn site to make professional contacts, click Skip this step; otherwise, click **Continue.**

If you skip the e-mail search at this point, you can perform the search later, after you finish creating your account.

5 If you clicked Continue, finish filling out the required information; otherwise, click Confirm my Windows Live Hotmail Account. In the Windows Live window, click Allow access. If a message displays indicating that your e-mail cannot be confirmed, follow the instructions to try again. When you see the LinkedIn Email Confirmation message, click the **Click here link** and follow the instructions to complete the process.

6 In the **Connect to more people you know and trust box**, add any e-mail addresses you want to include—separated by commas—or click skip this step.

7 In the **Your Account is Set Up—Choose Your Plan Level** window, under **What Do You Want to Do?**, point to *Create a professional profile and build your network* Compare your screen with Figure 3.36.

You can learn about all of the basic (free) and premium features of LinkedIn before you select your plan level.

Figure 3.36

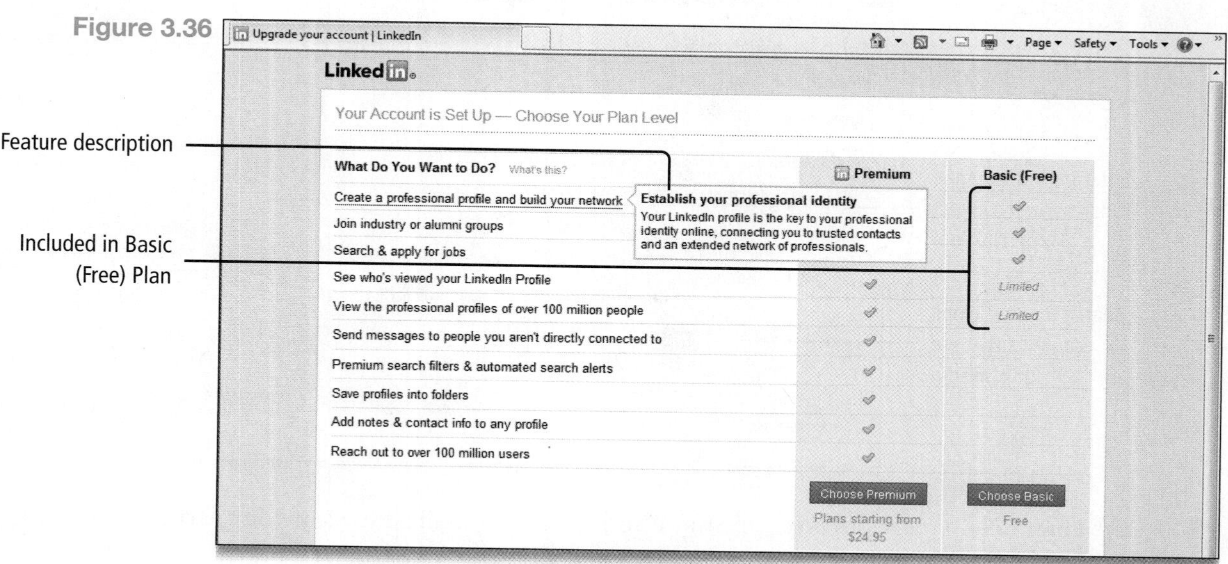

8 Review any other options, and then, under **Basic (Free)**, click **Choose Basic.**

9 On the LinkedIn menu, point to **Profile**, and then click **Edit Profile**. If you want to do so, upload a picture to identify yourself in your profile. Next to **Past**, add a past position. Add information to other sections of your profile to make it more complete.

Notice the profile completeness scale in the right column. Profile Completion tips are also displayed to guide you in creating an effective LinkedIn profile.

Note | To Import a Resume

In the right column, under Add another position, click Import your resume. In the Import your resume box, click the Browse button and upload a Word, PDF, or HTML file. When you import a resume, experience and education information are extracted from the resume and added to your profile.

10 At the top of the window, click the **View Profile tab**. Start the **Snipping Tool**, create a **Window Snip**, and then in your **All In One Chapter 3** folder, save the **JPEG** image as **Lastname_Firstname_3B_LinkedIn_Profile Close** the **Snipping Tool**. Hold this file until the end of this project.

11 Remain signed in for the next activity.

Activity 3.12 | Inviting LinkedIn Connections and Sharing an Update

Alert! | Working with a Partner

When completing Activity 3.12, identify a classmate or friend with a LinkedIn account with whom you can partner to complete this activity.

After you create a LinkedIn profile, you can build your connections by inviting contacts to connect with you using LinkedIn. In this activity, you will begin building your connections.

1 If necessary, sign in to your LinkedIn account. In the menu bar at the top of the screen, click **Contacts**, and then click the **Add Connections tab**. Compare your screen with Figure 3.37.

Here you can search your e-mail accounts to find people that you know on LinkedIn or you can enter e-mail addresses of people to invite them to be a connection.

Figure 3.37

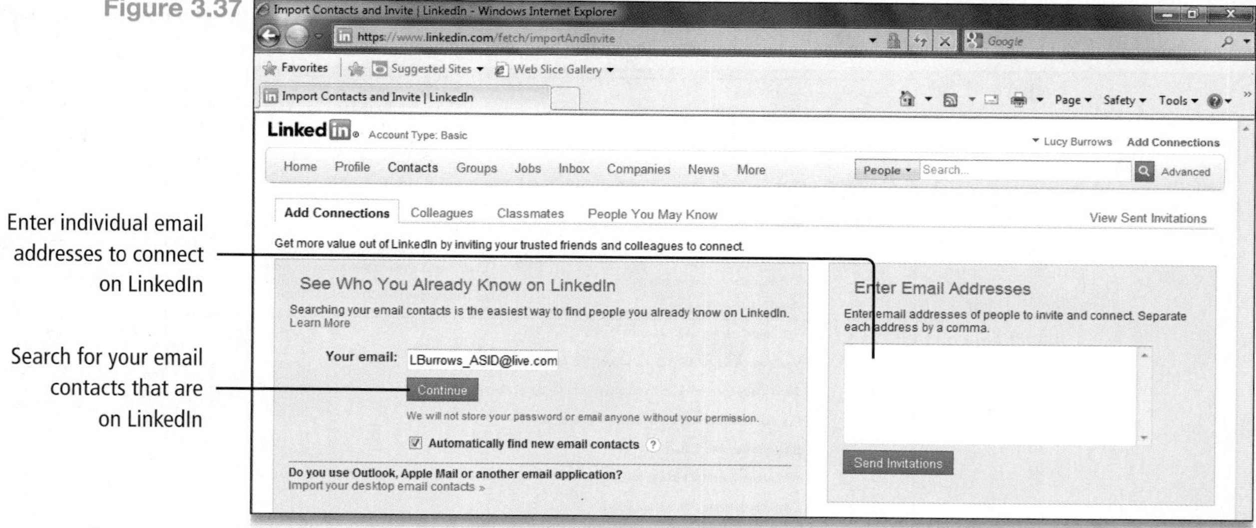

2 In the **Enter Email Addresses** box, type the Windows Live e-mail address of your partner, and then click **Send Invitations**.

After your invitation is accepted, you can click the Contacts menu and then click My Connections to see information about your contacts.

3 If necessary, in the menu bar, click **Home** to display your LinkedIn home page. Scroll down to the **Share an Update** box. Click inside the box, and type a short message about learning to use LinkedIn. Start the **Snipping Tool**, create a **Window Snip**, and then in your **All In One Chapter 3** folder, save the **JPEG** image as **Lastname_Firstname_3B_LinkedIn_Update Close** the **Snipping Tool**. Hold this file until you complete this project.

Use updates to share information with your connections. Because LinkedIn is a professional social networking site, be sure to write all your messages in a professional manner. Do not use the casual writing style that you might use on Facebook.

4 Below your update message, click **Share**. Scroll down to see any updates posted by your connections.

5 In the upper right corner of your screen, point to your name, and then click **Sign Out**. **Close** LinkedIn and **Close** Internet Explorer.

> **More Knowledge | Additional and Valuable Features in LinkedIn**
>
> As you build your career, try some other features of LinkedIn to connect with more people in your industry. For example, LinkedIn Groups enable you to follow influential people and join in groups in your area of interest. You can join a group or even start a group. Also try LinkedIn Answers to ask or answer questions. Finally, read and view the LinkedIn User Guides, especially the ones for New Users and for Students. There are many videos you can view to learn about getting started on your job search by using LinkedIn.

Objective 6 | Create and Maintain a Web Site and Blog with Squarespace

View the video on the Companion Web Site or in MyITLab

Blogs shaped early social media and are even more important now, because a blog is your online voice to tell the world about your business or your capabilities. ***Squarespace***, according to their own site, is "a fully hosted, completely managed environment for creating and maintaining a Web site, blog, or portfolio." Squarespace provides templates and tools to help you plan and create your site without hiring a Web designer. You can try Squarespace for free for a limited time, which provides you an opportunity to see if you like the platform. After the trial period, Squarespace charges for its services, but the price is quite affordable. Consider a platform like Squarespace if you have a business or service that requires an online presence.

> **Alert | Working with Web-Based Applications and Services**
>
> Computer programs and services on the Web receive continuous updates and improvements. Thus, the steps to complete this Web-based activity may differ from the ones shown. You can often look at the screens and the information presented to determine how to complete the activity.

Activity 3.13 | Creating a Squarespace Account and Blog Post

1 Open your browser, and then navigate to **www.squarespace.com** and compare your screen with Figure 3.38.

> **Note | For this Activity, you will create a free site that you can use for 14 days. No credit card information is required.**

Figure 3.38

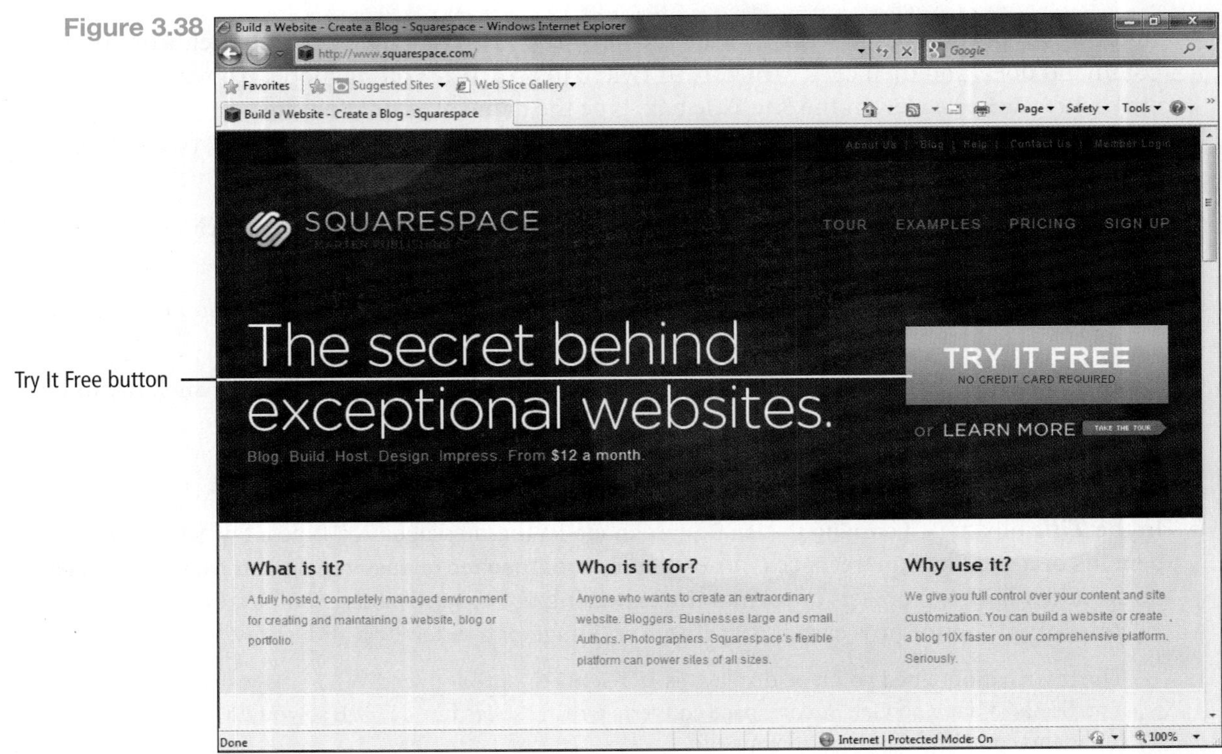

2 If you do not have a Squarespace account, click the **TRY IT FREE** button. In the first box, type your name or some variation of your name without spaces—for example, your initials and last name. Notice that as you type, *.squarespace.com* is added as part of your url.

The url you choose for your Web site will also be your log in. If this is going to be a personal Web site, you might consider using your name or an arrangement that includes part of your name.

3 In the next box, type a password—be sure to write it down or make it something easily remembered. In the third box, type your e-mail address—use your Windows Live address if you want to do so. Click **CREATE YOUR WEBSITE**. When the screen indicates *Your Squarespace Site is Ready!*, click the **VIEW WEBSITE** button, and then compare your screen with Figure 3.39.

Figure 3.39

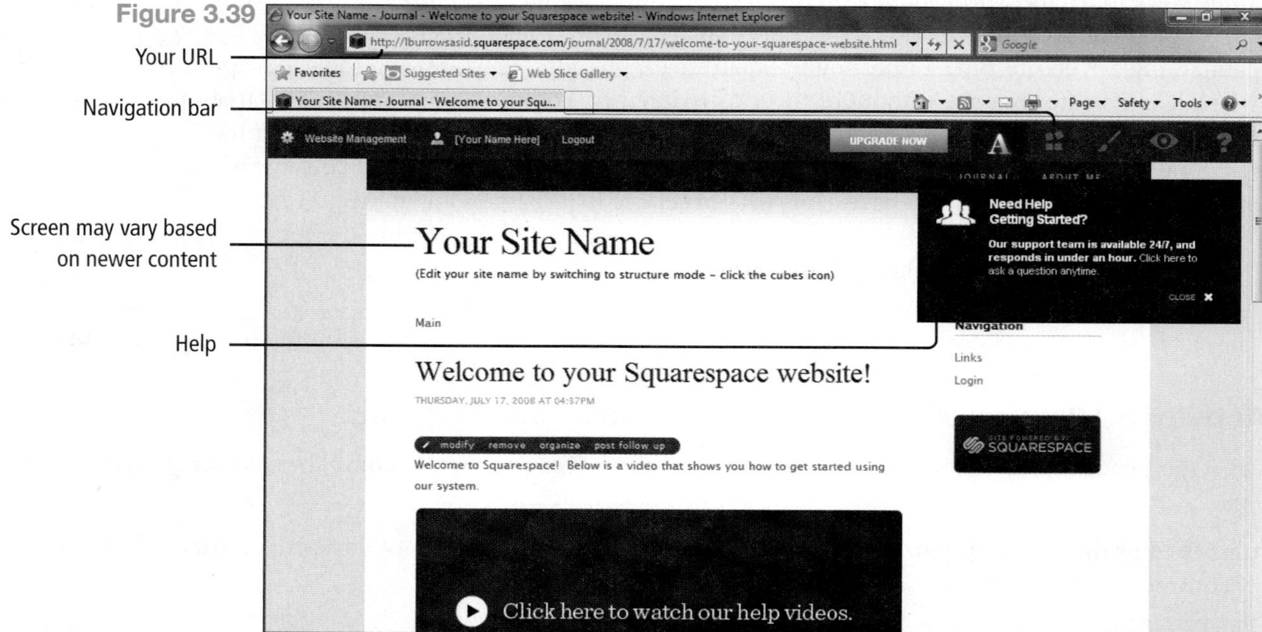

4 In the upper portion of the screen, locate the navigation bar, and then point to each icon to read what each command does, and then click **Structure** to switch to **Structure Editing** mode. Above the text *Your Site Name*, click **edit website header**. In the **Site Title** box, type the name of your Web site—something simple, for example *Susan's Design Service*. It is not necessary to complete the remaining. boxes, but if you want to complete them now, do so. At the bottom of the dialog box, click **Save & Close**.

5 On the navigation bar, click **Style** to display the **Appearance Editor**. Click the **Switch Templates** button to view the default options, and then select a template that you like.

You can make many other style changes by using the *Banner & Navigation*; *Fonts, Colors & Sizes*; *Custom CSS*; and *Advanced* options in the Appearance Editor.

6 On the navigation bar, click **Content**, and then in the upper portion of the screen, click the **Journal** button.

To modify information on your site, Content mode must be active.

7 Below your site title, click the **post new entry** button.

8 In the ***Title*** box, type **Learning to Use Squarespace** In the message box, type a few sentences about the benefits of a site like Squarespace—for example, **Squarespace is easy to use and free to try.** If you want to do so, add additional objects or format the text using the options in the toolbar. On the toolbar, point to the various icons—notice how easy it is to insert an image or a video or a slideshow.

The information typed you type displays as ***WYSIWYG***—pronounced WIZ-e-wig—which is an acronym for What You See Is What You Get. Squarespace converts writing styles into HTML so you do not have to learn HTML to build and code Web content on your site.

9 In the **Create a Post** window, click the **Save & Close** button. Then, locate and click the **Enable Style** button to complete your post.

10 On the navigation bar, click the **Preview** icon to display a preview of your Web site.

11 Start the **Snipping Tool**, create a **Window Snip**, and then in your **All In One Chapter 3** folder, save the **JPEG** image as **Lastname_Firstname_3B_Squarespace_Post Close** the **Snipping Tool**. In the upper left, click **Logout** to log out of your Squarespace account.

12 Submit your three snip files for this project to your instructor as directed:
Lastname_Firstname_3B_LinkedIn_Profile
Lastname_Firstname_LinkedIn_Update
Lastname_Firstname_3B_Squarespace_Post

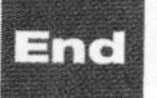

You have completed Project 3B

Content-Based Assessments

Summary

Microsoft Outlook 2010 is an e-mail program and personal information manager. Use Outlook to manage your schedule, store information about your contacts, keep track of tasks you need to complete, and send and receive e-mail messages. In this chapter, you started Outlook and navigated through its various components using the Navigation Pane and the folder list. You practiced using Outlook's contacts, calendar, and e-mail capabilities. You also learned about creating an online presence using the social media tool LinkedIn and about creating a professional Web site and blog by using Squarespace.

Key Terms

Appointment 98
Appointment area 98
Appointment form 98
At sign (@) 102
Busy 100
Calendar 95
Calendar folder 95
Carbon copy 103
Comments area 99
Connections 114
Contact 95
Contacts 95
Contacts folder 95
Courtesy copy 103
Date Navigator 98
Domain name 102
File tab 94
Free 100
Group names 94
LinkedIn 114
Memo style 108
Message header 105
Navigation Pane 94
Offline 102
Online 102
Out of Office 100
Personal information manager 91
Print style 108
Profile 92
Quick Access Toolbar 94
Range of recurrence .101
RE: 107
Reading Pane 103
Recurrence pattern ..101
Ribbon 94
Skype 110
Squarespace 117
Syntax 103
Tentative 100
Time Bar 98
Title bar 94
User account 91
Week view 99
Wizard 94
Wordwrap 104
Work Week view 99
WYSIWYG 118

Check Your Knowledge

Matching and Multiple Choice items are available in MyITLab and on the Companion Web Site.

Apply **3A** and **3B** skills from these Objectives:

1. Create an Outlook Account
2. Enter and Edit Contacts and Calendar Entries
3. Send and Receive E-mail
4. Make Calls Over the Internet Using Skype
5. Create a LinkedIn Account
6. Create and Maintain a Web site and Blog with Squarespace

Mastering Outlook | Project 3C LB Home Design

In the following Mastering Outlook project, you will add and modify contacts, create appointments, manage mail, and send an e-mail message for LB Home Design. You will also update the LinkedIn profile for Lucy Burrows. Your snips and printouts will look similar to Figure 3.40.

Project Files

For Project 3C, you will need the following file:

ou03C_LB_Home

You will save your files as:

Lastname_Firstname_3C_LBHD_Contacts
Lastname_Firstname_3C_Work_Week
Lastname_Firstname_3C_Forwarded_Message
Lastname_Firstname_3C_Deleted_Folder
Lastname_Firstname_3C_Updated_Profile

Project Results

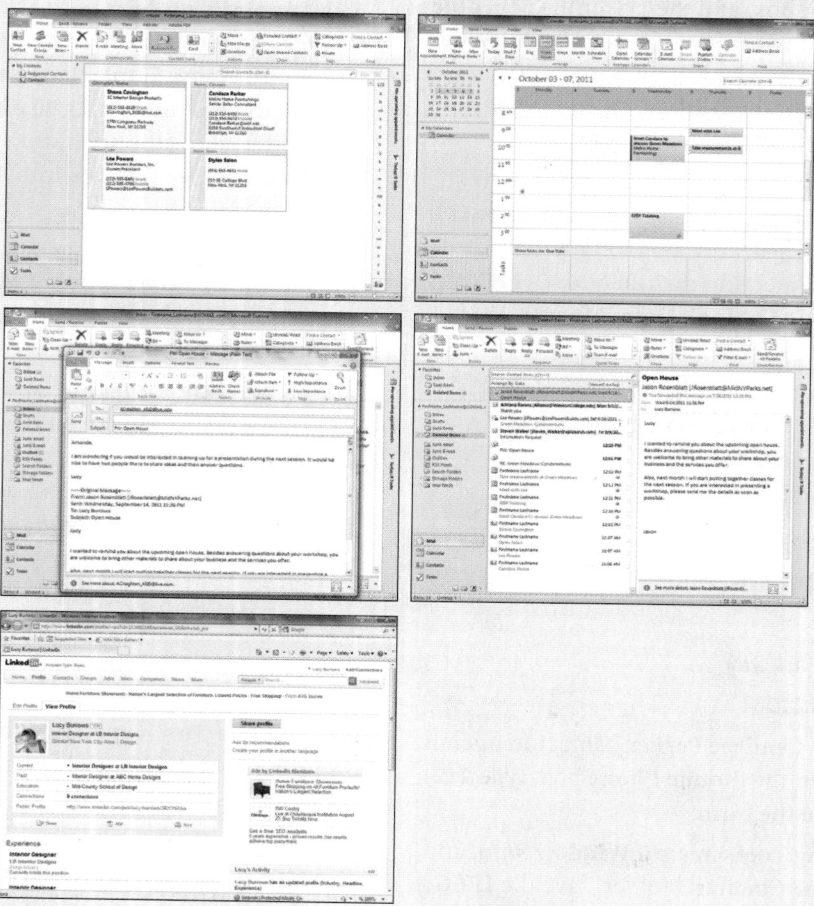

Figure 3.40

(Project 3C LB Home Design continues on the next page)

Mastering Outlook | Project 3C LB Home Design (continued)

1 Click the **Start** button, and then point to the **Shut down button arrow**. On the **Shut down** menu, click **Switch user** to display the Windows 7 desktop. Click your **Firstname Lastname** account. If the account does not exist, refer to Activities 3.01 and 3.02 to set up the Windows 7 user account and to configure Microsoft Outlook.

2 Start **Microsoft Outlook 2010**. In the **Navigation Pane**, under your GOMAIL.com e-mail address, click **Inbox**.

3 From the **Backstage** view, click **Options**. In the **Outlook Options** dialog box, on the left, click **Advanced**. Scroll down to the section **Send and receive**, *clear* the check mark from the **Send immediately when connected** check box, and then click the **Send/Receive** button. In the **Send/Receive Groups** dialog box, under **Setting for group "All Accounts"**, *clear* the **Include this group in send/receive (F9)** check box, and then *clear* the **Schedule an automatic send/receive every** check box. Under **When Outlook is Offline**, *clear* the two check boxes. Click the **Close** button, and then in the **Outlook Options** dialog box, click **OK** to close the dialog box.

4 With your **Inbox** selected, click the **File tab** to display **Backstage** view, click **Open**, and then **Import** the **Outlook Data File (.pst)** by navigating to your student data files and selecting the file **ou03C_LB_Home**. Import from the **Outlook Data File** into the **same folder**.

5 Display the **Contacts** folder, and open a **New Contact** form. Complete the form with the following information, and then **Save & Close** the form.

Shana Covington

SC Interior Design Products

SCovington_SCID@.live.com

212-555-0129

1750 Longview Parkway

New York, NY 11210

6 Double-click the **Candace Parker** contact to open it. In the **Contact** form, in the **Mobile Phone** box, type **212-555-0673** **Save & Close** the form.

7 Start the **Snipping Tool**, create a **Window Snip**, and then in your **All In One Chapter 3** folder, save the **JPEG** image as **Lastname_Firstname_3C_LBHD_Contacts** **Close** the **Snipping Tool**. Hold this file until you complete this project.

8 Display the **Calendar** folder. If you are working in a college lab or other classroom environment, clear all previous calendar entries made by others as follows: From the **View tab**, in the **Current View group**, click the **Change View** button, and then click **Active**. If any appointments display, press Ctrl + A, and then right-click on any of the selected appointments and on the displayed menu, click **Delete**. Return to the **Current View**, using the same steps, click **Change View**, and click **Calendar**.

9 If necessary, in the **Arrange group**, click **Day**. In the **Date Navigator**, click the right arrow next to the month name to advance the calendar one month. Click the **Wednesday** of the first full week. Open a new **Appointment** form, and as the **Subject**, type **Meet Candace to discuss Green Meadows** As the **Location**, type **Metro Home Furnishings** Set the **Start time** to **9:30 AM** and the **End time** to **11:00 AM**. Set the **Reminder** to **30 minutes**, show the appointment as **Out of Office**, and then **Save & Close** the appointment.

10 Open another new **Appointment** form. As the **Subject**, type **STEP Training** and set the **Start time** to **2:00 PM** and the **End time** to **3:30 PM**. Set the appointment as recurring every **1 week** to end after **4 occurrences**. **Save & Close** the appointment.

11 In the **Date Navigator**, click the **Thursday** of the same week in which you have been entering appointments. In the appointment area, click the **9:00 am** time slot and type **Meet with Lee** Click the **10:00 am** time slot and type **Take measurements at Green Meadows** Open both appointments and show the appointments as **Tentative**.

12 Display the **Work Week** arrangement. Start the **Snipping Tool**, create a **Window Snip**, and then in your **All In One Chapter 3** folder, save the **JPEG** image as **Lastname_Firstname_3C_Work_Week** **Close** the **Snipping Tool**. Hold this file until you complete the project.

13 Display the **Inbox**. Select the message from *Lee Powers*, and then **Reply** to the message.

(Project 3C LB Home Design continues on the next page)

Mastering Outlook | Project 3C LB Home Design (continued)

14 Using the format that you practiced in this chapter, type the following message. Refer to Figure 3.40 as an example for correct spacing.

Lee, Yes, I received the blueprints for Green Meadows. I have been in contact with Candace Parker at Metro Home Furnishings to start making plans. If you would like to talk to her, she can be reached at (214) 555-6400. Thanks, Lucy

15 Proofread the message, and correct any errors. **Send** the message.

16 Select the **Open House** message from *Jason Rosenblatt*. On the **Home tab**, in the **Respond** group, click the **Forward** button to forward the message to **ACreighton_ASID@live.com** In the message area, position the insertion point at the top of the message. Using the format that you practiced in this chapter, type the following message: **Amanda, I am wondering if you would be interested in teaming up for a presentation during the next session. It would be nice to have two people there to share ideas and then answer questions. Lucy**

17 Proofread the message and correct any errors. Start the **Snipping Tool**, create a **Window Snip**, and then in your **All In One Chapter 3** folder, save the **JPEG** image as **Lastname_Firstname_3C_Forwarded_Message Close** the **Snipping Tool**. Hold this file until you have completed this project.

18 **Send** the message.

19 Display the **Contacts** folder. Click the first contact, and then hold down Shift while clicking the last contact. Press Delete.

20 Display the **Calendar** folder. On the **View** tab, click **Change View**, and then click **Active**. Press Ctrl + A, right-click, and then click **Delete**.

21 Select and delete the items in the **Inbox** and **Outbox** folders.

22 Display the **Deleted Items** folder. Start the **Snipping Tool**, create a **Window Snip**, and then in your **All In One Chapter 3** folder, save the **JPEG** image as **Lastname_Firstname_3C_Deleted_Folder Close** the **Snipping Tool**. Hold this file until you complete the project. Empty the **Deleted Items** folder.

23 From **Backstage** view, click **Options**, and then click **Advanced**. Under **Send and receive**, select the **Send immediately when connected** check box. Click the **Send/Receive** button, and then in the **Send/Receive Groups** dialog box, under **Setting for group "All Accounts"**, select both the **Include this group in send/receive (F9)** and **Schedule an automatic send/receive every** check boxes. Under **When Outlook is Offline**, select the check box for **Include this group in send/receive (F9)** if this is a default setting on your computer. Click **Close**, and click **OK** to close all dialog boxes, and then **Exit** Outlook.

24 Sign in to your LinkedIn account. In the menu bar at the top of the screen, click **Profile**, and then click **Edit Profile**.

25 Add a section to your profile, and then add the related information; for example, recommend someone that you know. Save the changes, and then click the **View Profile tab**.

26 Start the **Snipping Tool**, create a **Window Snip**, and then in your **All In One Chapter 3** folder, save the **JPEG** image as **Lastname_Firstname_3C_Updated_Profile Close** the **Snipping Tool**. Sign out of LinkedIn and **Close** your browser. Submit the Snip files you created in the project to your instructor.

End **You have completed Project 3C**

© CandyBox Images/Shutterstock

Tasks Performed by a Freelance Interior Designer Using Windows 7 and Outlook

In this Unit Case Project, you will use Windows 7 and Microsoft Outlook to complete tasks that you might encounter working as a Freelance Interior Designer. You will work with computer files, e-mail, contacts, and calendar using Outlook. Your screen snips will look similar to the ones shown in Figure 1.1.

Project Files

For Unit 1 Case Project, you will need the following files:

ouU1_Inbox

You will save your files as

Lastname_Firstname_U1_Contacts
Lastname_Firstname_U1_Calendar
Lastname_Firstname_U1_Side_by_Side
Lastname_Firstname_U1_Reply_Message

Project Results

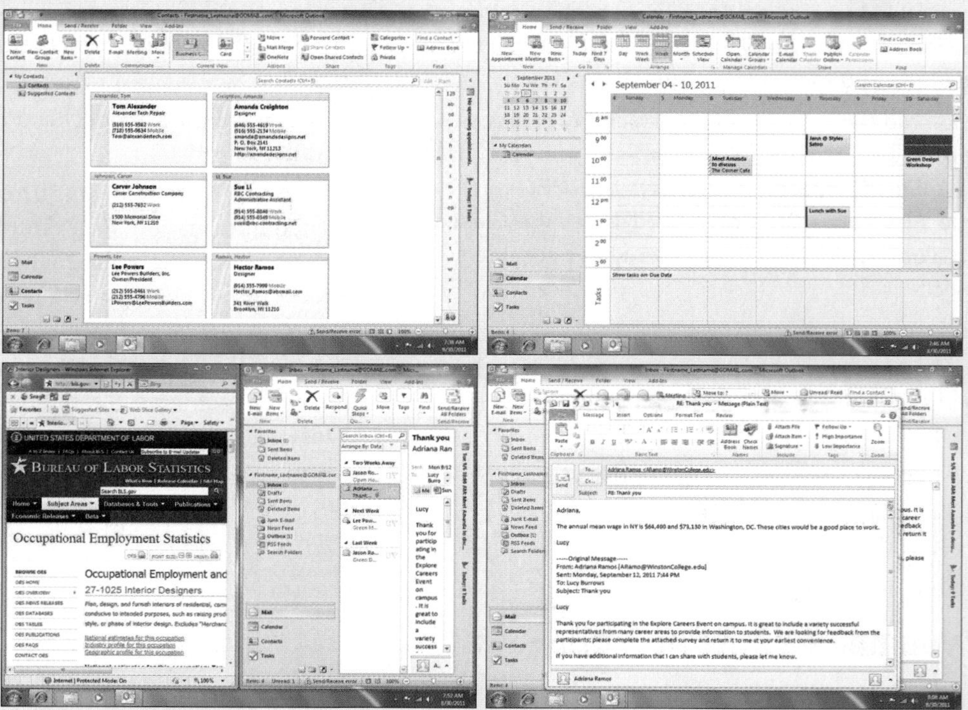

Figure 1.1

Tasks Performed by a Freelance Interior Designer using Windows 7 and Outlook (continued)

1 **Open** Windows Explorer. On your USB drive—not your hard drive—create a new folder named **All In One Unit 1** Locate the student data files that accompany this book, and copy them into the folder you just created.

2 Click the **Start** button, and then point to the **Shut down button arrow**. On the displayed menu, click **Switch user**, and then click the **Firstname Lastname** account that you created in Chapter 3; or, if necessary, refer to Chapter 3, Activities 3.01–3.02 to set up a new Windows 7 user account and to configure Microsoft Outlook. Recall that using a different Windows user account will protect your own Outlook account and will ensure that your results match this instruction.

3 From the **Start** menu, locate the **Microsoft Outlook** program. Point to the program name, and then drag the program to the taskbar. Release the mouse button when the ScreenTip *Pin to Taskbar* displays.

4 On the taskbar, click the **Microsoft Outlook** button to start Outlook. In the **Navigation Pane**, under your GOMAIL.com e-mail address, click **Inbox**. From **Backstage** view, click **Options**. In the **Outlook Options** dialog box, on the left, click **Advanced**. Scroll down to the section **Send and receive**, *clear* the check mark from the **Send immediately when connected** check box, and then click the **Send/Receive** button. In the **Send/Receive Groups** dialog box, under **Setting for group "All Accounts"** *clear* the **Include this group in send/receive (F9)** check box, and then *clear* the **Schedule an automatic send/receive every** check box. Under **When Outlook is Offline**, *clear* the two check boxes. Click the **Close** button, and then in the **Outlook Options** dialog box, click **OK** to close the dialog box.

5 With your **Inbox** selected, click the **File tab** to display **Backstage** view, click **Open**, and then **Import from another program or file** and click **Next**. Import from **Outlook Data File (.pst)**, click **Next**, click **Browse**, navigate to your USB drive, and then in your **All in One Unit 1** folder, select and open the **ouU1_Inbox** file. Click **Next**, import from the **Outlook Data File**, and then click the **Import items into the same folder** option button. Click **Finish**.

6 Display the **Contacts** folder, and open a **New Contact** form. Complete the form with the following information, and then **Save & Close** the form:

Carver Johnson
Carver Construction Company
212-555-7632
1500 Memorial Drive
New York, NY 11210

7 Double-click the **Sue Li** contact to open it. In the **Contact** form, in the **Mobile** box, type **914-555-0349** and then **Save & Close** the form.

8 Start the **Snipping Tool**, create a **Full-screen Snip**, and then in your **All In One Unit 1** folder, save the image as a **JPEG** with the file name **Lastname_Firstname_U1_Contacts Close** the Snipping Tool. Hold this file until you complete this project.

9 Display the **Calendar** folder. If necessary, clear all previous calendar entries made by you or others. In the **Date Navigator**, click the right arrow next to the month name to advance the calendar one month from the current month. In the **Arrange group**, click **Month**. Click the **Tuesday** of the first full week. Open a **New Appointment** form, and as the **Subject**, type **Meet Amanda to discuss workshop topics** As the **Location**, type **The Corner Cafe** Set the **Start time** to **10:00 AM** and the **End time** to **11:00 AM**. Show the appointment as **Tentative**, and then **Save & Close** the appointment.

10 In the **Date Navigator**, click the **Thursday** of the same week in which you have been entering appointments to display the Day view of this date. Set a new appointment for **Jenn @ Styles Salon** from **9:00 AM–10:00 AM** and one for **Lunch with Sue** from **12:30 PM–1:30 PM**. Show both appointments as **Out of Office**.

11 Click the **Saturday** of the same week in which you have been working, and open a **New Appointment** form. As the **Subject**, type **Green Design Workshop** and set the **Start time** to **10:00 AM** and the **End time** to **1:00 PM**. Set the appointment as recurring every **1 week** to end after **2 occurrences**. **Save & Close** the appointment.

(Unit 1 Case Project continues on the next page)

Unit 1 Case Project

Tasks Performed by a Freelance Interior Designer using Windows 7 and Outlook (continued)

12 Display the **Week** arrangement. Start the **Snipping Tool**, create a **Full-screen Snip**, and then in your **All In One Unit 1** folder, save the **JPEG** image as **Lastname_Firstname_U1_Calendar Close** the Snipping Tool. Hold this file until you complete this project.

13 Display the **Inbox**. Select the message from *Lee Powers*, and then **Reply** to the message using the format that you practiced by typing: **Lee, Thank you for including me in this event. I look forward to meeting more of the area realtors. Thanks, Lucy** Proofread the message, and correct any errors. **Send** the message.

14 Select the message from *Adriana Ramos* to display it in the Reading pane. **Open** Internet Explorer. Click in the **address bar** to select the URL text, and then type **bls.gov/oes/current/oes271025.htm** and press Enter. On the taskbar, point to an open area—an area where no buttons display—and right-click. On the displayed shortcut menu, click **Show windows side by side**. Create a **Full-screen Snip**, and then save the snip file in **JPEG** format in your **All In One Unit 1** folder as **Lastname_Firstname_U1_Side_by_Side** Hold this file until you complete this project.

15 Click in the Internet Explorer window to make it active, right-click in an empty area of the taskbar, and then click **Undo Show side by side**. Take a moment to read about interior design careers in New York, and then **Close** Internet Explorer. In the Outlook window, **Reply** to Adriana's e-mail by composing one or two sentences about the employment statistics for this career area so Adriana can provide it to students. For example, *Adriana, The annual mean wage in NY is $64,400 and $73,130 in Washington, DC. These cities would be a good place to work.*

16 Proofread the message, and correct any errors. Start the **Snipping Tool**, create a **Full-screen Snip**, and then in your **All In One Unit** folder, save the **JPEG** image as **Lastname_Firstname_U1_Reply_Message Close** the Snipping Tool. Hold this file until you complete this project.

17 **Send** the message. Display the **Contacts** folder. Click the first contact, and then press Ctrl + A to select all the contacts. Press Delete. Do the same for the **Suggested Contacts** folder. Display the **Calendar** folder. On the **View tab**, in the **Current View group**, click **Change View**, and then click **Active**. Press Ctrl + A to select all the appointments, right-click over the selected items, and then click **Delete**. Select and delete the items in the **Inbox** and **Outbox** folders. Empty the **Deleted Items** folder.

18 From **Backstage** view, click **Options**, and then click **Advanced**. Under **Send and receive**, reset the options to their original settings. Click **Close** and **OK**, and then **Exit** Outlook. On the taskbar, right-click the **Outlook** icon, and unpin it from your taskbar. If necessary, **Switch user** to return to your normal Windows 7 account. Submit your four snip files to your instructor as directed.

Copying and Moving Files

On the Internet, use the Bing or Google search engine to search for *copying and moving files in Windows 7*. In the search results, select a site from Microsoft about this topic. Create a Full-screen snip about this information. Submit your file as directed by your instructor.

Computers, Privacy, Office Common Features, and Word

Chapters in Unit 2:

© leedsn/Shutterstock

Job Focus: Production Manager for a Comic Book Publisher

View Unit 2 Video to meet a Comic Book Production Manager

At the end of this unit, you will have the opportunity to complete a case project that focuses on the job of a Production Manager for a comic book publisher. If you had a position like this, some of the things you might do are: manage publishing schedules, create art and pictures for the comic book, coordinate designers and authors to ensure timely production of the books, select computers for the production team, and manage projects for your organization such as producing newsletters and setting schedules.

Computer Hardware, Privacy, and Security

OUTCOMES

At the end of this chapter you will be able to:

Categorize computers based on size, application, and cost; and recognize the ethical and societal effects of computer use.

OBJECTIVES

Mastering these objectives will enable you to:

Job Focus: Comic Book Production Manager

In This Chapter

You are going to purchase a new communication device to help you in your position as a Production Manager for a comic book publisher. Do you need a laptop, desktop, netbook, or iPad? Or will a smartphone be enough? How will you protect your device and your data from accidental disasters, intentional intrusion, and harmful attacks?

In this chapter, you will look at different categories of computers, the various uses for computers, and the effect that using a computer has on you and on society in general. You will also consider issues that compromise your privacy and security, and then review appropriate methods to protect your privacy and security.

Objective 1 | Categorize Computers

In your job as a Production Manager for a comic book publisher, your company is providing you with a new computer. The IT Department has asked you to identify the type of computer equipment you need. Your daily tasks include scheduling projects, estimating the cost of projects, setting quality standards, monitoring production, communicating with other departments, and adjusting publishing schedules. When selecting a computer, you must evaluate how you use your computer—including security concerns—and then match that evaluation to computers that are available in the price range set by the IT Department. Where do you start?

Concept 4.01 | Identifying Computers for Individuals

Your ***personal computer***—usually referred to as a ***PC***—meets your individual computing needs or, when connected to a network, enables you to communicate and collaborate with others. The two most commonly used personal computers are categorized by their operating system—either the Microsoft Windows operating system or the Apple Macintosh (Mac) operating system. Computers that use the Microsoft Windows operating system are manufactured by companies such as Dell, Gateway, Sony, and Lenovo. Because the first PCs were made by IBM, they were termed IBM-compatible—and sometimes you still hear that term. Computers that use the Apple Macintosh operating system are made only by Apple.

You can categorize personal computers by size, power, and

Computers for Individual Use

Category	Size	Application	Cost	Example
Desktop Manufacturers: Dell, Gateway, Sony, Lenovo, Apple	Consist of a system unit that is about the size of a printer with an independent monitor and keyboard.	A home or office environment.	$300 to $5,000 depending on features	© Dmitry Melnikov/Shutterstock
All-in-one computer Manufacturers: **Apple iMac (trend leader), Lenovo, Sony, Dell**	Combines the system unit and monitor into one.	A home or office environment, good for small cubicles or apartments.	$700 to $5,000 depending on features	© Petinov Sergey Mihilovich/ Shutterstock
Notebook (also called laptop) Manufacturers: Dell, Sony, Gateway	The size of a spiral bound notebook; fits into a briefcase or backpack.	Designed for portability and popular with students and travelers.	$300 to $5,000	Notebook (also called laptop)

Figure 4.1

(continued)

Category	Size	Application	Cost	Example
Subnotebook Manufacturers: Apple, Dell, Sony, and Asus	Omits components such as DVDs, weighs 3 pounds or less, approximately 1-inch thick, runs a full operating system.	People that like full application features but have no need for all the peripheral devices.	$200 to $500	© John Joannides / Alamy
Tablet PC (convertible notebook) Manufacturers: Fujitsu, Lenovo, Dell	The size of a notebook with a screen that swivels and lies flat over the keyboard. You input with a stylus and use embedded handwriting recognition software to convert your handwritten input to digital text.	Designed for portability and ease of note taking. Used by salespersons and others who need to input data quickly.	$100 to $5,000	© Alexirius/Shutterstock

Figure 4.1 Continued

From either the Companion Web Site or MyITLab, try the Chapter 4 Types of Computers Simulation

function. View the table in Figure 4.1 for details.

After reviewing options, you might find that a system that is less powerful, less expensive, and more portable meets your needs. Figure 4.2 displays handheld computing device details.

Concept 4.02 | Identifying Enterprise Systems

An ***enterprise*** is a unit of economic organization or activity that provides goods, services, or both to individuals or to other enterprises; for example, a company or a college is considered to be an enterprise.

Handheld Computers for Individual Use

Category	Size	Application	Cost	Example
Netbook Manufacturers: Acer, Asus, Dell, HP, and Lenovo	Approximately 10 inches wide by 7 inches high, depth of 1.05 inches, and weight is 1.5 to 3 pounds	Web browsing, e-mail, and using online services.	$150 to $400	© francesco riccardo iacomino/Shutterstock
Tablet Manufacturers: iPad by Apple, Eee pad by Asus, Xoom by Motorola, and Galaxy by Samsung	7.47 inches wide by 9.56 inches high, depth of 0.5 inches, and weight is 1.5 to 1.6 pounds	Larger than a smartphone but smaller than a notebook; uses a touchscreen for input; can access the Web and e-mail; takes advantage of multimedia while on the move; can download a wide variety of apps.	$500 to $1,000	© Neil Fraser / Alamy

Figure 4.2

Category	Size	Application	Cost	Example
Handheld computers or personal digital assistants Manufacturers: Asus, Dell, and Sony	Fits in the palm of your hand or in a pocket	Designed for portability, uses a stylus or virtual keyboard to manage contacts, access e-mail, and schedule appointments.	\$200 to \$400	© BelleMedia/ Shutterstock
Smartphone Manufacturers: Apple iPhone, BlackBerry Curve, Motorola Droid, Samsung Focus Windows phone	Fits in the palm of your hand or in a pocket	Designed for use as a mobile phone, but with Web access and added features; becoming hard to distinguish it from a handheld computer.	\$100 to \$300	© Stefan Sollfors / Alamy
Dedicated Devices Example: Kindle DX Reader by Amazon, the Nook by Barnes and Noble, and the Sony Reader	Approximately 7.2 inches wide by 10.4 inches high, depth of 0.4 inches, and weight is 1.1 pounds	Dedicated to a specific activity: the Kindle DX Reader is an e-book reader (electronic book reader) on which you can download, display, and read books purchased through the Internet.	\$140 to \$400	© Ian Dagnall / Alamy

Figure 4.2 Continued

Because enterprise operations typically use more files and large databases for activities like customer transactions and employee information, enterprise employees need systems that compute faster and have more storage capacity.

Professional workstations (Figure 4.3) are high-end desktop computers with powerful processing and output capabilities that are used by engineers, architects, circuit designers, financial analysts, game developers, or other technical professionals. A professional workstation might function independently, but usually it is connected to a network. Because of its enhanced features, a professional workstation is more expensive than a consumer desktop PC such as one you might purchase at Best Buy. Manufacturers of professional workstations include HP, Dell, and Lenovo.

Servers (Figure 4.4) are computers equipped with the hardware and software that store and make programs and data available if you are connected to it via a

© kryczka/iStockphoto.com

FIGURE 4.3 Both desktop PCs and professional workstations are similar in appearance; however, the internal high-end components of a workstation can raise its price to \$2,000 or higher.

© luismmolina/iStockphoto.com

FIGURE 4.4 Server units are housed in secure, temperature-regulated environments to protect from deliberate or accidental damage.

network. A server is not designed for individual use. Servers are typically located in a centralized location and are about the size of a file cabinet. You connect to a network on a ***client***, which can be a desktop PC, a notebook, a netbook, a workstation, or a ***terminal***—an inexpensive input/output device consisting of a keyboard and video display but that has little processing capability. A client can be designated as a ***fat client*** if it accesses the server for data but does its own processing or a ***thin client*** if it relies on the server for its processing ability. When you use a client and a centralized server, your system is referred to as a ***client/server network***. The top two server manufacturers are Dell and IBM.

Minicomputers or ***midrange servers*** are servers that fall between workstations and mainframes and are about the size of a single- to four-drawer file cabinet. You would use this type of computer in situations that need to handle 4 to 200 clients. The demand for minicomputers has decreased as workstations have become more powerful and mainframes, less expensive. Minicomputer manufacturers include IBM and Sun Microsystems.

Mainframes or ***enterprise servers*** (Figure 4.5) are powerful servers that execute many computer instructions concurrently. This type of computer is stored in a secure, climate-controlled room and services hundreds of thousands of clients at the same time. Large mainframe computers process transactions such as airline reservations, bank transactions, or registrations for students at a college. Manufacturers include IBM, Fujitsu, and Amdahl.

FIGURE 4.5 Mainframes or enterprise servers connect thousands of clients concurrently, can cost from several thousand to millions of dollars, and can fill the wall of an average size room.

You probably have never seen a ***supercomputer*** (Figure 4.6), which is an ultrafast system that processes large amounts of scientific data, often for the purpose of identifying underlying patterns. A supercomputer can be a single computer or a series of computers working in parallel. You would find a supercomputer stored in secure, climate-controlled rooms, performing mathematical calculations at lightning speed. A supercomputer focuses on executing a few sets of instructions as fast as possible, and performance is measured in ***petaflops***—the equivalent of one quadrillion calculations per second or 150,000 calculations for every human being on the planet per second. Supercomputers are valuable in computing calculations for weather predictions and space flight.

FIGURE 4.6 A room-size supercomputer system can cost several million dollars.

Objective 2 | Understand and Relate Computers, Society, and You

In your job as a Production Manager for a comic book publisher, you must develop a presentation about using computers in the workplace for the members of your production team. You need to convey information about avoiding improper use of company computers, for example, inserting improper or confidential content into e-mail messages or posting—as an employee—on social media sites like Twitter and Facebook. You also want your team members to use the most current techniques to communicate with customers and with other employees. In your presentation, you want to focus on current trends, mobile computing, and the lifespan of digital information and its possible effect on current and future employment opportunities. Where do you start?

Computers are tools that should help you be more productive, creative, and efficient. Using a computer should reduce the amount of time you need to collect, organize, and process data and help you share the resulting information. Rather than going to the mall to buy the latest movie on DVD, you can purchase it or even view it online. Organizing your music or movie collection requires no physical actions—your computer and a database program make it possible to organize your entire collection by title, artist, release date, or genre while at a friend's house or on vacation. There is no need to wait for movie reviews to come out in the newspaper—you just go online to find the latest reviews from critics and other moviegoers, or watch the trailer yourself. You use a Facebook post, a blog entry, a Web page, or a tweet to invite or inform family and friends of your plans. Do you ever consider the amount of time you save and information you share during one day by using computer devices?

Your computer, with appropriate software, can carry out tasks on all types of data. That is why you see a penetration of computers into almost every occupational area and, as of 2009, into 80 percent of U.S. households. This is a significant increase from 49 percent in 2001 and 2002. In other words, four out of every five households in the United States have a computer. However, computers are still not readily accessible in some segments of society.

Concept 4.03 | Recognizing the Digital Divide

The more educated you are and the more money you make, the more likely you are to own a computer and have Internet access. The Pew Internet and American Life Project in December 2008 confirmed that 95 percent of college-educated individuals in the United States use the Internet, but only 53 percent of individuals with a high school education do so. Statistics also exist to support age and race as factors affecting U.S. computer use.

This disparity in computer ownership and Internet access, known as the ***digital divide***, is not limited to any single nation. It is a global social phenomenon that raises the ethical question of universal access for information. The ability to access this information places some individuals at an advantage, while those that cannot access it are at a disadvantage, thus creating the divide. You can research government and educational programs working to bridge this gap to get an idea of some attempts to provide computer access for all.

Concept 4.04 | Using Social Networks

Originally social networking seemed to be directed toward communication or entertainment—not toward increasing your information or learning. That has changed. Companies, universities, and nonprofit organizations now use social networking sites to gather input, collect your ideas for future products and events, and make use of videos and games to get you to connect with their brand. It would be a mistake for you to dismiss these types of sites or applications as child's play. You can review results from surveys provided by a Forrester Research Report in Figure 4.7. These summarizations substantiate that the contact between adults on these sites and the amount of information shared daily is real, on the rise, and reaching a population demographic that is significant.

Social networking sites are online services that initially were created to foster relationships among people but now have extended their usage to promote business, events, bands, and other such entities. Statistics from the June 2010

The Use of Social Network Sites by Adults

Statistics	Related Sites
A third of adults post at least once a week to a social site.	Popular social sites include Facebook, Twitter, LinkedIn, Google Circles, MySpace, eHarmony, Match.com, and Yahoo singles.
A quarter of adults publish a blog—entries that resemble journal notes—and upload video/audio they created.	YouTube is the most recognized and popular video broadcasting site. Others include Flickr Video, Vimeo, Metacafe, and Videojug.
Nearly 60 percent of adults maintain a profile on a social networking site.	The most popular social networking sites are Facebook and Twitter.
Approximately 70 percent of adults read blogs, tweets, and watch UGC (user-generated content) videos.	You can find blogs on almost any Web page and on any topic. Radio and TV stations, as well as political sites, are popular for hosting blogs to collect opinions. UGC videos can be posted on individually created Web pages or, for viewing by a larger audience, on YouTube.

SOURCE: http://www.socialnetworkingwatch.com/2010/01/adult-social-media-use-hits-new-highs.html

Figure 4.7

PEW Internet and American Life Project indicate that 47 percent of adults use social networking services. The most popular social networking sites include:

- ***Facebook***: The largest of the social networking sites, people use Facebook to keep in touch, post photos, share links, and distribute information with people you identify as friends. Businesses use Facebook to promote themselves and their products in a less formal manner and at a significantly lower cost than traditional advertising.
- ***LinkedIn***: A professional social networking site designed to post your professional profile, connect with colleagues, and seek advice from experts.
- ***MySpace***: A social network that promotes itself as a fan-powered social entertainment destination with a major focus on music.
- ***Twitter***: A free, real-time, ***microblogging*** system in which you can post small pieces of digital content like text, pictures, links, or short videos on the Internet. Twitter limits its messages to a maximum of 140 characters. You look up the Twitter accounts of friends or notable people and indicate that you want to become a follower and view their Twitter posts, which are called ***tweets***. For example, if you are a fan of major league baseball, you might follow sports newswriters who report on your favorite team.

Use Figure 4.8 to compare the features offered by two social networking sites, Facebook and MySpace.

Facebook Versus MySpace

Feature	Facebook	MySpace
Minimum age to join	13	14
Multilingual	✓	✓
Max photo size	4 MB	5 MB
Instant messaging	✓	✓
Chat rooms		✓
Privacy settings	✓	✓
Block users	✓	✓
Support music	✓	✓
Support music videos	✓	✓
Support commercial videos		✓
Games		✓

SOURCE: http://social-networking-websites-review.toptenreviews.com/

Figure 4.8

Concept 4.05 | Working Collaboratively

Collaboration is working together with others on a common endeavor, as when you and one or more of your classmates work together on a class project. Computers facilitate collaboration. For example, in law enforcement computers are used to communicate between jurisdictions permitting national and global exposure of events and to access and edit shared reports, files, and criminal databases like the Automated Fingerprint Identification System known as the AFIS (Figure 4.9).

Collaboration software—also referred to as ***groupware*** or ***workgroup support systems***—is software that helps people work together to complete a shared task or achieve a shared goal. By using collaboration software, you can share ideas, create documents, and conduct meetings, regardless of location or time zone. Examples of collaboration software include:

- ***Microsoft SharePoint****:* Collaboration software for an enterprise that makes use of Web sites so individuals can share information, manage documents, and publish reports.
- ***Google Docs****:* An online, real-time group of collaboration tools that provides access to a Web-based word processor, spreadsheet, graphic program, and a presentation program. Multiple approved users can edit the same file at the same time, assuring that you are always viewing the latest edits.
- ***Wiki****:* A collection of Web pages to which you can contribute or modify content if granted access. Wikipedia is one of the best known wikis.
- ***Google Groups****:* A free service provided by Google that permits group members interested in discussing a common topic to collaborate on shared Web pages; set group pictures, colors, and styles; and upload and share individually created work. You can save, print, and present the finished product on your own computer.

Concept 4.06 | Recognizing Advantages and Disadvantages of Computer Use

Computers offer you many advantages and communication options, but as a responsible computer user, you should also be aware of the disadvantages. Review both columns of the table in Figure 4.10.

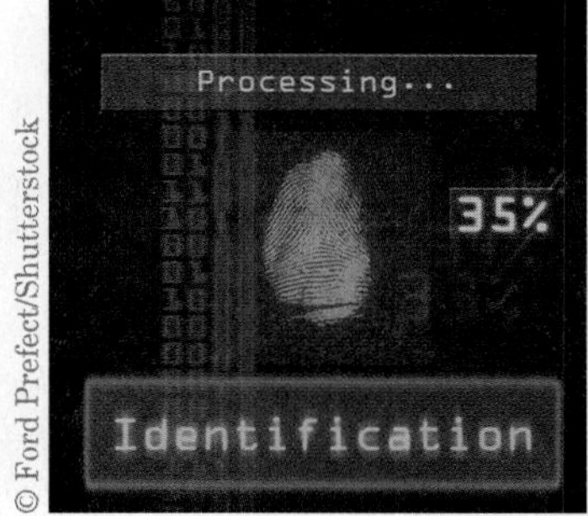

FIGURE 4.9 Converting a fingerprint into a digital image and sending it over the Internet to other law enforcement agencies enables quick comparisons and faster apprehension.

Speed is one of the greatest advantages of your computer. It can perform, in a few seconds, calculations that would take you days. So much information is generated from computers that it is easy for you to succumb to ***information overload***—a feeling of anxiety and incapacity when you are presented with more information than you can handle. According to research from the firm Basex, which chose information overload as its 2008 Workforce Problem of the Year, dealing with a constant stream of e-mail messages, phone calls, text messages, and tweets resulted in a loss of 28 percent of the workday in the United States This equates to eight to ten hours a week per worker and approximately $600 billion in lost productivity in a single year.

Cost is a factor you must weigh against your computer's performance—the combination of processing power and the amount of random access memory. In general, the faster your system runs and the more random access memory installed, the more your system will cost. You should weigh the costs against the benefits and needs on a case-by-case basis.

Hardware reliability and accuracy are two more advantages of computers. Computers almost always respond when turned on, and provide you with consistent results for repeated calculations. Your computer can transcribe your speech with an accuracy of 95 percent or more. In fact, almost all computer errors are actually caused by flaws in software or errors in the data supplied by the person using the computer.

Lastly is our need to be connected to the Internet as well as to each other. The

Advantages and Disadvantages of Computer Use

Advantages	Disadvantages
Speed	Information overload
Memory	Cost
Storage	Data inaccuracy
Hardware reliability and accuracy	Software unreliability
Connectivity	Security

Figure 4.10

FAST FORWARD

COURTROOMS OF THE FUTURE

Are you familiar with the sayings *Seeing is believing* and *A picture is worth a thousand words*? In the context of a courtroom, these words gain strength. Add the ability to use technology to magnify voices, provide testimony via webcam from a witness confined to a hospital bed, use a translator through videoconferencing, and digitally reproduce the scene to provide a reenactment of the event. Maybe it sounds like an episode from your favorite crime investigation show. But this is no television episode. With jurors traditionally having information organized for them in bulleted lists, slide shows, and presented in visual images, the atmosphere of the conventional courtroom, which is based on oral delivery and inaccurate sequencing of information, can be confusing. In the future, expect more visual aids in the courtroom to help jurors organize the data. Headsets will enable jurors to replay parts of the testimony, or using 3D goggles jurors can review a video clip or simulation or revisit the actual scene of the crime. Attorneys, paralegals, and administrative assistants of the future will have to combine their legal and technical skills to not only present the information, but to present it in a visual and audio manner that best suits their objective.

downside of all this digital information sharing is the security of that information and the headaches it can cause if it falls into the wrong hands. Along with computers' strengths and weaknesses, consider some additional points in your quest to become a responsible user.

Concept 4.07 | Using Computer Hardware

One way to get comfortable with your computer is to read any instructions on maintenance and operation that come with it. Then create a safe and healthy work area by following these tips:

- Place your computer equipment in a secure position so it will not fall or cause an accident, use a surge protector, and avoid plugging too many devices into the same electrical outlet.
- Leave plenty of space around your computer equipment for sufficient air circulation to prevent overheating.
- Make sure computer cables, cords, and wires are fastened securely and not left where you could trip over them or where they could cause a fire.
- Keep your computer area free of dust, food, and liquids. Moisture, static electricity, and magnetic interference affect your system's performance.

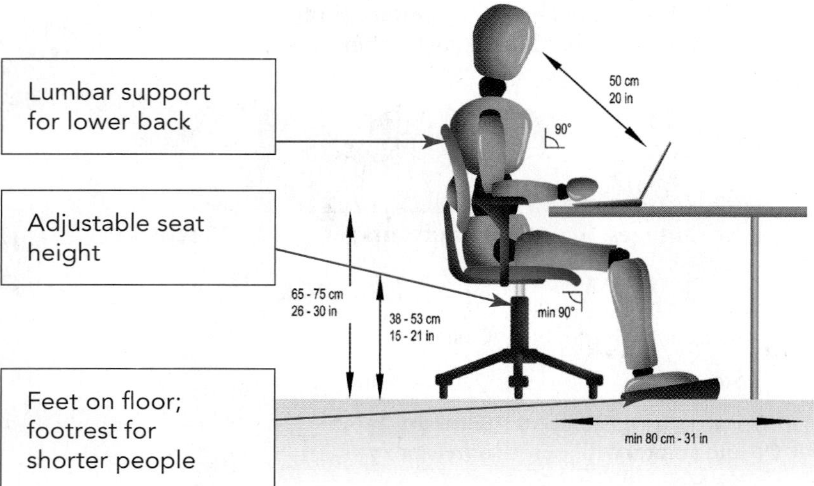

FIGURE 4.11 Keys to an ergonomically correct workstation.

Maluson/Shutterstock

Equally important to a safe working environment is the use and arrangement of your devices, equipment, and lighting. These can make a big impact on your physical health.

Ergonomics is the field of study that is concerned with matching your posture and body design to your equipment and your work environment. Ergonomics takes into account your limitations and capabilities to ensure that the tasks, equipment, and overall environment suit you (Figure 4.11). The most common injuries related to extended computer use occur to the wrist and back. *Carpal tunnel syndrome*—also known as cumulative trauma disorder or repetitive strain injury—is a condition caused by repeated motions that damage sensitive nerves in your hands, wrists, and arms and can be caused by prolonged keyboard use. This injury can be serious enough to require surgery. Using an ergonomically designed keyboard keeps your wrists flat, reducing—but not eliminating—your chance of an injury (Figure 4.12). You might also purchase an ergonomic desk chair if back injury is a concern. Go to **http://ergo.human.cornell.edu** to view a list that includes links to videos and worksheets that provide information to help you make healthy decisions. For guidance on a healthy setup, view the workspace planner at **www.ergotron.com/tabid/305/language/en-US/default.aspx**.

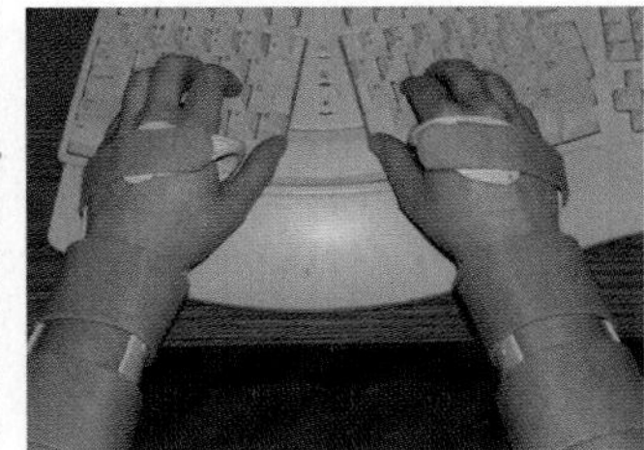

© Lanica Klein/iStockphoto.com

FIGURE 4.12 Using wrist guards with an ergonomic keyboard provides an extra level of protection to nerves in the wrist, arms, and hands.

© Regien Paassen/Shutterstock

FIGURE 4.14 Subway and train systems, like the Intercity Express (ICE) in Cologne, Germany, use safety-critical software for guidance that must be of the highest standards and bug free.

Concept 4.08 | Recognizing the Risks of Using Flawed Software

Computer hardware can be amazingly reliable, but software typically contains some errors, which are referred to as ***bugs***. Many programs contain millions of lines of computer programming language code (Figure 4.13). With so many lines of code, bugs are inevitable.

On average, commercial programs contain between 1 and 7 errors for every 1,000 lines of code. This means that your ATM program is likely to have approximately 360 errors in its code, and an IRS program over 400 thousand errors. Fortunately, most errors simply cause your programs to run slower or perform unnecessary tasks, but some errors cause miscalculations or cause your system to become nonresponsive.

Code Length for Key Programs

Program	Lines of Programming Code
Bank ATM	90,000
Air traffic control	900,000
Microsoft Windows 7	Over 50 million
Internal Revenue Service (IRS)	100 million

Figure 4.13

Bugs in a word processing program are not life threatening, but a bug in a mission-critical or safety-critical system, like air traffic control and commuter train guidance, can create a disastrous event (Figure 4.14). You might wonder how such events are avoided. Safety-critical systems are designed to higher quality standards and more intense testing to reduce errors and increase stability.

Concept 4.09 | Identifying the Impact of Computer Use

You would probably agree that computers and the Internet have improved your quality of life. Consider the effect of technological developments for the disabled (Figure 4.15).

While equipment in Figure 4.15 may not exist in your school, the integration of individuals with special needs into your regular classrooms and workforce environments requires that computer access be provided for these individuals. Advancements in this area include:

- The Americans with Disabilities Act of 1990: This act mandated that both

FIGURE 4.15 Technology provides options for individuals who cannot use traditional methods of input or output.

© Lisa F. Young/Shutterstock

public and private entities provide computer access to individuals with disabilities.

- Kindle 2: The release of this device by Amazon in 2009 took e-readers to a new height with the addition of the text-to-speech feature.
- Computer controlled devices: Individuals with physical disabilities benefit from the use of computer controlled treadmills and muscle stimulators, and by engaging in video game therapies that enhance coordination and muscle strength.
- Neurally controlled artificial limb: The Defense Advanced Research Projects Agency (DARPA) is working on an extremity that will hook up directly into severed nerves. It will feel, look, and perform like your natural arm and enable full motor and sensory capability.

What about general computer-based training and learning opportunities? Have you taken advantage of ***e-learning*** at your college? E-learning is the use of computers and computer programs to replace traditional classrooms and the time-place specificity of learning. How about taking an online class? These are newer computer-based approaches to learning. You might want to research the options offered at your school and see if any suit your learning style.

Concept 4.10 | Recognizing the Effects of Computers on Employment

Your computer skills are very important to your future. The use of computers creates new job opportunities, and thus creates a need for a computer proficient workforce. The state of Wyoming has a workforce planning Web site that contains computer skills needed by the workforce, and these are outlined in five proficiency levels. This list can help employers assess their needs and employees assess their skill level.

Using computers to complete your work is only one area of computer application in the workplace. Advanced technology can also free you from occupations with hazardous working conditions and ones with repetitive tasks, which make

TECHNOLOGY ON THE JOB

In many jobs, employers require you to accomplish tasks by using a computer. As a Production Manager for a comic book publisher, you not only need to know traditional planning techniques, but also how to use software applications to schedule and to organize and analyze tasks, deadlines, and resources. As a manager, you have the additional responsibility of keeping digital information confidential and secure. The Wyoming workforce planning Web site at http://wyomingworkforceplanning.state.wy.us/wyoming_competencies/analytical/basic_computer_skills.htm ranks the skills necessary for a Production Manager's position as a proficiency level 5, the highest level. In this ranking system, essential computer skills are associated with a specific computer application. For example:

- Word processing skills include: setting defaults, creating cross references, working with endnotes and footnotes, creating and using macros, and displaying content in tables.
- Spreadsheet skills include: knowing when and how to use functions and formulas, creating and using macros, using data analysis tools and advanced filters to sort through data and extract information, creating links to external sources of data for quick retrieval, and designing appropriate charts.
- Database skills include: designing, developing, protecting, and replicating complex databases with macro modules; using features like queries and reports to provide uncluttered and readable output; and controlling data accuracy through data validation tests.

Go to the Wyoming workforce planning Web site or search for other workforce development sites, and then evaluate your own computer skills against the information you find. In which proficiency level do you rank? What courses do you need to advance your proficiencies?

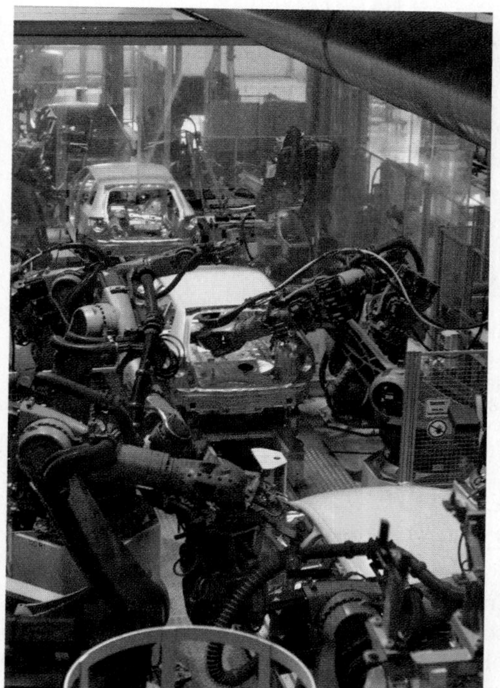

© Small Town Studio/Shutterstock

FIGURE 4.16 Computer-guided robots are taking over many manufacturing jobs that people once held.

workflow safer and more efficient and which increase productivity. ***Automation***, the replacement of human workers by machines and computer-guided robots, is taking over many manufacturing jobs once held by people (Figure 4.16).

In addition to seeing robots in an industrial and manufacturing setting, in your future, you will see robots playing a more important role in daily activities. The robot named ASIMO (Advanced Step in Innovative Mobility) is the result of more than two decades of experimentation by Honda engineers (Figure 4.17). It has human-like flexibility and endless possibilities. If you visit Disneyland in Anaheim, California, you can see ASIMO in action at the Honda ASIMO Theater in the Innoventions attraction. ASIMO is still a work in progress.

Another not so visible effect of technology on your employment is the globalization of jobs. An example is creating a product by assembling pieces of that product produced in different locations or in one or several different countries. The term ***outsourcing***, the subcontracting of portions of a job to a third party to reduce cost, time, and energy, is closely related to globalization. In December 2010, Investors.com cited that 1.3 million additional Western jobs will vanish by 2014 due to the accelerated movement of work to offshore locations. Outsourcing alone is not the only cause of job loss; some studies argue that increased productivity is an associated cause. Increasing U.S. productivity by as little as 1 percent can eliminate up to 1.3 million jobs per year. ***Structural unemployment*** results when technology makes an entire job category obsolete. If you lose a job because of structural unemployment, you most likely are not going to get it back; you will need to seek retraining.

Consider this: Half of all the jobs that you will see advertised in 10 years do not exist today. So, how will you survive—and flourish—in this changing computer-driven economy? To survive, you must understand technology, accept that education is a lifelong process, and adapt quickly to change.

© Paolo Patrizi / Alamy

FIGURE 4.17 ASIMO is a humanoid robot that stands 4 feet 3 inches and weighs 114 pounds. It can walk and run on two feet at rates of up to 4.3 miles per hour.

Concept 4.11 | Identifying Responsible and Ethical Computer Behavior

You probably use a computer and a cell phone to send e-mail, text messages, and maybe even tweets throughout the day. All of this seems fine within your own personal space. Do you stop to think about how your use of computer devices and the Internet really affects you and those in your school, your workplace, your family, your community, and the environment? Consider the following good practices:

- Do not talk on your phone or send text messages while driving.
- Be aware of the people around you; they do not want to hear your conversation,

read your text message, or see your e-mail.

- Recycle your paper and printer cartridges to protect the environment.
- Properly dispose of, recycle, or donate your obsolete computer equipment, also called ***e-waste*** (Figure 4.18).
- Extend your ethical standards of right and wrong to your use of computers. If you are unsure of an action, research ***computer ethics***, which is a branch of philosophy that deals with computer-related moral dilemmas to guide your decisions.
- Do not participate in ***digital piracy***, the unauthorized reproduction and distribution of computer-based media. This action is viewed in the same way as photocopying a book or taking a DVD from a store without paying, and is currently blamed for a global loss of more than $40 billion annually.
- Stay informed about software and hardware advances as well as legal issues related to technology.
- Monitor the amount of time you spend at your computer to avoid experiencing levels of depression and loneliness.

FIGURE 4.18 Responsible computer users and manufacturers recycle old computers, printers, monitors, batteries, and other types of e-waste.

Donating Old Computers

Is your old computer a good candidate for donation? Answer these questions to find out:

1. Is it less than five years old?
2. Does it still work?
3. Do you have the original software and documentation—operating system and other applications?
4. Have you used disk-cleaning software to remove your personal data?
5. Have you checked to be sure the organization to which you are donating your equipment can actually use it?

If you were able to answer yes to all these questions, it is likely your computer can be put to good use by someone else.

Objective 3 | Protect Privacy in Cyberspace

In your job as a Production Manager for a comic book publisher, you are in charge of planning, coordinating, and publishing a manuscript that will result in a finished comic book. You must use e-mail and other electronic tools to communicate with colleagues and independent contractors. You are concerned about sending sensitive and personal information—for example, contracts that contain social security numbers—and you want to maintain a high level of security on all communication. Where do you start?

Of all the social and ethical issues raised by the use of computers linked by the Internet, the threats to your privacy and anonymity are among the most serious. Government-sponsored sites, like the Identity Theft site hosted by the Federal Trade Commission (Figure 4.19) and **www.idtheft.gov**, your one stop source for government information about identity theft (Figure 4.20), offer you practical advice, display privacy alerts, and report on current privacy issues.

Privacy, as defined by U.S. Supreme Court Justice Louis Brandeis in 1928, is "the right to be left alone." Applied to technology, privacy refers to your ability to restrict or eliminate the collection, use, and sale of confidential personal information. Some privacy advocates, like the Electronic Frontier Foundation (EFF), have developed a Bill of Rights for Social Network Users. You can apply the principles in this bill to anyone who posts information on a server. The rights that the EFF proposes include:

- The right to informed decision making—You make the choices about who sees your data and how it is used, and

Web sites should provide a clear interface that allows you to do so.

- The right to control—You maintain control over the use and disclosure of your own data.
- The right to leave—You can transfer your data to another site in a usable format and delete, not just disable, all data or the entire account from the database.

Concept 4.12 | Collecting Information without Consent

You may be willing to divulge personal information when you see a need for doing so. For example, when you apply for a loan, the bank can reasonably ask you to list your other creditors to determine your ability to repay.

Companies that maintain databases may claim that they sell your information only to legitimate customers such as lending institutions, prospective employers, marketing firms, and licensed private investigators. They insist that these firms are highly ethical, have security measures in place, and do not release your information to the general public. However, no matter how secure data appears, there are always people seeking to violate your security. An open global forum called PCI Security Standards Council, founded by several financial organizations in 2006, develops and implements security standards to protect your bank account data. Go to **www.usa.gov/About/Privacy_Security.shtml** for information on use of data obtained from this government sponsored Web site (Figure 4.21).

Concept 4.13 | Exploring the Technology versus Anonymity Debate

Anonymity refers to your ability to convey a message without disclosing your name or identity. Anonymity can be good or bad. Marketing firms, snoops, and government officials can use computers and the Internet to collect information in ways that are hidden from you, which is counter to our country's strong belief in the protection of privacy. Courts acknowledge that anonymous works can raise

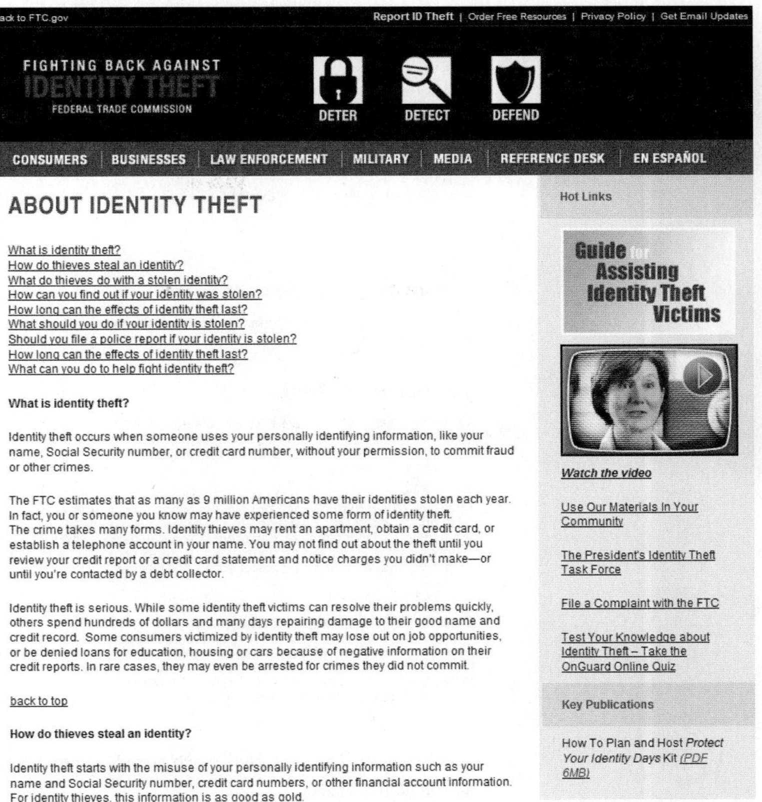

FIGURE 4.19 This Identity Theft site provides a link to file a complaint with the FTC and an online quiz to test your knowledge about identity theft.

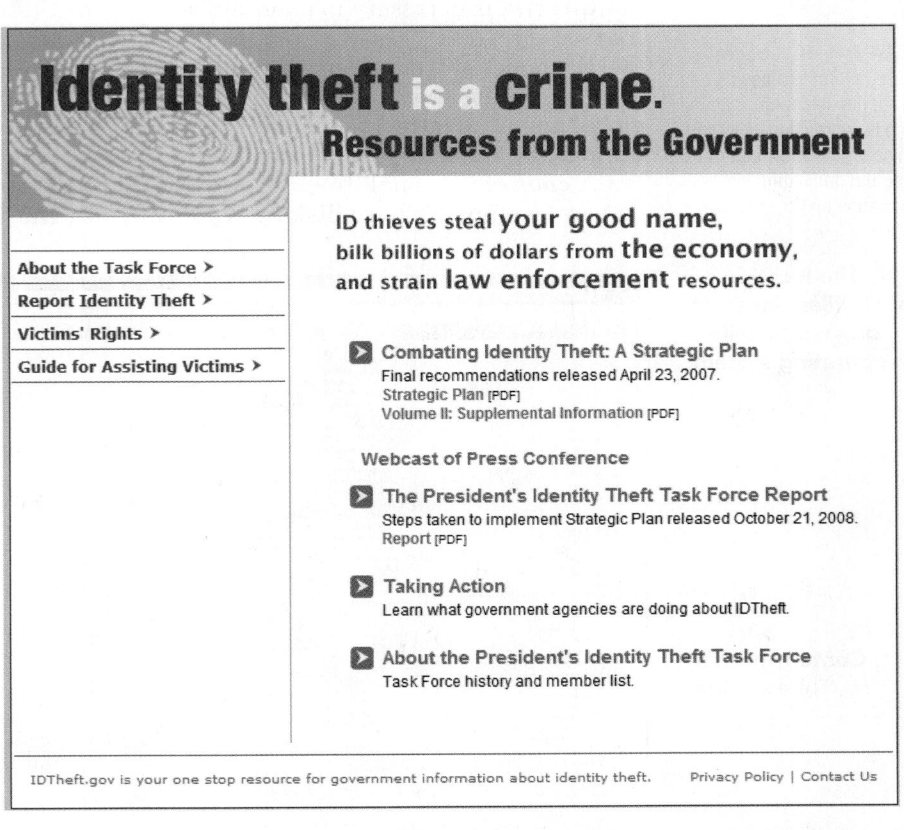

FIGURE 4.20 This site provides strategies for preventing identity theft in addition to outlining a victim's rights.
SOURCE: http://www.idtheft.gov/http://www.idtheft.gov/

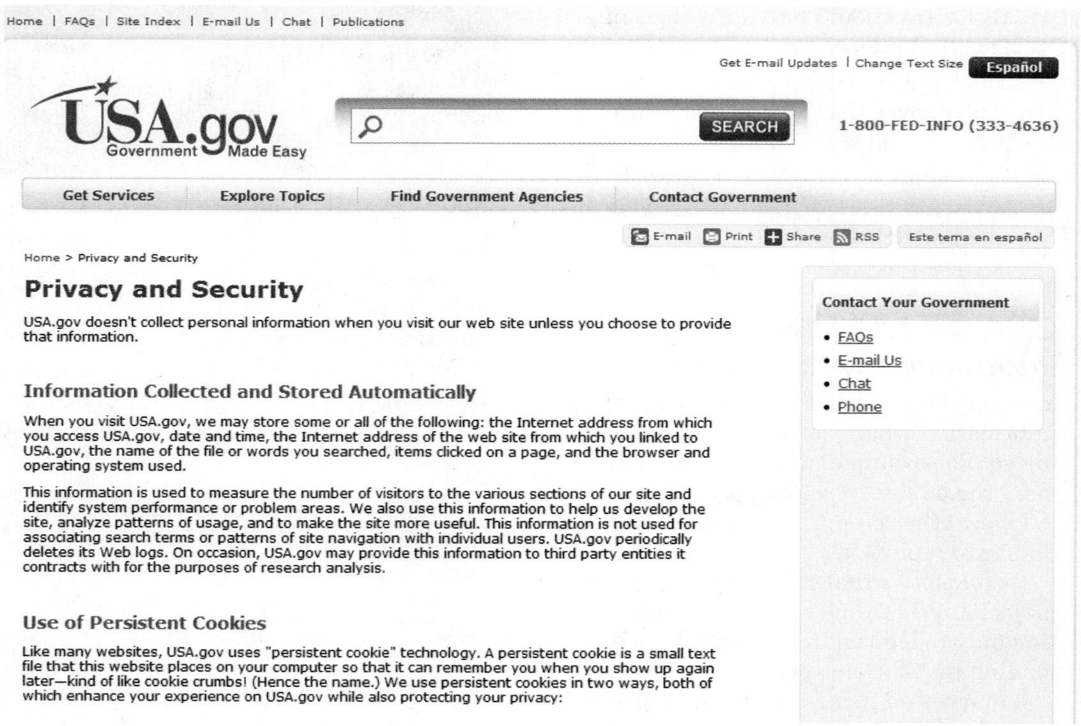

Home | FAQs | Site Index | E-mail Us | Chat | Publications

Get E-mail Updates | Change Text Size | Español

USA.gov Government Made Easy

SEARCH

1-800-FED-INFO (333-4636)

Get Services | Explore Topics | Find Government Agencies | Contact Government

E-mail | Print | Share | RSS | Este tema en español

Home > Privacy and Security

Privacy and Security

USA.gov doesn't collect personal information when you visit our web site unless you choose to provide that information.

Information Collected and Stored Automatically

When you visit USA.gov, we may store some or all of the following: the Internet address from which you access USA.gov, date and time, the Internet address of the web site from which you linked to USA.gov, the name of the file or words you searched, items clicked on a page, and the browser and operating system used.

This information is used to measure the number of visitors to the various sections of our site and identify system performance or problem areas. We also use this information to help us develop the site, analyze patterns of usage, and to make the site more useful. This information is not used for associating search terms or patterns of site navigation with individual users. USA.gov periodically deletes its Web logs. On occasion, USA.gov may provide this information to third party entities it contracts with for the purposes of research analysis.

Use of Persistent Cookies

Like many websites, USA.gov uses "persistent cookie" technology. A persistent cookie is a small text file that this website places on your computer so that it can remember you when you show up again later—kind of like cookie crumbs! (Hence the name.) We use persistent cookies in two ways, both of which enhance your experience on USA.gov while also protecting your privacy:

Contact Your Government

- FAQs
- E-mail Us
- Chat
- Phone

FIGURE 4.21 This Web site, which provides information on government services, clearly defines its privacy and security policy on its home page.

SOURCE: www.usa.gov/About/Privacy_Security.shtml

the potential for false or misleading ideas, but this risk is necessary to maintain a free society.

Examples of technologies that threaten online anonymity include cookies, global unique identifiers, ubiquitous computing, and radio frequency identification.

A ***cookie*** is a small text file stored on your computer's hard disk by Web sites that you visit. Cookies can be used to gather data on your browsing and shopping habits. You can locate the cookies on your hard disk (Figure 4.22) by searching for the word *cookie* from the search box located at the bottom of your Start menu. Each cookie contains a unique ID, which is assigned to you by the Web site on your first visit. On

FIGURE 4.22 Cookies can be helpful to a user by remembering login information and passwords; but, they can also act as an informant, providing the originating site with information on your browsing habits.

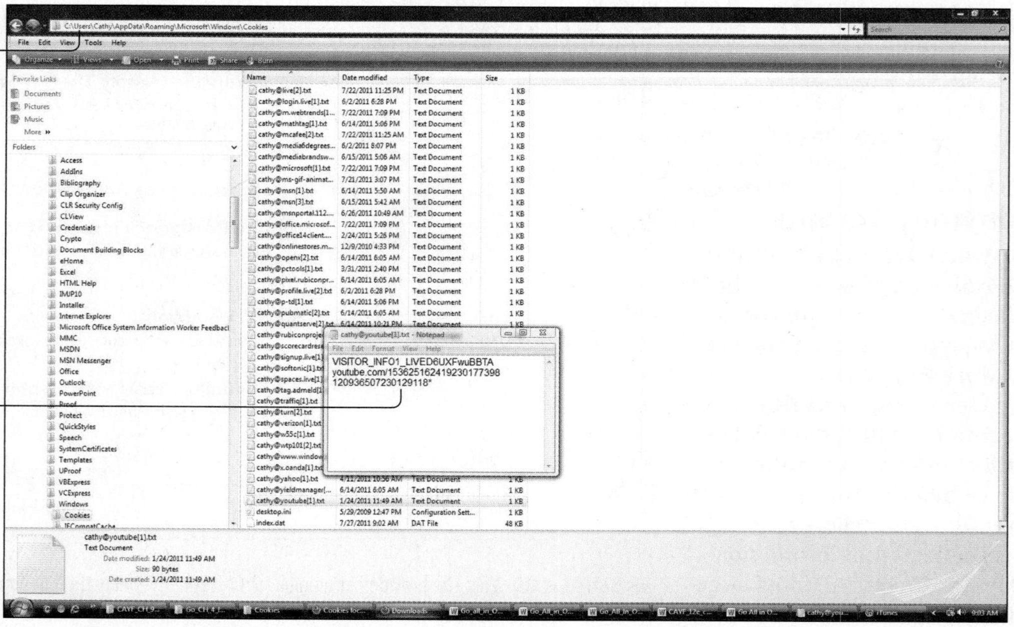

The location of cookie files depends on your installed operating system

Content from a YouTube cookie

VISITOR_INFO1_LIVED6UXFwuBBTA
youtube.com/153625162419230177398120936507230129118*

return visits to that Web site, your ID is used to record the visit in the Web site's database.

Although cookies are often perceived to be malicious, they are actually useful for legitimate tasks. For example:

- Cookies enable a Web site to obtain an actual count on the number of new and return visitors.
- Cookies can store your site preferences so that when you return to the site, your preferences are automatically applied.
- Online retail sites use cookies to implement "shopping carts," which enable you to make selections that will stay in your cart so that you can return to the online store for more browsing and shopping at a later time. After you make the purchase, the cookie is deleted and your purchases are stored in the database on a remote server associated with the Web page.

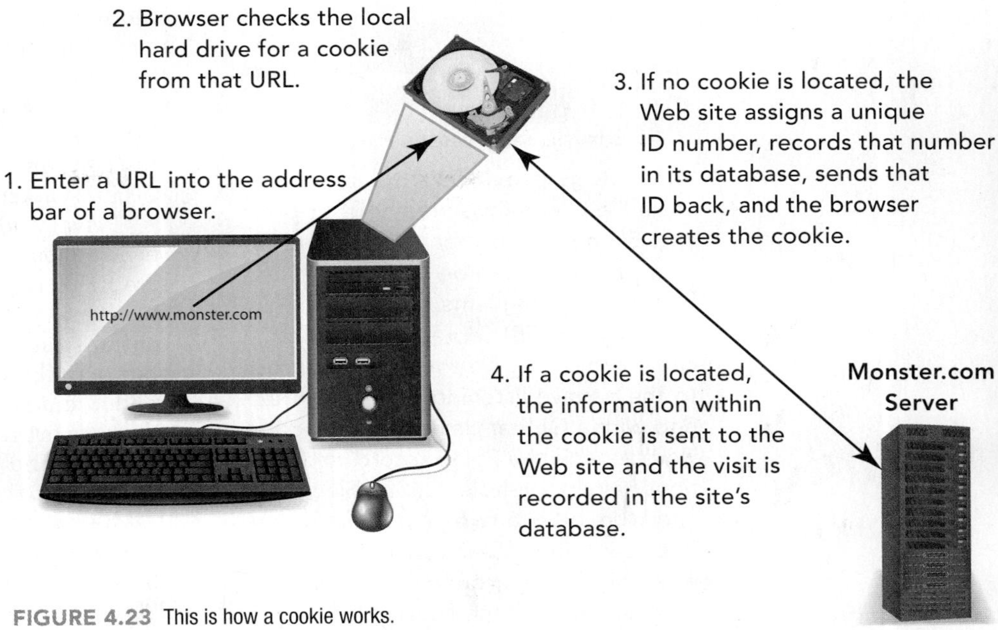

1. Enter a URL into the address bar of a browser.
2. Browser checks the local hard drive for a cookie from that URL.
3. If no cookie is located, the Web site assigns a unique ID number, records that number in its database, sends that ID back, and the browser creates the cookie.
4. If a cookie is located, the information within the cookie is sent to the Web site and the visit is recorded in the site's database.

http://www.monster.com

Monster.com Server

FIGURE 4.23 This is how a cookie works.

What troubles privacy advocates is the tactic of tracking cookies to gather data about your browsing and shopping habits—without your consent. Several Internet ad networks, for example DoubleClick, drop a cookie on your computer's hard drive that tracks your browsing habits and preferences as you move through Web sites that contract with the ad network. When you visit another site, the cookie is detected, read, and the ad network selects and displays a ***banner ad***—an ad that is not actually part of the Web page but is supplied separately by an ad network—that matches the products you were browsing.

In response to concerns that such tracking violates your privacy, ad networks claim that they do not link the collected information with your name or address. However, current technology would enable these firms to do so—and privacy advocates fear that some of them already have. If you are still confused about how cookies work, refer to Figure 4.23 or go to **http://computer.howstuffworks. com/cookie.htm**.

The term ***ubiquitous computing*** refers to a trend in which you no longer interact with one computer at a time but rather with multiple devices connected through an omnipresent network, enabling technology to become virtually embedded and enabling you to interact seamlessly with devices you use. The proponents of this technology say that this type of computing is more natural. They envision a system where billions of miniature, ubiquitous intercommunication devices are scattered worldwide. An example of the use of ubiquitous computing would be the automatic adjustment of an environmental setting, like heat, in your office.

An ***active badge*** is a small device you wear that transmits a unique infrared signal every 5 to 10 seconds. Networked sensors detect the signal and acknowledge your location, thus allowing e-mail, phone calls, or messages to be forwarded to you wherever you are. You already accept the idea of receiving e-mail anywhere; after all, that is already a feature of portable communication devices. However, have you thought about the electronic trails that your movement creates? You might be uncomfortable knowing that these trails can pinpoint your exact location through the day.

The use of radio waves to track a chip or tag placed in or on an object is referred to as ***radio frequency identification*** or ***RFID***. RFID tags (Figure 4.24) often substitute for bar codes for inventory control in

© Mr.Zach/Shutterstock

FIGURE 4.24 RFID tags are often hidden in products and used as antitheft devices or to track merchandise.

Surveillance versus Privacy

Technology provides a means of surveillance that is invisible and ever present. Even devices that are installed for your protection can be manipulated and become mechanisms of surveillance. Recently the FBI served OnStar with a court order to give the agency access to the passive listening feature embedded within OnStar devices. Such access would enable the FBI to record conversations held in a vehicle. OnStar filed a suit and won, after a two-year court battle. The ruling in OnStar's favor, however, was not on the grounds of invasion of privacy. Instead, the court ruled on the fact that the use of the passive listening feature would disable the emergency calling feature and this would constitute a breach of the consumers' contract. How do you feel about the use of such devices for surveillance? When do such actions become a violation of privacy? How private are your private conversations?

a retail environment. RFID does not require you to have direct contact or line-of-sight scanning. Instead, an antenna using radio frequency waves transmits a signal that activates the transponder—the tag. When activated, the tag transmits data back to the antenna. However, if the tag is not deactivated, the object's movements can continue to be tracked indefinitely.

Another example of this is the insertion of microchips into pets and other livestock. It has even been used for people. The RFID chip can include human contact information and health records; for an animal, the chip can contain owner information and vaccination data.

Privacy advocates have been concerned about the use of encrypted, passive RFID tags in your U.S. passports for several years (Figure 4.25). The tag contains the same information included on your actual passport—name, nationality, gender, date of birth, and place of birth of the passport holder—as well as a digitized signature and your photo. The government asserts that the RFID tag does not broadcast a signal and can be read only within close proximity of special scanning devices. However, a new passport card approved in 2008, as part of the Western Hemisphere Travel Initiative for travel to Mexico, Canada, Bermuda, and the Caribbean, has an unencrypted chip that can be read from up to 30 feet away. This raises serious concerns that your identity could easily be stolen or your location tracked without your consent or awareness.

Now that you can identify some of the privacy threats posed by technology and the Internet, consider ways to protect your own privacy.

Concept 4.14 | Protecting Your Privacy

Protecting your privacy rights as a U.S. citizen is a controversial topic. Marketing industry spokespeople and lobbyists argue that the U.S. government should not impose laws or regulations to protect consumers' privacy. They argue that the industry should regulate itself. Privacy advocates counter that technology has outpaced the industry's capability to regulate itself, as evidenced by the widespread availability of highly personal information on the Internet.

Most agree that your individual rights should be protected in some manner, but the definition of acceptable levels of protection

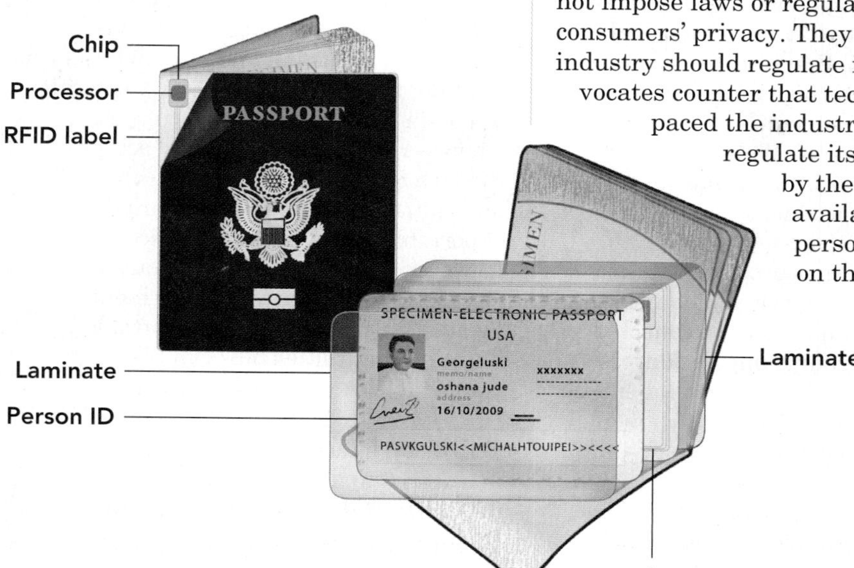

FIGURE 4.25 The insertion of RFID tags into credit cards and passports has raised suspicion about the ethics of their tracking potential.

Summary of Major U.S. Laws Concerning Privacy Issues

Year	Legislation	Objective
2003	CAN-SPAM Act	Combat Internet spammers.
2001	Children's Internet Protection Act (CIPA)	Address concerns about access to offensive content over the Internet on school and library computers.
1996	Health Insurance Portability and Accountability Act (HIPAA)	Establish standards for privacy and electronic transmission of health care data.
1974	Family Education Rights and Privacy Act (FERPA)	Protect the privacy of student education records.
1970	Fair Credit Reporting Act (FCRA)	Provide limited privacy protection for credit information.

Figure 4.26

varies widely. Some pieces of legislation currently in place are detailed in the table in Figure 4.26.

Some independent groups, such as the Direct Marketing Association (DMA), which is a leading global trade association with headquarters in New York City, are attempting to enforce a basic code of ethics among its membership. The organization tracks policy issues that affect the direct marketing community, operates the Web site ***https://www.dmachoice.org/dma/member/home.action*** that permits you to opt out of unwanted commercial mailing or opt in for mailing that you do want, and takes steps to ensure that your confidential information does not fall into the wrong hands.

Be aware that many of the most aggressive Internet-based marketing firms have no ties to or previous experience with the DMA, and several opt-out systems on the Internet are already used for fraudulent purposes. For example, e-mail spammers typically claim that you can opt out of mass e-mail marketing campaigns. But when you respond to such messages, you only succeed in validating your e-mail addresses, and the result is often a major increase in the volume of unsolicited e-mail you receive. A report from TRACE Laboratories at M86 Security for the week ending July 24, 2011, revealed that India and Russia (Figure 4.27) were the leaders in relaying ***spam***—unsolicited messages sent in bulk over electronic mailing systems—and that messages touting pharmaceutical products accounted for 58 percent of all spam.

In the United States, the CAN-SPAM Act of 2003 provided the tools to combat spammers. The Federal Trade Commission (FTC) and the Department of Justice have primary jurisdiction over spammers, but other agencies, including states and ISPs, can also prosecute them. The legislation has been criticized because it prevents states from enacting tougher laws, prevents you from individually suing spammers, and does not require e-mailers to request permission before sending messages. Additionally, it may be ineffective against foreign spammers who are outside U.S. jurisdiction. Although many contend that the act is just a drop in the bucket, the monetary threat the CAN-SPAM Act can impose on a violator can

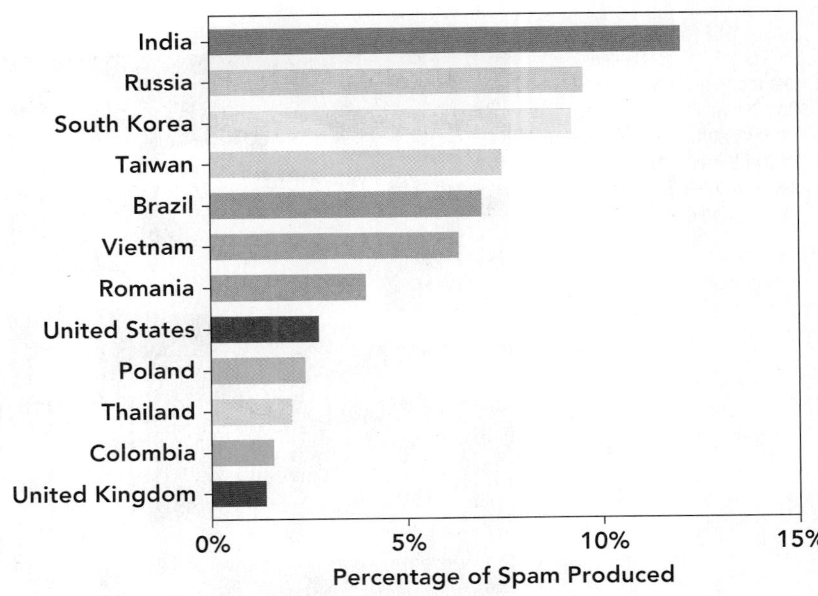

SOURCE: http://www.m86security.com/labs/spam_statistics.asp

FIGURE 4.27 The graph displays the countries that contributed the most spam for the week ending July 24, 2011.

itself be a deterrent. In 2008, MySpace successfully sued the so-called "Spam King" Sanford Wallace and a business partner for violations of the CAN-SPAM Act. A federal judge awarded MySpace close to $230 million; the award is significant although it is doubtful the money will ever be collected.

Although privacy on the Internet may be a concern for some, it has not slowed down e-commerce. The Internet retail sector continues to thrive. The Census Bureau records show that, despite economic issues, the estimate of U.S. retail e-commerce sales for the first quarter of 2010 was $38.7 billion, an increase of 1.5 percent from the fourth quarter of 2009. Most of the popular commercial Web sites try to relieve your online security fears by creating privacy policy pages that explain how they collect and use personal information about site visitors. Many also display privacy seals from third-party vendors such as TRUSTe, WebTrust, or the Better Business Bureau as a sign that they comply with the vendor's privacy standards and regulations.

Until laws are passed that will protect basic privacy rights, it is up to you to safeguard your data on the Internet. To do so, follow these suggestions:

- Surf the Web anonymously by using software products such as Anonymizer's Anonymous Surfing (**www.anonymizer.com**) or devices such as the IronKey Secure USB flash drive (**www.ironkey.com**), which includes special security software to protect your data and encrypt your online communications (Figure 4.28).
- Use a throwaway e-mail address from a free Web-based service such as Google's Gmail (**www.google.com**) for mailing lists and chat rooms.
- Instruct children not to divulge any personal information online without first asking a parent or teacher for permission. Reliable Web sites like **www.us-cert.gov** provide information on keeping children safe while on the Web and on other issues of Internet privacy and digital security (Figure 4.29).
- Do not fill out site registration forms unless you see a privacy policy statement indicating that the information you supply will not be sold.

Do you know that all new cell phones in the United States must have GPS awareness? This means that your phone can be located, usually within 30 feet, by law enforcement and emergency services personnel when you dial 911. Some services, such as Where (formerly known as uLocate) and BrickHouse Security child locator, provide the exact location of a cell phone. Such a service is useful when a parent is trying to keep track of a child, but it can be intrusive when an employer uses it to track an employee using a company cell phone.

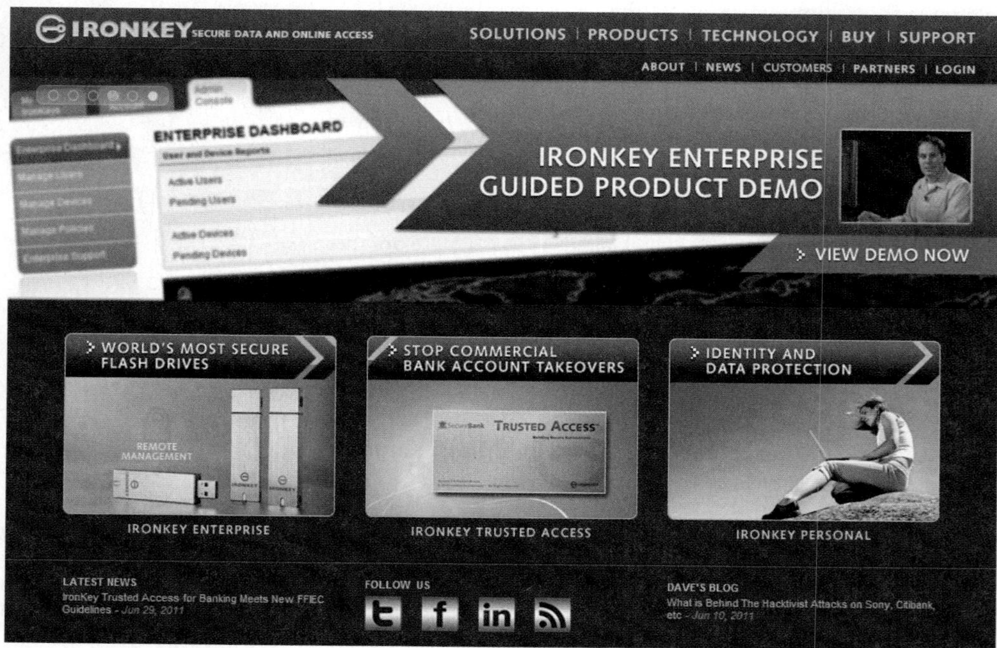

FIGURE 4.28 Devices like the IronKey Secure USB flash drive include special security software to allow you to surf the Web privately and securely while protecting your identity and data.

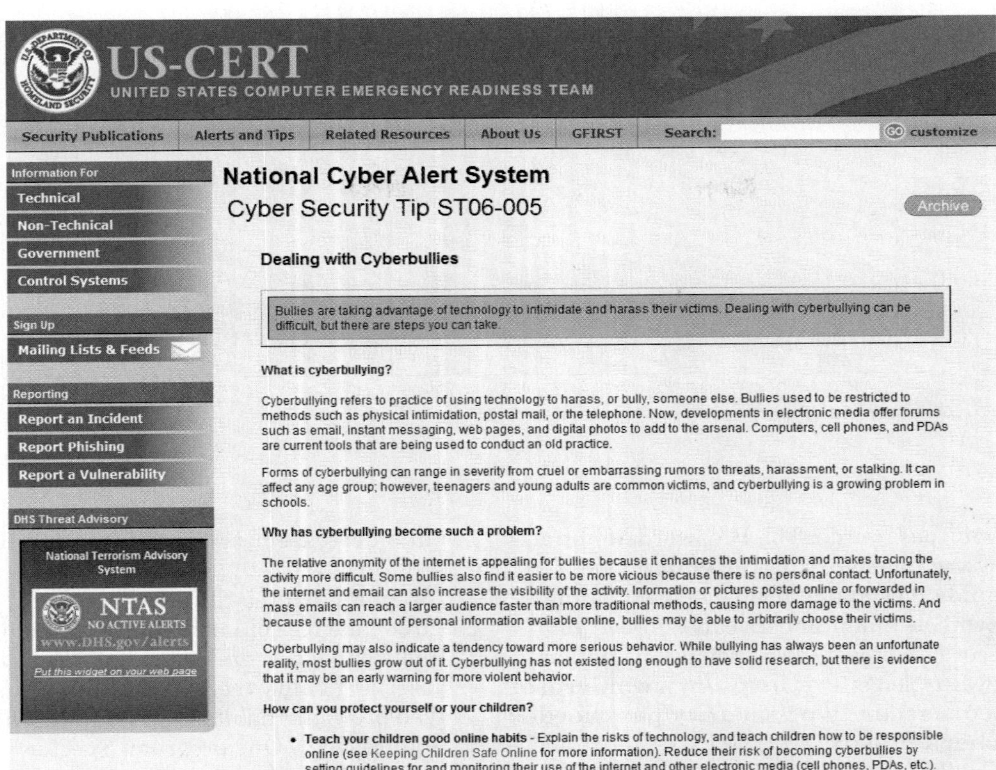

FIGURE 4.29 These sites act as portals and provide links to government and private sites that are related to Internet security and privacy.

Some software is so powerful that it will send a notification to the home unit whenever the cell phone leaves a designated geographic area. This type of location-aware tracking software is already in use by the criminal justice system to keep track of offenders who are sentenced to home detention. The subject is fitted with an ankle or wrist bracelet, and then the software is set to trigger an alarm if the wearer strays from the designated area. In the area of health care, these bracelets keep track of Alzheimer's patients. Recently MIT students developed programs using GPS capabilities for the Android mobile OS by Google. One program enables you to change your phone's settings as your location changes, so it will automatically be silent in a movie theater or classroom but will ring when you are outdoors. Another program will remind you that you need to pick up milk as you pass by the store.

When using a shared system, an important concern is creating and keeping your passwords private. A password is designated as a ***strong password*** if it contains a sequence of numbers and characters that is difficult for someone to guess. For example, your password should contain at least fourteen characters, include both uppercase and lowercase letters, and include some numbers and special characters. Additionally, your password should not be a recognizable word or phrase; not be the name of a person, pet, or item close to you, and not be a string of numbers like your social security number or birth date.

The longer the user login and password, the more time it takes for someone, or some program, to guess it (Figure 4.30). Use online strength testers to evaluate

Password Length Versus Guess Time

Length of Password Using Mixed Letters, Numerals, and Symbols	Time to Guess (@10,000 Passwords per Second)
2 characters	Instant
4 characters	2.25 hours
6 characters	2.5 years
8 characters	22,875 years

SOURCE: http://www.lockdown.co.uk/?pg=combi

Figure 4.30

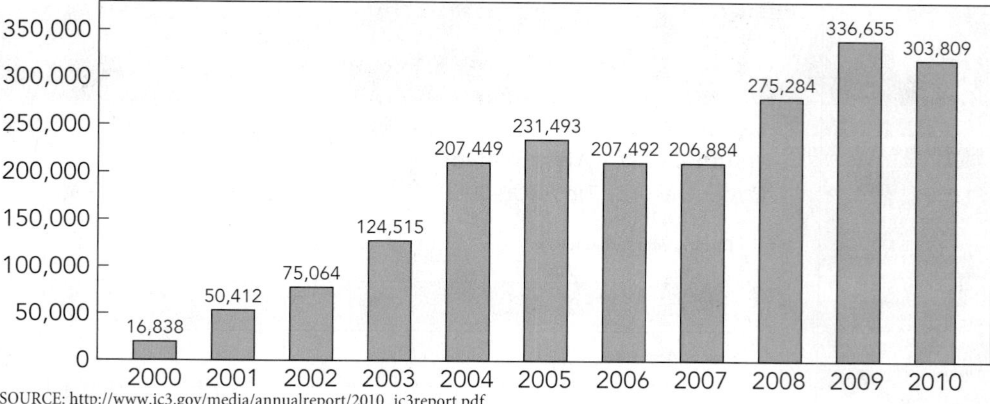

SOURCE: http://www.ic3.gov/media/annualreport/2010_ic3report.pdf

FIGURE 4.31 Complaints of Web crimes increased by 22.3 percent between 2008 and 2009 but decreased by 9.9 percent between 2009 and 2010.

your passwords. The Password Meter at **www.passwordmeter.com** provides guidelines and indicates how including symbols and numbers can improve your score. Microsoft also provides a similar evaluation site at **https://www.microsoft.com/security/pc-security/password-checker.aspx**.

The Internet Crime Complaint Center, also known as IC3, registers complaints for Web-related crimes. IC3 is a partnership between the FBI, the National White Collar Crime Center, and the Bureau of Justice Assistance. Complaints registered on their Web site, **www.ic3.gov**, for Web-related crimes show a significant increase between 2008 and 2009 but a decrease between 2009 and 2010 (Figure 4.31).

In the United States, more than three-quarters of large employers routinely engage in ***employee monitoring***, observing employees' phone calls, e-mails, Web browsing habits, and computer files (Figure 4.32). One program, Spector, provides employers with a report of everything you do online while at work by taking hundreds of screen snapshots per hour.

Why do companies monitor employees? Companies are concerned about employees who may offer trade secrets to competitors in hopes of landing an attractive job offer. Another concern is sexual harassment lawsuits. Employees who access pornographic

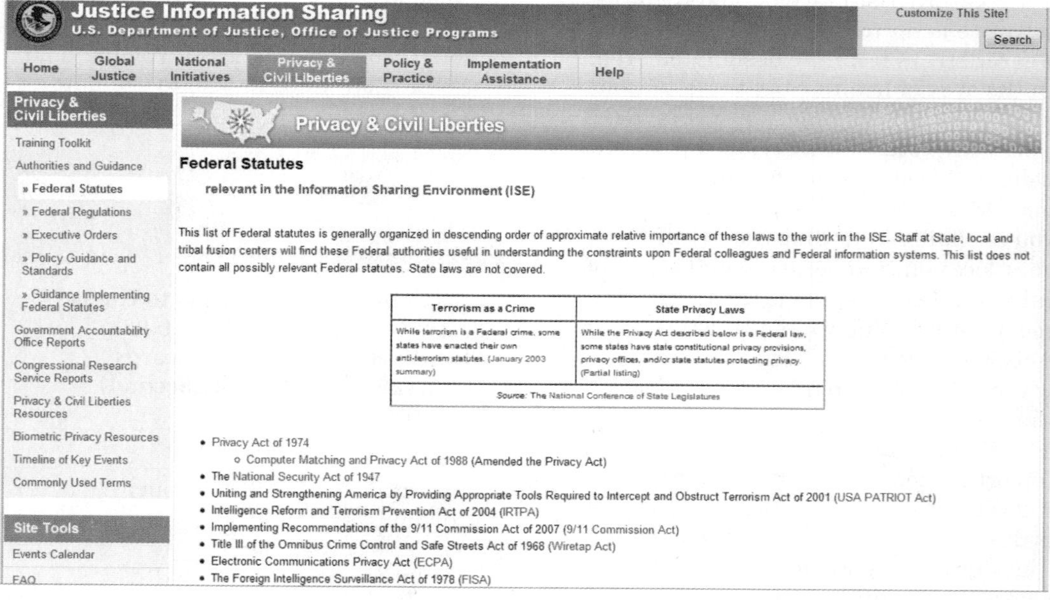

FIGURE 4.32 The Justice Information Sharing Web site, http://it.ojp.gov/ provides information on privacy and civil liberties protection.

Web sites or circulate offensive jokes via e-mail may be creating a hostile environment for other employees—and that could result in a lawsuit against the company.

To protect your privacy at work, consider the following measures:

- Do not use your employer's services like telephone or e-mail for personal purposes.
- Be aware of ***shoulder surfing***—the attempt by an individual to obtain information by watching your monitor and keyboard strokes—usually by looking over your shoulder.
- When entering a secured area that requires authorized access, be aware of anyone who is attempting to ***tailgate***—enter with you to avoid using the appropriate check-in or authorization procedure. Tailgating can also be extended to electronic entry and occurs when you do not log out of a system and another person sits down and begins to work under the guise of the authorized user.
- Assume that everything you do while you are at work may be monitored.

Check Your Knowledge: From either the Companion Web Site or MyITLab, take the quiz covering Objectives 1–3.

Objective 4 | Recognize Computer Crime in Cyberspace

In your job as a Production Manager at a comic book publisher, you have just learned that a malicious computer program was detected in several of the company's computing systems. As Production Manager, you must pass this alert to your team members and advise them of appropriate precautionary measures. Where do you start?

First, differentiate privacy issues, such as collecting personal information and employee monitoring, from ***computer crimes***—computer-based activities that violate state, federal, or international laws. ***Cybercrime*** refers to crimes carried out by means of the Internet. A new legal field—***cyberlaw***—is emerging to track and combat computer-related crime.

In 2006, the United States ratified a treaty known as the Convention on Cybercrime. This treaty, which was developed by the Council of Europe, is the first international treaty to address the issues and concerns surrounding cybercrime. Its goal is to provide guidelines for consistent cybercrime legislation that is compatible with other member countries and to encourage international cooperation in these areas. Many government agencies, such as the Department of Justice at **www.cybercrime.gov** and the FBI at **www.fbi.gov/cyberinvest/cyberhome.htm** have set up special sites to provide information and assistance to help combat cybercrime. The FTC's OnGuard Online site at **http://onguardonline.gov** collaborates with government agencies and technology organizations to provide tutorials and activities to educate individuals about the threats and risks posed by cybercriminals (Figure 4.33).

From either the Companion Web Site or MyITLab, try the Chapter 4 Security and Privacy Simulation

FIGURE 4.33 The FTC's OnGuard Online site provides many resources to educate you about types of cybercrime. You can view tutorials, explore topics, or file a complaint.

Concept 4.15 | Categorizing Computer Crime

Anyone who wants to invade or harm your computer system can use a variety of tools and tricks. If you pay close attention to your system's behavior and the activities of others that use it, you can avoid becoming a victim of computer crimes.

Imagine that your phone rings and the caller is a collection agency demanding immediate payment for a bill that is past due for a $5,000 stereo system. You cannot believe what you are hearing, because you always pay your bills on time, and you have not purchased any stereo equipment lately. What do you think is going on?

Such a call could indicate that you have been a victim of ***identity theft***, one of the fastest growing crimes in the United States and Canada. Identity theft happens when a criminal obtains enough personal information to impersonate you. With a few key pieces of information, such as your address and Social Security number, and possibly a credit card or bank account number, an identity thief can open a credit account, access your bank account, open accounts for utilities or cell phones, or apply for a loan or mortgage—all in your name!

How do criminals get this information? Some identity theft does not even involve computers. Disgruntled employees may physically steal information from their company, thieves may steal your mail or wallet, or a neighbor or business competitor may ***dumpster dive***—go through your garbage to obtain personal or sensitive data.

In a ***phishing*** attack, a "phisher" poses as a legitimate company, like a bank or credit agency, in an e-mail or on a Web site in an attempt to obtain personal information such as your Social Security number, user name, password, and account numbers. Because the communication looks legitimate, you comply and the phisher now gains access to your accounts.

Malware, short for *malicious software,* is a general term that describes software designed to damage or infiltrate a computer system without the owner's consent or knowledge. Malware is used to commit fraud, send spam, and steal your personal data. It includes spyware, computer viruses, worms, and Trojan horses. Although the United States was the biggest source of malware activity in 2009 (Figure 4.34), the exploits of those in other countries can have equally devastating consequences.

Spyware is software that can collect your personal information, monitor your Web surfing habits, and then distribute this information to a third party. Some of its less destructive activity can make your computer seem sluggish or crash more often, increase the frequency of pop-up ads, make unauthorized changes to your home or search pages, and cause the appearance of new browser toolbars.

Some spyware, such as ***adware***, generates pop-up ads and targeted banner ads, and is usually considered to be a nuisance rather than malicious. However, ***keyloggers***, which can record all the keystrokes you type—such as passwords, account numbers, or conversations—and then relay them to others, pose a more dangerous security threat.

How does spyware enter your system? It is often distributed when you download free software or infected files. File-sharing sites are notorious for this. However, clicking on a pop-up ad can also install spyware, and visiting an infected Web site can trigger a drive-by download.

Your best defense against spyware is to:

- Install an antispyware program and update it frequently.
- Use a ***firewall***, a program or device that allows you to access the

FIGURE 4.34 Sources of malware span the globe.

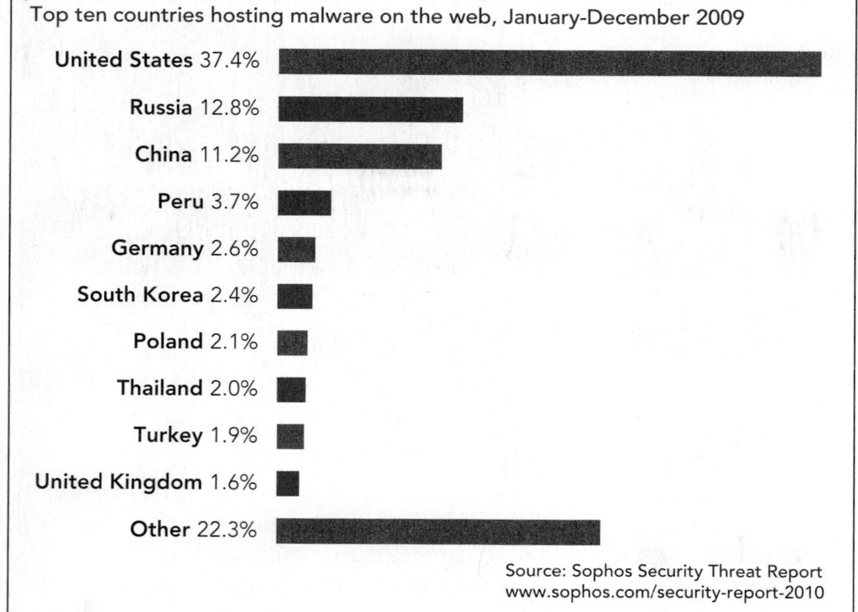

Internet but strictly limits the ability of outside users to access local, corporate, or personal data.

- Avoid visiting questionable Web sites; download software only from reputable sources.
- Never click on pop-up ads.

Two popular browsers, Internet Explorer (IE) and Mozilla Firefox, include pop-up blocking features identified by a yellow information bar that displays at the top or bottom of the browser window (Figure 4.35). Always read the message on the information bar, because it gives you options about how to handle the incident it is reporting. Both browsers also offer built-in antiphishing features to help protect you from known phishing sites. Firefox will display a warning dialog box when you attempt to access a phishing site, and IE uses a color-coded Security Status bar. In IE, a green security status bar indicates that the site is secure; yellow indicates the site might be suspicious; and red identifies a site known to pose a threat. A white status bar simply means that no identity information is available. However, the lack of a warning color or dialog box does not guarantee that a site is safe; you should still practice safe surfing methods.

Firefox blocker appears at the top of the browser's window.

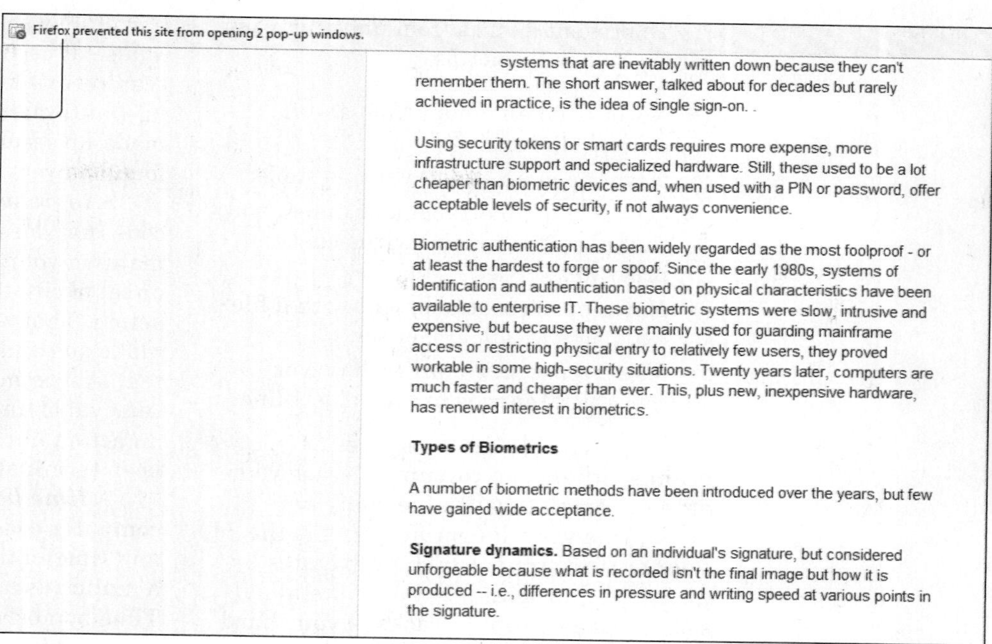

systems that are inevitably written down because they can't remember them. The short answer, talked about for decades but rarely achieved in practice, is the idea of single sign-on. .

Using security tokens or smart cards requires more expense, more infrastructure support and specialized hardware. Still, these used to be a lot cheaper than biometric devices and, when used with a PIN or password, offer acceptable levels of security, if not always convenience.

Biometric authentication has been widely regarded as the most foolproof - or at least the hardest to forge or spoof. Since the early 1980s, systems of identification and authentication based on physical characteristics have been available to enterprise IT. These biometric systems were slow, intrusive and expensive, but because they were mainly used for guarding mainframe access or restricting physical entry to relatively few users, they proved workable in some high-security situations. Twenty years later, computers are much faster and cheaper than ever. This, plus new, inexpensive hardware, has renewed interest in biometrics.

Types of Biometrics

A number of biometric methods have been introduced over the years, but few have gained wide acceptance.

Signature dynamics. Based on an individual's signature, but considered unforgeable because what is recorded isn't the final image but how it is produced -- i.e., differences in pressure and writing speed at various points in the signature.

IE blocker appears at the bottom of the browser window.

Internet Explorer blocked a pop-up from **www.ciol.com**. Information bar help Options ▾ ×

FIGURE 4.35 Most browsers allow users to decide whether they want to view a pop-up.

A ***computer virus*** is hidden code that attaches itself to a host, which can be a program, file, or e-mail message. Viruses that are attached to program files, like an Excel spreadsheet, are called ***file infectors*** and spread to other programs or files on your hard disk when the file is opened. E-mail viruses travel as attachments to e-mail messages and are spread when the attachment is opened. Some viruses are designed as a prank or to sabotage and damage or destroy the infected file. The dangerous actions the virus performs are referred to as its ***payload***.

On your own system, a virus spreads by simply opening an infected file or program. On a network or someone else's system, a virus spreads by copying an infected file or program to a USB drive, CD, or DVD and then giving it to someone. When the storage media with the infected program or file is inserted into the uninfected system, the infected file opens and the infection spreads to this system (Figure 4.36).

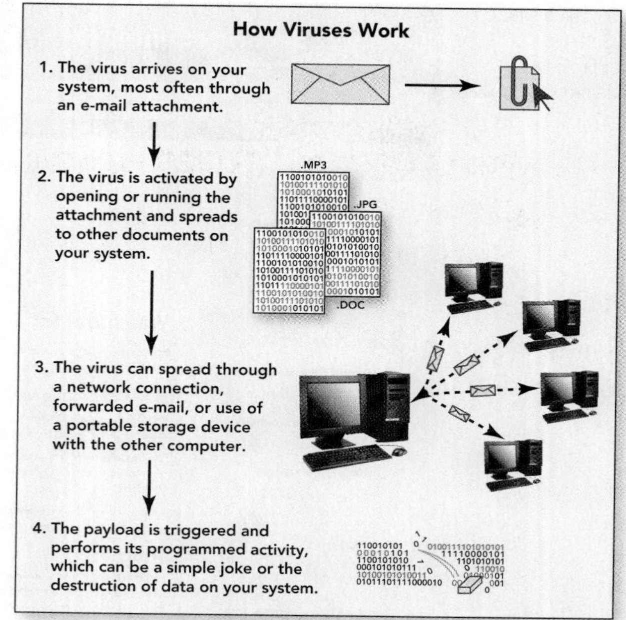

FIGURE 4.36 Safeguard your system and data by only viewing e-mails from reliable sources and running all attachments through an updated anti-virus program prior to opening.

To prevent a virus from infecting your system, follow these tips:

- Never open an e-mail from an unknown sender.
- Never open an e-mail with no subject.
- Never open an attachment unless you first pass it through a virus-checking program.
- Never open an attachment with a file extension of *dat*, *exe*, or *scr*.
- Never trust an e-mail with two or more "RE" entries in the subject line.

Some viruses are nuisances or pranks; others can corrupt or erase your data or completely disable your computer. One very dangerous virus is the ***boot sector virus***, which propagates by an infected program, but only installs itself on the beginning tracks of your hard drive where code is stored that automatically executes every time you start your computer. Another, named Disk Killer, can wipe out all of the data on your hard drive.

Spim is a spam text message sent on a cell phone or an instant messaging service. In March 2008, a spim message was sent to more than 200 million mobile phone users in China during just one day.

Rogue programs, which have gained attention in the last five years, are not harmful by themselves. Rather, they use a false advertisement or bogus malware scan results to scare you into purchasing a fake anti-malware program to remove the made-up security threats it claims to have found on your system (Figure 4.37).

A ***logic bomb*** is hidden computer code that does not replicate but sits dormant on your system until a certain event or set of circumstances triggers it into action. That action, or payload, is usually malicious and devastating to your system. An example of a trigger could be the removal of an employee from a database, an action implying that the employee has been terminated.

A ***time bomb*** is a hidden piece of computer code set to go off on some date and time in the future usually causing a malicious act to occur to your system. Time bombs are less sophisticated than logic bombs, because they are not programmed to be activated by a specific trigger.

A ***worm*** is a program that resembles a computer virus because it can spread from one computer to another. Unlike a virus, however, a worm can propagate over a computer network and does not require an unsuspecting individual to open a file or execute a program or macro. It takes control of affected computers and uses their resources to attack other network-connected systems. Newer worms

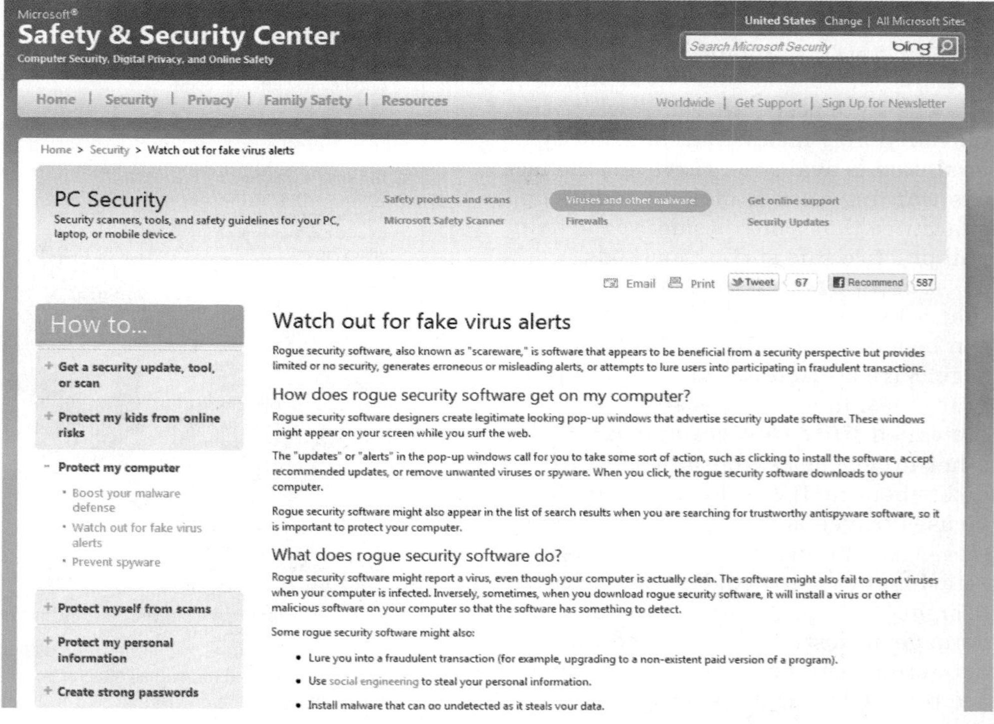

FIGURE 4.37 Web sites like Microsoft Safety & Security Center provide details on rogue programs.

have begun infecting social networking sites such as MySpace and Facebook, retrieving user information and passwords and then directing users to phishing sites.

A ***denial of service (DoS) attack*** is a form of network vandalism in which an attacker attempts to make network services unavailable to legitimate users of the service by bombarding the services with meaningless data. Because network administrators can easily block data from specific IP addresses and halt this type of attack, hackers commandeer as many unprotected computers—called ***zombies***—as possible to launch their attack swiftly and aggressively. The term *zombie* is appropriate because the computers do only what the controller, the zombie master, tells them to do (Figure 4.38). The commandeered computers form a ***botnet***, short for *robot network*, referred to as a zombie army. This, in turn, is controlled by a ***bot***—short for robot—which is an automated program that connects the commandeered computers to the controller. A controller is usually a server with some type of real time activity like Internet Relay Chat that is under the power of a botnet controller—the initiator of the attack. When multiple networked systems are involved in such an attack, it becomes a ***distributed denial of service (DDoS) attack***. Criminals also use botnets to send spam, host phishing attacks, and spread viruses and other malware. ***Syn flooding*** is a form of denial of service attack in which a hostile client repeatedly sends SYN (synchronization) packets to every port on the server, using fake IP addresses, which uses up all the available network connections and locks them up until they time out.

A ***rootkit*** is a malicious program disguised as a useful program; however, it enables the attacker to gain administrator-level access to a computer or network. Rootkits often facilitate the creation of a botnet by allowing an attacker repeated and undetected access to the compromised system.

A ***Trojan horse*** is a program disguised as a useful program, but instead, contains hidden instructions to perform a malicious task. Sometimes a Trojan horse is disguised as a game or a utility program that you find appealing. Then, when you begin running the game, you discover that an entirely different program was loaded.

1. Bot programs use the Internet to turn ordinary computers into zombies.

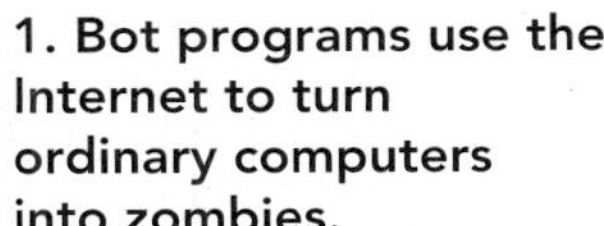

2. Bots connect zombies to controllers.
5. The zombies execute the commands, and a DDoS attack is launched or mass spam sent.
4. Commands are sent to the zombies.

3. Control servers are under the direction of botnet controllers.

FIGURE 4.38 In early 2011 a botnet attack was launched against large corporate investment groups and mining-related interests.

Detecting Illegal Copies of Videos

NEC Japan released a new identification technology capable of detecting, in a matter of seconds, copies of videos illegally uploaded to the Internet. The problem of video copyright infringement has traditionally been addressed by manual inspection. However, with the ever-growing quantity of pirated movies and TV programs, manual detection is impossible. According to NEC, their new technology has a detection rate of 96 percent and an error rate of 5 in 1 million. The technology uses a video's fingerprint or signature generated from each frame of the video based on the difference in luminescence between subregions on that frame. The signature of the suspected video is compared to the original, and an unauthorized duplicate is identified.

How do you feel about your uploaded videos automatically being scanned without your consent? Is it ethical? Are there ways this technology could be used that may not be as well intentioned? Because the sale, purchase, or even the use of pirated copies is illegal, how do you view this method of detection as a deterrent to piracy? Do you think this new technology is going to be enough to discourage the pirates, or will it just cause them to develop pirating techniques capable of circumventing this procedure?

Software piracy occurs when you, without authorization, copy or distribute copyrighted software. This can be done by copying, downloading, sharing, selling, or installing multiple copies onto your personal or work computer. What you might not realize—or not think about—is that when you purchase software, you are actually purchasing a license to use it, not the actual software. That license is what tells you how many times you can legally install the software.

Piracy can be intentional or unintentional. Regardless of intention, the Business Software Alliance (BSA), an antipiracy industry group, in its annual report issued on May 12, 2011, stated that the worldwide piracy rate doubled since 2003. In dollars, that means that software theft exceeded $59 billion in commercial value.

The Prioritizing Resources and Organization for Intellectual Property (Pro-IP) Act of 2008 strengthens civil and criminal penalties for copyright and trademark infringement, substantially increases fines, and allows officials to confiscate equipment. What about sharing programs without money changing hands? That is also illegal—and subject to similar penalties: Under the No Electronic Theft (NET) Act, profit does not have to be a motive in cases of criminal copyright infringement.

Some less known ways of using computers to perform crimes are detailed in the table in Figure 4.39.

Less Visible Crimes That Make Use of Computers

Crime	How It Works
Salami shaving	A program is edited to subtract a very small amount of money from thousands of accounts—say, two cents daily—and divert it to the embezzler's account. The amount is so small that no one individual notices, but over time the embezzler accumulated tens of thousands of dollars.
Data diddling	The modification of data by altering accounts or database records so that it is difficult or impossible to tell that the accounts have stolen funds or equipment.
Forgery	Making Internet data appear to come from one place when it is really coming from another.
Shilling	The use of a secret operative, on Internet auction sites, who bids on another seller's item to drive up the price.

Figure 4.39

Internet Scams

Crime	Definition	Example
Rip and tear	Accepting payment for goods that you have no intention of delivering.	A Seattle man posted ads for Barbie dolls and other goods on eBay, collected more than $32,000 in orders, and never delivered any goods.
Pumping and dumping	The use of Internet stock trading sites, chat rooms, and e-mail to give false praise to worthless companies in which an individual holds stock. After the false hype drives up the share prices, the individual dumps the stocks and makes a hefty profit.	In 2001, Enron participated in an elaborate pump-and-dump scheme by falsely reporting profits and inflating their stock price, then covering the real numbers with questionable accounting practices. More than $1 billion was sold in overvalued stocks.
Bogus goods	The deliberate selling of goods that do not perform the advertised function.	Two Miami residents were indicted on charges of mail and wire fraud after selling hundreds of "Go-boxes," which reportedly turned red traffic lights to green. The boxes, which were actually nothing more than strobe lights, sold for between $69 and $150.

Figure 4.40

Other types of activities that use the Internet to advertise or hype their scam are shown in Figure 4.40.

Concept 4.16 | Identifying the Attackers

A surprising variety of people can cause security problems, ranging from pranksters to hardened criminals. Some attackers are out for ego gratification and do not intend any harm. Others are out for money, on a misguided crusade, or are just plain malicious.

Accessing someone's computer without authorization is illegal, no matter what the motivation might be. ***Hackers*** are computer hobbyists who enjoy pushing computer systems—and themselves—to their limits. They experiment with programs to try to maximize performance and attack the weaknesses and loopholes in a system's security with the goal of improving security and closing the gaps. Hackers subscribe to an unwritten code of conduct, called the ***hacker ethic***, which forbids the destruction of data. ***Cybergangs*** are groups of hackers working together to coordinate attacks, post online graffiti, or engage in other malicious conduct. ***IP spoofing***, an activity associated with hackers, is done by sending a message with an IP address disguised as an incoming message from a trusted source. The hacker must first locate a ***packet header*** of a trusted source, a portion of an Internet protocol packet that precedes its body. After a trusted packet header is located, the hacker manipulates his own packet header to mimic that of the trusted source. The recipient is tricked into responding to a false source.

Hacking goes beyond public sites. A few years ago, a 23-year-old hacker known as *RaFa* downloaded about 43 MB of data from a top-security NASA server, including a 15-slide PowerPoint presentation of a future shuttle design. Then he sent the plans to a *Computerworld* reporter as proof that the NASA system was not secure. In many cases of hacking, the consequences can be damaging. Recognizing the danger, the federal government, through The United States Computer Emergency Readiness Team (US-CERT), has emergency-response teams ready to fend off attacks on critical systems. Internationally, a group of security specialists are using ***honeypots***—computers baited with fake data and purposely left vulnerable—to study how intruders operate in order to prepare stronger defenses (Figure 4.41).

Crackers, also called ***black hats***, are hackers who become obsessed—often uncontrollably—with gaining entry to highly secure computer systems. Their intent is to destroy data, steal information, and perform other malicious acts. In June 2007, Chinese crackers were able to breach an unclassified e-mail system in the Department of Defense, affecting more than 1,500 users and shutting down the network for more than a week. In an attack on the Epilepsy Foundation's forums, crackers posted hundreds of pictures and

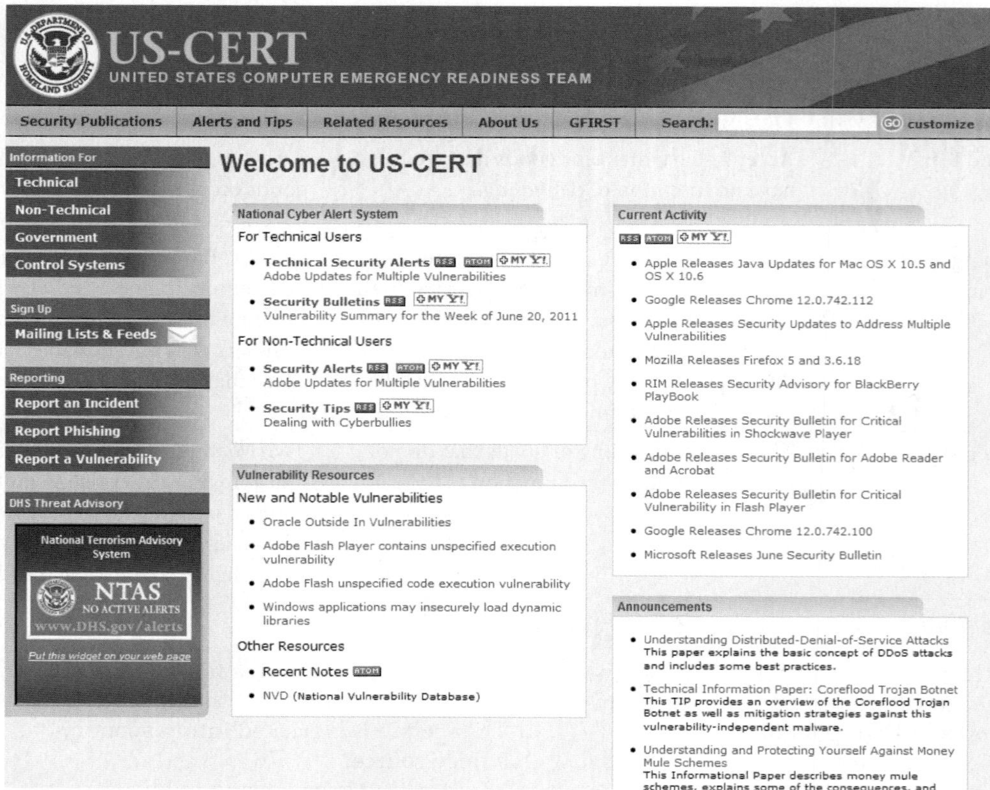

FIGURE 4.41 US-CERT provides defense support against cyberattacks and disseminates cybersecurity information to the public.

links to flashing animations that caused severe migraines and seizures in some visitors.

Anyone who tries to gain unauthorized access to a computer system is probably breaking one or more laws. However, ***ethical hackers*** or ***white hats*** are hackers or crackers that have turned professional, offering their services to companies that value such expertise to improve their computer systems' defenses.

For more information on hackers, crackers, threats, and current vulnerabilities, go to Kaspersky Lab's Securelist site at **www.securelist.com/en/**.

One of the newest and fastest growing crimes is ***cyberstalking***—using the Internet, social networking sites, e-mail, or other electronic communications to repeatedly harass or threaten a person and disrupt his or her life. Most perpetrators are men and most victims are women, particularly women in college. One in every 12 women and one in every 45 men will be stalked, including being watched, phoned, or e-mailed in obsessive and frightening ways, during his or her lifetime.

Cyberdating sites have become another avenue for predators to locate new victims. Most online dating sites use profiling to match potential mates. The downside is that it is difficult to check someone's cyberidentity against his or her actual identity because most are based on user-provided information (Figure 4.42).

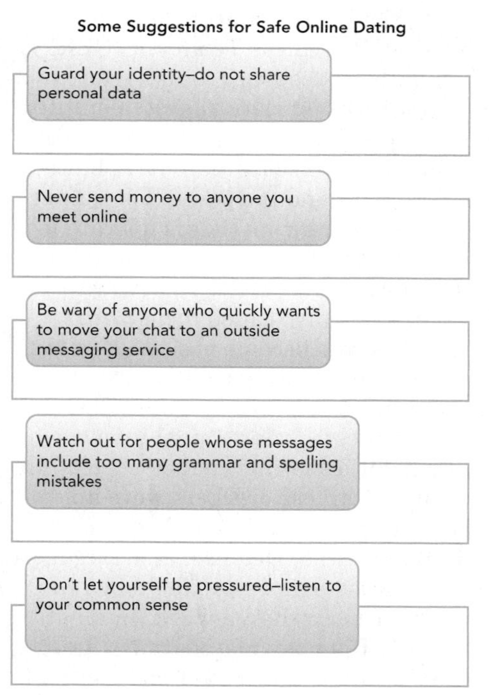

Some Suggestions for Safe Online Dating
Guard your identity–do not share personal data
Never send money to anyone you meet online
Be wary of anyone who quickly wants to move your chat to an outside messaging service
Watch out for people whose messages include too many grammar and spelling mistakes
Don't let yourself be pressured–listen to your common sense

FIGURE 4.42 Safe surfing along with common sense can prevent a Web experience from becoming a nightmare.

SOURCE: http://www.match.com/help/safetytips.aspx

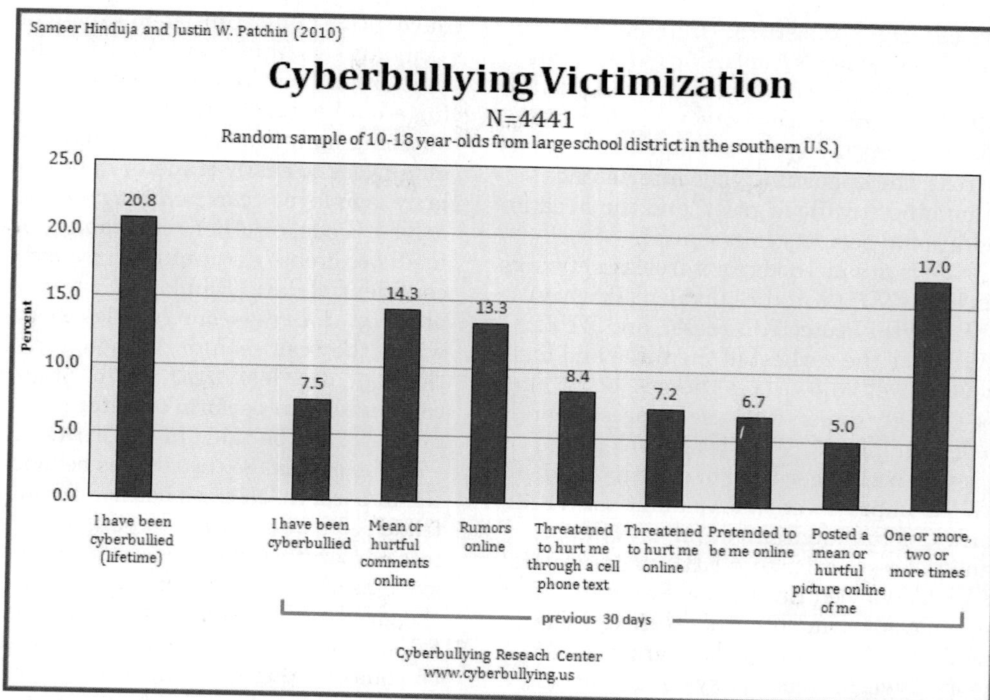

FIGURE 4.43 This survey used a random sample of approximately 4,000 youth between the ages of 12 and 18 from a district in the southern United States. Data was collected in February of 2010 from 41 different schools.

Cyberbullying involves situations in which one or more individuals harass or threaten another individual less capable of defending himself or herself by using the Internet or other forms of digital technology. Cyberbullying can include sending threatening e-mail or text messages or assuming someone else's online identity for the purpose of humiliating or misrepresenting him or her. In a weird twist of fate, the woman who created a fake MySpace profile of a 16-year-old boy to start an Internet relationship with Megan Meier, the Missouri teen who hanged herself after receiving hurtful messages, is now believed to be the victim of a cyberbullying impersonator herself. The online harassment laws that were passed after Meier's death may now be used to help the middle-aged woman, who many believe was responsible for the 13-year-old girl's suicide. This is not an isolated example. The Cyberbullying Research Center noted that 20 percent of the students they surveyed experienced cyberbullying in their lifetime (Figure 4.43).

Now that you have examined the types of perpetrators who pose a risk to your online privacy and safety, in the next objective, you will look more closely at the growing risks to equipment and data security.

Objective 5 | Make Security a Priority

As the Production Manager at a comic book publisher, you are required to hold meetings at hotels and conference centers away from corporate headquarters. At those meetings, you must use wireless networks that are not supported by your company. You want to write a memo to your team members regarding the security risks of logging into unsecured wireless networks and the necessity of installing a firewall on their portable devices. Where do you start?

Concept 4.17 | Recognizing Security Risks

A ***computer security risk*** is any event, action, or situation—intentional or not—that could lead to the loss or destruction of your computer system or the data it contains. Some research indicates that security breaches may cost billions of dollars per year because of their impact on customer service, worker productivity, and production delay.

Wireless LANs—local area networks—pose a challenge to the security of your systems. ***Hotspots***, locations like a coffee shop or restaurant that provide Internet access for devices fitted with wireless technology, are especially unsecure. Unlike wired networks, which send traffic over private dedicated lines, wireless LANs send traffic across shared space—airwaves. Because no one owns the space that airwaves travel across, the opportunity for interference from other traffic is great, and the need for additional security is essential.

Security methods for wireless networks include *WEP* (Wired Equivalent Privacy), *WPA* (WiFi Protected Access), and *WPA2*. WEP was the earliest of the three and has several well-known weaknesses, but it may be the only option for some devices or for older equipment. WPA was developed to provide a stronger level of security, and WPA2 improves on WPA's abilities. WPA2 provides confidentiality and data integrity and is far superior to WEP because it uses AES (Advanced Encryption Standard) to provide government-grade security. The need for wireless security is great, and more powerful security systems continue to be developed. If you access a wireless network, you should implement the security that is currently available so your system is at least protected from the casual hacker.

A new trend in Internet fraud is vacation hacking. Travelers are targeted by cybercriminals who create a phony WiFi hot spot, called an ***evil twin***, with names similar to a legitimate airport, hotel, or fast food hot spot. If you are on an evil twin and enter personal information, like a bank account number and password, your information will be captured by the evil twin's developers and can be used to access your account.

According to one estimate, 80 percent of all data loss is caused by company insiders. Unlike intruders, employees have many opportunities to sabotage a company's computer system, often in ways that are difficult to trace. Although incoming e-mail is routinely scanned for threats, outgoing mail is often overlooked, allowing employees to easily transfer data. Similarly, employees can ***pod slurp***—use USB drives, iPods, or other removable storage media to create an unauthorized copy of confidential data. Employees can also create ***trap doors***—security holes through which they can reenter, without authentication, after leaving the firm. Steps that companies can perform to deter data loss are listed in the table in Figure 4.44.

The espionage threat goes beyond national borders. Nations bent on acquiring trade secrets are always trying to break into corporate and government computer systems. According to a recent estimate, the governments of more than 125 countries are actively involved in industrial espionage. Congress enacted the Economic Espionage Act of 1996 to help companies protect themselves. But many companies do not take advantage of the Act, except as a last resort. Companies worry that news of such a theft may damage their reputation. To view a segment of an award-winning video on industrial espionage titled "The Red Balloon," go to **www.tscmvideo.com/**.

The use of information technologies to corrupt or destroy an enemy's information and industrial infrastructure is called ***information warfare***. A concerted enemy attack would include *electronic warfare*, which is the use of electronic devices to destroy or damage computer systems; *network warfare*, which is hacker-like attacks on a nation's network infrastructure, including

Company Actions to Prevent Security Breaches

Prevention	Action
Back up and protect data	Back up entire systems on a regular schedule and password protect individual files.
Reassess security policies frequently	Update policies to reflect current threats. Inform employees about new security policies and the consequences of violating security policies.
Perform audits	Perform both scheduled and random audits of files, backups, and security procedures to provide assurance of compliance.
Implement appropriate hardware and software	Install necessary hardware and software to protect systems and data from violations both from inside and outside sources.
Enforce password policies	Insist on the use of strong passwords. In a high-security environment, enforce changing passwords every five days or less.

Figure 4.44

Homeland Security

Tess
Seaman, USCG

About | Blog | Contact Us | Site Map
Search

Home | Counterterrorism | Border Security | Preparedness, Response, Recovery | Immigration | Cybersecurity | News

Preparedness, Response, Recovery
Activities & Programs
Committees & Working Groups
Laws & Regulations
Grants
Training & Technical Assistance
Local Resources

Cyber Storm: Securing Cyber Space

Cyber Storm, the Department of Homeland Security's biennial exercise series, provides the framework for the most extensive government-sponsored cybersecurity exercise of its kind.

Congress mandated the Cyber Storm exercise series to strengthen cyber preparedness in the public and private sectors. Securing cyber space is the National Cybersecurity Division's top priority.

Cyber Storm participants perform the following activities:

- Examine organizations' capability to prepare for, protect from, and respond to cyber attacks' potential effects;
- Exercise strategic decision making and interagency coordination of incident response(s) in accordance with national level policy and procedures;
- Validate information sharing relationships and communications paths for collecting and disseminating cyber incident situational awareness, response and recovery information; and
- Examine means and processes through which to share sensitive information across boundaries and sectors without compromising proprietary or national security interests.

Each Cyber Storm builds on lessons learned from previous real world incidents, ensuring that participants face more sophisticated and challenging exercises every two years.

Cyber Storm III: September 2010

Cyber Storm III built upon the success of previous exercises; however, enhancements in the nation's cybersecurity capabilities, an ever-evolving cyber threat landscape and the increased emphasis and extent of public-private collaboration and cooperation, made Cyber Storm III unique.

- **National Cyber Incident Response Plan**
  Cyber Storm III served as the primary vehicle to exercise the newly-developed National Cyber Incident Response Plan (NCIRP) - a blueprint for cybersecurity incident response - to examine the roles, responsibilities, authorities, and other key elements of the nation's cyber incident response and management capabilities and use those findings to refine the plan.
- **Increased Federal, State, International and Private Sector Participation**
  - *Administration-Wide* - Eight Cabinet-level departments including Commerce, Defense, Energy, Homeland Security, Justice, Transportation and Treasury, in addition to the White House and representatives from the intelligence and law enforcement communities.

FIGURE 4.45 Cyber Storm III was the third in a series of congressionally mandated exercises that examined the nation's cybersecurity preparedness and response capabilities.

the electronic banking system; and *structural sabotage*, which is attacks on computer systems that support transportation, finance, energy, and telecommunications. A country's information can also be destroyed by an attack with actual explosive bombs directed at computer centers. According to one expert, a well-coordinated bombing of only 100 key computer installations could bring the U.S. economy to a halt.

Once every two years, the DHS and US-CERT coordinate a national simulation known as Cyber Storm to assess the ability of the United States to identify and respond to a critical cyberattack. Cyber Storm III, held in September 2010, involved 8 cabinet level departments, 11 states, 12 international partners, and 60 private sector companies. The exercise simulated an attack on telecommunication centers, the Internet, and control systems and examined participants' strategic decision making ability in accordance with national procedure (Figure 4.45).

Concept 4.18 | Protecting Your Computer System

Several measures can safeguard computer systems, but none of them can make a computer system 100 percent secure. A trade-off exists between security and usability: The more restrictions imposed by security tools, the less useful the system can become.

Power surges caused by lightning storms or fluctuations in electrical currents and power outages can destroy sensitive electronic components and result in data loss. You should use an ***uninterruptible power supply (UPS)***, which is a battery-powered device that provides power to your computer for a limited time when it detects an outage or critical voltage drop, to safeguard your equipment and data (Figure 4.46). Many companies have electric generators to run large-scale computer systems when the power fails.

Because many security problems originate with stolen passwords, strong passwords and user authentication are required to control authorized access to computer systems. The most secure authentication approach is ***biometric authentication***, the use of a physical trait like hand geometry or a retinal scan to identify an individual (Figure 4.47).

A firewall is a computer program or device that permits your computer to access the Internet but severely limits the ability of outsiders to access

© Don Nichols/iStockphoto.com

FIGURE 4.46 A UPS is a battery-powered device that provides power to your computer for a limited time during a power outage.

© fStop / Alamy

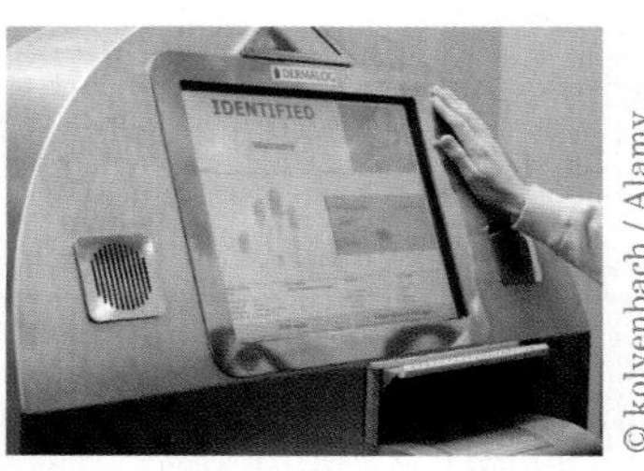

© kolvenbach / Alamy

FIGURE 4.47 Biometric authentication devices such as hand-geometry readers and fingerprint scanners are often used to provide access to restricted locations.

your internal data (Figure 4.48). You can implement a firewall through software, hardware, or a combination of both. Firewalls are a necessity, but they provide no protection against insider pilferage. Information and additional diagrams on how a firewall works or how to choose a firewall for your system is available at **http://computer.howstuffworks.com/firewall.htm** or **www.microsoft.com/security/firewalls/choosing.aspx**. To find out whether your firewall is configured properly, use the free ShieldsUP! service found at **www.grc.com**.

From either the Companion Web Site or MyITLab, watch Chapter 4 Video 1

Concept 4.19 | Safeguarding Yourself and Your Data

Besides protecting your system from intrusion or attack, it is just as important to shield your personal data from theft and yourself from a cyberattack. Following the old clichés of the real world, such as *Don't talk to strangers* and *If something sounds too good to be true, it usually is,* will also keep you out of trouble in the cyberworld.

FIGURE 4.48 A firewall permits an organization's internal computer users to access the Internet but limits the ability of outsiders to access internal data.

Communications leaving a network exists freely.
Internet
Communications entering network from an outside network must first pass firewall security options.

© Alex Slobodkin/iStockphoto

Objective 6 | Encrypt Data

In your job as a Production Manager at a comic book publishing company, you just learned that the company's computers experienced a security breach. Your supervisor wants all communications between managers and their support team members to be encrypted. You need to convey this information to all team members and include additional information on public key encryption, how it works, and why it is important. Where do you start?

Encryption refers to a coding or scrambling process that renders a message unreadable by anyone except the intended recipient. Until recently, encryption was used only by intelligence services, banks, and the military.

E-commerce requires strong, unbreakable encryption; otherwise, money could not be safely exchanged over the Internet. But now, powerful encryption software is available to the public, and U.S. law enforcement officials and defense agencies are concerned. Criminals, including drug dealers and terrorists, can use encryption to hide their activities. In the aftermath of the September 11 terrorist attacks, U.S. officials revealed that the terrorist network had used encrypted e-mail to keep their plans and activities secret.

Concept 4.20 | Understanding Encryption Basics

To understand encryption, try this simple exercise: Consider a short message such as *I love you*. Before it is encrypted, a readable message such as this one is in ***plaintext***—information a sender wants to send to someone. To encrypt the message, take each character and substitute the letter that is 13 positions to that character's right in the 26-letter alphabet. When you reach the end of the alphabet, continue counting from the beginning. This is an example of an ***encryption key***, a formula that makes a plaintext message unreadable. After applying the key, you get the coded message, which is now in ***ciphertext***—the result of encryption performed on plaintext. The ciphertext version of the original message looks like this:

```
V YBIR LBH
```

Of course this string of characters makes no sense; that is the purpose. No one who intercepts this message will know what it means. Your intended recipient, however, can tell what the message means if you give him or her the decoding key, in this instance, counting 13 characters down (Figure 4.49). When your recipient gets the message and decrypts it, your message displays as:

```
I LOVE YOU
```

With ***symmetric key encryption***, the same key is used for encryption and decryption. Some of the keys used by banks and military agencies are so complex that the world's most powerful computer would have to analyze the ciphertext for several hundred years to discover the key. However, there is one way to defeat symmetric key encryption: stealing the key, which is known as ***key interception***. Banks deliver decryption keys using trusted courier services; the military uses trusted personnel or agents.

Concept 4.21 | Using Public Key Encryption

Public key encryption is considered one of the greatest and also most troubling scientific achievements of the twentieth century. ***Public key encryption***, also called ***asymmetric key encryption***, is a computer security process in which two different keys are used. There is an encryption key—referred to as the ***public key***—and a decryption key—referred to as the ***private key***. The use of two different keys safeguards data and provides confidentiality. The way it works is that people who want to receive secret messages publish their public key, for example, by placing it on a Web page or sending it to those with whom they want to communicate. When the public key is used to encrypt a message, the message becomes unreadable. The message becomes readable only when the recipient applies his or her private key, which nobody else knows, and thus guarantees confidentiality (Figure 4.50).

Public key encryption is essential for e-commerce. For example, when you visit a secure site on the Web, your Web browser provides your public key to the Web server. In turn, the Web server provides the site's public key to your Web browser. After a secure communication channel is created, your browser displays a distinctive icon, such as a lock in the address bar; or, the address bar may turn green. Now you can supply confidential information, such as your credit card number, with a reasonable degree of confidence that this information will not be intercepted while it is traveling across the Internet.

You can use public key encryption to implement ***digital signatures***, a technique that guarantees a message has not been tampered with. Digital signatures are important to e-commerce because they enable computers to determine whether a received message or document is authentic and in its original form. A digital signature can be compared to the sealing of an envelope with a personal wax seal. Anyone can open the envelope, but the seal authenticates the sender.

Decoding Key for "I Love You."

A	1
B	2
C	3
D	4
E	5
F	6
G	7
H	8
I	9
J	10
K	11
L	12
M	13
N	14
O	15
P	16
Q	17
R	18
S	19
T	20
U	21
V	22
W	23
X	24
Y	25
Z	26

Figure 4.49

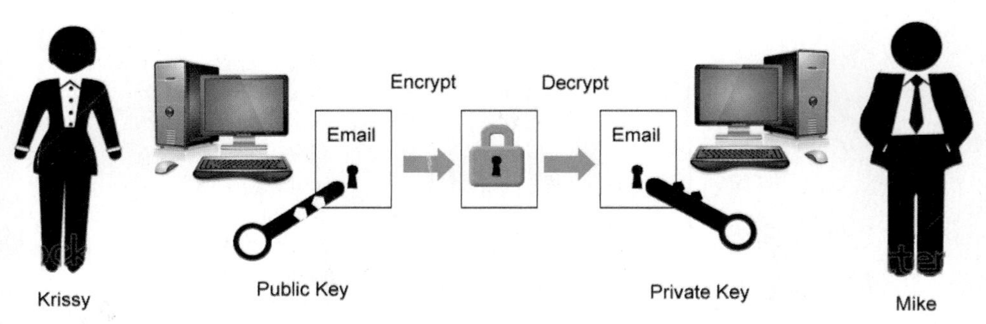

FIGURE 4.50 Krissy uses the public key, provided to her by Mike, to send an encrypted message to Mike. Mike uses his private key to decipher the message. The message would be unreadable to anyone intercepting it.

Public key encryption also enables ***digital certificates***—a method of validating a user, server, or Web site. For a user, a digital certificate validates identity in a manner similar to showing a driver's license when you cash a check. For example, to protect both merchants and customers from online credit card fraud, Visa, MasterCard, and American Express collaborated to create an online shopping security standard for merchants and customers called ***secure electronic transaction (SET)*** that uses digital certificates. They enable parties engaged in Internet-mediated transactions to confirm each other's identity. For a server or Web site, a digital certificate validates that the Web server or Web site is authentic, and the user can feel secure that his or her interaction with the Web site has no eavesdroppers and that the Web site is what it claims to be. This security is important for electronic commerce sites, especially ones that accept credit cards as a form of payment.

Objective 7 | Identify Technologies That Prosecute Computer Crime

In your job as a Production Manager for a comic book company, another manager informed you that a document related to a change in the layout of one of the company's projects was forwarded to an individual at a competitive firm who also happens to be one of your clients. You want to write an e-mail to members of your project group regarding the importance of document security. You want to make them aware of the irreversibility of actions like forwarding an e-mail to an inappropriate party. Where do you start?

Concept 4.22 | Defining E-Discovery

E-discovery, an abbreviated term for electronic discovery, is the process in which documents that exist in electronic form are searched for, located, and obtained for the purpose of being used in a civil or criminal case. Electronic documents include e-mails, voice mails, instant messages, e-calendars, audio files, data on handheld devices, animation, metadata, graphics, photographs, spreadsheets, Web sites, drawings, and other types of digital data. E-discovery is a $2 billion industry, and qualified professionals are in demand. E-discovery professionals use technology to identify, collect, process, review, and produce electronic evidence usable in court cases.

Concept 4.23 | Investigating Computer Forensics

Computer forensics, a complex branch of forensic science, pertains to legal evidence found in computers and digital storage media. This field requires careful preparation and procedural strictness. Because of the scope and technical requirements of this field, there are many subsections such as firewall forensics and mobile device forensics. However, all have the same purposes: to analyze computer systems related to court cases, evaluate a computer after a break-in, recover lost data, and gather evidence against an employee by an employer. Software developers have created several forensic tool kits to help in the logical and procedural accumulation of evidence in this field. These kits spell out proper procedure and contain forms to correctly document every action and event involving a piece of digital evidence, guaranteeing its authenticity, accuracy, and thus its reliability as evidence.

Check Your Knowledge: From either the Companion Web Site or MyITLab, take the quiz covering Objectives 4–7.

Chapter Summary

Computer Hardware, Privacy, and Security

- There are two major categories of computers: computers for individuals and those for organizations. Types of computers for individuals include personal computers (PCs), desktop computers, all-in-one computers, notebooks, subnotebooks, tablet PCs, and handheld computers including PDAs and smartphones. Types of computers for organizations include professional workstations, servers, minicomputers, mainframes, and supercomputers.
- Computers have advantages and disadvantages. Advantages include speed, memory, storage, hardware reliability, accuracy, and assistance to those with disabilities. Disadvantages include information overload, expense, data inaccuracy, unreliable software, viruses, software piracy, identity theft, loss of jobs, and health problems.
- The use of social networking sites such as Facebook, MySpace, LinkedIn, and Twitter is growing daily. Businesses realize the power of such sites and use them to analyze their customers, keep an eye on competitors, and connect customers with their brand.
- Computers are creating new job opportunities, shifting labor demand toward skilled workers, helping people complete their work, freeing workers from occupations with hazardous working conditions, making workflow safer and more efficient, and increasing productivity.
- Being a responsible computer user means respecting others when using technology and sharing resources, recycling computer hardware, being aware of technology overuse, and staying informed about changing technology and its effect on the environment.
- Sensitive personal information, such as Social Security numbers, can be collected through cookies and embedded RFID tags without informing the owner and countering your right of anonymity.
- Computer crimes include identity theft; malware, including spyware and viruses; rogue programs, time bombs, logic bombs, worms, botnets, zombies, and Trojan horses; fraud and theft; password theft; salami shaving and data diddling; forgery and blackmail; cyberstalking and cyberbullying. Internet crimes—cybercrime—include shilling, rip and tear, pump and dump, and bogus goods.
- Computer criminals include hackers, crackers, cybergangs, virus authors, swindlers, shills, cyberstalkers, cyberbullies, and sexual predators.
- No computer system is totally secure, but using safe surfing guides, an uninterruptible power supply (UPS), strong passwords, biometric authentication, encryption of sensitive data, and an installed firewall are all ways to increase your computer security.
- Encryption, essential for e-commerce and online banking, makes use of encryption keys to encode and decode information traveling over a network making it unreadable by anyone except the intended recipient.
- Electronic discovery and computer forensics are both facilitating the detection, apprehension, and conviction of cybercriminals.

Key Terms and Concepts

Active badge 143
Adware 150
All-In-One computer 129
Anonymity 141
Asymmetric key encryption 161
Automation 139
Banner ad 143
Biometric authentication 159
Black hat 155
Boot sector virus 152
Bot 153
Botnet 153
Bugs 137
Ciphertext 161
Client 132
Client/server network 132
Collaboration software 135
Computer crimes 149
Computer ethics 140
Computer forensics 162
Computer security risk 157
Computer virus 151
Cookie 142
Cracker 155
Cyberbullying 157
Cybercrime 149
Cybergangs 155
Cyberlaw 149
Cyberstalking 156
Data diddling 154
Dedicated devices 131
Denial of service (DoS) attack 153
Digital certificates 161
Digital divide 133
Digital piracy 140
Digital signatures 161
Distributed denial of service (DDoS) attack 153
Dumpster dive 150

Matching

Match each term in the second column with its correct definition in the first column by writing the letter of the term on the blank line in front of the correct definition.

____ 1. A computer system in which the system unit and the monitor are combined to reduce the amount of desk space needed to hold the system.

____ 2. A computer with a swivel screen that enables the monitor to lie flat over the keyboard and accept handwritten input.

____ 3. A portable, lightweight computer equipped with wireless technology and used for online services like e-mail, Web browsing, and cloud computing.

____ 4. A professional social network site that enables you to post your professional profile, connect with colleagues, and seek advice from experts.

____ 5. A social networking site designed for short messages that do not exceed 140 characters.

____ 6. Matching your posture and body design to your equipment and your work environment.

____ 7. The unauthorized reproduction and distribution of computer-based media.

____ 8. A small text file written to your computer's hard disk by Web sites you visit and used to gather data on your browsing and shopping habits.

A All-in-one computer
B Computer crime
C Cookie
D Cybercrime
E Digital piracy
F Ergonomics
G LinkedIn
H Netbook
I Payload
J Spim
K Tablet PC
L Time bomb
M Trojan horse
N Twitter
O Zombie

_____ 9. Computer-based activities that violate state, federal, or international laws.

_____ 10. Crimes carried out over the Internet.

_____ 11. The dangerous actions that a virus performs.

_____ 12. A spam text message.

_____ 13. A hidden piece of computer code, set to go off on some future date and time, which causes a malicious act to occur.

_____ 14. An unprotected computer commandeered by a hacker to be part of a denial of service (DoS) attack.

_____ 15. A program disguised as a useful program, but that contains hidden instructions to perform a malicious task.

Multiple Choice

Circle the correct answer.

1. A high-end desktop computer typically used by engineers, architects, circuit designers, financial analysts, game developers, or other technical professionals is a:
   A. professional workstation **C.** mainframe
   B. tablet PC
2. An ultrafast computer system that processes large amounts of scientific data and focuses on executing a few sets of instruction as fast as possible is a:
   A. workstation **C.** mainframe
   B. supercomputer
3. A social network in which individuals you want to connect with are identified as friends is:
   A. Twitter **B.** Google Docs **C.** Facebook
4. The replacement of human workers by machines and computer-guided robots is called:
   A. outsourcing **C.** structural unemployment
   B. automation
5. Obsolete computer equipment is referred to as:
   A. e-waste **B.** malware **C.** spam
6. Watching someone's monitor and keyboard strokes in an attempt to obtain information is called:
   A. tailgating **C.** shoulder surfing
   B. phishing
7. Subcontracting of portions of a job to a third party to reduce cost, time, and energy is called:
   A. automation **C.** outsourcing
   B. structural unemployment
8. The act of modifying data by altering accounts or database records so that it is difficult or impossible to tell if funds or equipment has been stolen is called:
   A. salami shaving **C.** software piracy
   B. data diddling
9. A computer hobbyist who enjoys pushing computer systems to their limit, trying to maximize performance and attack the weaknesses and loopholes in security without the destruction of data is called a:
   A. cracker **B.** hacker **C.** shill
10. A phony WiFi hot spot with a name similar to a legitimate airport, hotel, or fast food hot spot is referred to as:
    A. an evil twin **C.** a trap door
    B. a honeypot

Teamwork

1. **Ergonomics** As a team, use a search engine to locate three Web sites that contain information about the ergonomics of setting up computer workstations. Prepare a report that covers the following: 1) define the term *ergonomics*, and then list five items that should be ergonomically designed in a computer station for the user's health and comfort; 2) for three of the five items, find two retailers that sell suitable ergonomic products; 3) describe the products, explain how they will ergonomically correct or prevent a problem, and the cost. Cite your information sources.
2. **Database Security** As a team, develop a list of ten databases that team members use within a given week. Ask each team member to rank his or her login name and password for each database as strong, mild, or weak based on what you studied in this chapter. Additionally, ask each team member when he or she last changed passwords. Collect this information and organize it in a Word table or Excel worksheet. Summarize your findings on the use of databases, strength of passwords, and frequency of password changes below your table of data. Do you think your findings are representative of your age group and region as a whole?
3. **Electronic Monitoring** Traffic congestion in Hong Kong is a serious concern to commuters, environmentalists concerned about air-born pollution, and the government's Transport Department. Certain areas of the city that draw tourists get extremely congested at peak times during the day. One suggested solution is to charge the owners of private cars to drive in these tourist zones during peak times. Registered car owners would display a scannable chip in the car's windshield, and then the chip would be scanned when a vehicle enters a restricted zone and the individual would be billed. Extensive use of these roads could also result in additional charges for overuse. As a team, list three positive aspects of this system and three negative aspects. Discuss how this system might invade the privacy of a driver. Identify any barriers that might deter this plan. Report your team's stand on the plan in a one-page, double-spaced report.

On the Web

1. **Clean, Quarantine, or Delete?** Investigate three antivirus programs; state the options each provides, especially any option other than clean, quarantine, or delete; and then explain what each option actually does to the infected file. Determine the type of malware each option is best suited to contain. Present your research in a PowerPoint presentation of five to ten slides. Remember to cite the sources of your information.
2. **Red Flags Rules** Use a search engine to find information about the *Red Flags Rules*, which require financial institutions and creditors to develop and implement identity theft programs. Explain three components of the rules, who must comply, and any flexibility that there might be in this policy. Present your findings and cite the sources of your information in a one-page, double-spaced report.
3. **President's Task Force on Identity Theft** Use a search engine to identify the year that the President's Task Force on Identity Theft was created. What was the mission of this organization? Who are the members? What has the task force accomplished since its inception? Present your findings in a one-page, double-spaced report.

Ethics and Social Media

1. **Ethics and E-waste** Watch the Greenpeace video at **http://www.youtube.com/watch?v= 0JZey9GJQP0&NR=1**. After viewing the video, use a search engine to locate sources of information about how to dispose of e-waste properly. List three options that your community, local retailers, or nonprofit organizations provide. Indicate if their advertisements or Web pages display the environmental problems associated with improper disposal. Include such topics as fees associated for disposal, designated drop-off sites, and the method that each uses to dispose of collected e-waste. Present this information in a one- or two-page, double-spaced report.

2. **Are Privacy and Social Networking Incompatible?** Investigate the current security issues of Facebook or another popular social media site. Describe two security breaches involving social networking sites that occurred in the last two years and how long it took to identify them. Find statistics on the amount of information that was compromised and the response that the manager of the site issued. As a team, come to a consensus on the initial statement in this question: Are privacy and social networking incompatible? In a one-page, double-spaced paper, respond to the question.

Sources

http://www.marketingcharts.com/interactive/home-internet-access-in-us-still-room-for-growth-8280/nielsen-internet-access-household-income-february-2009jpg/

http://www.gadgetell.com/tech/comment/about-80-of-united-states-homes-has-a-computer/

http://blogs.forrester.com/jackie_rousseau_anderson/10-09-28-latest_global_social_media_trends_may_surprise_you

http://pewresearch.org/pubs/1484/social-media-mobile-internet-use-teens-millennials-fewer-blog

http://bits.blogs.nytimes.com/2007/12/20/is-information-overload-a-650-billion-drag-on-the-economy/

http://www.stevemcconnell.com/ieeesoftware/bp09.htm

http://gravitonus.com/lang/en-us/index/iclubby/ergonomics/

http://www.rttsweb.com/outsourcing/statistics/

http://www.city-data.com/forum/business-finance-investing/512597-productivity-vice-virtue.html

http://www.musicdish.com/mag/index.php3?id=12857

http://www.census.gov/retail/mrts/www/data/pdf/10Q1.pdf

http://www.sophos.com/sophos/docs/eng/papers/sophos-security-threat-report-jan-2010-wpna.pdf

http://www.theregister.co.uk/2011/03/09/gold_mine_site_botnet/

http://www.microsoft.com/security/pc-security/antivirus-rogue.aspx

http://www.eweek.com/c/a/Security/Software-Piracy-Costs-59-Bn-in-Lost-Revenue-May-Be-Even-Higher-Survey-272553/

http://www.tonyrogers.com/news/onstar.htm

http://www.humanevents.com/article.php?id=22244

http://www.dhs.gov/files/training/gc_1204738275985.shtm

http://5magazine.wordpress.com/2010/05/22/nec%E2%80%99s-new-technology-to-detect-pirated-videos-online/

Windows Explorer, File Management, Office Features, and Word Documents

OUTCOMES At the end of this chapter you will be able to:	**OBJECTIVES** Mastering these objectives will enable you to:
PROJECT 5A Create, save, and print a Microsoft Office 2010 file.	**1.** Locate and Start a Microsoft Office 2010 Program (p. 170) **2.** Enter and Edit Text in an Office 2010 Program (p. 171) **3.** Perform Commands from a Dialog Box (p. 173) **4.** Create a Folder, Save a File, and Close a File (p. 174) **5.** Add Document Properties and Print a File (p. 177)
PROJECT 5B Use the Ribbon and dialog boxes to perform common commands in a Microsoft Office 2010 file.	**6.** Open an Existing File and Save It with a New Name (p. 181) **7.** Explore Options for an Application (p. 182) **8.** Perform Commands from the Ribbon (p. 183) **9.** Apply Formatting in Office Programs (p. 187) **10.** Use the Microsoft Office 2010 Help System (p. 196) **11.** Compress Files (p. 196)
PROJECT 5C Create a flyer with a picture.	**12.** Create a New Document and Insert Text (p. 199) **13.** Insert and Format Graphics (p. 200) **14.** Insert and Modify Text Boxes and Shapes (p. 205) **15.** Preview and Print a Document (p. 208)
PROJECT 5D Format text, paragraphs, and documents.	**16.** Change Document and Paragraph Layout (p. 212) **17.** Create and Modify Lists (p. 216) **18.** Set and Modify Tab Stops (p. 219) **19.** Insert a SmartArt Graphic (p. 222)

© Joe Belanger/Shutterstock

© auremar/Shutterstock

Job Focus: Executive Chef and College Assistant

In This Chapter

In this chapter, you will learn how an Executive Chef manages her computer files and uses all the features in Office 2010. You will also learn how a College Assistant uses Word.

At the end of this Unit, following Chapter 6, you will have an opportunity to complete a case project that focuses on the career of a Production Manager for a comic book company.

Project 5A PowerPoint File

Project Activities

In Activities 5.01 through 5.05, you will create a PowerPoint file, save it in a folder that you create, and then print the file or submit it electronically as directed by your instructor. Your completed PowerPoint slide will look similar to Figure 5.1.

Project Files

For Project 5A, you will need the following file:

New blank PowerPoint presentation

You will save your file as:

Lastname_Firstname_5A_Menu_Plan

Project Results

Figure 5.1
Project 5A Menu Plan

Objective 1 | Locate and Start a Microsoft Office 2010 Program

View the video on the Companion Web Site or in MyITLab

Microsoft Office 2010 includes programs, servers, and services for individuals, small organizations, and large enterprises. A ***program***, also referred to as an ***application***, is a set of instructions used by a computer to perform a task, such as word processing or accounting.

Activity 5.01 | Locating and Starting a Microsoft Office 2010 Program

1 On the **Windows taskbar**, click the **Start** button to display the **Start** menu.

2 From the displayed **Start** menu, locate the group of **Microsoft Office 2010** programs on your computer—the Office program icons from which you can start the program may be located on your Start menu, in a Microsoft Office folder on the **All Programs** list, on your desktop, or any combination of these locations; the location will vary depending on how your computer is configured.

All Programs is an area of the Start menu that displays all the available programs on your computer system.

3 Click to open the program **Microsoft PowerPoint 2010**. Compare your screen with Figure 5.2, and then take a moment to study the description of these screen elements in the table in Figure 5.3.

Figure 5.2

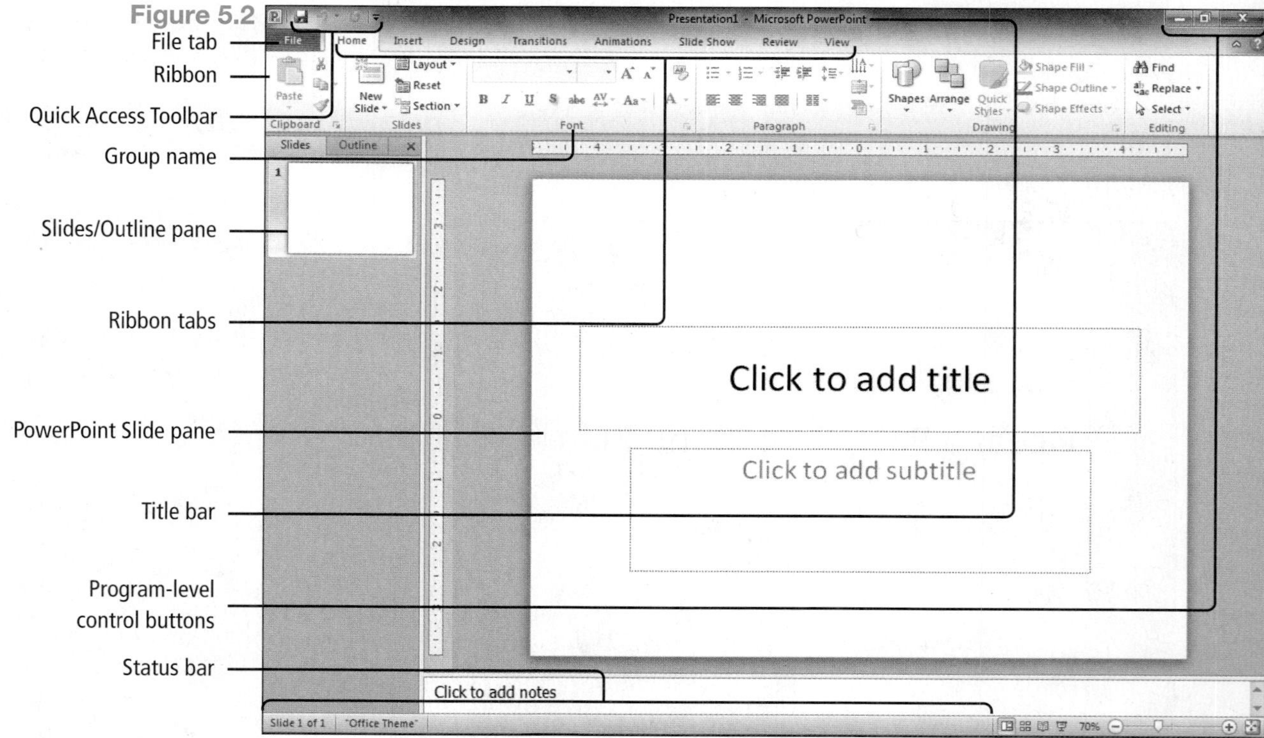

Screen Element	Description
File tab	Displays Microsoft Office Backstage view, which is a centralized space for all of your file management tasks such as opening, saving, printing, publishing, or sharing a file—all the things you can do *with* a file.
Group names	Indicate the name of the groups of related commands on the displayed tab.
PowerPoint Slide pane	Displays a large image of the active slide in the PowerPoint program.
Program-level control buttons	Minimizes, restores, or closes the program window.
Quick Access Toolbar	Displays buttons to perform frequently used commands and resources with a single click. The default commands include Save, Undo, and Redo. You can add and delete buttons to customize the Quick Access Toolbar.
Ribbon	Displays a group of task-oriented tabs that contain the commands, styles, and resources you need to work in an Office 2010 program. The look of your Ribbon depends on your screen resolution. A high resolution will display more individual items and button names on the Ribbon.
Ribbon tabs	Display the names of the task-oriented tabs relevant to the open program.
Slides/Outline pane	Displays either thumbnails of the slides in a PowerPoint presentation (Slides tab) or the outline of the presentation's content (Outline tab). In each Office 2010 program, different panes display in different ways to assist you.
Status bar	Displays file information on the left and View and Zoom on the right.
Title bar	Displays the name of the file and the name of the program. The program window control buttons—Minimize, Maximize/Restore Down, and Close—are grouped on the right side of the title bar.

Figure 5.3

Objective 2 | Enter and Edit Text in an Office 2010 Program

View the video on the Companion Web Site or in MyITLab

All of the programs in Office 2010 require some typed text. Your keyboard is still the primary method of entering information into your computer. Techniques to ***edit***—make changes to—text are similar among all of the Office 2010 programs.

Activity 5.02 | Entering and Editing Text in an Office 2010 Program

1 In the middle of the PowerPoint Slide pane, point to the text *Click to add title* to display the [I-beam] pointer, and then click one time.

The ***insertion point***—a blinking vertical line that indicates where text or graphics will be inserted—displays.

In Office 2010 programs, the mouse ***pointer***—any symbol that displays on your screen in response to moving your mouse device—displays in different shapes depending on the task you are performing and the area of the screen to which you are pointing.

2 Type **Oceana Grille Info** and notice how the insertion point moves to the right as you type. Point slightly to the right of the letter *e* in *Grille* and click to place the insertion point there.

3 On your keyboard, locate and press the Backspace key to delete the letter *e*.

Pressing Backspace removes a character to the left of the insertion point.

4 Point slightly to the left of the *I* in *Info* and click one time to place the insertion point there. Type **Menu** and then press Spacebar one time. Compare your screen with Figure 5.4.

By ***default***, when you type text in an Office program, existing text moves to the right to make space for new typing. Default refers to the current selection or setting that is automatically used by a program unless you specify otherwise.

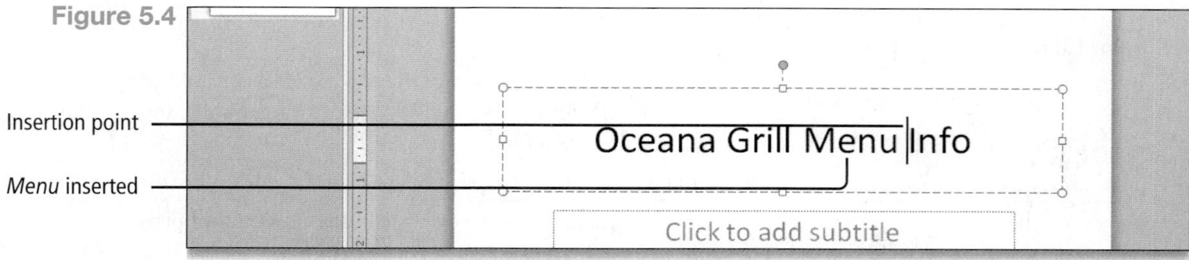

Figure 5.4

5 Press Delete four times to delete *Info* and then type **Plan**

Pressing Delete removes—deletes—a character to the right of the insertion point.

6 With your insertion point blinking after the word *Plan*, on your keyboard, hold down the Ctrl key. While holding down Ctrl, press ← three times to move the insertion point to the beginning of the word *Grill*.

This is a ***keyboard shortcut***—a key or combination of keys that performs a task that would otherwise require a mouse. This keyboard shortcut moves the insertion point to the beginning of the previous word. A keyboard shortcut is commonly indicated as Ctrl + ← (or some other combination of keys) to indicate that you hold down the first key while pressing the second key.

7 With the insertion point blinking at the beginning of the word *Grill*, type **Palm** and press Spacebar.

8 Click anywhere in the text *Click to add subtitle*. With the insertion point blinking, type the following and include the spelling error: **Prepered by Annabel Dunham**

9 With your mouse, point slightly to the left of the *A* in *Annabel*, hold down the left mouse button, and then ***drag***—hold down the left mouse button while moving your mouse—to the right to select the text *Annabel Dunham*, and then release the mouse button. Compare your screen with Figure 5.5.

The ***Mini toolbar*** displays commands that are commonly used with the selected object, which places common commands close to your pointer. When you move the pointer away from the Mini toolbar, it fades from view.

To ***select*** refers to highlighting, by dragging with your mouse, areas of text or data or graphics so that the selection can be edited, formatted, copied, or moved. The action of dragging includes releasing the left mouse button at the end of the area you want to select. The Office programs recognize a selected area as one unit, to which you can make changes.

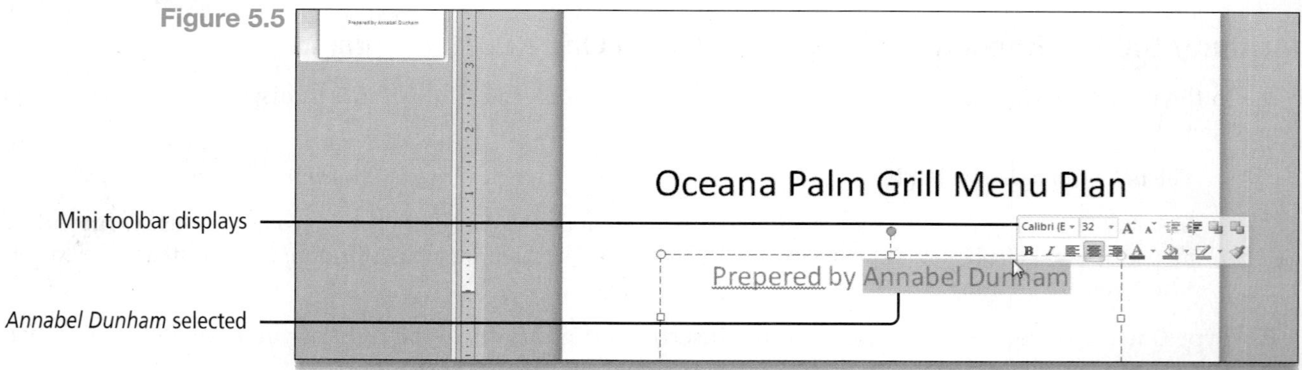

Figure 5.5

10 With the text *Annabel Dunham* selected, type your own firstname and lastname.

In any Windows-based program, such as the Microsoft Office 2010 programs, selected text is deleted and then replaced when you begin to type new text. You will save time by developing good techniques to select and then edit or replace selected text, which is easier than pressing the Delete key numerous times to delete text that you do not want.

11 Notice that the misspelled word *Prepered* displays with a wavy red underline; additionally, all or part of your name might display with a wavy red underline.

Office 2010 has a dictionary of words against which all entered text is checked. In Word and PowerPoint, words that are *not* in the dictionary display a wavy red line, indicating a possible misspelled word or a proper name or an unusual word—none of which are in the Office 2010 dictionary.

12 Point to *Prepered* and then ***right-click***—click your right mouse button one time.

The Mini toolbar and a ***shortcut menu*** display. A shortcut menu displays commands and options relevant to the selected text or object—known as ***context-sensitive commands*** because they relate to the item you right-clicked.

Here, the shortcut menu displays commands related to the misspelled word. You can click the suggested correct spelling *Prepared*, click Ignore All to ignore the misspelling, add the word to the Office dictionary, or click Spelling to display a ***dialog box***. A dialog box is a small window that contains options for completing a task. Whenever you see a command followed by an ***ellipsis*** (...), which is a set of three dots indicating incompleteness, clicking the command will always display a dialog box.

13 On the displayed shortcut menu, click **Prepared** to correct the misspelled word. If necessary, point to any parts of your name that display a wavy red underline, right-click, and then on the shortcut menu, click Ignore All so that Office will no longer mark your name with a wavy underline in this file.

Objective 3 | Perform Commands from a Dialog Box

In a dialog box, you make decisions about an individual object or topic. A dialog box also offers a way to adjust a number of settings at one time.

View the video on the Companion Web Site or in MyITLab

Activity 5.03 | Performing Commands from a Dialog Box

1 Point anywhere in the blank area above the title *Oceana Palm Grill Menu Plan* to display the pointer.

2 Right-click to display a shortcut menu. Notice the command *Format Background* followed by an ellipsis (...). Compare your screen with Figure 5.6.

Recall that a command followed by an ellipsis indicates that a dialog box will display if you click the command.

Figure 5.6

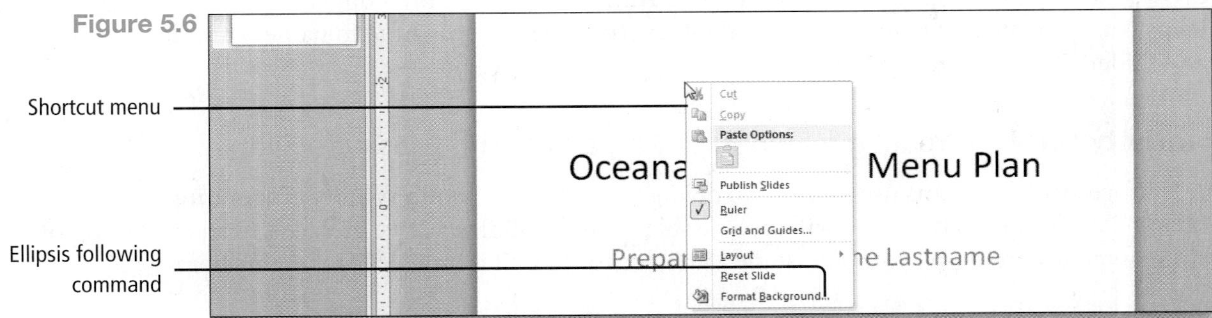

3 Click **Format Background** to display the **Format Background** dialog box.

4 On the left, if necessary, click **Fill** to display the **Fill** options. On the right, under **Fill**, click the **Gradient fill** option button.

Fill is the inside color of an object. Here, the dialog box displays the option group names on the left. The dialog box displays additional settings related to the gradient fill option. An ***option button*** is a round button that enables you to make one choice among two or more options. In a gradient fill, one color fades into another.

5 Click the **Preset colors arrow**—the arrow in the box to the right of the text *Preset colors*—and then in the gallery, in the second row, point to the fifth fill color to display the ScreenTip *Fog*.

A ***gallery*** is an Office feature that displays a list of potential results. A ***ScreenTip*** displays useful information about mouse actions, such as pointing to screen elements or dragging.

6 Click **Fog**, and then notice that the fill color is applied to your slide. Click the **Type arrow**, and then click **Rectangular** to change the pattern of the fill color. Compare your screen with Figure 5.7.

Figure 5.7

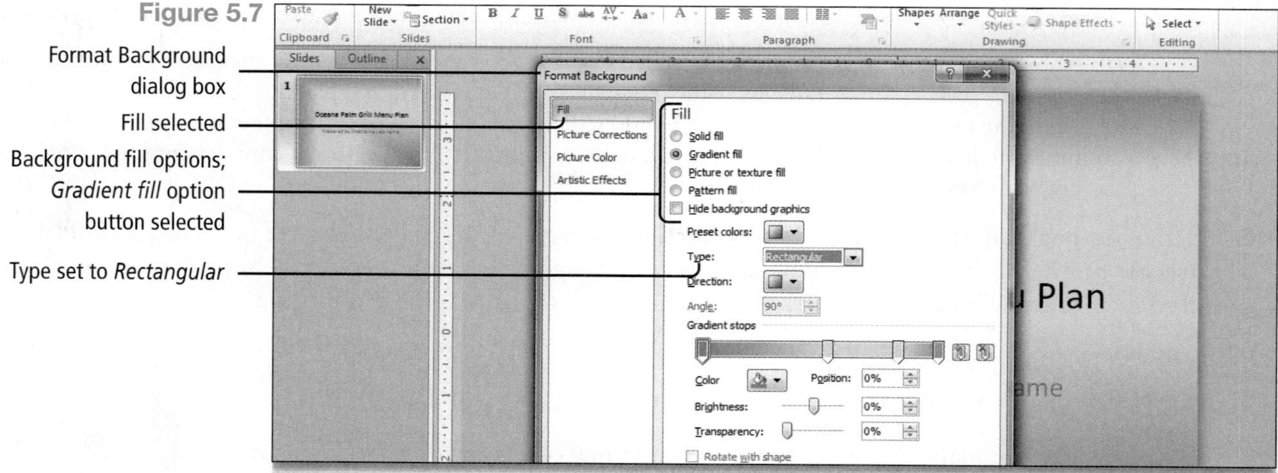

7 At the bottom of the dialog box, click **Close**.

Objective 4 | Create a Folder, Save a File, and Close a File

View the video on the Companion Web Site or in MyITLab

A ***location*** is any disk drive, folder, or other place in which you can store files and folders. Where you store your files depends on how and where you use your data. For example, for your classes, you might decide to store primarily on a removable USB flash drive so that you can carry your files with you. Although the Windows operating system helps you to create and maintain a logical folder structure, take the time to name your files and folders in a consistent manner.

Activity 5.04 | Creating a Folder, Saving a File, and Closing a File

Office 2010 programs use a common dialog box provided by the Windows operating system to assist you in saving files. In this activity, you will create a folder on a USB flash drive in which to store files. If you prefer to store on your hard drive, you can use similar steps to store files in your Documents library.

1 Insert a USB flash drive into your computer, and if necessary, **Close** the **AutoPlay** dialog box. If you are not using a USB flash drive, go to Step 2.

As the first step in saving a file, determine where you want to save the file, and if necessary, insert a storage device.

2 At the top of your screen, in the title bar, notice that *Presentation1 – Microsoft PowerPoint* displays.

Most Office 2010 programs open with a new unsaved file with a default name—*Presentation1*, *Document1*, and so on. As you create your file, your work is temporarily stored in the computer's memory until you initiate a Save command, at which time you must choose a file name and location in which to save your file.

3 In the upper left corner of your screen, click the **File tab** to display **Microsoft Office Backstage** view. Compare your screen with Figure 5.8.

Microsoft Office ***Backstage view*** is a centralized space for tasks related to *file* management; that is why the tab is labeled *File*. File management tasks include, for example, opening, saving, printing, publishing, or sharing a file. The ***Backstage tabs***—*Info*, *Recent*, *New*, *Print*, *Save & Send*, and *Help*—display along the left side. The tabs group file-related tasks together.

Above the Backstage tabs, ***Quick Commands***—*Save*, *Save As*, *Open*, and *Close*—display for quick access to these commands. When you click any of these commands, Backstage view closes and either a dialog box displays or the active file closes.

Here, the ***Info tab*** displays information—*info*—about the current file. In the center panel, various file management tasks are available in groups. For example, if you click the Protect Presentation button, a list of options that you can set for this file that relate to who can open or edit the presentation displays.

On the Info tab, in the right panel, you can also examine the ***document properties***. Document properties, also known as ***metadata***, are details about a file that describe or identify it, such as the title, author name, subject, and keywords that identify the document's topic or contents. On the Info page, a thumbnail image of the current file displays in the upper right corner, which you can click to close Backstage view and return to the document.

Figure 5.8

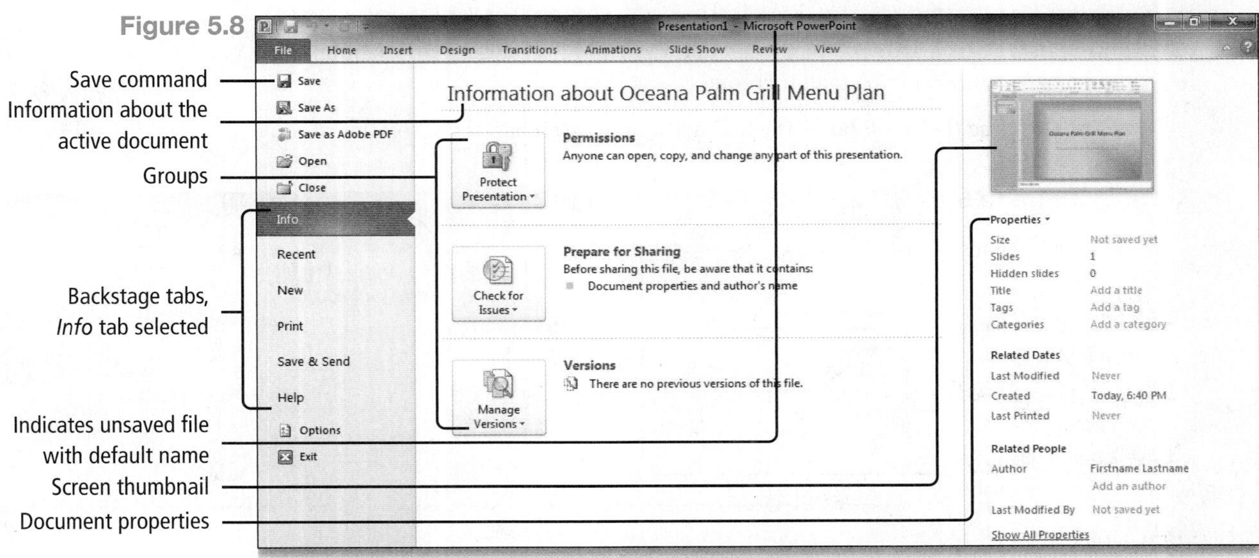

4 Above the **Backstage tabs**, click **Save** to display the **Save As** dialog box.

Backstage view closes and the Save As dialog box, which includes a folder window and an area at the bottom to name the file and set the file type, displays. When you are saving something for the first time, for example a new PowerPoint presentation, the Save and Save As commands are identical. That is, the Save As dialog box will display if you click Save or if you click Save As.

Note | Saving Your File

After you have named a file and saved it in your desired location, the Save command saves any changes you make to the file without displaying any dialog box. The Save As command will display the Save As dialog box and let you name and save a new file based on the current one—in a location that you choose. After you name and save the new document, the original document closes, and the new document—based on the original one—displays.

5 In the **Save As** dialog box, on the left, locate the **Navigation pane**; compare your screen with Figure 5.9.

By default, the Save command opens the Documents library unless your default file location has been changed.

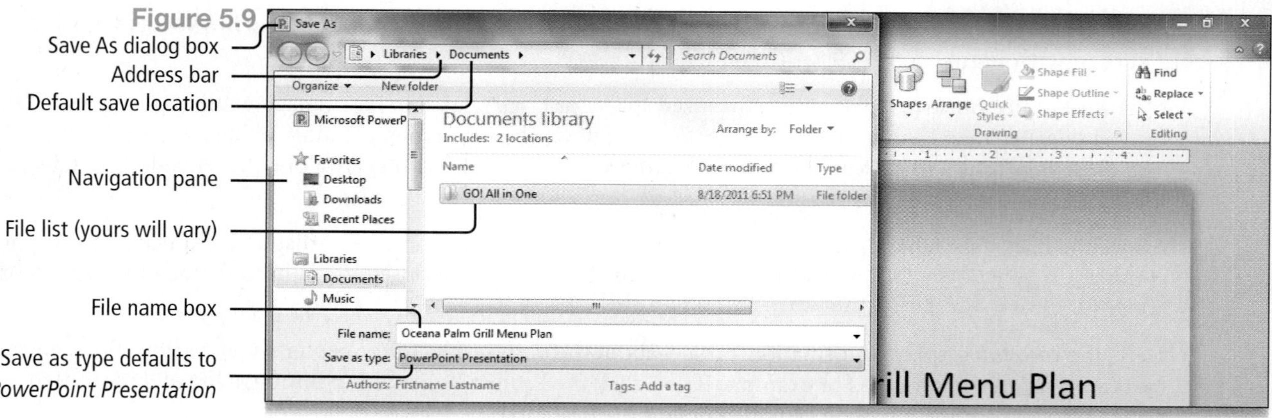

Figure 5.9

6 On the right side of the **Navigation pane**, point to the **scroll bar**. Click the **down scroll arrow** as necessary so that you can view the lower portion of the **navigation pane**, and then click the icon for your USB flash drive. Compare your screen with Figure 5.10. (If you prefer to store on your computer's hard drive instead of a USB flash drive, in the navigation pane, click Documents.)

A ***scroll bar*** displays when a window, or a pane within a window, has information that is not in view. You can click the up or down scroll arrows—or the left and right scroll arrows in a horizontal scroll bar—to scroll the contents up or down or left and right in small increments.

You can also drag the ***scroll box***—the box within the scroll bar—to scroll the window in either direction.

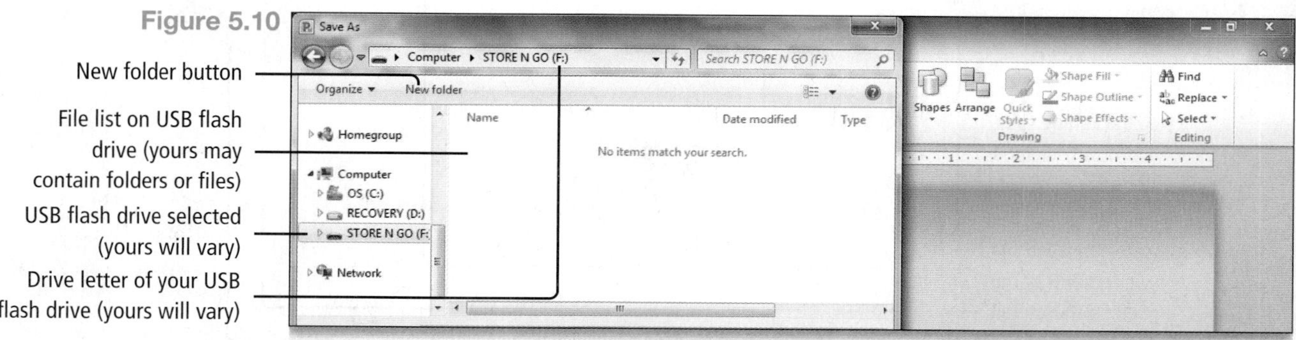

Figure 5.10

7 On the toolbar, click the **New folder** button.

In the file list, a new folder is created, and the text *New folder* is selected.

8 Type **All In One Chapter 5** and press Enter.

In Windows-based programs, the Enter key confirms an action.

9 In the **file list**, double-click the name of your new folder to open it and display its name in the **address bar**. In the lower portion of the dialog box, click in the **File name** box to select the existing text. Notice that Office inserts the text at the beginning of the presentation as a suggested file name.

10 On your keyboard, locate the - key. Notice that the Shift of this key produces the underscore character. With the text still selected, type **Lastname_Firstname_5A_Menu_Plan**

You can use spaces in file names; however, some individuals prefer not to use spaces. Some programs, especially when transferring files over the Internet, may not work well with spaces in file names. In this textbook, underscores are used instead of spaces in file names.

11 In the lower right corner, click **Save**; or press Enter. Compare your screen with Figure 5.11.

Your new file name displays in the title bar, indicating that the file has been saved to a location that you have specified.

Figure 5.11

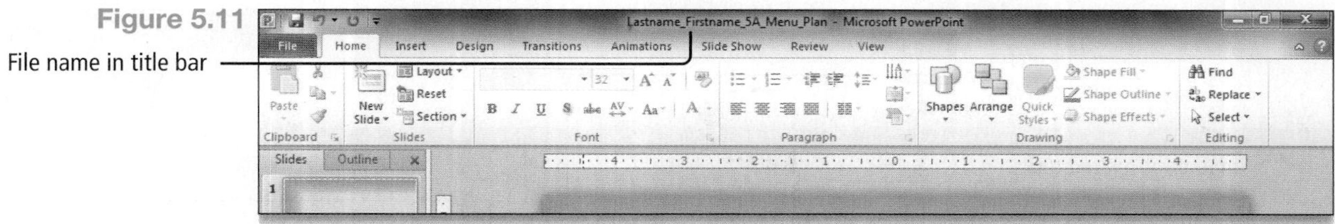

12 In the text that begins *Prepared by*, click to position the insertion point at the end of your name, and then press Enter to move to a new line. Type **For Laura Hernandez**

13 Click the **File tab** to display **Backstage** view. At the top of the center panel, notice that the path where your file is stored displays. Above the Backstage tabs, click **Close** to close the file. In the message box, click **Save** to save the changes you made and close the file. Leave PowerPoint open.

Because you have made additional changes to the file since your last Save operation, an Office program will always prompt you to save so that you do not lose any new data.

Objective 5 | Add Document Properties and Print a File

View the video on the Companion Web Site or in MyITLab

The process of printing a file is similar in all of the Office applications. There are differences in the types of options you can select. For example, in PowerPoint, you have the option of printing the full slide, with each slide printing on a full sheet of paper, or of printing handouts with small pictures of slides on a page.

Activity 5.05 | Adding Document Properties and Printing a File

Alert! | Are You Printing or Submitting Your Files Electronically?

If you are submitting your files electronically only, or have no printer attached, you can still complete this activity. Complete Steps 1-9, and then submit your file electronically as directed by your instructor.

1 In the upper left corner, click the **File tab** to display **Backstage** view. Notice that the **Recent tab** displays.

Because no file was open in PowerPoint, Office applies predictive logic to determine that your most likely action will be to open a PowerPoint presentation that you worked on recently. Thus, the Recent tab displays a list of PowerPoint presentations that were recently open on your system.

2 At the top of the **Recent Presentations** list, click your **Lastname_Firstname_5A_Menu_Plan** file to open it.

3 Click the **File tab** to redisplay **Backstage** view. On the right, under the screen thumbnail, click **Properties**, and then click **Show Document Panel**. In the **Author** box, delete the existing text, and then type your firstname and lastname. Notice that in PowerPoint, some variation of the slide title is automatically inserted in the Title box. In the **Subject** box, type your Course name and section number. In the **Keywords** box, type **menu plan** and then in the upper right corner of the **Document Properties** panel, click the **Close the Document Information Panel** button ☒.

Adding properties to your documents will make them easier to search for in systems such as Microsoft SharePoint.

4 Redisplay **Backstage** view, and then click the **Print tab**. Compare your screen with Figure 5.12.

On the Print tab in Backstage view, in the center panel, three groups of printing-related tasks display—Print, Printer, and Settings. In the right panel, the ***Print Preview*** displays, which is a view of a document as it will appear on the paper when you print it. At the bottom of the Print Preview area, on the left, the number of pages and arrows with which you can move among the pages in Print Preview display. On the right, ***Zoom*** settings enable you to shrink or enlarge the Print Preview. Zoom is the action of increasing or decreasing the viewing area of the screen.

Figure 5.12

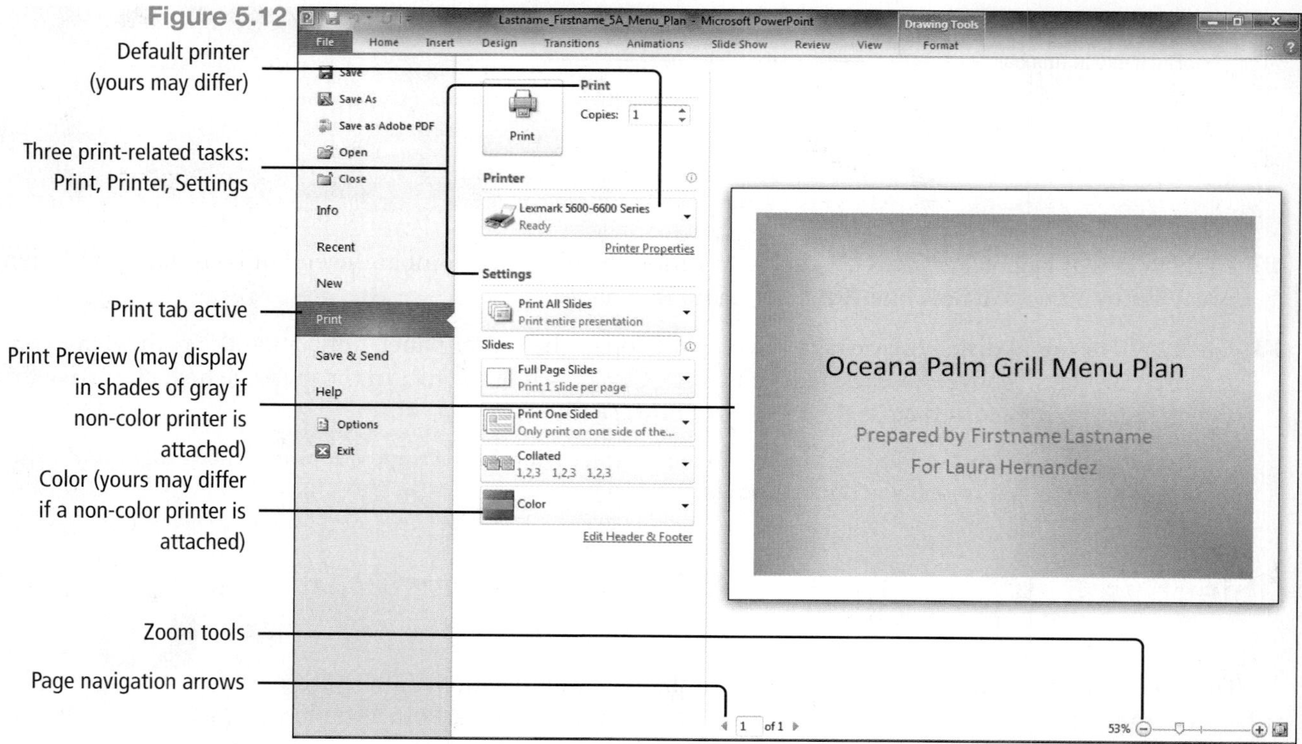

5 Locate the **Settings group**, and notice that the default setting is to **Print All Slides** and to print **Full Page Slides**—each slide on a full sheet of paper.

6 Point to **Full Page Slides**, notice that the button glows orange, and then click the button to display a gallery of print arrangements. Compare your screen with Figure 5.13.

Figure 5.13

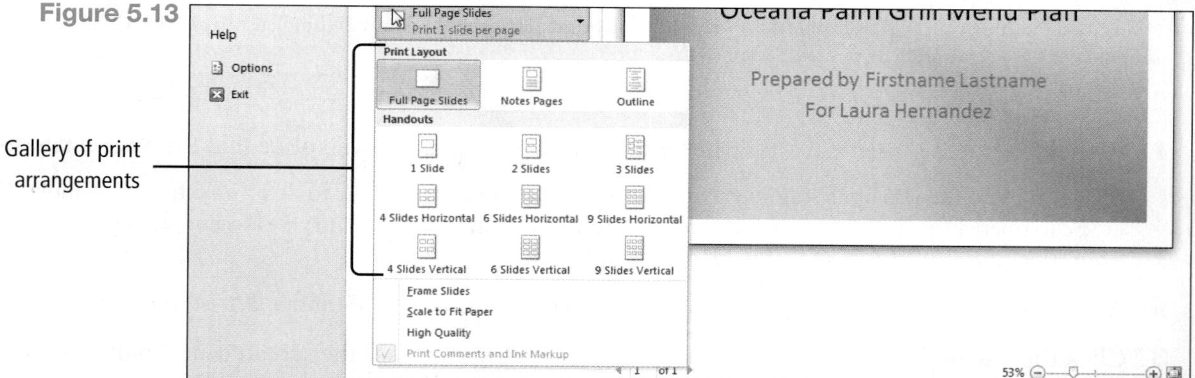

7 In the displayed gallery, under **Handouts**, click **1 Slide**.

The Print Preview changes to show how your slide will print on the paper in this arrangement.

8 To submit your file electronically, skip this step and move to Step 9. To print your slide, be sure your system is connected to a printer, and then in the **Print group**, click the **Print** button. On the Quick Access Toolbar, click **Save**, and then move to Step 10.

The handout will print on your default printer—on a black and white printer, the colors will print in shades of gray. Backstage view closes and your file redisplays in the PowerPoint window.

9 To submit your file electronically, above the **Backstage tabs**, click **Close** to close the file and close **Backstage** view, if necessary, click **Save** in the displayed message, and then either create a PDF as described in the More Knowledge box on the next page, or follow the instructions provided by your instructor to submit your file electronically.

10 Display **Backstage** view, and then below the **Backstage tabs**, click **Exit** to close your file and close PowerPoint.

More Knowledge | Creating a PDF as an Electronic Printout

From Backstage view, you can save an Office file as a *PDF file*. ***Portable Document Format*** (***PDF***) creates an image of your file that preserves the look of your file, but that cannot be easily changed. This is a popular format for sending documents electronically, because the document will display on most computers. From Backstage view, click Save & Send, and then in the File Types group, click Create PDF/XPS Document. Then in the third panel, click the Create PDF/XPS button, navigate to your chapter folder, and then in the lower right corner, click Publish.

End **You have completed Project 5A**

Project 5B Word File

Project Activities

In Activities 5.06 through 5.15, you will open, edit, save, and then compress a Word file. Your completed document will look similar to Figure 5.14.

Project Files

For Project 5B, you will need the following file:

w05B_Cheese_Promotion

You will save your Word document as:

Lastname_Firstname_5B_Cheese_Promotion

Project Results

Memo

TO:	Laura Mabry Hernandez, General Manager
FROM:	Donna Jackson, Executive Chef
DATE:	December 17, 2014
SUBJECT:	Cheese Specials on Tuesdays

To increase restaurant traffic between 4:00 p.m. and 6:00 p.m., I am proposing a trial cheese event in one of the restaurants, probably Orlando. I would like to try a weekly event on Tuesday evenings where the focus is on a good selection of cheese.

I envision two possibilities: a selection of cheese plates or a cheese bar—or both. The cheeses would have to be matched with compatible fruit and bread or crackers. They could be used as appetizers, or for desserts, as is common in Europe. The cheese plates should be varied and diverse, using a mixture of hard and soft, sharp and mild, unusual and familiar.

I am excited about this new promotion. If done properly, I think it could increase restaurant traffic in the hours when individuals want to relax with a small snack instead of a heavy dinner.

The promotion will require that our employees become familiar with the types and characteristics of both foreign and domestic cheeses. Let's meet to discuss the details and the training requirements, and to create a flyer that begins something like this:

Oceana Palm Grill Tuesday Cheese Tastings

Lastname_Firstname_5B_Cheese_Promotion

Figure 5.14
Project 5B Cheese Promotion

Objective 6 | Open an Existing File and Save It with a New Name

View the video on the Companion Web Site or in MyITLab

In any Office program, use the Open command to display the ***Open dialog box***, from which you can navigate to and then open an existing file that was created in that same program. The Open dialog box, along with the Save and Save As dialog boxes, are referred to as ***common dialog boxes***. These dialog boxes, which are provided by the Windows programming interface, display in all of the Office programs in the same manner. Thus, the Open, Save, and Save As dialog boxes will all look and perform the same in each Office program.

Activity 5.06 | Opening an Existing File and Saving It with a New Name

In this activity, you will display the Open dialog box, open an existing Word document, and then save it in your storage location with a new name.

1 Start the **Microsoft Word 2010** program on your system. On the Ribbon, click the **File tab** to display **Backstage** view, and then click **Open** to display the **Open** dialog box.

2 In the **Navigation pane** on the left, use the scroll bar to scroll as necessary, and then click the location of your student data files to display the location's contents in the **file list**.

3 Navigate to your student files. In the **file list**, point to the **Chapter_05** folder and double-click to open it. Compare your screen with Figure 5.15.

Figure 5.15

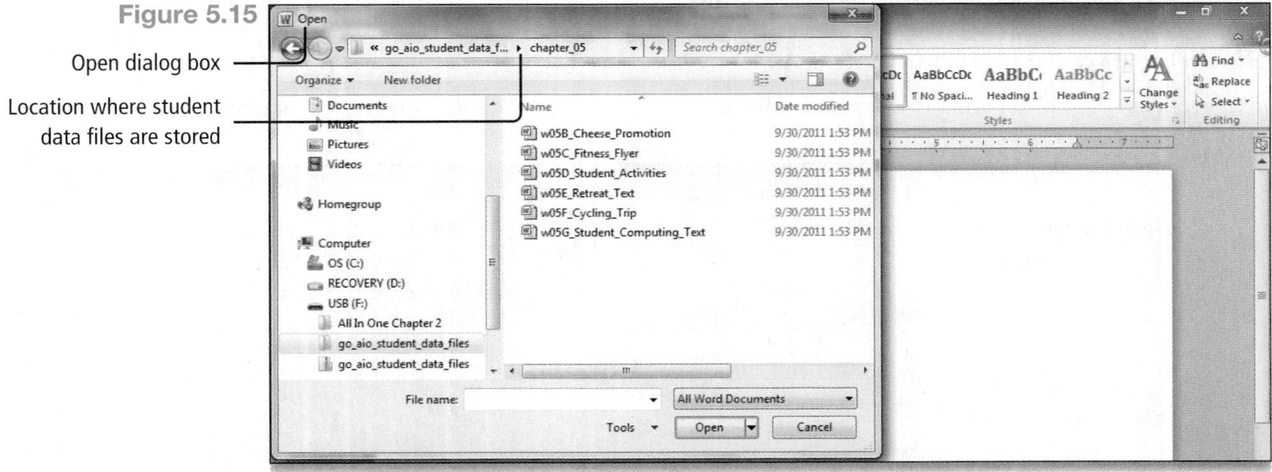

4 In the **file list**, point to Word file **w05B_Cheese_Promotion** and then double-click to open and display the file in the Word window. On the Ribbon, on the **Home tab**, in the **Paragraph group**, if necessary, click the **Show/Hide** button ¶ so that it is active. Compare your screen with Figure 5.16.

On the title bar at the top of the screen, the file name displays.

Figure 5.16

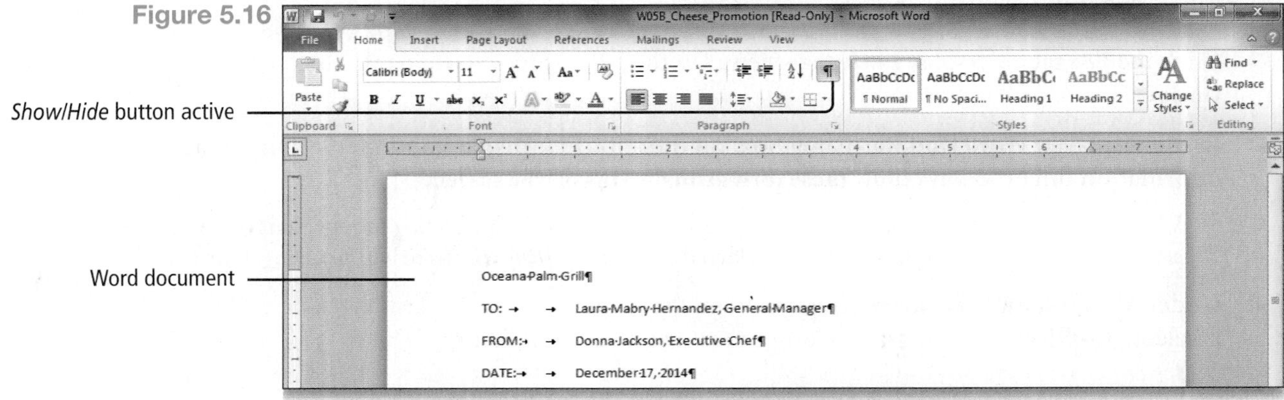

Alert! | Do You See a Message to Enable Editing or Enable Content?

In Office 2010, some files open in ***Protected View*** if the file appears to be from a potentially risky location, such as the Internet. Protected View is a new security feature in Office 2010 that protects your computer from malicious files by opening them in a restricted environment until you enable them. ***Trusted Documents*** is another security feature that remembers which files you have already enabled. You might encounter these security features if you open a file from an e-mail or download files from the Internet. So long as you trust the source of the file, click Enable Editing or Enable Content—depending on the type of file you receive—and then go ahead and work with the file.

5. Click the **File tab** to display **Backstage** view, and then click the **Save As** command to display the **Save As** dialog box.

   The Save As command displays the Save As dialog box where you can name and save a *new* document based on the currently displayed document. After you name and save the new document, the original document closes, and the new document—based on the original one—displays.

6. Navigate to the location in which you are storing your projects for this chapter—the location where you created your **All in One Chapter 5** folder. In the **file list**, double-click the necessary folders and subfolders until your **All in One Chapter 5** folder displays in the **address bar**.

7. Click in the **File name** box to select the existing file name, or drag to select the existing text, and then using your own name, type **Lastname_Firstname_5B_Cheese_Promotion**

   As you type, the file name from your 5A project might display briefly. Because your 5A project file is stored in this location and you began the new file name with the same text, Office predicts that you might want the same or similar file name. As you type new characters, the suggestion is removed.

8. In the lower right corner of the **Save As** dialog box, click **Save**; or press Enter. Compare your screen with Figure 5.17.

   The original document closes, and your new document, based on the original, displays with the name in the title bar.

Figure 5.17

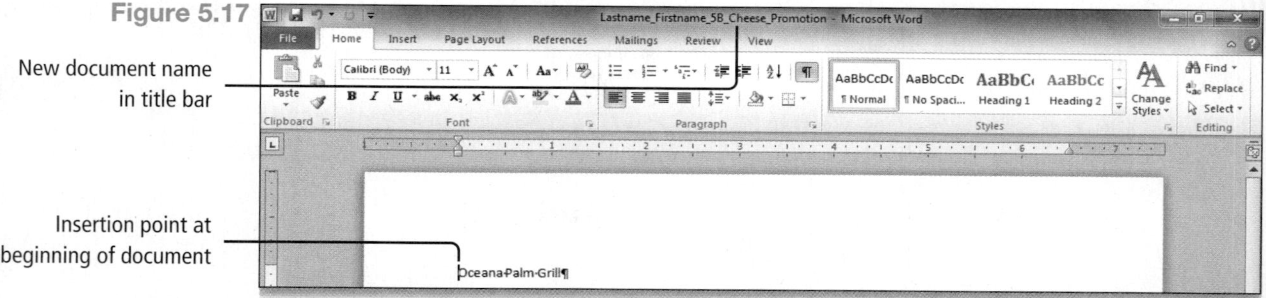

Objective 7 | Explore Options for an Application

Within each Office application, you can open an ***Options dialog box*** where you can select program settings and other options and preferences.

View the video on the Companion Web Site or in MyITLab

Activity 5.07 | Viewing Application Options

1. Click the **File tab** to display **Backstage** view. On the left, under the **Help tab**, click **Options**.

2. In the displayed **Word Options** dialog box, on the left, click **Display**, and then on the right, locate the information under **Always show these formatting marks on the screen.**

   When you press Enter, Spacebar, or Tab on your keyboard, characters display to represent these keystrokes. These screen characters do not print, and are referred to as ***formatting marks*** or ***nonprinting characters***.

3. Under **Always show these formatting marks on the screen**, be sure the last check box, **Show all formatting marks**, is selected—select it if necessary. Compare your screen with Figure 5.18.

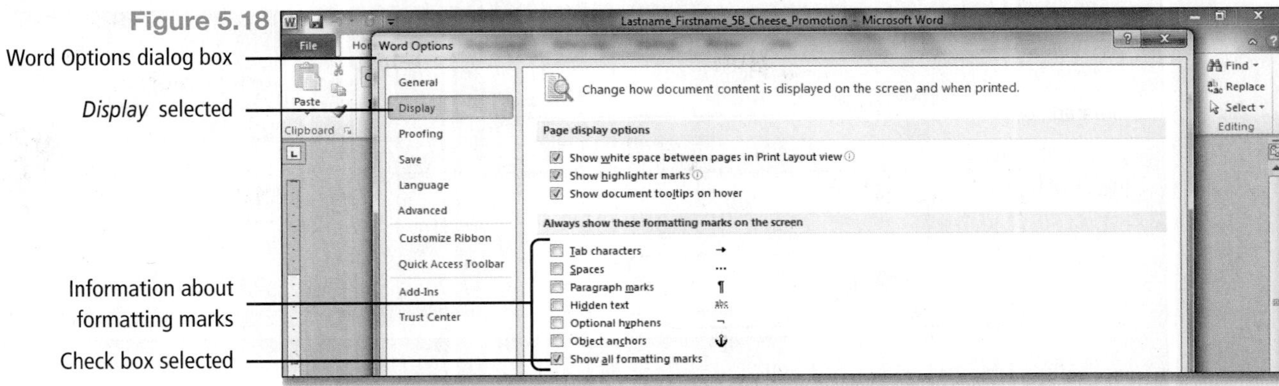

Figure 5.18

4 In the lower right corner of the dialog box, click **OK**.

Objective 8 | Perform Commands from the Ribbon

View the video on the Companion Web Site or in MyITLab

The ***Ribbon***, which displays across the top of the program window, groups commands and features in a manner that you would most logically use them. Each Office program's Ribbon is slightly different, but all contain the same three elements: ***tabs***, ***groups***, and ***commands***. Tabs display across the top of the Ribbon, and each tab relates to a type of activity; for example, laying out a page. Groups are sets of related commands for specific tasks. Commands—instructions to computer programs—are arranged in groups, and might display as a button, a menu, or a box in which you type information.

Activity 5.08 | Performing Commands from the Ribbon

1 On the Ribbon, click the **View tab**. In the **Show group**, if necessary, click to place a check mark in the **Ruler** check box, and then compare your screen with Figure 5.19.

When working in Word, display the rulers so that you can see how margin settings affect your document and how text aligns. Additionally, if you set a tab stop or an indent, its location is visible on the ruler.

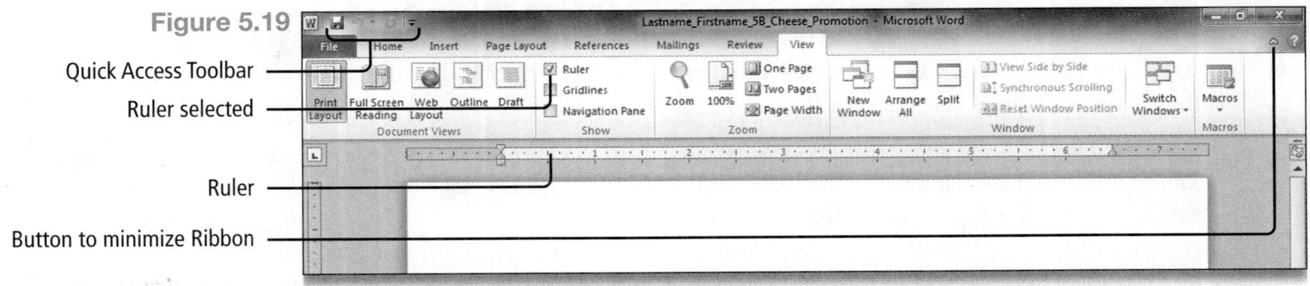

Figure 5.19

2 On the Ribbon, click the **Home tab**. In the **Paragraph group**, if necessary, click the **Show/Hide** button ¶ so that it glows orange and formatting marks display in your document. Point to the button to display information about the button, and then compare your screen with Figure 5.20.

When the Show/Hide button is active—glowing orange—formatting marks display. Because formatting marks guide your eye in a document—like road signs guide you along a highway—these marks will display throughout this instruction.

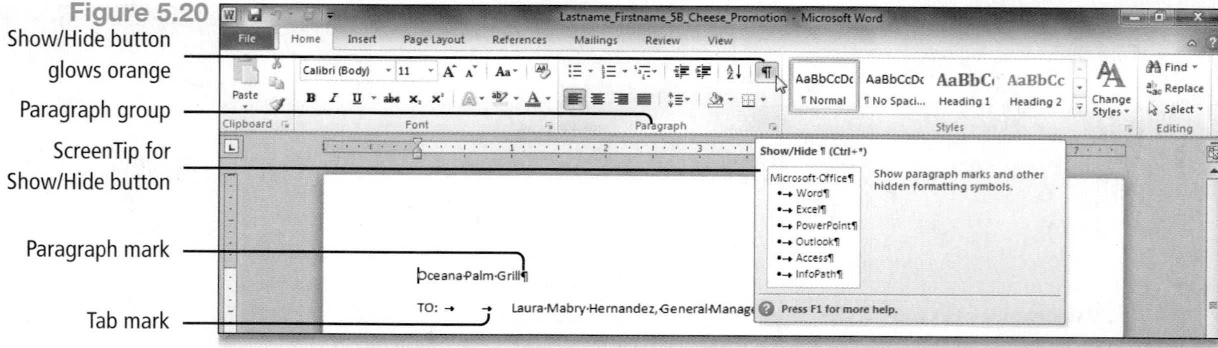

Figure 5.20

3 In the upper left corner of your screen, above the Ribbon, locate the **Quick Access Toolbar**.

The ***Quick Access Toolbar*** contains commands that you use frequently. By default, only the commands Save, Undo, and Redo display, but you can add and delete commands to suit your needs.

4 At the end of the Quick Access Toolbar, click the **Customize Quick Access Toolbar** button, and then compare your screen with Figure 5.21.

A list of commands that Office users commonly add to their Quick Access Toolbar displays, including *Open*, *E-mail*, and *Print Preview and Print*. Commands already on the Quick Access Toolbar display a check mark. Commands that you add to the Quick Access Toolbar are always just one click away.

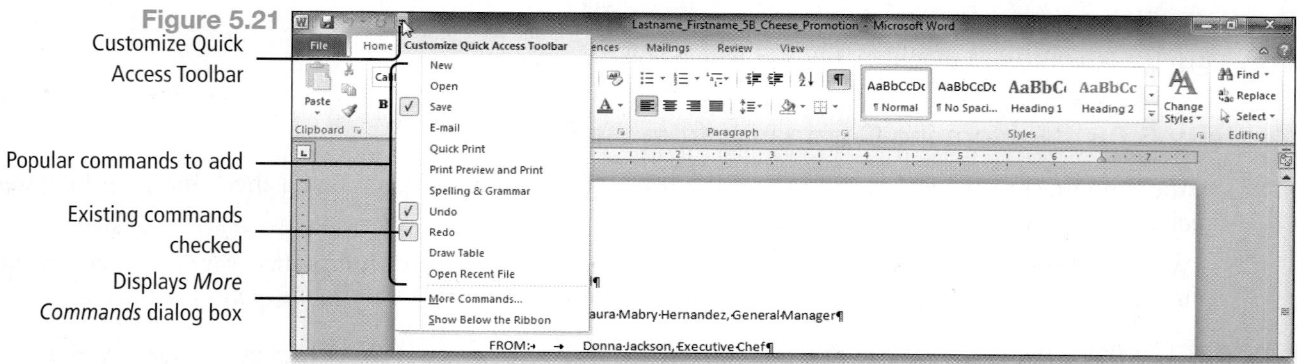

Figure 5.21

5 On the displayed list, click **Print Preview and Print**, and then notice that the icon is added to the **Quick Access Toolbar**. Compare your screen with Figure 5.22.

The icon that represents the Print Preview command displays on the Quick Access Toolbar. Because this is a command that you will use frequently while building Office documents, you might decide to have this command remain on your Quick Access Toolbar.

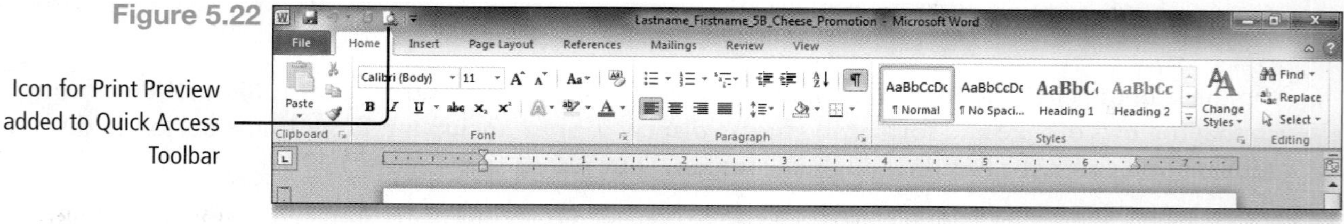

Figure 5.22

6 In the first line of the document, be sure your insertion point is blinking to the left of the *O* in *Oceana*. Press Enter one time to insert a blank paragraph, and then click to the left of the new paragraph mark (¶) in the new line.

The ***paragraph symbol*** is a formatting mark that displays each time you press Enter.

7 On the Ribbon, click the **Insert tab**. In the **Illustrations group**, point to the **Clip Art** button to display its ScreenTip.

Many buttons on the Ribbon have this type of ***enhanced ScreenTip***, which displays more descriptive text than a normal ScreenTip.

8 Click the **Clip Art** button.

The Clip Art ***task pane*** displays. A task pane is a window within a Microsoft Office application that enables you to enter options for completing a command.

9 In the **Clip Art** task pane, click in the **Search for** box, delete any existing text, and then type **cheese grapes** Under **Results should be:**, click the arrow at the right, if necessary click to *clear* the check mark for **All media types** so that no check boxes are selected, and then click the check box for **Illustrations**. Compare your screen with Figure 5.23.

Figure 5.23

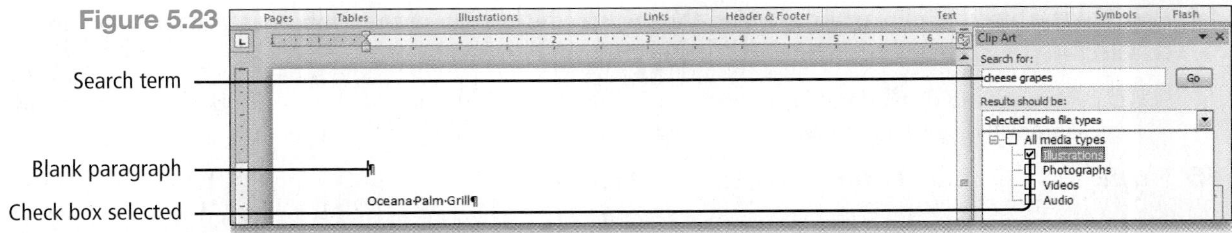

10 Click the **Results should be arrow** again to close the list, and then if necessary, click to place a check mark in the **Include Office.com content** check box.

By selecting this check box, the search for clip art images will include those from Microsoft's online collections of clip art at www.office.com.

11 At the top of the **Clip Art** task pane, click **Go**. Wait a moment for clips to display, and then locate the clip indicated in Figure 5.24.

Figure 5.24

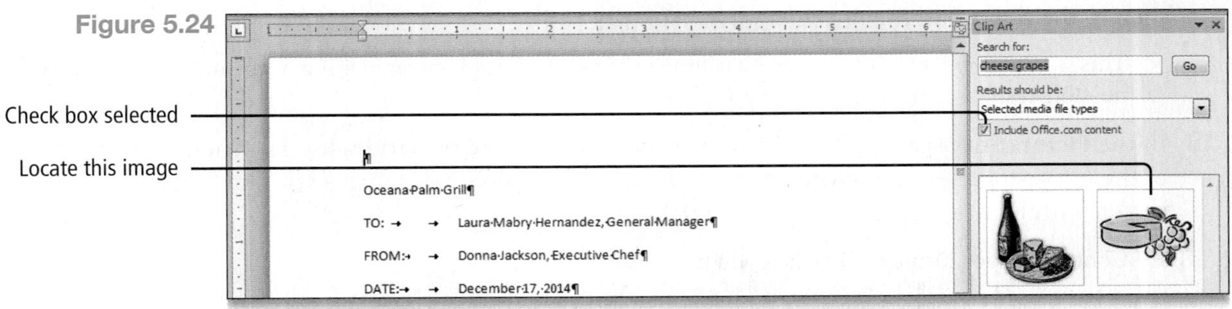

12 Click the image indicated in Figure 5.24 one time to insert it at the insertion point, and then in the upper right corner of the **Clip Art** task pane, click the **Close** [×] button.

> **Alert! | If You Cannot Locate the Image**
>
> If the image shown in Figure 5.24 is unavailable, select a different cheese image that is appropriate.

13 With the image selected—surrounded by a border—on the Ribbon, click the **Home tab**, and then in the **Paragraph group**, click the **Center** button [≡]. Click anywhere outside of the bordered picture to ***deselect***—cancel the selection. Compare your screen with Figure 5.25.

Figure 5.25

14 Point to the inserted clip art image, and then watch the last tab of the Ribbon as you click the image one time to select it.

The *Picture Tools* display and an additional tab—the *Format* tab—is added to the Ribbon. The Ribbon adapts to your work and will display additional tabs—referred to as ***contextual tabs***—when you need them.

15 On the Ribbon, under **Picture Tools**, click the **Format tab**.

> **Alert! | The Size of Groups on the Ribbon Varies with Screen Resolution**
>
> Your monitor's screen resolution might be set higher than the resolution used to capture the figures in this book. At a higher resolution, the Ribbon expands some groups to show more commands than are available with a single click, such as those in the Picture Styles group. Or, the group expands to add descriptive text to some buttons, such as those in the Arrange group. Regardless of your screen resolution, all Office commands are available to you. In higher resolutions, you will have a more robust view of the commands.

16 In the **Picture Styles group**, point to the first style to display the ScreenTip *Simple Frame, White*, and notice that the image displays with a white frame. Watch the image as you point to the second picture style, and then to the third, and then to the fourth.

This is ***Live Preview***, a technology that shows the result of applying an editing or formatting change as you point to possible results—*before* you actually apply it.

17 In the **Picture Styles group**, click the fourth style—**Drop Shadow Rectangle**—and then click anywhere outside of the image to deselect it. Notice that the Picture Tools no longer display on the Ribbon. Compare your screen with Figure 5.26.

Contextual tabs display only when you need them.

Figure 5.26

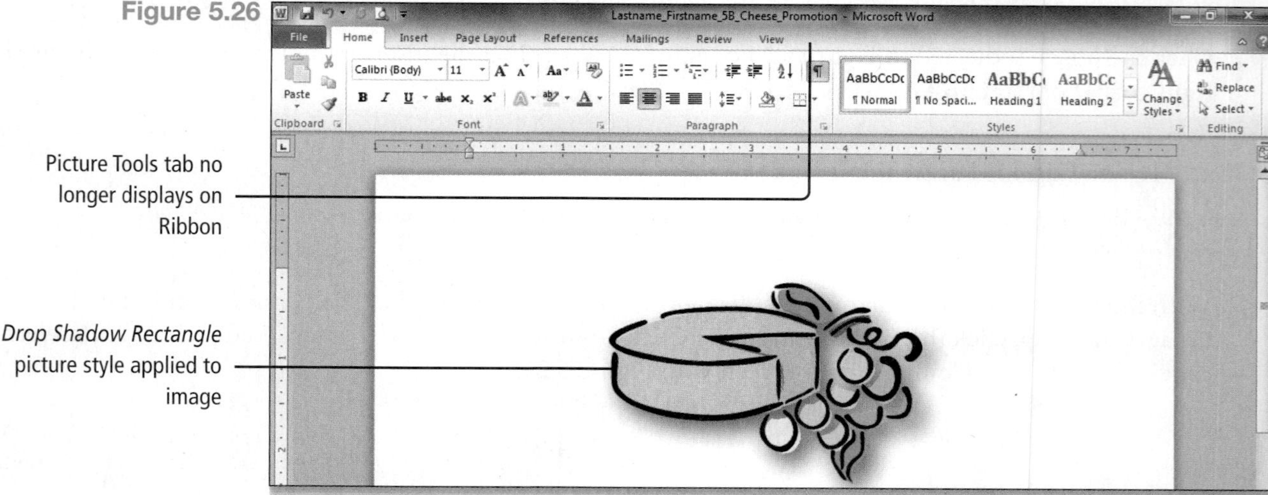

18 In the upper left corner of your screen, on the Quick Access Toolbar, click the **Save** button to save the changes you have made.

Activity 5.09 | Minimizing and Using the Keyboard to Control the Ribbon

Instead of a mouse, some individuals prefer to navigate the Ribbon by using keys on the keyboard. You can activate keyboard control of the Ribbon by pressing the Alt key. You can also minimize the Ribbon to maximize your available screen space.

1 On your keyboard, press the Alt key, and then on the Ribbon, notice that small labels display. Press N to activate the commands on the **Insert tab**, and then compare your screen with Figure 5.27.

Each label represents a ***KeyTip***—an indication of the key that you can press to activate the command. For example, on the Insert tab, you can press F to activate the Clip Art task pane.

Figure 5.27

KeyTips indicate that keyboard control of the Ribbon is active

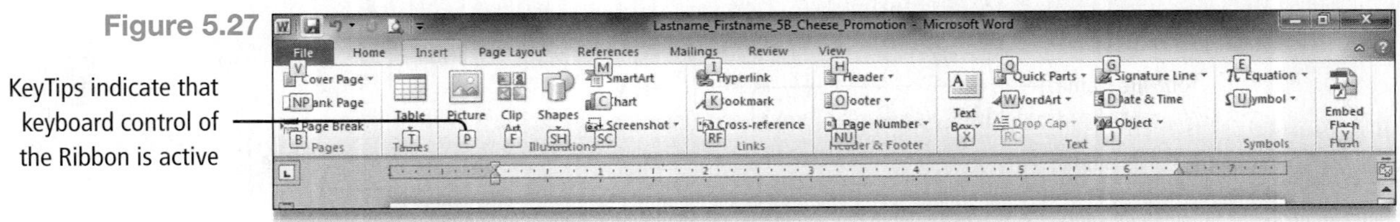

2 Press Esc to redisplay the KeyTips for the tabs. Then, press Alt again to turn off keyboard control of the Ribbon.

3 Point to any tab on the Ribbon and right-click to display a shortcut menu.

Here you can choose to display the Quick Access Toolbar below the Ribbon or minimize the Ribbon to maximize screen space. You can also customize the Ribbon by adding, removing, renaming, or reordering tabs, groups, and commands on the Ribbon, although this is not recommended until you become an expert Office user.

4 Click **Minimize the Ribbon**. Notice that only the Ribbon tabs display. Click the **Home tab** to display the commands. Click anywhere in the document, and notice that the Ribbon reverts to its minimized view.

5 Right-click any Ribbon tab, and then click **Minimize the Ribbon** again to turn the minimize feature off.

Most expert Office users prefer to have the full Ribbon display at all times.

Objective 9 | Apply Formatting in Office Programs

Formatting is the process of establishing the overall appearance of text, graphics, and pages in an Office file—for example, in a Word document.

View the video on the Companion Web Site or in MyITLab

Activity 5.10 | Formatting and Viewing Pages

In this activity, you will practice common formatting techniques used in Office applications.

1 On the Ribbon, click the **Insert tab**, and then in the **Header & Footer group**, click the **Footer** button.

2 At the top of the displayed gallery, under **Built-In**, click **Blank**. At the bottom of your document, with *Type text* highlighted in blue, using your own name type the file name of this document **Lastname_Firstname_5B_Cheese_Promotion** and then compare your screen with Figure 5.28.

Header & Footer Tools are added to the Ribbon. A ***footer*** is a reserved area for text or graphics that displays at the bottom of each page in a document. Likewise, a ***header*** is a reserved area for text or graphics that displays at the top of each page in a document. When the footer (or header) area is active, the document area is inactive (dimmed).

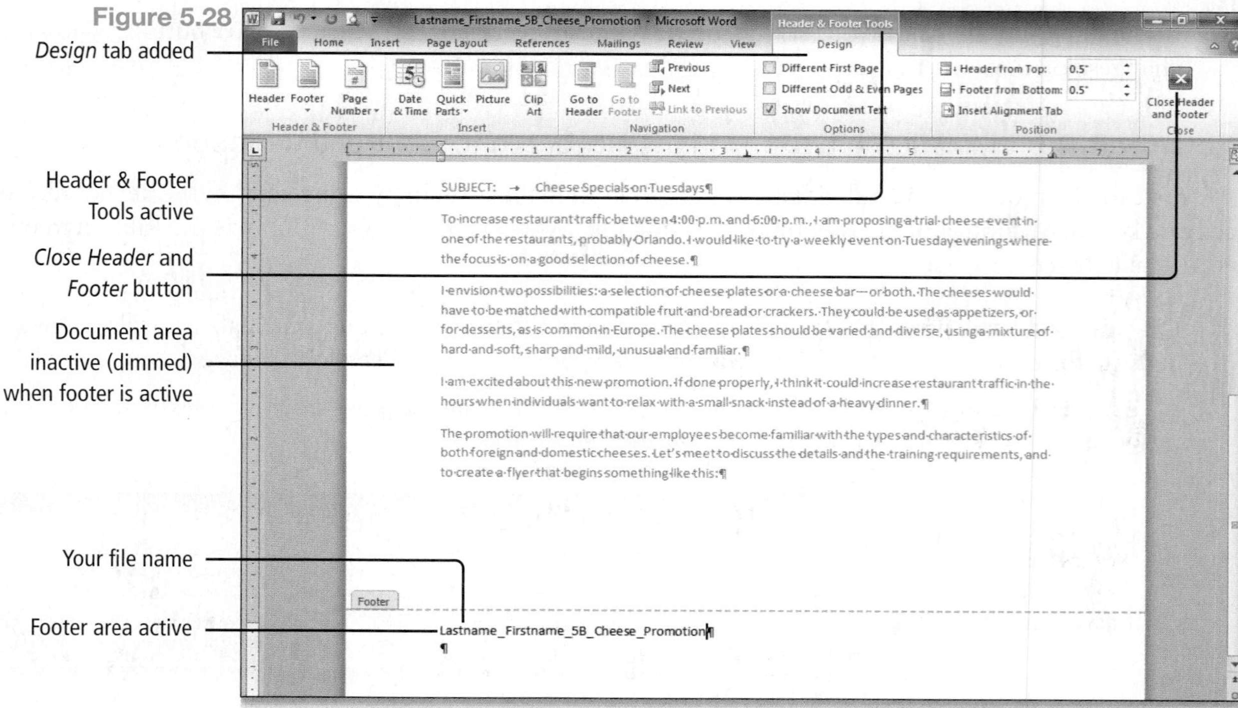

Figure 5.28

3 On the Ribbon, on the **Design tab**, in the **Close group**, click the **Close Header and Footer** button.

4 On the Ribbon, click the **Page Layout tab**. In the **Page Setup group**, click the **Orientation** button, and notice that two orientations display—*Portrait* and *Landscape*. Click **Landscape**.

In ***portrait orientation***, the paper is taller than it is wide. In ***landscape orientation***, the paper is wider than it is tall.

5 In the lower right corner of the screen, locate the **Zoom control** buttons. Drag the **Zoom slider** to the left until you have zoomed to approximately *60%*. Compare your screen with Figure 5.29.

To ***zoom*** means to increase or decrease the viewing area. You can zoom in to look closely at a section of a document, and then zoom out to see an entire page on the screen. You can also zoom to view multiple pages on the screen.

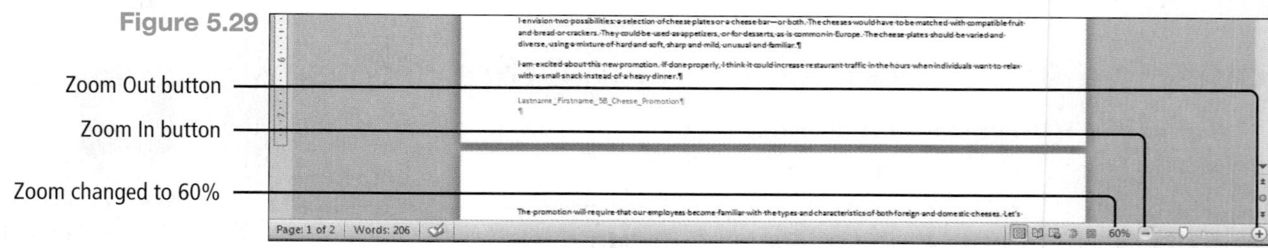

Figure 5.29

6 On the **Page Layout tab**, in the **Page Setup group**, click the **Orientation** button, and then click **Portrait**.

Portrait orientation is commonly used for business documents such as letters and memos.

7 In the lower right corner of your screen, click the **Zoom In** button as many times as necessary to return to the **100%** zoom setting. On the Quick Access Toolbar, click the **Save** button.

Use the zoom feature to adjust the view of your document for editing and for your viewing comfort.

Activity 5.11 | Formatting Text

1 To the left of *Oceana Palm Grill*, point in the margin area to display the [pointer] pointer and click one time to select the entire paragraph. Compare your screen with Figure 5.30.

Use this technique to select complete paragraphs from the margin area. Additionally, with this technique you can drag downward to select multiple-line paragraphs—which is faster and more efficient than dragging through text.

Figure 5.30

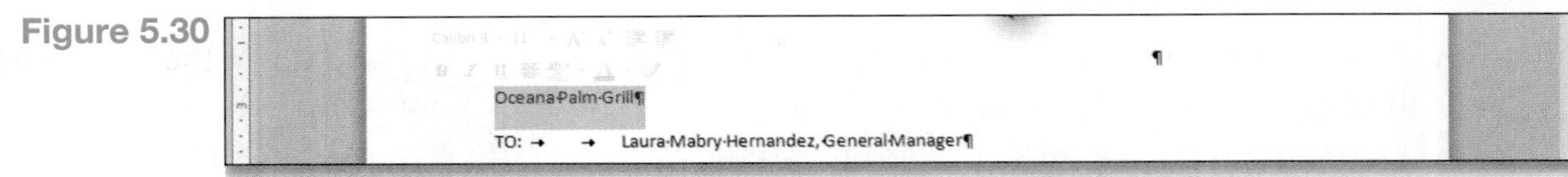

2 On the Ribbon, click the **Home tab**, and then in the **Paragraph group**, click the **Center** button [Center] to center the paragraph.

Alignment refers to the placement of paragraph text relative to the left and right margins. ***Center alignment*** refers to text that is centered horizontally between the left and right margins. You can also align text at the left margin, which is the default alignment for text in Word, or at the right margin.

3 On the **Home tab**, in the **Font group**, click the **Font button arrow** [Calibri (Body)]. At the top of the list, point to **Cambria**, and as you do so, notice that the selected text previews in the Cambria font.

A ***font*** is a set of characters with the same design and shape. The default font in a Word document is Calibri, which is a ***sans serif*** font—a font design with no lines or extensions on the ends of characters. The Cambria font is a ***serif*** font—a font design that includes small line extensions on the ends of the letters to guide the eye in reading from left to right.

The list of fonts displays as a gallery showing potential results. For example, in the Font gallery, you can see the actual design and format of each font as it would look if applied to text.

4 Point to several other fonts and observe the effect on the selected text. Then, at the top of the **Font** gallery, under **Theme Fonts**, click **Cambria**.

A ***theme*** is a predesigned set of colors, fonts, lines, and fill effects that look good together and that can be applied to your entire document or to specific items. A theme combines two sets of fonts—one for text and one for headings. In the default Office theme, Cambria is the suggested font for headings.

5 With the paragraph *Oceana Palm Grill* still selected, on the **Home tab**, in the **Font group**, click the **Font Size button arrow** [11], point to **36**, and then notice how Live Preview displays the text in the font size to which you are pointing. Compare your screen with Figure 5.31.

Figure 5.31

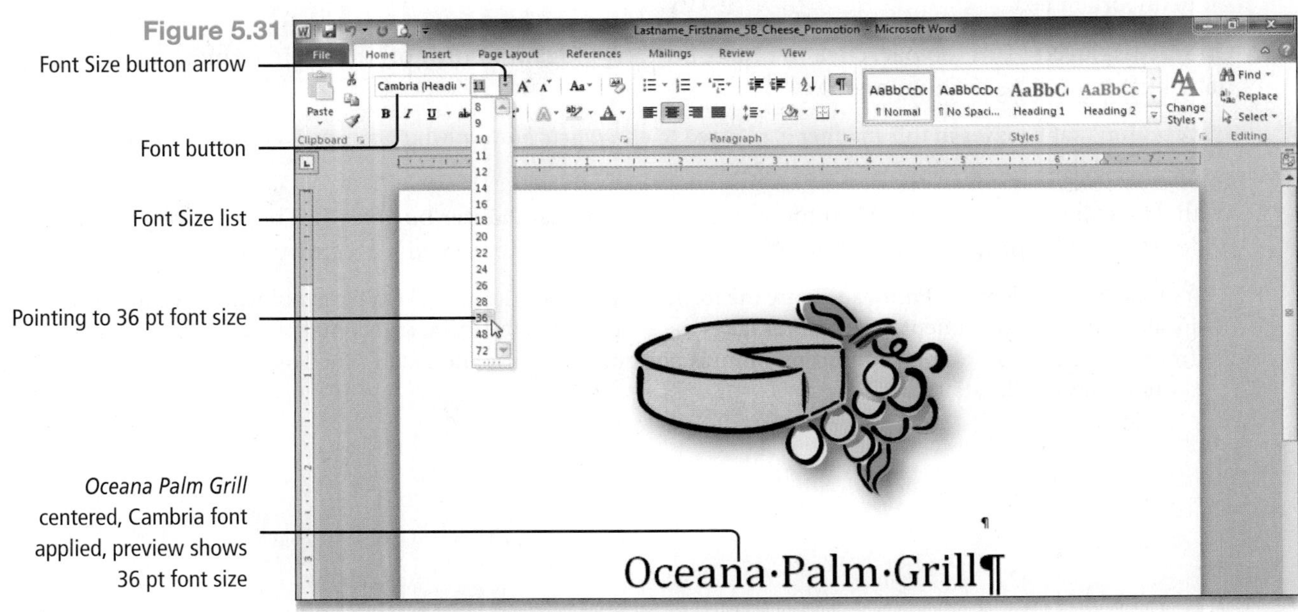

6 On the displayed list of font sizes, click **20**.

Fonts are measured in ***points***, with one point equal to 1/72 of an inch. A higher point size indicates a larger font size. Headings and titles are often formatted by using a larger font size. The word *point* is abbreviated as ***pt***.

7 With *Oceana Palm Grill* still selected, on the **Home tab**, in the **Font group**, click the **Font Color button arrow**. Under **Theme Colors**, in the seventh column, click the last color—**Olive Green, Accent 3, Darker 50%**. Click anywhere to deselect the text.

8 To the left of *TO:*, point in the left margin area to display the pointer, hold down the left mouse button, and then drag down to select the four memo heading lines. Compare your screen with Figure 5.32.

Figure 5.32

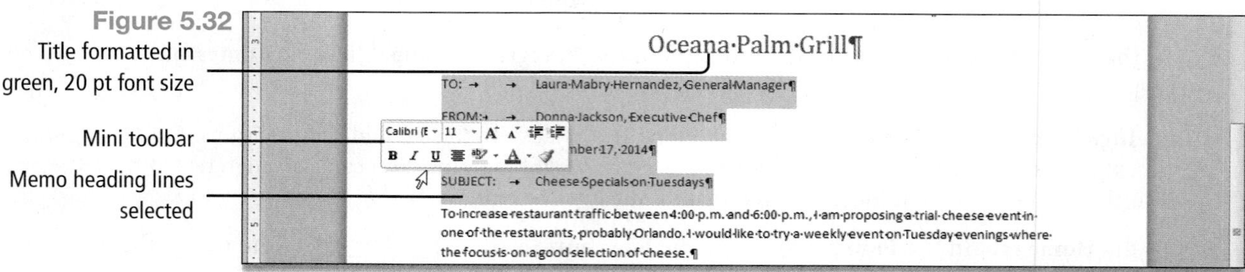

Title formatted in green, 20 pt font size
Mini toolbar
Memo heading lines selected
Oceana·Palm·Grill¶
TO: → → Laura·Mabry·Hernandez,·General·Manager¶
FROM: → → Donna·Jackson,·Executive·Chef¶
SUBJECT: → Cheese·Specials·on·Tuesdays¶
To·increase·restaurant·traffic·between·4:00·p.m.·and·6:00·p.m.,·I·am·proposing·a·trial·cheese·event·in·
one·of·the·restaurants,·probably·Orlando.·I·would·like·to·try·a·weekly·event·on·Tuesday·evenings·where·
the·focus·is·on·a·good·selection·of·cheese.¶

9 With the four paragraphs selected, on the Mini toolbar, click the **Font Color** button, which now displays a dark green bar instead of a red bar.

The font color button retains its most recently used color—Olive Green, Accent 3, Darker 50%.

The purpose of the Mini toolbar is to place commonly used commands close to text or objects that you select. By selecting a command on the Mini toolbar, you reduce the distance that you must move your mouse to access a command.

10 Click anywhere in the paragraph that begins *To increase*, and then ***triple-click***—click the left mouse button three times—to select the entire paragraph. If the entire paragraph is not selected, click in the paragraph and begin again.

11 With the entire paragraph selected, on the Mini toolbar, click the **Font Color button arrow**, and then under **Theme Colors**, in the sixth column, click the first color—**Red, Accent 2**.

12 Select the text *TO:* and then on the displayed Mini toolbar, click the **Bold** button and the **Italic** button.

Font styles include bold, italic, and underline. Font styles emphasize text and are a visual cue to draw the reader's eye to important text.

13 On the displayed Mini toolbar, click the **Italic** button again to turn off the Italic formatting. Notice that the Italic button no longer glows orange.

A button that behaves in this manner is referred to as a ***toggle button***, which means it can be turned on by clicking it once, and then turned off by clicking it again.

14 With *TO:* still selected, on the Mini toolbar, click the **Format Painter** button. Then, move your mouse under the word *Laura*, and notice the mouse pointer. Compare your screen with Figure 5.33.

You can use the ***Format Painter*** to copy the formatting of specific text or of a paragraph and then apply it in other locations in your document. The pointer takes the shape of a paintbrush, and contains the formatting information from the paragraph where the insertion point is positioned. Information about the Format Painter and how to turn it off displays in the status bar.

Figure 5.33

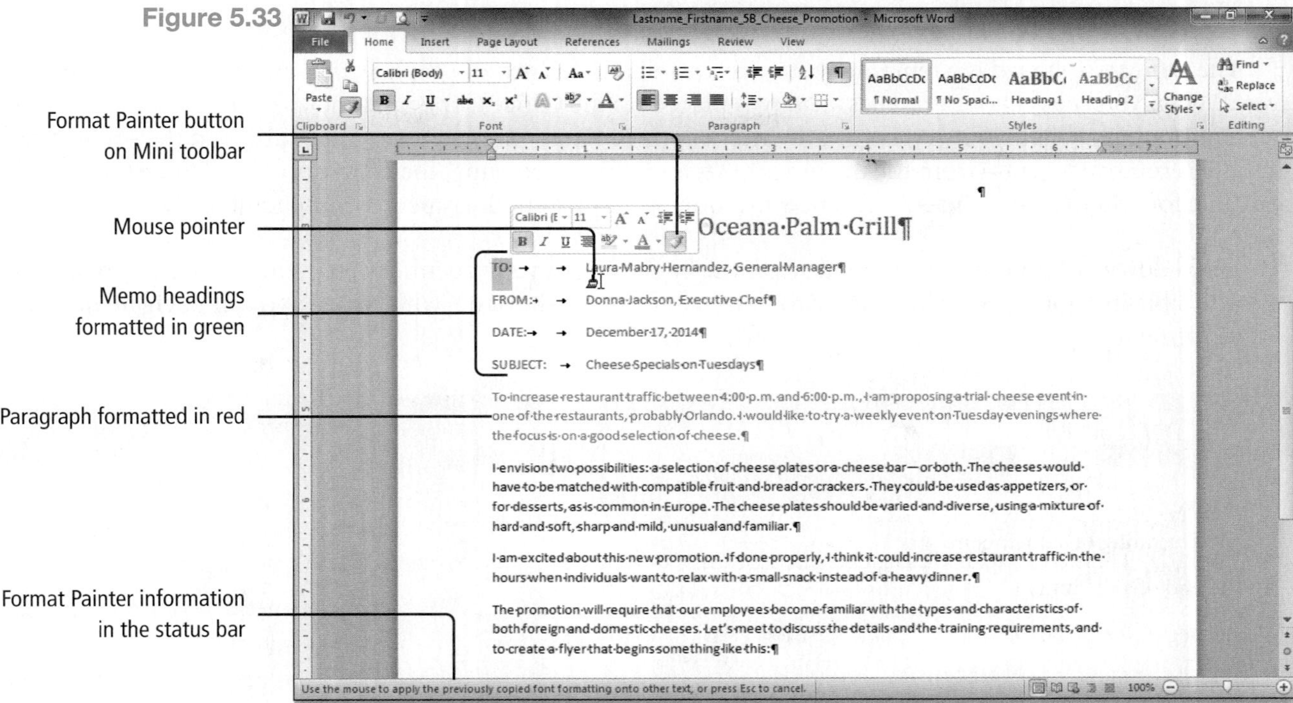

15 With the [Format Painter pointer] pointer, drag to select the text *FROM:* and notice that the Bold formatting is applied. Then, point to the selected text *FROM:* and on the Mini toolbar, *double-click* the **Format Painter** button [Format Painter].

16 Select the text *DATE:* to copy the Bold formatting, and notice that the pointer retains the [Format Painter pointer] shape.

When you *double-click* the Format Painter button, the Format Painter feature remains active until you either click the Format Painter button again, or press Esc to cancel it—as indicated on the status bar.

17 With Format Painter still active, select the text *SUBJECT:*, and then on the Ribbon, on the **Home tab**, in the **Clipboard group**, notice that the **Format Painter** button [Format Painter] is glowing orange, indicating that it is active. Compare your screen with Figure 5.34.

Figure 5.34

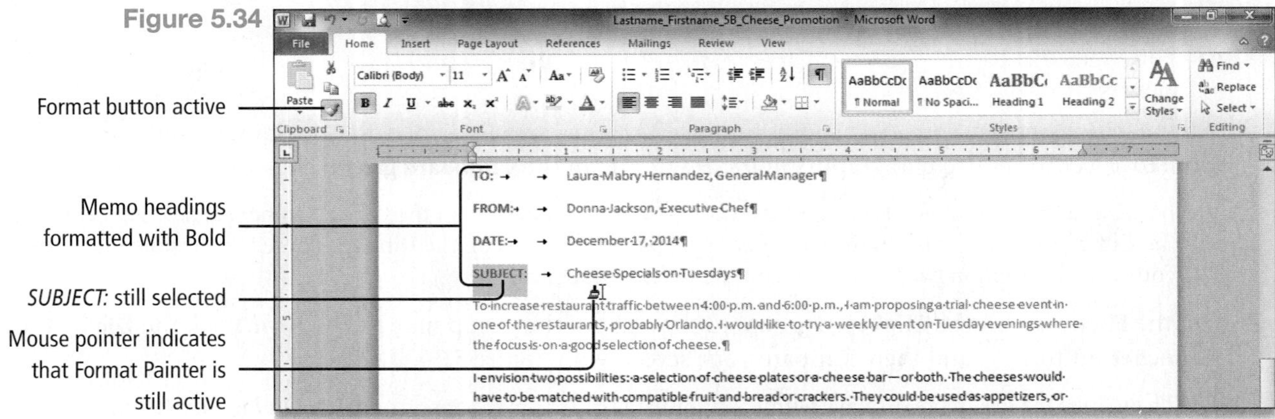

18 Click the **Format Painter** button [Format Painter] on the Ribbon to turn the command off.

19 In the paragraph that begins *To increase*, triple-click again to select the entire paragraph. On the displayed Mini toolbar, click the **Bold** button [B] and the **Italic** button [I]. Click anywhere to deselect.

20 On the Quick Access Toolbar, click the **Save** button [Save].

Activity 5.12 | Using the Office Clipboard to Cut, Copy, and Paste

The ***Office Clipboard*** is a temporary storage area that holds text or graphics that you select and then cut or copy. When you ***copy*** text or graphics, a copy is placed on the Office Clipboard and the original text or graphic remains in place. When you ***cut*** text or graphics, a copy is placed on the Office Clipboard, and the original text or graphic is removed—cut—from the document. After cutting or copying, the contents of the Office Clipboard are available for you to ***paste***—insert—in a new location in the current document, or into another Office file.

1 Hold down Ctrl and press Home to move to the beginning of your document, and then take a moment to study the table in Figure 5.35, which describes similar keyboard shortcuts with which you can navigate quickly in a document.

Keyboard Shortcuts to Navigate in a Document

To Move	Press
To the beginning of a document	Ctrl + Home
To the end of a document	Ctrl + End
To the beginning of a line	Home
To the end of a line	End
To the beginning of the previous word	Ctrl + ←
To the beginning of the next word	Ctrl + →
To the beginning of the current word (if insertion point is in the middle of a word)	Ctrl + ←
To the beginning of a paragraph	Ctrl + ↑
To the beginning of the next paragraph	Ctrl + ↓
To the beginning of the current paragraph (if insertion point is in the middle of a paragraph)	Ctrl + ↑
Up one screen	PageUp
Down one screen	PageDown

Figure 5.35

2 To the left of *Oceana Palm Grill*, point in the left margin area to display the pointer, and then click one time to select the entire paragraph. On the **Home tab**, in the **Clipboard group**, click the **Copy** button.

Because anything that you select and then copy—or cut—is placed on the Office Clipboard, the Copy command and the Cut command display in the Clipboard group of commands on the Ribbon. There is no visible indication that your copied selection has been placed on the Office Clipboard.

3 On the **Home tab**, in the **Clipboard group**, to the right of the group name *Clipboard*, click the **Dialog Box Launcher** button, and then compare your screen with Figure 5.36.

The Clipboard task pane displays with your copied text. In any Ribbon group, the ***Dialog Box Launcher*** displays either a dialog box or a task pane related to the group of commands. It is not necessary to display the Office Clipboard in this manner, although sometimes it is useful to do so. The Office Clipboard can hold 24 items.

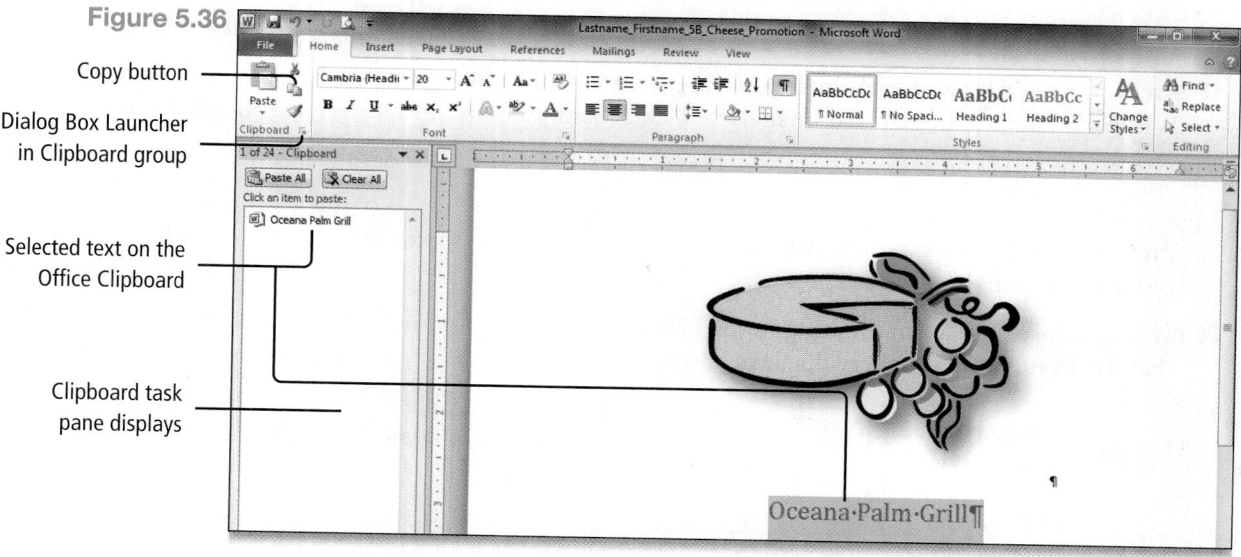

Figure 5.36

4 In the upper right corner of the **Clipboard** task pane, click the **Close** button [X].

5 Press Ctrl + End to move to the end of your document. Press Enter one time to create a new blank paragraph. On the **Home tab**, in the **Clipboard group**, point to the **Paste** button, and then click the *upper* portion of this split button.

The Paste command pastes the most recently copied item on the Office Clipboard at the insertion point location. If you click the lower portion of the Paste button, a gallery of Paste Options displays.

6 Click the **Paste Options** button that displays below the pasted text as shown in Figure 5.37.

Here you can view and apply various formatting options for pasting your copied or cut text. Typically you will click Paste on the Ribbon and paste the item in its original format. If you want some other format for the pasted item, you can do so from the ***Paste Options*** gallery. The Paste Options gallery provides a Live Preview of the various options for changing the format of the pasted item with a single click.

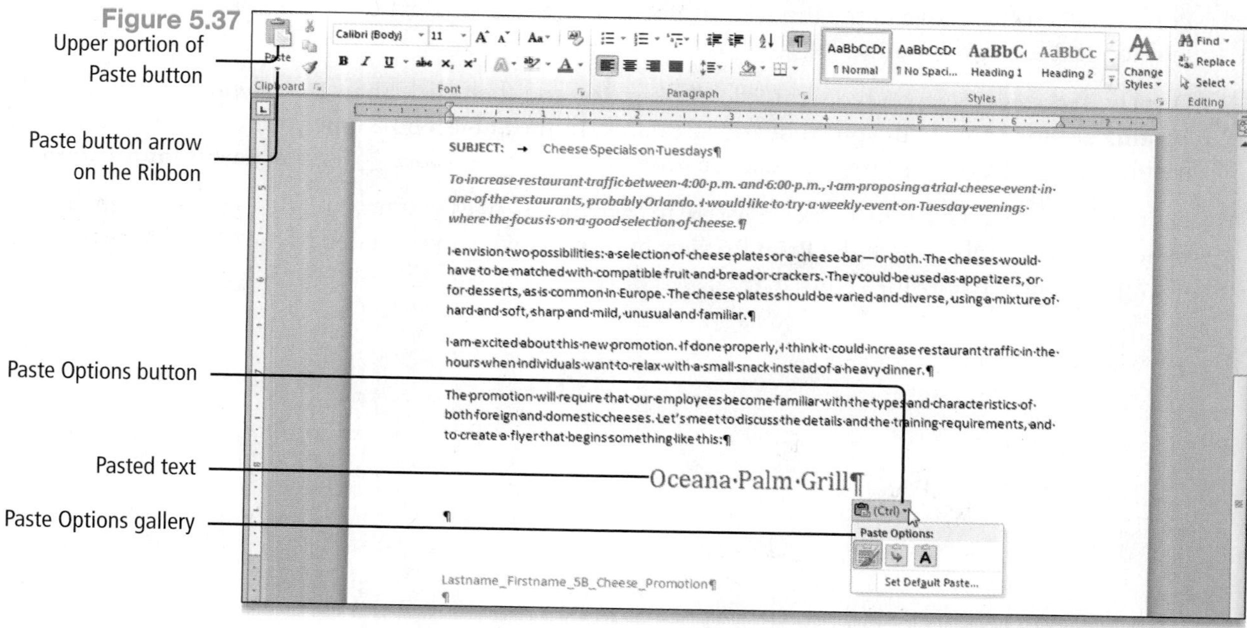

Figure 5.37

7 In the displayed **Paste Options** gallery, *point* to each option to see the Live Preview of the format that would be applied if you clicked the button.

The contents of the Paste Options gallery are contextual; that is, they change based on what you copied and where you are pasting.

8 Press Esc to close the gallery; the button will remain displayed until you take some other screen action.

9 Press Ctrl + Home to move to the top of the document, and then click the **cheese image** one time to select it. While pointing to the selected image, right-click, and then on the shortcut menu, click **Cut**.

Recall that the Cut command cuts—removes—the selection from the document and places it on the Office Clipboard.

10 Press Delete one time to remove the blank paragraph from the top of the document, and then press Ctrl + End to move to the end of the document.

11 With the insertion point blinking in the blank paragraph at the end of the document, right-click, and notice that the **Paste Options** gallery displays on the shortcut menu. Compare your screen with Figure 5.38.

Figure 5.38

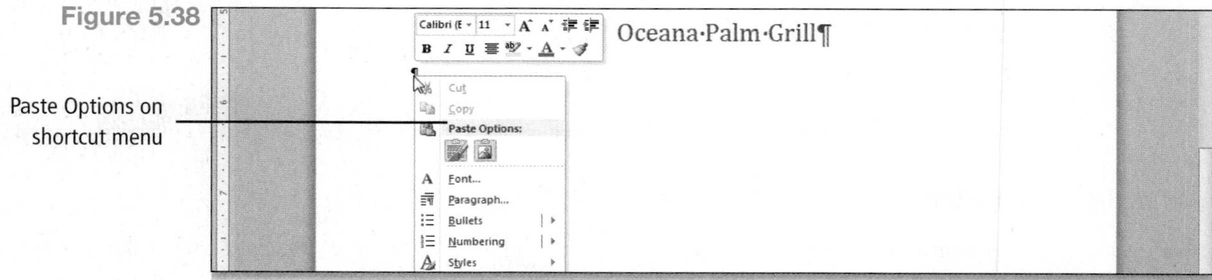

12 On the shortcut menu, under **Paste Options**, click the first button—**Keep Source Formatting**.

13 Click the picture to select it. On the **Home tab**, in the **Paragraph group**, click the **Center** button.

14 Above the cheese picture, click to position the insertion point at the end of the word *Grill*, press Spacebar one time, and then type **Tuesday Cheese Tastings**

Activity 5.13 | Viewing Print Preview and Printing a Word Document

1 Press Ctrl + Home to move to the top of your document. Select the text *Oceana Palm Grill*, and then replace the selected text by typing **Memo**

2 Display **Backstage** view, on the right, click **Properties**, and then click **Show Document Panel**. Replace the existing author name with your first and last name. In the **Subject** box, type your course name and section number, in the **Keywords** box, type **cheese promotion** and then **Close** the **Document Information Panel**.

3 On the Quick Access Toolbar, click **Save** to save the changes you have made to your document. On the Quick Access Toolbar, click the **Print Preview** button, which you added to the Quick Access Toolbar. Compare your screen with Figure 5.39.

Figure 5.39

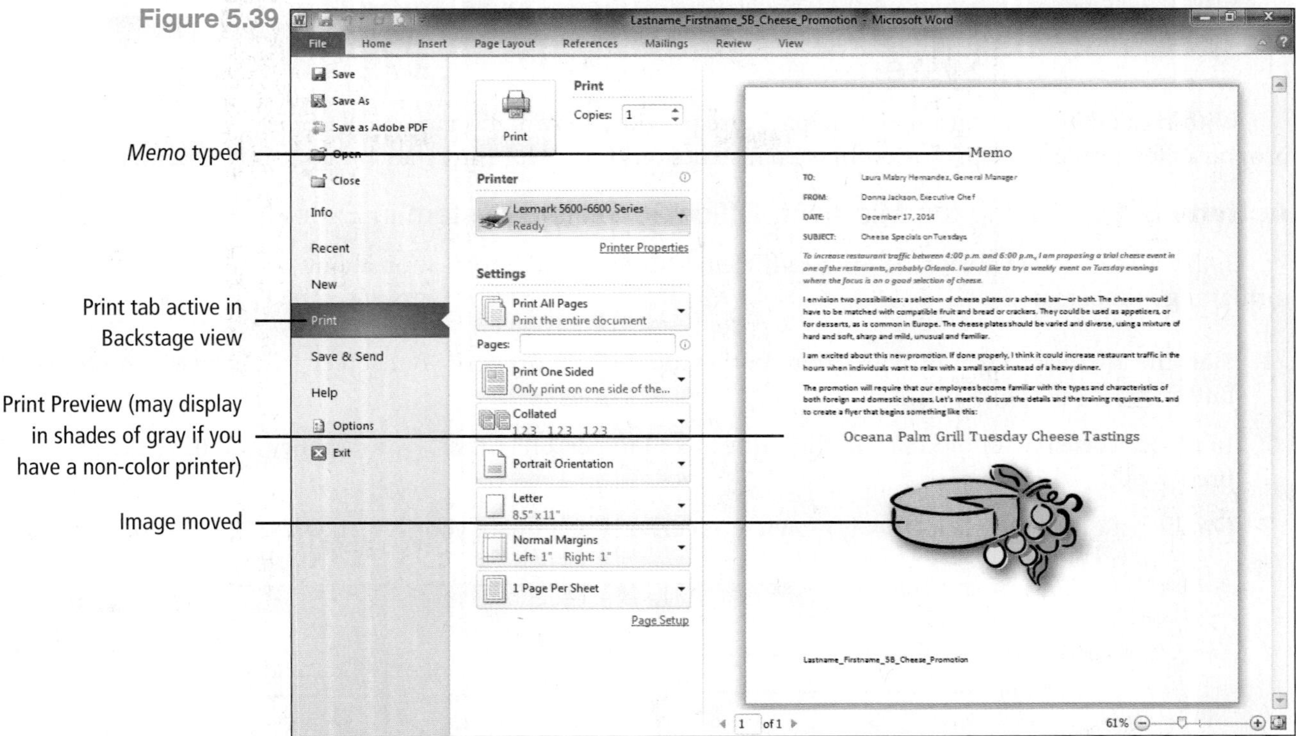

4 Examine the **Print Preview**. Under **Settings**, notice that in **Backstage** view, several of the same commands that are available on the Page Layout tab of the Ribbon also display.

For convenience, common adjustments to Page Layout display here, so that you can make last-minute adjustments without closing Backstage view.

5 If you need to make any corrections, click the Home tab to return to the document and make any necessary changes.

It is good practice to examine the Print Preview before printing or submitting your work electronically. Then, make any necessary corrections, re-save, and redisplay Print Preview.

6 If you are directed to do so, click Print to print the document; or, above the Info tab, click Close, and then submit your file electronically according to the directions provided by your instructor or according to the steps in the Note box below.

If you click the Print button, Backstage view closes and the Word window redisplays.

Note | Create a PDF Instead of a Paper Printout

To create a PDF electronic printout, from Backstage view, on the left, click the Save & Send tab, and then in the File Types group, click Create PDF/XPS Document. Then in the third panel, click the Create PDF/XPS button, navigate to your chapter folder, and then in the lower right corner, click Publish.

7 On the Quick Access Toolbar, point to the **Print Preview icon** you placed there, right-click, and then click **Remove from Quick Access Toolbar**.

If you are working on your own computer and you want to do so, you can leave the icon on the toolbar; in a lab setting, you should return the software to its original settings.

8 At the right end of the title bar, click the program **Close** button. If a message displays asking if you want the text on the Clipboard to be available after you quit Word, click No.

This message most often displays if you have copied some type of image to the Clipboard. If you click Yes, the items on the Clipboard will remain for you to use.

Objective 10 | Use the Microsoft Office 2010 Help System

View the video on the Companion Web Site or in MyITLab

Within each Office program, the Help feature provides information about all of the program's features and displays step-by-step instructions for performing many tasks.

Activity 5.14 | Using the Microsoft Office 2010 Help System in Excel

In this activity, you will use the Microsoft Help feature to find information about formatting numbers in Excel.

1. **Start** the **Microsoft Excel 2010** program. In the upper right corner of your screen, click the **Microsoft Excel Help** button.
2. In the **Excel Help** window, click in the white box in upper left corner, type **currency** and then click **Search** or press Enter.
3. On the list of results, click **Display numbers as currency**. Compare your screen with Figure 5.40.

Figure 5.40

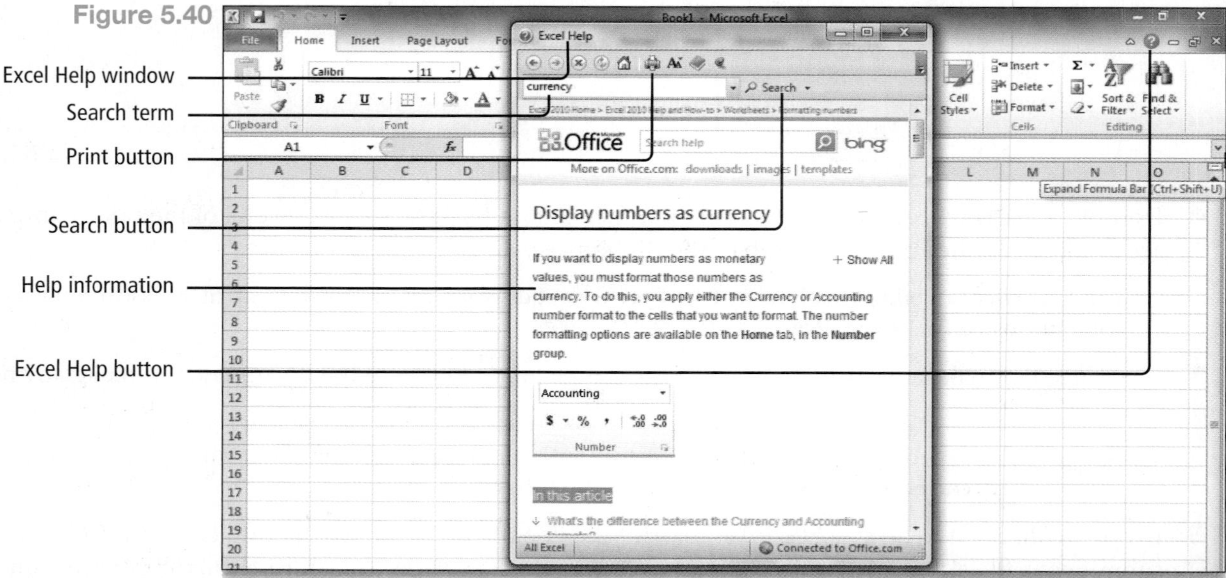

4. If you want to do so, on the toolbar at the top of the **Excel Help** window, click the Print button to print a copy of this information for your reference.
5. On the title bar of the Excel Help window, click the **Close** button. On the right side of the Microsoft Excel title bar, click the **Close** button to close Excel.

Objective 11 | Compress Files

View the video on the Companion Web Site or in MyITLab

A ***compressed file*** is a file that has been reduced in size. Compressed files take up less storage space and can be transferred to other computers faster than uncompressed files. You can also combine a group of files into one compressed folder, which makes it easier to share a group of files.

Activity 5.15 | Compressing Files

In this activity, you will combine the two files you created in this chapter into one compressed file.

1. On the Windows taskbar, click the **Start** button, and then on the right, click **Computer**. Navigate to your **All In One Chapter 5** folder.

2 In the **file list**, click your **Lastname_Firstname_5A_Menu_Plan** file one time to select it. Hold down Ctrl, and then click your **Lastname_Firstname_5B_Cheese_Promotion** file to select both files. Release Ctrl.

In any Windows-based program, holding down Ctrl while selecting enables you to select multiple items.

3 Point anywhere over the two selected files and right-click. On the shortcut menu, point to **Send to**, and then compare your screen with Figure 5.41.

Figure 5.41

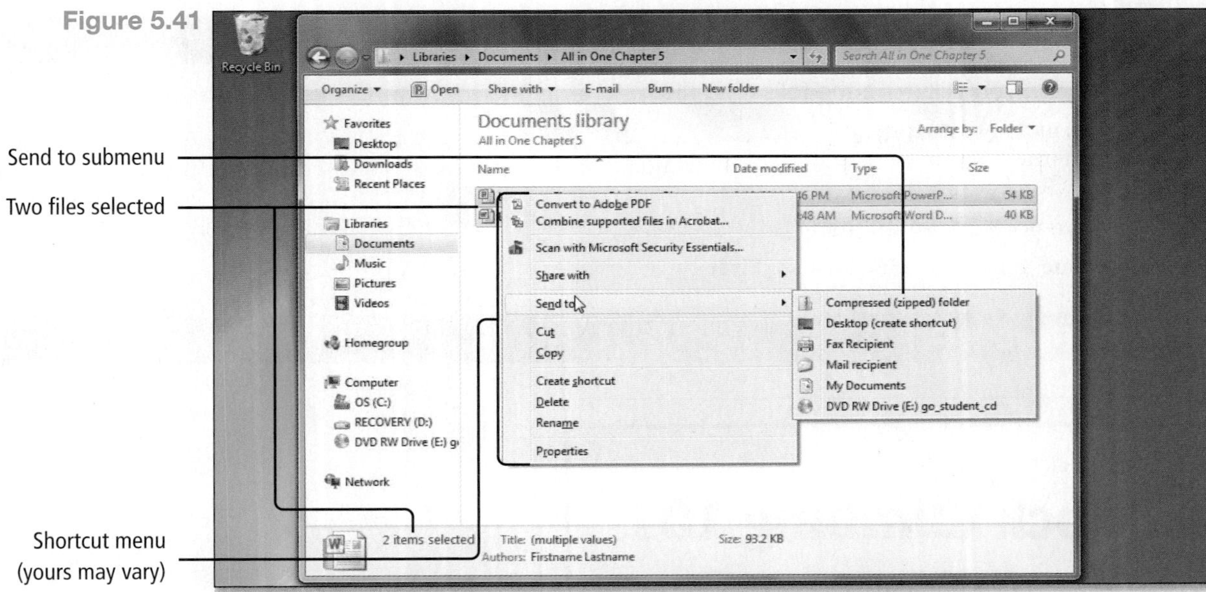

4 On the shortcut submenu, click **Compressed (zipped) folder**.

Windows creates a compressed folder containing a *copy* of each of the selected files. The folder name is the name of the file or folder to which you were pointing, and is selected—highlighted in blue—so that you can rename it.

5 Using your own name, type **Lastname_Firstname_Chapter_5** and press Enter.

The compressed folder is now ready to attach to an e-mail or share in some other electronic format.

6 **Close** the folder window. If directed to do so by your instructor, submit your compressed folder electronically.

More Knowledge | Extracting Compressed Files

Extract means to decompress, or pull out, files from a compressed form. When you extract a file, an uncompressed copy is placed in the folder that you specify. The original file remains in the compressed folder.

End **You have completed Project 5B**

Project 5C Flyer

Project Activities

In Activities 5.16 through 5.27, you will create a flyer announcing a new rock climbing class offered by the Physical Education Department at Laurel College. Your completed document will look similar to Figure 5.42.

Project Files

For Project 5C, you will need the following files:

New blank Word document
w05C_Fitness_Flyer
jpg05C_Rock_Climber

You will save your document as:

Lastname_Firstname_5C_Fitness_Flyer

Project Results

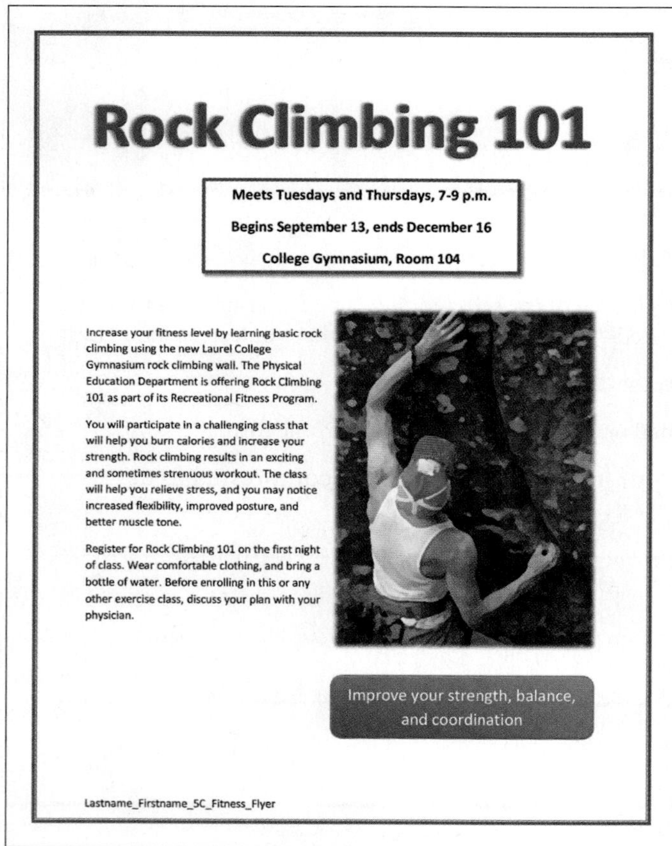

Figure 5.42
Project 5C Fitness Flyer

Objective 12 | Create a New Document and Insert Text

When you create a new document, you can type all of the text, or you can type some of the text and then insert additional text from another source.

View the video on the Companion Web Site or in MyITLab

Activity 5.16 | Starting a New Word Document and Inserting Text

1 **Start** Word and display a new blank document. On the **Home tab**, in the **Paragraph group**, if necessary click the Show/Hide button ¶ so that it is active to display the formatting marks. If the rulers do not display, click the View tab, and then in the Show group, select the Ruler check box.

2 Type **Rock Climbing 101** and then press Enter two times. As you type the following text, press the Spacebar only one time at the end of a sentence: **Increase your fitness level by learning basic rock climbing using the new Laurel College Gymnasium rock climbing wall. The Physical Education Department is offering Rock Climbing 101 as part of its Recreational Fitness Program.**

As you type, the insertion point moves to the right, and when it approaches the right margin, Word determines whether the next word in the line will fit within the established right margin. If the word does not fit, Word moves the entire word down to the next line. This feature is called ***wordwrap*** and means that you press Enter *only* when you reach the end of a paragraph—it is not necessary to press Enter at the end of each line of text.

Note | Spacing Between Sentences

Although you might have learned to add two spaces following end-of-sentence punctuation, the common practice now is to space only one time at the end of a sentence.

3 Press Enter one time. Take a moment to study the table in Figure 5.43 to become familiar with the default document settings in Microsoft Word, and then compare your screen with Figure 5.44.

Default Document Settings in a New Word Document

Setting	Default format
Font and font size	The default font is Calibri and the default font size is 11.
Margins	The default left, right, top, and bottom page margins are 1 inch.
Line spacing	The default line spacing is 1.15, which provides slightly more space between lines than single spacing does—an extra 1/6 of a line added between lines.
Paragraph spacing	The default spacing after a paragraph is 10 points, which is slightly less than the height of one blank line of text.
View	The default view is Print Layout view, which displays the page borders and displays the document as it will appear when printed.

Figure 5.43

Figure 5.44

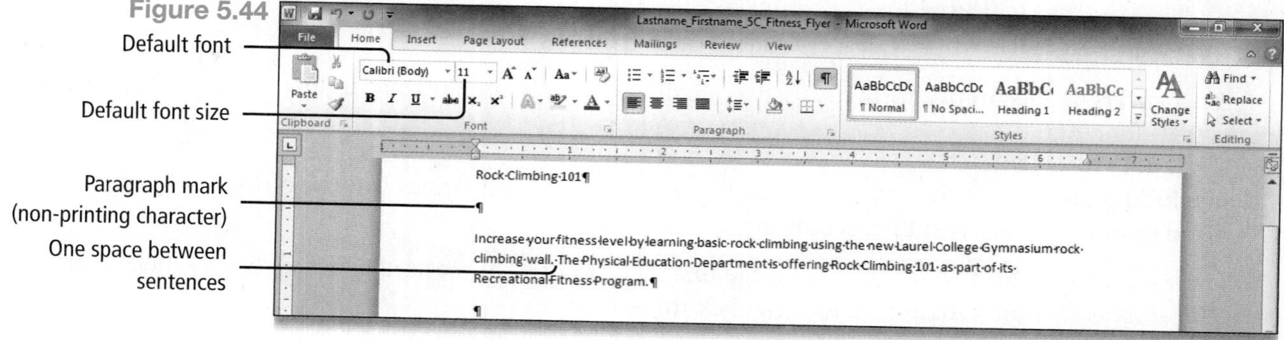

4 On the Ribbon, click the **Insert tab**. In the **Text group**, click the **Object button arrow**, and then click **Text from File**.

> **Alert! | Does the Object Dialog Box Display?**
>
> If the Object dialog box displays, you probably clicked the Object *button* instead of the Object *button arrow*. Close the Object dialog box, and then in the Text group, click the Object button arrow, as shown in Figure 5.45. Click *Text from File*, and then continue with Step 5.

5 In the **Insert File** dialog box, navigate to the student files that accompany this textbook, locate and select **w05C_Fitness_Flyer**, and then in the lower right corner of the dialog box, click **Insert**. Compare your screen with Figure 5.45.

A *copy* of the text from the w05C_Fitness_Flyer file displays at the insertion point location; the text is not removed from the original file.

Figure 5.45

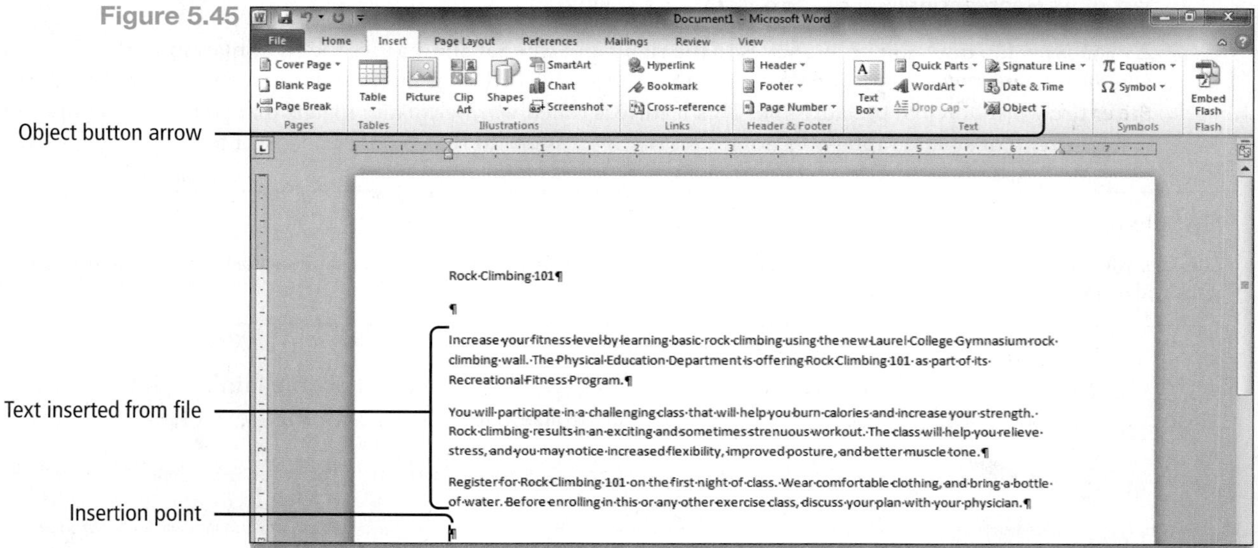

6 On the **Quick Access Toolbar**, click the **Save** button. In the **Save As** dialog box, navigate to your **All in One Chapter 5** folder. In the **File name** box, replace the existing text with **Lastname_Firstname_5C_Fitness_Flyer** and then click **Save**.

Objective 13 | Insert and Format Graphics

View the video on the Companion Web Site or in MyITLab

To add visual interest to a document, insert ***graphics***. Graphics include pictures, clip art, charts, and ***drawing objects***—shapes, diagrams, lines, and so on. For additional visual interest, you can convert text to an attractive graphic format; add, resize, move, and format pictures; and add an attractive page border.

Activity 5.17 | Formatting Text Using Text Effects

Text effects are decorative formats, such as shadowed or mirrored text, text glow, 3-D effects, and colors that make text stand out.

1 Including the paragraph mark, select the first paragraph of text—*Rock Climbing 101*. On the **Home tab**, in the **Font group**, click the **Text Effects** button.

2 In the displayed **Text Effects** gallery, in the first row, point to the second effect to display the ScreenTip *Fill - None, Outline - Accent 2* and then click this effect.

3 With the text still selected, in the **Font group**, click in the **Font Size** box to select the existing font size. Type **60** and then press Enter.

When you want to change the font size of selected text to a size that does not display in the Font Size list, type the number in the Font Size box and press Enter to confirm the new font size.

4 With the text still selected, in the **Paragraph group**, click the **Center** button to center the text.

5 With the text still selected, in the **Font group**, click the **Text Effects** button. Point to **Shadow**, and then under **Outer**, in the second row, click the third style—**Offset Left**.

6 With the text still selected, in the **Font group**, click the **Font Color button arrow**. Under **Theme Colors**, in the fourth column, click the first color—**Dark Blue, Text 2**.

7 Click anywhere in the document to deselect the text. **Save** your document, and then compare your screen with Figure 5.46.

Figure 5.46

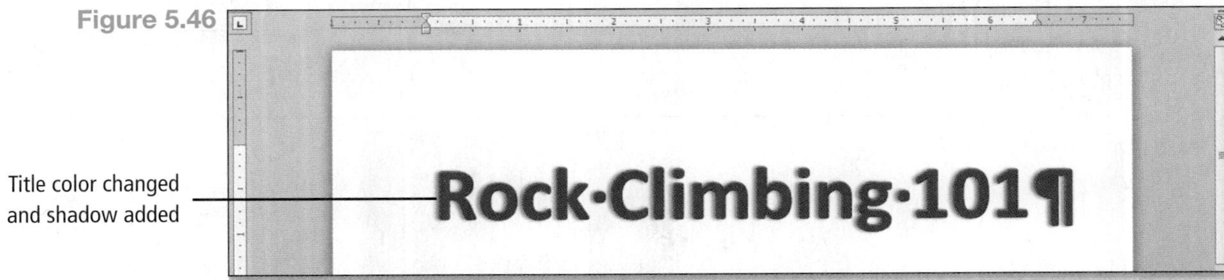

Activity 5.18 | Inserting and Resizing Pictures

1 In the paragraph that begins *Increase your fitness*, click to position the insertion point at the beginning of the paragraph.

2 On the **Insert tab**, in the **Illustrations group**, click the **Picture** button. In the **Insert Picture** dialog box, navigate to your student data files, locate and click **jpg05C_Rock_Climber**, and then click **Insert**.

Word inserts the picture as an ***inline object***; that is, the picture is positioned directly in the text at the insertion point, just like a character in a sentence. Sizing handles surround the picture indicating it is selected.

3 If necessary, scroll to view the entire picture. Notice the round and square sizing handles around the border of the selected picture, as shown in Figure 5.47.

The round corner sizing handles resize the graphic proportionally. The square sizing handles resize a graphic vertically or horizontally only; however, sizing with these will distort the graphic. A green rotate handle, with which you can rotate the graphic to any angle, displays above the top center sizing handle.

Figure 5.47

4 At the lower right corner of the picture, point to the round sizing handle until the pointer displays. Drag upward and to the left until the bottom of the graphic is aligned at approximately **4 inches on the vertical ruler**. Notice that the graphic is proportionally resized.

5 On the **Format tab**, in the **Adjust group**, click the **Reset Picture button arrow**, and then click **Reset Picture & Size**.

6 In the **Size group**, click the **Shape Height spin box up arrow** as necessary to change the height of the picture to **4.5"**. Scroll down to view the entire picture on your screen, compare your screen with Figure 5.48, and then **Save** your document.

When you use the Height and Width ***spin boxes*** to change the size of a graphic, the graphic will always resize proportionally; that is, the width adjusts as you change the height and vice versa.

Figure 5.48

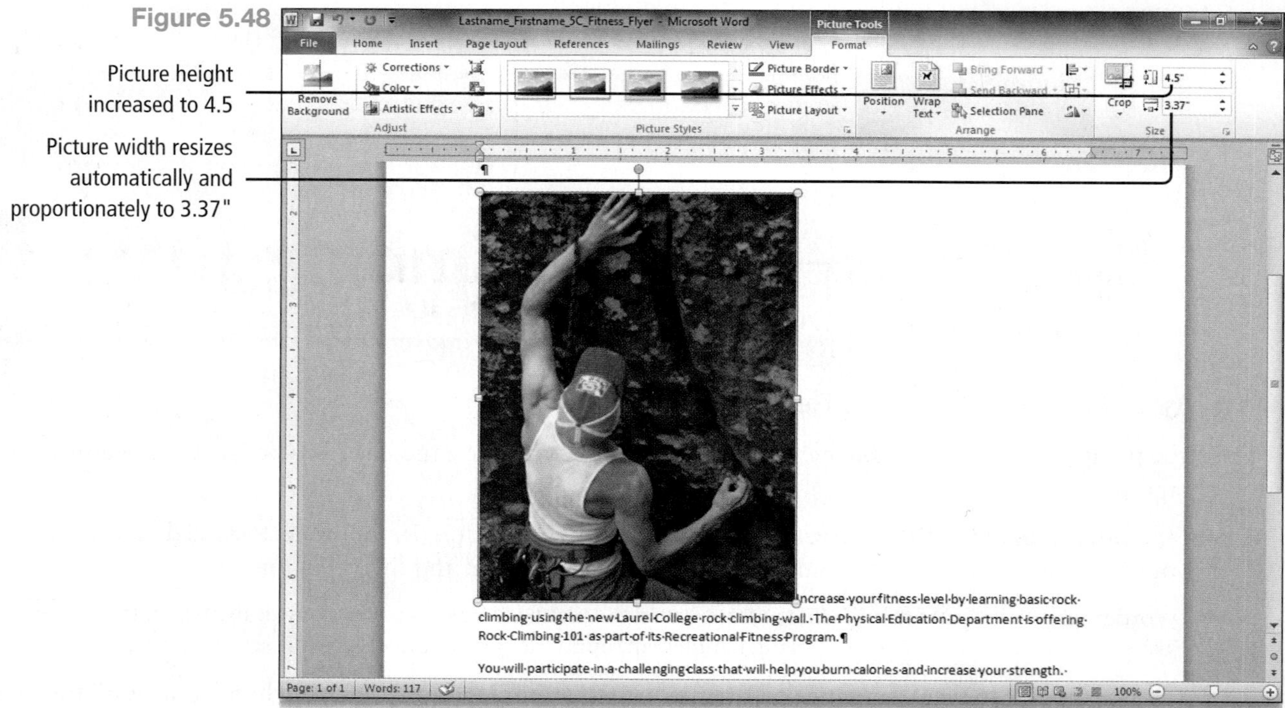

Activity 5.19 | Wrapping Text Around a Picture

Graphics inserted as inline objects are treated like characters in a sentence, which can result in unattractive spacing. You can change an inline object to a ***floating object***—a graphic that can be moved independently of the surrounding text characters.

1 Be sure the picture is selected—you know it is selected if the sizing handles display. On the **Format tab**, in the **Arrange group**, click the **Wrap Text** button to display a gallery of text wrapping arrangements.

Text wrapping refers to the manner in which text displays around an object.

2 From the gallery, click **Square** to wrap the text around the graphic, and then notice the ***anchor*** symbol to the left of the first line of the paragraph. If your anchor displays in white inside the picture, on the keyboard, press ↑ one time. Compare your screen with Figure 5.49.

Select square text wrapping when you want to wrap the text to the left or right of the image. When you apply text wrapping, the object is always associated with—anchored to—a specific paragraph.

Figure 5.49

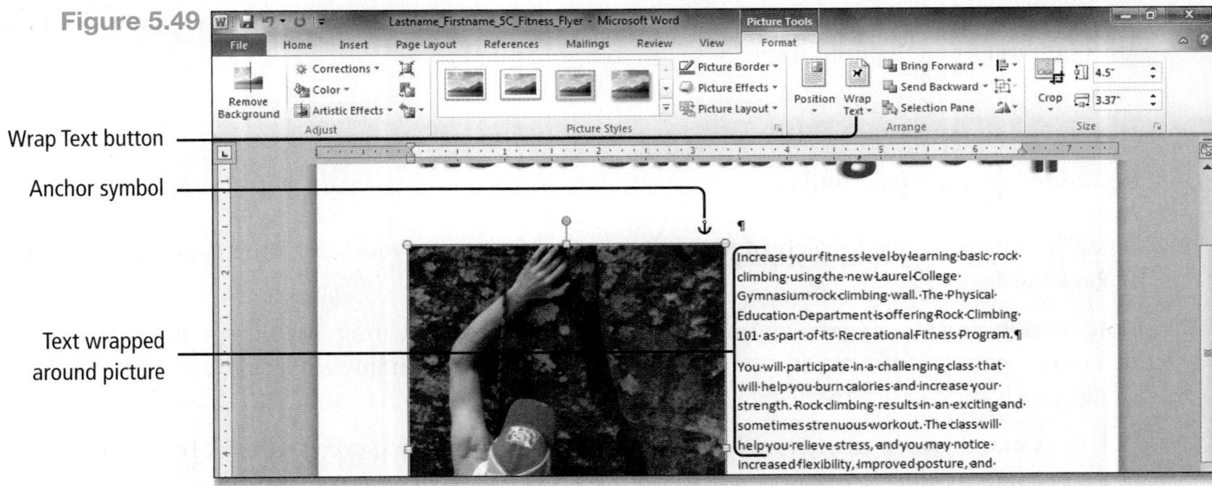

3 **Save** your document.

Activity 5.20 | Moving a Picture

1 Point to the rock climber picture to display the pointer.

2 Hold down Shift and drag the picture to the right until the right edge of the picture aligns at **6.5 inches on the horizontal ruler**. Notice that the picture moves in a straight line when you hold down Shift. Compare your screen with Figure 5.50.

Figure 5.50

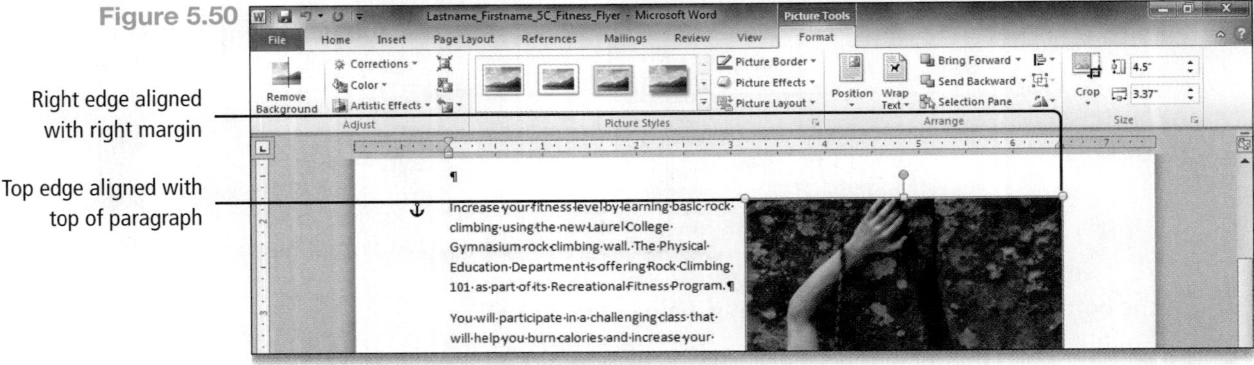

3 If necessary, press any of the arrow keys on your keyboard to ***nudge***—move in small increments—the picture in any direction so that the text wraps to match Figure 5.50. **Save** your document.

Activity 5.21 | Applying Picture Styles and Artistic Effects

Picture styles include shapes, shadows, frames, borders, and other special effects with which you can stylize an image. ***Artistic effects*** are formats that make pictures look more like sketches or paintings.

1 Be sure the rock climber picture is selected. On the **Format tab**, in the **Picture Styles group**, click the **Picture Effects** button. Point to **Soft Edges**, and then click **5 Point**.

The Soft Edges feature fades the edges of the picture. The number of points you choose determines how far the fade goes inward from the edges of the picture.

2 On the **Format tab**, in the **Adjust group**, click the **Artistic Effects** button. In the first row of the gallery, point to, but do not click, the third effect—**Pencil Grayscale**.

Live Preview displays the picture with the *Pencil Grayscale* effect added.

3 In the second row of the gallery, click the third effect—**Paint Brush**. Notice that the picture looks like a painting, rather than a photograph. **Save** your document.

Activity 5.22 | Adding a Page Border

Page borders frame a page and help to focus the information on the page.

1 Click anywhere outside the picture to deselect it. On the **Page Layout tab**, in the **Page Background group**, click the **Page Borders** button.

2 In the **Borders and Shading** dialog box, under **Setting**, click **Box**. Under **Style**, scroll down the list about a third of the way and click the heavy top line with the thin bottom line—check the **Preview** area to be sure the heavier line is the nearest to the edges of the page.

3 Click the **Color arrow**, and then in the fourth column, click the first color—**Dark Blue, Text 2**.

4 Under **Apply to**, be sure *Whole document* is selected, and then compare your screen with Figure 5.51.

Figure 5.51

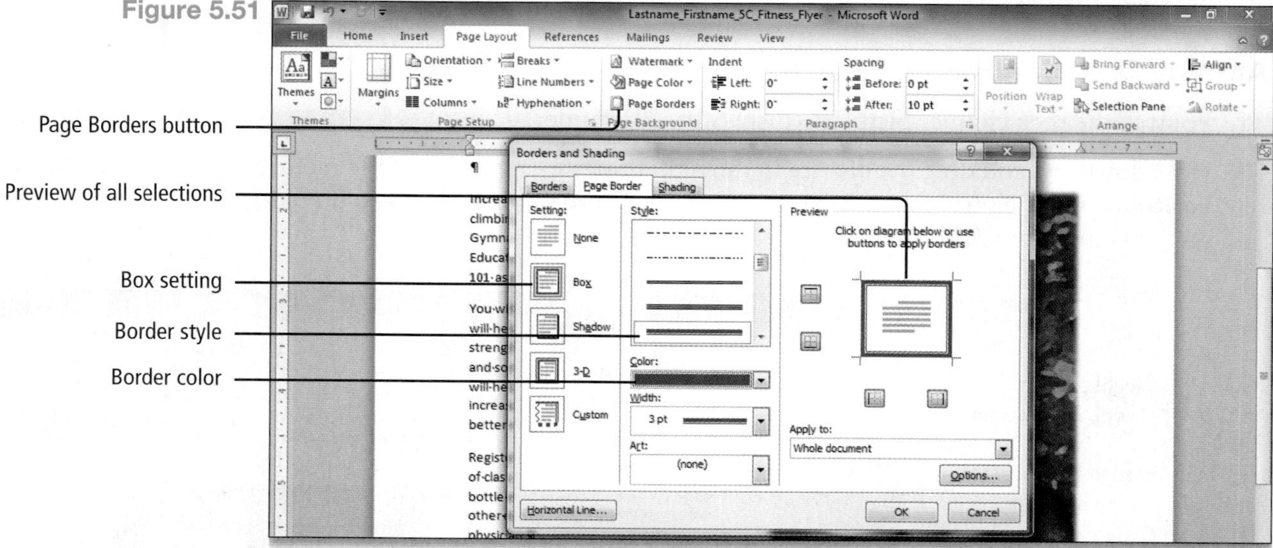

5 At the bottom of the **Borders and Shading** dialog box, click **OK**.

6 Press Ctrl + Home and then, if necessary, scroll up to view the top edge of your document. Compare your page border with Figure 5.52. **Save** your document.

Figure 5.52

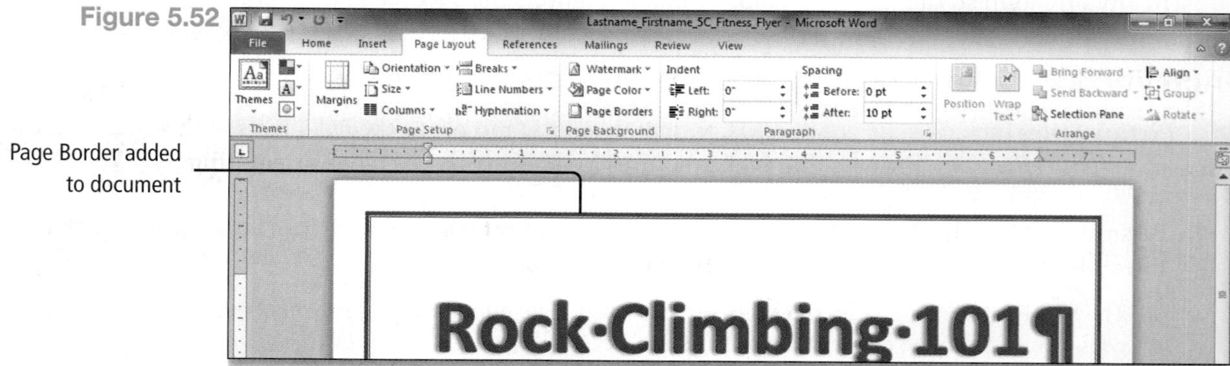

Objective 14 | Insert and Modify Text Boxes and Shapes

View the video on the Companion Web Site or in MyITLab

Word provides predefined ***shapes*** and ***text boxes*** that you can add to your documents. A shape is an object such as a line, arrow, box, callout, or banner. A text box is a movable, resizable container for text or graphics. Use these objects to add visual interest to your document.

Activity 5.23 | Inserting a Shape

1 Press ↓ one time to move the insertion point to the blank paragraph below the title. Press Enter four times to make space for a text box, and notice that the picture anchored to the paragraph moves with the text.

2 Press Ctrl + End to move to the bottom of the document, and notice that your insertion point is positioned in the empty paragraph at the end of the document.

3 Click the **Insert tab**, and then in the **Illustrations group**, click the **Shapes** button to display the gallery. Compare your screen with Figure 5.53.

Figure 5.53

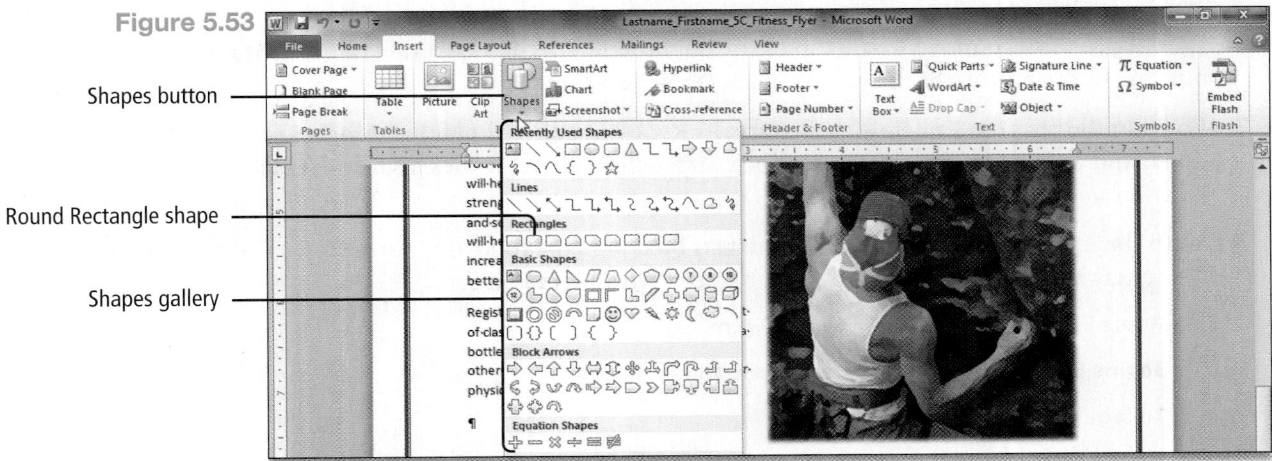

4 Under **Rectangles**, click the second shape—**Rounded Rectangle**, and then move your pointer. Notice that the + pointer displays.

5 Position the + pointer just under the lower left corner of the picture, and then drag down approximately **1 inch** and to the right edge of the picture. See Figure 5.55 as a guide, but the measurements need not be precise.

6 Point to the shape and right-click, and then on the shortcut menu, click **Add Text**. With the insertion point blinking inside the shape, point inside the shape and right-click, and then on the Mini toolbar, change the **Font Size** to **16**, and be sure **Center** alignment is selected.

7 Click inside the shape again, and then type **Improve your strength, balance, and coordination** If necessary, use the lower middle sizing handle to enlarge the shape to view your text. Compare your screen with Figure 5.54. **Save** your document.

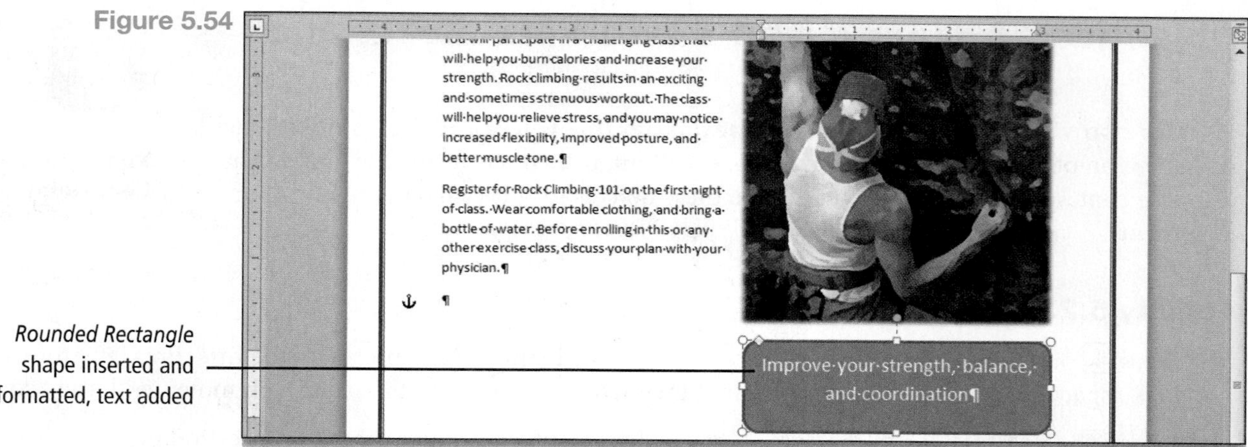

Figure 5.54

Activity 5.24 | Inserting a Text Box

A text box is useful to differentiate portions of text from other text on the page. You can move a text box anywhere on the page.

1. Press Ctrl + Home to move to the top of the document. On the **Insert tab**, in the **Text group**, click the **Text Box** button. At the bottom of the gallery, click **Draw Text Box**.
2. Position the pointer below the letter *k* in *Rock*—at approximately **1.5 inches on the vertical ruler**. Drag down and to the right to create a text box approximately **1.5 inches** high and **3 inches** wide—the exact size and location need not be precise.
3. With the insertion point blinking in the text box, type the following, pressing Enter after each line to create a new paragraph, and then compare your screen with Figure 5.55:

   Meets Tuesdays and Thursdays, 7-9 p.m.

   Begins September 13, ends December 16

   College Gymnasium, Room 104

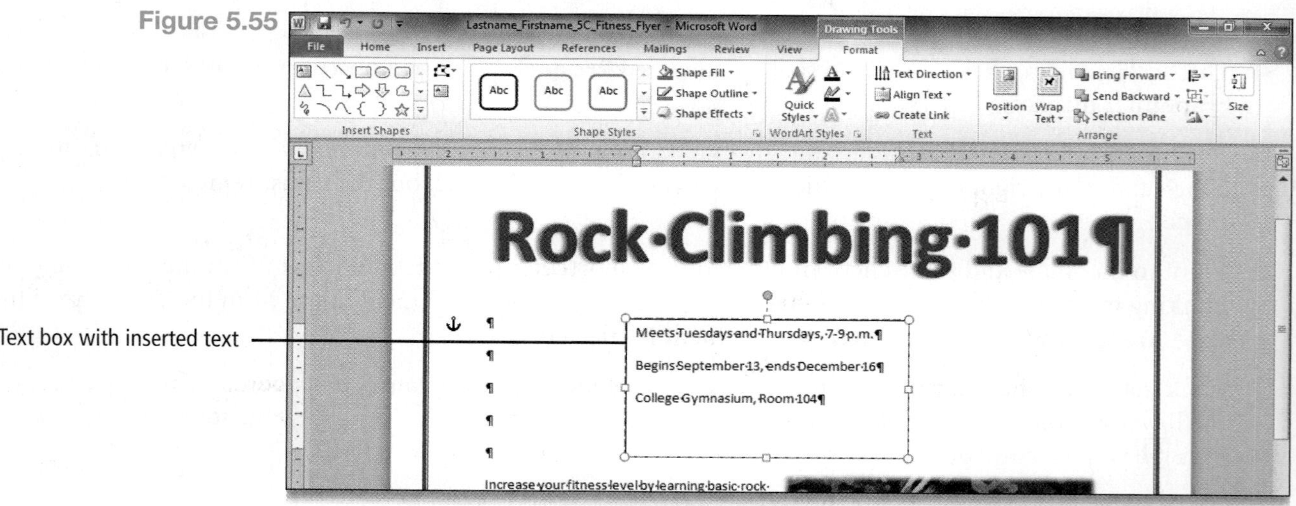

Figure 5.55

4. **Save** your document.

Activity 5.25 | Moving, Resizing, and Formatting Shapes and Text Boxes

1 In the text box you just created in the upper portion of the flyer, select all of the text. From the Mini toolbar, change the **Font Size** to **14**, apply **Bold** [B], and then **Center** [≡] the text.

2 On the **Format tab**, in the **Size group**, if necessary, click the **Size** button. Click the **Shape Height spin arrows** [1.5"] as necessary to set the height of the text box to **1.2"**. Click the **Shape Width spin arrows** [1.37"] as necessary to set the width of the text box to **4"**.

3 In the **Shape Styles group**, click the **Shape Effects** button. Point to **Shadow**, and then under **Outer**, in the first row, click the first style—**Offset Diagonal Bottom Right**.

4 In the **Shape Styles group**, click the **Shape Outline** button. In the fourth column, click the first color—**Dark Blue, Text 2** to change the color of the text box border. Click the **Shape Outline** button again, point to **Weight**, and then click **3 pt**.

5 Click anywhere in the document to deselect the text box. Notice that with the text box deselected, the full rulers redisplay.

6 Click anywhere in the text box and point to the text box border to display the [move] pointer. By dragging, visually center the text box vertically and horizontally in the space below the *Rock Climbing 101* title. Then, if necessary, press any of the arrow keys on your keyboard to nudge the text box in precise increments to match Figure 5.56.

Figure 5.56

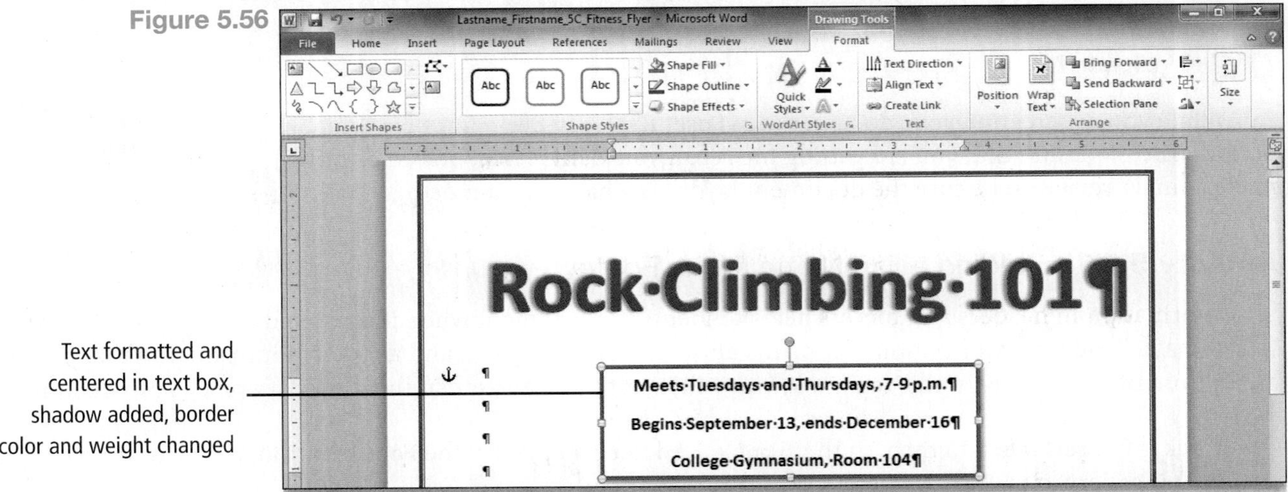

7 Press Ctrl + End to move to the bottom of the document. Click on the border of the rounded rectangular shape to select it.

8 On the **Format tab**, in the **Size group**, if necessary, click the **Size** button. Click the **Shape Height spin arrows** [1.5"] as necessary to change the height of the shape to **0.8"**.

9 In the **Shape Styles group**, click the **Shape Fill** button, and then at the bottom of the gallery, point to **Gradient**. Under **Dark Variations**, in the third row click the first gradient—**Linear Diagonal - Bottom Left to Top Right**.

10 In the **Shape Styles group**, click the **Shape Outline** button. In the sixth column, click the first color—**Red, Accent 2**.

11 Click the **Shape Outline** button again, point to **Weight**, and then click **1 1/2 pt**. Click anywhere in the document to deselect the shape. Compare your screen with Figure 5.57, and then **Save** [save] your document.

Figure 5.57

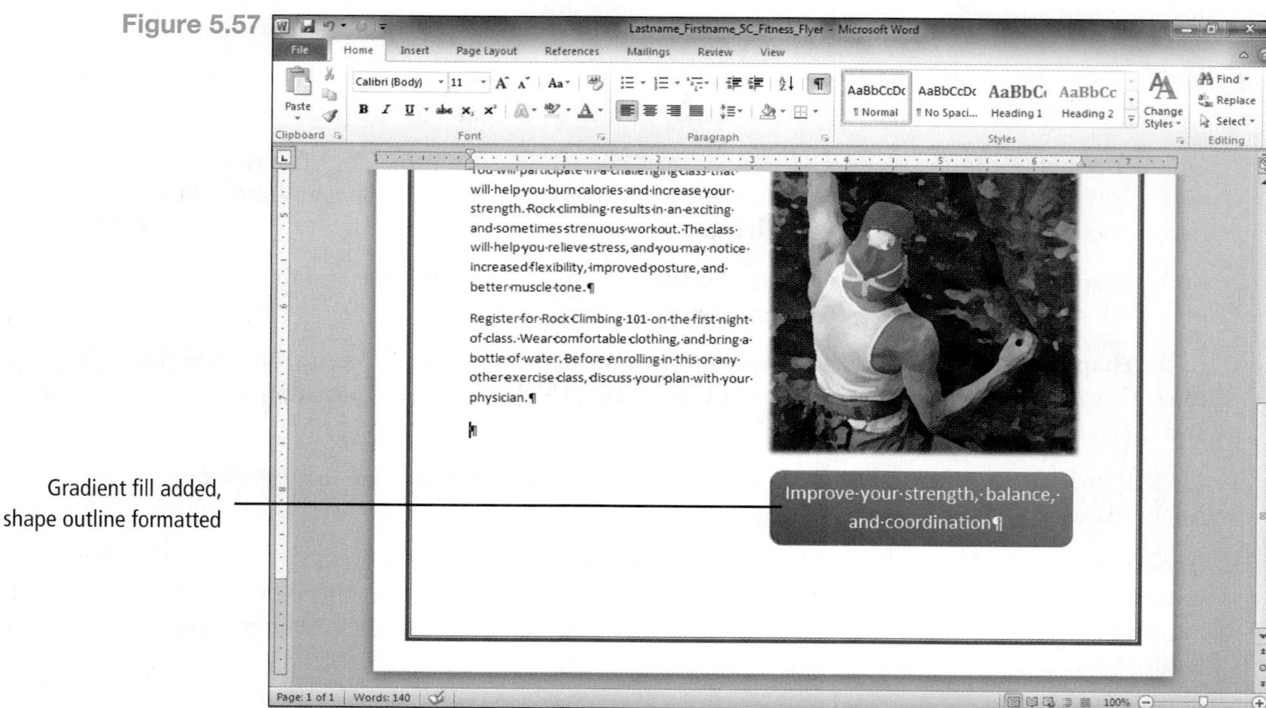

Objective 15 | Preview and Print a Document

While you are creating your document, it is useful to preview your document periodically to be sure that you are getting the result you want. Then, before printing, make a final preview to be sure the document layout is what you intended.

View the video on the Companion Web Site or in MyITLab

Activity 5.26 | Adding a File Name to the Footer

Information in headers and footers helps to identify a document when it is printed or displayed electronically. Recall that a header is information that prints at the top of every page, and a footer is information that prints at the bottom of every page. In this textbook, you will insert the file name in the footer of every Word document.

1 Click the **Insert tab**, and then, in the **Header & Footer group**, click the **Footer** button. At the bottom of the **Footer** gallery, click **Edit Footer**.

The footer area displays with the insertion point blinking at the left edge, and on the Ribbon, the Header & Footer Tools display and add the Design tab.

2 On the **Design tab**, in the **Insert group**, click the **Quick Parts** button, and then click **Field**. In the **Field** dialog box, under **Field names**, use the vertical scroll bar to examine the items that you can insert in a header or footer.

A ***field*** is a placeholder that displays preset content such as the current date, the file name, a page number, or other information already stored by your computer.

3 In the **Field names** list, scroll as necessary to locate and then click **FileName**. Compare your screen with Figure 5.58.

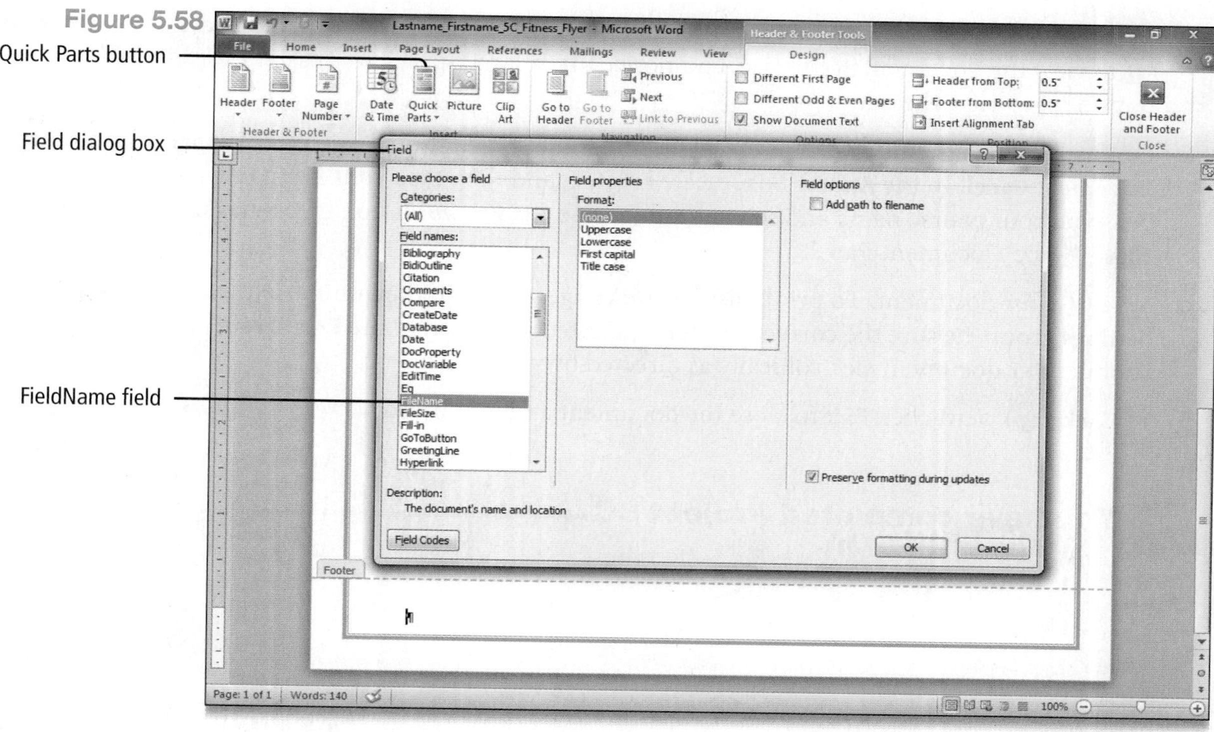

Figure 5.58

4 In the lower right corner of the **Field** dialog box, click **OK**, and then compare your screen with Figure 5.59.

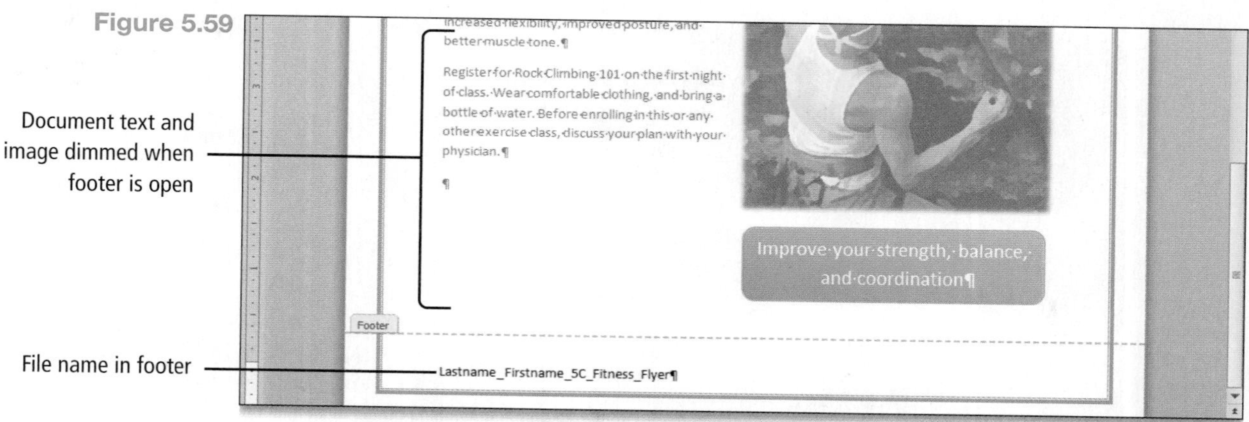

Figure 5.59

5 On the **Design tab**, at the far right in the **Close group**, click the **Close Header and Footer** button. **Save** your document.

When the body of the document is active, the footer text is dimmed—displays in gray. Conversely, when the footer area is active, the footer text is not dimmed; instead, the document text is dimmed.

Activity 5.27 | Previewing and Printing a Document

To ensure that you are getting the result you want, it is useful to periodically preview your document. Then, before printing, make a final preview to be sure the document layout is what you intended.

1 Press Ctrl + Home to move the insertion point to the top of the document. In the upper left corner of your screen, click the **File tab** to display **Backstage** view, and then on the left, click the **Print tab** to display the **Print Preview**.

The Print tab in Backstage view displays the tools you need to select your settings. On the right, Print Preview displays your document exactly as it will print; the formatting marks do not display.

2 In the lower right corner of the **Print Preview**, notice the zoom buttons that display. Click the **Zoom In** button to view the document at full size, and notice that a larger preview is easier to read. Click the **Zoom Out** button to view the entire page.

3 On the left, click the **Info tab**. On the right, under the screen thumbnail, click **Properties**, and then click **Show Document Panel**. In the **Author** box, delete any text and then type your firstname and lastname. In the **Subject** box type your course name and section number. In the **Keywords** box type **fitness, rock climbing** and then **Close** the Document Panel.

4 **Save** your document. To print, display **Backstage** view, and then on the left, click the **Print tab**. In the **Settings** group, be sure the correct printer is selected, and then in the **Print group**, click the **Print** button. Or, submit your document electronically as directed by your instructor.

5 In **Backstage** view, click **Exit** to close the document and exit Word.

End **You have completed Project 5C**

Project 5D Information Handout

Project Activities

In Activities 5.28 through 5.38, you will format and add lists to an information handout that describes student activities at Laurel College. Your completed document will look similar to Figure 5.60.

Project Files

For Project 5D, you will need the following file:

w05D_Student_Activities

You will save your document as:

Lastname_Firstname_5D_Student_Activities

Project Results

Every spring, students vote for the President, Vice President, Treasurer, Secretary, and Student Trustee for the following year. Executive Officers work with the college administration to manage campus activities and to make changes to policies and procedures. For example, the Student Trustee is a
consists of elected members from the
ollege budget, and employee hiring.
he Board to vote for a proposal to
ations in Laurelton and outlying areas.
bs and academic organizations vote for
information and applications on the
pus and in the student newspaper.
nterests, including academic, political,
urrently in existence at Laurel College. A
a club, you may enjoy being a member
you may decide to take a leadership role
e in the Campus Center, Room CC208, or
complete the form online. Clubs accept
ollowing are the first meeting dates and
October 8, 2:00 p.m., Room CC214
tober 5, 5:00 p.m., Computer Café
, 3:00 p.m., Field House, Room 2A
October 6, 2:00 p.m., Room CC212
4:00 p.m., Math Tutoring Lab, L35
October 8, 3:00 p.m., Room CC214
, 5:30 p.m., Photo Lab, Foster Hall
... October 8, 5:00 p.m., Room L24
October 7, 4:30 p.m., Room CC214
ctober 4, 3:00 p.m., Little Theater
ted here, are great, but your goals are
g a degree or certificate. Maybe you want
leave Laurel College. Whatever your
education, work experience, and
ones in which you had a leadership role,

Associated Students of Laurel College

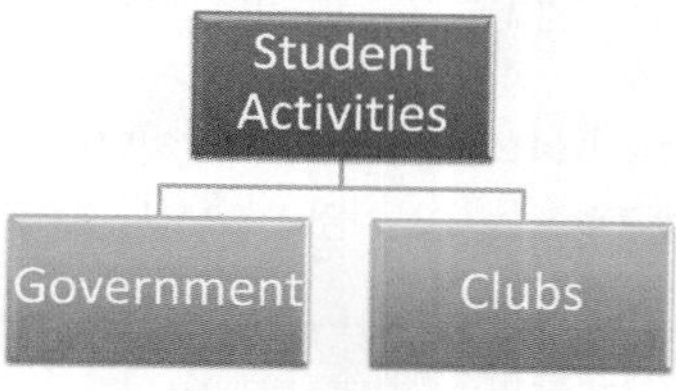

Get Involved in Student Activities

Your experience at Laurel College will be richer and more memorable if you get involved in activities that take you beyond the classroom. You will have the opportunity to meet other students, faculty, and staff members and will participate in organizations that make valuable contributions to your college and to the community.

Consider becoming involved in student government or joining a club. You might take part in activities such as these:

- ✓ Volunteering to help with a blood drive
- ✓ Traveling to a foreign country to learn about other cultures
- ✓ Volunteering to assist at graduation
- ✓ Helping to organize a community picnic
- ✓ Planning and implementing advertising for a student event
- ✓ Meeting with members of the state legislature to discuss issues that affect college students—for example, tuition costs and financial aid

Student Government

As a registered student, you are eligible to attend meetings of the Executive Officers of the Associated Students of Laurel College. At the meetings, you will have the opportunity to learn about college issues that affect students. At the conclusion of each meeting, the Officers invite students to voice their opinions. Eventually, you might decide to run for an office yourself. Running for office is a three-step process:

1. Pick up petitions at the Student Government office.
2. Obtain 100 signatures from current students.
3. Turn in petitions and start campaigning.

Lastname_Firstname_5D_Student_Activities

Figure 5.60
Project 5D Student Activities

Objective 16 | Change Document and Paragraph Layout

View the video on the Companion Web Site or in MyITLab

Document layout includes ***margins***—the space between the text and the top, bottom, left, and right edges of the paper. Paragraph layout includes line spacing, indents, and tabs. In Word, the information about paragraph formats is stored in the paragraph mark at the end of a paragraph. When you press Enter, the new paragraph mark contains the formatting of the previous paragraph, unless you take steps to change it.

Activity 5.28 | Setting Margins

1. **Start** Word. From **Backstage** view, display the **Open** dialog box. From your student files, locate and open the document **w05D_Student_Activities**. On the **Home tab**, in the **Paragraph group**, be sure the **Show/Hide** button is active—glows orange—so that you can view the formatting marks.

2. From **Backstage** view, display the **Save As** dialog box. Navigate to your **All in One Chapter 5** folder, and then **Save** the document as **Lastname_Firstname_5D_Student_Activities**

3. Click the **Page Layout tab**. In the **Page Setup group**, click the **Margins** button, and then take a moment to study the buttons in the Margins gallery.

   The top button displays the most recent custom margin settings, while the other buttons display commonly used margin settings.

4. At the bottom of the **Margins** gallery, click **Custom Margins**. In the **Page Setup** dialog box, press Tab as necessary to select the value in the **Left** box, and then, with *1.25"* selected, type **1**

   This action will change the left margin to 1 inch on all pages of the document. You do not need to type the inch (") mark.

5. Press Tab to select the margin in the **Right** box, and then type **1** At the bottom of the dialog box, notice that the new margins will apply to the **Whole document**. Compare your screen with Figure 5.61.

Figure 5.61

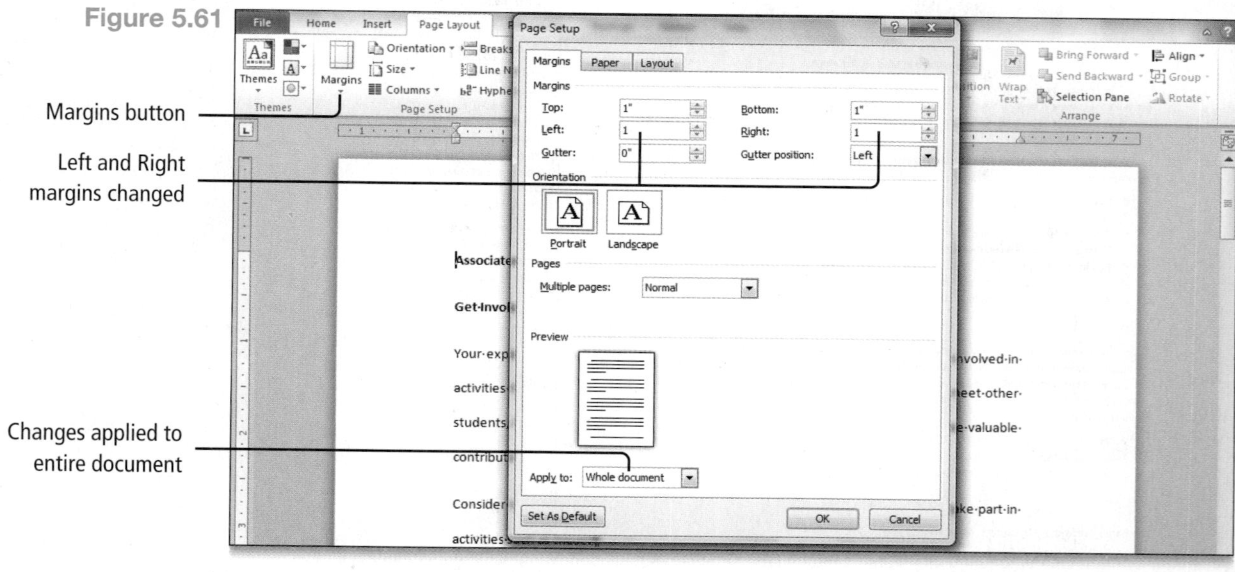

6. Click **OK** to apply the new margins and close the dialog box. If the ruler below the Ribbon is not displayed, at the top of the vertical scroll bar, click the View Ruler button.

7. Scroll to view the bottom of **Page 1** and the top of **Page 2**. Notice that the page edges display, and the page number and total number of pages display on the left side of the status bar.

8. Near the bottom edge of **Page 1**, point anywhere in the bottom margin area, right-click, and then click **Edit Footer** to display the footer area.

9 On the **Design tab**, in the **Insert group**, click the **Quick Parts** button, and then click **Field**. In the **Field** dialog box, under **Field names**, locate and click **FileName**, and then click **OK**.

10 Double-click anywhere in the document to close the footer area, and then **Save** [Save] your document.

Activity 5.29 | Aligning Text

Alignment refers to the placement of paragraph text relative to the left and right margins. Most paragraph text uses ***left alignment***—aligned at the left margin, leaving the right margin uneven. Three other types of paragraph alignment are: ***center alignment***—centered between the left and right margins; ***right alignment***—aligned at the right margin with an uneven left margin; and ***justified alignment***—text aligned evenly at both the left and right margins. See the table in Figure 5.62.

Paragraph Alignment Options

Alignment	Button	Description and Example
Align Text Left	[Align Text Left]	Align Text Left is the default paragraph alignment in Word. Text in the paragraph aligns at the left margin, and the right margin is uneven.
Center	[Center]	Center alignment aligns text in the paragraph so that it is centered between the left and right margins.
Align Text Right	[Align Text Right]	Align Text Right aligns text at the right margin. Using Align Text Right, the left margin, which is normally even, is uneven.
Justify	[Justify]	The Justify alignment option adds additional space between words so that both the left and right margins are even. Justify is often used when formatting newspaper-style columns.

Figure 5.62

1 Scroll to position the middle of **Page 2** on your screen, look at the left and right margins, and notice that the text is justified—both the right and left margins of multiple-line paragraphs are aligned evenly at the margins. On the **Home tab**, in the **Paragraph group**, notice that the **Justify** button [Justify] is active.

2 In the paragraph that begins *Every spring, students vote*, in the first line, look at the space following the word *Every*, and then compare it with the space following the word *Trustee* in the second line. Notice how some of the spaces between words are larger than others.

To achieve a justified right margin, Word adjusts the size of spaces between words in this manner, which can result in unattractive spacing in a document that spans the width of a page. Many individuals find such spacing difficult to read.

3 Press Ctrl + A to select all of the text in the document, and then on the **Home tab**, in the **Paragraph group**, click the **Align Text Left** button [Align Text Left].

4 Press Ctrl + Home. At the top of the document, in the left margin area, point to the left of the first paragraph—*Associated Students of Laurel College*—until the [pointer] pointer displays, and then click one time to select the paragraph. On the Mini toolbar, change the **Font Size** to **26**.

5 Point to the left of the first paragraph—*Associated Students of Laurel College*—to display the [pointer] pointer again, and then drag down to select the first two paragraphs, which form the title and subtitle of the document.

6 On the Mini toolbar, click the **Center** button [Center] to center the title and subtitle between the left and right margins, and then compare your screen with Figure 5.63.

Figure 5.63

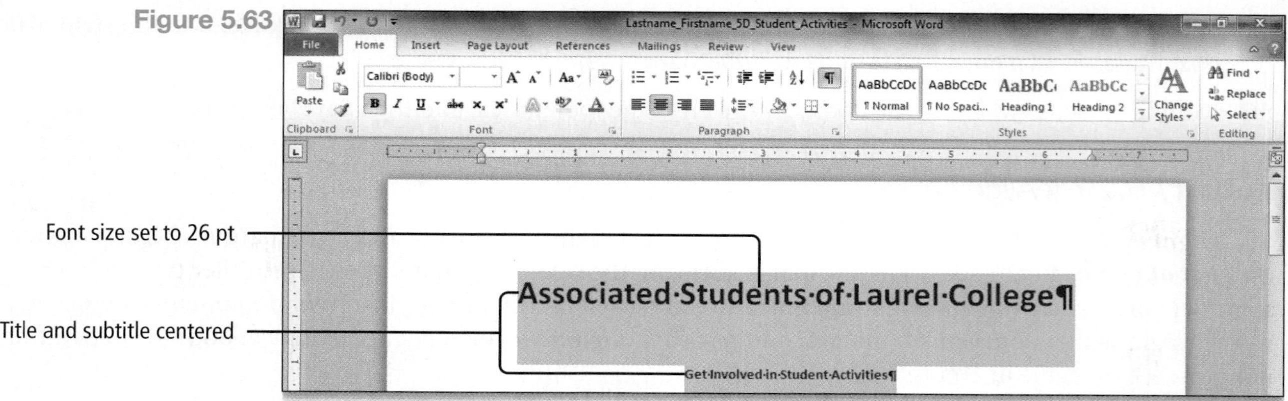

7 Scroll down to view the bottom of **Page 1**, and then locate the first bold subheading—*Student Government.* Point to the left of the paragraph to display the pointer, and then click one time.

8 With *Student Government* selected, use your mouse wheel or the vertical scroll bar to bring the lower portion of **Page 2** into view. Locate the subheading *Clubs*. Move the pointer to the left of the paragraph to display the pointer, hold down Ctrl, and then click one time.

Two subheadings are selected; in Windows-based programs, you can hold down Ctrl to select multiple items.

9 On the Mini toolbar, click the **Center** button to center both subheadings, and then click **Save**.

Activity 5.30 | Changing Line Spacing

Line spacing is the distance between lines of text in a paragraph. Three of the most commonly used line spacing options are shown in the table in Figure 5.64.

Line Spacing Options

Alignment	Description, Example, and Information
Single spacing	**The text in this example uses single spacing**. Single spacing was once the most commonly used spacing in business documents. Now, because so many documents are read on a computer screen rather than on paper, single spacing is becoming less popular.
Multiple 1.15 spacing	**The text in this example uses multiple 1.15 spacing.** The default line spacing in Microsoft Word 2010 is 1.15, which is equivalent to single spacing with an extra 1/6 line added between lines to make the text easier to read on a computer screen. Many individuals now prefer this spacing, even on paper, because the lines of text appear less crowded.
Double spacing	**The text in this example uses double spacing.** College research papers and draft documents that need space for notes are commonly double-spaced; there is space for a full line of text between each document line.

Figure 5.64

1 Press Ctrl + Home to move to the beginning of the document. Press Ctrl + A to select all of the text in the document.

2 With all of the text in the document selected, on the **Home tab**, in the **Paragraph group**, click the **Line Spacing** button, and notice that the text in the document is double spaced—**2.0** is checked. Compare your screen with Figure 5.65.

Figure 5.65

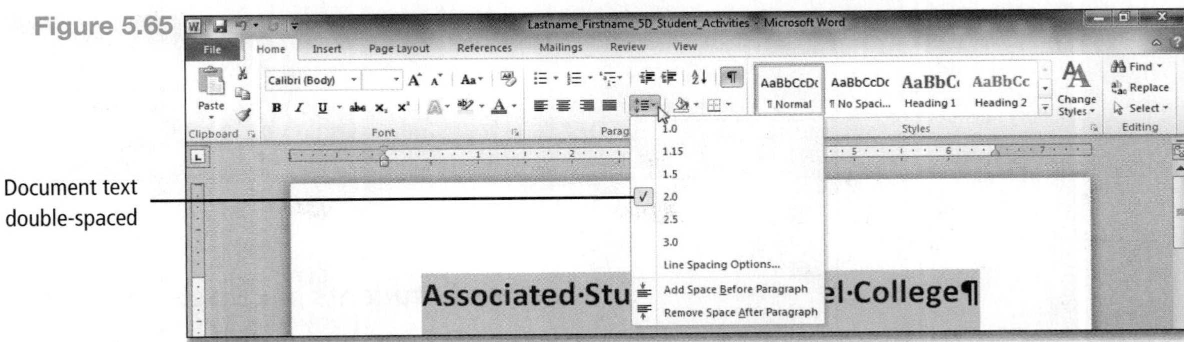

3 On the **Line Spacing** menu, click the *second* setting—**1.15**—and then click anywhere in the document. **Save** your document.

Activity 5.31 | Indenting Text and Adding Space After Paragraphs

Common techniques to distinguish paragraphs include adding space after each paragraph, indenting the first line of each paragraph, or both.

1 Below the title and subtitle of the document, click anywhere in the paragraph that begins *Your experience*. On the **Home tab**, in the **Paragraph group**, click the **Dialog Box Launcher**.

2 In the **Paragraph** dialog box, on the **Indents and Spacing tab**, under **Indentation**, click the **Special arrow**, and then click **First line** to indent the first line by 0.50, which is the default indent setting. Compare your screen with Figure 5.66.

Figure 5.66

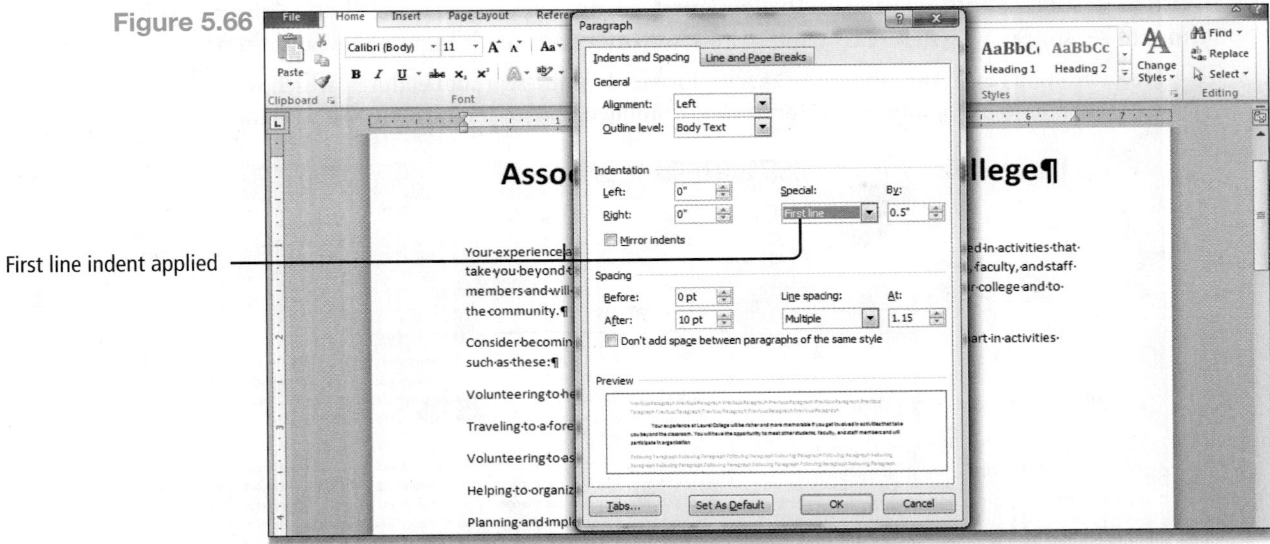

3 Click **OK**, and then click anywhere in the next paragraph, which begins *Consider becoming*. On the ruler under the Ribbon, drag the **First Line Indent** button to **0.5 inches on the horizontal ruler**, and then compare your screen with Figure 5.67.

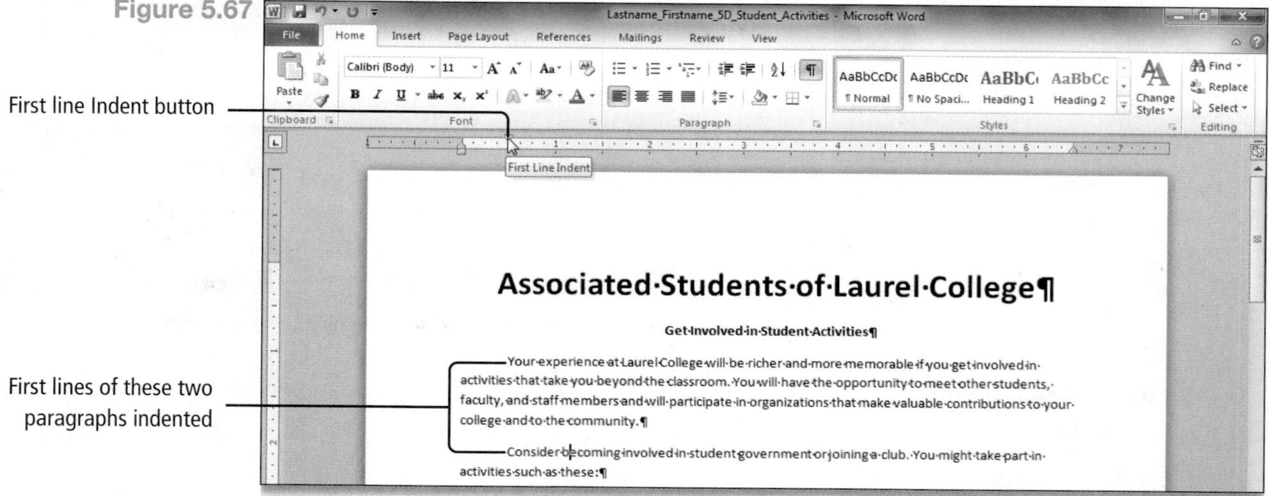

Figure 5.67

4 By using either of the techniques you just practiced, or by using the Format Painter, apply a first line indent of **0.5"** in the paragraph that begins *As a registered* to match the indent of the remaining paragraphs in the document.

5 Press Ctrl + A to select all of the text in the document. Click the **Page Layout tab**, and then in the **Paragraph group**, under **Spacing**, click the **After spin box down arrow** one time to change the value to **6 pt**.

To change the value in the box, you can also select the existing number, type a new number, and then press Enter. This document will use 6 pt spacing after paragraphs.

6 Scroll to view the lower half of **Page 1**. Select the subheading *Student Government*, including the paragraph mark following it, hold down Ctrl, and then select the subheading *Clubs*.

7 With both subheadings selected, in the **Paragraph group**, under **Spacing**, click the **Before up spin box arrow** two times to set the **Spacing Before** to **12 pt**. Compare your screen with Figure 5.68, and then **Save** your document.

This action increases the amount of space above each of the two subheadings, which will make them easy to distinguish in the document. The formatting is applied only to the two selected paragraphs.

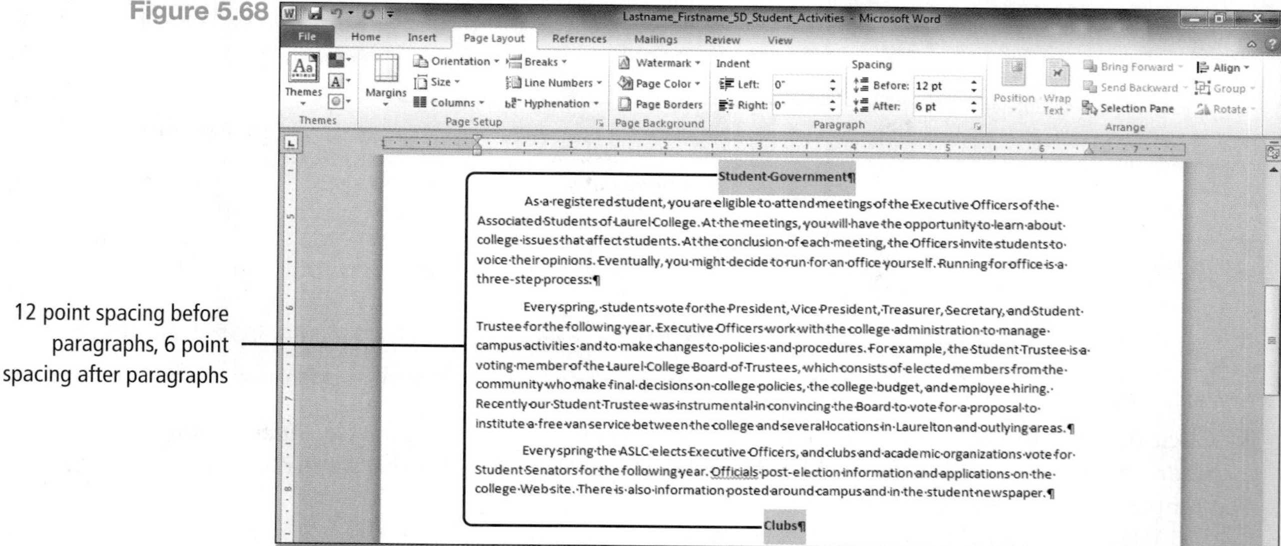

Figure 5.68

Objective 17 | Create and Modify Lists

View the video on the Companion Web Site or in MyITLab

To display a list of information, you can choose a ***bulleted list***, which uses ***bullets***—text symbols such as small circles or check marks—to introduce each item in a list. You can also choose a ***numbered list***, which uses consecutive numbers or letters to introduce each item in a list. Use a bulleted list if the items in the list can be introduced in any order; use a numbered list for items that have definite steps, a sequence of actions, or are in chronological order.

Activity 5.32 | Creating a Bulleted List

1 In the upper portion of **Page 1**, locate the paragraph that begins *Volunteering to help*, and then point to this paragraph from the left margin area to display the pointer. Drag down to select this paragraph and the next five paragraphs.

2 On the **Home tab**, in the **Paragraph group**, click the **Bullets** button to change the selected text to a bulleted list.

The spacing between each of the bulleted points changes to the spacing between lines in a paragraph—in this instance, 1.15 line spacing. The spacing after the last item in the list is the same as the spacing after each paragraph—in this instance, 6 pt. Each bulleted item is automatically indented.

3 On the ruler, point to the **First Line Indent** button and read the ScreenTip, and then point to the **Hanging Indent** button. Compare your screen with Figure 5.69.

By default, Word formats bulleted items with a first line indent of 0.250 and adds a Hanging Indent at 0.50. The hanging indent maintains the alignment of text when a bulleted item is more than one line, for example, the last bulleted item in this list.

Figure 5.69

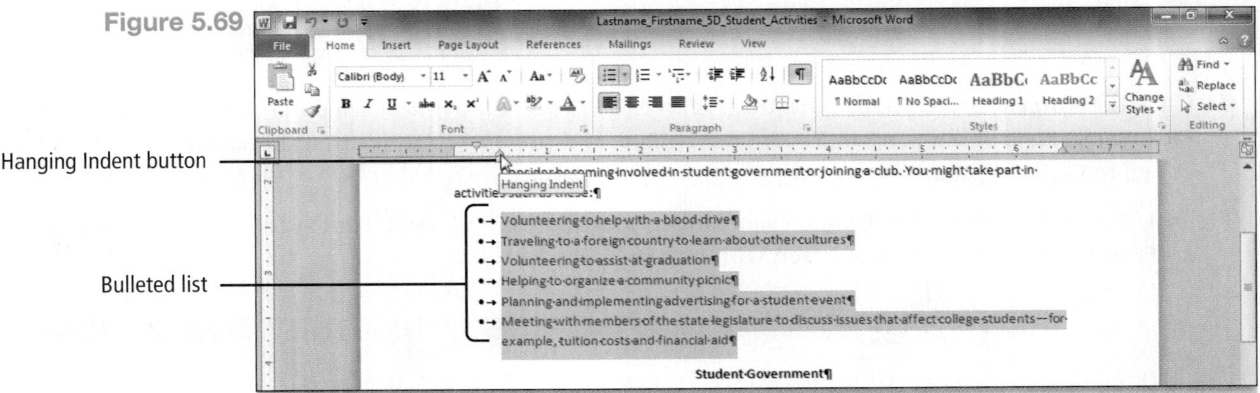

4 Scroll down to view **Page 2**. By using the pointer from the left margin area, select all of the paragraphs that indicate the club names and meeting dates, beginning with *Chess Club* and ending with *Theater Club*.

5 In the **Paragraph group**, click the **Bullets** button, and then **Save** your document.

Activity 5.33 | Creating a Numbered List

1 Scroll to view **Page 1**, and then under the subheading *Student Government*, in the paragraph that begins *As a registered student*, click to position the insertion point at the *end* of the paragraph following the colon. Press Enter one time to create a blank paragraph.

2 Notice that the paragraph is indented, because the First Line Indent from the previous paragraph carried over to the new paragraph.

3 To change the indent formatting for this paragraph, on the ruler, drag the **First Line Indent** button to the left so that it is positioned directly above the lower button.

4 Being sure to include the period, type **1.** and press Spacebar.

Word uses predictive logic to determine that this paragraph is the first item in a numbered list and formats the new paragraph accordingly, indenting the list in the same manner as the bulleted list. The space after the number changes to a tab, and the AutoCorrect Options button displays to the left of the list item. The tab is indicated by a right arrow formatting mark.

Alert! | Activating Automatic Numbered Lists

If a numbered list does not begin automatically, display Backstage view, and then click the Options tab. On the left side of the Word Options dialog box, click Proofing. Under AutoCorrect options, click the AutoCorrect Options button. In the AutoCorrect dialog box, click the AutoFormat As You Type tab. Under *Apply as you type*, select the *Automatic numbered lists* check box, and then click OK two times to close both dialog boxes.

5 Click the **AutoCorrect Options** button, and then compare your screen with Figure 5.70.

From the displayed list, you can remove the automatic formatting here, or stop using the automatic numbered lists option in this document. You also have the option to open the AutoCorrect dialog box to *Control AutoFormat Options*.

Figure 5.70

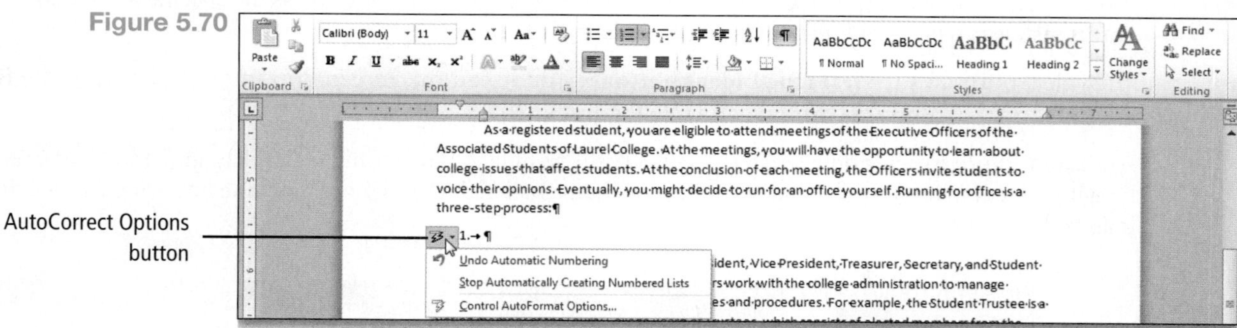

6 Click the **AutoCorrect Options** button again to close the menu without selecting any of the commands. Type **Pick up petitions at the Student Government office.** and press Enter. Notice that the second number and a tab are added to the next line.

7 Type **Obtain 100 signatures from current students.** and press Enter. Type **Turn in petitions and start campaigning.** and press Enter. Compare your screen with Figure 5.71.

Figure 5.71

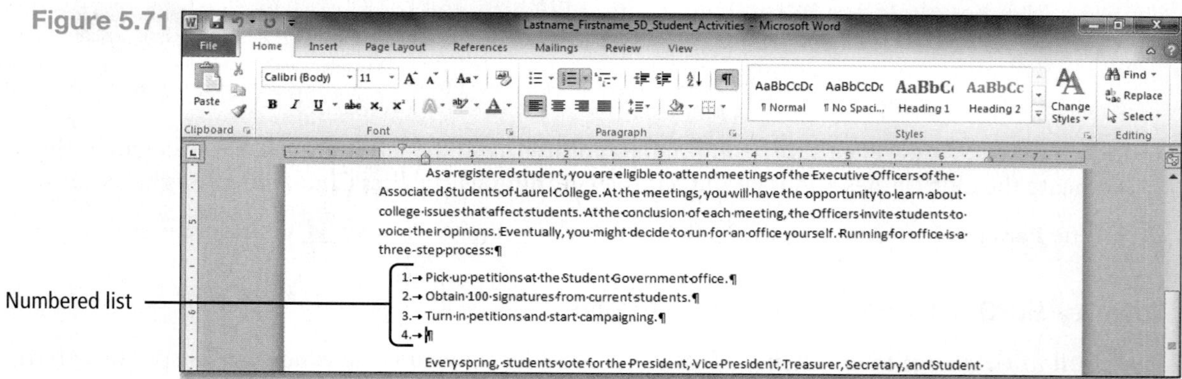

8 Press Backspace to turn off the list numbering. Then, press Backspace three more times to remove the blank paragraph. **Save** your document.

More Knowledge | To End a List

To turn a list off, you can press Backspace, click the Numbering or Bullets button, or press Enter a second time. Both list buttons—Numbering and Bullets—act as toggle buttons; that is, clicking the button one time turns the feature on, and clicking the button again turns the feature off.

Activity 5.34 | Customizing Bullets

1 Press Ctrl + End to move to the end of the document, and then scroll up as necessary to view the bulleted list containing the list of clubs. Point to the left of the first list item to display the [pointer] pointer, and then drag down to select all the clubs in the list—the bullet symbols are not highlighted.

2 Point to the selected list and right-click. From the shortcut menu, point to **Bullets**, and then compare your screen with Figure 5.72

Figure 5.72

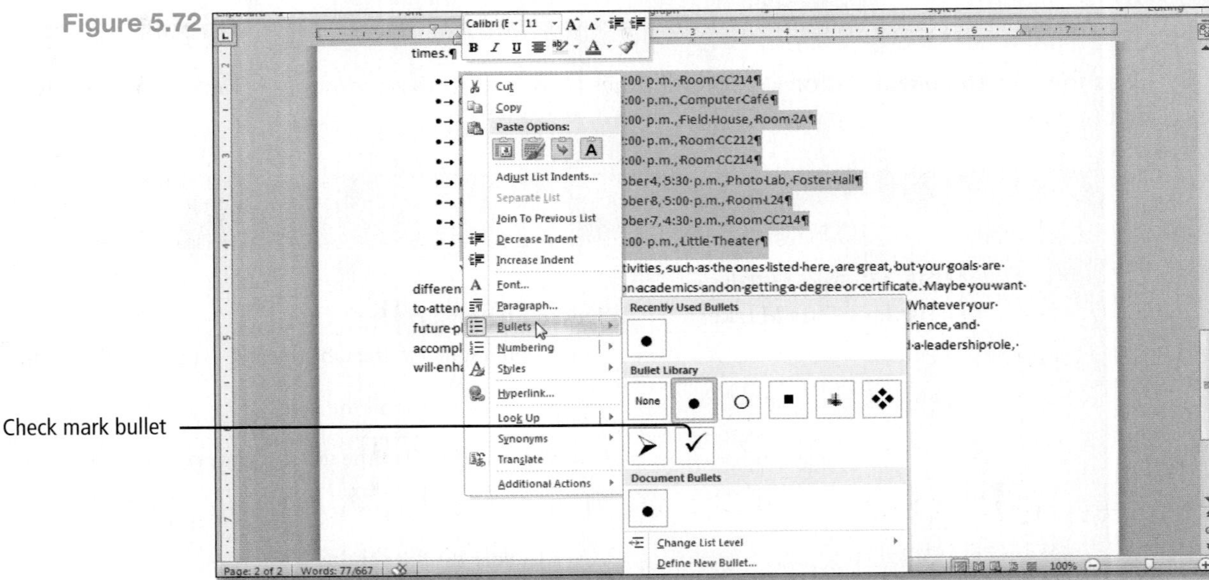

3 Under **Bullet Library**, click the **check mark** symbol. If the check mark is not available, choose another bullet symbol.

4 With the bulleted list still selected, right-click over the list, and then on the Mini toolbar, click the **Format Painter** button. Use the vertical scroll bar or your mouse wheel to scroll to view **Page 1**. Move the pointer to the left of the first item in the bulleted list to display the [pointer] pointer, and then drag down to select all of the items in the list and to apply the format of the second bulleted list to this list.

5 **Save** your document.

Objective 18 | Set and Modify Tab Stops

Tab stops mark specific locations on a line of text. Use tab stops to indent and align text, and use the Tab key to move to tab stops.

View the video on the Companion Web Site or in MyITLab

Activity 5.35 | Setting Tab Stops

1 Scroll to view the middle of **Page 2**, and then by using the [pointer] pointer at the left of the first item, select all of the items in the bulleted list. Notice that there is a tab mark between the name of the club and the date.

The arrow that indicates a tab is a nonprinting formatting mark.

2 To the left of the horizontal ruler, point to the **Tab Alignment** button to display the *Left Tab* ScreenTip, and then compare your screen with Figure 5.73.

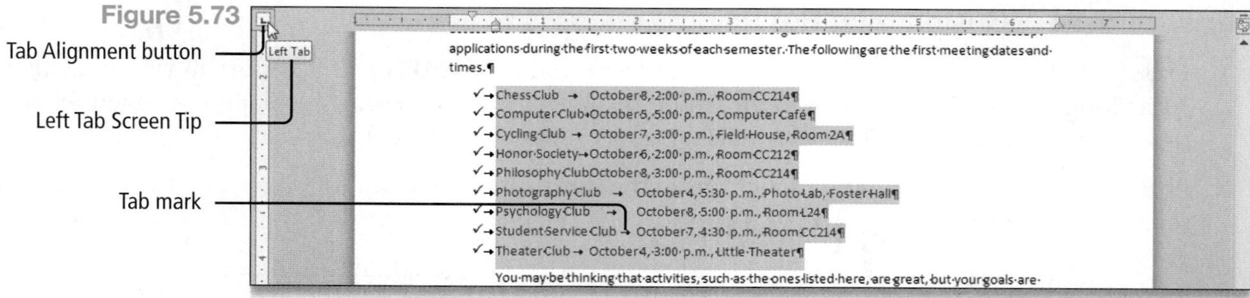

Figure 5.73

3 Click the **Tab Alignment** button several times to view the tab alignment options shown in the table in Figure 5.74.

Tab Alignment Options

Type	Tab Alignment Button Displays This Marker	Description
Left		Text is left aligned at the tab stop and extends to the right.
Center		Text is centered around the tab stop.
Right		Text is right aligned at the tab stop and extends to the left.
Decimal		The decimal point aligns at the tab stop.
Bar		A vertical bar displays at the tab stop.
First Line Indent		Text in the first line of a paragraph indents.
Hanging Indent		Text in all lines except the first line in the paragraph indents.

Figure 5.74

4 Display the **Left Tab** button. Along the lower edge of the horizontal ruler, point to and then click at **3 inches on the horizontal ruler**. Notice that all of the dates left align at the new tab stop location, and the right edge of the column is uneven.

5 Compare your screen with Figure 5.75, and then **Save** your document.

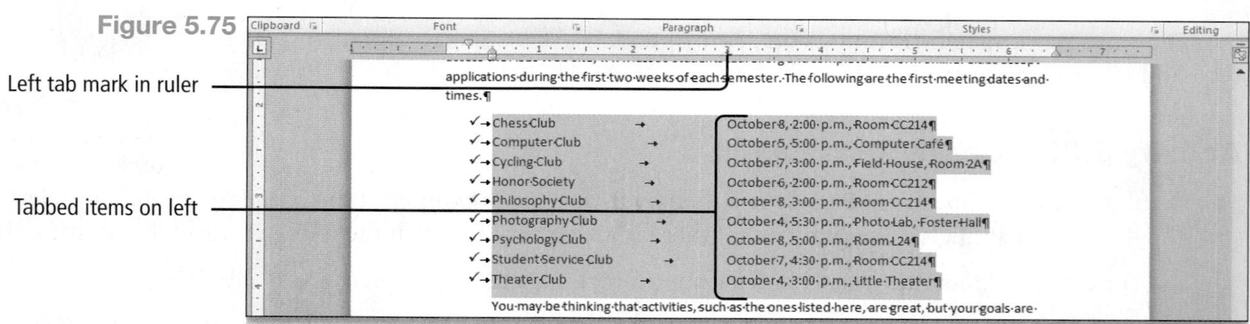

Figure 5.75

Activity 5.36 | Modifying Tab Stops

Tab stops are a form of paragraph formatting, and thus, the information about tab stops is stored in the paragraph mark in the paragraphs to which they were applied.

1 With the bulleted list still selected, on the ruler, point to the new tab marker that you just set at 3 inches, and then when the *Left Tab* ScreenTip displays, drag the tab marker to **3.5 inches on the horizontal ruler**.

In all of the selected lines, the text at the tab stop left aligns at 3.5 inches.

2 On the ruler, point to the tab marker to display the ScreenTip, and then double-click to display the **Tabs** dialog box.

3 In the **Tabs** dialog box, under **Tab stop position**, if necessary select *3.5″* and then type **6**

4 Under **Alignment**, click the **Right** option button. Under **Leader**, click the **2** option button. Near the bottom of the **Tabs** dialog box, click **Set**.

Because the Right tab will be used to align the items in the list, the tab stop at 3.50 is no longer necessary.

5 In the **Tabs** dialog box, in the **Tab stop position** box, click **3.5"** to select this tab stop, and then in the lower portion of the **Tabs** dialog box, click the **Clear** button to delete this tab stop, which is no longer necessary. Compare your screen with Figure 5.76.

Figure 5.76

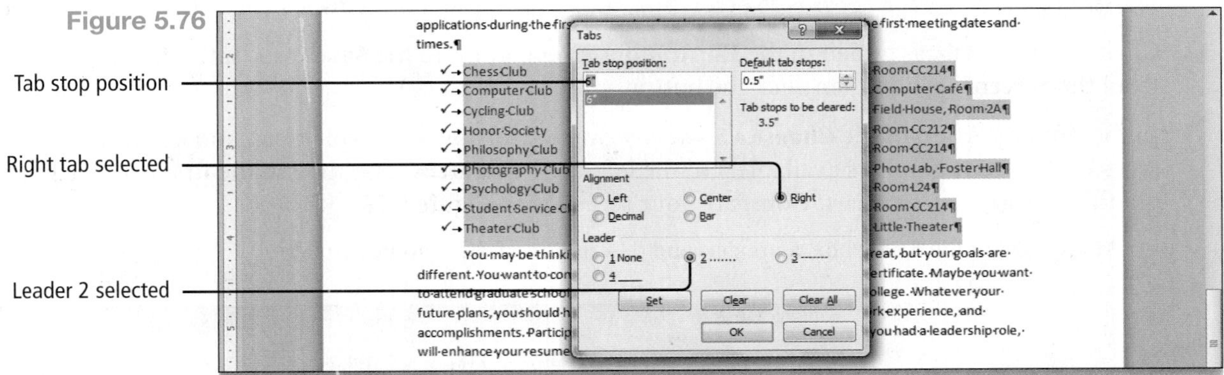

6 Click **OK**. On the ruler, notice that the left tab marker at *3.5″* no longer displays, a right tab marker displays at *6″*, and a series of dots—a ***dot leader***—displays between the columns of the list. Notice also that the right edge of the column is even. Compare your screen with Figure 5.77.

A ***leader character*** creates a solid, dotted, or dashed line that fills the space to the left of a tab character and draws the reader's eyes across the page from one item to the next. When the character used for the leader is a dot, it is commonly referred to as a dot leader.

Figure 5.77

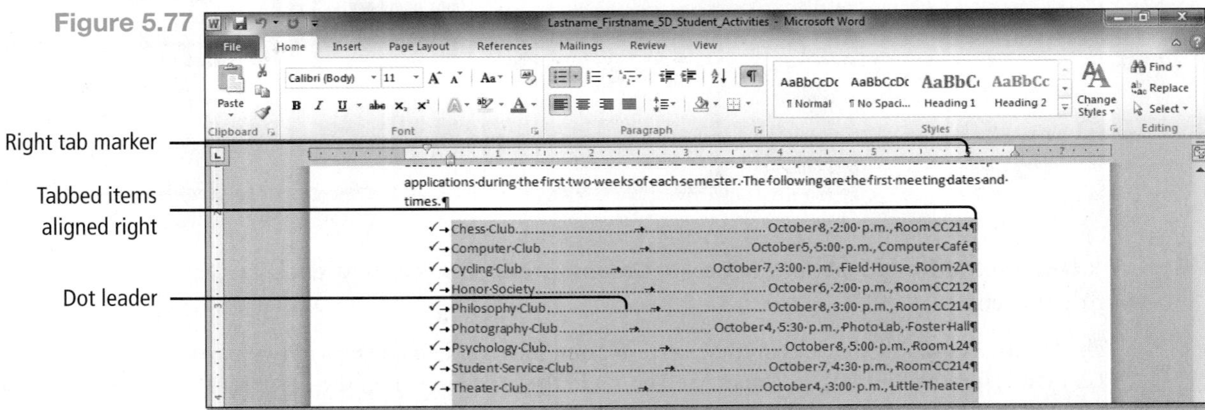

7 In the bulleted list that uses dot leaders, locate the *Honor Society* item, and then click to position the insertion point at the end of that line. Press Enter to create a new blank bullet item.

8 Type **Math Club** and press Tab. Notice that a dot leader fills the space to the tab marker location.

9 Type **October 6, 4:00 p.m., Math Tutoring Lab, L35** and notice that the text moves to the left to maintain the right alignment of the tab stop.

10 **Save** your document.

Objective 19 | Insert a SmartArt Graphic

View the video on the Companion Web Site or in MyITLab

SmartArt graphics are designer-quality visual representations of information, and Word provides many different layouts from which you can choose. A SmartArt graphic can communicate your messages or ideas more effectively than plain text and adds visual interest to a document or Web page.

Activity 5.37 | Inserting a SmartArt Graphic

1 Press Ctrl + Home to move to the top of the document. Press End to move to the end of the first paragraph—the title—and then press Enter to create a blank paragraph.

Because the paragraph above is 26 pt font size, the new paragraph mark displays in that size.

2 Click the **Insert tab**, and then in the **Illustrations group**, point to the **SmartArt** button to display its ScreenTip. Read the ScreenTip, and then click the button.

3 In the center portion of the **Choose a SmartArt Graphic** dialog box, scroll down and examine the numerous types of SmartArt graphics available. On the left, click **Hierarchy**, and then in the first row, click the first graphic—**Organization Chart**. Compare your screen with Figure 5.78.

At the right of the dialog box, a preview and description of the graphic display.

Figure 5.78

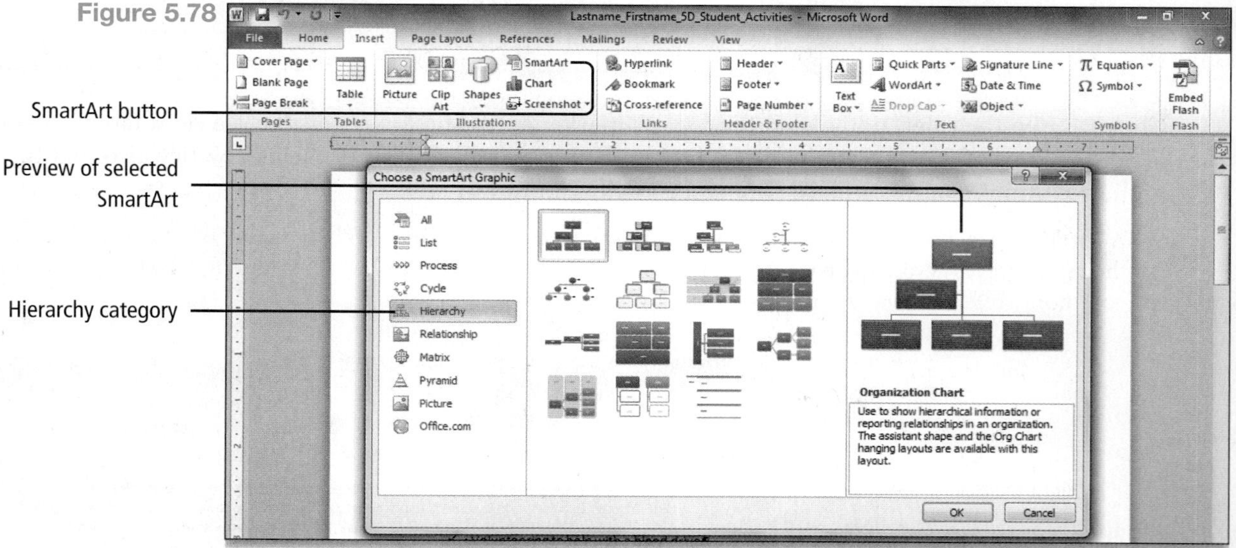

4 Click **OK**. On the **Design tab**, in the **Create Graphic group**, if necessary, click the **Text Pane** button. **Save** your document.

The SmartArt graphic displays at the insertion point location and consists of two parts—the graphic itself, and the Text Pane. On the Ribbon, the SmartArt Tools add the Design tab and the Format tab. You can type directly into the graphics, or type in the Text Pane.

Activity 5.38 | Modifying a SmartArt Graphic

1 In the SmartArt graphic, in the second row, click the border of the *[Text]* box to display a *solid* border and sizing handles, and then press Delete. Repeat this procedure in the bottom row to delete the middle *[Text]* box.

2 In the **Text Pane**, click in the top bulleted point, and then type **Student Activities** Notice that the first bulleted point aligns further to the left than the other points.

The ***top-level points*** are the main points in a SmartArt graphic. ***Subpoints*** are indented second-level bullet points.

3 Press ↓. Type **Government** and then press ↓ again. Type **Clubs** and then compare your screen with Figure 5.79.

Figure 5.79

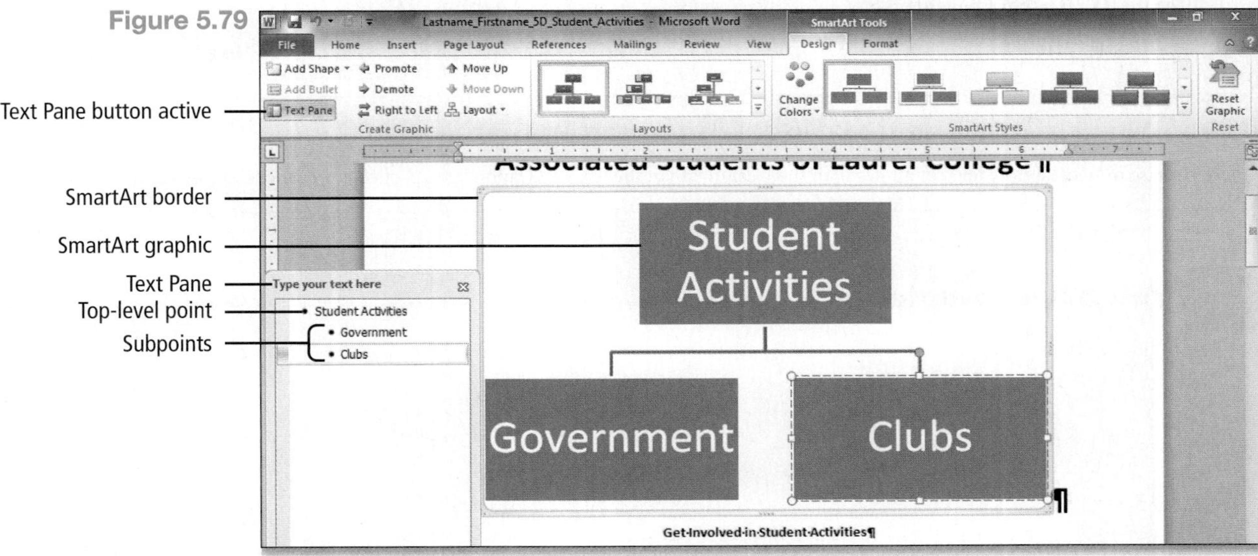

4 In the upper right corner of the **Text Pane**, click the **Close** button.

5 Click the border of the SmartArt graphic—a pale border surrounds it. Click the **Format tab**, and then in the **Size group**, if necessary click the **Size** button to display the **Shape Height** and **Shape Width** boxes.

6 Set the **Height** to **2.5"** and the **Width** to **4.2"**.

7 With the SmartArt graphic still selected, click the **Design tab**, and then in the **SmartArt Styles group**, click the **Change Colors** button. Under **Colorful**, click the second style—**Colorful Range - Accent Colors 2 to 3**.

8 On the **Design tab**, in the **SmartArt Styles group**, click the **More** button. Under **3-D**, click the first style—**Polished**. Compare your screen with Figure 5.80.

Figure 5.80

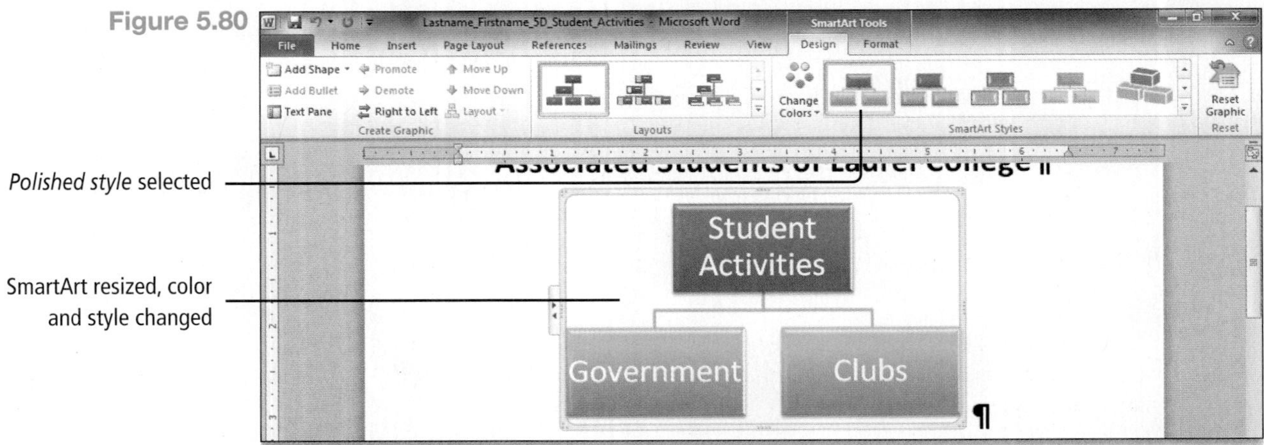

9 Click outside of the graphic to deselect it. Display **Backstage** view. On the right, under the screen thumbnail, click **Properties**, and then click **Show Document Panel**. In the **Author** box, delete any text and then type your firstname and lastname. In the **Subject** box, type your course name and section number, and in the **Keywords** box type **Student Activities, Associated Students Close** the Document Panel and **Save** your document.

10 Display **Backstage** view, and then click **Print** to display **Print Preview**. At the bottom of the preview, click the **Next Page** and **Previous Page** buttons to move between pages. If necessary, return to the document and make any necessary changes.

11 As directed by your instructor, print your document or submit it electronically. **Close** Word.

> More Knowledge | **Changing the Bullet Level in a SmartArt Graphic**
>
> To increase or decrease the level of an item, on the Design tab, in the Create Graphic group, click either the Promote or the Demote button.

End **You have completed Project 5D**

Content-Based Assessments

Summary

In this chapter, you used Windows Explorer to navigate the Windows file structure and the features that are common across the Microsoft Office 2010 programs. You also created documents in Microsoft Word using graphics, bullets, text boxes, tab stops, and SmartArt graphics.

Key Terms

Alignment 189
All Programs 170
Anchor 202
Application 170
Artistic effects 203
Backstage tabs 175
Backstage view 175
Bar tab stop 220
Bulleted list 216
Bullets 216
Center alignment 189
Center tab stop 220
Command 183
Common dialog boxes 181
Compressed file 196
Context-sensitive command 173
Contextual tabs 185
Copy 192
Cut 192
Decimal tab stop 220
Default 171
Deselect 185
Dialog box 173
Dialog Box Launcher 192
Document properties 175
Dot leader 221
Double-click 191
Drag 172
Drawing object 200
Edit 171
Ellipsis 173
Enhanced ScreenTip ..185
Field 208
Fill 173
Floating object 202
Font 189
Font styles 190
Footer 187
Format Painter 190
Formatting 186
Formatting marks 182
Gallery 174
Graphics 200
Groups 183
Header 187
Info tab 175
Inline object 201
Insertion point 171
Justified alignment ..213
Keyboard shortcut 172
KeyTip 187
Landscape orientation 188
Leader characters 221
Left alignment 213
Left tab stop 220
Line spacing 214
Live Preview 185
Location 174
Margins 212
Metadata 175
Microsoft Office 2010 170
Mini toolbar 172
Nonprinting characters 182
Nudge 203
Numbered list 216
Office Clipboard 192
Open dialog box 181
Option button 173
Options dialog box 182
Paragraph symbol 184
Paste 192
Paste Options 192
PDF (Portable Document Format) file 179
Picture styles 203
Pointer 171
Points 190
Portrait orientation ...188
Print Preview 177
Program 170
Program-level control buttons 171
Protected view 182
Pt. 190
Quick Access Toolbar 184
Quick Commands 175
Ribbon 183
Ribbon tabs 171
Right alignment 213
Right tab stop 220
Right-click 173
Sans serif 189
ScreenTip 174
Scroll bar 175
Scroll box 175
Select 172
Serif 189
Shape 205
Shortcut menu 173
SmartArt 222
Spin box 202
Status bar 171
Subpoints 223
Tab stop 219
Tabs 183
Task pane 185
Text box 205
Text effects 200
Text wrapping 202
Theme 189
Title bar 171
Toggle button 190
Top-level points 223
Triple-click 190
Trusted Documents ..182
Wordwrap 199
Zoom 177

Check Your Knowledge

Matching and Multiple Choice items are available in MyITLab and on the Companion Web Site.

Apply 5C skills from these Objectives:

12 Create a New Document and Insert Text
13 Insert and Format Graphics
14 Insert and Modify Text Boxes and Shapes
15 Preview and Print a Document

Mastering Word | Project 5E Retreat

In the following Mastering Word project, you will create a flyer announcing a retreat for the Associated Students of Laurel College Board. Your completed document will look similar to Figure 5.81.

Project Files

For Project 5E, you will need the following files:

New blank Word document
w05E_Retreat_Text
jpg05E_Retreat_Picture

You will save your document as:

Lastname_Firstname_5E_Retreat

Project Results

ALSC Board Retreat

College President Diane Gilmore is pleased to announce a retreat for the Board of Associated Students of Laurel College.

Invitees include the ASLC Board, consisting of the Executive Officers and their appointed directors, Student Senators, Club Presidents, and members of the Judicial Review Committee. The retreat will be held at the Fogelsville campus of Penn State University on Friday, November 12.

The morning session will begin with a continental breakfast at 8:30 a.m., and will include presentations on effective ways to set and achieve goals. Lunch will be served at noon. The afternoon session will begin at 1:30 p.m., and will include small breakout sessions for the sharing and development of goals and a series of exercises to facilitate group interaction.

In addition to goal setting, the retreat is organized to provide a means for Board members to get to know one another. Students are so busy with courses, student government duties, and personal responsibilities that they rarely get to interact with other Board members outside of their immediate circles. The afternoon will be devoted to a series of exercises specially designed for this retreat. It will enable all participants to meet every other person in attendance and to exchange ideas. We have hired the well-known group, Mountain Retreat Planners, to conduct this portion of the program. They have some entertaining activities planned that will help break down barriers to becoming acquainted with other participants.

Prize drawings at lunch include concert tickets, college football jerseys, coffee mugs, and restaurant gift cards.

Lastname_Firstname_5E_Retreat

Figure 5.81

(Project 5E Retreat continues on the next page)

Mastering Word | Project 5E Retreat (continued)

1 **Start** Word and display a new blank document. Be sure the formatting marks and rulers display. **Save** the document in your **All in One Chapter 5** folder as **Lastname_Firstname_5E_Retreat** and then add the file name to the footer. Close the Footer area.

2 As the first paragraph of the document, type **ASLC Board Retreat** and press Enter two times. Type **College President Diane Gilmore is pleased to announce a retreat for the Board of the Associated Students of Laurel College.** Press Enter one time. **Insert** the file **w05E_Retreat_Text**.

3 Select the title *ASLC Board Retreat*. On the **Home tab**, in the **Font group**, display the **Text Effects** gallery, and then in the third row, apply the first effect—**Fill - White, Gradient Outline - Accent 1**. Change the **Font Size** to **56** pt. Apply a **Shadow** text effect using the first effect under **Outer**—**Offset Diagonal Bottom Right**. Change the **Font Color** of the selected title to **Olive Green, Accent 3, Darker 25%**—in the seventh column, the fifth color.

4 Click to position the insertion point at the beginning of the paragraph that begins *College President*, and then from your student files, **Insert** the picture **jpg05E_Retreat_Picture**. Change the **Shape Height** of the picture to **2"**, and then set the **Wrap Text** to **Square**. Move the picture so that the right edge aligns with the right margin, and the top edge aligns with the top edge of the text that begins *College President*. Apply a **Film Grain Artistic Effect**—the third effect in the third row. From **Picture Effects**, add a **5 Point Soft Edge**.

5 Scroll to view the lower portion of the page. **Insert** and then draw a **Text Box** beginning at the left margin and at approximately **7 inches on the vertical ruler** that is approximately 1" high and 4.5" wide. Then, in the **Size group**, make the measurements exact by setting the **Height** to **1"** and the **Width** to **4.5"**. Type the following text in the text box: **Prize drawings at lunch include concert tickets, college football jerseys, coffee mugs, and restaurant gift cards.**

6 Select the text in the text box. Change the **Font Size** to **16** pt, apply **Bold**, and **Center** the text. Add a **Shape Fill** to the text box using the theme color **Olive Green, Accent 3, Lighter 40%**. Then apply a **Gradient** fill using the **Dark Variation Linear Right** gradient. Change the **Shape Outline** color to **White, Background 1**. Drag the text box as necessary to center it horizontally between the left and right margins, and vertically between the last line of text and the footer.

7 Display the **Document Panel**. Type your firstname and lastname in the **Author** box, your course name and section number in the **Subject** box, and then in the **Keywords** box type **retreat, ASLC**

8 **Close** the Document Panel. **Save** and preview your document, make any necessary adjustments, and then print your document or submit it electronically as directed. **Close** Word.

End **You have completed Project 5E**

Apply 5D skills from these Objectives:

16 Change Document and Paragraph Layout

17 Create and Modify Lists

18 Set and Modify Tab Stops

19 Insert a SmartArt Graphic

Mastering Word | Project 5F Cycling Trip

In the following Mastering Word project, you will create an informational handout about a planned trip by the Laurel College Cycling Club. Your completed document will look similar to Figure 5.82.

Project Files

For Project 5F, you will need the following file:

w05F_Cycling_Trip

You will save your document as:

Lastname_Firstname_5F_Cycling_Trip

Project Results

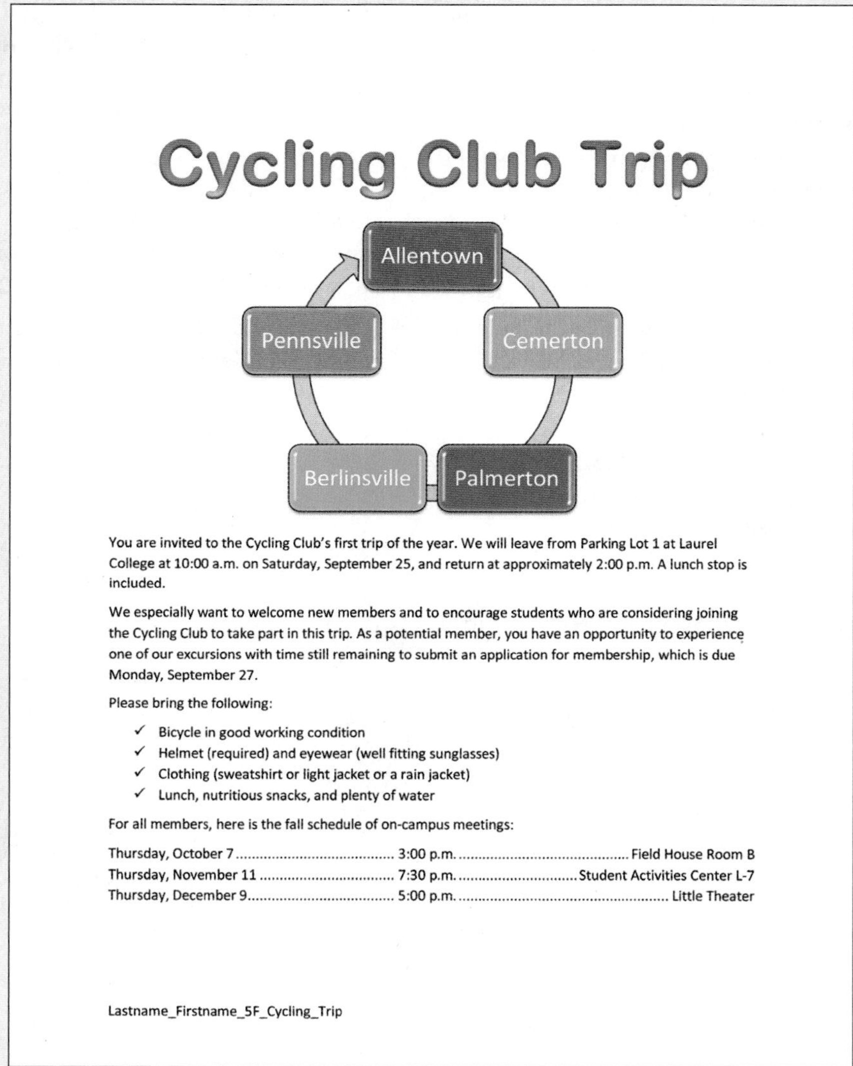

Figure 5.82

(Project 5F Cycling Trip continues on the next page)

Mastering Word | Project 5F Cycling Trip (continued)

1 **Start** Word and display formatting marks. From your student files open the document **w05F_Cycling_Trip**. **Save** the document in your **All in One Chapter 5** folder as **Lastname_Firstname_5F_Cycling_Trip** Add the file name to the footer. Close the Footer area.

2 On the **Page Layout tab**, in the **Page Setup group**, click the **Dialog Launcher** button to display the **Page Setup** dialog box. Set the **Top** margin to **1.25"** and the other three margins to **1"**. Select all of the text in the document, including the title. Add **6 pt** spacing after all paragraphs. From the **Home tab**, change the **Line Spacing** to **1.15**. Change the alignment to **Align Text Left**. **Center** the document title—*Cycling Club Trip*.

3 Locate the paragraph that begins *Bicycle in good*. Select that paragraph and the three paragraphs that follow it. Create a bulleted list from the selected text. Use the shortcut menu to display bullet options, and change the bullet character to a **check mark** or another symbol if the check mark is unavailable.

4 Position the insertion point in the blank paragraph at the end of the document. Add a **Right** tab stop at **3.5"**. Display the **Tabs** dialog box and add a dot leader to the existing tab. **Set** the tab stop, and then add and **Set** another **Right** tab stop with a dot leader at **6.5"**.

5 Type the text shown in **Table 1**, pressing Tab between columns and Enter at the end of each line. Refer to Figure 5.82.

6 Select the first two lines in the tabbed list and change the **Space After** to **0 pt**. Near the top of the document, position the insertion point in the blank line below the title. Display the **Choose a SmartArt Graphic** dialog box, select the **Cycle** category, and then in the second row, select the first style—**Continuous Cycle**.

7 Display the **Text Pane**. Add the following cities in this order: **Allentown** and **Cemerton** and **Palmerton** and **Berlinsville** and **Pennsville**

8 **Close** the **Text Pane**. Click the SmartArt border. On the **Format tab**, set the **Shape Width** of the SmartArt graphic to **6.5"** and the **Shape Height** to **3"**. On the **Design tab**, from the **SmartArt Styles** gallery, apply the **Cartoon 3-D** style, and change the colors to the first color under **Colorful**—**Colorful – Accent Colors**.

9 Display the **Document Panel**, type your firstname and lastname in the **Author** box, your course name and section number in the **Subject** box, and then in the **Keywords** box type **cycling, cycling club**

10 **Close** the Document Panel. **Save** your document. Preview your document, check for and make any adjustments, and then print your document or submit it electronically as directed. **Close** Word.

Table 1

Thursday, October 7	**3:00 p.m.**	**Field House Room B**
Thursday, November 11	**7:30 p.m.**	**Student Activities Center L-7**
Thursday, December 9	**5:00 p.m.**	**Little Theater**

--→ (Return to Step 6)

End **You have completed Project 5F**

Apply 5C and 5D skills from these Objectives:

12 Create a New Document and Insert Text

13 Insert and Format Graphics

14 Insert and Modify Text Boxes and Shapes

15 Preview and Print a Document

16 Change Document and Paragraph Layout

17 Create and Modify Lists

18 Set and Modify Tab Stops

19 Insert a SmartArt Graphic

Mastering Word | Project 5G Web Sites

In the following Mastering Word project, you will edit guidelines for club Web sites at Laurel College. Your completed document will look similar to Figure 5.83.

Project Files

For Project 5G, you will need the following files:

New blank Word document
jpg05G_WWW_Picture
w05G_Student_Computing_Text

You will save your document as:

Lastname_Firstname_5G_Web_Sites

Project Results

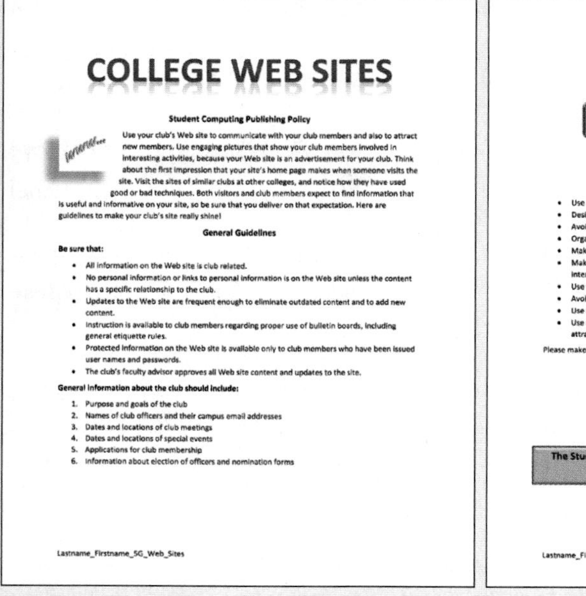

COLLEGE WEB SITES

Student Computing Publishing Policy

Use your club's Web site to communicate with your club members and also to attract new members. Use engaging pictures that show your club members involved in interesting activities, because your Web site is an advertisement for your club. Think about the first impression that your site's home page makes when someone visits the site. Visit the sites of similar clubs at other colleges, and notice how they have used good or bad techniques. Both visitors and club members expect to find information that is useful and informative on your site, so be sure that you deliver on that expectation. Here are guidelines to make your club's site really shine!

General Guidelines

Be sure that:

- All information on the Web site is club related.
- No personal information or links to personal information is on the Web site unless the content has a specific relationship to the club.
- Updates to the Web site are frequent enough to eliminate outdated content and to add new content.
- Instruction is available to club members regarding proper use of bulletin boards, including general etiquette rules.
- Protected information on the Web site is available only to club members who have been issued user names and passwords.
- The club's faculty advisor approves all Web site content and updates to the site.

General information about the club should include:

1. Purpose and goals of the club
2. Names of club officers and their campus email addresses
3. Dates and locations of club meetings
4. Dates and locations of special events
5. Applications for club membership
6. Information about election of officers and nomination forms

Lastname_Firstname_5G_Web_Sites

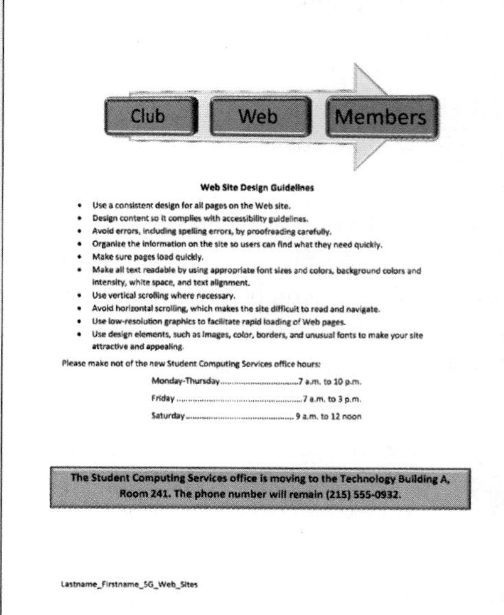

Club | Web | Members

Web Site Design Guidelines

- Use a consistent design for all pages on the Web site.
- Design content so it complies with accessibility guidelines.
- Avoid errors, including spelling errors, by proofreading carefully.
- Organize the information on the site so users can find what they need quickly.
- Make sure pages load quickly.
- Make all text readable by using appropriate font sizes and colors, background colors and intensity, white space, and text alignment.
- Use vertical scrolling where necessary.
- Avoid horizontal scrolling, which makes the site difficult to read and navigate.
- Use low-resolution graphics to facilitate rapid loading of Web pages.
- Use design elements, such as images, color, borders, and unusual fonts to make your site attractive and appealing.

Please make not of the new Student Computing Services office hours:

Monday-Thursday................7 a.m. to 10 p.m.
Friday................7 a.m. to 3 p.m.
Saturday................9 a.m. to 12 noon

The Student Computing Services office is moving to the Technology Building A, Room 241. The phone number will remain (215) 555-0932.

Lastname_Firstname_5G_Web_Sites

Figure 5.83

(Project 5G Web Sites continues on the next page)

Mastering Word | Project 5G Web Sites (continued)

1 **Start** Word and display a new blank document. Display formatting marks and rulers. **Save** the document in your **All in One Chapter 5** folder as **Lastname_Firstname_5G_Web_Sites** Add the file name to the footer.

Type **College Web Sites** and then press Enter. Select the title you just typed. From the **Text Effects** gallery, in the fourth row, apply the fifth effect—**Gradient Fill - Purple, Accent 4, Reflection**, change the **Font Size** to **48** pt, and **Center** the title.

2 Click in the blank line below the title. Locate and insert the file **w05G_Student_Computing_Text**. *Except* for the document title, select all of the document text. **Align Text Left**, change the **Line Spacing** to **1.15**, and change the **Spacing After** to **6 pt**. Locate and **Center** the document subtitles *Student Computing Publishing Policy, General Guidelines, and Web Site Design Guidelines.*

3 At the top of **Page 1**, under the subheading *Be sure that*, select the six paragraphs down to, but not including, the *General information* subheading. Format the selected text as a bulleted list. Near the bottom of **Page 1** and the top of **Page 2**, under the *Web Site Design Guidelines* subheading, select the ten paragraphs down to, but not including the blank paragraph at the end of the document, and create another bulleted list.

4 Under the subheading that begins *General information*, select the six paragraphs and apply **Numbering** to create a numbered list.

Near the top of the document, position the insertion point to the left of the paragraph that begins *Use your club's*. **Insert** the picture **jpg05G_WWW_Picture**. Set the **Wrap Text** to **Tight**. Decrease the picture **Width** to **1"**. From the **Picture Effects** gallery, apply the **Preset 5** effect.

5 Press Ctrl + End to move to the blank paragraph at the end of the document. Type **Please make note of the new Student Computing Services office hours:** and then press Enter. Set a **Left** tab stop at **1.5"**. Display the **Tabs** dialog box. At **5"** add a **Right** tab stop with a **dot leader** and click **Set**. Click **OK** to close the dialog box, press Tab to begin, and then type the following information; be sure to press Tab to begin each line and press Tab between the days and the times and press Enter at the end of each line:

Monday–Thursday	**7 a.m. to 10 p.m.**
Friday	**7 a.m. to 3 p.m.**
Saturday	**9 a.m. to 12 noon**

6 On **Page 1**, click to position the insertion point to the left of the subheading *Web Site Design Guidelines*. Hold down Ctrl and press Enter to break the page at that point. Press Enter one time, and then click in the blank paragraph you just created at the top of **Page 2**. **Insert** a **SmartArt** graphic, and then from the **Process** group, select the **Continuous Block Process**—in the third row, the first graphic. Click the border of the graphic, and then on the **Format tab**, set the **Shape Height** of the graphic to **2"** and the **Shape Width** of the graphic to **6.5"**. From the **Design tab**, display the **Text Pane**, and then type **Club** and **Web** and **Members Close** the **Text Pane**. Change the style to **3-D Metallic Scene** and the colors to **Colored Fill – Accent 4**, which is the second set of colors under **Accent 4**.

7 At the bottom of **Page 2**, in the empty space between the end of the text and the footer, **Insert** a **Text Box** and set the height to **0.7"** and the width to **7"**. By using the pointer, visually center the text box horizontally between the left and right margins and about one-half inch below the hours.

In the text box, type: **The Student Computing Services office is moving to the Technology Building A, Room 241. The phone number will remain (215) 555-0932.**

Select the text in the text box. From the Mini toolbar, change the **Font Size** to **14** pt, apply **Bold**, and **Center** the text. Change the **Shape Fill** to **Purple**, **Accent 4**, **Lighter 40%**. From the **Shape Effects** gallery, apply a **Circle Bevel**.

8 As the document properties, type your firstname and lastname in the **Author** box, your course name and section number in the **Subject** box, and then in the **Keywords** box type **Web sites, Student Computing Save** your document, examine the Print Preview, check for and make any adjustments, and then print your document or submit it electronically as directed. **Close** Word.

End **You have completed Project 5G**

Resumes, Cover Letters, Research Papers, Newsletters, and Merged Address Labels with Word

OUTCOMES At the end of this chapter you will be able to:	**OBJECTIVES** Mastering these objectives will enable you to:
PROJECT 6A Create a resume by using a Word table.	**1.** Create a Table (p. 234) **2.** Add Text to a Table (p. 235) **3.** Format a Table (p. 237)
PROJECT 6B Create a cover letter and resume by using a template.	**4.** Create a New Document from an Existing Document (p. 244) **5.** Change and Reorganize Text (p. 246) **6.** Use the Proofing Options (p. 251) **7.** Create a Document Using a Template (p. 254)
PROJECT 6C Create a research paper that includes citations and a bibliography.	**8.** Create a Research Paper (p. 260) **9.** Insert Footnotes in a Research Paper (p. 262) **10.** Create Citations and a Bibliography in a Research Paper (p. 265)
PROJECT 6D Create a multiple-column newsletter and merged mailing labels.	**11.** Format a Multiple-Column Newsletter (p. 271) **12.** Use Special Character and Paragraph Formatting (p. 275) **13.** Create Mailing Labels Using Mail Merge (p. 277)

© Douglas Freer/Shutterstock

© iQoncept/Shutterstock

Job Focus: Staffing Specialist and Sustainability Intern

In This Chapter

In this chapter, you will learn how a Staffing Specialist assists clients in preparing resumes and cover letters using Word. You will also learn how a Sustainability Intern for a recycling company uses Word to write research papers and newsletters, and to create address labels using Word's Mail Merge feature.

At the end of this Unit, following this chapter, you will have an opportunity to complete a case project that focuses on the career of a Production Manager for a comic book company.

Project 6A Resume

Project Activities

In Activities 6.01 through 6.09, you will create a table to use as the structure for a resume for one of Madison Staffing Services' clients. Your completed document will look similar to Figure 6.1.

Project Files

For Project 6A, you will need the following file:

w06A_Experience

You will save your document as:

Lastname_Firstname_6A_Resume

Project Results

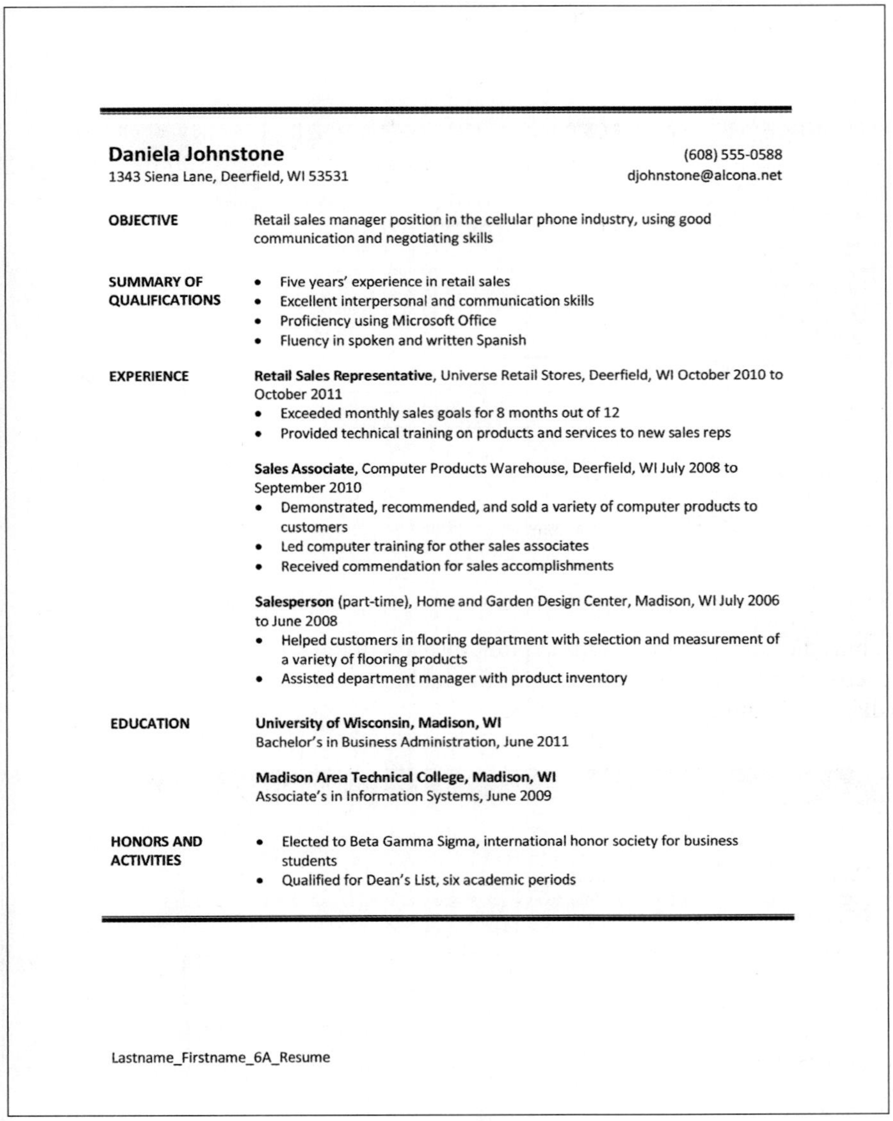

Daniela Johnstone (608) 555-0588
1343 Siena Lane, Deerfield, WI 53531 djohnstone@alcona.net

OBJECTIVE	Retail sales manager position in the cellular phone industry, using good communication and negotiating skills
SUMMARY OF QUALIFICATIONS	• Five years' experience in retail sales • Excellent interpersonal and communication skills • Proficiency using Microsoft Office • Fluency in spoken and written Spanish
EXPERIENCE	**Retail Sales Representative**, Universe Retail Stores, Deerfield, WI October 2010 to October 2011 • Exceeded monthly sales goals for 8 months out of 12 • Provided technical training on products and services to new sales reps **Sales Associate**, Computer Products Warehouse, Deerfield, WI July 2008 to September 2010 • Demonstrated, recommended, and sold a variety of computer products to customers • Led computer training for other sales associates • Received commendation for sales accomplishments **Salesperson** (part-time), Home and Garden Design Center, Madison, WI July 2006 to June 2008 • Helped customers in flooring department with selection and measurement of a variety of flooring products • Assisted department manager with product inventory
EDUCATION	**University of Wisconsin, Madison, WI** Bachelor's in Business Administration, June 2011 **Madison Area Technical College, Madison, WI** Associate's in Information Systems, June 2009
HONORS AND ACTIVITIES	• Elected to Beta Gamma Sigma, international honor society for business students • Qualified for Dean's List, six academic periods

Lastname_Firstname_6A_Resume

Figure 6.1
Project 6A Resume

Objective 1 | Create a Table

View the video on the Companion Web Site or in MyITLab

A ***table*** is an arrangement of information organized into rows and columns. The intersection of a row and a column in a table creates a box called a ***cell*** into which you can type. Tables are useful to present information in a logical and orderly manner.

Activity 6.01 | Creating a Table

1 **Start** Word, and in the new blank document, display formatting marks and rulers.

2 Click the **File tab**, and then in **Backstage** view, click **Save As**. In the **Save As** dialog box, navigate to the location where you are storing your projects for this chapter. Create a new folder named **All In One Chapter 6** Save the file in the **All In One Chapter 6** folder as **Lastname_Firstname_6A_Resume**

3 Scroll to the end of the document, right-click near the bottom of the page, and then click **Edit Footer**. On the **Design tab**, in the **Insert group**, click the **Quick Parts** button, and then click **Field**. Under **Field names**, scroll down, click **FileName**, and then click **OK**. **Close** the footer area.

4 On the **Insert tab**, in the **Tables group**, click the **Table** button. In the **Table** grid, in the fourth row, point to the second square, and notice that the cells display in orange and *2 × 4 Table* displays at the top of the grid. Compare your screen with Figure 6.2.

Figure 6.2

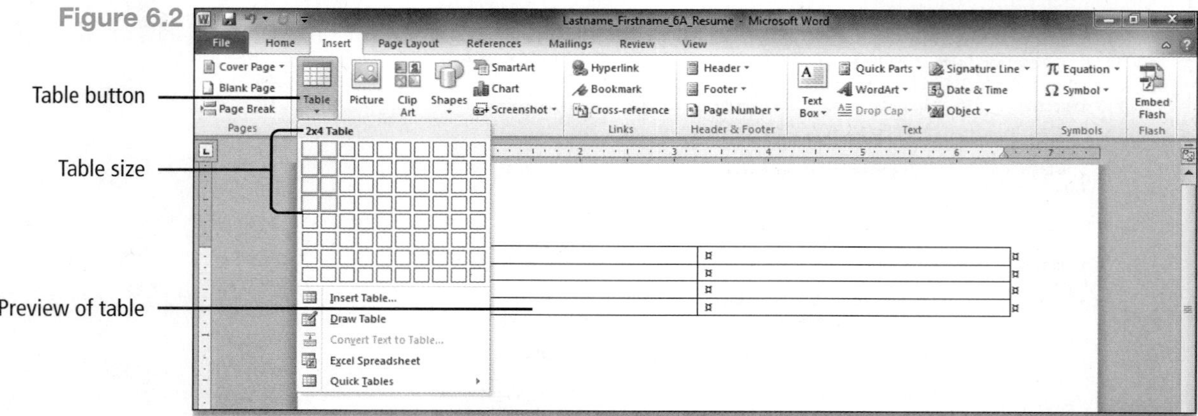

5 Click one time to create the table. **Save** your document, and then compare your screen with Figure 6.3.

A table with four rows and two columns displays, and the insertion point displays in the upper left cell. The table fills the width of the page, from the left margin to the right margin. On the Ribbon, Table Tools display and add two tabs—*Design* and *Layout*. Borders display around each cell in the table.

Figure 6.3

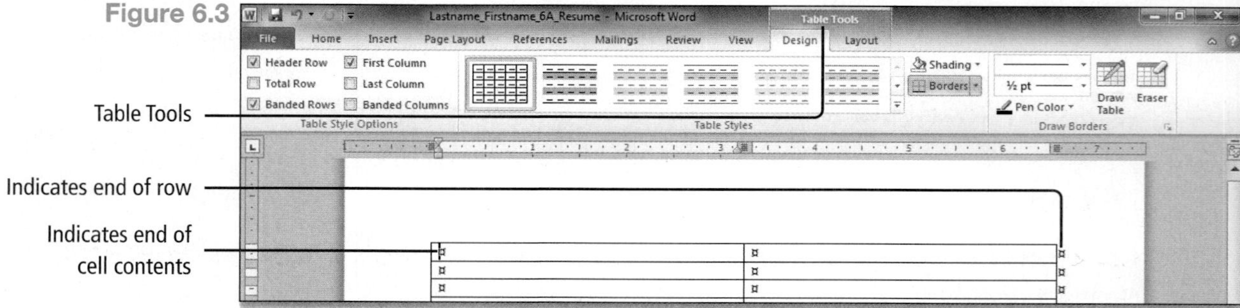

Objective 2 | Add Text to a Table

View the video on the Companion Web Site or in MyITLab

In a Word table, each cell behaves similarly to a document. For example, as you type in a cell, when you reach the right border of the cell, wordwrap moves the text to the next line. When you press Enter, the insertion point moves down to a new paragraph in the same cell. You can also insert text from another document into a table cell.

Activity 6.02 | Adding Text to a Table

There are numerous acceptable formats for resumes, many of which can be found in Business Communications textbooks. The layout used in this project is suitable for a recent college graduate and places topics in the left column and details in the right column.

1 With the insertion point blinking in the first cell in the first row, type **OBJECTIVE** and then press Tab.

Pressing Tab moves the insertion point to the next cell in the row, or, if the insertion point is already in the last cell in the row, pressing Tab moves the insertion point to the first cell in the following row.

2 Type **Retail sales manager position in the cellular phone industry, using good communication and negotiating skills**. Notice that the text wraps in the cell and the height of the row adjusts to fit the text.

3 Press Tab to move to the first cell in the second row. Type **SUMMARY OF QUALIFICATIONS** and then press Tab. Type the following, pressing Enter at the end of each line *except* the last line:

Five years' experience in retail sales

Excellent interpersonal and communication skills

Proficiency using Microsoft Office

Fluency in spoken and written Spanish

The default font and font size in a table are the same as for a document—Calibri 11 pt. The default line spacing in a table is single spacing with no space before or after paragraphs, which differs from the defaults for a document.

4 **Save** your document, and then compare your screen with Figure 6.4.

Figure 6.4

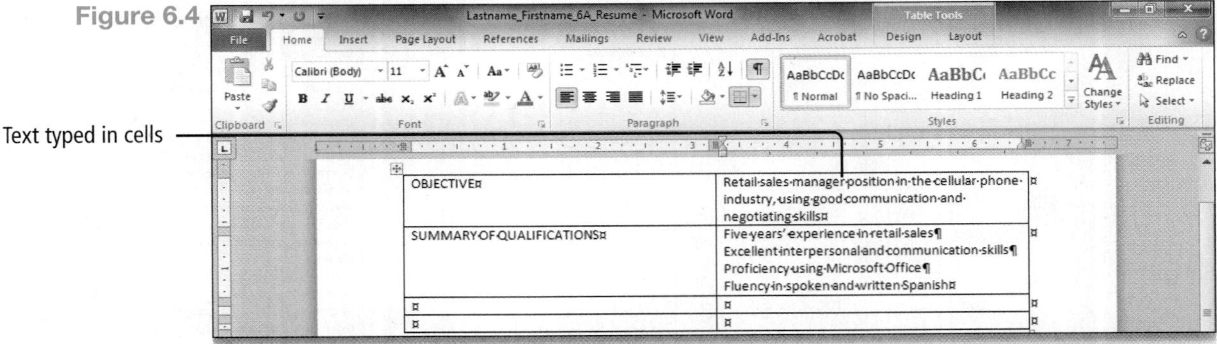

Activity 6.03 | Inserting Existing Text into a Table Cell

1 Press Tab to move to the first cell in the third row. Type **EXPERIENCE** and then press Tab.

2 Type the following, pressing Enter after each line:

Retail Sales Representative, Universe Retail Stores, Deerfield, WI October 2010 to October 2011

Exceeded monthly sales goals for 8 months out of 12

Provided technical training on products and services to new sales reps

3 Be sure your insertion point is still positioned in the second column below *sales reps*. Compare your screen with Figure 6.5.

Figure 6.5

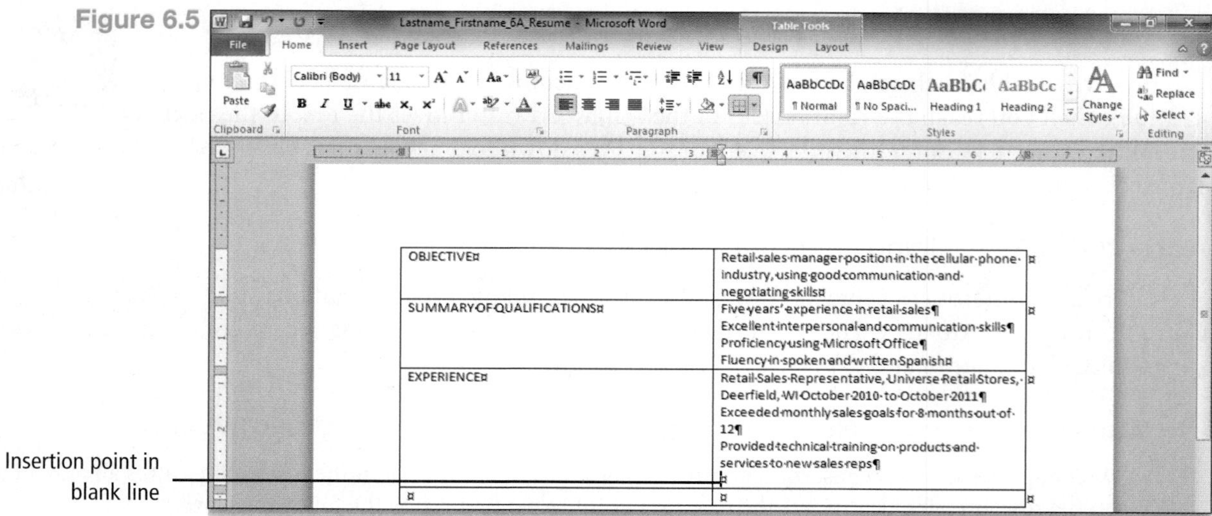

4 On the **Insert tab**, in the **Text group**, click the **Object button arrow**, and then click **Text from File**. Navigate to your student files, select **w06A_Experience**, and then click **Insert**.

5 Press Backspace one time to remove the blank line at the end of the inserted text.

6 Press Tab to move to the first cell in the fourth row. Type **EDUCATION** and then press Tab.

7 Type the following, pressing Enter at the end of each item except the last one:

University of Wisconsin, Madison, WI

Bachelor's in Business Administration, June 2011

Madison Area Technical College, Madison, WI

Associate's in Information Systems, June 2009

8 **Save** your document, and then compare your screen with Figure 6.6.

Figure 6.6

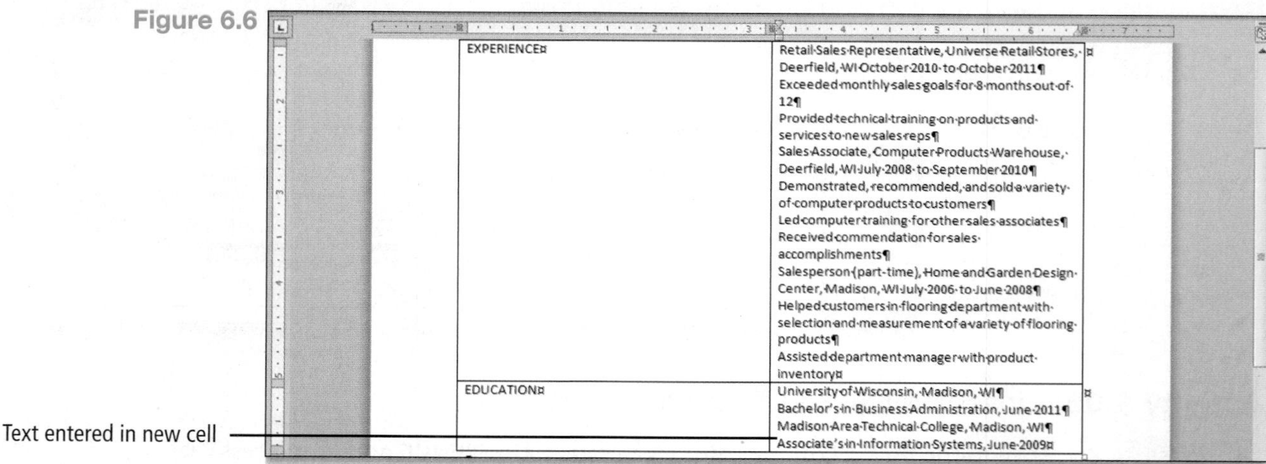

Activity 6.04 | Creating Bulleted Lists in a Table

1 Scroll to view the top of your document, and then in the cell to the right of *SUMMARY OF QUALIFICATIONS*, select all of the text. On the **Home tab**, in the **Paragraph group**, click the **Bullets** button.

The selected text displays as a bulleted list. Using a bulleted list in this manner makes each qualification more distinctive.

2 In the **Paragraph group**, click the **Decrease Indent** button one time to align the bullets at the left edge of the cell.

3 In the **Clipboard group**, double-click the **Format Painter** button. In the cell to the right of *EXPERIENCE*, select the second and third paragraphs—beginning *Exceeded* and *Provided*—to create the same style of bulleted list as you did in the previous step.

When you double-click the Format Painter button, it remains active until you turn it off.

4 In the same cell, under *Sales Associate*, select the three paragraphs that begin *Demonstrated* and *Led* and *Received* to create another bulleted list aligned at the left edge of the cell. In the same cell, select the paragraphs that begin *Helped* and *Assisted* to create the same type of bulleted list.

5 Press Esc to turn off the Format Painter. Click anywhere in the table to deselect the text, and then compare your screen with Figure 6.7.

Figure 6.7

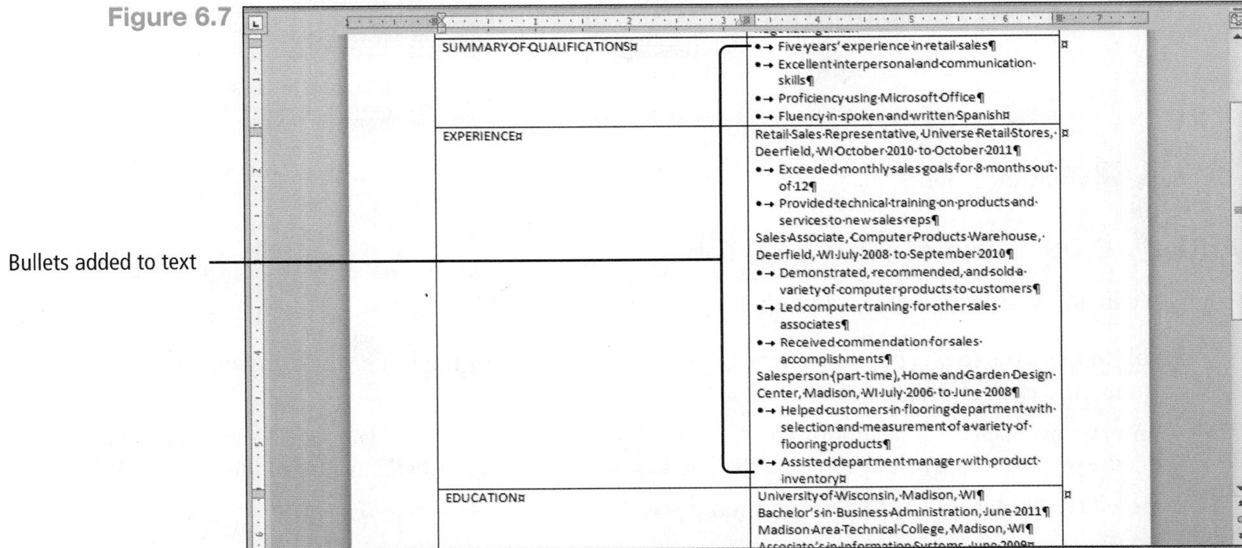

6 **Save** your document.

Objective 3 | Format a Table

Use Word's formatting tools to make your tables attractive and easy to read. Types of formatting you can add to a table include changing the row height and the column width, removing or adding borders, increasing or decreasing the paragraph or line spacing, or enhancing the text.

View the video on the Companion Web Site or in MyITLab

Activity 6.05 | Changing the Width of Table Columns

When you create a table, all of the columns are of equal width. In this activity, you will change the width of the columns.

1 In any row, point to the vertical border between the two columns to display the pointer. Drag the column border to the left to approximately **1.25 inches on the horizontal ruler**.

2 Scroll to the top of the document. Notice that in the second row, the text *SUMMARY OF QUALIFICATIONS* wraps to two lines to accommodate the new column width.

3 In the left column, click in any cell. On the Ribbon, under **Table Tools**, click the **Layout tab**.

4 In the **Cell Size group**, click the **Table Column Width button spin arrows** [button] as necessary to change the width of the first column to **1.40**. Compare your screen with Figure 6.8.

After dragging a border with your mouse, use the Width button to set a precise measurement if necessary.

Figure 6.8

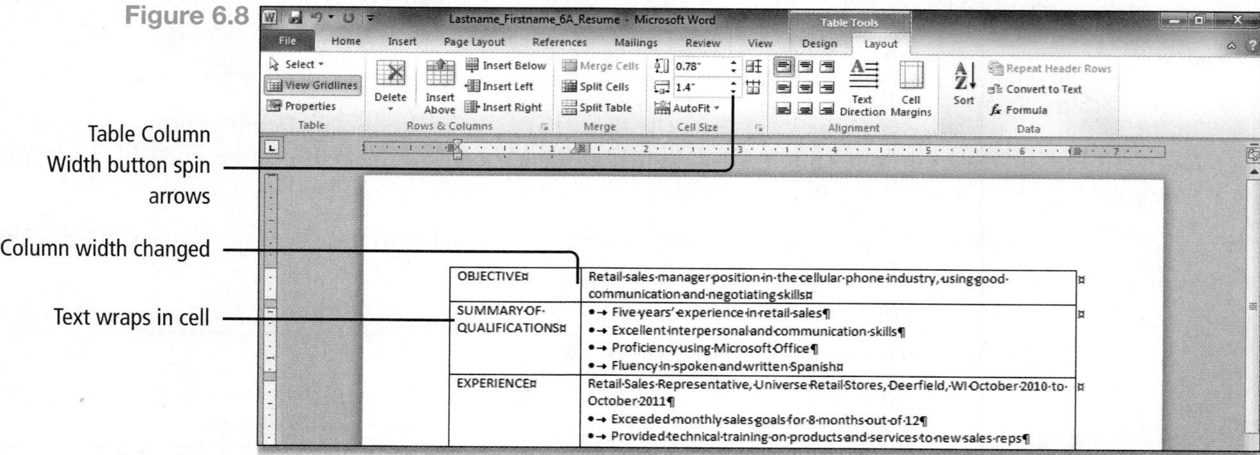

5 **Save** [icon] your document.

Activity 6.06 | Adding Rows to a Table

You can add rows or columns anywhere in a table.

1 Scroll to view the lower portion of the table. In the last row of the table, click anywhere in the *second* cell that contains the educational information, and then press Tab.

A new row displays at the bottom of the table. When the insertion point is in the last cell in the bottom row of a table, you can add a row by pressing the Tab key; the insertion point will display in the first cell of the new row.

2 Type **HONORS AND ACTIVITIES** and then press Tab.

3 Type the following, pressing Enter after the first item but not the second item:

Elected to Beta Gamma Sigma, international honor society for business students

Qualified for Dean's List, six academic periods

4 Select the text you typed in the last cell of the bottom row. On the **Home tab**, in the **Paragraph group**, click the **Bullets** button [icon], and then click the **Decrease Indent** button [icon] one time to align the bullets at the left edge of the cell.

5 Scroll up to view the entire table, and click anywhere in the top row of the table to deselect the text. On the **Layout tab**, in the **Rows & Columns group**, click the **Insert Above** button. Compare your screen with Figure 6.9.

Figure 6.9

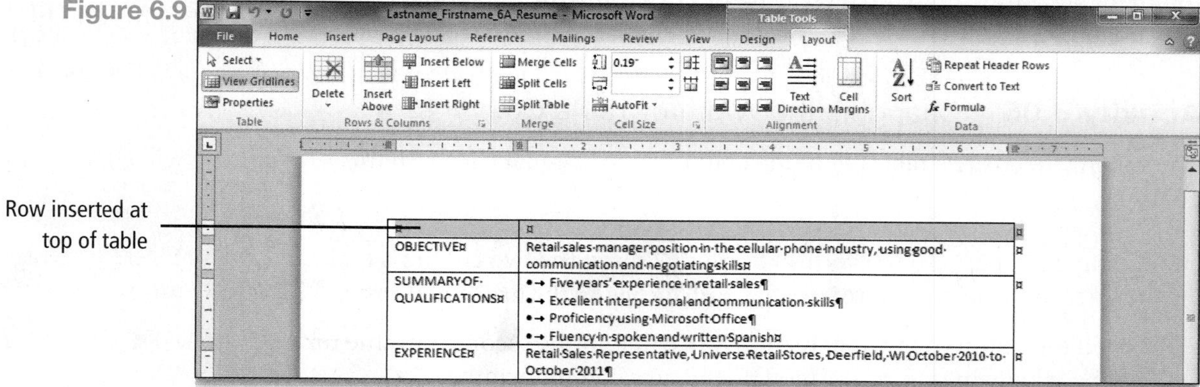

6 **Save** [icon] your document.

Activity 6.07 | Merging Cells

The title of a table typically spans all of the columns. In this activity, you will merge cells so that you can position the personal information across both columns.

1 Be sure the two cells in the top row are selected; if necessary, drag across both cells to select them. On the **Layout tab**, in the **Merge group**, click the **Merge Cells** button.

The cell border between the two cells no longer displays.

2 With the merged cell still selected, on the **Home tab**, in the **Paragraph group**, click the **Dialog Box Launcher** to display the **Paragraph** dialog box.

3 In the **Paragraph** dialog box, on the **Indents and Spacing tab**, in the lower left corner, click the **Tabs** button to display the **Tabs** dialog box.

4 In the **Tabs** dialog box, under **Tab stop position**, type **6.5** and then under **Alignment**, click the **Right** option button. Click **Set**, and then click **OK** to close the dialog box.

5 Type **Daniela Johnstone** Hold down Ctrl and then press Tab. Notice that the insertion point moves to the right-aligned tab stop at 6.50.

In a Word table, you must use Ctrl + Tab to move to a tab stop, because pressing Tab is reserved for moving the insertion point from cell to cell.

6 Type **(608) 555-0588** and then press Enter. Type **1343 Siena Lane, Deerfield, WI 53531**

7 Hold down Ctrl, press Tab, and then type **djohnstone@alcona.net**

8 **Save** your document.

Activity 6.08 | Formatting Text in Cells

1 In the first row of the table, select the name Daniela Johnstone, and then on the Mini toolbar, apply **Bold** and change the **Font Size** to **16**.

2 Under *Daniela Johnstone*, click anywhere in the second line of text, which contains the address and e-mail address. On the **Page Layout tab**, in the **Paragraph group**, click the **Spacing After up spin arrow** three times to add **18 pt** spacing between the first row of the table and the second row. Compare your screen with Figure 6.10.

These actions separate the personal information from the body of the resume and add focus to the applicant's name.

Figure 6.10

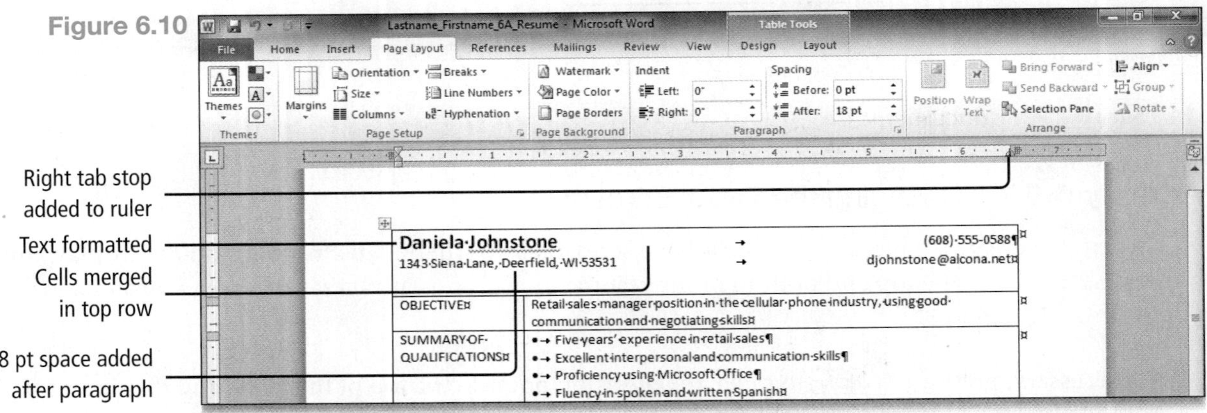

3 Using the technique you just practiced, in the second column, click in the last paragraph of every cell and add **18 pt Spacing After** the last paragraph of all rows including the last row; a border will be added to the bottom of the table, and spacing will be needed between the last row and the border.

4 In the second row, point to the word *OBJECTIVE*, hold down the left mouse button, and then drag downward in the first column only to select all the headings in uppercase letters. On the Mini toolbar, click the **Bold** button **B**.

> **Note | Selecting Only One Column**
> When you drag downward to select the first column, a fast mouse might also begin to select the second column when you reach the bottom. If this happens, drag upward slightly to deselect the second column and select only the first column.

5 In the cell to the right of *EXPERIENCE*, without selecting the following comma, select Retail Sales Representative and then on the Mini toolbar, click the **Bold** button **B**. In the same cell, apply **Bold** **B** to the other job titles—*Sales Associate* and *Salesperson*—but do not bold (*part time*).

6 In the cell to the right of *EDUCATION*, apply **Bold** **B** to *University of Wisconsin, Madison, WI* and *Madison Area Technical College, Madison, WI.*

7 In the same cell, click anywhere in the line beginning *Bachelor's*. On the **Page Layout tab**, in the **Paragraph group**, click the **Spacing After up spin arrow** two times to add **12 pt** spacing after the paragraph.

8 In the cell to the right of *EXPERIENCE*, under Retail Sales Representative, click anywhere in the second bulleted item, and then add **12 pt Spacing After** the item.

9 In the same cell, repeat this process for the last bulleted item under *Sales Associate*.

10 Scroll to the top of the table, and then compare your screen with Figure 6.11.

Figure 6.11

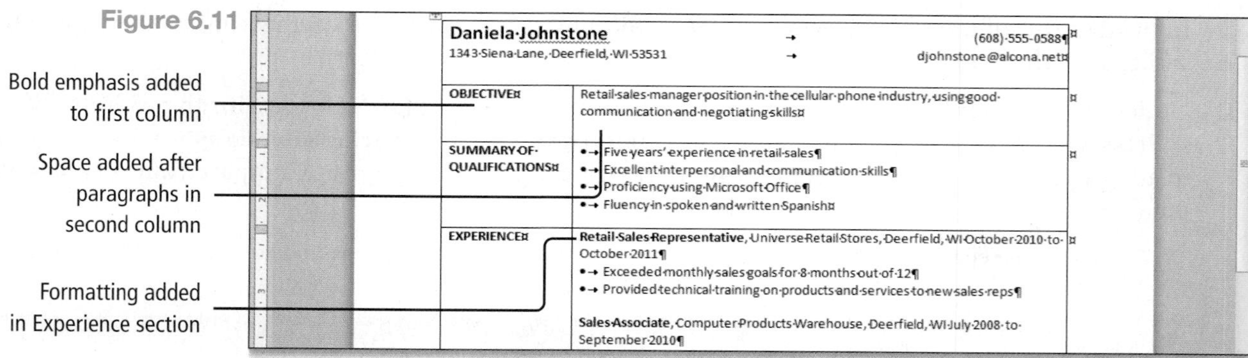

11 **Save** your document.

Activity 6.09 | Changing the Table Borders

When you create a table, all of the cells have solid, black borders. Most resumes do not display any cell borders. A border at the top and bottom of the resume, however, is attractive and adds a professional look to the document.

1 If necessary, press Ctrl + Home to move the insertion point to the top of the table, and then point slightly outside of the upper left corner of the table to display the **table move handle**. With the pointer, click one time to select the entire table.

Shaded row markers indicate that the entire row is selected.

2 Click the **Design tab**. In the **Table Styles group**, click the **Borders button arrow**, and then click **No Border**.

The black borders no longer display; instead, depending on your setup, either no borders—the default setting—or nonprinting blue dashed borders display.

3 Click the **Design tab**; be sure the table is still selected. In the **Table Styles group**, click the **Borders button arrow**, and then at the bottom of the **Borders** gallery, click **Borders and Shading**.

4 Under **Setting**, click the **Custom** button. Under **Style**, scroll down about a third of the way and click the style with the thick upper line and the thin lower line. In the **Preview** box at the right, point to the *top* border of the small preview and click one time.

5 Under **Style**, click the style with the thin upper line and the thick lower line, and then in the **Preview** box, click the *bottom* border of the preview. Compare your screen with Figure 6.12.

Figure 6.12

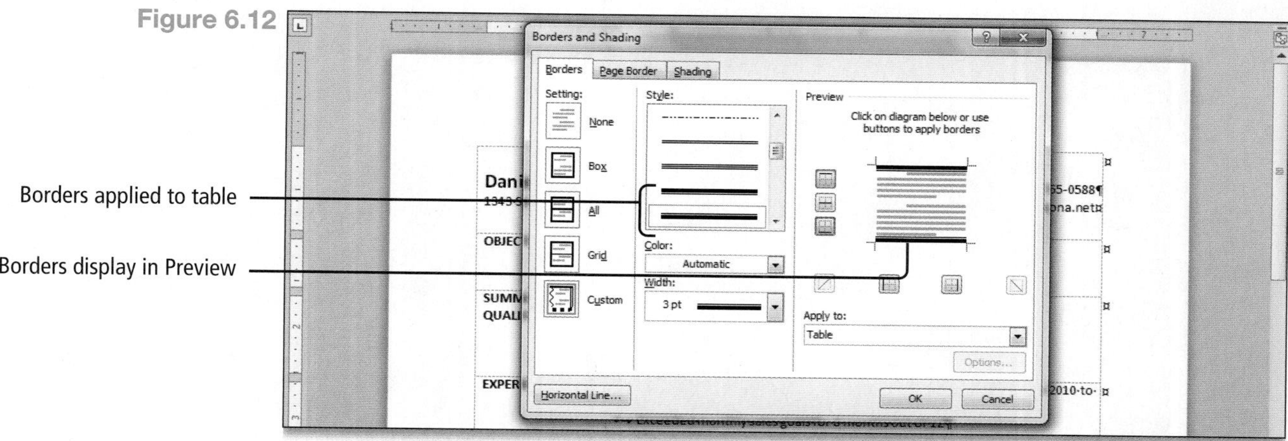

6 Click **OK**, click anywhere to cancel the selection, and then notice that there is only a small amount of space between the upper border and the first line of text.

7 Click anywhere in the text *Daniela Johnstone*, and then on the **Page Layout tab**, in the **Paragraph group**, click the **Spacing Before up spin arrow** as necessary to add **18 pt** spacing before the first paragraph.

8 Display **Backstage** view. Click the **Print tab** to preview the table. Compare your screen with Figure 6.13.

Figure 6.13

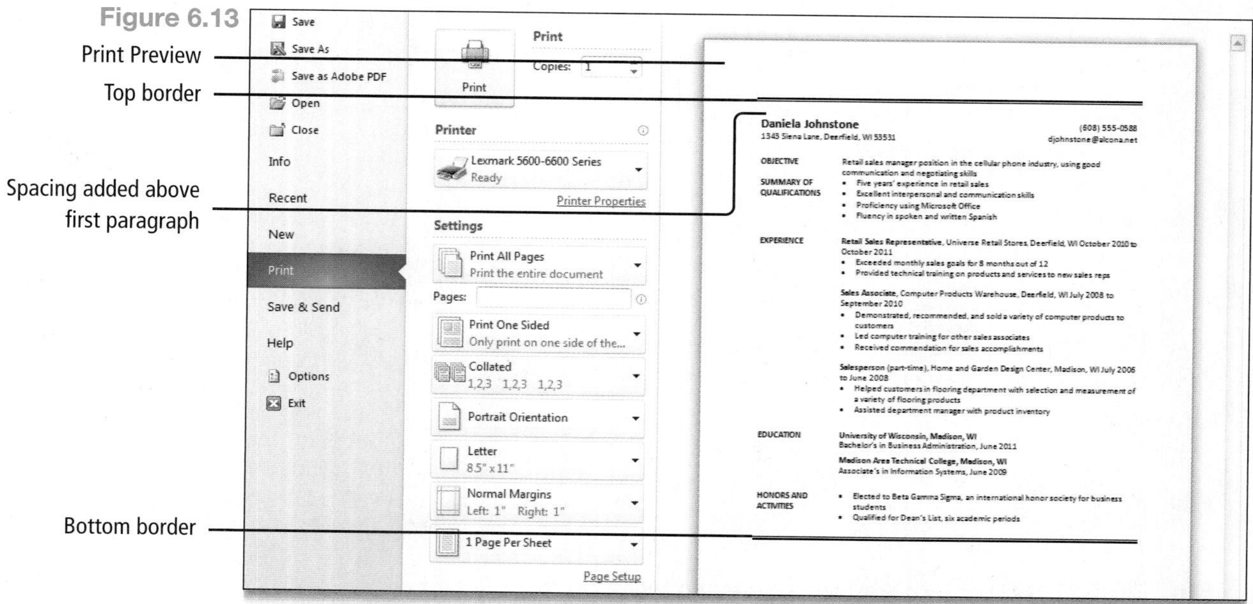

9 In **Backstage** view, click the **Info tab**. On the right, under the document thumbnail, click **Properties**, and then click **Show Document Panel**. In the **Author** box, delete any text and then type your firstname and lastname. In the **Subject** box, type your course name and section number, and in the **Keywords** box type **resume, Word table**

10 **Close** the **Document Panel**. **Save** and then print your document, or submit it electronically, as directed by your instructor. **Exit** Word.

End **You have completed Project 6A**

Project 6B Cover Letter and Resume

Project Activities

In Activities 6.10 through 6.22, you will create a letterhead, and then use the letterhead to create a cover letter. You will also create a short resume using a Microsoft template and save it as a Web page. Your completed documents will look similar to Figure 6.14.

Project Files

For Project 6B, you will need the following file:

w06B_Cover_Letter_Text

You will save your documents as:

Lastname_Firstname_6B_Letterhead
Lastname_Firstname_6B_Cover_Letter
Lastname_Firstname_6B_Brief_Resume
Lastname_Firstname_6B_HTML_Resume

Project Results

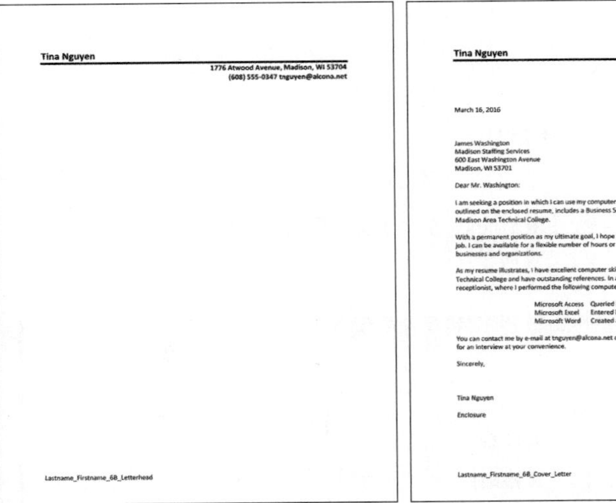

Tina Nguyen
1776 Atwood Avenue, Madison, WI 53704
(608) 555-0347 tnguyen@alcona.net

Lastname_Firstname_6B_Letterhead

Tina Nguyen
1776 Atwood Avenue, Madison, WI 53704
(608) 555-0347 tnguyen@alcona.net

March 16, 2016

James Washington
Madison Staffing Services
600 East Washington Avenue
Madison, WI 53701

Dear Mr. Washington:

I am seeking a position in which I can use my computer and communication skills. My education, outlined on the enclosed resume, includes a Business Software Applications Specialist certificate from Madison Area Technical College.

With a permanent position as my ultimate goal, I hope to use your staffing service to secure a temporary job. I can be available for a flexible number of hours or days and am willing to work in a variety of businesses and organizations.

As my resume illustrates, I have excellent computer skills. I was an honor student at Madison Area Technical College and have outstanding references. In addition, I have part-time work experience as a receptionist, where I performed the following computer activities:

Microsoft Access Queried inventory data
Microsoft Excel Entered budget data
Microsoft Word Created and mailed form letters

You can contact me by e-mail at tnguyen@alcona.net or by telephone at (818) 555-0837. I am available for an interview at your convenience.

Sincerely,

Tina Nguyen

Enclosure

Lastname_Firstname_6B_Cover_Letter

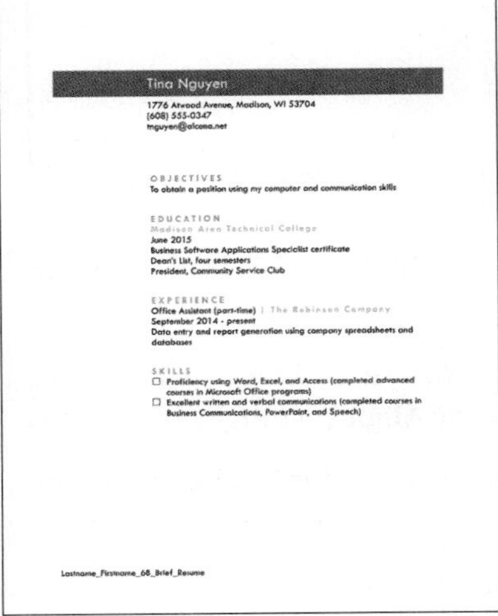

Tina Nguyen
1776 Atwood Avenue, Madison, WI 53704
(608) 555-0347
tnguyen@alcona.net

OBJECTIVES
To obtain a position using my computer and communication skills

EDUCATION
Madison Area Technical College
June 2015
Business Software Applications Specialist certificate
Dean's List, four semesters
President, Community Service Club

EXPERIENCE
Office Assistant (part-time) | The Robinson Company
September 2014 - present
Data entry and report generation using company spreadsheets and databases

SKILLS
- Proficiency using Word, Excel, and Access (completed advanced courses in Microsoft Office programs)
- Excellent written and verbal communications (completed courses in Business Communications, PowerPoint, and Speech)

Lastname_Firstname_6B_Brief_Resume

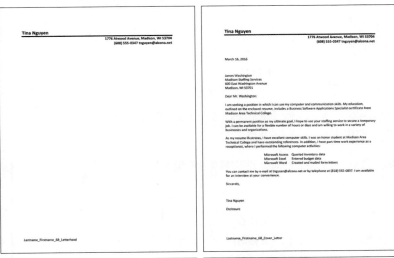

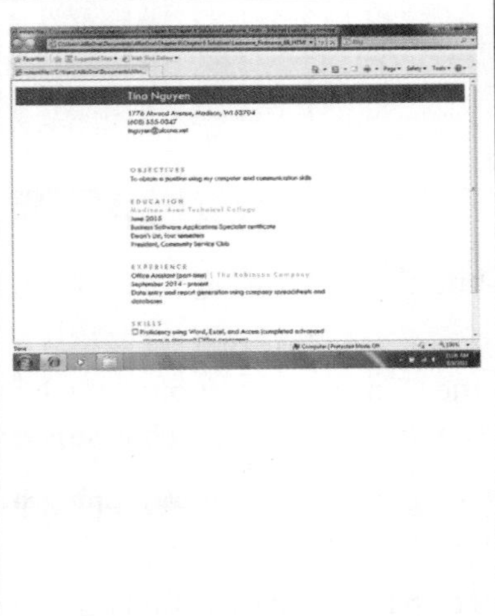

Figure 6.14
Project 6B Cover Letter and Resume

Objective 4 | Create a New Document from an Existing Document

View the video on the Companion Web Site or in MyITLab

A ***template*** is an *existing* document that you use as a starting point for a new document. The template document opens a copy of itself, unnamed, and then you use the structure—and possibly some content, such as headings—as the starting point for a new document. All documents are based on a template. When you create a new blank document, it is based on Word's ***Normal template***, which serves as the starting point for all new Word documents.

Activity 6.10 | Creating a Letterhead

A ***letterhead*** is the personal or company information that displays at the top of a letter, and commonly includes a name, address, and contact information. The term also refers to a piece of paper imprinted with such information at the top.

1 **Start** Word, and in the new blank document, be sure that formatting marks and rulers display. On the **Home tab**, in the **Styles group**, click the **More** button [▾]. In the displayed gallery, click the **No Spacing** button.

Recall that the default spacing for a new Word document is 10 points of blank space following a paragraph and line spacing of 1.15. The ***No Spacing style*** inserts no extra space following a paragraph and uses single spacing.

Using the No Spacing style allows you to format a letter as outlined in Business Communications texts.

2 Type the following, pressing Enter at the end of each item:

Tina Nguyen

1776 Atwood Avenue, Madison, WI 53704

(608) 555-0347 tnguyen@alcona.net

3 If the e-mail address changes to blue text, right-click the e-mail address, and then from the shortcut menu, click **Remove Hyperlink**. Compare your screen with Figure 6.15.

Figure 6.15

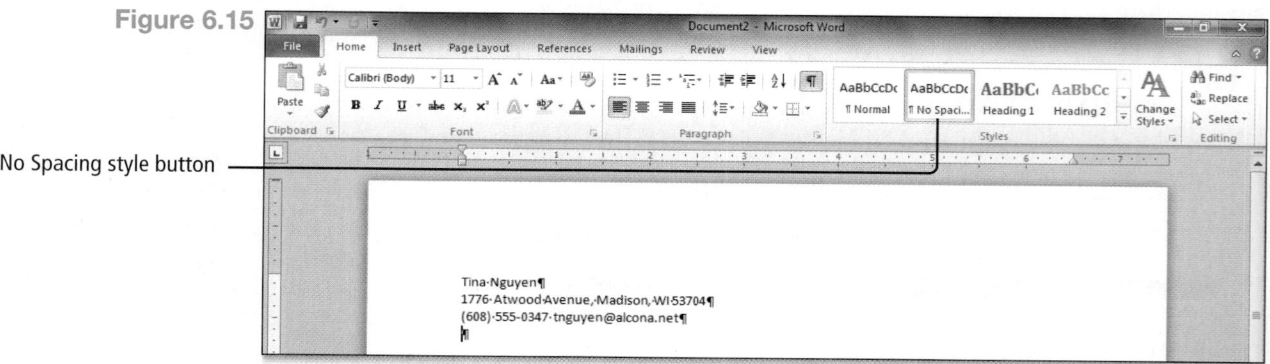

4 Select the first paragraph—*Tina Nguyen*—and then on the Mini toolbar, apply **Bold** [B] and change the **Font Size** to **16**

5 Select the second and third paragraphs. On the Mini toolbar, apply **Bold** [B] and change the **Font Size** to **12**. With the two paragraphs still selected, on the **Home tab**, in the **Paragraph group**, click the **Align Text Right** button [≡].

6 Click anywhere in the first paragraph—*Tina Nguyen*. In the **Paragraph group**, click the **Borders button arrow** [⊞▾], and then at the bottom, click **Borders and Shading**.

7 In the **Borders and Shading** dialog box, under **Style**, be sure the first style—a single solid line—is selected. Click the **Width arrow**, and then click **3 pt**. To the right, under **Preview**, click the bottom border of the diagram. Under **Apply to**, be sure *Paragraph* displays. Compare your screen with Figure 6.16.

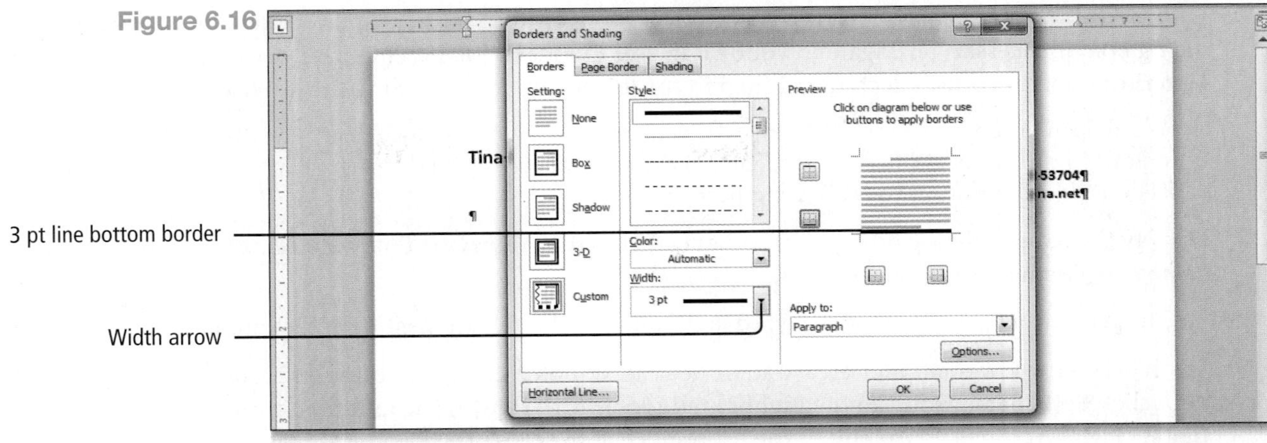

Figure 6.16

8 Click **OK** to display a 3 pt line below *Tina Nguyen*, which extends from the left margin to the right margin.

9 Display the **Save As** dialog box, **Save** the document in your **All In One Chapter 6** folder as **Lastname_Firstname_6B_Letterhead** and then add the file name to the footer.

10 Display **Backstage** view, click the **Info tab**, and then on the right, under the document thumbnail, click **Properties**. Click **Show Document Panel**. In the **Author** box, delete any text and then type your firstname and lastname. In the **Subject** box, type your course name and section number, and in the **Keywords** box type **personal letterhead Close** the **Document Panel**.

11 **Save** your document. Display **Backstage** view, and then click **Close** to close the document but leave Word open. Hold this file until you complete this project.

Activity 6.11 | Creating a Document from an Existing Document

To use an existing document as the starting point for a new document, Word provides the ***New from existing*** command.

1 Click the **File tab** to display **Backstage** view, and then click **New** to display the new document options. Compare your screen with Figure 6.17.

Here you can create a new document in a variety of ways, including from an existing document.

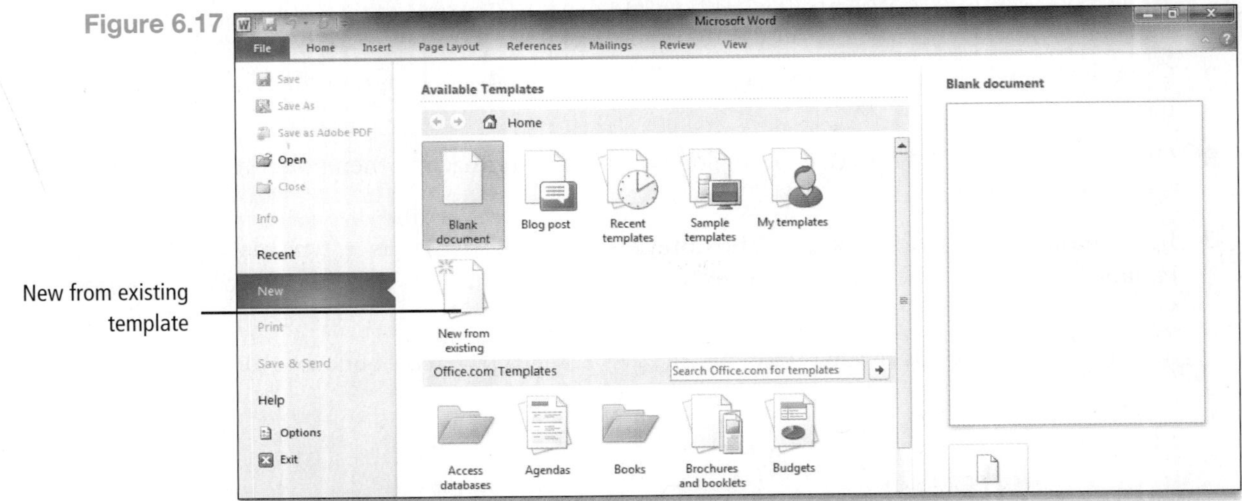

Figure 6.17

2 Under **Available Templates**, click the **New from existing** button. In the displayed **New from Existing Document** dialog box, if necessary, navigate to your **All In One Chapter 6** folder, click your **Lastname_Firstname_6B_ Letterhead** document to select it, and then in the lower right corner, click **Create New**.

Word opens a copy of your 6B_Letterhead document as a new Word document—the title bar indicates *Document* followed by a number. You are not opening the original document, and changes that you make to this new document will not affect your 6B_Letterhead document.

3 Display the **Save As** dialog box, and then navigate to your **All In One Chapter 6** folder. Save the file as **Lastname_Firstname_6B_Cover_Letter**

The personal information that you typed in the 6B_Letterhead Document Panel remains in the new document.

4 Scroll down to view the footer area, and notice that a footer displays. Point to the footer and right-click, and then click **Edit Footer**. Point to the highlighted footer text, right-click, and then from the shortcut menu, click **Update Field**. At the far right end of the Ribbon, click the **Close Header and Footer** button.

The footer displays because it was included in the document that you saved as a template. The *FileName* field does not automatically update to the new file name.

5 **Save** your document.

Objective 5 | Change and Reorganize Text

View the video on the Companion Web Site or in MyITLab

Business letters follow a standard format and contain the following parts: the current date, referred to as the ***date line***; the name and address of the person receiving the letter, referred to as the ***inside address***; a greeting, referred to as the ***salutation***; the text of the letter, usually referred to as the ***body*** of the letter; a closing line, referred to as the ***complimentary closing***; and the ***writer's identification***, which includes the name or job title (or both) of the writer, and which is also referred to as the ***writer's signature block***. Some letters also include the initials of the person who prepared the letter, an optional ***subject line*** that describes the purpose of the letter, or a list of ***enclosures***—documents included with the letter.

Activity 6.12 | Recording AutoCorrect Entries

You can correct commonly misspelled words automatically by using Word's ***AutoCorrect*** feature. Commonly misspelled words—such as *teh* instead of *the*—are corrected using a built-in list that is installed with Office. If you have words that you frequently misspell, you can add them to the list for automatic correction.

1 Click the **File tab** to display **Backstage** view. On the **Help tab**, click **Options** to display the **Word Options** dialog box.

2 On the left side of the **Word Options** dialog box, click **Proofing**, and then under **AutoCorrect options**, click the **AutoCorrect Options** button.

3 In the **AutoCorrect** dialog box, click the **AutoCorrect tab**. Under **Replace**, type **resumee** and under **With**, type **resume** Click **Add**. If the entry already exists, click Replace instead, and then click Yes. Compare your screen with Figure 6.18.

If another student has already added this AutoCorrect entry, a Replace button will display.

Figure 6.18

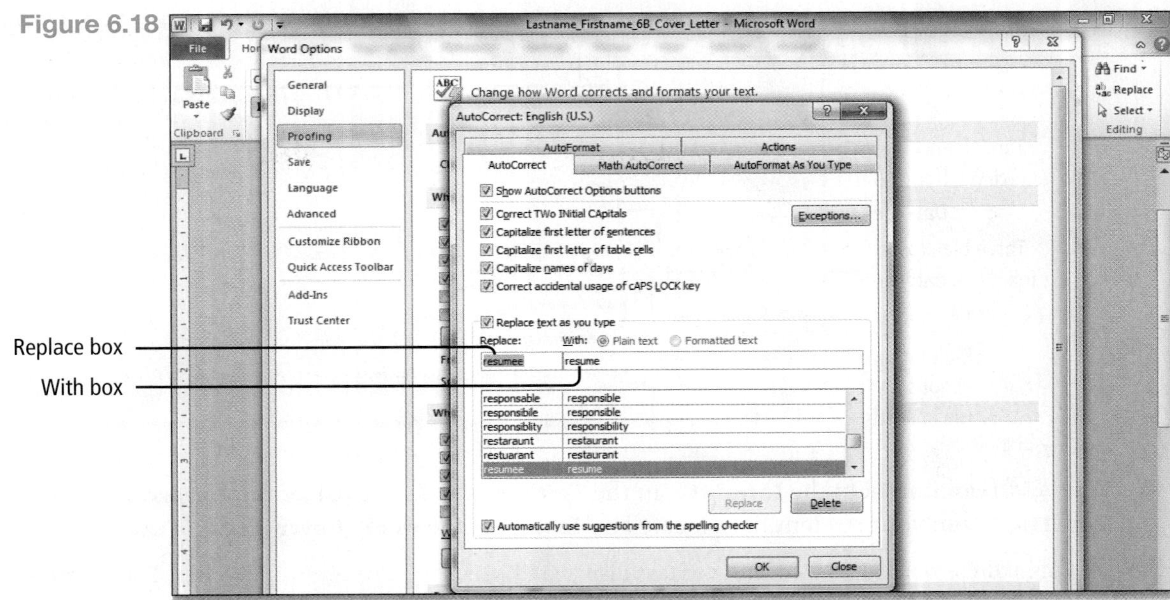

4 Click **OK** two times to close the dialog boxes.

Activity 6.13 | Creating a Cover Letter

There are a variety of accepted letter formats found in reference manuals and Business Communication texts. The one used in this chapter is a block style cover letter taken from *Business Communication Today*.

1 Press Ctrl + End to move the insertion point to the blank line below the letterhead. Press Enter three times, and then type **March 16, 2016** to create the dateline.

Most Business Communication texts recommend that the dateline be positioned at least 0.5 inch (3 blank lines) below the letterhead; or, position the dateline approximately 2 inches from the top edge of the paper.

2 Press Enter four times, which leaves three blank lines. Type the following inside address on four lines, but do not press Enter following the last line:

James Washington

Madison Staffing Services

600 East Washington Avenue

Madison, WI 53701

3 Press Enter two times to leave one blank line. Type the salutation **Dear Mr. Washington:** and then press Enter two times.

Always leave one blank line above and below the salutation.

4 Type the following, including the misspelled last word: **I am seeking a position in witch I can use my computer and communication skills. My education, outlined on the enclosed resumee** and then type **,** (a comma).

The AutoCorrect feature recognizes the misspelled word, and then changes *resumee* to *resume* when you press Spacebar, Enter, or a punctuation mark.

5 Press Spacebar. Complete the paragraph by typing **includes a Business Software Applications Specialist certificate from MATC.** Compare your screen with Figure 6.19.

Figure 6.19

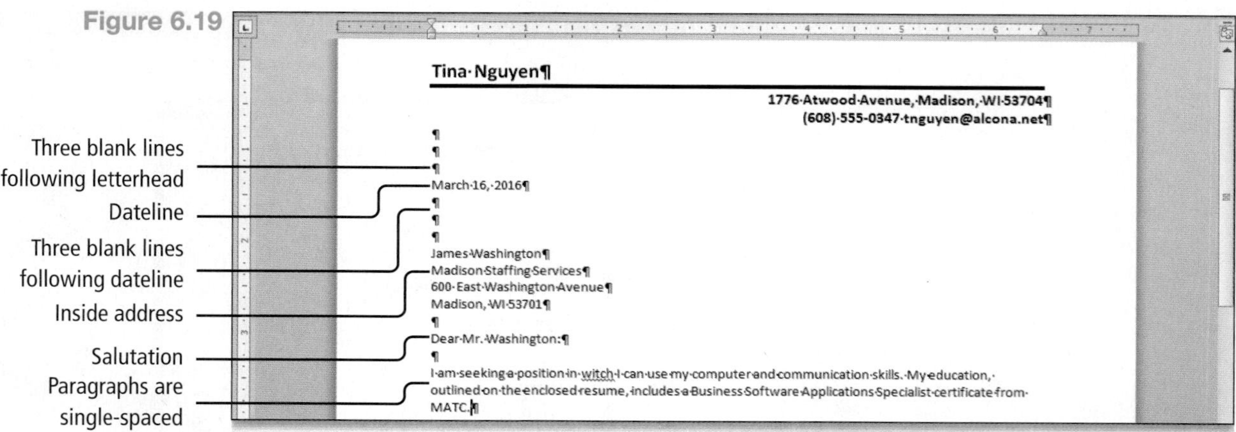

6 Press Enter two times. On the **Insert tab**, in the **Text group**, click the **Object button arrow**, and then click **Text from File**. From your student files, locate and **Insert** the file **w06B_Cover_Letter_Text**.

Some of the words in the cover letter text display red, green, or blue wavy underlines. These indicate potential spelling, grammar, or word usage errors, and you will correct them before the end of this project.

7 Scroll as necessary to display the lower half of the letter on your screen, and be sure your insertion point is positioned in the blank paragraph at the end of the document. Press Enter one time to leave one blank line between the last paragraph of the letter and the complimentary closing.

8 Type **Sincerely,** as the complimentary closing, and then press Enter four times to leave three blank lines between the complimentary closing and the writer's identification. Type **Tina Nguyen** as the writer's identification, and then press Enter two times.

9 Type **Enclosure** to indicate that a document is included with the letter. Save your document.

Activity 6.14 | Finding and Replacing Text

Use the Find command to locate text in a document quickly. Use the Find and Replace command to make the same change, or to make more than one change at a time, in a document.

1 Press Ctrl + Home to position the insertion point at the beginning of the document.

Because a find operation—or a find and replace operation—begins at the location of the insertion point and continues to the end of the document, it is good practice to position the insertion point at the beginning of the document before initiating the command.

2 On the **Home tab**, in the **Editing group**, click the **Find** button.

The Navigation Pane displays on the left side of the screen, with a search box at the top of the pane.

3 In the search box, type **ac** If necessary, scroll down in your document to view the entire body text of the letter, and then compare your screen with Figure 6.20.

In the document, the search letters ac are selected and highlighted in yellow for all three words that contain the letters ac together. In the Navigation Pane, the three instances are shown in context—ac displays in bold.

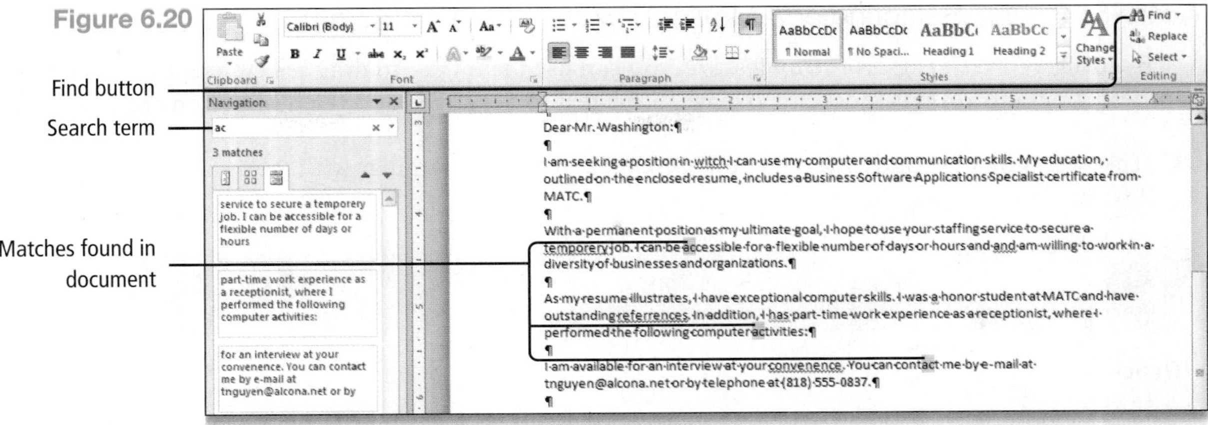

Figure 6.20

4 In the search box, complete the word **accessible**

One match for the search term displays in context in the Navigation Pane and is highlighted in the document.

5 In the document, point to the yellow highlighted word *accessible*, double-click, and then type **available** to replace the word. Notice that the list of results is now empty.

6 **Close** the **Navigation Pane**, and then on the **Home tab**, in the **Editing group**, click the **Replace** button.

7 In the **Find and Replace** dialog box, in the **Find what** box, replace the existing text by typing **MATC** In the **Replace with** box, type **Madison Area Technical College** and then compare your screen with Figure 6.21.

The acronym MATC appears in the document two times. The reader may not know what the acronym means, so you should include the full text.

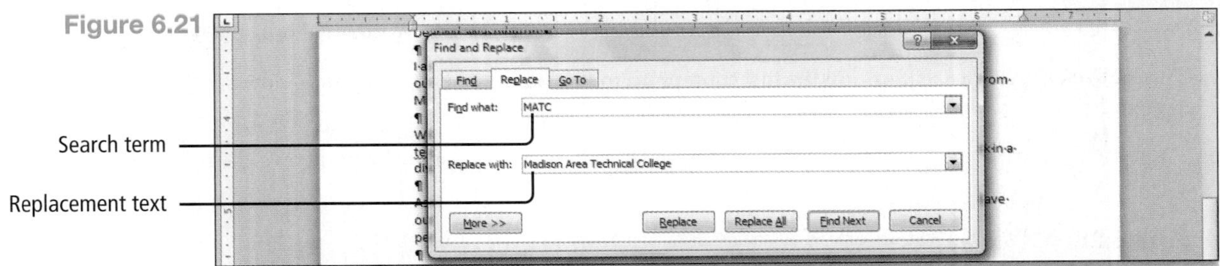

Figure 6.21

8 In the lower left corner of the dialog box, click the **More** button to expand the dialog box, and then under **Search Options**, select the **Match case** check box.

In this instance, you must select the Match case check box so that the replaced text will match the case you typed in the Replace with box, and *not* display in all uppercase letters like *MATC*.

9 In the **Find and Replace** dialog box, click the **Replace All** button to replace both instances of MATC. Click **OK** to close the message box.

10 In the **Find and Replace** dialog box, clear the **Match case** check box, click the **Less** button, and then **Close** the dialog box.

The Find and Replace dialog box opens with the settings used the last time it was open. Thus, it is good practice to reset this dialog box to its default settings each time you use it.

11 **Save** your document.

Activity 6.15 | Selecting and Moving Text to a New Location

By using Word's ***drag-and-drop*** feature, you can use the mouse to drag selected text from one location to another. Drag-and-drop is most effective when the text to be moved and the destination are on the same screen.

1 Take a moment to study the table in Figure 6.22 to become familiar with the techniques you can use to select text in a document quickly.

Selecting Text in a Document

To Select	Do This
A portion of text	Click to position the insertion point at the beginning of the text you want to select, hold down Shift, and then click at the end of the text you want to select. Alternatively, hold down the left mouse button and drag from the beginning to the end of the text you want to select.
A word	Double-click the word.
A sentence	Hold down Ctrl and click anywhere in the sentence.
A paragraph	Triple-click anywhere in the paragraph; or, move the pointer to the left of the line, into the margin area. When the pointer displays, double-click.
A line	Move the pointer to the left of the line. When the pointer displays, click one time.
One character at a time	Position the insertion point to the left of the first character, hold down Shift, and press ← or → as many times as desired.
A string of words	Position the insertion point to the left of the first word, hold down Shift and Ctrl, and then press ← or → as many times as desired.
Consecutive lines	Position the insertion point to the left of the first word, hold down Shift and press ↑ or ↓.
Consecutive paragraphs	Position the insertion point to the left of the first word, hold down Shift and Ctrl and press ↑ or ↓.
The entire document	Hold down Ctrl and press A. Alternatively, move the pointer to the left of any line in the document. When the pointer displays, triple-click.

Figure 6.22

2 Be sure you can view the entire body of the letter on your screen. In the paragraph that begins *With a permanent position*, in the second line, locate and double-click *days*.

3 Point to the selected word to display the pointer. Drag to the right until the dotted vertical line that floats next to the pointer is positioned to the right of the word *hours* in the same line, as shown in Figure 6.23.

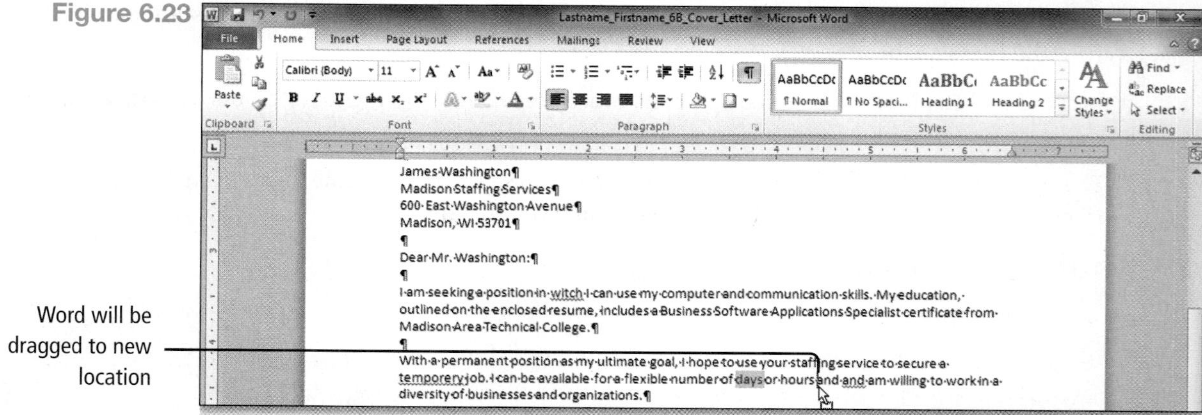

Figure 6.23

4 Release the mouse button to move the text. Select the word *hours* and drag it to the left of the word *or*—the previous location of the word *days*. Click anywhere in the document to deselect the text. Examine the text that you moved, and add or remove spaces as necessary.

5 Hold down Ctrl, and then in the paragraph that begins *I am available*, click anywhere in the first sentence to select the entire sentence. Drag the selected sentence to the end of the paragraph by positioning the small vertical line that floats with the pointer to the left of the paragraph mark.

6 **Save** your document.

Activity 6.16 | Inserting and Formatting a Table in a Document

1 Locate the paragraph that begins *As my resume*, and then click to position the insertion point in the blank line below that paragraph. Press Enter one time.

2 On the **Insert tab**, in the **Tables group**, click the **Table** button. In the **Table** grid, in the third row, click the second square to insert a 2 × 3 table.

3 In the first cell of the table, type **Microsoft Access** and then press Tab. Type **Queried inventory data** and then press Tab. Complete the table using the following information:

Microsoft Excel	**Entered budget data**
Microsoft Word	**Created and mailed form letters**

4 Point slightly outside of the upper left corner of the table to display the **table move handle** button. With the pointer, click one time to select the entire table.

5 On the **Layout tab**, in the **Cell Size group**, click the **AutoFit** button, and then click **AutoFit Contents** to have Word choose the best column widths for the two columns based on the text you entered.

6 On the **Home tab**, in the **Paragraph** group, click the **Center** button to center the table between the left and right margins.

7 On the **Design tab**, in the **Table Styles group**, click the **Borders button arrow**, and then click **No Border**. Click anywhere to cancel the selection of the table, and then compare your screen with Figure 6.24.

Figure 6.24

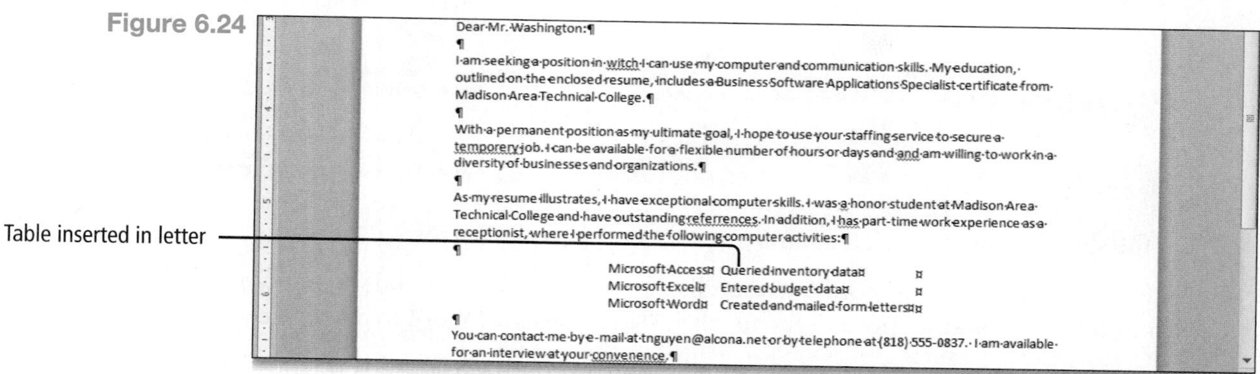
Dear Mr. Washington:

I am seeking a position in witch I can use my computer and communication skills. My education, outlined on the enclosed resume, includes a Business Software Applications Specialist certificate from Madison Area Technical College.

With a permanent position as my ultimate goal, I hope to use your staffing service to secure a temporery job. I can be available for a flexible number of hours or days and and am willing to work in a diversity of businesses and organizations.

As my resume illustrates, I have exceptional computer skills. I was a honor student at Madison Area Technical College and have outstanding referrences. In addition, I has part-time work experience as a receptionist, where I performed the following computer activities:

Microsoft Access	Queried inventory data
Microsoft Excel	Entered budget data
Microsoft Word	Created and mailed form letters

You can contact me by e-mail at tnguyen@alcona.net or by telephone at (818) 555-0837. I am available for an interview at your convenence.

8 **Save** your document.

Objective 6 | Use the Proofing Options

View the video on the Companion Web Site or in MyITLab

Word compares your typing to words in the Office dictionary and compares your phrases and punctuation to a list of grammar rules. Words that are not in the dictionary are marked with a wavy red underline. Phrases and punctuation that differ from the grammar rules are marked with a wavy green underline. Word also compares commonly misused words with a set of word usage rules, and marks misused words with a wavy blue underline; for example, the misuse of *their*, *there*, and *they're*. However, Word will not flag the word *sign* as misspelled even though you intended to type *sing a song* rather than *sign a song*, because both are words contained within Word's dictionary. Your own proofreading skills are still required to edit documents accurately.

Activity 6.17 | Checking Spelling and Grammar Errors

In this activity, you will practice with different methods to correct spelling and grammar errors.

> **Alert! | Spelling and Grammar Checking**
>
> If you do not see any wavy red, green, or blue lines under words, the automatic spelling and/or grammar checking has been turned off. To activate it, display Backstage view, click Options, click Proofing, and then under *When correcting spelling in Microsoft Office programs*, select the first four check boxes. Under *When correcting spelling and grammar in Word*, select the first four check boxes, and then click the Writing Style arrow and click Grammar Only. Under *Exceptions for*, clear both check boxes. To display the flagged spelling and grammar errors, click the Recheck Document button, and then close the dialog box.

1 Position the body of the letter on your screen, and then examine the text to locate green, red, and blue wavy underlines.

A list of grammar rules applied by a computer program like Word can never be exact, and a computer dictionary cannot contain all known words and proper names. Thus, you will need to check any words flagged by Word with wavy underlines, and you will also need to proofread for content errors.

2 In the paragraph that begins *With a permanent*, locate the word *temporery* with the wavy red underline. Point to the word and right-click to display the shortcut menu, and then compare your screen with Figure 6.25.

Figure 6.25

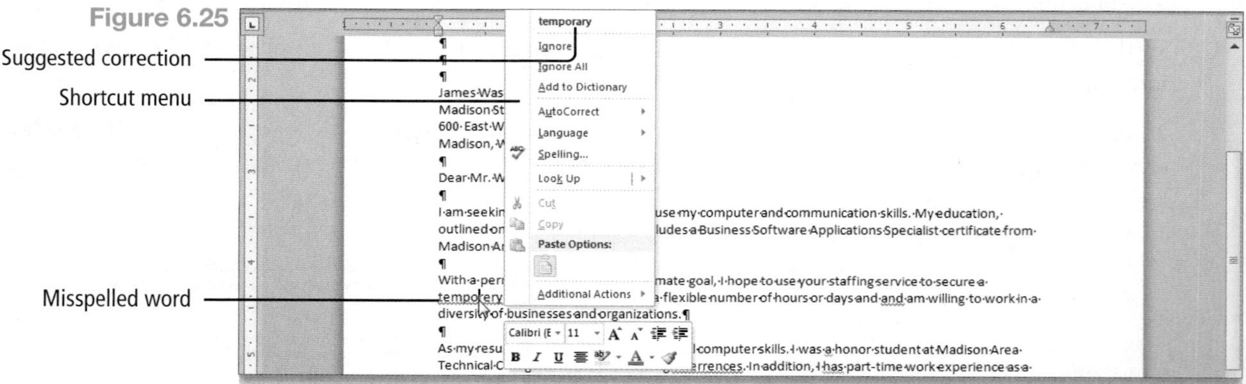

3 On the shortcut menu, click **temporary** to correct the spelling error.

4 In the next line, locate the word *and* that displays with a wavy red underline, point to the word and right-click, and then from the shortcut menu, click **Delete Repeated Word** to delete the duplicate word.

5 Press Ctrl + Home to move the insertion point to the beginning of the document. Click the **Review tab**, and then in the **Proofing group**, click the **Spelling & Grammar** button to check the spelling and grammar of the text in the document. Compare your screen with Figure 6.26.

The word *witch* is highlighted—a *Possible Word Choice Error*—and the sentence containing the potential error displays in the dialog box. A suggested change also displays.

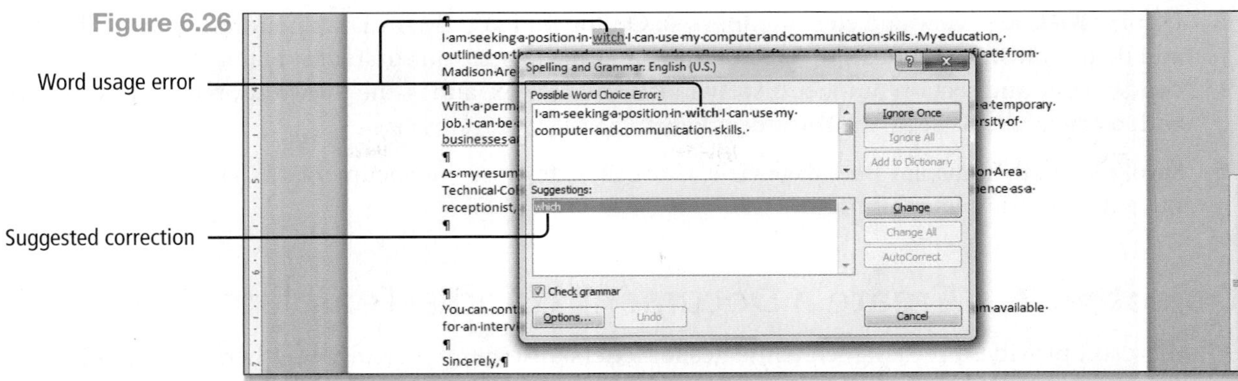

Figure 6.26

6 In the **Spelling and Grammar** dialog box, click the **Change** button to change to the correct usage *which*.

The next marked word—a possible spelling error—displays.

7 Click the **Change** button to change *referrences* to *references*. Click the **Change** button to change *a* to *an*. Continue the spelling and grammar check and change *has* to *have* and correct the spelling of *convenence*.

8 When Word indicates *The spelling and grammar check is complete*, click **OK**. **Save** your document.

Activity 6.18 | Using the Thesaurus

A ***thesaurus*** is a research tool that lists ***synonyms***—words that have the same or similar meaning to the word you selected.

1 Scroll so that you can view the body of the letter. In the paragraph that begins *With a permanent*, at the end of the second line, locate and right-click the word *diversity*. On the shortcut menu, point to **Synonyms**, and then compare your screen with Figure 6.27.

A list of synonyms displays; the list will vary in length depending on the selected word.

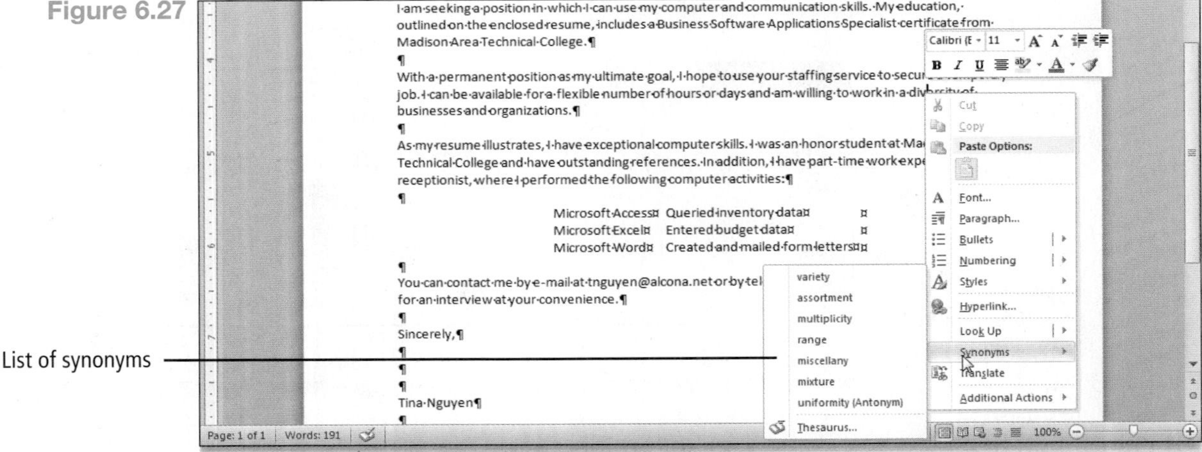

Figure 6.27

2 From the list of synonyms, click **variety** to replace *diversity* with *variety*.

3 In the paragraph that begins *As my resume*, point to the word *exceptional*, right-click, point to **Synonyms**, and then at the bottom of the shortcut menu, click **Thesaurus** to display the **Research** task pane.

4 In the **Research** task pane, under **Thesaurus**, point to the non-bold word *excellent*, and then click the **arrow**. On the menu, click **Insert**, and then **Close** the **Research** task pane.

The word *excellent* replaces the word *exceptional*.

5 Display **Backstage** view and click the **Info tab**. On the right, under the document thumbnail, click **Properties**, and then click **Show Document Panel**. In the **Author** box, type your firstname and lastname. Be sure your course name and section number display in the **Subject** box, and as the **Keywords**, replace any existing text with **cover letter**. **Close** [X] the **Document Panel**.

6 **Save** [Save icon], and then display **Backstage** view. Click **Close** to close the document but leave Word open. Hold this file until you complete this project.

Objective 7 | Create a Document Using a Template

View the video on the Companion Web Site or in MyITLab

Microsoft provides pre-designed templates for letters, resumes, invoices, and other types of documents. Recall that when you open a template, it opens unnamed so that you can reuse it as often as you need to do so.

Activity 6.19 | Locating and Opening a Template

If you need to create a short resume quickly, or if you need ideas about how to format your resume, Microsoft Word provides pre-designed resume templates on your computer and online. After opening a template, you can add text as indicated, modify the layout and design, and add or remove resume elements.

1 Close any open documents, and then from **Backstage** view, click **New**. Under **Available Templates**, click **Sample templates**.

2 Under **Available Templates**, scroll down, and then click **Median Resume**. Compare your screen with Figure 6.28.

Figure 6.28

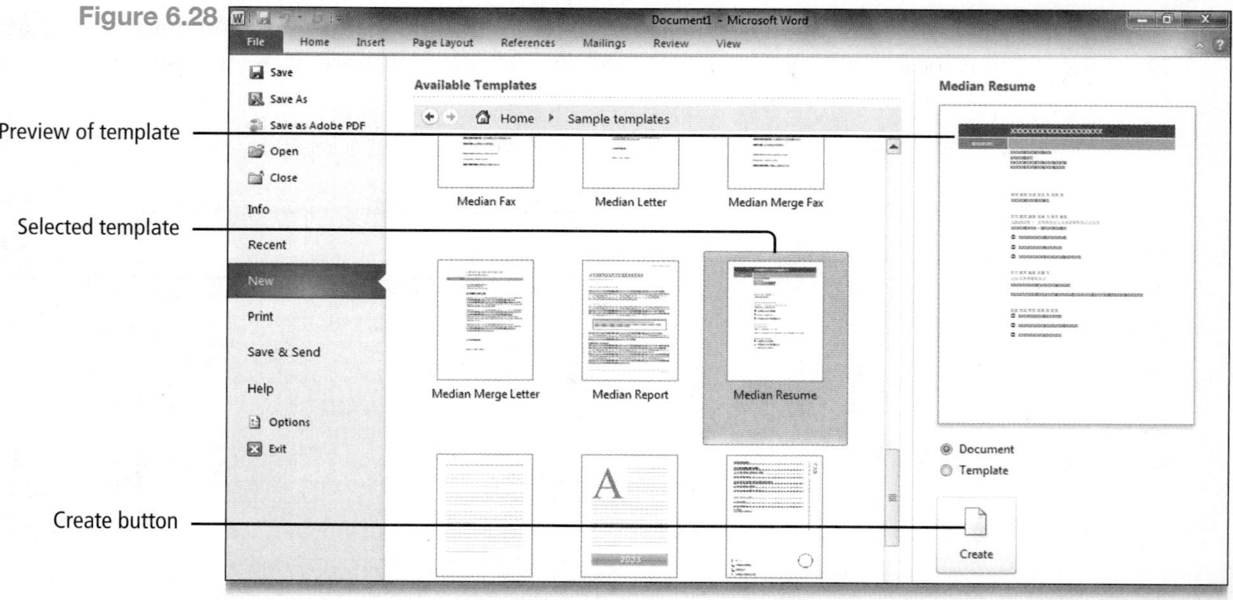

3 In the lower right corner, click the **Create** button.

The template opens a copy in the form of a new Word document—the title bar indicates *Document* followed by a number. Recall that you are not opening the template itself, and that changes you make to this new document will not affect the contents of the template file.

4 Display the **Save As** dialog box. Save the document in your **All In One Chapter 6** folder as **Lastname_Firstname_6B_Brief_Resume** and then add the file name to the footer—called the *First Page Footer* in this template. **Save** [Save icon] your document.

Activity 6.20 | Replacing Template Placeholder Text

After you save the template file as a Word document, you can begin to substitute your own information in the indicated locations. You can also remove unneeded resume elements that are included with the template.

1 Click on the picture, and notice that a Picture Tools tab is added to the Ribbon.

2 Click the **Layout tab**, and then in the **Table group**, click the **View Gridlines** button to display non-printing table borders.

This template consists of two Word tables, and the name in the first row of the upper table displays either the user name or the text [*Type your name*] in square brackets.

3 At the top of the upper table, click the **Resume Name tab arrow**, and then compare your screen with Figure 6.29.

There are two styles available with the Median template—with or without a photo. You should not include a picture on a resume unless physical appearance is directly related to the job for which you are applying—for example, for a job as an actor or a model.

Figure 6.29

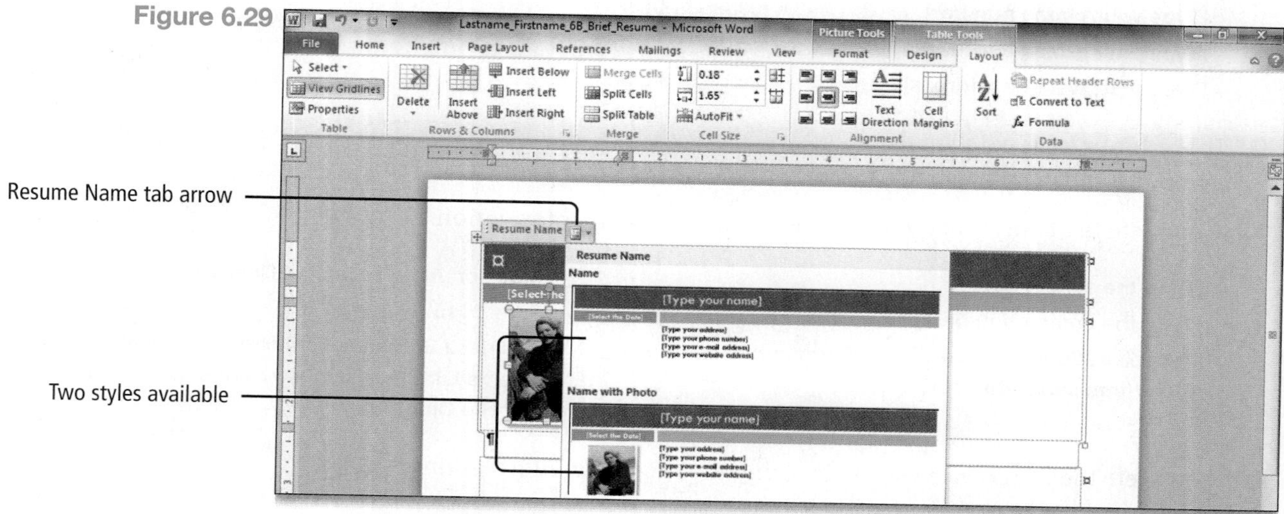

4 In the **Resume Name** gallery, click the first style—**Name**—to switch to the style with no picture.

5 In the first row of the table, select the displayed text and replace the text by typing **Tina Nguyen**

6 In the second row, click anywhere in the date control [*Select the Date*]. On the Ribbon, click the **Layout tab**. In the **Rows & Columns group**, click the **Delete** button, and then click **Delete Rows**.

Text surrounded by brackets is called a ***content control***. There are several different types of content controls, including date, picture, and ***text controls***. Because resumes do not typically include a date, you can delete this row.

7 Click anywhere in the content control [*Type your address*]. Compare your screen with Figure 6.30.

For the name and address at the top of the document, all of the text controls are grouped together. Each control has ***placeholder text***, text that indicates the type of information to be entered.

Figure 6.30

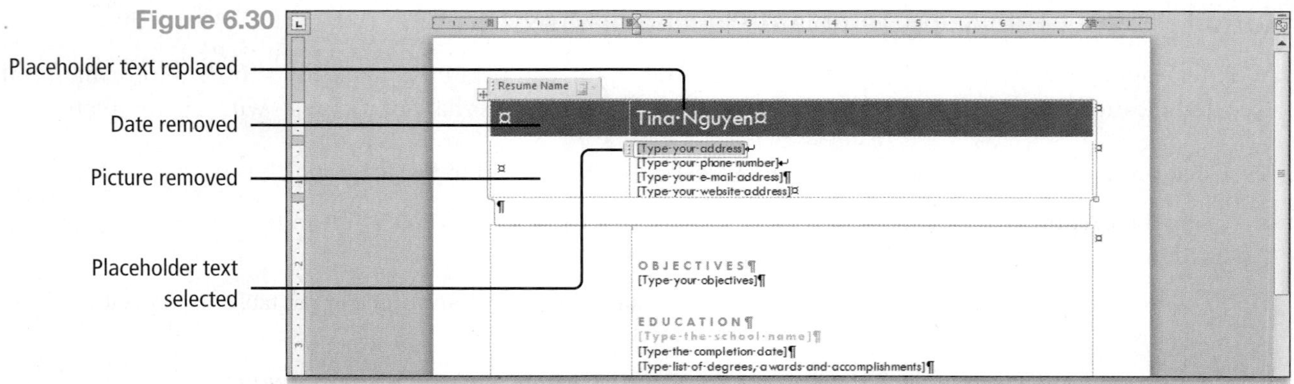

8 Complete the personal information by using the following information:

[Type your address]	**1776 Atwood Avenue, Madison, WI 53704**
[Type your phone number]	**(608) 555-0347**
[Type your e-mail address]	**tnguyen@alcona.net**
[Type your website address]	**(leave this blank)**

9 In the lower table, click in the [*Type your objectives*] control, and then type **To obtain a position using my computer and communications skills.**

10 Complete the **Education** section by using the following information:

[Type the school name]	**Madison Area Technical College**
[Type the completion date]	**June 2015**
[Type list of degrees, awards and accomplishments] (*type three separate lines*)	**Business Software Applications Specialist certificate Dean's List, four semesters President, Community Service Club**

11 Complete the **Experience** section by using the following information:

[Type the job title]	**Office Assistant (part-time)**
[Type the company name]	**The Robinson Company**
[Type the start date]	**September 2014**
[Type the end date]	**present**
[Type list of job responsibilities]	**Data entry and report generation using company spreadsheets and databases.**

12 Click in the [*Type list of skills*] control, type **Proficiency using Word, Excel, and Access (completed advanced courses in Microsoft Office programs)** and then press Enter.

13 As the second bulleted point, type **Excellent written and verbal communications (completed courses in Business Communications, PowerPoint, and Speech)** and then compare your screen with Figure 6.31. **Save** your document.

Figure 6.31

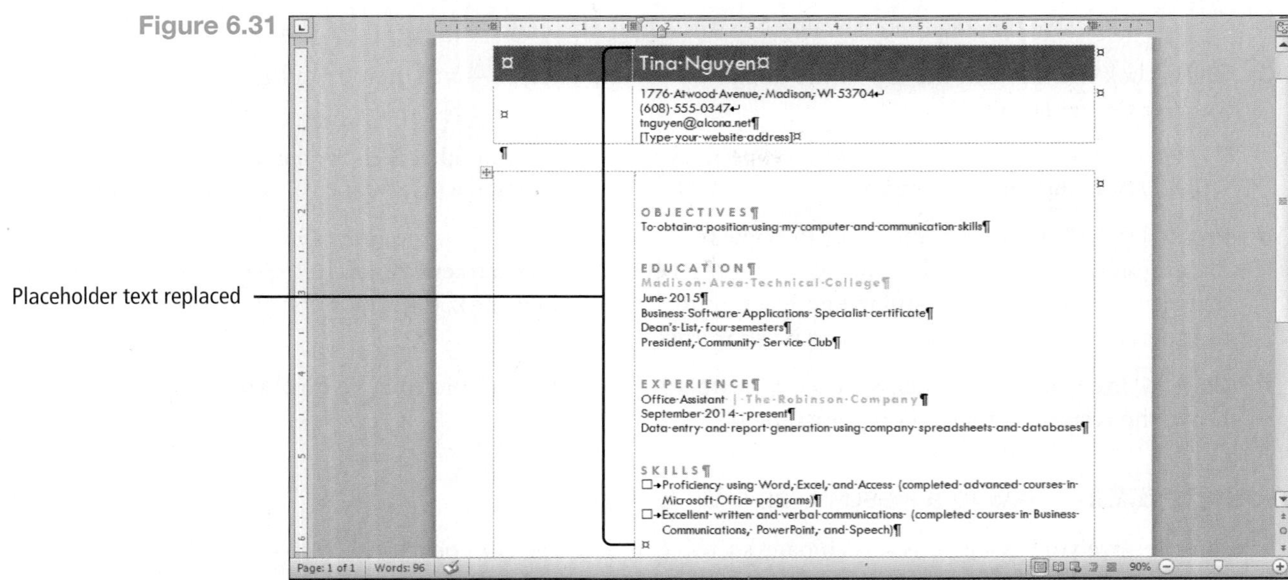

Activity 6.21 | Removing Template Controls and Formatting the Resume

1 Near the top of the document, point to the text control that you did not use—[*Type your website address*]. Right-click the control, and then from the shortcut menu, click **Remove Content Control**. Press Backspace as necessary to position the insertion point at the end of the e-mail address. Select the three lines with the address, phone, and e-mail information. On the Mini toolbar, click the **Font Size button arrow**, and then click **12**.

2 Click anywhere in the lower table—the table with the *Objectives* row at the top—and then point to the upper left corner of the active table to display the **table move handle** ⊞. Click one time to select the lower table. On the Mini toolbar, change the **Font Size** to **12** to match the table above.

3 Click anywhere to cancel the selection. On the **Page Layout tab**, in the **Page Setup group**, click the **Margins** button, and then click **Custom Margins**. Change the **Top margin** to **1.5** and the **Left** and **Right** margins to **1** to make this short resume better fill the page. Compare your screen with Figure 6.32.

Figure 6.32

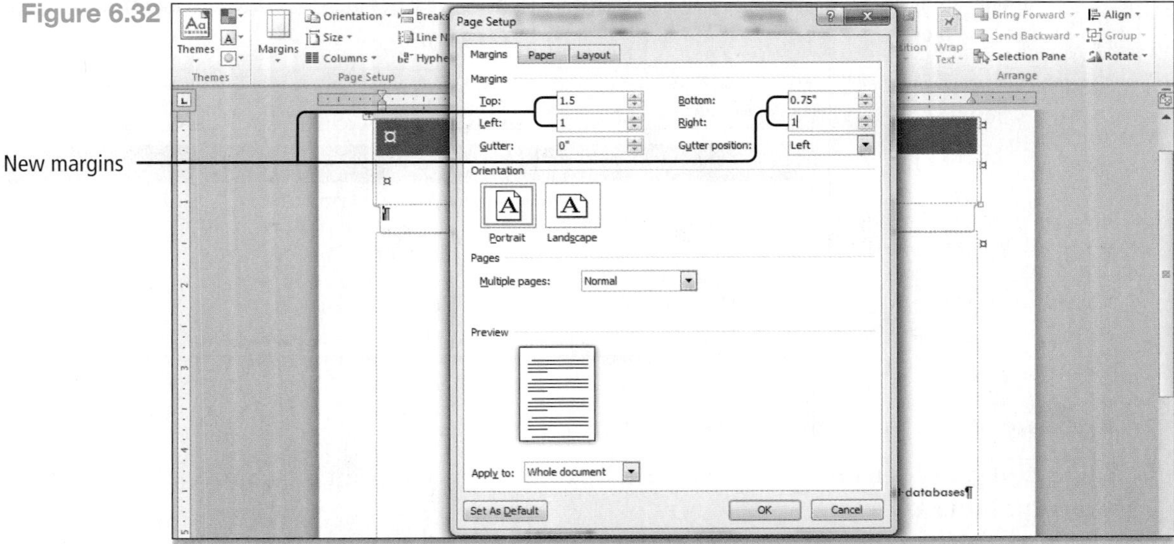

4 Click **OK** to close the **Page Setup** dialog box and apply the new margins.

5 Right-click the name at the top of the document—*Tina Nguyen*—and then from the shortcut menu, click **Remove Content Control**.

Remove the control if the Document Properties will have an author other than the name in this control so the name will not change to the name you type in the Author box. This action will leave the name but remove the control.

6 Press Ctrl + F2 to display the Print Preview in **Backstage** view. Click the **Info tab**. On the right, under the document thumbnail, click **Properties**, and then click **Show Document Panel**. In the **Author** box, delete any text and then type your firstname and lastname. In the **Subject** box, type your course name and section number, and in the **Keywords** box, type **short resume, template**

7 **Close** the **Document Panel**. **Save** your document, and then hold this file until you complete this project. Leave the resume displayed on your screen.

Activity 6.22 | Saving a Resume as a Web Page

You can save your resume as a Web page so you can post the Web page on a Web site and send it as an e-mail attachment that can be opened using any Web browser.

1 With your **6B_Brief_Resume** still open on your screen, click **Save** to be sure the current version of the document is saved.

2 Display the **Save As** dialog box. In the lower portion of the **Save As** dialog box, click the **Save as type arrow**, and then click **Single File Web Page**.

A ***Single File Web Page*** is a document saved using the ***Hypertext Markup Language*** (***HTML***). HTML is the language used to format documents that can be opened using a Web browser such as Internet Explorer.

3 In the **Save As** dialog box, in the **File name** box, type **Lastname_Firstname_6B_HTML_Resume** Click **Save**, and then click **Yes** if a message box displays. Notice that the Web page displays in Word.

4 **Exit** Word. From the **Start** menu, click **Computer**. Navigate to your **All In One Chapter 6** folder, and then double-click your **Lastname_Firstname_6B_HTML_Resume** file to open the resume in your Web browser.

Figure 6.33

Resume displayed in a Web browser

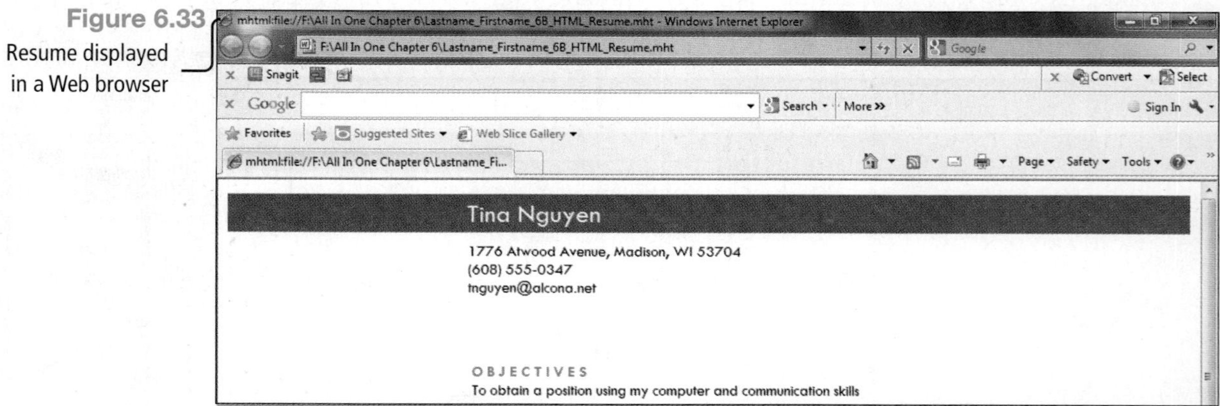

Compare your screen with Figure 6.33.

5 **Close** your Web browser. As directed by your instructor, print or submit electronically the four files from this project.

End **You have completed Project 6B**

Project 6C Research Paper

Project Activities

In Activities 6.23 through 6.29, you will edit and format a research paper that contains an overview of recycling activities in which businesses can engage. This paper was created by Elizabeth Freeman, a student intern working for Memphis Primary Metals, and will be included in a customer information packet. Your completed document will look similar to Figure 6.34.

Project Files

For Project 6C, you will need the following file:

w06C_Green_Business

You will save your document as:

Lastname_Firstname_6C_Green_Business

Project Results

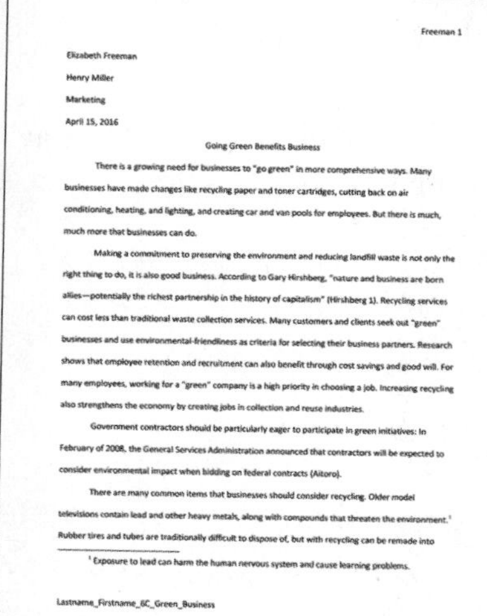

Freeman 1

Elizabeth Freeman

Henry Miller

Marketing

April 15, 2016

Going Green Benefits Business

There is a growing need for businesses to "go green" in more comprehensive ways. Many businesses have made changes like recycling paper and toner cartridges, cutting back on air conditioning, heating, and lighting, and creating car and van pools for employees. But there is much, much more that businesses can do.

Making a commitment to preserving the environment and reducing landfill waste is not only the right thing to do, it is also good business. According to Gary Hirshberg, "nature and business are born allies—potentially the richest partnership in the history of capitalism" (Hirshberg 1). Recycling services can cost less than traditional waste collection services. Many customers and clients seek out "green" businesses and use environmental-friendliness as criteria for selecting their business partners. Research shows that employee retention and recruitment can also benefit through cost savings and good will. For many employees, working for a "green" company is a high priority in choosing a job. Increasing recycling also strengthens the economy by creating jobs in collection and reuse industries.

Government contractors should be particularly eager to participate in green initiatives: In February of 2008, the General Services Administration announced that contractors will be expected to consider environmental impact when bidding on federal contracts (Aitoro).

There are many common items that businesses should consider recycling. Older model televisions contain lead and other heavy metals, along with compounds that threaten the environment.[1] Rubber tires and tubes are traditionally difficult to dispose of, but with recycling can be remade into

[1] Exposure to lead can harm the human nervous system and cause learning problems.

Lastname_Firstname_6C_Green_Business

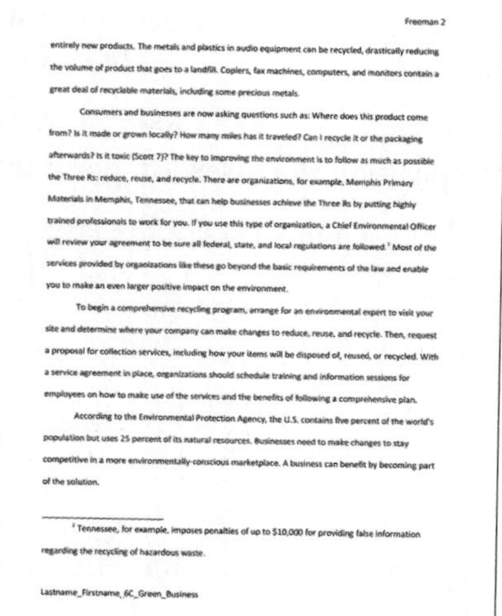

Freeman 2

entirely new products. The metals and plastics in audio equipment can be recycled, drastically reducing the volume of product that goes to a landfill. Copiers, fax machines, computers, and monitors contain a great deal of recyclable materials, including some precious metals.

Consumers and businesses are now asking questions such as: Where does this product come from? Is it made or grown locally? How many miles has it traveled? Can I recycle it or the packaging afterwards? Is it toxic (Scott 7)? The key to improving the environment is to follow as much as possible the Three Rs: reduce, reuse, and recycle. There are organizations, for example, Memphis Primary Materials in Memphis, Tennessee, that can help businesses achieve the Three Rs by putting highly trained professionals to work for you. If you use this type of organization, a Chief Environmental Officer will review your agreement to be sure all federal, state, and local regulations are followed.[2] Most of the services provided by organizations like these go beyond the basic requirements of the law and enable you to make an even larger positive impact on the environment.

To begin a comprehensive recycling program, arrange for an environmental expert to visit your site and determine where your company can make changes to reduce, reuse, and recycle. Then, request a proposal for collection services, including how your items will be disposed of, reused, or recycled. With a service agreement in place, organizations should schedule training and information sessions for employees on how to make use of the services and the benefits of following a comprehensive plan.

According to the Environmental Protection Agency, the U.S. contains five percent of the world's population but uses 25 percent of its natural resources. Businesses need to make changes to stay competitive in a more environmentally-conscious marketplace. A business can benefit by becoming part of the solution.

[2] Tennessee, for example, imposes penalties of up to $10,000 for providing false information regarding the recycling of hazardous waste.

Lastname_Firstname_6C_Green_Business

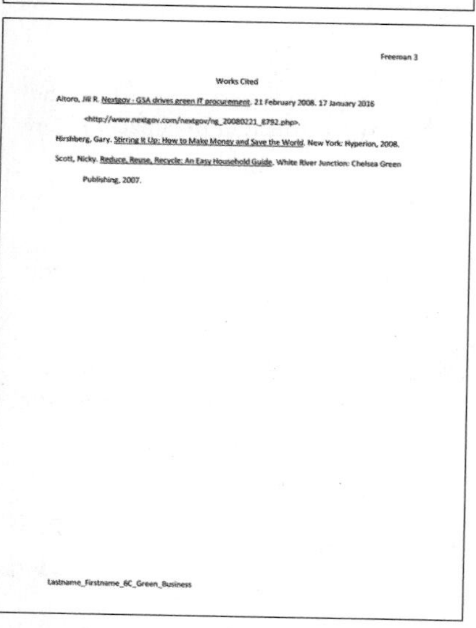

Freeman 3

Works Cited

Aitoro, Jill R. Nextgov - GSA drives green IT procurement. 21 February 2008. 17 January 2016 <http://www.nextgov.com/nextgov/ng_20080221_8792.php>.

Hirshberg, Gary. Stirring It Up: How to Make Money and Save the World. New York: Hyperion, 2008.

Scott, Nicky. Reduce, Reuse, Recycle: An Easy Household Guide. White River Junction: Chelsea Green Publishing, 2007.

Lastname_Firstname_6C_Green_Business

Figure 6.34
Project 6C Green Business

Objective 8 | Create a Research Paper

View the video on the Companion Web Site or in MyITLab

When you write a research paper or a report for college or business, follow a format prescribed by one of the standard ***style guides***—a manual that contains standards for the design and writing of documents. The two most commonly used styles for research papers are those created by the ***Modern Language Association*** (***MLA***) and the ***American Psychological Association (APA)***; there are several others.

Activity 6.23 | Formatting Text and Page Numbers in a Research Paper

When formatting the text for your research paper, refer to the standards for the style guide that you have chosen. In this activity, you will create a research paper using the MLA style. The MLA style uses 1-inch margins, a 0.5" first line indent, and double spacing throughout the body of the document, with no extra space above or below paragraphs.

1. **Start** Word. From your student files, locate and open the document **w06C_Green_Business**. If necessary, display the formatting marks and rulers. Save the file in the **All In One Chapter 6** folder as **Lastname_Firstname_6C_Green_Business**
2. Press Ctrl + A to select the entire document. On the **Home tab**, in the **Paragraph group**, click the **Line and Paragraph Spacing** button and then change the line spacing to **2.0**. On the **Page Layout tab**, in the **Paragraph group**, change the Spacing After to **0 pt**.
3. Press Ctrl + Home to deselect and move to the top of the document. Press Enter one time to create a blank line at the top of the document, and then click to position the insertion point in the blank line.
4. Type the following, pressing Enter at the end of each line except the last:

   Elizabeth Freeman

   Henry Miller

   Marketing

   April 15, 2016

   Going Green Benefits Business
5. Right-click anywhere in the last line you typed, and then on the Mini toolbar, click the **Center** button .

> **More Knowledge | Creating a Document Heading for a Research Paper**
>
> On the first page of an MLA-style research paper, on the first line, type the report author. On the second line, type the person for whom the report is prepared—for example, your professor or supervisor. On the third line, type the name of the class or department or organization. On the fourth line, type the date. On the fifth line, type the report title and center it.

6. At the top of the **Page 1**, point anywhere in the white top margin area, right-click, and then click **Edit Header**. In the header area, type **Freeman** and then press Spacebar.

   Recall that the text you insert into a header or footer displays on every page of a document. Within a header or footer, you can insert many different types of information, for example, automatic page numbers, the date, the time, the file name, or pictures.
7. On the **Design tab**, in the **Header & Footer group**, click the **Page Number** button, and then point to **Current Position**. In the displayed gallery, under **Simple**, click **Plain Number**. Compare your screen with Figure 6.35.

   Word will automatically number the pages using this number format.

Figure 6.35

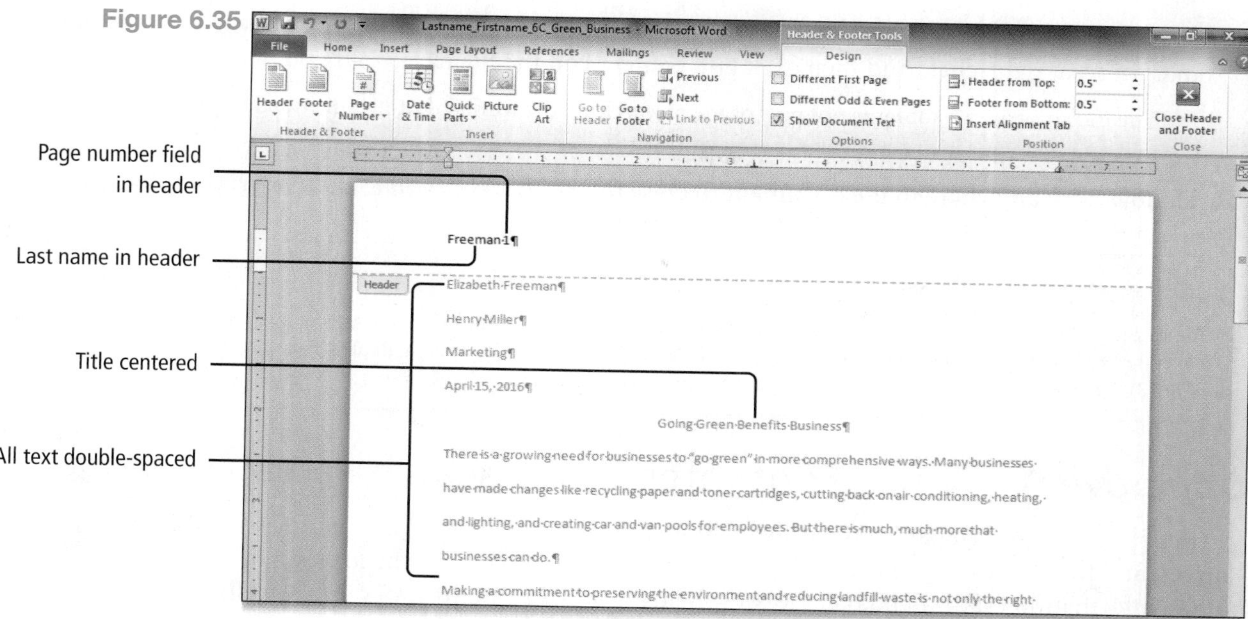

8 On the **Home tab**, in the **Paragraph group**, click the **Align Text Right** button. Double-click anywhere in the document to close the header area.

9 Near the top of **Page 1**, locate the paragraph beginning *There is a growing*, and then click to position the insertion point at the beginning of the paragraph. By moving the vertical scroll bar, scroll to the end of the document, hold down Shift, and then click to right of the last paragraph mark to select all of the text from the insertion point to the end of the document. Release Shift.

10 With the text selected, on the ruler, point to the **First Line Indent** button, and then drag the button to **0.5" on the horizontal ruler**. Compare your screen with Figure 6.36.

The MLA style uses 0.5-inch indents at the beginning of the first line of every paragraph. Indenting—moving the beginning of the first line of a paragraph to the right or left of the rest of the paragraph—provides visual cues to the reader to help divide the document text and make it easier to read.

Figure 6.36

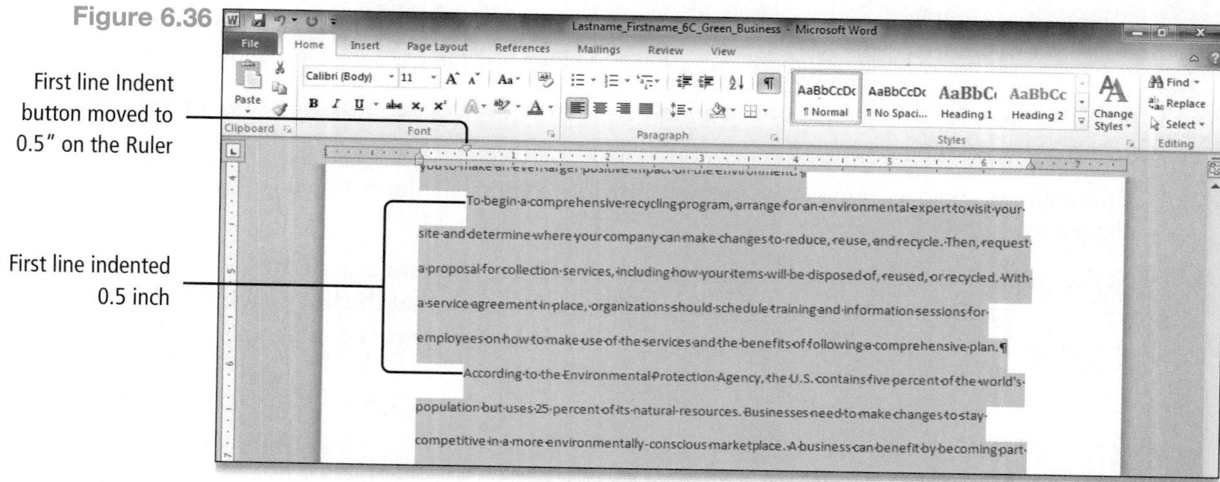

11 Click anywhere to deselect the text. Scroll to view the bottom of **Page 1**, point anywhere in the bottom white margin area, right-click, and then click **Edit Footer**. Add the file name to the footer.

The file name in the footer is not part of the research report format, but it is included in projects in this textbook so that you and your instructor can identify your work.

12 Double-click anywhere in the document to close the Footer area, and then **Save** your document.

> **More Knowledge | Suppressing the Page Number on the First Page**
>
> Some style guidelines require that the page number and other header and footer information on the first page be hidden from view—*suppressed*. To hide the information contained in the header and footer areas on Page 1 of a document, double-click in the header or footer area. Then, on the Design tab, in the Options group, select the Different First Page check box.

Objective 9 | Insert Footnotes in a Research Paper

View the video on the Companion Web Site or in MyITLab

Reports and research papers typically include information that you find in other sources, and these must be credited. Within report text, numbers mark the location of ***notes***—information that expands on the topic being discussed but that does not fit well in the document text. The numbers refer to ***footnotes***—notes placed at the bottom of the page containing the note, or to ***endnotes***—notes placed at the end of a document or chapter.

Activity 6.24 | Inserting Footnotes

Footnotes can be added as you type the document or after the document is complete. Word renumbers the footnotes automatically, so footnotes do not need to be entered in order; if one footnote is removed, the remaining footnotes renumber automatically.

1 Scroll to view the top of **Page 2**. Locate the paragraph that begins *Consumers and businesses*. In the seventh line of text, toward the end of the line, click to position the insertion point to the right of the period after *followed*.

2 On the **References tab**, in the **Footnotes group**, click the **Insert Footnote** button.

Word creates space for a footnote at the bottom of the page. Footnote 1 displays in the footnote area, and the insertion point moves to the right of the number. A short black line is added just above the footnote area.

3 Type **Tennessee, for example, imposes penalties of up to $10,000 for providing false information regarding the recycling of hazardous waste.**

This is an explanatory footnote; the footnote provides additional information that does not fit in the body of the report.

4 Click the **Home tab**, and then in the **Font group**, notice that the font size of the footer is *10 pt*. In the **Paragraph group**, click the **Line and Paragraph Spacing** button, and notice that the line spacing is *1.0*—single-spaced—even though the font size of the document text is 11 pt and the text is double-spaced, as shown in Figure 6.37.

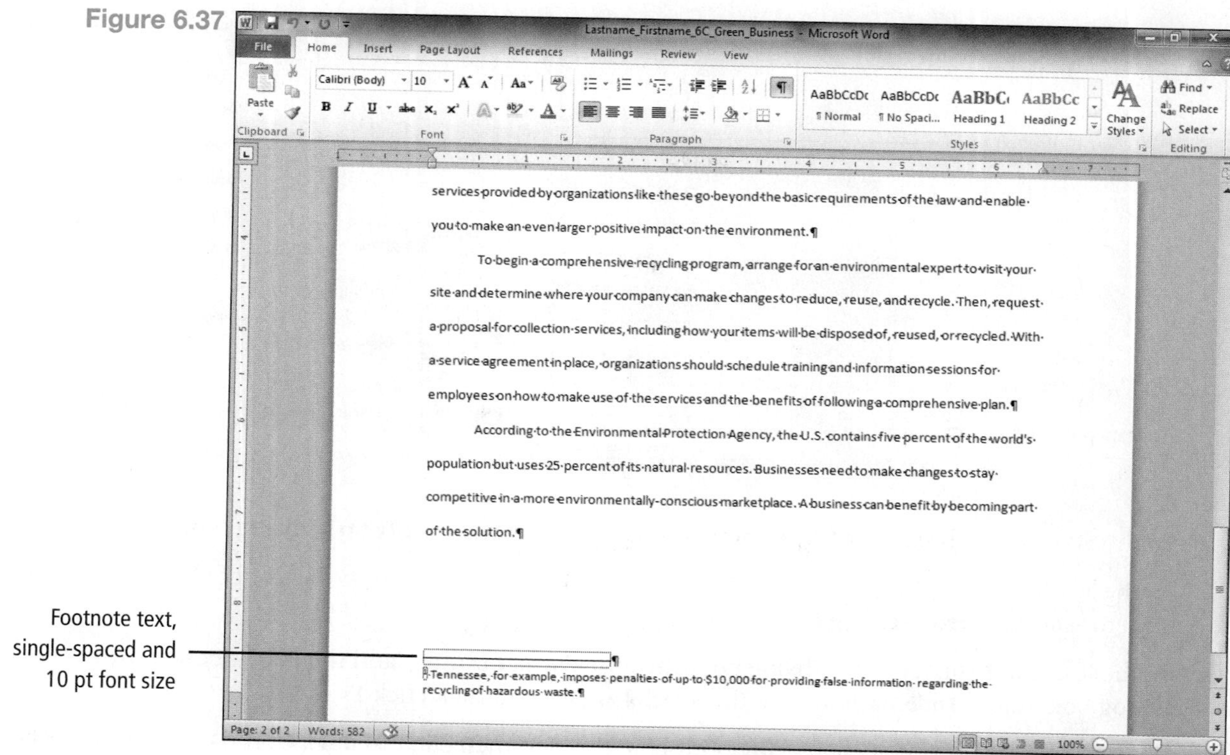

Figure 6.37

5 Scroll to view the bottom of **Page 1**, and then locate the paragraph that begins *There are many common*. At the end of the second line of text, click to position the insertion point to the right of the period following *environment*.

6 On the **References tab**, in the **Footnotes group**, click the **Insert Footnote** button. Type **Exposure to lead can harm the human nervous system and cause learning problems.** Notice that the footnote you just added becomes the new footnote 1.

The first footnote is renumbered as footnote 2.

7 **Save** your document.

Activity 6.25 | Modifying a Footnote Style

Microsoft Word contains built-in paragraph formats called ***styles***—groups of formatting commands, such as font, font size, font color, paragraph alignment, and line spacing—which can be applied to a paragraph with one command. The default style for footnote text is a single-spaced paragraph that uses a 10-point Calibri font and no paragraph indents. MLA style specifies double-spaced text in all areas of a research paper. According to the MLA style, first lines of footnotes must also be indented 0.5 inch and use the same font size as the report text.

1 Scroll to view the bottom of **Page 2**. Point anywhere in the footnote text and right-click, and then from the shortcut menu, click **Style**. Compare your screen with Figure 6.38.

The Style dialog box displays, listing the styles currently in use in the document, in addition to some of the word processing elements that come with special built-in styles. Because you right-clicked on the footnote text, the selected style is the Footnote Text style.

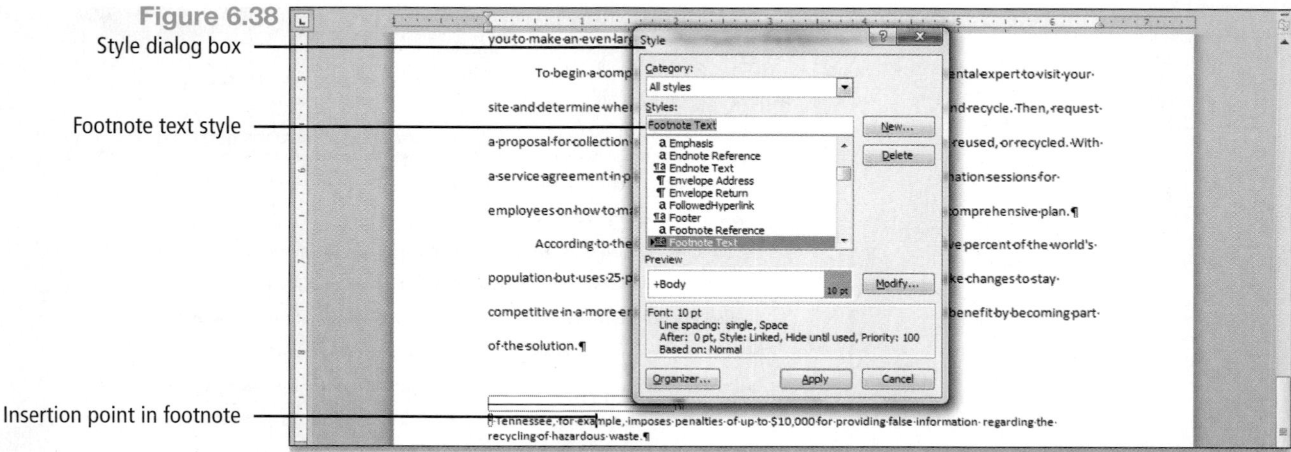

Figure 6.38

2 In the Style dialog box, click the **Modify** button to display the **Modify Style** dialog box.

3 In the **Modify Style** dialog box, locate the small **Formatting** toolbar in the center of the dialog box, click the **Font Size button arrow**, click **11**.

4 In the lower left corner of the dialog box, click the **Format** button, and then click **Paragraph**. In the **Paragraph** dialog box, under **Indentation**, click the **Special arrow**, and then click **First line**.

5 Under **Spacing**, click the **Line spacing** button arrow, and then click **Double**. Compare your dialog box with Figure 6.39.

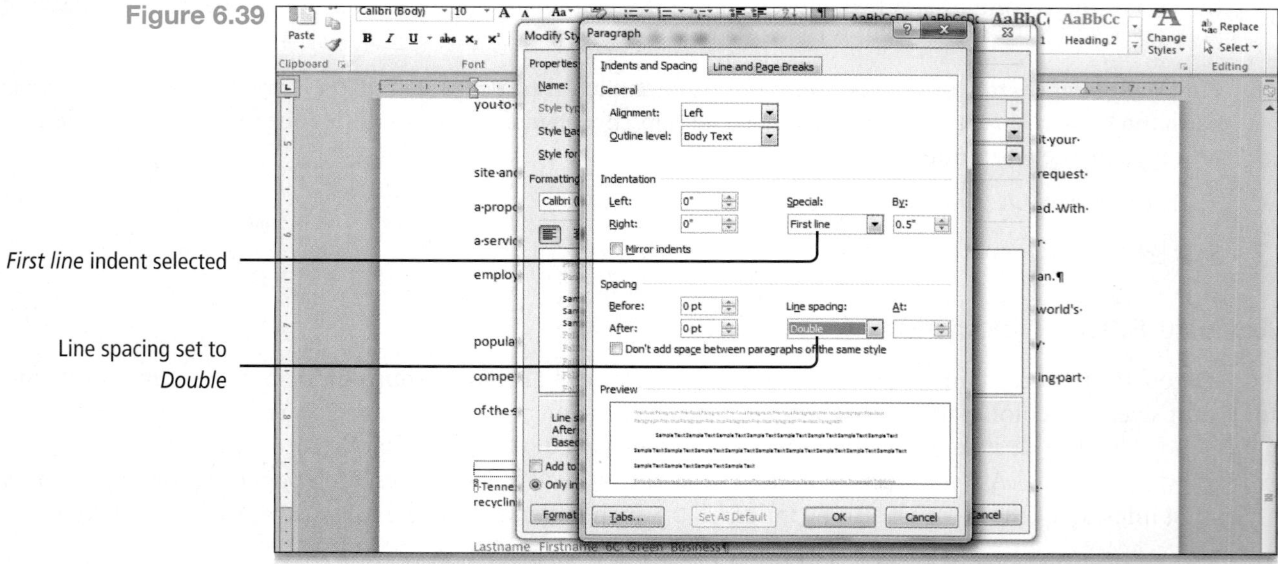

Figure 6.39

6 Click **OK** to close the **Paragraph** dialog box, click **OK** to close the **Modify Style** dialog box, and then click **Apply** to apply the new style. Notice that when you click Apply, the Style dialog box closes.

Your inserted footnotes are formatted with the new Footnote Text paragraph style; any new footnotes that you insert will also use this format.

7 **Save** your document.

Objective 10 | Create Citations and a Bibliography in a Research Paper

View the video on the Companion Web Site or in MyITLab

When you use quotations from or detailed summaries of other people's work, you must specify the source of the information. A ***citation*** is a note inserted into the text of a report or research paper that refers the reader to a source in the bibliography. Create a ***bibliography*** at the end of a document to list the sources referred to in the document. Such a list is typically titled ***Works Cited*** (in MLA style), *Bibliography*, *Sources*, or *References*.

Activity 6.26 | Adding Citations

When writing a research paper, you will likely reference books, articles, and Web sites. Some of your research sources may be referenced many times, and others only one time. It is necessary to create each source only one time, and it will be available for use throughout the document. Then, at the end of your paper, you will be able to generate the list of sources that must be included.

1. Press Ctrl + Home and then locate the paragraph that begins *Making a commitment*. In the third line, following the word *capitalism*, click to position the insertion point to the right of the quotation mark.

   The citation in the document points to the full source information in the bibliography, which typically includes the name of the author, the full title of the work, the year of publication, and other publication information.

2. On the **References tab**, in the **Citations & Bibliography group**, click the **Style button arrow**, and then click **MLA Sixth Edition** (or the latest edition) to insert a reference using MLA style.

3. Click the **Insert Citation** button, and then click **Add New Source**. Be sure *Book* is selected as the **Type of Source**. Add the following information, and then compare your screen with Figure 6.40:

Author:	**Hirshberg, Gary**
Title:	**Stirring it Up: How to Make Money and Save the World**
Year:	**2008**
City:	**New York**
Publisher:	**Hyperion**

   In the MLA style, citations that refer to items on the Works Cited page are placed in parentheses and are referred to as ***parenthetical references***—references that include the last name of the author or authors and the page number in the referenced source, which you add to the reference. No year is indicated, and there is no comma between the name and the page number.

Figure 6.40

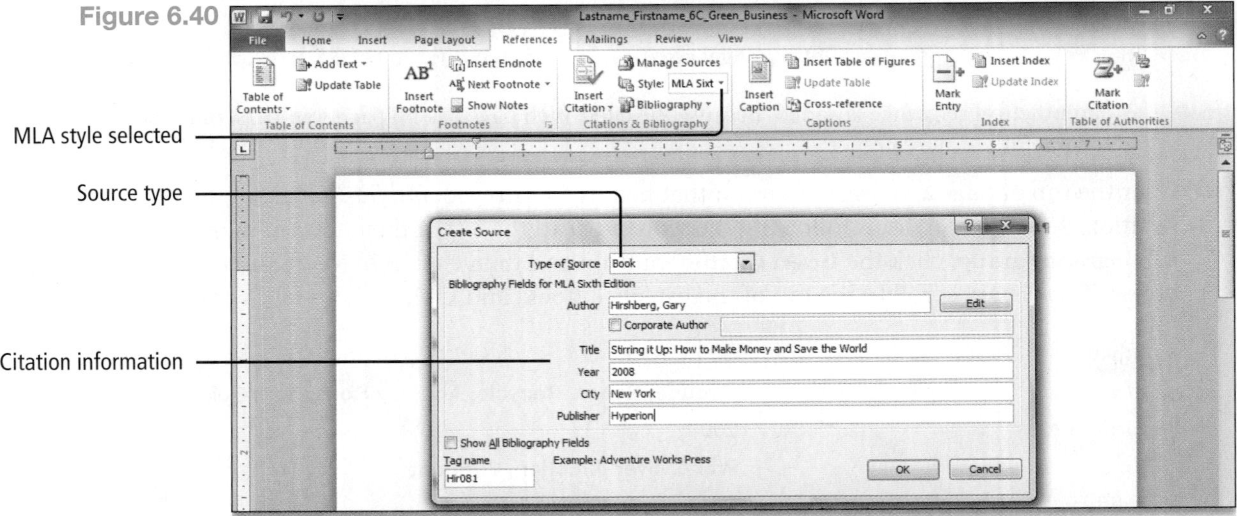

4 Click **OK** to insert the citation. In the paragraph, point to (*Hirshberg*) and click one time to select the citation.

5 In the lower right corner of the box that surrounds the reference, point to the small arrow to display the ScreenTip *Citation Options*. Click this **Citation Options arrow**, and then from the list of options, click **Edit Citation**.

6 In the **Edit Citation** dialog box, under **Add**, in the **Pages** box, type **1** to indicate that you are citing from page 1 of this source. Compare your screen with Figure 6.41.

Figure 6.41

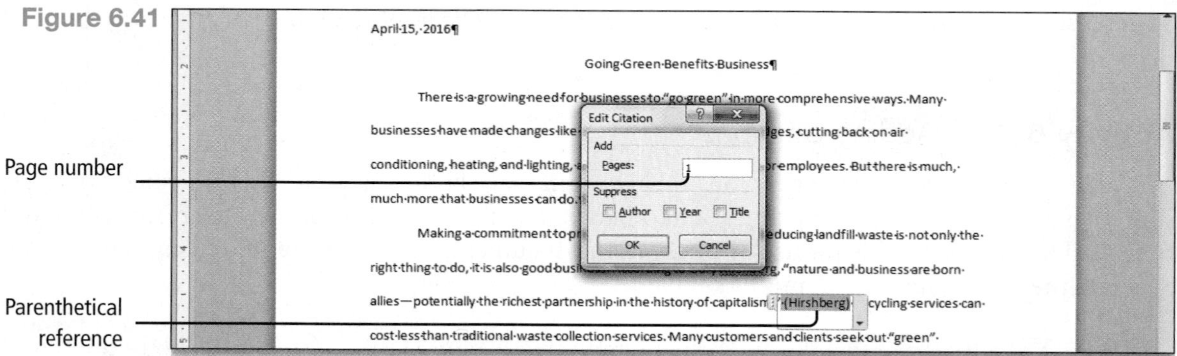

7 Click **OK** to display the page number of the citation. Click outside of the citation box to deselect it. Then type a period to the right of the citation, and delete the period to the left of the quotation mark.

In the MLA style, if the reference occurs at the end of a sentence, the parenthetical reference always displays to the left of the punctuation mark that ends the sentence.

8 In the next paragraph, which begins *Government contractors*, click to position the insertion point at the end of the paragraph, but before the period.

9 In the **Citations & Bibliography group**, click the **Insert Citation** button, and then click **Add New Source**. Click the **Type of Source arrow**, scroll down as necessary, and then click **Web site**. Add the following information, and then Click **OK** to close the **Create Source** dialog box and add the citation:

Author:	**Aitoro, Jill R.**
Name of Web Page:	**Nextgov - GSA drives green IT procurement**
Year:	**2008**
Month:	**February**
Day:	**21**
Year Accessed:	**2016**
Month Accessed:	**January**
Day Accessed:	**17**
URL:	**http://www.nextgov.com/nextgov/ng_20080221_8792.php**

A parenthetical reference is added. Because the cited Web page has no page numbers, only the author name is used in the parenthetical reference.

10 Near the top of **Page 2**, in the paragraph that begins *Consumers and businesses*, in the third line, click to position the insertion point following the word *toxic* to the left of the question mark. In the **Citations & Bibliography group**, click the **Insert Citation** button, and then click **Add New Source**. Click the **Type of Source arrow**, if necessary scroll to the top of the list, click **Book**, and then add the following information:

Author:	**Scott, Nicky**
Title:	**Reduce, Reuse, Recycle: An Easy Household Guide**
Year:	**2007**
City:	**White River Junction, Vermont**
Publisher:	**Chelsea Green Publishing**

11 Click **OK**. Click the inserted citation to select it, click the **Citation Options arrow**, and then click **Edit Citation**. In the **Edit Citation** dialog box, under **Add**, in the **Pages** box, type **7** to indicate that you are citing from page 7 of this source. Click **OK**.

12 **Save** your document.

Activity 6.27 | Inserting Page Breaks

In this activity you will insert a manual page break so that you can begin your bibliography on a new page.

1 Press Ctrl + End to move the insertion point to the end of the document. Notice that the insertion point displays at the end of the final paragraph, but above the footnote—the footnote is always associated with the page that contains the citation. Press Ctrl + Enter to insert a manual page break.

A ***manual page break*** forces a page to end at the insertion point location, and then places any subsequent text at the top of the next page. Recall that the new paragraph retains the formatting of the previous paragraph, so the first line is indented.

2 On the ruler, point to the **First Line Indent** button, and then drag the **First Line Indent** button to the left to **0 inches on the horizontal ruler**.

3 Scroll as necessary to position the bottom of **Page 2** and the top of **Page 3** on your screen. Compare your screen with Figure 6.42, and then **Save** your document.

A ***page break indicator***, which shows where a manual page break was inserted, displays at the bottom of the Page 2, and the footnote remains on the page that contains the citation, even though it displays below the page break indicator.

Figure 6.42

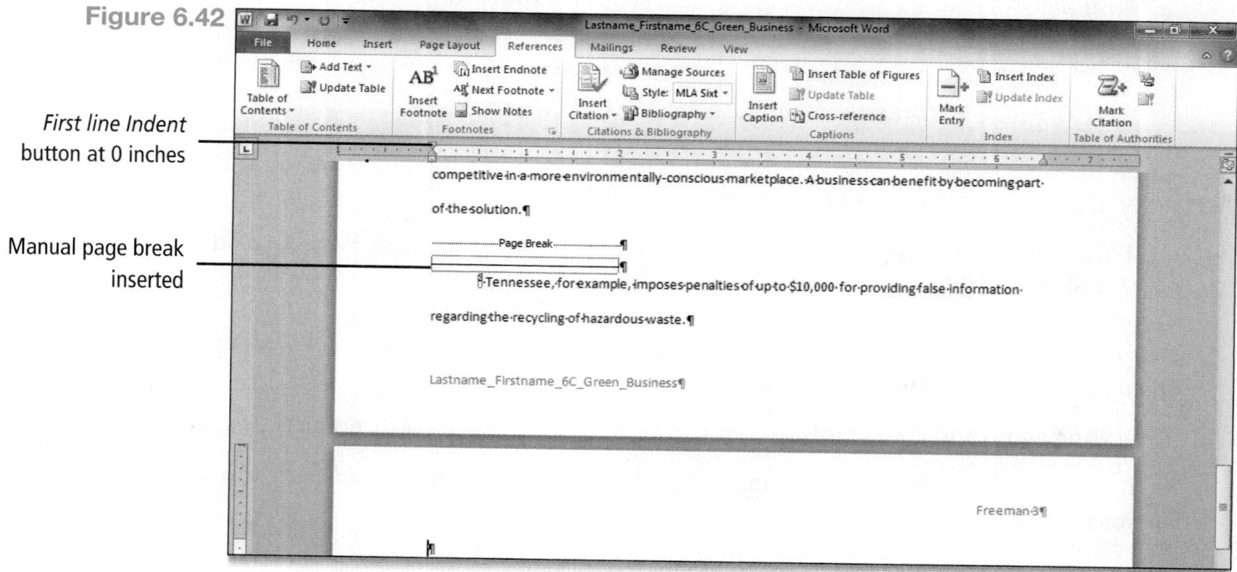

Activity 6.28 | Creating a Reference Page

At the end of a report or research paper, include a list of each source referenced. *Works Cited* is the reference page heading used in the MLA style guidelines. This information is always displayed on a separate page.

1 With the insertion point blinking in the first line of **Page 3**, type **Works Cited** and then press Enter. On the **References tab**, in the **Citations & Bibliography group**, in the **Style** box, be sure *MLA* displays.

2 In the **Citations & Bibliography group**, click the **Bibliography** button, and then near the bottom of the list, click **Insert Bibliography**.

3 Scroll as necessary to view the entire list of three references, and then click anywhere in the inserted text.

The bibliography entries that you created display as a field, which is indicated by the gray shading when you click in the text. The field links to the Source Manager for the citations. The references display alphabetically by the author's last name.

4 In the bibliography, point to the left of the first entry—beginning *Aitoro, Jill*—to display the pointer. Drag down to select all three references.

5 On the **Home tab**, in the **Paragraph group**, change the Line spacing to **2.0**, and then on the **Page Layout tab**, in the **Paragraph group**, change the **Spacing After** to **0 pt**.

The entries display according to MLA guidelines; the text is double-spaced, the extra space between paragraphs is removed, and each entry uses a ***hanging indent***—the first line of each entry extends 0.5 inch to the left of the remaining lines of the entry.

6 At the top of **Page 3**, right-click the *Works Cited* title, and then, on the Mini toolbar, click **Center**. Compare your screen with Figure 6.43, and then **Save** your document.

In MLA style, the Works Cited title is centered.

Figure 6.43

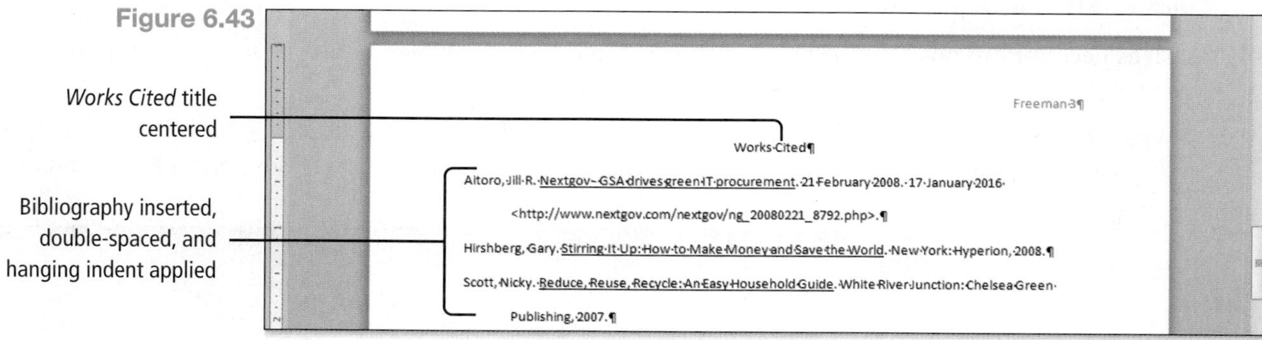

Activity 6.29 | Managing Document Properties

Recall that document property information is stored in the Document Panel. An additional group of property categories is also available.

1 Display **Backstage** view. On the right, under the document thumbnail, click **Properties**, and then click **Show Document Panel** to display the **Document Panel**.

2 Type your name and course information, and then add the keywords **green business, research paper**

3 In the upper left corner of the **Document Panel**, click the **Document Properties button arrow**, and then click **Advanced Properties**. Compare your screen with Figure 6.44.

Figure 6.44

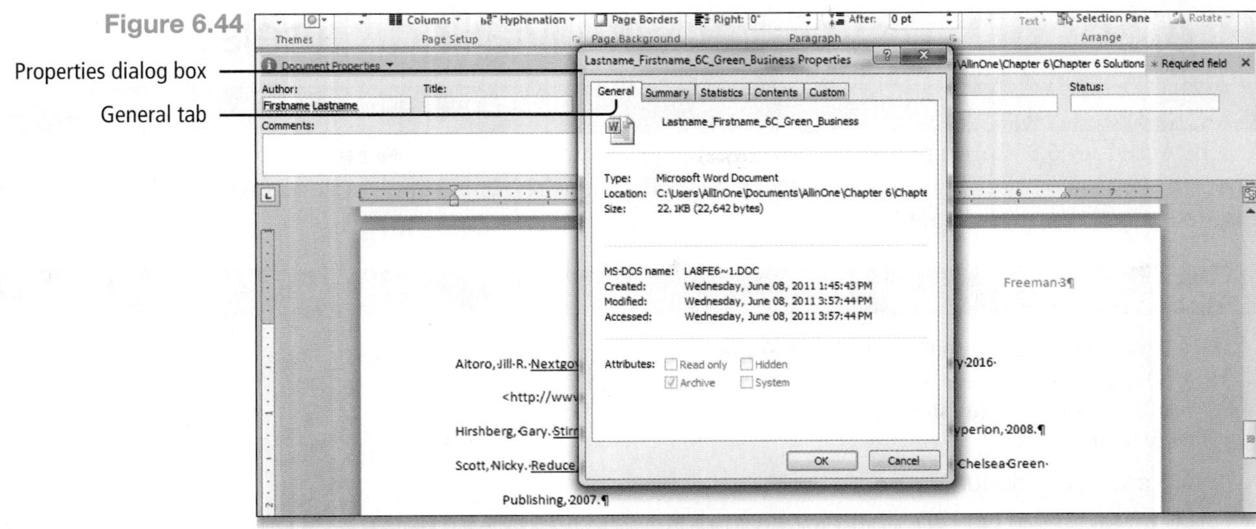

4 In the **Properties** dialog box, click the **Summary tab**. Click in the **Title** box and type **Going Green Benefits Business**

Some of the boxes may contain information from your computer system.

5 Click in the **Manager** box and type **Henry Miller** In the **Company** box, select and delete any existing text, and then type **Memphis Primary Materials** Click in the **Category** box and type **Marketing Documents**

6 Click in the **Comments** box and type **Draft copy of a research report that will be included in the marketing materials packet** and then compare your screen with Figure 6.45.

Figure 6.45

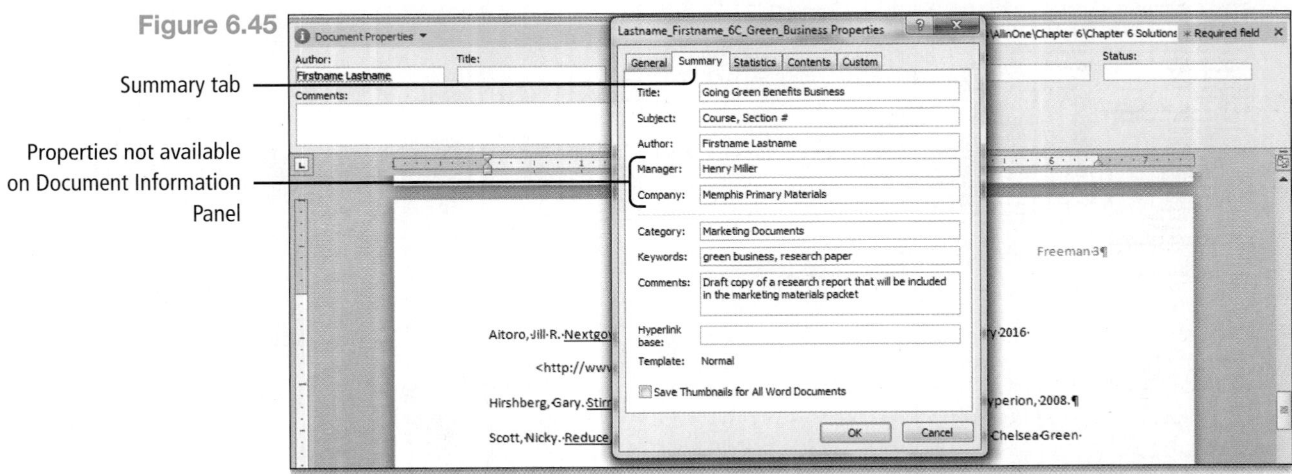

7 At the bottom of the **Properties** dialog box, click **OK**. **Close** the **Document Panel.**

8 **Save** your document, and then print or submit electronically as directed by your instructor. **Exit** Word.

End **You have completed Project 6C**

Project 6D Newsletter with Mailing Labels

Project Activities

In Activities 6.30 through 6.39, you will edit a newsletter that Memphis Primary Materials sends to its list of customers and subscribers and create a set of mailing labels. Your completed documents will look similar to Figure 6.46.

Project Files

For Project 6D, you will need the following files:

New blank Word document
w06D_Memphis_Newsletter
w06D_Addresses

You will save your documents as:

Lastname_Firstname_6D_Memphis_Newsletter
Lastname_Firstname_6D_Mailing_Labels
Lastname_Firstname_6D_Addresses

Project Results

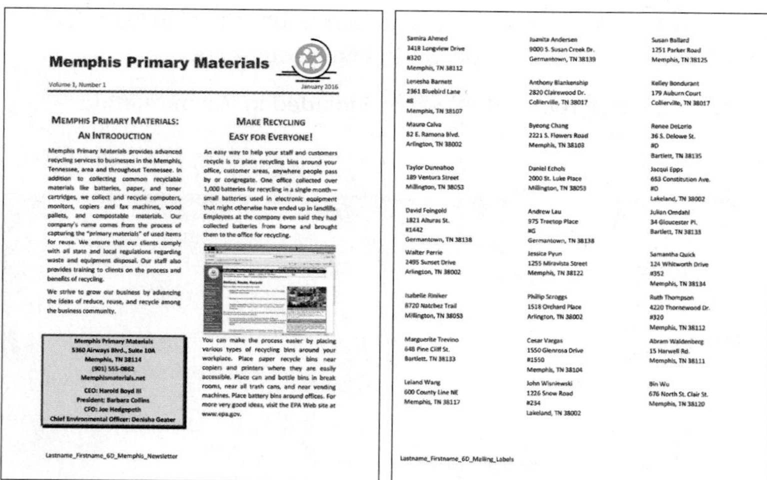

Figure 6.46
Project 6D Newsletter with Mailing Labels

Objective 11 | Format a Multiple-Column Newsletter

View the video on the Companion Web Site or in MyITLab

All newspapers and most magazines and newsletters use multiple columns for articles because text in narrower columns is easier to read than text that stretches across a page. Word has a tool with which you can change a single column of text into two or more columns, and then format the columns. If a column does not end where you want it to, you can end the column at a location of your choice by inserting a ***manual column break***.

Activity 6.30 | Changing One Column of Text to Two Columns

Newsletters are usually two or three columns wide.

1 **Start** Word. From your student files, locate and open the document **w06D_Memphis_Newsletter**. If necessary, display the formatting marks and rulers. **Save** the file in your **All In One Chapter 6** folder as **Lastname_ Firstname_6D_Memphis_Newsletter** and then add the file name to the footer.

2 Select the first paragraph of text—*Memphis Primary Materials*. From the Mini toolbar, change the **Font** to **Arial Black** and the **Font Size** to **24**.

3 Select the first two paragraphs—the title and the volume information and date. From the Mini toolbar, click the **Font Color button arrow**, and then under **Theme Colors**, in the fifth column, click the last color—**Blue, Accent 1, Darker 50%**.

4 With the text still selected, on the **Home tab**, in the **Paragraph group**, click the **Borders button arrow**, and then at the bottom, click **Borders and Shading**.

5 In the **Borders and Shading** dialog box, on the **Borders tab**, click the **Color arrow**, and then under **Theme Colors**, in the fifth column, click the last color—**Blue, Accent 1, Darker 50%**. Click the **Width arrow**, and then click **3 pt**. In the **Preview** box at the right, point to the *bottom* border of the small preview and click one time. Compare your screen with Figure 6.47.

Figure 6.47

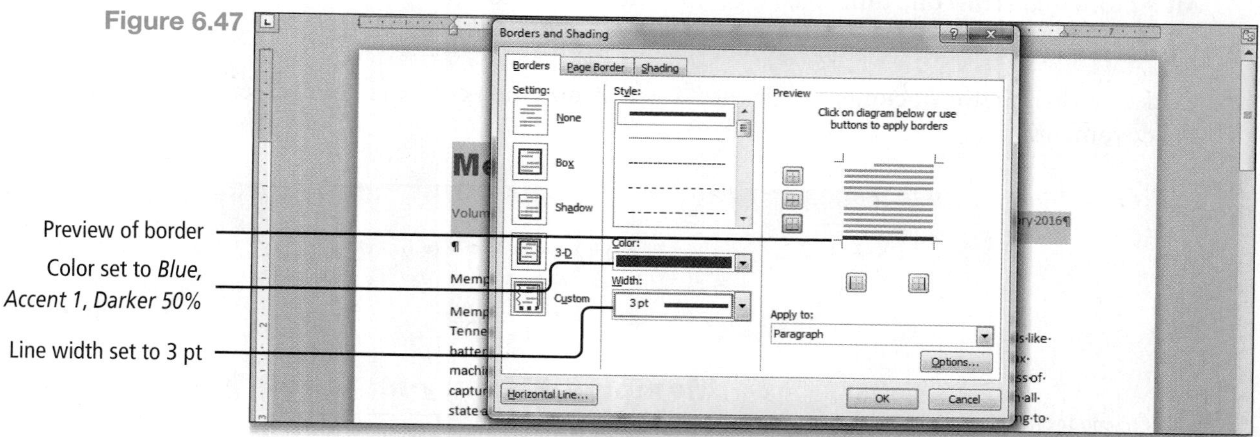

6 In the **Borders and Shading** dialog box, click **OK**.

The line visually defines the newsletter ***nameplate***—the banner on the front page of a newsletter that identifies the publication.

7 Below the nameplate, beginning with the paragraph *Memphis Primary Materials: An Introduction*, select all of the text to the end of the document, which extends to two pages.

8 On the **Page Layout tab**, in the **Page Setup group**, click the **Columns** button. From the **Columns** gallery, click **Two**. Scroll up to view the top of **Page 1**, and then compare your screen with Figure 6.48, and then **Save** the document.

Word divides the text into two columns, and inserts a ***section break*** below the nameplate, dividing the one-column section of the document from the two-column section of the document. A ***section*** is a portion of a document that can be formatted differently from the rest of the document. A section break marks the end of one section and the beginning of another section. Do not be concerned if your columns do not break at the same line as shown in the figure.

Figure 6.48

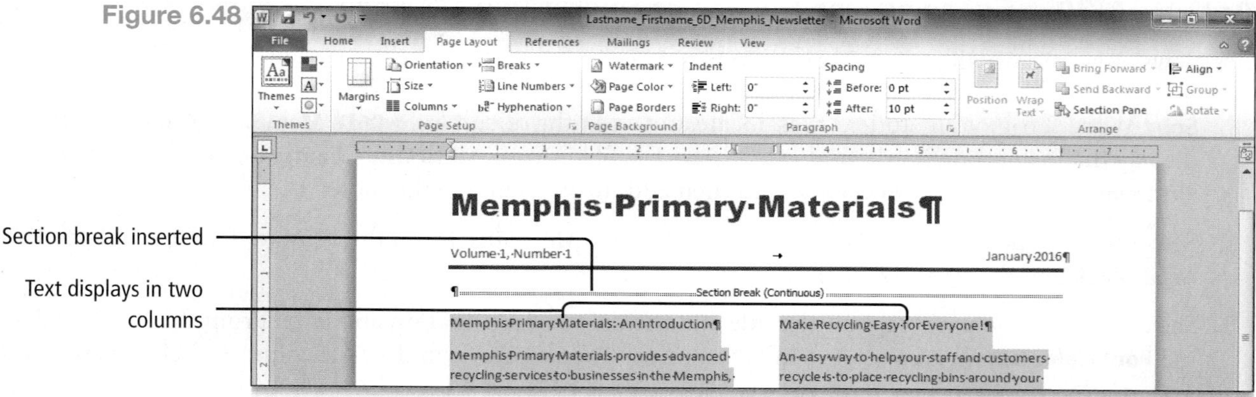

Activity 6.31 | Formatting Multiple Columns

The uneven right margin of a single page–width column is easy to read. When you create narrow columns, justified text is sometimes preferable.

1 With the two columns of text still selected, on the **Page Layout tab**, in the **Paragraph group**, click the **Spacing After down spin arrow** one time to change the spacing after to **6 pt**.

2 On the **Home tab**, in the **Paragraph group**, click the **Justify** button.

3 Click anywhere in the document to deselect the text, and then compare your screen with Figure 6.49. **Save** the document.

Figure 6.49

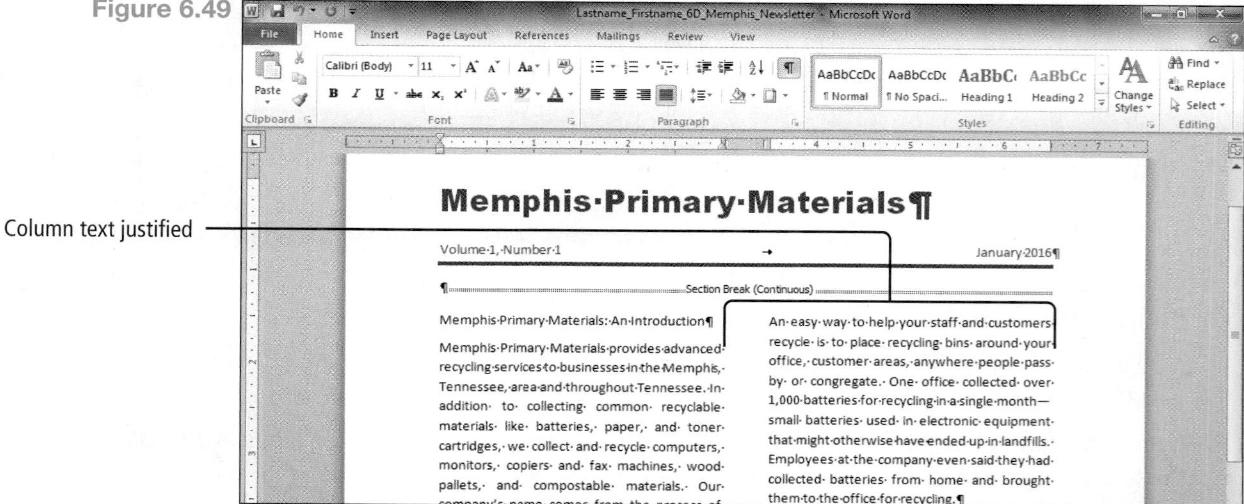

Activity 6.32 | Inserting a Column Break

1 Scroll down to view the lower portion of the page. In the first column, locate the company address that begins with the paragraph *Memphis Primary Materials*, and then select that paragraph and the three following paragraphs, ending with the telephone number. On the **Page Layout tab**, in the **Paragraph group**, click the **Spacing After down spin arrow** one time to change the spacing after to **0 pt**.

2 Select the three paragraphs that begin with *CEO* and end with *CFO*, and then in the **Paragraph group**, change the **Spacing After** to **0 pt**.

3 Near the bottom of the first column, click to position the insertion point at the beginning of the line that begins *Make Recycling*. On the **Page Layout tab**, in the **Page Setup group**, click the **Breaks** button to display the gallery of Page Breaks and Section Breaks.

4 Under **Page Breaks**, click **Column**. Scroll to view the bottom of the first column. Compare your screen with Figure 6.50, and then **Save** the document.

A ***column break indicator***—a dotted line containing the words *Column Break*—displays at the bottom of the column.

Figure 6.50

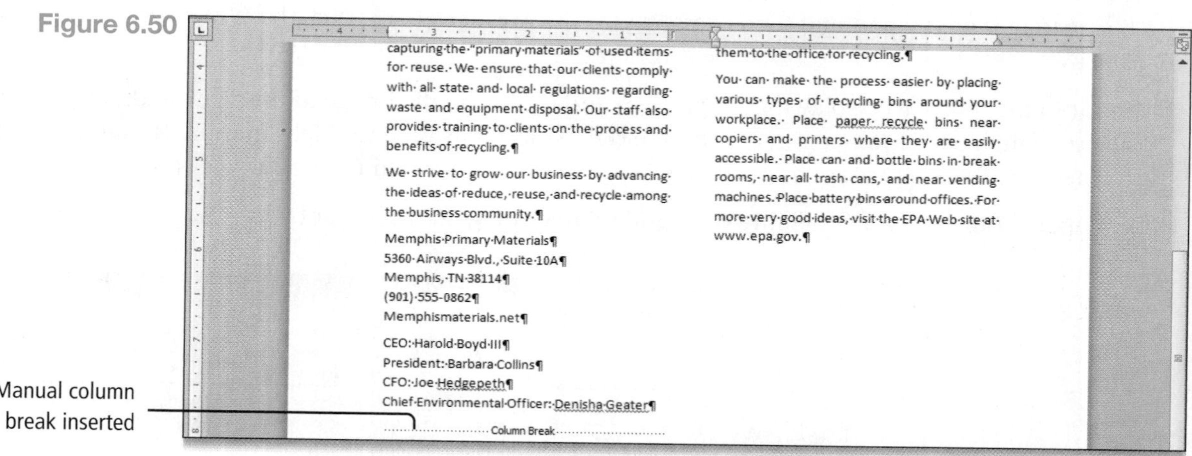
capturing·the·"primary·materials"·of·used·items·for·reuse.·We·ensure·that·our·clients·comply·with·all·state·and·local·regulations·regarding·waste·and·equipment·disposal.·Our·staff·also·provides·training·to·clients·on·the·process·and·benefits·of·recycling.¶
We·strive·to·grow·our·business·by·advancing·the·ideas·of·reduce,·reuse,·and·recycle·among·the·business·community.¶
Memphis·Primary·Materials¶
5360·Airways·Blvd.,·Suite·10A¶
Memphis,·TN·38114¶
(901)·555-0862¶
Memphismaterials.net¶
CEO:·Harold·Boyd·III¶
President:·Barbara·Collins¶
CFO:·Joe·Hedgepeth¶
Chief·Environmental·Officer:·Denisha·Geater¶
Column Break
them·to·the·office·for·recycling.¶
You·can·make·the·process·easier·by·placing·various·types·of·recycling·bins·around·your·workplace.·Place·paper·recycle·bins·near·copiers·and·printers·where·they·are·easily·accessible.·Place·can·and·bottle·bins·in·break·rooms,·near·all·trash·cans,·and·near·vending·machines.·Place·battery·bins·around·offices.·For·more·very·good·ideas,·visit·the·EPA·Web·site·at·www.epa.gov.¶
Manual column break inserted

Activity 6.33 | Inserting a ClipArt Image

Clip art images—predefined graphics included with Microsoft Office or downloaded from the Web—can make your document visually appealing and more interesting.

1 Press Ctrl + Home. On the **Insert tab**, in the **Illustrations group**, click the **Clip Art** button to display the **Clip Art** task pane on the right of your screen.

2 In the **Clip Art** task pane, click in the **Search for** box, and then replace any existing text with **environmental awareness** so that Word can search for images that contain the keywords *environmental* and *awareness*. Click the **Results should be arrow**. Be sure the **Illustrations** check box is selected, and then click as necessary to clear the *Photographs*, *Videos*, and *Audio* check boxes. Click the **Results should be arrow** again to collapse the list. Be sure the **Include Office.com content** check box is selected.

3 In the **Clip Art** task pane, click the **Go** button. Locate the image of the three white arrows in a blue circle. Click on the image to insert it, and then compare your screen with Figure 6.51.

Recall that when you insert a graphic, it is inserted as an inline object; that is, it is treated as a character in a line of text. Here, the inserted clip art becomes the first character in the nameplate.

Figure 6.51

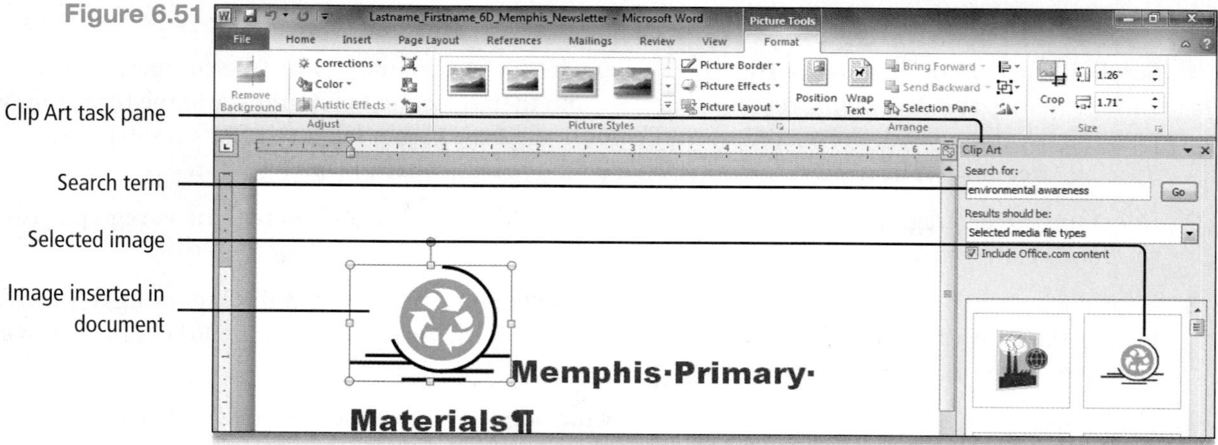

4 **Close** the **Clip Art** task pane. With the image still selected, on the **Format tab**, in the **Size group**, click in the **Shape Height** box, type **1** and then press Enter. In the **Arrange group**, click the **Wrap Text** button, and then click **Square**.

5 Point to the image to display the pointer, and then drag the image to the right so that the bottom edge aligns slightly above *January 2016*, and the right side aligns with the right margin. Recall that you can press the arrow keys as necessary to move the image in small, precise increments.

6 Compare your screen with Figure 6.52, and then **Save** the document.

Figure 6.52

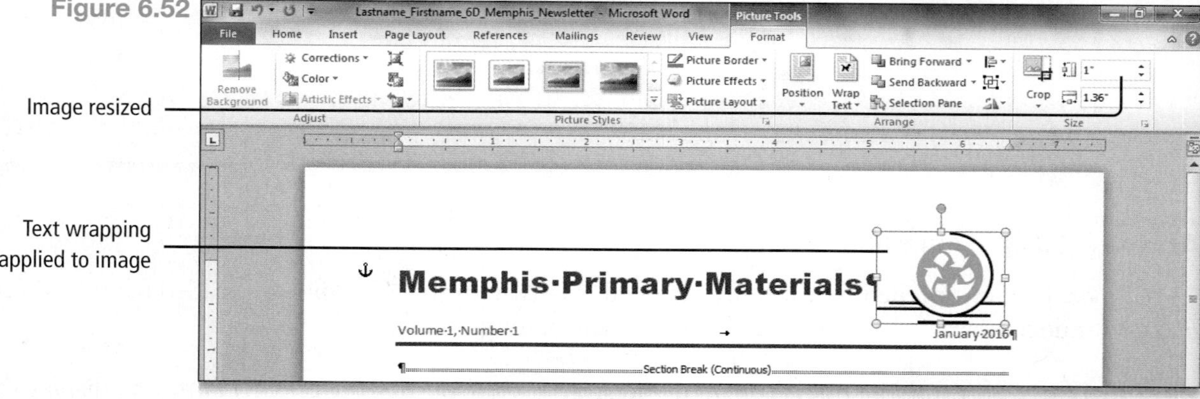

Activity 6.34 | Inserting a Screenshot

A ***screenshot*** is an image of an active window on your computer that you can paste into a document. You can insert a screenshot of any open window on your computer.

1 In the second column, click to position the insertion point at the beginning of the paragraph that begins *You can make*. Open your Internet browser, and then in the address bar type **www.epa.gov/osw/conserve/rrr** and press Enter. Maximize the browser window, if necessary

2 From the taskbar, redisplay your **6D_Memphis_Newletter** document.

3 On the **Insert tab**, in the **Illustrations group**, click the **Screenshot** button.

All of your open windows display in the Available Windows gallery and are available to paste into the document.

4 In the **Screenshot** gallery, click the browser window that contains the EPA site to insert the screenshot at the insertion point, and notice that the image resizes to fit between the column margins. Compare your screen with Figure 6.53. **Save** the document.

Figure 6.53

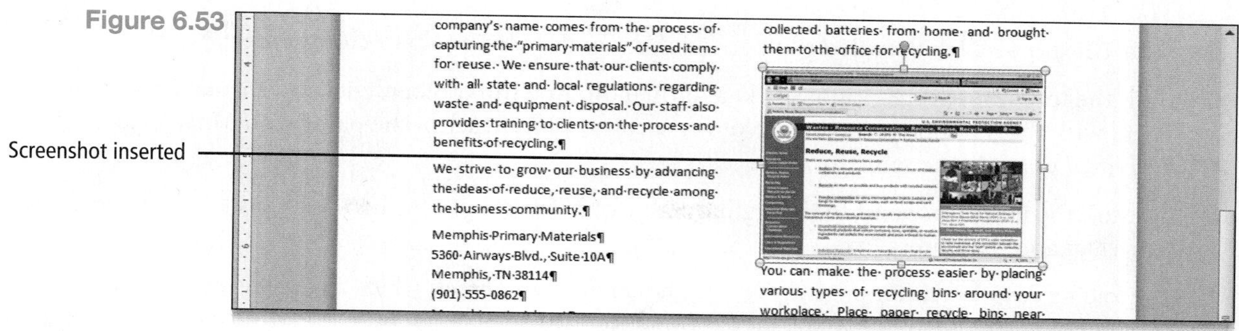
Screenshot inserted
company's name comes from the process of capturing the "primary materials" of used items for reuse. We ensure that our clients comply with all state and local regulations regarding waste and equipment disposal. Our staff also provides training to clients on the process and benefits of recycling.
We strive to grow our business by advancing the ideas of reduce, reuse, and recycle among the business community.
Memphis Primary Materials
5360 Airways Blvd., Suite 10A
Memphis, TN 38114
(901) 555-0862
collected batteries from home and brought them to the office for recycling.
You can make the process easier by placing various types of recycling bins around your workplace. Place paper recycle bins near

5 From the taskbar, redisplay your browser, and then **Close** the window.

Objective 12 | Use Special Character and Paragraph Formatting

View the video on the Companion Web Site or in MyITLab

Special text and paragraph formatting is useful to emphasize text, and it makes your newsletter look more professional.

Activity 6.35 | Applying the Small Caps Font Effect

For headlines and titles, ***small caps*** is an attractive font effect. The effect changes lowercase letters to uppercase letters, but with the height of lowercase letters.

1 At the top of the first column, select the paragraph *Memphis Primary Materials: An Introduction* including the paragraph mark.

2 Right-click the selected text, and then from the shortcut menu, click **Font**. In the **Font** dialog box, click the **Font color arrow**, and then under **Theme Colors**, in the fifth column, click the last color – **Blue, Accent 1, Darker 50%**.

3 Under **Font style**, click **Bold**. Under **Size**, click **18**. Under **Effects**, select the **Small caps** check box. Compare your screen with Figure 6.54.

The Font dialog box provides more options than are available on the Ribbon and enables you to make several changes at the same time. In the Preview box, the text displays with the selected formatting options applied.

Figure 6.54

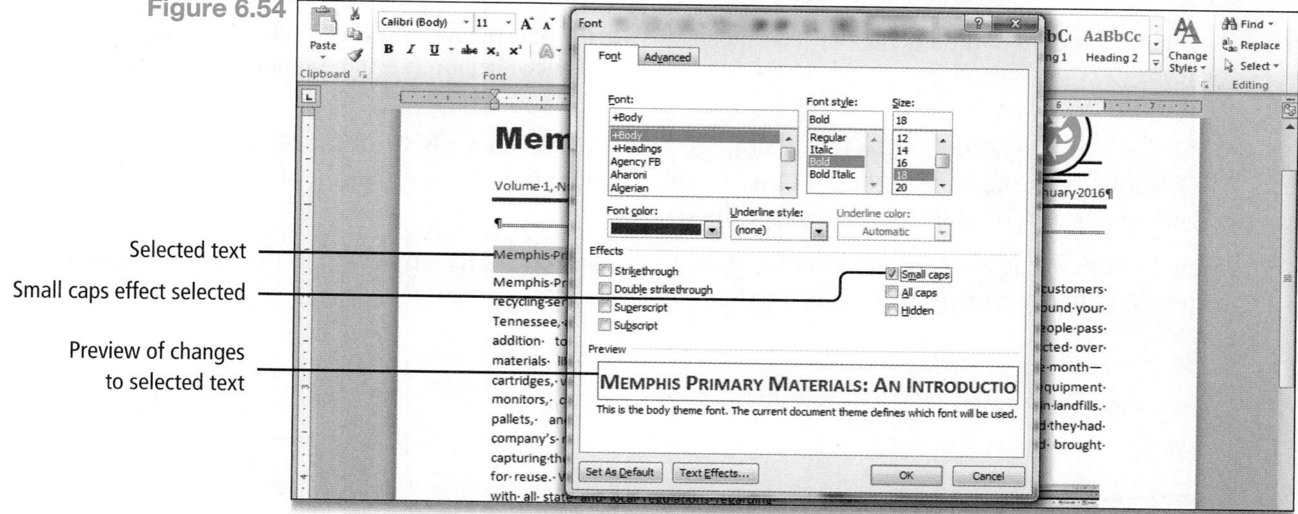
Selected text
Small caps effect selected
Preview of changes to selected text
Font
Font
Advanced
Font:
+Body
+Headings
Agency FB
Aharoni
Algerian
Font style:
Bold
Regular
Italic
Bold Italic
Size:
18
12
14
16
20
Font color:
Underline style:
(none)
Underline color:
Automatic
Effects
Strikethrough
Double strikethrough
Superscript
Subscript
Small caps
All caps
Hidden
Preview
MEMPHIS PRIMARY MATERIALS: AN INTRODUCTIO
This is the body theme font. The current document theme defines which font will be used.
Set As Default
Text Effects...
OK
Cancel

4 Click **OK**. Right-click the selected text, and then on the Mini toolbar, click **Center**.

5 With the text still selected, right-click, and then on the Mini toolbar, click the **Format Painter** button. Then, with the pointer, at the top of the second column, select the paragraph *Make Recycling Easy for Everyone!* to apply the same formats.

6 Position the insertion point to the right of the word *Recycling*, and then press Delete to remove the space. Hold down Shift and then press Enter.

Holding down Shift while pressing Enter inserts a ***manual line break***, which moves the text to the right of the insertion point to a new line while keeping the text in the same paragraph. A ***line break indicator***, in the shape of a bent arrow, indicates that a manual line break was inserted.

7 Compare your screen with Figure 6.55, and then **Save** the document.

Figure 6.55

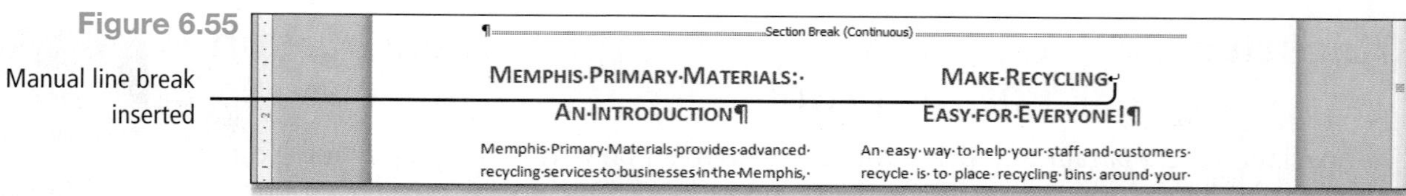

Activity 6.36 | Adding a Border and Shading to a Paragraph

Paragraph borders provide strong visual cues to the reader. Paragraph shading can be used with or without borders.

1 In the first column, in the paragraph that begins *We strive to grow*, click to position the insertion point at the end of the paragraph, and then press Enter one time.

2 At the bottom of the column, select the nine lines of company information, beginning with *Memphis Primary Materials* and ending with the paragraph that begins *Chief Environmental*. On the Mini toolbar, apply **Bold** and **Center**.

3 With the text still selected, on the **Home tab**, in the **Paragraph group**, click the **Borders button arrow**, and then click **Borders and Shading**.

4 In the **Borders and Shading** dialog box, be sure the **Borders tab** is selected. Under **Setting**, click **Shadow**. If necessary, click the **Color arrow**, and then in the fifth column, click the last color—**Blue, Accent 1, Darker 50%**. Click the **Width arrow**, and then click **3 pt**.

In the lower right portion of the Borders and Shading dialog box, the *Apply to* box displays *Paragraph*. The *Apply to* box directs where the border will be applied—in this instance, the border will be applied only to the selected paragraphs.

5 At the top of the **Borders and Shading** dialog box, click the **Shading tab**. Click the **Fill arrow**, and then in the fifth column, click the second color—**Blue, Accent 1, Lighter 80%**. Notice that the shading change is reflected in the Preview area on the right side of the dialog box.

6 At the bottom of the **Borders and Shading** dialog box, click **OK**. Click anywhere in the document to deselect the text, and then compare your screen with Figure 6.56.

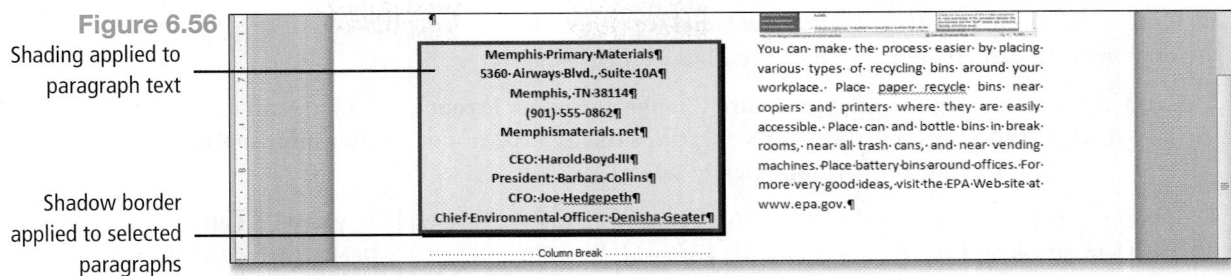

Memphis Primary Materials
5360 Airways Blvd., Suite 10A
Memphis, TN 38114
(901) 555-0862
Memphismaterials.net
CEO: Harold Boyd III
President: Barbara Collins
CFO: Joe Hedgepeth
Chief Environmental Officer: Denisha Geater
Column Break
You can make the process easier by placing various types of recycling bins around your workplace. Place paper recycle bins near copiers and printers where they are easily accessible. Place can and bottle bins in break rooms, near all trash cans, and near vending machines. Place battery bins around offices. For more very good ideas, visit the EPA Web site at www.epa.gov.
Shading applied to paragraph text
Shadow border applied to selected paragraphs

Figure 6.56

7 From **Backstage** view, display the **Document Panel**. In the **Author** box, delete any text and then type your firstname and lastname. In the **Subject** box, type your course name and section number, and in the **Keywords** box, type **newsletter, January Close** [X] the Document Panel.

8 Press Ctrl + F2 to view the **Print Preview**. **Close** the preview, make any necessary corrections, and then click **Save**. **Exit** Word; hold this file until you complete this Project.

Objective 13 | Create Mailing Labels Using Mail Merge

View the video on the Companion Web Site or in MyITLab

Word's ***mail merge*** feature joins a ***main document*** and a ***data source*** to create customized letters or labels. The main document contains the text or formatting that remains constant. The data source contains information that varies for each record, and it can be stored in a Word table, an Excel spreadsheet, or an Access database. The easiest way to perform a mail merge is to use the Mail Merge Wizard, which walks you step by step through the mail merge process.

Activity 6.37 | Opening the Mail Merge Wizard Template

In this activity, you will open the data source for the mail merge, a Word table containing names and addresses.

1 **Start** Word and display a new blank document. Display formatting marks and rulers. Save the document in your **All In One Chapter 6** folder as **Lastname_Firstname_6D_Mailing_Labels**

2 With your new document open on the screen, **Open** the file **w06D_Addresses**. Save the address file in your **All In One Chapter 6** folder as **Lastname_Firstname_6D_Addresses** and then add the file name to the footer.

This document contains a table of addresses. The first row contains the column names. The remaining rows contain the names and addresses.

3 Click to position the insertion point in the last cell in the table, and then press Tab to create a new row. Enter the following information:

First Name	**John**
Last Name	**Wisniewski**
Address 1	**1226 Snow Road**
Address 2	**#234**
City	**Lakeland**
State	**TN**
ZIP Code	**38002**

4 **Save**, and then **Close** the table of addresses. Be sure your blank **Lastname_Firstname_6D_Mailing_Labels** document displays.

5 Click the **Mailings tab**. In the **Start Mail Merge group**, click the **Start Mail Merge** button, and then click **Step by Step Mail Merge Wizard** to display the **Mail Merge** task pane.

6 Under **Select document type**, click the **Labels** option button. At the bottom of the task pane, click **Next: Starting document** to display Step 2 of 6 of the Mail Merge Wizard.

7 Under **Select starting document**, be sure **Change document layout** is selected, and then under **Change document layout**, click **Label options**. In the **Label Options** dialog box, under **Printer information**, click the **Tray arrow**, and then click **Default tray (Automatically Select)**.

8 Under **Label information**, click the **Label vendors arrow**, and then click **Avery US Letter**. Under **Product number**, scroll about halfway down the list, and then click **5160 Easy Peel Address Labels**. Compare your screen with Figure 6.57.

The Avery 5160 address label is a commonly used label. The precut sheets contain three columns of 10 labels each—for a total of 30 labels per sheet.

Figure 6.57

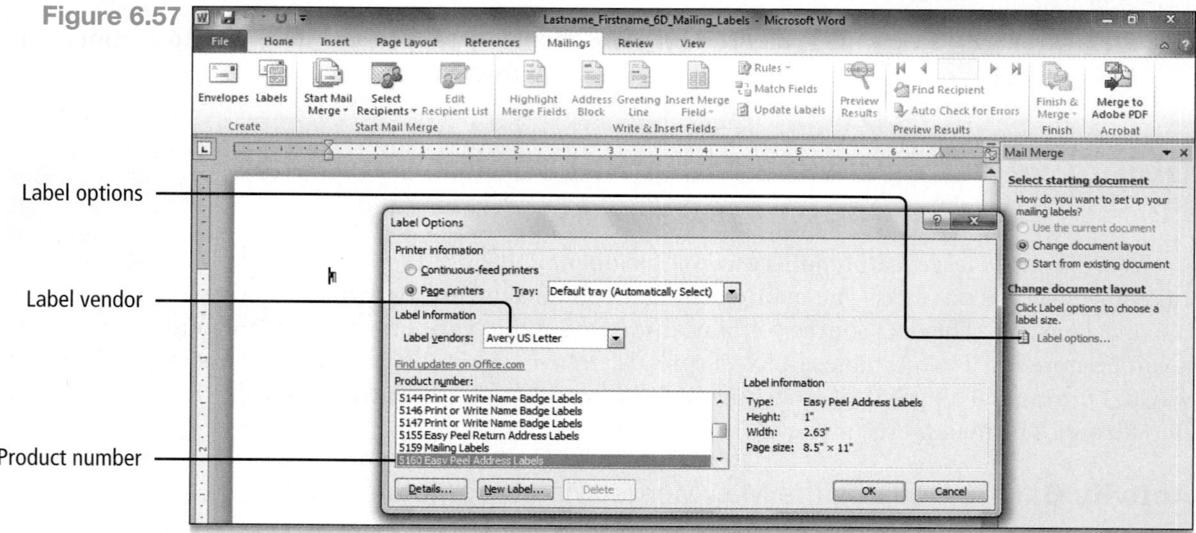

9 At the bottom of the **Label Options** dialog box, click **OK**. If a message box displays, click **OK** to set up the labels. At the bottom of the task pane, click **Next: Select recipients**.

The label page is set up with three columns and ten rows. The label borders may or may not display on your screen, depending on your settings. In Step 3 of the Mail Merge Wizard, the recipients or the data source is identified. It can be a list in an existing file or you can type a new list at this point in the wizard.

10 If gridlines do not display, click the **Layout tab**. In the **Table group**, click the **View Gridlines** button, and then notice that each label is outlined with a dashed line. If you cannot see the right and left edges of the page, in the status bar, click the **Zoom Out** button as necessary to see the entire label sheet on your screen.

11 Under **Select recipients**, be sure the **Use an existing list** option button is selected. Under **Use an existing list**, click **Browse**.

12 Navigate to your **All In One Chapter 6** folder, select your **Lastname_Firstname_6D_Addresses** file, and then click **Open** to display the **Mail Merge Recipients** dialog box.

In the Mail Merge Recipients dialog box, the column headings are formed from the text in the first row of your Word table of addresses. Each row of information that contains data for one person is referred to as a ***record***. The column headings—for example, *Last_Name* and *First_Name*—are referred to as ***fields***. An underscore replaces the spaces between the words in the field name headings.

13 Compare your screen with Figure 6.58.

Figure 6.58

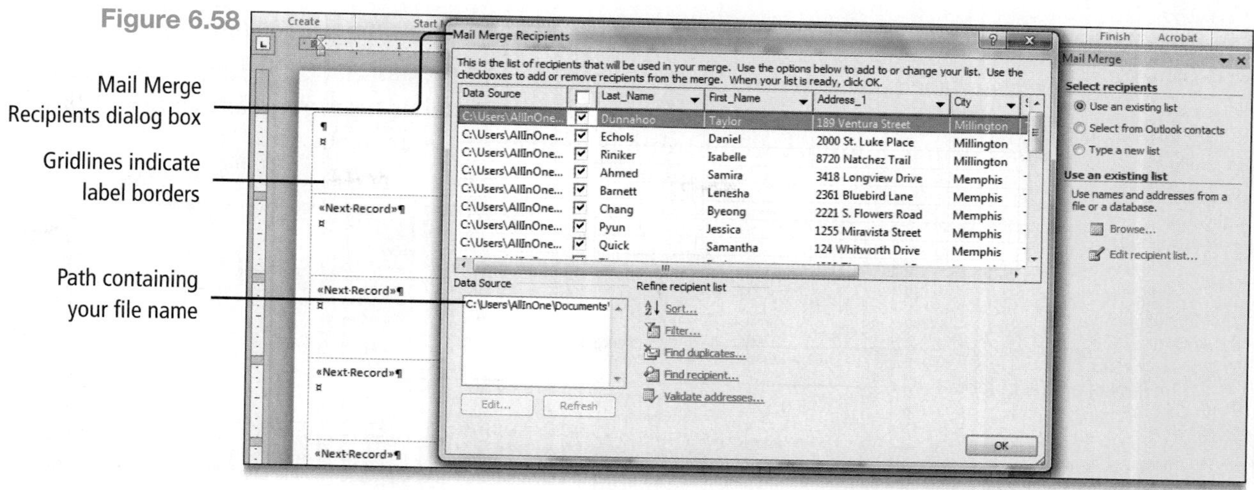

Activity 6.38 | Completing the Mail Merge Wizard

You can add or edit names and addresses while completing the Mail Merge Wizard. You can also match your column names with preset names used in Mail Merge.

1 In the lower left portion of the **Mail Merge Recipients** dialog box, in the **Data Source** box, click the path that contains your file name. Then, at the bottom of the **Mail Merge Recipients** dialog box, click **Edit**.

2 In the upper right corner of the **Data Form** dialog box, click **Add New**. In the blank record, type the following, pressing Tab to move from field to field, and then compare your **Data Form** dialog box with Figure 6.59.

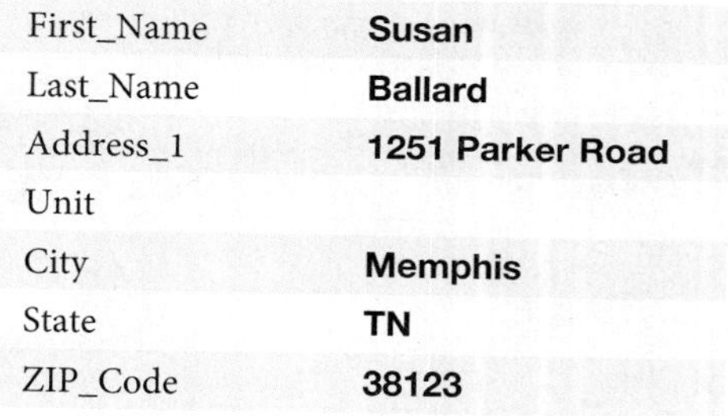

First_Name	**Susan**
Last_Name	**Ballard**
Address_1	**1251 Parker Road**
Unit	
City	**Memphis**
State	**TN**
ZIP_Code	**38123**

Figure 6.59

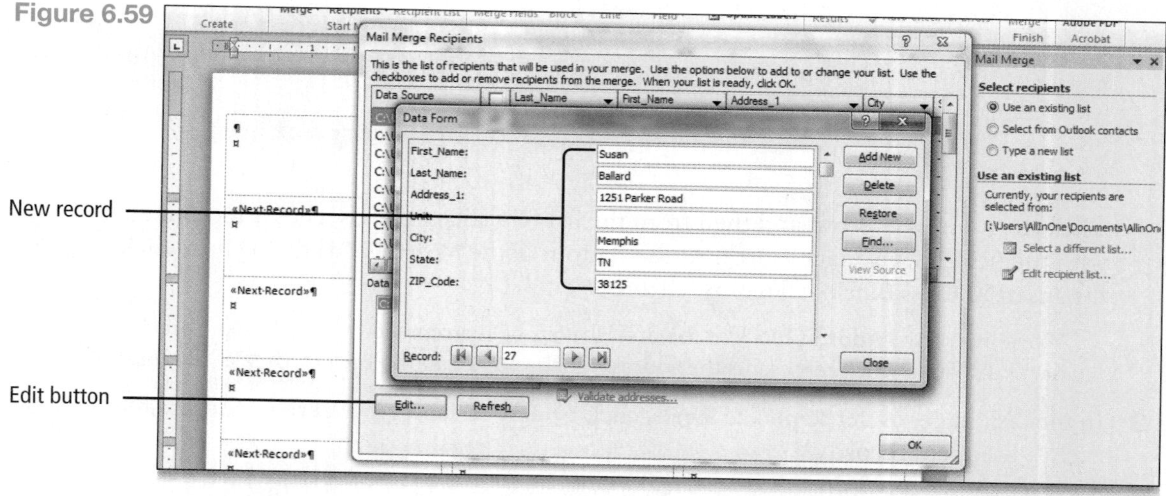

3 In the lower right corner of the **Data Form** dialog box, click **Close**. Scroll to the end of the recipient list to confirm that the record for *Susan Ballard* that you just added is in the list. At the bottom of the **Mail Merge Recipients** dialog box, click **OK**.

4 At the bottom of the **Mail Merge** task pane, click **Next: Arrange your labels.**

5 Under **Arrange your labels**, click **Address block**. In the **Insert Address Block** dialog box, under **Specify address elements**, examine the various formats for names. If necessary, under *Insert recipient's name in this format*, select the *Joshua Randall Jr.* format. Compare your screen with Figure 6.60.

Figure 6.60

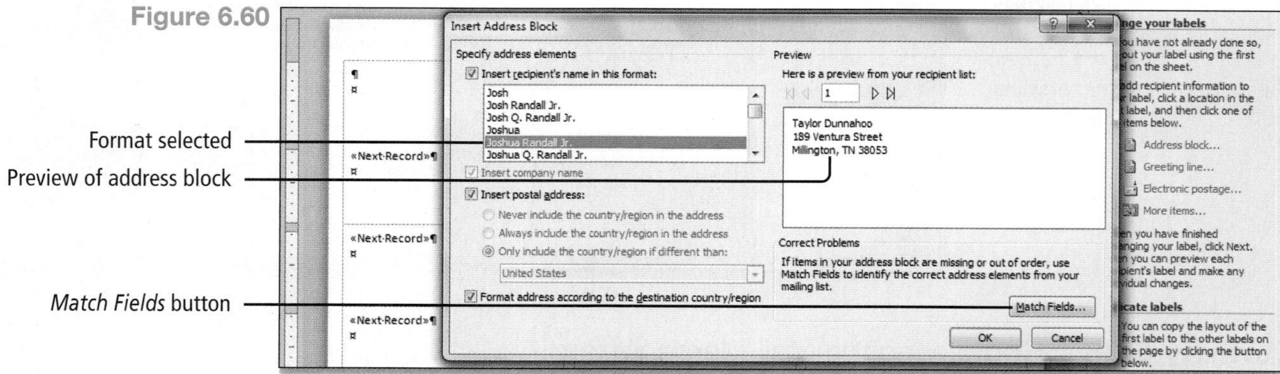

6 In the lower right corner of the **Insert Address Block** dialog box, click **Match Fields**. Scroll down and examine the dialog box, and then compare your screen with Figure 6.61.

If your field names are descriptive, the Mail Merge program will identify them correctly, as is the case with most of the information in the *Required for Address Block* section. However, the Address 2 field is unmatched—in the source file, this column is named *Unit*.

Figure 6.61

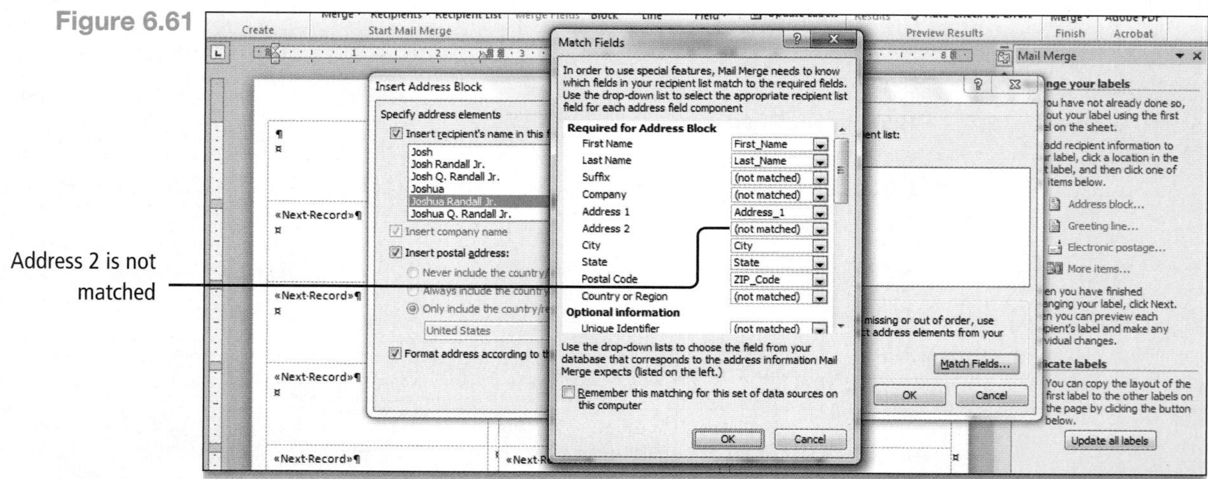

7 Click the **Address 2 arrow**, and then from the list of available fields, click **Unit** to match the Mail Merge field with the field in your data source. At the bottom of the **Match Fields** dialog box, click **OK**. At the bottom of the **Insert Address Block** dialog box, click **OK**.

Word inserts the Address block in the first label space surrounded by double angle brackets. The *AddressBlock* field name displays, which represents the address block you saw in the Preview area of the Insert Address Block dialog box.

8 In the task pane, under **Replicate labels**, click **Update all labels** to insert an address block in each label space for each subsequent record.

9 At the bottom of the task pane, click **Next: Preview your labels**. Notice that for addresses with four lines, the last line of the address is cut off.

10 Press Ctrl + A to select all of the label text, click the **Page Layout tab**, and then in the **Paragraph group**, click in the **Spacing Before** box. Type **3** and press Enter.

11 Click in any label to deselect, and notice that 4-line addresses are no longer cut off. Compare your screen with Figure 6.62.

Figure 6.62

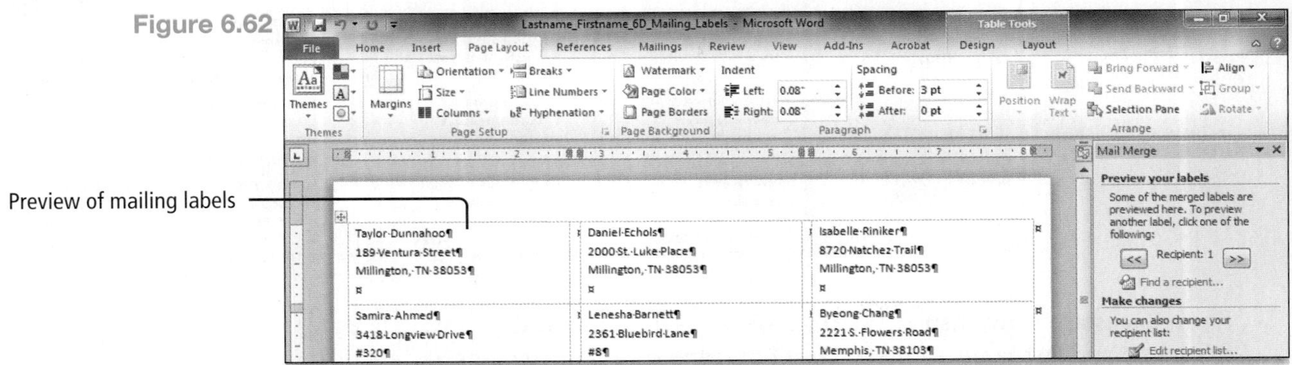

12 At the bottom of the task pane, click **Next: Complete the merge.**

Step 6 of the Mail Merge task pane displays. At this point you can print or edit your labels, although this is done more easily in the document window.

13 **Save** your labels, and then **Close** the Mail Merge task pane.

Activity 6.39 | Previewing and Printing the Mail Merge Document

If you discover that you need to make further changes to your labels, you can still make them even though the Mail Merge task pane is closed.

1 Add the file name to the footer, close the footer area, and then move to the top of Page 2. Click anywhere in the empty table row, click the **Layout tab**, in the **Rows & Columns group**, click the **Delete** button, and then click **Delete Rows**.

Adding footer text to a label sheet replaces the last row of labels on a page with the footer text, and moves the last row of labels to the top of the next page. In this instance, a blank second page is created, which you can delete by deleting the blank row.

2 Press Ctrl + F2 to display the **Print Preview**. Notice that the labels do not display in alphabetical order.

3 Click the **Mailings tab**, and then in the **Start Mail Merge group**, click the **Edit Recipient List** button to display the list of names and addresses.

4 In the **Mail Merge Recipients** dialog box, click the **Last_Name** field heading, and then click **OK**. Press Ctrl + Home, and then compare your screen with Figure 6.63.

Notice that the names are sorted alphabetically by the recipient's last name. Mailing labels are often sorted by either last name or by ZIP Code.

Figure 6.63

Labels in alphabetical order

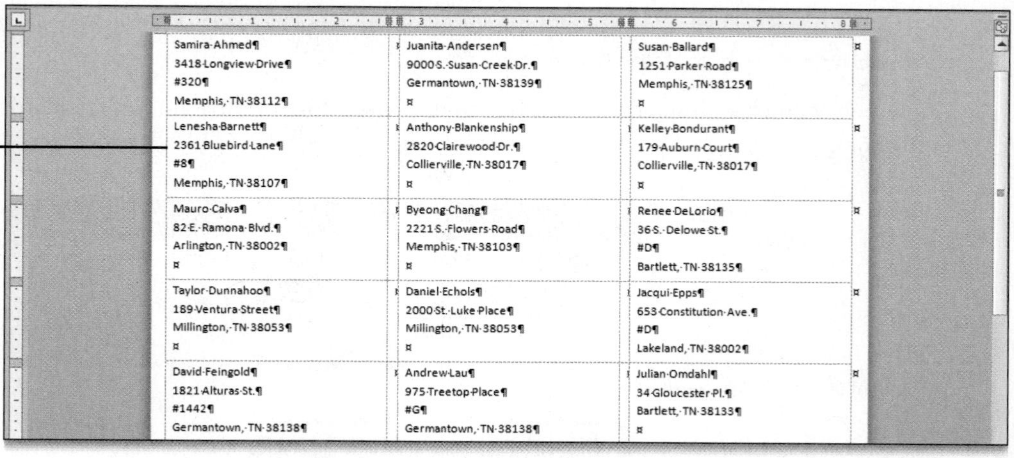

Samira Ahmed 3418 Longview Drive #320 Memphis, TN 38112	Juanita Andersen 9000 S. Susan Creek Dr. Germantown, TN 38139	Susan Ballard 1251 Parker Road Memphis, TN 38125
Lenesha Barnett 2361 Bluebird Lane #8 Memphis, TN 38107	Anthony Blankenship 2820 Clairewood Dr. Collierville, TN 38017	Kelley Bondurant 179 Auburn Court Collierville, TN 38017
Mauro Calva 82 E. Ramona Blvd. Arlington, TN 38002	Byeong Chang 2221 S. Flowers Road Memphis, TN 38103	Renee DeLorio 36 S. Delowe St. #D Bartlett, TN 38135
Taylor Dunnahoo 189 Ventura Street Millington, TN 38053	Daniel Echols 2000 St. Luke Place Millington, TN 38053	Jacqui Epps 653 Constitution Ave. #D Lakeland, TN 38002
David Feingold 1821 Alturas St. #1442 Germantown, TN 38138	Andrew Lau 975 Treetop Place #G Germantown, TN 38138	Julian Omdahl 34 Gloucester Pl. Bartlett, TN 38133

5 From **Backstage** view, display the **Document Panel**. In the **Author** box, delete any text and then type your firstname and lastname. In the **Subject** box, type your course name and section number, and in the **Keywords** box type **newsletter mailing labels Close** the Document Panel.

6 Click **Save**. Display **Backstage** view, and then click the **Print tab**. Examine the **Print Preview** on the right side of the window.

7 As directed by your instructor, print or submit electronically.

If you print, the labels will print on whatever paper is in the printer unless you have preformatted labels available. Printing the labels on plain paper enables you to proofread the labels before you print them on more expensive label sheets.

8 **Close** the document, click **Yes** to save the data source, and then, if necessary, click **Save** to save the labels.

9 In addition to your labels and address document, print or submit your **6D_Memphis_Newsletter** document as directed. **Exit** Word.

End **You have completed Project 6D**

Content-Based Assessments

Summary

In this chapter, you created a table, and then used the table to create a resume. You created a letterhead template, and then created a document using a copy of the letterhead template. You created a cover letter for the resume, moved text, corrected spelling and grammar, and used the built-in thesaurus. You also created a short resume using a template, and saved the resume as a Web page. You created a research paper using the MLA style, including a header, footnotes, citations, and a bibliography, and changed the footnote style. You created a newsletter that used multiple columns. You added a column break, a page break, and a manual line break. You added special font effects, and added a border and shading to a paragraph. Finally, you used the Mail Merge Wizard to create a set of mailing labels for the newsletter.

Key Terms

Check Your Knowledge

Matching and Multiple Choice items are available in MyITLab and on the Companion Web Site.

Apply 6A skills from these Objectives:

1. Create a Table
2. Add Text to a Table
3. Format a Table

Mastering Word | Project 6E Job Listings

In the following Mastering Word project, you will create an announcement for new job postings at Madison Staffing Services. Your completed document will look similar to Figure 6.64.

Project Files

For Project 6E, you will need the following files:

New blank Word document
w06E_New_Jobs

You will save your document as:

Lastname_Firstname_6E_Job_Listings

Project Results

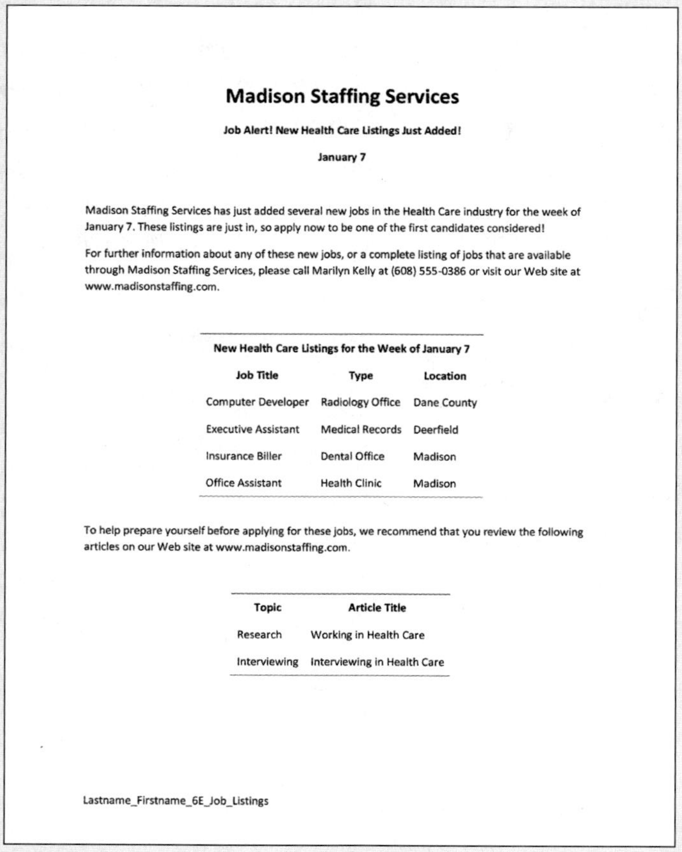

Madison Staffing Services

Job Alert! New Health Care Listings Just Added!

January 7

Madison Staffing Services has just added several new jobs in the Health Care industry for the week of January 7. These listings are just in, so apply now to be one of the first candidates considered!

For further information about any of these new jobs, or a complete listing of jobs that are available through Madison Staffing Services, please call Marilyn Kelly at (608) 555-0386 or visit our Web site at www.madisonstaffing.com.

New Health Care Listings for the Week of January 7

Job Title	Type	Location
Computer Developer	Radiology Office	Dane County
Executive Assistant	Medical Records	Deerfield
Insurance Biller	Dental Office	Madison
Office Assistant	Health Clinic	Madison

To help prepare yourself before applying for these jobs, we recommend that you review the following articles on our Web site at www.madisonstaffing.com.

Topic	Article Title
Research	Working in Health Care
Interviewing	Interviewing in Health Care

Lastname_Firstname_6E_Job_Listings

Figure 6.64

(Project 6E Job Listings continues on the next page)

Mastering Word | Project 6E Job Listings (continued)

1 **Start** Word and display a new blank document; display formatting marks and rulers. **Save** the document in your **All in One Chapter 6** folder as **Lastname_Firstname_6E_Job_Listings** and then add the file name to the footer.

2 Type **Madison Staffing Services** and press Enter. Type **Job Alert! New Health Care Listings Just Added!** and press Enter. Type **January 7** and press Enter two times. Insert the file **w06E_New_Jobs**.

3 At the top of the document, select and **Center** the three title lines. Select the title *Madison Staffing Services* and change the **Font Size** to **20 pt** and apply **Bold**. Apply **Bold** to the second and third title lines. Locate the paragraph that begins *For further information*, and then below that paragraph, click to position the insertion point in the second blank paragraph. **Insert** a **3 × 4** table. Enter the following:

Job Title	Type	Location
Executive Assistant	Medical Records	Deerfield
Insurance Biller	Dental Office	Madison
Office Assistant	Health Clinic	Madison

4 In the table, click anywhere in the second row, and then insert a row above. Add the following information so that the job titles remain in alphabetic order:

Computer Developer	Radiology Office	Dane County

5 Select the entire table. On the **Layout tab**, in the **Cell Size group**, use the **AutoFit** button to **AutoFit Contents**. With the table still selected, **Center** the table. With the table still selected, on the **Page Layout tab**, add **6 pt Spacing Before** and **6 pt Spacing After**.

6 With the table still selected, remove all table borders, and then add a **Custom 1 pt** solid line top border and bottom border. Select all three cells in the first row, apply **Bold**, and then **Center** the text. Click anywhere in the first row, and then insert a new row above. Merge the three cells in the new top row, and then type **New Health Care Listings for the Week of January 7** Notice that the new row keeps the formatting of the row from which it was created.

7 At the bottom of the document, **Insert** a **2 × 3** table. Enter the following:

Topic	Article Title
Research	Working in Health Care
Interviewing	Interviewing in Health Care

8 Select the entire table. On the **Layout tab**, in the **Cell Size group**, use the **AutoFit** button to **AutoFit Contents**. On the **Home tab**, **Center** the table. On the **Page Layout tab**, add **6 pt Spacing Before** and **6 pt Spacing After**.

9 With the table still selected, remove all table borders, and then add a **Custom 1 pt** solid line top border and bottom border. Select the cells in the first row, apply **Bold**, and then **Center** the text.

10 In the **Document Panel**, add your name and course information and the **Keywords new listings, health care Save** and then print or submit the document electronically as directed. **Exit** Word.

End **You have completed Project 6E**

Apply 6B skills from these Objectives:

4 Create a New Document from an Existing Document

5 Change and Reorganize Text

6 Use the Proofing Options

7 Create a Document Using a Template

Mastering Word | Project 6F Job Tips

In the following Mastering Word project, you will create a fax and a memo that includes job tips for Madison Staffing Services employees. Your completed documents will look similar to Figure 6.65.

Project Files

For Project 6F, you will need the following files:

w06F_Memo_Heading
w06F_Memo_Text
Origin Fax template from Word's installed templates

You will save your documents as:

Lastname_Firstname_6F_Job_Tips
Lastname_Firstname_6F_Fax

Project Results

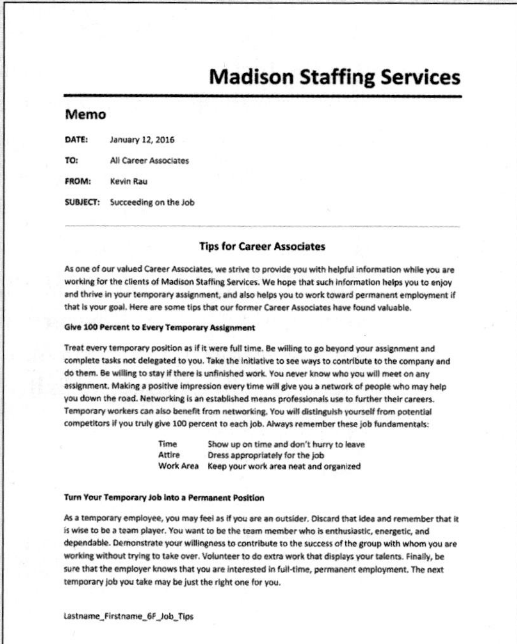

Madison Staffing Services

Memo

DATE: January 12, 2016

TO: All Career Associates

FROM: Kevin Rau

SUBJECT: Succeeding on the Job

Tips for Career Associates

As one of our valued Career Associates, we strive to provide you with helpful information while you are working for the clients of Madison Staffing Services. We hope that such information helps you to enjoy and thrive in your temporary assignment, and also helps you to work toward permanent employment if that is your goal. Here are some tips that our former Career Associates have found valuable.

Give 100 Percent to Every Temporary Assignment

Treat every temporary position as if it were full time. Be willing to go beyond your assignment and complete tasks not delegated to you. Take the initiative to see ways to contribute to the company and do them. Be willing to stay if there is unfinished work. You never know who you will meet on any assignment. Making a positive impression every time will give you a network of people who may help you down the road. Networking is an established means professionals use to further their careers. Temporary workers can also benefit from networking. You will distinguish yourself from potential competitors if you truly give 100 percent to each job. Always remember these job fundamentals:

Time	Show up on time and don't hurry to leave
Attire	Dress appropriately for the job
Work Area	Keep your work area neat and organized

Turn Your Temporary Job into a Permanent Position

As a temporary employee, you may feel as if you are an outsider. Discard that idea and remember that it is wise to be a team player. You want to be the team member who is enthusiastic, energetic, and dependable. Demonstrate your willingness to contribute to the success of the group with whom you are working without trying to take over. Volunteer to do extra work that displays your talents. Finally, be sure that the employer knows that you are interested in full-time, permanent employment. The next temporary job you take may be just the right one for you.

Lastname_Firstname_6F_Job_Tips

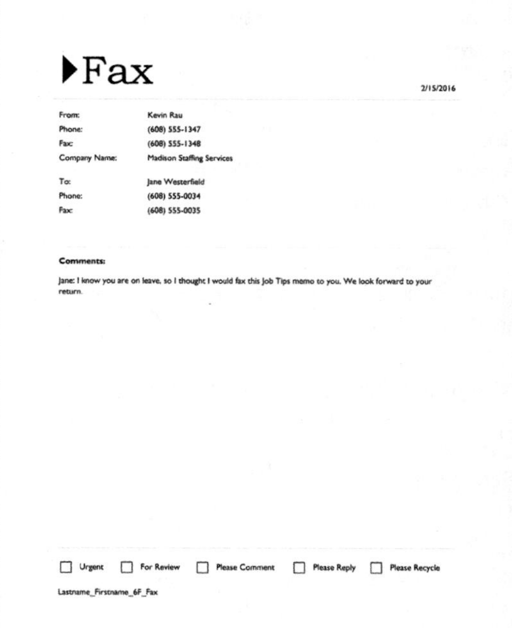

Fax

2/15/2016

From:	Kevin Rau
Phone:	(608) 555-1347
Fax:	(608) 555-1348
Company Name:	Madison Staffing Services
To:	Jane Westerfield
Phone:	(608) 555-0034
Fax:	(608) 555-0035

Comments:

Jane: I know you are on leave, so I thought I would fax this Job Tips memo to you. We look forward to your return.

☐ Urgent ☐ For Review ☐ Please Comment ☐ Please Reply ☐ Please Recycle

Lastname_Firstname_6F_Fax

Figure 6.65

(Project 6F Job Tips continues on the next page)

Mastering Word | Project 6F Job Tips (continued)

1 **Start** Word; display rulers and formatting marks. In **Backstage** view, create a **New** document using the **New from existing** template. In the **New from Existing Document** dialog box, navigate to your student files, click **w06F_Memo_Heading**, and then click **Create New**.

2 Display the **Document Panel**, add your name and course information and the **Keywords memo, associates**

3 **Save** the document in your **All in One Chapter 6** folder as **Lastname_Firstname_6F_Job_Tips** Add the file name to the footer.

4 At the top of your document, in the DATE paragraph, click to the right of the tab formatting mark, and then type **January 12, 2016** Use a similar technique to add the following information:

TO:	**All Career Associates**
FROM:	**Kevin Rau**
SUBJECT:	**Succeeding on the Job**

5 Position the insertion point in the blank paragraph below the memo heading. **Insert** the file **w06F_Memo_Text** and press Backspace to remove the blank line at the end of the inserted text.

6 Select and **Center** the title *Tips for Career Associates*. By using either the **Spelling and Grammar** dialog box, or by right-clicking selected words, correct all spelling, grammar, and word usage errors.

7 In the first line of the paragraph that begins *Treat every*, locate and right-click *provisional*. Use the shortcut menu to change the word to the synonym *temporary*. In the second line of the same paragraph, change *donate* to the synonym *contribute*.

8 At the end of the paragraph that begins *Treat every temporary*, create a blank paragraph. **Insert** a **2 × 3** table, and then type the following information:

Time	**Show up on time and don't hurry to leave**
Attire	**Dress appropriately for the job**
Work Area	**Keep your work area neat and organized**

9 Select the entire table. **AutoFit Contents**, **Center** the table, and remove the table borders. Display **Backstage** view and preview the document. **Save** and **Close** the document but leave Word open. Hold this file until you complete this project.

10 From **Sample templates**, create a document based on the **Origin Fax** template. **Save** the document in your **All in One Chapter 6** folder as **Lastname_Firstname_6F_Fax** and then add the file name to the footer—called the *First Page Footer* in this template.

11 Click the *Pick a date* placeholder, type **2/15/2016** and then type the following for the remaining controls:

From:	**Kevin Rau**
Phone:	**(608) 555-1347**
Fax:	**(608) 555-1348**
Company Name:	**Madison Staffing Services**
To:	**Jane Westerfield**
Phone:	**(608) 555-0034**
Fax:	**(608) 555-0035**

12 Locate and right-click *Kevin Rau*; remove the content control. Delete the lower *Company Name* text and remove the control to its right. In the *Type comments* control, type **Jane: I know you are on leave, so I thought I would fax this Job Tips memo to you. We look forward to your return.**

13 In the **Document Panel**, add your name and course information and the **Keywords job tips, fax Save** the document.

14 As directed by your instructor, print or submit electronically the two files that are the results of this project. **Exit** Word.

End **You have completed Project 6F**

Content-Based Assessments

Apply 6C skills from these Objectives:

8 Create a Research Paper

9 Insert Footnotes in a Research Paper

10 Create Citations and a Bibliography in a Research Paper

Mastering Word | Project 6G Hazards

In the following Mastering Word project, you will edit and format a research paper for Memphis Primary Materials, the topic of which is hazardous materials in electronic waste. Your completed document will look similar to Figure 6.66.

Project Files

For Project 6G, you will need the following file:

w06G_Hazards

You will save your document as:

Lastname_Firstname_6G_Hazards

Project Results

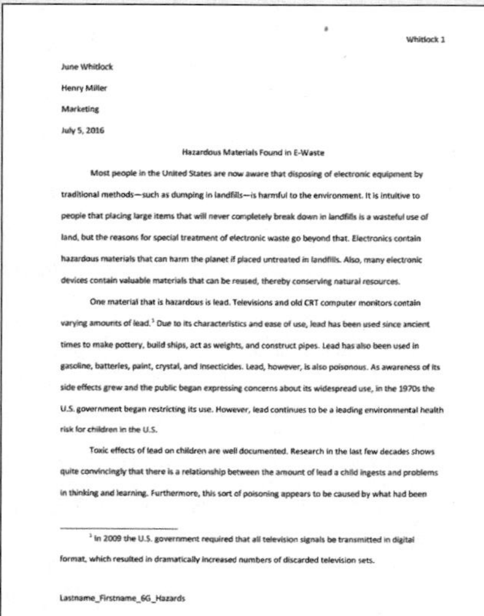

Whitlock 1

June Whitlock

Henry Miller

Marketing

July 5, 2016

Hazardous Materials Found in E-Waste

Most people in the United States are now aware that disposing of electronic equipment by traditional methods—such as dumping in landfills—is harmful to the environment. It is intuitive to people that placing large items that will never completely break down in landfills is a wasteful use of land, but the reasons for special treatment of electronic waste go beyond that. Electronics contain hazardous materials that can harm the planet if placed untreated in landfills. Also, many electronic devices contain valuable materials that can be reused, thereby conserving natural resources.

One material that is hazardous is lead. Televisions and old CRT computer monitors contain varying amounts of lead.[1] Due to its characteristics and ease of use, lead has been used since ancient times to make pottery, build ships, act as weights, and construct pipes. Lead has also been used in gasoline, batteries, paint, crystal, and insecticides. Lead, however, is also poisonous. As awareness of its side effects grew and the public began expressing concerns about its widespread use, in the 1970s the U.S. government began restricting its use. However, lead continues to be a leading environmental health risk for children in the U.S.

Toxic effects of lead on children are well documented. Research in the last few decades shows quite convincingly that there is a relationship between the amount of lead a child ingests and problems in thinking and learning. Furthermore, this sort of poisoning appears to be caused by what had been

[1] In 2009 the U.S. government required that all television signals be transmitted in digital format, which resulted in dramatically increased numbers of discarded television sets.

Lastname_Firstname_6G_Hazards

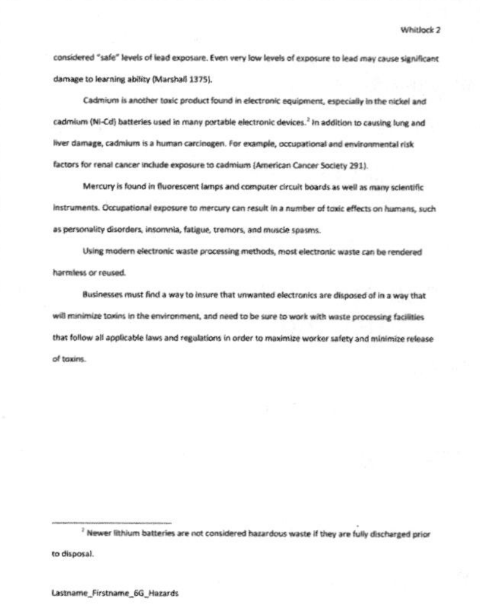

Whitlock 2

considered "safe" levels of lead exposure. Even very low levels of exposure to lead may cause significant damage to learning ability (Marshall 1375).

Cadmium is another toxic product found in electronic equipment, especially in the nickel and cadmium (Ni-Cd) batteries used in many portable electronic devices.[2] In addition to causing lung and liver damage, cadmium is a human carcinogen. For example, occupational and environmental risk factors for renal cancer include exposure to cadmium (American Cancer Society 291).

Mercury is found in fluorescent lamps and computer circuit boards as well as many scientific instruments. Occupational exposure to mercury can result in a number of toxic effects on humans, such as personality disorders, insomnia, fatigue, tremors, and muscle spasms.

Using modern electronic waste processing methods, most electronic waste can be rendered harmless or reused.

Businesses must find a way to insure that unwanted electronics are disposed of in a way that will minimize toxins in the environment, and need to be sure to work with waste processing facilities that follow all applicable laws and regulations in order to maximize worker safety and minimize release of toxins.

[2] Newer lithium batteries are not considered hazardous waste if they are fully discharged prior to disposal.

Lastname_Firstname_6G_Hazards

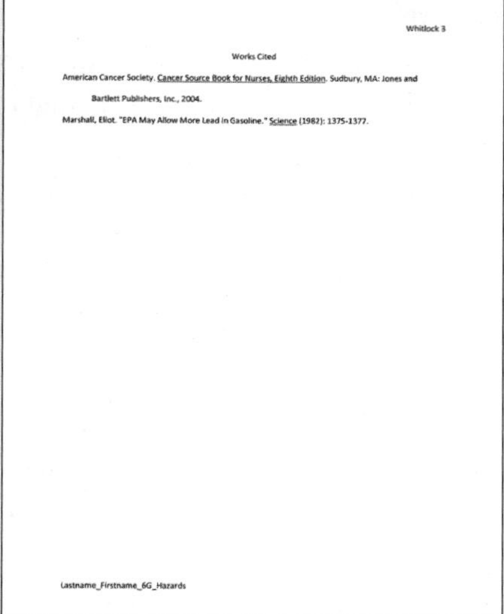

Whitlock 3

Works Cited

American Cancer Society. Cancer Source Book for Nurses, Eighth Edition. Sudbury, MA: Jones and Bartlett Publishers, Inc., 2004.

Marshall, Eliot. "EPA May Allow More Lead in Gasoline." Science (1982): 1375-1377.

Lastname_Firstname_6G_Hazards

Figure 6.66

(Project 6G Hazards continues on the next page)

Mastering Word | Project 6G Hazards (continued)

1 **Start** Word. From your student files open the document **w06G_Hazards**. Save the document in your **All In One Chapter 6** folder as **Lastname_Firstname_6G_Hazards** Display the header area, type **Whitlock** and then press Spacebar. Display the **Page Number gallery**, and then in the **Current Position**, add the **Plain Number** style. Apply **Align Text Right** formatting to the header. Add the file name to the footer.

2 Return to the beginning of the document, press Enter to insert a blank line, click in the blank line, type **June Whitlock** and then press Enter. Type **Henry Miller** and press Enter. Type **Marketing** and press Enter. Type **July 5, 2016**

3 Select all of the text in the document. Change the **Line Spacing** to **2.0**, and change the **Spacing After** to **0 pt**. Deselect the text, right-click anywhere in the title *Hazardous Materials Found in E-Waste*, and then **Center** the title.

Starting with the paragraph that begins *Most people*, select the text from that point to the end of the document, and then set the **First Line Indent** to **0.5"**.

4 Near the middle of **Page 1**, in the paragraph that begins *One material*, in the second line, click to position the insertion point to the right of the period following *lead*, and then add the following footnote:

> **In 2009 the U.S. government required that all television signals be transmitted in digital format, which resulted in dramatically increased numbers of discarded television sets.**

On **Page 2**, in the paragraph that begins *Cadmium is another*, in the second line, click to position the insertion point to the right of the period following *devices*, and then add the following footnote:

> **Newer lithium batteries are not considered hazardous waste if they are fully discharged prior to disposal.**

5 Right-click anywhere in the footnote, modify the **Style** to set the **Font Size** to **11**, and then change the **Format** of paragraphs to add a **First line** indent and use doublespacing.

Near the bottom of **Page 1**, locate the paragraph that begins *Toxic effects*, and then click to position the insertion point to the left of the period at the end of the paragraph, which displays at the top of **Page 2**. In the **MLA** format, add the following **Journal Article** citation (type the Title on one line):

Author:	**Marshall, Eliot**
Title:	**EPA May Allow More Lead in Gasoline**
Journal Name:	**Science**
Year:	**1982**
Pages:	**1375–1377**

6 Near the top of **Page 2**, locate the paragraph that begins *Cadmium*, and then click to position the insertion point to the left of the period at the end of the paragraph. Add the following **Book** citation, using a **Corporate Author** (type the Title on one line):

Corporate Author:	**American Cancer Society**
Title:	**Cancer Source Book for Nurses, Eighth Edition**
Year:	**2004**
City:	**Sudbury, MA**
Publisher:	**Jones and Bartlett Publishers, Inc.**

Select the *Marshall* citation and add the page number **1375** At the end of the next paragraph, select the *American Cancer Society* citation and add the page number **291**

7 Move to the end of the document, and then insert a manual page break to create a new page. Change the **First Line Indent** to **0"**. Add a **Works Cited** title, and then **Insert Bibliography**. Select the two references, apply double line spacing, and then remove spacing after the paragraphs. **Center** the *Works Cited* title.

8 Display the **Document Panel** and add your name and course information and the keywords **hazardous materials Save** your document. Display the Print Preview, make any necessary adjustments, and then print or submit electronically as directed. **Exit** Word.

End **You have completed Project 6G**

Content-Based Assessments

Apply 6D skills from these Objectives:

11 Format a Multiple-Column Newsletter

12 Use Special Character and Paragraph Formatting

13 Create Mailing Labels Using Mail Merge

Mastering Word | Project **6H** Spring Newsletter

In the following Mastering Word project, you will format a newsletter for Memphis Primary Materials, and then create a set of mailing labels for the newsletter. Your completed documents will look similar to Figure 6.67.

Project Files

For Project 6H, you will need the following files:

New blank Word document
w06H_Spring_Newsletter
w06H_Addresses

You will save your documents as:

Lastname_Firstname_6H_Spring_Newsletter
Lastname_Firstname_6H_Labels

Project Results

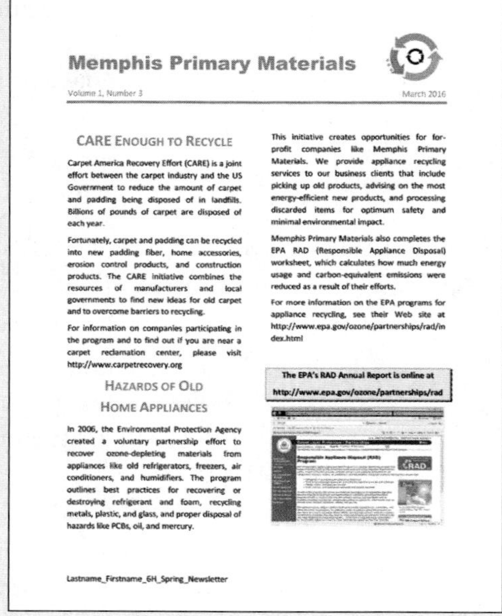

Memphis Primary Materials

Volume 1, Number 3 March 2016

CARE Enough to Recycle

Carpet America Recovery Effort (CARE) is a joint effort between the carpet industry and the US Government to reduce the amount of carpet and padding being disposed of in landfills. Billions of pounds of carpet are disposed of each year.

Fortunately, carpet and padding can be recycled into new padding fiber, home accessories, erosion control products, and construction products. The CARE initiative combines the resources of manufacturers and local governments to find new ideas for old carpet and to overcome barriers to recycling.

For information on companies participating in the program and to find out if you are near a carpet reclamation center, please visit http://www.carpetrecovery.org

Hazards of Old Home Appliances

In 2006, the Environmental Protection Agency created a voluntary partnership effort to recover ozone-depleting materials from appliances like old refrigerators, freezers, air conditioners, and humidifiers. The program outlines best practices for recovering or destroying refrigerant and foam, recycling metals, plastic, and glass, and proper disposal of hazards like PCBs, oil, and mercury.

This initiative creates opportunities for for-profit companies like Memphis Primary Materials. We provide appliance recycling services to our business clients that include picking up old products, advising on the most energy-efficient new products, and processing discarded items for optimum safety and minimal environmental impact.

Memphis Primary Materials also completes the EPA RAD (Responsible Appliance Disposal) worksheet, which calculates how much energy usage and carbon-equivalent emissions were reduced as a result of their efforts.

For more information on the EPA programs for appliance recycling, see their Web site at http://www.epa.gov/ozone/partnerships/rad/index.html

The EPA's RAD Annual Report is online at http://www.epa.gov/ozone/partnerships/rad

Lastname_Firstname_6H_Spring_Newsletter

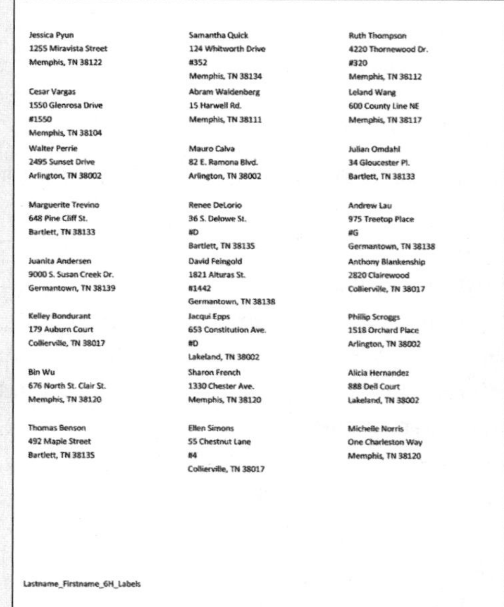

Jessica Pyun 1255 Miravista Street Memphis, TN 38122	Samantha Quick 124 Whitworth Drive #352 Memphis, TN 38134	Ruth Thompson 4220 Thornewood Dr. #320 Memphis, TN 38112
Cesar Vargas 1550 Glenrosa Drive #1550 Memphis, TN 38104	Abram Waldenberg 15 Harwell Rd. Memphis, TN 38111	Leland Wang 600 County Line NE Memphis, TN 38117
Walter Perrie 2495 Sunset Drive Arlington, TN 38002	Mauro Calva 82 E. Ramona Blvd. Arlington, TN 38002	Julian Omdahl 34 Gloucester Pl. Bartlett, TN 38133
Marguerite Trevino 648 Pine Cliff St. Bartlett, TN 38133	Renee DeLorio 36 S. Delowe St. #D Bartlett, TN 38135	Andrew Lau 975 Treetop Place #G Germantown, TN 38138
Juanita Andersen 9000 S. Susan Creek Dr. Germantown, TN 38139	David Feingold 1821 Alturas St. #1442 Germantown, TN 38138	Anthony Blankenship 2820 Clairewood Collierville, TN 38017
Kelley Bondurant 179 Auburn Court Collierville, TN 38017	Jacqui Epps 653 Constitution Ave. #D Lakeland, TN 38002	Phillip Scroggs 1518 Orchard Place Arlington, TN 38002
Bin Wu 676 North St. Clair St. Memphis, TN 38120	Sharon French 1330 Chester Ave. Memphis, TN 38120	Alicia Hernandez 888 Dell Court Lakeland, TN 38002
Thomas Benson 492 Maple Street Bartlett, TN 38135	Ellen Simons 55 Chestnut Lane #4 Collierville, TN 38017	Michelle Norris One Charleston Way Memphis, TN 38120

Lastname_Firstname_6H_Labels

Figure 6.67

(Project 6H Spring Newsletter continues on the next page)

Mastering Word | Project 6H Spring Newsletter (continued)

1 **Start** Word. Open **w06H_Spring_Newsletter**, and then save it in your **All In One Chapter 6** folder as **Lastname_Firstname_6H_Spring_Newsletter** Add the file name to the footer. Display the rulers and formatting marks.

Select the first line of text—*Memphis Primary Materials*. Change the **Font** to **Arial Black**, the **Font Size** to **24**, and the **Font Color** to **Orange, Accent 6, Darker 25%**.

Select the second line of text—the date and volume. Change the **Font Color** to **Orange, Accent 6, Darker 25%**. Display the **Borders and Shading** dialog box, and then add an **Orange, Accent 6, Darker 25%**, **3 pt** line below the selected text.

2 Click at the beginning of the newsletter title. Display the **Clip Art** task pane, search for **recycle earth** and then insert the image of the orange and tan recycle arrows. Change the **Height** to **1** and then apply **Square** text wrapping. Close the **Clip Art** task pane. Drag the image to the location shown in Figure 6.67.

Starting with the paragraph that begins *CARE enough*, select all of the text from that point to the end of the document. Change the **Spacing After** to **6 pt**, format the text in two columns, and apply the **Justify** alignment.

3 At the top of the first column, select the paragraph *CARE Enough to Recycle*. From the **Font** dialog box, change the **Font Size** to **20**, apply **Bold**, add the **Small caps** effect, and change the **Font color** to **Orange, Accent 6, Darker 25%**. **Center** the paragraph. Near the bottom of the same column, apply the same formatting to the paragraph that begins *Hazards of Old*. Add a manual line break between *Old* and *Home*.

Move to the blank line at the bottom of the second column. Open your Web browser and open the **www.epa.gov/ozone/partnerships/rad/** Web site. Maximize the browser window and return to your Word document. Insert a **Screenshot** of the EPA Web page. **Close** your Web browser.

4 Select the two lines of text above the inserted screenshot. **Center** the text and apply **Bold**. Add a **Shadow** border, change the **Color** to **Tan, Background 2, Darker 25%**, the **Width** to **1 1/2 pt**, and then on the **Shading tab** of the dialog box, apply a **Fill** of **Tan, Background 2** shading—in the third column, the first color.

Display the **Document Panel** and add your name, course information, and the **Keywords Spring newsletter** Display the **Print Preview**, return to your document and make any necessary corrections, and then **Save** and **Close** the document. Hold this document until you complete the project.

5 Display a **New** blank document. **Save** the document in your **All In One Chapter 6** folder as **Lastname_Firstname_6H_Labels** On the **Mailings tab**, start the **Step by Step Mail Merge Wizard**.

In **Step 1**, select **Labels** as the document type. In **Step 2**, set **Label options** to use the **Auto default** tray (yours may vary) and **Avery US Letter 5160**.

In **Step 3**, use an existing list, browse to select **w06H_Addresses**. In **Step 4**, add an **Address block** to the labels, use the *Joshua Randall Jr.* format, and then **Match Fields** by matching *Address 2* to *Unit*.

Update all labels and **Preview**. Select all of the label text, and then on the **Page Layout tab**, click in the **Spacing Before** box, type **4** and press Enter to ensure that the four-line addresses will fit on the labels. On the **Layout tab**, in the **Table group**, if necessary click **View Gridlines** to check the alignment of the labels.

Complete the merge, and then **Close** the **Mail Merge** task pane. Delete the last two empty rows of the table, and then add the file name to the footer.

6 Display the **Document Panel**, and then add your name and course information and the keywords **mailing labels** Display the **Print Preview**, return to your document and make any necessary corrections, and then **Save**. Print or submit electronically your two files that are the results of this project. **Exit** Word.

End **You have completed Project 6H**

Content-Based Assessments

Apply **6A** and **6B** skills from these Objectives:

1. Create a Table
2. Add Text to a Table
3. Format a Table
4. Create a New Document from an Existing Document
5. Change and Reorganize Text
6. Use the Proofing Options
7. Create a Document Using a Template

Mastering Word | Project 6I Job Letter

In the following Mastering Word project, you will create a new document from an existing document, format a table, and then create a fax cover using a template. Your completed documents will look similar to Figure 6.68.

Project Files

For Project 6I, you will need the following files:

w06I_Letter_Text
w06I_Letterhead
w06I_Resume
Equity Fax template from Word's installed templates

You will save your documents as:

Lastname_Firstname_6I_Job_Letter
Lastname_Firstname_6I_Resume
Lastname_Firstname_6I_Fax

Project Results

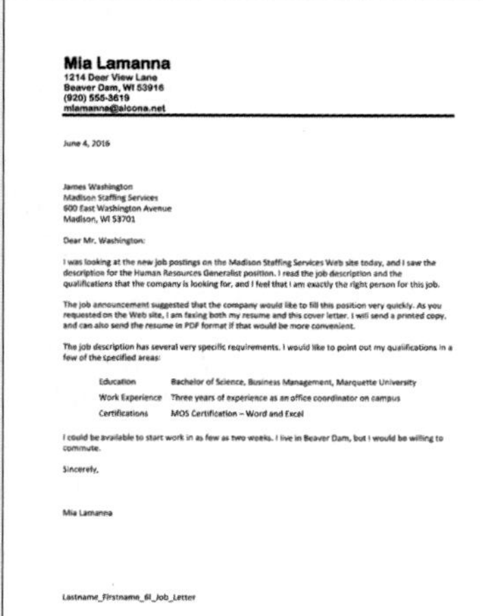

Mia Lamanna
1214 Deer View Lane
Beaver Dam, WI 53916
(920) 555-3619
mlamanna@alcona.net

June 4, 2016

James Washington
Madison Staffing Services
600 East Washington Avenue
Madison, WI 53701

Dear Mr. Washington:

I was looking at the new job postings on the Madison Staffing Services Web site today, and I saw the description for the Human Resources Generalist position. I read the job description and the qualifications that the company is looking for, and I feel that I am exactly the right person for this job.

The job announcement suggested that the company would like to fill this position very quickly. As you requested on the Web site, I am faxing both my resume and this cover letter. I will send a printed copy, and can also send the resume in PDF format if that would be more convenient.

The job description has several very specific requirements. I would like to point out my qualifications in a few of the specified areas:

Education	Bachelor of Science, Business Management, Marquette University
Work Experience	Three years of experience as an office coordinator on campus
Certifications	MOS Certification – Word and Excel

I could be available to start work in as few as two weeks. I live in Beaver Dam, but I would be willing to commute.

Sincerely,

Mia Lamanna

Lastname_Firstname_6I_Job_Letter

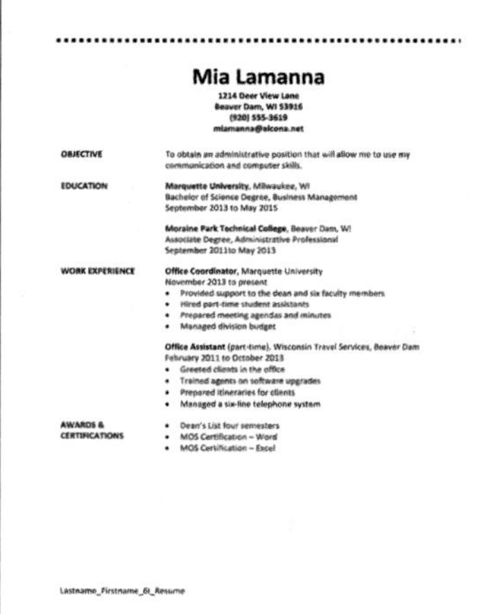

Mia Lamanna
1214 Deer View Lane
Beaver Dam, WI 53916
(920) 555-3619
mlamanna@alcona.net

OBJECTIVE	To obtain an administrative position that will allow me to use my communication and computer skills.
EDUCATION	**Marquette University**, Milwaukee, WI Bachelor of Science Degree, Business Management September 2013 to May 2015 **Moraine Park Technical College**, Beaver Dam, WI Associate Degree, Administrative Professional September 2011to May 2013
WORK EXPERIENCE	**Office Coordinator**, Marquette University November 2013 to present • Provided support to the dean and six faculty members • Hired part-time student assistants • Prepared meeting agendas and minutes • Managed division budget **Office Assistant** (part-time), Wisconsin Travel Services, Beaver Dam February 2011 to October 2013 • Greeted clients in the office • Trained agents on software upgrades • Prepared itineraries for clients • Managed a six-line telephone system
AWARDS & CERTIFICATIONS	• Dean's List four semesters • MOS Certification – Word • MOS Certification – Excel

Lastname_Firstname_6I_Resume

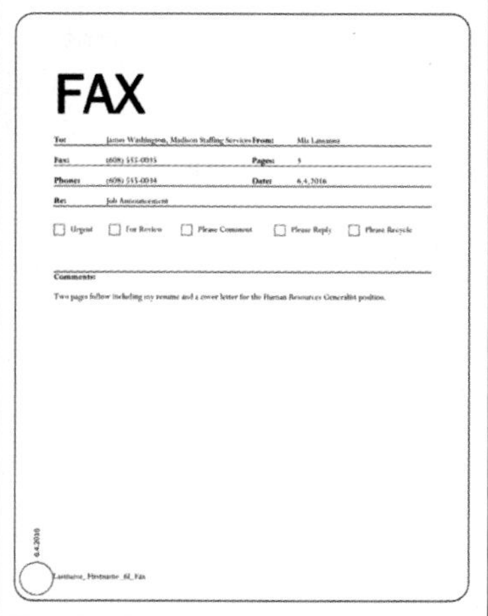

FAX

To:	James Washington, Madison Staffing Services	**From:**	Mia Lamanna
Fax:	(608) 555-0095	**Pages:**	3
Phone:	(608) 555-0034	**Date:**	6.4.2016
Re:	Job Announcement		

☐ Urgent ☐ For Review ☐ Please Comment ☐ Please Reply ☐ Please Recycle

Comments:

Two pages follow including my resume and a cover letter for the Human Resources Generalist position.

6.4.2016

Lastname_Firstname_6I_Fax

Figure 6.68

(Project 6I Job Letter continues on the next page)

Mastering Word | Project 6I Job Letter (continued)

1 **Start** Word and display rulers and formatting marks. By using the **New from existing** template, create a document from the file **w06I_Letterhead**. **Save** the document in your **All in One Chapter 6** folder as **Lastname_Firstname_6I_Job_Letter** Add the file name to the footer. Move to the end of the document, and then on the **Home tab**, apply the **No Spacing** style. Type **June 4, 2016** and then press Enter four times. Type the following:

> **James Washington**
>
> **Madison Staffing Services**
>
> **600 East Washington Avenue**
>
> **Madison, WI 53701**

2 Press Enter two times, type **Dear Mr. Washington:** and press Enter two times. Insert the text from the file **w06I_Letter_Text** and remove the blank line at the bottom of the selected text.

3 Move to the top of the document, and then by using either the **Spelling and Grammar** dialog box, or by right-clicking selected words, correct spelling, grammar, and word usage errors. In the first paragraph, in the third line, locate and right-click *correct*. Use the shortcut menu to open the **Thesaurus** and change the word to the synonym *right*. In the next paragraph, in the first line, change *notice* to the synonym *announcement*.

4 In the paragraph that begins *I live*, select the first sentence of the paragraph and drag it to the end of the same paragraph. In the second blank line below the paragraph that begins *The job description*, insert a **2 × 3** table, and then type the text shown in **Table 1** below.

5 Select the entire table. **AutoFit Contents**, **Center** the table, remove the table borders, and then add **3 pt** spacing before and after by typing **3** in the **Spacing** boxes and pressing Enter.

6 In the **Document Panel**, add your name and course information and the **Keywords job letter** Preview the document. **Save** and **Close** the document but leave Word open. Hold the file until you complete this project.

7 From your student files, open **w06I_Resume**. **Save** the document in your **All in One Chapter 6** folder as **Lastname_Firstname_6I_Resume** Add the file name to the footer.

8 **Insert** a new second row in the table. In the first cell of the new row, type **OBJECTIVE** and then press Tab. Type **To obtain an administrative position that will use my communication and computer skills.** In the same cell, add **12 pt Spacing After**.

9 Select the entire table. On the **Layout tab**, **AutoFit Contents**. Remove the table borders, and then display the **Borders and Shading** dialog box. With the table selected, create a **Custom** dotted line **4 1/2 pt** top border.

10 In the first row of the table, select both cells and then **Merge Cells**. **Center** the five lines and apply **Bold**. In the first row, select *Mia Lamanna* and change the **Font Size** to **28 pt** and add **24 pt Spacing Before**. In the e-mail address at the bottom of the first row, add **18 pt Spacing After**. In the cell to the right of *OBJECTIVE*, add **12 pt Spacing After** the paragraph displayed

11 In the first column, apply **Bold** to the four headings. In the cell to the right of *EDUCATION*, **Bold** the names of the two schools, and add **12 pt Spacing After** the two lines that begin *September*. In the cell to the right of *WORK EXPERIENCE*, bold the names of the two jobs—*Office Coordinator* and *Office Assistant*. In the same cell, below the line that begins *November 2013*, apply bullets to the four lines that comprise the job duties. Decrease the indent applied to the bulleted list. Create a similar bulleted list for the duties as an Office Assistant. Add **12 pt Spacing After** to the last line of each of the bulleted lists.

12 In the cell to the right of *AWARDS & CERTIFICATIONS*, select all three lines and create a bulleted list. Decrease the indent applied to the bulleted list. In the **Document Panel**, add your name and course information and the **Keywords HR generalist resume** and then submit your document as directed. **Save** and **Close** the document but leave Word open.

Table 1

Education	**Bachelor of Science, Business Management, Marquette University**
Work Experiencee	**Three years of experience as an office coordinator on campus**
Certifications	**MOS Certification - Word and Excel**

Return to Step 5

(Project 6I Job Letter continues on the next page)

Mastering Word | Project 6I Job Letter (continued)

13 From **Sample templates**, create a document based on the **Equity Fax** template. **Save** the document in your **All in One Chapter 6** folder as **Lastname_Firstname_6I_Fax** and then add the file name to the footer—called a *First Page Footer* in this template.

14 Type the text shown in **Table 2** for the content controls.

Table 2

To:	**James Washington, Madison Staffing Services**
Fax:	**(608) 555-0035**
Phone:	**(608) 555-0034**
Re:	**Job Announcement**
From:	**Mia Lamanna**
Pages:	**3**
Date:	**6/4/2016**
CC:	Remove this content control and row heading
Comments:	**Two pages follow including my resume and a cover letter for the Human Resources Generalist position.**

Return to Step 15

15 Locate and right-click *Mia Lamanna*; remove the content control. In the **Document Panel**, add your name and course information and the **Keywords fax cover page** As directed by your instructor, print or submit electronically the three files from this project. **Exit** Word.

End You have completed Project 6I

Content-Based Assessments

Apply 6C and 6D skills from these Objectives:

8 Create a Research Paper
9 Insert Footnotes in a Research Paper
10 Create Citations and a Bibliography in a Research Paper
11 Format a Multiple-Column Newsletter
12 Use Special Character and Paragraph Formatting
13 Create Mailing Labels Using Mail Merge

Mastering Word | Project 6J Economics

In the following Mastering Word project, you will edit and format a newsletter and a research paper for Memphis Primary Materials on the topic of environmental economics. Your completed documents will look similar to Figure 6.69.

Project Files

For Project 6J, you will need the following files:

New blank Word document
w06J_E-Waste
w06J_Addresses
w06J_June_Newsletter

You will save your documents as:

Lastname_Firstname_6J_June_Newsletter
Lastname_Firstname_6J_E-Waste
Lastname_Firstname_6J_Labels

Project Results

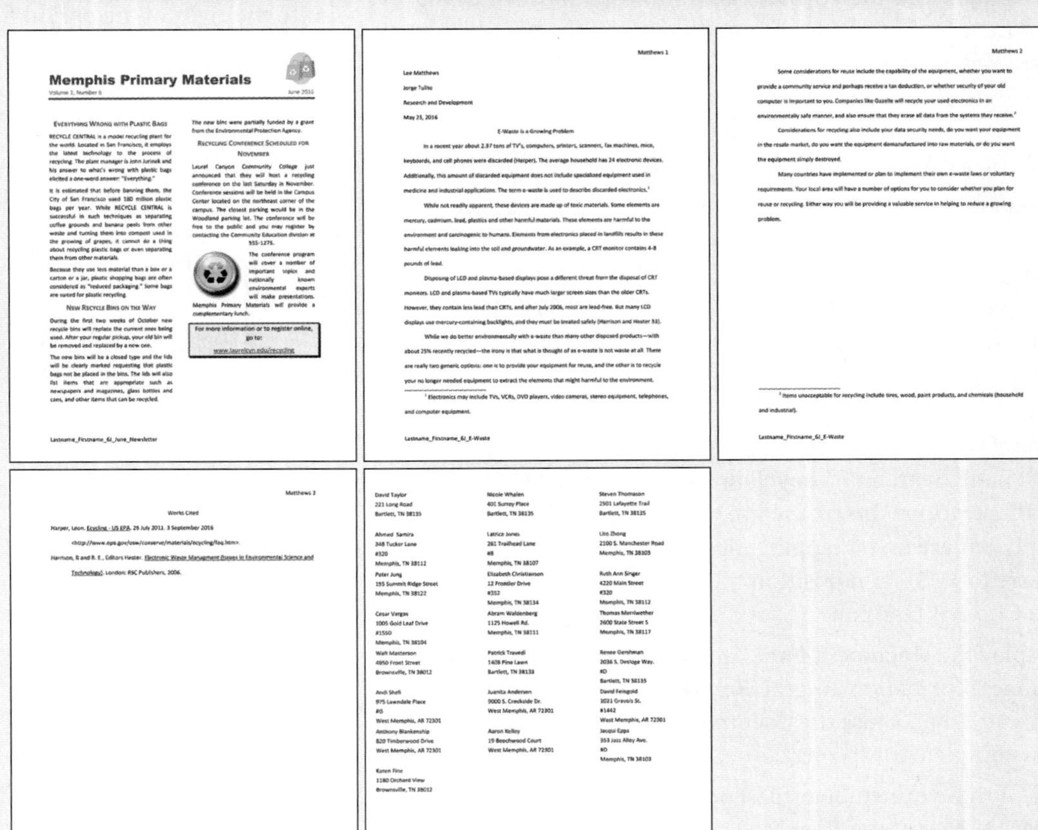

Figure 6.69

(Project 6J Economics continues on the next page)

Mastering Word | Project 6J Economics (continued)

1 **Start** Word. Open the document **w06J_June_Newsletter**, and then save the document in your **All In One Chapter 6** folder as **Lastname_Firstname_6J_June_Newsletter** Add the file name to the footer. Starting with the paragraph that begins *Everything Wrong with Plastic Bags*, select all of the text from that point to the end of the document—the document text extends to two pages. Set the **Spacing After** to **6 pt**, format the selected text as two columns, and set the alignment to **Justify**.

2 Near the bottom of the first column, click to position the insertion point to the left of *The new bins*. Insert a column break. At the top of the first column, select the paragraph *Everything Wrong with Plastic Bags*.

Display the **Font** dialog box, set the **Font Size** to **14**, apply **Bold**, set the **Font color** to **Olive Green, Accent 3, Darker 50%**, and then add the **Small caps** effect. **Center** the paragraph. Use the Format Painter to copy the formatting and then apply the same formatting to the paragraph *New Recycle Bins on the Way* located near the bottom of the first column and to *Recycling Conference Scheduled for November* in the second column.

3 At the bottom of the second column, select the last two paragraphs of text. From the **Borders and Shading** dialog box, apply a **2 1/4 pt, Shadow** border using the **Dark Blue, Text 2** color, and then on the **Shading tab**, apply a **Fill** of **Olive Green, Accent 3, Lighter 80%**. **Center** the paragraphs, and set the **Font Size** to **12**.

In the second column, click to position the insertion point at the beginning of the paragraph that begins *Laurel Canyon Community College*. Display the **Clip Art** task pane. Search for **recycling** and limit your search to **Illustrations**. **Insert** the image shown in Figure 6.69, apply **Square** text wrapping, decrease the **Height** of the image to **1.25"**, and position the image as shown. **Close** the Clip Art task pane.

Display the **Document Panel** and add your name and course information and the **Keywords June newsletter** **Save** and then **Close** the document. Hold this file until you complete this project.

4 From your student files, open the document **w06J_E-Waste**, and then save it in your **All In One Chapter 6** folder as **Lastname_Firstname_6J_E-Waste** Display the header area, type **Matthews** and then press Spacebar. In the **Header & Footer group**, add a **Plain Number** from the **Current Position** gallery. Apply **Align Text Right** formatting to the header. Move to the footer area and add the file name to the footer.

Select all of the text in the document. Change the **Line Spacing** to **2.0**, and change the **Spacing After** to **0**. Near the top of the document, **Center** the title *E-Waste is a Growing Problem*. Beginning with the text below the centered title, select the text from that point to the end of the document, and then set a **First Line Indent** at **0.5"**.

5 In the last line of the first paragraph, click to position the insertion point to the right of the period following *electronics*, and then insert the following footnote:

> **Electronics may include TVs, VCRs, DVD players, video cameras, stereo equipment, telephones, and computer equipment.**

On the next page, in the paragraph that begins *Some considerations for*, in the last line, position the insertion point to the right of the period following *receive*, and then insert the following footnote:

> **Items unacceptable for recycling include tires, wood, paint products, and chemicals (household and industrial).**

Right-click in the footnote, and then modify the style to set the **Font Size** to **11** and the format of the paragraph to include a **First line** indent and double-spacing. **Save** your document.

6 In the first paragraph, at the end of the first sentence, position the insertion point to the left of the period following *discarded*. Using **MLA** format, add the following **Web site** citation:

Author:	**Harper, Leon**
Name of Web Page	**Ecycling – US EPA**
Year:	**2011**
Month:	**July**
Day:	**26**
Year Accessed	**2016**
Month Accessed	**September**
Day Accessed	**3**
URL	**http://www.epa.gov/osw/conserve/materials/ecycling/faq.htm**

Near the bottom of **Page 1**, in the paragraph that begins *Disposing of LCD*, click to position the insertion point to the left of the period at the end of the paragraph. Add the

(Project 6J Economics continues on the next page)

Mastering Word | Project 6J Economics (continued)

following **Book** citation in **MLA** format (type the Title on one line):

Author:	**Harrison, R; Hester, R. E., Editors**
Title:	**Electronic Waste Management (Issues in Environmental Science and Technology)**
Year:	**2006**
City:	**London**
Publisher:	**RSC Publishers**

7 Select the *Harrison* citation and add the page number **33** Insert a manual page break at the end of the document. On the new **Page 3**, on the ruler, set the **First Line Indent** to **0"**. Type **Works Cited** and then press Enter.

On the **References tab**, in the **Citations & Bibliography group**, be sure *MLA* displays in the **Style** box. Insert the bibliography. Select the inserted references, set the **Line Spacing** to **2.0**, and then set **Spacing After** to **0 pt**. Center the *Works Cited* title.

Display the **Document Panel** and add your name and course information and the **Keywords e-waste** Display the **Print Preview** to check your document, make any necessary adjustments, **Save**, and then **Close** the document. Hold this file until you complete this project.

8 Display a **New** blank document. **Save** the document in your **All In One Chapter 6** folder as **Lastname_Firstname_6J_Labels** On the **Mailings tab**, start the **Step by Step Mail Merge Wizard**. In **Step 1**, select **Labels** as the document type. In **Step 2**, set **Label options** to use the **Auto default** tray (yours may vary) and **Avery US Letter 5160**. If you cannot see the gridlines, on the **Layout tab**, in the **Table group**, click **View Gridlines**. In **Step 3**, use an existing list, browse to select **w06J_Addresses**, and then click **OK**.

In **Step 4**, add an **Address block** to the labels, use the *Joshua Randall Jr.* format, and then **Match Fields** by matching *Address 2* to *Unit*. **Update all labels** and then **Preview**. Select all of the label text, and then on the **Page Layout tab**, click in the **Spacing Before** box, type **4** and press Enter. Complete the merge, and then **Close** the **Mail Merge** task pane. Delete the last two empty rows of the table, and then add the file name to the footer.

Display the **Document Panel**, and then add your name, course information, and the keywords **address labels** Click **Save**. Print or submit electronically your three files that are the results of this project. **Exit** Word.

End **You have completed Project 6J**

Unit 2 Case Project

© Jeedsn/Shutterstock

Documents Created by a Production Manager for a Comic Book Publisher; Your Own Personal Resume

In this Unit Case Project, you will create and modify Word documents that you might encounter while working as a Production Manager for a comic book publisher. You will modify a company newsletter, which includes company and industry news. Then, you will create a flyer to promote an upcoming event for aspiring comic book writers and a fax cover sheet using a template. Finally, you will complete your own personal resume. Your completed documents will look similar to the ones shown in Figure 2.1.

Project Files

For Unit 2 Case Project, you will need the following files:

- wU2_Company_Newsletter
- wU2_Workshop_Text
- Equity Fax template from Word's installed templates
- New blank Word document

You will save your files as:

- Lastname_Firstname_U2_Modified_Newsletter
- Lastname_Firstname_U2_Workshop_Flyer
- Lastname_Firstname_U2_Fax
- Lastname_Firstname_U2_Personal_Resume

Project Results

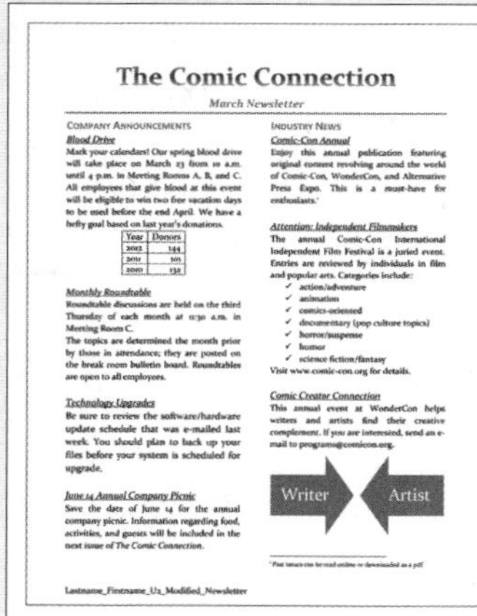

The Comic Connection

March Newsletter

COMPANY ANNOUNCEMENTS

Blood Drive

Mark your calendars! Our spring blood drive will take place on March 23 from 10 a.m. until 4 p.m. in Meeting Rooms A, B, and C. All employees that give blood at this event will be eligible to win two free vacation days to be used before the end April. We have a hefty goal based on last year's donations.

Year	Donors
2012	144
2011	101
2010	132

Monthly Roundtable

Roundtable discussions are held on the third Thursday of each month at 11:30 a.m. in Meeting Room C.

The topics are determined the month prior by those in attendance; they are posted on the break room bulletin board. Roundtables are open to all employees.

Technology Upgrades

Be sure to review the software/hardware update schedule that was e-mailed last week. You should plan to back up your files before your system is scheduled for upgrade.

June 14 Annual Company Picnic

Save the date of June 14 for the annual company picnic. Information regarding food, activities, and guests will be included in the next issue of *The Comic Connection*.

INDUSTRY NEWS

Comic-Con Annual

Enjoy this annual publication featuring original content revolving around the world of Comic-Con, WonderCon, and Alternative Press Expo. This is a must-have for enthusiasts.[1]

Attention: Independent Filmmakers

The annual Comic-Con International Independent Film Festival is a juried event. Entries are reviewed by individuals in film and popular arts. Categories include:

- ✓ action/adventure
- ✓ animation
- ✓ comics-oriented
- ✓ documentary (pop culture topics)
- ✓ horror/suspense
- ✓ humor
- ✓ science fiction/fantasy

Visit www.comic-con.org for details.

Comic Creator Connection

This annual event at WonderCon helps writers and artists find their creative complement. If you are interested, send an e-mail to programs@comicon.org.

Writer Artist

Lastname_Firstname_U2_Modified_Newsletter

Comic Books as a Career

The Comic Studio, Inc. is a presenting the *Becoming a Comic Book Writer* series on the Laurel Valley College campus. The event includes panel discussions, instructional workshops, and portfolio reviews to assist aspiring comic book writers.

The series will be presented over six weeks, on Tuesday evenings from 7 p.m. to 9 p.m. beginning on January 14. The workshops will be held in the College Conference Center and include the following topics:

- Submitting Proposals, January 14
- Developing Content, January 21
- Thinking Visually, January 28
- Writing for the Comic Reader, February 4
- Comic Book Art, February 11
- Professional Resources, February 18

Advance registration is recommended through the Student Activities office. Admission is free for students and $10 per session for the public.

For additional information or to register, visit the Student Activities office in ADM 210.

Monday-Thursday........8 a.m. to 8 p.m.
Friday........8 a.m. to 4 p.m.
Saturday........9 a.m. to 1 p.m.

Lastname_Firstname_U2_Workshop_Flyer

FAX

To: Terrell Emiko | From: Olivia Cockrell
Fax: (314) 555-2157 | Pages: 2
Phone: (314) 555-3300 | Date: 1.1.2014
Re: Audio Visual Needs

☐ Urgent ☐ For Review ☐ Please Comment ☒ Please Reply ☐ Please Recycle

Comments:

[Type comments]

Lastname_Firstname_U2_Fax

Figure 2.1

Documents Created by a Production Manager for a Comic Book Publisher; Your Own Personal Resume (continued)

1 **Start** Word and display formatting marks. Download and open the file **wU2_Company_Newsletter**. In your storage location, create a new folder named **All In One Unit 2** and then, using your own name, **Save** the document as **Lastname_Firstname_U2_Modified_Newsletter** Add the file name to the footer.

2 Change the top, bottom, left, and right margins to **1** inch. Select the entire document, and then change the **Line Spacing** to **1.15**.

3 Select the title *The Comic Connection* and the paragraph mark that follows it. Format the text using the **Gradient Fill – Blue, Accent 1** text effect.

4 Select the text beginning with *Company Announcements* and ending with the blank paragraph at the end of the document, and then change the format to two columns. Set the alignment to **Justify**.

5 Insert a **column break** before the heading *Industry News*.

6 In the blank paragraph above the heading *Monthly Roundtable*, **Insert** a **2x3** table, and then type the following text into the table:

2012	**144**
2011	**101**
2010	**132**

7 Under the heading *Attention: Independent Filmmakers*, format the seven paragraphs beginning with *action/adventure* and ending with *science fiction* as a **bulleted list** using the checkmark bullet style.

8 In the paragraph that begins *Enjoy this annual*, immediately following the period after the last sentence that ends *enthusiasts*, insert a footnote and type **Past issues can be read online or downloaded as a pdf.** Modify the font size of the **Footnote style** to **8 pt.** and apply it to your footnote.

9 **Insert** a new first row in the table. In the new row type **Year** press Tab and then type **Donors**

10 Select the three cells in the table that contain the number of donors and apply **Align Text Right** alignment.

11 Select the entire table and **AutoFit** the contents. **Center** the table within the first column of the newsletter.

12 Select the headings *Company Announcements* and *Industry News* and set **Spacing Before** to **6 pt**.

13 Add a **Box** page border to the document using the default settings.

14 Press Ctrl + End. In the blank paragraph at the end of the document, insert a **SmartArt** graphic, and then from the **Relationship** group, select the **Converging Arrows Relationship**. Type **Writer** in the left arrow and **Artist** in the right arrow. Change the height of the **SmartArt** graphic to **1.5**.

15 Display the **Document Panel**, add your name, course information and modify the **Title** to include **March 2013 Newsletter** as the Title. **Close** the Document Panel.

16 **Save** your document, examine the Print Preview, check for and make any adjustments, and then print your document or submit it electronically.

17 Create a new Word document and save it in your **All In One Unit 2** folder as **Lastname_Firstname_U2_Workshop_Flyer**

18 Type **Comic Books as a Career** and press Enter. Select the title, and then from the **Text Effects** gallery, apply the **Gradient Fill – Orange, Accent 6, Inner Shadow** effect. **Center** the title, and change the **Font Size** to **36 pt**.

19 Click in the blank line below the title. Locate and insert the file **wU2_Workshop_Text**.

20 Select the list of six workshop topics, and format the selected text as a bulleted list.

21 Position the insertion point to the left of the paragraph that begins *The series*. Search for and then insert a clip art image of your choice that relates to *comic book*. Apply **Square** text wrapping and one of the white frame picture styles to the image. Set the image height to **2.25"**.

22 Press Ctrl + End to move to the end of the document, and type **For additional information or to register, visit the Student Activities office in ADM 210.** Press Enter.

23 Set a **Left** tab stop at **1.5"** and a **Right** tab stop with a **dot leader** at **5"**. As you type the following text, be sure to press Tab to begin each line and press Tab between

(Unit 2 Case Project continues on the next page)

Documents Created by a Production Manager for a Comic Book Publisher; Your Own Personal Resume (continued)

the days and the times. Press Enter at the end of each line.

Monday-Thursday	8 a.m. to 8 p.m.
Friday	8 a.m. to 4 p.m.
Saturday	9 a.m. to 1 p.m.

24 Add the file name to the footer. As the Document Properties, add your name, your course name and section number, and the keywords **comic, workshop** **Close** the Document Panel.

25 **Save** your document, examine the Print Preview, check for and make any adjustments, and then print your document or submit it electronically. Close the document.

26 From **Sample templates**, create a document based on the **Equity Fax** template. **Save** the document in your **All In One Unit 2** folder as **Lastname_Firstname_U2_Fax** and then add the file name to the footer.

27 Type the text shown in the table below as the content controls.

To:	**Terrell Faulks**
Fax:	**(314) 555-2357**
Phone:	**(314) 555-3300**
Re:	**Audio Visual Needs**
From:	**Olivia Cockrell**
Pages:	**2**
Date:	**1/3/2014**
CC:	**Remove content control and heading**

28 Click in the box to the left of *Please Reply* and type **X**

29 Add your name, your course name and section number, and the keywords **fax, template** to the Properties area.

30 **Save** your document, examine the Print Preview, check for and make any adjustments, and then print your document or submit it electronically.

Your Personal Resume

Locate and print the information for a job for which you would like to apply, and then create your own personal resume using a table and a cover letter. Include any information that is appropriate, including your objective for a specific job, your experience, skills, education, honors or awards. Create your own letterhead and cover letter, using the skills you practiced in this Unit as your guide.

To complete the assignment, be sure to format the text appropriately, resize the table columns in the resume to best display the information, and check both documents for spelling and grammar errors. Save your resume as **Lastname_Firstname_U2_Personal_Resume** and the cover letter as **Lastname_Firstname_U2_Personal_Cover_Letter** Add the file name to the footer, and add your name, your course name and section number, and the keywords **my resume** and **cover letter** to the Properties area. Submit your files as directed.

Computer Hardware and Microsoft Excel

Chapters in Unit 3:

CHAPTER 7

Concepts: System Components, Input / Output Devices, and Storage Devices

CHAPTER 8

Applications: Excel Worksheets, Charts, Formulas, Functions, and Tables

CHAPTER 9

Applications: Excel Pie Charts, Line Charts, and What-If Analysis Tools

© beboy/Shutterstock

Job Focus: Marketing Assistant for an Entertainment Company

View Unit 3 Video to meet a Marketing Assistant for an Entertainment Company

At the end of this unit, you will have the opportunity to complete a case project that focuses on the job of a Marketing Assistant for an entertainment company. If you had a position like this, some of the things you might do are: use Microsoft Excel to plan and track budgets for events, award shows, parties, and tours; plan and budget for computer systems to support marketing events and marketing team members; and use Microsoft Excel to maintain expense records for events and talent contracts.

System Components, Input / Output Devices, and Storage Devices

OUTCOMES

At the end of this chapter you will be able to:

Recognize the components, functions, and interaction of the elements inside a computer's system unit.
Identify the input, output, and storage devices for a computer system.

OBJECTIVES

Mastering these objectives will enable you to:

Job Focus:
Marketing Assistant for an Entertainment Company

In This Chapter

As a Marketing Assistant for an entertainment company, some of your responsibilities will include coordinating events, creating media campaign packets, and tracking a project's progress and budget. Your computer will need to have wireless communication, audio and visual output, and the ability to store data on different types of storage devices. It is useful to know what your computer needs are and understand how to explain them, so that when you ask your Information Technology department for support, you can explain the problem or situation to them accurately.

In this chapter, you will study the hardware components of a computer system and explore how they operate. This information will help you understand the workings and limitations of your system, and make you more comfortable talking about technology on a professional level.

Objective 1 | Recognize the Difference Between Human and Computer Representation of Input

In your job as a Marketing Assistant for an entertainment company, the Marketing Director has e-mailed you some questions about the compatibility of your notebook computer system with the newly purchased software that tracks projects. You were a little uncertain on the terms *bit*, *byte*, *megahertz*, *gigahertz*, *RAM*, and *cache*. After reading the e-mail, you decide to investigate the relation of these terms to your system's components. Where do you start?

Computers need data to work with, and that data must be represented in a specific way for the computer's hardware to accept and use it. The normal characters or sentences you input are not actually what the computer reads. For example, when you press a key on your keyboard and the letter Z displays on your monitor, the information does not actually move through your computer as the letter Z. Instead, the letter Z is passed through your system as a unit of information called a ***bit***, which is a contraction of the term ***binary digit***. A bit is a single circuit, or path, that either contains a current or does not. To visualize a bit, the binary digits of 0 and 1 are used. The *Off* state, the mode when current is not flowing through the circuit, is represented by the digit 0. The *On* state, the mode when current is flowing through the circuit, is represented by the digit 1. A bit is the smallest piece of data a computer can process. The use of 0 and 1 help you visualize the on and off state. For the computer, however, it is the presence or absence of current flowing through the circuitry that the computer system detects (Figure 7.1).

Concept 7.01 | Representing Data as Bits and Bytes

Computers represent numbers and characters by sensing the current as it moves through a *group* of bits. When you press a key on your keyboard, an off/on pattern of current, unique to that character, passes through this bit group. The representation of this pattern, a string of 0s and 1s, is called its ***binary number representation*** (Figure 7.2).

A Bit Has Two States: Current (On represented by 1) and No Current (Off represented by 0)		
Binary Digit	0	1
Bit (circuitry)	○ no current	● current
Status	Off	On

Figure 7.1

Think of a bit as a light switch. Both a light switch and a bit have the same two states, *off* and *on*. If a computer system used one bit—one switch—to transfer data, your keyboard would be limited to two keys—one key whose value would be represented by the number 0 and no current in the circuit (off) and another key represented by the number 1 and current passing through the circuit (on). If your system had two switches, your keyboard would be limited to four keys representing the four possible states of current in the two circuits—both switches on, both switches off, the first switch on and the second switch off, or the first switch off and the second switch on. How do you determine the number of possible combinations of on/off patterns? The result of the formula 2^n, where n is the number of switches, will provide you with the number of possible combinations of circuit states for n switches. Consider that your keyboard can contain from 128 to 256 different characters, including all the letters of the alphabet in both uppercase

Common Keyboard Characters and Their Equivalent Binary Number Representation	
Keyboard Character	**Binary Number Representation**
R	01010010
S	01010011
T	01010100
L	01001100
N	01001110
E	01000101

Figure 7.2

Units of Data Transfer Rates

Unit	Abbreviation	Transfer Rate	Text Equivalent
Kilobits per second	Kbps	1 thousand bits per second	125 characters
Megabits per second	Mbps	1 million bits per second	125 pages
Gigabits per second	Gbps	1 billion bits per second	125,000 pages

Figure 7.3

and lowercase, the numbers 0 through 9, and punctuation marks. So how many switches, or bits, are needed to represent your entire keyboard? The answer is 8 because $2^8 = 256$.

A ***byte***, a group of eight bits, is used to represent one character of data, such as the letters of the alphabet (like the character Z uppercase and lowercase), the numbers 0 – 9, and the most common punctuation symbols. Because one byte represents one character on your keyboard, the byte is used as the unit to express the amount of information your computer's storage device can hold. For example, one of your typical college essays contains 250 words per page, and each word contains, on average, 5.5 characters. Therefore, one page contains approximately 1,375 characters. In other words, you will need about 1,375 bytes of storage to save one page of your essay.

Because a *bit* is one component of a *byte*, you might ask if the terms are interchangeable. The terms are used to present different types of information. Bytes express storage capacity, and bits—1s and 0s—are commonly used for measuring the data transfer rate of computer communications devices such as modems. You may have heard of terms such as ***kilobits per second (Kbps)***, ***megabits per second (Mbps)***, and ***gigabits per second (Gbps)***. These are the terms, or measurement units, that describe rapid data transfer rates. These units correspond roughly to 1 thousand, 1 million, and 1 billion bits per second. These terms refer to *bits* per second, not *bytes* per second (Figure 7.3).

Bytes commonly measure data storage. The measurements—***kilobyte (KB)*** for one thousand bytes, ***megabyte (MB)*** for one million bytes, ***gigabyte (GB)*** for one billion bytes, and ***terabyte (TB)*** for one trillion bytes—describe the amount of data a computer is managing either in RAM memory or in longer-term storage such as a hard disk, CD, DVD, or USB drive. Figure 7.4 displays these units and the approximate value of text data for each. For these units, the equivalents of a thousand, a million, and so on, are not exact; rounding numbers has become acceptable. For example, a kilobyte is actually 1,024 bytes.

This information is useful when you buy a new computer and you need to determine the size of the storage devices you need. Most hard drives on computers available for sale hold gigabytes and terabytes of data. In anticipation of continued data use and storage needs, terms already exist for representing even larger units. A ***petabyte*** is 1 quadrillion bytes, an ***exabyte*** is 1 quintillion bytes, a ***zettabyte*** is 1 sextillion bytes, and a ***yottabyte*** is 1 septillion bytes (Figure 7.5).

Current Units of Data Storage

Unit	Abbreviation	Storage Amount	Text Equivalent
Byte	B	8 bits	1 character
Kilobyte	KB	1 thousand bytes	1 page
Megabyte	MB	1 million bytes	1,000 pages
Gigabyte	GB	1 billion bytes	1,000 books
Terabyte	TB	1 trillion bytes	1 million books

Figure 7.4

Larger Units of Data Storage			
Unit	**Abbreviation**	**Storage Amount**	**Text Equivalent**
Petabyte	PB	1 quadrillion bytes	1 billion books
Exabyte	EB	1 quintillion bytes	7,500 libraries the size of the Library of Congress
Zettabyte	ZB	1 sextillion bytes	Not able to estimate
Yottabyte	YB	1 septillion bytes	Not able to estimate

Figure 7.5

Concept 7.02 | Processing Very Large and Very Small Numbers

When you need to represent and process numbers with fractional parts such as 1.25 or numbers that are extremely large such as in the billions and trillions, computers use ***floating point standard***. The term *floating point* suggests how this notation system works: There is no fixed number of digits before or after the decimal point—thus the word *float*, so the computer can work with very large and very small numbers by shifting the decimal point. Floating point standard requires special processing circuitry embedded within the CPU—the processor or microprocessor.

Concept 7.03 | Converting Characters

Most of your daily communication uses written text not numbers. So how are characters converted into bytes?

Character code is an established procedure used to create bit patterns for the letters, numbers, and symbols on your keyboard called ***characters***. Depending on your system, the conversion from your visible keyboard character to the internal bit pattern used by the computer for that character is done by one of three different character coding formats: ***ASCII***, ***EBCDIC***, or ***Unicode***.

The most widely used character code is ASCII (pronounced ASK-ee)—the ***American Standard Code for Information Interchange***. The ASCII character code is used in computers that make information available over the Internet. ASCII uses seven bits and can thus represent 128 ($2^7 = 128$) different characters. A variation of ASCII code, called ***Extended ASCII*** (see Figure 7.6), uses eight bits and allows 128 additional characters—logical symbols such as >= and the fractions 1/2 and 1/4— for a total of 256 ($2^8 = 256$). In both systems, the first 128 codes represent the same characters. Go to **www.asciitable.com** to view the complete ASCII and Extended ASCII listings. EBCDIC (pronounced EBB-see-dic)—***Extended Binary Coded Decimal Interchange Code***—is another eight-bit character code format used in IBM mainframe computers and some midrange systems.

Although ASCII and EBCDIC provide enough bits to represent all characters in the English language and some foreign language symbols, neither one has enough binary combinations for some Eastern languages and historic symbols that exceed 256 characters. A new coding system—Unicode—is becoming popular. Unicode uses 16 bits, can represent over 65,000 characters, and can symbolize the entire world's written languages. The first 128 codes in the Unicode system represent

Sample of a Section of Extended ASCII Code					
Character	**ASCII Code**	**Character**	**ASCII Code**	**Character**	**ASCII Code**
!	00100001	E	01000101	e	01100101
#	00100011	P	01010000	p	01110000
$	00100100	A	01000001	a	01100001
space	00100000	Y	01011001	y	01111001

Figure 7.6

© Emrah Turudu/iStockphoto

FIGURE 7.7 The Automated Fingerprint Identification System (AFIS) smoothes and converts fingerprints to binary code.

the same characters as the first 128 in the ASCII and Extended ASCII systems.

How is non-character input like images or biometric data like a fingerprint converted? All data, no matter what the source, is converted into patterns of binary digits (Figure 7.7). Specialized programs are usually used to convert and interpret data that is not keyboard generated.

Objective 2 | List the Elements of the System Unit

In your position of Marketing Assistant in an entertainment company, you make use of both a desktop unit at your office and a laptop computer when you are on site at a client's office or trade show. The media packets developed for media events seem to sound better on your newer laptop than when presented on your older desktop system. When you called the IT department for help with this issue, they wanted to know how many available expansion slots your desktop system unit has. They say that adding a sound board and subwoofer to your desktop unit will improve the sound. You are a little unsure about how to respond to their question. Where do you start?

© Dino Ablakovic/iStockphoto

FIGURE 7.9 This fingerprint reader is one of several devices that provide biometric authentication.

FIGURE 7.8 Every kind of computer has a system unit: all-in-one, notebook, smartphone, and desktop.

© Goldmund Lukic/iStockphoto.com

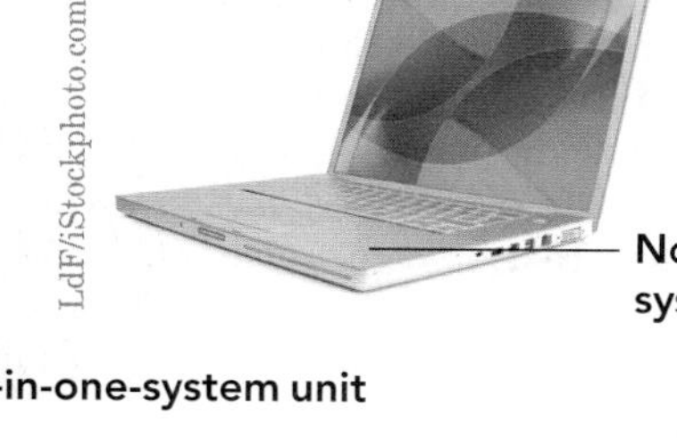

LdF/iStockphoto.com

© amriphoto/iStockphoto

© Ayaaz Rattansi/iStockphoto

The ***system unit*** is the boxlike metal or plastic case that provides a clean and cool environment for your computer's main hardware elements and a sturdy frame for mounting internal components (Figure 7.8).

The system unit case was originally a horizontal design created to lie on top of your desk. Today, non-mobile system units are housed in a ***tower case***, which has a vertical design enabling it to sit on the floor next to or under your desk. A smaller version of the tower that has less internal space for components is called a ***mini-tower case***.

In a laptop computer or a personal digital assistant (PDA), the system unit contains all the computer's components, including input components such as a keyboard and output components such as the display. If you need to ensure access, identification, and security, biometric authentication devices such as fingerprint readers, retina scanners, and face recognition systems can be embedded into your system unit (Figure 7.9).

System units also vary in their ***form factor***—a specification for how internal components such as the motherboard are mounted inside the system unit.

Concept 7.04 | Looking Inside the System Unit

If you open your system unit, regardless of the manufacturer or type of computer you own, you will see the motherboard, power supply, cooling fan, internal speakers, internal drive bays, external drive bays, and various expansion cards (see Figures 7.10 and 7.11).

The following overview of these basic components will help you identify and clarify the purpose of each:

- ***Motherboard***: This is the large circuit board located within your system unit to which all other components are connected. It contains a chip referred to as the computer's ***central processing unit*** (***CPU***)—the brain of the computer. All other components, such as disk drives, monitors, and printers, exist only to bridge the gap between you and the CPU.
- ***Power supply***: This transforms the alternating current (AC) from standard

wall outlets into the direct current (DC) needed for the computer's operation. It also steps the voltage down to the low level required by the motherboard.

- ***Cooling fan***: This keeps your system unit cool. The fan is often part of the power supply, although many systems include auxiliary fans to provide additional cooling.
- ***Internal speaker***: This is useful only for the beeps you hear when the computer starts up or encounters an error. For other sound, such as playing music or watching YouTube, your computer includes a sound card and external speakers for better quality sound.
- ***Drive bays***: These are the slots that accommodate your computer's storage devices such as the hard disk drive, CD drive, or DVD drive. Internal drive bays accommodate hard disks that are permanently contained in the system unit and have no outside access. External drive bays accommodate drives that are accessible from the outside—a necessity if you need to insert and remove a DVD from the drive.
- ***Expansion slots***: These are receptacles that accept additional circuit boards or expansion cards. ***Expansion cards***—also referred to as ***expansion boards***, ***adapter cards***, or ***adapters***—contain the circuitry for peripheral devices that are not normally included as standard equipment. Examples of expansion cards are additional memory modules, enhanced sound cards, modem cards, network interface cards (NICs), video cards, and wireless network cards (Figure 7.12).

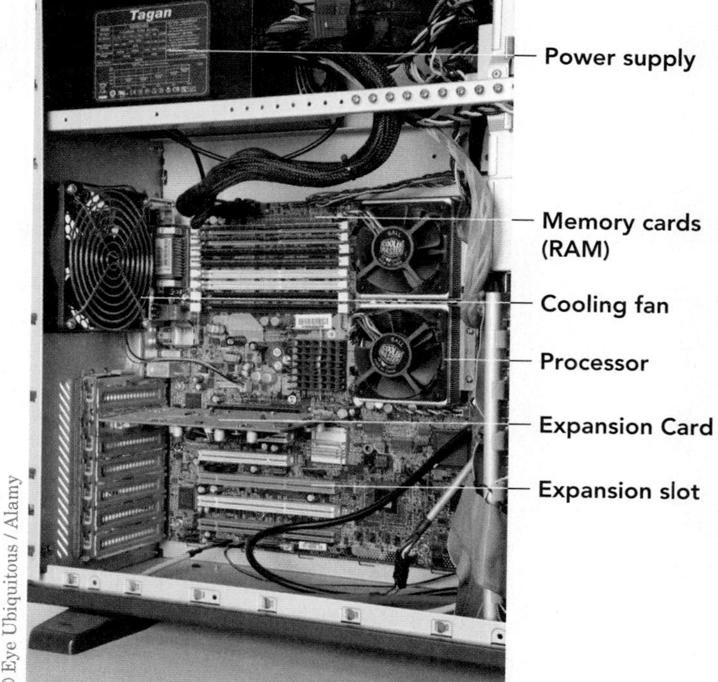

FIGURE 7.10 The Location of the Components of the System Unit in a Tower

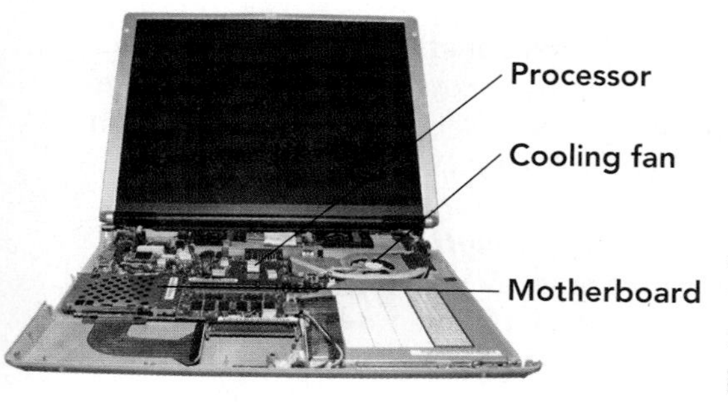

FIGURE 7.11 The Location of the Components of the System Unit in a Notebook

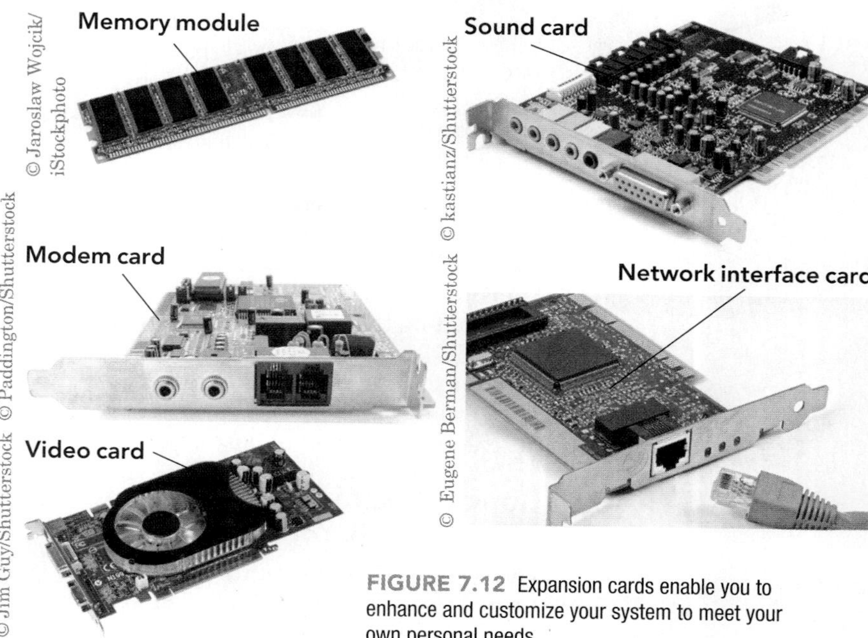

FIGURE 7.12 Expansion cards enable you to enhance and customize your system to meet your own personal needs.

Objective 3 | Identify Components of the Motherboard

In your job as a Marketing Assistant with an entertainment company, you have received an e-mail from the Marketing Director listing new software specifications for systems in the Marketing Division. You know that the components of your portable system need to meet or exceed the software specifications. Where do you start?

The motherboard within your system unit is a circuit board—a large flat piece of plastic or fiberglass that contains thousands of electrical circuits etched onto its surface. The circuits connect numerous plug-in receptacles that accommodate your computer's most important components, such as the CPU and RAM, which communicate through the centralized circuitry embedded within the motherboard. Most of the components on your motherboard are an ***integrated circuit (IC)***, also called a ***chip***. They carry an electrical current and contain millions of ***transistors***. A transistor is an electronic switch, like the light switch discussed earlier in this chapter, which controls the flow of electrical signals through a circuit. Transistors are made out of layers of special material, called a ***semiconductor***, that either conducts electrical current or blocks its passage through the circuit. Semiconductor material, like silicone, produces the off and on impulses that represent your keyboard characters within your system. To view a short video about how chips are created, go to **www97.intel.com/en/TheJourneyInside/ExploreTheCurriculum/EC_Microprocessors/MPLesson4**.

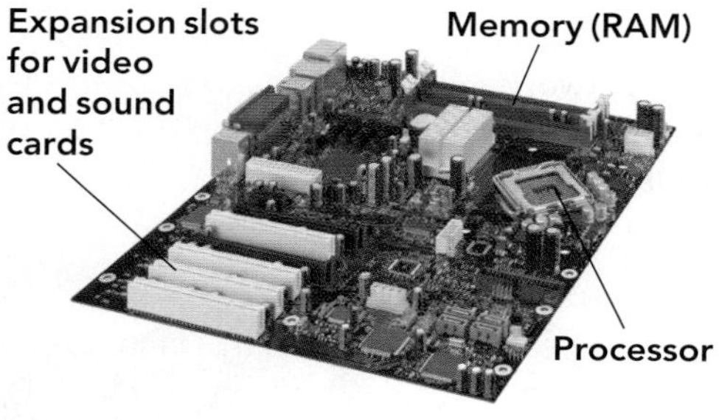

FIGURE 7.13 This typical PC motherboard shows the system unit's main components and their location on the motherboard.

What do these chips do? Examine Figure 7.13 to see some of the most important components on the motherboard: the CPU (or microprocessor), the system clock, the chipset, input/output buses, and memory.

Concept 7.05 | Examining the CPU: The Microprocessor

The central processing unit (CPU) is a ***microprocessor***—also referred to a ***processor***—that is an incredibly complex integrated circuit chip that performs many different functions depending on the instructions sent to it by the program you are running. The CPU is the most important element of a computer in terms of its overall performance. Many electronic and mechanical devices you use daily, such as smartphones, calculators, automobile engines, and industrial and medical equipment, contain ***embedded processors***. These processors are programmed to perform only the tasks intended to be done by that specific device.

Concept 7.06 | Checking Processor Slots and Sockets

The CPU is an integrated circuit of incredible complexity that plugs into a motherboard in much the same way that other integrated circuits do—through a series of pins that extend out from the bottom of the chip. However, only special slots and sockets can accommodate CPUs, because CPUs are larger and have more pins than most other chips. Additionally, CPUs generate so much heat that they could destroy themselves or other system components. The CPU is generally covered by a ***heat sink***, a heat-dissipating component that drains heat from the chip through a small auxiliary cooling fan. The latest high-end CPUs include their own built-in refrigeration systems to keep these speedy processors cool.

Concept 7.07 | Understanding the Instruction Set

Every processor performs a fixed set of operations, called instructions. One instruction might be to retrieve a character from the computer's memory and another might be to compare two numbers to see which is larger. A processor's list of instructions is called its ***instruction set***, and is unique for that processor. This is why a program that runs on a Windows-based PC may not run on an Apple Mac—the two computers have a different type of processor.

Concept 7.08 | Moving Through the Machine Cycle

Every CPU contains two subcomponents—the control unit and the arithmetic logic unit. Both components play a part in the four-step process called the ***processing cycle*** or ***machine cycle***. The ***control unit***, under the direction of an embedded program, switches from one stage to the next and performs the action of that stage. The four steps of the machine cycle are:

- ***Fetch*** retrieves the next instruction from the program stored in the computer's RAM memory located on the motherboard.
- ***Decode*** takes the fetched instruction and translates it into a form that the control unit understands.
- ***Execute*** performs the requested instruction using the ***arithmetic logic unit (ALU)*** to perform ***arithmetic operations***, which include addition, subtraction, multiplication, and division, and ***logical operations*** that involve the comparison of two or more data items. Arithmetic operations return a numeric value, whereas logical operations return a value of true or false.
- ***Store*** holds the results in an internal register—a location on the CPU—for further use by the CPU or a location in RAM.

Registers are temporary storage areas located within a microprocessor. Even though the word *store* is used when describing their function, they are not considered as part of memory and act more like a digital scratch pad. Some registers accept, hold, and transfer instructions or data, and others perform arithmetic or logical comparisons at high speed. Registers work extremely fast, in fact at the same speed as the CPU into which they are embedded.

These four steps of the machine cycle, or processing cycle, can be grouped into two phases: the ***instruction cycle*** (fetch and decode) and the ***execution cycle*** (execute and store). Today's microprocessors work so fast that they can go through this entire four-step process billions of times per second (Figure 7.14).

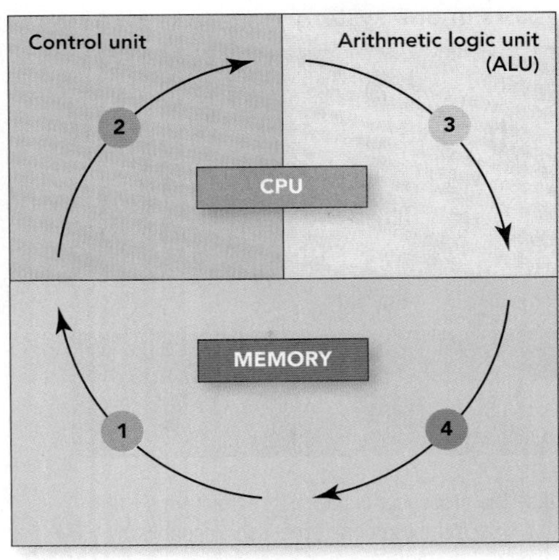

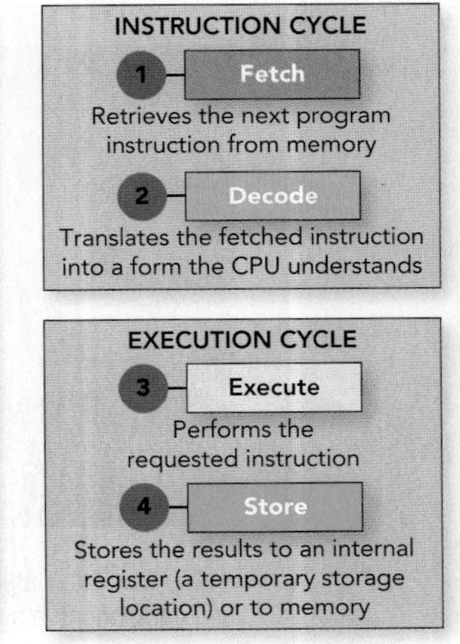

FIGURE 7.14 The four steps of the machine cycle are the same in all systems, from personal computers to mainframes. What differs is the speed at which the cycle is performed.

Concept 7.09 | Enhancing the Microprocessor's Performance

The number of transistors and the closer they are in proximity to each other within a processor have a large effect on the performance speed of that processor. Some additional features that affect the processor's performance include:

- ***Pipelining***: A technique that feeds a new instruction into the CPU at every step of the processing cycle so that four or more instructions are worked on simultaneously. Pipelining can be compared to an auto assembly line in which more than one car is being worked on at once. Before the first instruction is finished, the next one is started. Figure 7.15 visually

From either the Companion Web Site or MyITLab, watch Chapter 7 Video 1

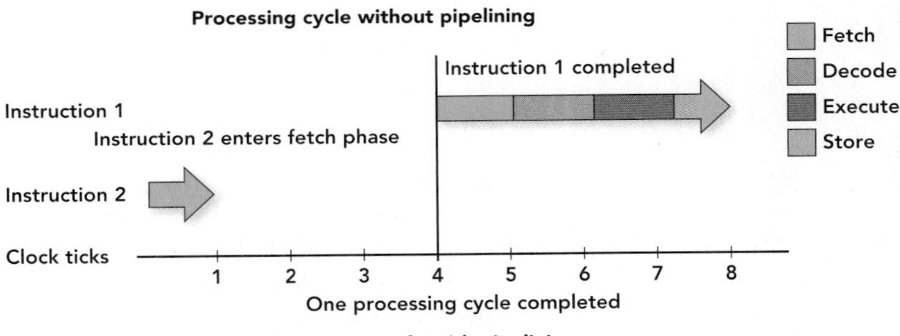

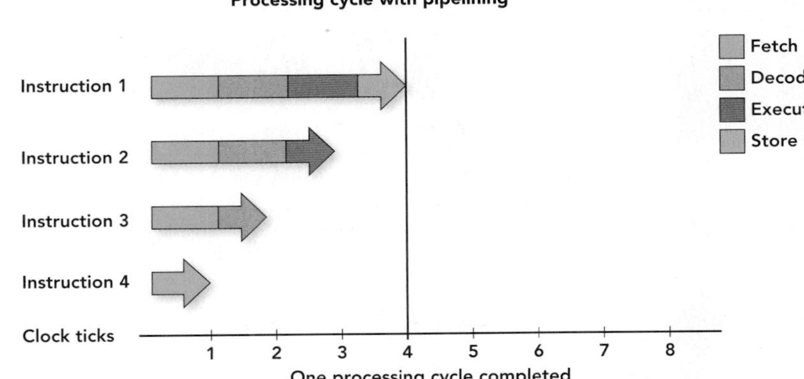

FIGURE 7.15 Without pipelining, one instruction goes through the fetch–decode–execute–store cycle before another one begins the cycle. With pipelining, when an instruction moves from one phase of the processing cycle to the next, another instruction moves into the vacated phase, greatly reducing processing time.

Two processors in one system

© cello / Alamy

FIGURE 7.16 Because the processor is the most expensive system unit component, a system with more than one processor, capable of parallel processing, is costly.

differentiates between a processing cycle *without* pipelining and *with* pipelining.

- ***Parallel processing***: A technique in which more than one processor executes two or more portions of a program at the same time. You will find parallel processing on systems that run programs that perform many computations, such as simulations or graphic processing software. These processors might be within one system, on the same motherboard, or on independent systems networked with sophisticated distributed processing software (Figure 7.16). The idea is to speed up the execution of a program by dividing the program into multiple fragments that can execute simultaneously, each on its own processor. Parallel processing should not be confused with ***multitasking***, a process by which the CPU gives you the illusion of performing instructions from multiple programs at once when in reality, the CPU is rapidly switching between the programs and instructions. Most computers that you use at home and at work have one CPU.
- ***Multi-core processors***: These systems attempt to correct the slowdown that occurs in the processing cycle when the CPU is held up by waiting for instructions and data from slower-running RAM or a hard disk. In dual-core and quad-core processors, access time is reduced and overall processing time improved because while one core is busy executing an instruction, another can handle incoming streams of data or instructions. The idea is that "two hands are better than one." AMD and Intel offer multi-core 64-bit processors. To use a dual-core or quad-core processor to full capacity, your system must use a compatible operating system and application software. Otherwise only one core will be recognized, and the processor will never work to its full potential.

Concept 7.10 | Reviewing Popular Microprocessors

The most commonly used microprocessors are those in IBM-compatible computers, also called PCs, and Macs. Most PCs are powered by chips produced by Intel and AMD. Figure 7.17 shows how popular microprocessors for PCs have improved over time.

In 2010, Intel released the Core i7 Extreme Edition microprocessor with a clock speed of 3.3GHz. Since 2003, Intel has been concentrating on producing processors that are suited for specific computing

Evolution of Intel Microprocessors

Year	Chip	Bus Width	Clock Speed	Transistors
1971	4004	4 bits	108 KHz	2,300
1993	Pentium	32 bits	Up to 66 MHz	3.1 million
2000	Pentium 4	32 bits	Up to 2 GHz	42 million
2006	Core Duo	32 bits	Up to 2 GHz	151 million
2007	Core 2 Quad	64 bits	Up to 2.4 GHz	582 million
2008	Core 2 Extreme, Quad Processor	64 bits	3.2 GHz	820 million
2010	Core i7 Extreme Edition	64 bits	3.3 GHz	732 Million

Figure 7.17

needs—such as the Centrino processor for mobile computing and the Core Extreme family of processors for multimedia and gaming. For articles, videos, forums, and charts that provide detailed information about current processors and other hardware elements, go to **www.tomshardware.com/cpu**.

Concept 7.11 | Deciphering the Chipset and the Input/Output Bus

Another key motherboard component is the ***chipset***, which is a collection of chips that work together to provide the switching circuitry needed by the microprocessor to move data throughout the computer. One of the jobs handled by the chipset is linking the microprocessor's system bus with the computer's ***input/output (I/O) bus***, which refers specifically to the electrical pathway that extends beyond your microprocessor to communicate with your input and output devices. Typically, the I/O bus contains expansion slots to accommodate plug-in expansion cards.

Modern PCs use the ***PCI (peripheral component interconnect) bus***, a slower bus that connects devices like hard drives and sound cards to the faster microprocessor system bus. Many motherboards still contain an Industry Standard Architecture (ISA) bus and have one or two ISA slots available. Most include an accelerated graphics port (AGP) designed for video and graphics display. The microprocessor is just one of several chips on your computer's motherboard. Among the others are those that provide the computer with various types of memory.

PENN STATE IS BLUE, WHITE, AND GREEN

Penn State's electricity bill totals $2 million a month and the annual total cost of energy for the university, including electricity, natural gas, coal, and heating oil, is $49 million a year.

In an effort to decrease utility costs and address environmental concerns Penn state is:

- Purchasing 20 percent of its energy needs from renewable resources
- Using solar power in its Center for Sustainability
- Initiating a natural gas combustion turbine with a heat recovery steam boiler project at the East Campus Steam Plant that will generate electricity equivalent to 5,110 homes in a year

Do you know of any actions on your campus to go green?

Concept 7.12 | Understanding Memory

Memory refers to the chips, located on your motherboard or within your CPU, that retain instructions and data to be accessed by the CPU. As you run a program, the instructions and data are loaded from a permanent storage device, such as your hard drive, into memory chips on your motherboard. From here, other components of your system access this information via the data bus. So you might ask, is information actually in a system in two places at the same time? Yes, the main reason for what appears as a double set of information is that the access time from memory on your motherboard is significantly less than the access time from your storage device, like a hard drive, and decreased access time improves overall system performance.

Concept 7.13 | Recognizing the Importance of RAM

The large, rectangular memory modules housed on your computer's motherboard contain ***random access memory (RAM)***. RAM is nonpermanent memory; its contents are erased when the computer's power is switched off either on purpose or accidentally. RAM is used to:

- Receive and hold the program instructions and data you are currently using
- Provide those instructions and data to the CPU when needed
- Hold the results of the CPU's processing until an instruction is received to transfer it to a printer or permanent storage device

RAM is referred to as *random access* because any storage location can be accessed directly without having to go from the first location to the last in sequential order. RAM organization is often compared

FIGURE 7.18 The addressing scheme used to identify RAM locations makes storage and retrieval fast and easy.

to post office boxes (Figure 7.18). Each location has a memory address that enables the location to be found and the content within to be accessed directly. Other forms of storage, such as the hard disk and CD-ROM, are also accessed directly or randomly—out of sequential order—but the term *random access* is never applied to these forms of storage.

Of the different types of RAM available, the newest and fastest PCs contain either DDR2-SDRAM (double-data-rate two synchronous dynamic RAM) or DDR3-SDRAM. RAM appears in the form of ***memory modules*** or ***memory cards***, which are small circuit boards that hold several RAM chips and lock into special slots on the motherboard. RAM modules are usually ***dual inline memory modules (DIMM)*** that have a 168-pin connector and a 64-bit data transfer rate. Their predecessor, ***single inline memory modules (SIMM)***, used a 72-pin connector and a 32-bit data transfer rate.

How much RAM does a computer need? In general, the more RAM the better. Current operating systems require a minimum of approximately 600 MB of RAM but most systems come with 2 GB and an option to have more installed.

If your RAM fills up, what happens? Your operating system will make use of ***virtual memory***, whereby the operating system looks at the contents of RAM to identify data that has not been used recently and copies this data onto a section of the hard disk that the operating system delegates for this purpose. This action frees up space in RAM so you can load a new application or add more data to a program currently in use. However, accessing data on a disk drive is much slower than using RAM, so when virtual memory kicks in, your computer may seem to slow to a crawl. To avoid using virtual memory, choose a system with at least 2 GB of RAM.

Concept 7.14 | Understanding Cache Memory

RAM is not fast enough to support the processing speeds of newer superfast microprocessors such as the Intel Core i7 Extreme Edition or the AMD Phenom X4. These microprocessors use ***cache memory*** to function at maximum speed. Cache memory is a small unit of ultrafast memory built into or near the processor that stores frequently or recently accessed program instructions and data. Cache—pronounced CASH—memory is faster than RAM, but it is also more expensive. Although the amount of cache that comes on a system is relatively small compared with RAM, cache memory greatly improves the computer system's overall performance because the CPU retrieves data more quickly from cache than from RAM.

Cache is identified by its location relative to the CPU. There can be three levels of cache in a system:

- ***Level 1 (L1) cache***: Also called ***primary cache***, this is a unit of 4 KB to 16 KB of ultrafast memory included in the microprocessor chip that runs at approximately 10 ***nanoseconds***. A nanosecond is one-billionth of a second. Primary cache is the fastest memory.
- ***Level 2 (L2) cache***: Also called ***secondary cache***, this is a unit of up to 512 KB of ultrafast memory that can be located within the microprocessor but further from the registers than Level 1 cache, or on a separate cache chip located on the motherboard very close to the microprocessor. It runs at 20 to 30 nanoseconds.
- ***Level 3 (L3) cache***: This cache is found on some systems with newer microprocessors like Intel's Xeon processor that are in some servers and workstations. It is located outside of the processor on a separate cache chip on the motherboard very close to the microprocessor.

Keeping the Level 2 and Level 3 cache as close as possible to the microprocessor improves overall system performance (Figure 7.19).

Now that you know the different levels of cache that can be embedded within your system and where they can be located, how does your computer access the information in cache? There is a sequence that the CPU (microprocessor) follows when looking for an instruction or data. If the next instruction or data to be fetched is not already in a register, the CPU—the microprocessor—attempts to locate that instruction in Level 1 cache. If it is not located in Level 1 cache, the CPU checks Level 2 cache. If the instruction is not in Level 2 cache, then it checks Level 3 cache if any

FIGURE 7.19 The close proximity of cache to the CPU is one reason why accessing information from cache is quicker than from RAM.

Level 3 cache exists on the system. If the command is not already loaded into one of the cache chips, then the CPU must make the longer and slower trip and check RAM.

Because cache is part of the microprocessor or the motherboard, it cannot be upgraded. For this reason, it is important to check the amount of the various levels of cache on a system when you buy a computer.

Concept 7.15 | Examining ROM and Other Types of Memory on the Motherboard

If everything in your RAM chips is erased when the power is turned off, how does the computer start up again? The answer is ***read-only memory (ROM)***, a type of nonvolatile memory in which essential startup instructions are prerecorded by the manufacturer of your system and not erased when the system is shut down. Here are some of the more recognized programs stored in ROM:

- ***BIOS***: The ***basic input/output system***—the first code to run when your system is powered on. BIOS checks and initializes devices such as your keyboard, display screen, and disk drives.
- ***Bootstrap Loader***: A program that locates the operating system on your hard drive and loads it into RAM.
- ***CMOS*** or ***complementary metal-oxide semiconductor***: Controls a variety of actions including starting the power-on self-test and verifying that other components of the system are functioning correctly.
- ***POST***, also called the ***power-on self-test***: A program, activated by CMOS, that checks the circuitry and RAM, marking any locations that are defective so that they are not used.

Objective 4 | Identify Connectors Located Outside the System Unit

In your job as a Marketing Assistant for an entertainment company, you observed at a recent convention that many attendees were using smartphones, notebooks, and netbooks to take notes and record segments of the presentations. They had microphones and other external devices plugged into connectors on the side or back of their portable computers. You want to be able to use some of these at the next convention you attend but do not know what devices plug into which connectors. Where do you start?

On the outside of a typical tower computer system unit, you most likely will find:

- The front panel with some buttons and some lights
- The power switch
- Connectors and ports for plugging in keyboards, mice, monitors, and speakers

Your front panel may have a ***drive activity light***, which lights up when your computer is reading from or writing to the hard disk, and the power switch, which turns your system on.

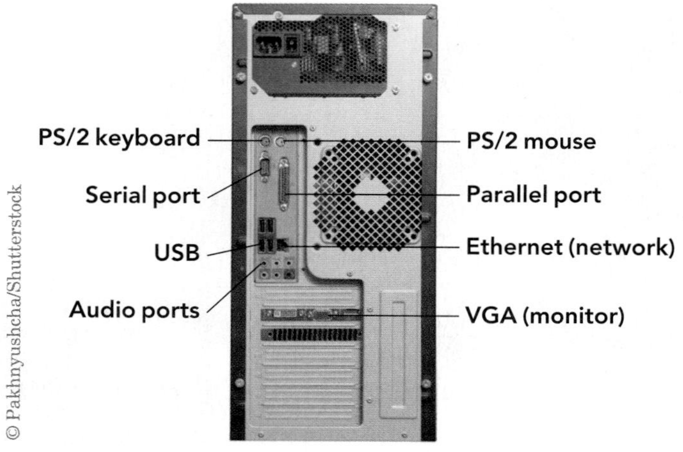

FIGURE 7.20 The connectors on the outside of a system unit enable you to connect peripherals such as a printer, keyboard, or mouse.

FIGURE 7.22 USB ports and connectors will be the standard for years to come because of their universal connectivity.

Concept 7.16 | Distinguishing Between Connectors and Ports

A ***connector*** is a physical receptacle either on the system unit or extending from an expansion card. Plugs for different devices are inserted into the connectors and are sometimes secured to the connector by ***thumbscrews***—small screws that are usually attached to the plug and secure the plug to the system unit or expansion card. Figure 7.20 summarizes the connectors you may find on your computer's case. Most of these connectors are on the back of the case, but on laptop and notebook computers (Figure 7.21), it is common to find connectors on the front or side to provide easier access.

The word *connector* and *port* are often confused. A ***port*** is the electronic pathway or interface for getting information into and out of the computer. A port almost always uses a connector, but a connector may not be a port. For example, a telephone jack is just a connector—not a port. The two words are often used interchangeably.

Concept 7.17 | Recognizing the Versatility of USB Ports

You can connect a variety of devices with ***USB (universal serial bus) ports***, including keyboards, mice, printers, and digital cameras. A single USB port can connect up to 127 different peripheral devices, eliminating the need for ports that work only with specific devices (Figure 7.22).

USB 2.0 ports, the current standard, use an external bus specification that supports data transfer rates of 480 Mbps—480 million bits per second—between the computer and its peripheral devices. A USB port does not transfer data between devices within the system. Some advantages of USB ports include ***hot swapping*** and support for ***Plug-and-Play (PnP)***. Hot swapping is the ability to connect and disconnect devices without shutting down your computer. This is convenient when you are using portable devices that you want to disconnect often, such as a digital camera. Plug-and-Play refers to a set of standards, jointly developed by Intel Corporation and Microsoft, which enable a computer to automatically detect the brand, model, and characteristics of a device when you plug it in and configure the system accordingly.

If your computer does not have enough USB ports for your devices, you can

FIGURE 7.21 The location of connectors on a notebook may vary. Many are located on the sides, and some might even be on the front.

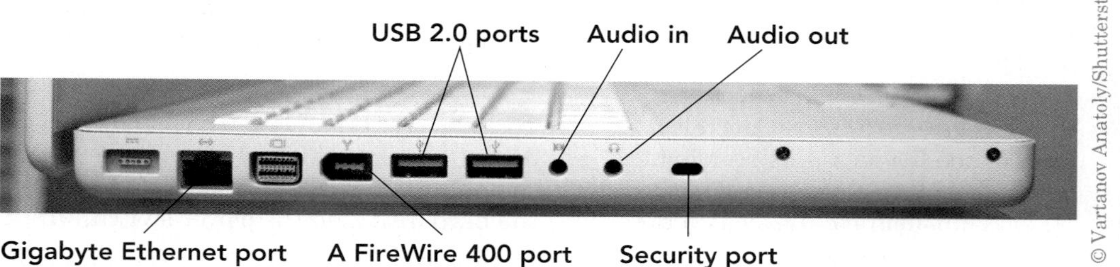

purchase a ***USB hub***—a device that plugs into an existing USB port and contains four or more additional ports (Figure 7.23).

What is next in USB development? Look for USB 3.0 standard in the near future. Known as *SuperSpeed USB*, USB 3.0 is expected to use a fiber optic link to attain a data transfer rate of 4.8 Gbps—up to 10 times faster than USB 2.0, be compatible with older versions, and continue to provide the same benefits while consuming less power.

© Tatiana Melikhova/iStockphoto

FIGURE 7.23 If your computer needs more USB ports, a USB hub can expand the number of ports.

Concept 7.18 | Using FireWire (1394 Port)

In 1995 Apple introduced ***FireWire***, an interface Apple created and standardized as the IEEE 1394 High Performance Serial Bus specification. A FireWire connector, similar to a USB connector, offers a high-speed connection for dozens of different peripheral devices (up to 63 of them) and enables hot swapping and PnP. However, it is more expensive than USB and is used only for certain high-speed peripherals such as digital video cameras and audio data that need greater throughput (data transfer capacity) than USB provides (Figure 7.24).

FireWire 400 has a data transfer rate of 400 Mbps; FireWire 800 offers 800 Mbps. The next generation, FireWire S3200, is expected to transfer data at 3.2 Gbps. Although some experts consider FireWire technologically superior to USB, the popularity and affordability of USB 2.0, coupled with the promise of the faster USB 3.0 interface in the near future, lead most to believe that the 1394 FireWire standard may fade away.

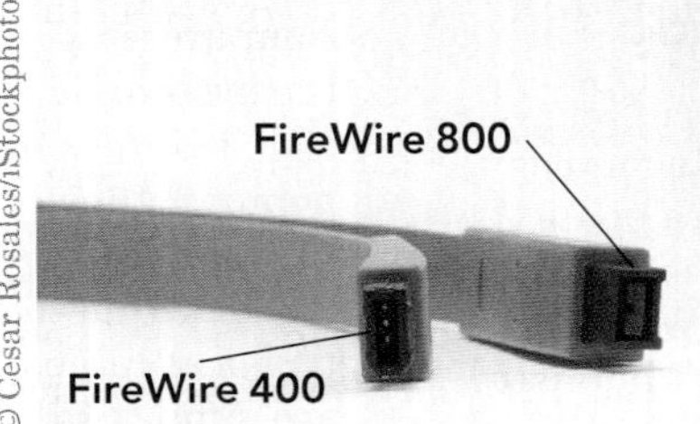

© Cesar Rosales/iStockphoto

FIGURE 7.24 FireWire cables are used with FireWire ports to transmit digital video or audio files at high rates of speed.

Concept 7.19 | Understanding Video Connectors

Most computers use a video adapter—also referred to as a video card—to generate the output that is displayed on the computer's screen or monitor. On the back of the adapter, you will find a standard ***VGA (video graphics array) connector***, a 15-pin connector that works with standard cathode ray tube (CRT) monitors. With LCD monitors, a ***DVI (digital visual interface) port*** is used. On some computers this video circuitry is built into the motherboard and is called ***onboard video*** with a connector that extends from the back of the system unit case.

Concept 7.20 | Managing Additional Ports and Connectors

You may find additional ports and connectors on the exterior of a computer's case or on one of the computer's expansion cards:

- *Telephone connector*: The typical modem interface, a telephone connector—called RJ-11—is a standard modular telephone jack that will work with an ordinary telephone cord.
- *Network connector*: Provided with networking adapters, the network connector—called an RJ-45 or Ethernet port—looks like a standard telephone jack but is bigger and capable of much faster data transfer.
- *PC card / Express Card slots*: Normally found on laptop computers, PC Cards originally known as the PCMCIA card (short for Personal Computer Memory Card International Association) or its successor the ***ExpressCard***, are credit card–sized devices that fit into a designated slot to provide expanded capabilities such as wireless communication, additional memory, multimedia, or security features.
- *Sound card connectors*: PCs equipped with sound cards—adapters that provide stereo sound and sound synthesis—as well as Macs with built-in sound, offer two or more sound connectors. These connectors, also

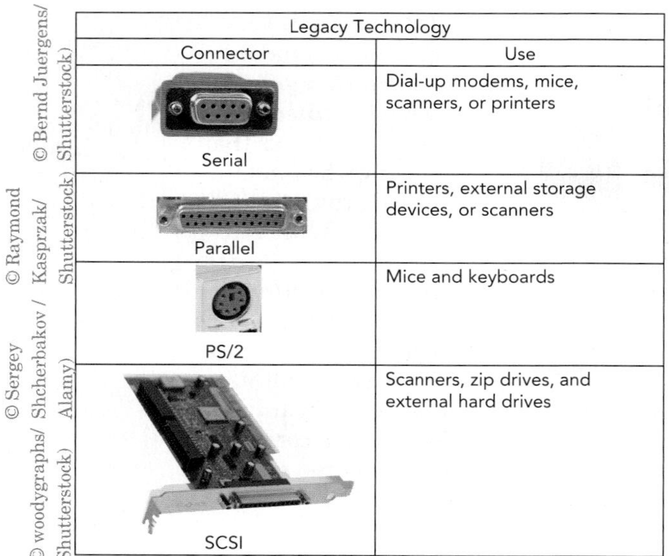

Legacy Technology	
Connector	Use
Serial	Dial-up modems, mice, scanners, or printers
Parallel	Printers, external storage devices, or scanners
PS/2	Mice and keyboards
SCSI	Scanners, zip drives, and external hard drives

(© Bernd Juergens/ Shutterstock) (© Raymond Kasprzak/ Shutterstock) (© Sergey Shcherbakov / Alamy) (© woodygraphs/ Shutterstock)

FIGURE 7.25 Legacy Technologies

called jacks, accept the same stereo miniplug used by portable CD players.

- *Game card*: Game cards provide connectors for high-speed access to the CPU and RAM for graphics-intensive interaction.
- *TV/sound capture board connectors*: If your computer is equipped with TV and video capabilities, you will see additional connectors that look like those found on a television monitor. These include a connector for a coaxial cable, which can be connected to a video camera or cable TV system.

Concept 7.21 | Reviewing Legacy Technology

Legacy technology refers to technology, devices, or applications that are being phased out in favor of more suitable replacements like USB and FireWire ports that provide greater flexibility and faster data transfer rates. Although legacy technology may still work on older systems, it may not work on newer ones. Figure 7.25 displays and explains the use of ports that are considered legacy technology.

Check Your Knowledge: From either the Companion Web Site or MyITLab, take the quiz covering Objectives 1, 2, 3, and 4

Objective 5 | Recognize Input Devices

In your job as a Marketing Assistant for an entertainment company, at a recent management meeting you noticed that a colleague was making use of several input devices on her laptop computer. You noticed she was using a wireless optical mouse and a virtual laser keyboard. Because the portability of both would enhance your presentation to clients, you want to find out more about these devices. Where do you start?

Input refers to entering data and instructions into your computer for processing. You can do this through several ***input devices***, hardware components that make it possible for you to get data and instructions into RAM, or temporary memory, where it is held while you work with it (Figure 7.26).

Concept 7.22 | Examining Keyboards

A ***keyboard*** is an input device that uses switches and circuits to translate keystrokes into a signal a computer understands. Most keyboards have the same 80 keys—the letters of the alphabet, numbers, punctuation marks, control keys, and function keys. The purpose of function keys change with the program in use. ***Enhanced keyboards*** contain additional keys, such as media control buttons that adjust speaker volume and access the optical disc drive, and Internet controls that open e-mail, a browser, or a search window with a single keystroke (Figure 7.27).

How is a keyboard connected to your computer system? Keyboards are usually connected to the computer through a cable with a connector. Laptop and notebook computers, in which the keyboard is part of the system unit, use internal connectors.

Wireless keyboards are increasingly popular; they connect to your computer through infrared (IR), radio frequency (RF), or Bluetooth connections instead of physical cables. IR and RF connections are similar to what you would find in your television remote control. Wireless keyboards are battery powered and the signals they emit are detected by either a built-in receiver or a receiver that is plugged into a USB port.

Applications can make use of special keys on your keyboard to facilitate scrolling, cursor movement, and increase your productivity. Figure 7.28 displays a list of these keys and their associated function.

Additional keys you might be familiar with and use on a regular basis include:

- ***Cursor-movement keys***, also called ***arrow keys***: A set of four keys located to the left of the number pad that move the insertion point up, down, left, or right.

© OtnaYdur/Shutterstock

© wavebreakmedia ltd/hutterstock

© carlosseller/Shutterstock

© Photosani/Shutterstock

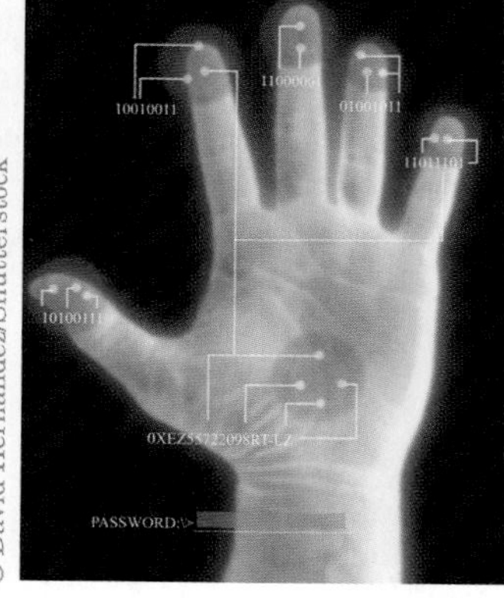

PASSWORD:\>

© David Hernandez/Shutterstock

© Evgeny Tyzhinov/Shutterstock

© Martin Kawalski/iStockphoto

© Chase Swift/iStockphoto

FIGURE 7.26 Input devices today can vary depending on the type of computing device, user preference, and application in use.

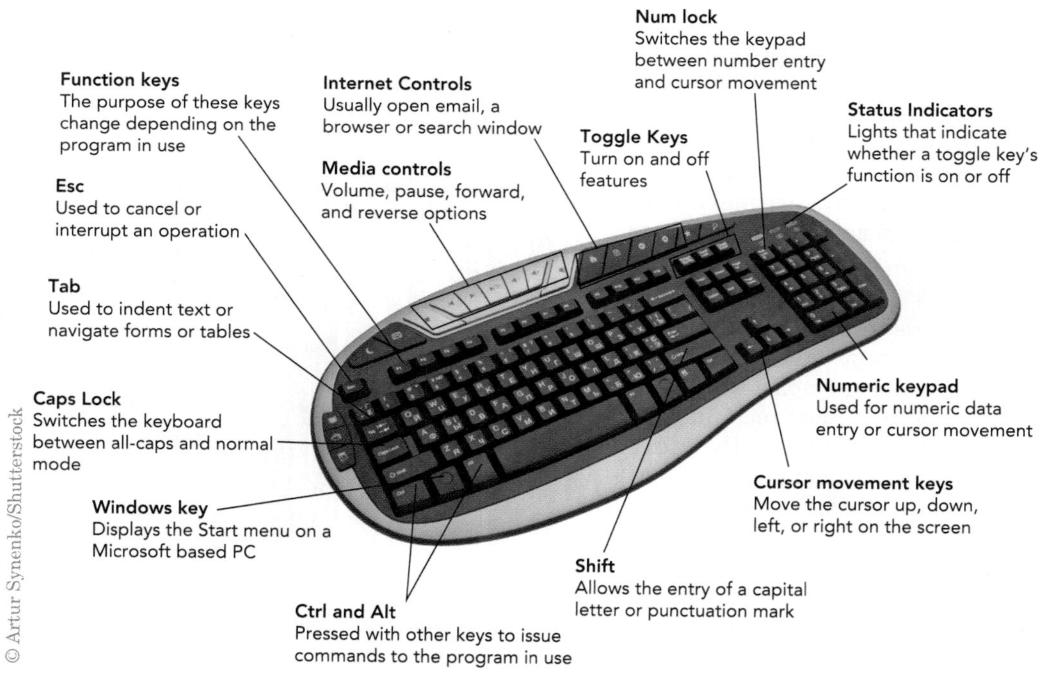

Function keys
The purpose of these keys change depending on the program in use
Internet Controls
Usually open email, a browser or search window
Num lock
Switches the keypad between number entry and cursor movement
Status Indicators
Lights that indicate whether a toggle key's function is on or off
Toggle Keys
Turn on and off features
Media controls
Volume, pause, forward, and reverse options
Esc
Used to cancel or interrupt an operation
Tab
Used to indent text or navigate forms or tables
Caps Lock
Switches the keyboard between all-caps and normal mode
Windows key
Displays the Start menu on a Microsoft based PC
Ctrl and Alt
Pressed with other keys to issue commands to the program in use
Shift
Allows the entry of a capital letter or punctuation mark
Numeric keypad
Used for numeric data entry or cursor movement
Cursor movement keys
Move the cursor up, down, left, or right on the screen

© Artur Synenko/Shutterstock

FIGURE 7.27 Most keyboards include a number pad and special keys to facilitate Internet access and control media.

Special Keys on a PC Keyboard

Key Name	Typical Function
Alt	In combination with another key, enters a command.
Caps Lock	Toggles Caps Lock mode on or off.
Ctrl	In combination with another key, enters a command.
End	Moves the insertion point to the end of the current line.
F1	Displays the Help system for the application.
Home	Moves the insertion point to the beginning of the current line.
Insert	Toggles between Insert mode and Overwrite mode if these modes are available in the program you are using.
Print Screen	Captures the image on the screen and places it in memory. Also labeled as PrtScn, Prt Scr, or PrintScrn.
Windows key	Displays the Start menu in Microsoft Windows.

Figure 7.28

- ***Toggle keys***: A key that has only two positions—on and off. The Caps Lock and Num Lock keys are toggle keys.
- ***Function keys***: A row of keys labeled F1 through F12 or F15 located above the letters and numbers on your keyboard. The action performed by each key depends on the program in use but F1, referred to as the *Help key*, is usually associated with activating the help window.
- ***Modifier keys***: Keys like Shift, Windows, Alt, and Ctrl, have no effect unless you hold them down and press another key. By keeping a modifier key pressed down and hitting another key, you modify the meaning of that key. For example, if you are using a Microsoft Office application, pressing Ctrl + S (the + notation means to hold down the Ctrl key while pressing the S key) saves an active document, and Windows + L locks the screen quickly.
- Because of their smaller size, some laptops and netbooks have more compact keyboards. All of the same functionality is provided through the use of an additional Function key labeled as *Fn* in combination with other keys. One noticeably missing element of these keyboards is a numeric keypad. Instead, the keys labeled 7, 8, 9, U, I, O, J, K, L, and M typically act as a number pad when they are struck while the Fn function key is held down (Figure 7.29).

A keyboard that displays on a touch-sensitive screen is referred to as a ***soft keyboard*** or ***on-screen keyboard***. With such keyboards, a full set of keys displays, and when you tap the key on the screen with a stylus or your finger, the outcome is the same as if you pressed a key on a traditional keyboard. The iPhone uses an onscreen keyboard and includes software that makes it appear to be an ***intelligent keyboard*** by providing such features as: suggestions for misspelled words and corrections for grammar mistakes; magnification of text being entered or modified; visual confirmation of your keystroke by

© terekhov igor/Shutterstock

FIGURE 7.29 Some notebooks and laptops use a series of adjacent keys that double as a number pad when a special function key is used.

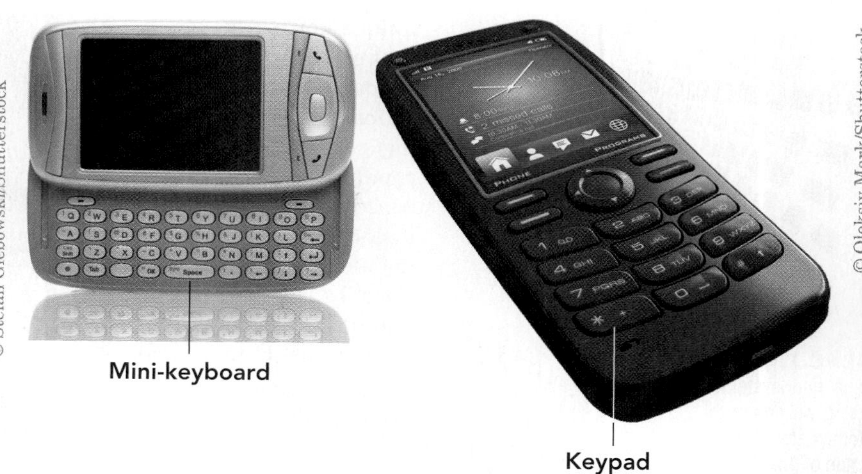

FIGURE 7.30 Mobile devices are equipped with several keyboard options.

displaying an enlarged image of the key you hit on the screen; and permitting editing features such as cut, copy, and paste with a simple touch on the screen. These features make texting and using your smartphone an easier and more intuitive experience.

A ***mini-keyboard*** is an option available on many smartphones and portable devices. This is a keyboard that has a key for each letter of the alphabet. It is usually hidden when the phone is held in a vertical position, but slides out when you reposition the phone horizontally.

A ***keypad*** is a smaller and more compact keyboard found on smartphones. On this device, each key represents multiple letters. You need to strike a key one to four times to get the desired character entered as input. Figure 7.30 illustrates the keyboard options on smartphones. With a 107 percent increase in text messaging from 2008 to 2009, and 2.5 billion text messages being sent daily in the United States alone, it is no surprise that when you choose a smartphone, the type of keyboard might be an important factor.

A ***virtual laser keyboard*** is a full-size keyboard projected on almost any surface by a device about the size of a small cellular phone and works with portable devices like PDAs and smartphones. It works by monitoring the motion of your finger movements to determine the key that you struck. You can set it to generate the clicking sound produced on a regular keyboard. Virtual laser keyboards are currently not very common; however, they are another alternative to enhance productivity when using a portable device (Figure 7.31).

FIGURE 7.31 A virtual laser keyboard projects a full-sized keyboard onto almost any surface.

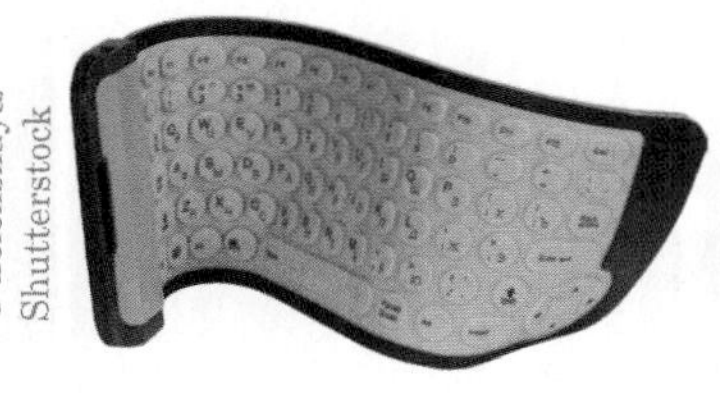

FIGURE 7.32 A flexible keyboard is perfect for travel. It is lightweight, can be equipped with 85 or 109 keys, costs around $25, and can be rolled or flexed to fit any suitcase space.

There are substitutes available if a conventional keyboard does not work for you; for example:

- A flexible keyboard has the size and layout of a standard PC keyboard but weighs only 250 grams, is foldable, and completely sealed making it perfect for use in factories, wet areas, and retail environments (Figure 7.32).
- The Ergodex DX1 is a recently developed input system that differs from your standard keyboard. It is available with 25 to 50 keys and an 11-inch × 9.3-inch pad you connect to your computer through a high-speed USB connector. Using its Manager application, you can manipulate the location of the keys to create a

FIGURE 7.33 Innovations in input systems are allowing individuals to customize the location and function of input keys.

unique key arrangement that conforms to the shape of your hand and assign an action to execute by pressing a single key. This is rapidly becoming the keyboard of choice for gamers, task-oriented professionals, and developers of applications for young children and physically impaired individuals (Figure 7.33).

- An ergonomically designed keyboard—one engineered for comfort, ease of use, and injury avoidance—can prevent repetitive strain injuries (Figure 7.34).
- Keyboards that are stylish, unobtrusive, wireless, and combine a cursor control pad with a miniature keyboard are necessary to manage a ***Media center PC***—an all-in-one entertainment device that provides easy access to photos, TV, movies, and the latest in online media—all from the comfort of your couch (Figure 7.35).

FIGURE 7.34 Ergonomic keyboards usually have a raised surface, a wrist rest, and a key display split down the middle.

FIGURE 7.35 Keyboards for PC home entertainment systems are compact and allow you to control various media components by keyboard or touchpad.

Concept 7.23 | Using Your Mouse and Other Pointing Devices

A ***pointing device*** (Figure 7.36) is an input device with which you control the movements of the ***pointer***—a symbol that shows the current location of on-the-screen activity. The most common actions performed by a pointing device include: clicking, double-clicking, selecting, and dragging. Such actions give commands

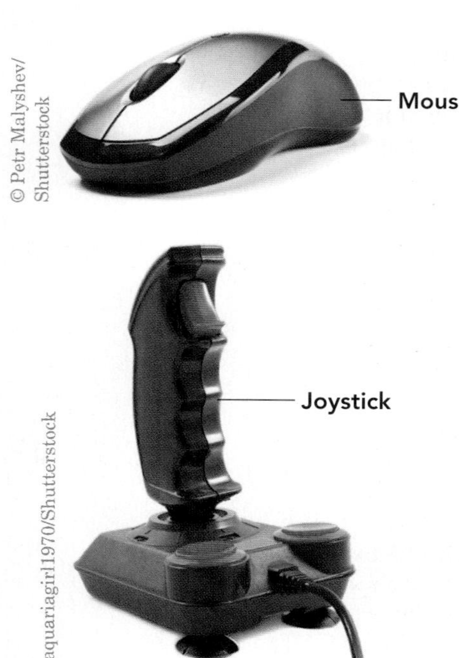

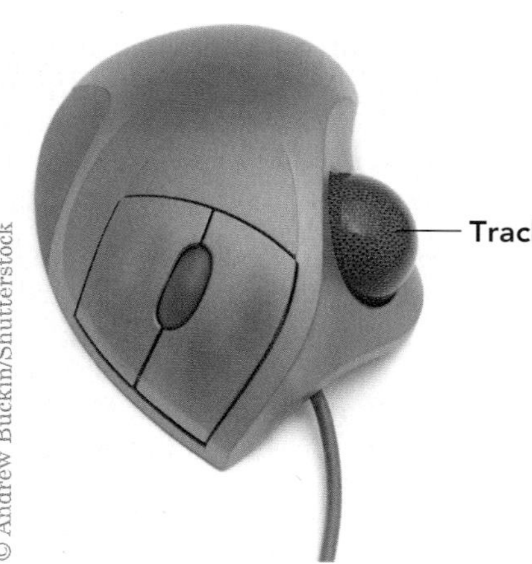

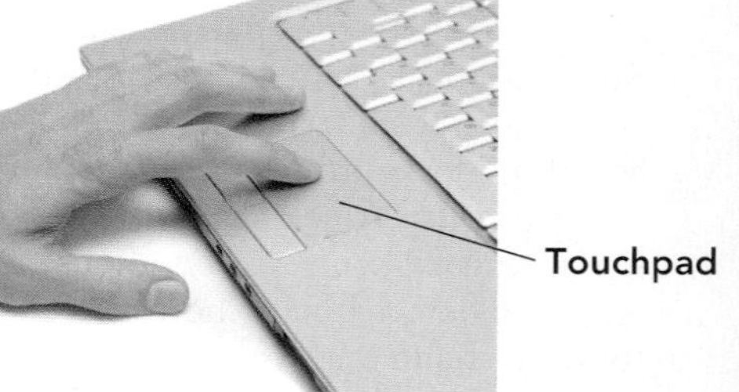

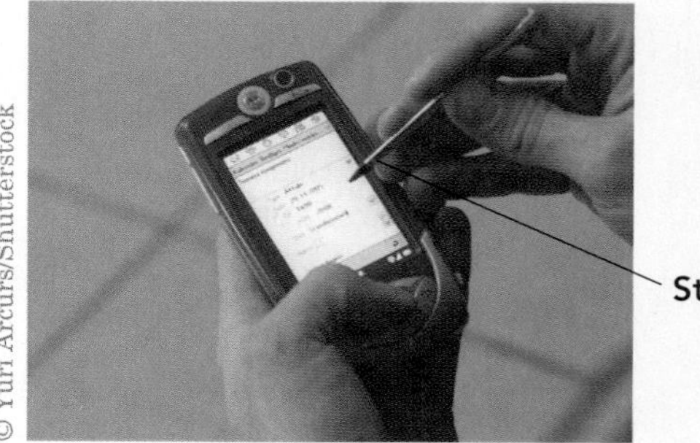

FIGURE 7.36 Pointing devices come in many shapes and styles and are located in a variety of devices.

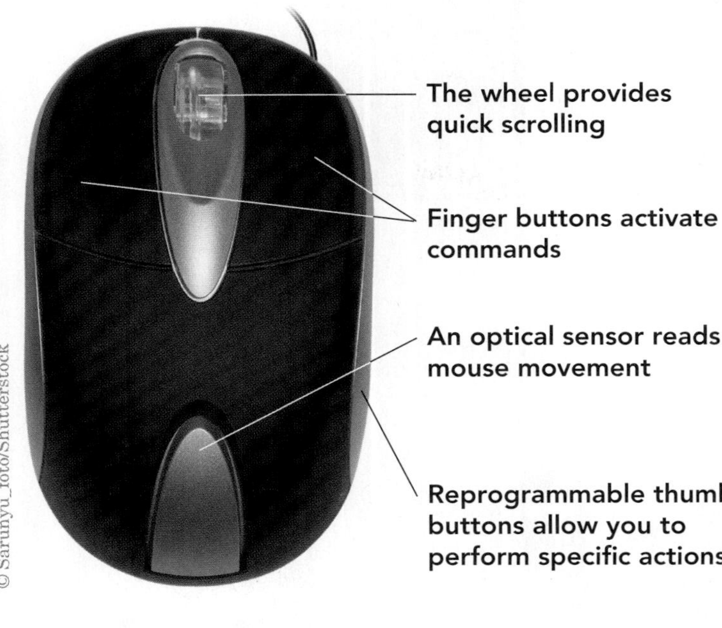
The wheel provides quick scrolling
Finger buttons activate commands
An optical sensor reads mouse movement
Reprogrammable thumb buttons allow you to perform specific actions
© Sarunyu_foto/Shutterstock

FIGURE 7.37 An optical mouse can be equipped with thumb buttons to move between Web pages, zoom in on photos, or reassign actions.

and respond to the program you are using. Pointing devices can also be used as a pencil or brush to input lines and shapes in graphic programs.

The most widely used pointing device is the ***mouse***; a palm-sized device that moves about on a clean, flat surface. The direction and speed of the mouse is mirrored by the on-screen pointer, and other actions are initiated by using buttons located on the top or on the side of the mouse.

Variations of the mouse include:

- An ***optical mouse***, which makes use of an LED (light-emitting diode) light on the underside of the mouse and a small camera that takes continuous images of the changes in the surface under the mouse as it is moved (Figure 7.37).
- Notebook users may like the ***travel mouse***, a pointing device half the size of a normal mouse, but with all the same capabilities.
- The ***wheel mouse***, developed by Microsoft, includes a rotating wheel to scroll text vertically within a document or on a Web page.
- The ***wireless mouse***, also called a ***cordless mouse***, eliminates the cord and transmits infrared or radio signals (RF) to a base station receiver on the computer. The infrared mouse requires line of sight to the receiver, whereas the RF variety uses radio waves that transmit in a wider pattern allowing the mouse to be positioned further from the system unit.
- An ***air mouse*** is a motion-sensing device that recognizes the typical forward, back, left, and right motions made by a mouse. This device does not need to rest on a surface to function. Instead, it works as it moves through the air. This allows for other directions of motion, like up and down, to be programmed to control such media elements as volume and fast forward.

Although the mouse is the most popular pointing device, there are alternatives that work well when desktop space is limited or nonexistent or for actions that are associated with gaming, ATMs, and managing handheld devices. You might be familiar with some of the following input alternatives:

- A ***trackball*** is a stationary pointing device that contains a movable ball held in a cradle. The on-screen pointer moves by rotating the ball with your fingers or palm. From one to three keys can be located in various positions to perform the equivalent of a click and right-click.
- A ***pointing stick*** is a pointing device that looks like a pencil eraser usually positioned between the G, H, and B keys on notebook computers.
- A ***touchpad***, also called a ***trackpad***, is a small, stationary, pressure-sensitive, flat surface located on a notebook. An area is set aside along the right and bottom edges of the pad to accommodate vertical or horizontal scroll operations created when you slide your finger in these reserved sections.
- A variation of the touchpad is the ***click wheel***, a pad that looks like a circle and uses a circular motion to move through song lists, movie lists, or photos. The click wheel is the method of navigation on the iPod and the iPod touch.
- A ***joystick*** is a pointing device that navigates the on-screen pointer or

© Jim West / Alamy

© Baloncici/Shutterstock

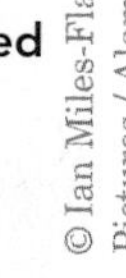
© Ian Miles-Flashpoint Pictures / Alamy

© kaczor58/Shutterstock

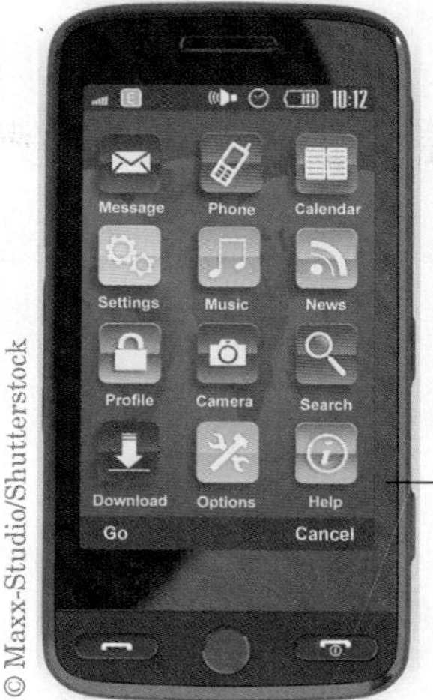

© Maxx-Studio/Shutterstock

FIGURE 7.38 Touch-screen technology is often used to display special-purpose programs. There are usually fewer choices on a screen and larger on-screen buttons to accommodate individual touch.

object through the movement of a vertical rod mounted on a base with one or two buttons. Joysticks are most often used with computer games, training simulators, or CAD (computer-aided design) systems.

- A ***stylus***, which looks like an ordinary pen except that the tip is dry and semi-blunt, is commonly used as an alternative to fingers on touch-screen devices such as smartphones and with pressure-sensitive graphics tablets used for sketching complex images in graphics applications.
- A ***touch screen*** is a display screen that is sensitive to the touch of a finger or stylus. Figure 7.38 displays several uses of touch-screen applications. Microsoft's Surface Display, the latest in touch-screen technology, enables input from multiple sources simultaneously on a high-resolution display (Figure 7.39). The prototype, designed for restaurant use, displays the menu items on the table's surface, allowing the customer to order by simply dragging choices into a center ordering ring. To see the surface in action, go to **http://cnettv.cnet.com/microsoft-unveils-touch-screen-computing/9742-1_53-27807.html** and watch the demonstration video.

FIGURE 7.39 The Surface Display, with multi-touch capability, could revolutionize input in many industries.

Concept 7.24 | Reviewing Alternative Input Devices

Although you probably use a keyboard and mouse most frequently to input data, specialized input devices are also available.

Speech recognition, also called ***voice recognition***, is the conversion of spoken words into computer text. Your spoken word, received through a microphone, is digitized and then matched against a dictionary of coded voice waves. The matches are converted into text as if your words were typed on the keyboard. This method

FAST FORWARD

The next generation of touch-screen input is being jointly developed by Carnegie Mellon University and Microsoft. Known as *Skinput*, the technology uses your body as the touch interface for computer and portable media input (Figure 7.40). Computers and computer embedded devices are becoming smaller, yet input devices like keyboards and output devices like monitors have *not* gotten smaller. Through the use of acoustic and impact-sensing software, along with a *pico projector*, a very small projection system attached to an armband, images are projected onto your skin, making your wrist and hand the equivalent of a touch screen. No electronics are attached to the skin; instead, you wear a sensing array. When you tap your body with a finger, bone densities, soft tissues, and joint proximity change, resulting in a sound pattern made by the motion. The software recognizes these different acoustic patterns and interprets them as function commands with accuracies as high as 95.5 percent. Imagine, you will be able to answer your phone by pressing a location on your own wrist, text message on a keypad displayed on your arm, and play video games with your fingers. For a demonstration, go to **www.gizmag.com/skinput-body-touch-screen-keypad/14408/** to view a video of the prototype.

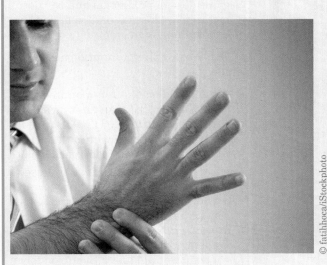

© fatihhoca/iStockphoto

FIGURE 7.40 A small pico projector will display choices on your skin. The selection you make is detected by a device that senses the sound generated by touching skin, muscle, or bone.

of input is favored by individuals for whom traditional input devices are not an option; for example, those with limited hand movement.

There are three types of voice recognition systems:

- Command systems recognize only a few hundred words and eliminate using the mouse or keyboard for repetitive commands like open file or close file.
- Discrete voice recognition systems are used for dictation but require a pause between each word. You might have used this technology in a customer-service routing system, where a voice prompts you to answer a question with a one-word reply like yes or no.
- Continuous voice recognition understands natural speech without pauses and is the most process intensive.

A speech recognition system that works with Microsoft's mainstream applications is included in the Microsoft Vista and Windows 7 operating systems. It requires no speech training and allows you to dictate documents and e-mails, use voice commands to start and switch between applications, control the operating system, fill out forms on the Web, and dictate content into compatible applications. Go to **www.youtube.com/watch?v=N3VZnyKViC4** to view a simple demonstration. The system is fairly easy to set up.

Speech recognition systems have improved over the years but are still not perfect. Some of the weaknesses and flaws include: intensive use of processing power, background noise that can introduce humming or hissing and distort words, group situations with more than one individual talking, and the inability to distinguish between homonyms.

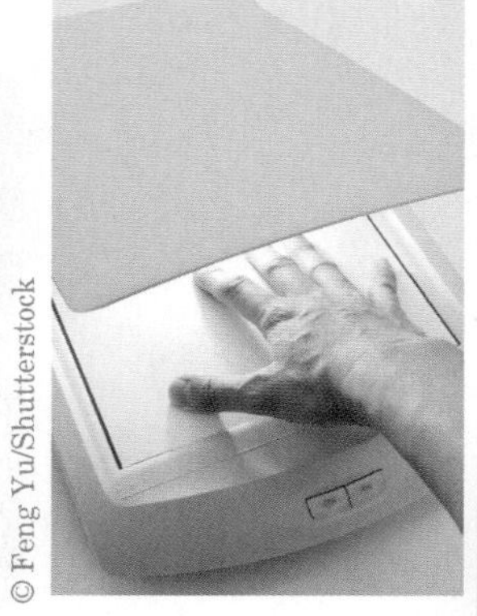
© Feng Yu/Shutterstock

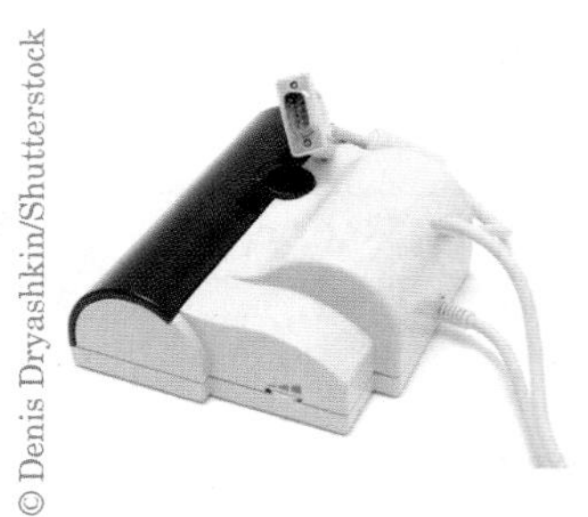
© Denis Dryashkin/Shutterstock

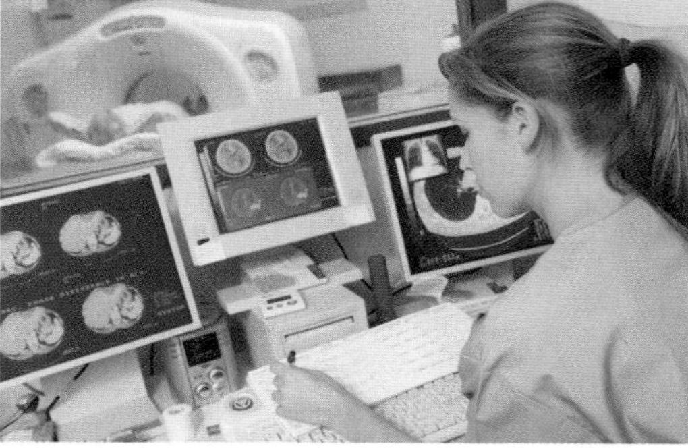
© Monkey Business Images/ Shutterstock

FIGURE 7.41 Scanners convert not only written or printed documents into digital data, but also convert other items like photos and film negatives.

A ***scanner*** is an automated form of input that copies anything you enter on a sheet of paper, including artwork, handwriting, and typed or printed text, and converts the content into a graphic image for input into a computer. The scanner does not recognize or differentiate the type of material it is scanning. Everything is converted by default into a graphic ***bitmapped image***, a representation of an image as a matrix of dots called picture elements (pixels). All images acquired by your digital camera and camcorder, scanner, and screen capture program are bitmapped images. Scanners can use ***optical character recognition (OCR)*** software to convert scanned text into a text file instead of a bitmapped image.

There are several types of scanners (Figure 7.41):

- Flatbed scanners copy items placed on a stationary glass surface. They are good for books or other bulky objects or documents that you do not want to bend.
- Sheet-fed scanners use a roller mechanism to draw in multiple sheets of paper, one sheet at a time, and are useful for high-volume scanning.
- Film scanner takes an image from a film negative or a slide, digitizes it into bitmap format, and sends it to the computer to be edited, enhanced, saved, and outputted.
- Handheld scanners are similar to sheet-fed scanners in that the item to be copied must pass through the scanner. They are small, portable, and used to copy business cards, receipts, magazine articles, small photos, or business documents.
- 3D scanners analyze real-world input by collecting information on the item being scanned, including shape, appearance, and color. A three-dimensional model of the image is generated by the scanner. This type of scanner is popular in video game design, production quality control, medicine, industrial design, and in the entertainment and movie industry.

Other examples of input devices include:

- A handheld or desktop-mounted ***bar code reader*** can scan an item's Universal Product Code (UPC). Bar codes are used to update inventory, ensure correct pricing, and track packages.
- Have you ever taken a test and used a no. 2 pencil to fill in your answers on a grid-like Scantron test form? A special scanning device called an ***optical mark reader (OMR)*** scans the marks made by your pencil and compares your answer against a Scantron form with the correct answers submitted by your instructor.
- Radio frequency identification technology uses an ***RFID reader*** to detect radio signals emitted from a tag placed on an item. The signal emitted by the tag is picked up by RFID readers mounted on a wall and does not have to be scanned by a handheld scanning device. The tags are inexpensive and can be embedded within the packaging of the product (Figure 7.42).
- Magnetic-ink character recognition employs an ***MICR reader*** to scan and

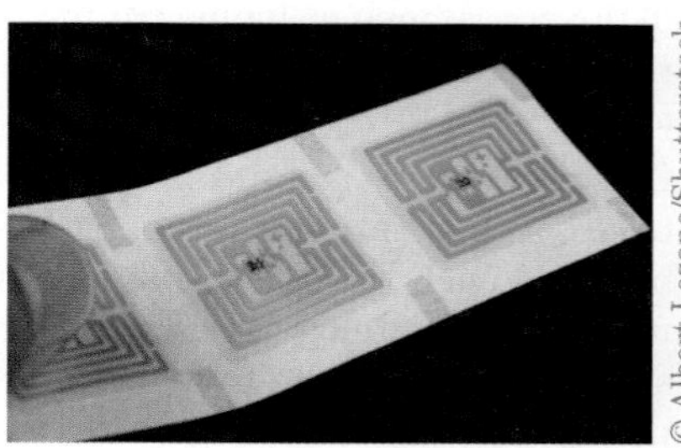
© Albert Lozano/Shutterstock

FIGURE 7.42 New RFID tags are embedded in packaging and allow merchandise to be scanned as you walk through the checkout.

input characters printed with special ink like those on the bottom of your checks and some billing statements. When the check or statement is returned to the creator, the numbers are scanned by an MICR reader and input into the company's data system. No human entry is needed and thus no human error occurs.

- A ***magnetic stripe card reader*** can detect and read information stored on magnetic strips that are usually located on the back of credit cards, gift cards, and other cards of similar use.
- A ***biometric input device*** uses physical or chemical features of an individual's body to provide a unique method of identification. The device analyzes a feature, for example, a fingerprint, retinal pattern, or voice pattern, to identify the owner as a legitimate user (Figure 7.43). Many laptops are equipped with biometric fingerprint to serve as a means of identification and authentication, and also to act as a theft deterrent.
- Devices like a ***digital camera*** and ***digital video camera*** input images and video into your system directly through a USB or FireWire port.
- A ***webcam***, an inexpensive camera attached or embedded within your computer, can be used to hold live chat sessions and make video phone calls.

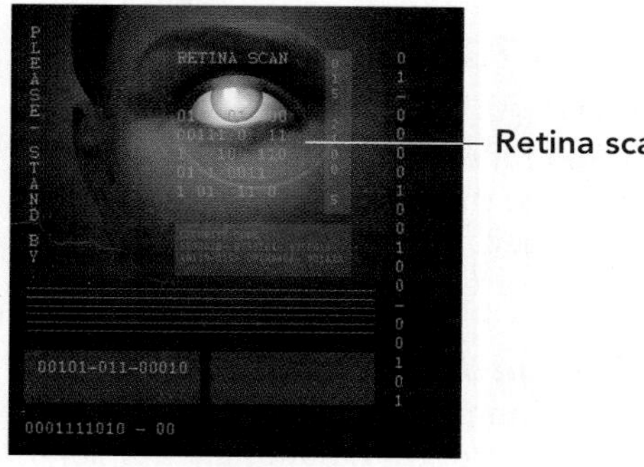
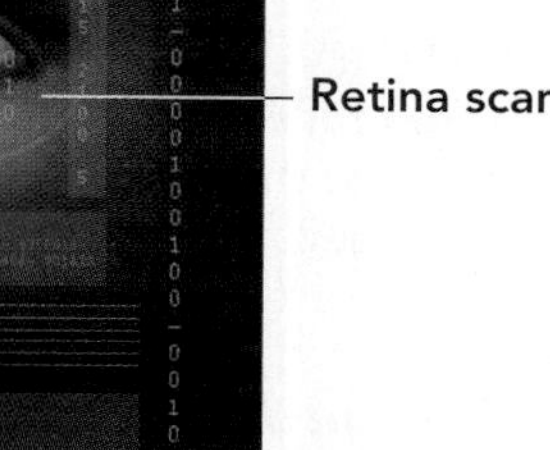

© Bruce Rolff/Shutterstock

© Daniel Halvorson/iStockphoto

FIGURE 7.43 Biometric input devices use retinal scans to match the shape and pattern of an individual's eye and fingerprint readers to detect the shape, curve, and unique pattern of lines on a finger.

Objective 6 | Describe Output Devices and How They Engage Your Senses

In your job as a Marketing Assistant for an entertainment company, you will be presenting to the regional sales staff the media packet that you developed for clients. You want several forms of output for the meeting attendees to reference. You ask your manager for some help and she suggests a large LCD monitor, projection system, and possible colored laser printouts of some of the less interactive material. Where do you start?

Output devices enable people to see, hear, and even feel the results of processing operations. The most widely used output devices are monitors and printers.

Concept 7.25 | Analyzing Monitors

Monitors are screens that display your data and processed information, which is called ***output***. The screen display, called ***soft copy***, is not a permanent record. To permanently keep the information displayed on your screen, you must save it to a storage device or print it. Printed output is often called ***hard copy***.

There are two basic types of monitors: the big cathode-ray tube (CRT) monitors that are very bulky and are usually connected to older desktop computers, and the thin, popular liquid crystal display—LCD—monitors like those that accompany newer desktops and all-in-one units. The LCD is also incorporated on notebooks, handheld computers, and smartphones (Figure 7.44).

Liquid crystal displays (LCDs), or ***flat-panel displays***, have largely replaced

FIGURE 7.44 LCD monitors are lightweight and thin, making them ideal for small portable devices.

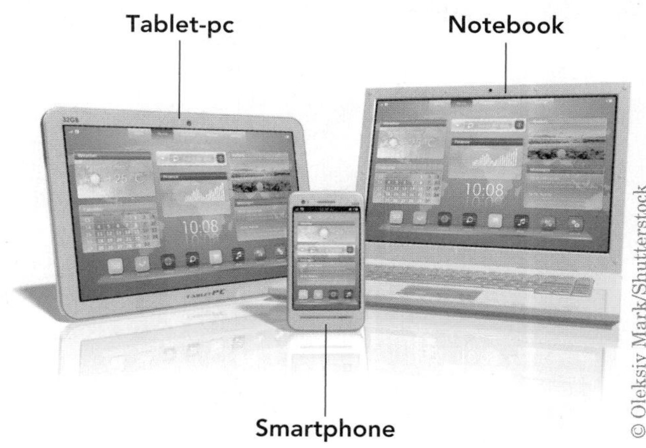

© Oleksiy Mark/Shutterstock

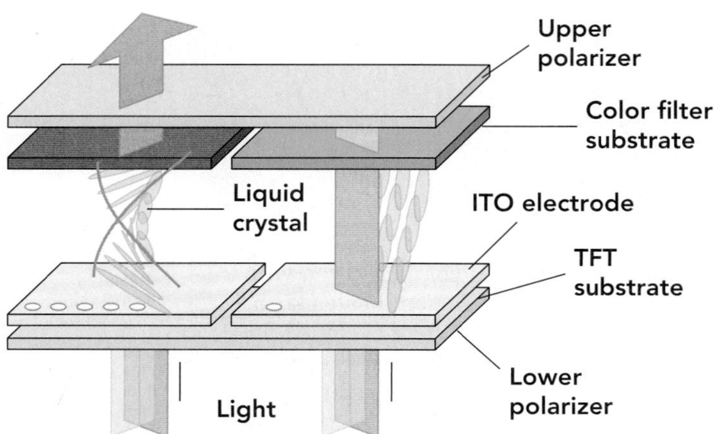

FIGURE 7.45 LCD technology allows the display to be an inch or less in thickness, making it usable in small work areas and with portable devices.

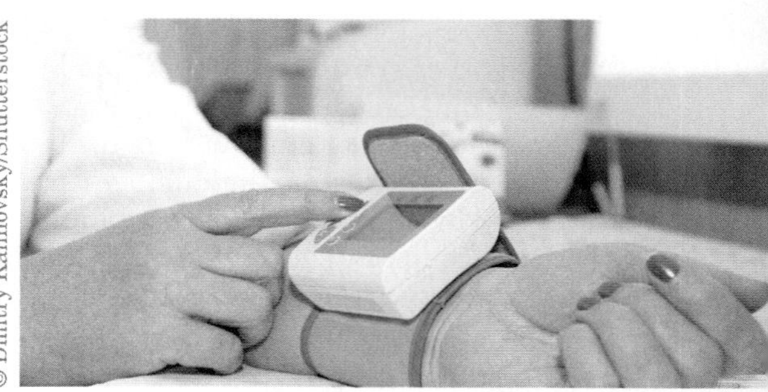

FIGURE 7.47 Paper thin OLED displays will, in the future, replace bulky displays, like the one shown, that are awkward and cumbersome.

CRT monitors. An LCD screen is a grid of *pixels*—a term shortened from the words *picture element*. A pixel is the smallest single element of a display. A florescent panel at the back of the system generates light waves to make the images and colors. These waves pass through a layer of crystal solution. The electric current moves the crystals and either blocks the light or lets it through, thus creating the images and colors viewable on the display (Figure 7.45).

You might be surprised to find that an LCD display is not your only option. ***OLED (organic light emitting diode) displays*** are becoming popular. Unlike LCDs, which require backlighting, OLED displays are emissive devices, meaning they emit light rather than modulate transmitted or reflected light. The light is produced when electric current passes through carbon-based material that is sandwiched between two conductors—an anode and cathode—that are pressed together between two plates of glass called the seal and substrate (Figure 7.46). These displays are extremely thin and lightweight, and produce outstanding color, contrast, brightness, and viewing angles. Sales for OLED displays hit 1 billion in 2009 and are predicted to exceed 6 billion by 2015.

Flexible OLED displays (FOLED) will revolutionize the advertising and motion picture industries and increase the ease and portability of output (Figure 7.47). FOLED displays can be paper-thin and appear as posters on walls. In addition, these displays can be made so small and flexible that they can be worn on your wrist and used to watch a movie or surf the Web. If you think that the possibilities for entertainment are endless, just imagine the military and security applications that will develop from this technology.

FIGURE 7.46 OLED displays consume less energy and are extremely thin.

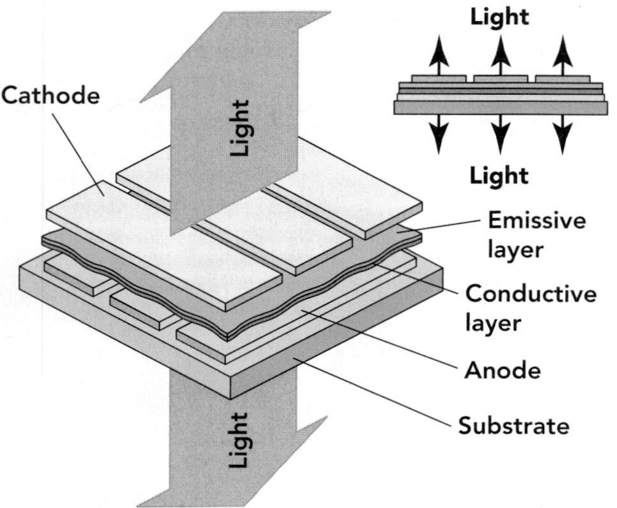

Concept 7.26 | Classifying Printers

Printers produce a permanent version, or hard copy, of the output on the computer's display screen. Some of the most popular printers are inkjet printers and laser printers.

Inkjet printers are relatively inexpensive nonimpact printers that produce excellent color output, making them popular choices for home users (Figure 7.48). They spray ionized ink from a series of

FIGURE 7.48 Inkjet printers produce high-quality color output.

© Jeff Metzger/Shutterstock

FIGURE 7.49 Black-and-white laser printers provide quick output at affordable prices.

small jets onto a sheet of paper, creating the desired character shapes.

A ***laser printer*** is a high-resolution nonimpact printer that uses an electrostatic reproductive technology similar to that used by copiers (Figure 7.49). Under the printer's computerized control, a laser beam creates electrical charges on a rotating print drum. These charges attract toner, which is transferred to the paper and fused to its surface by a heat process. Laser printers print faster than inkjets; some laser printers can produce 60 or more pages per minute. Black-and-white laser printers are increasingly affordable and generally have a lower per-page print cost than inkjet printers.

Thermal-transfer printers use a heat process to transfer an impression onto paper. There are two types of thermal printers. Thermal-wax transfer printers adhere a wax-based ink onto paper, whereas direct thermal printers burn dots onto coated paper when the paper passes over a line of heating elements. Thermal printers are popular for mobile printing, for example, generating an instant receipt for a car rental or a traffic ticket by police officer (Figure 7.50).

© IDAL/Shutterstock

FIGURE 7.50 Thermal printers are small and portable, making them useful for issuing tickets or receipts.

© Moreno Soppelsa/Shutterstock

FIGURE 7.51 Plotters are useful for printing oversized output such as maps, charts, and blueprints.

Photo printers are either inkjet or laser printers and use special inks and good-quality photo paper to produce pictures that are as good as those generated by commercial photo developers.

A ***plotter*** is a printer that produces high-quality images by physically moving ink pens over the surface of the paper. A continuous-curve plotter draws maps from stored data such as those used by cartographers and weather analysts (Figure 7.51).

Concept 7.27 | Examining Additional Output Devices

In addition to monitors and printers, several other methods of obtaining output from your computer system exist, including the following:

- Speakers: All computer systems include basic built-in speakers to transmit the

More than 700 million inkjet and laser toner cartridges are sold every year. What happens when they are empty? Although many organizations and retail stores have recycling programs, every second nearly eight used cartridges are thrown away in the United States—approximately 875 million pounds of environmental waste each year! So what can you do? Take advantage of your local recycling program. Keeping them out of the waste stream reduces toxicity levels and saves landfill space. Additionally, a half-gallon of oil is saved for every toner cartridge you recycle!

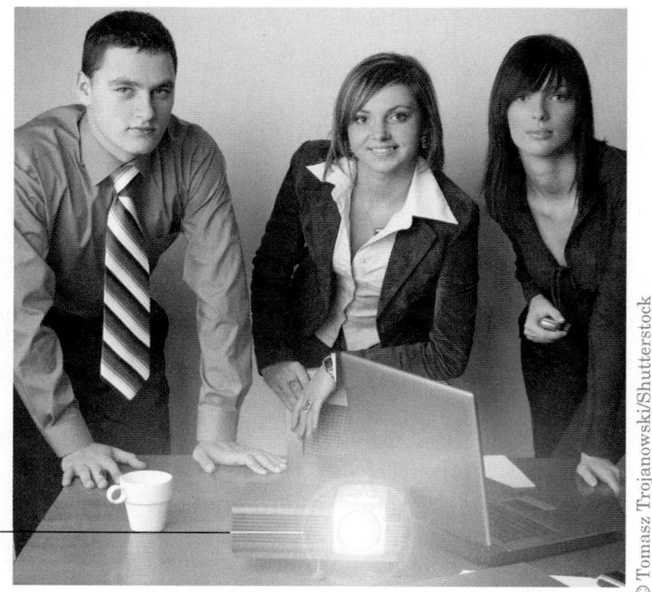
Projection Unit – A device that displays the content of the computer it is connected to.

© Tomasz Trojanowski/Shutterstock

FIGURE 7.52 Projection systems and colored handouts make lecture material and discussion more dynamic and visually stimulating.

Printer, copier, and scanner all in one unit

© ra3rn/Shutterstock

FIGURE 7.53 Multifunction devices are common in home office environments.

beeps normally made during processing. These speakers, however, are not designed for playing CDs. You will have to purchase speakers to listen to computer-generated sound such as music and synthesized speech, unless higher-end speakers were included with your system. Like microphones, speakers require a sound card to function and may include surround sound (systems set up so that they surround you with sound as in a theatre) and subwoofer (speakers that produce only low bass sounds) effects. Speaker output, like monitor output, is soft copy.

- ***Data projectors***: These projection systems display your computer's video output on a screen for an audience to view (Figure 7.52).
- ***Interactive white boards***: These are popular in educational settings. When connected to a computer and a large video display, they enable the video display to become touch sensitive allowing it to be used to control the computer. SmartBoard is a trademarked brand of a popular interactive white board.
- Computers can be equipped with a fax modem and fax software, enabling them to receive incoming faxes and transmit outgoing faxes. The incoming document displays on the screen, and can be printed or saved. To send a fax using your computer, you must save your document using a special format that is compatible with the fax program. The fax program then sends the document through the telephone system to the destination fax machine. This eliminates printing the document and using a traditional fax machine.
- ***Multifunction devices*** combine ink-jet or laser printers with a scanner, a fax machine, and a copier, enabling home office users to obtain all of these devices without spending a great deal of money (Figure 7.53).

Objective 7 | Evaluate Methods for Storing Data

In your job as Marketing Assistant for an entertainment company, the Marketing Director has asked you to attend a local trade show and record the names, phone numbers, and relative information of people you meet there. You plan to take your laptop computer, but the hard disk drive is nearly full. You will need to make space by copying data to another portable storage device. Additionally, as a precaution, you want to back up important documents to ensure that if your laptop is damaged, you have a reliable copy of your data. Where do you start?

Storage—also referred to as ***mass storage, auxiliary storage***, or ***secondary storage***—refers to the ways your computer system can keep software and data for future use. Storage relies on hardware components, called ***storage devices***, such as hard disks, flash memory, USB drives, CDs, and DVDs, on which data is held for future use (Figure 7.54). For photos and descriptions of current storage devices, go to **www.warepin.com/computer-storage-devices-4/**.

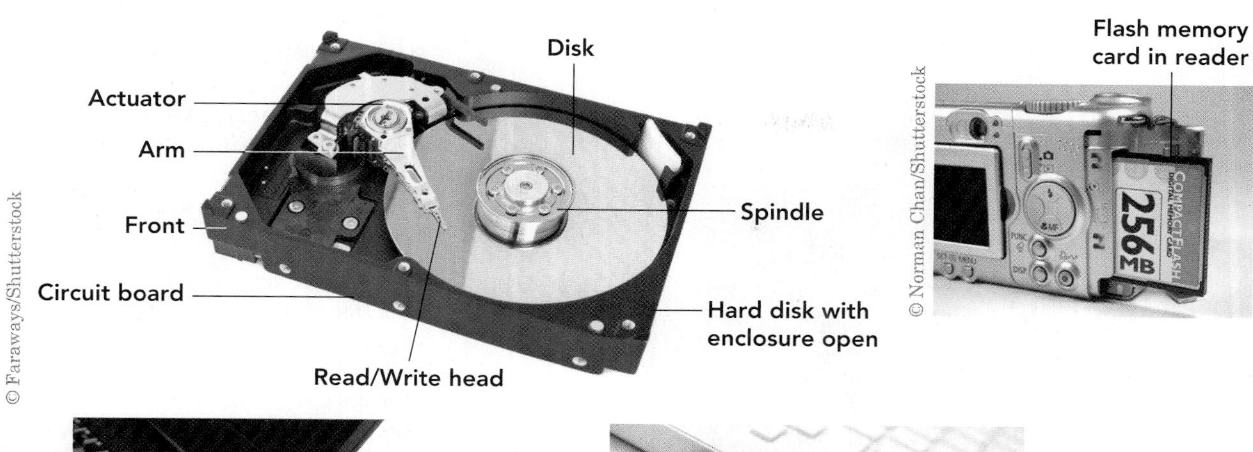

FIGURE 7.54 Many types of recording media are common on most portable and non-portable systems.

Concept 7.28 | Distinguishing Between Memory and Storage

To understand the distinction between memory and storage, think of the last time you worked at your desk. In your file drawer, you store all your personal items and papers, such as your checking account statements. The file drawer is good for long-term storage. When you decide to work on one or more of these items, you take it out of storage and put it on your desk. Computers work the same way. When you want to work with the contents of a file, the computer transfers the file from storage to a temporary workplace called RAM (random access memory).

Concept 7.29 | Understanding Hard Disk Drives

On almost all computers, the hard disk drive is by far the most important storage device. A ***hard disk drive***—or simply ***hard drive***—is a high-capacity, high-speed storage device, usually housed in the system unit, that consists of several high capacity, rapidly rotating, magnetically coated disks called ***platters*** on which your programs, data, and processed results are stored. To communicate with the CPU, hard disks require a ***hard disk controller***, which is an electronic circuit board that provides an interface between the CPU and the hard disk's electronics. The controller may be located on the computer's motherboard, on an expansion card, or within the hard disk.

The computer's hard disk, also referred to as secondary storage or ***fixed storage***, can also be categorized as both random access and magnetic storage. A ***random access storage device*** can go directly to the requested data without having to go through a sequential order. ***Magnetic storage devices*** use disks that are coated with magnetically sensitive material and use a ***read/write head*** to record information by transforming electrical impulses into a varying magnetic field. As the magnetic materials pass beneath the read/write head, this varying field forces the particles to be rearranged in a meaningful pattern of positive and negative magnetic indicators that represent the off and on bit patterns used to represent data. This operation is called *writing*. When *reading*, the read/write head senses the recorded pattern and transforms this pattern into electrical impulses that are decoded into text characters.

How does the read/write head know where to look for data in order to access it randomly? To answer this question, you need to know a little about how stored data is organized on a disk. Disks are formatted—physically laid out—in circular bands called ***tracks***. Each track is divided into pie-shaped wedges called ***sectors***. Two or more sectors combine to form a ***cluster*** (Figure 7.55).

To keep track of where specific files are located, the computer's operating

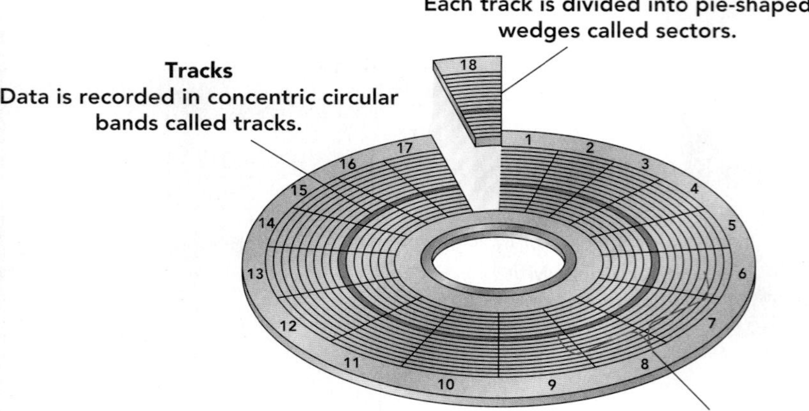
Sector
Each track is divided into pie-shaped wedges called sectors.
Tracks
Data is recorded in concentric circular bands called tracks.
Clusters
Two or more sectors form a cluster.
18
1
2
3
4
5
6
7
8
9
10
11
12
13
14
15
16
17

FIGURE 7.55 Disks are configured into tracks and sectors, similar to a street name and house number, to provide an addressing scheme that facilitates quick access to the data.

system records a table of information, like a directory, on the disk. This table contains the name of each file and the file's exact location, actually the cluster, sector, and track it is located on the disk. The current system for Windows NT, 2000, XP, Vista, and Windows 7 is known as ***NTFS (new technology file system)***. Its improved security and encryption ability provide another layer of protection for stored data.

Factors that affect a hard disk's performance include:

- Obstacles, such as a dust or smoke particle, on the disk surface that cause the read/write head to bounce on the disk surface, preventing accurate reading or writing.
- Major jolts, such as one caused by dropping or severely bumping a computer while the hard disk is running. This action could cause a head crash, the dragging of the read/write head across the hard disk surface, resulting in ***bad sectors***—areas of the disk that have become damaged and can no longer reliably hold data.
- ***Access time***, which is the amount of time it takes a device from the request for the information to the delivery of that information. Access time includes the ***seek time***, the time it takes the read/write head to locate the data before reading begins.
- ***Positioning performance***, which is the time that elapses from the initiation of drive activity until the hard disk has positioned the read/write head so that it can begin transferring data.
- ***Transfer performance,*** which is the time it takes the read/write head to transfer data from the disk to random access memory.

Besides a hard drive being used for storage in your personal computer, it can also be used on a larger scale as network attached storage (NAS) and remote storage. ***Network attached storage (NAS)*** devices are becoming more popular as the demands for data storage increase. NAS devices consist primarily of hard drives or other media used for data storage, are attached directly to a network, and are accessed by computers on the network. ***Remote storage***, sometimes referred to as an ***Internet hard drive***, is storage space on a server that is accessible from the Internet. In most cases, you subscribe to the storage service and agree to rent a block of storage space for a specific period of time. Instead of sending e-mail attachments to share with family and friends, you might simply post the files to the remote storage site and then allow them to be viewed or retrieved by others. You might save backup copies of critical files or all the data on your hard disk to your Internet hard drive.

The key advantage of this type of remote storage is the ability to access data from any location and from any device that connects with the Internet. The concerns about using remote storage center on such issues as data security, data corruption, and the possibility that the company offering the Internet storage may go out of business.

Concept 7.30 | Examining Portable Storage Options

Although hard disks are currently the main storage media on most systems, newer portable devices are important in our mobile society. ***Portable storage (removable storage)*** means that you can remove the device from one computer and insert it into another computer. A ***flash drive*** refers to a type of storage device that uses solid-state circuitry and has no moving parts (Figure 7.56). A

FIGURE 7.56 Flash drives provide a durable, lightweight alternative to hard disks.

TECHNOLOGY ON THE JOB

As a Marketing Assistant in the field of entertainment, you need both marketing skills and technology skills. Because companies are striving to understand their customers and respond to customer needs quickly, you also need Internet skills and social networking skills. Review the list of technology skills recently posted for a position of Marketing Assistant. Are you surprised at the level of technology required? Do you already possess any of these skills? Individuals in this type of position often travel, so knowledge of portable devices, backup procedures, and network attached storage (NAS) or Internet storage is critical in order to maintain communication with team members and guarantee the availability of data. Try to gain as much experience in these areas as possible.

Technology skills recently posted for a Marketing Assistant position include:

- Developing media packs and organizing conferences and trade shows.
- Serving as liaison between advertising agencies and the company, print suppliers, freelance talent, and various marketing services.
- Preparing press releases, company newsletters, and event announcements.
- Updating company headlines and news in the corporate Web site.
- Assisting in promotional strategies.

Flash drive is also known as a solid-state drive (SSD) and uses ***flash memory***, which is nonvolatile, memory that stores data electronically on a chip in sections known as *blocks*. Rather than erasing data byte by byte, flash memory uses an electrical charge to delete all of the data on the chip or just the data contained in a specific block, which is a much faster method than other types of storage use. Because of their lack of moving parts, lower power consumption, and lighter weight, flash drives are becoming an alternative to hard drives.

USB flash drives, also known as ***memory sticks, thumb drives***, or ***jump drives***, are one of the most popular portable secondary storage devices because of their small size and universal ease of use. USB flash drives work with both the PC and the Mac. No power supply or device instructions are needed; just plug it into a USB port and it is ready to read and write. USB flash drives come in different designs and novelty shapes; many include security and encryption software to help protect your data in case the drive is lost (Figure 7.57).

CD drives and ***DVD drives*** are referred to as ***optical storage devices***. Optical storage devices use tightly focused laser beams to read minute patterns of data encoded on the surface of plastic discs (Figure 7.58). The format of a CD or DVD includes microscopic indentations called ***pits*** that scatter the laser's light in certain areas. The drive's light-sensing device receives no light from these areas, so it sends a signal to the computer that corresponds to a 0 in the computer's binary numbering system. Flat reflective areas called ***lands*** bounce the light back to a light-sensing device, which sends a signal equivalent to a binary 1.

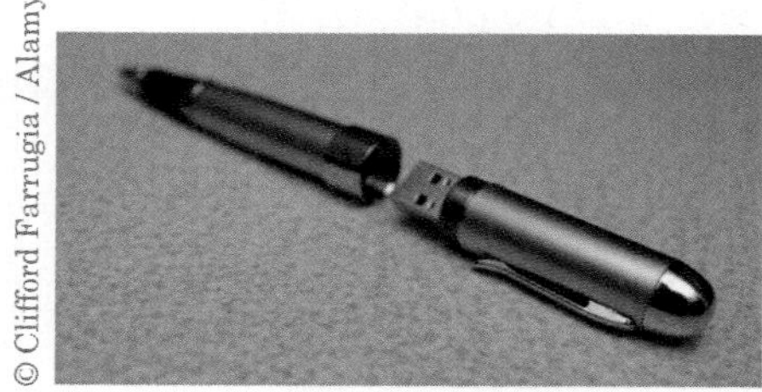

© Clifford Farrugia / Alamy

© Studio 101 / Alamy

FIGURE 7.57 The look of USB flash drives varies from the ordinary to ones disguised as key chains and pens, to still others that are caricatures of favorite TV or sport personalities.

Several types of optical read/write media and devices are available. Many PCs include a combination drive that reads and writes CDs and DVDs. For this reason, these storage devices are a popular, cost-effective alternative medium for backup and storage purposes. Looking at each a little closer should help you clarify their features. Notice that when the storage medium is optical, the correct spelling is *disc*. Magnetic storage media are spelled with a *k—disk*. Consider the following devices:

- ***CD-ROM*** (short for ***compact disc read-only memory***) is an optical storage media from which data can be read many times; it cannot be changed or erased. This type of CD can store up to 700 MB of data.
- ***DVD-ROM*** (digital video *[*or ***versatile****]* ***disc read-only memory****)* is

From either the Companion Web Site or MyITLab, watch Chapter 7 Video 2

Ethics

USB flash drives are very popular, but many experts worry that they pose a great security risk. Some companies are so concerned about corporate espionage that they disable USB ports to prevent the unauthorized copying of data. Even so, many people carry a lot of critical or personal data on their USB flash drives. What are the implications if the device is lost? Should USB drive manufacturers be required to provide a means of securing these devices or some type of registration process? With such processes in place, a lost device could be returned to the manufacturer and matched to the owner. What actions should individuals take to safeguard their data? Is hooking a USB flash drive to your backpack or keychain a very good idea? If you found a USB flash drive and did not know who it belonged to, what would you do? What should you do?

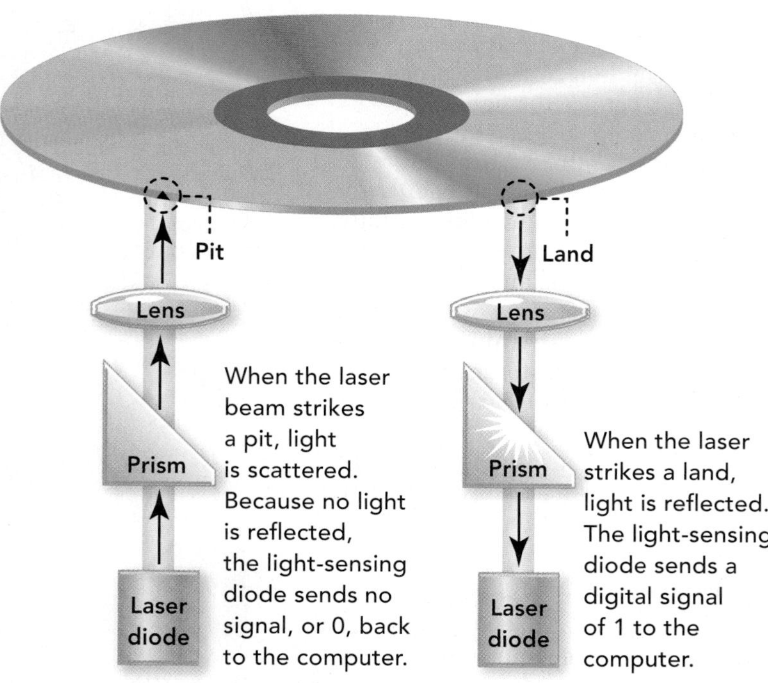
Pit
Land
Lens
Lens
Prism
Prism
Laser diode
Laser diode
When the laser beam strikes a pit, light is scattered. Because no light is reflected, the light-sensing diode sends no signal, or 0, back to the computer.
When the laser strikes a land, light is reflected. The light-sensing diode sends a digital signal of 1 to the computer.

FIGURE 7.58 In optical storage devices such as CD and DVD drives, a tightly focused laser beam reads data encoded on the disc's surface. Some optical devices write data as well as read it.

another optical storage media from which data can only be read. A double-sided, double-layer DVD-ROM can store up to 17.08 GB of data—enough for an entire digitized movie.

- ***CD-R*** (short for ***compact disc–recordable***) is an optical storage media to which you "write-once" but read many times. This means that after data has been written to the disc, you cannot erase or write over it but you can read it as many times as needed. An advantage of CD-Rs is that they are relatively inexpensive.
- ***CD-RW*** (short for ***compact disc–rewritable***), allows data that has been saved to be erased and rewritten.
- DVDs come in two standards. The first (newer) format is the DVD+ (DVD plus) standard. This standard employs two types of discs, DVD+R and the DVD+RW. ***DVD+R*** is a recordable format that enables the disc to be written to one time and read many times. The ***DVD+RW*** is a recordable format that enables the disc to be rewritten to many times.
- The second DVD format, which is older, is the DVD– (DVD dash) standard. ***DVD-R*** operates the same way as CD-R; you can write to the disc once and read from it many times. With ***DVD-RW***, you can write to, erase, and read from the disc many times.

One of the newest forms of optical storage is Blu-ray, also known as Blu-ray Disc. The name is derived from the blue-violet laser beams (blue rays) used to read and write data. The ***Blu-ray Disc (BD)*** format was developed to enable recording, rewriting, and playing back of high-definition video (HD), as well as storing large amounts of data. The format offers more than five times the storage capacity of a traditional DVD.

A ***solid-state storage device*** is another portable storage option that consists of nonvolatile memory chips, which retain the data stored in them even if the chips are disconnected from a computer or power source. The term *solid state* indicates that these devices have no moving parts; they consist only of semiconductors. Some solid-state storage devices, in addition to a flash drive, include:

- ExpressCard: A credit card–sized accessory typically used with notebook

FIGURE 7.59 ExpressCards are about the size of a credit card and fit into ExpressCard slots, which are standard in most notebooks.

© Daniel Dempster Photography / Alamy

© David Chapman / Alamy

© Hugh Threlfall / Alamy

FIGURE 7.60 Flash memory cards are thin, portable solid-state storage systems that use a flash memory reader to transfer data into your system's RAM memory.

computers (Figure 7.59), and which can function as modems, network adapters, and portable storage.

- ***Flash memory card*** (Figure 7.60): A card that uses nonvolatile flash memory chips, are wafer-thin, highly portable solid-state storage systems, and are capable of storing as much as 64 GB of data. They are used with smartphones, MP3 players, digital video cameras, and other portable digital devices. To use a flash memory card, the device must have a compatible ***flash memory reader***—a slot or compartment into which the flash memory card is inserted.
- A ***smart card***: Also known as a ***chip card*** or an ***integrated circuit card (ICC)***. This credit card–sized device combines flash memory with a tiny microprocessor, enabling the card to process as well as store information. It is viewed as a replacement for magnetic stripe cards, from which data is eventually lost (Figure 7.61).

Concept 7.31 | Anticipating Future Storage Options and Problems

In response to the explosive demand for more storage capacity, designers are creating storage media and devices that store larger amounts of data and retrieve it more quickly. Examples of these trends are:

- ***Holographic storage*** uses two laser beams to create a pattern on photosensitive media, resulting in a three-dimensional image similar to the holograms you can buy in a novelty shop. Although still under development, it is anticipated that this 3-D approach will enable much higher-density storage capacities enabling you to store 50,000 music files on an object the size of a postage stamp!
- The Eye-Fi ***wireless memory card*** is a storage device for digital photography that uses wireless circuitry to connect with your PC or send pictures directly from your digital camera to your favorite online photo site.
- ***Racetrack memory***, under development by Stuart Parkin and his colleagues at IBM's Almaden Research Center, uses the spin of electrons to store information. This allows the memory to operate at much higher speeds than today's storage media, which is a boon for transferring and retrieving data. It is anticipated that racetrack memory will consume much less power, and could enable iPods to store 500,000 songs instead of the 40,000 that the largest units can handle today.

Any secondary storage device, like a USB drive or a hard drive, will at some point get damaged or lost and be irretrievable. As a wise computer user, you must have a backup strategy in place and use it. A ***backup*** is a copy of programs, data, and information saved on one secondary storage medium that is duplicated to another. Backing up on a regular schedule could avoid the loss of critical data and information that, in a business environment, could lead to lost revenue.

Check Your Knowledge: From either the Companion Web Site or MyITLab, take the quiz covering Objectives 5, 6, and 7

From either the Companion Web Site or MyITLab, try the Chapter 7 Hardware Simulation

© nobeastsofierce/Shutterstock

FIGURE 7.61 Smart cards can be used for quick transactions, to identify the user, or to access electronically controlled doors.

Chapter Summary

System Components, Input/Output Devices, and Storage Devices

- The basic unit of information in a computer is the bit—a single circuit whose electrical state is represented by the binary digits of 0 or 1. A sequence of eight bits, called a byte, represents the basic letters, numbers, and punctuation marks of most languages. Bits are used to describe data transfer rates, whereas bytes describe storage capacity.
- The system unit contains the motherboard, memory, circuits, power supply, cooling fan(s), internal speakers, drive bays for storage devices, and expansion cards.
- The computer's motherboard contains the microprocessor, the system clock, the chipset, memory modules, and expansion slots.
- The computer's central processing unit (CPU) processes data in a four-step machine cycle using two components: the control unit and the arithmetic logic unit (ALU).
- The performance of the microprocessor is determined by the number of transistors, their proximity to each other, processing speed, the data bus width and word size, clock speed, operations performed per microprocessing cycle, the use of parallel processing, and the type of chip.
- The computer's main memory is random access memory known as RAM, and holds programs, data, and instructions currently in use for quick access by the processor.
- Level 1, Level 2, and Level 3 cache, physically positioned within or close to the CPU, operates at speeds faster than RAM and holds data accessed by the processor.
- Read-only memory (ROM) holds prerecorded start-up operating instructions.
- A variety of ports and connectors enable peripheral devices, such as USB drives, external hard drives, digital cameras, and iPods, to function effectively.
- The computer's main input devices are the keyboard and mouse.
- Monitors display data and processed information. Types of monitors include CRT, LCD, and OLED.
- Printers are output devices that produce hard copy. The most popular printers use inkjet or laser technology.
- Storage devices save programs, data, and information on storage media that retain information even when the power is switched off. Storage devices include hard disk, CDs, DVDs, and solid-state devices as USB, flash drives, ExpressCards, flash memory cards, and smart cards.

Key Terms and Concepts

Matching

Match each term in the second column with its correct definition in the first column by writing the letter of the term on the blank line in front of the correct definition.

	Definition		Term
_____	1. A unit of measurement for computer memory and disk capacity approximately equal to one million bytes.	**A**	Extended ASCII
_____	2. A unit of measurement for computer memory and disk capacity approximately equal to one billion bytes.	**B**	Gigabyte
_____	3. A character coding format that uses eight bits and can represent 256 different characters.	**C**	Hard copy
_____	4. A 16-bit character coding format that can represent over 65,000 characters.	**D**	Inkjet printer
_____	5. Fast temporary storage areas located only within a microprocessor.	**E**	Laser printer
_____	6. Nonpermanent memory, located on the motherboard, whose contents are erased when the computer's power is switched off.	**F**	Megabyte
_____	7. Memory located on the motherboard in which essential start-up instructions are prerecorded and that does not erase when the system is switched off.	**G**	Pit
_____	8. Output displayed on a monitor or played through speakers.	**H**	Plotter
_____	9. Output viewed in printed form.	**I**	Ram
_____	10. An inexpensive nonimpact printer that produces excellent color output by spraying ionized ink from a series of small jets onto a sheet of paper.	**J**	Registers
_____	11. A high-resolution nonimpact printer that uses an electrostatic reproductive technology similar to that used by copiers.	**K**	ROM
_____	12. A printer that produces high-quality output by physically moving ink pens over the surface of the paper.	**L**	Sectors
_____	13. Concentric circular bands on a hard disk or platter where data is recorded.	**M**	Soft copy
_____	14. The pie-shaped divisions of a track on a hard disk or platter.	**N**	Tracks
_____	15. An indentation on an optical disk that corresponds to the binary digit 0.	**O**	Unicode

Multiple Choice

Circle the correct answer:

1. The technique, used in CPUs built with superscalar architecture, that feeds a new instruction into the CPU at every step of the processing cycle so that four or more instructions are worked on simultaneously is:
   A. multitasking **C.** Plug-and-Play
   B. pipelining

2. The technique that uses more than one processor to run two or more portions of a program at the same time is:
   A. parallel processing **C.** Plug-and-Play
   B. hot swapping

3. The portion of a hard disk that the operating system treats like RAM when RAM is full is:
   A. cache **B.** virtual memory **C.** a cluster

4. The ability to connect and disconnect devices without shutting down your computer is referred to as:
   A. cache **C.** hot swapping
   B. virtual memory

5. The set of standards that detects the brand, model, and characteristics of a device when you plug it in and configure the system accordingly is:
   A. hot swapping **C.** Plug-and-Play
   B. multitasking

6. A pointing device that is half the size of a normal mouse, but with all the same capabilities is:
   A. a travel mouse **C.** an air mouse
   B. an optical mouse
7. An inexpensive camera attached to or embedded within your computer that can be used to hold live chat sessions and make video phone calls is a:
   A. data projector **C.** webcam
   B. digital camera
8. A solid-state portable storage device that is also referred to as a jump drive or memory stick is:
   A. a CD-RW **C.** an ExpessCard
   B. a USB flash drive
9. A 3-D approach to portable storage that will enable much higher-density storage capacities and promoted for its backup capabilities is called:
   A. holographic **C.** ExpessCard
   B. racetrack
10. A type of memory that uses the spin of electrons to store information is:
   A. ROM **C.** Level 3 cache
   B. racetrack

Teamwork

1. **Dream Machine** As a team, use the information in this chapter and a list of your computing needs and desires to identify the technical specifications and price for your dream computer. Include the name and details of the processor you select, the amount of RAM, the type and amount of cache, and the type of video and sound card you want installed. Additionally, cite the purposes for which you and your team members intend to use the system. Use an Excel spreadsheet to display each component, its technical specifications, and its associated price. Provide a total cost for the dream system. Below the technical specifications, include the list of purposes that the team proposed in ranked order from the use that most members cited to the one that was cited the least.
2. **Buy New or Upgrade?** Whether to buy a new computer or upgrade is a question that every computer owner faces at some time. As a team, locate several references on this topic. Make a list of some of the behaviors that a computer can exhibit that might indicate that the system is old or malfunctioning. In a one-page, double-spaced report, use your list of behaviors to support a decision to buy a new system or to simply upgrade a current one. Remember to cite your references.
3. **Portable Memory Choices** As a team, research portable memory devices. Include memory sticks, memory cards (used in digital cameras), and USB flash drives. As a group, list each device in a table with its current manufacturer, and compare each device's cost per megabyte and maximum storage capacity. Include a picture of each device, if possible. Come to a group consensus as to which portable device the team prefers. Present the table, your conclusion, and the reasons for your decision in a one-page, double-spaced report.

On the Web

1. **The Base of Mobility** In mobile devices, the brain or processor is one of the most important components. Use a search engine to locate information about processors for mobile devices. Locate several Web sites that either give you information about the new AMD processors or direct you to articles about this topic. In a one-page, double-spaced report, provide information about the competition in this mobile market. Who are the key players? Which devices use which processors? What are the capabilities of competing processors? Remember to cite your Web references.
2. **Apps, Apps, and More Apps?** A smartphone has the ability to input data through several types of input devices and even act as a portable storage device for your digital data. Using the Web and observing other smartphone users, create an Excel spreadsheet listing the input and storage options such phones offer. Then investigate the applications you can download to enhance your phone's ability. Add a section to the spreadsheet listing the name of these apps, their cost, and the additional input or features they enable. For example, you can download an app that allows the picture you took of a bar code to be-

come the content of a Web search. At the bottom of the spreadsheet, list models of smartphones that are capable of becoming a storage device for data on a notebook or desktop and the amount of storage space they provide. Submit the Excel spreadsheet; remember to cite your references.

3. **Talk, Talk, Talk** One of the features of Windows 7 and Microsoft Vista is the embedded speech recognition feature. Go to your favorite search engine and type in the keywords **Windows 7 Speech Recognition** and **Vista Speech Recognition** to learn about this method of entering input. Go to the Microsoft site **www.microsoft.com** and enter the same keywords in the search box there. On the basis of your research, describe the commands to set up and activate speech recognition in Windows 7. What three actions can speech recognition help users perform? What types of users will benefit from this technology? What are two suggestions for minimizing speech recognition errors? Cite your references and present your findings in a one-page, double-spaced paper.

Ethics and Social Media

1. **Do You Really Recycle?** Using the Internet and your favorite Web browser, research the recycling and disposal options available in your community to dispose of an aging computing device. Indicate the cost of recycling, if any, and whether the owner of the device, the manufacturer, or the recycling source pays the cost. Then create a brief survey that asks questions on the disposal of computing devices; include ink cartridges and cell phones. Make sure that you do not request that a name be placed on the survey, as you want honest results, and distribute it to at least 20 individuals. Present your disposal/recycle options and cumulative survey results in a PowerPoint slide show of at least 5 slides and remember to cite your references.

2. **Add Social Media Apps to Your Mobile Tool Box** On the Internet, locate at least five apps for mobile devices, for example Instagram, that facilitate social networking. In a Word processing table, state the name of the app, the mobile devices it is available on, its cost, features, and reviews. Remember to cite your references.

Sources

www.asciitable.com

http://www.intel.com/pressroom/kits/quickrefyr.htm

http://ark.intel.com/

http://www.usb.org/developers/ssusb

http://www.textmessageblog.mobi/2009/02/19/text-message-statistics-usa/

http://ergodex.com/mainpage.htm

http://www.oled-display.net/oled-display-revenues-expected-to-reach-us6-billion-in-2015/

Excel Worksheets, Charts, Formulas, Functions, and Tables

OUTCOMES

At the end of this chapter you will be able to:

OBJECTIVES

Mastering these objectives will enable you to:

PROJECT 8A
Create a sales report with an embedded column chart and sparklines.

1. Create, Save, and Navigate an Excel Workbook (p. 341)
2. Enter Data in a Worksheet (p. 344)
3. Construct and Copy Formulas and Use the SUM Function (p. 348)
4. Format Cells with Merge & Center and Cell Styles (p. 351)
5. Chart Data to Create a Column Chart and Insert Sparklines (p. 353)
6. Print, Display Formulas, and Close Excel (p. 357)

PROJECT 8B
Calculate the value of an inventory.

7. Check Spelling in a Worksheet (p. 362)
8. Enter Data by Range (p. 364)
9. Construct Formulas for Mathematical Operations (p. 365)
10. Edit Values in a Worksheet (p. 368)
11. Format a Worksheet (p. 370)

PROJECT 8C
Analyze inventory by applying statistical and logical calculations to data and by sorting and filtering data.

12. Use the SUM, AVERAGE, MEDIAN, MIN, and MAX Functions (p. 375)
13. Move Data, Resolve Error Messages, and Rotate Text (p. 378)
14. Use COUNTIF and IF Functions and Apply Conditional Formatting (p. 380)
15. Use Date & Time Functions and Freeze Panes (p. 384)
16. Create, Sort, and Filter an Excel Table (p. 386)
17. Format and Print a Large Worksheet (p. 388)

PROJECT 8D
Summarize the data on multiple worksheets.

18. Navigate a Workbook and Rename Worksheets (p. 392)
19. Enter Dates, Clear Contents, and Clear Formats (p. 393)
20. Copy and Paste by Using the Paste Options Gallery (p. 396)
21. Edit and Format Multiple Worksheets at the Same Time (p. 397)
22. Create a Summary Sheet with Column Sparklines (p. 401)
23. Format and Print Multiple Worksheets in a Workbook (p. 403)

© Jason Stitt/Shutterstock

© Paul Hakimata Photography/Shutterstock

Job Focus: Manager of a cell phone store and Owner of a specialty food store

In This Chapter

In this chapter, you will learn how the manager of a cell phone store and the owner of a retail and Internet specialty food store use Excel.

At the end of this Unit, following Chapter 9, you will have an opportunity to complete a case project that focuses on the career of a Marketing Assistant for an entertainment company.

Project 8A Sales Report with Embedded Column Chart and Sparklines

Project Activities

In Activities 8.01 through 8.16, you will create an Excel worksheet for Roslyn Thomas, the President of Texas Spectrum Wireless. The worksheet displays the first quarter sales of wireless accessories for the current year, and includes a chart to visually represent the data. Your completed worksheet will look similar to Figure 8.1.

Project Files

For Project 8A, you will need the following file:

New blank Excel workbook

You will save your workbook as:

Lastname_Firstname_8A_Quarterly_Sales

Project Results

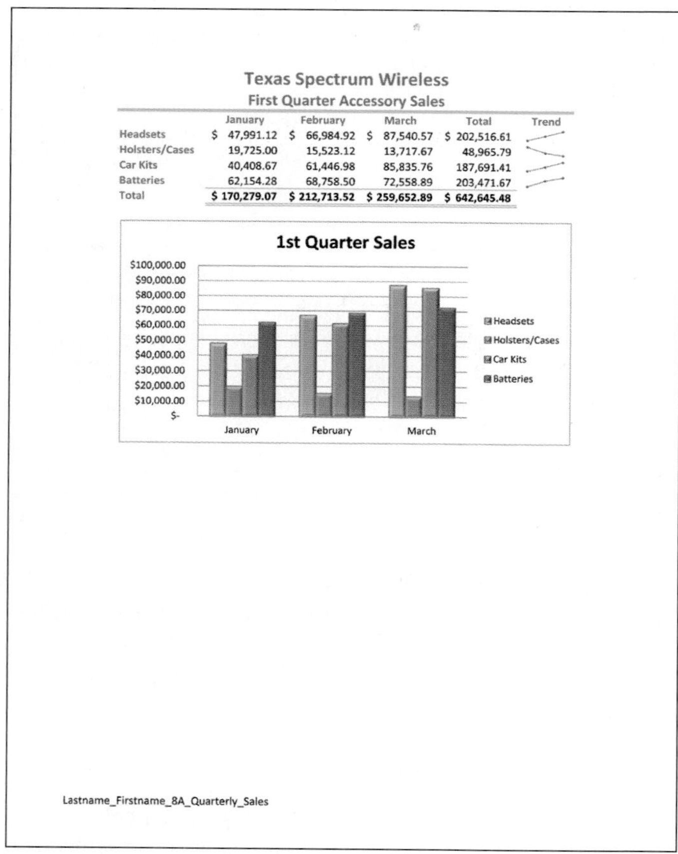

Texas Spectrum Wireless

First Quarter Accessory Sales

	January	February	March	Total	Trend
Headsets	$ 47,991.12	$ 66,984.92	$ 87,540.57	$ 202,516.61	
Holsters/Cases	19,725.00	15,523.12	13,717.67	48,965.79	
Car Kits	40,408.67	61,446.98	85,835.76	187,691.41	
Batteries	62,154.28	68,758.50	72,558.89	203,471.67	
Total	$ 170,279.07	$ 212,713.52	$ 259,652.89	$ 642,645.48	

Figure 8.1
Project 8A Quarterly Sales

Objective 1 | Create, Save, and Navigate an Excel Workbook

View the video on the Companion Web Site or in MyITLab

On startup, Excel displays a new blank ***workbook***—the Excel document that stores your data—which contains one or more pages called a ***worksheet***. A worksheet—or ***spreadsheet***—is stored in a workbook, and is formatted as a pattern of uniformly spaced horizontal rows and vertical columns. The intersection of a column and a row forms a box referred to as a ***cell***.

Activity 8.01 | Starting Excel and Naming and Saving a Workbook

1 **Start** Excel. In the lower right corner of the window, if necessary, click the **Normal** button, and then to the right, locate the zoom—magnification—level.

Your zoom level should be 100%, although some figures in this textbook may be shown at a higher zoom level.

2 In the upper left corner of your screen, click the **File tab** to display **Backstage** view, click **Save As**, and then in the **Save As** dialog box, navigate to the location where you will store your workbooks for this chapter.

3 In your storage location, create a new folder named **All In One Chapter 8** Open the new folder to display its folder window, and then in the **File name** box, notice that *Book1* displays as the default file name.

4 In the **File name** box, with *Book1* selected, and then using your own name, type **Lastname_Firstname_8A_Quarterly_Sales** Compare your screen with Figure 8.2.

Figure 8.2

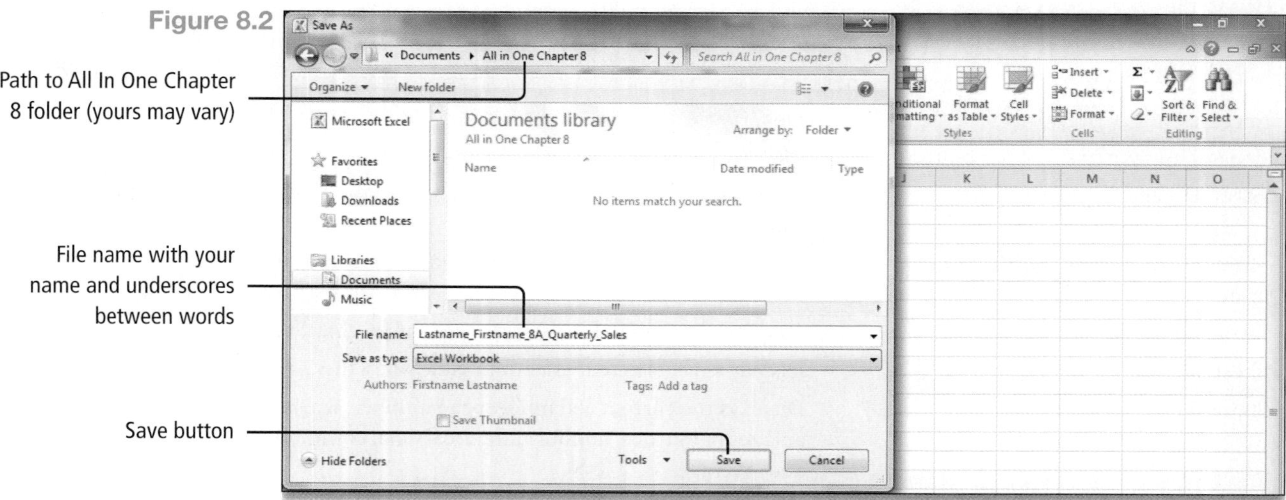

5 Click **Save**. Compare your screen with Figure 8.3, and then take a moment to study the Excel window parts in the table in Figure 8.4.

Figure 8.3

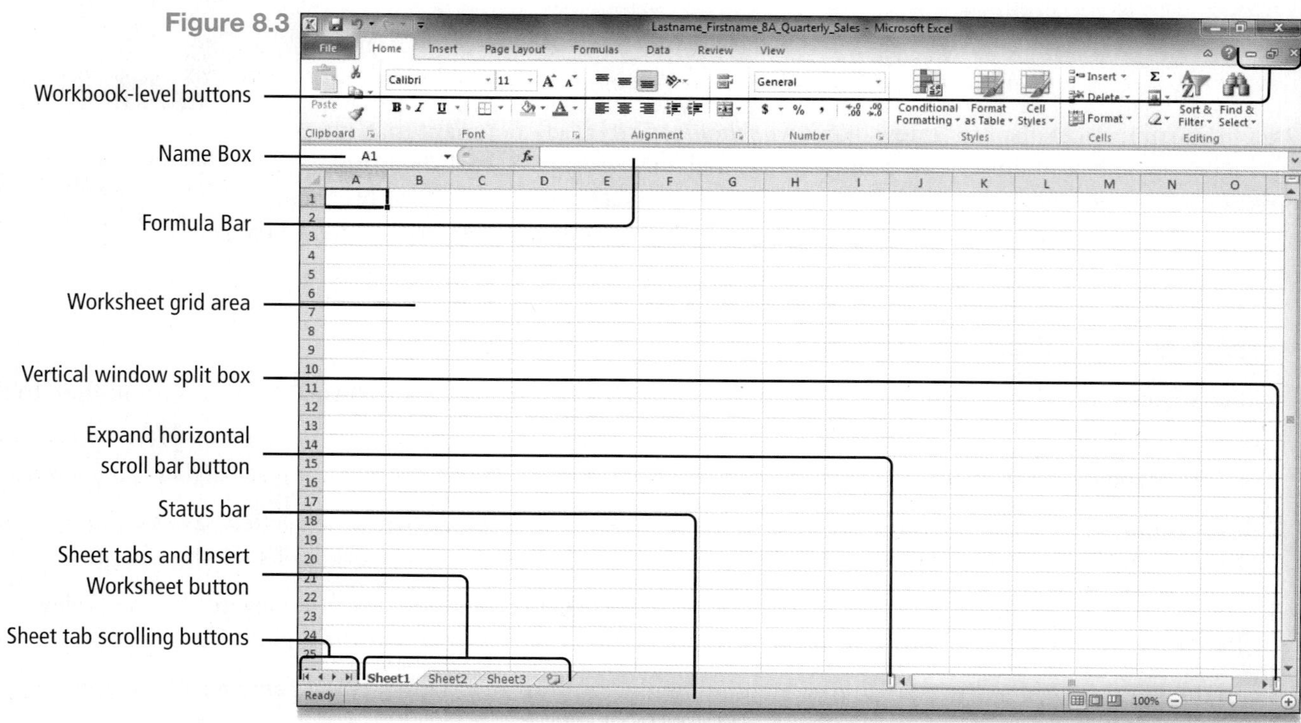

Parts of the Excel Window

Screen Part	Description
Expand horizontal scroll bar button	Increases the width of the horizontal scroll bar.
Formula Bar	Displays the value or formula contained in the active cell; also permits entry or editing.
Sheet tabs and Insert Worksheet button	Identify the worksheets in a workbook and inserts an additional worksheet.
Name Box	Displays the name of the selected cell, table, chart, or object.
Sheet tab scrolling buttons	Display sheet tabs that are not in view when there are numerous sheet tabs.
Status bar	Displays the current cell mode, page number, worksheet information, view and zoom buttons, and for numerical data, common calculations such as Sum and Average.
Vertical window split box	Splits the worksheet into two vertical views of the same worksheet.
Workbook-level buttons	Minimize, close, or restore the previous size of the displayed workbook.
Worksheet grid area	Displays the columns and rows that intersect to form the worksheet's cells.

Figure 8.4

Activity 8.02 | Navigating a Worksheet and a Workbook

1 Take a moment to study Figure 8.5 and the table in Figure 8.6 to become familiar with the Excel workbook window.

Figure 8.5

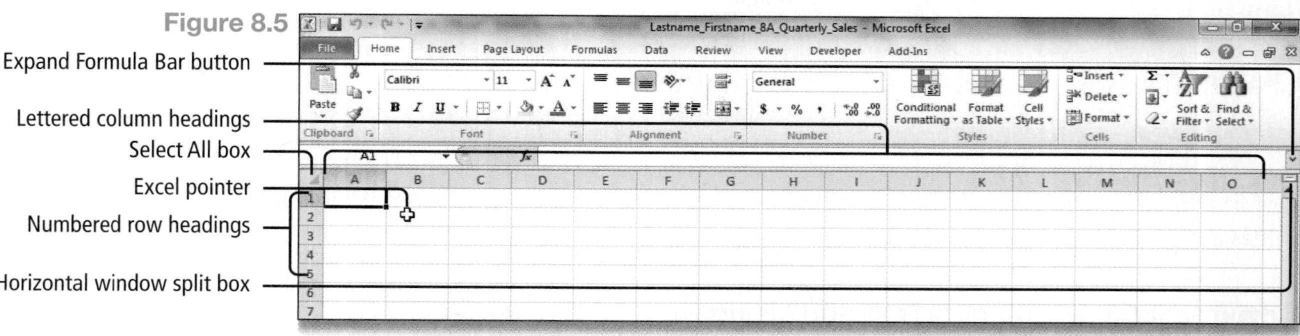

Excel Workbook Window Elements

Workbook Window Element	Description
Excel pointer	Displays the pointer in Excel.
Expand Formula Bar button	Increases the height of the Formula Bar to display lengthy cell content.
Horizontal window split box	Splits the worksheet into two horizontal views of the same worksheet.
Lettered column headings	Indicate the column letter.
Numbered row headings	Indicate the row number.
Select All box	Selects all the cells in a worksheet.

Figure 8.6

2 In the lower right corner of the screen, in the horizontal scroll bar, click the **right scroll arrow** one time to shift **column A** out of view.

A ***column*** is a vertical group of cells in a worksheet. Beginning with the first letter of the alphabet, *A*, a unique letter identifies each column—this is called the ***column heading***. Clicking one of the horizontal scroll bar arrows shifts the window either left or right one column at a time.

3 Point to the **right scroll arrow**, and then hold down the left mouse button until the columns begin to scroll rapidly to the right; release the mouse button when you begin to see pairs of letters as the column headings.

4 Slowly drag the horizontal scroll box to the left, and notice that just above the scroll box, ScreenTips with the column letters display as you drag. Drag the horizontal scroll box left or right—or click the left or right scroll arrow—as necessary to position **column Z** near the center of your screen.

Column headings after column Z use two letters starting with AA, AB, and so on through ZZ. After that, columns begin with three letters beginning with AAA. This pattern provides 16,384 columns. The last column is XFD.

5 In the lower left portion of your screen, click the **Sheet2 tab**.

The second worksheet displays and is the active sheet. Column A displays at the left.

6 In the vertical scroll bar, click the **down scroll arrow** one time to move **Row 1** out of view.

A ***row*** is a horizontal group of cells. Beginning with number 1, a unique number identifies each row—this is the ***row heading***, located at the left side of the worksheet. A single worksheet has 1,048,576 rows.

7 In the lower left corner, click the **Sheet1 tab**. Use the skills you just practiced to scroll horizontally to display **column A**, and if necessary, **row 1**.

The first worksheet in the workbook becomes the active worksheet. By default, new workbooks contain three worksheets. When you save a workbook, the worksheets are contained within it and do not have separate file names.

Objective 2 | Enter Data in a Worksheet

View the video on the Companion Web Site or in MyITLab

Cell content, which is anything you type in a cell, can be one of two things: either a ***constant value***—referred to simply as a ***value***—or a ***formula***. A formula is an equation that performs mathematical calculations on values in your worksheet. The most commonly used values are ***text values*** and ***number values***, but a value can also include a date or a time of day.

Activity 8.03 | Entering Text and Using AutoComplete

A text value, also referred to as a ***label***, usually provides information about number values in other worksheet cells. For example, a title such as First Quarter Accessory Sales gives the reader an indication that the data in the worksheet relates to information about sales of accessories during the three-month period January through March.

1 Click the **Sheet1 tab** to make it the active sheet, if necessary. Point to and then click the cell at the intersection of **column A** and **row 1** to make it the ***active cell***—the cell is outlined in black and ready to accept data.

The intersecting column letter and row number form the ***cell reference***—also called the ***cell address***. When a cell is active, its column letter and row number are highlighted. The cell reference of the selected cell, *A1*, displays in the Name Box.

2 With cell **A1** as the active cell, type the title **Texas Spectrum Wireless** and then press Enter. Compare your screen with Figure 8.7.

Text or numbers in a cell are referred to as ***data***. You must confirm the data you type in a cell by pressing Enter or by some other keyboard movement, such as pressing Tab or an arrow key. Pressing Enter moves the active cell to the cell below.

Figure 8.7

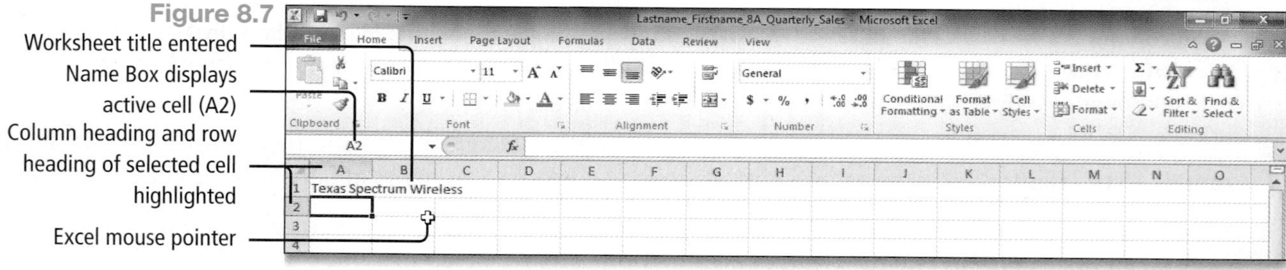

3 In cell **A1**, notice that the text does not fit; the text spills over and displays in cells **B1** and **C1** to the right.

If text is too long for a cell and cells to the right are empty, the text will display. If the cells to the right contain other data, only the text that will fit in the cell displays.

4 In cell **A2**, type the worksheet subtitle **First Quarter Accessory Sales** and then press Enter.

5 Press Enter again to make cell **A4** the active cell. In cell **A4**, type **Headsets** which will form the first row title, and then press Enter.

The text characters that you typed align at the left edge of the cell—referred to as ***left alignment***—and cell A5 becomes the active cell. Left alignment is the default for text values.

6 In cell **A5**, type **H** and notice the text from the previous cell displays.

If the first characters you type in a cell match an existing entry in the column, Excel fills in the remaining characters for you. This feature, called ***AutoComplete***, assists only with alphabetic values.

7 Continue typing the remainder of the row title **olsters/Cases** and press Enter.

The AutoComplete suggestion is removed when the entry you are typing differs from the previous value.

8 In cell **A6**, type **Car Kits** and press Enter. In cell **A7**, type **Batteries** and press Enter. In cell **A8**, type **Total** and press Enter. On the Quick Access Toolbar, click **Save**.

Activity 8.04 | Using Auto Fill and Keyboard Shortcuts

1 Click cell **B3**. Type **J** and notice that when you begin to type in a cell, on the **Formula Bar**, the **Cancel** and **Enter** buttons become active, as shown in Figure 8.8.

Figure 8.8

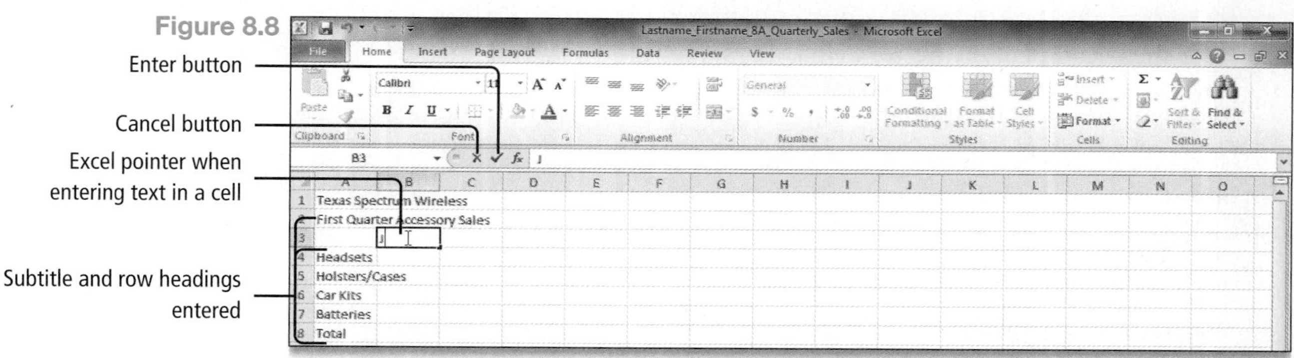

2 Continue to type **January** On the **Formula Bar**, notice that values you type in a cell also display there. Then, on the **Formula Bar**, click the **Enter** button to confirm the entry and keep cell **B3** active.

3 With cell **B3** active, locate the small black square in the lower right corner of the selected cell.

You can drag this ***fill handle***—the small black square in the lower right corner of a selected cell—to adjacent cells to fill the cells with values based on the first cell.

4 Point to the **fill handle** until the + pointer displays, hold down the left mouse button, drag to the right to cell **D3**, and as you drag, notice the ScreenTips *February* and *March*. Release the mouse button.

5 Under the text that you just filled, click the **Auto Fill Options** button that displays, and then compare your screen with Figure 8.9.

Auto Fill generates and extends a ***series*** of values into adjacent cells based on the value of other cells. A series is a group of things that come one after another in succession; for example, *January*, *February*, *March*. The Auto Fill Options button displays options to fill the data; options vary depending on the content and program from which you are filling, and the format of the data you are filling. *Fill Series* is selected, indicating the action that was taken. Because the options are related to the current task, the button is referred to as being ***context sensitive***.

Figure 8.9

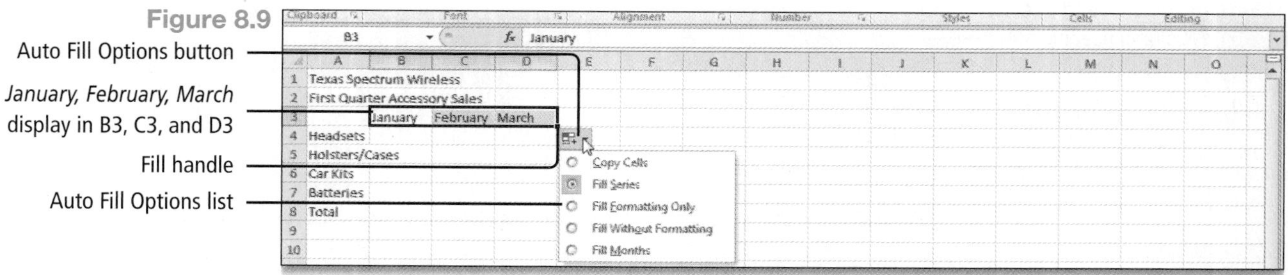

6 Click in any cell to cancel the display of the Auto Fill Options list.

The list no longer displays; the button will display until you perform some other screen action.

7 Press Ctrl + Home, which is the keyboard shortcut to make cell **A1** active.

8 On the Quick Access Toolbar, click **Save** to save the changes you have made to your workbook, and then take a moment to study the table in Figure 8.10 to become familiar with additional keyboard shortcuts with which you can navigate the Excel worksheet.

Keyboard Shortcuts to Navigate the Excel Window

To Move the Location of the Active Cell:	Press:
Up, down, right, or left one cell	↑, ↓, →, ←
Down one cell	Enter
Up one cell	Shift + Enter
Up one full screen	PageUp
Down one full screen	PageDown
To column A of the current row	Home
To the last cell in the last column of the active area (the rectangle formed by all the rows and columns in a worksheet that contain entries)	Ctrl + End
To cell A1	Ctrl + Home
Right one cell	Tab
Left one cell	Shift + Tab

Figure 8.10

Activity 8.05 | Aligning Text and Adjusting the Size of Columns

1 In the **column heading area**, point to the vertical line between **column A** and **column B** to display the pointer, press and hold down the left mouse button, and then compare your screen with Figure 8.11.

A ScreenTip displays information about the width of the column. The default width of a column is 64 ***pixels***. A pixel, short for ***picture element***, is a point of light measured in dots per square inch. Sixty-four pixels equal 8.43 characters, which is the average number of digits that will fit in a cell using the default font. The default font in Excel is Calibri and the default font size is 11.

Figure 8.11

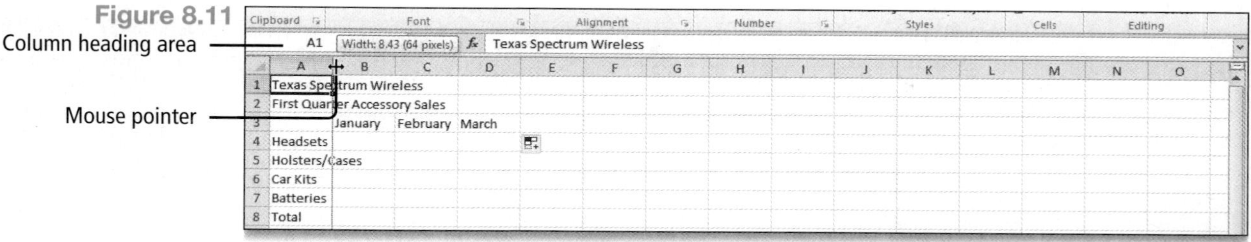

2 Drag to the right, and when the number of pixels indicated in the ScreenTip reaches **100 pixels**, release the mouse button. If you are not satisfied with your result, click Undo on the Quick Access Toolbar and begin again.

This width accommodates the longest row title in cells A4 through A8—*Holsters/Cases*. The worksheet title and subtitle in cells A1 and A2 span more than one column and still do not fit in column A.

3 Point to cell **B3** and then drag across to select cells **B3**, **C3**, and **D3**. Compare your screen with Figure 8.12.

The three cells, B3 through D3, are selected and form a ***range***—two or more cells on a worksheet that are adjacent (next to each other) or nonadjacent (not next to each other). This range of cells is referred to as *B3:D3*. When you see a colon (:) between two cell references, the range includes all the cells between the two cell references. A range of cells that is selected in this manner is indicated by a dark border, and Excel treats the range as a single unit so you can make the same changes to more than one cell at a time. The selected cells in the range are highlighted except for the first cell in the range, which displays in the Name Box.

Figure 8.12

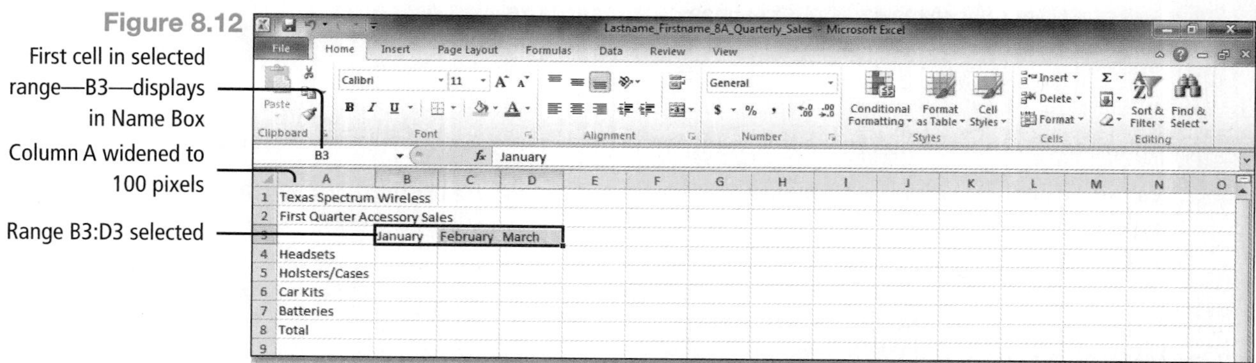

4 With the range **B3:D3** selected, point anywhere over the selected range, right-click, and then on the Mini toolbar, click the **Center** button. On the Quick Access Toolbar, click **Save**.

The column titles *January, February, March* align in the center of each cell.

Activity 8.06 | Entering Numbers

To type number values, use either the number keys across the top of your keyboard or the numeric keypad if you have one—laptop computers may not have a numeric keypad.

1 Under *January*, click cell **B4**, type **47991.12** and then on the **Formula Bar**, click the **Enter** button to maintain cell **B4** as the active cell. Compare your screen with Figure 8.13.

By default, *number* values align at the right edge of the cell. The default ***number format***—a specific way in which Excel displays numbers—is the ***general format***. In the default general format, whatever you type in the cell will display, with the exception of trailing zeros to the right of a decimal point. Data that displays in a cell is the ***displayed value***. Data that displays in the Formula Bar is the ***underlying value***. Calculations on numbers will always be based on the underlying value, not the displayed value.

Figure 8.13

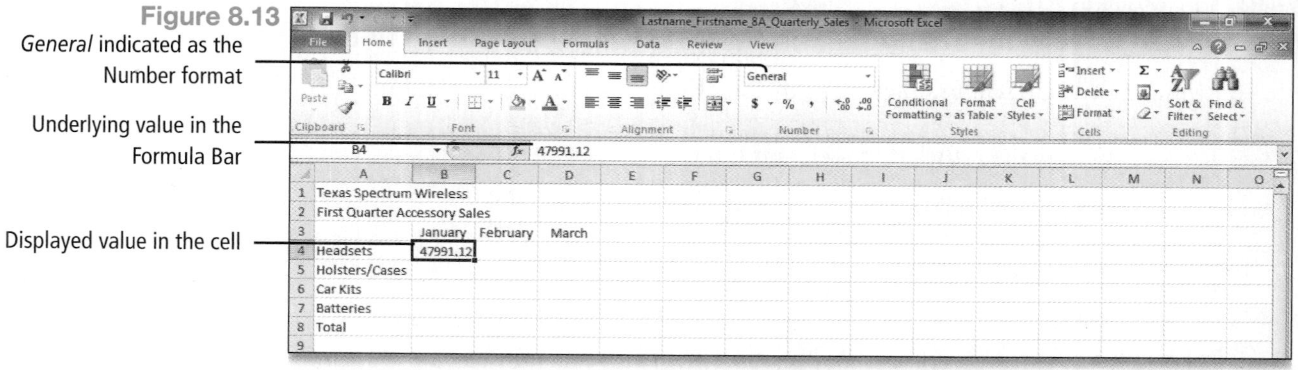

2 Press Tab to make cell **C4** active. Then, enter the remaining sales numbers as shown by using the following technique: Press Tab to confirm your entry and move across the row, and then press Enter at the end of a row to move to the next row.

	January	February	March
Headsets	47991.12	**66984.92**	**87540.57**
Holsters/Cases	**19725**	**15523.12**	**13717.67**
Car Kits	**40408.67**	**61446.98**	**85835.76**
Batteries	**62154.28**	**68758.50**	**72558.89**

3 Compare the numbers you entered with Figure 8.14 and then **Save** your workbook.

In the default general format, trailing zeros to the right of a decimal point will not display. For example, when you type *68758.50*, the cell displays 68758.5 instead.

Figure 8.14

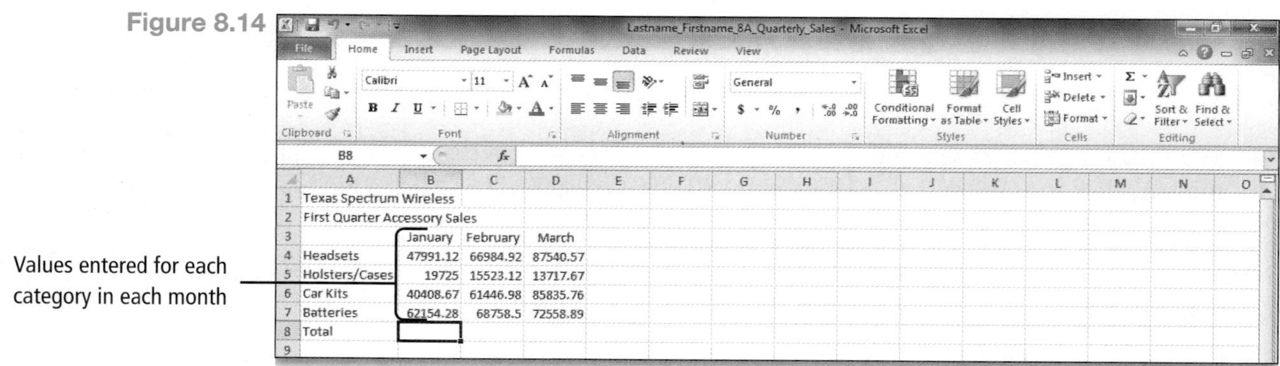

Objective 3 | Construct and Copy Formulas and Use the SUM Function

View the video on the Companion Web Site or in MyITLab

A cell contains either a constant value (text or numbers) or a formula. A formula is an equation that performs mathematical calculations on values in other cells, and then places the result in the cell containing the formula. You can create formulas or use a ***function***—a prewritten formula that looks at one or more values, performs an operation, and then returns a value.

Activity 8.07 | Constructing a Formula and Using the SUM Function

In this activity, you will practice three different ways to sum a group of numbers in Excel.

1 Click cell **B8** to make it the active cell and type =

The equal sign (=) displays in the cell with the insertion point blinking, ready to accept more data. All formulas begin with the = sign, which signals Excel to begin a calculation. The Formula Bar displays the = sign, and the Formula Bar Cancel and Enter buttons display.

2 At the insertion point, type **b4** and then compare your screen with Figure 8.15.

A list of Excel functions that begin with the letter *B* may briefly display—as you progress in your study of Excel, you will use functions of this type. A blue border with small corner boxes surrounds cell B4, which indicates that the cell is part of an active formula. The color used in the box matches the color of the cell reference in the formula.

Figure 8.15

Cell B4 outlined in blue to show it is part of an active formula

Cell B8 displays the beginning of the formula, with *b4* in blue to match the outlined cell

	A	B	C	D
1	Texas Spectrum Wireless			
2	First Quarter Accessory Sales			
3		January	February	March
4	Headsets	47991.12	66984.92	87540.57
5	Holsters/Cases	19725	15523.12	13717.67
6	Car Kits	40408.67	61446.98	85835.76
7	Batteries	62154.28	68758.5	72558.89
8	Total	=b4		

3 At the insertion point, type **+** and then type **b5**

A border of another color surrounds cell B5, and the color matches the color of the cell reference in the active formula. When typing cell references, it is not necessary to use uppercase letters.

4 At the insertion point, type **+b6+b7** and then press Enter.

The result of the formula calculation—*170279.1*—displays in the cell. Recall that in the default General format, trailing zeros do not display.

5 Click cell **B8** again, look at the **Formula Bar**, and then compare your screen with Figure 8.16.

The formula adds the values in cells B4 through B7, and the result displays in cell B8. In this manner, you can construct a formula by typing. Although cell B8 displays the *result* of the formula, the formula itself displays in the Formula Bar. This is referred to as the ***underlying formula***. Always view the Formula Bar to be sure of the exact content of a cell—*a displayed number may actually be a formula.*

Figure 8.16

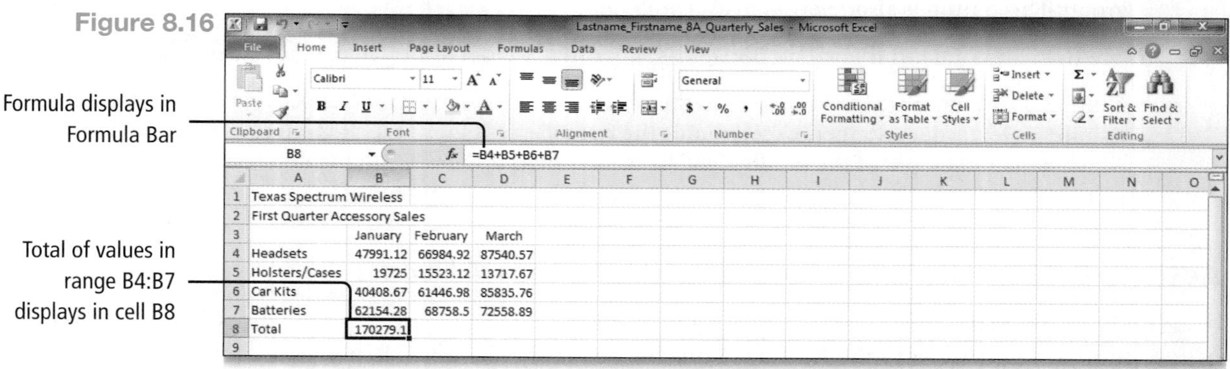

6 Click cell **C8** and type **=** to signal the beginning of a formula. Then, point to cell **C4** and click one time.

The reference to the cell C4 is added to the active formula. A moving border surrounds the referenced cell, and the border color and the color of the cell reference in the formula are color coded to match.

7 At the insertion point, type **+** and then click cell **C5**. Repeat this process to complete the formula to add cells **C6** through **C7**, and then press Enter.

The result of the formula calculation—*212713.5*—displays in the cell. This method of constructing a formula is the ***point and click method***.

8 Click cell **D8**. On the **Home tab**, in the **Editing group**, click the **Sum** button Σ, and then compare your screen with Figure 8.17.

SUM is an Excel function—a prewritten formula. A moving border surrounds the range D4:D7 and *=SUM(D4:D7)* displays in cell D8. The = sign signals the beginning of a formula, *SUM* indicates the type of calculation that will take place (addition), and *(D4:D7)* indicates the range of cells on which the sum calculation will be performed. A ScreenTip provides additional information about the action.

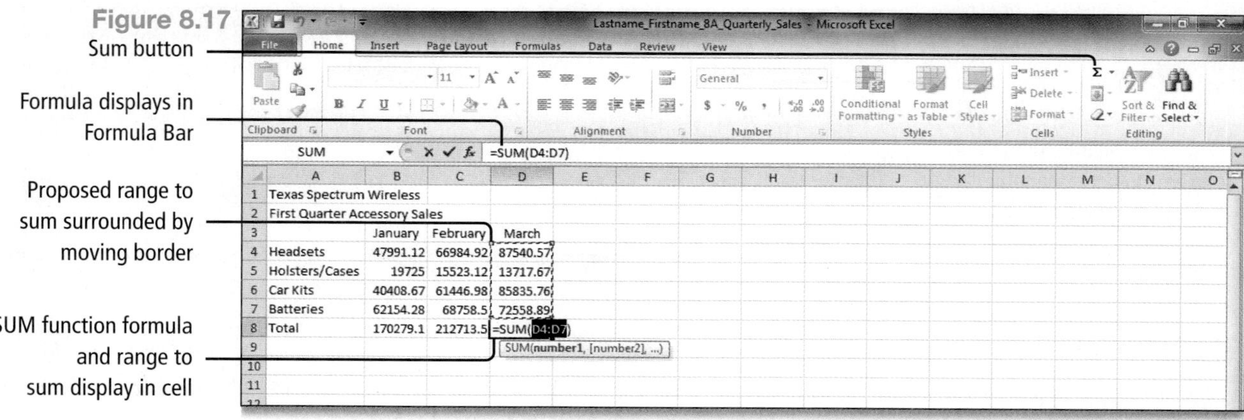

Figure 8.17

9 Look at the **Formula Bar**, and notice that the formula also displays there. Then, look again at the cells surrounded by the moving border.

When you activate the Sum function, Excel first looks *above* the active cell for a range of cells to sum. If no range is above the active cell, Excel will look to the *left* for a range of cells to sum. If the proposed range is not what you want to calculate, you can select a different group of cells.

10 Press Enter to construct a formula by using the prewritten SUM function.

Your total is *259652.9*. Because the Sum function is frequently used, it has its own button in the Editing group on the Home tab of the Ribbon. A larger version of the button also displays on the Formulas tab in the Function Library group. This button is also referred to as ***AutoSum***.

11 Notice that the totals in the range **B8:D8** display only *one* decimal place. Click **Save**.

Number values that are too long to fit in the cell do *not* spill over into the unoccupied cell to the right in the same manner as text values. Rather, Excel rounds the number to fit the space. ***Rounding*** is a procedure that determines which digit at the right of the number will be the last digit displayed and then increases it by one if the next digit to its right is 5, 6, 7, 8, or 9.

Activity 8.08 | Copying a Formula by Using the Fill Handle

You have practiced three ways to create a formula—by typing, by using the point-and-click technique, and by using a function button from the Ribbon. You can also copy formulas. When you copy a formula from one cell to another, Excel adjusts the cell references to fit the new location of the formula.

1 Click cell **E3**, type **Total** and then press Enter.

The text in cell E3 is centered because the centered format continues from the adjacent cell.

2 With cell **E4** as the active cell, hold down Alt, and then press =. Compare your screen with Figure 8.18.

Alt + = is the keyboard shortcut for the Sum function. Recall that Excel first looks above the selected cell for a proposed range of cells to sum, and if no data is detected, Excel looks to the left and proposes a range of cells to sum.

Figure 8.18

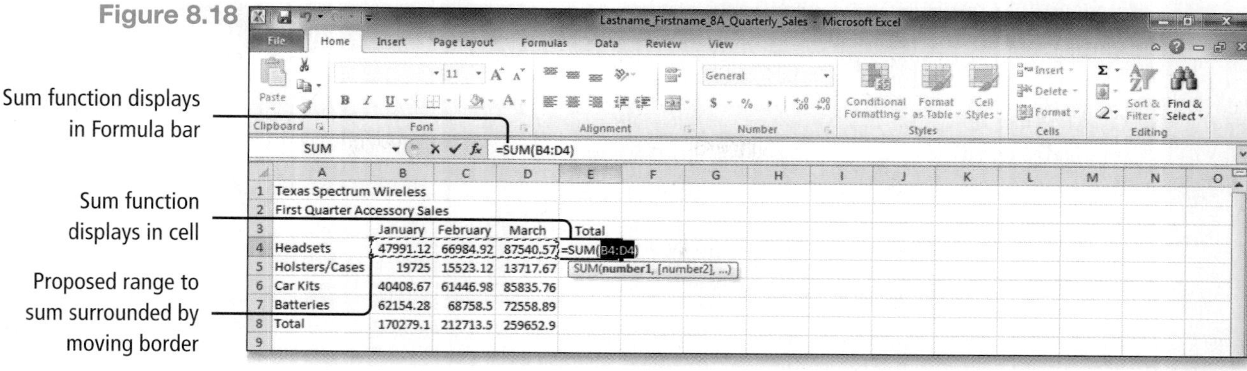

3 On the **Formula Bar**, click the **Enter** button ☑ to display the result and keep cell **E4** active.

The total dollar amount of *Headsets* sold in the quarter is *202516.6*. In cells E5:E8, you can see that you need a formula similar to the one in E4, but formulas that refer to the cells in row 5, row 6, and so on.

4 With cell **E4** active, point to the fill handle in the lower right corner of the cell until the + pointer displays. Then, drag down through cell **E8**; if you are not satisfied with your result, on the Quick Access Toolbar, click Undo and begin again. Compare your screen with Figure 8.19.

Figure 8.19

Totals display in the selected cells

Auto Fill Options button displays

E4 =SUM(B4:D4)

	A	B	C	D	E
1	Texas Spectrum Wireless				
2	First Quarter Accessory Sales				
3		January	February	March	Total
4	Headsets	47991.12	66984.92	87540.57	202516.6
5	Holsters/Cases	19725	15523.12	13717.67	48965.79
6	Car Kits	40408.67	61446.98	85835.76	187691.4
7	Batteries	62154.28	68758.5	72558.89	203471.7
8	Total	170279.1	212713.5	259652.9	642645.5

5 Click cell **E5**, look at the **Formula Bar**, and notice the formula *=SUM(B5:D5)*. Click cell **E6**, look at the **Formula Bar**, and then notice the formula *=SUM(B6:D6)*.

In each row, Excel copied the formula but adjusted the cell references *relative to* the row number. This is called a ***relative cell reference***—a cell reference based on the relative position of the cell that contains the formula and the cells referred to.

6 Click cell **F3**, type **Trend** and then press Enter. **Save** your workbook.

Objective 4 | Format Cells with Merge & Center and Cell Styles

Format—change the appearance of—cells to make your worksheet attractive and easy to read.

View the video on the Companion Web Site or in MyITLab

Activity 8.09 | Using Merge & Center and Applying Cell Styles

1 Select the range **A1:F1**, and then, on the **Home tab**, in the **Alignment group**, click the **Merge & Center** button. Then, select the range **A2:F2** and click the **Merge & Center** button.

The ***Merge & Center*** command joins selected cells into one larger cell and centers the contents in the new cell; individual cells in the range B1:F1 and B2:F2 can no longer be selected—they are merged into cells A1 and A2, respectively.

2 Click cell **A1**. In the **Styles group**, click the **Cell Styles** button, and then compare your screen with Figure 8.20.

A ***cell style*** is a defined set of formatting characteristics, such as font, font size, font color, cell borders, and cell shading.

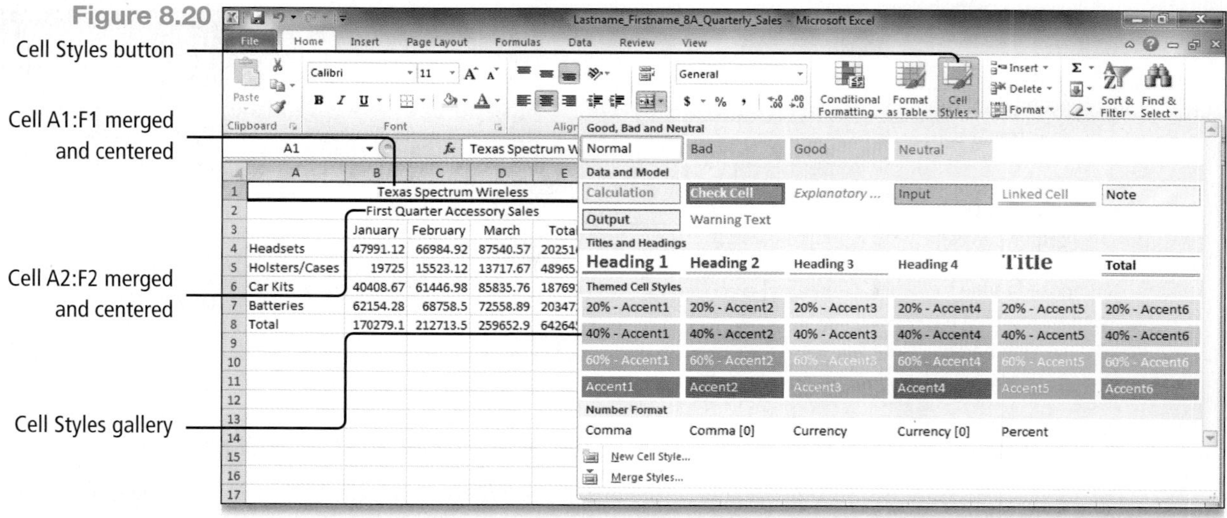

3 In the displayed gallery, under **Titles and Headings**, click **Title** and notice that the row height adjusts to accommodate this larger font size.

4 Click cell **A2**, display the **Cell Styles** gallery, and then under **Titles and Headings**, click **Heading 1**.

Use cell styles to maintain a consistent look in a worksheet and across worksheets in a workbook.

5 Select the range **B3:F3**, hold down Ctrl, and then select the range **A4:A8** to select the column titles and the row titles.

Use this technique to select two or more ranges that are nonadjacent—not next to each other.

6 Display the **Cell Styles** gallery, click **Heading 4** to apply this cell style to the column titles and row titles, and then **Save** your workbook.

Activity 8.10 | Formatting Financial Numbers

1 Select the range **B4:E4**, hold down Ctrl, and then select the range **B8:E8**.

This range is referred to as *b4:e4,b8:e8* with a comma separating the references to the two nonadjacent ranges.

2 On the **Home tab**, in the **Number group**, click the **Accounting Number Format** button $. Compare your screen with Figure 8.21.

The ***Accounting Number Format*** applies a thousand comma separator where appropriate, inserts a fixed U.S. dollar sign aligned at the left edge of the cell, applies two decimal places, and leaves a small amount of space at the right edge of the cell to accommodate a parenthesis when negative numbers are present. Excel widens the columns to accommodate the formatted numbers.

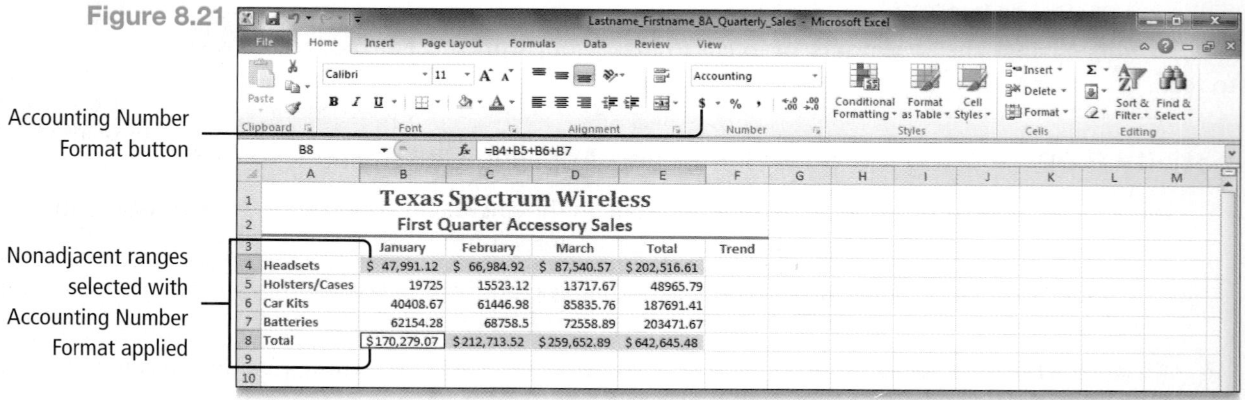

3 Select the range **B5:E7**, and then in the **Number group**, click the **Comma Style** button [,].

The ***Comma Style*** inserts thousand comma separators where appropriate and applies two decimal places. Comma Style also leaves space at the right to accommodate a parenthesis when negative numbers are present.

When preparing worksheets with financial information, the first row of dollar amounts and the total row of dollar amounts are formatted in the Accounting Number Format. Rows that are *not* the first row or the total row should be formatted with the Comma Style.

4 Select the range **B8:E8**. From the **Styles group**, display the **Cell Styles** gallery, and then under **Titles and Headings**, click **Total**. Click any blank cell to cancel the selection, and then compare your screen with Figure 8.22.

This is a common way to apply borders to financial information. The single border indicates that calculations were performed on the numbers above, and the double border indicates that the information is complete.

Figure 8.22

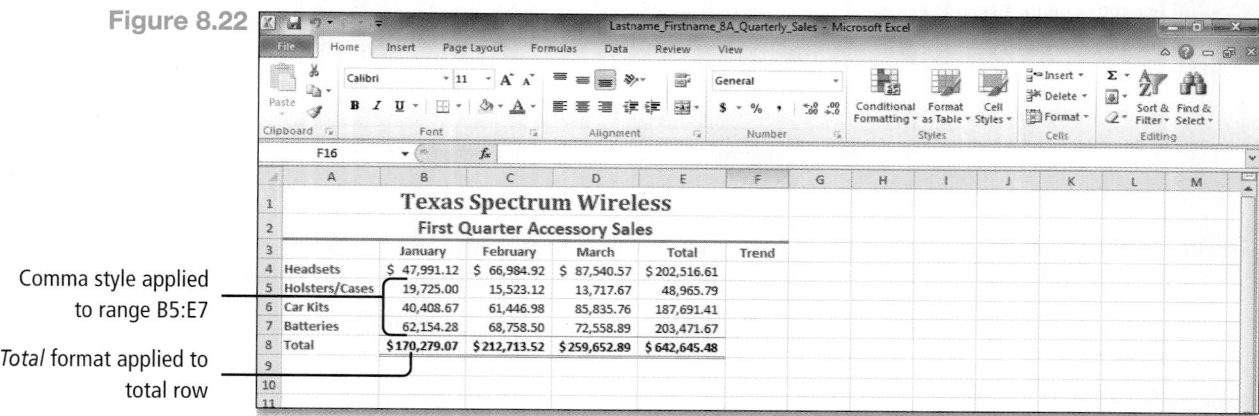

5 Click the **Page Layout tab**, and then in the **Themes group**, click **Themes**. Click the **Composite** theme, and notice that the cell styles change to match the new theme. Click **Save** [Save].

Recall that a theme is a predefined set of colors, fonts, lines, and fill effects that look good together.

Objective 5 | Chart Data to Create a Column Chart and Insert Sparklines

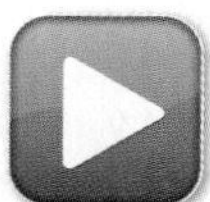

View the video on the Companion Web Site or in MyITLab

A ***chart*** is a graphic representation of data in a worksheet. Data presented as a chart is easier to understand than a table of numbers. ***Sparklines*** are tiny charts embedded in a cell and give a visual trend summary alongside your data. A sparkline makes a pattern more obvious to the eye.

Activity 8.11 | Charting Data in a Column Chart

In this activity, you will create a ***column chart*** showing the monthly sales of accessories by category during the first quarter. A column chart is useful for illustrating comparisons among related numbers.

1 Select the range **A3:D7**. Click the **Insert tab**, and then in the **Charts group**, click **Column** to display a gallery of Column chart types.

When charting data, typically you should *not* include totals—include only the data you want to compare. By using different ***chart types***, you can display data in a way that is meaningful to the reader—common examples are column charts, pie charts, and line charts.

2 On the gallery of column chart types, under **2-D Column**, point to the first chart to display the ScreenTip *Clustered Column*, and then click to select it. Compare your screen with Figure 8.23.

A column chart displays in the worksheet, and the charted data is bordered by colored lines.

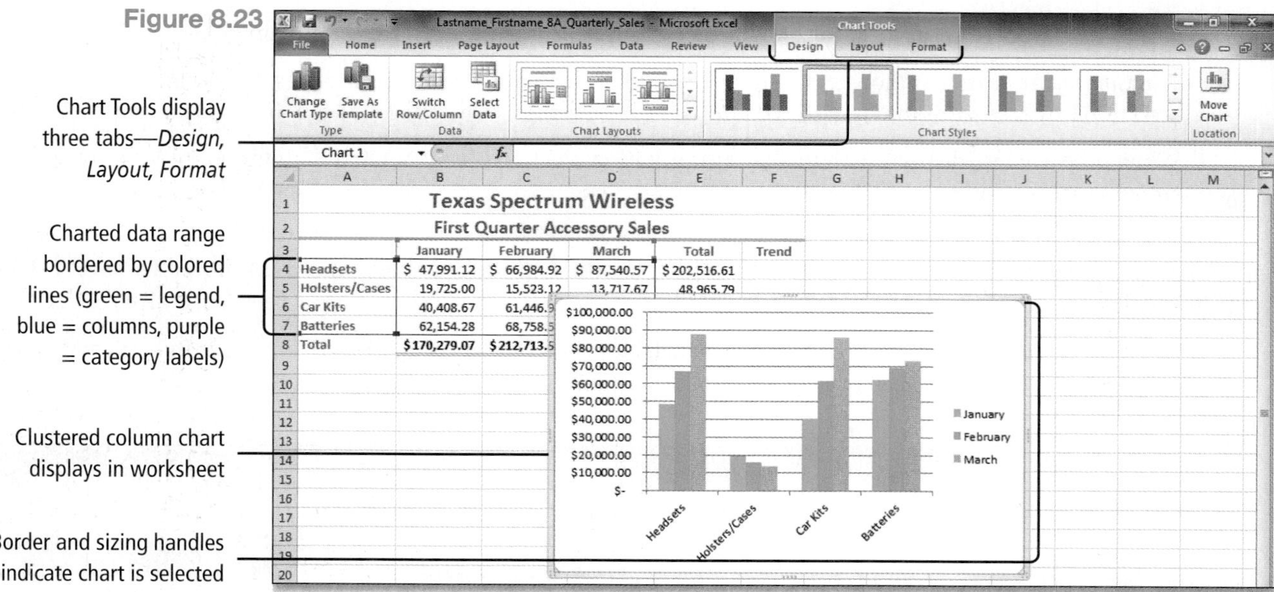

Figure 8.23

3 Point to the top border of the chart to display the pointer, and then drag the upper left corner of the chart just inside the upper left corner of cell **A10**, approximately as shown in Figure 8.24.

Based on the data you selected in your worksheet, Excel constructs a column chart and adds ***category labels***—the labels that display along the bottom of the chart to identify the category of data. This area is referred to as the ***category axis*** or the ***x-axis***. Excel uses the row titles as the category names. On the left, Excel includes a numerical scale on which the charted data is based; this is the ***value axis*** or the ***y-axis***. On the right, a ***legend***, which identifies the patterns or colors that are assigned to the categories in the chart, displays.

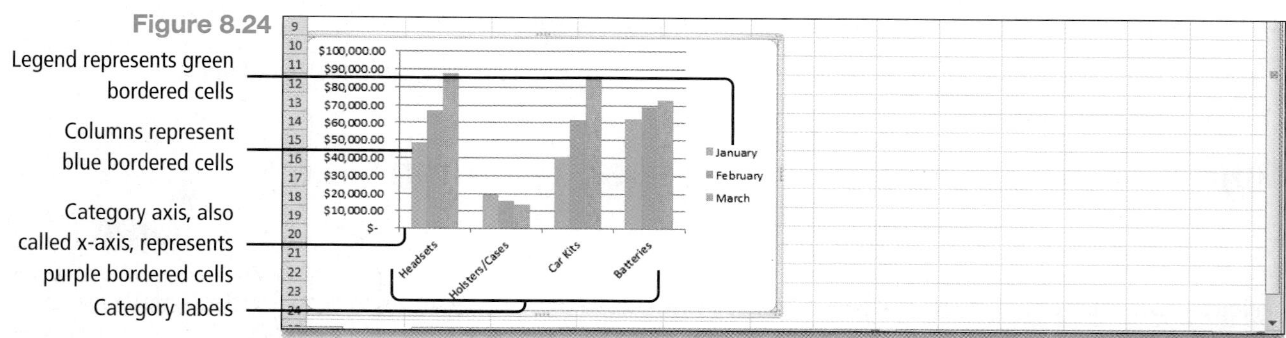

Figure 8.24

4 On the Ribbon, locate the contextual tabs under **Chart Tools—Design**, **Layout**, and **Format**.

When a chart is selected, Chart Tools become available and three tabs provide commands for working with the chart.

5 Locate the group of cells bordered in blue.

Each of the twelve cells bordered in blue is referred to as a ***data point***—a value that originates in a worksheet cell. Each data point is represented in the chart by a ***data marker***—a column, bar, area, dot, pie slice, or other symbol in a chart that represents a single data point. Related data points form a ***data series***; for example, there is a data series for *January*, for *February*, and for *March*. Each data series has a unique color or pattern represented in the chart legend.

6 On the **Design tab** of the Ribbon, in the **Data group**, click the **Switch Row/Column** button, and then compare your chart with Figure 8.25.

In this manner, you can easily change the categories of data from the row titles, which is the default, to the column titles. Whether you use row or column titles as your category names depends on how you want to view your charted data. Here, the president wants to see monthly sales and the breakdown of product categories within each month.

Figure 8.25

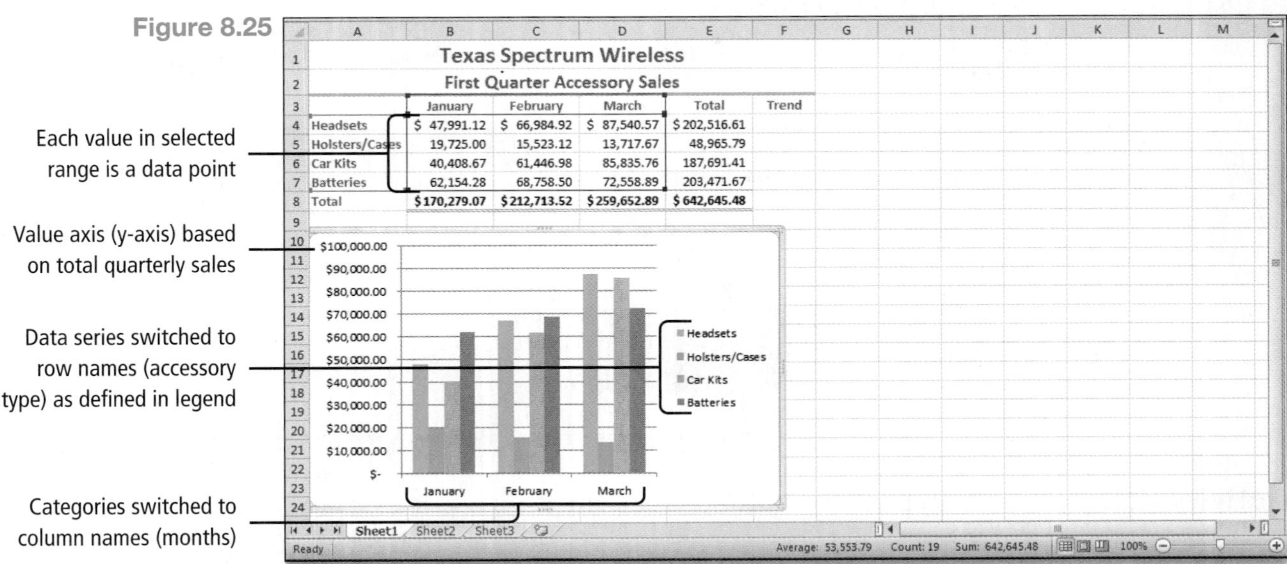

7 On the **Design tab**, in the **Chart Layouts group**, locate and click the **More** button. Compare your screen with Figure 8.26.

In the ***Chart Layouts gallery***, you can select a predesigned ***chart layout***—a combination of chart elements, which can include a title, legend, labels for the columns, and the table of charted cells.

Figure 8.26

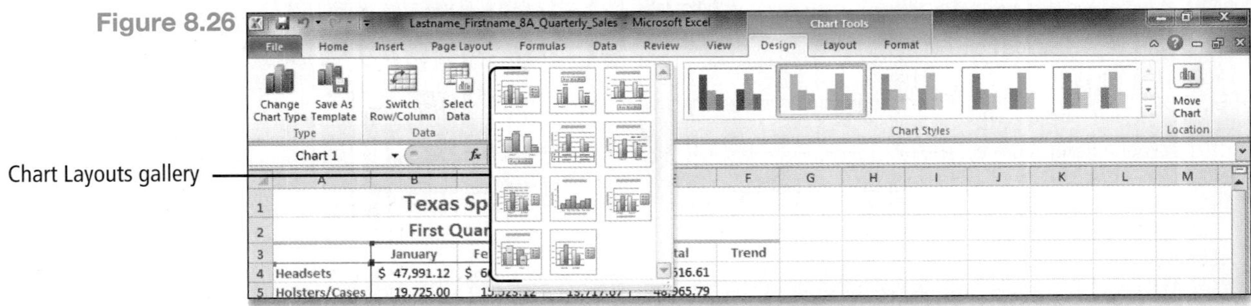

8 Click several different layouts to see the effect on your chart, and then using the ScreenTips as your guide, locate and click **Layout 1**.

9 In the chart, click anywhere in the text *Chart Title* to select the title box, watch the **Formula Bar** as you type **1st Quarter Sales** and then press Enter to display the new chart title.

10 Click in a white area just slightly *inside* the chart border to deselect the chart title. On the **Design tab**, in the **Chart Styles group**, click the **More** button.

The ***Chart Styles gallery*** displays an array of pre-defined ***chart styles***—the overall visual look of the chart in terms of its colors, backgrounds, and graphic effects such as flat or beveled columns.

11 Using the ScreenTips as your guide, locate and click **Style 26**.

This style uses a white background, formats the columns with theme colors, and applies a beveled effect. With this clear visual representation of the data, you can see the sales of all product categories in each month and that the sale of headsets and car kits has risen quite markedly during the quarter.

12 Click any cell to deselect the chart, and notice that the *Chart Tools* no longer display in the Ribbon. Click **Save**, and then compare your screen with Figure 8.27.

Contextual tabs display when an object is selected, and then are removed from view when the object is deselected.

Figure 8.27

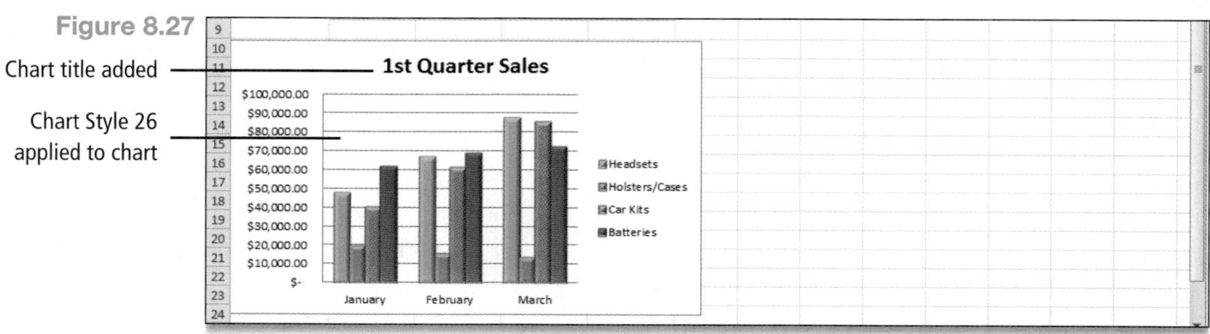

Activity 8.12 | Creating and Formatting Sparklines

By creating sparklines, you provide a context for your numbers. Your readers will be able to see the relationship between a sparkline and its underlying data quickly.

1 Select the range **B4:D7**. Click the **Insert tab**, and then in the **Sparklines group**, click **Line**. In the displayed **Create Sparklines** dialog box, notice that the selected range *B4:D7* displays.

2 With the insertion point blinking in the **Location Range** box, type **f4:f7** Compare your screen with Figure 8.28.

Figure 8.28

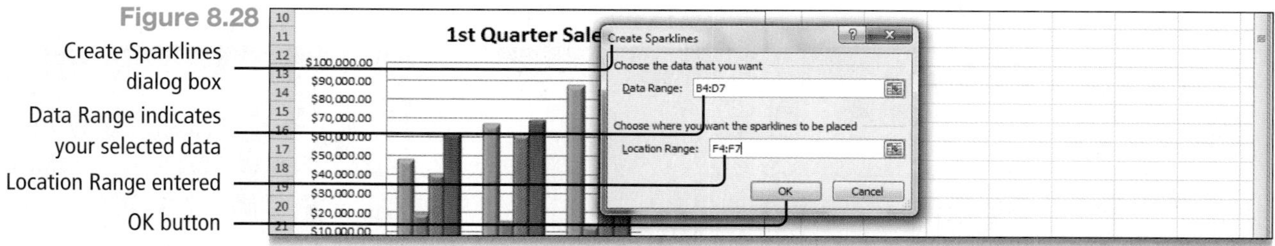

3 Click **OK** to insert the sparklines in the range F4:F7, and then on the **Design tab**, in the **Show group**, click the **Markers** check box to select it.

Alongside each row of data, the sparkline provides a quick visual trend summary for sales of each accessory item over the three-month period. For example, you can see instantly that of the four items, only Holsters/Cases had declining sales for the period.

4 In the **Style group**, click the **More** button. In the second row, click the fourth style—**Sparkline Style Accent 4, Darker 25%**. Click cell **A1** to deselect the range. Click **Save**. Compare your screen with Figure 8.29.

Use markers, colors, and styles in this manner to further enhance your sparklines.

Figure 8.29

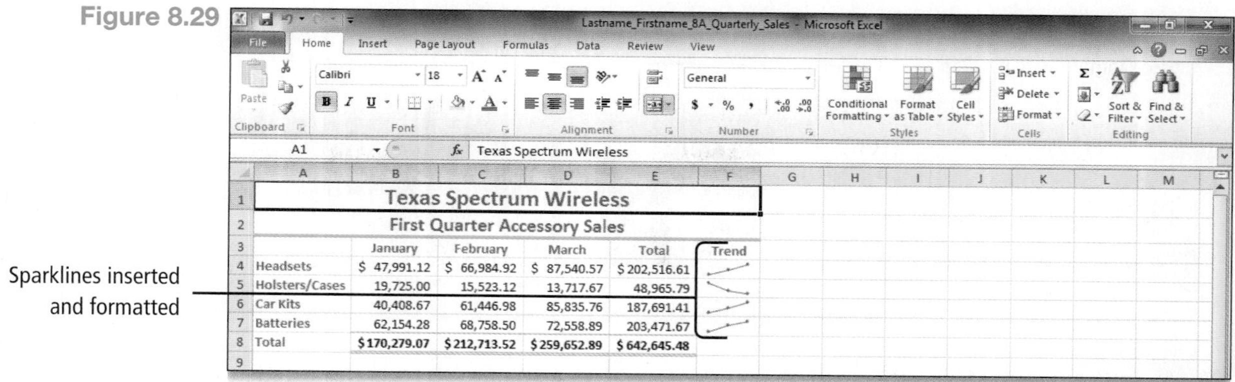

Objective 6 | Print, Display Formulas, and Close Excel

View the video on the Companion Web Site or in MyITLab

Use ***Page Layout view*** and the commands on the Page Layout tab to prepare for printing.

Activity 8.13 | Changing Views, Creating a Footer, and Using Print Preview

For each Excel project in this textbook, you will create a footer containing your name and the project name.

1 Be sure the chart is *not* selected. Click the **Insert tab**, and then in the **Text group**, click the **Header & Footer** button to switch to Page Layout view and open the **Header area**. Compare your screen with Figure 8.30.

In Page Layout view, you can see the edges of the paper of multiple pages, the margins, and the rulers. You can also insert a header or footer by typing in the areas indicated and use the Header & Footer Tools.

Figure 8.30

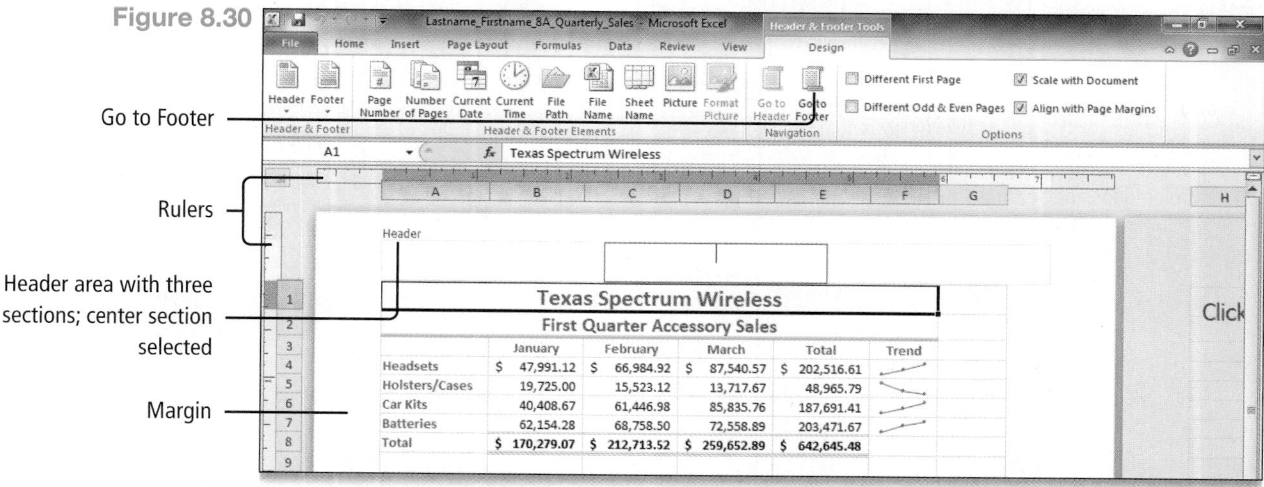

2 On the **Design tab**, in the **Navigation group**, click **Go to Footer** to open the **Footer area**, and then click just above the word *Footer* to place the insertion point in the **left section** of the **Footer area**.

3 In the **Header & Footer Elements group**, click the **File Name** button to add the name of your file to the footer—&[File] displays in the left section of the **Footer area**. Then, click in a cell just above the footer to exit the **Footer area** and view your file name.

4 Scroll up to see your chart, click a corner of the chart to select it, and then see if the chart is centered under the data. *Point* to the small dots on the right edge of the chart; compare your screen with Figure 8.31.

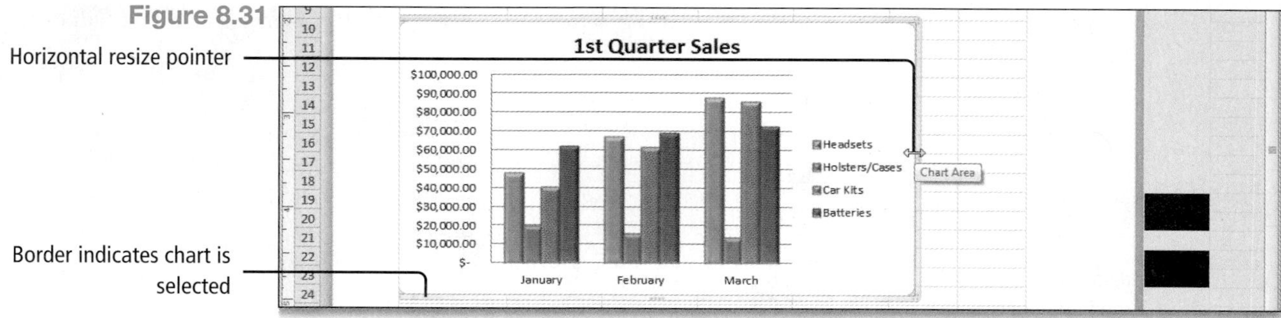

Figure 8.31

5 Drag the pointer to the right so that the right border of the chart is just inside the right border of **column F**. Be sure the left and right borders of the chart are just slightly **inside** the left border of **column A** and the right border of **column F**—adjust as necessary.

6 Click any cell to deselect the chart. Click the **Page Layout tab**, in the **Page Setup group**, click the **Margins** button, and then at the bottom of the **Margins** gallery, click **Custom Margins**. In the **Page Setup** dialog box, under **Center on page**, select the **Horizontally** check box.

This action will center the data and chart horizontally on the page, as shown in the Preview area.

7 Click **OK**. In the upper left corner of your screen, click the **File tab** to display **Backstage** view. On the **Info tab**, on the right under the screen thumbnail, click **Properties**, and then click **Show Document Panel**.

8 In the **Author** box, replace the existing text with your firstname and lastname. In the **Subject** box, type your course name and section number. In the **Keywords** box type **accessory sales** and then **Close** the **Document Information Panel**.

9 Click the **File tab** to redisplay **Backstage** view, and then on the left, click the **Print tab** to view the Print commands and the **Print Preview**. Compare your screen with Figure 8.32.

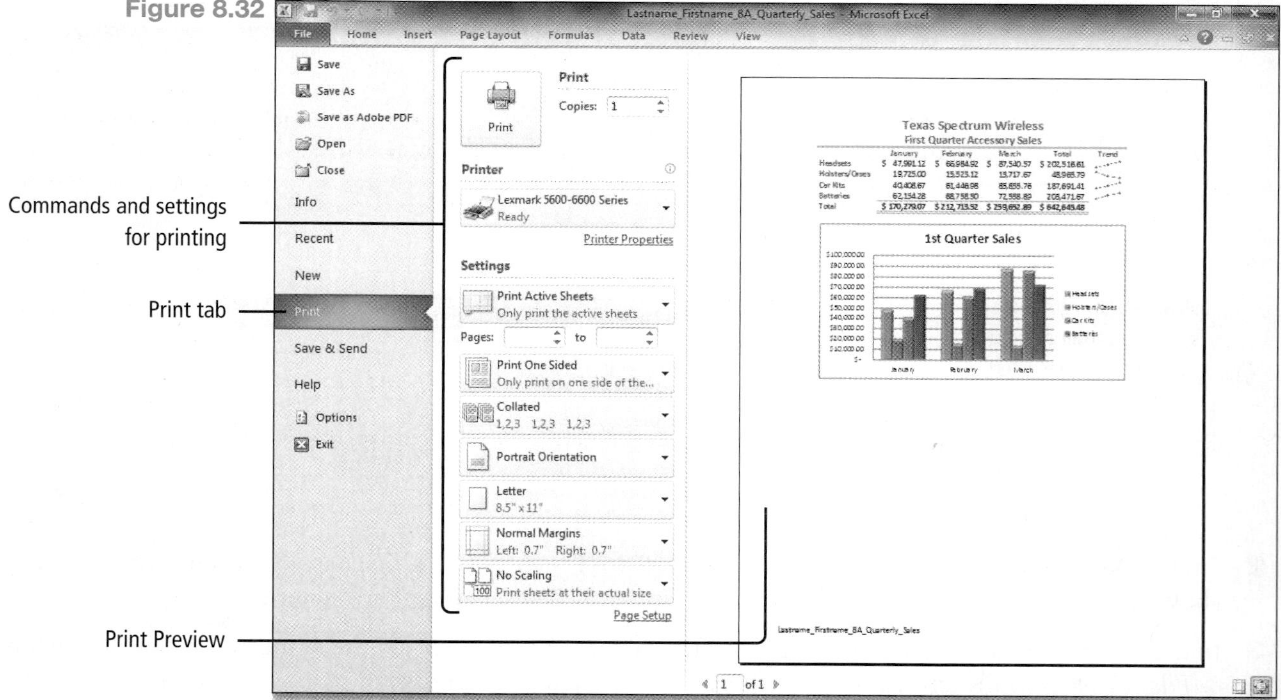

Figure 8.32

10 Note any adjustments that need to be made, and then on the Ribbon, click the **Home tab** to close Backstage view and return to the worksheet. In the lower right corner of your screen, click the **Normal** button to return to the Normal view, and then press Ctrl + Home to return to cell **A1**.

The ***Normal view*** maximizes the number of cells visible on your screen and keeps the column letters and row numbers closer. The vertical dotted line between columns indicates that as currently arranged, only the columns to the left of the dotted line will print on the first page. The exact position of the vertical line may depend on your default printer setting.

11 Make any necessary adjustments, and then **Save** your workbook.

Activity 8.14 | Deleting Unused Sheets in a Workbook

A new Excel workbook contains three blank worksheets. It is not necessary to delete unused sheets, but doing so saves storage space and removes any doubt that additional information is in the workbook.

1 At the bottom of your worksheet, click the **Sheet2 tab** to display the second worksheet in the workbook and make it active.

2 Hold down Ctrl, and then click the **Sheet3 tab**. Release Ctrl, and then with both sheets selected (the tab background is white), point to either of the selected sheet tabs, right-click, and then on the shortcut menu, click **Delete**.

Excel deletes the two unused sheets from your workbook. If you attempt to delete a worksheet with data, Excel will display a warning and permit you to cancel the deletion. ***Sheet tabs*** are labels along the lower border of the Excel window that identify each worksheet.

Activity 8.15 | Printing a Worksheet

1 Click **Save** .

2 Display **Backstage** view and on the left, click the Print tab. Under **Print**, be sure **Copies** indicates *1*. Under **Settings**, verify that *Print Active Sheets* displays.

3 To print, be sure that a printer is available to your system, and then click the **Print** button. To create an electronic printout, on the Backstage tabs, click the **Save & Send tab**, under **File Types** click **Create PDF/XPS Document**, and then on the right, click **Create PDF/XPS**. In the **Publish as PDF or XPS** dialog box, navigate to your storage location, and then click the **Publish** button to create the PDF file. Close the Adobe window.

Activity 8.16 | Displaying, Printing, and Hiding Formulas

When you type a formula in a cell, the cell displays the *results* of the formula calculation. Recall that this value is called the displayed value. You can view and print the underlying formulas in the cells. When you do so, a formula often takes more horizontal space to display than the result of the calculation.

1 If necessary, redisplay your worksheet. Because you will make some temporary changes to your workbook, on the Quick Access Toolbar, click **Save** to be sure your work is saved up to this point.

2 On the **Formulas tab**, in the **Formula Auditing group**, click the **Show Formulas** button. Then, in the **column heading area**, point to the **column A** heading to display the pointer, hold down the left mouse button, and then drag to the right to select columns **A:F**. Compare your screen with Figure 8.33.

Figure 8.33

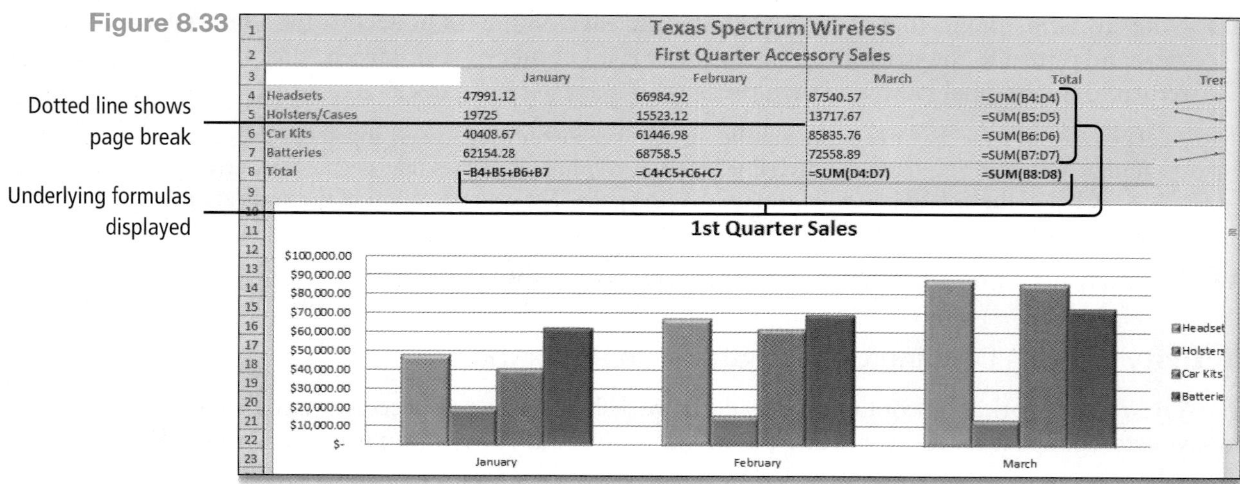

> **Note | Turning the Display of Formulas On and Off**
>
> The Show Formulas button is a toggle button. Clicking it once turns the display of formulas on—the button will glow orange. Clicking the button again turns the display of formulas off.

3 Point to the column heading boundary between any two of the selected columns to display the [pointer icon] pointer, and then double-click to AutoFit the selected columns.

AutoFit adjusts the width of a column to fit the cell content of the *widest* cell in the column.

4 On the **Page Layout tab**, in the **Page Setup group**, click **Orientation**, and then click **Landscape**. In the **Scale to Fit** group, click the **Width arrow**, and then click **1 page** to scale the data to fit onto one page.

Scaling shrinks the width (or height) of the printed worksheet to fit a maximum number of pages, and is convenient for printing formulas.

5 In the **Page Setup group**, click the **Dialog Box Launcher** button [icon]. In the **Page Setup** dialog box, click the **Margins tab**, and then under **Center on page**, if necessary, click to select the **Horizontally** check box.

6 Click **OK** to close the dialog box. Check to be sure your chart is centered below the data and the left and right edges are slightly inside column A and column F—drag a chart edge and then deselect the chart if necessary. Display the **Print Preview**, and then submit your worksheet with formulas displayed, either printed or electronically, as directed by your instructor.

7 Click the **File tab** to display **Backstage** view, click **Close**, and when prompted, click **Don't Save** so that you do *not* save the changes you made—displaying formulas, changing column widths and orientation, and scaling—to print your formulas.

8 In the upper right corner of your screen, click the **Close** button [X] to exit Excel.

End You have completed Project 8A

Project 8B Inventory Valuation

Project Activities

In Activities 8.17 through 8.24, you will create a workbook for Josette Lovrick, Operations Manager, which calculates the retail value of an inventory of car convenience products. Your completed worksheet will look similar to Figure 8.34.

Project Files

For Project 8B, you will need the following file:

New blank Excel workbook

You will save your workbook as:

Lastname_Firstname_8B_Car_Products

Project Results

Texas Spectrum Wireless
Car Products Inventory Valuation
As of December 31

	Warehouse Location	Quantity In Stock	Retail Price	Total Retail Value	Percent of Total Retail Value
Antenna Signal Booster	Dallas	1,126	$ 19.99	$ 22,508.74	8.27%
Car Power Point Adapter	Dallas	3,546	19.49	69,111.54	25.39%
Repeater Antenna	Houston	1,035	39.99	41,389.65	15.21%
SIM Card Reader and Writer	Houston	2,875	16.90	48,587.50	17.85%
Sticky Dash Pad	Houston	3,254	11.99	39,015.46	14.33%
Window Mount GPS Holder	Dallas	2,458	20.99	51,593.42	18.95%
Total Retail Value for All Products				**$ 272,206.31**	

Lastname_Firstname_8B_Car_Products

Figure 8.34
Project 8B Car Products

Objective 7 | Check Spelling in a Worksheet

View the video on the Companion Web Site or in MyITLab

In Excel, the spelling checker performs similarly to the other Microsoft Office programs.

Activity 8.17 | Checking Spelling in a Worksheet

1 **Start** Excel and display a new blank workbook. In cell **A1**, type **Texas Spectrum Wireless** and press Enter. In cell **A2**, type **Car Products Inventory** and press Enter.

2 On the Ribbon, click the **File tab** to display **Backstage** view, click **Save As**, and then in the **Save As** dialog box, navigate to your **All In One Chapter 8** folder. As the **File name**, type **Lastname_Firstname_8B_Car_Products** and then click **Save**.

3 Press Tab to move to cell **B3**, type **Quantity** and press Tab. In cell **C3**, type **Average Cost** and press Tab. In cell **D3**, type **Retail Price** and press Tab.

4 Click cell **C3**, and then look at the **Formula Bar**. Notice that in the cell, the displayed value is cut off; however, in the **Formula Bar**, the entire text value—the underlying value—displays. Compare your screen with Figure 8.35.

Text that is too long to fit in a cell spills over to cells on the right only if they are empty. If the cell to the right contains data, the text in the cell to the left is truncated. The entire value continues to exist, but is not completely visible.

Figure 8.35

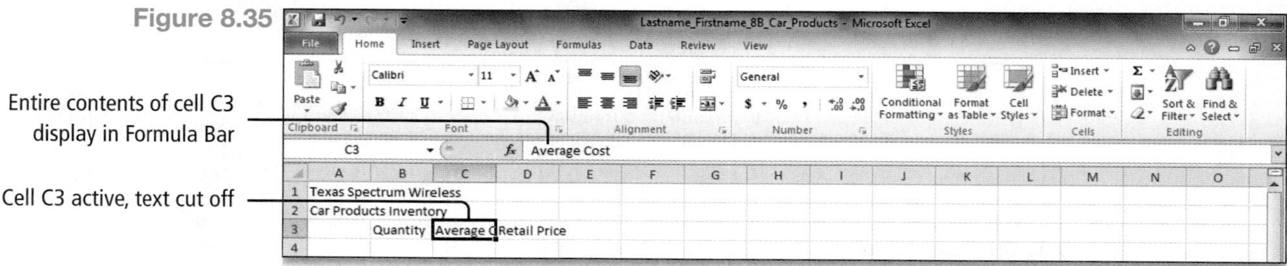

5 Click cell **E3**, type **Total Retail Value** and press Tab. In cell **F3**, type **Percent of Total Retail Value** and press Enter.

6 Click cell **A4**. *Without* correcting the spelling error, type **Antena Signal Booster** Press Enter. In the range **A5:A10**, type the remaining row titles shown below. Then compare your screen with Figure 8.36.

Car Power Port Adapter

Repeater Antenna

SIM Card Reader and Writer

Sticky Dash Pad

Window Mount GPS Holder

Total Retail Value for All Products

Figure 8.36

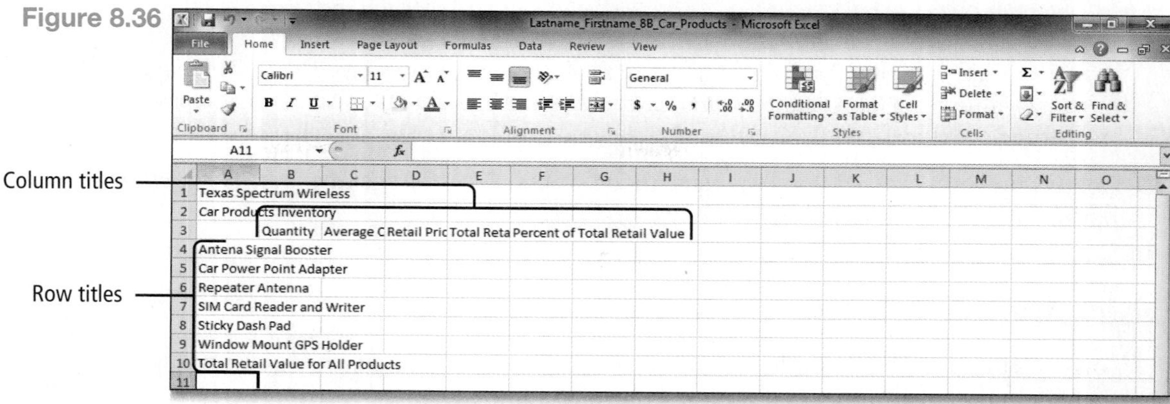

7 In the **column heading area**, point to the right boundary of **column A** to display the [+] pointer, and then drag to the right to widen **column A** to **215** pixels.

8 Select the range **A1:F1**, **Merge & Center** the text, and then from the **Cell Styles** gallery, apply the **Title** style.

9 Select the range **A2:F2**, **Merge & Center** the text, and then from the **Cell Styles** gallery, apply the **Heading 1** style. Press Ctrl + Home to move to the top of your worksheet.

10 With cell **A1** as the active cell, click the **Review tab**, and then in the **Proofing group**, click the **Spelling** button. Compare your screen with Figure 8.37.

Figure 8.37

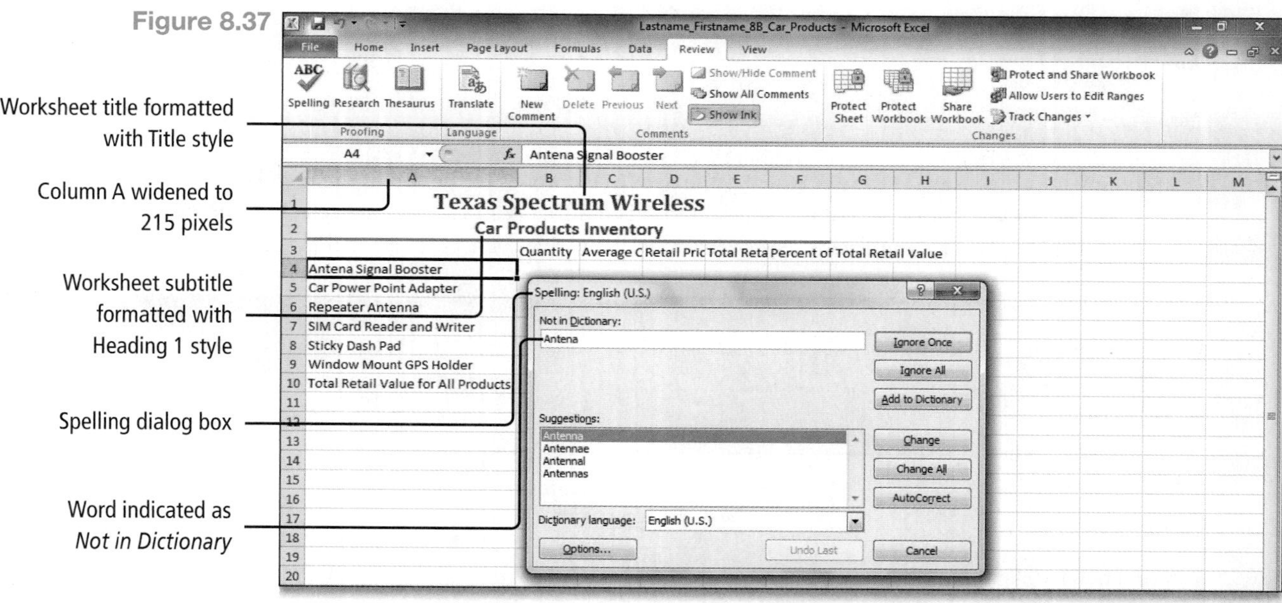

Alert! | Does a Message Display Asking if You Want to Continue Checking at the Beginning of the Sheet?

If a message displays asking if you want to continue checking at the beginning of the sheet, click Yes. The Spelling command begins its checking process with the currently selected cell and moves to the right and down. Thus, if your active cell was a cell after A4, this message may display.

11 In the **Spelling** dialog box, under **Not in Dictionary**, notice the word *Antena*.

The spelling tool does not have this word in its dictionary. Under *Suggestions*, Excel provides a list of suggested spellings.

12 Under **Suggestions**, click **Antenna**, and then click the **Change** button.

Antena, a typing error, is changed to *Antenna*. A message box displays *The spelling check is complete for the entire sheet*—unless you have additional unrecognized words. Because the spelling check begins its checking process starting with the currently selected cell, it is good practice to return to cell A1 before starting the Spelling command.

13 Correct any other errors you may have made. When the message displays, *The spelling check is complete for the entire sheet*, click **OK**. **Save** your workbook.

Objective 8 | Enter Data by Range

You can enter data by first selecting a range of cells. This is a time-saving technique, especially if you use the numeric keypad to enter the numbers.

View the video on the Companion Web Site or in MyITLab

Activity 8.18 | Entering Data by Range

1 Select the range **B4:D9**, type **1126** and then press Enter.

The value displays in cell B4, and cell B5 becomes the active cell.

2 With cell **B5** active in the range, and pressing Enter after each entry, type the following, and then compare your screen with Figure 8.38:

4226
1035
2875
3254
2458

After you enter the last value and press Enter, the active cell moves to the top of the next column within the selected range. Although it is not required to enter data in this manner, you can see that selecting the range before you enter data saves time because it confines the movement of the active cell to the selected range.

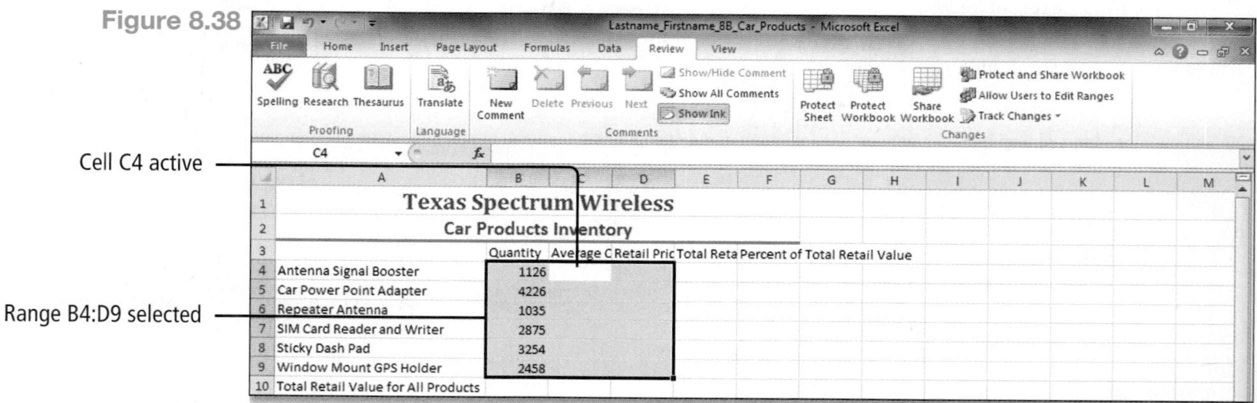

Figure 8.38

3 With the selected range still active, from the following table, beginning in cell **C4** and pressing Enter after each entry, enter the data for the **Average Cost** column and then the **Retail Price** column.

Average Cost	Retail Price
9.75	19.99
9.25	19.49
16.90	39.99
9.55	16.90
4.20	12.99
10.45	20.99

Recall that the default number format for cells is the *General* number format, in which numbers display exactly as you type them and trailing zeros do not display, even if you type them.

4 Click any blank cell. Correct any errors you may have made while entering data, and then click **Save**.

Objective 9 | Construct Formulas for Mathematical Operations

View the video on the Companion Web Site or in MyITLab

Operators are symbols with which you can specify the type of calculation you want to perform in a formula.

Activity 8.19 | Using Arithmetic Operators

1 Click cell **E4**, type **=b4*d4** and notice that the two cells are outlined as part of an active formula. Then press Enter.

The *Total Retail Value* of all *Antenna Signal Booster* items in inventory—*22508.74*—equals the *Quantity* (1,126) times the *Retail Price* (selling price) of 19.99. In Excel, the asterisk (*) indicates multiplication.

2 Take a moment to study the symbols you will use to perform basic mathematical operations in Excel, as shown in the table in Figure 8.39, which are referred to as ***arithmetic operators***.

Symbols Used in Excel for Arithmetic Operators

Operator Symbol	Operation
+	Addition
-	Subtraction (also negation)
*	Multiplication
/	Division
%	Percent
^	Exponentiation

Figure 8.39

3 Click cell **E4**.

You can see that in cells E5:E9, you need a formula similar to the one in E4, but one that refers to the cells in row 5, row 6, and so forth. Recall that you can copy formulas and the cell references will change *relative to* the row number.

4 With cell **E4** selected, position your pointer over the fill handle in the lower right corner of the cell until the + pointer displays. Then, drag down through cell **E9** to copy the formula.

5 Select the range **B4:B9**, and then on the **Home tab**, in the **Number group**, click the **Comma Style** button [,]. Then, in the **Number group**, click the **Decrease Decimal** button [.00→.0] two times to remove the decimal places from these values.

Comma Style formats a number with two decimal places; because these are whole numbers referring to quantities, no decimal places are necessary.

6 Select the range **E4:E9**, and then at the bottom of your screen, in the status bar, notice the displayed values for **Average**, **Count**, and **Sum**—*48118.91833*, *6* and *288713.51*.

When you select numerical data, three calculations display in the status bar by default—Average, Count, and Sum.

7 Click cell **E10**, in the **Editing group**, click the **Sum** button [Σ], notice that Excel selects a range to sum, and then press Enter to display the total *288713.5*.

8 Select the range **C5:E9** and apply the **Comma Style** [,]; notice that Excel widens **column E**.

9 Select the range **C4:E4**, hold down Ctrl, and then click cell **E10**. Release Ctrl and then apply the **Accounting Number Format** [$]. Notice that Excel widens the columns as necessary.

10 Click cell **E10**, and then from the **Cell Styles** gallery, apply the **Total** style. Click any blank cell, and then compare your screen with Figure 8.40.

Figure 8.40

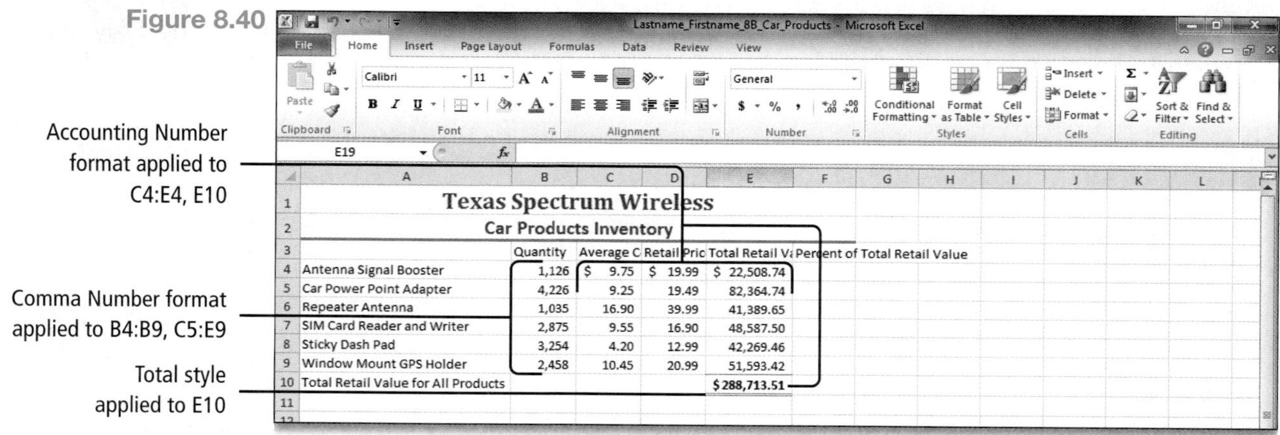

11 **Save** your workbook.

More Knowledge | Multiple Status Bar Calculations

You can display a total of six calculations on the status bar. To add additional calculations—Minimum, Maximum, and Numerical Count (the number of selected cells that contain a number value)—right-click on the status bar, and then click the additional calculations that you want to display.

Activity 8.20 | Copying Formulas Containing Absolute Cell References

In a formula, a relative cell reference refers to a cell by its position *in relation to* the cell that contains the formula. An ***absolute cell reference***, on the other hand, refers to a cell by its *fixed* position in the worksheet, for example, the total in cell E10.

A relative cell reference automatically adjusts when a formula is copied. In some calculations, you do *not* want the cell reference to adjust; rather, you want the cell reference to remain the same when the formula is copied.

1 Click cell **F4**, type = and then click cell **E4**. Type / and then click cell **E10**.

The formula *=E4/E10* indicates that the value in cell E4 will be *divided* by the value in cell E10 to display the percentage by which each product's Total Retail Value makes up the Total Retail Value for All Products.

The result will be a percentage expressed as a decimal.

2 Press Enter. Click cell **F4** and notice that the formula displays in the **Formula Bar**. Then, point to cell **F4** and double-click.

The formula, with the two referenced cells displayed in color and bordered with the same color, displays in the cell. This feature, called the ***range finder***, is useful for verifying formulas because it visually indicates which workbook cells are included in a formula calculation.

3 Press Enter to redisplay the result of the calculation in the cell, and notice that approximately 8% of the total retail value of the inventory is made up of Antenna Signal Boosters.

4 Click cell **F4** again, and then drag the fill handle down through cell **F9**. Compare your screen with Figure 8.41.

Each cell displays an error message—*#DIV/0!* and a green triangle in the upper left corner of each cell indicates that Excel detects an error. Like a grammar checker, Excel uses rules to check for formula errors and flags errors in this manner. Additionally, the Auto Fill Options button displays, from which you can select formatting options for the copied cells.

Figure 8.41

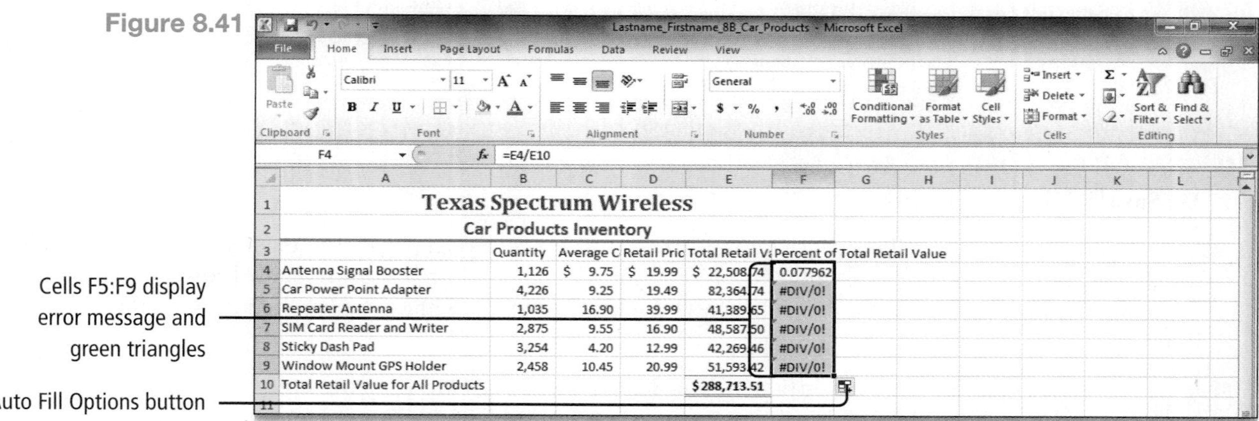

5 Click cell **F5**, and to the left of the cell, point to the **Error Checking** button to display its ScreenTip—*The formula or function used is dividing by zero or empty cells.*

In this manner, Excel suggests the cause of an error.

6 Look at the **Formula Bar** and examine the formula.

The formula is *=E5/E11*. The cell reference to *E5* is correct, but the cell reference following the division operator (/) is *E11*, and E11 is an *empty* cell.

7 Click cell **F6**, point to the **Error Checking** button, and in the **Formula Bar** examine the formula.

Because the cell references are relative, Excel builds the formulas by increasing the row number for each equation. But in this calculation, the divisor must always be the value in cell E10—the Total Retail Value for All Products.

8 Point to cell **F4**, and then double-click to place the insertion point within the cell. Within the cell, use the arrow keys as necessary to position the insertion point to the left of *E10*, and then press F4. Compare your screen with Figure 8.42.

Dollar signs ($) display, which changes the reference to cell E10 to an absolute cell reference. The use of the dollar sign to denote an absolute reference is not related in any way to whether or not the values you are working with are currency values. It is simply the symbol that Excel uses to denote an absolute cell reference.

Figure 8.42

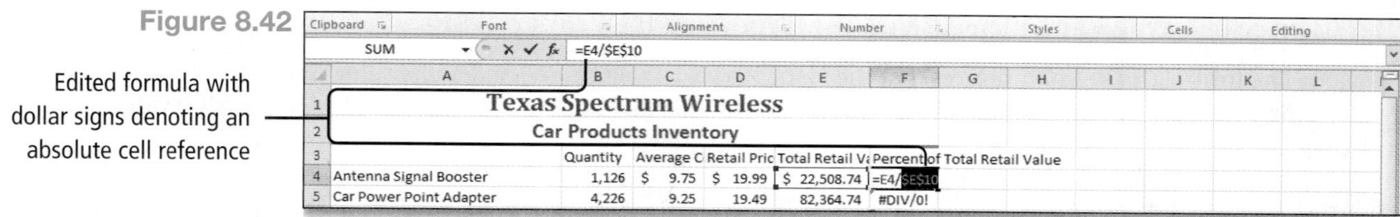

9 On the **Formula Bar**, click the **Enter** button so that **F4** remains the active cell. Then, drag the fill handle to copy the new formula down through cell **F9**. Compare your screen with Figure 8.43.

Figure 8.43

Formula containing absolute cell reference for the first cell in selected range

Percentage of total (E10) calculated for each product

Lastname_Firstname_8B_Car_Products - Microsoft Excel

F4 =E4/$E$10

Texas Spectrum Wireless

Car Products Inventory

	A	B	C	D	E	F
3		Quantity	Average C	Retail Pric	Total Retail Va	Percent of Total Retail Value
4	Antenna Signal Booster	1,126	$ 9.75	$ 19.99	$ 22,508.74	0.077962
5	Car Power Point Adapter	4,226	9.25	19.49	82,364.74	0.285282
6	Repeater Antenna	1,035	16.90	39.99	41,389.65	0.143359
7	SIM Card Reader and Writer	2,875	9.55	16.90	48,587.50	0.16829
8	Sticky Dash Pad	3,254	4.20	12.99	42,269.46	0.146406
9	Window Mount GPS Holder	2,458	10.45	20.99	51,593.42	0.178701
10	Total Retail Value for All Products				$288,713.51	

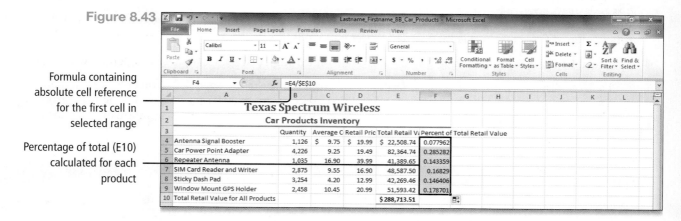

10 Click cell **F5**, examine the formula in the **Formula Bar**, and then examine the formulas for cells **F6**, **F7**, **F8**, and **F9**. **Save** your workbook.

For each formula, the cell reference for the *Total Retail Value* of each product changed relative to its row; however, the value used as the divisor—*Total Retail Value for All Products* in cell F10—remained absolute. Thus, using either relative or absolute cell references, it is easy to duplicate formulas without typing them.

> **More Knowledge | Calculate a Percentage if You Know the Total and the Amount**
>
> Using the equation *amount/total = percentage*, you can calculate the percentage by which a part makes up a total—with the percentage formatted as a decimal. For example, if on a test you score 42 points correctly out of 50, your percentage of correct answers is 42/50 = 0.84 or 84%.

Objective 10 | Edit Values in a Worksheet

Excel performs calculations on numbers; that is why you use Excel. If you make changes to the numbers, Excel automatically *re*-calculates. This is one of the most powerful and valuable features of Excel.

View the video on the Companion Web Site or in MyITLab

Activity 8.21 | Editing Values in a Worksheet

You can edit text and number values directly within a cell or on the Formula Bar.

1 In cell **E10**, notice the column total *$288,713.51*. Then, click cell **B5**, and to change its value type **3546** Watch cell **E5** and press Enter.

Excel formulas *re-calculate* if you change the value in a cell that is referenced in a formula. It is not necessary to delete the old value in a cell; selecting the cell and typing a new value replaces the old value with your new typing.

The *Total Retail Value* of all *Car Power Port Adapters* items recalculates to *69,111.54* and the total in cell E10 recalculates to *$275,460.31*. Additionally, all of the percentages in column F recalculate.

2 Point to cell **D8**, and then double-click to place the insertion point within the cell. Use the arrow keys to move the insertion point to the left or right of *2*, and use either Delete or Backspace to delete *2* and then type **1** so that the new Retail Price is *11.99*.

3 Watch cell **E8** and **E10** as you press Enter, and then notice the recalculation of the formulas in those two cells.

Excel recalculates the value in cell E8 to *39,015.46* and the value in cell E10 to *$272,206.31*. Additionally, all of the percentages in column F recalculate because the *Total Retail Value for All Products* recalculated.

4 Point to cell **A2** so that the pointer is positioned slightly to the right of the word *Inventory*, and then double-click to place the insertion point in the cell. Edit the text to add the word **Valuation** pressing Spacebar as necessary, and then press Enter.

5 Click cell **B3**, and then in the **Formula Bar**, click to place the insertion point after the letter *y*. Press Spacebar one time, type **In Stock** and then on the **Formula Bar**, click the **Enter** button ✓. Click **Save**, and then compare your screen with Figure 8.44.

Recall that if text is too long to fit in the cell and the cell to the right contains data, the text is truncated—cut off—but the entire value still exists as the underlying value.

Figure 8.44

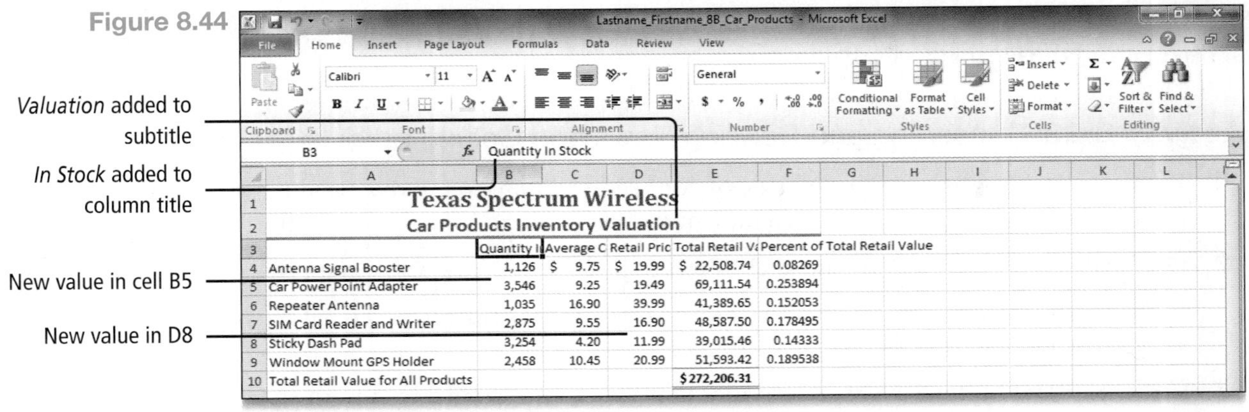

Valuation added to subtitle

In Stock added to column title

New value in cell B5

New value in D8

Activity 8.22 | Formatting Cells with the Percent Style

A percentage is part of a whole expressed in hundredths. For example, 75 cents is the same as 75 percent of one dollar. The Percent Style button formats the selected cell as a percentage rounded to the nearest hundredth.

1 Click cell **F4**, and then in the **Number group**, click the **Percent Style** button %.

Your result is 8%, which is *0.08269* rounded to the nearest hundredth and expressed as a percentage. Percent Style displays the value of a cell as a percentage.

2 Select the range **F4:F9**, right-click over the selection, and then on the Mini toolbar, click the **Percent Style** button %, click the **Increase Decimal** button two times, and then click the **Center** button.

Percent Style may not offer a percentage precise enough to analyze important financial information—adding additional decimal places to a percentage makes data more precise.

3 Click any cell to cancel the selection, **Save** your workbook, and then compare your screen with Figure 8.45.

Figure 8.45

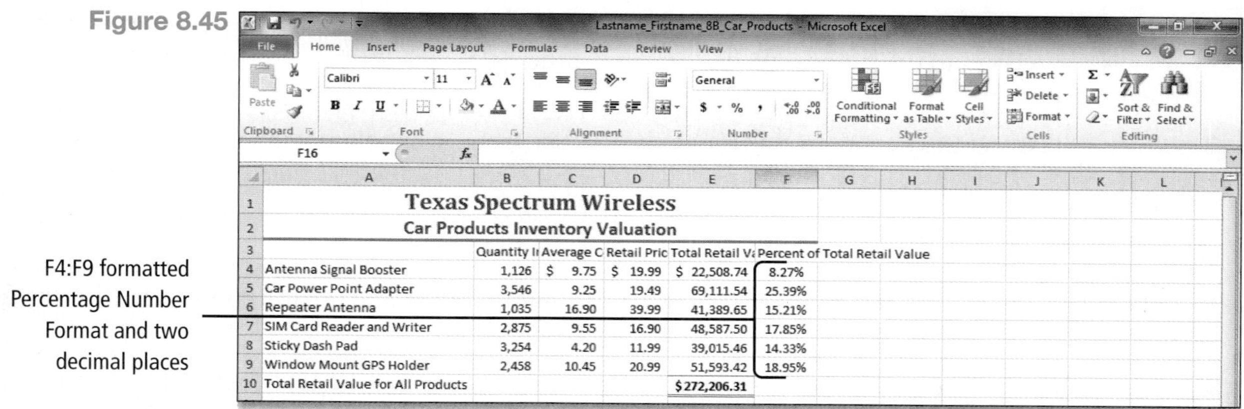

Objective 11 | Format a Worksheet

View the video on the Companion Web Site or in MyITLab

Formatting refers to the process of specifying the appearance of cells and the overall layout of your worksheet. Formatting is accomplished through various commands on the Ribbon, for example, applying Cell Styles, and also from shortcut menus, keyboard shortcuts, and the Format Cells dialog box.

Activity 8.23 | Inserting and Deleting Rows and Columns

1 In the **row heading area** on the left side of your screen, point to the row heading for **row 3** to display the [→] pointer, and then right-click to simultaneously select the row and display a shortcut menu.

2 On the displayed shortcut menu, click **Insert** to insert a new **row 3**.

The rows below the new row 3 move down one row, and the Insert Options button displays. By default, the new row uses the formatting of the row *above*.

3 Click cell **E11**. On the **Formula Bar**, notice that the range changed to sum the new range **E5:E10**. Compare your screen with Figure 8.46.

If you move formulas by inserting additional rows or columns in your worksheet, Excel automatically adjusts the formulas. Excel adjusted all of the formulas in the worksheet that were affected by inserting this new row.

Figure 8.46

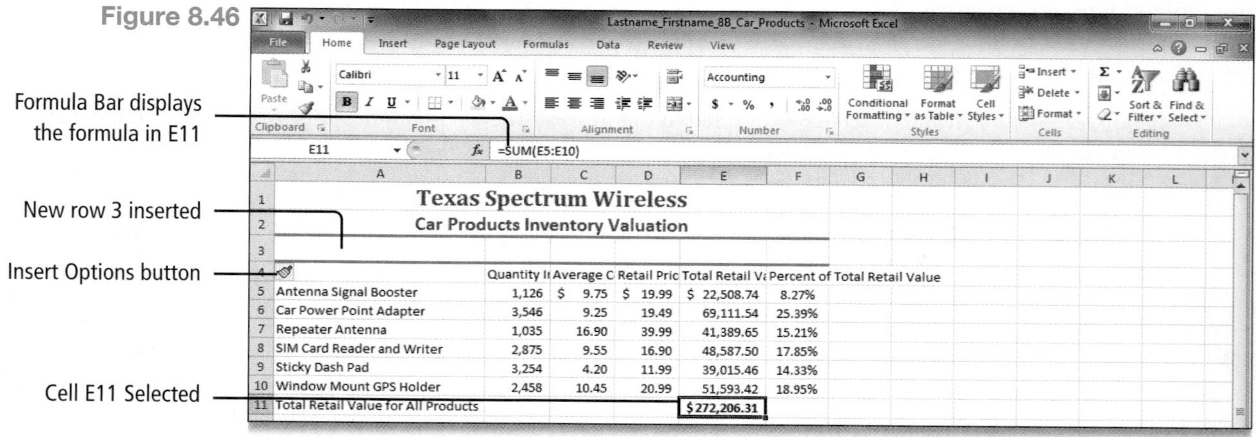

4 Click cell **A3**, type **As of December 31** and then on the **Formula Bar**, click the **Enter** button [✓] to maintain **A3** as the active cell. **Merge & Center** [⊞] the text across the range **A3:F3**, and then apply the **Heading 2** cell style.

5 In the **column heading area**, point to **column B** to display the [↓] pointer, right-click, and then click **Insert**.

By default, the new column uses the formatting of the column to the *left*.

6 Click cell **B4**, type **Warehouse Location** and then press Enter.

7 In cell **B5**, type **Dallas** and then type **Dallas** again in cells **B6** and **B10**. Use AutoComplete to speed your typing by pressing Enter as soon as the AutoComplete suggestion displays. In cells **B7**, **B8**, and **B9**, type **Houston**

8 In the **column heading area**, point to **column D**, right-click, and then click **Delete**.

The remaining columns shift to the left, and Excel adjusts all the formulas in the worksheet accordingly. You can use a similar technique to delete a row in a worksheet.

9 Compare your screen with Figure 8.47, and then **Save** your workbook.

Figure 8.47

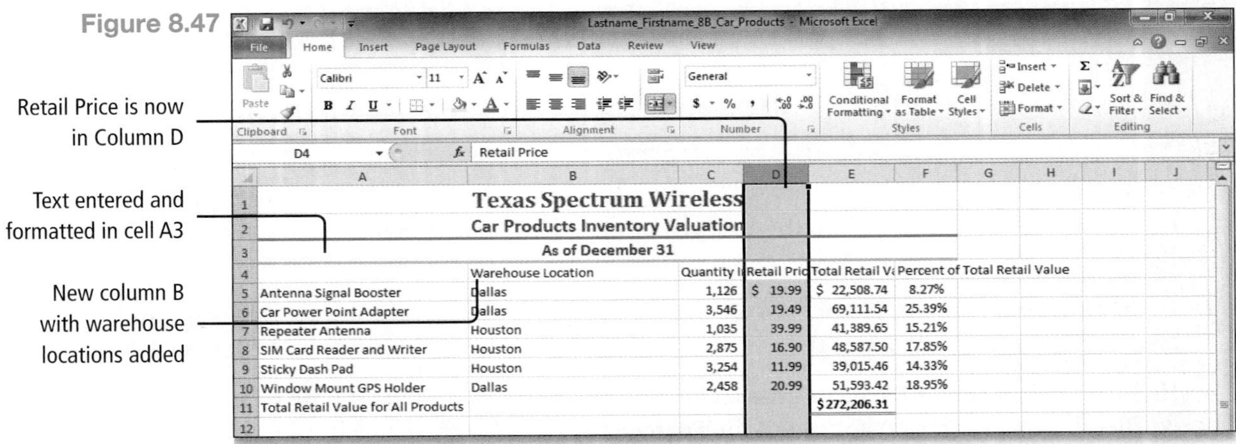

Activity 8.24 | Adjusting Column Widths and Wrapping Text

Use the Wrap Text command to display the contents of a cell on multiple lines.

1 In the **column heading area**, point to the **column B** heading to display the pointer, and then drag to the right to select **columns B:F**.

2 With the columns selected, in the **column heading area**, point to the right boundary of any of the selected columns to display the pointer, and then drag to set the width to **90 pixels**.

Use this technique to format multiple columns or rows simultaneously.

3 Select the range **B4:F4** that comprises the column headings, and then on the **Home tab**, in the **Alignment group**, click the **Wrap Text** button. Notice that the row height adjusts.

4 With the range **B4:F4** still selected, in the **Alignment group**, click the **Center** button and the **Middle Align** button. With the range **B4:F4** still selected, apply the **Heading 4** cell style.

The Middle Align command aligns text so that it is centered between the top and bottom of the cell.

5 Select the range **B5:B10**, right-click, and then on the Mini toolbar click the **Center** button. Click cell **A11**, and then from the **Cell Styles** gallery, under **Themed Cell Styles**, click **40% - Accent1**. Click any blank cell, and then compare your screen with Figure 8.48.

Figure 8.48

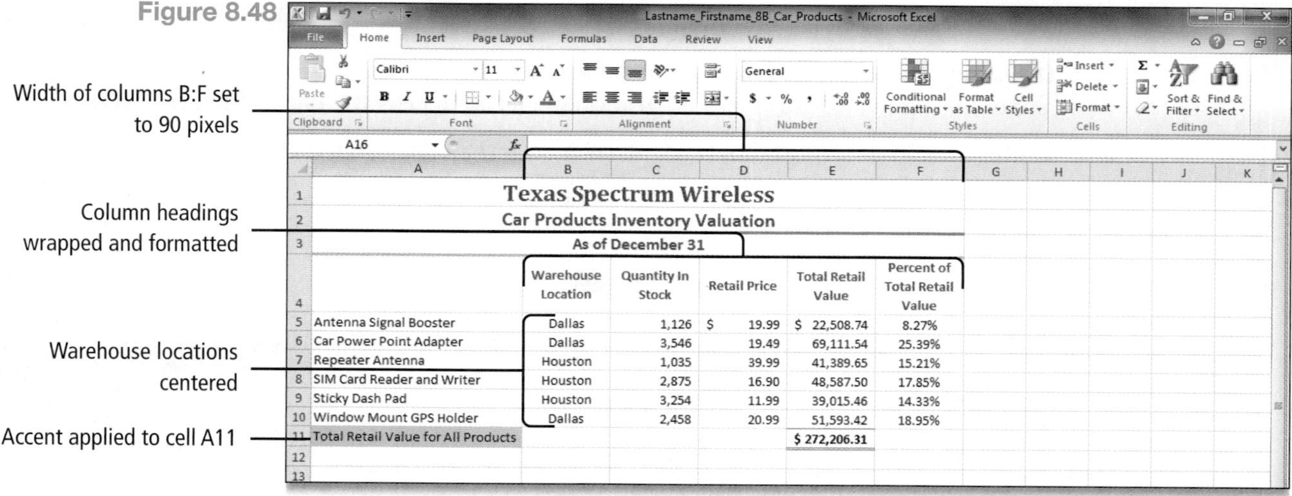

6 Click the **Insert tab**, and then in the **Text group**, click **Header & Footer** to switch to Page Layout view and open the **Header area**.

7 In the **Navigation group**, click the **Go to Footer** button to move to the bottom of the page and open the **Footer area**, and then click just above the word *Footer* to place the insertion point in the **left section** of the **Footer area**.

8 In the **Header & Footer Elements group**, click the **File Name** button to add the name of your file to the footer—*&[File]* displays in the left section of the **Footer area**. Then, click in a cell above the footer to exit the **Footer area** and view your file name.

9 Click the **Page Layout tab**, in the **Page Setup group**, click the **Margins** button, and then at the bottom of the **Margins gallery**, click **Custom Margins**. In the **Page Setup** dialog box, under **Center on page**, select the **Horizontally** check box; click **OK**.

10 In the upper left corner of your screen, click **File** to display **Backstage** view. On the **Info tab**, on the right under the screen thumbnail, click **Properties**, and then click **Show Document Panel**.

11 In the **Author** box, replace the existing text with your firstname and lastname. In the **Subject** box, type your course name and section number. In the **Keywords** box, type **car products, inventory** and then **Close** [X] the **Document Information Panel**.

12 Press Ctrl + F2 to view the **Print Preview**. At the bottom of the **Print Preview**, click the **Next Page** button [▶], and notice that as currently formatted, the worksheet occupies two pages.

13 In the center panel, under **Settings**, click **Portrait Orientation**, and then click **Landscape Orientation**.

You can change the orientation on the Page Layout tab, or here, in the Print Preview. Because it is in the Print Preview that you will often see adjustments that need to be made, commonly used settings display on the Print tab in Backstage view.

14 Note any additional adjustments or corrections that need to be made, and then on the Ribbon, click **Home** to redisplay your worksheet. In the lower right corner of your screen, on the right side of the status bar, click the **Normal** button [▦] to return to the Normal view, and then press Ctrl + Home to return to cell **A1**.

15 Make any necessary corrections. Then, at the bottom of your worksheet, click the **Sheet2 tab** to make it the active worksheet. Hold down Ctrl, and then click the **Sheet3 tab**. Release Ctrl, and then with both sheets selected (tab background is white), point to either of the selected sheet tabs, right-click, and click **Delete** to delete the unused sheets in the workbook.

16 **Save** [💾] your workbook.

17 Print or submit your worksheet electronically as directed by your instructor. If required by your instructor, print or create an electronic version of your worksheet with formulas displayed using the instructions in Activity 8.16 in Project 8A.

18 Close your workbook and close Excel.

End **You have completed Project 8B**

Project 8C Inventory Status Report

Project Activities

In Activities 8.25 through 8.39, you will edit a worksheet for Laura Morales, President, detailing the current inventory of flavor products at the Oakland production facility. Your completed worksheet will look similar to Figure 8.49.

Project Files

For Project 8C, you will need the following file:

e08C_Flavor_Inventory

You will save your workbook as

Lastname_Firstname_8C_Flavor_Inventory

Project Results

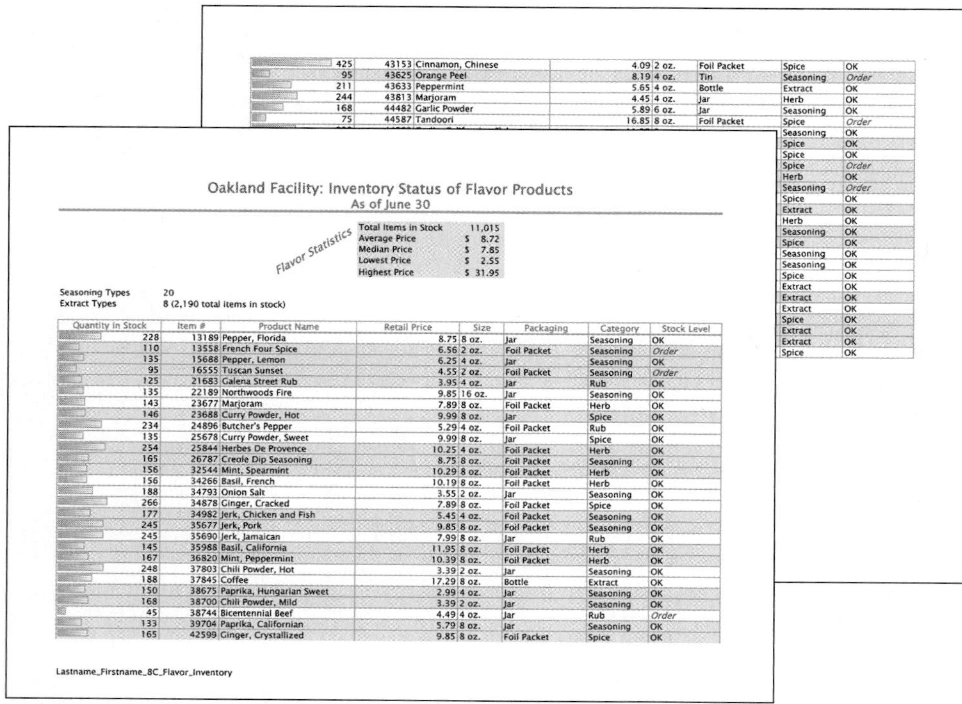

Quantity in Stock	Item #	Product Name	Retail Price	Size	Packaging	Category	Stock Level
425	43153	Cinnamon, Chinese	4.09	2 oz.	Foil Packet	Spice	OK
95	43625	Orange Peel	8.19	4 oz.	Tin	Seasoning	*Order*
211	43633	Peppermint	5.65	4 oz.	Bottle	Extract	OK
244	43813	Marjoram	4.45	4 oz.	Jar	Herb	OK
168	44482	Garlic Powder	5.89	6 oz.	Jar	Seasoning	OK
75	44587	Tandoori	16.85	8 oz.	Foil Packet	Spice	*Order*
						Seasoning	OK
						Spice	OK
						Spice	OK
						Spice	*Order*
						Herb	OK
						Seasoning	*Order*
						Spice	OK
						Extract	OK
						Herb	OK
						Seasoning	OK
						Spice	OK
						Seasoning	OK
						Seasoning	OK
						Spice	OK
						Extract	OK
						Extract	OK
						Extract	OK
						Spice	OK
						Extract	OK
						Extract	OK
						Spice	OK

Oakland Facility: Inventory Status of Flavor Products

As of June 30

Flavor Statistics

Total Items in Stock	11,015
Average Price	$ 8.72
Median Price	$ 7.85
Lowest Price	$ 2.55
Highest Price	$ 31.95

Seasoning Types	20
Extract Types	8 (2,190 total items in stock)

Quantity in Stock	Item #	Product Name	Retail Price	Size	Packaging	Category	Stock Level
228	13189	Pepper, Florida	8.75	8 oz.	Jar	Seasoning	OK
110	13558	French Four Spice	6.56	2 oz.	Foil Packet	Seasoning	*Order*
135	15688	Pepper, Lemon	6.25	4 oz.	Jar	Seasoning	OK
95	16555	Tuscan Sunset	4.55	2 oz.	Foil Packet	Seasoning	*Order*
125	21683	Galena Street Rub	3.95	4 oz.	Jar	Rub	OK
135	22189	Northwoods Fire	9.85	16 oz.	Jar	Seasoning	OK
143	23677	Marjoram	7.89	8 oz.	Foil Packet	Herb	OK
146	23688	Curry Powder, Hot	9.99	8 oz.	Jar	Spice	OK
234	24896	Butcher's Pepper	5.29	4 oz.	Foil Packet	Rub	OK
135	25678	Curry Powder, Sweet	9.99	8 oz.	Jar	Spice	OK
254	25844	Herbes De Provence	10.25	4 oz.	Foil Packet	Herb	OK
165	26787	Creole Dip Seasoning	8.75	8 oz.	Foil Packet	Seasoning	OK
156	32544	Mint, Spearmint	10.29	8 oz.	Foil Packet	Herb	OK
156	34266	Basil, French	10.19	8 oz.	Foil Packet	Herb	OK
188	34793	Onion Salt	3.55	2 oz.	Jar	Seasoning	OK
266	34878	Ginger, Cracked	7.89	8 oz.	Foil Packet	Spice	OK
177	34982	Jerk, Chicken and Fish	5.45	4 oz.	Foil Packet	Seasoning	OK
245	35677	Jerk, Pork	9.85	8 oz.	Foil Packet	Seasoning	OK
245	35690	Jerk, Jamaican	7.99	8 oz.	Jar	Rub	OK
145	35988	Basil, California	11.95	8 oz.	Foil Packet	Herb	OK
167	36820	Mint, Peppermint	10.39	8 oz.	Foil Packet	Herb	OK
248	37803	Chili Powder, Hot	3.39	2 oz.	Jar	Seasoning	OK
188	37845	Coffee	17.29	8 oz.	Bottle	Extract	OK
150	38675	Paprika, Hungarian Sweet	2.99	4 oz.	Jar	Seasoning	OK
168	38700	Chili Powder, Mild	3.39	2 oz.	Jar	Seasoning	OK
45	38744	Bicentennial Beef	4.49	4 oz.	Jar	Rub	*Order*
133	39704	Paprika, Californian	5.79	8 oz.	Jar	Seasoning	OK
165	42599	Ginger, Crystallized	9.85	8 oz.	Foil Packet	Spice	OK

Lastname_Firstname_8C_Flavor_Inventory

Figure 8.49
Project 8C Flavor Inventory

Objective 12 | Use the SUM, AVERAGE, MEDIAN, MIN, and MAX Functions

View the video on the Companion Web Site or in MyITLab

A ***function*** is a predefined formula—a formula that Excel has already built for you—that performs calculations by using specific values in a particular order or structure. ***Statistical functions***, which include the AVERAGE, MEDIAN, MIN, and MAX functions, are useful to analyze a group of measurements.

Activity 8.25 | Using the SUM and AVERAGE Functions

In this activity, you will use the SUM and AVERAGE functions to gather information about the product inventory.

1 **Start** Excel. From **Backstage** view, display the **Open** dialog box, and then from the student files that accompany this textbook, locate and open **e08C_Flavor_Inventory**. Click the **File tab** to redisplay **Backstage** view, and then click **Save As**. In the **Save As** dialog box, navigate to your **All In One Chapter 8** folder, and save the workbook as **Lastname_Firstname_8C_Flavor_Inventory**

2 Scroll down. Notice that the worksheet contains data related to types of flavor products in inventory, including information about the *Quantity in Stock, Item #, Product Name, Retail Price, Size, Packaging,* and *Category.*

3 Leave row 3 blank, and then in cell **A4**, type **Total Items in Stock** In cell **A5**, type **Average Price** In cell **A6**, type **Median Price**

4 Click cell **B4**. Click the **Formulas tab**, and then in the **Function Library group**, click the **AutoSum** button. Compare your screen with Figure 8.50.

The *SUM function* that you have used is a predefined formula that adds all the numbers in a selected range of cells. Because it is frequently used, there are several ways to insert the function.

Figure 8.50

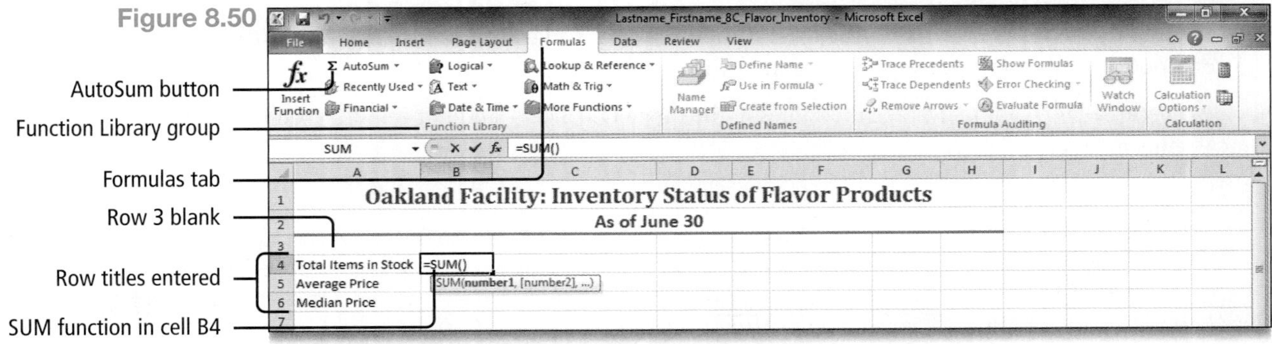

5 With the insertion point blinking in the function, select the range A11:A65, dragging down as necessary, and then press Enter. Scroll up to view the top of your worksheet, and notice your result in cell **B4**, *11015*.

6 Click cell **B4** and look at the **Formula Bar**: Compare your screen with Figure 8.51.

SUM is the name of the function. The values in parentheses are the ***arguments***—the values that an Excel function uses to perform calculations or operations. In this instance, the argument consists of the values in the range A11:A65.

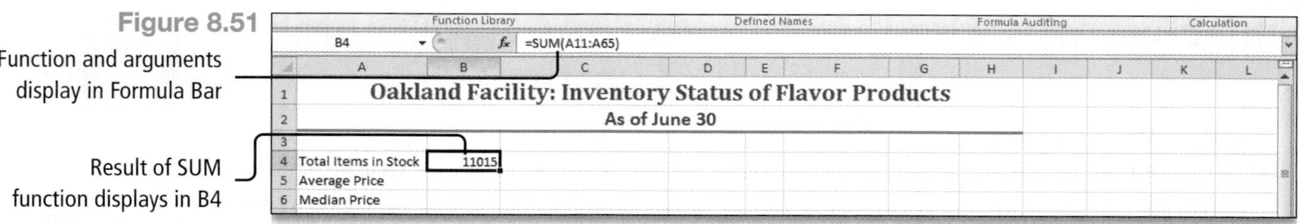

Figure 8.51

7 Click cell **B5**. In the **Function Library group**, click the **More Functions** button, point to **Statistical**, point to **AVERAGE**, and notice the ScreenTip. Compare your screen with Figure 8.52.

The ScreenTip describes how the AVERAGE function will compute the calculation.

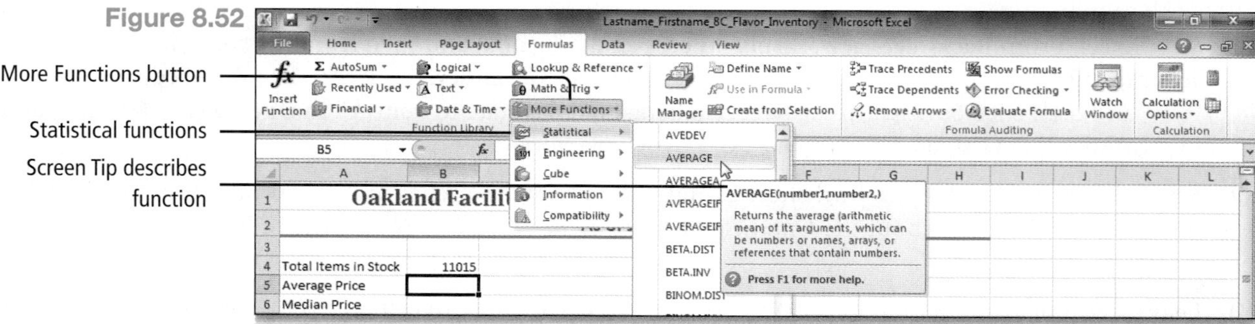

Figure 8.52

8 Click **AVERAGE**, and then if necessary, drag the title bar of the **Function Arguments** dialog box down and to the right so you can view the **Formula Bar** and cell **B5**.

The ***AVERAGE function*** adds a group of values, and then divides the result by the number of values in the group.

In the cell, the Formula Bar, and the dialog box, Excel proposes to average the value in cell B4. Recall that Excel functions will propose a range if data is above or to the left of a selected cell.

9 In the **Function Arguments** dialog box, notice that *B4* is highlighted. Press Delete to delete the existing text, type **d11:d65** and then compare your screen with Figure 8.53.

Because you want to average the values in the range D11:D65—and not cell B4—you must edit the proposed range in this manner.

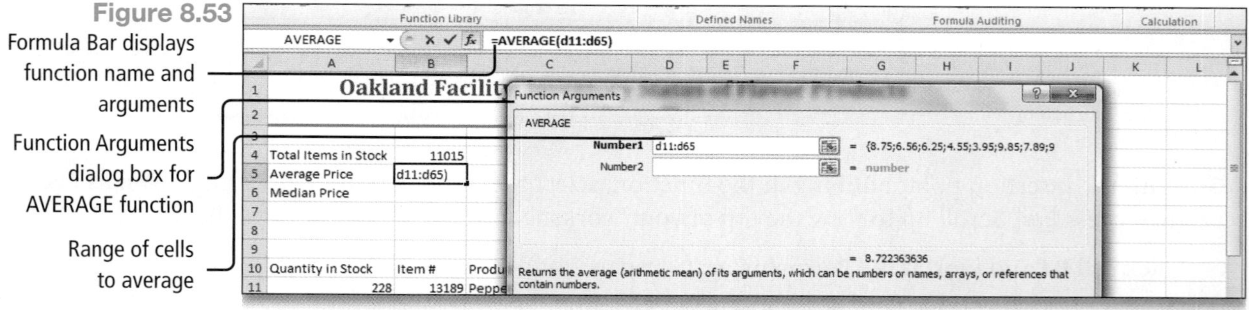

Figure 8.53

10 In the **Function Arguments** dialog box, click **OK**, and then **Save**.

The result indicates that the average Retail Price of all products is *8.72*.

Activity 8.26 | Using the MEDIAN Function

The ***MEDIAN function*** is a statistical function that describes a group of data. The MEDIAN function finds the middle value that has as many values above it in the group as are below it. It differs from AVERAGE in that the result is not affected as much by a single value that is greatly different from the others.

1. Click cell **B6**. In the **Function Library group**, click the **More Functions** button, display the list of **Statistical** functions, scroll down as necessary, and then click **MEDIAN**.
2. In the **Function Arguments** dialog box, to the right of the **Number 1** box, click the **Collapse Dialog** button.

   The dialog box collapses to a small size with space only for the first argument so you can see more of your data.
3. Select the range **D11:D65**, and then compare your screen with Figure 8.54.

   When indicating which cells you want to use in the function's calculation—known as *defining the arguments*—you can either select the values with your mouse or type the range of values, whichever you prefer.

Figure 8.54

Formula Bar displays function and arguments

Collapsed dialog box displays selected range

Selected range surrounded by moving border

MEDIAN | =MEDIAN(D11:D65)

Function Arguments: D11:D65

	A	B	C	D	E	F	G
49	265	46532	Oregano	10.19	8 oz.	Jar	Herb
50	73	49652	Rojo T[illegible]	[illegible]	[illegible]	[illegible]	[illegible]
51	185	52164	Cloves [illegible]	[illegible]	[illegible]	[illegible]	[illegible]
52	165	53634	Vanilla, [illegible]	[illegible]	[illegible]	[illegible]	[illegible]
53	325	54635	Dill Weed	2.65	4 oz.	Paper Envelope	Herb
54	195	55255	Sea Salt, Pacific	2.55	8 oz.	Tin	Seasoning
55	312	56853	Peppercorns, Indian	4.59	2 oz.	Jar	Spice
56	152	64525	Onion Powder	4.85	4 oz.	Jar	Seasoning
57	215	78655	Garlic Salt	2.58	6 oz.	Jar	Seasoning
58	540	85655	Peppercorns, Red	3.69	2 oz.	Tin	Spice
59	225	92258	Vanilla	15.95	4 oz.	Bottle	Extract
60	368	93157	Almond	7.33	4 oz.	Bottle	Extract
61	285	93553	Lemon	24.90	6 oz.	Bottle	Extract
62	126	94236	Cumin	3.55	4 oz.	Paper Envelope	Spice
63	423	96854	Vanilla	31.95	6 oz.	Bottle	Extract
64	325	98225	Orange	24.19	6 oz.	Bottle	Extract
65	211	98655	Cloves, Ground	4.55	6 oz.	Jar	Spice

4. At the right end of the collapsed dialog box, click the **Expand Dialog** button to expand the dialog box to its original size, and then click **OK** to display *7.85*.

   In the range of prices, 7.85 is the middle value. Half of all flavor products are priced *above* 7.85 and half are priced *below* 7.85.
5. Scroll up to view **row 1**. Select the range **B5:B6** and right-click over the selection. On the Mini toolbar, click the **Accounting Number Format** button.
6. Right-click cell **B4**, and then on the Mini toolbar, click the **Comma Style** button one time and the **Decrease Decimal** button two times. Click **Save** and compare your screen with Figure 8.55.

Figure 8.55

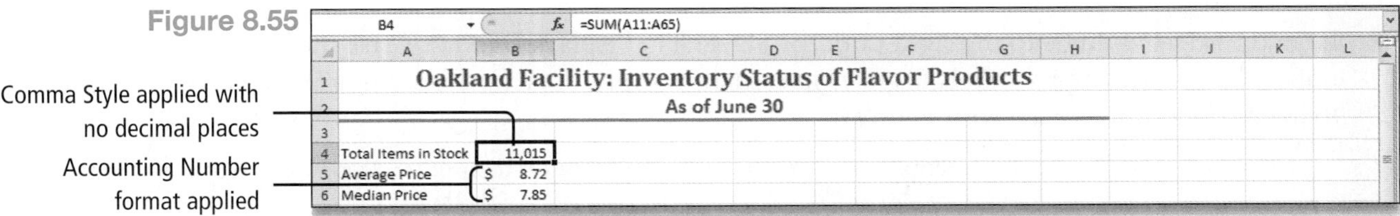

Activity 8.27 | Using the MIN and MAX Functions

The statistical ***MIN function*** determines the smallest value in a selected range of values. The statistical ***MAX function*** determines the largest value in a selected range of values.

1. In cell **A7**, type **Lowest Price** and then in cell **A8**, type **Highest Price**

2 Click cell **B7**. On the **Formulas tab**, in the **Function Library group**, click the **More Functions** button, display the list of **Statistical** functions, scroll as necessary, and then click **MIN**.

3 At the right end of the **Number1** box, click the **Collapse Dialog** button, select the range **D11:D65**, and then click the **Expand Dialog** button. Click **OK**.

The lowest Retail Price is *2.55*.

4 Click cell **B8**, and then by using a similar technique, insert the **MAX** function to determine the highest **Retail Price**—*31.95*.

5 Select the range **B7:B8** and apply the **Accounting Number Format** $, click **Save**, and then compare your screen with Figure 8.56.

Figure 8.56

MIN function calculates lowest price

MAX function calculates highest price

B7 =MIN(D11:D65)

	A	B
4	Total Items in Stock	11,015
5	Average Price	$ 8.72
6	Median Price	$ 7.85
7	Lowest Price	$ 2.55
8	Highest Price	$ 31.95

Objective 13 | Move Data, Resolve Error Messages, and Rotate Text

View the video on the Companion Web Site or in MyITLab

When you move a formula, the cell references within the formula do not change, no matter what type of cell reference you use. If you move cells into a column that is not wide enough to display number values, Excel will display a message so that you can adjust as necessary. You can reposition data within a cell at an angle by rotating the text.

Activity 8.28 | Moving Data and Resolving a # # # # # Error Message

1 Select the range **A4:B8**. Point to the right edge of the selected range to display the pointer, and then compare your screen with Figure 8.57.

Figure 8.57

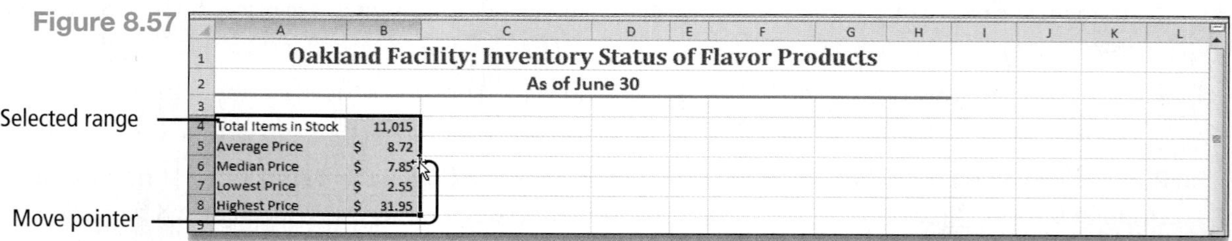

2 Drag the selected range to the right until the ScreenTip displays *D4:E8*, release the mouse button, and then notice that a series of # symbols displays in **column E**. Point to any of the cells that display # symbols, and then compare your screen with Figure 8.58.

Using this technique, cell contents can be moved from one location to another; this is referred to as ***drag and drop***.

If a cell width is too narrow to display the entire number, Excel displays the ##### error, because displaying only a portion of a number would be misleading. The underlying values remain unchanged and are displayed in the Formula Bar for the selected cell. An underlying value also displays in the ScreenTip if you point to a cell containing # symbols.

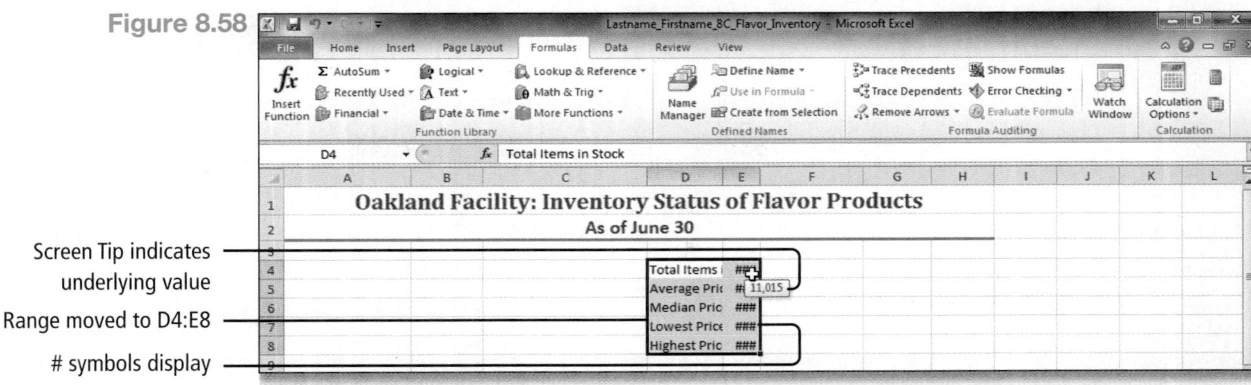

Figure 8.58

3 Select **column E** and widen it to **50** pixels, and notice that two cells are still not wide enough to display the cell contents.

4 In the **column heading area**, point to the right boundary of **column E** to display the pointer. Double-click to AutoFit the column to accommodate the widest entry.

5 Using the same technique, AutoFit **column D** to accommodate the widest text entry.

6 Select the range **D4:E8**. On the **Home tab**, in the **Styles group**, display the **Cell Styles** gallery. Under **Themed Cell Styles**, click **20%-Accent1**. Click **Save**.

Activity 8.29 | Rotating Text

Rotated text is useful to draw attention to data on your worksheet.

1 In cell **C6**, type **Flavor Statistics** Select the range **C4:C8**, right-click over the selection, and then on the shortcut menu, click **Format Cells**. In the **Format Cells** dialog box, click the **Alignment tab**. Under **Text control**, select the **Merge cells** check box.

2 In the upper right portion of the dialog box, under **Orientation**, point to the **red diamond**, and then drag the diamond upward until the **Degrees** box indicates **30**. Compare your screen with Figure 8.59.

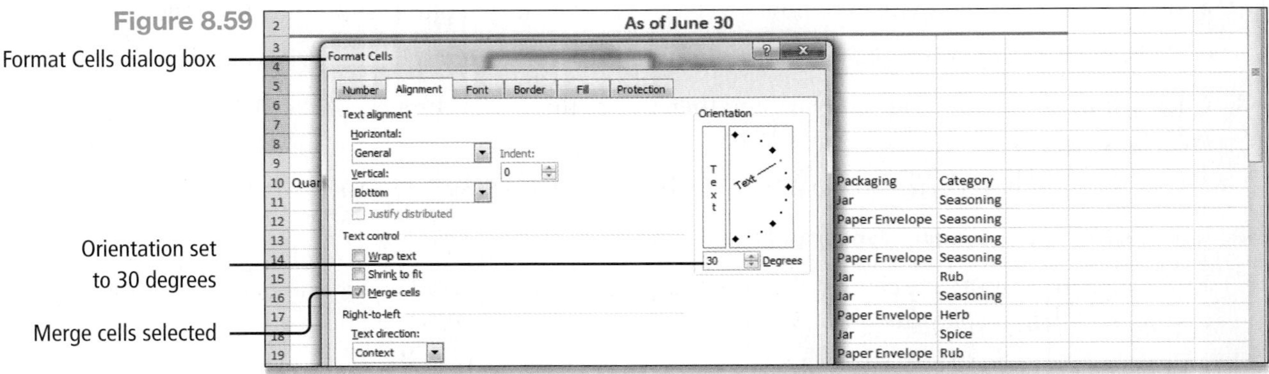

Figure 8.59

3 In the lower right corner of the **Format Cells** dialog box, click **OK**.

4 With the merged cell still selected, on the **Home tab**, in the **Font group**, change the **Font Size** to **14**, and then apply **Bold** and **Italic**. Click the **Font Color arrow**, and then in the fourth column, click the first color—**Dark Blue, Text 2**.

5 In the **Alignment group**, apply **Align Text Right**. Click cell **A1**, **Save** your workbook, and then compare your screen with Figure 8.60.

Figure 8.60

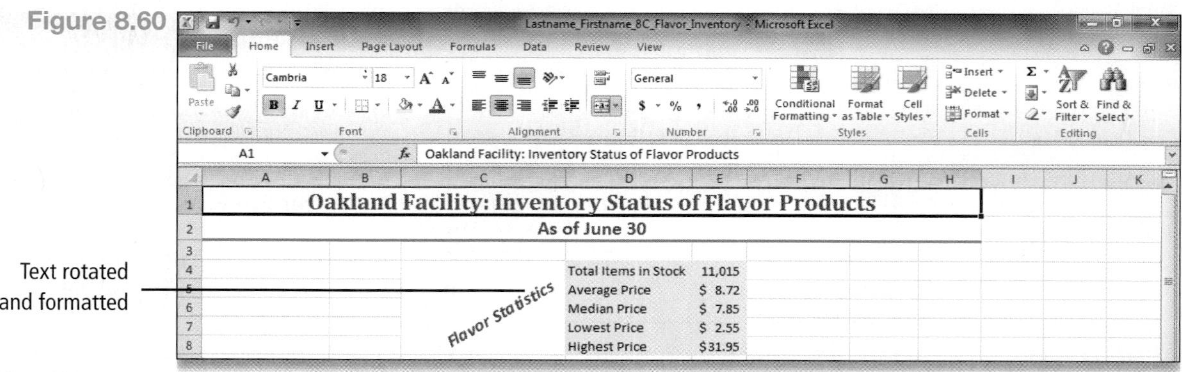

Objective 14 | Use COUNTIF and IF Functions and Apply Conditional Formatting

View the video on the Companion Web Site or in MyITLab

Recall that statistical functions analyze a group of measurements. Another group of Excel functions, referred to as ***logical functions***, test for specific conditions. Logical functions typically use conditional tests to determine whether specified conditions—called ***criteria***—are true or false.

Activity 8.30 | Using the COUNTIF Function

The ***COUNTIF function*** is a statistical function that counts the number of cells within a range that meet the given condition—the criteria that you provide. The COUNTIF function has two arguments—the range of cells to check and the criteria. In this activity, you will use the COUNTIF function to determine the number of *seasoning* products currently available in inventory.

1. In the **row heading area**, point to **row 9** and right-click to select the row and display the shortcut menu. Click **Insert**, and then press F4 two times to repeat the last action and thus insert three blank rows.

   F4 is useful to repeat commands in Microsoft Office programs. Most commands can be repeated in this manner.

2. From the **row heading area**, select rows **9:11**. On the **Home tab**, in the **Editing group**, click the **Clear** button, and then click **Clear Formats** to remove the blue accent color in columns D and E from the new rows.

   When you insert rows or columns, formatting from adjacent rows or columns repeats in the new cells.

3. Click cell **E4**, look at the **Formula Bar**, and then notice that the arguments of the **SUM** function adjusted and refer to the appropriate cells in rows 14:68.

   Excel adjusts the cell references to *A14:A68* after you insert the three new rows.

4. In cell **A10**, type **Seasoning Types:** and then press Tab.

5. With cell **B10** as the active cell, on the **Formulas tab**, in the **Function Library group**, click the **More Functions** button, and then display the list of **Statistical** functions. Click **COUNTIF**.

   Recall that the COUNTIF function counts the number of cells within a range that meet the given condition.

6. In the **Range** box, click the **Collapse Dialog** button, select the range **G14:G68**, and then at the right end of the collapsed dialog box, click the **Expand Dialog** button. Click in the **Criteria** box, type **Seasoning** and then compare your screen with Figure 8.61.

Figure 8.61

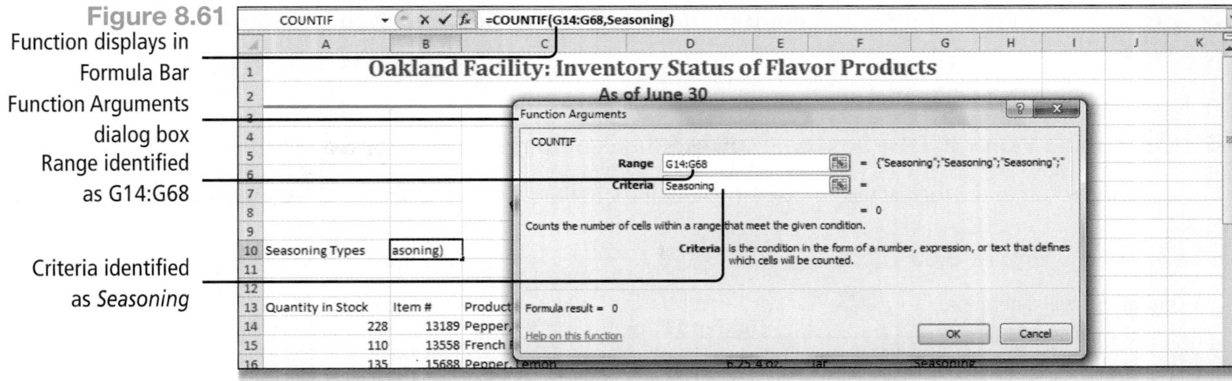

7 In the lower right corner of the **Function Arguments** dialog box, click **OK**.

There are *20* different *Seasoning* products available to feature on the TV show.

8 On the **Home tab**, in the **Alignment group**, click **Align Text Left** to place the result closer to the row title. **Save** your workbook.

Activity 8.31 | Using the IF Function

A ***logical test*** is any value or expression that you can evaluate as being true or false. The ***IF function*** uses a logical test to check whether a condition is met, and then returns one value if true, and another value if false. For example, *C14=228* is an expression that can be evaluated as true or false. If the value in cell C14 is equal to 228, the expression is true. If the value in cell C14 is not 228, the expression is false. In this activity, you will use the IF function to determine the inventory levels and determine if more products should be ordered.

1 Click cell **H13**, type **Stock Level** and then press Enter.

2 In cell **H14**, on the **Formulas tab**, in the **Function Library group**, click the **Logical** button, and then in the list, click **IF**. Drag the title bar of the **Function Arguments** dialog box up or down to view **row 14** on your screen.

3 With the insertion point in the **Logical_test** box, click cell **A14**, and then type **<125**

This logical test will look at the value in cell A14, which is *228*, and then determine if the number is less than 125. The expression *<125* includes the < ***comparison operator***, which means *less than*. Comparison operators compare values.

4 Examine the table in Figure 8.62 for a list of comparison operator symbols and their definitions.

Comparison Operators

Comparison Operator	Symbol Definition
=	Equal to
>	Greater than
<	Less than
>=	Greater than or equal to
<=	Less than or equal to
<>	Not equal to

Figure 8.62

5 Press Tab to move the insertion point to the **Value_if_true** box, and then type **Order**

If the result of the logical test is true—the Quantity in Stock is less than 125—cell H14 will display the text *Order* indicating that additional product must be ordered.

6 Click in the **Value_if_false** box, type **OK** and then compare your dialog box with Figure 8.63.

If the result of the logical test is false—the Quantity in Stock is *not* less than 125—then Excel will display *OK* in the cell.

Figure 8.63

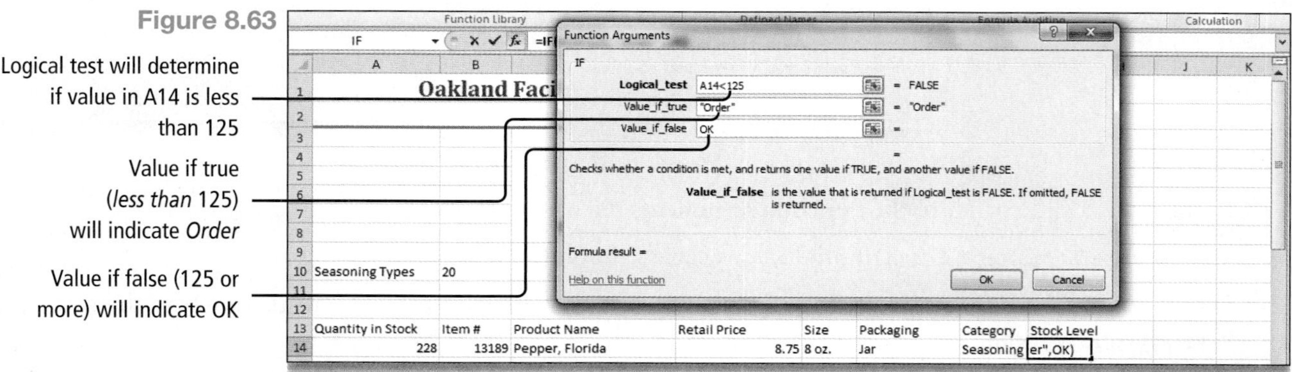

7 Click **OK** to display the result *OK* in cell **H14**.

8 Using the fill handle, copy the function in cell **H14** down through cell **H68**. Then scroll as necessary to view cell **A18**, which contains *125*. Look at cell **H18** and notice that the **Stock Level** is indicated as *OK*. **Save** your workbook.

The comparison operator indicated <125 (less than 125) and thus a value of *exactly* 125 is indicated as OK.

Activity 8.32 | Applying Conditional Formatting by Using Highlight Cells Rules and Data Bars

A ***conditional format*** changes the appearance of a cell based on a condition—a criteria. If the condition is true, the cell is formatted based on that condition; if the condition is false, the cell is not formatted. In this activity, you will use conditional formatting as another way to draw attention to the Stock Level of products.

1 Be sure the range **H14:H68** is selected. On the **Home tab**, in the **Styles group**, click the **Conditional Formatting** button. In the list, point to **Highlight Cells Rules**, and then click **Text that Contains**.

2 In the **Text That Contains** dialog box, with the insertion point blinking in the first box, type **Order** and notice that in the selected range, the text *Order* displays with the default format—Light Red Fill with Dark Red Text.

3 In the second box, click the arrow, and then in the list, click Custom Format.

In the Format Cells dialog box, you can select any combination of formats to apply to the cell if the condition is true, in this example, if it contains the text *Order*.

4 On the **Font tab**, under **Font style**, click **Bold Italic**. Click the **Color arrow**, and then under **Theme Colors**, in the sixth column, click the first color—**Red, Accent 2**. Click **OK**. Compare your screen with Figure 8.64.

In the range, if the cell meets the condition of containing *Order*, the font color will change to Bold Italic, Red, Accent 2.

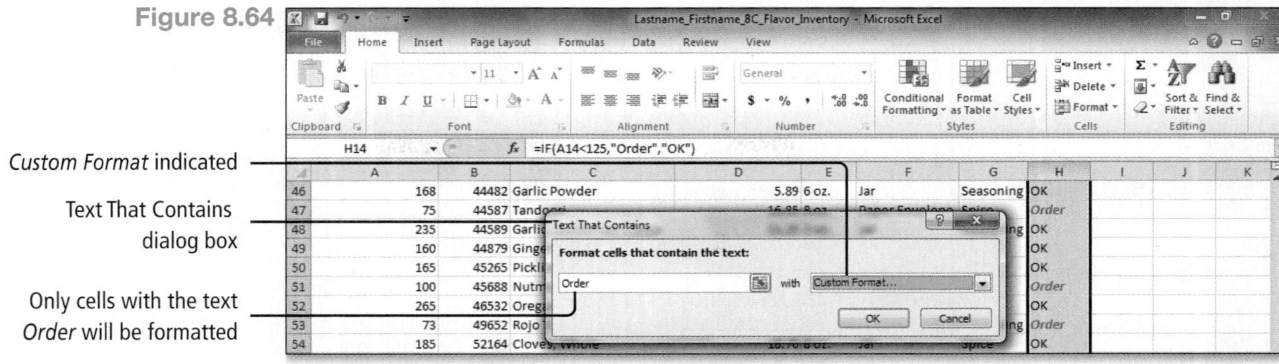

Figure 8.64

5 In the **Text That Contains** dialog box, click **OK**.

6 Select the range **A14:A68**. In the **Styles group**, click the **Conditional Formatting** button. Point to **Data Bars**, and then under **Gradient Fill**, click **Orange Data Bar**. Click anywhere to cancel the selection; click [Save]. Compare your screen with Figure 8.65.

A ***data bar*** provides a visual cue to the reader about the value of a cell relative to other cells. The length of the data bar represents the value in the cell. A longer bar represents a higher value and a shorter bar represents a lower value. Data bars are useful for identifying higher and lower numbers quickly within a large group of data, such as very high or very low levels of inventory.

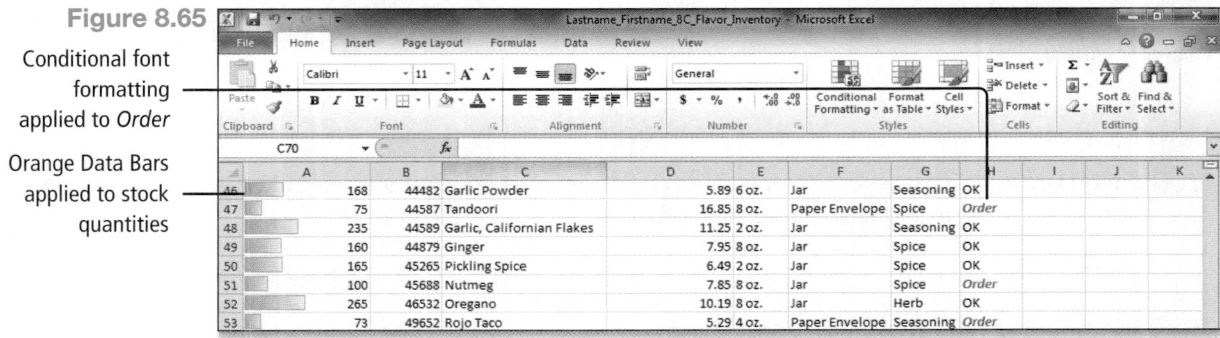

Figure 8.65

Activity 8.33 | Using Find and Replace

The ***Find and Replace*** feature searches the cells in a worksheet—or in a selected range—for matches, and then replaces each match with a replacement value of your choice. In this activity, you will replace all occurrences of Paper Envelope with Foil Packet.

1 Select the range **F14:F68**.

Restrict the find and replace operation to a specific range in this manner, especially if there is a possibility that the name occurs elsewhere.

2 On the **Home tab**, in the **Editing group**, click the **Find & Select** button, and then click **Replace**.

3 Type **Paper Envelope** to fill in the **Find what** box. In the **Replace with** box, type **Foil Packet** and then compare your screen with Figure 8.66.

Figure 8.66

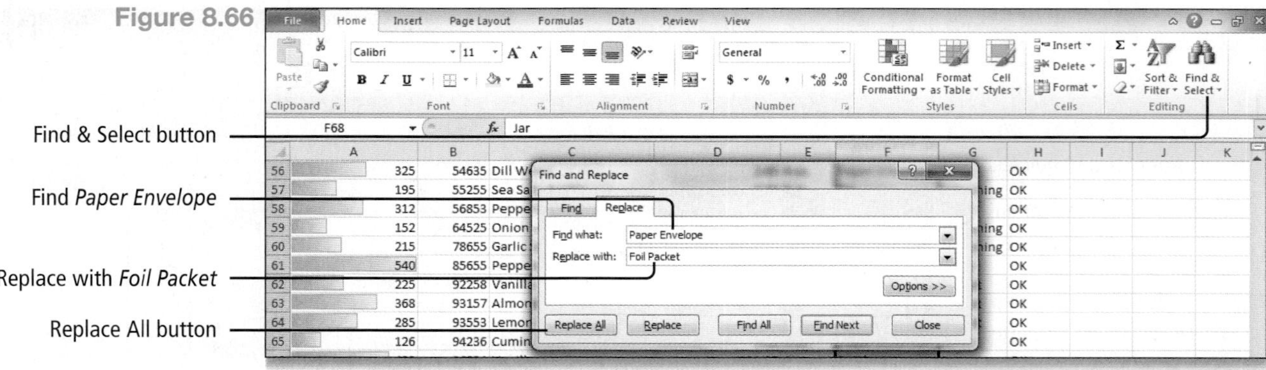

4 Click the **Replace All** button. In the message box, notice that 19 replacements were made, and then click **OK**. In the lower right corner of the **Find and Replace** dialog box, click the **Close** button. Click **Save** [Save icon].

Objective 15 | Use Date & Time Functions and Freeze Panes

View the video on the Companion Web Site or in MyITLab

Excel can obtain the date and time from your computer's calendar and clock and display this information on your worksheet. By freezing or splitting panes, you can view two areas of a worksheet and lock rows and columns in one area. When you freeze panes, you select the specific rows or columns that you want to remain visible when scrolling in your worksheet.

Activity 8.34 | Using the NOW Function to Display a System Date

The ***NOW function*** retrieves the date and time from your computer's calendar and clock and inserts the information into the selected cell. The result is formatted as a date and time.

1 Scroll down as necessary, and then click cell **A70**. Type **Edited by Frank Barnes** and then press Enter.

2 With cell **A71** as the active cell, on the **Formulas tab**, in the **Function Library group**, click the **Date & Time** button. In the list of functions, click **NOW**. Compare your screen with Figure 8.67.

Figure 8.67

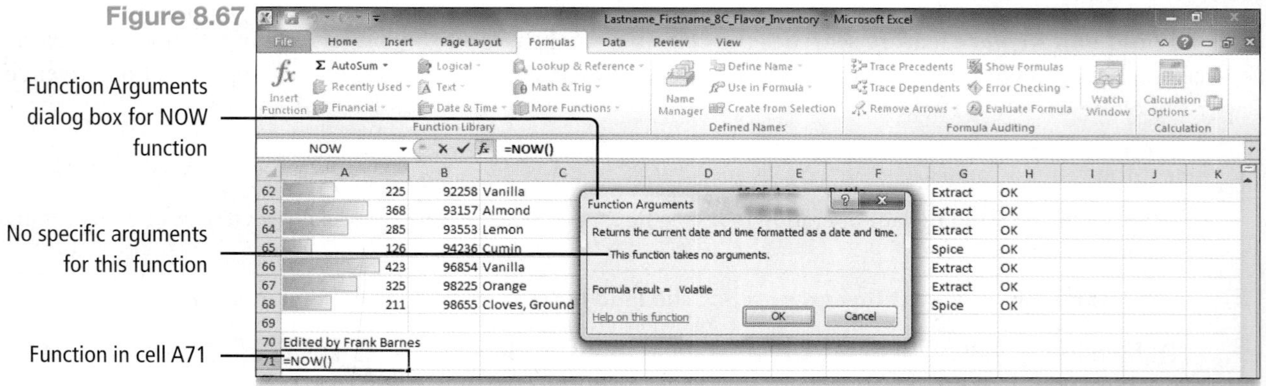

3 Read the description in the **Function Arguments** dialog box, and notice that this result is *Volatile*.

The Function Arguments dialog box displays a message indicating that this function does not require an argument. It also states that this function is ***volatile***, meaning the date and time will not remain as entered, but rather the date and time will automatically update each time you open this workbook.

4 In the **Function Arguments** dialog box, click **OK** to close the dialog box to display the current date and time in cell **A71**. **Save** your workbook.

> **More Knowledge | NOW Function Recalculates Each Time a Workbook Opens**
>
> The NOW function updates each time the workbook is opened. With the workbook open, you can force the NOW function to update by pressing 9, for example, to update the time.

Activity 8.35 | Freezing and Unfreezing Panes

In a large worksheet, if you scroll down more than 25 rows or scroll beyond column O (the exact row number and column letter varies, depending on your screen resolution), you will no longer see the top rows or first column of your worksheet where identifying information about the data is usually placed. The ***Freeze Panes*** command enables you to select one or more rows or columns and then freeze (lock) them into place. The locked rows and columns become separate panes. A ***pane*** is a portion of a worksheet window bounded by and separated from other portions by vertical or horizontal bars.

1 Press Ctrl + Home to make cell **A1** the active cell. Scroll down until **row 40** displays at the top of your Excel window, and notice that all of the identifying information in the column titles is out of view.

2 Press Ctrl + Home again, and then from the **row heading** area, select **row 14**. Click the **View tab**, and then in the **Window group**, click the **Freeze Panes** button. In the list, click **Freeze Panes**. Click any cell to deselect the row, and then notice that a line displays along the upper border of **row 14**.

By selecting row 14, the rows above—rows 1 - 13—are frozen in place and will not move as you scroll down.

3 Watch the row numbers below **row 13**, and then begin to scroll down to bring **row 40** into view again. Notice that rows 1:13 are frozen in place. Compare your screen with Figure 8.68.

The remaining rows of data continue to scroll. Use this feature when you have long or wide worksheets.

Figure 8.68

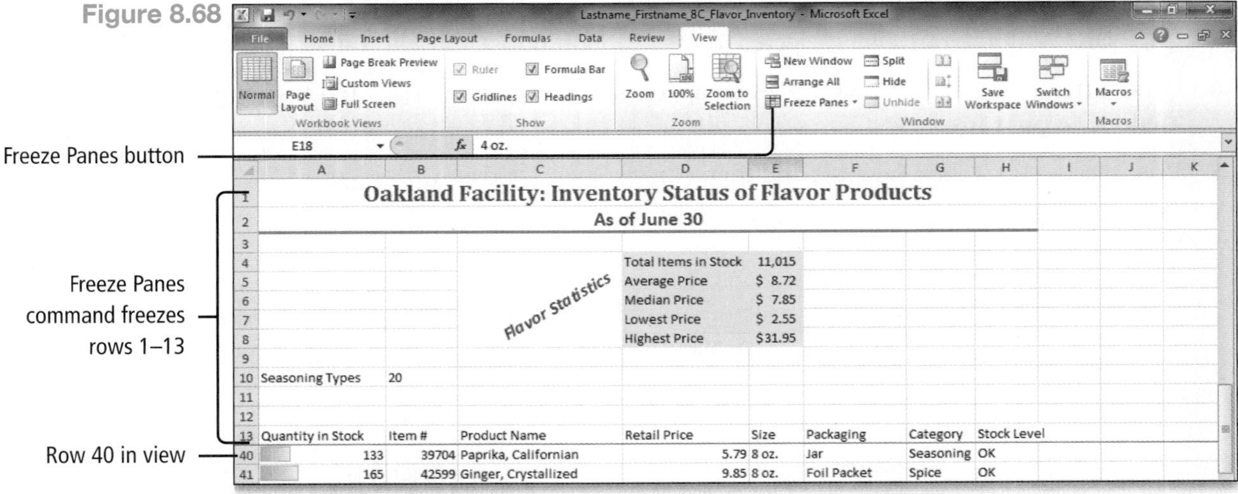

4 In the **Window group**, click the **Freeze Panes** button, and then click **Unfreeze Panes** to unlock all rows and columns. **Save** your workbook.

> **More Knowledge | Freeze Columns or Freeze both Rows and Columns**
>
> You can freeze columns that you want to remain in view on the left. Select the column to the right of the column(s) that you want to remain in view while scrolling to the right, and then click the Freeze Panes command. You can also use the command to freeze both rows and columns; click a cell to freeze the rows above the cell and the columns to the *left* of the cell.

Objective 16 | Create, Sort, and Filter an Excel Table

To analyze a group of related data, you can convert a range of cells to an ***Excel table***. An Excel table is a series of rows and columns that contains related data that is managed independently from the data in other rows and columns in the worksheet.

View the video on the Companion Web Site or in MyITLab

Activity 8.36 | Creating an Excel Table

1 Be sure that you have applied the Unfreeze Panes command—no rows on your worksheet are locked. Then, click any cell in the data below row 13.

2 Click the **Insert tab**. In the **Tables group**, click the **Table** button. In the **Create Table** dialog box, if necessary, click to select the **My table has headers** check box, and then compare your screen with Figure 8.69.

The column titles in row 13 will form the table headers. By clicking in a range of contiguous data, Excel will suggest the range as the data for the table. You can adjust the range if necessary.

Figure 8.69

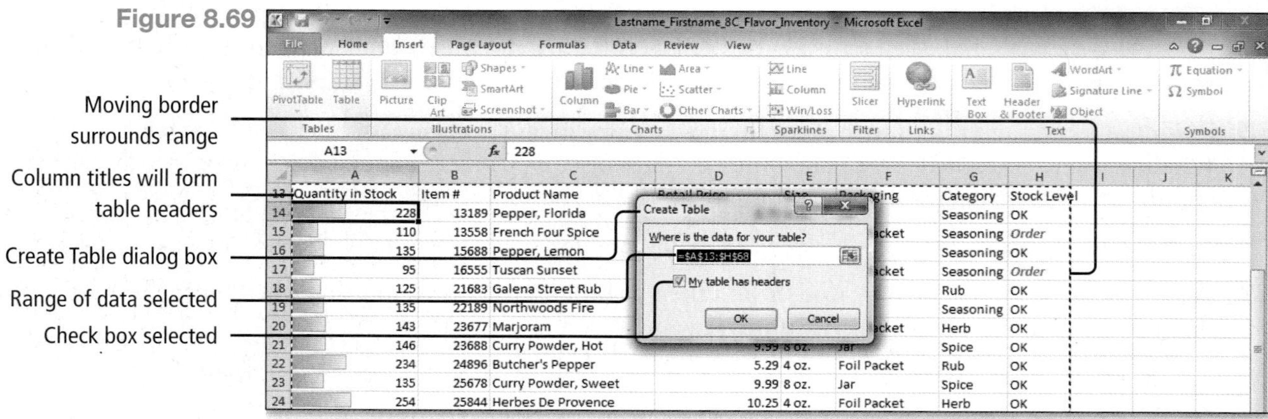

3 Click **OK**. With the range still selected, on the Ribbon notice that the **Table Tools** are active.

4 On the **Design tab**, in the **Table Styles group**, click the **More** button, and then under **Light**, locate and click **Table Style Light 16**.

5 Press Ctrl + Home. Click **Save**, and then compare your screen with Figure 8.70.

Sorting and filtering arrows display in the table's header row.

Figure 8.70

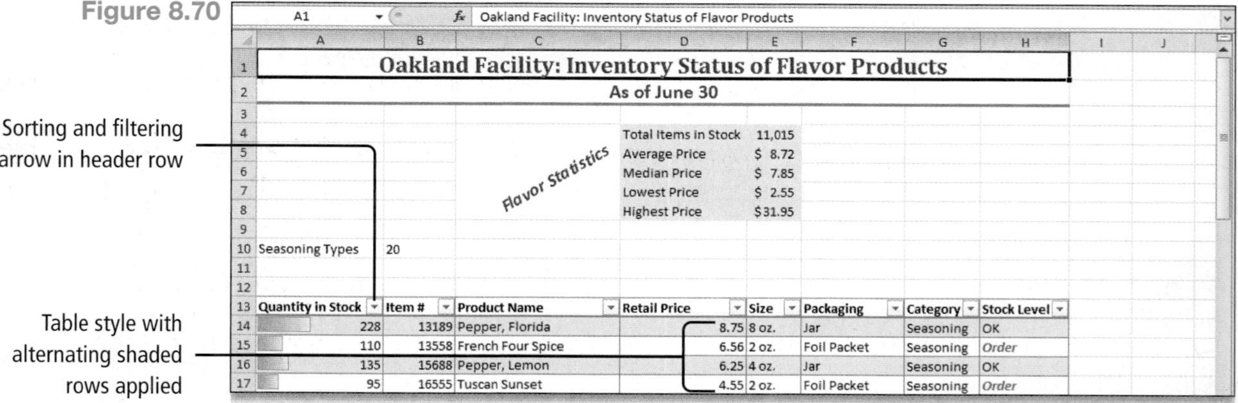

Activity 8.37 | Sorting and Filtering an Excel Table

You can ***sort*** tables—arrange all the data in a specific order—in ascending or descending order. You can ***filter*** tables—display only a portion of the data based on matching a specific value—to show only the data that meets the criteria that you specify.

1 In the header row of the table, click the **Retail Price** arrow, and then on the menu, click **Sort Smallest to Largest**. Next to the arrow, notice the small **up arrow** indicating an ascending (smallest to largest) sort.

The rows in the table are sorted from the lowest retail price to highest retail price.

2 In the table's header row, click the **Category arrow**. On the menu, click **Sort A to Z**. Next to the arrow, notice the small **up arrow** indicating an ascending (A to Z) sort.

The rows in the table are sorted alphabetically by Category.

3 Click the **Category arrow** again, and then sort from **Z to A**.

The rows in the table are sorted in reverse alphabetic order by Category name, and the small arrow points downward, indicating a descending (Z to A) sort.

4 Click the **Category arrow** again. On the menu, click the (**Select All**) check box to clear all the check boxes. Click to select only the **Extract** check box, and then click **OK**. Compare your screen with Figure 8.71.

Only the rows containing *Extract* in the Category column display—the remaining rows are hidden from view. A small funnel—the filter icon—indicates that a filter is applied to the data in the table. Additionally, the row numbers display in blue to indicate that some rows are hidden from view. A filter hides entire rows in the worksheet.

Figure 8.71

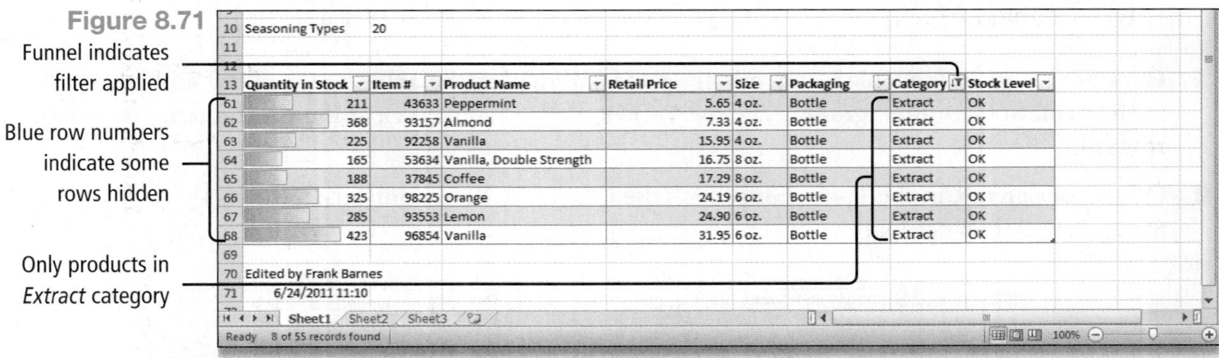

5 Point to the **Category arrow**, and notice that *Equals "Extract"* displays to indicate the filter criteria.

6 Click any cell in the table so that the table is selected. On the Ribbon, click the **Design tab**, and then in the **Table Style Options group**, select the **Total Row** check box.

Total displays in cell A69. In cell H69, the number *8* indicates that eight rows currently display.

7 Click cell **A69**, click the **arrow** that displays to the right of cell **A69**, and then in the list, click **Sum**.

Excel sums only the visible rows in Column A, and indicates that 2190 products in the Extract category are in stock. In this manner, you can use an Excel table to quickly find information about a group of data.

8 Click cell **A11**, type **Extract Types:** and press Tab. In cell **B11**, type **8 (2,190 total items in stock)** and then press Enter.

9 In the table header row, click the **Category arrow**, and then on the menu, click **Clear Filter From "Category"**.

All the rows in the table redisplay. The Z to A sort on Category remains in effect.

10 Click the **Packaging arrow**, click the (**Select All**) check box to clear all the check boxes, and then click to select the **Foil Packet** check box. Click **OK**.

11 Click the **Category arrow**, click the (**Select All**) check box to clear all the check boxes, and then click the **Herb** check box. Click **OK**, and then compare your screen with Figure 8.72.

By applying multiple filters, Laura can quickly determine that seven items in the Herb category are packaged in foil packets with a total of 1,346 such items in stock.

Figure 8.72

Seven items in *Herb* category are packaged in *Foil Packets*

12								
13	Quantity in Stock	Item #	Product Name	Retail Price	Size	Packaging	Category	Stock Level
52	325	54635	Dill Weed	2.65	4 oz.	Foil Packet	Herb	OK
54	143	23677	Marjoram	7.89	8 oz.	Foil Packet	Herb	OK
55	156	34266	Basil, French	10.19	8 oz.	Foil Packet	Herb	OK
57	254	25844	Herbes De Provence	10.25	4 oz.	Foil Packet	Herb	OK
58	156	32544	Mint, Spearmint	10.29	8 oz.	Foil Packet	Herb	OK
59	167	36820	Mint, Peppermint	10.39	8 oz.	Foil Packet	Herb	OK
60	145	35988	Basil, California	11.95	8 oz.	Foil Packet	Herb	OK
69	1346							7
70	Edited by Frank Barnes							

12 Click the **Category arrow**, and then click **Clear Filter From "Category"**. Use the same technique to remove the filter from the **Packaging** column.

13 In the table header row, click the **Item # arrow**, and then click **Sort Smallest to Largest**, which will apply an ascending sort to the data using the *Item#* column. **Save** your workbook.

Activity 8.38 | Converting a Table to a Range of Data

When you are finished answering questions about the data in a table by sorting, filtering, and totaling, you can convert the table into a normal range. Doing so is useful if you want to use the feature only to apply an attractive Table Style to a range of cells.

1 Click anywhere in the table to activate the table and display the **Table Tools** on the Ribbon. On the **Design tab**, in the **Table Style Options group**, click the **Total Row** check box to clear the check mark and remove the Total row from the table.

2 On the **Design tab**, in the **Tools group**, click the **Convert to Range** button. In the message box, click **Yes**. Click **Save**, and then compare your screen with Figure 8.73.

Figure 8.73

Table converted to a normal range, color and shading formats remain

13	Quantity in Stock	Item #	Product Name	Retail Price	Size	Packaging	Category	Stock Level
14	228	13189	Pepper, Florida	8.75	8 oz.	Jar	Seasoning	OK
15	110	13558	French Four Spice	6.56	2 oz.	Foil Packet	Seasoning	Order
16	135	15688	Pepper, Lemon	6.25	4 oz.	Jar	Seasoning	OK
17	95	16555	Tuscan Sunset	4.55	2 oz.	Foil Packet	Seasoning	Order
18	125	21683	Galena Street Rub	3.95	4 oz.	Jar	Rub	OK
19	135	22189	Northwoods Fire	9.85	16 oz.	Jar	Seasoning	OK
20	143	23677	Marjoram	7.89	8 oz.	Foil Packet	Herb	OK
21	146	23688	Curry Powder, Hot	9.99	8 oz.	Jar	Spice	OK

Objective 17 | Format and Print a Large Worksheet

View the video on the Companion Web Site or in MyITLab

A worksheet might be too wide, too long—or both—to print on a single page. Use Excel's ***Print Titles*** and ***Scale to Fit*** commands to create pages that are attractive and easy to read.

The Print Titles command enables you to specify rows and columns to repeat on each printed page. Scale to Fit commands enable you to stretch or shrink the width, height, or both, of printed output to fit a maximum number of pages.

Activity 8.39 | Printing Titles and Scaling to Fit

1 Press Ctrl + Home to display the top of your worksheet. Select the range **A13:H13**. On the **Home tab**, from the **Styles group**, apply the **Heading 4** cell style, and then apply **Center**.

2 On the **Insert tab**, in the **Text group**, click **Header & Footer**. In the **Navigation group**, click the **Go to Footer** button, and then click just above the word *Footer*. In the **Header & Footer Elements group**, click the **File Name** button to add the name of your file to the footer—*&[File]* displays. Then, click in a cell just above the footer to exit the Footer and view your file name.

3 Delete the unused sheets **Sheet2** and **Sheet3**. On the right edge of the status bar, click the **Normal** button, and then press Ctrl + Home to display the top of your worksheet.

Dotted lines indicate where the pages would break if printed as currently formatted; these dotted lines display when you switch from Page Layout view to Normal view.

4 On the **Page Layout tab**, in the **Themes group**, click the **Themes** button, and then click **Concourse**.

5 In the **Page Setup group**, click **Margins**, and then at the bottom, click **Custom Margins**. In the **Page Setup** dialog box, under **Center on page**, select the **Horizontally** check box, and then click **OK**.

6 In the **Page Setup group**, click **Orientation**, and then click **Landscape**. Press Ctrl + F2 to display the **Print Preview**. At the bottom of the **Print Preview**, click the **Next Page** button. Compare your screen with Figure 8.74.

As currently formatted, the worksheet will print on five pages, and the columns will span multiple pages. Additionally, after Page 1, no column titles are visible to identify the data in the columns.

Figure 8.74

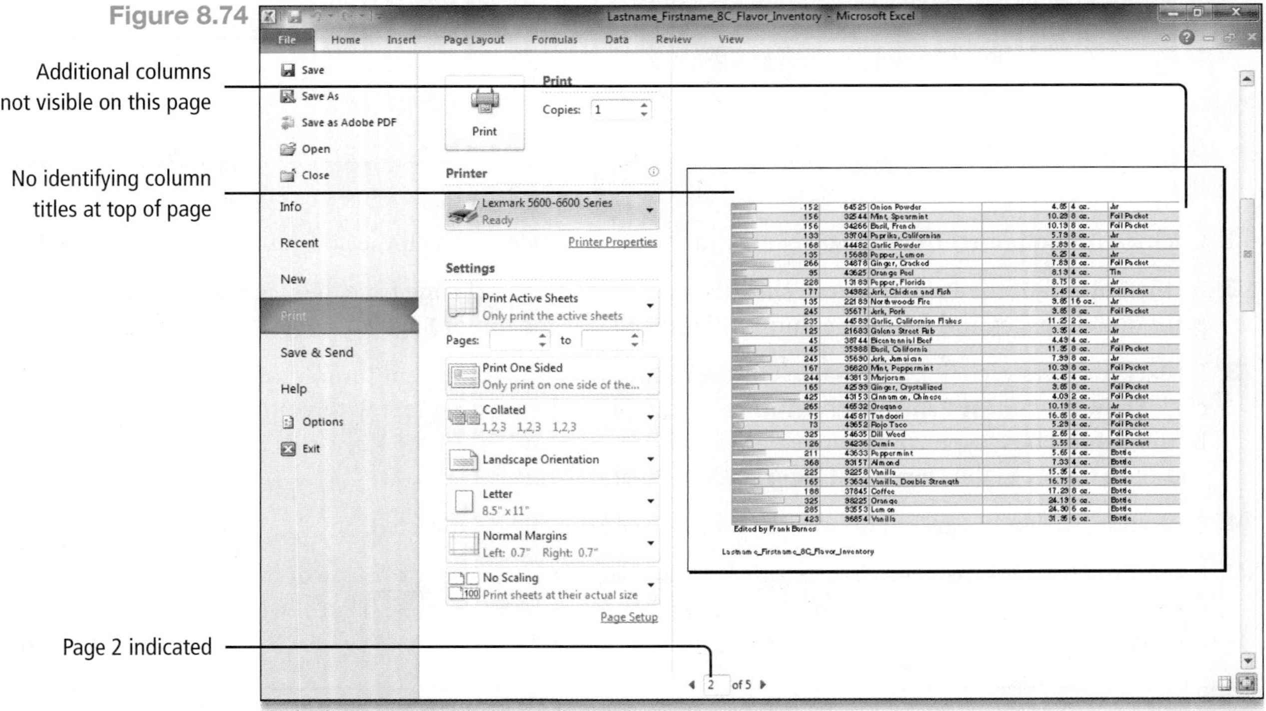

7 Click **Next Page** two times to display **Page 4**, and notice that two columns move to an additional page.

8 On the Ribbon, click **Page Layout** to redisplay the worksheet. In the **Page Setup group**, click the **Print Titles** button. Under **Print titles**, click in the **Rows to repeat at top** box, and then at the right, click the **Collapse Dialog** button.

9 From the **row heading area**, select **row 13**, and then click the **Expand Dialog** button. Click **OK** to print the column titles in row 13 at the top of every page.

Adding the titles on each page increases the number of pages to 6.

10 Press Ctrl + F2 to display the **Print Preview**. In the center panel, at the bottom of the **Settings group**, click the **Scaling** button, and then on the displayed list, point to **Fit All Columns on One Page**. Compare your screen with Figure 8.75.

This action will shrink the width of the printed output to fit all the columns on one page. You can make adjustments like this on the Page Layout tab, or here, in the Print Preview.

Figure 8.75

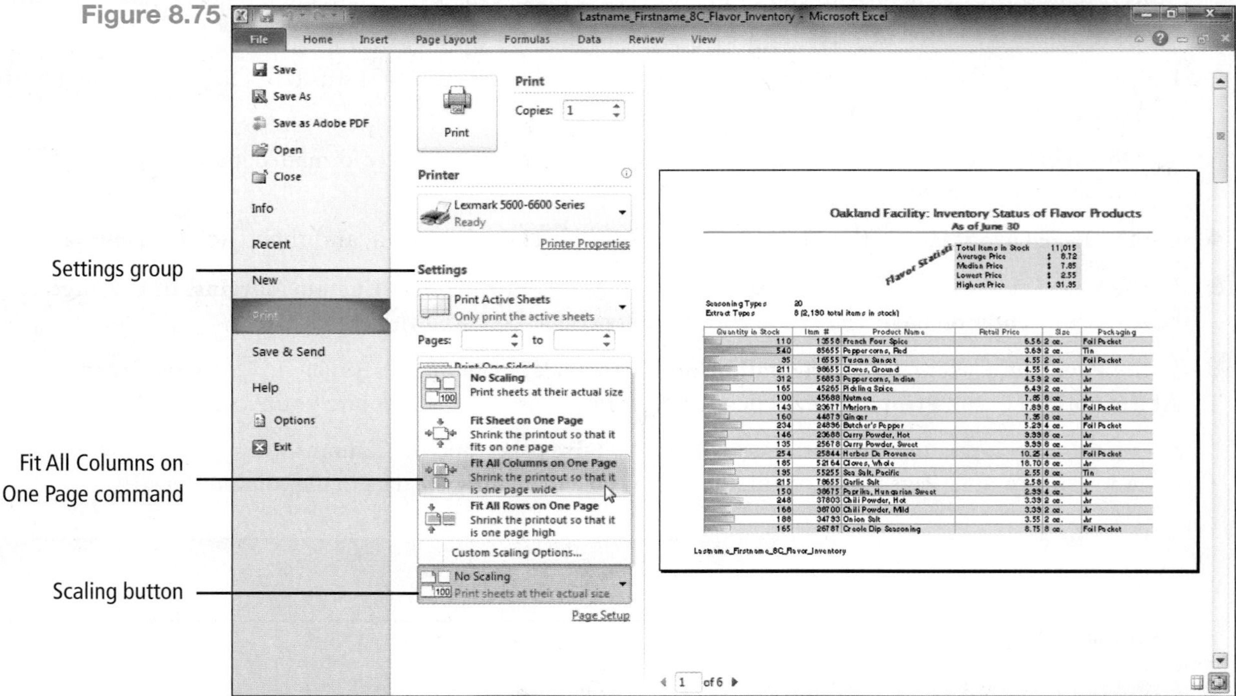

11 Click **Fit All Columns on One Page**. Notice in the **Print Preview** that all the columns display on one page.

12 At the bottom of the **Print Preview**, click the **Next Page** button ▶ one time. Notice that the output will now print on two pages and that the column titles display at the top of **Page 2**.

13 In **Backstage** view, click the **Info tab**. On the right, under the document thumbnail, click **Properties**, and then click **Show Document Panel**. In the **Author** box, replace the existing text with your firstname and lastname. In the **Subject** box, type your course name and section number. In the **Keywords** box, type **inventory, Oakland** and then **Close** ✕ the **Document Information Panel**.

14 **Save** your workbook, and then print or submit electronically as directed.

15 If required by your instructor, print or create an electronic version of your worksheets with formulas displayed by using the instructions in Activity 8.16, and then **Close** ✕ Excel without saving so that you do not save the changes you made to print formulas.

More Knowledge | Scaling for Data That Is Slightly Larger Than the Printed Page

If your data is just a little too large to fit on a printed page, you can scale the worksheet to make it fit. Scaling reduces both the width and height of the printed data to a percentage of its original size or by the number of pages that you specify. To adjust the printed output to a percentage of its actual size, for example to 80%, on the Page Layout tab, in the Scale to Fit group, click the Scale arrows to select a percentage.

End **You have completed Project 8C**

Project 8D Weekly Sales Summary

Project Activities

In Activities 8.40 through 8.50, you will edit an existing workbook for Laura Morales. The workbook summarizes the online and in-store sales of products during a one-week period in July. The worksheets of your completed workbook will look similar to Figure 8.76.

Project Files

For Project 8D, you will need the following file:

e08D_Weekly_Sales

You will save your workbook as

Lastname_Firstname_8D_Weekly_Sales

Project Results

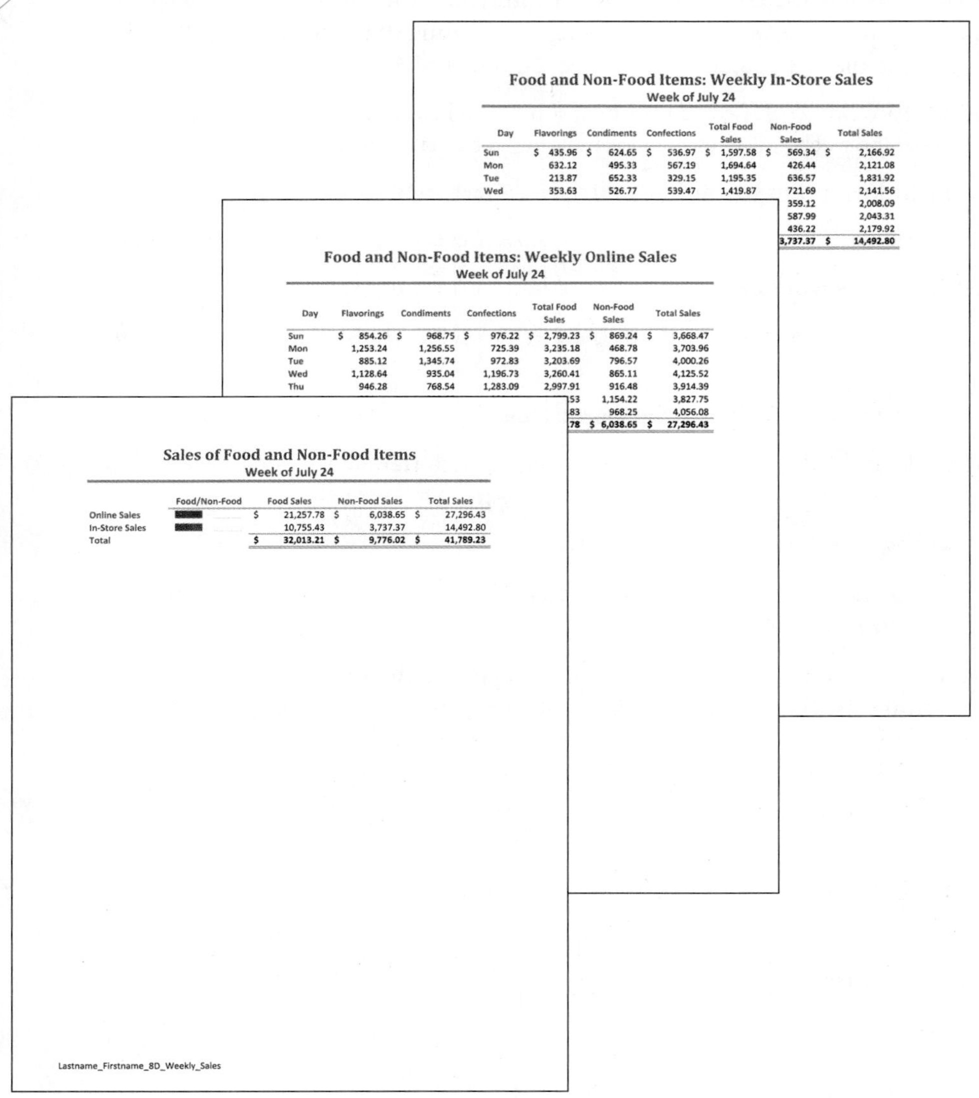

Food and Non-Food Items: Weekly In-Store Sales
Week of July 24

Day	Flavorings	Condiments	Confections	Total Food Sales	Non-Food Sales	Total Sales
Sun	$ 435.96	$ 624.65	$ 536.97	$ 1,597.58	$ 569.34	$ 2,166.92
Mon	632.12	495.33	567.19	1,694.64	426.44	2,121.08
Tue	213.87	652.33	329.15	1,195.35	636.57	1,831.92
Wed	353.63	526.77	539.47	1,419.87	721.69	2,141.56
					359.12	2,008.09
					587.99	2,043.31
					436.22	2,179.92
					3,737.37	$ 14,492.80

Food and Non-Food Items: Weekly Online Sales
Week of July 24

Day	Flavorings	Condiments	Confections	Total Food Sales	Non-Food Sales	Total Sales
Sun	$ 854.26	$ 968.75	$ 976.22	$ 2,799.23	$ 869.24	$ 3,668.47
Mon	1,253.24	1,256.55	725.39	3,235.18	468.78	3,703.96
Tue	885.12	1,345.74	972.83	3,203.69	796.57	4,000.26
Wed	1,128.64	935.04	1,196.73	3,260.41	865.11	4,125.52
Thu	946.28	768.54	1,283.09	2,997.91	916.48	3,914.39
				53	1,154.22	3,827.75
				83	968.25	4,056.08
				78	$ 6,038.65	$ 27,296.43

Sales of Food and Non-Food Items
Week of July 24

	Food/Non-Food	Food Sales	Non-Food Sales	Total Sales
Online Sales		$ 21,257.78	$ 6,038.65	$ 27,296.43
In-Store Sales		10,755.43	3,737.37	14,492.80
Total		$ 32,013.21	$ 9,776.02	$ 41,789.23

Lastname_Firstname_8D_Weekly_Sales

Figure 8.76
Project 8D Weekly Sales

Objective 18 | Navigate a Workbook and Rename Worksheets

View the video on the Companion Web Site or in MyITLab

Use multiple worksheets in a workbook to organize data in a logical arrangement. When you have more than one worksheet in a workbook, you can ***navigate*** (move) among worksheets by clicking the ***sheet tabs***. Sheet tabs identify each worksheet in a workbook and are located along the lower left edge of the workbook window. When you have more worksheets in the workbook than can be displayed in the sheet tab area, use the four sheet tab scrolling buttons to move sheet tabs into and out of view.

Activity 8.40 | Navigating Among Worksheets, Renaming Worksheets, and Changing the Tab Color of Worksheets

Excel names the first worksheet in a workbook *Sheet1* and each additional worksheet in order—*Sheet2*, *Sheet3*, and so on. Most Excel users rename the worksheets with meaningful names. In this activity, you will navigate among worksheets, rename worksheets, and change the tab color of sheet tabs.

1. **Start** Excel. From **Backstage** view, display the **Open** dialog box. From your student files, open **e08D_Weekly_Sales**. From **Backstage** view, display the **Save As** dialog box, navigate to your **All In One Chapter 8** folder, and then using your own name, save the file as **Lastname_Firstname_8D_Weekly_Sales**

   In the displayed workbook, there are two worksheets into which some data has already been entered. For example, on the first worksheet, the days of the week and sales data for the one-week period displays.

2. Along the bottom of the Excel window, point to and then click the **Sheet2 tab**.

   The second worksheet in the workbook displays and becomes the active worksheet. Sheet2 displays in bold.

3. In cell **A1**, notice the text *In-Store*—this worksheet will contain data for in-store sales.

4. Click the **Sheet1 tab**. Then, point to the **Sheet1 tab**, and double-click to select the sheet tab name. Type **Online Sales** and press Enter.

   The first worksheet becomes the active worksheet, and the sheet tab displays Online Sales.

5. Point to the **Sheet2 tab**, right-click, and then from the shortcut menu, click **Rename**. Type **In-Store Sales** and press Enter.

   You can use either of these methods to rename a sheet tab.

6. Point to the **In-Store Sales sheet tab** and right-click. On the shortcut menu, point to **Tab Color**, and then in the last column, click the first color—**Orange, Accent 6**.

7. Using the technique you just practiced, change the tab color of the **Online Sales sheet tab** to **Aqua, Accent 5**—in the next to last column, the first color. Compare your screen with Figure 8.77 and **Save** your workbook.

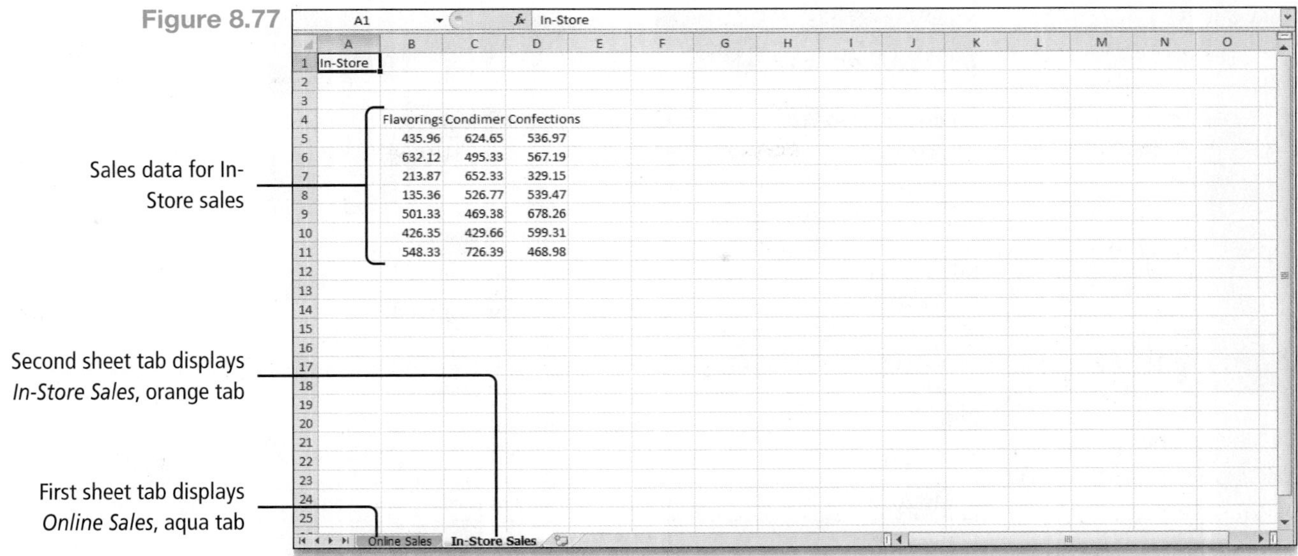

Objective 19 | Enter Dates, Clear Contents, and Clear Formats

View the video on the Companion Web Site or in MyITLab

Dates represent a type of value that you can enter in a cell. When you enter a date, Excel assigns a serial value—a number—to the date. This makes it possible to treat dates like other numbers. For example, if two cells contain dates, you can find the number of days between the two dates by subtracting the older date from the more recent date.

Activity 8.41 | Entering and Formatting Dates

In this activity, you will examine the various ways that Excel can format dates in a cell. Date values entered in any of the following formats will be recognized by Excel as a date:

Format	Example
m/d/yy	7/4/12
d-mmm	4-Jul
d-mmm-yy	4-Jul-12
mmm-yy	Jul-12

On your keyboard, - (the hyphen key) and / (the forward slash key) function identically in any of these formats and can be used interchangeably. You can abbreviate the month name to three characters or spell it out. You can enter the year as two digits, four digits, or even leave it off. When left off, the current year is assumed but does not display in the cell.

A two-digit year value of 30 through 99 is interpreted by the Windows operating system as the four-digit years of 1930 through 1999. All other two-digit year values are assumed to be in the 21st century. If you always type year values as four digits, even though only two digits may display in the cell, you can be sure that Excel interprets the year value as you intended. Examples are shown in Figure 8.78.

How Excel Interprets Dates

Date Typed As:	Completed by Excel As:
7/4/12	7/4/2012
7-4-98	7/4/1998
7/4	4-Jul (current year assumed)
7-4	4-Jul (current year assumed)
July 4	4-Jul (current year assumed)
Jul 4	4-Jul (current year assumed)
Jul/4	4-Jul (current year assumed)
Jul-4	4-Jul (current year assumed)
July 4, 1998	4-Jul-98
July 2012	Jul-12 (first day of month assumed)
July 1998	Jul-98 (first day of month assumed)

Figure 8.78

1 On the **Online Sales** sheet, click cell **A16** and notice that the cell indicates *8/3* (August 3). In the **Formula Bar**, notice that the full date of August 3, 2014 displays in the format *8/3/2014*.

2 With cell **A16** selected, on the **Home tab**, in the **Number group**, click the **Number Format arrow**. At the bottom of the menu, click **More Number Formats** to display the **Number tab** of the **Format Cells** dialog box.

Under Category, *Date* is selected, and under Type, *3/14* is selected. Cell A16 uses this format type; that is, only the month and day display in the cell.

3 In the displayed dialog box, under **Type**, click several other date types and watch the **Sample** area to see how applying the selected date format would format your cell. When you are finished, click the **3/14/01** type, and then compare your screen with Figure 8.79.

Figure 8.79

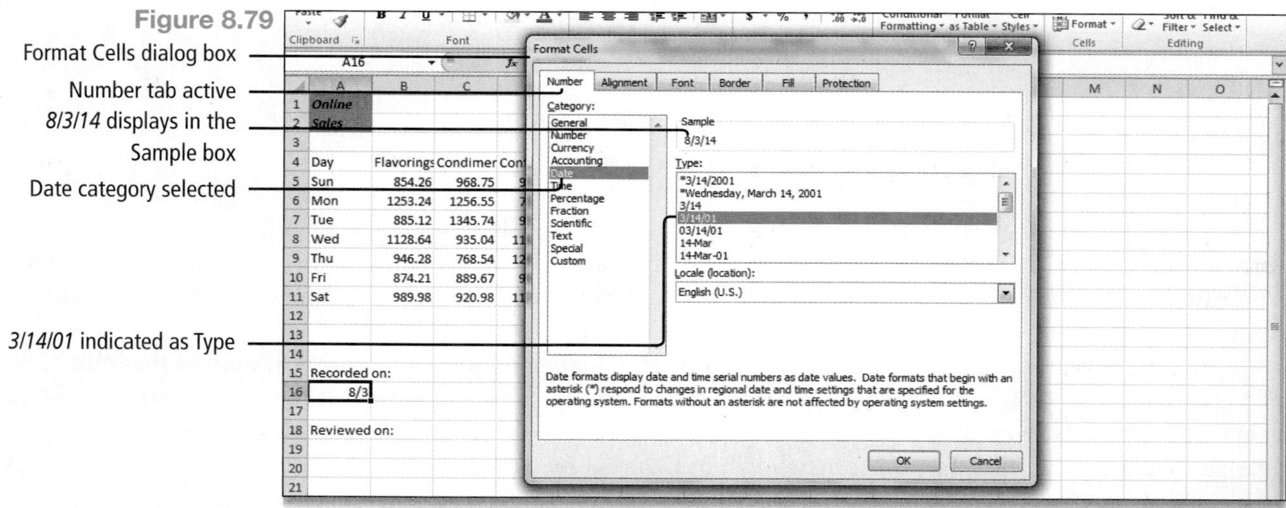

4 At the bottom of the dialog box, click **OK**. Click cell **A19**, type **8-7-14** and then press Enter.

Cell A19 has no special date formatting applied, and thus displays in the default date format *8/7/2014*.

> **Alert! | The Date Does Not Display as 8/7/2014?**
>
> Settings in your Windows operating system determine the default format for dates. If your result is different, it is likely that the formatting of the default date was adjusted on the computer at which you are working.

5 Click cell **A19** again. Hold down Ctrl and press ; (semicolon) on your keyboard. Press Enter to confirm the entry.

Excel enters the current date, obtained from your computer's internal calendar, in the selected cell using the default date format. Ctrl + ; is a quick method to enter the current date.

6 Click cell **A19** again, type **8/7/14** and then press Enter.

Because the year *14* is less than 30, Excel assumes a 21st century date and changes *14* to *2014* to complete the four-digit year.

7 Click cell **A16**, and then on the **Home tab**, in the **Clipboard group**, click the **Format Painter** button. Click cell **A19**, and notice that the date format from cell **A16** is copied to cell **A19**. **Save** your workbook.

Activity 8.42 | Clearing Cell Contents and Formats

A cell has *contents*—a value or a formula—and a cell may also have one or more *formats* applied, for example, bold and italic font styles, fill color, font color, and so on. You can choose to clear—delete—the *contents* of a cell, the *formatting* of a cell, or both. Clearing the contents of a cell deletes the value or formula typed there, but it does *not* clear formatting applied to a cell. In this activity, you will clear the contents of a cell and then clear the formatting of a cell that contains a date to see its underlying content.

1 In the **Online Sales** worksheet, click cell **A1**. In the **Editing group**, click the **Clear** button. On the displayed list, click **Clear Contents** and notice that the text is cleared, but the orange formatting remains.

2 Click cell **A2**, and then press Delete.

You can use either of these two methods to delete the contents of a cell. Deleting the contents does not, however, delete the formatting of the cell; you can see that the orange fill color format applied to the two cells still displays.

3 In cell **A1**, type **Online Sales** and then on the **Formula Bar**, click the **Enter** button so that cell **A1** remains the active cell.

In addition to the orange fill color, the bold italic text formatting remains with the cell.

4 In the **Editing group**, click the **Clear** button, and then click **Clear Formats**.

Clearing the formats deletes formatting from the cell—the orange fill color and the bold and italic font styles—but does not delete the cell's contents.

5 Use the same technique to clear the orange fill color from cell **A2**. Click cell **A16**, click the **Clear** button, and then click **Clear Formats**. In the **Number group**, notice that *General* displays as the number format of the cell.

The box in the Number group indicates the current Number format of the selected cell. Clearing the date formatting from the cell displays the date's serial number. The date, August 3, 2014, is stored as a serial number that indicates the number of days since January 1, 1900. This date is the 41,854th day since the reference date of January 1, 1900.

6 On the Quick Access Toolbar, click the **Undo** button to restore the date format. **Save** your workbook, and then compare your screen with Figure 8.80.

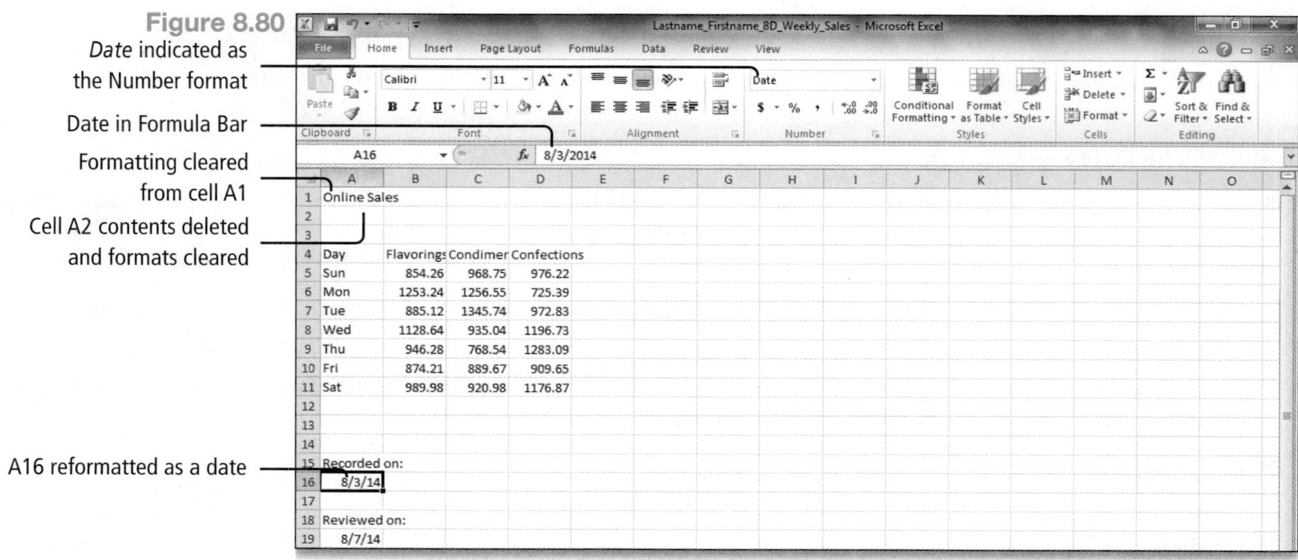

Figure 8.80

Objective 20 | Copy and Paste by Using the Paste Options Gallery

View the video on the Companion Web Site or in MyITLab

Data in cells can be copied to other cells in the same worksheet, to other sheets in the same workbook, or to sheets in another workbook. The action of placing cell contents that have been copied or moved to the Office Clipboard into another location is called ***paste***.

Activity 8.43 | Copying and Pasting by Using the Paste Options Gallery

Recall that the Office Clipboard is a temporary storage area maintained by your Windows operating system. When you select one or more cells, and then perform the Copy command or the Cut command, the selected data is placed on the Office Clipboard. From the Office Clipboard storage area, the data is available for pasting into other cells, other worksheets, other workbooks, and even into other Office programs. When you paste, the ***Paste Options gallery*** displays, which includes Live Preview to preview the Paste formatting that you want.

1. With the **Online Sales** worksheet active, select the range **A4:A19**. Right-click over the selection, and then click **Copy** to place a copy of the cells on the Office Clipboard. Notice that the copied cells display a moving border.
2. At the bottom of the workbook window, click the **In-Store Sales sheet tab** to make it the active worksheet. Point to cell **A4**, right-click, and then on the shortcut menu, under **Paste Options**, *point* to the first button—**Paste**. Compare your screen with Figure 8.81.

   Live Preview displays how the copied cells will be placed in the worksheet if you click the Paste button. In this manner, you can experiment with different paste options, and then be sure you are selecting the paste operation that you want. When pasting a range of cells, you need only point to or select the cell in the upper left corner of the ***paste area***—the target destination for data that has been cut or copied using the Office Clipboard.

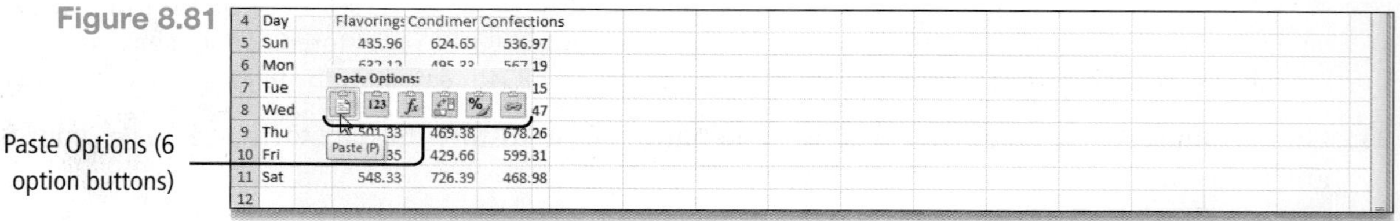

Figure 8.81

3 Click the first button, **Paste**. In the status bar, notice that the message still displays, indicating that your selected range remains available on the Office Clipboard.

4 Display the **Online Sales** worksheet. Press Esc to cancel the moving border. **Save** your workbook.

The status bar no longer displays the message.

Objective 21 | Edit and Format Multiple Worksheets at the Same Time

View the video on the Companion Web Site or in MyITLab

You can enter or edit data on several worksheets at the same time by selecting and grouping multiple worksheets. Data that you enter or edit on the active sheet is reflected in all selected sheets. If you apply color to the sheet tabs, the name of the sheet tab will be underlined in the color you selected. If the sheet tab displays with a background color, you know the sheet is not selected.

Activity 8.44 | Grouping Worksheets for Editing

In this activity, you will group the two worksheets, and then format both worksheets at the same time.

1 With the **Online Sales** sheet active, press Ctrl + Home to make cell **A1** the active cell. Point to the **Online Sales sheet tab**, right-click, and then from the shortcut menu, click **Select All Sheets**.

2 At the top of your screen, notice that [*Group*] displays in the title bar. Compare your screen with Figure 8.82.

Both worksheets are selected, as indicated by [*Group*] in the title bar and the sheet tab names underlined in the selected tab color. Data that you enter or edit on the active sheet will also be entered or edited in the same manner on all the selected sheets in the same cells.

Figure 8.82

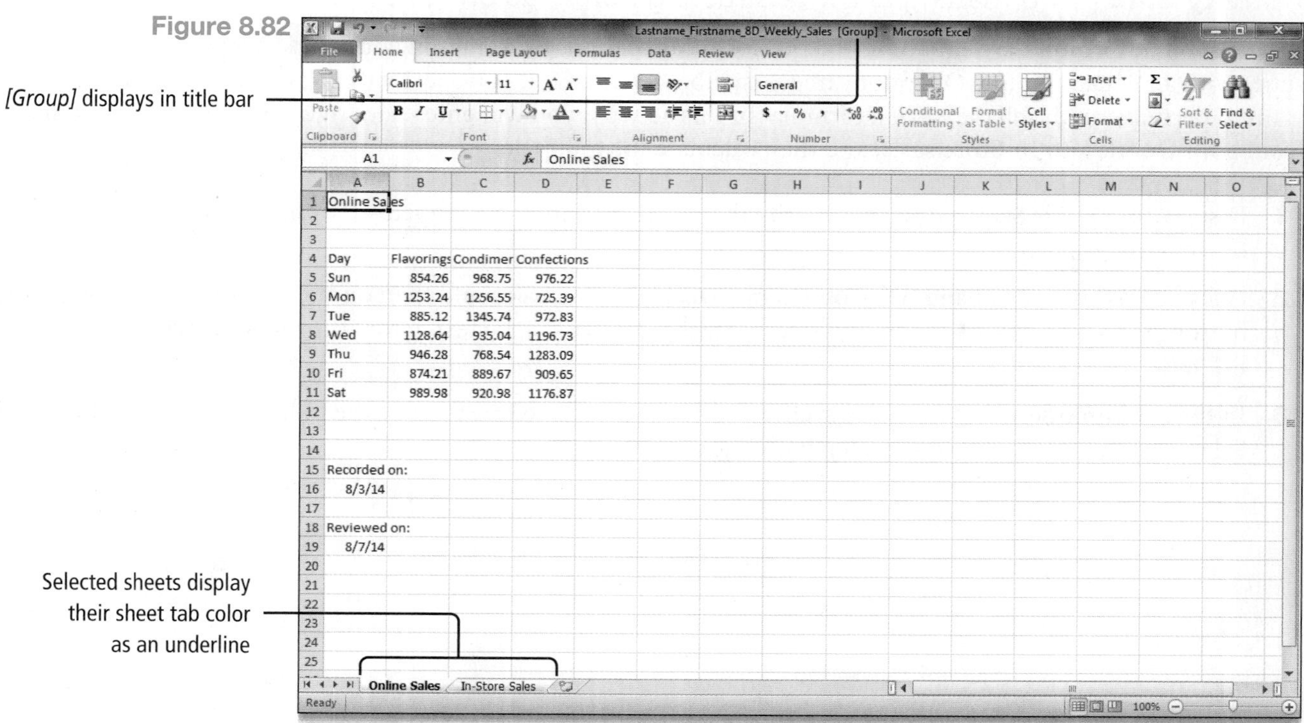

3 Select **columns A:G**, and then set their width to **85 pixels**.

4 Click cell **A2**, type **Week of July 24** and then on the **Formula Bar**, click the **Enter** button to keep cell **A2** as the active cell. **Merge & Center** the text across the range **A2:G2**, and then apply the **Heading 1** cell style.

5 Click cell **E4**, type **Total Food Sales** and then press Tab. In cell **F4**, type **Non-Food Sales** and then press Tab. In cell **G4**, type **Total Sales** and then press Enter.

6 Select the range **A4:G4**, and then apply the **Heading 3** cell style. In the **Alignment group**, click the **Center**, **Middle Align**, and **Wrap Text** buttons. **Save** your workbook.

7 Display the **In-Store Sales** worksheet to cancel the grouping, and then compare your screen with Figure 8.83.

As soon as you select a single sheet, the grouping of the sheets is canceled and [*Group*] no longer displays in the title bar. Because the sheets were grouped, the same new text and formatting was applied to both sheets. In this manner, you can make the same changes to all the sheets in a workbook at one time.

Figure 8.83

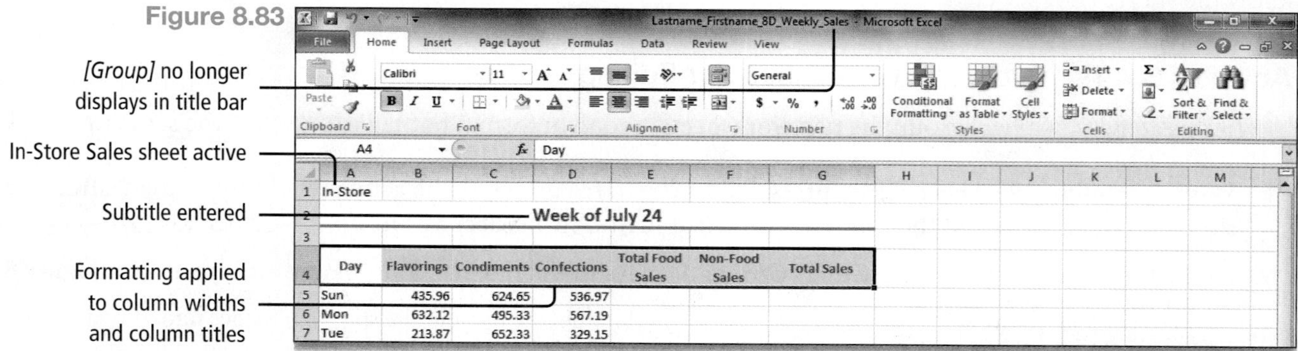

Activity 8.45 | Formatting and Constructing Formulas on Grouped Worksheets

Recall that formulas are equations that perform calculations on values in your worksheet and that a formula starts with an equal sign (=). Operators are the symbols with which you specify the type of calculation that you want to perform on the elements of a formula. In this activity, you will enter sales figures for Non-Food items from both Online and In-Store sales, and then calculate the total sales.

1 Display the **Online Sales** worksheet. Verify that the sheets are not grouped—[*Group*] does *not* display in the title bar.

2 Click cell **A1**, type **Food and Non-Food Items: Weekly Online Sales** and then on the **Formula Bar**, click the **Enter** button to keep cell **A1** as the active cell. **Merge & Center** the text across the range **A1:G1**, and then apply the **Title** cell style.

3 In the column titled *Non-Food Sales*, click cell **F5**, in the range **F5:F11**, type the following data for Non-Food Sales, and then compare your screen with Figure 8.84.

	Non-Food Sales
Sun	**869.24**
Mon	**468.78**
Tue	**796.57**
Wed	**865.11**
Thu	**916.48**
Fri	**1154.22**
Sat	**968.25**

Figure 8.84

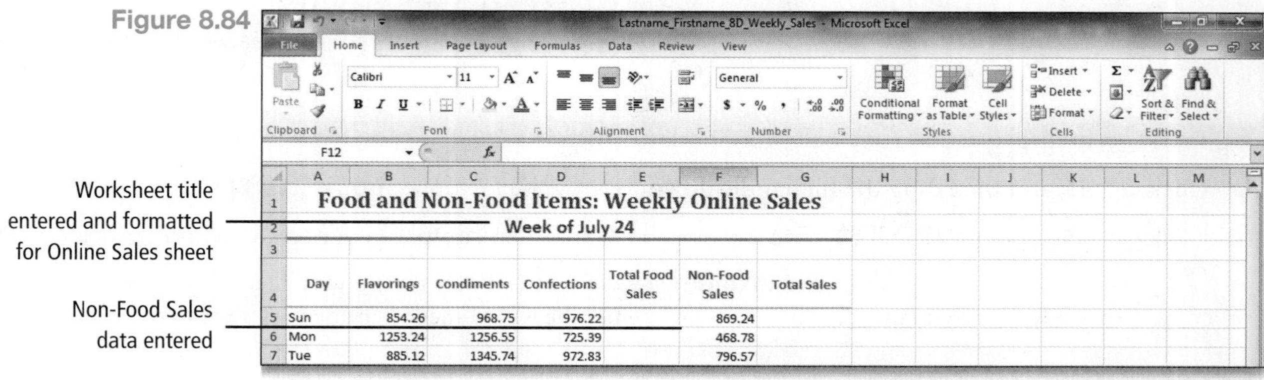

4 Display the **In-Store Sales** sheet. In cell **A1**, replace *In-Store* by typing **Food and Non-Food Items: Weekly In-Store Sales** and then on the **Formula Bar**, click the **Enter** button to keep cell **A1** as the active cell. **Merge & Center** the text across the range **A1:G1**, and then apply the **Title** cell style.

5 In the column titled *Non-Food Sales*, click cell **F5**, in the range **F5:F11**, type the following data for Non-Food Sales.

	Non-Food Sales
Sun	**569.34**
Mon	**426.44**
Tue	**636.57**
Wed	**721.69**
Thu	**359.12**
Fri	**587.99**
Sat	**436.22**

6 **Save** your workbook. Right-click the **Online Sales sheet tab**, and then from the shortcut menu, click **Select All Sheets**.

The first worksheet becomes the active sheet, and the worksheets are grouped. [*Group*] displays in the title bar, and the sheet tabs are underlined in the tab color to indicate they are selected as part of the group. Recall that when grouped, any action that you perform on the active worksheet is *also* performed on any other selected worksheets.

7 With the sheets *grouped* and the **Online Sales** sheet active, click cell E5. On the **Home tab**, in the **Editing group**, click the **Sum** button Σ. Compare your screen with Figure 8.85.

Recall that when you enter the SUM function, Excel looks first above and then left for a proposed range of cells to sum.

Figure 8.85

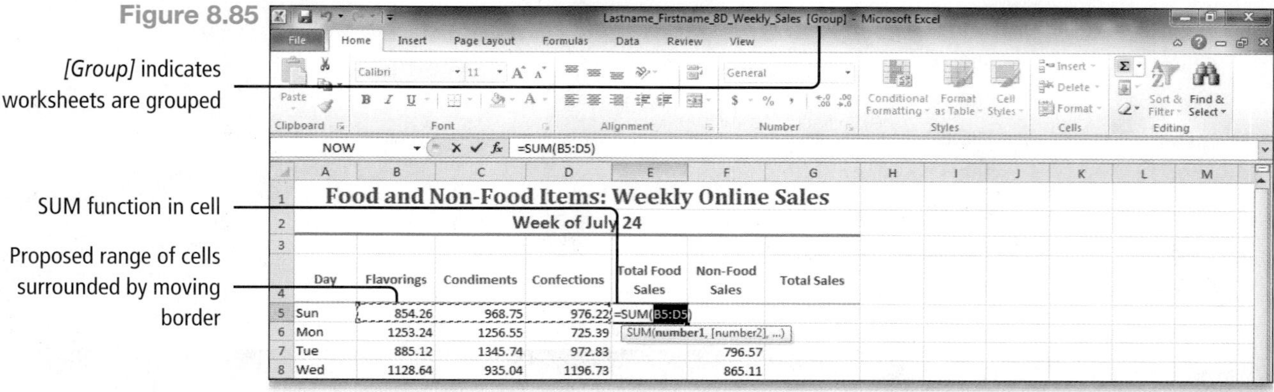

8 Press Enter to display Total Food Sales for Sunday, which is *2799.23*.

9 Click cell **E5**, and then drag the fill handle down to copy the formula through cell **E11**.

10 Click cell **G5**, type = click cell **E5**, type + click cell **F5**, and then compare your screen with Figure 8.86.

Using the point-and-click technique to construct this formula is only one of several techniques you can use. Alternatively, you could use any other method to enter the SUM function to add the values in these two cells.

Figure 8.86

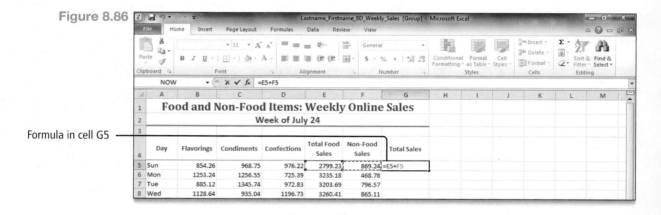

Formula in cell G5

Day	Flavorings	Condiments	Confections	Total Food Sales	Non-Food Sales	Total Sales
Sun	854.26	968.75	976.22	2799.23	869.24	=E5+F5
Mon	1253.24	1256.55	725.39	3235.18	468.78	
Tue	885.12	1345.74	972.83	3203.69	796.57	
Wed	1128.64	935.04	1196.73	3260.41	865.11	

11 Press Enter to display the result *3668.47*, and then copy the formula down through cell **G11**.

12 In cell **A12**, type **Total** and then select the range **B5:G12**, which is all of the sales data and the empty cells at the bottom of each column of sales data.

13 With the range **B5:G12** selected, hold down Alt and press = to enter the **SUM** function in each empty cell.

Selecting a range in this manner will place the Sum function in the empty cells at the bottom of each column.

14 Select the range **A5:A12**, and then apply the **Heading 4** cell style.

15 To apply financial formatting to the worksheets, select the range **B5:G5**, hold down Ctrl, and then select the range **B12:G12**. With the nonadjacent ranges selected, apply the **Accounting Number Format** $.

16 Select the range **B6:G11** and apply **Comma Style** ,. Select the range **B12:G12** and apply the **Total** cell style.

17 Press Ctrl + Home to move to the top of the worksheet. Click the **In-Store Sales sheet tab** to cancel the grouping and display the second worksheet. Click **Save**, and then compare your screen with Figure 8.87.

With your worksheets grouped, the calculations on the first worksheet were also performed on the second worksheet.

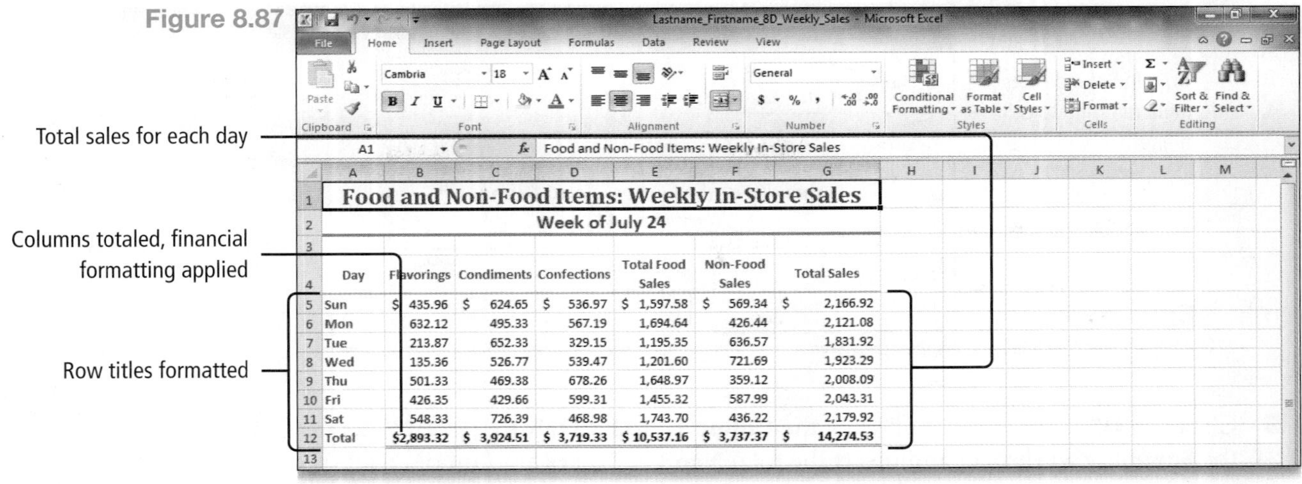

Objective 22 | Create a Summary Sheet with Column Sparklines

A ***summary sheet*** is a worksheet where totals from other worksheets are displayed and summarized. Recall that sparklines are tiny charts within a single cell that show a data trend.

View the video on the Companion Web Site or in MyITLab

Activity 8.46 | Constructing Formulas that Refer to Cells in Another Worksheet

In this activity, you will insert a new worksheet in which you will place the totals from the Online Sales worksheet and the In-Store Sales worksheet. You will construct formulas in the Summary worksheet to display the total sales for both online sales and in-store sales that will update the Summary worksheet whenever changes are made to the other worksheet totals.

1. To the right of the **In-Store Sales sheet tab**, click the **Insert Worksheet** button.
2. Rename the new worksheet tab **Summary** Change the **Tab Color** to **Olive Green, Accent 3**.
3. Widen columns **A:E** to **110** pixels. In cell **A1**, type **Sales of Food and Non-Food Items Merge & Center** the title across the range **A1:E1**, and then apply the **Title** cell style.
4. In cell **A2**, type **Week of July 24** and then **Merge & Center** across **A2:E2**; apply the **Heading 1** cell style.
5. Leave **row 3** blank. To form column titles, in cell **B4**, type **Food/Non-Food** and press Tab. In cell **C4**, type **Food Sales** and press Tab. In cell **D4**, type **Non-Food Sales** and press Tab. In cell **E5**, type **Total Sales** Press Enter. Select the range **B4:E4**. Apply the **Heading 3** cell style and **Center**.
6. To form row titles, in cell **A5**, type **Online Sales** In cell **A6**, type **In-Store Sales** and then press Enter.
7. Click cell **C5**. Type = Click the **Online Sales sheet tab**. On the **Online Sales** worksheet, click cell **E12**, and then press Enter to redisplay the **Summary** worksheet and insert the total **Food Sales** amount of *$21,257.78*.
8. Click cell **C5** to select it again. Look at the **Formula Bar**, and notice that instead of a value, the cell contains a formula that is equal to the value in another cell in another worksheet. Compare your screen with Figure 8.88.

   The value in this cell is equal to the value in cell E12 of the *Online Sales* worksheet. The Accounting Number Format applied to the referenced cell is carried over. By using a formula of this type, changes in cell E12 on the *Online Sales* worksheet will be automatically updated in this *Summary* worksheet.

Figure 8.88

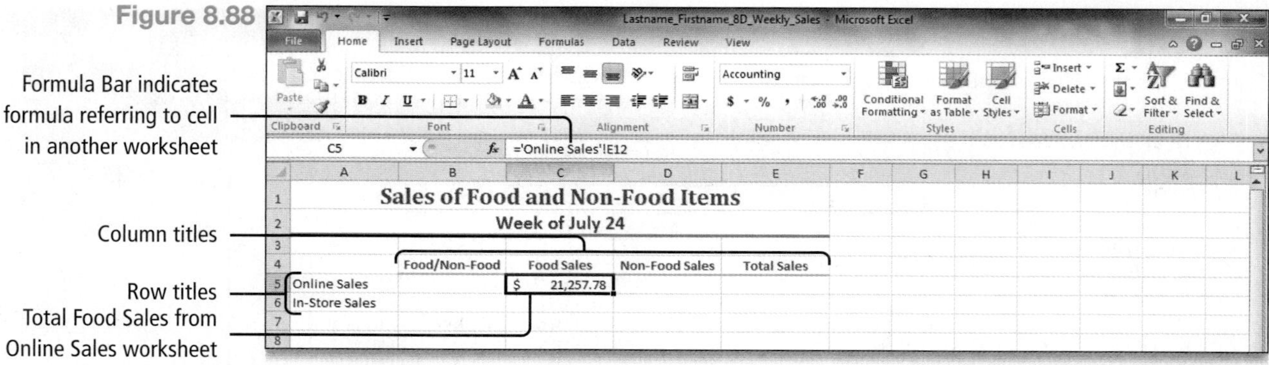

9 Click cell **D5**. Type = and then click the **Online Sales sheet tab**. Click cell **F12**, and then press Enter to redisplay the **Summary** worksheet and insert the total **Non-Food Sales** amount of *$6,038.65*.

10 By using the techniques you just practiced, in cells **C6** and **D6** insert the total **Food Sales** and **Non-Food Sales** data from the **In-Store Sales** worksheet. Click **Save**, and then compare your screen with Figure 8.89.

Figure 8.89

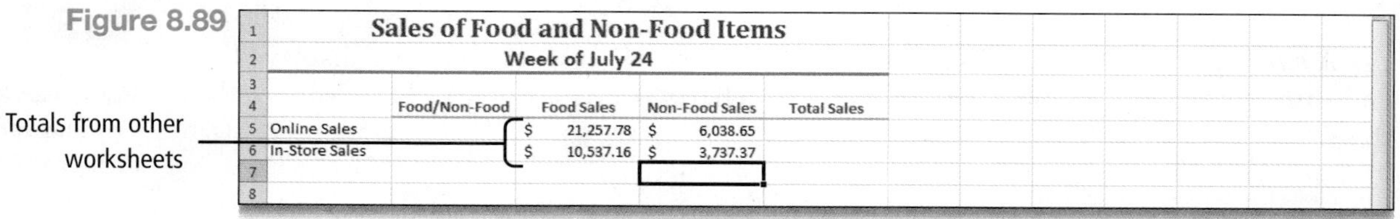

Activity 8.47 | Changing Values in a Detail Worksheet to Update a Summary Worksheet

The formulas in cells C5:D6 display the totals from the other two worksheets. Changes made to any of the other two worksheets—sometimes referred to as ***detail sheets*** because the details of the information are contained there—that affect their totals will display on this Summary worksheet. In this manner, the Summary worksheet accurately displays the current totals from the other worksheets.

1 In cell **A7**, type **Total** Select the range **C5:E6**, and then click the **Sum** button Σ to total the two rows.

This technique is similar to selecting the empty cells at the bottom of columns and then inserting the SUM function for each column. Alternatively, you could use any other method to sum the rows. Recall that cell formatting carries over to adjacent cells unless two cells are left blank.

2 Select the range **C5:E7**, and then click the **Sum** button Σ to total the three columns. Compare your screen with Figure 8.90.

Figure 8.90

Sales of Food and Non-Food Items

Week of July 24

	Food/Non-Food	Food Sales	Non-Food Sales	Total Sales
Online Sales		$ 21,257.78	$ 6,038.65	$ 27,296.43
In-Store Sales		$ 10,537.16	$ 3,737.37	$ 14,274.53
Total		$ 31,794.94	$ 9,776.02	$ 41,570.96

Rows and columns totaled

3 In cell **C6**, notice that total **Food Sales** for **In-Store Sales** is *$10,537.16*, and in cell **C7**, notice the total of *$31,794.94*.

4 Display the **In-Store Sales** worksheet, click cell **B8**, type **353.63** and then press Enter. Notice that the formulas in the worksheet recalculate.

5 Display the **Summary** worksheet, and notice that in the **Food Sales** column, both the total for the *In-Store Sales* location and the *Total* also recalculated.

In this manner, a Summary sheet recalculates any changes made in the other worksheets.

6 Select the range **C6:E6** and change the format to **Comma Style**. Select the range **C7:E7**, and then apply the **Total** cell style. Select the range **A5:A7** and apply the **Heading 4** cell style. **Save** your workbook.

Activity 8.48 | Inserting Sparklines

In this activity, you will insert column sparklines to visualize the ratio of Food to Non-Food sales for both Online and In-Store sales.

1 Click cell **B5**. On the **Insert tab**, in the **Sparklines group**, click **Column**. In the **Create Sparklines** dialog box, with the insertion point blinking in the **Data Range** box, select the range **C5:D5**. Compare your screen with Figure 8.91.

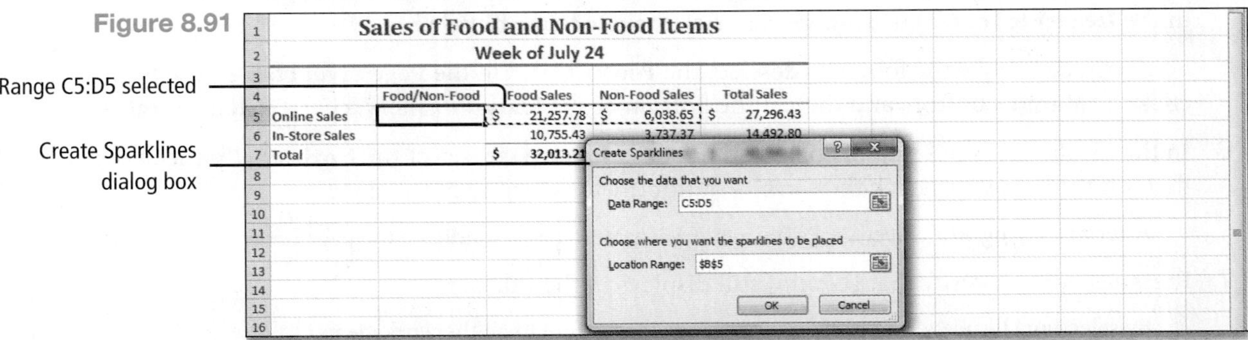

2 Click **OK**. Click cell **B6**, and then **Insert** a **Column Sparkline** for the range **C6:D6**. In the **Style group**, apply **Sparkline Style Accent 2, Darker 25%**—in the second row, the second style. Press Ctrl + Home, click **Save**, and then compare your screen with Figure 8.92.

You can see, at a glance, that for both Online and In-Store sales, Food sales are much greater than Non-Food sales.

Figure 8.92

Column sparklines compare sales of Food to Non-Food in both Online and In-Store

Sales of Food and Non-Food Items

Week of July 24

	Food/Non-Food	Food Sales	Non-Food Sales	Total Sales
Online Sales		$ 21,257.78	$ 6,038.65	$ 27,296.43
In-Store Sales		10,755.43	3,737.37	14,492.80
Total		$ 32,013.21	$ 9,776.02	$ 41,789.23

Objective 23 | Format and Print Multiple Worksheets in a Workbook

View the video on the Companion Web Site or in MyITLab

Each worksheet within a workbook can have different formatting, for example, different headers or footers. If all the worksheets in the workbook will have the same header or footer, you can select all the worksheets and apply formatting common to all of the worksheets; for example, you can set the same footer in all of the worksheets.

Activity 8.49 | Moving and Formatting Worksheets in a Workbook

In this activity, you will move the Summary sheet to become the first worksheet in the workbook. Then you will format and prepare your workbook for printing. The three worksheets containing data can be formatted simultaneously.

1 Point to the **Summary sheet tab**, hold down the left mouse button to display a small black triangle—a caret—and then notice that a small paper icon attaches to the mouse pointer.

2 Drag to the left until the caret and mouse pointer are to the left of the **Online Sales sheet tab**, as shown in Figure 8.93, and then release the left mouse button.

Use this technique to rearrange the order of worksheets within a workbook.

Figure 8.93

Caret moved to the left; mouse pointer with paper icon attached

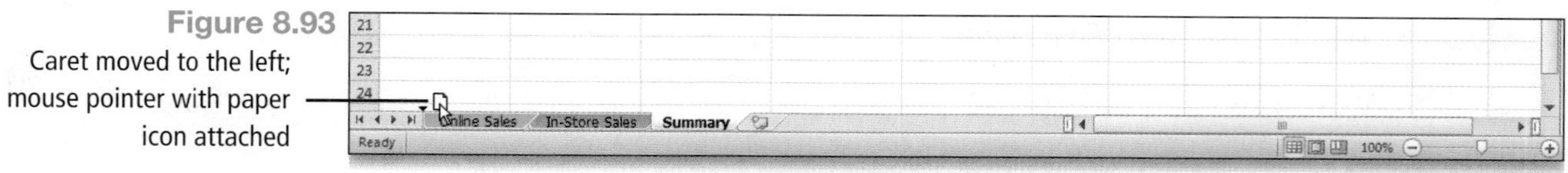

3 Be sure the **Summary** worksheet is the active sheet, point to its sheet tab, right-click, and then click **Select All Sheets** to display [*Group*] in the title bar. On the **Insert tab**, in the **Text group**, click **Header & Footer**.

4 In the **Navigation group**, click the **Go to Footer** button, click in the **left section** above the word *Footer*, and then in the **Header & Footer Elements group**, click the **File Name** button.

5 Click in a cell above the footer to deselect the **Footer area**. On the **Page Layout tab**, in the **Page Setup group**, click the **Margins** button, and then at the bottom of the **Margins** gallery, click **Custom Margins**.

6 In the displayed **Page Setup** dialog box, under **Center on page**, select the **Horizontally** check box. Click **OK**, and then on the status bar, click the **Normal** button to return to Normal view.

After displaying worksheets in Page Layout View, dotted lines indicate the page breaks in Normal view.

7 Press Ctrl + Home; verify that [*Group*] still displays in the title bar.

By selecting all sheets, you can apply the same formatting to all the worksheets at the same time.

8 Display **Backstage** view, show the **Document Panel**, type your firstname and lastname in the Author box, and then type your course name and section number in the **Subject** box. As the Keywords type **weekly sales, online, in-store** and then **Close** the **Document Information Panel**.

9 Press Ctrl + F2.

By grouping, you can view all sheets in Print Preview. If you do not see *1 of 3* at the bottom of the Preview, click the Home tab, select all the sheets again, and then redisplay Print Preview.

10 At the bottom of the **Print Preview**, click the **Next Page** button as necessary and take a moment to view each page of your workbook.

Activity 8.50 | Printing All the Worksheets in a Workbook

1 In **Backstage** view, click the **Save** button to save your workbook before printing. To submit your workbook electronically, follow the instructions provided by your instructor. To print your workbook, continue to Step 2.

2 Display **Backstage** view, click the **Print tab**, verify that the worksheets in your workbook are still grouped—[*Group*] displays in the title bar—and then in the center panel, in the **Print group**, click the **Print** button.

3 If required, print or create an electronic version of your worksheets with formulas displayed by using the instructions in Activity 8.16, and then **Close** [x] Excel without saving so that you do not save the changes you made to print formulas.

End **You have completed Project 8D**

Content-Based Assessments

Summary

In this chapter, you used Microsoft Excel 2010 to create and analyze data organized into columns and rows and to chart and perform calculations on the data. By organizing your data with Excel, you will be able to make calculations and create visual representations of your data in the form of charts. Also, you used the Statistical, Logical, and Date & Time functions from the Function Library. You created a table and analyzed the table's data by sorting and filtering. You also created a workbook with multiple worksheets, and then summarized all the worksheets on a summary worksheet.

Key Terms

Absolute cell reference 366
Accounting Number Format 352
Active cell 344
Arguments 375
Arithmetic operators 365
Auto Fill 345
AutoComplete 344
AutoFit 360
AutoSum 350
AVERAGE function 376
Category axis 354
Category labels 354
Cell 341
Cell address 344
Cell content 344
Cell reference 344
Cell style 351
Chart 353
Chart layout 355
Chart Layouts gallery 355
Chart styles 355
Chart Styles gallery ..355
Chart types 353
Column 343
Column chart 353
Column heading 343
Comma Style 353
Comparison operator 381
Conditional format ...382
Constant value 344
Context sensitive 345
COUNTIF function 380
Criteria 380
Data 344
Data bar 383
Data marker 354
Data point 354
Data series 354
Detail sheets 402
Displayed value 347
Drag and drop 378
Excel table 386
Expand Formula Bar button 343
Expand horizontal scroll bar button ...342
Fill handle 345
Filter 387
Find and Replace 383
Format 351
Formula 344
Formula Bar 342
Freeze Panes 385
Function 348
General format 347
Horizontal window split box 343
IF function 381
Insert Worksheet button 342
Label 344
Left alignment 344
Legend 354
Lettered column headings 343
Logical functions 380
Logical test 381
MAX function 377
MEDIAN function 377
Merge & Center 351
MIN function 377
Name Box 342
Navigate 392
Normal view 359
NOW function 384
Number format 347
Number values 344
Numbered row headings 343
Operators 365
Page Layout view 357
Pane 385
Paste 396
Paste area 396
Paste Options gallery 396
Picture element 346
Pixels 346
Point and click method 349
Print Titles 388
Range 347
Range finder 367
Relative cell reference 351
Rounding 350
Row 343
Row heading 343
Scale to Fit 388
Scaling 360
Select All box 343
Series 345
Sheet tab 359
Sheet tab scrolling buttons 342
Sheet tabs 392
Sort 387
Sparklines 353
Spreadsheet 341
Statistical functions 375
Status bar 342
SUM function 349
Summary Sheet 401
Text values 344
Underlying formula ...349
Underlying value 347
Value 344
Value axis 354
Vertical window split box 342
Volatile 384
Workbook 341
Workbook-level buttons 342
Worksheet 341
X-axis 354
Y-axis 354

Check Your Knowledge

Matching and Multiple Choice items are available in MyITLab and on the Companion Web Site.

Apply 8A skills from these Objectives:

1. Create, Save, and Navigate an Excel Workbook
2. Enter Data in a Worksheet
3. Construct and Copy Formulas and Use the SUM Function
4. Format Cells with Merge & Center and Cell Styles
5. Chart Data to Create a Column Chart and Insert Sparklines
6. Print, Display Formulas, and Close Excel

Mastering Excel | Project 8E Benefits Fair

In the following Mastering Excel project, you will create a worksheet comparing the sales of different types of external hard drives sold in the second quarter. Your completed worksheet will look similar to Figure 8.94.

Project Files

For Project 8E, you will need the following file:

New blank Excel workbook

You will save your workbook as:

Lastname_Firstname_8E_Hard_Drives

Project Results

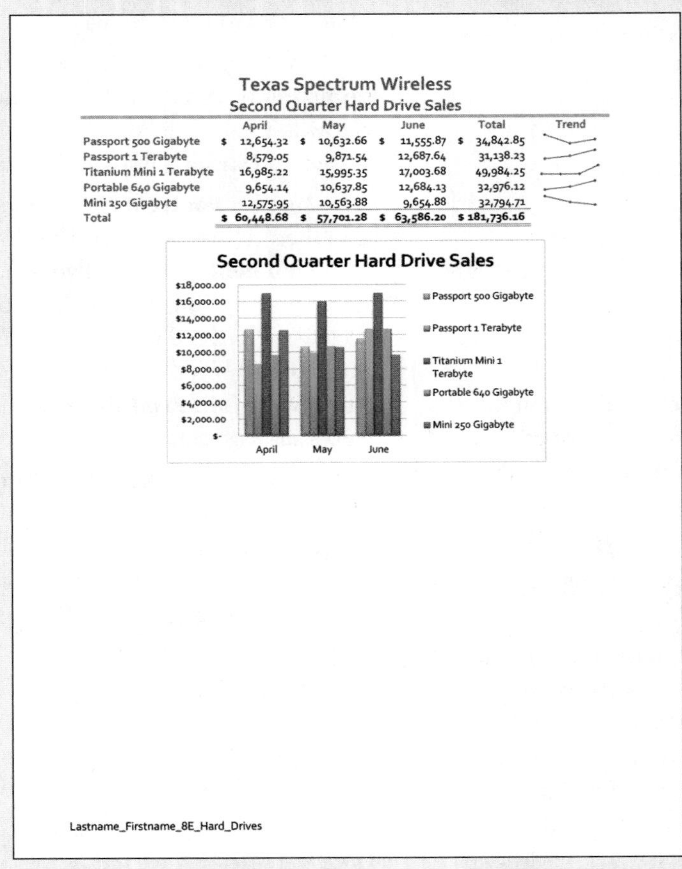

Texas Spectrum Wireless

Second Quarter Hard Drive Sales

	April	May	June	Total	Trend
Passport 500 Gigabyte	$ 12,654.32	$ 10,632.66	$ 11,555.87	$ 34,842.85	
Passport 1 Terabyte	8,579.05	9,871.54	12,687.64	31,138.23	
Titanium Mini 1 Terabyte	16,985.22	15,995.35	17,003.68	49,984.25	
Portable 640 Gigabyte	9,654.14	10,637.85	12,684.13	32,976.12	
Mini 250 Gigabyte	12,575.95	10,563.88	9,654.88	32,794.71	
Total	$ 60,448.68	$ 57,701.28	$ 63,586.20	$ 181,736.16	

Lastname_Firstname_8E_Hard_Drives

Figure 8.94

(Project 8E Benefits Fair continues on the next page)

Mastering Excel | Project 8E Benefits Fair (continued)

1 **Start** Excel. In cell **A1**, type **Texas Spectrum Wireless** and in cell **A2**, type **Second Quarter Hard Drive Sales** Change the **Theme** to **Module**, and then **Save** the workbook in your **All In One Chapter 8** folder as **Lastname_Firstname_8E_Hard_Drives**

2 In cell **B3**, type **April** and then use the fill handle to enter the months *May* and *June* in the range **C3:D3**. In cell **E3**, type **Total** and in cell **F3**, type **Trend**

3 **Center** the column titles in the range **B3:F3**. **Merge & Center** the title across the range **A1:F1**, and apply the **Title** cell style. **Merge & Center** the subtitle across the range **A2:F2**, and apply the **Heading 1** cell style.

4 Widen **column A** to **170 pixels**, and then in the range **A4:A9**, type the following row titles:

Passport 500 Gigabyte

Passport 1 Terabyte

Titanium Mini 1 Terabyte

Portable 640 Gigabyte

Mini 250 Gigabyte

Total

5 Widen columns **B:F** to **100 pixels**, and then in the range **B4:D8**, enter the monthly sales figures for each type of hard drive, as shown in **Table 1** at the bottom of the page.

6 In cell **B9**, **Sum** the *April* hard drive sales, and then copy the formula across to cells **C9:D9**. In cell **E4**, **Sum** the *Passport 500 Gigabyte sales*, and then copy the formula down to cells **E5:E9**.

7 Apply the **Heading 4** cell style to the row titles and the column titles. Apply the **Total** cell style to the totals in the range **B9:E9**. Apply the **Accounting Number Format** to the first row of sales figures and to the total row. Apply the **Comma Style** to the remaining sales figures.

8 To compare the monthly sales of each product visually, select the range that represents the sales figures for the three months, including the month names, and for each product name—do not include any totals in the range. With this data selected, **Insert** a **2-D Clustered Column** chart. Switch the Row/Column data so that the months display on the category axis and the types of hard drives display in the legend.

9 Position the upper left corner of the chart in the approximate center of cell **A11** so that the chart is visually centered below the worksheet, as shown in Figure 8.94. Apply **Chart Style 26**, and then modify the **Chart Layout** by applying **Layout 1**. Change the **Chart Title** to **Second Quarter Hard Drive Sales**

10 In the range **F4:F8**, insert **Line** sparklines that compare the monthly data. Do not include the totals. Show the sparkline **Markers** and apply **Sparkline Style Accent 2, Darker 50%**—in the first row, the second style.

11 Insert a **Footer** with the **File Name** in the **left section**, and then return the worksheet to **Normal** view. Display the **Document Panel**, add your name, your course name and section, and the keywords **hard drives, sales** Delete the unused sheets, and then center the worksheet **Horizontally** on the page. Check your worksheet by previewing it in **Print Preview**, and then make any necessary corrections.

12 **Save** your workbook, and then print or submit electronically as directed. If required by your instructor, print or create an electronic version of your worksheets with formulas displayed by using the instructions in Activity 8.16. **Exit** Excel without saving so that you do not save the changes you made to print formulas.

	April	May	June
Passport 500 Gigabyte	12654.32	10632.66	11555.87
Passport 1 Terabyte	8579.05	9871.54	12687.64
Titanium Mini 1 Terabyte	16985.22	15995.35	17003.68
Portable 640 Gigabyte	9654.14	10637.85	12684.13
Mini 250 Gigabyte	12575.95	10563.88	9654.88

Return to Step 6

End You have completed Project 8E

Apply 8B skills from these Objectives:

7 Check Spelling in a Worksheet
8 Enter Data by Range
9 Construct Formulas for Mathematical Operations
10 Edit Values in a Worksheet
11 Format a Worksheet

Mastering Excel | Project 8F Camera Accessories

In the following Mastering Excel project, you will create a worksheet that summarizes the sale of digital camera accessories. Your completed worksheet will look similar to Figure 8.95.

Project Files

For Project 8F, you will need the following file:

New blank Excel workbook

You will save your workbook as:

Lastname_Firstname_8F_Camera_Accessories

Project Results

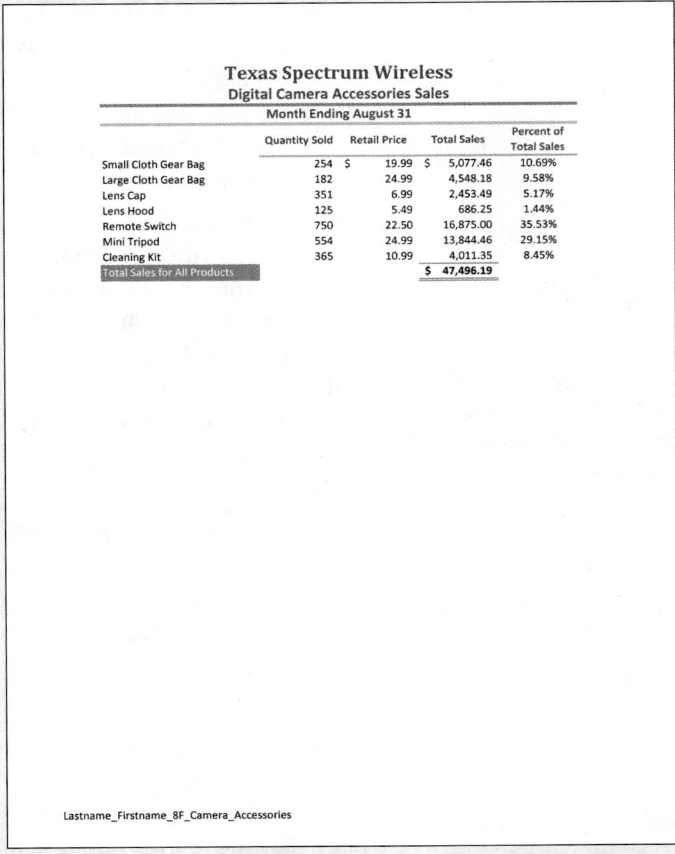

Texas Spectrum Wireless
Digital Camera Accessories Sales
Month Ending August 31

	Quantity Sold	Retail Price	Total Sales	Percent of Total Sales
Small Cloth Gear Bag	254	$ 19.99	$ 5,077.46	10.69%
Large Cloth Gear Bag	182	24.99	4,548.18	9.58%
Lens Cap	351	6.99	2,453.49	5.17%
Lens Hood	125	5.49	686.25	1.44%
Remote Switch	750	22.50	16,875.00	35.53%
Mini Tripod	554	24.99	13,844.46	29.15%
Cleaning Kit	365	10.99	4,011.35	8.45%
Total Sales for All Products			$ 47,496.19	

Lastname_Firstname_8F_Camera_Accessories

Figure 8.95

(Project 8F Camera Accessories continues on the next page)

Mastering Excel | Project 8F Camera Accessories (continued)

1 **Start** Excel and display a new blank workbook. **Save** the workbook in your **All In One Chapter 8** folder as **Lastname_Firstname_8F_Camera_Accessories** In cell **A1**, type **Texas Spectrum Wireless** In cell **A2**, type **Digital Camera Accessories Sales** and then **Merge & Center** the title and the subtitle across **columns A:F**. Apply the **Title** and **Heading 1** cell styles respectively.

2 Beginning in cell **B3**, type the following column titles: **Product Number** and **Quantity Sold** and **Retail Price** and **Total Sales** and **Percent of Total Sales**

3 Beginning in cell **A4**, type the following row titles, including misspelled words:

Small Cloth Gear Bag

Large Cloth Gear Bag

Lens Cap

Lens Hood

Remote Switch

Mini Tripod

Cleening Kit

Total Sales for All Products

4 Make cell **A1** the active cell, and then check spelling in your worksheet. Correct *Cleening* to **Cleaning**, and make any other necessary corrections. Widen **column A** to **180 pixels** and **columns B:F** to **90 pixels**.

5 In the range **B4:D10**, type the data shown in the following table:

	Product Number	Quantity Sold	Retail Price
Small Cloth Gear Bag	CGB-3	254	19.99
Large Cloth Gear Bag	CGB-8	182	24.99
Lens Cap	LC-2	351	6.99
Lens Hood	LH-4	125	5.49
Remote Switch	RS-5	677	22.50
Mini Tripod	MTP-6	554	29.99
Cleaning Kit	CK-8	365	10.99

6 In cell **E4**, construct a formula to calculate the *Total Sales* of the *Small Cloth Gear Bags* by multiplying the *Quantity Sold* times the *Retail Price*. Copy the formula down for the remaining products. In cell **E11**, use the **SUM** function to calculate the *Total Sales for All Products*, and then apply the **Total** cell style to the cell.

7 Using absolute cell references as necessary so that you can copy the formula, in cell **F4**, construct a formula to calculate the *Percent of Total Sales* for the first product by dividing the *Total Sales* of the *Small Cloth Gear Bags* by the *Total Sales for All Products*. Copy the formula down for the remaining products. To the computed percentages, apply **Percent Style** with two decimal places, and then **Center** the percentages.

8 Apply the **Comma Style** with no decimal places to the *Quantity Sold* figures. To cells **D4**, **E4**, and **E11** apply the **Accounting Number Format**. To the range **D5:E10**, apply the **Comma Style**.

9 Change the *Retail Price* of the *Mini Tripod* to **24.99** and the *Quantity Sold* of the *Remote Switch* to **750** Delete **column B**, and then **Insert** a new **row 3**. In cell **A3**, type **Month Ending August 31** and then **Merge & Center** the text across the range **A3:E3**. Apply the **Heading 2** cell style. To cell **A12**, apply the **Accent1** cell style. Select the four column titles, apply **Wrap Text**, **Middle Align**, and **Center** formatting, and then apply the **Heading 3** cell style.

10 Insert a **Footer** with the **File Name** in the **left section**, and then return to **Normal** view. Display the **Document Panel**, add your name, your course name and section, and the keywords **digital camera accessories, sales**

11 Delete the unused sheets, and then center the worksheet **Horizontally** on the page. Preview the worksheet in **Print Preview**, and make any necessary corrections.

12 **Save** your workbook, and then print or submit electronically as directed. If required by your instructor, print or create an electronic version of your worksheets with formulas displayed by using the instructions in Activity 8.16. **Exit** Excel without saving so that you do not save the changes you made to print formulas.

End **You have completed Project 8F**

Content-Based Assessments

Apply 8C skills from these Objectives:

12 Use the SUM, AVERAGE, MEDIAN, MIN, and MAX Functions
13 Move Data, Resolve Error Messages, and Rotate Text
14 Use COUNTIF and IF Functions and Apply Conditional Formatting
15 Use Date & Time Functions and Freeze Panes
16 Create, Sort, and Filter an Excel Table
17 Format and Print a Large Worksheet

Mastering Excel | Project 8G Desserts

In the following Mastery project, you will edit a worksheet for Laura Morales, President, detailing the current inventory of desserts produced at the San Diego facility. Your completed worksheet will look similar to Figure 8.96

Project Files

For Project 8G, you will need the following file:
e08G_Desserts

You will save your workbook as:
Lastname_Firstname_8G_Desserts

Project Results

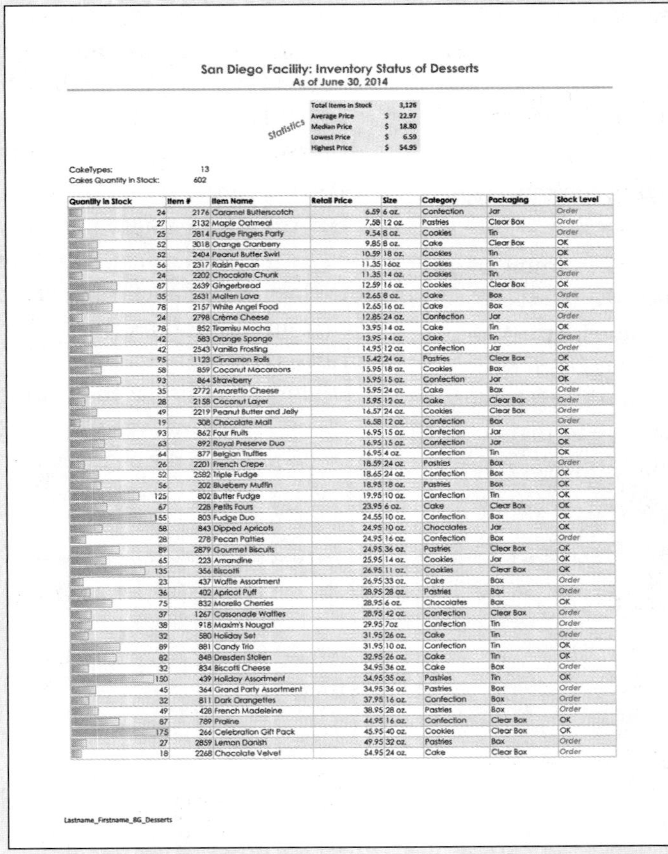

San Diego Facility: Inventory Status of Desserts
As of June 30, 2014

Statistics

Total Items in Stock		3,126
Average Price	$	22.97
Median Price	$	18.80
Lowest Price	$	6.59
Highest Price	$	54.95

CakeTypes: 13
Cakes Quantity in Stock: 602

Quantity in Stock	Item #	Item Name	Retail Price	Size	Category	Packaging	Stock Level
24	2176	Caramel Butterscotch	6.59	6 oz.	Confection	Jar	Order
27	2132	Maple Oatmeal	7.58	12 oz.	Pastries	Clear Box	Order
25	2814	Fudge Fingers Party	9.54	8 oz.	Cookies	Tin	Order
52	3018	Orange Cranberry	9.85	8 oz.	Cake	Clear Box	OK
52	2404	Peanut Butter Swirl	10.59	18 oz.	Cookies	Tin	OK
56	2317	Raisin Pecan	11.35	16oz	Cookies	Tin	OK
24	2202	Chocolate Chunk	11.35	14 oz.	Cookies	Tin	Order
87	2639	Gingerbread	12.59	16 oz.	Cookies	Clear Box	OK
35	2631	Molten Lava	12.65	8 oz.	Cake	Box	Order
78	2157	White Angel Food	12.65	16 oz.	Cake	Box	OK
24	2798	Crème Cheese	12.85	24 oz.	Confection	Jar	Order
78	852	Tiramisu Mocha	13.95	14 oz.	Cake	Tin	OK
42	583	Orange Sponge	13.95	14 oz.	Cake	Tin	Order
42	2543	Vanilla Frosting	14.95	12 oz.	Confection	Jar	Order
95	1123	Cinnamon Rolls	15.42	24 oz.	Pastries	Clear Box	OK
58	859	Coconut Macaroons	15.95	18 oz.	Cookies	Box	OK
93	864	Strawberry	15.95	15 oz.	Confection	Jar	OK
35	2772	Amaretto Cheese	15.95	24 oz.	Cake	Box	Order
28	2158	Coconut Layer	15.95	12 oz.	Cake	Clear Box	Order
49	2219	Peanut Butter and Jelly	16.57	24 oz.	Cookies	Clear Box	Order
19	308	Chocolate Malt	16.58	12 oz.	Confection	Box	Order
93	862	Four Fruits	16.95	15 oz.	Confection	Jar	OK
63	892	Royal Preserve Duo	16.95	15 oz.	Confection	Jar	OK
64	877	Belgian Truffles	16.95	4 oz.	Confection	Tin	OK
26	2201	French Crepe	18.59	24 oz.	Pastries	Box	Order
52	2582	Triple Fudge	18.65	24 oz.	Confection	Box	OK
56	202	Blueberry Muffin	18.95	18 oz.	Pastries	Box	OK
125	802	Butter Fudge	19.95	10 oz.	Confection	Tin	OK
67	228	Petits Fours	23.95	6 oz.	Cake	Clear Box	OK
155	803	Fudge Duo	24.55	10 oz.	Confection	Box	OK
58	843	Dipped Apricots	24.95	10 oz.	Chocolates	Jar	OK
28	278	Pecan Patties	24.95	16 oz.	Confection	Box	Order
89	2879	Gourmet Biscuits	24.95	36 oz.	Pastries	Clear Box	OK
65	223	Amandine	25.95	14 oz.	Cookies	Jar	OK
135	356	Biscotti	26.95	11 oz.	Cookies	Clear Box	OK
23	437	Waffle Assortment	26.95	33 oz.	Cake	Box	Order
36	402	Apricot Puff	28.95	28 oz.	Pastries	Box	Order
75	832	Morello Cherries	28.95	6 oz.	Chocolates	Box	OK
37	1267	Cassonade Waffles	28.95	42 oz.	Confection	Clear Box	Order
38	918	Maxim's Nougat	29.95	7oz	Confection	Tin	Order
32	580	Holiday Set	31.95	26 oz.	Cake	Tin	Order
89	881	Candy Trio	31.95	10 oz.	Confection	Tin	OK
82	848	Dresden Stollen	32.95	26 oz.	Cake	Tin	OK
32	834	Biscotti Cheese	34.95	36 oz.	Cake	Box	Order
150	439	Holiday Assortment	34.95	35 oz.	Pastries	Tin	OK
45	364	Grand Party Assortment	34.95	36 oz.	Pastries	Box	Order
32	811	Dark Orangettes	37.95	16 oz.	Confection	Box	Order
49	428	French Madeleine	38.95	28 oz.	Pastries	Box	Order
87	789	Praline	44.95	16 oz.	Confection	Clear Box	OK
175	266	Celebration Gift Pack	45.95	40 oz.	Cookies	Clear Box	OK
27	2859	Lemon Danish	49.95	32 oz.	Pastries	Box	Order
18	2268	Chocolate Velvet	54.95	24 oz.	Cake	Clear Box	Order

Lastname_Firstname_8G_Desserts

Figure 8.96

(Project 8G Desserts continues on the next page)

Content-Based Assessments

Mastering Excel | Project 8G Desserts (continued)

1 **Start** Excel, from your student files, locate and open **e08G_Desserts**, and then **Save** the file in your **All In One Chapter 8** folder as **Lastname_Firstname_8G_Desserts**

2 In cell **B4**, calculate the **Total Items in Stock** by summing the **Quantity in Stock** data, and then apply **Comma Style** with zero decimal places to the result. In each cell in the range **B5:B8**, insert formulas to calculate the Average, Median, Lowest, and Highest retail prices, and then apply the **Accounting Number Format** to each result.

3 Move the range **A4:B8** to the range **D4:E8**, and then apply the **20% - Accent1** cell style. Widen **column D** to **130** pixels. In cell **C6**, type **Statistics** select the range **C4:C8**, and then from the **Format Cells** dialog box, merge the selected cells. Change the text **Orientation** to **25 Degrees**, and then apply **Bold** and **Italic**. Change the **Font Size** to **14** and the **Font Color** to **Pink, Accent 1, Darker 25%**. Apply **Middle Align** and **Align Text Right**.

4 In cell **B10**, use the **COUNTIF** function to count the number of **Cake** items. In the **Packaging** column, **Replace All** occurrences of **Cellophane** with **Clear Box**

5 In cell **H14**, enter an **IF** function to determine the items that must be ordered. If the **Quantity in Stock** is less than **50** the **Value_if_true** is **Order** Otherwise the **Value_if_false** is **OK** Fill the formula down through cell **H65**. Apply **Conditional Formatting** to the **Stock Level** column so that cells that contain the text *Order* are formatted with **Bold Italic** and with a **Color** of **Orange, Accent 5**. Apply conditional formatting to the **Quantity in Stock** column by applying a **Gradient Fill Orange Data Bar**.

6 Format the range **A13:H65** as a table with headers, and apply the **Table Style Light 16** style. Sort the table from smallest to largest by **Retail Price**, and then filter on the **Category** column to display the **Cake** types. Display a **Total Row** in the table and then in cell **A66**, **Sum** the **Quantity in Stock** for the **Cake** items. Type the result in cell **B11**, and apply appropriate number formatting. Click in the table, and then on the **Design tab**, remove the total row from the table. Clear the **Category** filter and convert the table to a range.

7 Change the theme to **Composite**. Display the footer area, and insert the **File Name** in the **left section**. Center the worksheet **Horizontally**, and then use the **Scale to Fit** option to change the **Width** to **1 page**. Return to **Normal** view and make cell **A1** the active cell. In **Backstage** view, display the **Print Preview**, and then make any necessary corrections.

8 Add your name, your course name and section, and the keywords desserts **inventory, San Diego** to the Document Panel. **Save**, and then print or submit electronically as directed. If required by your instructor, print or create an electronic version of your worksheets with formulas displayed by using the instructions in Activity 8.16, and then **Close** Excel without saving so that you do not save the changes you made to print formulas.

End **You have completed Project 8G**

Content-Based Assessments

Apply **8D** skills from these Objectives:

- **18** Navigate a Workbook and Rename Worksheets
- **19** Enter Dates, Clear Contents, and Clear Formats
- **20** Copy and Paste by Using the Paste Options Gallery
- **21** Edit and Format Multiple Worksheets at the Same Time
- **22** Create a Summary Sheet with Column Sparklines
- **23** Format and Print Multiple Worksheets in a Workbook

Mastering Excel | Project 8H Compensation

In the following Mastery project, you will edit a workbook that summarizes the Laurales Herb and Spices salesperson compensation for the month of November. Your completed worksheet will look similar to Figure 8.97.

Project Files

For Project 8H, you will need the following file:

e08H_Compensation

You will save your workbook as:

Lastname_Firstname_8H_Compensation

Project Results

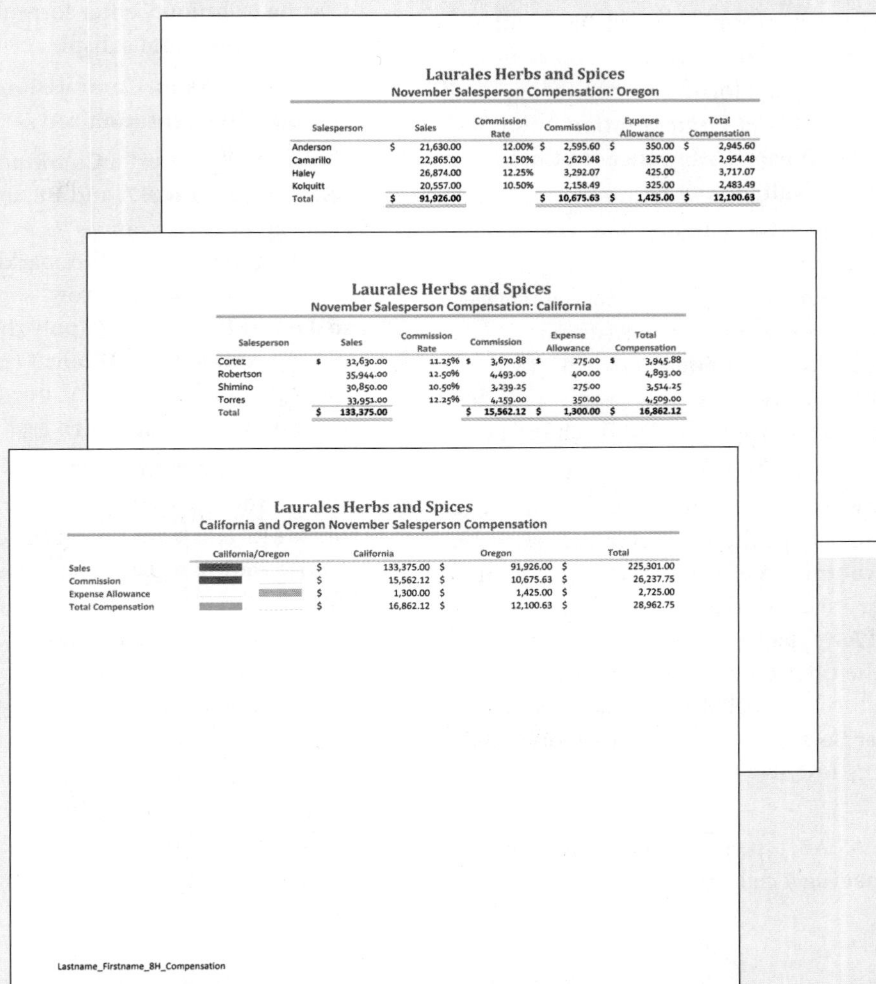

Laurales Herbs and Spices
November Salesperson Compensation: Oregon

Salesperson	Sales	Commission Rate	Commission	Expense Allowance	Total Compensation
Anderson	$ 21,630.00	12.00%	$ 2,595.60	$ 350.00	$ 2,945.60
Camarillo	22,865.00	11.50%	2,629.48	325.00	2,954.48
Haley	26,874.00	12.25%	3,292.07	425.00	3,717.07
Kolquitt	20,557.00	10.50%	2,158.49	325.00	2,483.49
Total	$ 91,926.00		$ 10,675.63	$ 1,425.00	$ 12,100.63

Laurales Herbs and Spices
November Salesperson Compensation: California

Salesperson	Sales	Commission Rate	Commission	Expense Allowance	Total Compensation
Cortez	$ 32,630.00	11.25%	$ 3,670.88	$ 275.00	$ 3,945.88
Robertson	35,944.00	12.50%	4,493.00	400.00	4,893.00
Shimino	30,850.00	10.50%	3,239.25	275.00	3,514.25
Torres	33,951.00	12.25%	4,159.00	350.00	4,509.00
Total	$ 133,375.00		$ 15,562.12	$ 1,300.00	$ 16,862.12

Laurales Herbs and Spices
California and Oregon November Salesperson Compensation

	California/Oregon	California	Oregon	Total
Sales		$ 133,375.00	$ 91,926.00	$ 225,301.00
Commission		$ 15,562.12	$ 10,675.63	$ 26,237.75
Expense Allowance		$ 1,300.00	$ 1,425.00	$ 2,725.00
Total Compensation		$ 16,862.12	$ 12,100.63	$ 28,962.75

Lastname_Firstname_8H_Compensation

Figure 8.97

(Project 8H Compensation continues on the next page)

Mastering Excel | Project 8H Compensation (continued)

1 **Start** Excel, from your student files, open **e08H_Compensation**, and then save the file in your **All In One Chapter 8** folder as **Lastname_Firstname_8H_Compensation**

2 Rename **Sheet1** as **California** and change the **Tab Color** to **Green, Accent 1**. Rename **Sheet2** as **Oregon** and change the **Tab Color** to **Gold, Accent 3**.

3 Click the **California sheet tab** to make it the active sheet, and then group the worksheets. In cell **A1**, type **Laurales Herbs and Spices** and then **Merge & Center** the text across the range **A1:F1**. Apply the **Title** cell style. **Merge & Center** the text in cell **A2** across the range **A2:F2**, and then apply the **Heading 1** cell style.

4 With the sheets still grouped, in cell **D5** calculate **Commission** for *Cortez* by multiplying the **Sales** by the **Commission Rate**. Copy the formula down through cell **D8**. In cell **F5**, calculate **Total Compensation** by summing the **Commission** and **Expense Allowance** for *Cortez*. Copy the formula down through the cell **F8**.

5 In **row 9**, sum the **Sales**, **Commission**, **Expense Allowance**, and **Total Compensation** columns. Apply the **Accounting Number Format** with two decimal places to the appropriate cells **in row 5** and **row 9** (do not include the percentages). Apply the **Comma Style** with two decimal places to the appropriate cells in **rows 6:8** (do not include the percentages). Apply the **Total** cell style to the appropriate cells in the Total row.

6 Insert a new worksheet. Change the sheet name to **Summary** and then change the **Tab Color** to **Periwinkle, Accent 5**. Widen **columns A:E** to **165** pixels, and then move the **Summary** sheet so that it is the first sheet in the workbook. In cell **A1**, type **Laurales Herbs and Spices** **Merge & Center** the title across the range **A1:E1**, and then apply the **Title** cell style. In cell **A2**, type **California and Oregon November Salesperson Compensation** and then **Merge & Center** the text across the range **A2:E2**. Apply the **Heading 1** cell style.

7 In the range **A5:A8**, type the following row titles and then apply the **Heading 4** cell style:

Sales

Commission

Expense Allowance

Total Compensation

8 In the range **B4:E4**, type the following column titles, and then **Center** and apply the **Heading 3** cell style.

California/Oregon

California

Oregon

Total

9 In cell **C5**, enter a formula that references cell **B9** in the **California** worksheet so that the total sales for California display in **C5**. Create similar formulas to enter the total **Commission**, **Expense Allowance** and **Total Compensation** for California in the range **C6:C8**. Using the same technique, enter formulas in the range **D5:D8** so that the **Oregon** totals display.

10 Sum the **Sales**, **Commission**, **Expense Allowance**, and **Total Compensation** rows.

11 In cell **B5**, insert a **Column Sparkline** for the range **C5:D5**. In cells **B6**, **B7**, and **B8**, insert **Column** sparklines for the appropriate ranges to compare California totals with Oregon totals. To the sparkline in **B6**, apply the second style in the third row—**Sparkline Style Accent 2**, (**no dark or light**). In **B7** apply the third style in the third row—**Sparkline Style Accent 3** (**no dark or light**). In **B8** apply the fourth style in the third row—**Sparkline Style Accent 4**, (**no dark or light**).

12 **Group** the three worksheets, and then insert a footer in the left section with the **File Name**. Center the worksheets **Horizontally** on the page, and then change the **Orientation** to **Landscape**. Return the document to **Normal** view.

13 Display the **Document Panel**. Add your name, your course name and section, and the keywords **November sales** **Save** your workbook, and then print or submit electronically as directed. If required by your instructor, print or create an electronic version of your worksheets with formulas displayed by using the instructions in Activity 8.16, and then **Close** Excel without saving so that you do not save the changes you made to print formulas.

End **You have completed Project 8H**

Apply 8A and 8B skills from these Objectives:

1 Create, Save, and Navigate an Excel Workbook
2 Enter Data in a Worksheet
3 Construct and Copy Formulas and Use the SUM Function
4 Format Cells with Merge & Center and Cell Styles
5 Chart Data to Create a Column Chart and Insert Sparklines
6 Print, Display Formulas, and Close Excel
7 Check Spelling in a Worksheet
8 Enter Data by Range
9 Construct Formulas for Mathematical Operations
10 Edit Values in a Worksheet
11 Format a Worksheet

Mastering Excel | Project 8I Accessory Sales

In the following Mastering Excel project, you will create a new worksheet that compares annual accessory sales by store location. Your completed worksheet will look similar to Figure 8.98.

Project Files

For Project 8I, you will need the following file:

New blank Excel workbook

You will save your workbook as:

Lastname_Firstname_8I_Accessory_Sales

Project Results

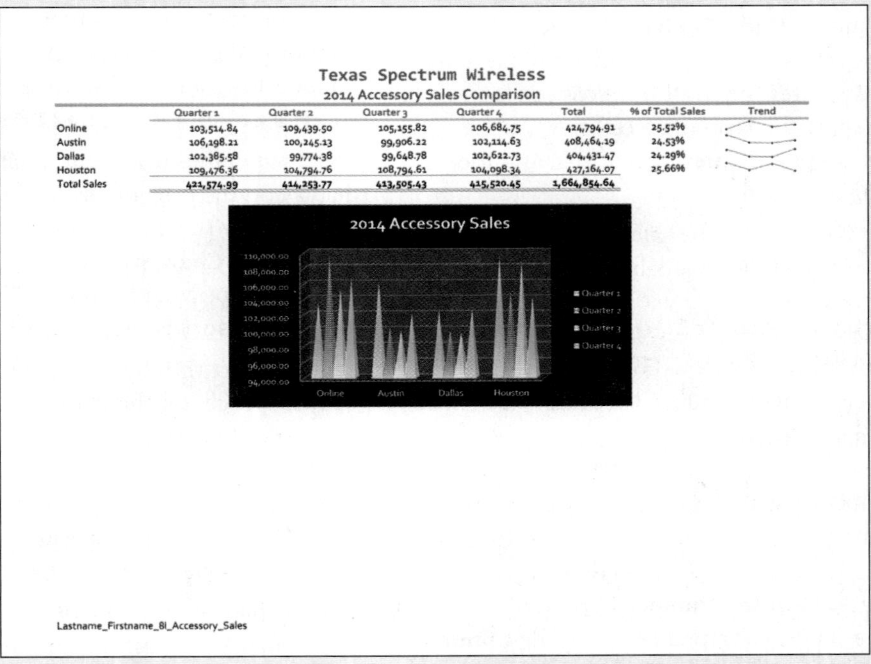

Texas Spectrum Wireless

2014 Accessory Sales Comparison

	Quarter 1	Quarter 2	Quarter 3	Quarter 4	Total	% of Total Sales	Trend
Online	103,514.84	109,439.50	105,155.82	106,684.75	424,794.91	25.52%	
Austin	106,198.21	100,245.13	99,906.22	102,114.63	408,464.19	24.53%	
Dallas	102,385.58	99,774.38	99,648.78	102,622.73	404,431.47	24.29%	
Houston	109,476.36	104,794.76	108,794.61	104,098.34	427,164.07	25.66%	
Total Sales	421,574.99	414,253.77	413,505.43	415,520.45	1,664,854.64		

Figure 8.98

(Project 8I Accessory Sales continues on the next page)

Mastering Excel | Project 8I Accessory Sales (continued)

1 **Start** Excel. In a new blank workbook, as the worksheet title, in cell **A1**, type **Texas Spectrum Wireless** As the worksheet subtitle, in cell **A2**, type **2014 Accessory Sales Comparison by Location** and then **Save** the workbook in your **All In One Chapter 8** folder as **Lastname_Firstname_8I_Accessory_Sales**

2 In cell **B3**, type **Quarter 1** and then use the fill handle to enter *Quarter 2*, *Quarter 3*, and *Quarter 4* in the range **C3:E3**. In cell **F3**, type **Total** In cell **G3**, type **% of Total Sales** In cell **H3**, type **Trend**

3 In the range **A4:A7**, type the following row titles: **Online** and **Austin** and **Houston** and **Total Sales**

4 Widen columns **A:H** to **115 pixels**. **Merge & Center** the title across the range **A1:H1**, and then apply the **Title** cell style. **Merge & Center** the subtitle across the range **A2:H2**, and then apply the **Heading 1** cell style. Select the seven column titles, apply **Center** formatting, and then apply the **Heading 3** cell style.

5 In the range **B4:E6**, enter the sales values for each Quarter as shown in the following table:

	Quarter 1	**Quarter 2**	**Quarter 3**	**Quarter 4**
Online	103514.84	109439.50	105155.82	106684.75
Austin	106198.21	100245.13	99906.22	102114.63
Houston	109476.36	104794.76	108794.61	104098.34

6 **Sum** the *Quarter 1* sales, and then copy the formula across for the remaining quarters. **Sum** the sales for the *Online* sales, and then copy the formula down through cell **F7**. Apply the **Accounting Number Format** to the first row of sales figures and to the total row, and the **Comma Style** to the remaining sales figures. Format the totals in **row 7** with the **Total** cell style.

7 **Insert** a new **row 6** with the row title **Dallas** and the following sales figures for each quarter: **102385.58** and **99774.38** and **99648.78** and **102622.73** Copy the formula in cell **F5** down to cell **F6** to sum the new row.

8 Using absolute cell references as necessary so that you can copy the formula, in cell **G4** construct a formula to calculate the *Percent of Total Sales* for the first location by dividing the *Total* for the *Online* sales by the *Total Sales* for all Quarters. Copy the formula down for the remaining locations. To the computed percentages, apply **Percent Style** with two decimal places, and then **Center** the percentages.

9 Insert **Line** sparklines in the range **H4:H7** that compare the quarterly data. Do not include the totals. Show the sparkline **Markers** and apply the first style in the second row—**Sparkline Style Accent 1, Darker 25%**.

10 **Save** your workbook. To chart and then compare the quarterly sales of each location visually, select the range that represents the sales figures for the four quarters, including the quarter names and each location—do not include any totals in the range. With this data selected, **Insert** a **Column**, **Clustered Pyramid** chart.

11 Switch the row/column data so that the locations display on the category axis. Position the top edge of the chart in **row 10** and visually center it below the worksheet data. Apply **Chart Style 42**, and then modify the **Chart Layout** by applying **Layout 1**. Above the chart, display **2014 Accessory Sales** as the **Chart Title**.

12 Deselect the chart. Change the **Orientation** to **Landscape**, center the worksheet **Horizontally** on the page, and then change the **Theme** to **Metro**. Scale the worksheet so that the **Width** fits to **1 page**. Insert a **Footer** with the **File Name** in the **left section**. Return the worksheet to **Normal** view and make **A1** the active cell so that you can view the top of your worksheet.

13 Display the **Document Panel**, add your name, your course name and section, and the keywords **accessories, sales** Delete the unused sheets, preview your worksheet in **Print Preview**, and then make any necessary corrections.

14 **Save** your workbook, and then print or submit electronically as directed. If required by your instructor, print or create an electronic version of your worksheets with formulas displayed by using the instructions in Activity 8.16. **Exit** Excel without saving so that you do not save the changes you made to print formulas.

End **You have completed Project 8I**

Apply 8C and 8D skills from these Objectives:

12 Use the SUM, AVERAGE, MEDIAN, MIN, and MAX Functions

13 Move Data, Resolve Error Messages, and Rotate Text

14 Use COUNTIF and IF Functions and Apply Conditional Formatting

15 Use Date & Time Functions and Freeze Panes

16 Create, Sort, and Filter an Excel Table

17 Format and Print a Large Worksheet

18 Navigate a Workbook and Rename Worksheets

19 Enter Dates, Clear Contents, and Clear Formats

20 Copy and Paste by Using the Paste Options Gallery

21 Edit and Format Multiple Worksheets at the Same Time

22 Create a Summary Sheet with Column Sparklines

23 Format and Print Multiple Worksheets in a Workbook

Mastering Excel | Project 8J Inventory Summary

In the following Mastery project, you will edit a worksheet that summarizes the inventory status at the San Rafael production facility. Your completed workbook will look similar to Figure 8.99.

Project Files

For Project 8J, you will need the following file:

e08J_Inventory_Summary

You will save your workbook as:

Lastname_Firstname_8J_Inventory_Summary

Project Results

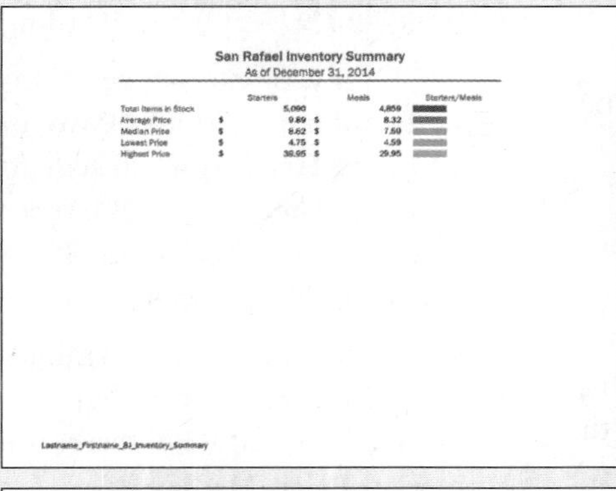

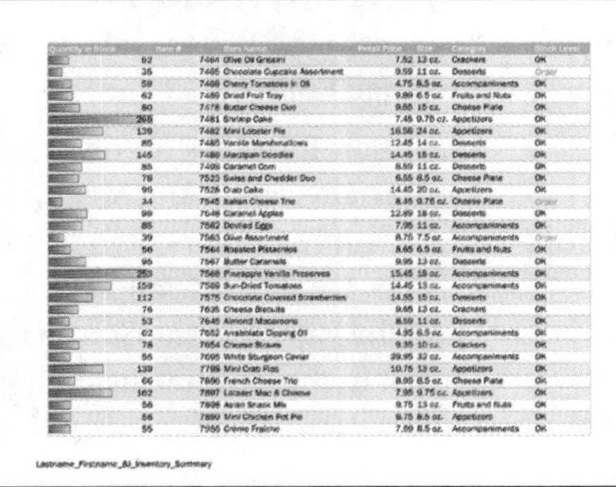

Figure 8.99

(Project 8J Inventory Summary continues on the next page)

Content-Based Assessments

Mastering Excel | Project 8J Inventory Summary (continued)

1 **Start** Excel. From your student files, open **e08J_Inventory_Summary**. Save the file in your **All In One Chapter 8** folder as **Lastname_Firstname_8J_Inventory_Summary**

2 Rename **Sheet1** as **Starters** and **Sheet2** as **Meals** Make the following calculations in each of the two worksheets *without* grouping the sheets:

- In cell **B4**, enter a formula to sum the **Quantity in Stock** data, and then apply **Comma Style** with zero decimal places to the result.
- In cells **B5:B8**, enter formulas to calculate the Average, Median, Lowest, and Highest retail prices, and then apply the **Accounting Number Format**.

3 In each of the two worksheets, make the following calculations without grouping the sheets:

- In cell **B10**, enter a COUNTIF function to determine how many different types of **Crackers** products are in stock on the **Starters** sheet and how many different types of **Salad** products are in stock on the **Meals** worksheet.
- In cell **G15**, enter an **IF** function to determine the items that must be ordered. If the **Quantity in Stock** is less than **40** the **Value_if_true** is **Order** Otherwise the **Value_if_false** is **OK** Fill the formula down through all the rows.
- Apply **Conditional Formatting** to the **Stock Level** column so that cells that contain the text *Order* are formatted with **Bold Italic** with a **Font Color** of **Green, Accent 5, Darker 25%**. Apply **Gradient Fill Red Data Bars** to the **Quantity in Stock** column.

4 In the **Starters** sheet, format the range **A14:G64** as a table with headers and apply **Table Style Medium 6**. Insert a **Total Row**, filter by **Category** for **Crackers**, and then **Sum** the **Quantity in Stock** column. Record the result in cell **B11**.

5 Select the table, clear the filter, **Sort** the table on the **Item #** column from **Smallest to Largest**, remove the **Total Row**, and then convert the table to a range. On the **Page Layout tab**, set **Print Titles** so that **row 14** repeats at the top of each page.

6 In the **Meals** sheet, format the range **A14:G61** as a table with headers and apply **Table Style Light 20**. Insert a **Total Row**, filter by **Category** for **Salad**, and then **Sum** the **Quantity in Stock** column. Record the result in cell **B11**.

7 Select the table, clear the filter, **Sort** the table on the **Item #** column from **Smallest to Largest**, remove the **Total Row**, and then convert the table to a range.

8 On the **Page Layout tab**, set **Print Titles** so that **row 14** repeats at the top of each page, and then **Save** your workbook. **Group** the two worksheets. **Center** the worksheets **Horizontally**, and then use the **Scale to Fit** option to change the **Width** to **1 page**.

9 Insert a new worksheet. Change the sheet name to **Summary** and then widen **columns A:D** to **170** pixels. Move the **Summary** sheet so that it is the first sheet in the workbook. In cell **A1**, type **San Rafael Inventory Summary** **Merge & Center** the title across the range **A1:D1**, and then apply the **Title** cell style. In cell **A2**, type **As of December 31, 2014** and then **Merge & Center** the text across the range **A2:D2**. Apply the **Heading 1** cell style.

10 On the **Starters sheet**, **Copy** the range **A4:A8**. Display the **Summary sheet** and **Paste** the selection to cell **A5**. Apply the **Heading 4** cell style to the selection. In the **Summary sheet**, in cell **B4**, type **Starters** In cell **C4**, type **Meals** and in cell **D4**, type **Starters/Meals Center** the column titles, and then apply the **Heading 4** cell style.

11 In cell **B5**, enter a formula that references cell **B4** in the **Starters sheet** so that the **Starters Total Items in Stock** displays in **B5**. Create similar formulas to enter the **Average Price**, **Median Price**, **Lowest Price**, and **Highest Price** from the **Starters sheet** into the **Summary** sheet in the range **B6:B9**.

12 Enter formulas in the range **C5:C9** that reference the appropriate cells in the **Meals** worksheet. To the range **B5:C5**, apply **Comma Style** with zero decimal places. In cells **D5**, **D6**, **D7**, **D8**, and **D9**, insert **Column** sparklines using the values in the *Starters* and *Meals* columns. Format each sparkline using the first five Sparkline styles in the second row.

13 Center the **Summary** worksheet **Horizontally** and change the **Orientation** to **Landscape**. **Group** the worksheets and insert a footer in the left section with the **File Name**. In **Normal** view, make cell **A1** the active cell. Display the **Document Panel**. Add your name, your course name and section, and the keywords **San Rafael inventory**

14 **Save** your workbook, and then print or submit electronically as directed. If required by your instructor, print or create an electronic version of your worksheets with formulas displayed by using the instructions in Activity 8.16, and then **Close** Excel without saving so that you do not save the changes you made to print formulas.

End **You have completed Project 8J**

Excel Pie Charts, Line Charts, and What-If Analysis Tools

OUTCOMES At the end of this chapter you will be able to:	**OBJECTIVES** Mastering these objectives will enable you to:
PROJECT 9A Present budget data in a pie chart.	**1.** Chart Data with a Pie Chart (p. 421) **2.** Format a Pie Chart (p. 423) **3.** Edit a Workbook and Update a Chart (p. 429) **4.** Use Goal Seek to Perform What-If Analysis (p. 430)
PROJECT 9B Make projections using what-if analysis and present projections in a line chart.	**5.** Design a Worksheet for What-If Analysis (p. 435) **6.** Answer What-If Questions by Changing Values in a Worksheet (p. 440) **7.** Chart Data with a Line Chart (p. 442)

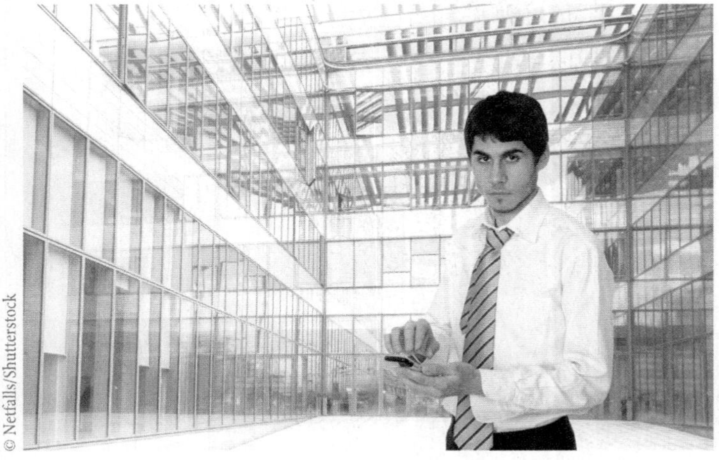

Job Focus: Assistant to a City Manager

In This Chapter

In this chapter, you will learn how an Assistant to a City Manager uses Excel to create pie charts and line charts—two commonly used charts in city management to visualize budget and population data. You will also learn how to use parentheses in a formula, calculate the percentage rate of an increase, and answer what-if questions to provide information to city residents.

At the end of this Unit, following this chapter, you will have an opportunity to complete a case project that focuses on the career of a Marketing Assistant at an entertainment company.

Project 9A Budget Pie Chart

Project Activities

In Activities 9.01 through 9.11, you will edit a worksheet for Lila Darius, City Manager, that projects expenses from the city's general fund for the next fiscal year, and then present the data in a pie chart. Your completed worksheet will look similar to Figure 9.1.

Project Files

For Project 9A, you will need the following file:

e09A_Fund_Expenses

You will save your workbook as:

Lastname_Firstname_9A_Fund_Expenses

Project Results

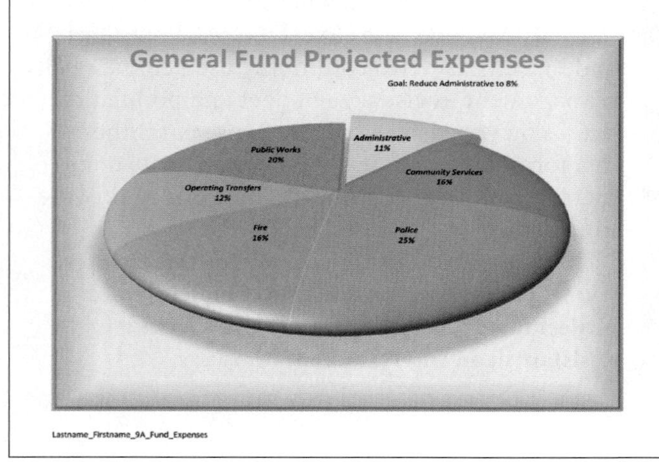
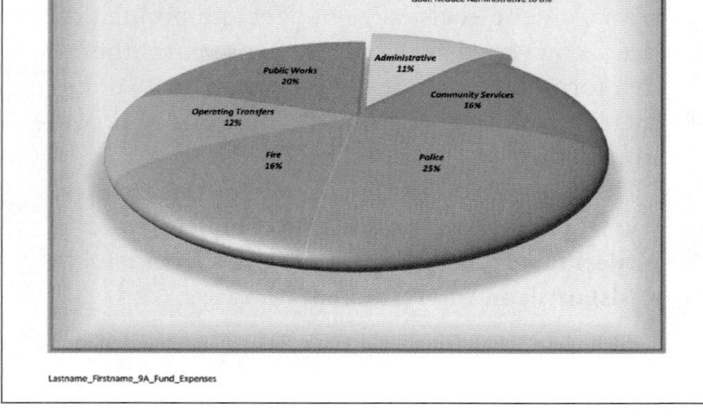

City of Orange Blossom Beach

General Fund Expenses by Program

Projected Increase for Next Fiscal Year Budget

	Current Year Expenses	Projected Expenses for Next Fiscal Year	% of Total Projected Budget
Police	$ 54,815,128	$ 62,200,388	25%
Fire	35,840,661	38,707,913	16%
Operating Transfers	27,407,564	29,600,169	12%
Public Works	46,382,032	50,092,594	20%
Administrative	25,299,290	27,070,240	11%
Community Services	37,948,935	40,225,871	16%
Total	$ 227,693,610	$ 247,897,175	

GENERAL FUND EXPENSES

Goal: To Reduce Administrative Expenses from 11% to 8% of Total Expenses

Goal Amount	19,831,774	8%

Lastname_Firstname_9A_Fund_Expenses

Figure 9.1
Project 9A Fund Expenses

Objective 1 | Chart Data with a Pie Chart

View the video on the Companion Web Site or in MyITLab

A ***pie chart*** shows the relationship of each part to a whole. The size of each pie slice is equal to its value compared to the total value of all the slices. The pie chart displays data that is arranged in a single column or single row, and shows the size of items in a single data series proportional to the sum of the items. Consider using a pie chart when you have only one data series to plot, you do not have more than seven categories, and the categories represent parts of a total value.

Activity 9.01 | Creating a Pie Chart and a Chart Sheet

A ***fund*** is a sum of money set aside for a specific purpose. In a municipal government like the City of Orange Blossom Beach, the ***general fund*** is money set aside for the normal operating activities of the city, such as police, fire, and administering the everyday functions of the city.

1. **Start** Excel. From the student files that accompany this textbook, open **e09A_Fund_Expenses**. From **Backstage** view, display the **Save As** dialog box. Navigate to the location where you are storing projects for this chapter.
2. Create a new folder named **All In One Chapter 9** and open the new folder. In the **File name** box, type **Lastname_Firstname_9A_Fund_Expenses** Click **Save** or press Enter.

   The worksheet indicates the expenses for the current year and the projected expenses for the next fiscal year.
3. Click cell **D5**, and then type **=** to begin a formula.
4. Click cell **C5**, which is the first value that is part of the total Projected Expenses, to insert it into the formula. Type **/** to indicate division, and then click cell **C11**, which is the total Projected Expenses.

   Recall that to determine the percentage by which a value makes up a total, you must divide the value by the total. The result will be a percentage expressed as a decimal.
5. Press F4 to make the reference to the value in cell **C11** absolute, which will enable you to copy the formula. Compare your screen with Figure 9.2.

   Recall that an ***absolute cell reference*** refers to a cell by its fixed position in the worksheet. The reference to cell C5 is a ***relative cell reference***, because when you copy the formula, you want the reference to change relative to its row.

   Recall also that dollar signs display to indicate that a cell reference is absolute.

Figure 9.2

	A	B	C	D
1	City of Orange Blossom Beach			
2	General Fund Expenses by Program			
3	Projected Increase for Next Fiscal Year Budget			
4		Current Year Expenses	Projected Expenses for Next Fiscal Year	% of Total Projected Budget
5	Police	$ 54,815,128	$ 59,200,338	=C5/$C$11
6	Fire	35,840,661	38,707,913	
7	Operating Transfers	27,407,564	29,600,169	
8	Public Works	46,382,032	50,092,594	
9	Administrative	25,299,290	27,070,240	
10	Community Services	37,948,935	40,225,871	
11	Total	$ 227,693,610	$ 244,897,125	

6. On the **Formula Bar**, click the **Enter** button ✓ to confirm the entry and to keep cell **D5** the active cell. Copy the formula down through cell **D10**, and then compare your screen with Figure 9.3.

Figure 9.03

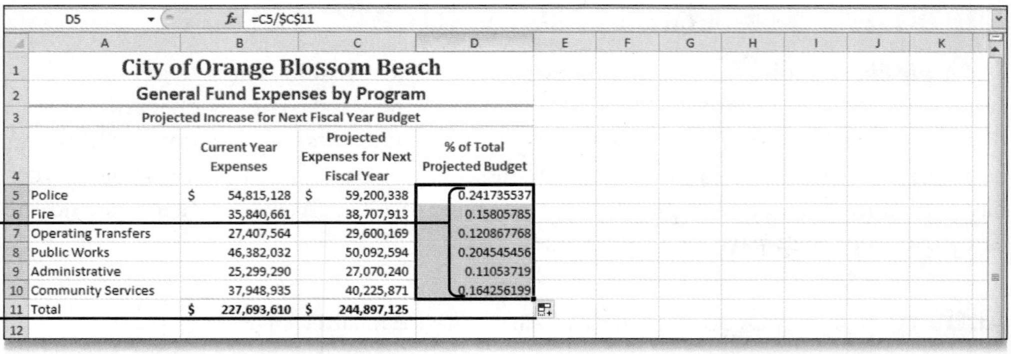

Percentages, expressed as decimals

Auto Fill Options button displays

D5 | =C5/$C$11

	A	B	C	D
1	City of Orange Blossom Beach			
2	General Fund Expenses by Program			
3	Projected Increase for Next Fiscal Year Budget			
4		Current Year Expenses	Projected Expenses for Next Fiscal Year	% of Total Projected Budget
5	Police	$ 54,815,128	$ 59,200,338	0.241735537
6	Fire	35,840,661	38,707,913	0.15805785
7	Operating Transfers	27,407,564	29,600,169	0.120867768
8	Public Works	46,382,032	50,092,594	0.204545456
9	Administrative	25,299,290	27,070,240	0.11053719
10	Community Services	37,948,935	40,225,871	0.164256199
11	Total	$ 227,693,610	$ 244,897,125	
12				

7 With the range **D5:D10** still selected, right-click over the selection, and then on the Mini toolbar, click the **Percent Style** button [%] and the **Center** button. Click cell **A1** to cancel the selection, and then **Save** your workbook. Compare your screen with Figure 9.4.

Figure 9.4

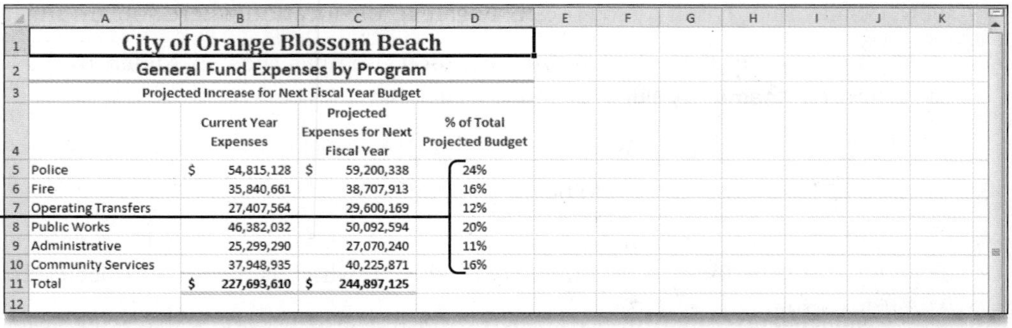

Percentage of Total for each program calculated, expressed as percentages

	A	B	C	D
1	City of Orange Blossom Beach			
2	General Fund Expenses by Program			
3	Projected Increase for Next Fiscal Year Budget			
4		Current Year Expenses	Projected Expenses for Next Fiscal Year	% of Total Projected Budget
5	Police	$ 54,815,128	$ 59,200,338	24%
6	Fire	35,840,661	38,707,913	16%
7	Operating Transfers	27,407,564	29,600,169	12%
8	Public Works	46,382,032	50,092,594	20%
9	Administrative	25,299,290	27,070,240	11%
10	Community Services	37,948,935	40,225,871	16%
11	Total	$ 227,693,610	$ 244,897,125	
12				

8 Select the range **A5:A10**, hold down Ctrl, and then select the range **C5:C10** to select the nonadjacent ranges with the program names and the projected expense for each program.

To create a pie chart, you must select two ranges. One range contains the labels for each slice of the pie chart, and the other range contains the values that add up to a total. The two ranges must have the same number of cells and the range with the values should not include the cell with the total. The program names (Police, Fire, and so on) are the category names and will identify the slices of the pie chart. Each projected expense is a ***data point***—a value that originates in a worksheet cell and that is represented in a chart by a data marker. In a pie chart, each pie slice is a ***data marker***. Together, the data points form the ***data series***—related data points represented by data markers—and determine the size of each pie slice.

9 With the nonadjacent ranges selected, click the **Insert tab**, and then in the **Charts group**, click **Pie**. Under **3-D Pie**, click the first chart—**Pie in 3-D**—to create the chart on your worksheet.

10 On the **Design tab**, at the right end of the Ribbon in the **Location group**, click the **Move Chart** button. In the **Move Chart** dialog box, click the **New sheet** option button.

11 In the **New sheet** box, replace the highlighted text *Chart1* by typing **Projected Expenses Chart** and then click **OK** to display the chart on a separate worksheet in your workbook. Compare your screen with Figure 9.5.

The pie chart displays on a separate new sheet in your workbook, and a ***legend*** identifies the pie slices. Recall that a legend is a chart element that identifies the patterns or colors assigned to the categories in the chart.

A ***chart sheet*** is a workbook sheet that contains only a chart; it is useful when you want to view a chart separately from the worksheet data. The sheet tab indicates *Projected Expenses Chart*.

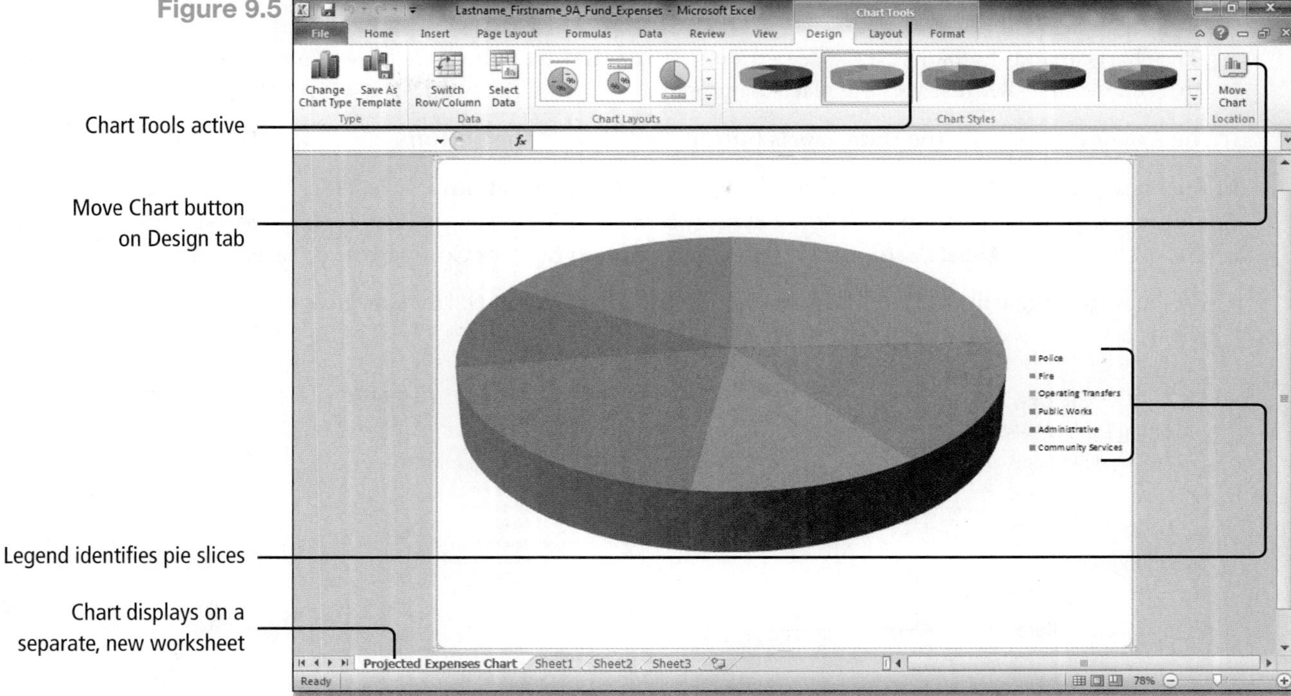

Figure 9.5

Objective 2 | Format a Pie Chart

Activity 9.02 | Applying Percentages to Labels in a Pie Chart

View the video on the Companion Web Site or in MyITLab

In your worksheet, for each expense, you calculated the percent of the total in column D. These percentages can also be calculated by the Chart feature and added to the pie slices as labels.

1. On the Ribbon under **Chart Tools**, click the **Layout tab**, and then in the **Labels group**, click the **Chart Title** button. On the displayed list, click **Above Chart**.
2. With the **Chart Title** box selected, watch the **Formula Bar** as you type **General Fund Projected Expenses** and then press Enter to create the new chart title in the box.
3. Point to the chart title text, right-click to display the Mini toolbar, and then change the **Font Size** to **36** and the **Font Color** to **Olive Green, Accent 1, Darker 25%**—in the fifth column, the fifth color. Compare your screen with Figure 9.6.

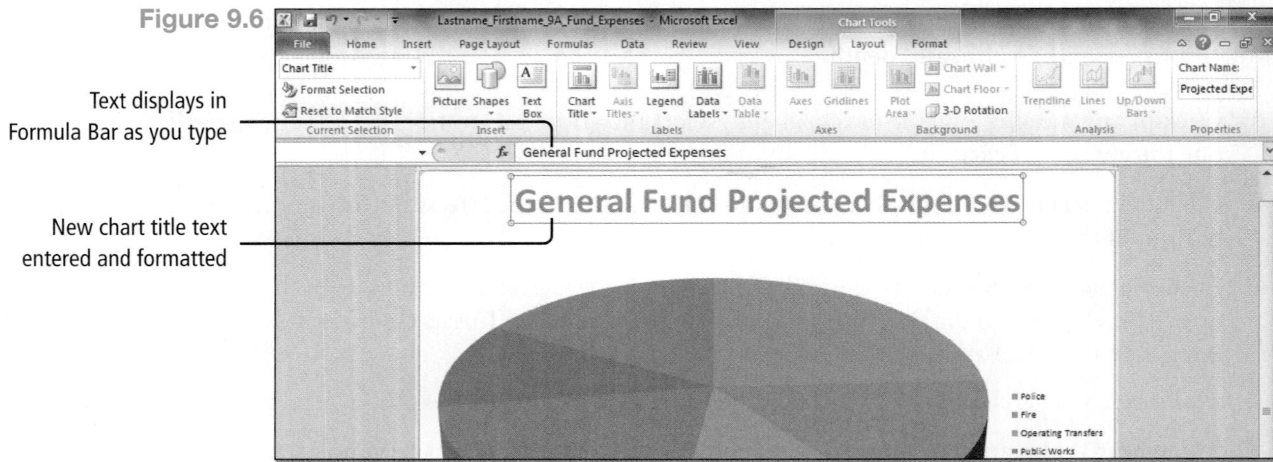

Figure 9.6

4 In the **Labels group**, click the **Legend** button, and then click **None**.

The chart expands to fill the new space. In a pie chart, it is usually more effective to place the labels within, or close to, each pie slice. Because you will place the program names (the categories) on the pie slices, a legend is unnecessary.

5 In the **Labels group**, click the **Data Labels** button, and then at the bottom, click **More Data Label Options**.

6 In the **Format Data Labels** dialog box, on the left, be sure **Label Options** is selected. On the right, under **Label Contains**, click as necessary to select the **Category Name** and **Percentage** check boxes. *Clear* any other check boxes in this group. Under **Label Position**, click the **Center** option button. Compare your screen with Figure 9.7.

In the worksheet, you calculated the percent of the total in column D. Here, the percentage will be calculated by the Chart feature and added to the chart as a label.

Figure 9.7

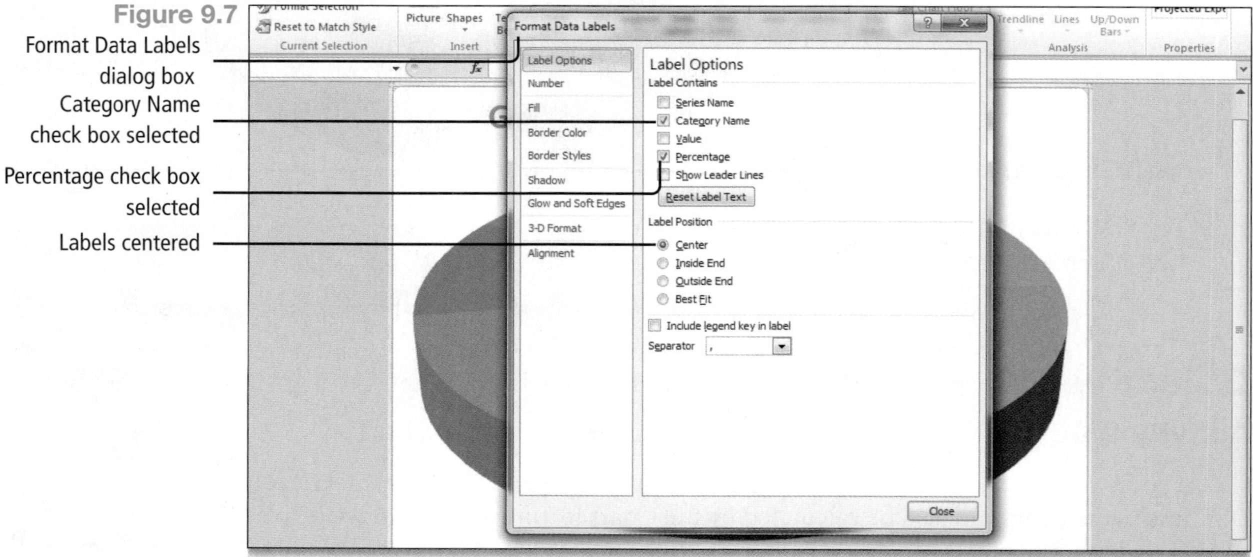

7 In the lower right corner of the **Format Data Labels** dialog box, click **Close**, and notice that all of the data labels are selected and display both the category name and the percentage.

8 Point to any of the selected labels, right-click to display the Mini, and then change the **Font Size** to **11**, apply **Bold** [B], and apply **Italic** [I].

9 Press Esc to deselect the labels, and **Save** your workbook.

Activity 9.03 | Formatting a Pie Chart with 3-D

3-D, which is short for *three-dimensional*, refers to an image that appears to have all three spatial dimensions—length, width, and depth.

1 Click in any pie slice outside of the label to select the entire pie; notice that selection handles display on the outside corners of each slice.

2 Click the **Format tab**. In the **Shape Styles group**, click the **Shape Effects** button, point to **Bevel**, and then at the bottom of the gallery, click **3-D Options**.

3 In the **Format Data Series** dialog box, on the right, under **Bevel**, click the **Top** button. In the displayed gallery, under **Bevel**, point to the first button to display the ScreenTip *Circle*. Click the **Circle** button. Then click the **Bottom** button, and apply the **Circle** bevel.

Bevel is a shape effect that uses shading and shadows to make the edges of a shape appear to be curved or angled.

4 In the four **Width** and **Height** spin boxes, type **512 pt** and then compare your screen with Figure 9.8.

Figure 9.8

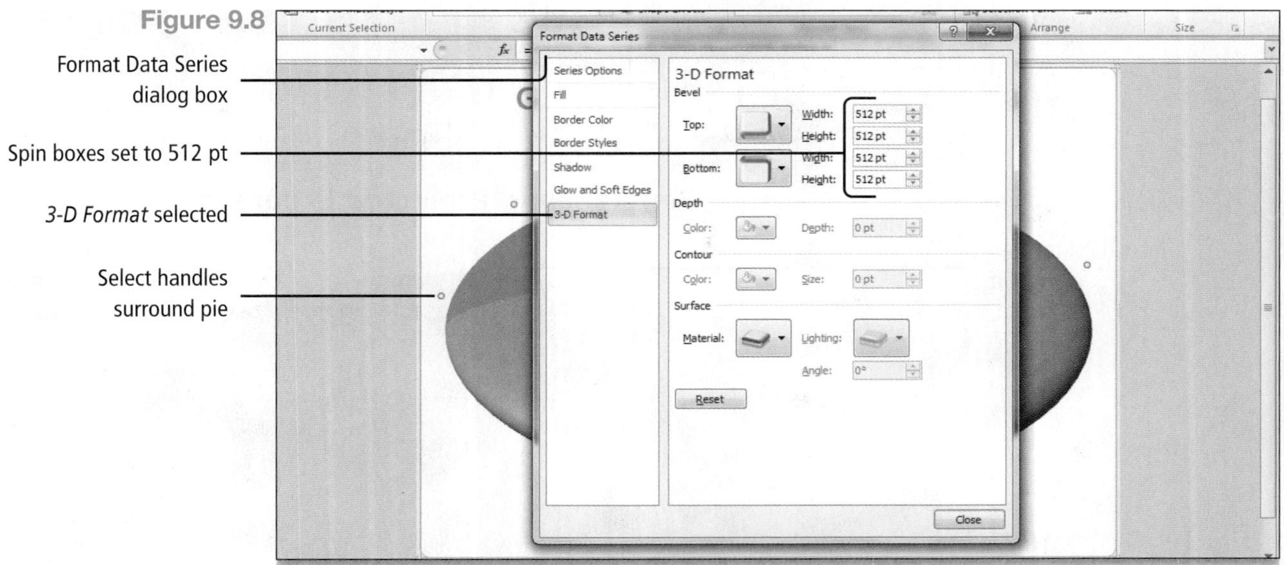

5 In the lower portion of the dialog box, under **Surface**, click the **Material** button. Under **Standard**, click the third button—**Plastic**. In the lower right corner, click **Close**.

6 With the pie still selected, on the **Format tab**, in the **Shape Styles group**, click **Shape Effects**, and then point to **Shadow**. At the bottom of the displayed gallery, scroll if necessary, and then under **Perspective**, click the third button, which displays the ScreenTip Below to display a shadow below the pie chart. Click **Save**.

Activity 9.04 | Rotating a Pie Chart

The order in which the data series in pie charts are plotted in Excel is determined by the order of the data on the worksheet. To gain a different view of the chart, you can rotate the chart within the 360 degrees of the circle of the pie shape to present a different visual perspective of the chart.

1 Notice the position of the **Fire** and **Police** slices in the chart. Then, with the pie chart still selected—sizing handles surround the pie—point anywhere in the pie and right-click. On the displayed shortcut menu, click **Format Data Series**.

2 In the **Format Data Series** dialog box, on the left, be sure **Series Options** is selected. On the right, under **Angle of first slice**, click in the box and type **100** to rotate the chart 100 degrees to the right.

3 Close the **Format Data Series** dialog box. Click **Save**, and then compare your screen with Figure 9.9.

Rotating the chart can provide a better perspective to the chart. Here, rotating the chart in this manner emphasizes that the Fire and Police programs represent a significant portion of the total expenses.

Figure 9.9

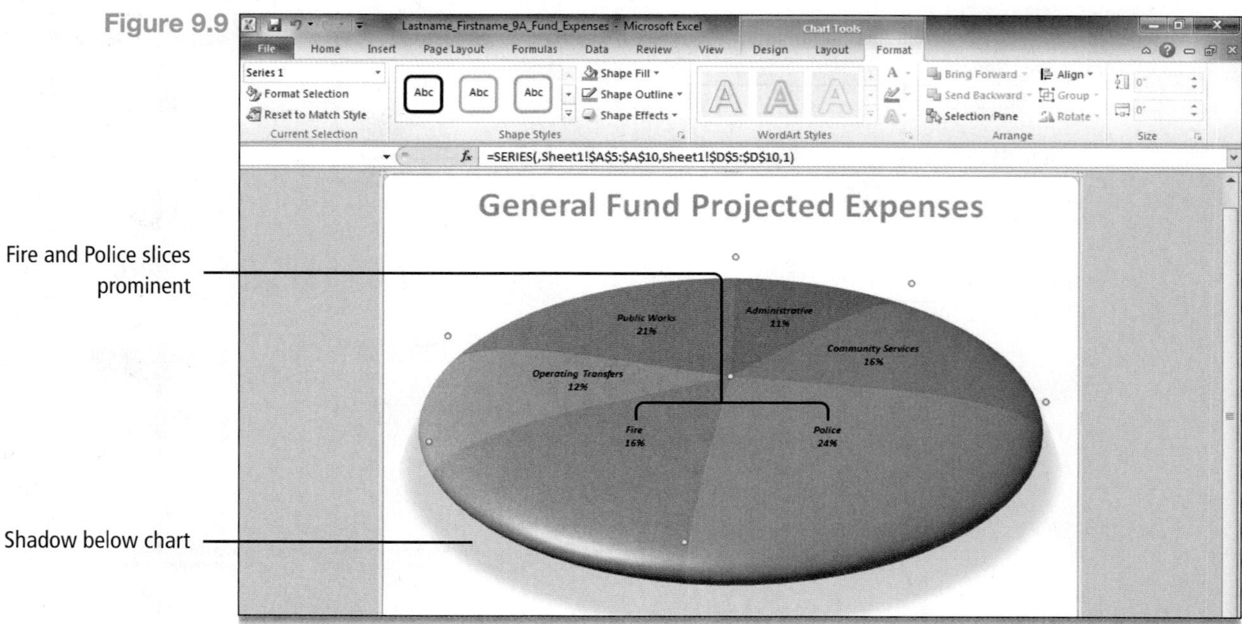

Activity 9.05 | Exploding and Coloring a Pie Slice

You can pull out—***explode***—one or more slices of a pie chart to emphasize a specific slice or slices. Additionally, there is a different chart type you can select if you want *all* the slices to explode and emphasize all the individual slices of a pie chart—the exploded pie or exploded pie in 3-D chart type. The exploded pie chart type displays the contribution of *each* value to the total, while at the same time emphasizing individual values.

1 Press Esc to deselect all chart elements. Click any slice to select the entire pie, and then click the **Administrative** slice to select only that slice. Compare your screen with Figure 9.10.

Figure 9.10

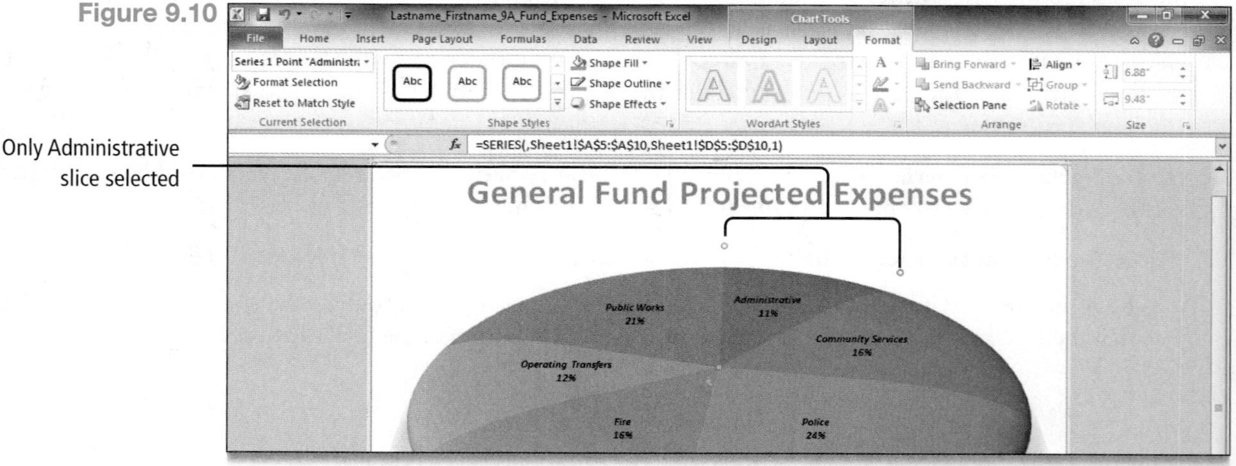

2 Point to the **Administrative** slice to display the pointer, and then drag the slice slightly upward and away from the center of the pie, as shown in Figure 9.11, and then release the mouse button.

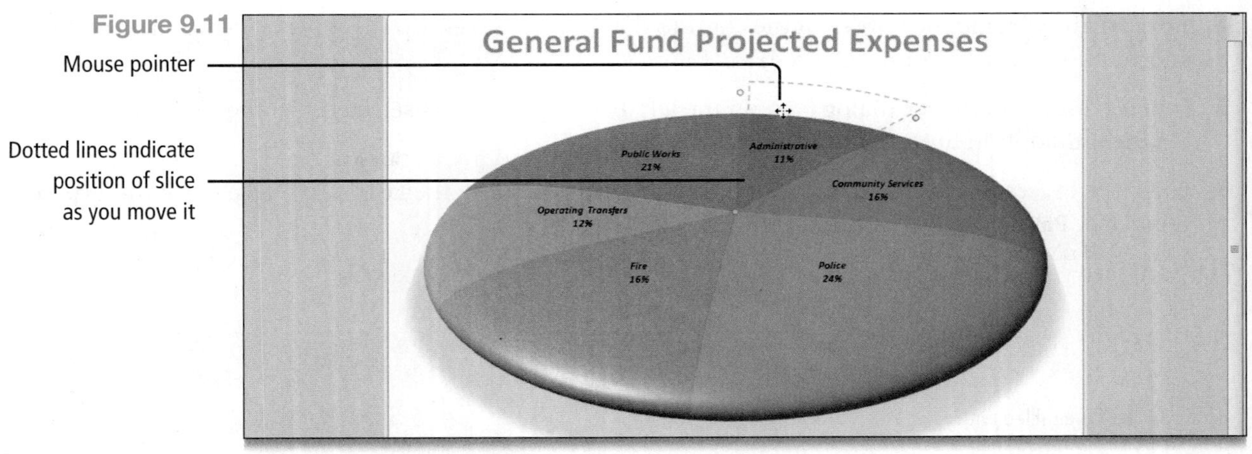

Figure 9.11

3 With the **Administrative** slice still selected, point to the slice and right-click, and then on the shortcut menu, click **Format Data Point**.

4 In the **Format Data Point** dialog box, on the left, click **Fill**. On the right, under **Fill**, click the **Solid fill** option button.

5 Click the **Color arrow**, and then under **Theme Colors**, in the seventh column, click the fourth color—**Gold, Accent 3, Lighter 40%**.

6 In the lower right corner of the **Format Data Point** dialog box, click the **Close** button.

Activity 9.06 | Formatting the Chart Area

The entire chart and all of its elements comprise the ***chart area***.

1 Point to the white area just inside the border of the chart to display the ScreenTip *Chart Area*. Click one time.

2 On the **Format tab**, in the **Shape Styles group**, click the **Shape Effects** button, point to **Bevel**, and then under **Bevel**, in the second row, click the third bevel—**Convex**.

3 Press Esc to deselect the chart element and view this effect—a convex beveled frame around your entire chart—and then compare your screen with Figure 9.12.

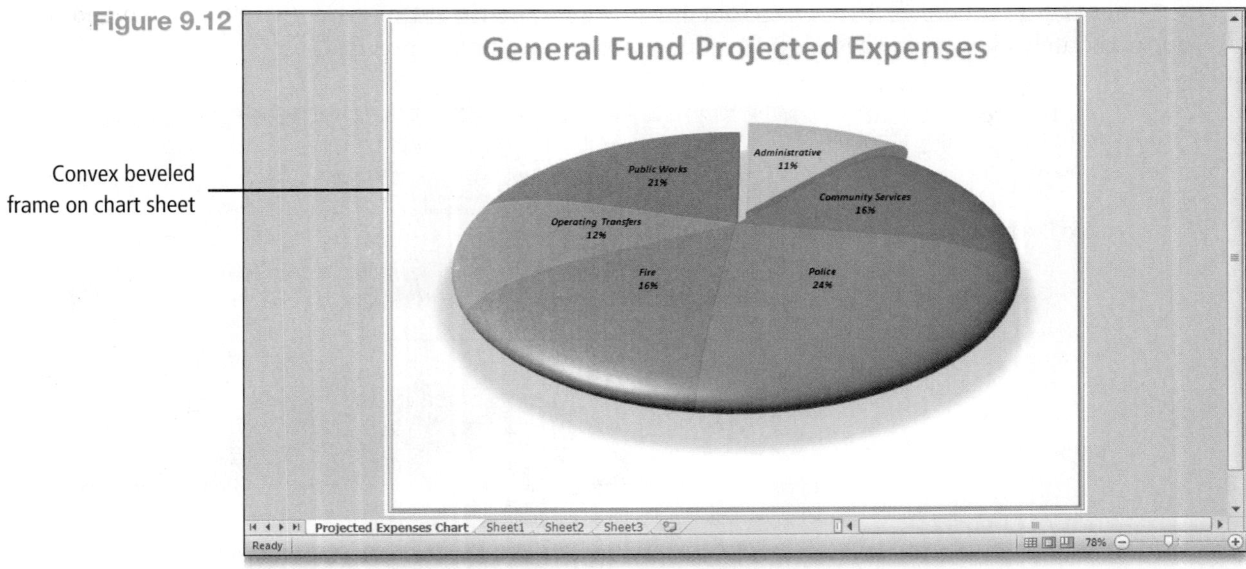

Figure 9.12

4 Point slightly inside the border of the chart to display the ScreenTip *Chart Area*, right-click, and then on the shortcut menu, click **Format Chart Area**.

5 In the **Format Chart Area** dialog box, on the left, be sure that **Fill** is selected. On the right, under **Fill**, click the **Gradient fill** option button.

6 Click the **Preset colors** arrow, and then in the second row, click the last preset, **Fog**. Click the **Type arrow**, and then click **Path**. Click the **Close** button.

7 Compare your screen with Figure 9.13, and then **Save** your workbook.

Figure 9.13

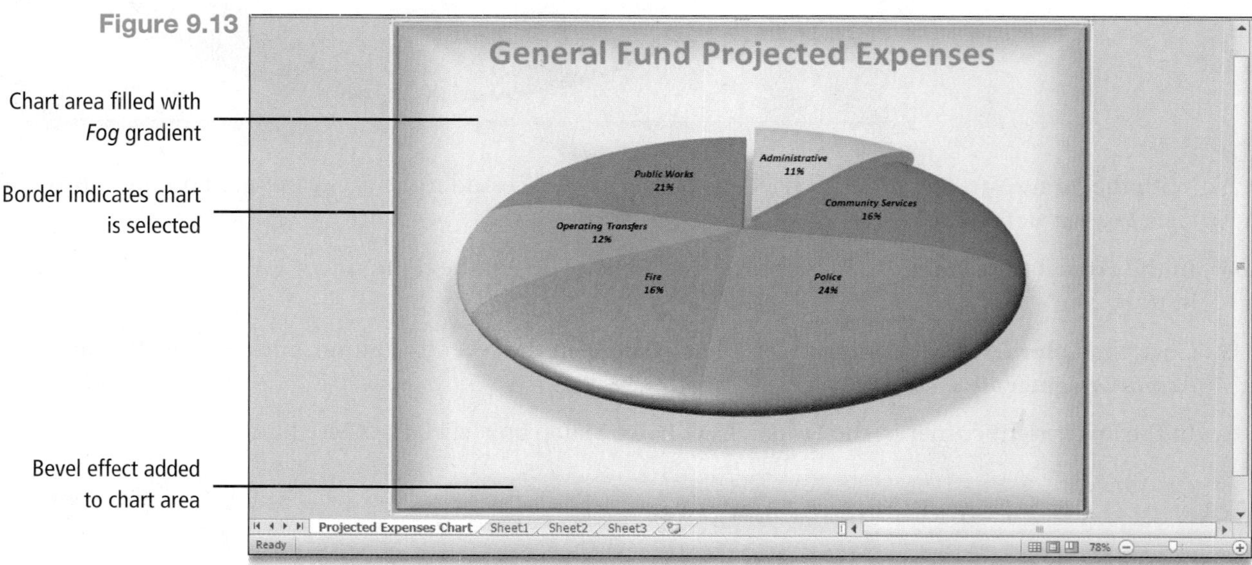

Chart area filled with *Fog* gradient

Border indicates chart is selected

Bevel effect added to chart area

Activity 9.07 | Inserting a Text Box in a Chart

A ***text box*** is a movable, resizable container for text or graphics.

1 With the Chart Area still selected, click the **Layout tab**, in the **Insert group**, click the **Text Box** button, and then move the pointer into the chart area.

2 Position the displayed pointer under the *c* in *Projected* and about midway between the title and the pie—above the *Administrative* slice. Hold down the left mouse button, and then drag down and to the right approximately as shown in Figure 9.14; your text box need not be precise.

Figure 9.14

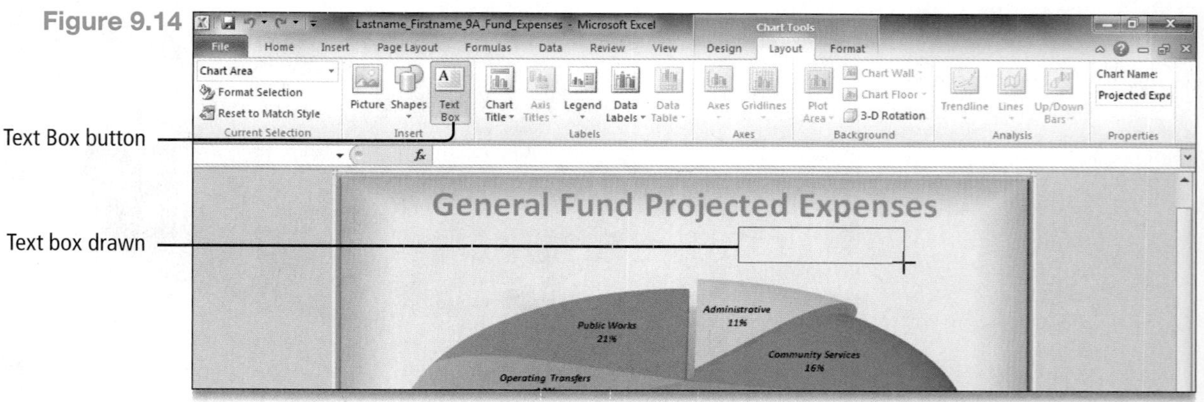

Text Box button

Text box drawn

3 With the insertion point blinking inside the text box, type **Goal: Reduce Administrative to 8%** Press Esc or click outside the chart area to deselect the chart element, and then compare your screen with Figure 9.15.

Figure 9.15

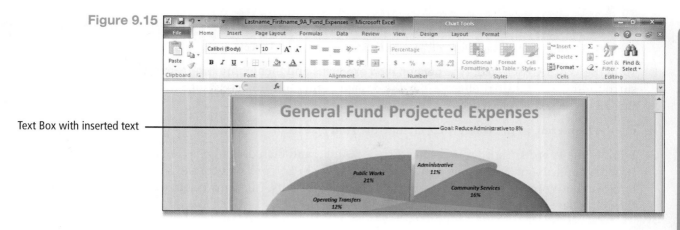

Text Box with inserted text

4 If necessary, select and then adjust or move your text box. **Save** your workbook.

Objective 3 | Edit a Workbook and Update a Chart

View the video on the Companion Web Site or in MyITLab

Activity 9.08 | Editing a Workbook and Updating a Chart

If you edit the data in your worksheet, the chart data markers—in this instance the pie slices—will adjust automatically to accurately represent the new values.

1 On the pie chart, notice that *Police* represents 24% of the total projected expenses.

2 In the sheet tab area at the bottom of the workbook, click the **Sheet1 tab** to redisplay the worksheet.

3 Click cell **C5**, and then in Formula Bar, change *59,200,338* to **62200388**

4 Press Enter, and notice that the total in cell **C11** recalculates to *$247,897,175* and the percentages in **column D** also recalculate.

5 Display the **Projected Expenses Chart** sheet. Notice that the pie slices adjust to show the recalculation—*Police* is now *25%* of the projected expenses. Click **Save**, and then compare your screen with Figure 9.16.

Figure 9.16

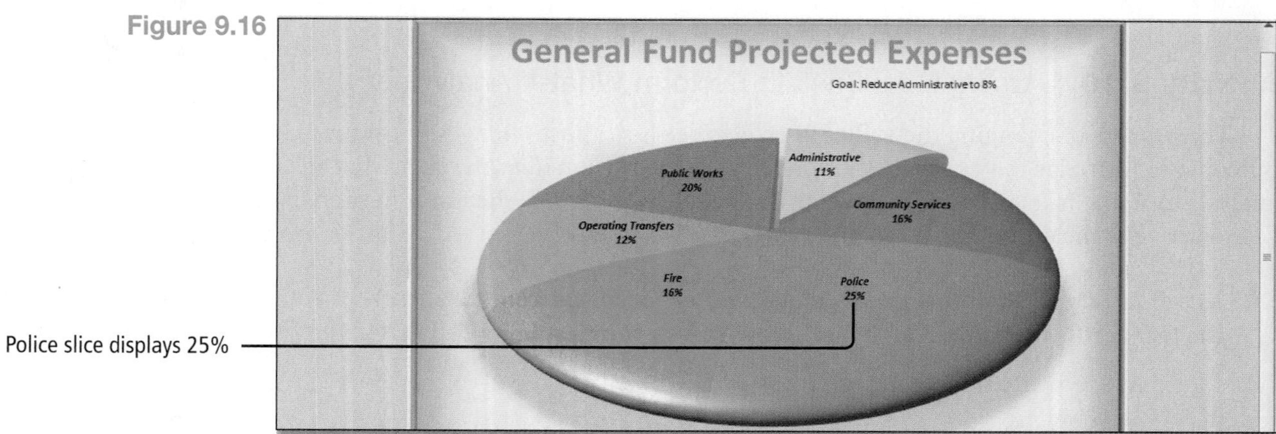

Activity 9.09 | Inserting WordArt in a Worksheet

WordArt is a gallery of text styles with which you can create decorative effects, such as shadowed or mirrored text. In an Excel worksheet, WordArt can be effective if you plan to display your worksheet in a PowerPoint presentation, or if readers will be viewing the worksheet data online.

1 In the sheet tab area at the bottom of the workbook, click the **Sheet1 tab** to redisplay the worksheet. Click the **Insert tab**, and then in the **Text group**, click the **WordArt** button.

2 In the WordArt gallery, in the last row, click the last style—**Fill – Olive Green, Accent 1, Metal Bevel, Reflection**.

The WordArt indicating *YOUR TEXT HERE* displays in the worksheet.

3 With the WordArt selected, type **general fund expenses** and then point anywhere on the dashed border surrounding the WordArt object. Click the dashed border one time to change it to a solid border, indicating that all of the text is selected.

4 On the **Home tab**, in the **Font group**, change the **Font Size** to **28**.

5 Point to the WordArt border to display the pointer, and then drag to position the upper left corner of the WordArt approximately as shown in Figure 9.17. If necessary, press any of the arrow keys on your keyboard to move the WordArt object into position in small increments. Click any cell to deselect the WordArt, and then click **Save**.

Figure 9.17

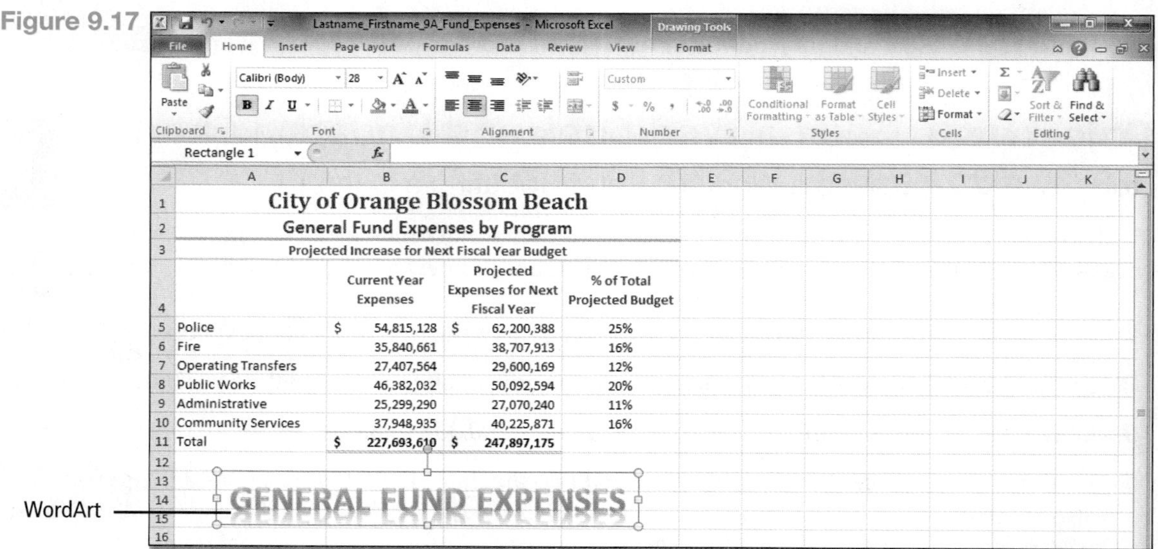

Objective 4 | Use Goal Seek to Perform What-If Analysis

View the video on the Companion Web Site or in MyITLab

Activity 9.10 | Using Goal Seek to Perform What-If Analysis

The process of changing the values in cells to see how those changes affect the outcome of formulas in your worksheet is referred to as ***what-if analysis***. A what-if analysis tool that is included with Excel is ***Goal Seek***, which finds the input needed in one cell to arrive at the desired result in another cell.

1 In cell **A17**, type **Goal: To Reduce Administrative Expenses from 11% to 8% of Total Expenses** Merge & Center the text across the range **A17:D17**, and then apply the **Heading 3** Cell Style.

2 In cell **A18**, type **Goal Amount:** and press Enter.

3 Select the range **C9:D9**, right-click over the selection, and then click **Copy**. Point to cell **B18**, right-click, and then under **Paste Options**, click the **Paste** button.

4 Press Esc to cancel the moving border, click cell **C18**, and then compare your screen with Figure 9.18.

Figure 9.18

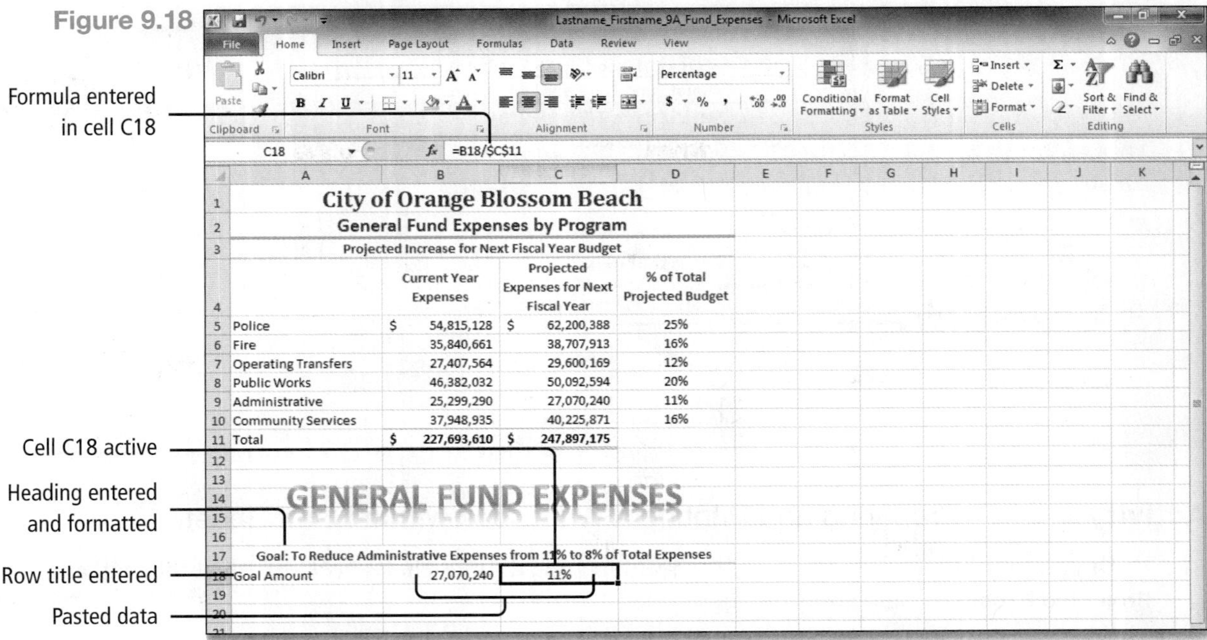

5 Be sure cell **C18** is the active cell. On the **Data tab**, in the **Data Tools group**, click the **What-If Analysis** button, and then click **Goal Seek**.

6 In the **Goal Seek** dialog box, notice that the active cell, **C18**, is indicated in the **Set cell** box. Press Tab to move to the **To value** box, and then type **8%**

C18 is the cell in which you want to set a specific value; 8% is the percentage of the total expenses that you want to budget for Administrative expenses. The Set cell box contains the formula that calculates the information you seek.

7 Press Tab to move the insertion point to the **By changing cell** box, and then click cell **B18**. Compare your screen with Figure 9.19.

Cell B18 contains the value that Excel changes to reach the goal. Excel formats this cell as an absolute cell reference.

Figure 9.19

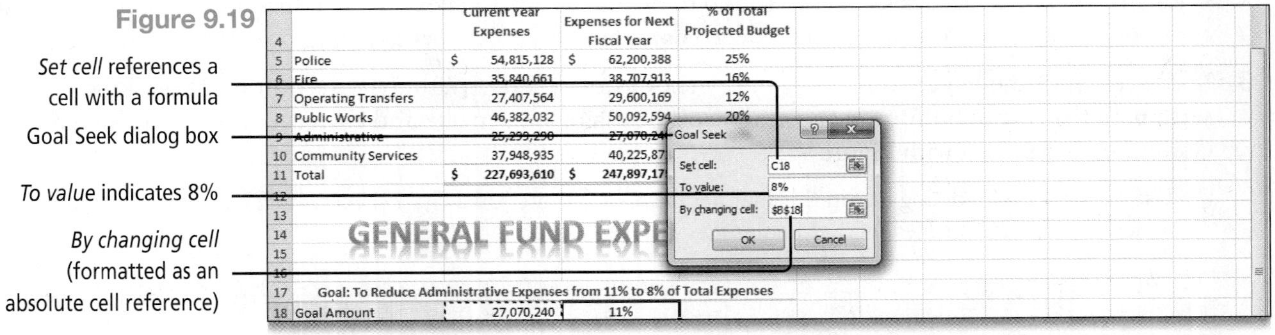

Set cell references a cell with a formula

Goal Seek dialog box

To value indicates 8%

By changing cell (formatted as an absolute cell reference)

8 Click **OK**. In the displayed **Goal Seek Status** dialog box, click **OK**.

9 Select the range **A18:C18**. From the **Home tab**, display the **Cell Styles** gallery. Under **Themed Cell Styles**, apply **20% - Accent3**. Click cell **B18**, and then from the **Cell Styles** gallery, at the bottom of the gallery under **Number Format**, apply the **Currency [0]** cell style.

10 Press Ctrl + Home, click **Save**, and then compare your screen with Figure 9.20.

Excel calculates that the City must budget for *$19,831,774* in Administrative expenses in order for this item to become 8% of the total projected budget.

Figure 9.20

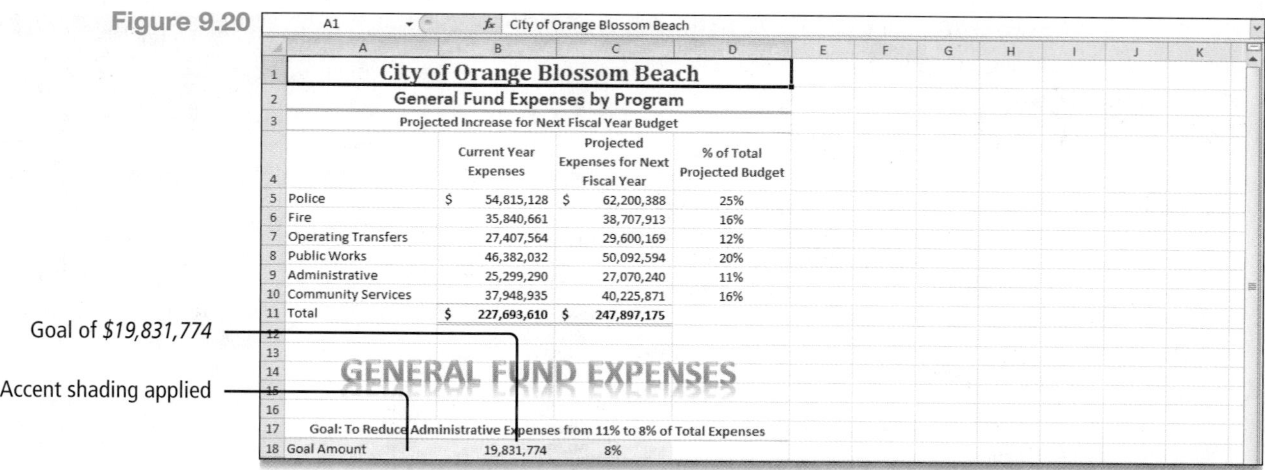

Activity 9.11 | Preparing and Printing a Workbook with a Chart Sheet

1 With your worksheet displayed, in the sheet tab area, double-click *Sheet1* to select the text, and then type **Projected Expenses Data** and press Enter.

2 Select **Sheet2** and **Sheet3**, right-click over the selected tabs, and then click **Delete** to delete the unused sheets.

3 On the **Insert tab**, click **Header & Footer**. In the **Navigation group**, click the **Go to Footer** button, click in the left section above the word **Footer**, and then in the **Header & Footer Elements group**, click the **File Name** button.

4 Click in a cell above the footer to deselect the **Footer area** and view your file name. On the **Page Layout tab**, in the **Page Setup group**, click the **Margins** button, and then at the bottom click **Custom Margins**.

5 In the displayed **Page Setup** dialog box, under **Center on page**, select the **Horizontally** check box. Click **OK**, and then on the status bar, click the **Normal** button to return to Normal view.

Recall that after displaying worksheets in Page Layout View, dotted lines display to indicate the page breaks when you return to Normal view.

6 Press Ctrl + Home to move to the top of the worksheet.

7 Click the **Projected Expenses Chart** sheet tab to display the chart sheet. On the **Insert tab**, in the **Text group**, click **Header & Footer** to display the **Header/Footer tab** of the **Page Setup** dialog box.

8 In the center of the **Page Setup** dialog box, click **Custom Footer**. With the insertion point blinking in the **Left section**, in the row of buttons in the middle of the dialog box, locate and click the **Insert File Name** button. Compare your screen with Figure 9.21.

Use the Page Setup dialog box in this manner to insert a footer on a chart sheet, which has no Page Layout view in which you can see the Header and Footer areas.

Figure 9.21

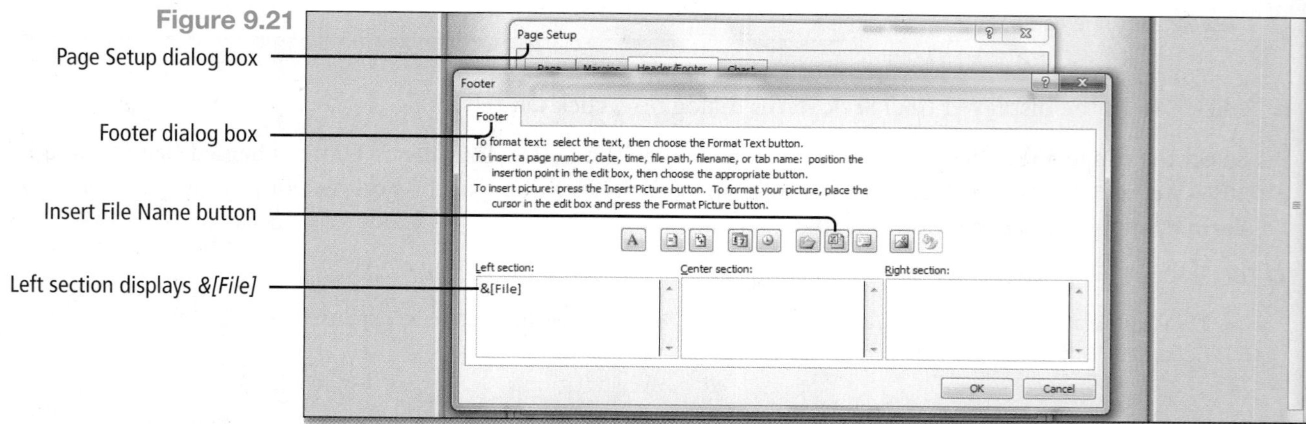

9 Click **OK** two times. Display **Backstage** view, on the right under the thumbnail, click **Properties**, and then click **Show Document Panel**. In the **Author** box, replace the existing text with your firstname and lastname. In the **Subject** box, type your course name and section number. In the **Keywords** box type **general fund, expenses, pie chart** and then **Close** [X] the **Document Information Panel**.

10 Right-click either of the sheet tabs, and then click **Select All Sheets**. Verify that [*Group*] displays in the title bar.

Recall that by selecting all sheets, you can view all of the workbook pages in Print Preview.

11 Press Ctrl + F2 to display the **Print Preview**. Examine the first page, and then at the bottom of the **Print Preview**, click the **Next Page** [▶] button to view the second page of your workbook.

Note | Printing a Chart Sheet Uses More Toner

Printing a chart that displays on a chart sheet will use more toner or ink than a small chart that is part of a worksheet. If you are printing your work, check with your instructor to verify whether or not you should print the chart sheet.

12 Click **Save** to redisplay the workbook. Print or submit electronically as directed by your instructor.

13 If you are directed to submit printed formulas, refer to Activity 8.16 in Project 8A to do so.

14 If you printed your formulas, be sure to redisplay the worksheet by clicking the Show Formulas button to turn it off. **Close** the workbook. If you are prompted to save changes, click **No** so that you do not save the changes to the worksheet that you used for printing formulas. **Close** [X] Excel.

More Knowledge | Setting the Default Number of Sheets in a New Workbook

By default, the number of new worksheets in a new workbook is three, but you can change this default number. From Backstage view, display the Excel Options dialog box, click the General tab, and then under When creating new workbooks, change the number in the Include this many sheets box.

End You have completed Project 9A

Project 9B Growth Projection with Line Chart

Project Activities

In Activities 9.12 through 9.19, you will assist Lila Darius, City Manager, in creating a worksheet to estimate future population growth based on three possible growth rates. You will also create a line chart to display past population growth. Your resulting worksheet and chart will look similar to Figure 9.22.

Project Files

For Project 9B, you will need the following files:

e09B_Population_Growth
jpg09B_Beach

You will save your document as:

Lastname_Firstname_9B_Population_Growth

Project Results

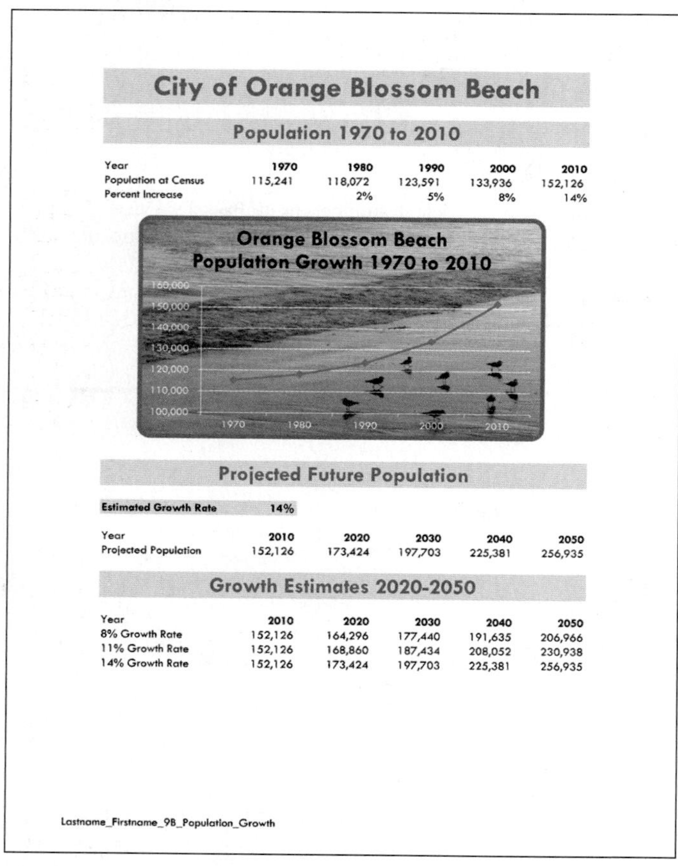

City of Orange Blossom Beach

Population 1970 to 2010

Year	1970	1980	1990	2000	2010
Population at Census	115,241	118,072	123,591	133,936	152,126
Percent Increase		2%	5%	8%	14%

Projected Future Population

Estimated Growth Rate	14%

Year	2010	2020	2030	2040	2050
Projected Population	152,126	173,424	197,703	225,381	256,935

Growth Estimates 2020-2050

Year	2010	2020	2030	2040	2050
8% Growth Rate	152,126	164,296	177,440	191,635	206,966
11% Growth Rate	152,126	168,860	187,434	208,052	230,938
14% Growth Rate	152,126	173,424	197,703	225,381	256,935

Lastname_Firstname_9B_Population_Growth

Figure 9.22
Project 9B Population Growth

Objective 5 | Design a Worksheet for What-If Analysis

View the video on the Companion Web Site or in MyITLab

If you change the value in a cell referenced in a formula, Excel automatically recalculates the result of the formula. Thus, you can change cell values to see *what* would happen *if* you tried different values. Recall the process of changing the values in cells to see how those changes affect the outcome of formulas in your worksheet is referred to as what-if analysis.

Activity 9.12 | Using Parentheses in a Formula to Calculate a Percentage Rate of Increase

Ms. Darius has the city's population figures for the past five 10-year census periods. In each 10-year census period, the population has increased. In this activity, you will construct a formula to calculate the ***percentage rate of increase***—the percent by which one number increases over another number—for each 10-year census period since 1970. From this information, future population growth can be estimated.

1. **Start** Excel. From your student files, open the file **e09B_Population_Growth**. From **Backstage** view, display the **Save As** dialog box, and navigate to your **All In One Chapter 9** folder. In the **File name** box, type **Lastname_Firstname_9B_Population_Growth** and then click **Save** or press Enter.
2. Leave **row 4** blank, and then click cell **A5**. Type **Year** and then press Tab. In cell **B5**, type **1970** and then press Tab.
3. In cell **C5**, type **1980** and then press Tab. Select the range **B5:C5**, and then drag the fill handle to the right through cell **F5** to extend the series to 2010.

   By establishing a pattern of 10-year intervals with the first two cells, you can use the fill handle to continue the series. The AutoFill feature will do this for any pattern that you establish with two or more cells.
4. With the range **B5:F5** still selected, right-click over the selection, and then on the Mini toolbar, click **Bold** B. Compare your screen with Figure 9.23.

Figure 9.23

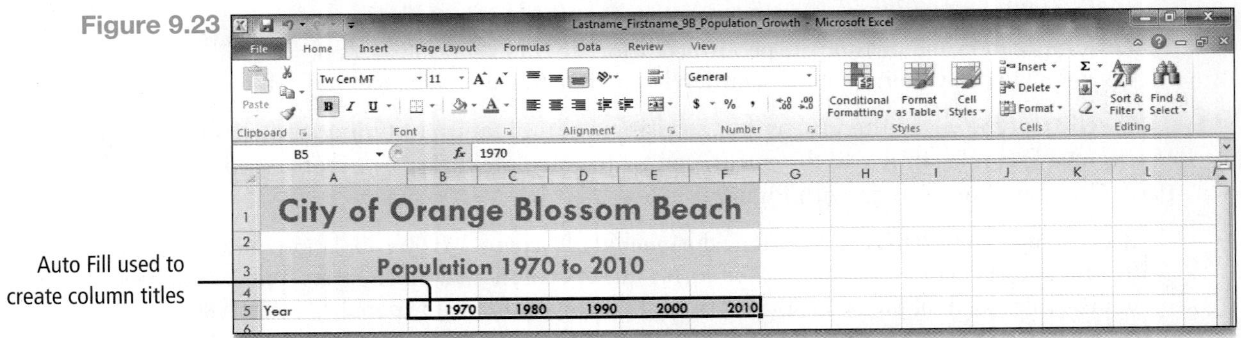

5. In cell **A6**, type **Population at Census** and press Enter. In cell **A7**, type **Percent Increase** and press Enter.
6. Click cell **B6**, and then beginning in cell **B6**, and pressing Tab to move across the row, enter the following values for the population in the years listed:

1970	1980	1990	2000	2010
115241	**118072**	**123591**	**133936**	**152126**

7. Select the range **B6:F6**, right-click, on the Mini toolbar, click **Comma Style** , and then click **Decrease Decimal** .00→.0 two times.
8. Click cell **C7**. Being sure to include the parentheses, type **=(c6-b6)/b6** and then on the **Formula Bar**, click the **Enter** button to keep cell **C7** active; your result is *0.02456591* (or *0.02*). Compare your screen with Figure 9.24.

   Recall that as you type, a list of Excel functions that begin with the letter *C* and *B* may briefly display. This is ***Formula AutoComplete***, an Excel feature which, after typing an = (equal sign) and the beginning letter or letters of a function name, displays a list of function names that match the typed letter(s). In this instance, the letters represent cell references, *not* the beginning of a function name.

Figure 9.24

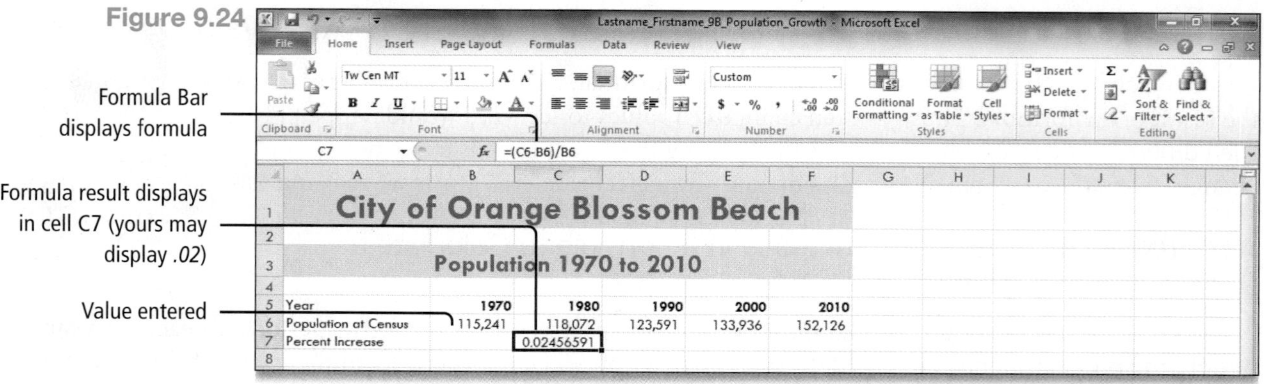

9 With cell **C7** active, on the **Home tab**, in the **Number group**, click the **Percent Style** button [%], and then examine the formula in the **Formula Bar**.

The mathematical formula ***rate* = *amount of increase/base*** is used to calculated the percentage rate of population increase from 1970 to 1980. The formula is applied as follows: First, determine the *amount of increase* by subtracting the ***base***—the starting point represented by the 1970 population—from the 1980 population. Thus, the *amount of increase* = 118,072 – 115,241 or 2,831. Between 1970 and 1980, the population increased by 2,831 people. In the formula, this calculation is represented by *C6-B6*. Second, calculate the *rate*—what the amount of increase (2,831) represents as a percentage of the base (1970's population of 115,241). Determine this by dividing the amount of increase (2,831) by the base (115,241). Thus, 2,831 divided by 115,241 is equal to 0.02456591 or, when formatted as a percent, 2%.

10 In the **Formula Bar**, locate the parentheses enclosing **C6-B6**.

Excel follows a set of mathematical rules called the ***order of operations***, which has four basic parts:

- Expressions within parentheses are processed first.
- Exponentiation, if present, is performed before multiplication and division.
- Multiplication and division are performed before addition and subtraction.
- Consecutive operators with the same level of precedence are calculated from left to right.

11 Click cell **D7**, type = and then by typing, or using a combination of typing and clicking cells to reference them, construct a formula similar to the one in cell **C7** to calculate the rate of increase in population from 1980 to 1990. Compare your screen with Figure 9.25.

Recall that the first step is to determine the *amount of increase*—1990 population minus 1980 population—and then to write the calculation so that Excel performs this operation first; that is, place it in parentheses. The second step is to divide the result of the calculation in parentheses by the *base*—the population for 1980.

Figure 9.25

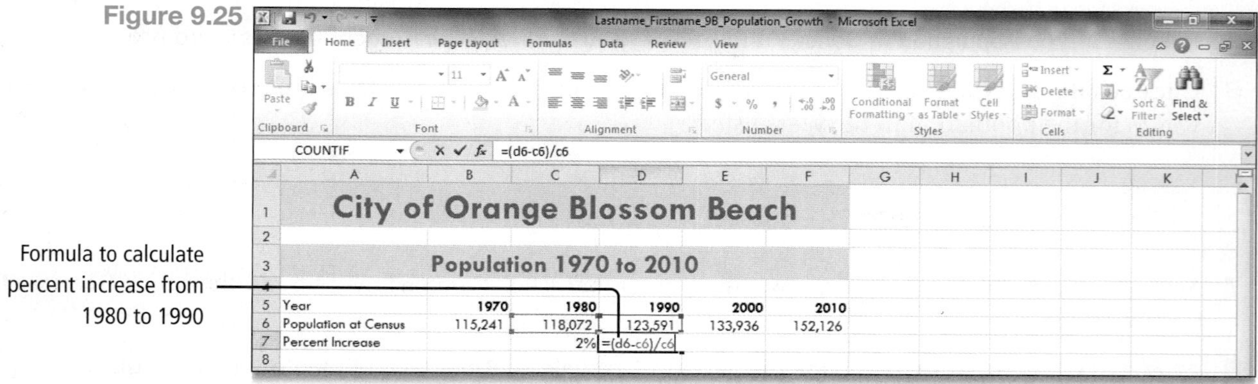

12 Press [Enter]; your result is *0.04674267* (or *0.05*). Format cell **D7** with the **Percent Style** [%].

Your result is *5%*; Excel rounds up or down to format percentages.

13 With cell **D7** selected, drag the fill handle to the right through cell **F7**. Click any empty cell to cancel the selection, **Save** your workbook, and then compare your screen with Figure 9.26.

Because this formula uses relative cell references—that is, for each year, the formula is the same but the values used are relative to the formula's location—you can copy the formula in this manner. For example, the result for 1990 uses the 1980 population as the base, the result for 2000 uses the 1990 population as the base, and the result for 2010 uses the 2000 population as the base. The formula results show the percent of increase for each 10-year period between 1970 and 2010. You can see that in each 10-year period, the population has grown as much as 14%—from 2000 to 2010—and as little as 2%—from 1970 to 1980.

Figure 9.26

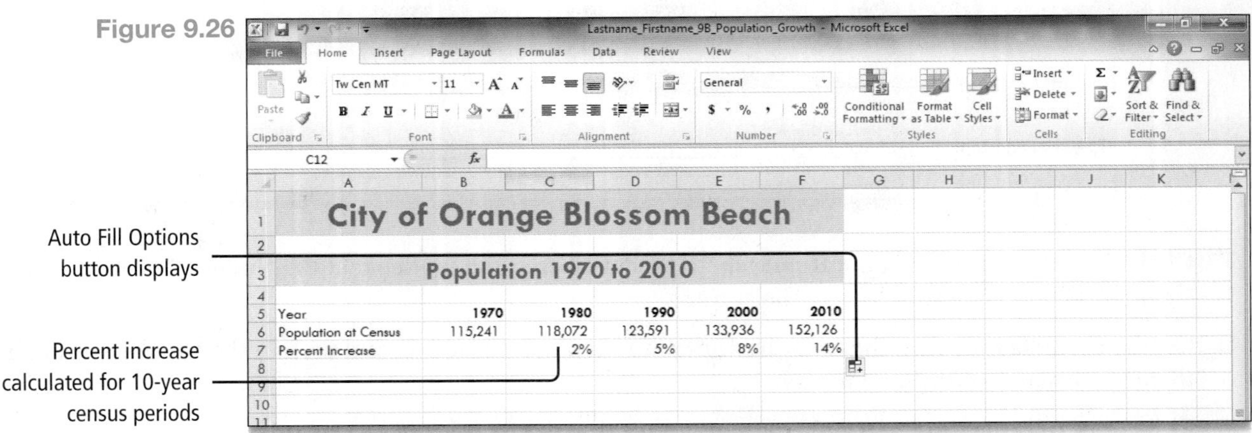

> **More Knowledge | Use of Parentheses in a Formula**
>
> When writing a formula in Excel, use parentheses to communicate the order in which the operations should occur. For example, to average three test scores of 100, 50, and 90 that you scored on three different tests, you would add the test scores and then divide by the number of test scores in the list. If you write this formula as =100+50+90/3, the result would be 180, because Excel would first divide 90 by 3 and then add 100+50+30. Excel would do so because the order of operations states that multiplication and division are calculated before addition and subtraction.
>
> The correct way to write this formula is =(100+50+90)/3. Excel will add the three values, and then divide the result by 3, or 240/3 resulting in a correct average of 80. Parentheses play an important role in ensuring that you get the correct result in your formulas.

Activity 9.13 | Using Format Painter and Formatting as You Type

You can format numbers as you type them. When you type numbers in a format that Excel recognizes, Excel automatically applies that format to the cell. Recall that once applied, cell formats remain with the cell, even if the cell contents are deleted. In this activity, you will format cells by typing the numbers with percent signs and use Format Painter to copy text (non-numeric) formats.

1 Leave **row 8** blank, and then click cell **A9**. Type **Projected Future Population** and then press Enter.

2 Point to cell **A3**, right-click, on the Mini toolbar click the **Format Painter** button, and then click cell **A9**.

The format of cell A3 is *painted*—applied to—cell A9, including the merging and centering of the text across the range A9:F9.

3 Leave **row 10** blank, and then click cell **A11**, type **Estimated Growth Rate** and then press Enter.

4 Leave **row 12** blank, and then click cell **A13**. Type **Year** and then in cell **A14**, type **Projected Population**

5 In cell **B13**, type **2010** and then press Tab. In cell **C13**, type **2020** and then press Tab.

6 Select the range **B13:C13**, and then drag the fill handle through cell **F13** to extend the pattern of years to *2050*. Apply **Bold** to the selected range. Compare your screen with Figure 9.27.

Figure 9.27

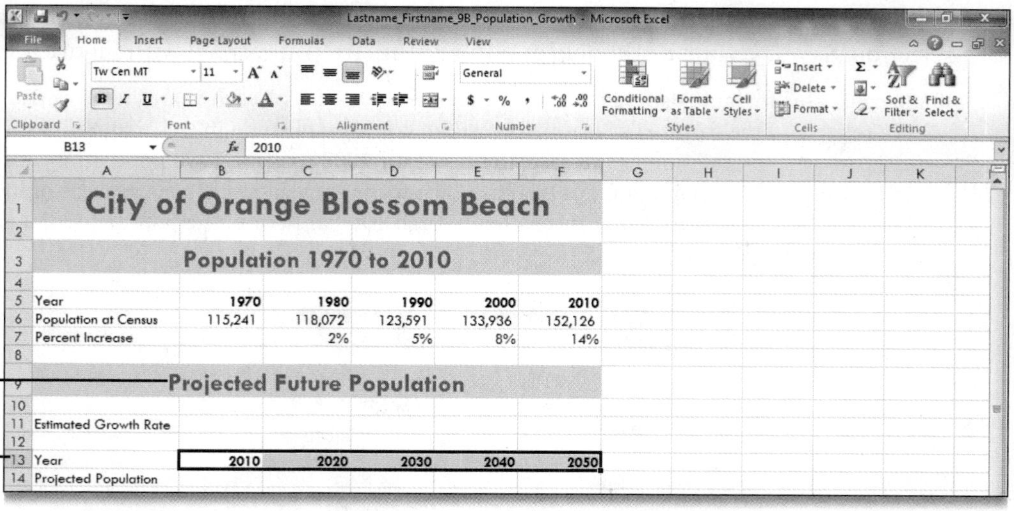

New title entered

Row and column titles entered

7 Click cell **B14**, and then on the **Home tab**, in the **Number group**, notice that the **Number Format** box indicates *General*. Then, being sure to type the comma, type **152,126**

8 On the **Formula Bar**, click the **Enter** button ✓ to keep the cell active, and then in the **Number group**, notice that the format changed to *Number*.

9 Press Delete, and then in the **Number group**, notice that the *Number* format is still indicated.

Recall that deleting the contents of a cell does not delete the cell's formatting.

10 *Without* typing a comma, in cell **B14**, type **152126** and then press Enter.

The comma displays even though you did not type it. When you type a number and include a formatting symbol such as a comma or dollar sign, Excel applies the format to the cell. Thus, if you delete the contents of the cell and type in the cell again, the format you established remains applied to the cell. This is referred to as ***format as you type***.

11 Examine the format of the value in cell **B14**, and then compare it to the format in cell **B6** where you used the **Comma Style** button to format the cell. Notice that the number in cell **B14** is flush with the right edge of the cell, but the number in cell **B6** leaves a small amount of space on the right edge.

When you type commas as you enter numbers, Excel applies the *Number* format, which does not leave a space at the right of the number for a closing parenthesis in the event of a negative number. This is different from the format that is applied when you use the *Comma Style* button on the Ribbon or Mini toolbar, as you did for the numbers entered in row 6. Recall that the Comma Style format applied from either the Ribbon or the Mini toolbar leaves space on the right for a closing parenthesis in the event of a negative number.

12 In cell **B11**, type **8%** Select the range **A11:B11**, and then from the Mini toolbar, apply **Bold** B. **Save** your workbook.

More Knowledge | Percentage Calculations

When you type a percentage into a cell—for example 8%—the percentage format, without decimal points, displays in both the cell and the Formula Bar. Excel will, however, use the decimal value of 0.08 for actual calculations.

Activity 9.14 | Calculating a Value After an Increase

A growing population results in increased use of city services. Thus, city planners in Orange Blossom Beach must estimate how much the population will increase in the future. The calculations you made in the previous activity show that the population has increased at varying rates during each 10-year period from 1970 to 2010, ranging from a low of 2% to a high of 14% per 10-year census period.

Population data estimates suggest that future growth will trend close to that of the recent past. To plan for the future, Ms. Darius wants to prepare three forecasts of the city's population based on the percentage increases in 2000, in 2010, and for a percentage increase halfway between the two; that is, for 8%, 11%, and 14%. In this activity, you will calculate the population that would result from an 8% increase.

1 Click cell **C14**. Type **=b14*(100%+b11)** and then on the **Formula Bar**, click the **Enter** button to display a result of *164296.08*. Compare your screen with Figure 9.28.

This formula calculates what the population will be in the year 2020 assuming an increase of 8% over 2010's population. Use the mathematical formula ***value after increase* = *base* × *percent for new value*** to calculate a value after an increase as follows:

First, establish the *percent for new value*. The ***percent for new value* = *base percent* + *percent of increase***. The *base percent* of 100% represents the base population and the *percent of increase* in this instance is 8%. Thus, the population will equal 100% of the base year plus 8% of the base year. This can be expressed as 108% or 1.08. In this formula, you will use 100% + the rate in cell B11, which is 8%, to equal 108%.

Second, enter a reference to the cell that contains the *base*—the population in 2010. The base value resides in cell B14—*152,126*.

Third, calculate the *value after increase*. Because in each future 10-year period the increase will be based on 8%—an absolute value located in cell B11—this cell reference can be formatted as absolute by typing dollar signs.

Figure 9.28

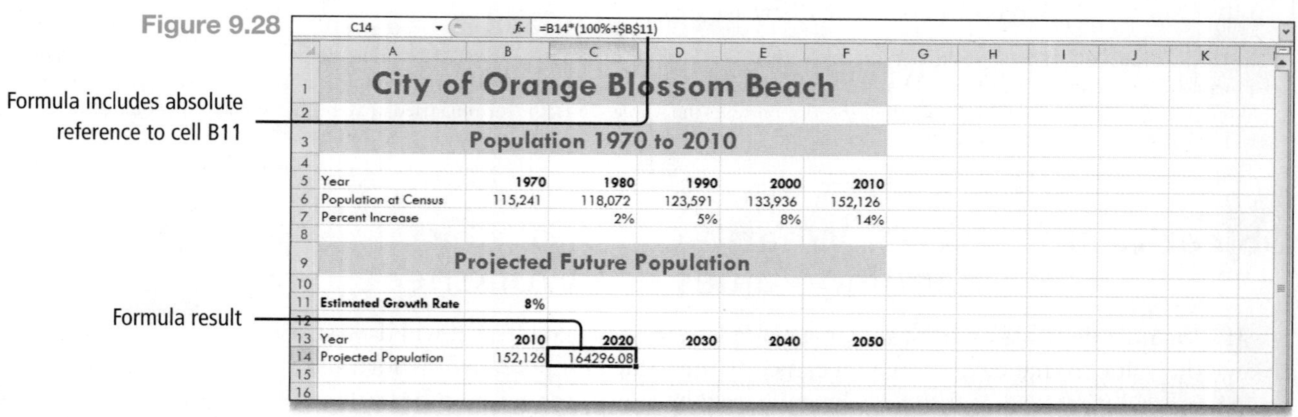

2 With cell **C14** as the active cell, drag the fill handle to copy the formula to the range **D14:F14**.

3 Point to cell **B14**, right-click, click the **Format Painter** button, and then select the range **C14:F14**. Press Esc to cancel the selection, click **Save** and then compare your screen with Figure 9.29.

This formula uses a relative cell address—B14—for the *base*; the population in the previous 10-year period is used in each of the formulas in cells D14:F14 as the *base* value. Because the reference to the *percent of increase* in cell B11 is an absolute reference, each *value after increase* is calculated with the value from cell B11. The population projected for 2020—*164,296*—is an increase of 8% over the population in 2010. The projected population in 2030—*177,440*—is an increase of 8% over the population in 2020 and so on.

Figure 9.29

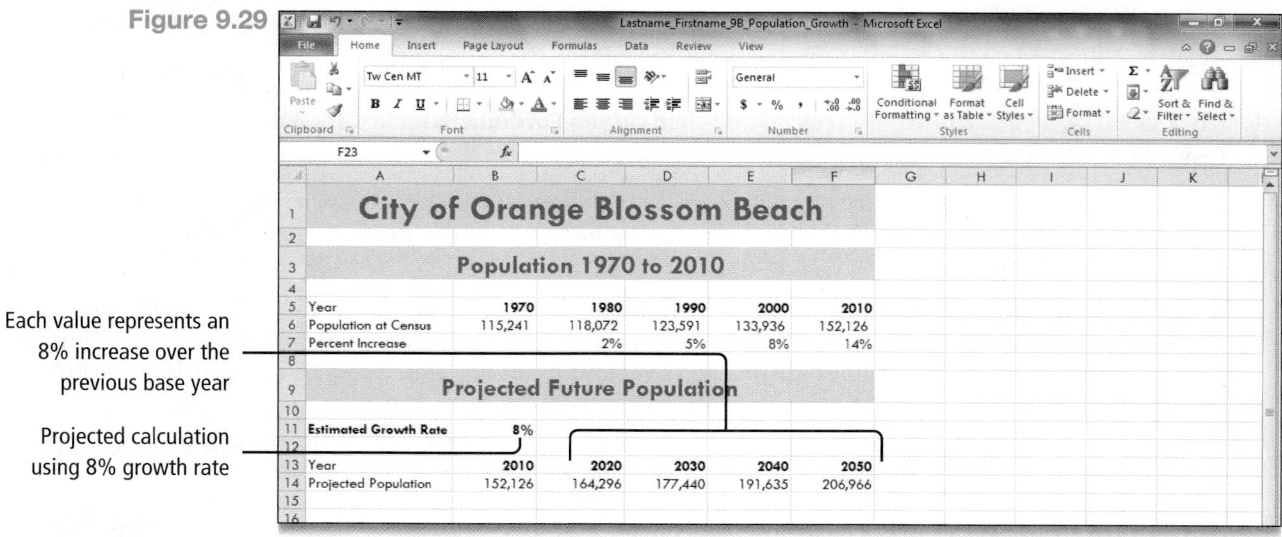

> **More Knowledge | Percent Increase or Decrease**
>
> The basic formula for calculating an increase or decrease can be done in two parts. First, determine the percent by which the base value will be increased or decreased, and then add or subtract the results to the base. The formula can be simplified by using (1+amount of increase) or (1–amount of decrease), where 1, rather than 100%, represents the whole. Thus, the formula used in Step 1 of Activity 9.14 could also be written =b14*(1+b11), or =(b14*b11)+b14.

Objective 6 | Answer What-If Questions by Changing Values in a Worksheet

View the video on the Companion Web Site or in MyITLab

If a formula depends on the value in a cell, you can see what effect it will have if you change the value in that cell. Then, you can copy the value computed by the formula and paste it into another part of the worksheet where you can compare it to other values.

Activity 9.15 | Answering What-If Questions and Using Paste Special

A growth rate of 8% in each 10-year period will result in a population of almost 207,000 people by 2050. The city planners will likely ask: *What if* the population grows at the highest rate (14%)? *What if* the population grows at a rate that is halfway between the 2000 and 2010 rates (11%)?

Because the formulas are constructed to use the growth rate displayed in cell B11, Ms. Darius can answer these questions quickly by entering different percentages into that cell. To keep the results of each set of calculations so they can be compared, you will paste the results of each what-if question into another area of the worksheet.

1. Leave **row 15** blank, and then click cell **A16**. Type **Growth Estimates 2020 to 2050** and then press Enter. Use **Format Painter** to copy the format from cell **A9** to cell **A16**.
2. Select the range **A11:B11**, right-click to display the Mini toolbar, click the **Fill Color button arrow**, and then under **Theme Colors**, in the first column, click the third color—**White, Background 1, Darker 15%**.
3. Leave **row 17** blank, and then in the range **A18:A21**, type the following row titles:

   Year

   8% Growth Rate

   11% Growth Rate

   14% Growth Rate

4 Select the range **B13:F13**, right-click over the selection, and then on the shortcut menu, click **Copy**.

5 Point to cell **B18**, right-click, and then on the shortcut menu, under **Paste Options**, click the **Paste** button.

Recall that when pasting a group of copied cells to a target range, you need only point to or select the first cell of the range.

6 Select and **Copy** the range **B14:F14**, and then **Paste** it beginning in cell **B19**.

7 Click cell **C19**. On the **Formula Bar**, notice that the *formula* was pasted into the cell, as shown in Figure 9.30.

This is *not* the desired result. The actual *calculated values*—not the formulas—are needed in the range.

Figure 9.30

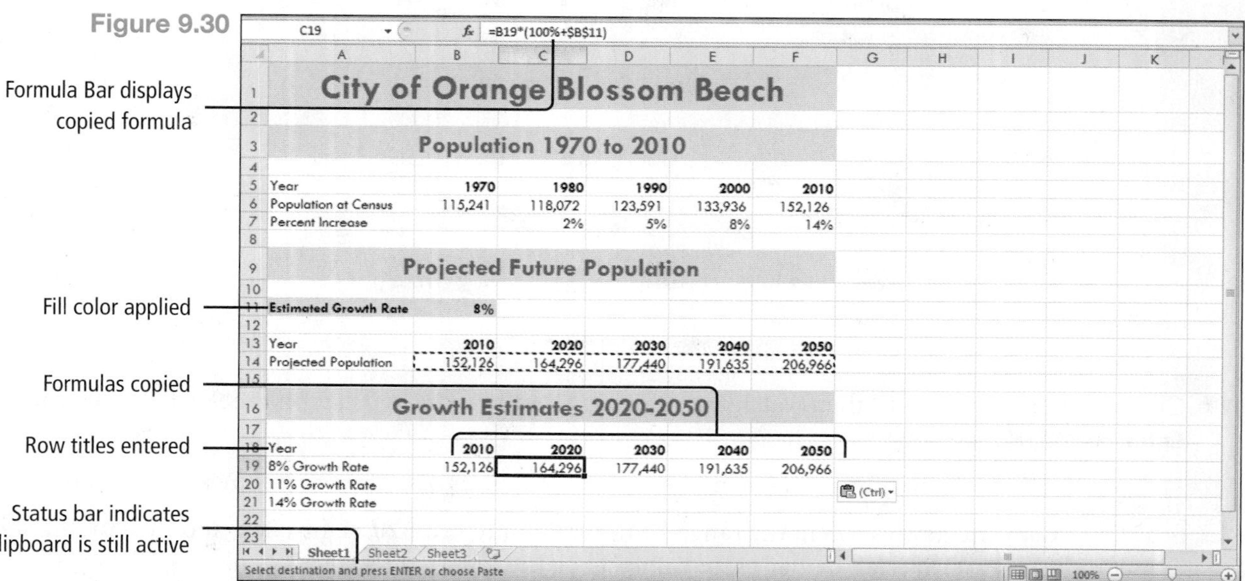

8 On the Quick Access Toolbar, click the **Undo** button. With the range **B14:F14** still copied to the Clipboard—as indicated by the message in the status bar and the moving border—point to cell **B19**, and then right-click to display the shortcut menu.

9 Under **Paste Options**, point to **Paste Special** to display another gallery, and then under Paste Values, point to the **Values & Number Formatting** button to display the ScreenTip as shown in Figure 9.31.

The ScreenTip *Values & Number Formatting (A)* indicates that you can paste the *calculated values* that result from the calculation of formulas along with the formatting applied to the copied cells. (*A*) is the keyboard shortcut for this command.

Figure 9.31

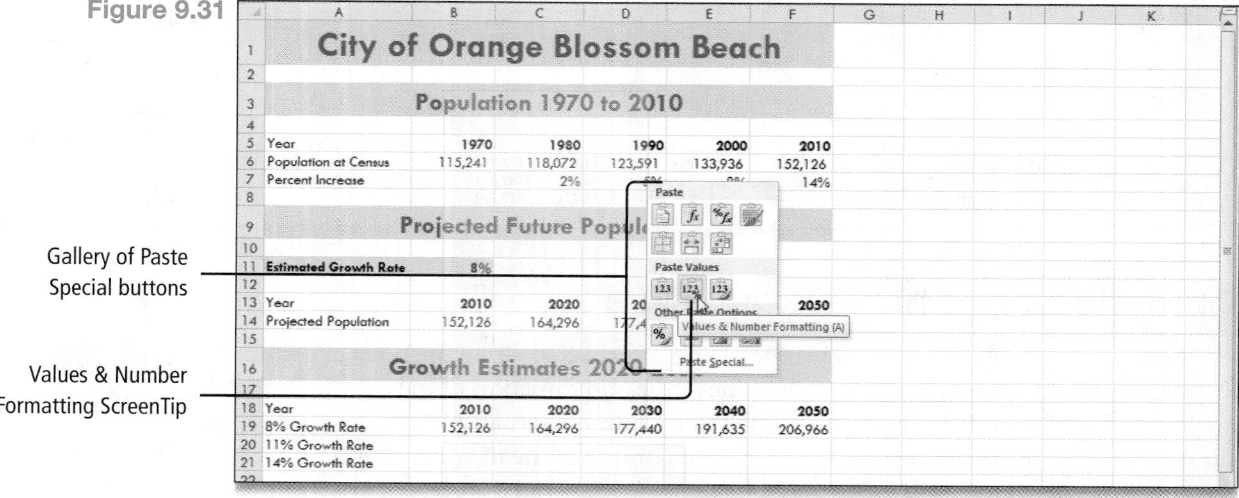

10 Click the **Values & Number Formatting** button, click cell **C19** and notice on the **Formula Bar** that the cell contains a value, not a formula. Press Esc to cancel the moving border. Compare your screen with Figure 9.32.

The calculated estimates based on an 8% growth rate are pasted along with their formatting.

Figure 9.32

Formula Bar indicates the value

C19 | f_x 164296.08

	A	B	C	D	E	F
1	City of Orange Blossom Beach					
2						
3	Population 1970 to 2010					
4						
5	Year	1970	1980	1990	2000	2010
6	Population at Census	115,241	118,072	123,591	133,936	152,126
7	Percent Increase		2%	5%	8%	14%
8						
9	Projected Future Population					
10						
11	Estimated Growth Rate	8%				
12						
13	Year	2010	2020	2030	2040	2050
14	Projected Population	152,126	164,296	177,440	191,635	206,966
15						
16	Growth Estimates 2020-2050					
17						
18	Year	2010	2020	2030	2040	2050
19	8% Growth Rate	152,126	164,296	177,440	191,635	206,966
20	11% Growth Rate					
21	14% Growth Rate					

11 Click cell **B11**. Type **11** and then watch the values in **C14:F14** *recalculate* as, on the **Formula Bar**, you click the **Enter** button.

The value *11%* is halfway between 8% and 14%—the growth rates from the two most recent 10-year periods.

12 Select and **Copy** the new values in the range **B14:F14**. Point to cell **B20**, right-click, and then on the shortcut menu, point to **Paste Special**. Under **Paste Values**, click the **Values & Number Formatting** button.

13 In cell **B11**, change the percentage by typing **14** and then press Enter. Notice that the projected values in **C14:F14** recalculate.

14 Using the skills you just practiced, select and copy the recalculated values in the range **B14:F14**, and then paste the **Values & Number Formatting** to the range **B21:F21**.

15 Press Esc to cancel the moving border, click cell **A1**, click **Save**, and then compare your screen with Figure 9.33.

With this information, Ms. Darius can answer several what-if questions about the future population of the city and provide a range of population estimates based on the rates of growth over the past 10-year periods.

Figure 9.33

Values copied for each what-if question

	A	B	C	D	E	F
9	Projected Future Population					
10						
11	Estimated Growth Rate	14%				
12						
13	Year	2010	2020	2030	2040	2050
14	Projected Population	152,126	173,424	197,703	225,381	256,935
15						
16	Growth Estimates 2020-2050					
17						
18	Year	2010	2020	2030	2040	2050
19	8% Growth Rate	152,126	164,296	177,440	191,635	206,966
20	11% Growth Rate	152,126	168,860	187,434	208,052	230,938
21	14% Growth Rate	152,126	173,424	197,703	225,381	256,935
22						

Objective 7 | Chart Data with a Line Chart

A ***line chart*** displays trends over time. Time is displayed along the bottom axis and the data point values connect with a line. The curve and direction of the line make trends obvious to the reader. Whereas the columns in a column chart and the pie slices in a pie chart emphasize the distinct values of each data point, the line in a line chart emphasizes the flow from one data point value to the next.

View the video on the Companion Web Site or in MyITLab

Activity 9.16 | Inserting Multiple Rows and Creating a Line Chart

So that city council members can see how the population has increased over the past five census periods, in this activity, you will chart the actual population figures from 1970 to 2010 in a line chart.

1 In the **row header** area, point to **row 8** to display the pointer, click and then drag down to select rows **8:24**. Right-click over the selection, and then click **Insert** to insert the same number of blank rows as you selected. Compare your screen with Figure 9.34.

Use this technique to insert multiple rows quickly.

Figure 9.34

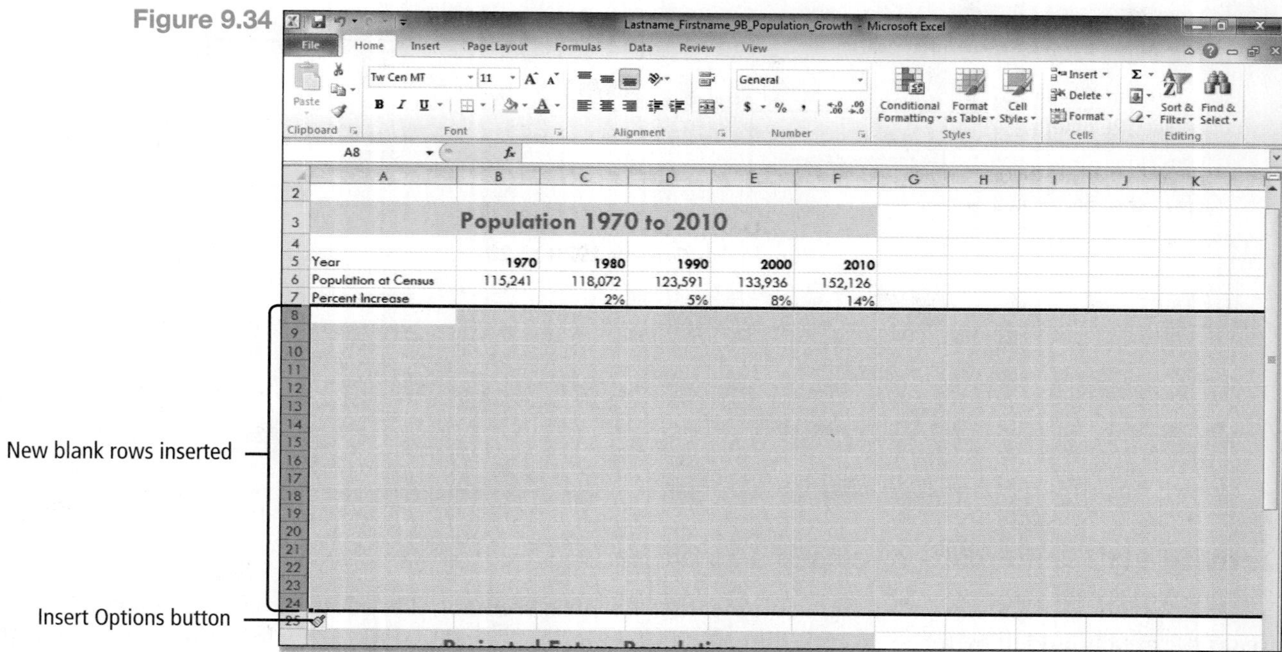

2 Near **row 25**, click the **Insert Options** button, and then click the **Clear Formatting** option button to clear any formatting from these rows.

You will use this blank area in which to position your line chart.

3 Select the range **A6:F6**. On the **Insert tab**, in the **Charts group**, click the **Line** button.

4 In the displayed gallery of line charts, in the second row, point to the first chart type to display the ScreenTip *Line with Markers*. Compare your screen with Figure 9.35.

Figure 9.35

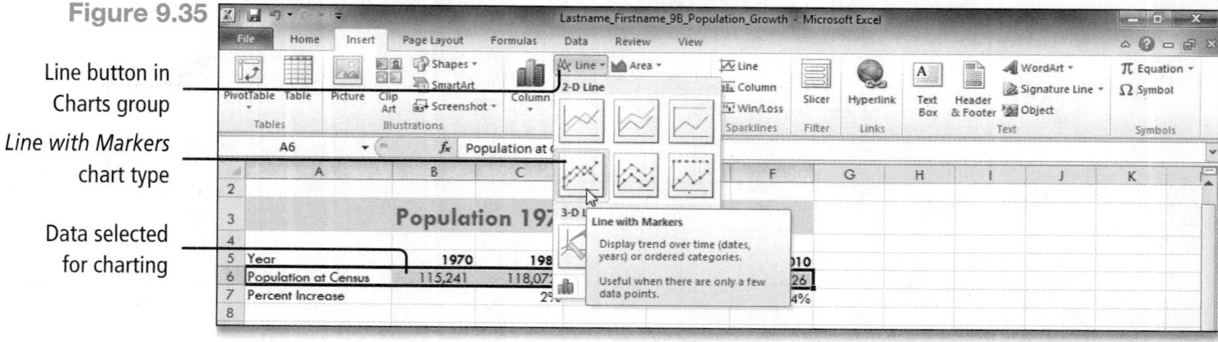

5 Click the **Line with Markers** chart type to create the chart as an embedded chart in the worksheet.

6 Point to the border of the chart to display the pointer, and then drag the chart so that its upper left corner is positioned in cell **A9**, aligned approximately under the *t* in the word *Percent* above.

7 On the **Layout tab**, in the **Labels group**, click the **Legend** button, and then click **None**.

8 Click the chart title one time to select it and display a solid border around the title. Watch the **Formula Bar** as you type **Orange Blossom Beach** and then press Enter.

9 In the chart title, click to position the insertion point following the *h* in *Beach*, and then press Enter to begin a new line. Type **Population Growth 1970 to 2010** Click the dashed border around the chart title to change it to a solid border, right-click, and then on the Mini toolbar, change the **Font Size** of the title to **20**.

Recall that a solid border around an object indicates that the entire object is selected.

10 **Save** your workbook, and then compare your screen with Figure 9.36.

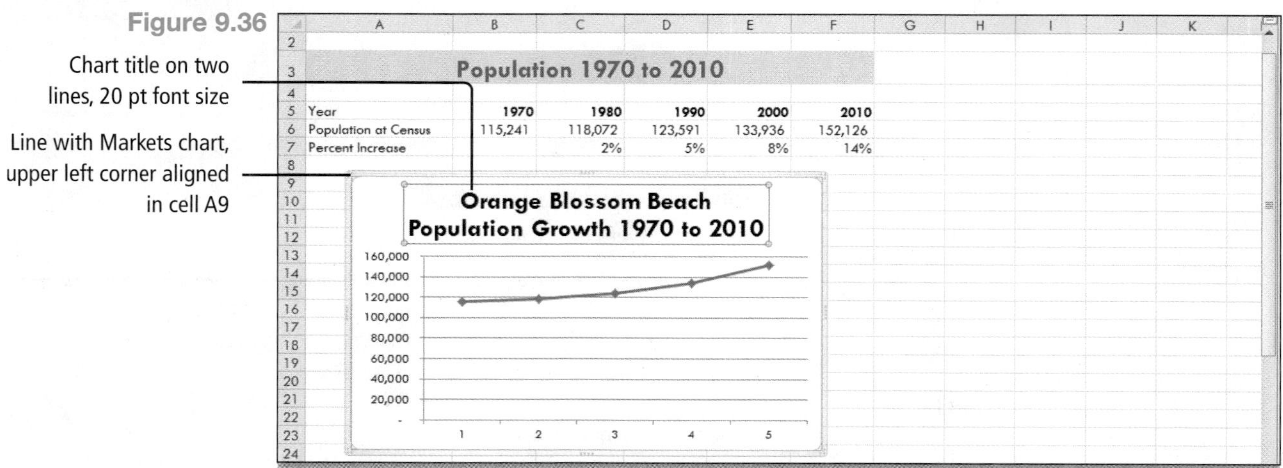

Figure 9.36

Activity 9.17 | Formatting Axes in a Line Chart

An ***axis*** is a line that serves as a frame of reference for measurement; it borders the chart ***plot area***. The plot area is the area bounded by the axes, including all the data series. Recall that the area along the bottom of a chart that identifies the categories of data is referred to as the ***category axis*** or the ***x-axis***. Recall also that the area along the left side of a chart that shows the range of numbers for the data points is referred to as the ***value axis*** or the ***y-axis***. In this activity, you will change the category axis to include the names of the 10-year census periods and adjust the numeric scale of the value axis.

1 Be sure the chart is still selected—a pale frame surrounds the chart area. Click the **Design tab**, and then in the **Data group**, click the **Select Data** button.

2 On the right side of the displayed **Select Data Source** dialog box, under **Horizontal (Category) Axis Labels**, locate the **Edit** button, as shown in Figure 9.37.

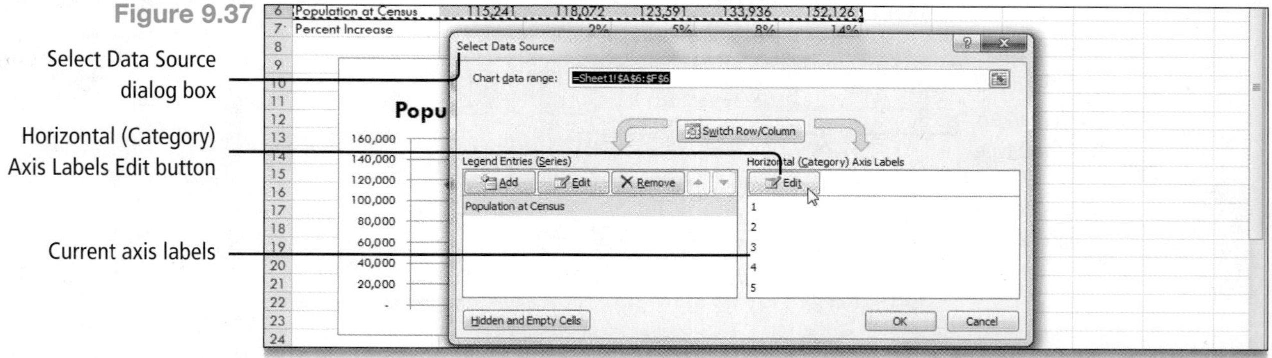

Figure 9.37

3 In the right column, click the **Edit** button. If necessary, drag the title bar of the **Axis Labels** dialog box to the right of the chart so that it is not blocking your view of the data, and then select the years in the range **B5:F5**. Compare your screen with Figure 9.38.

Figure 9.38

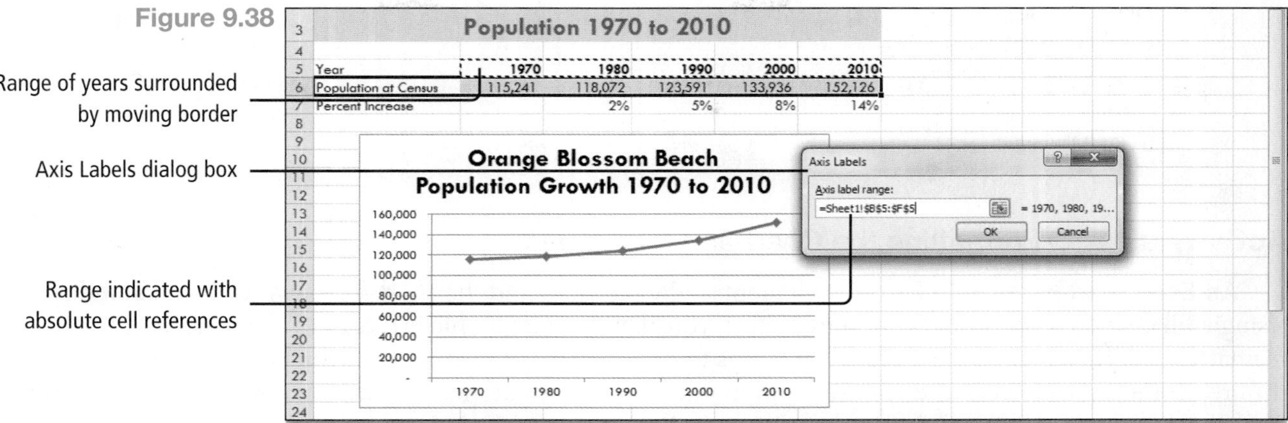

4 In the **Axis Labels** dialog box, click **OK**, and notice that in the right column of the **Select Data Source** dialog box, the years display as the category labels. Click **OK** to close the **Select Data Source** dialog box. Compare your screen with Figure 9.39.

Figure 9.39

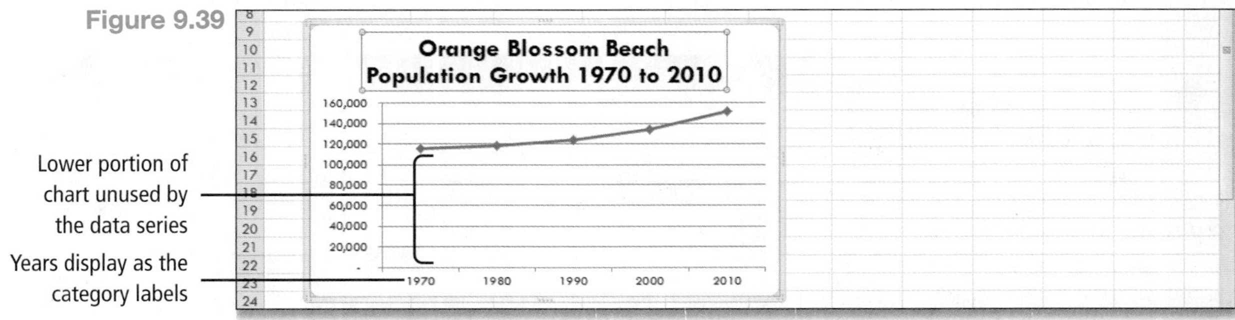

5 On the chart, notice that the blue line—the data series—does not display in the lower portion of the chart. Then, on the **Layout tab**, in the **Axes group**, click the **Axes** button. Point to **Primary Vertical Axis**, and then click **More Primary Vertical Axis Options**.

6 In the **Format Axis** dialog box, on the left, be sure **Axis Options** is selected. On the right, in the **Minimum** row, click the **Fixed** option button. In the box to the right, select the existing text *0.0*, and then type **100000**

Because none of the population figures are under 100,000, changing the Minimum number to 100,000 will enable the data series to occupy more of the plot area.

7 In the **Major unit** row, click the **Fixed** option button, select the text in the box to the right, and then type **10000** In the lower right corner, click **Close**. **Save** your workbook, and then compare your screen with Figure 9.40.

The ***Major unit*** value determines the spacing between ***tick marks*** and thus between the gridlines in the plot area. Tick marks are the short lines that display on an axis at regular intervals. By default, Excel started the values at zero and increased in increments of 20,000. By setting the Minimum value on the value axis to 100,000 and changing the Major unit from 20,000 to 10,000, the line chart shows a clearer trend in the population growth.

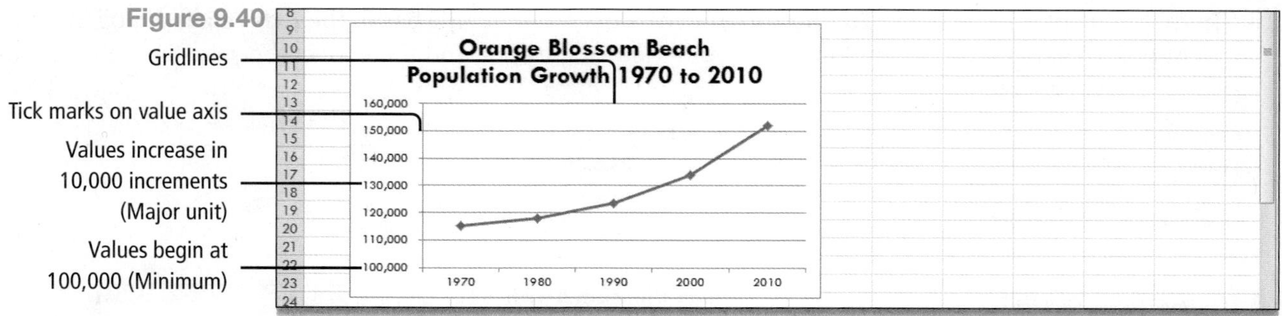

Figure 9.40

Activity 9.18 | Formatting the Chart and Plot Areas

An Excel chart has two background elements—the plot area and the chart area—which by default display a single fill color. To add visual appeal to a chart, you can insert a graphic image as the background. When formatting chart elements, there are several ways to display the dialog boxes that you need. You can right-click the area you want to format and choose a command on the shortcut menu. In this activity, you will use the Chart Elements box in the Current Selection group on the Format tab of the Ribbon, which is convenient if you are changing the format of a variety of chart elements.

1 Click the **Format tab**, and then in the **Current Selection group**, point to the small arrow to the right of the first item in the group to display the ScreenTip *Chart Elements*. Compare your screen with Figure 9.41.

From the ***Chart Elements*** box, you can select a chart element so that you can format it.

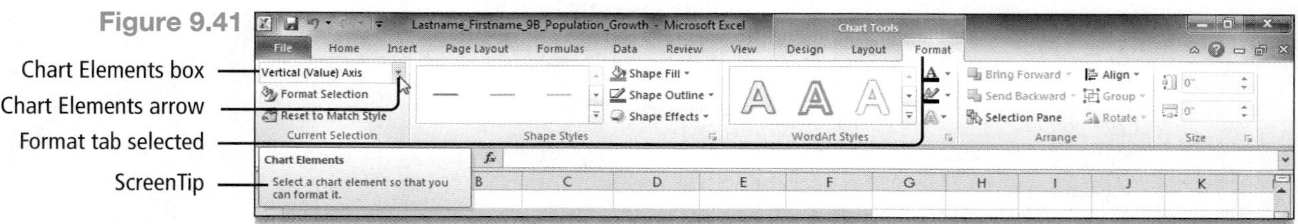

Figure 9.41

2 Click the **Chart Elements arrow**, and then from the displayed list, click **Chart Area**. Directly below the **Chart Elements** box, click the **Format Selection** button.

The Format Chart Area dialog box displays. Use this technique to select the chart element that you want to format, and then click the Format Selection button to display the appropriate dialog box.

3 In the **Format Chart Area** dialog box, on the left, be sure that **Fill** is selected.

4 On the right, under **Fill**, click the **Picture or texture fill** option button, and then under **Insert from**, click the **File** button. In the **Insert Picture** dialog box, navigate to your student files, and then insert the picture **jpg09B_Beach**. Leave the dialog box open, and then compare your screen with Figure 9.42.

Figure 9.42

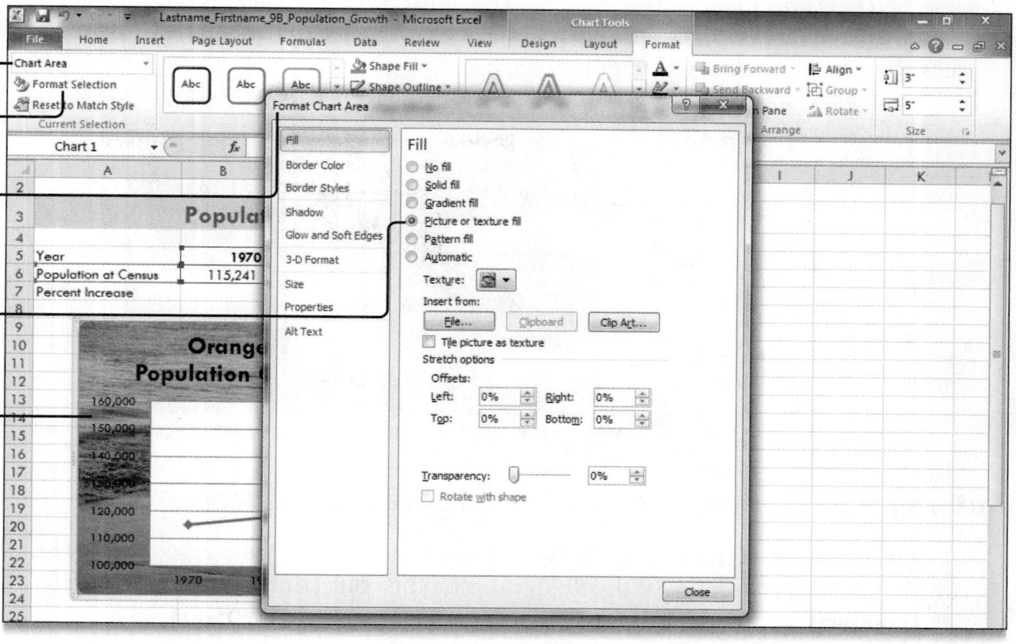

Chart Area selected

Format Selection button

Format Chart Area dialog box

Picture or texture fill option

Beach picture displays in the chart

5 In the **Format Chart Area** dialog box, on the left, click **Border Color**, on the right click the **Solid line** option button, click the **Color arrow**, and then under **Theme Colors**, in the fourth column, click the first color—**Dark Teal, Text 2**.

6 On the left, click **Border Styles**. On the right, select the text in the **Width** box and type **4 pt** At the bottom select the **Rounded corners** check box, and then **Close** the dialog box.

A 4 pt teal border with rounded corners frames the chart.

7 In the **Current Selection group**, click the **Chart Elements arrow**, on the list click **Plot Area**, and then click the **Format Selection** button.

8 In the **Format Plot Area** dialog box, on the left, be sure that **Fill** is selected, and then on the right, click the **No fill** option button. **Close** the dialog box.

The fill is removed from the plot area so that the picture is visible as the background.

9 Click the **Chart Elements arrow**, on the list click **Vertical (Value) Axis**, and then click the **Format Selection** button.

10 In the **Format Axis** dialog box, on the left click **Line Color**, on the right click the **Solid line** option button, click the **Color arrow**, and then click the first color—**White, Background 1**.

The vertical line with tick marks displays in white.

11 **Close** the dialog box. From the **Chart Elements** box, select the **Vertical (Value) Axis Major Gridlines**, and then click **Format Selection**. Change the **Line Color** to a **Solid line**, and then apply the **White, Background 1** color. **Close** the dialog box.

12 From the **Chart Elements** list, select the **Horizontal (Category) Axis**, and then click **Format Selection**. In the **Format Axis** dialog box, change the **Line Color** to a **Solid line**, and then apply the **White, Background 1** color. **Close** the dialog box.

13 Point to any of the numbers on the vertical value axis, right-click, and then on the Mini toolbar, change the **Font Color** [A] to **White, Background 1**. Point to any of the years on the horizontal category axis, right-click, and then change the **Font Color** [A] to **White, Background 1**.

For basic text-formatting changes—for example changing the size, font, style, or font color—you must leave the Chart Tools on the Ribbon and use commands from the Home tab or the Mini toolbar.

14 Click any cell to deselect the chart, Ctrl + Home to move to the top of your worksheet, click **Save**, and then compare your screen with Figure 9.43.

Figure 9.43

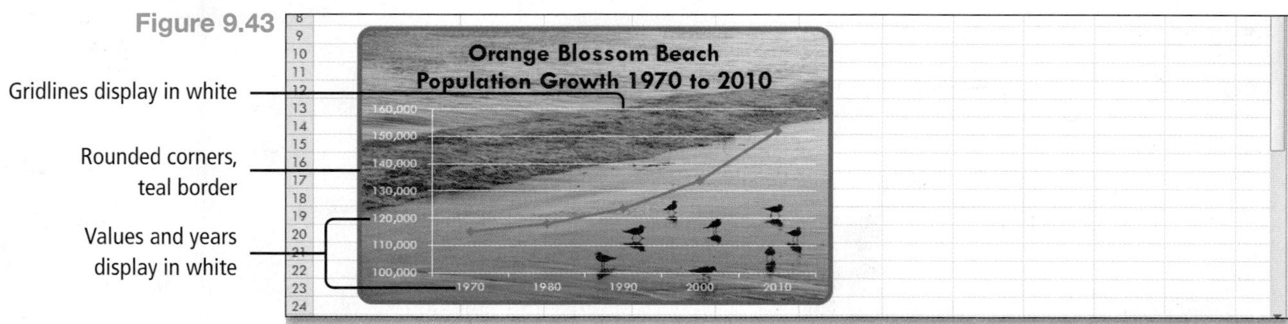

Activity 9.19 | Preparing and Printing Your Worksheet

1 From **Backstage** view, display the **Document Panel**. In the **Author** box, replace the existing text with your firstname and lastname. In the **Subject** box, type your course name and section number. In the **Keywords** box, type **population** and then **Close** the **Document Information Panel**.

2 Click the **Insert tab**, and then in the **Text group**, click the **Header & Footer** button to switch to **Page Layout View** and open the **Header area**.

3 In the **Navigation group**, click the **Go to Footer** button, click just above the word *Footer*, and then in the **Header & Footer Elements** group, click the **File Name** button. Click in a cell just above the footer to exit the **Footer area** and view your file name.

4 Click the **Page Layout tab**. In the **Page Setup group**, click the **Margins** button, and then at the bottom of the **Margins** gallery, click **Custom Margins**. In the dialog box, under **Center on page**, select the **Horizontally** check box. Click **OK** to close the dialog box.

5 On the status bar, click the **Normal** button to return to Normal view, and then press Ctrl + Home to move to the top of your worksheet.

6 At the lower edge of the window, click to select the **Sheet2 tab**, hold down Ctrl, and then click the **Sheet3 tab** to select the two unused sheets. Right-click over the selected sheet tabs, and then on the displayed shortcut menu, click **Delete**.

7 **Save** your workbook before printing or submitting. Press Ctrl + F2 to display the **Print Preview** to check your worksheet. If necessary, return to the worksheet to make any necessary adjustments or corrections, and then **Save**.

8 Print or submit electronically as directed. If you are directed to submit printed formulas, refer to Activity 8.16 to do so.

9 If you printed your formulas, be sure to redisplay the worksheet by clicking the Show Formulas button to turn it off. From **Backstage** view, click **Close**. If the dialog box displays asking if you want to save changes, click **No** so that you do not save the changes you made for printing formulas. **Close** Excel.

End **You have completed Project 9B**

Content-Based Assessments

Summary

In this chapter, you created a pie chart to show how the parts of a budget contribute to a total budget. Then you formatted the pie chart attractively and used Goal Seek. You also practiced using parentheses in a formula, calculating the percentage rate of an increase, answering what-if questions, and charting data in a line chart to show the flow of data over time.

Key Terms

Check Your Knowledge

Matching and Multiple Choice items are available in MyITLab and on the Companion Web Site.

Content-Based Assessments

Apply 9A skills from these Objectives:

1. Chart Data with a Pie Chart
2. Format a Pie Chart
3. Edit a Workbook and Update a Chart
4. Use Goal Seek to Perform What-If Analysis

Mastering Excel | Project 9C Investments

In the following project, you will you will edit a worksheet for Jennifer Carson, City Finance Manager, that summarizes the investment portfolio of the City of Orange Blossom Beach. Your completed worksheets will look similar to Figure 9.44.

Project Files

For Project 9C, you will need the following file:

e09C_Investments

You will save your workbook as:

Lastname_Firstname_9C_Investments

Project Results

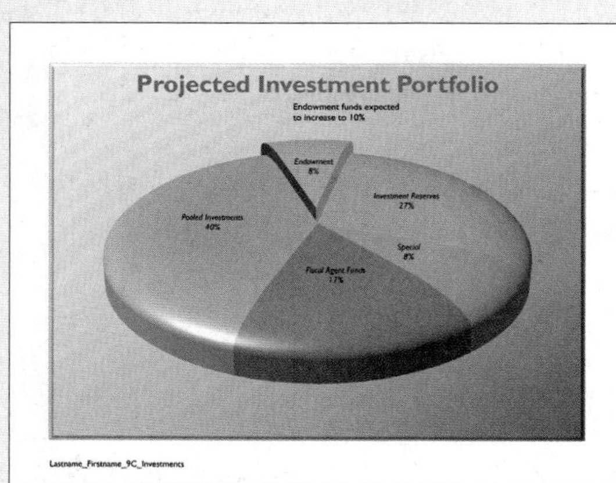

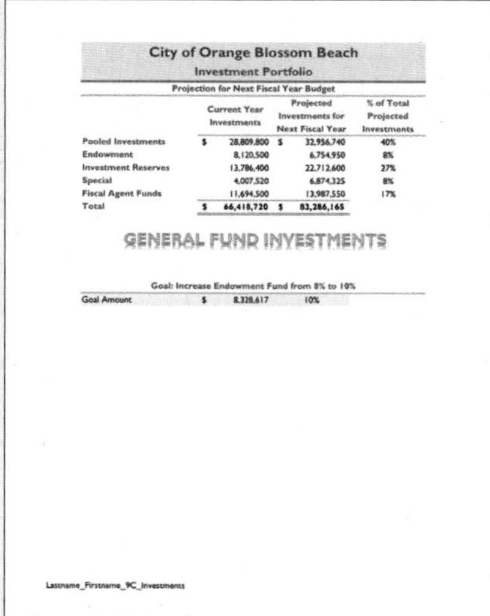

City of Orange Blossom Beach

Investment Portfolio

Projection for Next Fiscal Year Budget

	Current Year Investments	Projected Investments for Next Fiscal Year	% of Total Projected Investments
Pooled Investments	$ 28,809,800	$ 32,956,740	40%
Endowment	8,120,500	6,754,950	8%
Investment Reserves	13,786,400	22,712,600	27%
Special	4,007,520	6,874,325	8%
Fiscal Agent Funds	11,694,500	13,987,550	17%
Total	$ 66,418,720	$ 83,286,165	

GENERAL FUND INVESTMENTS

Goal: Increase Endowment Fund from 8% to 10%

Goal Amount	$ 8,328,617	10%

Lastname_Firstname_9C_Investments

Figure 9.44

(Project 9C Investments continues on the next page)

Mastering Excel | Project 9C Investments (continued)

1 **Start** Excel. From your student files, locate and open **e09C_Investments**. **Save** the file in your **All In One Chapter 9** folder as **Lastname_Firstname_9C_Investments**

2 In cells **B10** and **C10**, enter formulas to calculate totals for each column. Then, in cell **D5**, enter a formula to calculate the % of Total Projected Investments for Pooled Investments by dividing the **Projected Investments for Next Fiscal Year** for the **Pooled Investments** by the **Total Projected Investments for Next Fiscal Year**. Use absolute cell references as necessary, format the result in **Percent Style**, and **Center** the percentage. Fill the formula down through cell **D9**.

3 Select the nonadjacent ranges **A5:A9** and **C5:C9**, and then insert a **Pie in 3-D** chart. Move the chart to a **New sheet** named **Projected Investment Chart** Insert a **Chart Title** above the chart with the text **Projected Investment Portfolio** Change the chart title **Font Size** to **32** and change the **Font Color** to **Brown, Accent 6**—in the last column, the first color.

4 Remove the **Legend** from the chart, and then add **Data Labels** formatted so that only the **Category Name** and **Percentage** display positioned in the **Center**. Change the data labels **Font Size** to **11**, and then apply **Italic**.

5 Select the entire pie, display the **Shape Effects** gallery, point to **Bevel**, and then at the bottom of the gallery, click **3-D Options**. Change the **Top** and **Bottom** options to the last **Bevel** type—**Art Deco**. Set the **Top Width** and **Height** boxes to **256** and then set the **Bottom Width** and **Height** boxes to **0** Change the **Material** to the third **Standard** type—**Plastic**.

6 With the pie chart selected, display the shortcut menu, and then click **Format Data Series**. Change the **Angle of first slice** to **200** to move the *Endowment* slice to the top of the pie. Select the **Endowment** slice, and then explode the slice slightly.

7 Change the **Fill Color** of the **Pooled Investments** slice to **Gray-50%, Accent 1, Lighter 40%**. Format the **Chart Area** by applying a **Convex Bevel**. To the **Chart Area**, apply the **Moss, Preset Gradient** fill. In the **Angle** box, type **45**

8 **Insert** a **Text Box** positioned approximately halfway between the *Endowment* pie slice and the *v* in the word *Investment* in the title. In the text box, type **Endowment funds expected to increase to 10%** Select the text and then, on the Mini toolbar, change the **Font Size** to **12**. Size the text box as necessary so that the text displays on two lines as shown in Figure 9.44.

9 Rename **Sheet1** as **Projected Investment Data** Insert a **WordArt**—in the fifth row, insert the last WordArt style—**Fill – Gray-50%, Accent 1, Plastic Bevel, Reflection**. Type **General Fund Investments** and then change the **Font Size** to **20**. Drag to position the upper left corner of the WordArt in cell **A12**, centered below the worksheet.

10 In cell **A16**, type **Goal: Increase Endowment Fund from 8% to 10%** and then **Merge & Center** the text across the range **A16:D16**. Apply the **Heading 3** cell style. In cell **A17**, type **Goal Amount**

11 **Copy** the range **C6:D6** to cell **B17**. Click cell **C17**, and then use **Goal Seek** to determine the projected amount of endowment funds in cell **B17** if the value in **C17** is **10%**.

12 Select the range **A17:C17**, and then apply the **20% - Accent2** cell style. In **B17**, from the **Cell Styles** gallery, apply the **Currency [0]** cell style.

13 Insert a **Header & Footer** with the file name in the **left section** of the footer. In Page Layout view, check that the WordArt is centered under the worksheet data. Center the worksheet **Horizontally** on the page, and then return to **Normal** view. Display the **Projected Investment Chart** sheet and insert a **Custom Footer** with the file name in the **Left section**.

14 Display the **Document Panel**. Add your name, your course name and section, and the keywords **investment portfolio**

15 **Save** your workbook. Print or submit electronically as directed by your instructor. If required by your instructor, print or create an electronic version of your worksheets with formulas displayed by using the instructions in Activity 8.16, and then **Close** Excel without saving so that you do not save the changes you made to print formulas.

End **You have completed Project 9C**

Content-Based Assessments

Apply 9B skills from these Objectives:

5 Design a Worksheet for What-If Analysis

6 Answer What-If Questions by Changing Values in a Worksheet

7 Chart Data with a Line Chart

Mastering Excel | Project 9D Benefit Analysis

In the following project, you will edit a worksheet that Jeffrey Lovins, Human Resources Director, will use to prepare a five-year forecast of the annual cost of city employee benefits per employee. Your completed worksheet will look similar to Figure 9.45.

Project Files

For Project 9D, you will need the following file:

e09D_Benefit_Analysis

You will save your workbook as:

Lastname_Firstname_9D_Benefit_Analysis

Project Results

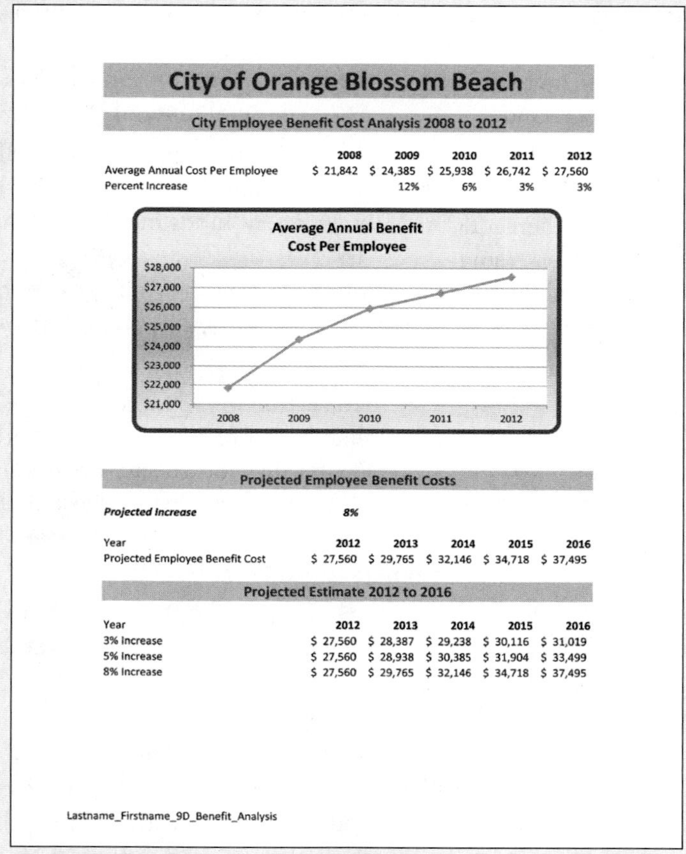

City of Orange Blossom Beach

City Employee Benefit Cost Analysis 2008 to 2012

	2008	2009	2010	2011	2012
Average Annual Cost Per Employee	$ 21,842	$ 24,385	$ 25,938	$ 26,742	$ 27,560
Percent Increase		12%	6%	3%	3%

Projected Employee Benefit Costs

Projected Increase		8%			
Year	2012	2013	2014	2015	2016
Projected Employee Benefit Cost	$ 27,560	$ 29,765	$ 32,146	$ 34,718	$ 37,495

Projected Estimate 2012 to 2016

Year	2012	2013	2014	2015	2016
3% Increase	$ 27,560	$ 28,387	$ 29,238	$ 30,116	$ 31,019
5% Increase	$ 27,560	$ 28,938	$ 30,385	$ 31,904	$ 33,499
8% Increase	$ 27,560	$ 29,765	$ 32,146	$ 34,718	$ 37,495

Lastname_Firstname_9D_Benefit_Analysis

Figure 9.45

(Project 9D Benefit Analysis continues on the next page)

Mastering Excel | Project 9D Benefit Analysis (continued)

1 **Start** Excel. From your student files, open the file **e09D_Benefit_Analysis**. Save the file in your **All In One Chapter 9** folder as **Firstname_Lastname_9D_Benefit_Analysis**

2 In cell **C7**, construct a formula to calculate the percent of increase in employee annual benefit costs from 2008 to 2009. Format the result with the **Percent Style** and then fill the formula through cell **F7**.

3 In cell **A9**, type **Projected Employee Benefit Costs** and then use **Format Painter** to copy the formatting from cell **A3** to cell **A9**. In cell **A11**, type **Projected Increase** and then in cell **A13**, type **Year** In cell **A14**, type **Projected Employee Benefit Cost** and then in the range **B13:F13**, use the fill handle to enter the years 2012 through 2016. Apply **Bold** to the years. In cell **B14**, type **27560** and then from the **Cell Styles** gallery, apply the **Currency [0]** format. In cell **B11**, type **3%** which is the percent of increase from 2011 to 2012. To the range **A11:B11**, apply **Bold** and **Italic**.

4 In cell **C14**, construct a formula to calculate the annual cost of employee benefits for the year 2013 after the projected increase of 3% is applied. Fill the formula through cell **F14**, and then use **Format Painter** to copy the formatting from cell **B14** to the range **C14:F14**.

5 In cell **A16**, type **Projected Estimates 2012 to 2016** and then use **Format Painter** to copy the format from cell **A9** to cell **A16**. In cells **A18:A21**, type the following row titles:

Year
3% Increase
5% Increase
8% Increase

6 **Copy** the range **B13:F13**, and then **Paste** the selection to **B18:F18**. Copy the range **B14:F14** and then paste the **Values & Number Formatting** to the range **B19:F19**. Complete the Projected Estimates section of the worksheet by changing the *Projected Increase* in **B11** to **5%** and then to **8%** copying and pasting the **Values & Number Formatting** to the appropriate ranges in the worksheet.

7 Select **rows 8:24**, and then **Insert** the same number of blank rows as you selected. **Clear Formatting** from the inserted rows. By using the data in **A5:F6**, insert a **Line with Markers** chart in the worksheet. Move the chart so that its upper left corner is positioned in cell **A9** and centered under the data above. Remove the **Legend**, and then replace the existing chart title with the two-line title **Average Annual Benefit Cost Per Employee** The text *Cost per Employee* should display on the second line. Change the title **Font Size** to **14**.

8 Format the **Primary Vertical Axis** so that the **Minimum** is **21000** and the **Major unit** is **1000** Format the **Chart Area** with a **Gradient fill** by applying the third **Preset color** in the third row—**Wheat**. Change the **Border Color** by applying a **Solid line—Orange, Accent 1, Darker 50%**. Change the **Width** of the border to **4** and apply the **Rounded corners** option.

9 Deselect the chart, and then insert a **Header & Footer** with the file name in the **left section** of the footer; center the worksheet **Horizontally** on the page. In the **Document Panel**, add your name, your course name and section, and the keywords **employee benefits, forecast**

10 **Save** your workbook. Print or submit electronically as directed by your instructor. If required by your instructor, print or create an electronic version of your worksheets with formulas displayed by using the instructions in Activity 8.16, and then **Close** Excel without saving so that you do not save the changes you made to print formulas.

End **You have completed Project 9D**

Content-Based Assessments

Apply 9A and 9B skills from these Objectives:

1. Chart Data with a Pie Chart
2. Format a Pie Chart
3. Edit a Workbook and Update a Chart
4. Use Goal Seek to Perform What-If Analysis
5. Design a Worksheet for What-If Analysis
6. Answer What-If Questions by Changing Values in a Worksheet
7. Chart Data with a Line Chart

Mastering Excel | Project 9E Operations Analysis

In the following project, you will you will edit a workbook for Andrew Rivera, City Finance Manager, that summarizes the city expenses. Your completed worksheets will look similar to Figure 9.46.

Project Files

For Project 9E, you will need the following file:

e09E_Expense_Analysis

You will save your workbook as:

Lastname_Firstname_9E_Expense_Analysis

Project Results

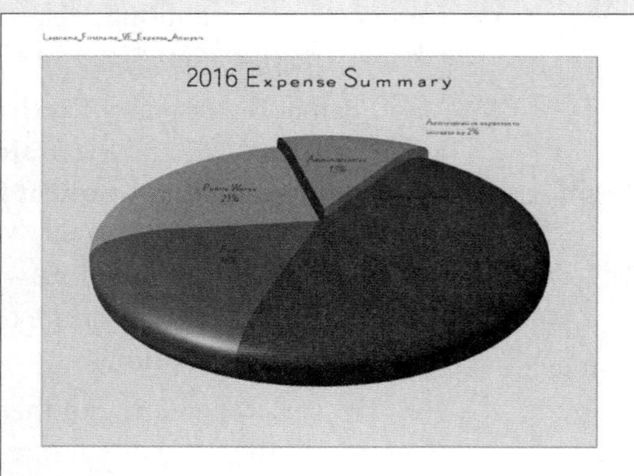

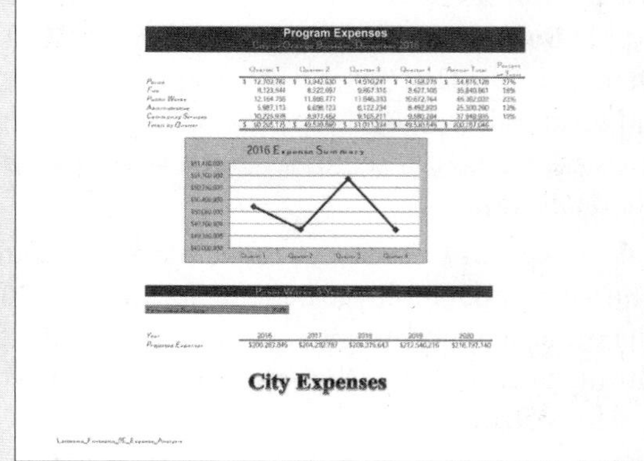

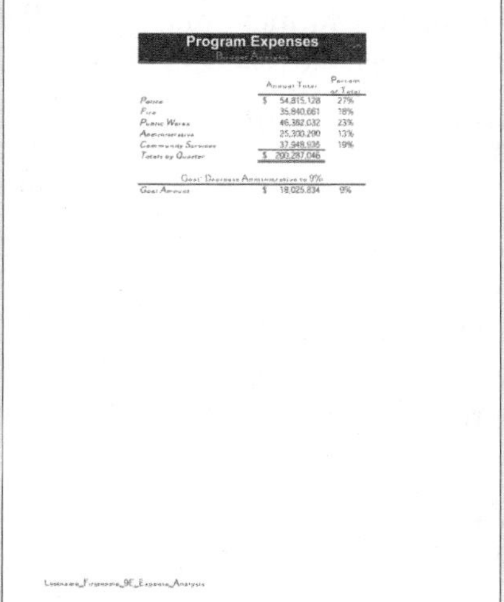

Figure 9.46

(Project 9E Operations Analysis continues on the next page)

Mastering Excel | Project 9E Operations Analysis (continued)

1 **Start** Excel. From your student files, open **e09E_Expense_Analysis**. Save the file as in your **All In One Chapter 9** folder as **Lastname_Firstname_9E_Expense_Analysis**

2 In the **Program Expenses** sheet, calculate totals in the ranges **F5:F9** and **B10:F10**. In cell **G5**, construct a formula to calculate the **Percent of Total** by dividing the **Annual Total** for **Police** in cell **F5** by the **Annual Total** for all quarters in cell **F10**. Use absolute cell references as necessary, format the result in **Percent Style**, and then **Center**. Fill the formula down through cell **G9**.

3 Select the nonadjacent ranges **A5:A9** and **F5:F9**, and then insert a **Pie in 3-D** chart. Move the chart to a **New sheet** with the name **Expense Summary Chart** Insert a **Chart Title** above the chart with the text **2016 Expense Summary** and then change the **Font Size** to **32**.

4 Remove the **Legend** from the chart and then add **Data Labels** formatted so that only the **Category Name** and **Percentage** display positioned in the **Center**. Change the data labels **Font Size** to **12**, and apply **Bold** and **Italic**.

5 Select the chart, and then modify the pie chart **Shape Effects** by changing the **Bevel**, **3-D Options**. Change the **Top** and **Bottom** options to the first **Bevel** type in the second row—**Angle**. Set the **Top Width** and **Height** boxes to **256 pt** and then set the **Bottom Width** and **Height** boxes to **50 pt** Change the **Material** to the third **Standard Effect** type—**Plastic**.

6 In the displayed **Format Data Series** dialog box, on the left, click **Series Options**, and then change the **Angle of first slice** to **100** Explode the **Administrative** slice slightly away from the pie. Format the **Chart Area** with a **Solid fill**—**Gray, 25%, Background 2**—in the third column, the first color.

7 Insert a **Text Box** positioned outside the upper corner of the **Administration** pie slice extending to the edge of the chart area and that is about one-half inch in height. In the text box, type **Administrative expenses to increase by 2%** Change the **Font Size** to **10.5** Size the text box so that the text displays on two lines. On this chart sheet, insert a **Custom Footer** with the file name in the **left section**.

8 In the **Program Expenses** sheet, using the data in the nonadjacent ranges **B4:E4** and **B10:E10**, insert a **Line with Markers** chart in the worksheet. Move the chart so that its upper left corner is positioned in cell **A12**, aligned approximately under the word *Services* above. Remove the **Legend** and then add a **Chart Title** above the chart with the text **2016 Expense Summary** Edit the **Primary Vertical Axis** so that the **Minimum** is **Fixed** at **49000000** and the **Major unit** is **Fixed** at **350000** Format the **Chart Area** with a **Solid fill** by applying **Dark Red, Accent 1, Lighter 80%**—in the fifth column, the second color.

9 In cell **B35**, type **200287046** and then apply the **Currency [0]** cell style. In cell **C35**, construct a formula to calculate the **Projected Expense Costs** after the forecasted increase is applied. Fill the formula through cell **F35**, and then use **Format Painter** to copy the formatting from cell **B35** to the range **C35:F35**.

10 Insert a **WordArt** using the second style in the last row—**Fill – Dark Red, Accent 6, Warm Matte Bevel**. Type **City Expenses** and then change the **Font Size** to **36**. Drag to position the WordArt in cell **B38**, centered below the worksheet.

11 Change the **Orientation** to **Landscape**, and then use the **Scale to Fit** options to fit the **Height** to **1 page**. Insert a **Header & Footer** with the file name in the left area of the footer. In **Page Layout** view, check and adjust if necessary the visual centering of the chart and the WordArt. Center the worksheet **Horizontally** on the page, and then return to **Normal** view.

12 Display the **Projected Decrease** sheet. In cell **C5**, calculate the **Percent of Total** by dividing the *Police Annual Total* by the *Totals by Quarter*, using absolute cell references as necessary. Apply **Percent Style** and then fill the formula from **C5:C9**.

13 **Copy** cell **B8**, and then use **Paste Special** to paste the **Values & Number Formatting** to cell **B13**. **Copy** and **Paste** cell **C8** to **C13**. With cell **C13** selected, use **Goal Seek** to determine the goal amount of administrative expenses in cell **B13** if the value in **C13** is set to **9%**

14 On the **Projected Decrease** sheet, insert a **Header & Footer** with the file name in the **left section** of the footer, and then center the worksheet **Horizontally** on the page. Show the **Document Panel**. Add your name, your course name and section, and the keywords **city expenses**

15 **Save** your workbook. Print or submit electronically as directed by your instructor. If required by your instructor, print or create an electronic version of your worksheets with formulas displayed by using the instructions in Activity 8.16, and then **Close** Excel without saving so that you do not save the changes you made to print formulas.

End **You have completed Project 9E**

Unit 3 Case Project

Excel Workbooks Created by a Marketing Assistant; Personal Expenses Projected for a Year

In this Unit Case Project, you will work with multiple worksheets and enter formulas and functions to calculate totals and other statistics that you might encounter as a Marketing Assistant for an entertainment company. You will also format cells, insert charts and sparklines, and use Goal Seek in the workbook. Your completed worksheets will look similar to the ones shown in Figure 3.1.

Project Files

For Unit 3 Case Project, you will need the following file:

eU3_Festival_Entertainment

You will save your file as:

Lastname_Firstname_U3_Festival_Entertainment

Project Results

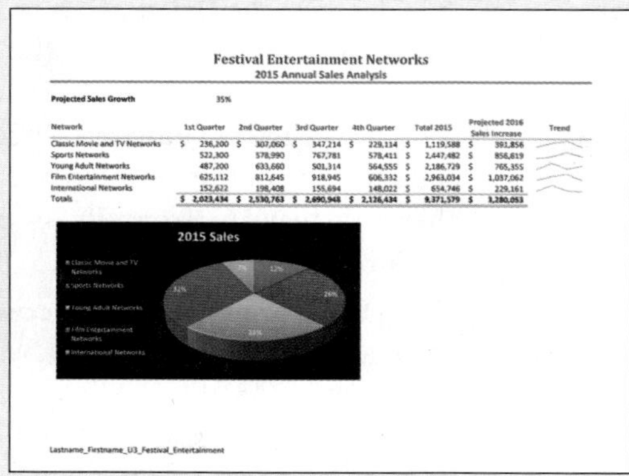

Festival Entertainment Networks
2015 Annual Sales Analysis

Projected Sales Growth 35%

Network	1st Quarter	2nd Quarter	3rd Quarter	4th Quarter	Total 2015	Projected 2016 Sales Increase	Trend
Classic Movie and TV Networks	$ 236,200	$ 307,060	$ 347,214	$ 229,114	$ 1,119,588	$ 391,856	
Sports Networks	522,300	578,990	767,781	578,411	$ 2,447,482	$ 856,619	
Young Adult Networks	487,200	633,660	501,314	564,555	$ 2,186,729	$ 765,355	
Film Entertainment Networks	625,112	812,645	918,945	606,332	$ 2,963,034	$ 1,037,062	
International Networks	152,622	198,408	155,694	148,022	$ 654,746	$ 229,161	
Totals	$ 2,023,434	$ 2,530,763	$ 2,690,948	$ 2,126,434	$ 9,371,579	$ 3,280,053	

Lastname_Firstname_U3_Festival_Entertainment

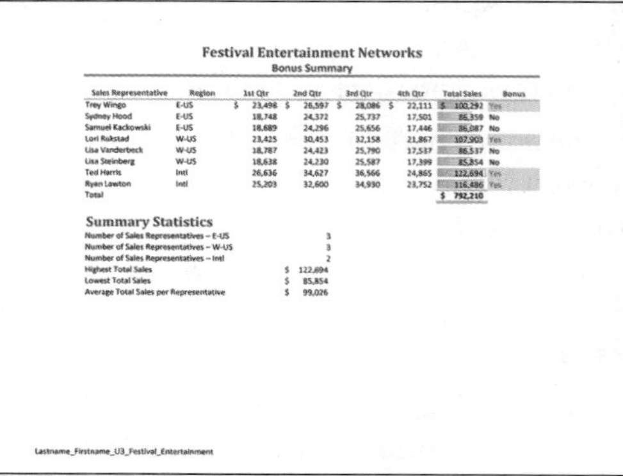

Festival Entertainment Networks
Bonus Summary

Sales Representative	Region	1st Qtr	2nd Qtr	3rd Qtr	4th Qtr	Total Sales	Bonus
Trey Wingo	E-US	$ 23,498	$ 26,597	$ 28,086	$ 22,111	$ 100,292	Yes
Sydney Hood	E-US	18,748	24,372	25,737	17,501	86,359	No
Samuel Kackowski	E-US	18,689	24,296	25,656	17,446	86,087	No
Lori Rukstad	W-US	23,425	30,453	32,158	21,867	107,903	Yes
Lisa Vanderbeck	W-US	18,787	24,423	25,790	17,537	86,537	No
Lisa Steinberg	W-US	18,638	24,230	25,587	17,399	85,854	No
Ted Harris	Intl	26,636	34,627	36,566	24,865	122,694	Yes
Ryan Lawton	Intl	25,203	32,600	34,930	23,752	116,486	Yes
Total						$ 792,210	

Summary Statistics

Number of Sales Representatives – E-US	3
Number of Sales Representatives – W-US	3
Number of Sales Representatives – Intl	2
Highest Total Sales	$ 122,694
Lowest Total Sales	$ 85,854
Average Total Sales per Representative	$ 99,026

Lastname_Firstname_U3_Festival_Entertainment

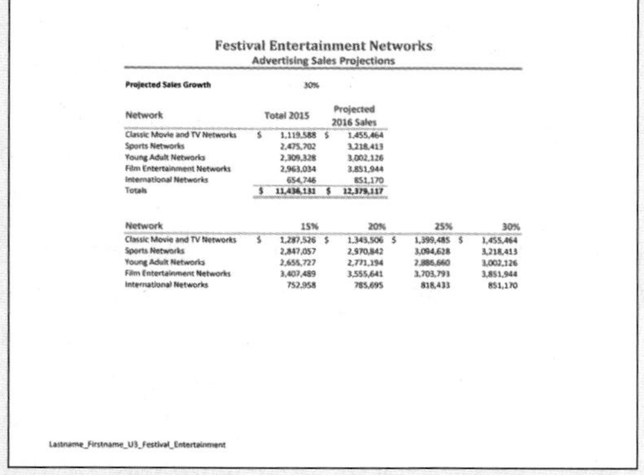

Festival Entertainment Networks
Advertising Sales Projections

Projected Sales Growth 30%

Network	Total 2015	Projected 2016 Sales
Classic Movie and TV Networks	$ 1,119,588	$ 1,455,464
Sports Networks	2,475,702	3,218,413
Young Adult Networks	2,309,328	3,002,126
Film Entertainment Networks	2,963,034	3,851,944
International Networks	654,746	851,170
Totals	$ 11,436,131	$ 12,379,117

Network	15%	20%	25%	30%
Classic Movie and TV Networks	$ 1,287,526	$ 1,343,506	$ 1,399,485	$ 1,455,464
Sports Networks	2,847,057	2,970,842	3,094,628	3,218,413
Young Adult Networks	2,655,727	2,771,194	2,886,660	3,002,126
Film Entertainment Networks	3,407,489	3,555,641	3,703,793	3,851,944
International Networks	752,958	785,695	818,433	851,170

Lastname_Firstname_U3_Festival_Entertainment

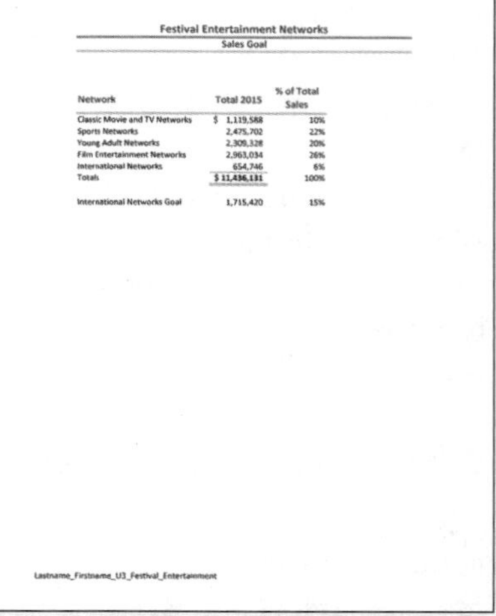

Festival Entertainment Networks
Sales Goal

Network	Total 2015	% of Total Sales
Classic Movie and TV Networks	$ 1,119,588	10%
Sports Networks	2,475,702	22%
Young Adult Networks	2,309,328	20%
Film Entertainment Networks	2,963,034	26%
International Networks	654,746	6%
Totals	$ 11,436,131	100%
International Networks Goal	1,715,420	15%

Lastname_Firstname_U3_Festival_Entertainment

Figure 3.1

Unit 3 Case Project

Excel Workbooks Created by a Marketing Assistant; Personal Expenses Projected for a Year (continued)

1 **Start** Excel. From your student files, open Excel file **eU3_Festival_Entertainment**. On your storage device, create a new folder named **All In One Unit 3** and then **Save** the workbook as **Lastname_Firstname_U3_Festival_Entertainment**

2 Familiarize yourself with the workbook by displaying each worksheet, and then display the **Quarterly Sales Summary** worksheet. Click cell **F7**, and construct a formula to calculate the **Sum** of **Classic Movie and TV Networks** for all quarters of 2015. Fill the formula down to cell **F11**.

3 In cell **G7**, construct a formula to calculate the projected 2016 sales increase using the projected sales growth rate in cell **B4** and the total 2015 sales in cell **F7**. Use absolute cell references as necessary, and then fill the formula down through cell **G11**. With the range **G7:G11** selected, display the **Cell Styles** gallery, and then at the bottom of the gallery, apply the **Currency [0]** style.

4 In cell **A12** type **Totals** and then in cell **B12**, construct a formula to sum the **1st Quarter** sales for all networks. Fill the formula across through cell **G12**. Apply the **Total** cell style to the range **B12:G12**.

5 In cell **H6** type **Trend** and apply the **Heading 3** cell style. In the range **H7:H11**, insert **Line** sparklines to represent the trend of each network's sales across the four quarters. Apply **Sparkline Style Dark #6**.

6 Select the nonadjacent ranges **A7:A11** and **F7:F11**, and then insert a **Pie in 3-D** chart. Insert a **Chart Title** above the chart with the text **2015 Sales** Add **Data Labels** formatted so that only the **Percentage** displays positioned at the **Inside End** of each pie slice. Move the **Legend** to the left of the chart. Apply the **Style 42** chart style. Move the chart so that the top left corner of the chart is inside the upper left corner of cell **A14**. Click cell **A1** and then **Save**.

7 On the **Bonuses** worksheet, in cell **H5**, enter an **IF** function to determine whether or not an employee receives a bonus based on the following: if an employee's **Total Sales** are greater than **$100,000** the **Value_if_true** is **Yes** Otherwise the **Value_if_false** is **No** Fill the formula down through cell **H12**.

8 With the range still selected, apply **Conditional Formatting** so that cells with a value of *Yes* are formatted as **Light Green Fill with Dark Green Text**. Select the range **G5:G12** and apply conditional formatting using **Gradient Fill Orange Data Bar**.

9 In cell **D16**, enter a **COUNTIF** function to determine the number of sales representatives from **E-US**. In the appropriate cells, use the same function to determine the number of sales representatives from **W-US** and **Intl**.

10 In the range **D19:D21**, using the values in the range **G5:G12**, enter appropriate functions to determine which sales representative had the **Highest Total Sales** (MAX function), the **Lowest Total Sales** (MIN function), and then determine the **Average Sales per Representative**.

11 On the **Sales Projections** worksheet, change the value in cell **B4** to **15%** to recalculate the projected sales at that rate. **Copy** the range **C7:C11** and **Paste** the **Values & Number Formatting**—not the formulas—in the range **B16:B20**. Change cell **B4** to **20% Copy** the range **C7:C11**, and then **Paste** the **Values & Number Formatting** in the range **C16:C20**. By using the same technique, project the sales for each network using a 25% growth rate and then a 30% growth rate. Press Esc to cancel the selection. Click cell **A1** and then save.

12 Insert a new worksheet. Change the sheet name to **Sales Analysis** and change the tab color to **Purple, Accent 4**.

13 In cell **A1**, type **Festival Entertainment Networks** Merge and center the title across the range **A1:E1**, and then apply the **Heading 1** cell style. In cell **A2**, type **Sales Goal** Merge and center the subtitle across the range **A2:E2**, and then apply the **Heading 2** cell style.

14 From the **Sales Projections** worksheet, copy the range **A6:B12**, and then paste it into the **Sales Analysis** worksheet in the range **A6:B12**. Then select columns **A:B** and AutoFit the column widths.

15 Select **column C** and set the width to **90 pixels**. Click cell **C6**, and then on the **Home tab**, in the **Alignment group**, apply **Wrap Text**. Type **% of Total Sales** Apply the **Heading 2** cell style and **Center** the text.

(Unit 3 Case Project continues on the next page)

Excel Workbooks Created by a Marketing Assistant; Personal Expenses Projected for a Year (continued)

16 In cell **C7**, construct a formula to calculate the **% of Total Sales** by dividing the **Total 2015** for **Classic Movie and TV Networks** by the total for all networks in cell **B12**. Use absolute cell references as necessary. Format the result in **Percent Style** and fill the formula down through cell **C11**.

17 In cell **A14**, type **International Networks Goal Copy** the range **B11:C11** into the range **B14:C14**. In cell **C14**, use **Goal Seek** to determine a goal sales amount in cell **B14** if the goal is to have International Networks contribute 15% of total sales.

18 **Center** the **Sales Analysis** worksheet **Horizontally**. **Group** the worksheets and insert a footer in the left section with the **File Name**. In **Normal** view, make cell **A1** the active cell. Display the **Document Panel**. Add your name, your course name and section number, and the keywords **sales, bonuses**

19 Check the print preview of the entire workbook and make any necessary changes. **Save** your workbook, and then print or submit electronically as directed. If required by your instructor, create an electronic version of your worksheets with formulas displayed, and then close Excel without saving so that you do not save the changes you made to print formulas.

Annual Expenses

Develop a workbook that details the expenses you expect to incur during the current year. Create four worksheets, one for each quarter of the year, and enter your expenses by month. For example, the Quarter 1 sheet will contain expense information for January, February, and March. Some of these expenses might include, but are not limited to, Mortgage, Rent, Utilities, Phone, Food, Entertainment, Tuition, Childcare, Clothing, and Insurance. Include monthly and quarterly totals for each category of expense. Insert a worksheet that summarizes the total expenses for each quarter. Format the worksheet by adjusting column width and wrapping text, and by applying appropriate financial number formatting and cell styles. Insert a footer with the file name and center the worksheet horizontally on the page. Save your file as **Lastname_Firstname_U3_Annual_Expenses** and submit as directed.

Application and Productivity Software, Including Microsoft PowerPoint

Chapters in Unit 4:

CHAPTER 10

Concepts: Using Application Software as Productivity Tools

CHAPTER 11

Applications: PowerPoint Presentation Creation; Enhancing Presentations with Pictures, Transitions, Objects, Backgrounds, and SmartArt

© Juriah Mosin/Shutterstock

Job Focus: Sales Operations Manager for a Sporting Goods Company

View Unit 4 Video to meet a Sales Operations Manager for a sporting goods company

At the end of this unit, you will have the opportunity to complete a case project that focuses on the job of a Sales Operations Manager for a sporting goods company. If you had a position like this, some of the things you might do are: track and then report sales figures by week and month; make presentations to sales reps and sales managers using PowerPoint; and assist in selecting the application software used in the retail stores.

Using Application Software as Productivity Tools

OUTCOMES

At the end of this chapter you will be able to:

Recognize the computer application skills you should acquire to be successful in the job market and to organize your everyday life.

List applications necessary to complete a task and be able to categorize, install, manage, license, and register them.

OBJECTIVES

Mastering these objectives will enable you to:

Job Focus:
Sales Operations Manager
for a Sporting Goods Company

In This Chapter

As the Sales Operations Manager for a sporting goods company, some of your responsibilities include the supervision of sales performance and profitability objectives. This includes resolving technical problems; confirming that hardware and software is updated, licensed, and properly maintained; and anticipating technical and sales problems to take proactive measures. Additionally, you must use productivity applications to forward data and communicate with corporate headquarters, regional directors, and sales personnel.

In this chapter, you will review popular productivity programs, examine the capabilities of each program, and differentiate between commercial, shareware, freeware, and public domain software. This knowledge will help you to determine the right application for all the tasks at your job and in your day-to-day life.

Objective 1 | Identify General Purpose Applications

As the Sales Operations Manager at a sporting goods company, you know that you will make use of word processing, spreadsheet, and database programs every day. You also want to understand the purpose and use of other types of applications and determine if they can help you decrease repetitive tasks and quicken your response time to communications. Where do you start?

Concept 10.01 | Identifying General Purpose Applications

General purpose applications are programs you use to accomplish frequently performed tasks. These tasks include writing documents, working with numbers, keeping track of information, developing multimedia and graphic content, and using the Internet. These applications were once found only on home and business computers, but now they are on your mobile devices and media-specific technology such as iPods. Figure 10.1 lists types of general-purpose application software, including some applications that work through and run from the Internet.

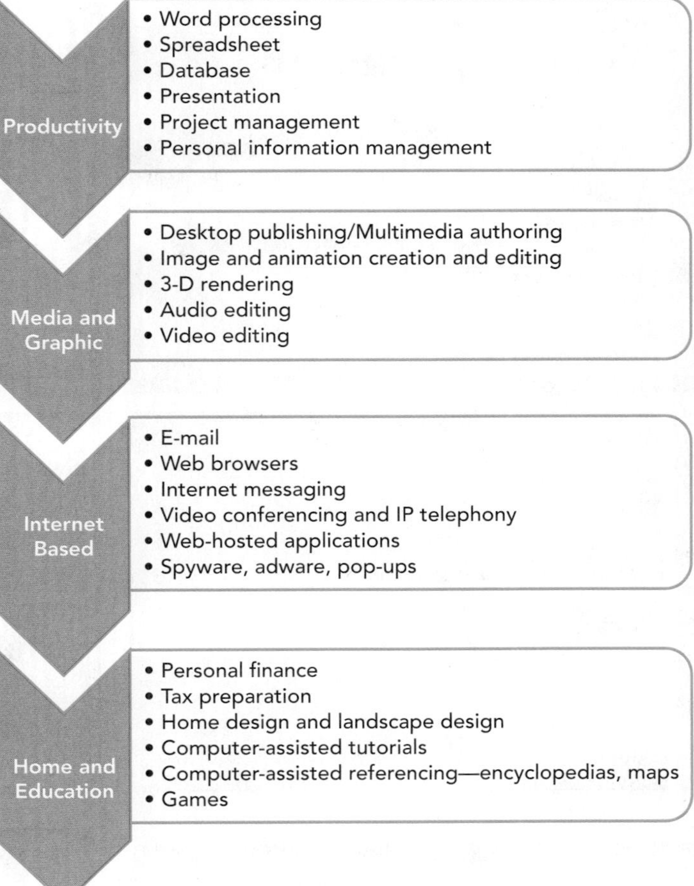

FIGURE 10.1 Application software can be categorized based on use.

Objective 2 | Differentiate Between Productivity Programs

As the Sales Operations Manager at a sporting goods company, you have just been assigned two assistants to help with the new sales promotion in the northeast and southwest regions. Both assistants are knowledgeable about computers and are adept with mobile devices. Both will travel extensively within their respective regions. To communicate with these assistants when they are traveling, you want to use a shared calendar and programs that are accessible on portable devices. To manage the new sales promotion, you want to use computer programs to allocate responsibility for tasks, to collaboratively edit promotional material, and to view and adjust milestones for this project. Where do you start?

The most popular general-purpose applications are ***productivity programs***, which help you work more efficiently and effectively on both personal and business-related documents. Productivity software includes word processors, spreadsheets, databases, presentation, project management, and personal information management programs (Figure 10.2). These programs are valuable regardless of the subject matter. For example, a word processor is equally valuable for typing a term paper for your history class, writing a letter to a family member, or creating the agenda for an important meeting for your job.

Learn to use the right application for the task. You could use Excel for a presentation, but it is much better to use PowerPoint as the presentation program and import Excel spreadsheets and charts into it. There are several companies that create programs for home and business productivity.

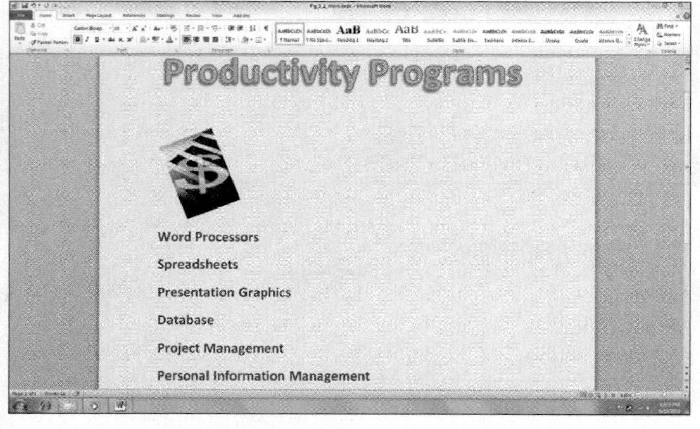

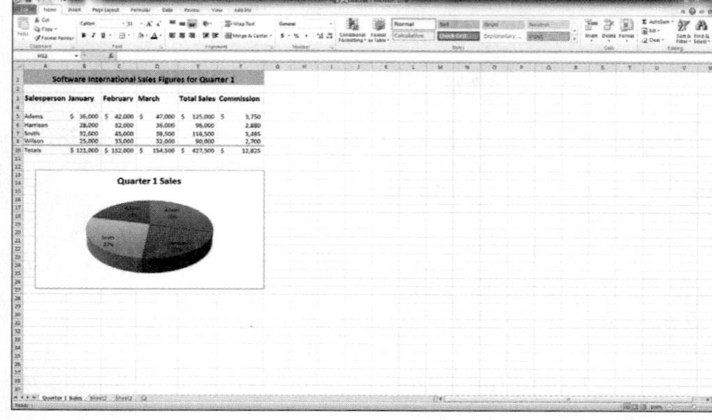

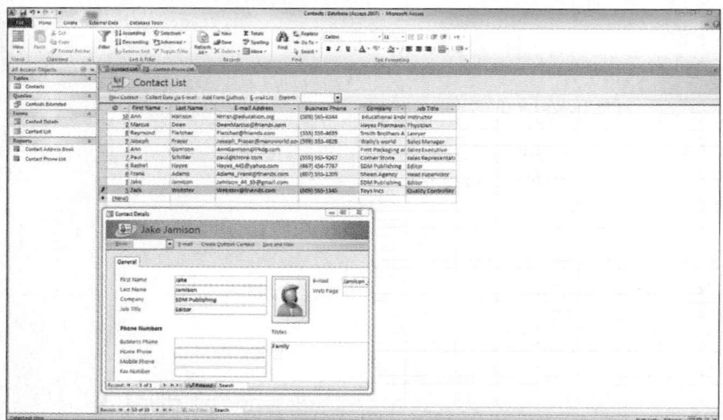

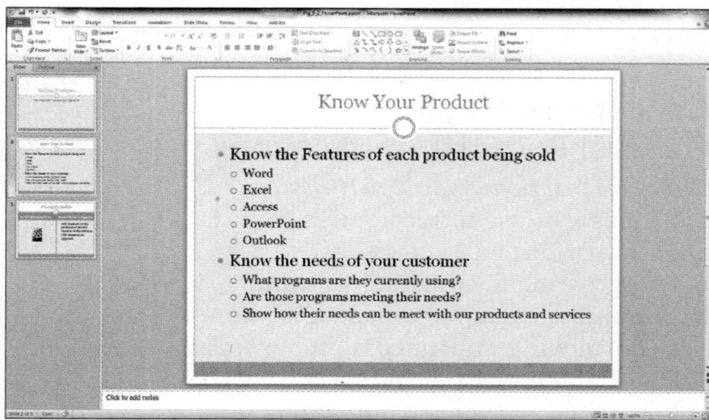

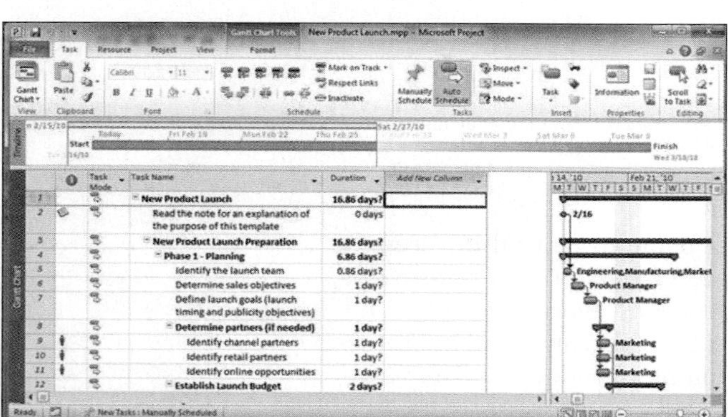

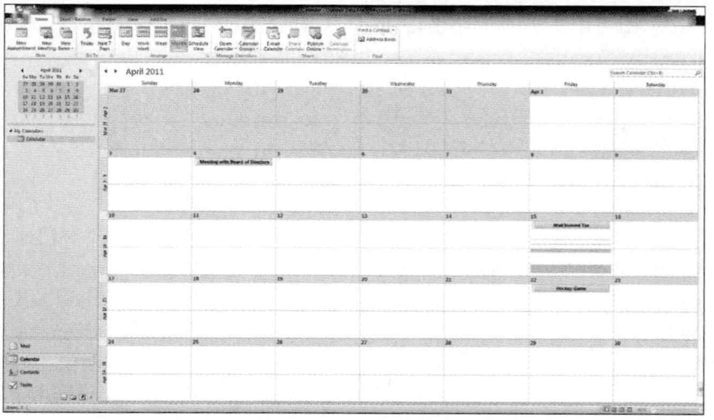

FIGURE 10.2 Productivity programs include Microsoft Word for word processing, Microsoft Excel to create a spreadsheet, Microsoft Access to create and manage a database, Microsoft PowerPoint to develop presentations, Microsoft Project to oversee project progress, and Microsoft Outlook to manage your e-mail and calendar.

Figure 10.3 lists these applications by type, along with some of the manufacturers, and is followed by a brief overview of Microsoft Office 2010, a group of productivity applications chosen most often by home and business users. Microsoft Office, according to Microsoft, is installed on over 1 billion computers worldwide.

Concept 10.02 | Reviewing Microsoft Office 2010

The latest version of the popular application known simply as "Office" is Microsoft Office 2010. Some of its new features include:

- The change of the Office Button to a tab on the Ribbon labeled "File"
- The ability to customize the Ribbon
- The option to capture and insert screen shots
- Enhanced multimedia editing in PowerPoint
- Stronger security settings that include "Restrict Editing" and "Block Author" modes, both added to enable or restrict users working on a collaborative project

These are just some of the upgrades included in Office 2010 productivity programs. One feature that has not changed significantly is the shared office interface that most Office applications possess (Figure 10.4).

Productivity Applications

Productivity Category	Example Programs	Manufacturer	Uses
Word Processing	Pages WordPerfect Documents Word	Apple Corel Google Docs Microsoft	Write, format, and print documents and reports
Spreadsheet	Numbers Quatro Pro Spreadsheets Excel	Apple Corel Google Docs Microsoft	Enter and manipulate numeric data through the use of formulas
Database	FileMaker Pro and Bento Paradox Access	Apple (FileMaker, Inc., a subsidiary of Apple) Corel Microsoft	Manage and connect data between related tables to produce queries, reports, and forms
Presentation	Keynote Presentation Presentation PowerPoint	Apple Corel Google Docs Microsoft	Create slide shows
Project Management	Project Tenrox	Microsoft Tenrox	Manage and schedule resources among multiple projects
Personal Information Manager	Calendar Lotus Organizer Entourage Outlook	Google IBM Microsoft—for the Mac OS Microsoft	Keep e-mails, contact lists, schedules, and calendars of appointments

Figure 10.3

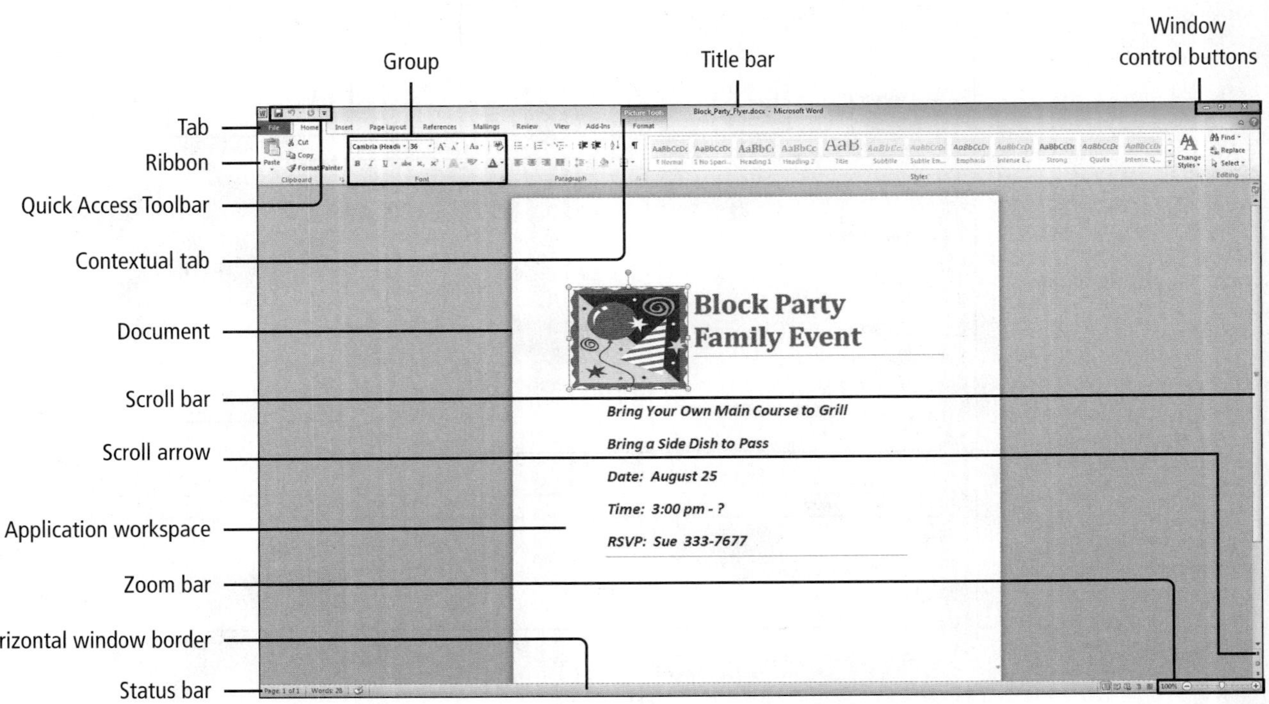

FIGURE 10.4 These display components are found in most Microsoft Office 2010 applications.

Microsoft Word is a full-featured word processing program that, along with other Office applications, uses a common user interface—the Ribbon. Word's opening screen mimics a blank sheet of paper on which you create your document. Word is often the first application you learn, and using it at a basic level to create short letters, memos, and reports is an easy process.

Microsoft Excel, a popular business and personal spreadsheet program, also uses the common user interface—the Ribbon. A spreadsheet program records numeric data used it in calculations and performs ***modeling***—also referred to as ***what-if analysis***—to take current information and use it to predict things that could happen in the future. Perhaps you have already used popular Excel features such as formulas, functions, charts, PivotTables, and PivotCharts.

Microsoft Access is a database management system (DBMS), a software application designed to store your data in tables, create relationships between tables, and then generate forms, queries, and reports to present your data in an informative and attractive manner. The power of Access is its ability to connect data in different tables and in different databases. This connectivity eliminates repeated searches in different locations, saves time, and enables you to generate a single report from multiple sources.

You might be familiar with Microsoft PowerPoint, a popular program among students and individuals who need to create and deliver presentations. When you open PowerPoint, you will see the common user interface—the Ribbon—and a blank slide. The slide acts like a canvas on which you organize text boxes and graphics to present your ideas. Be careful not to get caught up with all of the animation and transition effects offered by this application. The slideshow is a backdrop and enhancement to your content; it should not be the main feature.

Microsoft Project is often a requirement in graduate management programs. It is a productivity program that has more utility for a business user than the home user. It provides an environment for the overall management of one or more projects that can vary in complexity. This program offers such features as:

- A timeline that tracks due dates, milestones, and deadlines
- A team-planning capability that, by simply dragging and dropping, creates a team with the right individuals and resources
- A portfolio manager that monitors the allocation of scarce resources and current project costs

Project 2010 includes the Ribbon user interface (Figure 10.5).

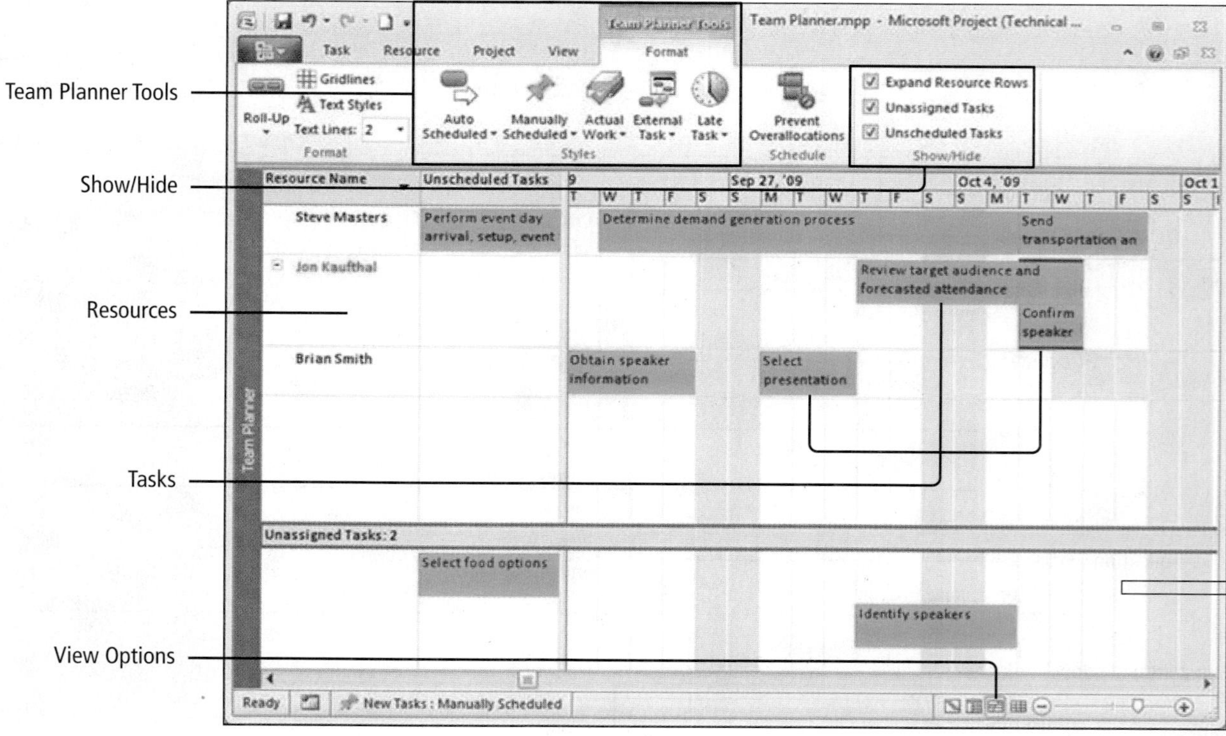

FIGURE 10.5 The new Team Planner Tools feature in Project 2010 displays tasks and resources—including people—in a view similar to an Outlook calendar.

Microsoft Outlook manages your e-mail, your contacts, and your calendar. Recent features include conversation grouping and a "think before you send" warning that displays when you select the "Reply to All" option in an e-mail. A large majority of enterprises worldwide use and depend on Outlook for both internal and external communication. With Microsoft's acquisition of Skype, you can use Outlook for video conferencing. You will be surprised at how easy it is to let Outlook organize your life.

Objective 3 | Identify Media and Graphic Software

As the Sales Operations Manager for a sporting goods company, you must oversee all new sales campaigns. The latest products target the young adult market and the campaign is filled with multimedia advertisements and computer-enhanced images of the products. You need more information on graphic formats and the application programs required to edit and enhance images. Where do you start?

When discussing applications, ***media*** refers to the technology that encompasses pictures, sound, and video. Most media and graphic software applications are referred to as ***multimedia*** programs, because they enable you to incorporate more than one of these technologies. Do you think that graphics, sounds, animations, and video do a better job than simple text to engage you in a topic? These features, which once were considered entertainment or amusement, are now standard components of business, advertising, and educational programs (Figure 10.6).

Some multimedia applications offer interactivity by which you can choose your own path through the presentation. This creates different outcomes for each viewer, enabling the learner to view the possible outcomes of decisions and the associated consequences. Interactivity is a big factor in the popularity of the Web. In fact, the Web could be viewed as a gigantic interactive multimedia presentation.

Concept 10.03 | Clarifying Compression and Decompression

Your computer can work with art, photographs, videos, and sounds. When these multimedia resources are stored in digitized files on your computer, they require large amounts of storage space. To use the space on your hard disk efficiently and improve file transfer speeds over the Internet, most multimedia software programs reduce file size by using ***codecs***, the technical name for compression/decompression or code/decode algorithms.

Codecs use two different approaches to compression. By using ***lossless compression***, the original file is compressed so that it can be completely restored, without flaw, when it is decompressed. By using ***lossy compression***, the original file is processed so that some information is permanently removed from the file. Lossy compression techniques eliminate information that is not perceived when you see pictures or hear sounds, such as very high musical notes that are outside of the frequency range for most users. A hybrid of these two techniques is used in the area of medical imaging. For these images, a lossless compression scheme is needed in the region of interest while a lossy

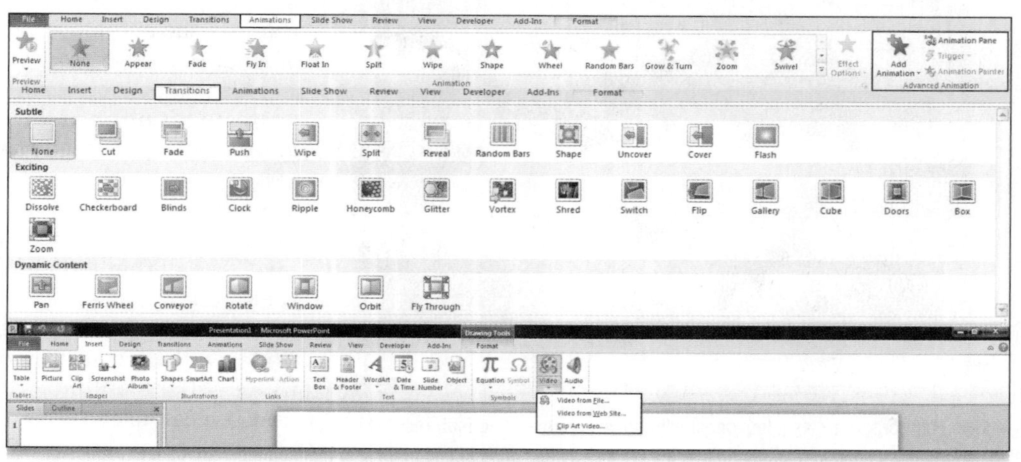

FIGURE 10.6 PowerPoint 2010 reduces the difficulty of adding multimedia features to a presentation with the addition of the animation painter, 3-D transitions, and video options.

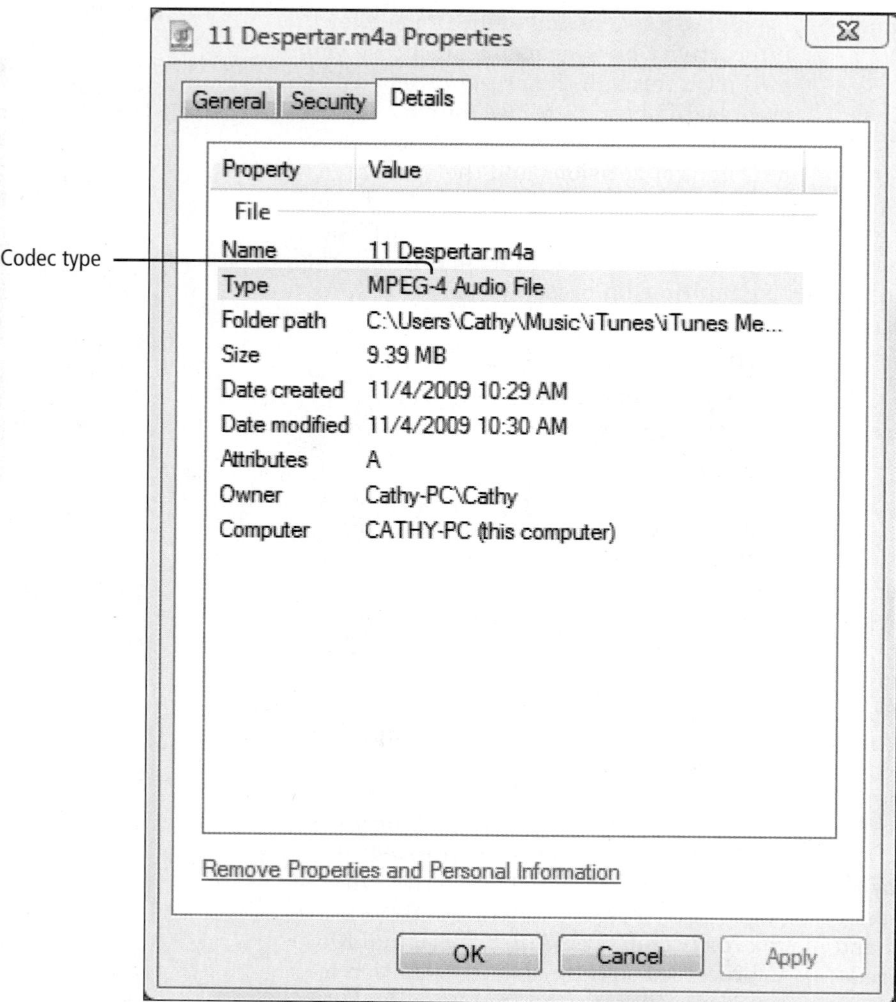

FIGURE 10.7 Locate the codec in the Properties dialog box. If the codec is not already downloaded to your system, obtain it from a Web site like **www.fourcc.org/fcccodec.htm**.

FIGURE 10.8 The Microsoft Windows Paint program has a tool panel with basic image-editing features and is an easy way to create or edit bitmapped graphics.

compression scheme is suitable for image sections in nonregions of interest.

Why do we need codecs? Without the use of codecs, downloads would take three to five times longer than they do now because the files would be significantly larger. How many codecs are there? Unfortunately, there are hundreds of codecs; some are for audio and video compression, whereas others reduce the size of streaming media over the Internet. If you download frequently, you probably use five to ten different codecs on a regular basis. Common codecs you might recognize include MP3, WMA, RealVideo, DivX, and XviD.

How do you know which codec decodes which files? Right-click the file and select *Properties*; in the Properties dialog box, the Details tab indicates the file type and thus the codec (Figure 10.7). If your system cannot open the file, record this code and then use a search engine to locate a download.

Concept 10.04 | Designing with Desktop Publishing and Paint Programs

Programs in this category create newsletters, product catalogs, advertising brochures—documents that require unusual design and layout not normally provided by a word processor. From these types of programs, you can print or save documents in formats that you can send to a professional printer. Microsoft Publisher is an entry-level desktop publishing program that has the familiar interface of other Microsoft products.

Use paint programs to create ***bitmapped graphics***—also called ***raster graphics***—which are images composed of tiny squares or dots that correspond to one pixel. Recall that a ***pixel*** is the smallest addressable element of a display device. The Windows operating system includes the Paint program that you can use to create this type of graphic (Figure 10.8).

FIGURE 10.9 This enlargement is an illustration of pixels.

Paint is great for beginners and provides a tool panel with features that allow an image to be cropped, colors altered, and areas erased. If you are looking for more advanced features, you can purchase a professional paint program to create a wider scope of effects through a more enhanced tool panel.

Editing a pixel-based image requires you make a selection before applying an edit or change. This action is similar to selecting text in a Word document and then applying bold formatting; however, selecting a graphic or a portion of a graphic is not as straightforward as making a selection in a Word document. Enhanced graphic programs have tools to ease this selection process. When editing an image, you need to zoom in at a high viewing level as seen in Figure 10.9. Then the pixels become more apparent and appear to have the *jaggies*, a jagged edge between contrasting colors. When you resize a bitmapped or raster image, the computer must calculate or "guess"—either where to add pixels when enlarging the image size—or where to throw away pixels when shrinking the size of an image. Thus, the image can lose clarity because it is losing image information as the computer makes its best "guess" based on surrounding pixel information.

Is it possible to convert an image from one graphic format to another? Yes, it is possible, in some graphic applications, to convert a graphic in one format to another format through the Save As command. Figure 10.10 provides a list of the standard formats in which the Paint programs can save your work.

Use ***image editors***—sophisticated versions of graphic programs—to edit and create images and save them in a variety of file formats. Free programs like Picasa and GIMP, designed for personal and home use, incorporate automated image-processing algorithms to add a variety of special effects, remove blemishes, crop portions, and adjust coloring to photographic images. Programs like Adobe Photoshop, which include the capability of paint software and image editors, in the past were used primarily by professionals. But the popularity of photo editing has forced companies to create simpler interfaces such as Adobe's Photoshop Elements that enable you to create a professional finished photo or image without the cost and learning curve of complex software (Figure 10.11).

Concept 10.05 | Using Graphic Programs

Vector graphic programs that create ***vector graphics*** are math based. If you remember your high school days of math, a line segment was defined as having at least two points. Therefore, the rules for

Standard Graphic File Format

Format	File Extension	Description
Graphics Interchange Format	***GIF*** (pronounced "jiff" or "giff")	A 256-color graphic file format that uses lossless compression and is best for simple images with large areas of solid color. This file format is a Web standard for images with a limited amount of colors.
Joint Photographic Experts Group	***JPEG*** or ***JPG*** (pronounced "JAY-peg")	A graphic format that can store up to 16.7 million colors, is best for complex images such as photographs, uses lossy compression, and is also a Web standard.
Portable Network Graphics	***PNG*** (pronounced "ping")	A patent-free graphic format alternative to GIF, PNG produces images that use lossless compression and is best suited to Web use only.
Windows Bitmap	***BMP***	This standard graphic format was developed for Microsoft Windows. Compression is optional, so BMP files tend to be very large.
Tag Image File Format	***TIFF*** or ***TIF***	A lossless graphic format, used in publishing because it allows specific instructions to be embedded within the file to retain image quality. The drawback is the resulting large file size.

Figure 10.10

drawing in a vector program require that you define the points to draw line segments which are known as paths. The graphic program stores the paths as mathematical equations. When you enlarge or shrink a vector graphic, the program needs only to recalculate the math for the line segments or paths you created. Thus, clarity is perfectly maintained regardless of resized dimensions. For this reason, illustrations such as clip art and logos are often designed in vector programs (Figure 10.12).

Professional drawing programs such as CorelDRAW Graphics Suite and Adobe Illustrator save files by outputting instructions in ***PostScript***, which is an automated page-description language (PDL). Page description languages describe image elements as geometric objects such as lines and arcs and consist of commands given by the program and carried out by the printer to precisely re-create the computer image on a printed page. PostScript is the printing and image standard used by corporations and publishers.

FIGURE 10.11 Current releases of image editors include the ability to adjust overall color and remove markings like fold lines and water marks.

FIGURE 10.12 The cat eye is a vector image generated by defining points that the program uses to create lines or paths.

© AptTone/Shutterstock

FIGURE 10.13 Ray tracing is a technique that uses color and color intensity to create the illusion of light and makes drawn images appear more realistic.

Concept 10.06 | Simplifying Three-Dimensional Rendering Programs

A 3-D rendering program adds three-dimensional effects to graphic objects. The results are strikingly realistic. Objects can be rotated in any direction to achieve the exact result the artist is looking for.

Rendering software no longer requires a high-powered engineering workstation; high-end desktop computers are suitable. One rendering technique, ***ray tracing***, adds amazing realism to a simulated three-dimensional object by manipulating variations in color intensity that would be produced by light falling on the object from multiple directions, which is the norm in the real world (Figure 10.13). Detailed steps to create night lighting using ray tracing can be found at **www.cgdigest.com/index.php/night-rendering-tutorial-vray/**.

Concept 10.07 | Appreciating Computer-Aided Design (CAD) Programs

Programs in this category create sophisticated 3-D rendering images frequently used by engineers to design entire structures and by scientists to display cell structure. These computer-generated diagrams (Figure 10.14) can range from something as simple as the design of a new nut or bolt to the design of a bridge, security system, shopping complex, or visual representation of DNA molecules. These are more complicated drawing programs and usually require some practice to become proficient. Figure 10.15 lists some current applications for drawing, image editing, and photo editing.

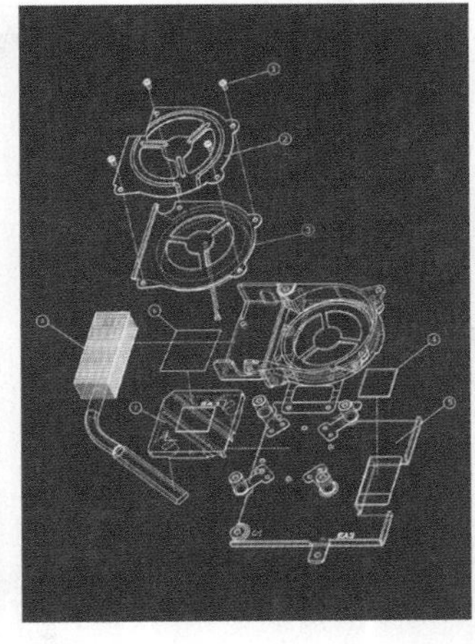

© ImageDJ/Alamy

FIGURE 10.14 CAD diagrams vary in complexity and purpose but provide detail and depth that other drawing programs lack.

Concept 10.08 | Experiencing Animation Programs

When you see a movie at a theater, you are actually looking at still images shown at a frame rate—images per second—which when sufficiently high tricks the eye into seeing continuous motion. Like a movie, computer animation consists of the same concept: images that appear to move. Computer animators create each of the still images separately in its own frame with the help of computer programs

Drawing, Image Editing, and Photo Editing Applications

Category	Example	Company	Use
Desktop publishing	Publisher	Microsoft	Home/ educational
	InDesign	Adobe	Professional
Image editing	Painter	Corel	Professional
	Paint	Microsoft	Home/ educational
	Photoshop	Adobe	Professional
	Photoshop Elements	Adobe	Home/ educational
	PaintShop Photo Pro	Corel	Home/ educational
	Picassa	Google	Home/ educational
	GIMP	Open Source	Home/ educational
Vector programs	Illustrator	Adobe	Professional
	AutoCAD	Autodesk	Professional
	CorelDraw Graphics	Corel	Professional
	Visio	Microsoft	Professional

Figure 10.15

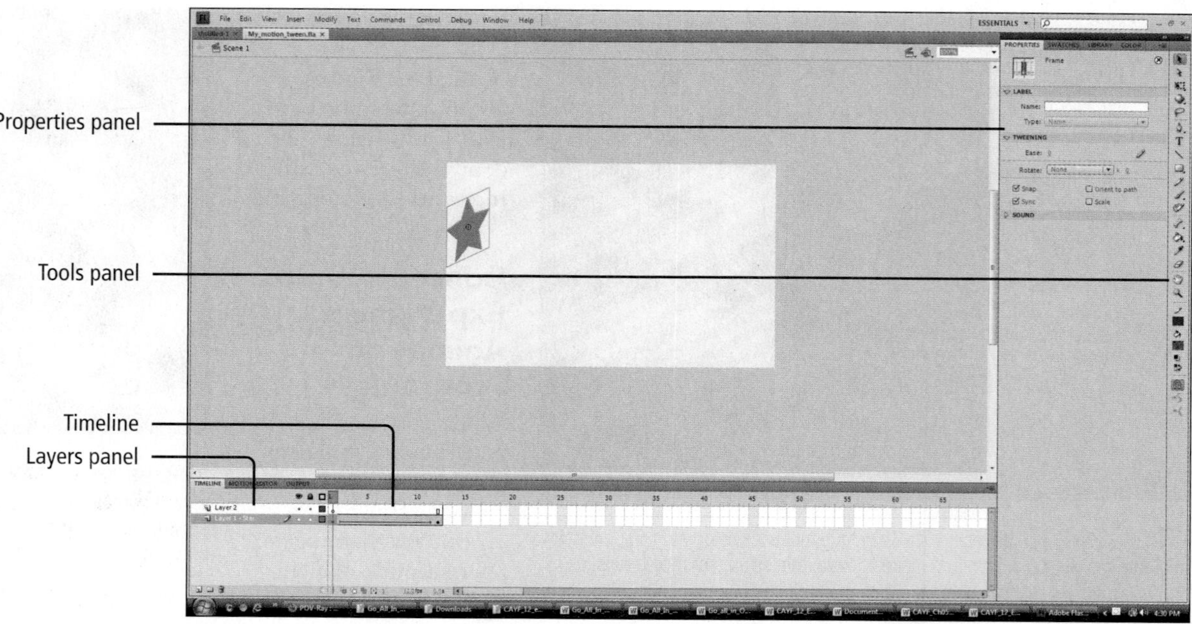

FIGURE 10.16 Animation applications provide user friendly interfaces and incorporate layers, a tool panel, and an animation timeline with which you can increase image complexity and add animation.

that contain tools to facilitate the image creation as well as animation.

Professional animation programs like Adobe Flash provide sophisticated tools for creating animations (Figure 10.16). The main restricting feature of this program is that it creates a ***proprietary file***, a file whose format is patented or copyright protected and controlled by a single company. To view these files on the Web, you need a special free ***plug-in*** program, a program downloaded from a Web site that extends the ability of your Web browser usually to enable multimedia features. Shockwave Player and Flash Player from Adobe and Silverlight from Microsoft are examples of common plug-ins.

Concept 10.09 | Using Audio Editing Software

A variety of programs are available for capturing and processing sound for multimedia presentations, including sound mixers, compression software, bass enhancers, synthesized stereo, and even onscreen music composition programs. Most programs include options to create unique music mixes, record podcasts, convert between file formats, filter out background noise and static, and edit content through cut, copy, and paste features. Recent reviews at **http://audio-editing-software-review.toptenreviews.com/index.html** favor Magix Music Maker, WavePad, Dexter Audio Editor, and GoldWave.

Sound files contain digitized data in the form of recorded live sounds or music, which are saved in one of several standardized sound formats. These formats, displayed in Figure 10.17, specify how sounds should be digitally represented and generally include some type of data compression.

There are over a dozen formats for ***streaming audio***, accessing sounds that play almost immediately after you click an audio link on a Web page, without waiting for the entire file to download. Popular formats include RealNetworks' RealAudio, streaming MP3, Macromedia's Flash, Director Shockwave, Microsoft's Windows Media, and Apple's QuickTime. More recent streaming audio formats synchronize sounds with events on a Web page, such as RealMedia G2 with SMIL and Beatnik's Rich Music Format (RMF). To hear some popular snips of commercials, movies, TV series, and special sound effects visit **www.wavcentral.com**.

Concept 10.10 | Using Video Editing

Video editors are programs that enable you to modify digitized videos. With a video editor, you can cut segments, resequence frames, add transitions, compress a file, and determine a video's frame rate—the number of still images displayed per second. To view a list of video editing programs and a brief description of some of their capabilities, go to **www.video-editing-software-guide.com/video-software.html**. Among the preferred home and educational programs are PowerDirector, Video Studio Pro, Premier

Audio Formats

Format	Description
MP3	A patented audio sound file format that uses lossy compression and enables you to compress CD-quality digital audio by a ratio of 12:1.
Windows Media Audio (WMA)	A Microsoft proprietary data compression file format, similar to the MP3 format, that produces files smaller in size, requires less processing power, but generates the same audio quality. WMA is one of the most popular audio file formats.
WAV	The default Microsoft Windows sound file format uses the .wav extension (short for "Wave Sounds"). It can be saved with a variety of quality levels, from low-fidelity mono to CD-quality stereo. WAV sounds usually are not compressed, so they tend to take up a lot of disk space.
Ogg Vorbis	An open source, patent-free, professional audio encoding format similar to MP3 but about 20 percent smaller.
Musical Instrument Digital Interface (MIDI)	A language that enables the creation of an electronic instrument sound out of an acoustical instrument. MIDI files, generally small in size, contain a text-based description that tells a synthesizer when and how to play individual musical notes. MIDI sound samples of an instrument can be added to a MIDI song file, allowing overlapping and stacking of instrument sounds.

Figure 10.17

Elements, and Creator. Video editors also enable you to save video files to some or all of the following video file formats:

- Moving Picture Experts Group (MPEG): A family of video file formats and lossy compression standards for full- motion video.
- QuickTime: A video file format developed by Apple Computer. It plays full-screen, broadcast-quality video as well as CD- and DVD-quality audio. It is widely used in multimedia CD-ROM productions.
- Video for Window: The original video file format for Microsoft Windows, Video for Windows is often called AVI (Audio Video Interleave). This format is still widely used but is inferior to the new MPEG-4 standard.

Because a huge amount of data must be stored to create realistic-looking video on a computer, all video file formats use codec techniques. For the best playback, your computer should have a special ***video adapter***, an expansion board that provides display capabilities. These adapters have hardware that decodes videos at high speed.

Streaming video, accessing video clips almost immediately after you click a video link on a Web page, without waiting for the entire file to download, is made possible by streaming video formats. These formats rely on compression, low frame rates, and small image size to deliver your video over the Internet, which does not have sufficient bandwidth—signal-carrying capacity—to disseminate broadcast-quality video. A popular streaming video site is YouTube.

Concept 10.11 | Using Multimedia Authoring Systems

Use authoring tools to create multimedia presentations. These tools enable you to specify which multimedia objects to use, how to display them in relation to each other, how long to display them, and how to enable the end user to interact with the presentation (Figure 10.18). To take full advantage of an authoring tool's capabilities, you might have to learn a scripting language—a simple programming language. Leading authoring packages for home or educational purposes include iMovie by Apple and Windows Live Movie Maker; at the professional level, Adobe Director is state of the art.

Many commercial authoring tools, such as Adobe Director, save output in proprietary file formats. To view Adobe presentations on a Web site, you must download and install a plug-in. The World Wide Web Consortium (W3C), the organization that sets Web standards, recently approved a simple multimedia scripting language called ***Synchronized Multimedia Integration Language (SMIL)***. This language displays Web pages in a standard manner without the use of plug-ins. Although the idea is a good one, multimedia formats that use plug-ins, like Shockwave, are still in wide use.

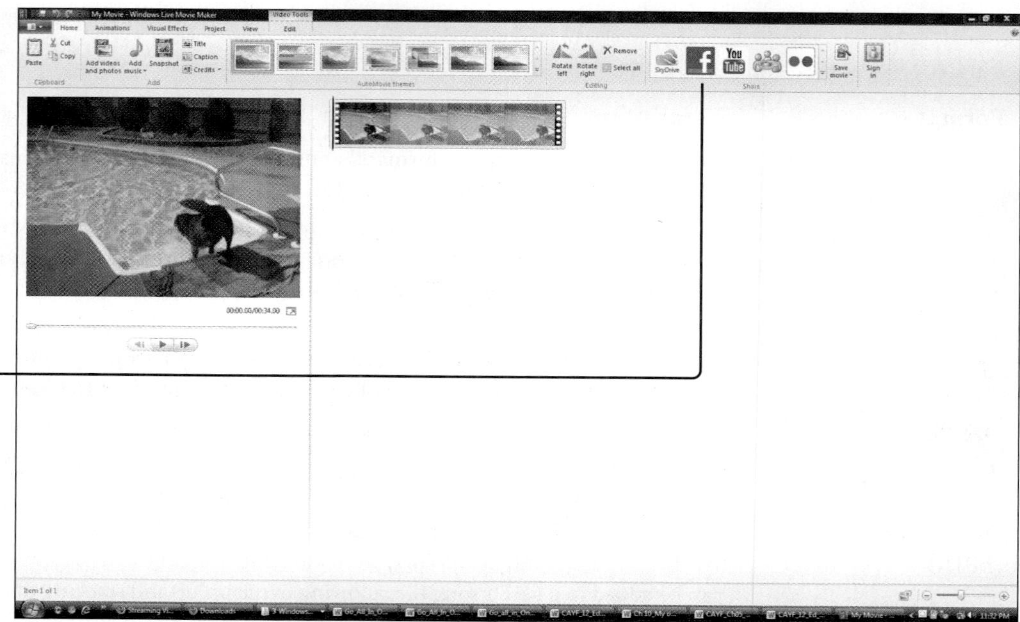
Options to upload your movie to popular Web sites are in the Ribbon

FIGURE 10.18 Using Windows Live Movie Maker, you can convert photos, video, and music into a movie and upload the movie to SkyDrive, YouTube, Facebook, Windows Live Groups, and Flickr.

Concept 10.12 | Reviewing Web Page Authoring Programs

The Adobe Creative Suite media development kit is a combination of programs that create multimedia Internet applications. Productivity programs like Word and Excel have options to save your work as a Web page, and this works fine for a beginner. Adobe Creative Suite has three core programs with advanced capabilities for Web page development:

- Dreamweaver: An environment in which you develop Web pages visually or directly in code and provide the connectivity to other languages used in Web interactivity and design.
- Flash: A platform to create animation and interactivity that can be added to Web pages.
- Fireworks: A program that provides an interface that enables the creation of highly optimized graphics that can be embedded within Web pages and portable devices.

If you are a Mac user, visit **www.apple.com/ilife** to learn about Apple's multimedia iLife suite, with which you can create music with GarageBand; integrate and organize your music, photos, and home videos with iTunes, iPhoto, and iMovie; and share your creations over the Internet on a Web site created with iWeb.

Programs of this type are frequently updated and new ones are always entering the market. The lines between many are blurred because video editors can now edit sound and sound editors can edit video. Figure 10.19 provides a list of some of the products available in this advanced media authoring and editing group.

Objective 4 | Recognize Applications That Run from the Internet

As the Sales Operations Manager for a sporting goods company, you are excited that the sales resulting from your promotional event exceeded corporate projections. You have been assigned two new assistants to help you expand the promotion. You and your new assistants must be in contact throughout the day and you must all be able to share and update documents and data. You want to be able to do this by using Web-based applications. Where do you start?

There are many types of Internet applications. Some work through the Internet, using it as the transport medium. Others actually run from the Internet, using programs that reside there.

Concept 10.13 | Relying on Web-Based Applications

Many applications are Web based; that is, they are accessed over a network like the Internet. Examples include e-mail clients

Animation, Sound, Video, and Multimedia Applications

Category	Example Program	Manufacturer	Use
Animation	Flash	Adobe	Professional
	GIF Animator	Microsoft	Home/educational
Sound editing	Soundbooth	Adobe	Professional
	Music Maker	MAGIX	Home/educational
	Media Player	Microsoft	Home/educational
	Dexster Audio Editor	Softdiv Software	Home/educational
Video editing	Premier Elements	Adobe	Home/educational
	Premier Pro	Adobe	Professional
	Final Cut Pro	Apple	Home/educational
	Studio Pro	Corel	Home/educational
Multimedia authoring	Director	Adobe	Professional
	iMovie	Apple	Home/educational
	Video Studio	Corel	Home/educational
	Windows Live Movie Maker	Microsoft	Home/educational
Web authoring	Dreamweaver	Adobe	Professional
	Fireworks	Adobe	Professional
	Flash	Adobe	Professional

Figure 10.19

like Hotmail, instant messaging programs like Windows Live messenger, and video-conferencing software like Skype. These are general-purpose applications because they facilitate your communication, learning, and interaction.

Concept 10.14 | Running Applications from the Internet

Web-based applications are applications that reside on a remote server and are accessed by you through the Internet. Often the provider of the application also supplies

From either the Companion Web Site or MyITLab, watch Chapter 10 Video 1

FIGURE 10.20 Web-based applications are popular with individuals who travel and work on collaborative projects.

From either the Companion Web Site or MyITLab, try the Chapter 10 Digital Devices Multimedia Simulation

you with a limited amount of storage on their server. If you save a file on the provider's server, you will be able to access and edit it from anywhere. Web-based applications improve file sharing and collaboration. Office Web Apps and Google Docs are two examples of sites that offer these capabilities (Figure 10.20). Most of these services are free, but you must create an account and sign in.

Check Your Knowledge: From either the Companion Web Site or MyITLab, take the quiz covering Objectives 1, 2, 3, and 4.

Objective 5 | Categorize Home and Educational Programs

As the Sales Operations Manager for a sporting goods company, you and your team have just ended a meeting about marketing strategies for the new line of young adult, ecofriendly products. Your assistants support a viral marketing campaign that includes street teams in the major targeted cities. The street teams will be selected from Facebook subscribers who like your company's Facebook page. Each team will have a leader who will receive communication and guidance from a promotional staff member through either a popular home or educational program or a social media site. The idea of using a Web-based game centered on the street team's location and activities was suggested as a means of getting consumers involved in promoting the products. Where do you start?

General-purpose software also includes ***home and educational programs***. Programs in this category are useful for less complex or more personal activities like personal finance and tax preparation software, home design and landscaping software, computerized reference information such as encyclopedias, street maps (Figure 10.21), computer-assisted tutorials, and games.

Best sellers in the reference CD/DVD-ROM market include multimedia versions of dictionaries, language learning software, encyclopedias, and how-to guides.

Concept 10.15 | Interacting through Computer Games

Computer games are a large and growing business. The worldwide video game industry predicts a continuation of the video game boom, with total sales growing to $68.4 billion by 2012. This highly profitable industry got its start in the 1970s, when the earliest computer video games appeared in lounges and gaming arcades. Then video games entered the living room with the advent of Atari, Nintendo, and Sega console game players, which are special-purpose computers designed to display their output on a TV screen. Games soon migrated to personal computers—and from there, to the Internet.

Multiplayer online gaming (MMO or MMOG) is technology that, through the Internet, connects hundreds of

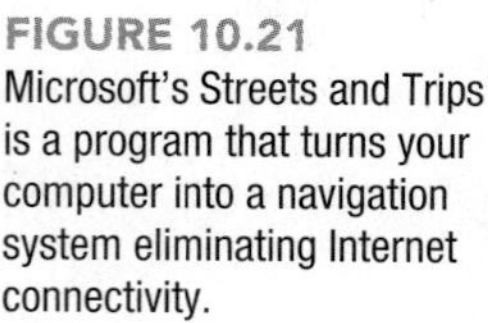

FIGURE 10.21
Microsoft's Streets and Trips is a program that turns your computer into a navigation system eliminating Internet connectivity.

Ethics and Gaming

Does the video gaming industry have an ethical obligation to produce games that have less violent and addictive content? Gaming has become a method of entertainment, with at least half of the individuals that you meet having tried to play one at least once. But is it really entertainment? Entertainment is an act that should relax people and take their mind off their troubles. Serious gamers, the ones that play for hours, do not seem to be getting entertainment in the traditional sense of the word. Watching some "gamers" as they are called, you might see signs of frustration and irritation.

Often the games have activities that are not legal in the real world, for example, stealing or abuse of another individual. Consider these questions: Is the difference between the ethics in the real world and gaming world one of the problems with serious gaming? Is it possible for an individual to transfer the rules of the gaming world into the real world and begin to exhibit these unethical behaviors in his or her real life? Is it possible to become addicted to the gaming world environment and stay there for longer and longer periods of time? When is it enough? How should the games be rated so that parents can distinguish violent games from ones that are truly entertainment? Can the gaming industry change its strategy and develop games that encourage a healthier mind-set—one that promotes the ethics of a nonviolent society? Individuals must understand the responsibility and accept the consequences when the behavior of a game is transferred to the real world and some innocent bystander is injured.

FAST FORWARD

Using Technology to Protect Air Space

After September 11, 2001, programmers went to work creating a software program that would prevent aircraft from being used as weapons. The concept of *Soft Walls* was developed at the University of Berkeley under Professor Edward A. Lee. A Soft Wall would behave like a virtual bubble around forbidden air space. The software consists of a database of forbidden zones. The plane's computer would check the GPS against the database. If the plane were approaching a forbidden zone, the pilot would be notified and given the opportunity to change course. If the pilot did not cooperate, the plane would meet with resistance, similar to a forceful wind, causing the plane to change paths (Figure 10.22). Soft Walls are independent of ground controls, but that does not make the system less vulnerable to tampering. There are still safety and security issues to iron out, but in the future individuals attempting to use planes as weapons might come up against this invisible shield of defense.

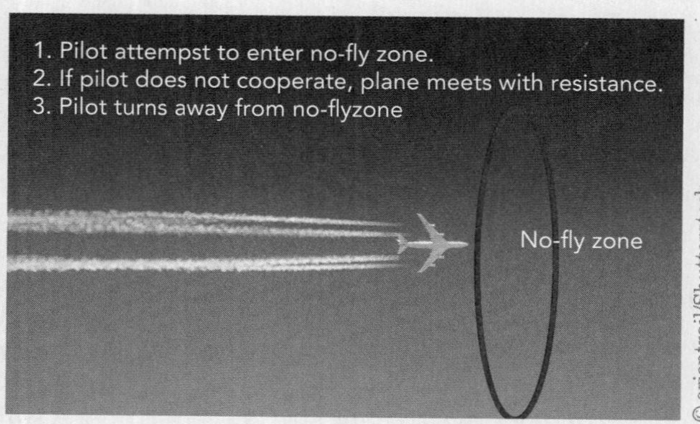
1. Pilot attempst to enter no-fly zone.
2. If pilot does not cooperate, plane meets with resistance.
3. Pilot turns away from no-flyzone
No-fly zone
© oriontrail/Shutterstock

FIGURE 10.22 Soft Walls software creates the equivalent of a virtual shield around the forbidden zone and guides the plane in another direction.

thousands of game players located anywhere in the world simultaneously in a virtual world that continues to exist even after the player has signed off. In these games, the graphical images are controlled by other players rather than by a computer. Combining a rich 3-D graphical virtual environment with multiplayer thrills, these types of games are attracting increasing numbers of users. ***Massively multiplayer online role-playing games (MMORPGs)*** are an extension of multiplayer online gaming in which the participants assume the characteristics of a predesigned character or a self-designed character and play the game as that character. These virtual worlds are often hosted on servers maintained by the software publisher. You can access some of these games directly online without any special equipment other than a Web browser, whereas others require a locally installed game package to speed up processing. An interesting positive element of MMORPGs is that they encourage the player to progress to higher levels, promote team building, and frequently necessitate seeking other players whose skills and abilities complement those of your character to attain a strategic advantage. Examples of such games include *EverQuest* and *World of WarCraft*.

Objective 6 | Differentiate Between Application Types

As the Sales Operations Manager for a sporting goods company, the idea of incorporating a game into the next sales promotion with the street team and perhaps some use of GPS monitoring seems feasible. You schedule a meeting with your team to determine if any marketing promotions have tried this type of activity. If so, you want to know who developed the game, did it come packed with other computer-based activities relative to the promotion, and was the campaign successful? Where do you start?

Concept 10.16 | Separating Custom from Packaged Software

Custom software is written for specialized fields or businesses and is tailor-made to suit their exact needs. Custom applications can be created by an in-house software development team or commissioned to an external developer. Either way, the cost of a custom program is much higher than general-purpose, off-the-shelf applications. Examples of areas that make use of custom software include military projects, billing needs of medical offices, restaurant management systems, and occupational injury tracking software.

On your own computer, you probably use ***packaged software***, which is software purchased off the shelf that is aimed at fulfilling the needs of the general public including the basic home and business user. Although packaged software provides settings to customize certain features, it is immediately useful in a wide variety of contexts. Packaged software is much cheaper than custom software.

In addition to the choices of custom or packaged software, you have three other options when purchasing software: standalone programs, integrated programs, and software suites.

Concept 10.17 | Evaluating Standalone Programs, Integrated Programs, and Software Suites

A ***standalone program*** is a program that does not require any software other than the operating system to run. Many software programs like Word and Excel can be considered standalone programs. A plug-in, which will not run unless another program is already installed, is not a standalone program.

An ***integrated program*** is a single program that manages an entire business or set of related tasks. It combines the most commonly used functions of many productivity software programs, like word processing, database management, spreadsheet, accounting, and customer service, into one single application. Integrated programs, such as Microsoft Works, offer easy-to-learn and easy-to-use versions of basic productivity software. The functions offered by an integrated program, called ***modules***, share the same interface, enable you to switch among them quickly, and are not available as standalone programs (Figure 10.23). A complaint about these integrated modules is that they lack features that provide advanced capabilities.

A ***software suite***, sometimes called an ***office suite***, is a collection of individual, full-featured, standalone programs possessing a similar interface and a common command structure, which are bundled and sold

Works Quick launch menu provides easy access to a word processor, spreadsheet, and database module

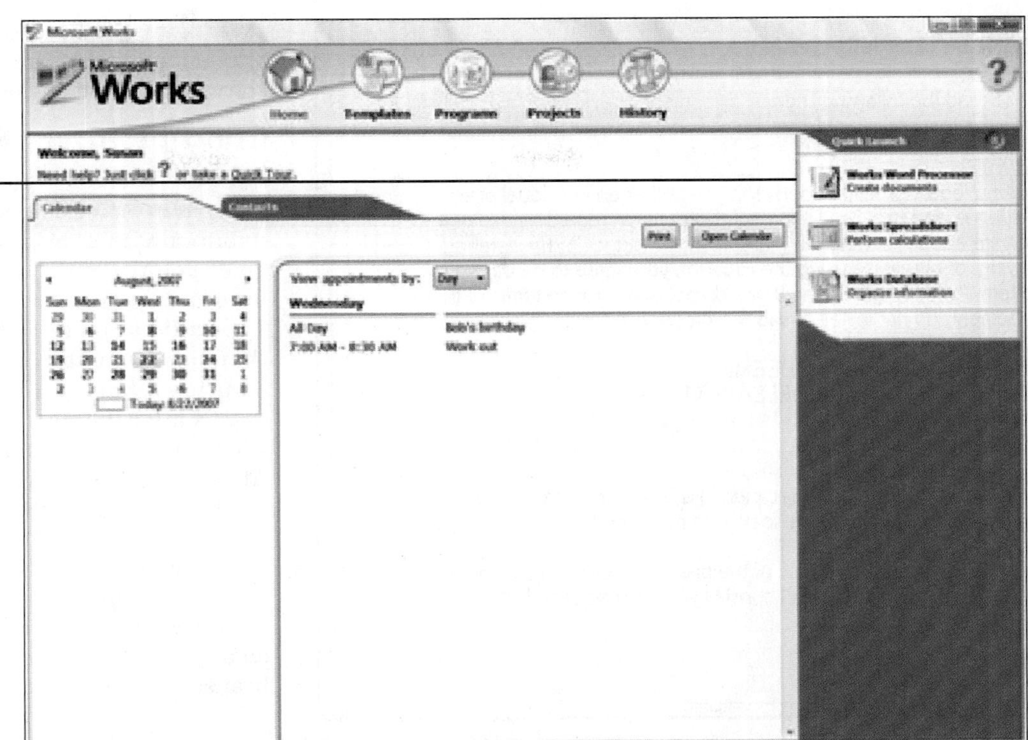

FIGURE 10.23 Microsoft Works modules provide basic productivity tools that are helpful for new users.

together. The cost of purchasing a suite is usually less than buying each program individually. Most personal productivity software is sold in office suites, such as Corel WordPerfect Office, IBM Lotus SmartSuite, and the market leader, Microsoft Office.

TECHNOLOGY ON THE JOB

As the Sales Operations Manager for a sporting goods company, it is important to have current knowledge of software programs and technology trends. A company that produces antivirus software recently posted a job description for the following position on an Internet job site with the desired qualifications listed below. Review the qualifications, focusing on those related to technology, and see how many you have and how many you are lacking for such a position. Does the level of technology for a sales-related job surprise you?

Posted requirements for Sales Operations Specialist:

- Work cross-functionally with various business units, partners, and vendors to create and maintain sales and merchandising strategies
- Perform a variety of moderately complex and detailed operational tasks to support the online storefronts
- Proactively identify potential operational issues, consult management, and make recommendations for improving the processes/tools
- Receive and manage requests and escalations from the sales teams; perform ongoing quality assurance of Web site and sales strategy; participate in the testing of new functionality and pages
- Two to four years of experience in an e-commerce environment
- Experience with Excel, Outlook, various Web browsers, and a general knowledge of using online applications
- Able to understand and use professional concepts, company/team policies, and standard procedures to practically and creatively solve a variety of problems
- Able to learn and thrive in a moderately complex and ambiguous environment, within a diverse and global team

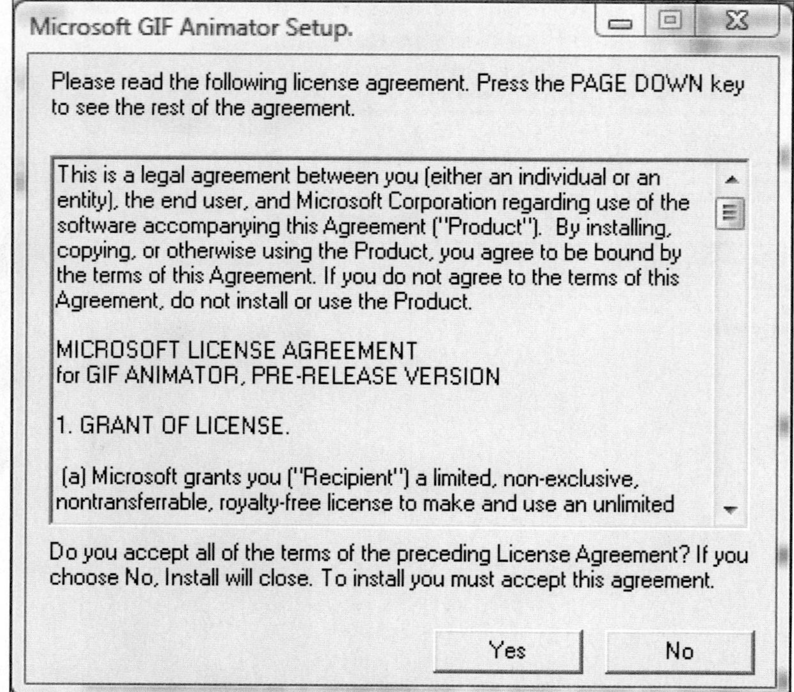

FIGURE 10.24 The license agreement usually appears at the beginning of the installation sequence.

Objective 7 | Respect Software Licenses and Registration Agreements

As the Sales Operations Manager of a sporting goods company, the idea of the interactive game software in the new sales promotion has been accepted by your company, and management has asked you to investigate the license and registration agreements necessary to deploy the software. Where do you start?

Concept 10.18 | Reviewing Licenses and Registration

A ***software license*** is a contract distributed with a program that typically gives you the right to install and use the program on one computer (Figure 10.24). Typically, to install a program on more than one computer, you must purchase additional licenses. However, some programs allow home users to install software on one or two additional computers. Always read the license to be sure.

Organizations such as colleges and universities often purchase ***site licenses***, a contract between the software publisher and the organization that enables the organization to install copies of a program on a specified number of computers. Site licenses offer large organizations multiple software licenses at a slightly reduced cost.

You usually have to ***validate*** your software—verify that it is a legal copy by providing a special code or product key before you can use it. You may also be asked to register your software. Doing so may provide you with product news, upgrade notices, and qualify you for technical assistance.

Concept 10.19 | Commercial Software, Shareware, Freeware, and Public Domain Software

Public domain software is software that is expressly free from copyright. You can do anything you want with it, including modify it or sell it to others. ***Copy-protected software*** programs include some mechanism to ensure that you do not make or run unauthorized copies. There are three types of copy-protected software:

- ***Commercial software***, which must be purchased. The current trend is to make these programs available as an online download or initially as shareware, to give the potential customer a trial period. After the trial period is over, you can pay for the program directly on the Web site and download an official copy.

FIGURE 10.25 A site known for its large library of shareware is ***www.tucows.com***. Click the Looking for Downloads link in the upper right corner.

- ***Shareware***, which is more of a marketing method than a type of software. You are permitted to have a set period of time in which to "try before buying" the program (Figure 10.25). If you like the program after using it for a specified trial period, you must pay a registration fee.
- ***Freeware***, which is given away for no charge but with the restriction that you cannot sell it for profit.

Objective 8 | Connect System Requirements and Software Versions

As the Sales Operations Manager for a sporting goods company and the individual directly responsible for the viral marketing campaign, the Information Technology Department has asked you to set the minimum system requirements that the street team game in development should require. You need to do some research before you reply. Where do you start?

When you buy software, your computer system must meet the program's ***system requirements***—the minimal level of equipment that a program needs in order to run. For example, a program may be designed to run on a PC with an Intel Core i3 processor, a CD or DVD drive, at least 1 GB of RAM, and 50 GB of free hard disk space. If you are shopping for software, you will find the system requirements printed somewhere on the outside of the box or online through a link that is usually called "system requirements." It is usually better if your system exceeds these requirements, especially when it comes to memory and disk space.

Software Going Green

A recent survey by PricewaterhouseCoopers revealed that 60 percent of technology manufacturers are developing green products and services, using recycled or recyclable materials, and creating packaging that meets or exceeds global environmental standards. For example, Microsoft has eliminated the use of PVC in their packaging, and McAfee encourages users to *download* their software, thereby eliminating the need for packaging. Do you want to do your part? If you have old copies of software on CD, stacks of obsolete floppy disks, or other unwanted computer accessories, GreenDisk at **www.greendisk.com** will safely and responsibly dispose of them for you for a small fee.

You have probably noticed that most program names include a number, such as 6.0, or a year, such as 2010. Software publishers often introduce new versions of their programs, and these numbers help you determine whether you have the latest version. In a version number, the whole number, such as 6 in 6.0, indicates a major program revision. A decimal number indicates a ***maintenance release***—a minor revision that corrects bugs or adds minor features. The year 2010 would indicate the year the software was published.

Beta versions of forthcoming programs are versions in the final phases of testing, and are sometimes available for free. Beta users are usually sophisticated users that try out these preliminary versions and tell the publisher about any major issues so they can be fixed before the applications are officially released.

From either the Companion Web Site or MyITLab, try the Chapter 10 Application Software Simulation

Concept 10.20 | Installing Software Upgrades

Software upgrading describes the process of keeping your version of an application current with the marketplace. Some upgrades are small changes called patches; sometimes they are major fixes called service releases or service packs. Microsoft software has a built-in capability to automatically check with Microsoft's Web site to determine whether updates are available.

Concept 10.21 | Distribution and Documentation

Before high-speed Internet connections became commonplace, most software was available only in shrink-wrapped packages that included floppy disks or CD-ROMs containing the program installation files. Using high-speed Internet connections to distribute software is cheaper for the company and often more convenient for you.

Most software provides some type of ***documentation***, a collection of printed or online material that provides instructions and brief tutorials. Many programs also have Help screens that enable you to consult all or part of the documentation on your computer screen.

Check Your Knowledge: From either the Companion Web Site or MyITLab, take the quiz covering Objectives 5, 6, 7, and 8.

Chapter Summary

Using Application Software as Productivity Tools

- General-purpose applications are useful to accomplish frequently performed tasks.
- Productivity programs are general-purpose applications that help you work more efficiently and effectively on both personal and business-related documents.
- Media refers to technology that presents information. This technology encompasses pictures, sound, and video. Most media and graphic software are referred to as multimedia programs because they enable you to incorporate more than one of these technologies.
- Most multimedia software programs reduce file size by using *codecs*, the technical name for compression/decompression or code/decode algorithms. Two common codes are lossy and lossless.
- Applications that run from the Internet reside on a remote server and are accessed through the Internet. This technology makes file sharing and collaboration easier. Examples include Windows Office Live and Google Docs.
- Home and educational programs are used for less complex or more personal activities like personal finance and tax preparation software, home design and landscaping software, computerized reference information, and games.
- Custom software is tailor-made for specialized fields or businesses, while packaged software is purchased off the shelf and fulfills the needs of the general public.
- Types of applications include standalone programs, integrated programs, and software suites.
- Software must be licensed, validated, and usually registered.
- Publishers introduce new or updated versions of their software periodically. In a version number, the whole number, such as 6 in 6.0, indicates a major program revision. A decimal number indicates a maintenance release.
- Software that is public domain software—free from copyright or copy protection—contains some mechanism to ensure that you do not make or run unauthorized copies.

Key Terms and Concepts

Matching

Match each term in the second column with its correct definition in the first column by writing the letter of the term on the blank line in front of the correct definition.

_____ 1. A compression technique that allows a file to be completely restored without any flaws.

_____ 2. Sophisticated versions of graphic programs used to edit and create images and save them in a variety of file formats.

_____ 3. A collection of printed or online material that provides instructions and brief tutorials.

_____ 4. A program that enables you to modify digitized videos.

_____ 5. A compression technique that permanently removes some data from the file.

_____ 6. A single program that manages an entire business or set of related tasks.

_____ 7. A program purchased and installed separately that functions independently and is fully self-contained.

_____ 8. Software purchased off the shelf for the needs of the general public including the basic home and business user.

_____ 9. A program downloaded from a Web site that extends the ability of your Web browser to enable multimedia features.

_____ 10. Software designed for specialized fields or businesses and that is tailor-made to suit their exact needs.

_____ 11. The functions offered by an integrated program that share the same interface, enable you to switch among them quickly, and are not available as standalone programs.

_____ 12. The term that refers to a "try before buying" program.

_____ 13. A compression/decompression algorithm.

_____ 14. An automated page-description language (PDL) that describes image elements as geometric objects such as lines and arcs and consists of commands given by the program and carried out by the printer to precisely re-create the computer image on a printed page.

_____ 15. Software given away for no charge but with the restriction that you cannot resell it for profit.

A Codec
B Custom software
C Documentation
D Freeware
E Image editors
F Integrated program
G Lossless
H Lossy
I Modules
J Packaged software
K Plug-in
L PostScript
M Shareware
N Standalone program
O Video editor

Multiple Choice

Circle the correct answer.

1. An image formed by a pattern of tiny dots, each corresponding to one pixel on the computer's display is a:
   A. vector graphic **C.** plug-in
   B. bitmapped graphic
2. An image generated by a program that requires you to define points to draw line segments that are known as paths and are stored as mathematical equations by the graphic program is a:
   A. vector graphic **C.** module
   B. bitmapped graphic
3. An image-rendering technique that adds vivid realism to a simulated three-dimensional object by manipulating variations in color intensity that would be produced by light falling on the object from multiple directions is called:
   A. modeling **C.** PostScript
   B. ray tracing
4. A technology that, through the Internet, connects hundreds of thousands of players, located anywhere in the world, simultaneously in a virtual world that continues to exist even after the player has signed off is:
   A. modeling **C.** multiplayer online gaming
   B. ray tracing
5. A collection of individual, full-featured, standalone programs bundled and sold together and that employ a similar user interface and a common command structure is:
   A. a software suite **C.** an integrated program
   B. a module
6. Contracts between an enterprise and a software publisher permitting the installation of a program on a specified number of computers is:
   A. documentation **C.** an integrated program
   B. a site license
7. Software that is expressly free from copyright is:
   A. shareware **C.** public domain
   B. commercial
8. Programs that include some mechanism to ensure that you do not make or run unauthorized copies is:
   A. shareware **C.** public domain
   B. copy protected
9. The minimum level of equipment that a program needs to run is referred to as the:
   A. system requirements **C.** maintenance release
   B. system updates
10. The preliminary version of a software program in the final testing phase is referred to as the:
    A. alpha version **C.** bitmap version
    B. beta version

Teamwork

1. **Applications for a Web Developer** As a team, consult the college catalog and interview faculty in the computer and graphic art departments of your college to create a list of courses and applications that a student interested in developing Web pages or becoming a Web developer should take. Use a Word table to list the courses, the prerequisites, the software for the course, and the number of credit hours. Then, consult local job listings and list at least five jobs in Web development, the name of the employer, and the required skills. Do you think your college's offerings match up with the job requirements? Present your findings at the bottom of the Word table.
2. **Use a Photo Editor** Download the current version of Google's Picasa photo editor. Then, use a digital camera to take a series of photos or use a team member's photos and experiment with some of Picasa's photo editing features. After making a change to a photo, save it with a new name so that the original is unaltered so that you can compare the before and after versions. Select at least five photos and record the changes made to each photo, the Picasa feature you used, the level of difficulty your team assigned to the use of that feature, and what your team thought of the finished image. Attempt to make at least one collage, and learn how to create an album. Insert before and after pictures, a summary of the features you used, and their level of difficulty in a PowerPoint slide show. Conclude the show with the features your team thought produced the best results.
3. **It Takes More Than the Application** As a team, research the qualities of a good business presentation. From the ones located, select eight that the team believes would have the greatest effect on the overall quality of a business presentation. Use your findings to create, as a team, a high-quality PowerPoint presentation demonstrating your eight features. Remember to cite your references.

On the Web

1. **A Look Back in Time** It is easy to take for granted the programs that we use today and complain about all of the features that they lack. Visit **http://royal.pingdom.com/2009/06/17/first-version-of-todays-most-popular-applications-a-visual-tour/**, and review the 1.0 version of today's popular programs. From this site, select five programs with which you are familiar, and then in a table or spreadsheet, list each program and the features of each that are still in use today. In the same table list the features that have changed or been added to make the programs suitable for today's users. Finally, make a wish list of the features that you would like to see each application include in future versions. Explain how your suggested features would improve the overall objective of the application. Appropriately title your report, and submit your table or spreadsheet with your insights and assessments.
2. **Gaming Popularity** Using your favorite search engine, locate references that contain statistics on gaming. Present your findings in a one-page, double-spaced report. Remember to cite your references. Attempt to locate such information as:
   - The average hours a week a gamer spends playing video games
   - The number of female versus male gamers
   - The percent of U.S. households that play video games
   - The average age of a gamer
   - Some of the benefits of gaming
   - Some of the problems associated with gaming
3. **Free Personal Information Managers** Do you want some free or inexpensive software? The Internet is frequently used to distribute shareware and freeware applications. Go to **www.yahoo.com** and type *freeware* in the Search box at the top of the window. Browse some of the more than 242 million sites returned by your search. Perform a more limited search to zero in on free personal information management programs. Download two programs. Use both and critically compare their interfaces, e-mail, contacts, and calendars. Include the product names, the URLs from which you downloaded the product, the file size, comparisons of the interfaces, and your assessment of functionality in a one-page, double-spaced summary report.

Ethics and Social Media

1. **Shareware** Have you ever downloaded shareware software or the beta of a program and after the free preview period realized that it still worked; so you continued to use it? In both cases, you probably had to agree to some type of usage statement limiting the time you can use the program to the specified free period. By continuing to use the program, you are violating this agreement. Using your favorite search engine, find three actions software companies are taking to reduce this violation of shareware agreements. Include your ethical stand on the continued use of a shareware program that has expired and an explanation of the three steps you located that are being taken by software companies to deter this behavior in a one-page, double-spaced summary report.

2. **Viral Marketing** The use of viral marketing as a multimedia and interactive method of promoting products has become popular. Both its successes and failures have been documented. First, locate a valid definition for viral marketing. Then, using a search engine, locate three viral marketing attempts that were successful and three that were not successful. In a slide show of five or more slides, indicate the year of each event and how success or failure was determined. Conclude your slide show with your views on this type of multimedia advertising.

Sources

http://www.microsoft.com/presspass/press/2010/jun10/06-152010officelaunchpr.mspx

http://www.engagelearning.eu/wiki/doku.php?id=decision_making_tool:games_industry

http://softwalls.eecs.berkeley.edu/

http://www.greenbang.com/tech-companies-its-time-to-exploit-the-green-shoppers_2324.html

PowerPoint Presentation Creation; Enhancing Presentations with Pictures, Transitions, Objects, Backgrounds, and SmartArt

OUTCOMES
At the end of this chapter you will be able to:

OBJECTIVES
Mastering these objectives will enable you to:

PROJECT 11A
Create a new PowerPoint presentation.

1. Create a New Presentation (p. 487)
2. Edit a Presentation in Normal View (p. 489)
3. Add Pictures to a Presentation (p. 493)
4. Print and View a Presentation (p. 496)

PROJECT 11B
Edit and format a PowerPoint presentation.

5. Edit an Existing Presentation (p. 500)
6. Format a Presentation (p. 503)
7. Use Slide Sorter View (p. 505)
8. Apply Slide Transitions (p. 506)

PROJECT 11C
Format a presentation to add visual interest and clarity.

9. Format Numbered and Bulleted Lists (p. 510)
10. Insert Clip Art (p. 513)
11. Insert Text Boxes and Shapes (p. 516)
12. Format Objects (p. 519)

PROJECT 11D
Enhance a presentation with WordArt and diagrams.

13. Remove Picture Backgrounds and Insert WordArt (p. 524)
14. Create and Format a SmartArt Graphic (p. 528)

© AISPIX/Shutterstock

© evgeny varlamov/Shutterstock

Job Focus: Hawaiian Tour Director and Amusement Park Assistant Manager

In This Chapter

In this chapter, you will learn how a Tour Director in Hawaii uses PowerPoint presentations to introduce tour services. You will also learn how an Assistant Manager at an amusement park uses PowerPoint for employee training and community announcements.

At the end of this unit, following this chapter, you will have an opportunity to complete a case project that focuses on the career of a Sales Manager for a sports retail chain.

Project 11A Company Overview

Project Activities

In Activities 11.01 through 11.13, you will create the first four slides of a new presentation that Lehua Hawaiian Adventures tour manager Carl Kawaoka is developing to introduce the tour services that the company offers. Your completed presentation will look similar to Figure 11.1.

Project Files

For Project 11A, you will need the following files:

New blank PowerPoint presentation
jpg11A_Helicopter
jpg11A_Beach

You will save your presentation as:

Lastname_Firstname_11A_LHA_Overview

Project Results

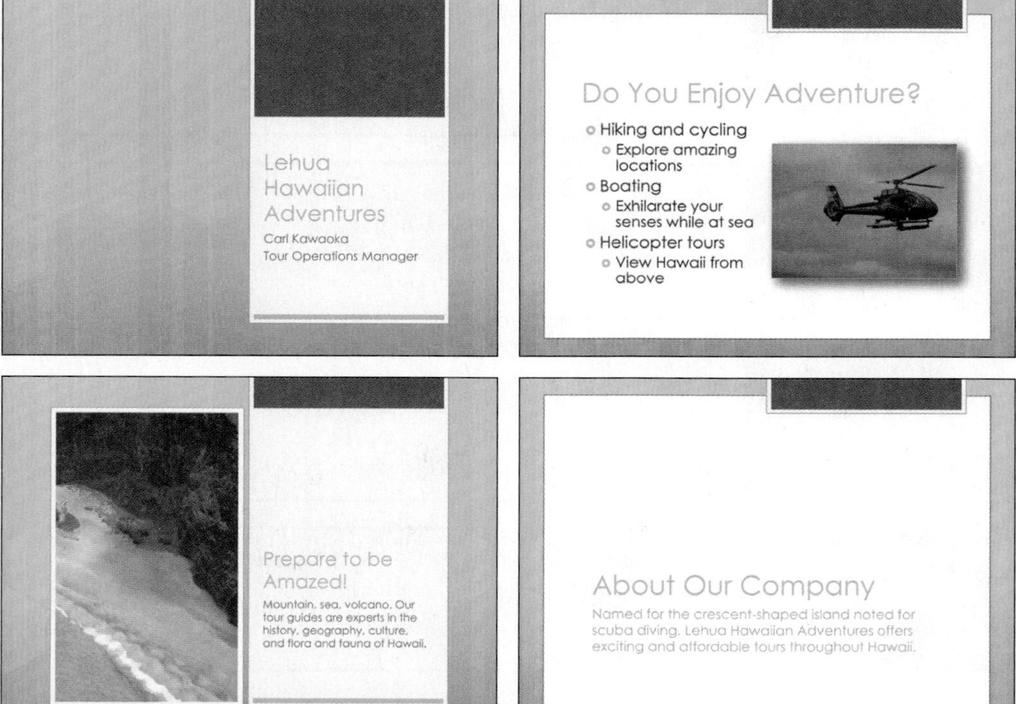

Figure 11.1
Project 11A LHA Overview

Objective 1 | Create a New Presentation

Microsoft PowerPoint 2010 is software with which you can present information to your audience effectively. You can edit and format a blank presentation by adding text, a presentation theme, and pictures.

View the video on the Companion Web Site or in MyITLab

Activity 11.01 | Identifying Parts of the PowerPoint Window

In this activity, you will start PowerPoint and identify the parts of the PowerPoint window.

1 **Start** PowerPoint to display a new blank presentation in Normal view, and then compare your screen with Figure 11.2.

Normal view is the primary editing view in PowerPoint where you write and design your presentations. Normal view includes the Notes pane, the Slide pane, and the Slides/Outline pane.

Figure 11.2

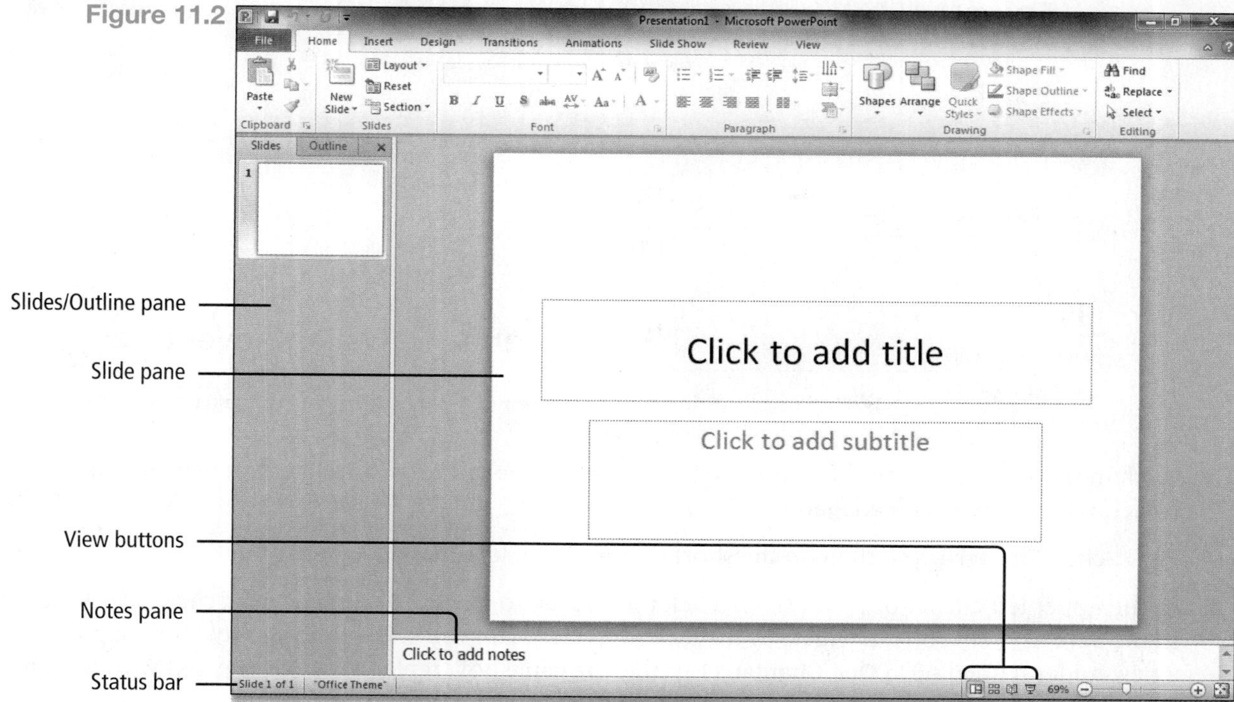

2 Take a moment to study the parts of the PowerPoint window described in the table in Figure 11.3.

Microsoft PowerPoint Screen Elements

Screen Element	Description
Notes pane	Displays below the Slide pane and provides space for you to type notes regarding the active slide.
Slide pane	Displays a large image of the active slide.
Slides/Outline pane	Displays either the presentation in the form of miniature images called ***thumbnails*** (Slides tab) or the presentation outline (Outline tab).
Status bar	Displays, in a horizontal bar at the bottom of the presentation window, the current slide number, number of slides in a presentation, theme, View buttons, Zoom slider, and Fit slide to current window button; you can customize this area to include additional helpful information.
View buttons	Control the look of the presentation window with a set of commands.

Figure 11.3

Activity 11.02 | Entering Presentation Text and Saving a Presentation

On startup, PowerPoint displays a new blank presentation with a single ***slide***—a ***title slide*** in Normal view. A presentation slide—similar to a page in a document—can contain text, pictures, tables, charts, and other multimedia or graphic objects. The title slide is the first slide in a presentation and provides an introduction to the presentation topic.

1 In the **Slide pane**, click in the text *Click to add title*, which is the title ***placeholder***.

A placeholder is a box on a slide with dotted or dashed borders that holds title and body text or other content such as charts, tables, and pictures. This slide contains two placeholders, one for the title and one for the subtitle.

2 Type **Lehua Hawaiian Adventures** point to *Lehua*, and then right-click. On the shortcut menu, click **Ignore All** so *Lehua* is not flagged as a spelling error in this presentation. Compare your screen with Figure 11.4.

Recall that a red wavy underline indicates that the underlined word is not in the Microsoft Office dictionary.

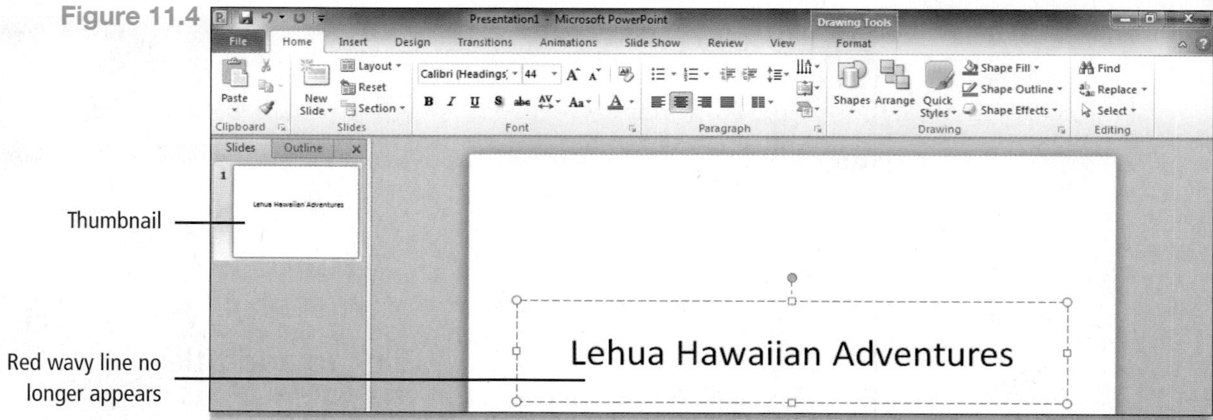

Figure 11.4

3 Click in the subtitle placeholder, and then type **Carl Kawaoka** Press Enter to create a new line in the subtitle placeholder. Type **Tour Manager**

4 Right-click **Kawaoka**, and then on the shortcut menu, click **Ignore All**.

5 In the upper left corner of your screen, click the **File tab** to display **Backstage** view, click **Save As**, and then in the **Save As** dialog box, navigate to the location where you will store your files for this chapter. Create a new folder named **All In One Chapter 11** In the **File name** box, replace the existing text with **Lastname_Firstname_11A_LHA_Overview** and then click **Save**.

Activity 11.03 | Applying a Presentation Theme

A ***theme*** is a set of unified design elements that provides a look for your presentation by applying colors, fonts, and effects.

1 On the Ribbon, click the **Design tab**. In the **Themes group**, click the **More** button to display the **Themes** gallery. Compare your screen with Figure 11.5.

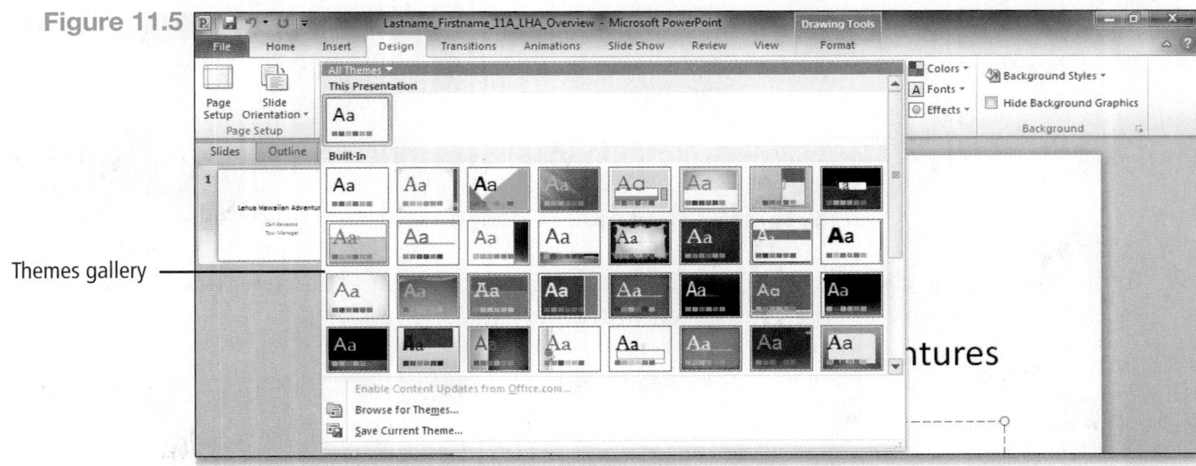

Figure 11.5

2 Under **Built-In**, point to several of the themes and notice that a ScreenTip displays the name of each theme and the Live Preview feature displays how each theme would look if applied to your presentation.

The first theme that displays is the Office theme. Subsequent themes are arranged alphabetically.

3 Use the ScreenTips to locate the theme with the green background—**Austin**—as shown in Figure 11.6.

Figure 11.6

4 Click the **Austin** theme to change the presentation theme and then **Save** your presentation.

Objective 2 | Edit a Presentation in Normal View

View the video on the Companion Web Site or in MyITLab

Editing is the process of modifying a presentation by adding and deleting slides or by changing the contents of individual slides.

Activity 11.04 | Inserting a New Slide

To insert a new slide in a presentation, display the slide that will precede the slide that you want to insert.

1 On the **Home tab**, in the **Slides group**, point to the **New Slide** button. Compare your screen with Figure 11.7.

The New Slide button is a split button. Recall that clicking the main part of a split button performs a command and clicking the arrow opens a menu, list, or gallery. The upper, main part of the New Slide button, when clicked, inserts a slide without displaying any options. The lower part—the New Slide button arrow—when clicked, displays a gallery of slide ***layouts***. A layout is the arrangement of elements, such as title and subtitle text, lists, pictures, tables, charts, shapes, and movies, on a slide.

Figure 11.7

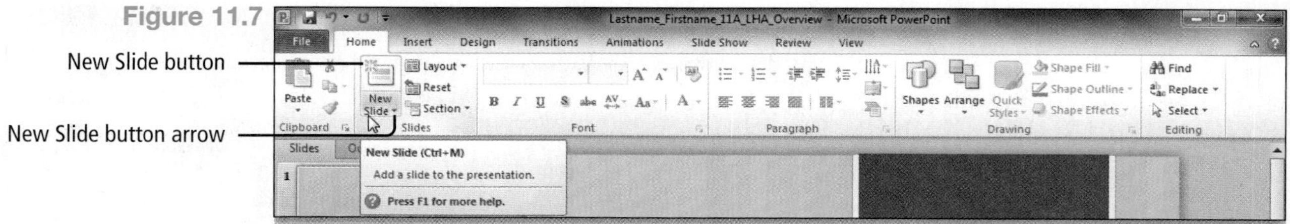

2 In the **Slides group**, click the lower portion of the New Slide button—the **New Slide button arrow**—to display the gallery, and then compare your screen with Figure 11.8.

Figure 11.8

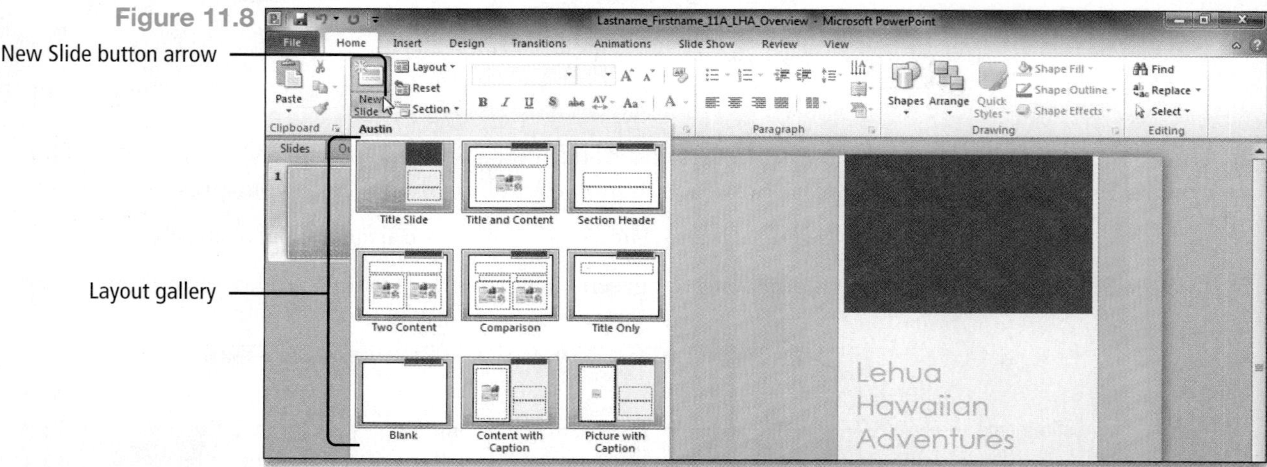

3 In the gallery, click the **Two Content** layout to insert a new slide. Notice that the new blank slide displays in the **Slide pane** and in the **Slides/Outline pane**.

4 In the **Slide pane**, click the text *Click to add title*, and then type **Do You Enjoy Adventure?** On the left side of the slide, click anywhere in the content placeholder. Type **Hiking and cycling** and then press Enter.

5 Type **Explore locations** and then compare your screen with Figure 11.9.

Figure 11.9

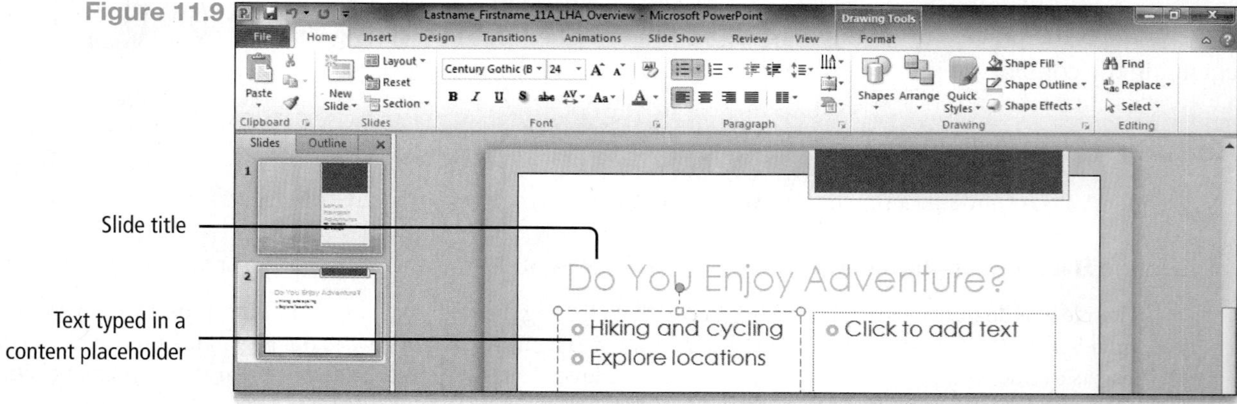

6 **Save** your presentation.

Activity 11.05 | Increasing and Decreasing List Levels

Text in a PowerPoint presentation is organized according to ***list levels***. List levels, each represented by a bullet symbol, are similar to outline levels. On a slide, list levels are identified by the bullet style, indentation, and the size of the text. The first level on an individual slide is the title. Increasing the list level of a bullet point increases its indent and results in a smaller text size. Decreasing the list level of a bullet point decreases its indent and results in a larger text size.

1. On **Slide 2**, if necessary, click at the end of the last bullet point after the word *locations*, and then press Enter to insert a new bullet point.
2. Type **Boating excursions** and then press Enter. Press Tab, and then notice that the green bullet is indented. Type **Exhilarate your senses while at sea**

   By pressing Tab at the beginning of a bullet point, you can increase the list level and indent the bullet point.
3. Press Enter. Notice that a new bullet point displays at the same level as the previous bullet point. Then, on the **Home tab**, in the **Paragraph group**, click the **Decrease List Level** button. Type **Helicopter tours** and then compare your screen with Figure 11.10.

   The Decrease List Level button promotes the bullet point. The text size increases and the text is no longer indented.

Figure 11.10

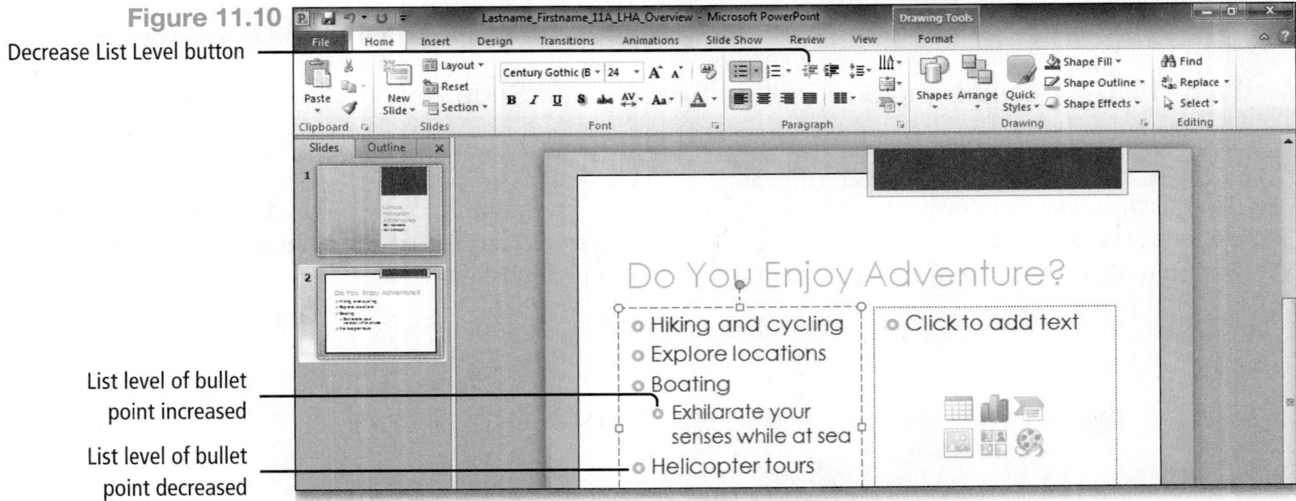

4. Press Enter, and then press Tab to increase the list level. Type **View Hawaii from above**
5. Click anywhere in the second bullet point—*Explore locations*. On the **Home tab**, in the **Paragraph group**, click the **Increase List Level** button.

   The bullet point is indented and the size of the text decreases.
6. **Save** your presentation.

Activity 11.06 | Adding Speaker's Notes to a Presentation

Recall that when a presentation is displayed in Normal view, the Notes pane displays below the Slide pane. Use the Notes pane to type speaker's notes that you can print below a picture of each slide. Then, while making your presentation, you can refer to these printouts to remind you of the important points that you want to discuss during the presentation.

1. With **Slide 2** displayed, on the **Home tab**, in the **Slides group**, click the **New Slide button arrow** to display the **Slide Layout** gallery, and then click **Section Header**.

   The section header layout changes the look and flow of a presentation by providing text placeholders that do not contain bullet points.

2 Click in the title placeholder, and then type **About Our Company** Click in the content placeholder below the title, and then type **Named for the crescent-shaped island noted for scuba diving, Lehua Hawaiian Adventures offers exciting and affordable tours throughout Hawaii.**

3 Below the slide, click in the **Notes pane**. Type **Lehua Hawaiian Adventures is based in Honolulu but has offices on each of the main Hawaiian islands.** Compare your screen with Figure 11.11, and then **Save** your presentation.

Figure 11.11

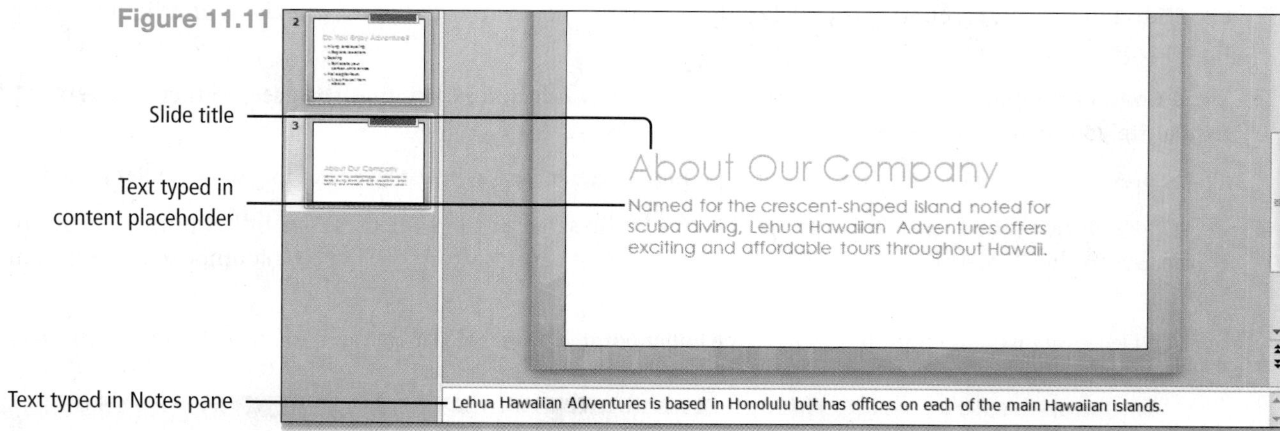

Activity 11.07 | Displaying and Editing Slides in the Slide Pane

To edit a presentation slide, display the slide in the Slide pane.

1 Look at the **Slides/Outline pane**, and then notice that the presentation contains three slides. At the right side of the PowerPoint window, in the vertical scroll bar, point to the scroll box, and then hold down the left mouse button to display a ScreenTip indicating the slide number and title.

2 Drag the scroll box up until the ScreenTip displays *Slide: 2 of 3 Do You Enjoy Adventure?* Compare your slide with Figure 11.12, and then release the mouse button to display **Slide 2**.

Figure 11.12

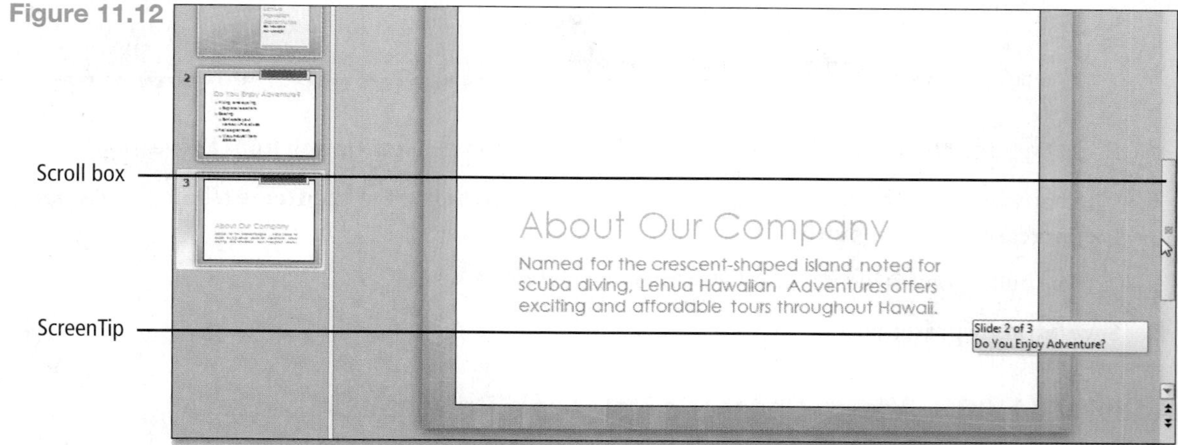

3 In the second bullet point, click at the end of the word *Explore*. Press Spacebar, and then type **amazing** Compare your screen with Figure 11.13.

The placeholder text is resized to fit within the placeholder. The AutoFit Options button displays.

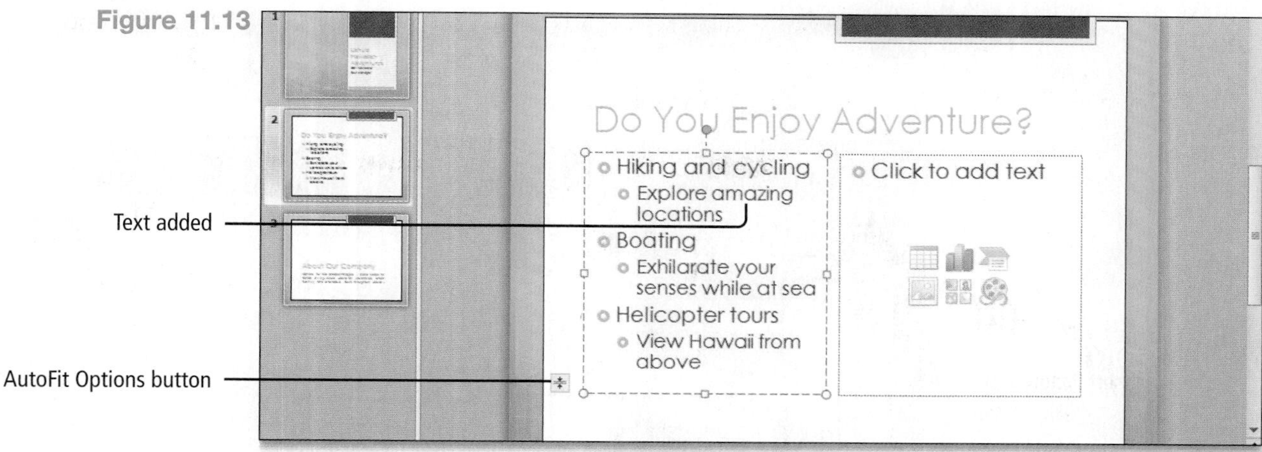

Figure 11.13

4 Click the **AutoFit Options** button, and then click **AutoFit Text to Placeholder**.

The *AutoFit Text to Placeholder* option keeps the text contained within the placeholder by reducing the size of the text. The *Stop Fitting Text to This Placeholder* option turns off the AutoFit option so that the text can flow beyond the placeholder border; the text size remains unchanged.

5 On the left side of the PowerPoint window, in the **Slides/Outline pane**, point to **Slide 1**, and then notice that a ScreenTip displays the slide title. Compare your screen with Figure 11.14.

In the Slides/Outline pane, the slide numbers display to the left of the slide thumbnails.

Figure 11.14

6 Click **Slide 1** to display it in the **Slide pane**, and then in the slide subtitle, click at the end of the word *Tour*. Press Spacebar, and then type **Operations**

Clicking a slide thumbnail is the most common method used to display a slide in the Slide pane.

7 **Save** your presentation.

Objective 3 | Add Pictures to a Presentation

Photographic images add impact to a presentation and help the audience visualize the messages you are trying to convey.

View the video on the Companion Web Site or in MyITLab

Activity 11.08 | Inserting a Picture from a File

1 In the **Slides/Outline pane**, click **Slide 2** to display it in the **Slide pane**. On the **Home tab**, in the **Slides group**, click the **New Slide button arrow** to display the **Slide Layout** gallery. Click **Picture with Caption** to insert a new **Slide 3**. Compare your screen with Figure 11.15.

Figure 11.15

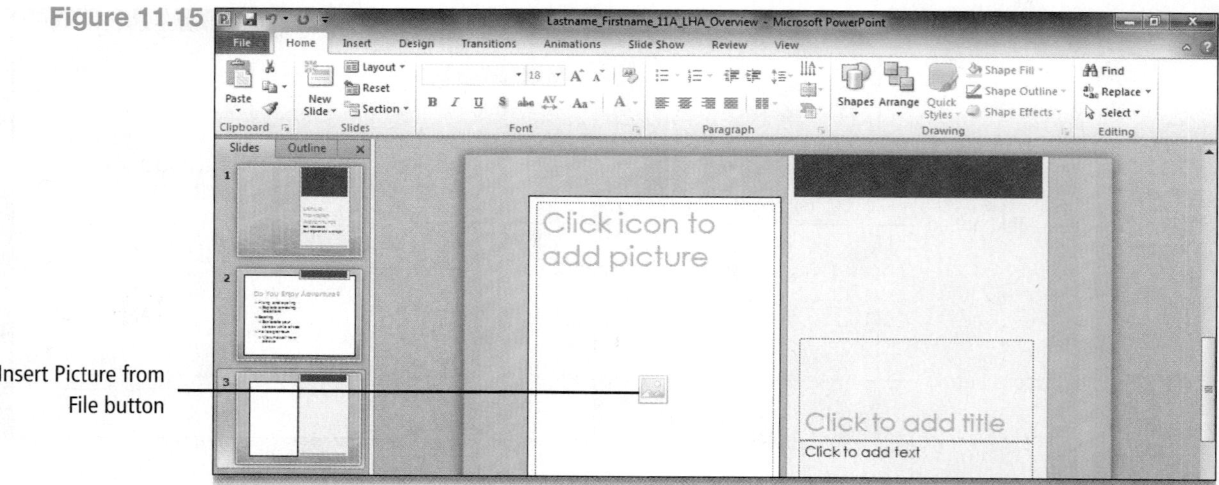

2 In the picture placeholder, click the **Insert Picture from File** button to open the **Insert Picture** dialog box. Navigate to the location in which your student files are stored, click **jpg11A_Beach**, and then click **Insert** to insert the picture in the placeholder.

3 To the right of the picture, click in the title placeholder. Type **Prepare to be Amazed!** Below the title, click in the caption placeholder, and then type **Mountain, sea, volcano. Our tour guides are experts in the history, geography, culture, and flora and fauna of Hawaii.** Compare your screen with Figure 11.16.

Figure 11.16

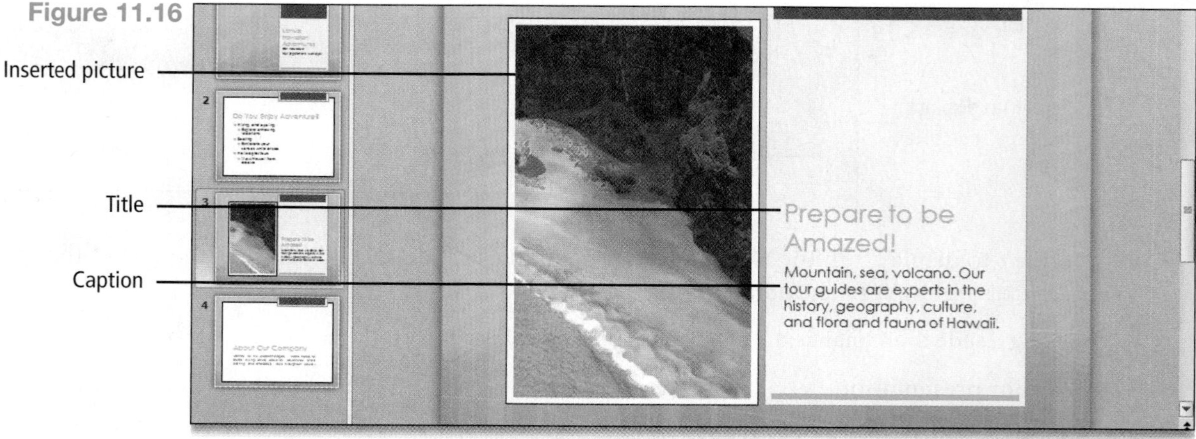

4 Display **Slide 2**. In the placeholder on the right side of the slide, click the **Insert Picture from File** button. Navigate to your student files, and then click **jpg11A_Helicopter**. Click **Insert**.

Activity 11.09 | Applying a Style to a Picture

The Picture Tools add the Format tab to the Ribbon, which provides numerous ***styles*** that you can apply to a picture, text, or an object.

1 With **Slide 2** displayed, if necessary, click the picture of the helicopter to select it. On the Ribbon, notice that the Picture Tools are active and the Format tab displays.

Small circles and squares—***sizing handles***—surround the inserted picture and indicate that the picture is selected and can be modified or formatted. The ***rotation handle***—a green circle above the picture—provides a way to rotate a selected image.

2 On the **Format tab**, in the **Picture Styles group**, click the **More** button to display the **Picture Styles** gallery, and then compare your screen with Figure 11.17

Figure 11.17

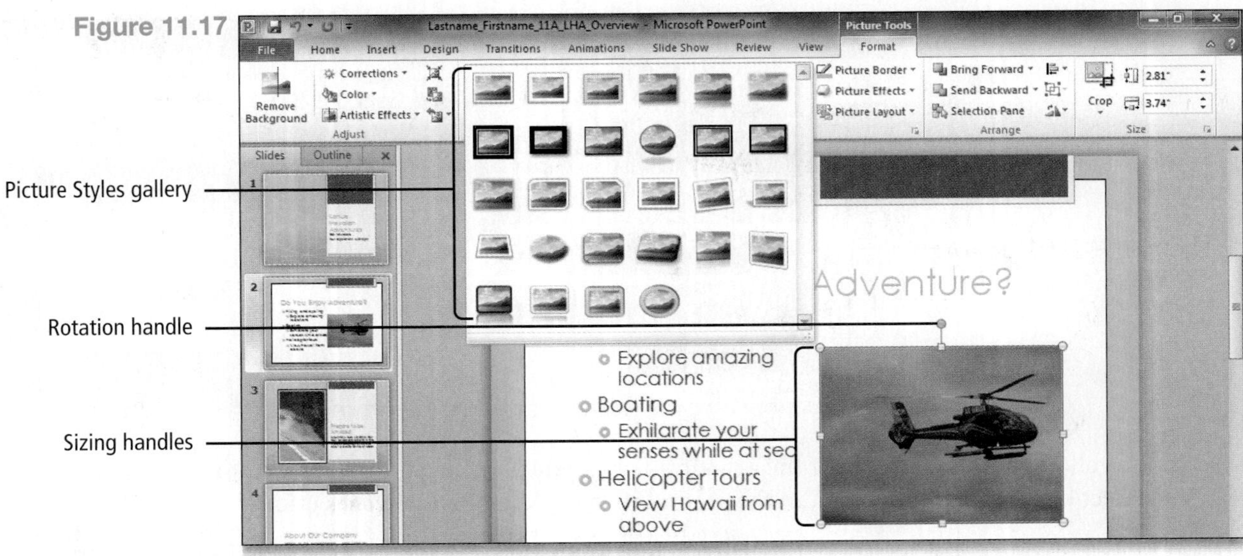

3 In the gallery, point to several of the picture styles to display the ScreenTips and to view the effect on your picture. In the first row, click **Drop Shadow Rectangle**. Click in a blank area of the slide, and then compare your screen with Figure 11.18.

Figure 11.18

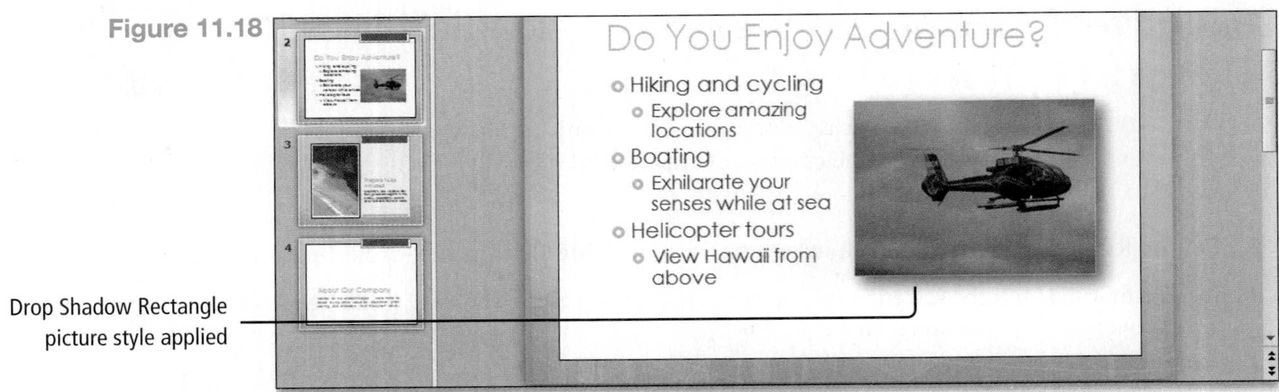

4 **Save** the presentation.

Activity 11.10 | Applying and Removing Picture Artistic Effects

Artistic effects are formats applied to images that make pictures resemble sketches or paintings.

1 With **Slide 2** displayed, select the picture of the helicopter.

2 Click the **Format tab**, and then in the **Adjust group**, click the **Artistic Effects** button to display the **Artistic Effects** gallery. Compare your screen with Figure 11.19.

Figure 11.19

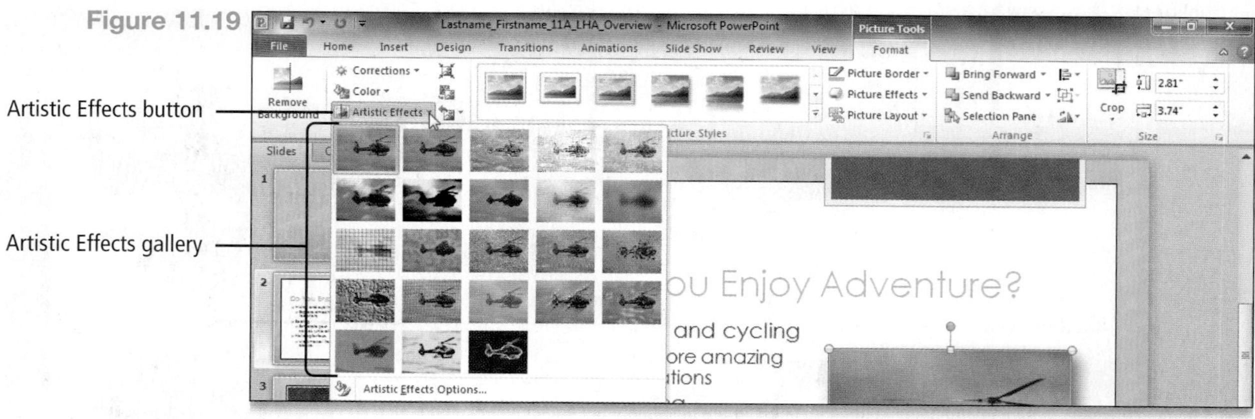

3 In the gallery, point to several of the artistic effects to display the ScreenTips and to have Live Preview display the effect on your picture. Then, in the second row, click the **Paint Strokes** effect.

4 With the picture still selected, on the **Format tab**, in the **Adjust group**, click the **Artistic Effects** button to display the gallery. In the first row, click the first effect—**None**—to remove the effect from the picture and restore the previous formatting.

5 **Save** your presentation.

Objective 4 | Print and View a Presentation

View the video on the Companion Web Site or in MyITLab

Activity 11.11 | Viewing a Slide Show

When you view a presentation as an electronic slide show, the entire slide fills the computer screen, and an audience can view your presentation if your computer is connected to a projection system.

1 On the Ribbon, click the **Slide Show tab**. In the **Start Slide Show group**, click the **From Beginning** button.

The first slide fills the screen, displaying the presentation as the audience would see it if your computer was connected to a projection system.

2 Click the left mouse button or press Spacebar to advance to the second slide. Continue to click or press Spacebar until the last slide displays, and then click or press Spacebar one more time to display a black slide.

After the last slide in a presentation, a ***black slide*** displays, indicating that the presentation is over.

3 With the black slide displayed, click the left mouse button or press Spacebar to exit the slide show and return to the presentation.

Activity 11.12 | Inserting Headers and Footers

A ***header*** is text that prints at the top of each sheet of ***slide handouts*** or ***notes pages***. Slide handouts are printed images of slides on a sheet of paper. Notes pages are printouts that contain the slide image on the top half of the page and notes that you have created on the Notes pane in the lower half of the page. In addition to headers, you can insert ***footers***—text that displays at the bottom of every slide or that prints at the bottom of a sheet of slide handouts or notes pages.

1 Click the **Insert tab**, and then in the **Text group**, click the **Header & Footer** button to display the **Header and Footer** dialog box.

2 In the **Header and Footer** dialog box, click the **Notes and Handouts tab**. Under **Include on page**, select the **Date and time** check box, and as you do so, watch the Preview box in the lower right corner of the Header and Footer dialog box.

The Preview box indicates the placeholders on the printed Notes and Handouts pages. When you select the Date and time check box, the placeholder in the upper right corner is outlined, indicating the location in which the date will display.

3 If necessary, click the Update automatically option button so that the current date prints on the notes and handouts each time the presentation is printed. If necessary, *clear* the Header check box to omit this element.

4 Select the **Page number** and **Footer** check boxes, and then notice that the insertion point displays in the **Footer** box. Using your own name, type **Lastname_Firstname_11A_LHA_Overview** so that the file name displays as a footer, and then compare your dialog box with Figure 11.20.

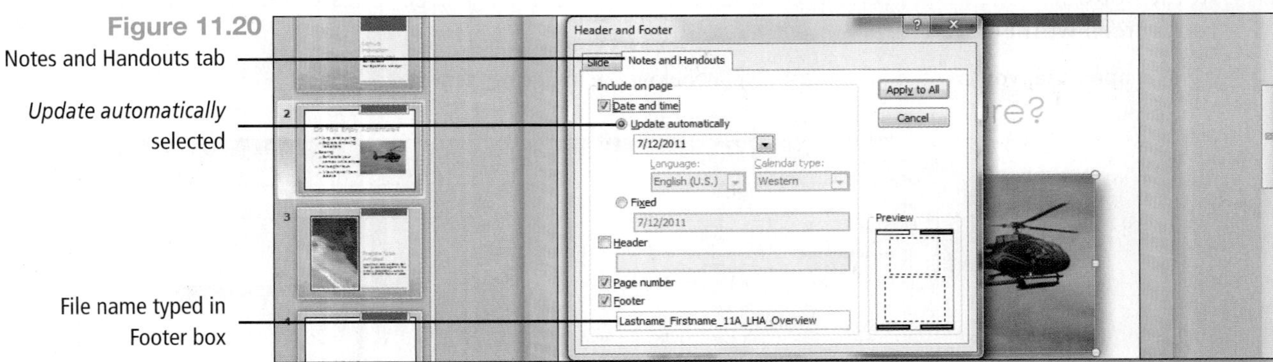

5 In the upper right corner of the dialog box, click **Apply to All**. **Save** your presentation.

Activity 11.13 | Printing a Presentation

Use Backstage view to preview the arrangement of slides on the handouts and notes pages.

1 Display **Slide 1**. Click the **File tab** to display **Backstage** view, and then click the **Print tab**.

The Print tab in Backstage view displays the tools you need to select your settings and also to view a preview of your presentation. On the right, Print Preview displays your presentation exactly as it will print.

2 In the **Settings group**, click **Full Page Slides**, and then compare your screen with Figure 11.21.

The gallery displays either the default print setting—Full Page Slides—or the most recently selected print setting.

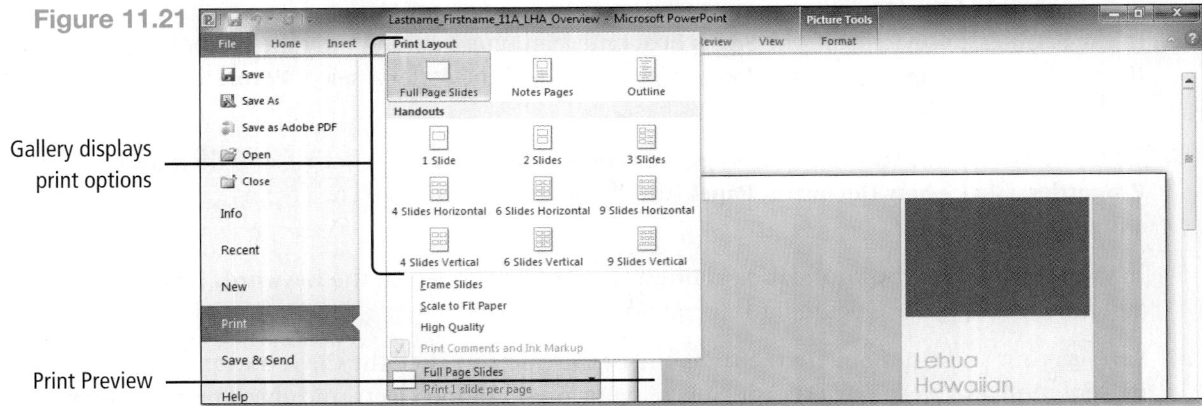

3 In the gallery, under **Handouts**, click **4 Slides Horizontal**. Notice that the **Print Preview** on the right displays the slide handout, and that the current date, file name, and page number display in the header and footer.

In the Settings group, the Portrait Orientation option displays so that you can change the print orientation from Portrait to Landscape. The Portrait Orientation option does not display when Full Page Slides is chosen.

4 To print your handout, be sure your system is connected to a printer, and then in the **Print group**, click the **Print** button.

Backstage view closes and your file redisplays in the PowerPoint window.

5 Click the **File tab** to display **Backstage** view, and then click the **Print tab**. In the **Settings group**, click **4 Slides Horizontal**, and then under **Print Layout**, click **Notes Pages** to view the presentation notes for **Slide 1**; recall that you created notes for **Slide 4**.

Indicated below the Notes page are the current slide number and the number of pages that will print when Notes page is selected. You can use the Next Page and Previous Page arrows to display each Notes page in the presentation.

6 At the bottom of the **Print Preview**, click the **Next Page** button three times so that **Page 4** displays. Compare your screen with Figure 11.22.

The notes that you created for Slide 4 display below the image of the slide.

Figure 11.22

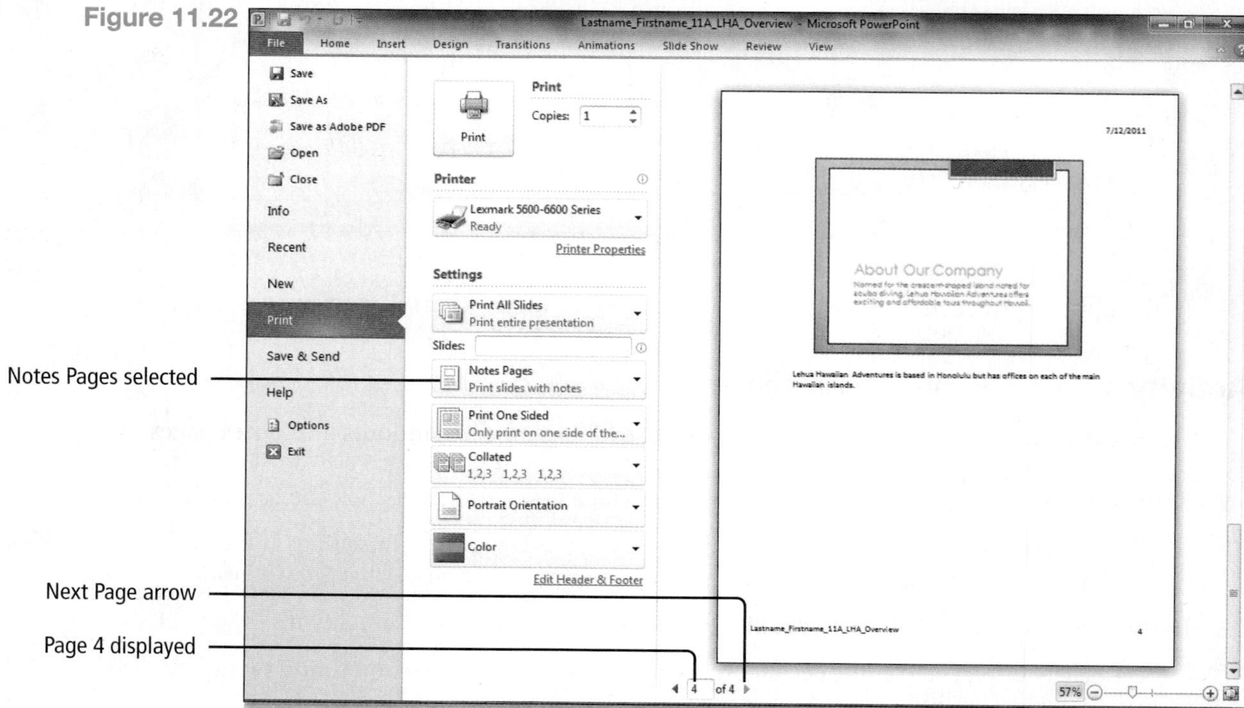

7 In the **Settings group**, click in the **Slides** box, and then type **4** so that only the Notes pages for **Slide 4** will print. In the **Settings group**, click **Notes Pages**, and then below the gallery, select **Frame Slides**. In the **Print group**, click the **Print** button to print the Notes page.

8 Click the **File tab** to redisplay **Backstage** view, be sure the **Info tab** is active, and then in the third panel, click **Properties**. Click **Show Document Panel**, and then in the **Author** box, delete any text and type your firstname and lastname.

9 In the **Subject** box, type your course name and section number. In the **Keywords** box, type **company overview** and then **Close** the Document Information Panel.

10 **Save** your presentation. On the right end of the title bar, click the **Close** button to close the presentation and close PowerPoint. Submit your presentation electronically or print **Handouts, 4 Slides Horizontal**, as directed by your instructor.

End **You have completed Project 11A**

Project 11B New Product Announcement

Project Activities

In Activities 11.14 through 11.23, you will combine two presentations that the marketing team at Lehua Adventure Travels developed describing their new Ecotours. You will combine the presentations by inserting slides from one presentation into another, and then you will rearrange and delete slides. You will also apply font formatting and slide transitions to the presentation. Your completed presentation will look similar to Figure 11.23.

Project Files

For Project 11B, you will need the following files:

p11B_Ecotours
p11B_Slides

You will save your presentation as:

Lastname_Firstname_11B_Ecotours

Project Results

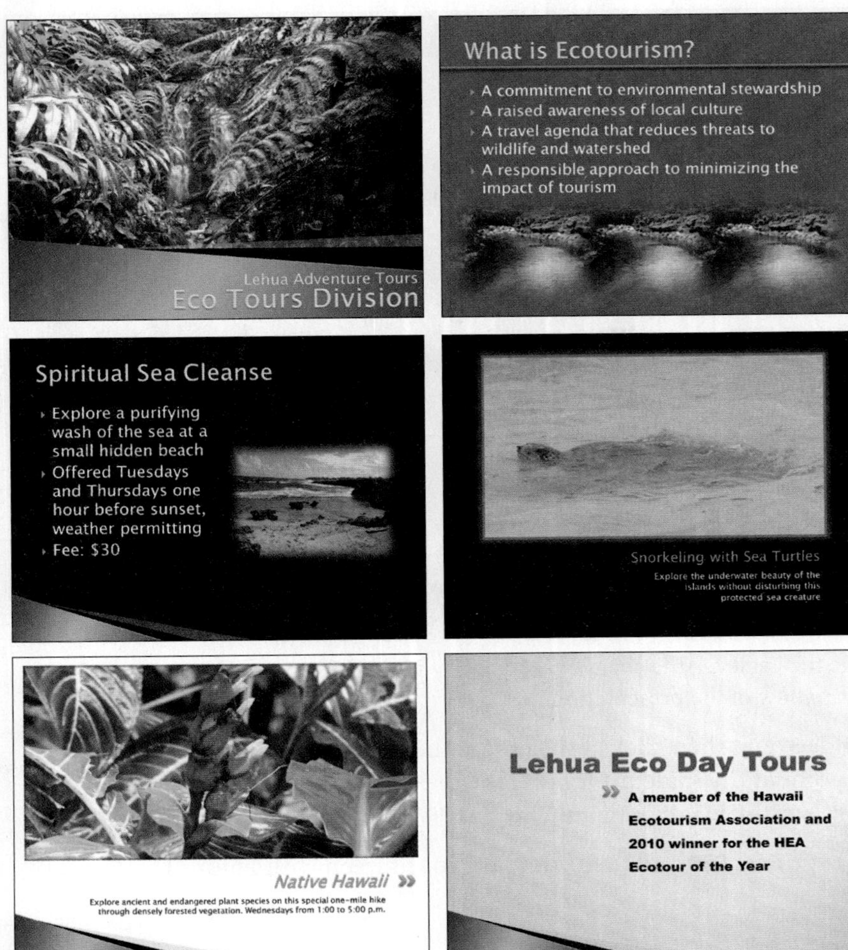

Figure 11.23
Project 11B Ecotours

GO! All In One | Chapter 11

Objective 5 | Edit an Existing Presentation

View the video on the Companion Web Site or in MyITLab

Recall that editing refers to the process of adding, deleting, and modifying presentation content. You can edit presentation content in either the Slide pane or the Slides/Outline pane.

Activity 11.14 | Displaying and Editing the Presentation Outline

You can display the presentation outline in the Slides/Outline pane and edit the presentation text. Changes that you make in the outline are immediately displayed in the Slide pane.

1 **Start** PowerPoint. From your student files, open **p11B_Ecotours**. On the **File tab**, click **Save As**, navigate to your **All In One Chapter 11** folder, and then using your own name, save the file as **Lastname_Firstname_11B_Ecotours**

2 In the **Slides/Outline pane**, click the **Outline tab** to display the presentation outline. If necessary, below the Slides/Outline pane, drag the scroll box all the way to the left so that the slide numbers display. Compare your screen with Figure 11.24.

Each slide in the outline displays the slide number, slide icon, and the slide title in bold.

Figure 11.24

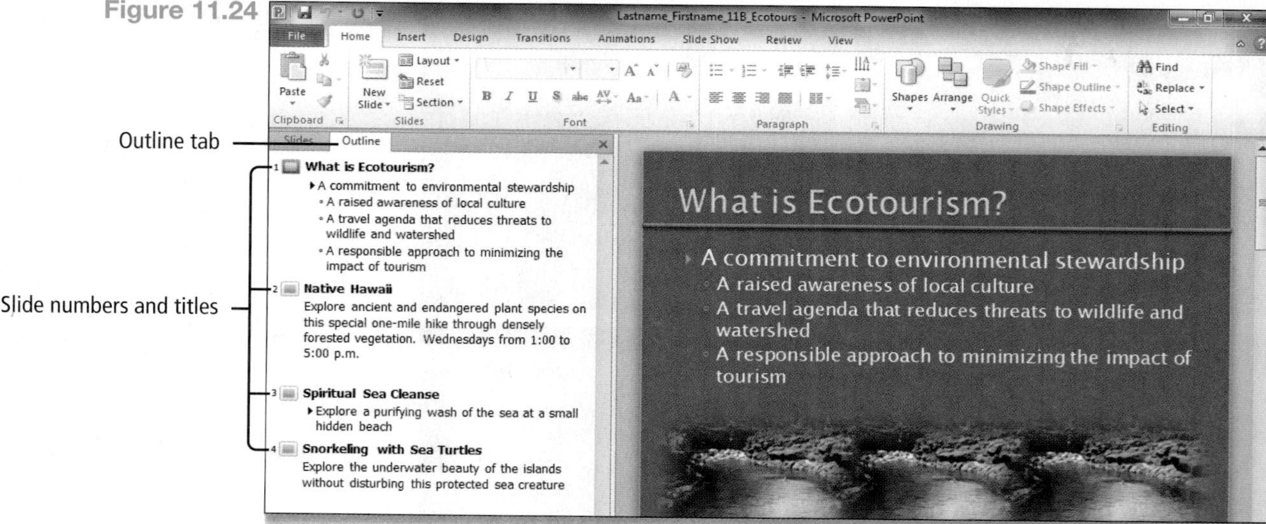

3 In the **Outline tab**, in **Slide 1**, select the last three bullet points. On the **Home tab**, in the **Paragraph group**, click the **Decrease List Level** button one time to decrease the list level of the selected bullet points.

When you type in the outline or change the list level, the changes also display in the Slide pane. Displaying the Outline tab enables you to view the entire flow of the presentation.

4 In the **Outline tab**, click anywhere in **Slide 3**, and then click at the end of the last bullet point after the word *beach*. Press Enter to create a new bullet point at the same list level as the previous bullet point. Type **Offered Tuesdays and Thursdays one hour before sunset, weather permitting**

5 Press Enter to create a new bullet point. Type **Fee: $30** and then compare your screen with Figure 11.25.

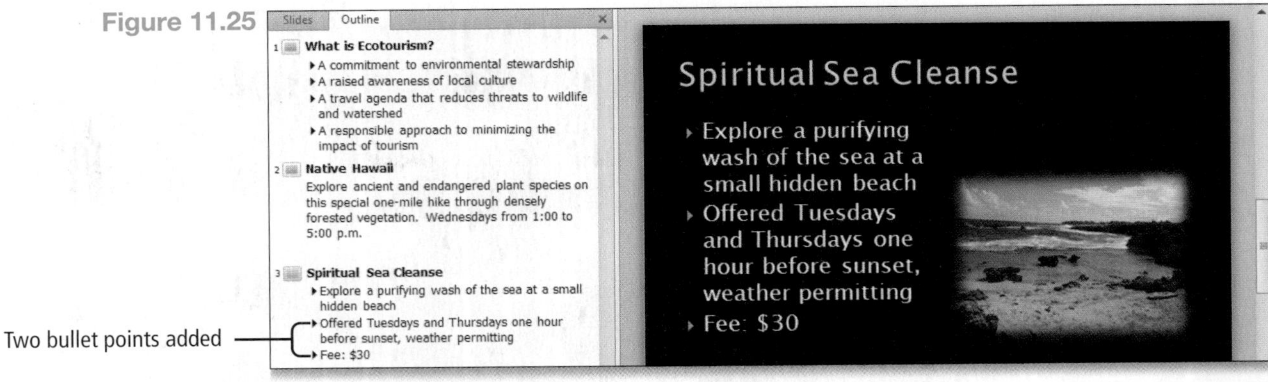

Figure 11.25

6 In the **Slides/Outline pane**, click the **Slides tab** to display the slide thumbnails, and then **Save** the presentation.

Activity 11.15 | Inserting Slides from an Existing Presentation

In this activity, you will insert slides from an existing presentation into your 11B_Ecotours presentation.

1 Display **Slide 1**. On the **Home tab**, in the **Slides group**, click the **New Slide button arrow** to display the **Slide Layout** gallery and additional commands for inserting slides. Compare your screen with Figure 11.26.

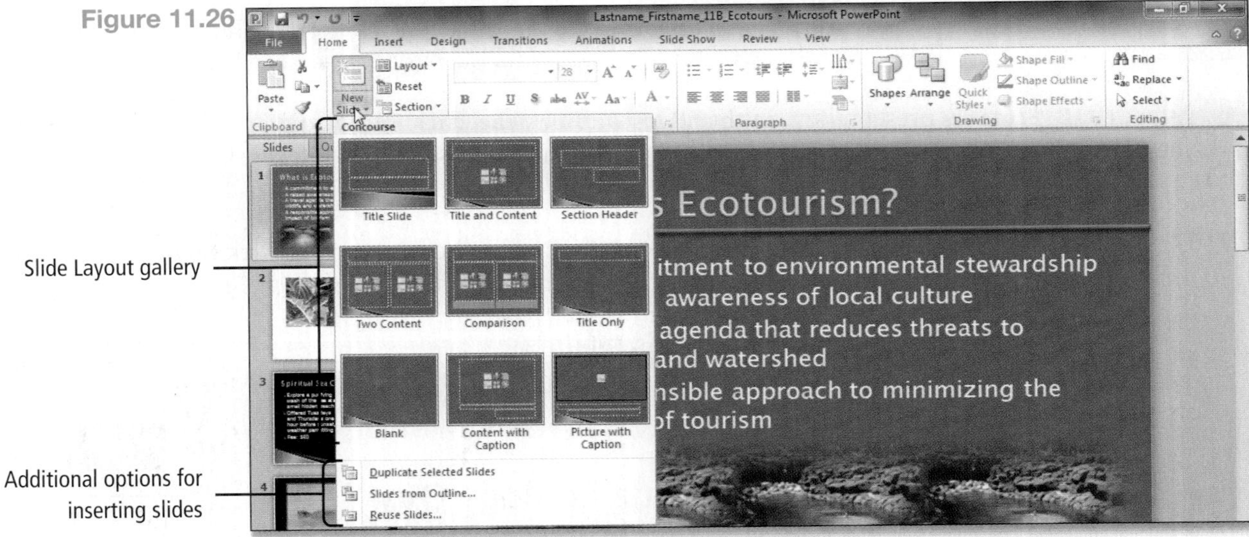

Figure 11.26

2 Below the gallery, click **Reuse Slides** to open the Reuse Slides pane on the right side of the PowerPoint window.

3 In the **Reuse Slides** pane, click the **Browse** button, and then click **Browse File**. In the **Browse** dialog box, navigate to the location where your student files are stored, and then double-click **p11B_Slides** to display the slides in the Reuse Slides pane.

4 At the bottom of the **Reuse Slides** pane, select the **Keep source formatting** check box, and then compare your screen with Figure 11.27.

By selecting the *Keep source formatting* check box, you retain the existing formatting applied to the slides when inserted into the current presentation. When the *Keep source formatting* check box is cleared, the theme formatting of the presentation in which the slides are inserted is applied.

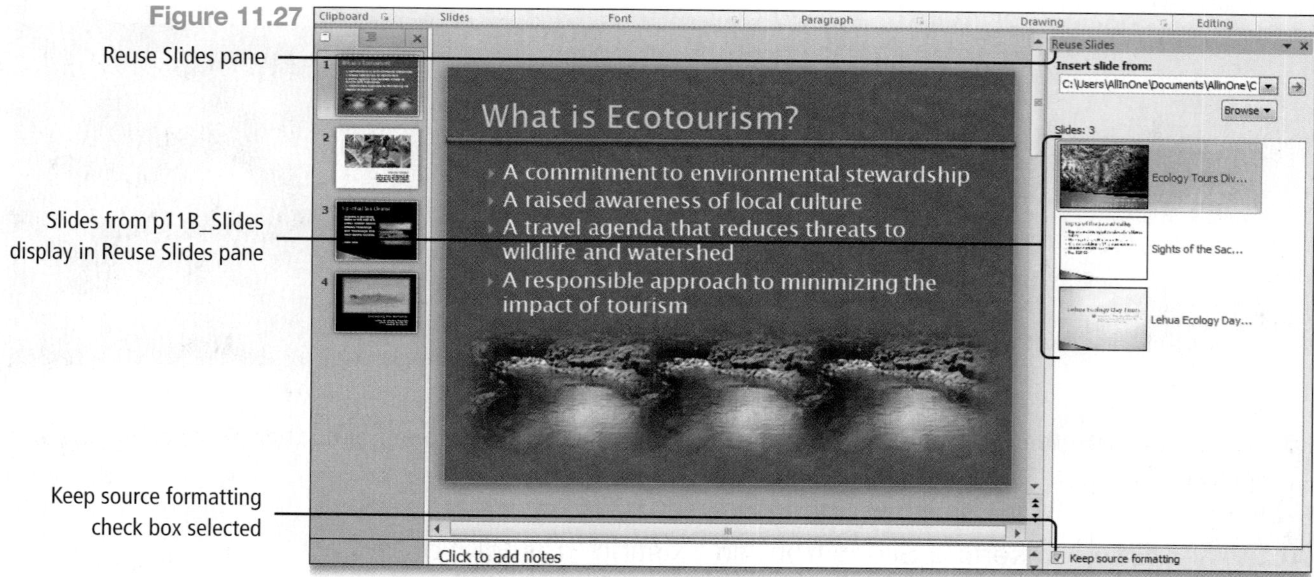

Figure 11.27

5 In the **Reuse Slides** pane, click the first slide—**Ecology Tours Division**—to insert the slide into the current presentation after Slide 1, and then notice that the original slide background formatting is retained.

> **Note | Inserting Slides**
>
> You can insert slides into your presentation in any order; remember to display the slide that will precede the slide that you want to insert.

6 In your **11B_Ecotours** presentation, in the **Slides/Outline pane**, click **Slide 5** to display it in the **Slide pane**. In the **Reuse Slides** pane, click the second slide and then click the third slide to insert both slides after **Slide 5**.

Your presentation now contains seven slides.

7 On **Slide 7**, point to *Lehua*, and then right-click to display the shortcut menu. Click **Ignore all**. Use the same technique to ignore the spelling of the word *Ecotour*. Compare your screen with Figure 11.28.

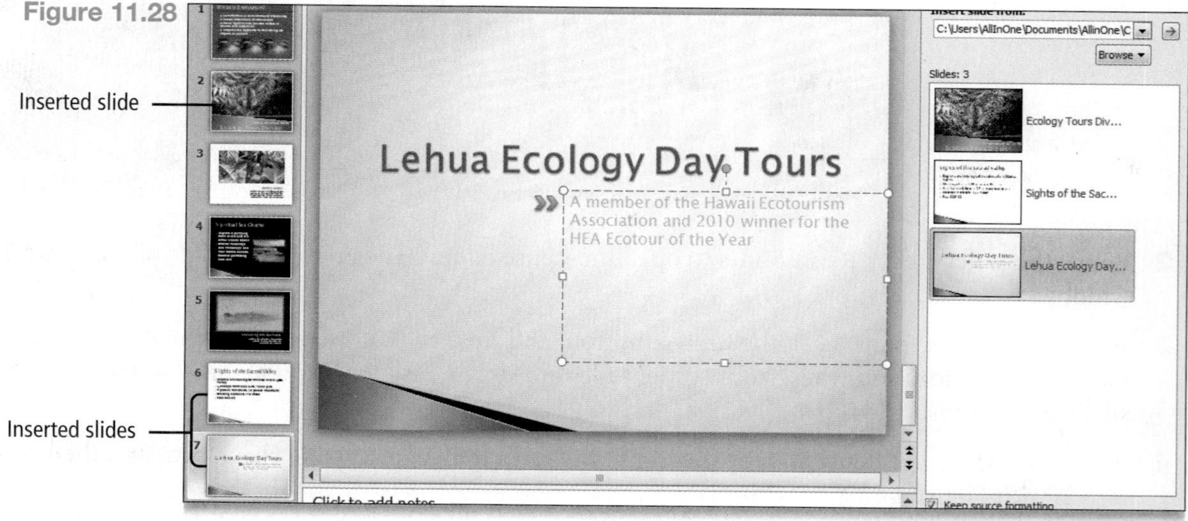

Figure 11.28

8 **Close** the **Reuse Slides** pane; click **Save**.

Activity 11.16 | Finding and Replacing Text

The Replace command enables you to locate all occurrences of specified text and replace it with alternative text.

1 Display **Slide 1**. On the **Home tab**, in the **Editing group**, click the **Replace** button. In the **Replace** dialog box, in the **Find what** box, type **Ecology** and then in the **Replace with** box, type **Eco** Compare your screen with Figure 11.29.

Figure 11.29

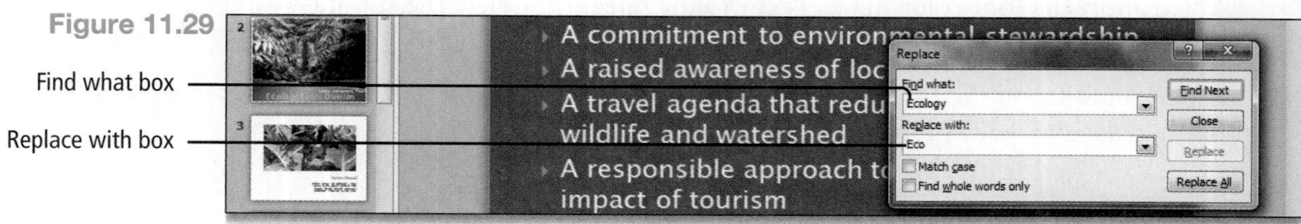

2 In the **Replace** dialog box, click the **Replace All** button.

A message box displays indicating the number of replacements (2) that were made.

3 In the message box, click **OK**, **Close** the **Replace** dialog box, and then click **Save**.

Objective 6 | Format a Presentation

Formatting refers to changing the appearance of the text, layout, and design of a slide. You will find it easiest to do most of your formatting changes in PowerPoint in the Slide pane.

View the video on the Companion Web Site or in MyITLab

Activity 11.17 | Changing Fonts, Font Sizes, Font Styles, and Font Colors

Font styles include bold, italic, and underline. You can apply any combination of these styles to presentation text to draw the reader's eye to important text.

1 On the right side of the **Slides/Outline pane**, drag the scroll box down until **Slide 7** displays, and then click **Slide 7** to display it in the **Slides** pane.

2 Select the title text—*Lehua Eco Day Tours.* Point to the Mini toolbar, and then click the **Font button arrow** [Calibri (Headings)] to display the available fonts. Click **Arial Black**.

3 Select the light green text in the placeholder below the title, and then on the Mini toolbar, change the **Font** to **Arial Black** and the **Font Size** to **23**. Then, click the **Font Color button arrow**, and compare your screen with Figure 11.30.

The colors in the top row of the color gallery are the colors associated with the presentation theme—*Concourse*. The colors in the rows below the first row are light and dark variations of the theme colors.

Figure 11.30

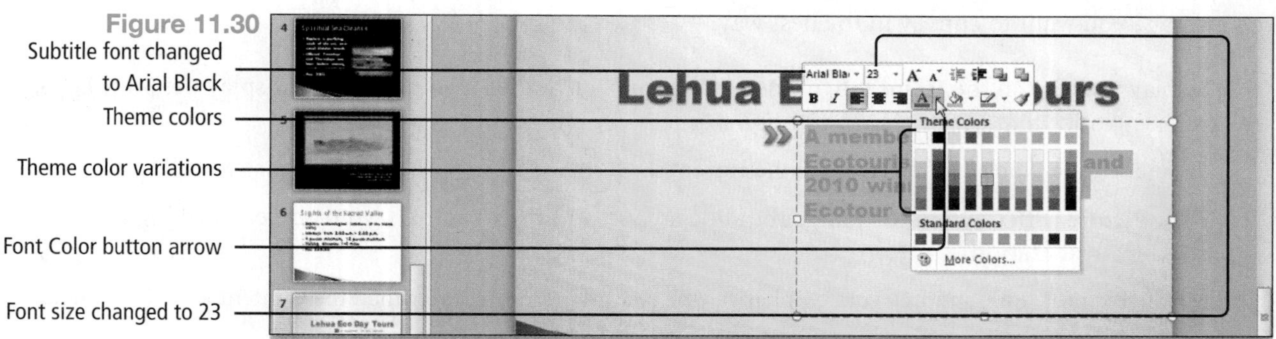

4 In the second column of colors, click the first color—**Black, Text 1**—to change the font color. Notice that on the Home tab and Mini toolbar, the lower part of the Font Color button displays the most recently applied font color—Black.

When you click the Font Color button instead of the Font Color button arrow, the color displayed in the lower part of the Font Color button is applied to selected text without displaying the color gallery.

5 Display **Slide 2**, and then select the title *Eco Tours Division*. On the Mini toolbar, click the **Font Color button** to apply the font color **Black, Text 1** to the selection. Select the subtitle—*Lehua Adventure Tours*—and then change the **Font Color** to **Black, Text 1**.

6 Display **Slide 3**, and then select the title—*Native Hawaii*. From the Mini toolbar, apply **Bold** and **Italic**, and then **Save** your presentation.

Activity 11.18 | Aligning Text and Changing Line Spacing

In PowerPoint, ***text alignment*** refers to the horizontal placement of text within a placeholder. You can align left, centered, right, or justified.

1 Display **Slide 2**. Click anywhere in the title—*Eco Tours Division*. On the **Home tab**, in the **Paragraph group**, click the **Align Text Right** button to right align the text within the placeholder.

2 Display **Slide 7**. Click anywhere in the text below the title. In the **Paragraph group**, click the **Line Spacing** button. In the list, click **1.5** to change from single-spacing between lines to one-and-a-half spacing between lines. **Save** your presentation, and then compare your screen with Figure 11.31.

Figure 11.31

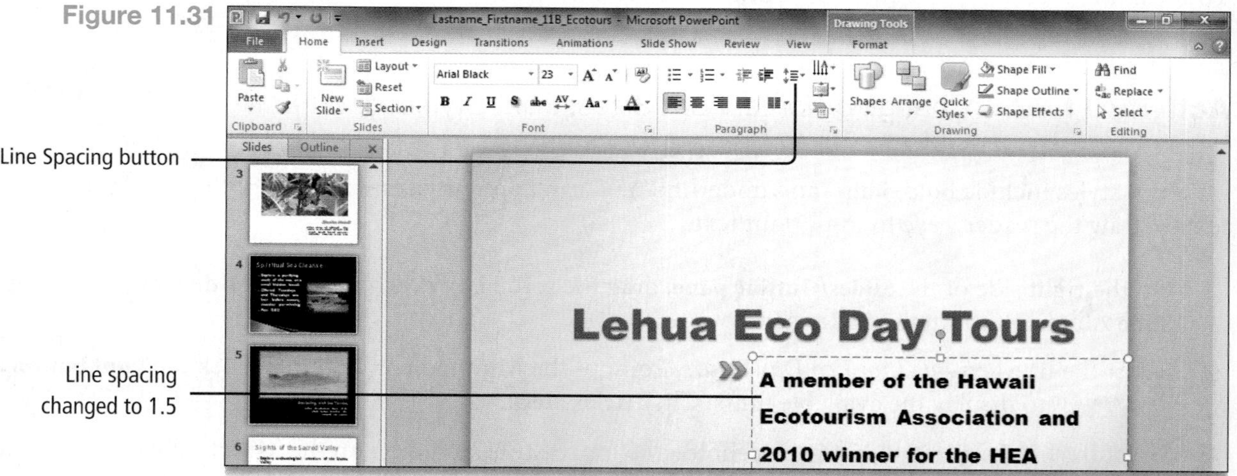

Activity 11.19 | Modifying Slide Layout

Recall that the slide layout defines the placement of the content placeholders on a slide. When you design your slides, consider the content that you want to include, and then choose a layout with the elements that will display the message you want to convey in the best way.

1 Display **Slide 3**. On the **Home tab**, in the **Slides group**, click the **Layout** button to display the **Slide Layout** gallery. Notice that *Content with Caption* is selected.

The selection indicates the layout of the current slide.

2 Click **Picture with Caption** to change the slide layout, and then compare your screen with Figure 11.32. **Save** your presentation.

The Picture with Caption layout emphasizes the picture more effectively than the Content with Caption layout.

Figure 11.32

Objective 7 | Use Slide Sorter View

View the video on the Companion Web Site or in MyITLab

Slide Sorter view displays thumbnails of all of the slides in a presentation. Use Slide Sorter view to rearrange and delete slides and to apply formatting to multiple slides.

Activity 11.20 | Deleting Slides in Slide Sorter View

1 In the lower right corner of the PowerPoint window, click the **Slide Sorter** button to display all of the slide thumbnails. Compare your screen with Figure 11.33.

Your slides may display larger or smaller than those shown in Figure 11.33.

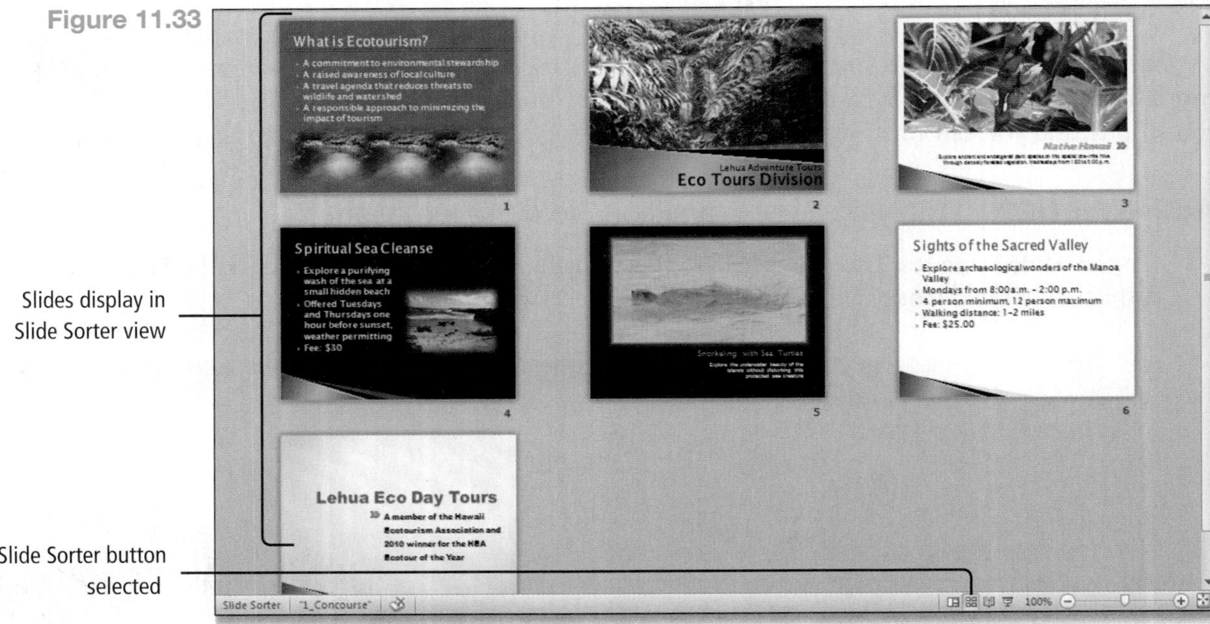

Figure 11.33

2 Click **Slide 6**, and notice that a thick outline surrounds the slide, indicating that it is selected. On your keyboard, press Delete to delete the slide. Click **Save**.

Activity 11.21 | Moving Slides in Slide Sorter View

1 With the presentation displayed in Slide Sorter view, point to **Slide 2**. Hold down the left mouse button, and then drag the slide to the left until the vertical move bar and pointer indicating the position to which the slide will be moved is positioned to the left of **Slide 1**, as shown in Figure 11.34.

Figure 11.34

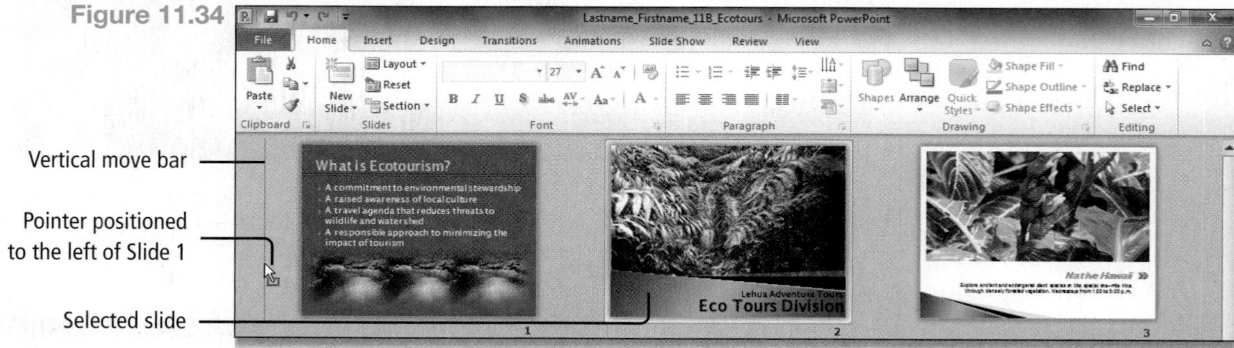

2 Release the mouse button to move the slide to the Slide 1 position in the presentation.

3 Click **Slide 4**, hold down Ctrl, and then click **Slide 5**.

Both slides are outlined, indicating that both are selected. By holding down Ctrl, you can create a group of selected slides.

4 Point to either of the selected slides, hold down the left mouse button, and then drag to position the vertical move bar to the left of **Slide 3**. Release the mouse button to move the two slides.

5 In the status bar, click the **Normal** button to return to Normal view. **Save** your presentation.

Objective 8 | Apply Slide Transitions

Slide transitions are the motion effects that occur in Slide Show view when you move from one slide to the next during a presentation. You can choose from a variety of transitions, and you can control the speed and method with which the slides advance.

View the video on the Companion Web Site or in MyITLab

Activity 11.22 | Applying Slide Transitions to a Presentation

1 Display **Slide 1**. On the **Transitions tab**, in the **Transition to This Slide group**, click the **More** button to display the **Transitions** gallery. Compare your screen with Figure 11.35.

Figure 11.35

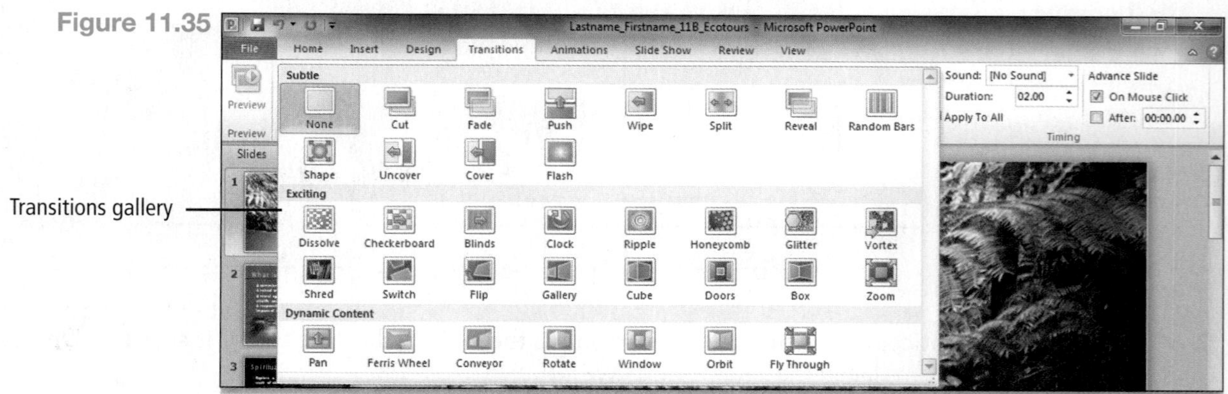

2 Under **Exciting**, click **Doors** to apply and view the transition. In the **Transition to This Slide group**, click the **Effect Options** button to display the directions from which the slide enters the screen. Click **Horizontal**.

The Effect Options vary depending upon the selected transition and include the direction from which the slide enters the screen or the shape in which the slide displays during the transition.

3 In the **Timing group**, notice that the **Duration** box displays *01.40*, indicating that the transition lasts 1.40 seconds. Click the **Duration** box **up spin arrow** two times so that *01.75* displays. Under **Advance Slide**, verify that the **On Mouse Click** check box is selected; select it if necessary. Compare your screen with Figure 11.36.

When the On Mouse Click option is selected, the presenter controls when the current slide advances to the next slide by clicking the mouse button or by pressing s.

Figure 11.36

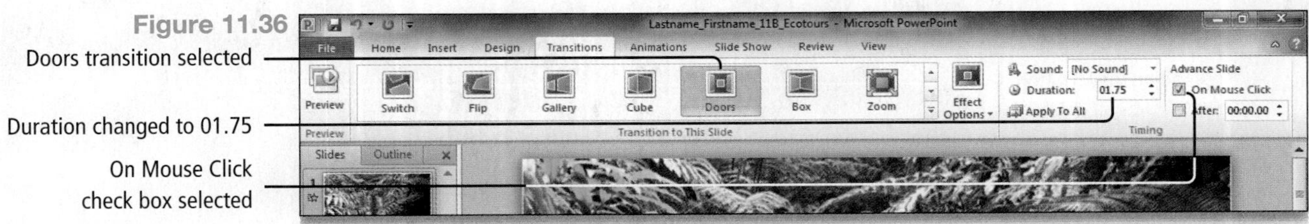

4 In the **Timing group**, click the **Apply To All** button so that the Doors, Horizontal with a Duration of 1.75 seconds transition is applied to all of the slides in the presentation.

Notice that in the Slides/Outline pane, a star displays below the slide number providing a visual cue that a transition has been applied to the slide.

5 Click the **Slide Show tab**. In the **Start Slide Show group**, click the **From Beginning** button, and then view your presentation, clicking the mouse button to advance through the slides. When the black slide displays, click the mouse button one more time to display the presentation in Normal view. **Save** your presentation.

Activity 11.23 | Displaying a Presentation in Reading View

Organizations frequently conduct online meetings when participants are unable to meet in one location. The ***Reading View*** in PowerPoint displays a presentation in a manner similar to a slide show but the taskbar, title bar, and status bar remain available in the presentation window. Thus, a presenter can easily facilitate an online conference by switching to another window without closing the slide show.

1 In the lower right corner of the PowerPoint window, click the **Reading View** button. Compare your screen with Figure 11.37.

In Reading View, the status bar contains the Next and Previous buttons, which are used to navigate in the presentation, and the Menu button which is used to print, copy, and edit slides.

Figure 11.37

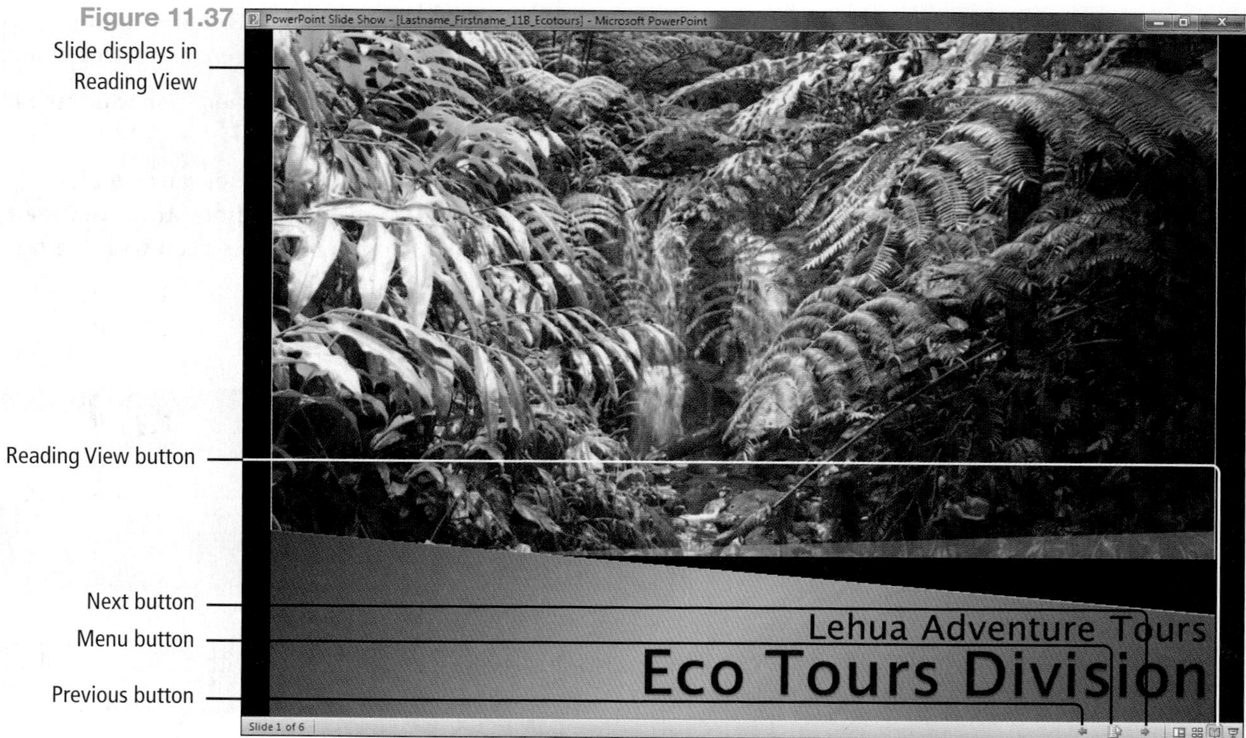

2 In the status bar, click the **Next** button to display **Slide 2**. Press Spacebar to display **Slide 3**. Click the left mouse button to display **Slide 4**. In the status bar, click the **Previous** button to display **Slide 3**.

3 In the status bar, click the **Menu** button to display the Reading View menu, and then click **End Show** to return to Normal view.

4 On the **Insert tab**, in the **Text group**, click the **Header & Footer** button, and then click the **Notes and Handouts tab**. Under **Include on page**, select the **Date and time** check box, and if necessary, select **Update automatically**. Clear the **Header** check box, and then select the **Page number** and **Footer** check boxes. In the **Footer** box, using your own name, type **Lastname_Firstname_11B_Ecotours** and then click **Apply to All**.

5 Display **Backstage** view, and then on the right, click **Properties**. Click **Show Document Panel**, and then in the **Author** box, delete any text and type your firstname and lastname. In the **Subject** box, type your course name and section number, and in the **Keywords** box, type **ecotours, ecotourism** **Close** the Document Information Panel.

6 **Save** your presentation. Submit your presentation electronically or print **Handouts, 6 Slides Horizontal**, as directed by your instructor.

7 **Close** the presentation and **Exit** PowerPoint.

End **You have completed Project 11B**

Project 11C Employee Training Presentation

Project Activities

In Activities 11.24 through 11.37, you will format a presentation that describes important safety guidelines for employees at Fascination Entertainment Group. Your completed presentation will look similar to Figure 11.38.

Project Files

For Project 11C, you will need the following file:

p11C_Safety

You will save your presentation as:

Lastname_Firstname_11C_Safety

Project Results

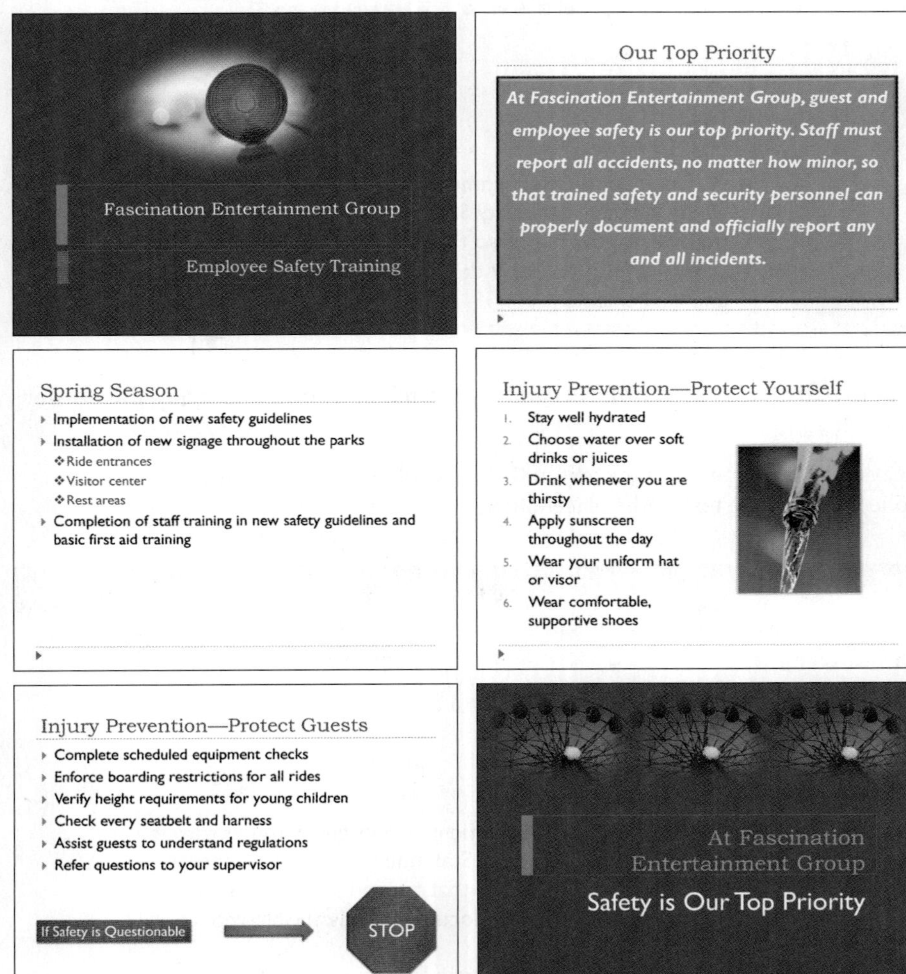

Figure 11.38
Project 11C Safety

Objective 9 | Format Numbered and Bulleted Lists

You can format slide content by changing the bulleted and numbered list styles and colors.

Activity 11.24 | Selecting Placeholder Text

View the video on the Companion Web Site or in MyITLab

You can format placeholder contents by selecting text or by selecting the entire placeholder.

1 **Start** PowerPoint. From your student files, open **p11C_Safety**. On the **File tab**, click **Save As**, navigate to your **All In One Chapter 11** folder, and then using your own name, save the file as **Lastname_Firstname_11C_Safety** Take a moment to become familiar with the contents of this presentation.

2 Display **Slide 2**. Click anywhere in the content placeholder with the single bullet point, and then compare your screen with Figure 11.39.

A dashed border displays, indicating that you can make editing changes to the placeholder text.

Figure 11.39

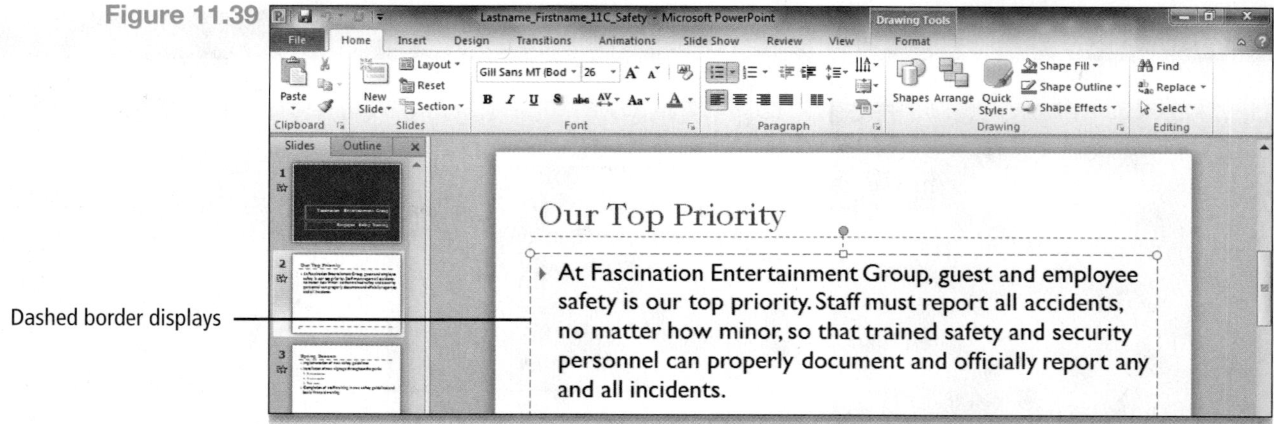

3 Point anywhere on the dashed border to display the pointer, and then click one time to display the border as a solid line. Compare your screen with Figure 11.40.

When a placeholder's border displays as a solid line, all of the text in the placeholder is selected, and any formatting changes that you make will be applied to *all* of the text in the placeholder.

Figure 11.40

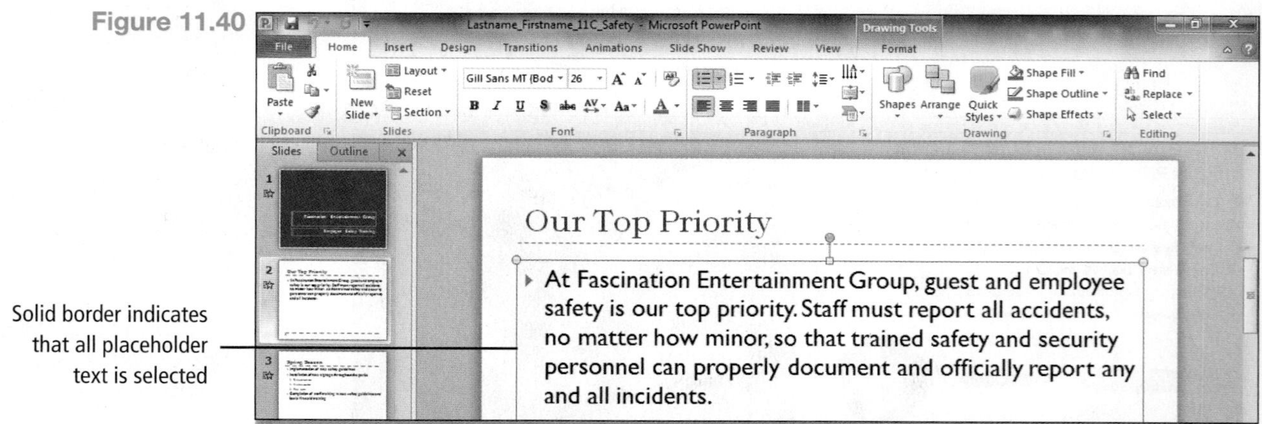

4 With the border of the placeholder displaying as a solid line, click in the **Font Size** box 44 to select the number, and then type **30** and press Enter. Notice that the font size of *all* of the placeholder text increases. **Save** your presentation.

Activity 11.25 | Changing a Bulleted List to a Numbered List

1 Display **Slide 4**, and then click anywhere in the bulleted list. Point to the blue dashed border to display the pointer, and then click one time to display the border as a solid line indicating that all of the text is selected.

2 On the **Home tab**, in the **Paragraph group**, click the **Numbering** button. Compare your slide with Figure 11.41, and then **Save** your presentation.

All of the bullet symbols are converted to numbers. The color of the numbers is determined by the presentation theme.

Figure 11.41

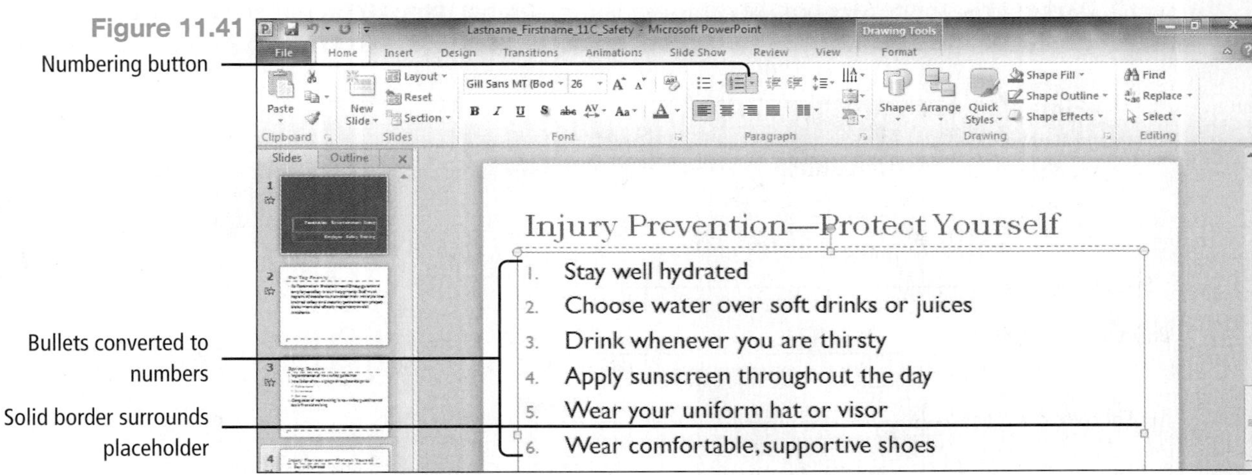

> **Alert! | Did You Display the Numbering Gallery?**
>
> If you clicked the Numbering button arrow instead of the Numbering button, the Numbering gallery displays. Click the Numbering button arrow again to close the gallery, and then click the Numbering button to convert the bullets to numbers.

Activity 11.26 | Modifying a Bulleted List Style

The presentation theme includes default styles for the bullet points in content placeholders. You can customize a bullet by changing its style, color, and size.

1 Display **Slide 3**, and then select the three second-level bullet points—*Ride entrances*, *Visitor center*, and *Rest areas.*

2 On the **Home tab**, in the **Paragraph group**, click the **Bullets button arrow** to display the **Bullets** gallery, and then compare your screen with Figure 11.42.

The Bullets gallery displays several bullet characters that you can apply to the selection.

Figure 11.42

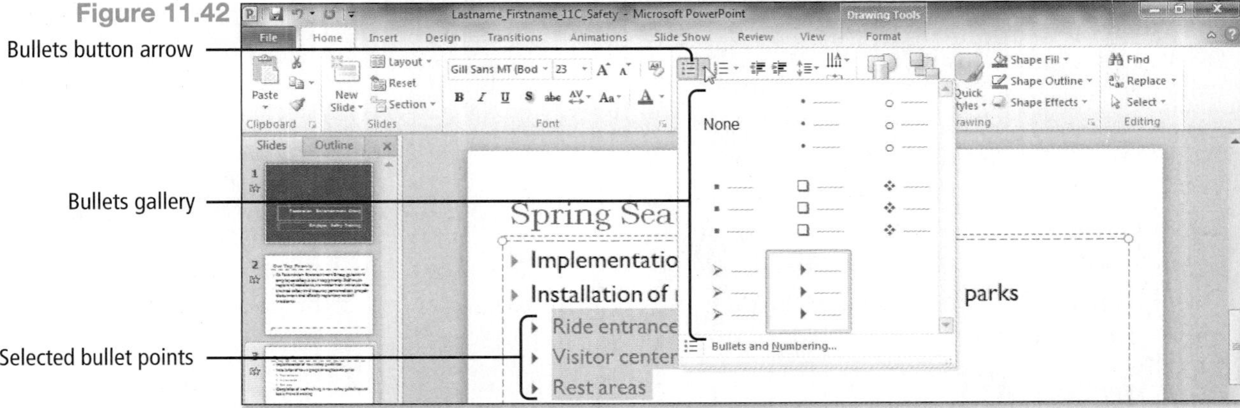

> **Alert! | Were the Bullets Removed?**
>
> If the bullets were removed, then you clicked the Bullets button instead of the Bullets button arrow. Click the Bullets button arrow, and then continue with Step 3.

3 At the bottom of the **Bullets** gallery, click **Bullets and Numbering**. In the **Bullets and Numbering** dialog box, point to each bullet style to display its ScreenTip. Then, in the second row, click **Star Bullets**.

4 Below the gallery, click the **Color** button. Under **Theme Colors**, in the sixth column, click the fifth color—**Red, Accent 2, Darker 25%**. In the **Size** box, select the existing number, type **100** and then compare your dialog box with Figure 11.43.

Figure 11.43

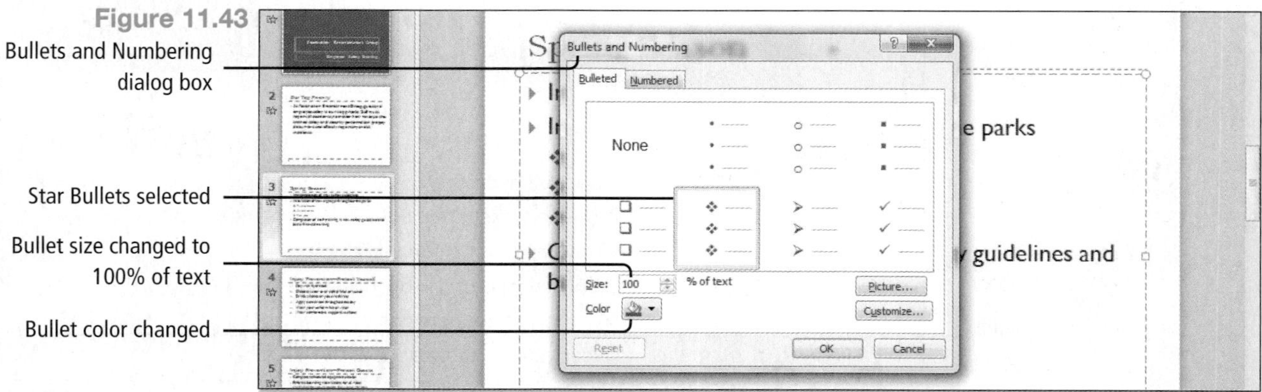

5 Click **OK** to apply the bullet style, and then **Save** your presentation.

Activity 11.27 | Removing a Bullet Symbol from a Bullet Point

The Bullet button is a toggle button, enabling you to turn the bullet symbol on and off. A slide that contains a single bullet point can be formatted as a single paragraph *without* a bullet symbol.

1 Display **Slide 2**, and then click in the paragraph. On the **Home tab**, in the **Paragraph group**, click the **Bullets** button.

The bullet symbol no longer displays, and the bullet button is no longer selected. Additionally, the indentation associated with the list level is removed.

2 **Center** the paragraph. On the **Home tab**, in the **Paragraph group**, click the **Line Spacing** button, and then click **1.5**.

3 Click the dashed border to display the solid border and to select all of the text in the paragraph, and then apply **Bold** and **Italic**. Click in the slide title, and then click the **Center** button. **Save** your presentation, and then compare your screen with Figure 11.44.

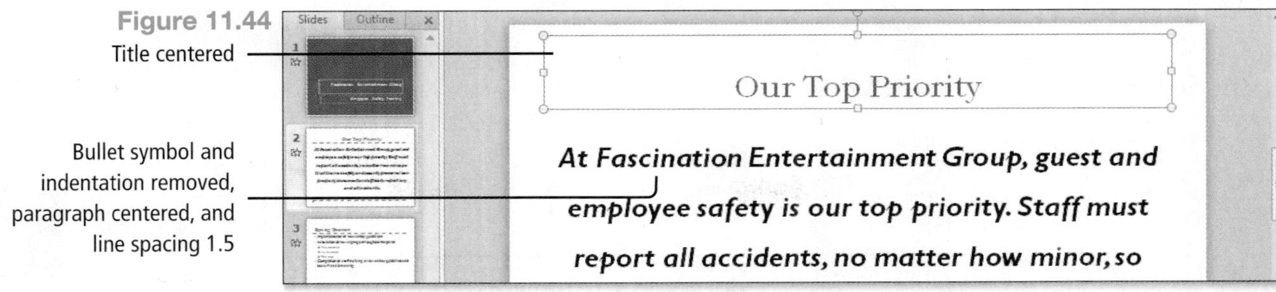

Figure 11.44

Objective 10 | Insert Clip Art

There are many sources from which you can insert images into a presentation. One type of image that you can insert is a ***clip***—a single media file such as art, sound, animation, or a movie.

View the video on the Companion Web Site or in MyITLab

Activity 11.28 | Inserting Clip Art

1 Display **Slide 4**, and then on the **Home tab**, in the **Slides group**, click the **Layout** button. Click **Two Content** to change the slide layout.

2 In the placeholder on the right side of the slide, click the **Clip Art** button to display the **Clip Art** pane.

3 In the **Clip Art** pane, click in the **Search for** box, and then replace any existing text with **bottled water** so that PowerPoint can search for images that contain the keyword *bottled water*.

4 Click the **Results should be arrow**, and then click as necessary to *clear* the **Illustrations**, **Videos**, and **Audio** check boxes and to select only the **Photographs** check box. Compare your screen with Figure 11.45.

With the Photographs check box selected, PowerPoint will search for images that were created with a digital camera or a scanner.

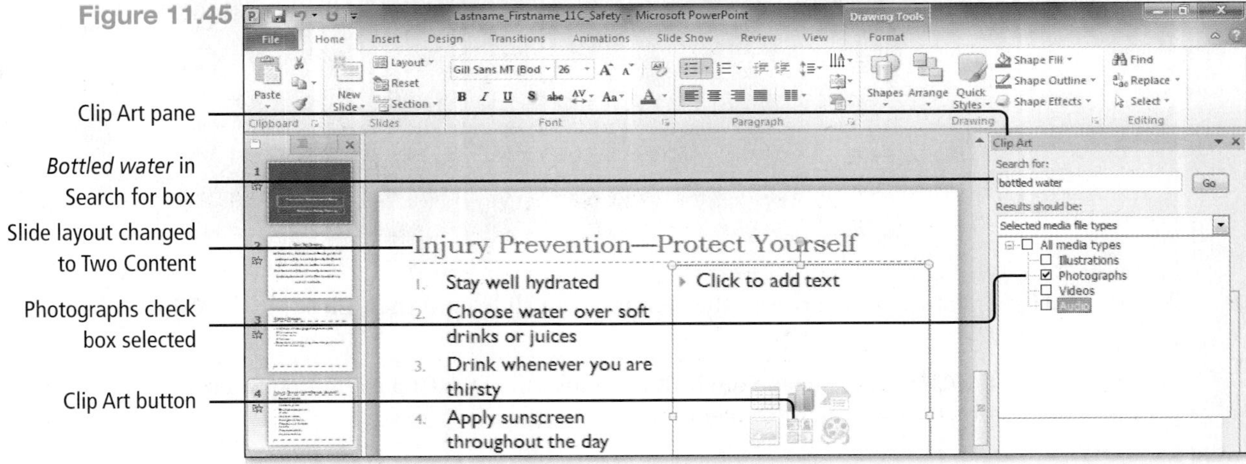

Figure 11.45

5 In the **Clip Art** pane, click the **Results should be arrow** to close the list. Then, if necessary, select the **Include Office.com content** check box so that images available on Office.com are included in the search.

6 In the **Clip Art** pane, click **Go** to display clips in the Clip Art pane. Scroll through the clips, and then locate and point to the image of the water pouring from a glass water bottle on a blue background. Compare your screen with Figure 11.46.

Figure 11.46

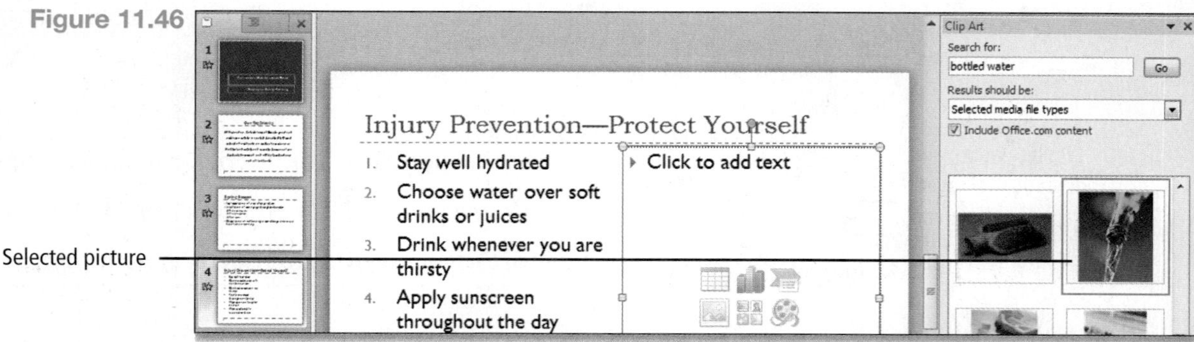

Alert! | Is the Water Bottle Picture Unavailable?

If you are unable to locate the suggested picture, choose another similar image.

7 Click the water bottle picture to insert it in the content placeholder on the right side of the slide. **Close** [X] the **Clip Art** pane.

On the Ribbon, the Picture Tools display, and the water bottle image is surrounded by sizing handles, indicating that it is selected.

8 Display **Slide 1**. Click the **Insert tab**, and then in the **Images group**, click **Clip Art**.

9 In the **Clip Art** pane, in the **Search for** box, search for **red lights** and then click **Go**. Scroll as necessary to locate the picture of the single red warning light. Point to the picture, and then compare your screen with Figure 11.47.

If you cannot locate the picture, select another appropriate image.

Figure 11.47

10 Click the **red light** picture to insert it in the center of the slide, and then **Close** [X] the **Clip Art** pane. **Save** your presentation.

When you use the Clip Art command on the Ribbon instead of the Clip Art button in a content placeholder, PowerPoint inserts the image in the center of the slide.

Activity 11.29 | Moving and Sizing Images

Recall that when an image is selected, it is surrounded by sizing handles that you can drag to resize the image. You can also resize an image using the Shape Height and Shape Width boxes on the Format tab. When you point to the image, rather than pointing to a sizing handle, the move pointer—a four-headed arrow—displays, indicating that you can move the image.

1 If necessary, select the picture of the red light. On the **Format tab**, in the **Size group**, click in the **Shape Height** box, and then replace the selected number with **3.5**

2 Press Enter to resize the image. Notice that the picture is resized proportionately, and the **Width** box displays *5.26*. Compare your screen with Figure 11.48.

When a picture is resized in this manner, the width adjusts in proportion to the picture height.

Figure 11.48

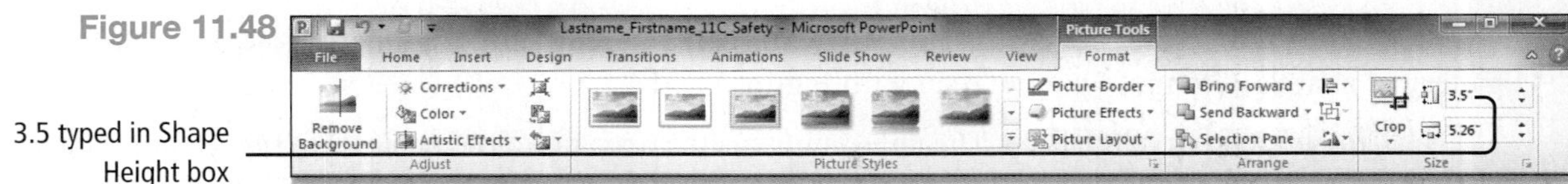

3 Display the **View tab**. In the **Show group**, verify that the **Ruler** check box is selected and, if necessary, select it. On the horizontal and vertical rulers, notice that *0* displays in the center.

Horizontally, the PowerPoint ruler indicates measurements from the center *out* to the left and to the right. Vertically, the PowerPoint ruler indicates measurements from the center up and down.

4 Point to the picture to display the pointer. Hold down Shift, and then drag the picture to the right until the left edge of the picture is aligned with the **left half of the horizontal ruler at 3 inches**. If necessary, hold down Ctrl and press an arrow key to move the picture in small increments in any direction for a more precise placement. Compare your screen with Figure 11.49.

Pressing Shift while dragging an object constrains object movement in a straight line either vertically or horizontally.

Figure 11.49

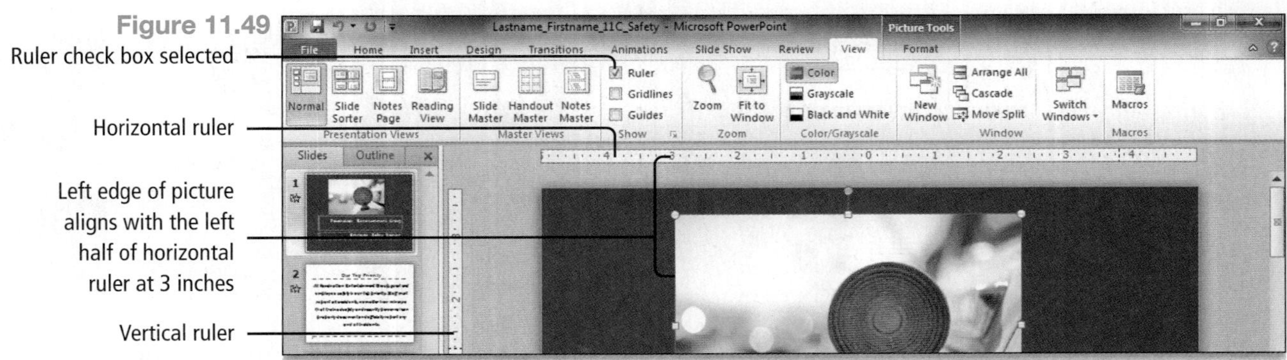

5 Display **Slide 6**. On the **Insert tab**, in the **Images group**, click the **Clip Art** button. In the **Clip Art** pane, search for **amusement park** and then click **Go**. Locate and click the picture of the Ferris wheel with the sky in the background, and then compare your slide with Figure 11.50.

Figure 11.50

6 **Close** the **Clip Art** pane, and be sure that the picture is still selected. On the **Format tab**, in the **Size group**, click in the **Shape Height** box. Replace the displayed number with **2.5** and then press Enter to resize the picture. **Save** your presentation.

Activity 11.30 | Changing the Shape of a Picture

An inserted picture is rectangular in shape; however, you can modify a picture by changing its shape.

1. Display **Slide 1**, and then select the picture.
2. On the **Format tab**, in the **Size group**, click the **Crop button arrow**, and then point to **Crop to Shape** to display a gallery of shapes. Compare your screen with Figure 11.51.

   The Crop button is a split button. The upper section—the Crop button—enables the ***crop*** feature, which reduces the size of a picture by removing vertical or horizontal edges. The lower section—the Crop arrow—displays cropping options, such as the option to crop a picture to a shape.

Figure 11.51

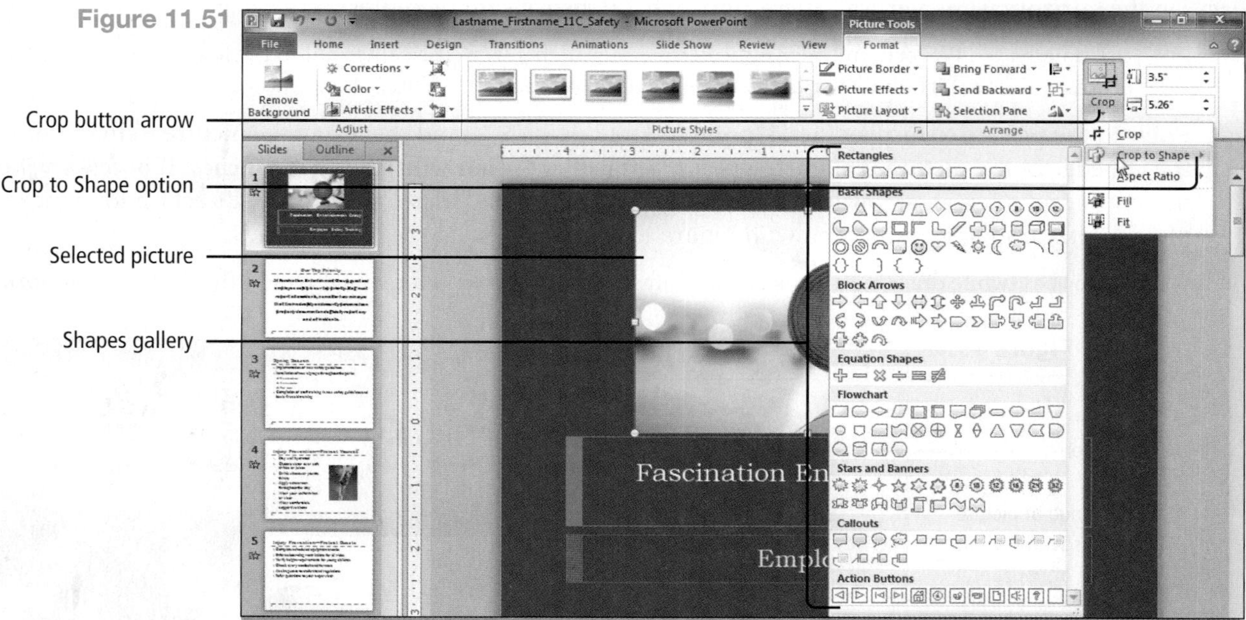

3. Under **Basic Shapes**, in the first row, click the first shape—**Oval**—to change the picture's shape to an oval. **Save** your presentation.

Objective 11 | Insert Text Boxes and Shapes

You can use objects, including text boxes and shapes, to draw attention to important information or to serve as containers for slide text.

View the video on the Companion Web Site or in MyITLab

Activity 11.31 | Inserting a Text Box

A ***text box*** is an object with which you can position text anywhere on a slide.

1. Display **Slide 5** and verify that the rulers display. Click the **Insert tab**, and then in the **Text group**, click the **Text Box** button.
2. Move the pointer to several different places on the slide, and as you do so, in the horizontal and vertical rulers, notice that ***ruler guides***—dotted vertical and horizontal lines that display in the rulers indicating the pointer's position—move also.

   Use the ruler guides to help you position objects on a slide.
3. Position the pointer so that the ruler guides are positioned on the **left half of the horizontal ruler at 4.5 inches** and on the **lower half of the vertical ruler at 1.5 inches**, and then compare your screen with Figure 11.52.

Figure 11.52

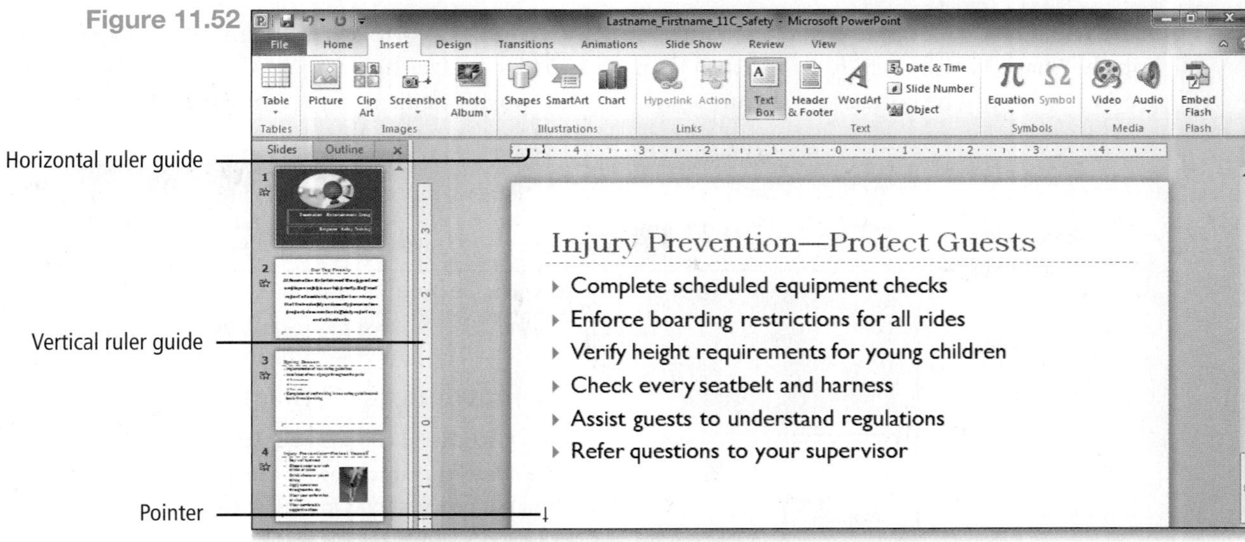
Lastname_Firstname_11C_Safety - Microsoft PowerPoint
Horizontal ruler guide
Vertical ruler guide
Pointer
Injury Prevention—Protect Guests
Complete scheduled equipment checks
Enforce boarding restrictions for all rides
Verify height requirements for young children
Check every seatbelt and harness
Assist guests to understand regulations
Refer questions to your supervisor

4 Click one time to create a narrow rectangular text box. With the insertion point blinking inside the text box, type **If Safety is Questionable** Notice that as you type, the width of the text box expands to accommodate the text.

> **Alert! | Does the Text in the Text Box Display Vertically, One Character at a Time?**
>
> If you move the pointer when you click to create the text box, PowerPoint sets the width of the text box and does not widen to accommodate the text. If this happened to you, your text may display vertically instead of horizontally or it may display on two lines. Click Undo, and then repeat the steps again, being sure that you do not move the mouse when you click to insert the text box.

5 Select the text that you typed, change the **Font Size** to **24** and then **Save** your presentation.

You can format the text in a text box by using the same techniques that you use to format text in any other placeholder.

Activity 11.32 | Inserting, Sizing, and Positioning Shapes

Shapes include lines, arrows, stars, banners, ovals, rectangles, and other basic shapes you can use to illustrate an idea, a process, or a workflow. Shapes can be sized and moved using the same techniques that you use to size and move clip art images.

1 With **Slide 5** displayed, click the **Insert tab**, and then in the **Illustrations group**, click the **Shapes** button to display the **Shapes** gallery. Under **Block Arrows**, click the first shape—**Right Arrow**. Move the pointer into the slide until the pointer—called the ***crosshair pointer***—displays, indicating that you can draw a shape.

2 Move the pointer to position the ruler guides at approximately **zero on the horizontal ruler** and on the **lower half of the vertical ruler at 1.5 inches**.

3 Click the mouse button to insert the arrow. Click the **Format tab**, and then in the **Size group**, click in the **Shape Height** box to select the number. Type **.5** and then click in the **Shape Width** box. Type **2** and then press Enter to resize the arrow.

4 On the **Format tab**, in the **Insert Shapes group**, click the **More** button. In the gallery, under **Basic Shapes**, in the first row, click the second to last shape—**Octagon**.

5 Move the pointer to position the ruler guides on the **right half of the horizontal ruler at 2.5 inches** and on the **lower half of the vertical ruler at 1 inch**, and then click one time to insert an octagon.

6 On the **Format tab**, in the **Size group**, click in the **Shape Height** box to select the number. Type **2** and then click in the **Shape Width** box. Type **2** and then press Enter to resize the octagon. Compare your slide with Figure 11.53. Do not be concerned if your shapes are not positioned exactly as shown in the figure.

Figure 11.53

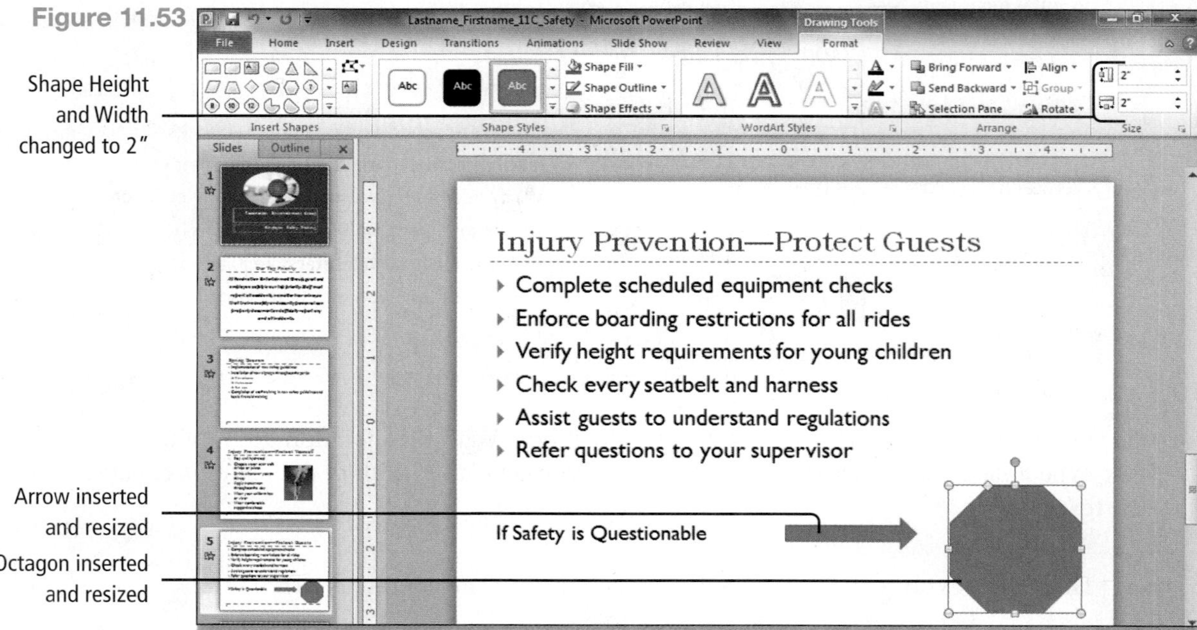

7 **Save** your presentation.

Activity 11.33 | Adding Text to Shapes

Shapes can serve as a container for text. After you add text to a shape, you can change the font and font size, apply font styles, and change text alignment.

1 On **Slide 5**, if necessary, click the octagon so that it is selected. Type **STOP** and notice that the text is centered within the octagon.

2 Select the text *STOP*, and then on the Mini toolbar, change the **Font Size** to **32**. Compare your screen with Figure 11.54, and then **Save** your presentation.

Figure 11.54

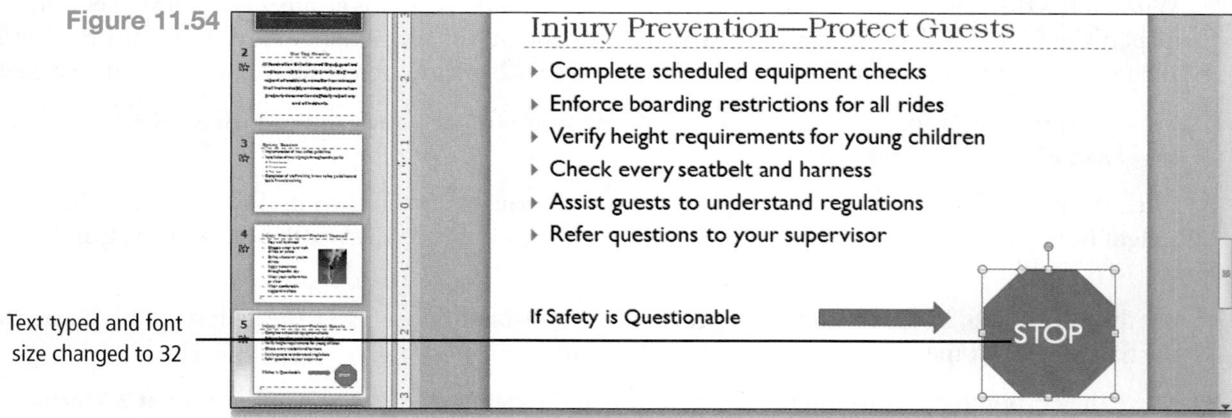

Objective 12 | Format Objects

Apply styles and effects to clip art, shapes, and text boxes to complement slide backgrounds and colors.

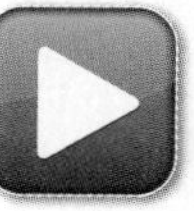

View the video on the Companion Web Site or in MyITLab

Activity 11.34 | Applying Shape Fills, Outlines, and Styles

Changing the inside ***fill color*** and the outside line color is a distinctive way to format a shape. A fill color is the inside color of text or of an object. Use the Shape Styles gallery to apply predefined combinations of these fill and line colors and also to apply other effects.

1. On **Slide 5**, click anywhere in the text *If Safety is Questionable* to select the text box. On the **Format tab**, in the **Shape Styles group**, click the **More** button to display the **Shape Styles** gallery.
2. In the last row, click the third style—**Intense Effect - Red, Accent 2**. Select the **octagon** shape, and then apply the same style you applied to the text box—**Intense Effect - Red, Accent 2**.
3. Select the **arrow**, and then display the **Shape Styles** gallery. In the last row, click the second style—**Intense Effect - Blue, Accent 1**.
4. Click in a blank part of the slide so that no objects are selected, and then compare your screen with Figure 11.55.

Figure 11.55

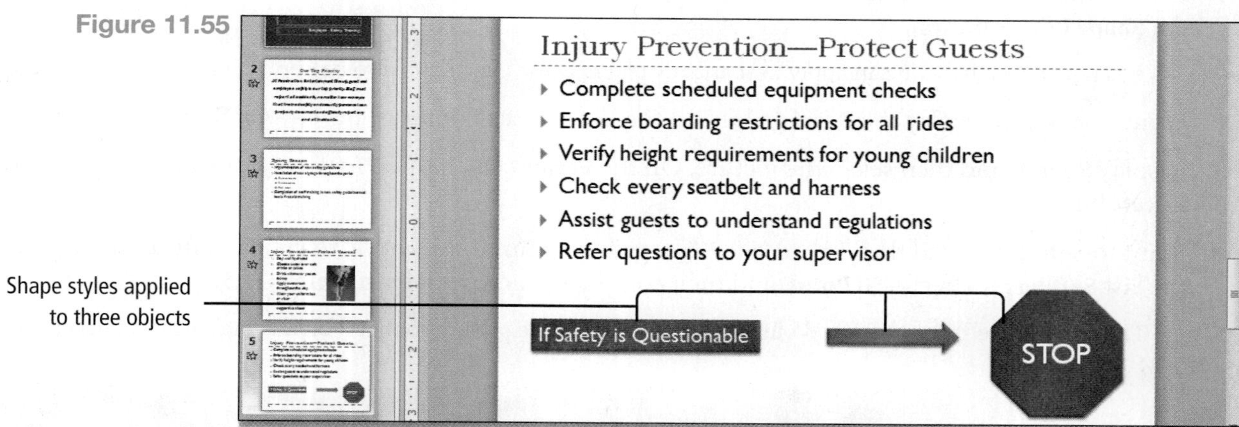
Shape styles applied to three objects
Injury Prevention—Protect Guests
Complete scheduled equipment checks
Enforce boarding restrictions for all rides
Verify height requirements for young children
Check every seatbelt and harness
Assist guests to understand regulations
Refer questions to your supervisor
If Safety is Questionable
STOP

5. Display **Slide 2**, and then click anywhere in the paragraph of text to select the content placeholder.
6. On the **Format tab**, in the **Shape Styles group**, click the **Shape Fill** button, and then, in the fifth column, click the first color—**Blue, Accent 1**.
7. In the **Shape Styles group**, click the **Shape Outline** button. Point to **Weight**, click **3 pt**, and notice that a thick outline surrounds the text placeholder. Click in a blank area of the slide so that nothing is selected, and then compare your slide with Figure 11.56.

   You can use combinations of shape fill, outline colors, and weights to format an object.

Figure 11.56

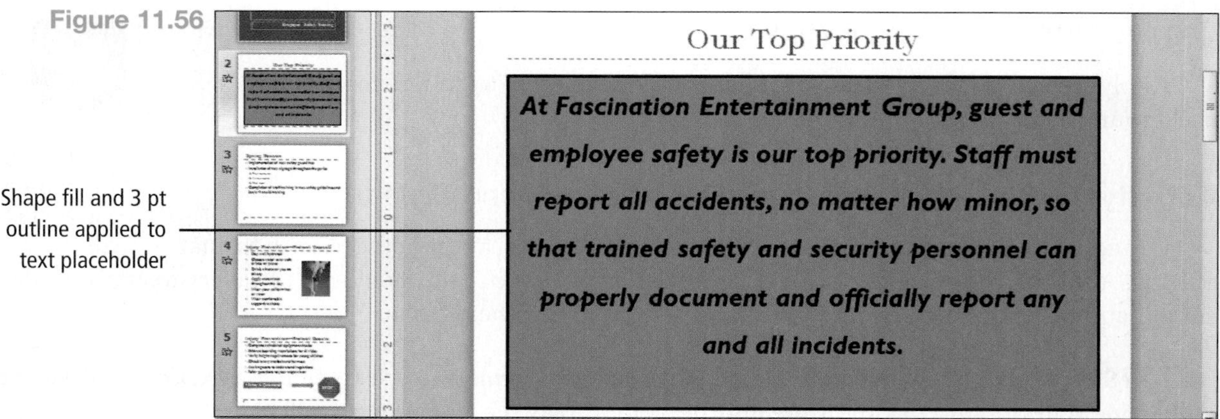

8 Click in the paragraph, and then press Ctrl + A to select all of the paragraph text, right-click in the selection to display the Mini toolbar, and then click the **Font Color button arrow** to display the **Theme Colors** gallery. Click the first color—**White, Background 1**. **Save** your presentation.

Activity 11.35 | Applying Shape and Picture Effects

1 On **Slide 2**, if necessary, select the blue content placeholder. On the **Format tab**, in the **Shape Styles group**, click the **Shape Effects** button.

A list of effects that you can apply to shapes displays. These effects can also be applied to pictures and text boxes.

2 Point to **Bevel** to display the **Bevel** gallery. In the last row, click the last bevel—**Art Deco**.

3 Display **Slide 1**, and then select the picture. On the **Format tab**, in the **Picture Styles group**, click the **Picture Effects** button.

4 Point to **Soft Edges**, and then in the **Soft Edges** gallery, point to each style to view its effect on the picture. Click the last **Soft Edges** effect—**50 Point**, and then compare your screen with Figure 11.57.

The soft edges effect softens and blurs the outer edge of the picture so that it blends into the slide background.

Figure 11.57

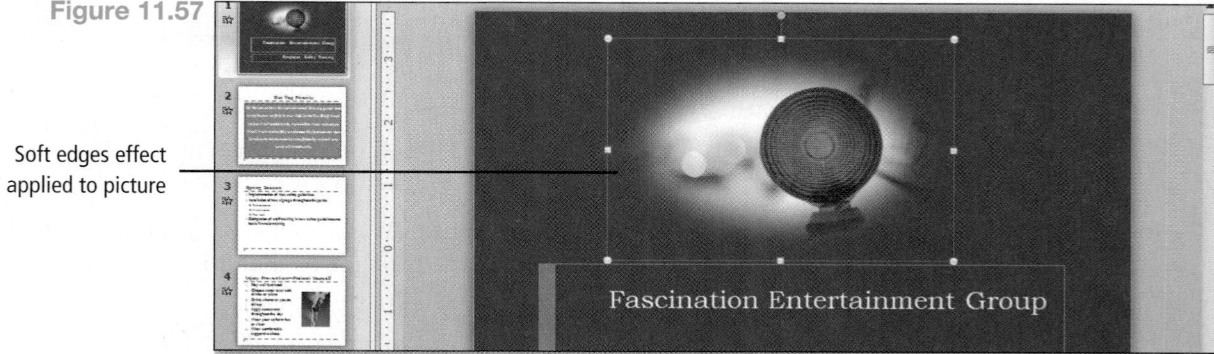

5 Display **Slide 4**, and then select the picture. On the **Format tab**, in the **Picture Styles group**, click the **Picture Effects** button, and then point to **Glow**.

6 Under **Glow Variations**, in the second row, click the second glow effect—**Red, 8 pt glow, Accent color 2**. **Save** your presentation.

The glow effect applies a colored, softly blurred outline to the selected object.

Activity 11.36 | Duplicating Objects

1 Display **Slide 6**, point to the picture to display the [pointer icon] pointer, and then drag up and to the left so that the upper left corner of the picture aligns with the upper left corner of the slide.

2 Press and hold down Ctrl, and then press D one time. Release Ctrl.

A duplicate of the picture overlaps the original picture and the duplicated image is selected.

3 Point to the duplicated picture to display the [pointer icon] pointer, and then drag down and to the right approximately 1 inch in both directions so that both pictures are visible. Compare your screen with Figure 11.58. Do not be concerned if your pictures are not positioned exactly as shown in the figure.

Figure 11.58

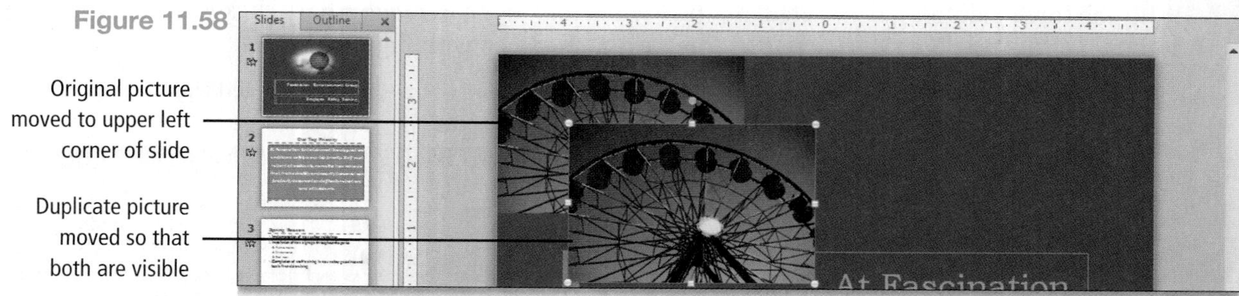

4 With the duplicated image selected, hold down Ctrl, and then press D to insert a third copy of the image. Using the same technique, drag down and to the right approximately 1 inch in both directions.

5 Click anywhere on the slide so that none of the three pictures are selected. **Save** [Save icon] your presentation.

Activity 11.37 | Aligning and Distributing Objects

When you insert multiple objects on a slide, you can use commands on the Ribbon to align and distribute the objects precisely.

1 With **Slide 6** displayed, position the pointer in the gray area of the Slide pane just outside the upper left corner of the slide to display the [pointer icon] pointer. Drag down and to the right to draw a transparent blue rectangle that encloses the three pictures. Compare your slide with Figure 11.59.

Figure 11.59

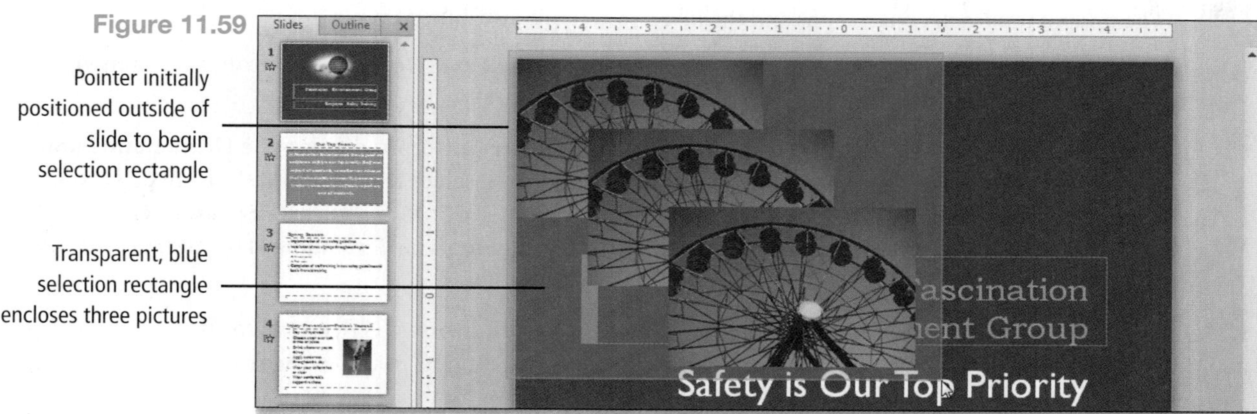

2 Release the mouse button to select the three objects.

Objects completely enclosed by a selection rectangle are selected when the mouse button is released.

3 Click the **Format tab**, and then in the **Arrange group**, click the **Align** button [Align icon]. Toward the bottom of the menu, click **Align to Slide** to activate this setting.

When you select an alignment option, this setting will cause the objects to align with the edges of the slide.

4 On the **Format tab**, in the **Arrange group**, click the **Align** button again, and then click **Align Top**.

The top of each of the three pictures aligns with the top edge of the slide.

5 Click in a blank area of the slide so that nothing is selected. Then, click the third picture. Point to the picture so that the pointer displays, and then drag to the right so that its upper right corner aligns with the upper right corner of the slide.

6 Hold down Shift and click the remaining two pictures so that all three pictures are selected. On the **Format tab**, in the **Arrange group**, click the **Align** button. Click **Align Selected Objects** to activate this setting.

When you select an alignment option, this setting will cause the objects that you select to align relative to each other.

7 With the three pictures still selected, on the **Format tab**, in the **Arrange group**, click the **Align** button again, and then click **Distribute Horizontally**. Compare your screen with Figure 11.60.

The three pictures are spaced and distributed evenly across the top of the slide and aligned with the top edge of the slide.

Figure 11.60

8 With the three pictures selected, on the **Format tab**, in the **Picture Styles group**, click the **Picture Effects** button. Point to **Soft Edges**, and then click **50 Point** to apply the picture effect to all three images.

9 Display **Slide 5**, select all three objects. On the **Format tab**, in the **Arrange group**, click the **Align** button. Be sure that **Align Selected Objects** is still active—a check mark displays to its left. Then, click **Align Middle**. Click the **Align** button again, and then click **Distribute Horizontally**.

The midpoint of each object aligns and the three objects are distributed evenly.

10 On the **Slide Show tab**, in the **Start Slide Show group**, click the **From Beginning** button, and then view the slide show. Press Esc when the black slide displays.

11 On the **Insert tab**, in the **Text group**, click the **Header & Footer** button to display the **Header and Footer** dialog box. Click the **Notes and Handouts tab**. Under **Include on page**, select the **Date and time** check box, and then select **Update automatically**. If necessary, clear the Header check box. Select the **Page number** and **Footer** check boxes. In the **Footer** box, using your own name, type **Lastname_Firstname_11C_Safety** and then click **Apply to All**.

12 Display the **Document Properties**. Replace the text in the **Author** box with your own firstname and lastname, in the **Subject** box, type your course name and section number, and in the **Keywords** box, type **safety, injury prevention Close** the **Document Information Panel**.

13 **Save** your presentation. Print **Handouts 6 Slides Horizontal**, or submit your presentation electronically as directed by your instructor. **Close** the presentation and exit PowerPoint.

End **You have completed Project 11C**

Project 11D Event Announcement

Project Activities

In Activities 11.38 through 11.47, you will format slides in a presentation for the Fascination Entertainment Group Marketing Director that informs employees about upcoming events at the company's amusement parks. You will enhance the presentation using SmartArt and WordArt graphics. Your completed presentation will look similar to Figure 11.61.

Project Files

For Project 11D, you will need the following files:

p11D_Celebrations
jpg11D_Canada_Contact
jpg11D_Mexico_Contact
jpg11D_US_Contact

You will save your presentation as:

Lastname_Firstname_11D_Celebrations

Project Results

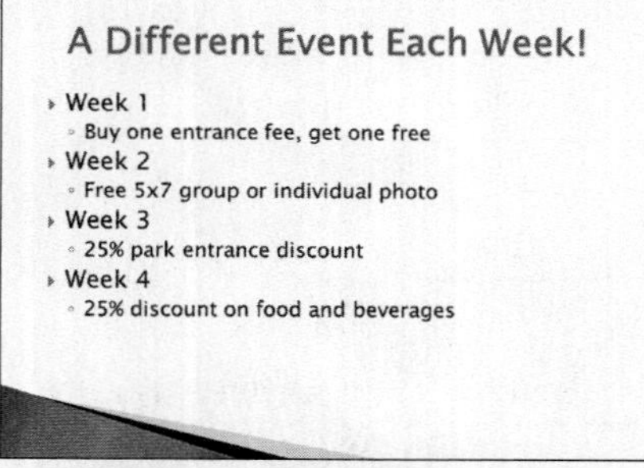

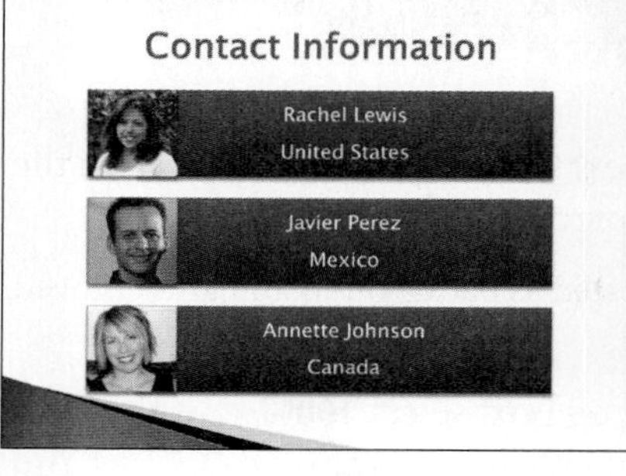

Figure 11.61
Project 11D Celebrations

Objective 13 | Remove Picture Backgrounds and Insert WordArt

View the video on the Companion Web Site or in MyITLab

To avoid the boxy look that results when you insert an image into a presentation, use ***Background Removal*** to flow a picture into the content of the presentation. Background Removal removes unwanted portions of a picture so that the picture does not appear as a self-contained rectangle.

WordArt is a gallery of text styles with which you can create decorative effects, such as shadowed or mirrored text. You can choose from the gallery of WordArt styles to insert a new WordArt object or you can customize existing text by applying WordArt formatting.

Activity 11.38 | Removing the Background from a Picture and Applying Soft Edge Options

1. **Start** PowerPoint. From your student files, open **p11D_Celebrations**. On the **View tab**, in the **Show group**, if necessary, select the Ruler check box. In your **All In One Chapter 11** folder, save the file as **Lastname_Firstname_11D_Celebrations**

2. Display **Slide 6**. Notice how the picture is a self-contained rectangle and that it has a much darker black background than the presentation. Click the picture to select it, and then on the **Format tab**, in the **Adjust group**, click the **Remove Background** button. Compare your screen with Figure 11.62.

   PowerPoint determines what portion of the picture is the foreground—the portion to keep—and which portion is the background—the portion to remove. The background is overlaid in magenta. A rectangular selection area displays that can be moved and sized to select additional areas of the picture. The Background Removal options display in the Refine group on the Ribbon.

Figure 11.62

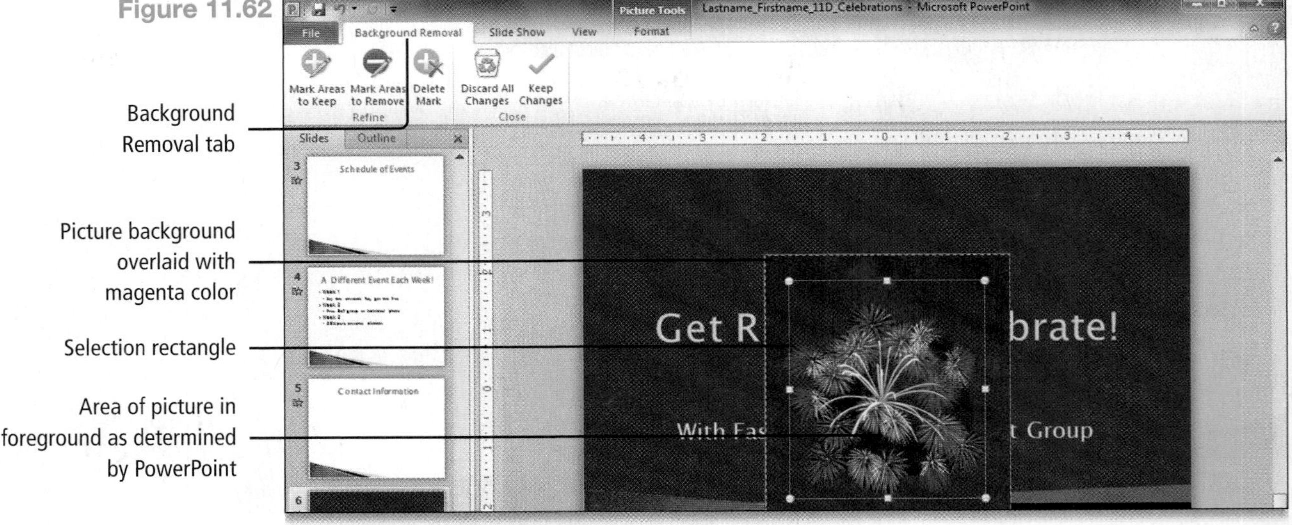

3. On the **selection rectangle**, point to the left center sizing handle to display the ⟺ pointer, and then drag to the left so that the left edge of the selection area aligns with the dashed border surrounding the picture.

   When you move or size the selection area, the areas outside the selection are treated as background and are removed. Thus, you have control over which portions of the picture that you keep.

4. On the **View tab**, in the **Zoom group**, click the **Zoom** button. In the **Zoom** dialog box, select **100%**, and then click **OK** to increase the size of the slide in the Slide pane. Notice on the right side of the fireworks picture the dark red shadowing in a triangular shape that is visible between some of the outer flowers of the fireworks display. Compare your slide with Figure 11.63.

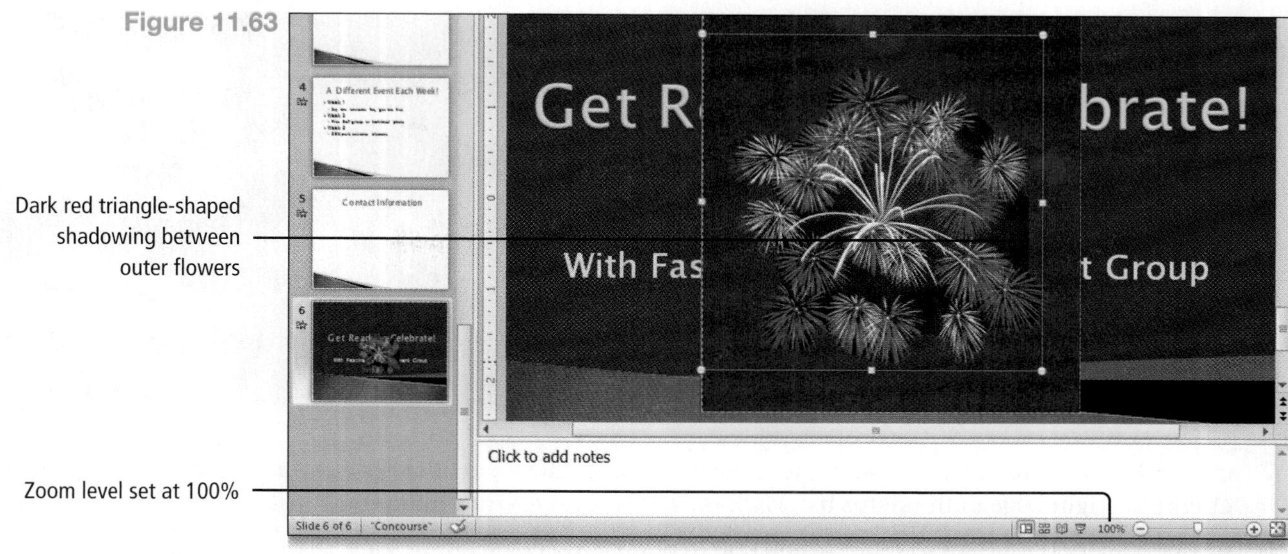

Figure 11.63

5 On the **Background Removal tab**, in the **Refine group**, click the **Mark Areas to Remove** button, and then position the pencil pointer so that the ruler guides align on the **right half of the horizontal ruler at 1 inch** and on the **lower half of the vertical ruler at 0.5 inch**. Click one time to insert a deletion mark, and then compare your screen with Figure 11.64. If your mark is not positioned as shown in the figure, click Undo and begin again.

You can surround irregular-shaped areas that you want to remove with deletion marks. Here, you can begin to surround the dark red shadow by placing a deletion mark in one corner of the red triangular area.

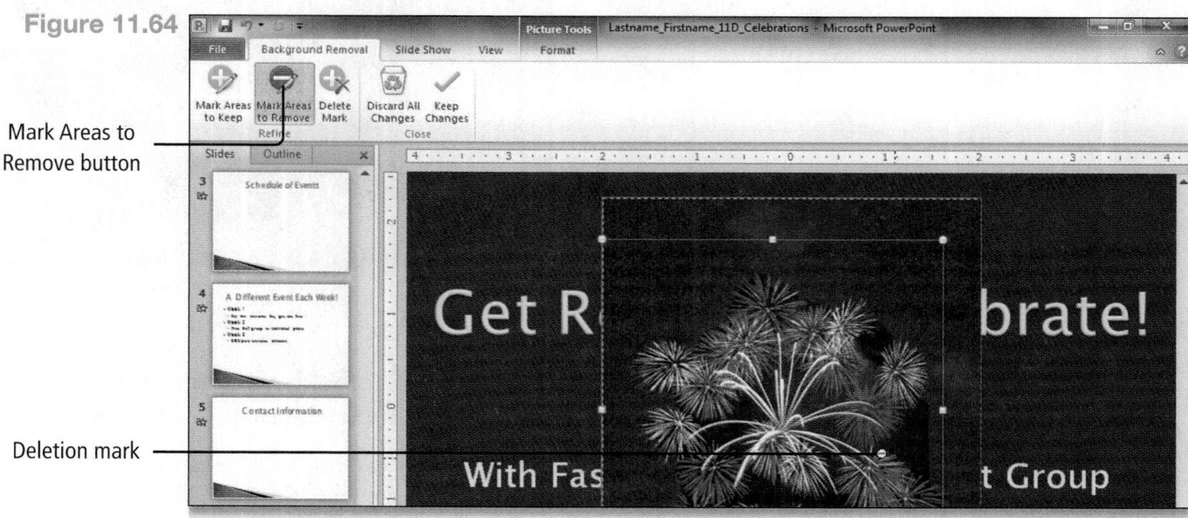

Figure 11.64

6 With the pencil pointer still active, position the pointer to align the ruler guides on the **right half of the horizontal ruler at approximately 1.5 inches** and on the **lower half of the vertical ruler to 0.75 inch** so that the pointer is aligned on the right edge of the dark red triangle. Click one time to insert another mark, and then compare your screen with Figure 11.65.

The two inserted marks provide PowerPoint sufficient information to remove the triangular-shaped red and black shadowed area. If the area is not removed as shown in the figure, insert additional deletion marks as necessary.

Figure 11.65

7 On the **Background Removal tab**, in the **Close group**, click the **Keep Changes** button to remove the background. On the far right edge of the status bar, click the **Fit slide to current window** button.

8 With the picture selected, on the **Format tab**, in the **Picture Styles group**, click the **Picture Effects** button, point to **Soft Edges**, and then click **50 Point**. In the **Adjust group**, click the **Artistic Effects** button, and then in the fourth row, click the third effect—**Crisscross Etching**.

9 In the **Size group**, click in the **Shape Height** box, replace the number with **3.5** and then press Enter. In the **Arrange group**, click the **Align** button, and then click **Align Center**. Click the **Align** button again, and then click **Align Middle**. Compare your slide with Figure 11.66, and then **Save** your presentation.

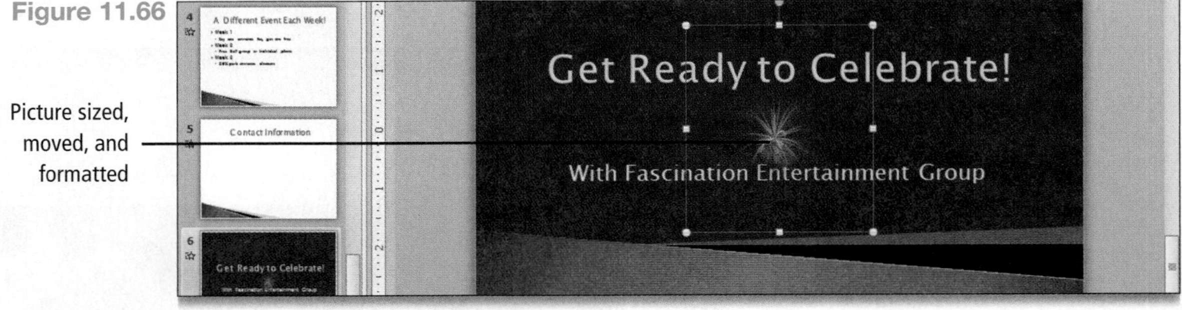

Figure 11.66

Activity 11.39 | Applying WordArt Styles to Existing Text

1 On **Slide 6**, click anywhere in the word *Get* to activate the title placeholder, and then select the title—*Get Ready to Celebrate!* Click the **Format tab**, and then in the **WordArt Styles group**, click the **More** button.

The WordArt Styles gallery displays in two sections. If you choose a WordArt style in the Applies to Selected Text section, you must first select all of the text to which you want to apply the WordArt. If you choose a WordArt style in the Applies to All Text in the Shape section, the WordArt style is applied to all of the text in the placeholder or shape.

2 Under **Applies to Selected Text**, in the first row, click the fourth style—**Fill – White, Outline – Accent 1**, and then compare your screen with Figure 11.67.

Figure 11.67

3 With the text still selected, in the **WordArt Styles group**, click the **Text Fill button arrow** [A]. Under **Theme Colors**, in the sixth column, click the fourth color—**Dark Red, Accent 2, Lighter 40%**, and then compare your screen with Figure 11.68.

Figure 11.68

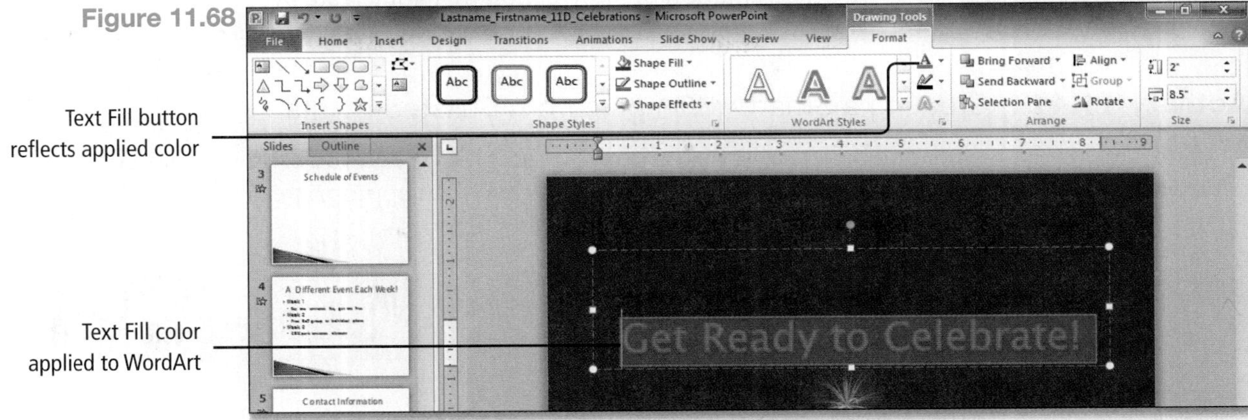

4 Display **Slide 1**, and then click anywhere in the title—*Fascination Entertainment Group*.

5 Click the **Format tab**, and then in the **WordArt Styles group**, click the **More** button to display the **WordArt Styles** gallery. Under **Applies to All Text in the Shape**, in the first row, click the third style—**Fill – Dark Red, Accent 2, Warm Matte Bevel**, and then **Save** your presentation.

Activity 11.40 | Inserting a WordArt Object

In addition to formatting existing text using WordArt, you can insert a new WordArt object anywhere on a slide.

1 Display **Slide 2**. Click the **Insert tab**, and then in the **Text group**, click the **WordArt** button. In the gallery, in the last row, click the third WordArt style—**Fill – Dark Red, Accent 2, Matte Bevel.**

In the center of your slide, a WordArt placeholder displays *Your text here*. Text that you type will replace this text and the placeholder will expand to accommodate the text.

2 Type **Get Ready for 2014!** to replace the WordArt placeholder text.

3 Point to the WordArt border to display the pointer. Hold down Shift, and then drag down to position the WordArt between the picture and the text at the bottom of the slide and centered between the left and right edge of the slide. Use Ctrl + any of the arrow keys to move the WordArt in small increments. Compare your slide with Figure 11.69 and move the WordArt again if necessary. **Save** your presentation.

Recall that holding down Shift when dragging an object constrains the horizontal and vertical movement so that the object is moved in a straight line.

Figure 11.69

Objective 14 | Create and Format a SmartArt Graphic

View the video on the Companion Web Site or in MyITLab

A ***SmartArt graphic*** is a visual representation of information that you create by choosing from among various layouts to communicate your message or ideas effectively.

Activity 11.41 | Creating a SmartArt Graphic from Bulleted Points

You can convert an existing bulleted list into a SmartArt graphic. When you create a SmartArt graphic, consider the message that you are trying to convey, and then choose an appropriate layout. The table in Figure 11.70 describes types of SmartArt layouts and suggested purposes.

Microsoft PowerPoint SmartArt Graphic Types

Graphic Type	Purpose of Graphic
List	Shows nonsequential information
Process	Shows steps in a process or timeline
Cycle	Shows a continual process
Hierarchy	Shows a decision tree or displays an organization chart
Relationship	Illustrates connections
Matrix	Shows how parts relate to a whole
Pyramid	Shows proportional relationships with the largest component on the top or bottom
Picture	Includes pictures in the layout to communicate messages and ideas

Figure 11.70

1. Display **Slide 4**, and then click anywhere in the bulleted list placeholder. On the **Home tab**, in the **Paragraph group**, click the **Convert to SmartArt** button. Below the gallery, click **More SmartArt Graphics**.

   Three sections comprise the Choose a SmartArt Graphic dialog box. The left section lists the SmartArt graphic types. The center section displays the SmartArt graphics according to type. The third section displays the selected SmartArt graphic, its name, and a description of its purpose.

2. On the left side of the **Choose a SmartArt Graphic** dialog box, click **List**. Use the ScreenTips to locate and then click **Vertical Bullet List**.

3. In the **Choose a SmartArt Graphic** dialog box, click **OK**. If the Text Pane displays to the right of the SmartArt graphic, click its Close button. Compare your screen with Figure 11.71, and then **Save** your presentation.

   It is not necessary to select all of the text in the list. By clicking in the list, PowerPoint converts all of the bullet points to the selected SmartArt graphic.

Figure 11.71

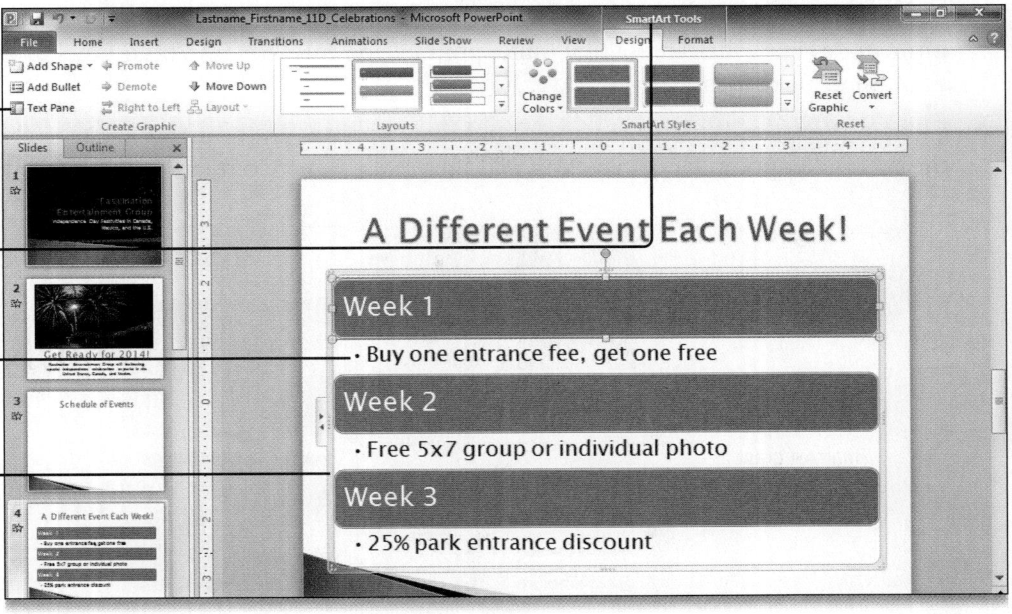

Text pane button not selected

SmartArt Tools display Design and Format tabs

Text converted to Vertical Bullet List SmartArt graphic

Border indicates SmartArt selected

Activity 11.42 | Adding Shapes in a SmartArt Graphic

If a SmartArt graphic does not have enough shapes to illustrate a concept or display the relationships, you can add more shapes.

1 Click in the shape that contains the text *Week 3*. In the **SmartArt Tools**, click the **Design tab**. In the **Create Graphic group**, click the **Add Shape arrow**, and then click **Add Shape After** to insert a shape at the same level. Type **Week 4**

The text in each of the SmartArt shapes resizes to accommodate the added shape.

2 On the **Design tab**, in the **Create Graphic group**, click the **Add Bullet** button to add a bullet below the *Week 4* shape.

3 Type **25% discount on food and beverages** Compare your slide with Figure 11.72, and then **Save** your presentation.

Figure 11.72

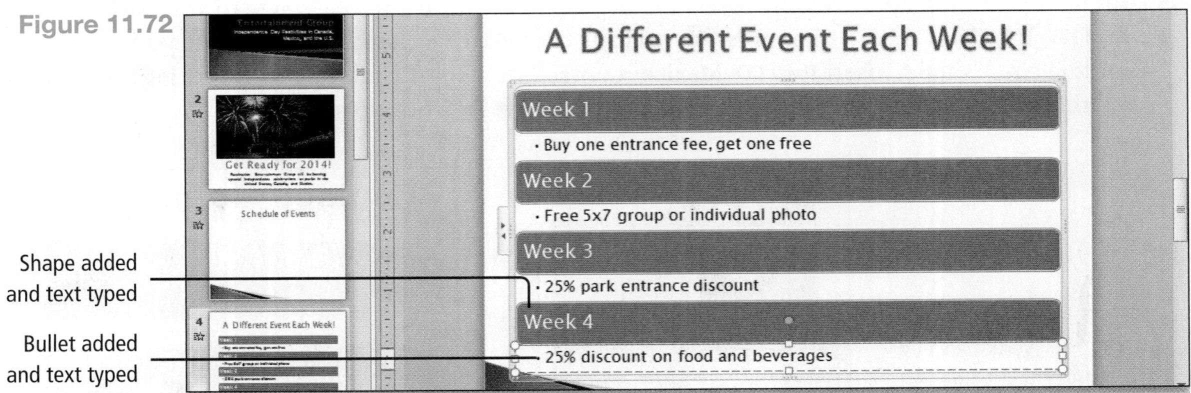

Activity 11.43 | Creating a SmartArt Graphic Using a Content Layout

1 Display **Slide 3**. In the center of the content placeholder, click the **Insert SmartArt Graphic** button to open the **Choose a SmartArt Graphic** dialog box.

2 On the left, click **Process**, and then scroll as necessary and use the ScreenTips to locate **Vertical Arrow List**. Click **Vertical Arrow List**. Click **OK** to insert the SmartArt graphic.

The SmartArt graphic displays with two rounded rectangle shapes and two arrow shapes. You can type text directly into the shapes or you can type text in the Text Pane, which may display to the left of your SmartArt graphic. You can display the Text Pane by clicking the Text Pane tab on the left side of the SmartArt graphic border, or by clicking the Text Pane button in the Create Graphic group.

3 In the SmartArt graphic, click in the first orange rectangle, and then type **Canada** In the arrow shape to the immediate right, click in the first bullet point. Type **July 2014** and then press Delete to remove the second bullet point in the arrow shape.

4 Click in the second orange rectangle, and then type **U.S.** In the arrow shape to the immediate right, click in the first bullet point. Type **July 2014** and then press Delete. Compare your slide with Figure 11.73.

Figure 11.73

5 Click in the *U.S.* rectangle. On the **Design tab**, in the **Create Graphic group**, click the **Add Shape arrow**. Click **Add Shape After** to insert a new rectangle and arrow. Type **Mexico** and then in the arrow shape to the right, type **September 2014**

6 Display **Slide 5**. In the center of the content placeholder, click the **Insert SmartArt Graphic** button. In the **Choose a SmartArt Graphic** dialog box, click **Picture**, and then scroll as necessary to locate **Vertical Picture Accent List**. Click **Vertical Picture Accent List**, and then click **OK** to insert the graphic.

7 In the SmartArt graphic, in the top rectangle shape, type **Rachel Lewis** and then press Enter. Type **United States** and then click in the middle rectangle shape. Type **Javier Perez** and then press Enter. Type **Mexico** and then click in the last rectangle shape, type **Annette Johnson** and then press Enter. Type **Canada**

8 In the top circle shape, click the **Insert Picture from File** button. Navigate to your student files, click **jpg11D_US_Contact**, and then press Enter to insert the picture. Using the technique you just practiced, in the middle circle shape, insert **jpg11D_Mexico_Contact**. In the last circle shape, insert **jpg11D_Canada_Contact**. Compare your screen with Figure 11.74, and then **Save** your presentation.

Figure 11.74

Activity 11.44 | Changing the SmartArt Layout

1. Display **Slide 3**, and then click anywhere in the SmartArt graphic. In the **SmartArt Tools**, click the **Design tab**. In the **Layouts group**, click the **More** button [▼], and then click **More Layouts**. In the **Choose a SmartArt Graphic** dialog box, click **Hierarchy**. Locate and click **Hierarchy List**, and then click **OK**.
2. **Save** [💾] the presentation.

Activity 11.45 | Changing the Color and Style of a SmartArt graphic

SmartArt Styles are combinations of formatting effects that you can apply to SmartArt graphics.

1. With **Slide 3** displayed and the SmartArt graphic selected, on the **Design tab**, in the **SmartArt Styles group**, click the **Change Colors** button. In the color gallery, under **Colorful**, click the first style—**Colorful - Accent Colors**—to change the color.
2. On the **Design tab**, in the **SmartArt Styles group**, click the **More** button [▼] to display the **SmartArt Styles gallery**. Under **3-D**, click the second style, **Inset**. Compare your slide with Figure 11.75.

Figure 11.75

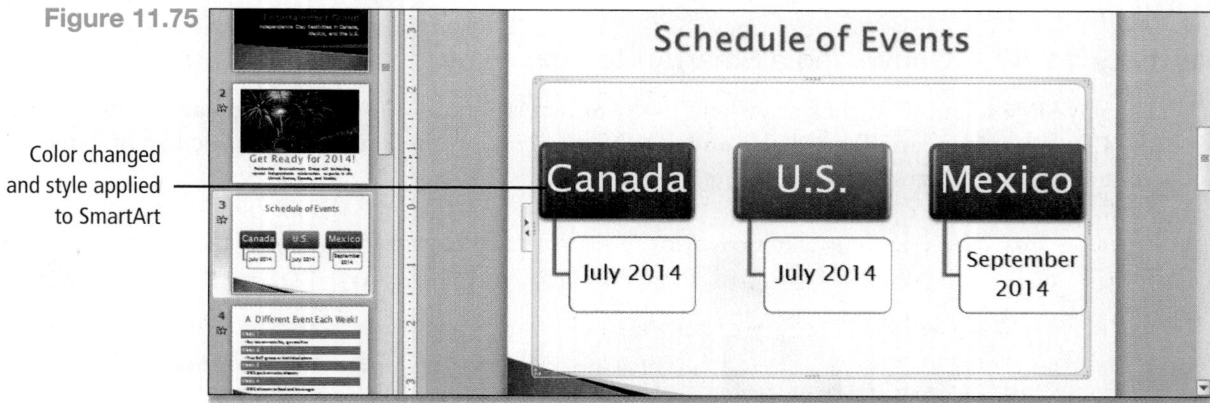

3. Display **Slide 5**, and select the SmartArt. On the **Design tab**, in the **SmartArt Styles group**, click the **Change Colors** button. Under **Accent 2**, click the second style—**Colored Fill - Accent 2**. On the **Design tab**, in the **SmartArt Styles group**, click the **More** button [▼]. Under **Best Match for Document**, click the last style, **Intense Effect**. **Save** [💾] the presentation.

Activity 11.46 | Customizing the Size and Shape of a SmartArt Graphic

You can select individual or groups of shapes in a SmartArt graphic and make them larger or smaller, and you can change selected shapes to another type of shape.

1. With **Slide 5** displayed, click in the upper red shape that contains the text *Rachel Lewis*. Hold down Shift, and then click in each of the two remaining red shapes containing the text *Javier Perez* and *Annette Johnson* so that all three text shapes are selected.
2. On the **Format tab**, in the **Shapes group**, click the **Larger** button two times to increase the size of the three selected shapes.
3. With the three shapes selected, on the **Home tab**, in the **Font group**, increase the **Font Size** to **23**.
4. Select the first circle picture, and then hold down Shift and click the remaining two circles so that all three circles are selected. In the **SmartArt Tools**, on the **Format tab**, in the **Shapes group**, click the **Change Shape** button. Under **Rectangles**, click the first shape—**Rectangle**—to change the circles to rectangles. With the three shapes selected, in the **Shapes group**, click the **Larger** button two times. Compare your screen with Figure 11.76, and then **Save** [💾] the presentation.

Figure 11.76

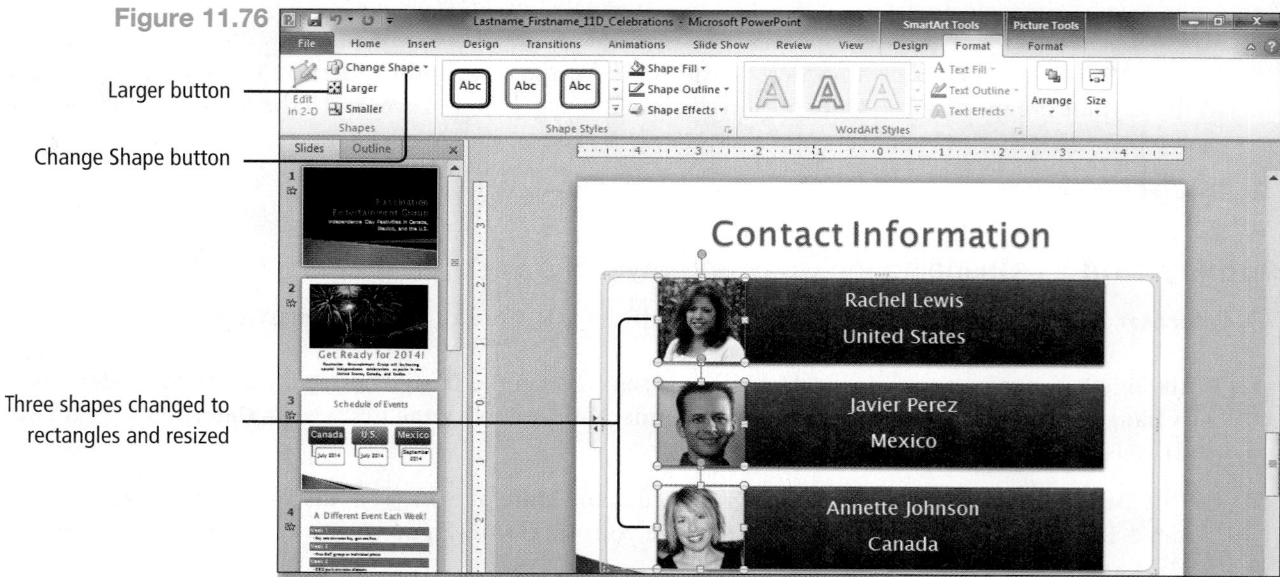

Activity 11.47 | Converting a SmartArt to Text

1 Display **Slide 4**, and then click anywhere in the SmartArt graphic. On the **Design tab**, in the **Reset group**, click the **Convert** button, and then click **Convert to Text** to convert the SmartArt graphic to a bulleted list. Compare your screen with Figure 11.77.

Figure 11.77

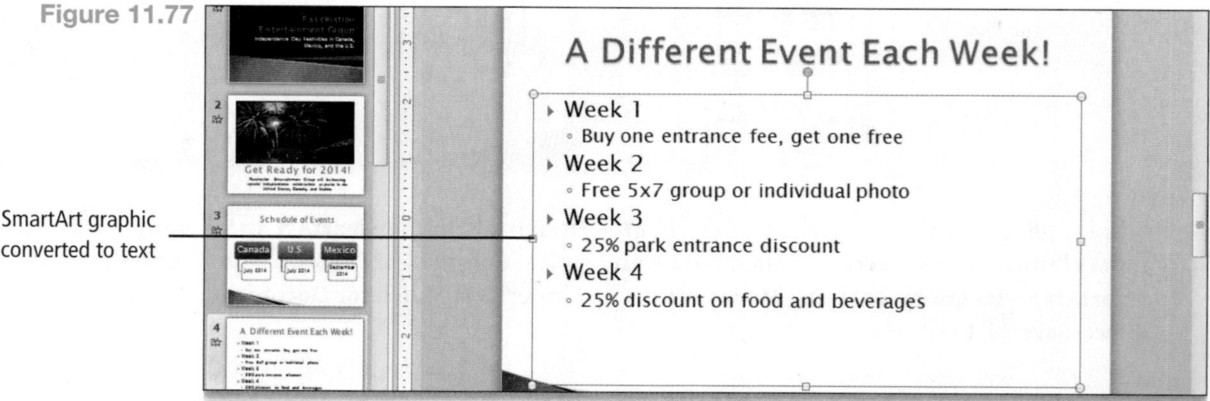

2 Display the **Document Properties**. Replace the text in the **Author** box with your own firstname and lastname, in the **Subject** box, type your course name and section number, and in the **Keywords** box, type **Independence day, celebrations Close** [X] the **Document Information Panel**.

3 Insert a **Header & Footer** on the **Notes and Handouts**. Include the **Date and time updated automatically**, the **Page number**, and a **Footer** with the text **Lastname_Firstname_11D_Celebrations** Apply to all the slides. View the presentation from the beginning, and then make any necessary adjustments.

4 **Save** your presentation. Print **Handouts 6 Slides Horizontal**, or submit your presentation electronically as directed by your instructor. **Close** the presentation and close PowerPoint.

Content-Based Assessments

Summary

In this chapter, you created a new PowerPoint presentation and edited an existing presentation by reusing slides from another presentation. You entered, edited, and formatted text in Normal view; worked with slides in Slide Sorter view; and viewed the presentation as a slide show. You also added emphasis to your presentations by inserting pictures, applying font formatting, and modifying layout, alignment, and line spacing.

Key Terms

Artistic effects 495
Background Removal 524
Black slide 496
Clip 513
Crop 516
Crosshair pointer 517
Editing 489
Fill Color 519
Footer 496
Formatting 503
Header 496
Layout 489
List level 491
Normal view 487
Notes page 496
Notes pane 487
Placeholder 488
Reading View 507
Rotation handle 494
Ruler guides 516
Shapes 517
Sizing handles 494
Slide 488
Slide handouts 496
Slide pane 487
Slide Sorter view 505
Slide transitions 506
Slides/Outline pane ...487
SmartArt graphic 528
SmartArt Styles 531
Style 494
Text alignment 504
Text box 516
Theme 488
Thumbnails 487
Title slide 488
WordArt 524

Check Your Knowledge

Matching and Multiple Choice items are available in MyITLab and on the Companion Web Site.

Apply **11A** skills from these Objectives:

1. Create a New Presentation
2. Edit a Presentation in Normal View
3. Add Pictures to a Presentation
4. Print and View a Presentation

Mastering PowerPoint | Project 11E Boat Tours

In the following Mastering PowerPoint project, you will create a new presentation describing the types of boat tours offered by Lehua Hawaiian Adventures. Your completed presentation will look similar to Figure 11.78.

Project Files

For Project 11E, you will need the following files:

New blank PowerPoint presentation
jpg11E_Catamaran
jpg11E_Raft

You will save your presentation as:

Lastname_Firstname_11E_Boat_Tours

Project Results

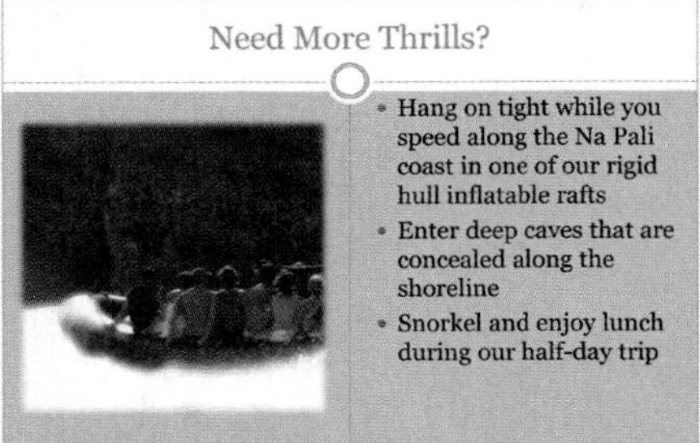

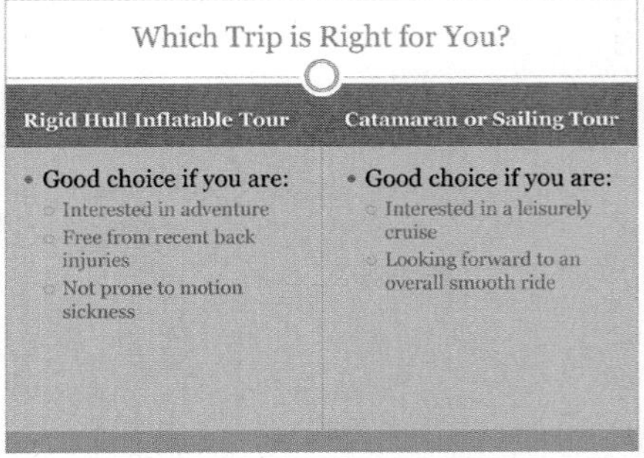

Figure 11.78

(Project 11E Boat Tours continues on the next page)

Mastering PowerPoint | Project 11E Boat Tours (continued)

1 **Start** PowerPoint to display a new blank presentation, and then change the **Design** by applying the **Civic** theme. As the title of this presentation type **Viewing Na Pali by Sea** and as the subtitle type **With Lehua Hawaiian Adventures**

2 Correct spelling errors on this slide by choosing the **Ignore All** option for the words *Pali* and *Lehua*. Save the presentation in your **All In One Chapter 11** folder as **Lastname_Firstname_11E_Boat_Tours**

3 Insert a **New Slide** using the **Content with Caption** layout. In the title placeholder, type **Looking to Relax?** In the large content placeholder on the right side of the slide, from your student files, insert the picture **jpg11E_Catamaran**. Format the picture with the **Compound Frame, Black** picture style and the **Texturizer** artistic effect.

4 In the text placeholder, type **If an easy day of sailing is your style, consider a morning or sunset cruise on our forty-person catamaran. Our experienced crew will sail our vessel along the Na Pali coast for a view of waterfalls, caves, and beaches. Spinner dolphins often swim alongside and whales can be spotted January through March.**

5 Insert a **New Slide** using the **Two Content** layout. In the title placeholder, type **Need More Thrills?** In the content placeholder on the left side of the slide, from your student files, insert the picture **jpg11E_Raft**. Format the picture with the **Soft Edge Rectangle** picture style and the **Glow Diffused** artistic effect. In the content placeholder on the right side of the slide, type the following three bullet points:

Hang on tight while you speed along the Na Pali coast in one of our rigid hull inflatable rafts

Enter deep caves that are concealed along the shoreline

Snorkel and enjoy lunch during our half-day trip

6 Insert a **New Slide** using the **Comparison** layout. In the title placeholder, type **Which Trip is Right for You?** In the orange placeholder on the left side of the slide, type **Rigid Hull Inflatable Tour** and in the orange placeholder on the right side of the slide, type **Catamaran or Sailing Tour**

7 In the content placeholder on the left, type each of the following bullet points, increasing the list level for the last three bullet points as indicated:

Good choice if you are:

Interested in adventure

Free from recent back injuries

Not prone to motion sickness

8 In the content placeholder on the right, type each of the following bullet points, increasing the list level for the last two bullet points as indicated:

Good choice if you are:

Interested in a leisurely cruise

Looking forward to an overall smooth ride

9 On **Slide 4**, type the following notes in the **Notes pane**: **If you need assistance deciding which boat tour is right for you, we'll be happy to help you decide.** Insert a **New Slide** using the **Section Header** layout. In the title placeholder, type **Book Your Trip Today!** In the text placeholder, type **Contact Lehua Hawaiian Adventures**

10 Insert a **Header & Footer** on the **Notes and Handouts**. Include the **Date and time** updated automatically, the **Page number**, and a **Footer**—using your own name—with the text **Lastname_Firstname_11E_Boat_Tours** and apply to all the slides.

11 Display the **Document Information Panel**. Replace the text in the **Author** box with your own firstname and lastname. In the **Subject** box, type your course name and section number, and in the **Keywords** box, type **Na Pali, boat tours, sailing** **Close** the Document Information Panel.

12 **Save** your presentation, and then view the slide show from the beginning. Submit your presentation electronically or print **Handouts, 6 Slides Horizontal** as directed by your instructor. **Close** the presentation.

End **You have completed Project 11E**

Content-Based Assessments

Apply 11B skills from these Objectives:

5 Edit an Existing Presentation

6 Format a Presentation

7 Use Slide Sorter View

8 Apply Slide Transitions

Mastering PowerPoint | Project **11F** Helicopter Tour

In the following Mastering PowerPoint project, you will edit a presentation describing the helicopter tours offered by Lehua Hawaiian Adventures. Your completed presentation will look similar to Figure 11.79.

Project Files

For Project 11F, you will need the following files:

p11F_Helicopter_Tour
p11F_Aerial_Views

You will save your presentation as:

Lastname_Firstname_11F_Helicopter_Tour

Project Results

Figure 11.79

(Project 11F Helicopter Tour continues on the next page)

Mastering PowerPoint | Project 11F Helicopter Tour (continued)

1 **Start** PowerPoint, and then from your student data files, open the file **p11F_Helicopter_Tour**. In your **All In One Chapter 11** folder, **Save** the file as **Lastname_Firstname_11F_Helicopter_Tour**

2 Display the presentation **Outline**. In the **Outline tab**, in **Slide 2**, increase the list level of the bullet point that begins *Formed by erosion*. In the **Outline tab**, click at the end of the second bullet point after the word *Kauai*. Press Enter, and then decrease the list level of the new bullet point. Type **Lava flows changed the canyon landscape over the course of centuries**

3 In the **Slides/Outline pane**, click the **Slides tab** to display the slide thumbnails, and then display **Slide 1**. Display the **Reuse Slides** pane, and then click the **Browse** button. Click **Browse File**, and then in the **Browse** dialog box, from your student files, open **p11F_Aerial_Views**. Select the **Keep source formatting** check box, and then from this group of slides, insert the first and second slides—*Aerial View of Kauai* and *Dramatic Overhead.*

4 In the **Slides/Outline pane**, click **Slide 4** to display it in the **Slide pane**, and then from the **Reuse Slides** pane, insert the third, fourth, fifth, and sixth slides—*Na Pali Coast, Honopu Beach, Amazing Shorelines, Tunnels Beach*. **Close** the **Reuse Slides** pane.

5 Display **Slide 1**, and then select the title—*Maui from the Sky*. Change the **Font** to **Arial**, and the **Font Size** to **44**. Change the **Font Color** to **White, Text 1**. Display the **Replace** dialog box. **Replace All** occurrences of the word **Maui** with **Kauai** and then **Close** the **Replace** dialog box.

6 Display **Slide 5**, and then select the paragraph in the content placeholder. Apply **Bold** and **Italic**, and then **Center** the text. Change the **Line Spacing** to **1.5**. Display **Slide 7**, and then change the **Slide Layout** to **Section Header**. **Center** the text in both placeholders.

7 In **Slide Sorter** view, delete **Slide 2**. Then select **Slides 6** and **7** and move both slides so that they are positioned after **Slide 3**. In **Normal** view, display **Slide 1**. Apply the **Split** transition and change the **Effect Options** to **Horizontal Out**. Apply the transition to all of the slides in the presentation. View the slide show from the beginning.

8 **Insert** a **Header & Footer** on the **Notes and Handouts**. Include the **Date and time** updated automatically, the **Page number**, and a **Footer** with the text **Lastname_Firstname_11F_Helicopter_Tour** Apply to all the slides.

9 Check spelling in the presentation. If necessary, select the Ignore All option if proper names are indicated as misspelled.

10 Display the **Document Information Panel**. Replace the text in the **Author** box with your own firstname and lastname. In the **Subject** box, type your course name and section number, and in the **Keywords** box, type **helicopter, Kauai Close** the Document Information Panel.

11 **Save** your presentation, and then submit your presentation electronically or print **Handouts, 4 Slides Horizontal** as directed by your instructor. **Close** the presentation.

End **You have completed Project 11F**

Apply 11C skills from these Objectives:

9 Format Numbered and Bulleted Lists
10 Insert Clip Art
11 Insert Text Boxes and Shapes
12 Format Objects

Mastering PowerPoint | Project 11G Roller Coasters

In the following Mastering PowerPoint project, you will format a presentation describing new roller coaster attractions at the Fascination Entertainment Group theme parks. Your completed presentation will look similar to Figure 11.80.

Project Files

For Project 11G, you will need the following file:

p11G_Roller_Coasters

You will save your presentation as:

Lastname_Firstname_11G_Roller_Coasters

Project Results

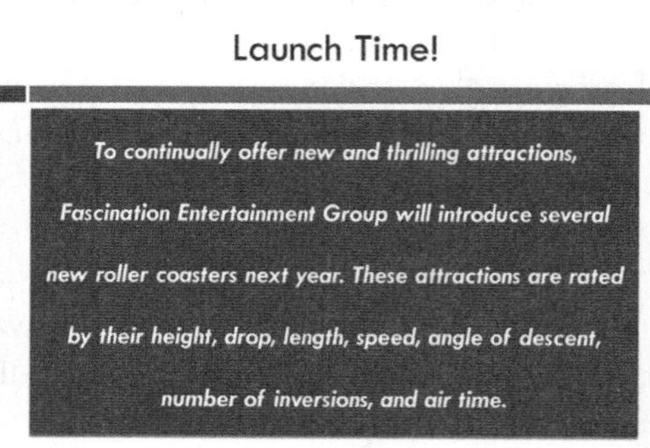

New Coasters for 2016

1. Intensity
   - 2,933 foot steel coaster
   - Scheduled for completion in March
   - Merrillville Park
2. Hang Time
   - 7,438 foot steel coaster
   - Scheduled for completion in May
   - Montreal Park
3. Last Chance
   - 4,564 foot steel coaster
   - Scheduled for completion in July
   - Atlanta Park

Hold Your Breath!

And Let the Excitement Begin!

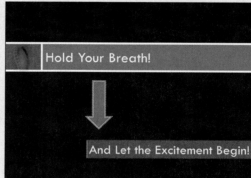

Figure 11.80

(Project 11G Roller Coasters continues on the next page)

Mastering PowerPoint | Project 11G Roller Coasters (continued)

1 **Start** PowerPoint. From the student files that accompany this textbook, locate and open **p11G_Roller_Coasters**. In your **All In One Chapter 11** folder, **Save** the file as **Lastname_Firstname_11G_Roller_Coasters**

2 On **Slide 2**, remove the bullet symbol from the paragraph. **Center** the paragraph, apply **Bold** and **Italic** to the text, and then set the **Line Spacing** to **2.0**. With the content placeholder selected, display the **Shape Styles** gallery, and then in the fifth row, apply the third style—**Moderate Effect - Red, Accent 2**.

3 On **Slide 3**, apply **Numbering** to the first-level bullet points—*Intensity, Hang Time,* and *Last Chance*. Under each of the numbered items, change all of the hollow circle bullet symbols to **Filled Square Bullets**, and then change the bullet color to **Dark Blue, Text 2**—the first color in the fourth column.

4 In the content placeholder on the right side of the slide, insert a **Clip Art** photograph by searching for **roller coaster** Insert the close-up picture of the roller coaster with the red cars on the blue sky background, as shown in Figure 11.80 at the beginning of this project. Crop the picture shape to **Rounded Rectangle**, and then modify the **Picture Effect** by applying the last **Bevel** style—**Art Deco**.

5 On **Slide 4**, insert the picture of the white looped roller coaster on the lighter blue sky background. Change the picture **Height** to **1.5** and then apply a **25 Point Soft Edges** effect. Drag the picture up and to the left to position it in the center of the red rectangle to the left of the slide title. Deselect the picture.

6 From the **Shapes** gallery, under **Block Arrows**, insert a **Down Arrow** aligned with the **left half of the horizontal ruler at 1 inch** and the **upper half of the vertical ruler at 0.5 inches**. On the **Format tab**, from the **Shape Styles** gallery, in the third row, apply the second style—**Light 1 Outline, Colored Fill - Blue, Accent 1**. Change the **Shape Height** to **2** and the **Shape Width** to **1**

7 Insert a **Text Box** aligned with the **left half of the horizontal ruler at 1.5 inches** and with the **lower half of the vertical ruler at 2 inches**. On the **Format tab**, from the **Shape Styles** gallery, in the last row, apply the third style—**Intense Effect - Red, Accent 2**. In the inserted text box, type **And Let the Excitement Begin!** Change the **Font Size** to **40**, and then if necessary, drag the text box so that its right edge aligns with the right edge of the slide. Select the arrow and the text box, and then apply **Align Left** alignment using the **Align Selected Objects** option.

8 Select the title, the arrow, and the text box. Distribute the objects vertically using the **Align Selected Objects** option. Apply the **Box** transition to all of the slides in the presentation, and then view the slide show from the beginning.

9 **Insert** a **Header & Footer** on the **Notes and Handouts**. Include the **Date and time updated automatically**, the **Page number**, and a **Footer** with the text **Lastname_Firstname_11G_Roller_Coasters** Apply to all.

10 Display the **Document Properties**. Replace the text in the **Author** box with your own firstname and lastname, in the **Subject** box, type your course name and section number, and in the **Keywords** box, type **roller coasters, new attractions** **Close** the **Document Information Panel**.

11 **Save** your presentation. Submit your presentation electronically or print **Handouts 4 Slides Horizontal** as directed by your instructor. **Close** the presentation and exit PowerPoint.

End **You have completed Project 11G**

Apply **11D** skills from these Objectives:

13 Remove Picture Backgrounds and Insert WordArt

14 Create and Format a SmartArt Graphic

Mastering PowerPoint | Project 11H Coaster Club

In the following Mastering PowerPoint project, you will format a presentation describing an event sponsored by Fascination Entertainment Group for roller coaster club members. Your completed presentation will look similar to Figure 11.81.

Project Files

For Project 11H, you will need the following file:

p11H_Coaster_Club

You will save your presentation as:

Lastname_Firstname_11H_Coaster_Club

Project Results

About Coaster Enthusiasts

Coaster enthusiasts travel the world to find the tallest, fastest, and longest coasters. They will expect park employees to understand coaster terminology and be able to answer questions about the coasters at all of our park locations and also those at competing parks.

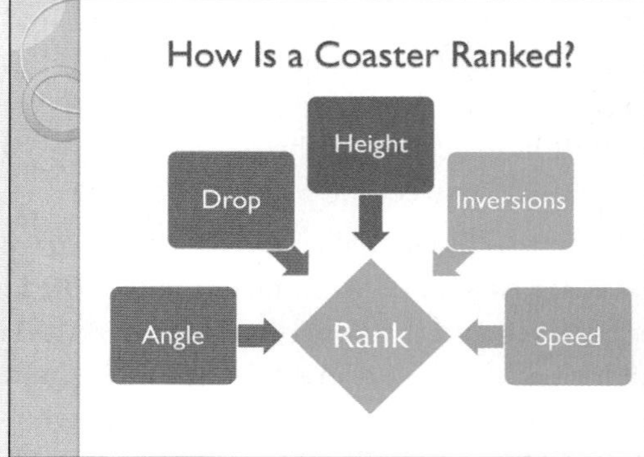

KNOW THE FOLLOWING INFORMATION FOR EACH OF OUR ROLLER COASTERS!

- Angle
  - Degree of steepest angle
- Drop
  - Distance from top of largest drop to bottom
- Height
  - Distance from highest point of track to ground
- Inversions
  - Number of times rider goes upside-down
- Speed
  - Maximum speed achieved by coaster

Figure 11.81

(Project 11H Coaster Club continues on the next page)

Mastering PowerPoint | Project 11H Coaster Club (continued)

1 **Start** PowerPoint. From the student files that accompany this textbook, open **p11H_Coaster_Club**, and then **Save** the file in your **All In One Chapter 11** folder as **Lastname_Firstname_11H_Coaster_Club**

2 On **Slide 1**, select the title and display the **WordArt** gallery. In the last row, apply the third WordArt style—**Fill - Aqua, Accent 2, Matte Bevel**. On **Slide 2**, convert the bulleted list to a **SmartArt** graphic by applying the **Vertical Bracket List** graphic. Change the SmartArt color to **Colorful Range - Accent Colors 3 to 4**, and then apply the **Inset 3-D** style.

3 On **Slide 4**, in the content placeholder, insert a **Relationship** type **SmartArt** graphic—**Converging Radial**. In the circle shape, type **Rank** In the left rectangle, type **Angle** in the middle rectangle, type **Drop** and in the right rectangle type **Height** Add a shape after the *Height* rectangle, and then type **Inversions** Add a shape after the *Inversions* rectangle, and then type **Speed** so that your SmartArt contains five rectangular shapes pointing to the circle shape.

4 Change the SmartArt color to **Colorful Range - Accent Colors 3 to 4**, and then apply the **3-D Flat Scene** style. Change the circle shape to the **Diamond** basic shape. On the **Format tab**, in the **Shapes group**, click the **Larger** button two times to increase the size of the diamond.

5 On **Slide 5**, select the content placeholder, and then from the **Shape Styles** gallery, in the last row, apply the third style—**Intense Effect - Aqua, Accent 2**. Change the **Font Color** of all the text in the content placeholder to **Black, Text 1**.

6 On **Slide 6**, insert a **WordArt**—the third style in the last row—**Fill - Aqua, Accent 2, Matte Bevel**. Replace the WordArt text with **Mark Your Calendars!** Change the **Font Size** to **48**, and align the right edge of the WordArt placeholder with the right edge of the slide.

7 **Insert** a **Header & Footer** on the **Notes and Handouts**. Include the **Date and time updated automatically**, the **Page number**, and a **Footer** with the text **Lastname_Firstname_11H_Coaster_Club** Apply to all.

8 Display the **Document Properties**. Replace the text in the **Author** box with your own firstname and lastname, in the **Subject** box, type your course name and section number, and in the **Keywords** box, type **roller coasters, coaster club, events** Close the **Document Information Panel**.

9 **Save** your presentation, and then view the slide show from the beginning. Submit your presentation electronically or print **Handouts 6 Slides Horizontal** as directed by your instructor. **Close** the presentation and exit PowerPoint.

End **You have completed Project 11H**

Content-Based Assessments

Apply 11A and 11B skills from these Objectives:

1. Create a New Presentation
2. Edit a Presentation in Normal View
3. Add Pictures to a Presentation
4. Print and View a Presentation
5. Edit an Existing Presentation
6. Format a Presentation
7. Use Slide Sorter View
8. Apply Slide Transitions

Mastering PowerPoint | Project 11I Island Tour

In the following Mastering PowerPoint project, you will edit an existing presentation that describes the tour of the islands offered by Lehua Hawaiian Adventures. Your completed presentation will look similar to Figure 11.82.

Project Files

For Project 11I, you will need the following files:

p11I_Island_Tour
jpg11I_Rocky_Shore
p11I_Scenic_Cruise

You will save your presentation as:

Lastname_Firstname_11I_Island_Tour

Project Results

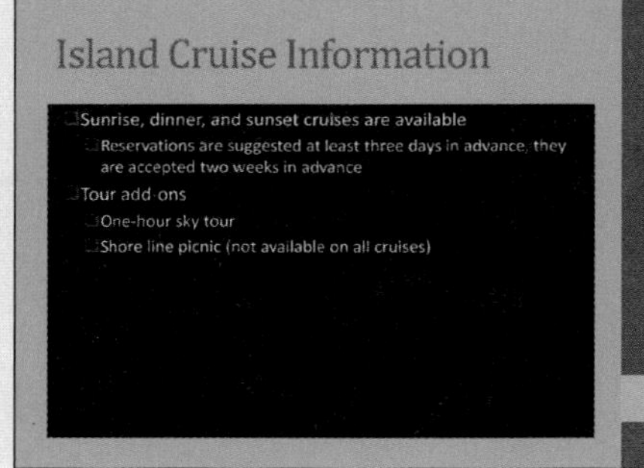

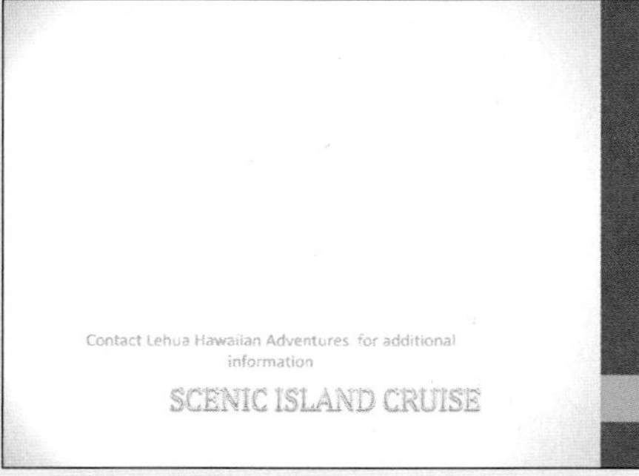

Figure 11.82

(Project 11I Island Tour continues on the next page)

Mastering PowerPoint | Project 11I Island Tour (continued)

1 **Start** PowerPoint, and then from your student files, open the file **p11I_Island_Tour**. In your **All In One Chapter 11** folder, **Save** the file as **Lastname_Firstname_11I_Island_Tour**

2 Replace all occurrences of the text **Hawaiian Shore** with **Island Cruise** Display **Slide 3**, open the **Reuse Slides** pane, and then from your student files browse for and display the presentation **p11I_Scenic_Cruise**. If necessary, clear the Keep source formatting check box, and then insert both slides from the **p11I_Scenic_Cruise** file. **Close** the **Reuse Slides** pane.

3 Display the presentation outline, and then in **Slide 3**, increase the list level of the bullet point beginning *Reservations are suggested*. In either the **Slide pane** or the **Outline**, click at the end of the last bullet point after the word *advance*, and then insert a new bullet point. Decrease its list level. Type **Tour add-ons** and then press Enter. Increase the list level, and then type the following two bullet points.

One-hour sky tour

Shore line picnic (not available on all cruises)

4 Display the slide thumbnails. In **Slide 1**, select the subtitle—*The Big Island's Shore Line*—and then change the **Font Color** to **Lime, Accent 1, Darker 25%** and the **Font Size** to **30** On **Slide 2**, apply **Bold** and **Italic** formatting to the caption text located below the slide title. Change the **Line Spacing** to **1.5**. Click in the content placeholder at the top, and then from your student files, insert the picture **jpg11H_Rocky_Shore**. Format the picture with the **Snip Diagonal Corner, White** picture style and the **Paint Brush** artistic effect.

5 In **Slide Sorter** view, move **Slide 5** between **Slides 3** and **4**. In **Normal** view, on **Slide 5**, change the slide **Layout** to **Section Header**, and then type the following notes in the **Notes pane**: **Other cruises and tours are also available.** Apply the **Blinds** transition and change the **Effect Options** to **Horizontal**. Change the **Timing** by increasing the **Duration** to **01.75**. Apply the transition effect to all of the slides. View the slide show from the beginning.

6 **Insert** a **Header & Footer** on the **Notes and Handouts**. Include the **Date and time updated automatically**, the **Page number**, and a **Footer**, using your own name, with the text **Lastname_Firstname_11I_Island_Tour**

7 Check spelling in the presentation. If necessary, select the Ignore All option if proper names are indicated as misspelled.

8 Display the **Document Information Panel**. Replace the text in the **Author** box with your own firstname and lastname. In the **Subject** box, type your course name and section number, and in the **Keywords** box, type **scenic island tour** **Close** the Document Information Panel.

9 **Save** your presentation. Submit your presentation electronically or print **Handouts, 6 Slides Horizontal** as directed by your instructor. **Close** the presentation.

End **You have completed Project 11I**

Apply 11C and 11D skills from these Objectives:

9 Format Numbered and Bulleted Lists
10 Insert Clip Art
11 Insert Text Boxes and Shapes
12 Format Objects
13 Remove Picture Backgrounds and Insert WordArt
14 Create and Format a SmartArt Graphic

Mastering PowerPoint | Project 11J Corporate Events

In the following Mastering PowerPoint project, you will edit an existing presentation that is shown to promote corporate events at Fascination Entertainment Group. Your completed presentation will look similar to Figure 11.83.

Project Files

For Project 11J, you will need the following files:

p11J_Corporate_Events
p11J_Orientation
p11J_Maya_Ruiz
p11J_David_Jensen
Jp11J_Ken_Lee

You will save your presentation as:

Lastname_Firstname_11J_Corporate_Events

Project Results

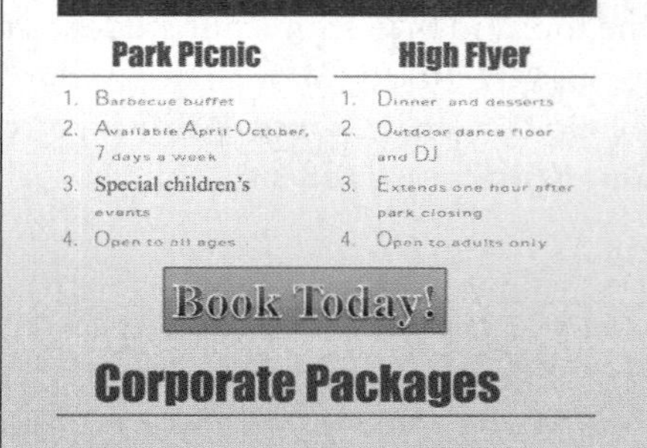

Figure 11.83

(Project 11J Corporate Events continues on the next page)

Mastering PowerPoint | Project 11J Corporate Events (continued)

1 **Start** PowerPoint, and then from your student data files, open the file **p11J_Corporate_Events**. In your **All In One Chapter 11** folder, **Save** the file as **Lastname_Firstname_11J_Corporate_Events**

2 On **Slide 1**, format the title as a **WordArt** using the fifth style in the sixth row—**Fill – Dark Red, Accent 1, Metal Bevel, Reflection**. Select all three pictures, and then using the **Align to Slide** option, align the pictures using the **Distribute Horizontally** and **Align Middle** commands. On **Slide 2**, change the **Shape Style** of the text content placeholder to the second style in the fourth row—**Subtle Effect – Dark Red, Accent 1**.

3 On **Slide 3**, convert the bulleted list to the **Picture** type **SmartArt** graphic—**Vertical Picture List**. Change the color to **Gradient Range - Accent 1**, and then apply the **3-D Powder** style. In the three picture placeholders, from your student files insert the following pictures: **jpg11J_Sondra_Hernandez**, **jpg11J_Jason_Thomas**, and **jpg11J_Lee_Wang**.

4 On **Slide 4**, change the two bulleted lists to **Numbering**. Then, insert a **WordArt** using the **Gradient Fill – Dark Red, Accent 1, Outline – White** style with the text **Book Today!** and position the WordArt centered below the two content placeholders. Apply a **Shape Style** to the WordArt using **Subtle Effect – Blue-Gray, Accent 5**.

5 On **Slide 5**, change the bullet symbols to **Checkmark Bullets**, and then in the placeholder on the right, insert a **Clip Art** photograph by searching for **ticket** Insert the picture of the two raffle tickets on green background, and then remove the background from the picture so that only the tickets display. Mark areas to keep and remove as necessary. Change the **Shape Height** to **3** and then apply the **Blue-Gray, 18 pt glow, Accent color 4** picture effect.

6 On **Slide 5**, insert a **Text Box** aligned with the **left half of the horizontal ruler at 3 inches** and with the **lower half of the vertical ruler at 2.5 inches**. In the text box, type **All attendees will enjoy these benefits!** Apply **Italic**, and then **Align Center** the text box using the **Align to Slide** option.

7 Insert a **New Slide** with the **Blank** layout. From the **Shapes** gallery, under **Rectangles**, insert a **Rounded Rectangle** of any size anywhere on the slide. Then, resize the rectangle so that its **Shape Height** is **5** and its **Shape Width** is **7** Using the **Align to Slide** option, apply the **Align Center**, and **Align Middle** alignment commands. Apply the **Moderate Effect – Blue-Gray, Accent 5** shape style to the rectangle, and then in the rectangle, type **Fascination Entertainment Group Welcomes Your Group!** Change the **Font Size** to **54**, and then apply the **Soft Round Bevel** effect to the rectangle shape.

8 **Insert** a **Header & Footer** on the **Notes and Handouts**. Include the **Date and time updated automatically**, the **Page number**, and a **Footer** with the text **Lastname_Firstname_11J_Corporate_Events** Apply to all.

9 Display the **Document Properties**. Replace the text in the **Author** box with your own firstname and lastname, in the **Subject** box, type your course name and section number, and in the **Keywords** box, type **corporate events** **Close** the **Document Information Panel**.

10 **Save** your presentation, and then view the slide show from the beginning. Submit your presentation electronically or print **Handouts 6 Slides Horizontal** as directed by your instructor. **Close** the presentation and exit PowerPoint.

End **You have completed Project 11J**

Unit 4 Case Project

© Juriah Mosin/Shutterstock

PowerPoint Presentations Created by a Sales Operations Manager for a Sporting Goods Company; Your Own Presentation about Sports

In this Unit Case Project, you will modify PowerPoint presentations for Front Range Action Sports regarding promotions for sports activities and a new location. You will also create your own PowerPoint presentation about your favorite sports. Your completed presentations for Front Range Action Sports will look similar to the ones shown in Figure 4.1.

Project Files

For Unit 4 Case Project, you will need the following files:

pU4_Bicycling
pU4_Company_Info
jpgU4_Picture1
jpgU4_Picture2

You will save your file as:

Lastname_Firstname_U4_Biking

Project Results

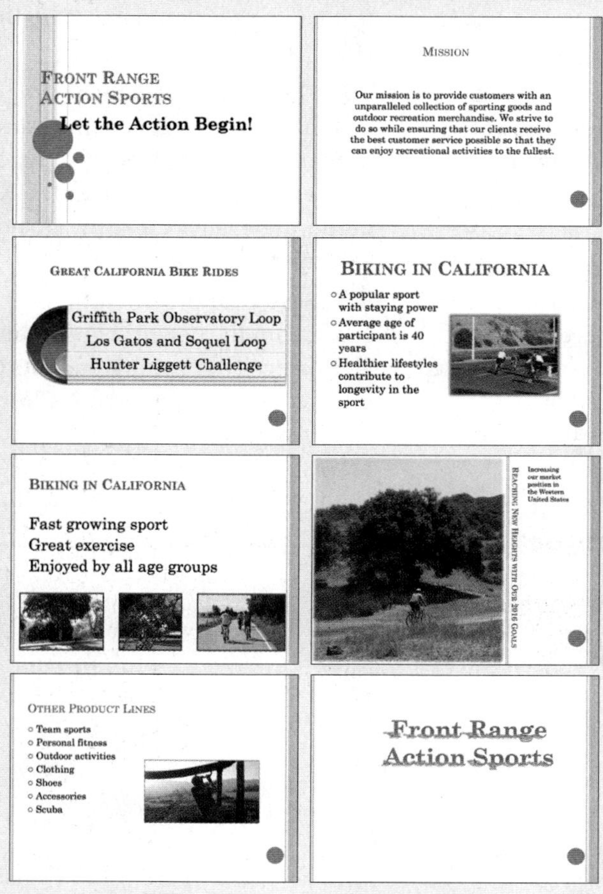

Figure 4.1

PowerPoint Presentations Created by a Sales Operations Manager for a Sporting Goods Company; Your Own Presentation about Sports (continued)

1 **Start** PowerPoint. From your student data files, open the file **pU4_Bicycling**. On your storage device, create a new folder named **All In One Unit 4** and then **Save** the presentation as **Lastname_Firstname_U4_Bicycling**

2 Apply the **Oriel** design theme to all slides in the presentation.

3 After **Slide 1**, insert **Slide 2** from the student data file **pU4_Company_Info**. Close the **Reuse Slides** pane. On **Slide 2**, remove the bullet symbol from the paragraph and **Center** the text.

4 On **Slide 3**, apply the picture style **Soft Edge Rectangle** to the picture.

5 On **Slide 4**, convert the text in the content placeholder to a **Target List** SmartArt diagram. Change the color to **Colorful Range – Accent Colors 3 to 4** and then apply the **3-D Polished** style.

6 Change the slide layout of **Slide 5** to **Two Content**. In the right placeholder, insert the **jpgU4_Picture1** picture.

7 In **Slide Sorter** view. Move **Slide 3** into the **Slide 6** position.

8 In **Normal** view, on **Slide 5**, select the three pictures, and **Align** them at the bottom. With the three pictures selected, **Distribute Horizontally**.

9 Insert a new **Two Content** slide after **Slide 6**. As the title text, type **Other Product Lines** In the first placeholder, type the following bullet points:

Team sports
Personal fitness
Outdoor activities
Clothing
Shoes
Accessories
Scuba

10 In the second placeholder, insert the picture **jpgU4_Picture2**.

11 In the **Notes** pane on **Slide 7**, add the following speaker note: **With the increase in travel to the western U.S. for sports, the opportunities are great.**

12 Delete **Slide 8** from the presentation.

13 To the title *Front Range Action Sports* on **Slide 8**, apply the WordArt style **Gradient Fill – Orange, Accent 1** and then from the **Text Effects**, apply the **Shadow** effect **Perspective Diagonal Upper Left Shadow**.

14 Apply the **Fade** transition effect with the **Through Black** option to all slides in the presentation at a duration of **1.5**.

15 **Insert** a **Header & Footer** on the **Notes and Handouts**. Include the **Date and time** updated automatically, the **Page number**, and a **Footer**, using your own name, with the text **Lastname_Firstname_U4_Bicycling**

16 Display the Properties area, and add your name, your course name and section number, and the keywords **bicycling, California**

17 View your presentation from the beginning. When the black slide displays, click the mouse button one more time, and then correct any errors.

18 **Save** and **Close** the presentation. Submit as directed by your instructor.

Favorite Sports

Pick one or two of your favorite sporting or outdoor activities. Create a presentation with six or more slides that describes the sport, the equipment required, your ideal location in which to participate in the sport, and famous athletes who have exceled at the sports you like. Choose an appropriate theme, slide layouts, and pictures from Microsoft clipart, and then format the presentation attractively. Save your presentation as **Lastname_Firstname_U4_Favorite_Sports** and submit as directed.

The Internet, Web Apps, and Microsoft Access

Chapters in Unit 5:

CHAPTER 12

Concepts: The Internet and World Wide Web

CHAPTER 13

Applications: Create, Query, and Sort an Access Database; Create Forms and Reports

CHAPTER 14

Applications: Explore Cloud Computing Using Windows Live and Microsoft Office Web Apps

Job Focus: Library Assistant at a College

View Unit 5 Video to meet a College Librarian

At the end of this unit, you will have the opportunity to complete a case project that focuses on the job of a Library Assistant at a college. If you had a position like this, some of the things you might do are: assist students in the library with Internet and Web searches; assist students in using computer databases in the library; conduct meetings with students and faculty; and help students save and store documents in the cloud.

The Internet and World Wide Web

OUTCOMES

At the end of this chapter you will be able to:

Access the Internet, differentiate the Web from the Internet, recognize quality Web sites, and practice online etiquette and safe surfing.

Evaluate the possibilities of e-commerce and cloud computing.

OBJECTIVES

Mastering these objectives will enable you to:

Job Focus:
Library Assistant for a College

In This Chapter

As a Library Assistant at a college, some of your responsibilities are related to the Internet and online research. For example, you are expected to provide information about online sources, demonstrate to others the use of the online library, and assist students and faculty in the use of subscription databases like business directories and encyclopedias.

In this chapter, you will learn the overall structure of the Internet and the Web. You will also learn about polite online behavior, safe surfing strategies, e-commerce, and cloud computing. This knowledge will help you expand your Internet use by recognizing quality Web sites and using good search tools to reduce your search time—all while staying safe and keeping your data secure.

Objective 1 | Understand the Internet

As a Library Assistant at a college, you frequently conduct a presentation entitled *Introduction to the Library*, which is required for all new students. You want the Internet portion of your presentation to include an overview of the Internet's architecture. You also want to emphasize how easy it is to access the Internet regardless of computer type or computer operating system. Where do you start?

The ***Internet***, also called the ***Net***, is a global computer network made up of thousands of privately and publicly owned computers and networks that grew and interlinked, over time, into one giant network. In short, the Internet is a network of networks.

The idea of connecting computers of different designs and over distant locations started in the 1960s with the U.S. Department of Defense and a project called ARPANET, which stands for Advanced Research Projects Agency Network. The purpose of the project was to create a form of secure communication for military and scientific purposes and to create a method for transferring such communications between computers. The outcome of the project was a network that consisted of four computers located at the University of California at Los Angeles, the University of California at Santa Barbara, the University of Utah, and Stanford Research Institute. In turn, each of these four computers—referred to as nodes—connected hundreds of other computers to the network. What you know as the Internet is the offspring of the ARPANET project. To learn more about the history of the Internet, go to **www.isoc.org/internet/history/brief.shtml**.

The Internet is composed of more than 750 million ***hosts***. A host is a computer that can receive requests and reply to those requests. These hosts are interconnected and geographically spread out over the world. Figure 12.1 provides a simplified image of a single network that is set up to provide its users with access to the Internet and any of the Internet's hosts. A study done by the Internet Systems Consortium substantiates the rapid growth of the Internet by citing an increase of over 208 million hosts between 2008 and 2010.

The Internet began as a communication and file exchange network for government agencies, scientific research groups, and academic institutions. Now the Internet has grown into a tool for everyone to discover and explore information, buy and sell products, take classes, and socialize with friends. As a global leader in measuring the digital world, comScore, Inc. indicates from its surveys that the global Internet audience—defined as users ages 15 and older—exceeded 2 billion unique visitors as of March 2011. This includes the use of both home and work computers. The leap to 3 billion users is expected to come quickly.

Concept 12.01 | Exploring the Internet

Nobody owns the Internet. It is a network in which every connected computer can exchange data with any other computer on the network. The term ***cyberspace*** captures the concept of the intangible, nonphysical territory that the Internet encompasses. The networks that make up the Internet are not maintained by one company or organization. Instead, the

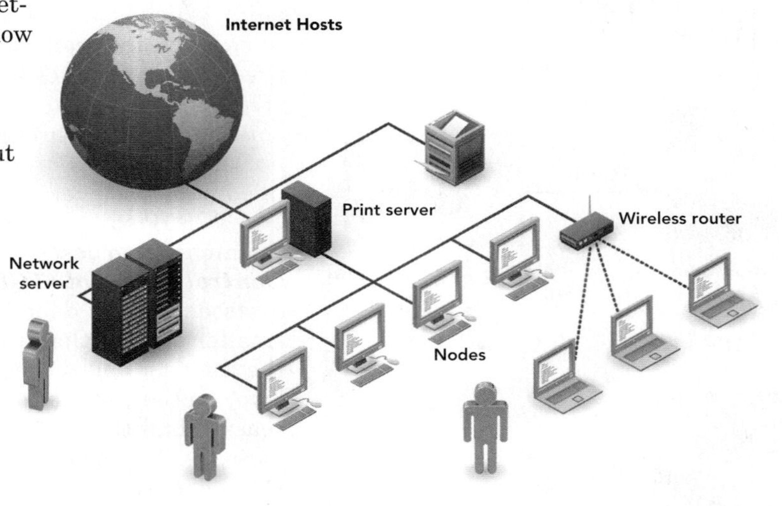

FIGURE 12.1 Both wired and wireless technologies connect to the Internet.

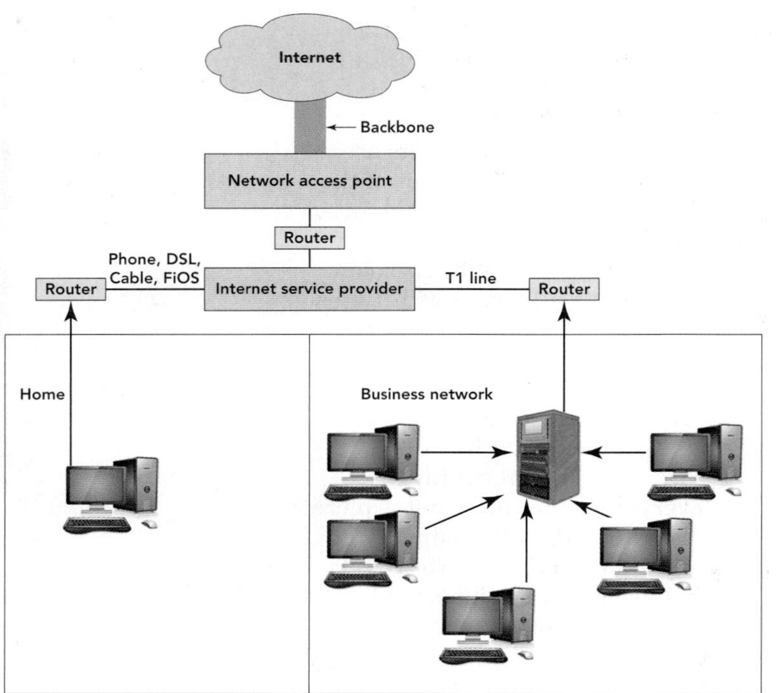

FIGURE 12.2 The path data takes from your computer to the Internet.

Internet is maintained by a conglomerate of volunteers across the world. Some governing bodies restrict control and/or provide equipment. But the majority of network servers and connectivity equipment are provided by universities, telecommunications companies, businesses, corporations, and services that sell Internet access. It really is amazing that it all works!

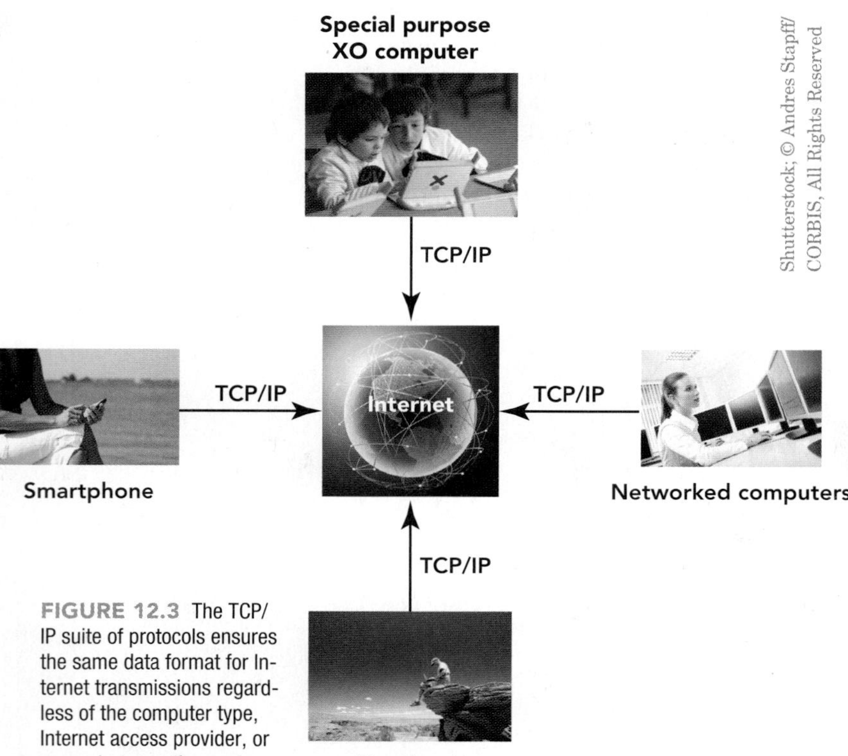

FIGURE 12.3 The TCP/IP suite of protocols ensures the same data format for Internet transmissions regardless of the computer type, Internet access provider, or computer operating system.

Concept 12.02 | Investigating Internet Architecture

The ***Internet backbone***, the main high-speed routes through which data travels, is maintained by ***network service providers (NSPs)*** such as AT&T, Sprint, Verizon, BBN, and UUNET. The equipment of these providers is linked at ***network access points (NAPs)*** so that data may, for example, begin its journey on a segment maintained by AT&T but cross over to a Sprint segment in order to reach its destination. Between your computer or business network and the Internet backbone are ***routers***, specialized devices that connect networks, locate the best path of transmission, and ensure that your data reaches its destination (Figure 12.2).

Concept 12.03 | Understanding Interoperability

The Internet does more than allow you to freely exchange data among millions of computers; it provides you with the ability to exchange data regardless of the brand, model, or operating system of the computer you are using. This capability is called ***interoperability***. When you access the Internet using a Mac, for example, you contact a number of computers that may include other Macs, Windows PCs, UNIX systems, smartphones, and even mainframe computers. You do not know what type of computer you are accessing and it makes no difference.

How is the Internet's interoperability achieved? The ***TCP/IP (Transmission Control Protocol/ Internet Protocol)*** suite, which is a set of standard methods to package and transmit information on the Internet, enables interoperability (Figure 12.3). When you access the Internet, usually through an Internet access provider, your computer is supplied with a copy of the TCP/IP programs. The TCP/IP suite employs a two-layer communication design. The ***Transmission Control Protocol (TCP)***, manages the disassembling of a message or file into smaller packets that are transmitted over the Internet and then received by a TCP layer on the destination computer that reassembles the packets into the original message. The lower layer, the ***Internet Protocol (IP)***, handles the address part of each packet so that it gets to the right recipient.

Objective 2 | Evaluate Internet Connectivity Options

As a Library Assistant at a college, you serve on the college's Technology Committee. The committee is investigating methods to establish Internet connectivity on a new rural extension site designed to reach a community approximately 60 miles from the main campus. The committee wants to be sure that the Internet connection can support all of the college services and accommodate all students, especially those using older computers. Where do you start?

When you access the Internet, it is referred to as *going online*. You usually do not connect directly to the Internet backbone. Instead, you usually connect to an Internet access provider that in turn connects you to the backbone via some type of wired or wireless connection.

Concept 12.04 | Investigating Internet Access Providers

Internet access providers are companies or businesses that provide access to the Internet either for free, for a fixed monthly charge, or for an itemized per use fee. Some of the roles and responsibilities of an access provider include:

- Providing and maintaining a connection to the Internet
- Supporting the hardware and software needed to service the connection
- Protecting their site and network from external threats such as viruses, hacker attacks, and other illegal activities
- Providing 24-hour customer service and technical support

Access providers fall into three categories: Internet service providers, online service providers, and wireless Internet service providers.

An ***Internet service provider (ISP)*** is a company that provides access to the Internet. Initially, they provided no additional services, but now ISPs have features to make them a one-stop source for Internet services. There are both local and national ISPs, each having various services and pricing. If you are looking for an Internet service provider, consider *The List*, a buyer's guide to ISPs that you can access at **www.thelist.com**.

Energy-Aware Computing

It is easy to think of the Internet as just something out there, an intangible, having no effect on our physical world. In reality, 2009 estimates indicate that Internet data centers worldwide consumed 2 percent of global electricity production. Most of the energy was used to power forced-air cooling systems in the data centers. One data center operator compared the heat emitted from a rack of servers in a data center to the amount of heat emitted by a 7-foot stack of toaster ovens. The energy to cool such centers probably did not come from green sources and cost $30 billion.

Another way to cool the data centers is under development. This new idea is to use water, not air, to cool the computing environment. Water cooled to 60°C–70°C (158°F), which is cool enough to keep the processing chips below their maximum heat of 85°C (185°F), will be pumped through tiny channels in the computer systems of the data centers and will absorb heat from the metal along the way. The working model, named Aquasar, developed by IBM Zurich and the Swiss Federal Institute of Technology Zurich (ETH), will be located on the ETH campus. In this prototype, the water used to absorb the heat from the computer systems will release that heat into the building and then recirculate to cool the computer system. It is estimated that this system will reduce the carbon footprint of the ETH campus by 85 percent and save up to 30 tons of carbon emissions a year. For more information, go to **www.youtube.com/watch?v=FbGyAXsLzlc** to view a video on this new cooling concept.

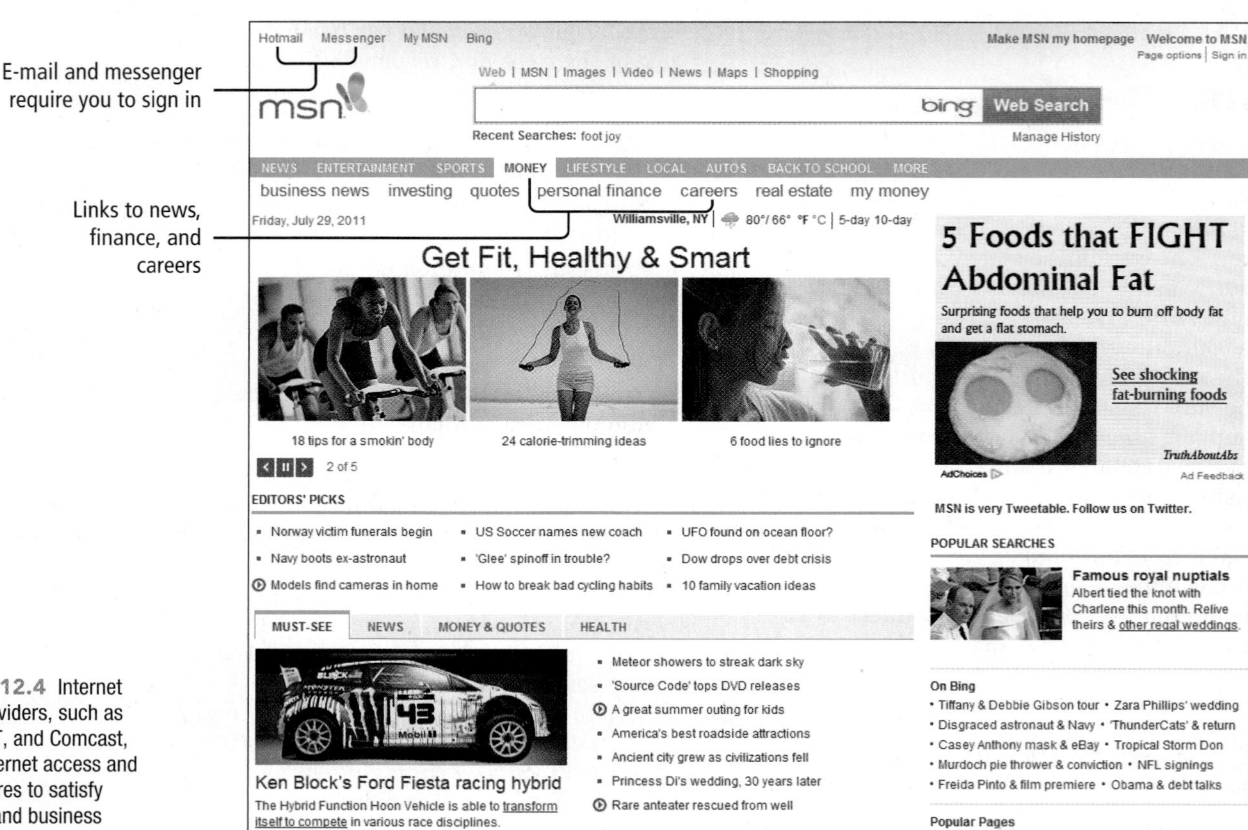

FIGURE 12.4 Internet access providers, such as MSN, AT&T, and Comcast, provide Internet access and extra features to satisfy individual and business subscribers.

An ***online service provider (OSP)*** is a for-profit firm that provides a proprietary network and offers special services that are available only to subscribers. Members may participate in instant messaging, chat rooms, and discussions, and take advantage of fee-based content such as magazines and newspapers. When they began, online services provided a large amount of content that was accessible only by those who subscribed to that online service, whereas ISPs predominantly served to provide access to the Internet and generally provided little exclusive content of their own. The distinction between these two services has become less defined as OSPs today offer Internet access and ISPs offer more user services. Popular OSPs are MSN and AOL (Figure 12.4).

A ***wireless Internet service provider*** is a local or national company that provides wireless Internet access to computers and other mobile devices, such as notebooks and smartphones. Some familiar providers are AT&T, T-Mobile, and Verizon Wireless. Requirements for a wireless connection include a portable device, an internal wireless adapter or a USB port for connecting an external adapter, and a wireless Internet access plan from a provider. Wireless connectivity for portable devices in your home or office is usually provided through a wireless router located in close proximity and connected to your provider.

From either the Companion Web Site or MyITLab, watch Chapter 12 Video 1

Your access provider furnishes you with a modem, or some other type of hardware, that enables access to the Internet backbone. Essentially, the provider acts as your access ramp to a highway; in this case, the highway is the Internet backbone. Your provider usually charges a monthly fee for Internet access, like the fee you pay to use some expressways.

Now that you can distinguish between access providers, focus on the types of physical connections used to gain entry to the Internet.

Concept 12.05 | Understanding Connection Options

In addition to obtaining an Internet account, you must decide how you will access the Internet. Be aware that the access speed advertised by an Internet access provider is often a maximum and your usage will probably never reach the advertised figure. Your

Types of Internet Access

Type	Price Range per Month	Speed of Access (receiving data)	Advantages	Disadvantages
Dial-up	$5 to $20	Slow: 56 kilobits per second (Kbps)	Availability Low user cost	Slow speed
DSL	$10 to $30	Average: 1.5 megabits per second (Mbps) Maximum: 7+ Mbps	Speed Reliability	Availability High user cost
Cable	$30 to $60	Average: 3 Mbps Maximum: 30+ Mbps	Speed Reliability	Availability High user cost
Satellite	$60 to $100	Average: 700 Kbps Maximum: 1.5 Mbps	Availability Speed	High user cost Reliability
Fiber-optic service	$40 to $140	Average: 15 Mbps Maximum: 50+ Mbps	Speed	Availability High user cost

Figure 12.5

access choices typically include the options shown in Figure 12.5.

- Dial-up access: If you are searching for an affordable connection solution and speed is not a high priority, then a dial-up provider will likely meet your needs. A dial-up connection does not require any special hardware; it uses your existing phone jack and dial-up modem configurations. The downside of this type of access is the speed; it is the slowest of all Internet services.
- Digital subscriber line (DSL): A DSL connection offers faster access speeds than dial-up, while making use of ordinary phone lines with the addition of a special external modem. One drawback of DSL is that service does not extend more than a few miles from a telephone switching station or central office (CO).
- Cable access: Many cable TV companies provide permanent online connections and offer high-speed Internet access, comparable to—and sometimes surpassing—DSL speeds. No phone line is needed, but a cable modem is required.
- Satellite access: If your geographical area has been overlooked by DSL and cable providers, go outside. If you have a clear view of the sky, then you can most likely get high-speed satellite Internet service! The connection to your high-speed satellite service is comprised of both indoor and outdoor equipment. Outside, there is an antenna and electronics to transmit and receive data, along with a connection to a small, unobtrusive dish. This equipment connects to an indoor receive unit (IRU) and indoor transmit unit (ITU) that connect to your computer through a simple USB connector. Satellite is more costly than cable or DSL, but if you live in a rural area, it might be a viable alternative to dial-up.
- Fiber-optic service: Fiber-optic lines running directly to the home provide users with an incredibly fast Internet connection, easily surpassing other access methods. ***Fiber-optic service*** is rapidly becoming a challenger to DSL and cable providers, especially in the suburbs. However, this service is still unavailable in many cities and rural areas and is usually offered by a limited number of providers. No modem is needed, but fiber-optic cable may have to be installed to and within your home.

If you do not need a constant, daily Internet connection, some businesses offer special leased lines for companies, educational institutions, and large organizations. Internet access is attained through the organization's network and is usually free to the users because the company or institution pays the bill.

Objective 3 | Differentiate Between the Internet and the Web

As a Library Assistant at a college, your presentation to students must include information about how to navigate the Web and you want to encourage students to try different browsers. Where do you start?

What is the difference between saying *I'm on the Internet* and saying *I'm on the Web*? The Internet and the Web are not the same thing, although we think of them that way. Recall that the Internet is a network of hardware—computers, cables, and routers—through which any computer can directly access other computers and exchange data. The ***World Wide Web***—or ***Web*** or ***WWW***—is a portion of the Internet that contains billions of documents. Think of the Internet as the physical connection of millions of networks, like an interstate highway. The Web *uses* the Internet as its transport mechanism to distribute its collection of documents or resources. The Web uses the Internet architecture to move information in the same way that cars and trucks use an interstate to move goods and people (Figure 12.6).

Just like the Internet, no one owns the Web. Standards and guidelines related to all aspects of the Web are published by the World Wide Web Consortium (W3C), an international organization based in Cambridge, Massachusetts. Visit **www.w3.org** to review the mission of the W3C, a list of its 316 members, and Internet standards. Besides the W3C, Figure 12.7 lists organizations that contribute to the development of the Internet and Web and describes the organization's mission.

Concept 12.06 | Viewing Content on the Web

The documents that comprise the World Wide Web and are transported over the Internet are called ***Web pages***. Each page is a document or information resource created using ***Hypertext Markup Language (HTML)*** or ***Extensible Hypertext Markup Language (XHTML)***. HTML is a language that uses a tag system of code to create Web pages. In this system, text is surrounded by a pair of markers called *tags*. One tag starts the feature and another indicates where it is to stop. The pair of tags describes how the text located

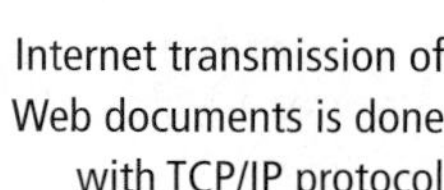
Internet transmission of
Web documents is done
with TCP/IP protocol

© Glenn Millington / Alamy

FIGURE 12.6 TCP/IP protocol is used to transport data, information, and Web pages over the Internet.

Internet and Web Management Organizations

Name	Description and Purpose
ICANN: Internet Corporation for Assigned Names and Numbers **www.icann.org**	Nonprofit, international organization responsible for coordinating the Internet's Domain Name System and assigning IP addresses.
IETF: Internet Engineering Task Force **www.ietf.org**	International community of information technology (IT) professionals—including network designers, operators, vendors, and researchers—responsible for developing Internet standards, best practices, and informational documents.
ISOC: Internet Society **www.isoc.org**	Nonprofit, international association of over 80 organizations and 28,000 individual members, formed to provide leadership in Internet-related standards, education, and policy for the benefit of people throughout the world.
IAB: Internet Architecture Board **www.iab.org**	Advisory body to the ISOC, this international committee of the IETF is comprised of 13 volunteers from the IT community who oversee the development of Internet architecture, protocols, procedures, and standards.
IRTF: Internet Research Task Force **www.irtf.org**	A task force of individual contributors from the research community working together in small, long-term research groups that report to the IAB and explore important topics related to the evolution of the Internet.

Figure 12.7

between them should display. For example, a line surrounded by h1 (level 1 heading) tags would be coded as:

```
<h1>Welcome to GO! All In
One</h1>
```

This text would display in your browser as bold, in a larger font size used for level 1 headings, and left aligned.

XHTML combines the flexibility of HTML with the addition of ***Extensible Markup Language (XML)***, a language that enables Web page developers to create their own set of rules to define how data is to be represented on the Web. The rules created are included in the Web page and used by your browser to interpret the code correctly and display the page accurately.

A ***Web browser*** is a free program installed on your computer that displays a Web document by interpreting the HTML or XHTML format, enabling you to view and activate features that appear on that page. One of the most used features of markup languages is ***hypertext***, a feature that enables objects like text, pictures, music, and programs to be linked to each other. It works by means of ***hyperlinks***—also called ***links***—which are elements in an electronic document that act as the connector to another place in the same document or to an entirely different document. Typically, you click on the hyperlink to bring another object into view (Figure 12.8). When related Web pages are linked together by hyperlinks they create a ***Web site***. A Web site typically contains a ***home page***—also called an ***index page***—which is a default page that displays automatically when you enter a site at its top level.

Concept 12.07 | Choosing a Browser

There are several browsers that you can use to navigate the Internet. You might even have more than one installed on your system and alternate between them. Figure 12.9 displays the five top browsers in use worldwide from June 2011 to July 2011. Each browser has variations in terms of its interface and features as described in Figure 12.10.

FIGURE 12.8 Hyperlinks, often displayed in blue characters and underlined, are perfect for tutorial Web sites.

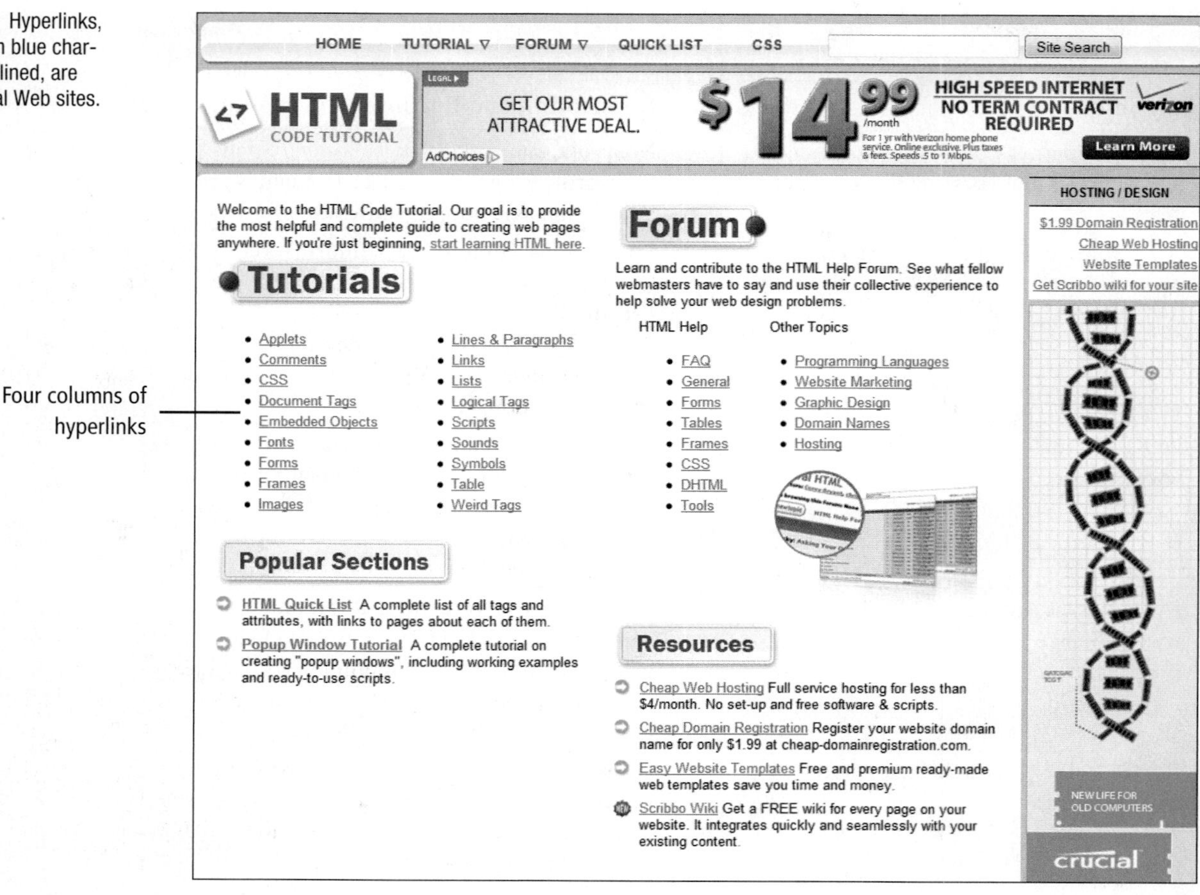

FIGURE 12.9 Although Internet Explorer is still the favorite browser, Firefox and Google Chrome provide viable competition.

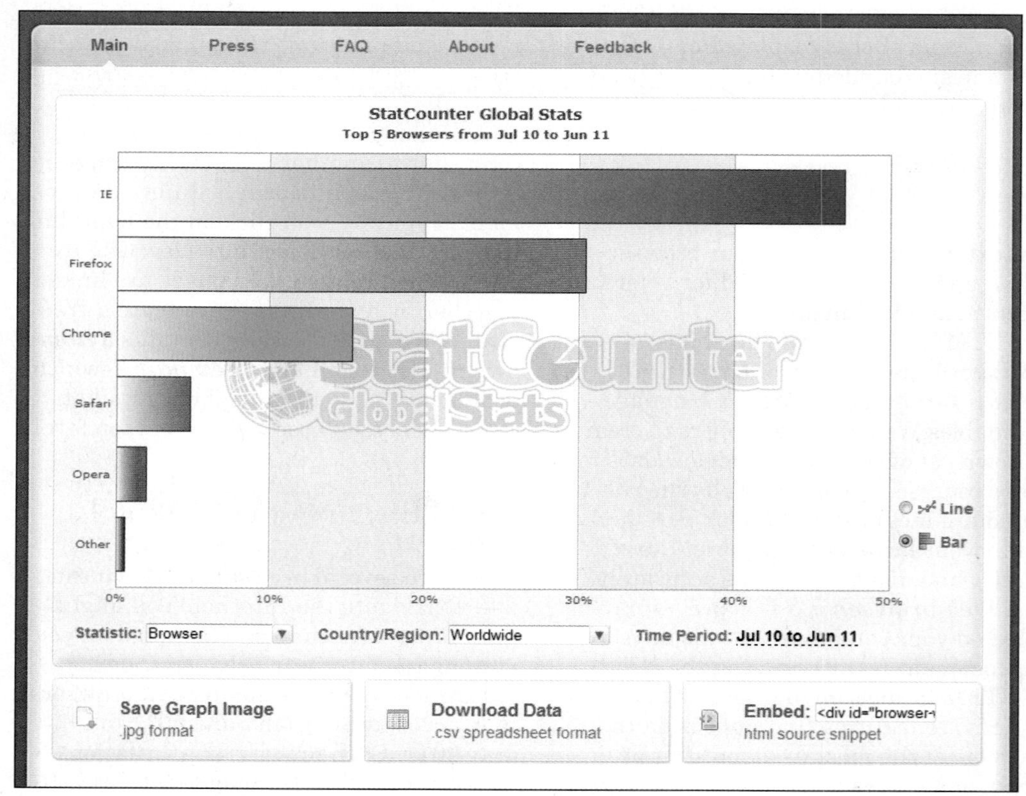

SOURCE: http://gs.statcounter.com/#browser-ww-monthly-201007-201106-bar

Popular Browsers and Their Features

Browser	Features
Internet Explorer (IE)	Internet Explorer, the browser installed on most newly purchased computers, offers some premier features: • Extensive parental controls that can be customized. • A variety of security and entertainment add-ons. • A smart toolbar that offers search suggestions. • The ability to pull a tab off the browser and pin it to the taskbar, if you are using Windows 7.
Firefox	Firefox, known for its speed and intuitive interface, also includes: • The ability to group tabs together without opening a new window. • Pin tabs as apps, which shrinks the tab to the size of an icon and moves it to the left of the tab bar. Pinned tabs can remain pinned over browser sessions. • Consolidated menus to give the site more space.
Google Chrome	Chrome touts its speed and ability to make complex features easy to use. Features include: • Visual sampling of your most visited sites every time you open a new tab including most used search engines, recently bookmarked pages, and closed tabs. (Internet Explorer 9 includes a similar feature.) • Tabs can be rearranged or dragged out of the browser to gather multiple tabs into one window. • Every tab you use is run independently in the browser, so if one application crashes, others are unaffected. • Bookmarking is accomplished by clicking a star icon at the left edge of the address bar.
Safari	Safari, which lacks some features like parental and antiphishing controls, was originally for Macs but is now also available for PCs. Features include: • The Mac look and feel in the Internet environment. • Tabbed browsing. • Spell checking for all fields. • Snapback—a temporary marker that enables you to return to a Web page.
Opera	Some features unique to Opera include: • *Duplicate this tab*, a feature that avoids cutting and pasting the URL in the address bar. • Fit to window width. • Nicknames for collections of sites.

Figure 12.10

All five browser programs open the same way and use similar features, such as tabbed browsing, navigation buttons, a search box, an address bar, and a status bar, as shown in Figure 12.11. All browsers also have the ability to cache—meaning store—Web page files and graphics on a computer's hard drive. When you browse a Web page for the first time, a copy of the page is stored on your hard drive in a storage space referred to as ***browser cache***. If you attempt to retrieve the page again, the browser does not go back to the Internet, but instead retrieves the page from the browser's cache. This eliminates excessive round trips to the server, displays the page for you faster, and reduces Internet traffic. However, if you are visiting a news provider's Web site that is constantly updating current stories, browser cache is not an advantage, because you do not want to view old news. This problem has been solved by including directives, referred to as freshness indicators, at the beginning of Web pages, images, and other features, that specify how long the page

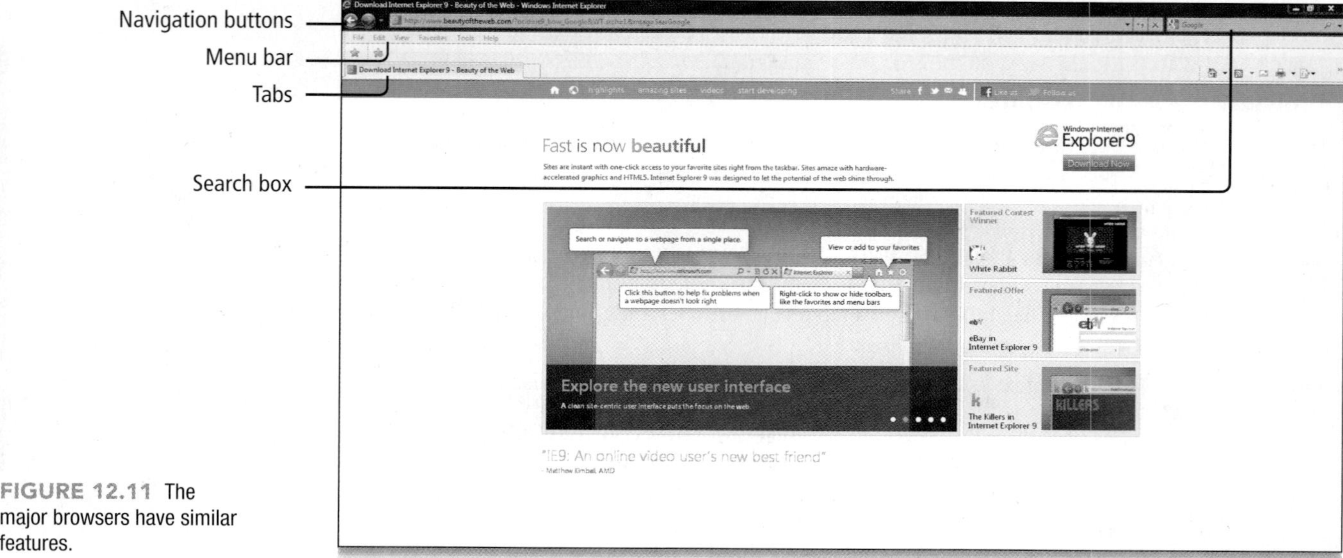

FIGURE 12.11 The major browsers have similar features.

or item is considered fresh. If you retrieve the page within the allotted time, the page is retrieved from the browser's cache; otherwise the round trip is made back to the originating server and a new page displays for you.

A few problems still exist in the distribution of Web content; for example:

- Some HTML tags are only viewable in one browser or another. The only solutions that an HTML writer has are to avoid using those tags, use those tags and provide a message that the page is meant for one browser or another, or write multiple pages and direct readers to the appropriate pages. With XHTML, however, if you need to define a tag for clarity across different browsers or create a new markup tag, you define the tag in an XHTML module and use it in your page as you would any other HTML tag. The browser interpreting the page reads the definition of the tag and presents it as defined. This feature

FAST FORWARD

Anticipating Network Demands

Video-on-demand (VOD) delivered wirelessly over the Internet is creating network slowdowns and congestion. There was a 63 percent increase in VOD users in the fourth quarter of 2009. Due to the increased demand for this service, its large swings in bandwidth, and excessive demands on a server, VOD can affect the performance of not only the video customer but also network applications. To accommodate this form of transmission, wireless networks need higher frequencies and wider bandwidth. Electrical engineers from the University of California San Diego are working to develop technologies for the network of the future. The key to creating higher frequencies and wider bandwidth is advances in silicon-based circuits that operate at millimeter and microwave frequencies. Research at the university is focused on advanced radio-frequency CMOS chips, planar antennas, and system-level design that will increase data transfer 10 to 100 times, yet maintain the same energy consumption. Lawrence Larson, who leads the Radio Frequency Integrated Circuit (RFIC) group, captures the potential of the new technology by comparing the current connection and transport ability between your smartphone and tower to a drinking straw. He claims that this technology will be the equivalent of replacing the straw with a fire hose. This analogy provides a visual image for the projected increased bandwidths and speed that research promises.

makes a page truly compatible with all browsers. As stated earlier, the agency responsible for standardizing HTML and XHTML is the World Wide Web Consortium (W3C).

- Not all links work. The author of a Web page can delete the link or move it at any time without notice. For this reason, ***dead links***—also called ***broken links***—which are links to documents or features that have disappeared or been moved, are common on the Web.
- No individual or organization validates information posted on the Web. When you create a hyperlink to a Web site you did not create, investigate the credentials of the source and the accuracy of the content. This is critical to the integrity of your own Web site or Web page.
- Basic Web pages are not expensive to create or host. This has led to the proliferation of Web content and to information overload. The Web content creator can supply too much data, more than what is necessary to substantiate a point. You, as a Web searcher, can get caught up in a search and become saturated with content and lose focus.

Concept 12.08 | Connecting with Web Servers

Web sites and their associated images and scripts are housed on ***Web servers***, a computer running special software that enables it to respond to requests for information or accept information. Millions of Web servers are located all over the world. When you enter the Web address of a Web site or click a hyperlink on a Web page, you are requesting information, a Web page, from a server. More complex is a request from an online shopping site for a list of sweatshirts available in size Medium. In this case the server accepts your information, searches a database of products stored on the server or a storage device connected to the server, and then displays the products that correspond to your request. If the information is not found, the server responds with an error message.

Objective 4 | Locate and Authenticate Information on the Web

From either the Companion Web Site or MyITLab, try the Chapter 12 Internet Simulation

As a Library Assistant at a college, you want to create a Web page that explains how to determine the validity of Web information and provide examples and tips on effective search techniques. This information will be helpful to both students and faculty when they are conducting Web searches. Where do you start?

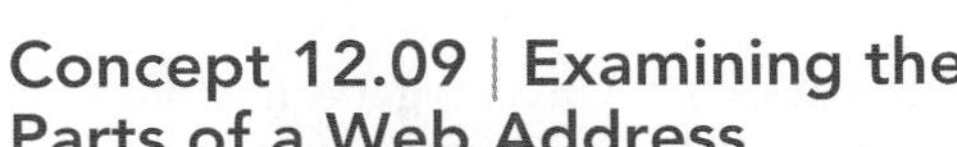

Concept 12.09 | Examining the Parts of a Web Address

To locate a resource on the Web, you must know how to find the Web server on which it resides. Every host, computer, server, device, and application that communicates over the Internet is assigned an ***Internet Protocol address (IP address)***—a numerical identification and logical address assigned to devices participating in a computer network. The IP address consists of four groups of numbers separated by periods. The value in each group ranges from 0 to 255. As an example, *64.12.107.131* is one of the IP addresses *for www.aol.com*.

IP addresses are either static or dynamic. A static IP address never changes and is the type used by most major Web sites. A dynamic IP address is automatically assigned to a computer when you log on to a network. Internet service providers (ISPs) are assigned dynamic IP addresses that they, in turn, dispense to you, their customer. Although this numeric system works well for computers, it does not work as well for people. It is much easier to use a ***Uniform Resource Locator (URL)***—a string of characters that precisely identifies an Internet resource's type and location. Typing *www.aol.com* is easier than remembering and typing *64.12.107.131*.

A complete URL has four parts: protocol, domain name, path, and resource/filename. Each component provides a piece of data needed to locate the site (Figure 12.12).

Protocol, the first part of a complete URL, specifies the ***Hypertext Transfer Protocol (HTTP)***, which is the Internet standard that supports the exchange of information on the Web. The protocol name is followed by a colon and two forward

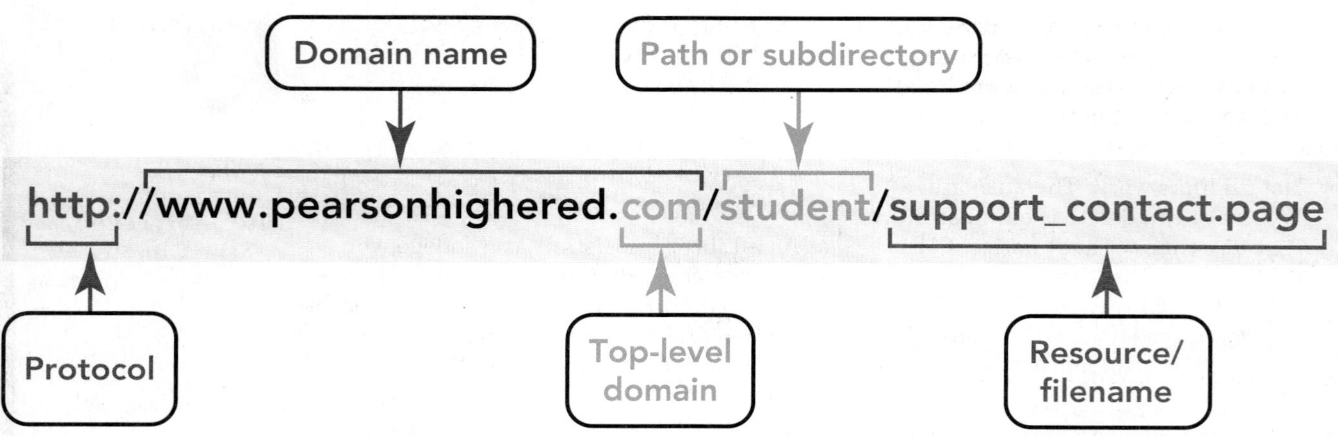

FIGURE 12.12 A complete URL has four parts: protocol, domain name, path, and resource/ filename. This is the URL for the Pearson student support and contact page.

slash marks (//). You can generally omit the *http://* protocol designation when you are typing the URL of a Web page, because the browser assumes that you are browsing an unsecured hypertext Web page. For example, you can access Pearson's Web site for the GO! series by typing **www.pearsonhighered.com/go**. Most browsers can also access information using other protocols such as FTP (File Transfer Protocol), which transfers files from one computer on the Internet to another; POP (Post Office Protocol), which is used to receive e-mail; and HTTPS (Hypertext Transfer Protocol Secure), which is used when the content being transferred requires encryption and a secure identification of the server such as is required for financial transactions.

The second part of a complete URL specifies the Web site's ***domain name***, which correlates to the Web server's IP address. The domain name has two parts: a host name and a top-level domain name. Some domain names also include a prefix, the most common of which is *www*. The ***host name*** is usually the name of the group or institution hosting the site. The ***top-level domain (TLD) name*** is the extension—such as .com or .edu—following the host name and indicates the type of group or institution to which the site belongs. This two-part identifier is used by the Internet in the ***Domain Name System (DNS)***, which is a system that links domain names with their corresponding numerical IP addresses and functions like a phone book for the Internet. The Domain Name System enables you to type an address that includes letters as well as numbers; for example *pearsonhighered.com* instead of 165.193.140.24, its IP numerical address. Through a process called ***domain name registration***, individuals and organizations register a *unique* domain name with a service organization such as InterNIC, and are assigned a *unique* Internet address (IP address) that will be associated with that domain name. You can use your favorite search engine to search for domain name registrars to find sites that provide this service. One example is **www.hover.com**—a registrar that is inexpensive and easy to use.

A domain reveals a great deal about where a computer is located. For Web sites hosted in the United States, top-level domain names—the *last* part of the domain name—indicate the type of organization to which the Web site belongs (Figure 12.13). Outside the United States, the top-level domain indicates the name of the country from which the Web site is published or of which the owner is a citizen, such as .ca (Canada), .uk (United Kingdom), and .mx (Mexico). For more information on domain names, visit the Internet Corporation for Assigned Names and Numbers (ICANN) at **www.icann.org**.

The third part of a complete URL, the ***path***, specifies the location of the

Common Top-Level Domain Names

Top-Level Domain Name	Used By
.biz	Businesses
.com	Commercial sites
.co	Commercial sites
.edu	Educational institutions
.gov	Government agencies
.info	Information
.mil	Military
.mobi	Mobile Websites
.name	Individuals
.net	Network organizations (such as ISPs)
.org	Nonprofit organizations

Figure 12.13

document on the server. It contains the document's location on the computer, including the names of subfolders if any. In the example in Figure 12.12, the path to the student contact page on the Web server at **www.pearsonhighered.com** is *student*.

The last part of a complete URL, the ***resource*** or ***filename***, gives the name of the file resource you are accessing. A resource is a file, such as an HTML file, a sound file, a video file, or a graphics file. The resource's extension—the part of the file name after the period—indicates the type of resource it is. For example, HTML documents have the .html or .htm extension. Many URLs do not include a resource name because they reference the Web site's home or index page.

Concept 12.10 | Surfing the Web

Once you have subscribed and connected to an Internet service provider and downloaded and opened a browser, you are ready to surf the Web. To access a Web page, you can do any of the following, as illustrated in Figure 12.14:

- Type a URL in the address bar.
- Click a tab in the browser window. Most major browsers offer ***tabbed browsing***, which is a feature that opens new Web pages as tabs within one window instead of a new window for each page. This enables you to have several Web pages open at once and switch quickly between them. The tabs are not visible in Figure 12.14 because the History list is extended.
- Click a hyperlink. Hyperlinks are usually underlined, but sometimes they are embedded in graphics or highlighted in other ways, such as with shading or colors. Most browsers indicate the presence of a hyperlink by changing the on-screen pointer to a hand shape when it is over a hyperlink.
- Use the ***History list***, which is a list of previously visited Web pages. It is accessed in Internet Explorer by clicking the arrow to the right of the address bar and in Firefox by selecting the History option on the menu bar. Both browsers then display a drop-down list from which you can select a Web page.
- Make use of the Favorites or Bookmarks feature. This feature, called Favorites in IE and Bookmarks in Firefox, is located on the menu bar. When selected, you can mark a Web page that you visit frequently. To return to that page later, click the Favorite or Bookmarks option and select the Web page name from the drop-down list. Favorites can be grouped into categories.

After you have browsed the Web and accessed Web pages, you may want to download or upload data. In the process called ***downloading***, a document or file is transferred from another computer to your computer, for example when downloading music from iTunes. Your computer is the destination; the other computer is the source. In the process called ***uploading***, you transfer files from your computer to another computer, for example, when

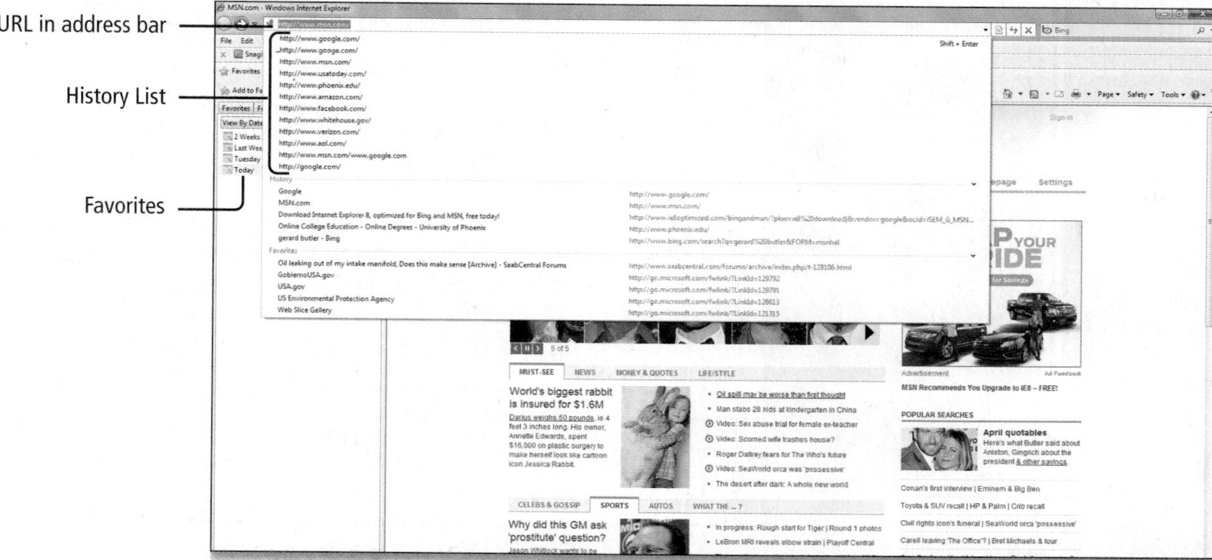

FIGURE 12.14 There are many ways to access a Web page.

you upload a video you created to YouTube. When uploading, your computer is the source and the other computer is the destination. You download and upload files when using a Web-based course management system such as Blackboard or MyItLab. These systems allow you and the instructor to interact in classes delivered entirely online or to supplement a face-to-face class. As a student using one of these systems, you can download course notes or application files to your own computers. When you complete an assignment, you can upload the completed assignment to a drop box folder for your instructor to grade.

No matter how familiar you are with the source, you should use caution when downloading files of unknown origin from the Web. If you download software from a site that does not inspect files using up-to-date antivirus software, you could infect your own computer with a virus. Be sure to use an antivirus program to check any software or data files that you download. For a Windows-based PC, use Microsoft Security Essentials, which is a free program.

Concept 12.11 | Getting and Sharing Information on the Internet

Sometimes the best way to get information online is from an individual or agency that is also online and communicating or contributing through an online feed, conversation, or Web posting.

One way to keep up with news, weather, and sports is by using ***Really Simple Syndication (RSS)***. After you set up a connection to a Web site that provides an RSS feed, you will receive constant updates over the Internet from that site without any further action on your part. The URL or Web page that allows its up-to-date information to be published on another Web site is said to be *syndicated*.

So how does RSS work? A Web page that displays constantly changing data maintains a list of RSS feeds. Individuals interested in getting updated information from locations on the list can, through an RSS feed, select sources from the list and receive the updated information on their own Web page. There are hundreds of Web sites that provide RSS feeds, for example, the *New York Times*, the BBC, Reuters, and many blogs. If your site will be updating several feeds, you can use an RSS ***aggregator***—a program that remembers your subscription list, checks each site on a regular basis, alerts you if new information has been published, and organizes the results for you (Figure 12.15). Many RSS aggregators are available through your browser. Some are even integrated into your e-mail, and others are standalone applications. For example, Outlook 2010 includes an RSS aggregator.

Want to share information fast through the Web, for either personal or professional reasons? A wiki, a blog, or a podcast might be just what you need. A ***wiki***—short for *wiki-wiki*, the Hawaiian

FIGURE 12.15 Google Reader is a free aggregator that can be set up by going to www.google.com/reader/view/.

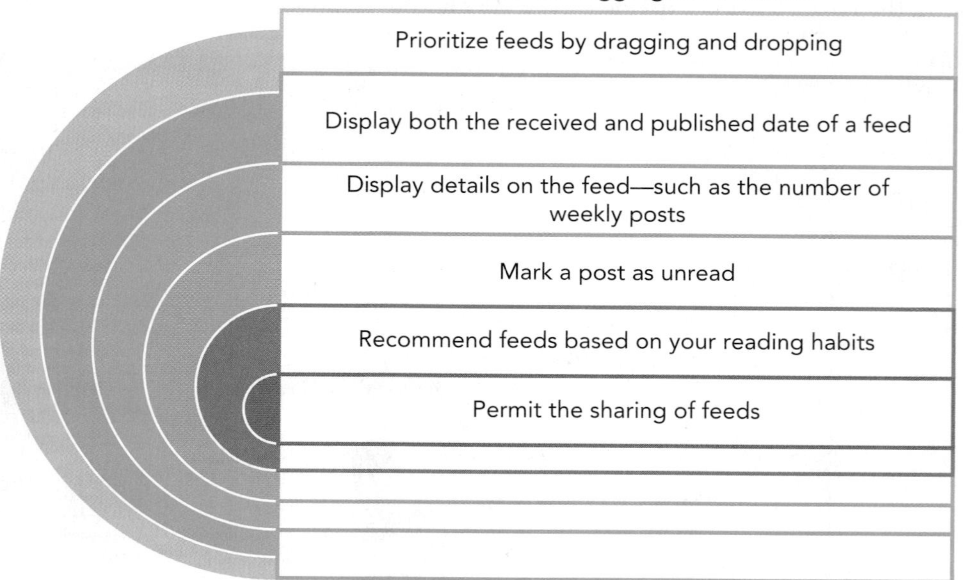

Common RSS Aggregator Features
Prioritize feeds by dragging and dropping
Display both the received and published date of a feed
Display details on the feed—such as the number of weekly posts
Mark a post as unread
Recommend feeds based on your reading habits
Permit the sharing of feeds

SOURCE: http://www.makeuseof.com/tag/7-cool-google-reader-features-which-you-might-have-missed/

word for *fast*—is a simple Web page that can be public or restricted to specific members, and on which any visitor or member can post text or images, read previous posts, change posted information, and track earlier changes. No elaborate coding is needed; just click to post, click to refresh the page, and you are done. Information referenced from a public wiki should be verified through another source because entries can be made by anyone and the content is not always verified.

Another way to share information online is by using a ***blog***, which is short for Web log. A blog is the Internet equivalent of a journal or diary. Bloggers post their thoughts and opinions, along with photos or links to interesting Web sites, for the entire world to see. Over 1 million blogs are posted on the Web. Some are meant for family and friends; some offer running commentary on politics and other timely topics, and others are written by employees about their jobs. At **http://microsoftjobsblog.com/blog/** you will find information posted from individuals that have been interviewed for jobs at Microsoft and include everything from sample categories of questions to advice on how to dress (Figure 12.16). If you are interested in creating a free blog, Google's site **www.blogger.com/start** is a place to begin.

If you would rather get your information in an audio or video format, podcasts may be just what you need! A ***podcast*** is a digital file that contains audio, images, and video and is available as a download from the Internet or is released periodically by means of Web syndication, a delivery method that makes use of ***podcatchers*** such as Apple Inc.'s iTunes or Nullsoft's Winamp. A podcatcher is an application that can automatically identify and retrieve new files in a given series and make them available through a centrally maintained Web site. You can listen to podcasts on your computer or most portable devices—including smartphones. You can go to sites that provide podcasts or sign up for one using an RSS feed. Check the Podcast Directory at **http://podcast.com** and hear what's new!

Concept 12.12 | Clicking Hyperlinks to Surf the Web

Although browsing or surfing the Web is easy and fun, it falls short as a means of information research. When you are looking for specific and reliable data, you must use more targeted methods.

From either the Companion Web Site or MyITLab, try the Chapter 12 Communicating and Sharing on the Web Simulation

GO! All In One | Chapter 12

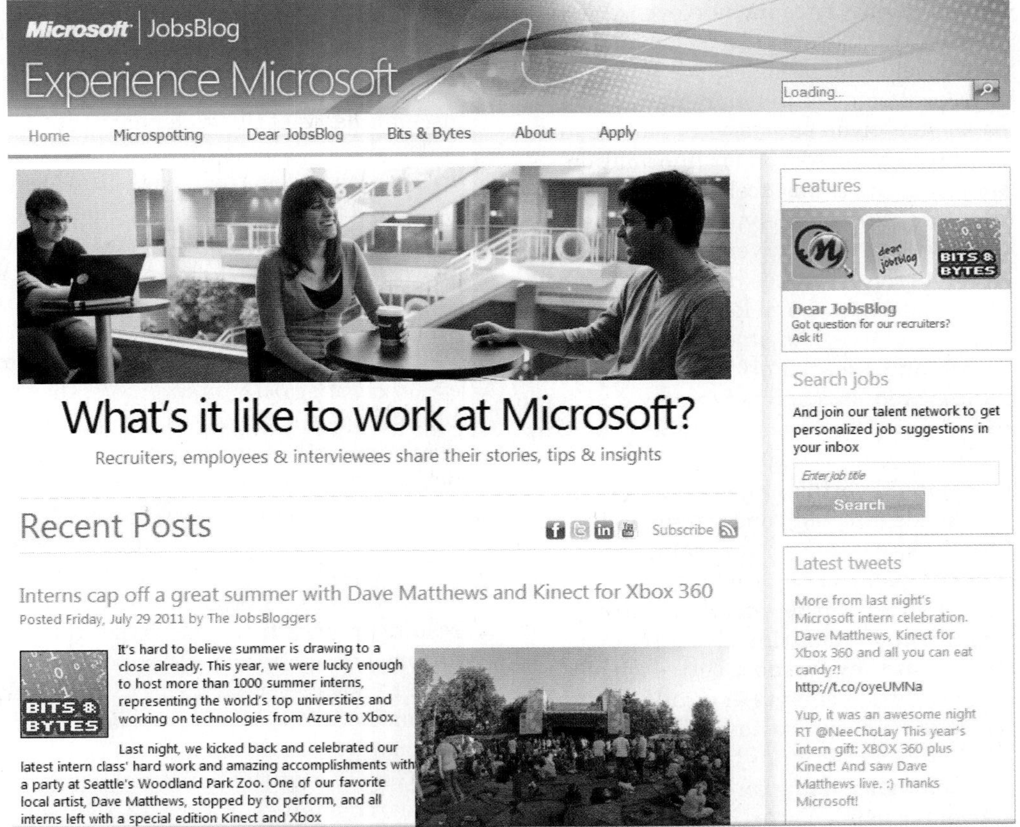

FIGURE 12.16 Blogs from individuals who have gone through the Microsoft job interview process can provide valuable hints and advice for a future interviewee.

FIGURE 12.17 Subject guides can help you find the information you seek quickly.

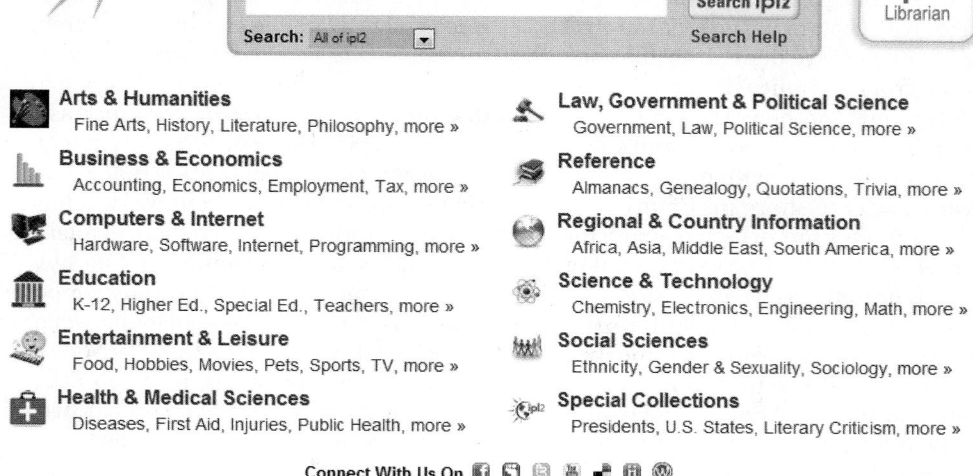

Using hyperlinks on a reliable Web page could be a start. Some Web sites offer a ***subject guide***, a list of subject-related categories such as business, news, or trends that, when selected, displays a page of related links (Figure 12.17). These guides do not try to include every Web page on the World Wide Web, but they offer a selection of high-quality pages that represent some of the more useful Web pages in a given category. If you are just beginning your search for information, a subject guide is an excellent place to start.

A ***portal*** is a Web page that acts as a gateway to many diverse resources and presents those sources in an organized way. It enables you to locate fast-breaking news, local weather, stock quotes, sports scores, and e-mail. Portal sites usually use indexes and lists of links to provide a jumping-off point for your search. Sites such as MSNBC, AOL, iGoogle, and USA.gov are examples of portals (Figure 12.18).

A side effect of your search method is the ***clickstream*** you generate, the trail of Web links you followed to get to a particular site. Internet merchants are quite interested in analyzing clickstream activity so that they can do a better job of targeting advertisements and tailoring Web pages to potential customers.

If you cannot find the information you are looking for using any of the methods above, try using a search engine.

Concept 12.13 | Using Search Engines

You have probably heard of Google, Yahoo!, Bing, and Ask. Knowing how to use these search engines effectively, and also knowing their limitations, can greatly increase your chances of finding the specific information you want.

Search engines are programs that use databases of the Web pages they have indexed to locate information you requested in a search bar on their Web site. To add pages to their databases, search engines make use of computer programs, referred to as ***spiders***, to roam the World Wide Web via the Internet, visit sites and databases, and keep the search engine's database of Web pages up to date. Also known as *crawlers*, *knowledge bots*, or *knowbots*, they obtain new pages, update known pages, and delete obsolete ones from the database's index. Most large search engines operate several spiders all the time. Even so, the Web is so enormous that it can take six months to cover the content, resulting in a certain degree of antiquated results. Such outdated results produce ***link rot***—hyperlinks that no longer work because Web pages have been removed or restructured. Such links can make a Web search frustrating and tedious.

Google is at the top of the list of favorite search engines. Figure 12.19 displays

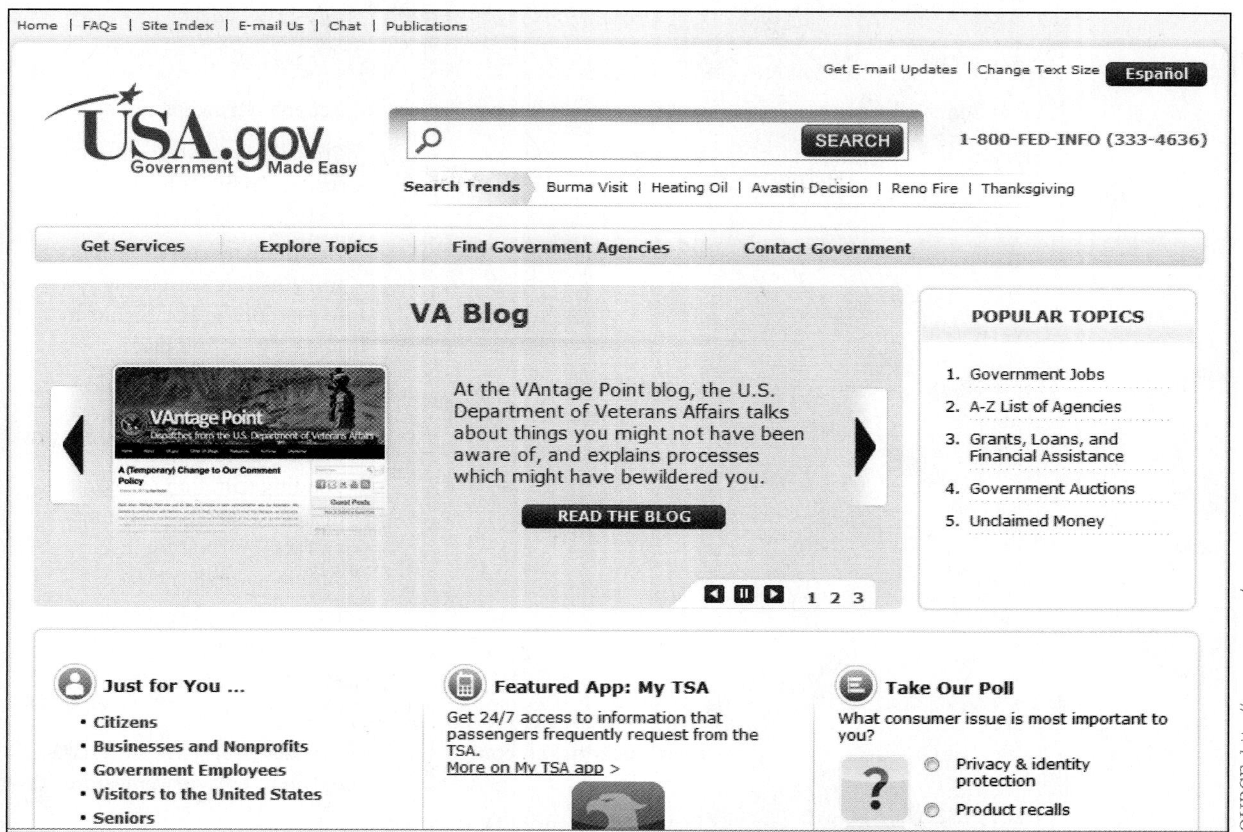

SOURCE: http://www.usa.gov/

FIGURE 12.18 Government portals can provide citizens with current information and resources.

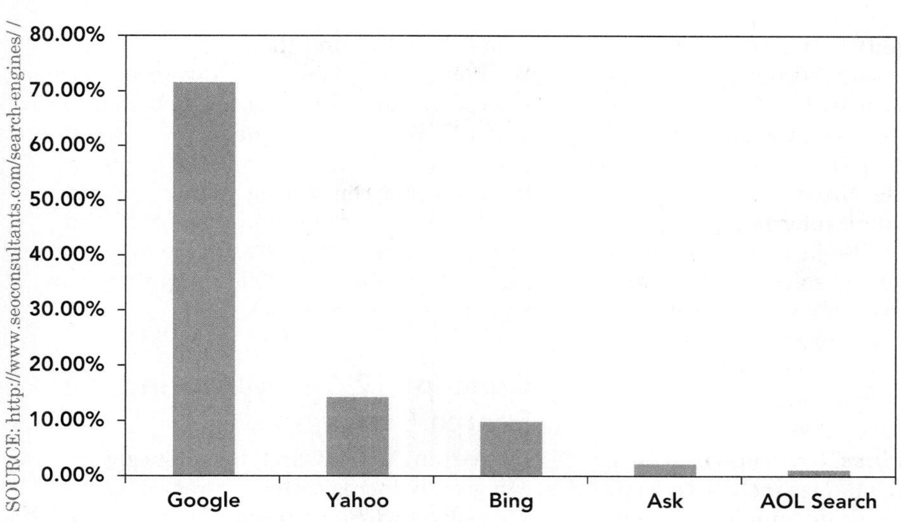

SOURCE: http://www.seoconsultants.com/search-engines/ /

FIGURE 12.19 Google use far exceeded any of the others, with Yahoo! a distant second.

August 2010 statistics on the popularity of the five core search engines. You might wonder why there is more than one search engine. Each search engine uses a different strategy to locate Web content and thus return different results. Some search engines are special purpose engines and only return search results for a specific target like music, movies, or employment. Refer to the list of search engines in Figure 12.20, try a few, and see if the results are what you expect.

To use a search engine, type one or more words that describe the subject you are looking for into the search text box and click *Search* or press *Enter*. Generally, it is a good idea to type several words—four or five—to reduce the results displayed.

Why do search engines sometimes produce unsatisfactory results? The problem

Search Engine Comparisons

Web Search Engine	URL	Search Strategy
Mahalo	**www.mahalo.com**	Provides a knowledge-sharing service; useful for how-to videos on many different topics.
Dogpile	**www.dogpile.com**	Accumulates search results from leading search engines to present the best results in one easy-to-find place
FindSounds	**www.findsounds.com**	Locates sound effects and musical instrument samples.
SurfWax	**www.surfwax.com**	Makes use of a patent-pending spiraling matrix design to search, sort, and extract information in a simple natural interface.
BlogPulse	**www.blogpulse.com**	Uses machine learning and natural language to provide a search engine that focuses on blogs.
DuckDuckGo	**www.duckduckgo.com**	Provides an easy-to-use interface and an instant answer feature.

Figure 12.20

lies in the ambiguity of the English language. Suppose you are searching for information on the Great Wall of China. You will find some information on the ancient Chinese defensive installation, but you may also get the menu of the Great Wall of China, a Chinese restaurant; information on the Great Wall hotel in Beijing; or the lyrics of *Great Wall of China*, a song by Billy Joel.

Full Web search engines generally do not index specialized information such as names and addresses, job advertisements, quotations, or newspaper articles. To find such information, you need to use ***specialized search engines***. Examples of such specialized search engines include Indeed, a database of more than 1 million jobs, and Infoplease, which contains the full text of an encyclopedia and an almanac (Figure 12.21).

You can save the results of your searches—the Web pages you visit by following the resulting links of a search engine—to your hard drive by using your browser's File, Save As menu sequence. If you do not want or need the entire Web page, you can right-click the elements of the page and choose from a variety of options; for example, Save Target As, Save Picture As, Print Target, Print Picture, E-mail Picture. You can also use your mouse to select and then copy text on a Web page for pasting into a word processing file or other document. The benefit of saving a Web page offline to your own storage device is that you can view the page later without connecting to the Internet.

Often a search produces a large and varied number of results. There are some search techniques that can help zero in on your target information.

Concept 12.14 | Mastering Search Basics

By learning a few search techniques, you can greatly increase the accuracy of your Web searches. ***Search operators***, which are symbols or words used to refine a search, can be helpful. Although specific methods may vary, some or all of the following techniques will work with most search engines.

Wildcards, also called ***truncation symbols***, are symbols such as * and ? that take the place of characters in a search. Wildcards help you improve the accuracy of your searches and are useful if you are unsure of the exact spelling of a word. For example, the search term *bank** might return *bank*, *banks*, *banking*, *bankruptcy*, *bank account*, and so on.

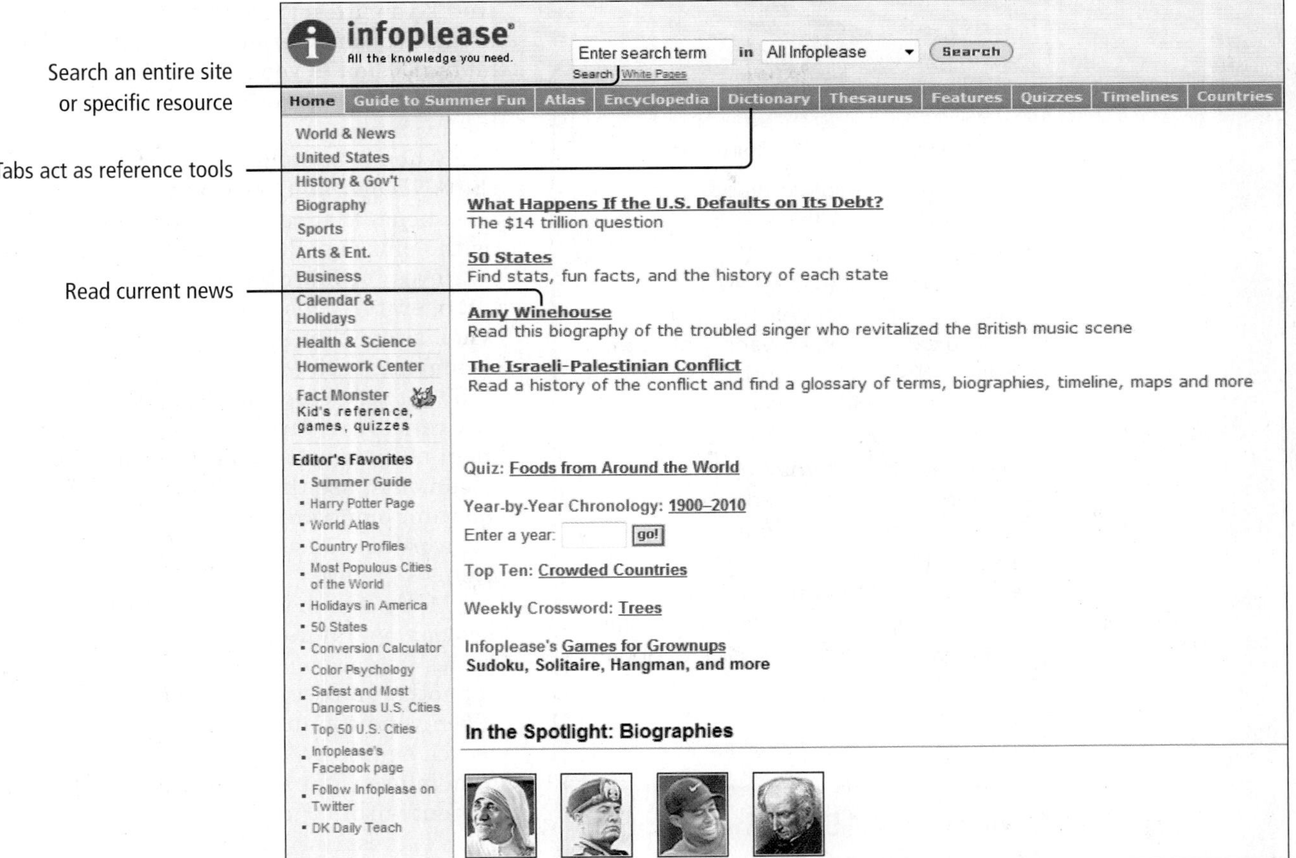

FIGURE 12.21 Specialized search engines, like Infoplease, provide access to selected reference tools and resources.

Another way to improve the accuracy of your searches is through ***phrase searching***, which is generally performed by typing a phrase within quotation marks. This tells the search engine to retrieve only those documents that contain the exact phrase rather than some or all of the words anywhere in the document.

With many search engines, you can improve search performance by specifying an ***inclusion operator***—a symbol in a Web search string, usually a plus sign—that instructs the search software to display only results that contain the word or phrase following the inclusion operator. By listing several key terms with this search operator, you can isolate pages that contain only one or more of your target terms. If the list of retrieved documents contains many items that you do not want, you can use the ***exclusion operator***—a symbol in a Web search string, usually a minus sign—that instructs the search software to omit displaying results that contain the word or phrase following the exclusion operator (Figure 12.22).

Improving Your Search Results with Search Operators

Operator/Symbol	Example	Result
Inclusion/Plus sign (+)	CD+Radiohead	Web pages that contain all search terms listed, in any order. In this instance, pages would include *both* the word CD *and* the word Radiohead.
Exclusion/Minus sign (–)	CD+Radiohead–eBay	Web pages that contain all included search terms listed, but not the excluded term. In this instance, pages would include *both* the word CD *and* the word Radiohead but *not* the word eBay.
Wildcards (*)	CD*	Web pages that include variations of the search term or additional words. For example, pages could include the terms CD, CDs, CD Ripping, CD Files, etc.
Quotation Marks (“ ”)	“Radiohead concert”	Web pages that contain the exact phrase in the order listed.

Figure 12.22

Search Engines Going Green

Environmental concerns generate a lot of interest. Now there is even a *green* search engine—Green Maven at **www.greenmaven.com**. Use it to find environmentally conscious Web sites and news.

You can also find a variety of ecologically and socially conscious search engines that donate to causes based on the searches people run. Two such engines are Ecosearch at **www.ecosearch.org** powered by Google and GoodSearch at **www.goodsearch.com** powered by Yahoo! There are, however, many other such sites. Use them as you would your normal search engine, and you will get great results. Do not just click to donate. Without attempting a legitimate search, you will jeopardize the relationships that enable such sites to fund their initiatives.

Concept 12.15 | Conducting Boolean Searches

In most search engines, you can conduct ***Boolean searches***, which use logical operators—AND, OR, and NOT—to link the words you are searching for. By using Boolean operators, you can add precision to your search results. The table in Figure 12.23 provides a few examples.

When used to link two search words, the AND operator returns only those documents that contain both words, just as the plus sign does. If your search retrieves too few documents, try the OR operator. This may be helpful when a topic has several common synonyms, such as *car*, *auto*, *automobile*, and *vehicle*. Using the OR operator usually retrieves a larger quantity of documents. If you want to exclude unwanted documents, use the NOT operator. This operator omits any documents containing the word preceded by NOT, just as the minus sign does.

Many search engines that support Boolean operators allow you to use parentheses to place one search string inside of another, a process called ***nesting***. When you nest an expression, the search engine evaluates the expression from left to right and searches for the content within the parentheses first. Such expressions enable you to conduct a search with unmatched accuracy. To learn more about search engines, their specialized capabilities, and specific examples go to **www.internettutorials.net/**.

Use These Boolean Search Operators to Refine Your Search

Search Operator	Example	Search Result
AND	CD AND Radiohead	Returns the same result as using the plus sign (+), which are sites that contain both words CD and Radiohead.
OR	CD OR Radiohead	Web pages that include either or both of the search terms listed, usually providing a large number of hits. For this example, results would include *either* the word CD *or* the word Radiohead or *both*.
NOT	CD AND Radiohead NOT eBay	Returns the same results as using the minus sign (–) thus eliminating results containing eBay.
Parenthesis ( )	(CD OR MP3 OR Record) AND Radiohead	Search terms in parenthesis are located first, using the search operator provided. In this instance, results would include pages that included any combination of CD, MP3, or RECORD *and* the word Radiohead

Figure 12.23

Concept 12.16 | Critically Evaluating Web Pages

After you have found information on the Web, you must evaluate it critically. Anyone can publish information on the Web; many Web pages are not subject to the fact-checking standards of newspapers or magazines. Although you can find excellent and reliable information on the Web, you can also find pages that are biased or blatantly incorrect.

As you are evaluating a Web page for possible use or reference, read with a critical eye and ask yourself these questions:

- Who is the *author* of this page? Is the author affiliated with a recognized institution, such as a university or a well-known company? Is there any evidence that the author is qualified and possesses credentials with respect to this topic?
- Does the author *reference* his or her sources? If so, do they appear to be from recognized and respected publications?
- Who is the Web page *affiliated* with? Who pays for this page? The association between the page server, sponsor, and author should be credible.
- Is the language *objective* and dispassionate, or is it strident and argumentative? Is it written in a form and level that suits the target population?
- What is the *purpose* of this page? Is the author trying to sell something or promote a biased idea? Who would profit if this page's information were accepted as true? Does the site include links to external information, or does it reference only other pages within the site itself?
- Does the information appear to be *accurate*? Is the page free of sweeping generalizations or other signs of shoddy thinking? Do you see any misspellings or grammatical errors that would indicate a poor educational background?
- Is this page *current*? The information should be up to date.

Concept 12.17 | Using the Web for Your College Assignments

Finding information on the Web can help you as a consumer to locate products, and it can also help you as a student to locate authoritative online sources and material in published works.

Many respected magazines and journals have established Web sites where you can search back issues, which gives you the power and convenience of the Internet, plus material that is more reliable than the average Web page.

Keep in mind that the Web is only one of several sources you can and should use for research. Many high-level research tools can be found in your institution's library such as EBSCOhost, LexisNexis, and other professional databases. Check your library's home page to find out what Internet services are available.

Also, try Google Scholar at **http://scholar.google.com** to search for scholarly literature from many academic disciplines and www.USA.gov for information on government agencies and services (Figure 12.24).

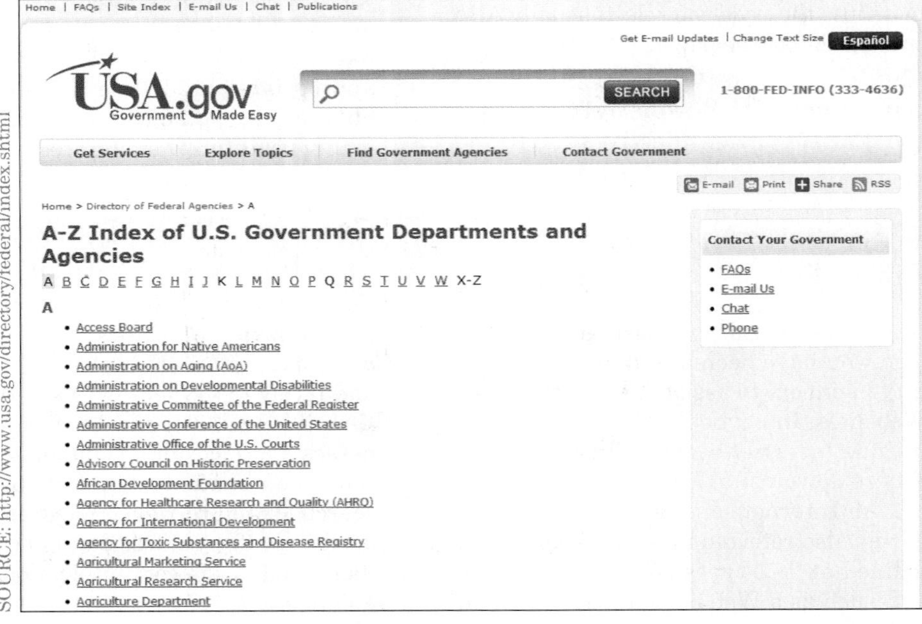

SOURCE: http://www.usa.gov/directory/federal/index.shtml

FIGURE 12.24 For accurate government references and information try www.usa.gov/directory/federal/index.shtml

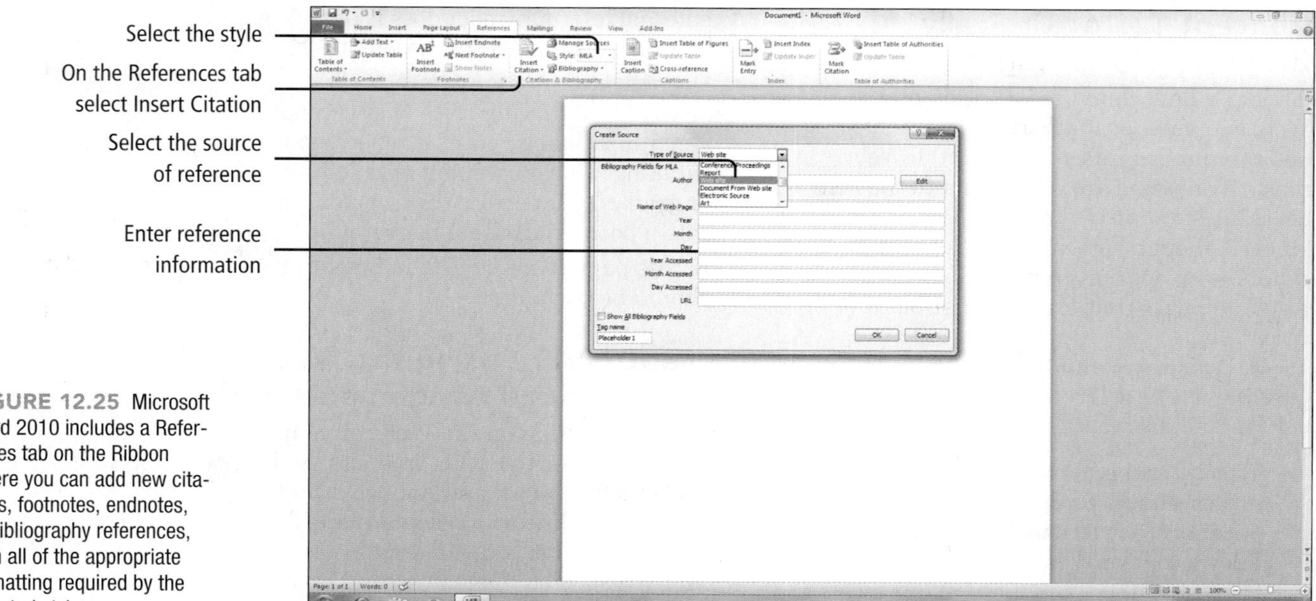

FIGURE 12.25 Microsoft Word 2010 includes a References tab on the Ribbon where you can add new citations, footnotes, endnotes, or bibliography references, with all of the appropriate formatting required by the selected style.

Concept 12.18 | Citing Online and Offline References

Including citations in your work is an important way to honor copyright and avoid accusations of plagiarism. Because citing Internet-based sources is not the same as citing traditional references, visit University of California Berkeley's General Guides site at **www.lib.berkeley.edu/Help/guides.html** to learn how to cite online and electronic resources properly.

Application developers like Microsoft include reference options within their current word processing programs. Such features prompt you to input the necessary information into a form that the application then formats into the style you select, usually APA or MLA for college papers (Figure 12.25).

Check Your Knowledge: From either the Companion Web Site or MyITLab, take the quiz covering Objectives 1, 2, 3, and 4.

Objective 5 | Explore Internet Services

In your job as Library Assistant at a college, you have been asked by several faculty members to assist them with their Web sites. In particular, they want to include ***Internet services*** in their sites. Where do you start?

An Internet service is a set of standards, also referred to as protocols, that define how two types of programs—a client, such as a Web browser that runs on the user's computer, and a server—can communicate with each other through the Internet. By using the service's protocols, the client requests information from a server program that is located on some other computer on the Internet.

In the past, browsers such as Netscape Navigator and the Mozilla Suite were distributed as software suites that included client programs to handle e-mail, newsgroups, and chat services, as well as browsing. Current browsers, including Internet Explorer, Firefox, Google Chrome, and Safari for Macs, operate as standalone programs. Although it is still possible to obtain client software for some of these services, many of them are Web based and do not require any special software to use. However, you may need to install an appropriate plug-in to ensure full functionality. Figure 12.26 lists a selection of commonly used Internet services.

Concept 12.19 | Staying in Touch by Using E-Mail

The most popular Internet service is e-mail. ***E-mail***, which is short for ***electronic mail***, is a system that enables you to send and receive messages over a network. E-mail is an indispensable tool for businesses and individuals due to its speed, convenience, and its ability to be saved, searched, and retrieved. Text messaging is often preferred over e-mail because of its immediacy in communication. Both e-mail and text messaging are preferred

Commonly Used Internet Services			
Service	**Client**	**Web-Based**	**Comments**
E-mail			
AOL Mail	✓	✓	Available with AOL Desktop installation or as Web-based service
Google Mail		✓	
Microsoft Outlook	✓		Part of the Microsoft Office suite
Instant Message			
AOL AIM	✓	✓	Available with AOL Desktop installation or as a Web-based service
Google Talk	✓	✓	Available for download or as Web-based service
Yahoo! Messenger		✓	
Windows Live Messenger		✓	Formerly MSN Messenger

Figure 12.26

for interpersonal written communication, far outpacing the old-fashioned paper letter sent by the U.S. Postal Service.

When you receive an e-mail, you can reply to the message, forward it to someone else, store it for later action, or delete it. In addition to writing the text of the e-mail message, you can format the text, check its spelling, organize your e-mail into folders, and include an e-mail attachment (Figure 12.27). An ***e-mail attachment*** can be any type of computer file—document, photo, audio, or video—that is included with an e-mail message. If you receive an e-mail message containing an attachment, your e-mail program displays a distinctive icon, such as a paper clip, to notify you. E-mail usually arrives at the destination server in a few seconds. It is then stored on the server until the recipient logs on to the server and downloads the message.

To send an e-mail, you need to know the recipient's e-mail address. An ***e-mail address*** is a unique cyberspace identity for a particular recipient that follows the form myname@somedomain.com. The components of an e-mail address are the user name or other identifier, the name of the domain that is hosting the e-mail service, and the top-level domain that identifies the provider's type of institution. For instance, you can send mail to the president of the United States at the e-mail address

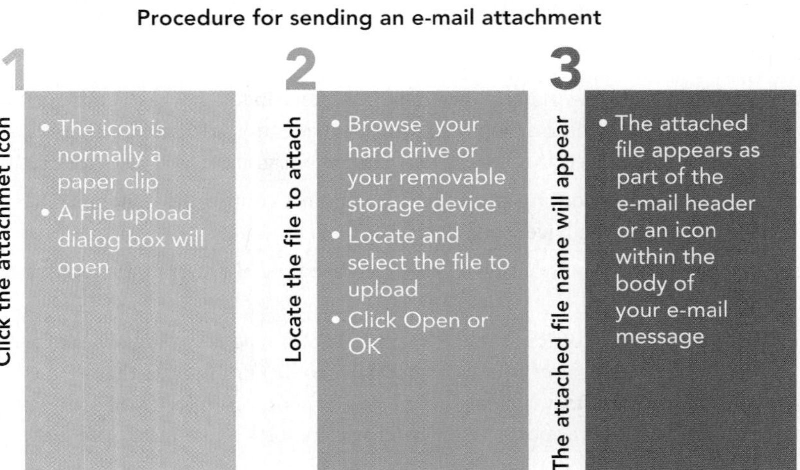

Procedure for sending an e-mail attachment
1
Click the attachmet icon
• The icon is normally a paper clip
• A File upload dialog box will open
2
Locate the file to attach
• Browse your hard drive or your removable storage device
• Locate and select the file to upload
• Click Open or OK
3
The attached file name will appear
• The attached file appears as part of the e-mail header or an icon within the body of your e-mail message

FIGURE 12.27 The size of an e-mail attachment might be limited by your e-mail service provider. Yahoo! and Gmail both have a 20MB limit.

president@whitehouse.gov. In this instance, the user name is *president*, the domain is *whitehouse*, and the top-level domain is *.gov*, which indicates government. Seeing someone's e-mail address can be very revealing!

If you typically send e-mails to the same group of people frequently, consider creating a distribution list, which is a grouping of individuals in your list of contacts, all of whom you want to send the same e-mails.

E-mail has many benefits: It is inexpensive, fast, and easy to access; enables collaboration; creates an electronic paper trail; and saves paper.

Be aware of potential problems with e-mail. Sometimes e-mail systems fail to properly send or receive mail. Attachments may not be delivered or they may be blocked by e-mail system administrators as potentially unsafe. Messages can become corrupt and may not display properly. Sometimes, if you do not regularly check your mail, your Inbox may overflow, which causes messages received past the overflow point to be bounced out of the box and never delivered.

Perhaps the worst thing that can happen with e-mail is that you hastily send a message that you later wished you had not. Or, you use the Reply All or Forward feature to send inappropriate or irrelevant messages that can embarrass you or that inconvenience the receiver.

Concept 12.20 | Using Instant Messaging

What is faster than e-mail and more convenient than picking up the phone? The answer is instant messaging—referred to as IM—systems that alert you when a friend or business associate who also uses the IM system is online. You can then contact this person and exchange messages and attachments, including multimedia files.

To use IM, you must install instant messenger software from an instant messenger service, such as AOL's AIM or Microsoft's Live Messenger, on your computer. You can use IM systems on any type of computer, including handhelds. Many IM services also give you access to information such as daily news, stock prices, sports scores, and the weather, and you can keep track of your appointments. There is no standard IM protocol, which means that you can send messages only to people who are using the same IM service that you are.

A threat to the use of IM is a phenomenon known as ***spimming***, spam that targets users of instant messaging. Spimming is to IM as spam is to e-mail. Be very careful about opening files or clicking on a link sent in an instant message by an unknown sender.

Concept 12.21 | Connecting by Using Social Networks

Social networking is a way to build and expand online communities. Originally such sites were created to foster relationships among people but since have extended their usage to promote business. On a social networking site like Facebook, Google+, or MySpace, you can create an online profile, invite friends and acquaintances to join your network, and invite their friends to join too. The table in Figure 12.28 provides a brief description of the most popular social network sites.

Popular Social Networking Sites

Social Site	Description
Facebook	The largest of the social networking sites and useful to keep in touch with friends and family, post photos, share links, and distribute information with people you identify as friends. Businesses use Facebook to promote themselves and their products in a less formal manner for significantly lower cost than traditional advertising.
LinkedIn	A professional social networking site on which you post your professional profile and resume, connect with colleagues, and seek advice from experts.
MySpace	A social network that promotes itself as a fan-powered social entertainment destination with a major focus on music.
Twitter	A free, real-time blogging system in which you send and read short messages of up to 140 characters. You look up the Twitter accounts of friends or notable people and indicate that you want to become a follower and view their Twitter posts, which are called *tweets*. For example, if you are a fan of major league baseball, you might follow a sports news writer who reports on your favorite team.

Figure 12.28

Options for Creating Your Own Social Network Site

Option	Web site	Description	Charge
Ning	www.ning.com	Provides customized themes and design settings	Free and pay options
Pligg	www.pligg.com	An open source content management system that provides social publishing software; often criticized for poor security	Free
CrowdVine	www.crowdvine.com	An easy way to build a community around your event or conference	Free and pay options
Groupsite	www.groupsite.com	Communicate via subgroups and forums, group calendars, and share files and media	Free and pay options
Drupal	www.drupal.org	An open source content management system that provides modules to enable the creation of everything from a personal blog to enterprise applications	Free

Figure 12.29

Tired of Facebook? Why not start your own social network? Ning at **www.ning.com** is just one site that encourages people to start their own social networking community (Figure 12.29). Artists, hobbyists, educators, athletes—the list continues to grow. Find a community to join or start your own!

Many privacy and security concerns surround the use and access of social networking sites. Statistics from a Pew Internet 2011 report cites that 83 percent of American adults 29 years of age and younger use social networking Web sites. Statistics like this fuel the concern over security and the need to educate young adults on the use and possible repercussion of postings placed on such sites. Once posted, pictures and content are easily shared and distributed to others, sometimes with detrimental effects. You should give thought to the information you publicly display and consider the possible consequences. If you are searching for employment, make sure that your social networking site is not offensive. Employers are researching candidates' Facebook sites to gain insight into a potential employee's personality and behavior.

Concept 12.22 | Joining Online Discussions on Usenet

Usenet is a worldwide computer-based discussion system accessible through the Internet. It consists of thousands of topically named ***newsgroups***, which are discussion groups devoted to a single topic. A newsgroup typically requires participants to use a program called a news reader. Each newsgroup contains articles that users have posted for all to see. Users can respond to specific articles by posting follow-up articles. Over time, a discussion thread develops as people reply to the replies. A ***thread*** is a series of articles that offer a continuing commentary on the same specific subject.

Usenet newsgroups are organized into the following main categories:

- Standard newsgroups: You are most likely to find rewarding, high-quality discussions in the standard

Standard Newsgroup Subcategories

Subcategory Name	Description of Topics Covered
Comp	Everything related to computers and computer networks, including applications, compression, databases, multimedia, and programming.
Misc	Subjects that do not fit into other standard newsgroup hierarchies, including activism, books, business, consumer issues, health, investing, jobs, and law.
Sci	The sciences and social sciences, including anthropology, archaeology, chemistry, economics, math, physics, and statistics.
Soc	Social issues, including adoption, college-related issues, human rights, and world cultures.
Talk	Debate on controversial subjects, including euthanasia, gun control, and religion.
News	Usenet itself, including announcements and materials for new users.
Rec	All aspects of recreation, including aviation, backcountry sports, bicycles, boats, gardening, and scouting.

Figure 12.30

newsgroups—also called world newsgroups. Figure 12.30 lists the standard newsgroup subcategories.

- Alt newsgroups: The alt category is much more freewheeling. Anyone can create an alt newsgroup, which explains why so many of them have silly or offensive names.
- Biz newsgroups: These newsgroups are devoted to the commercial uses of the Internet.

© AJSlife / Alamy

FIGURE 12.31 VoIP can be used on most computer-based devices, even smartphones, so long as they have Internet connectivity.

The easiest way to access Usenet is through Google Groups **http://groups.google.com**. You can read and post messages, but be careful what you post on Usenet. When you post an article, you are publishing in the public domain. Sometimes articles are stored for long periods in Web-accessible archives.

A ***message board*** is similar to a newsgroup, but it is easier to use and does not require a newsreader. Many colleges and universities have switched to message boards for this reason.

Concept 12.23 | Using Electronic Mailing Lists

Electronic mailing lists are a variation of e-mail that allows for the automatic distribution of messages to all individuals on a mailing list. It consists of a list of e-mail addresses of the subscribers, the e-mail messages sent to those subscribers, and a reflector—a single e-mail address that receives or creates the e-mail and sends a copy of it to all subscribers. Because the messages are transmitted as e-mail, only individuals who are subscribers to the mailing list receive and view the messages. Some colleges and universities host electronic mailing lists that include all registered student and staff to provide notification of security issues on campus or weather closings.

Concept 12.24 | Making Phone Calls Using VoIP

VoIP (Voice over Internet Protocol) enables you to speak to others over a broadband Internet connection instead of over a traditional analog phone line (Figure 12.31). One advantage of VoIP is that the telephone calls over the Internet do not incur a surcharge beyond what the user is paying for Internet access, much in the same way that you do not pay for sending individual e-mails over the Internet. What do you need to use VoIP? This form of communication requires a broadband Internet connection, a VoIP service provider, and a normal telephone with a VoIP adapter or a computer with supporting software. Calls to others using the same service are usually free, whereas calls to those using other services can vary. Many businesses are

TECHNOLOGY ON THE JOB

Job descriptions for librarians and library assistants include the use of the Internet and Web. In Figure 12.32, you can see the job description for a librarian over 35 years ago. On the right is the way the task could be accomplished today.

Can you think of other professions that have had such changes in their job descriptions due to technology, the Internet, and the World Wide Web?

Comparison of Old and New Job Description for a Librarian

Old Task	New Task
Assist in the use of the card catalog files	Use the online card catalog
Create a booklet on how to use the library	Create a Web page with the library information
Phone other local branch libraries to locate a book for a customer	Use e-mail, or a direct messaging system in the library's proprietary network
Stay in touch with other professionals	Use LinkedIn to connect with other professionals

Figure 12.32

using VoIP services, like Skype, to reduce their communication bills and operating expenses.

Concept 12.25 | Transferring Files Using File Transfer Protocol

File Transfer Protocol (FTP) is one way to transfer files over the Internet, and it is especially useful for transferring files that are too large to send by e-mail. Although you can use special FTP client software, such as WS_FTP Home, you can also transfer files to and from an FTP server simply by using your browser or Windows Explorer. FTP can transfer two types of files: ASCII and binary. ASCII files are text files while binary files are files saved in the file format of the application used to created them.

In most cases, you need a user name and a password to access an FTP server. FTP services are built into such academic interfaces as Blackboard and used by a student to upload his or her assignment to the designated link or drop box for your course.

Objective 6 | Evaluate E-Commerce Sites

In your job as a Library Assistant at a college, many students are interested in ***e-commerce***—the use of networks or the Internet to carry out business. You have been asked to create a slide presentation to demonstrate the use of e-commerce for students. Where do you start?

A large portion of Internet traffic and Web sites are associated with e-commerce. ***Commerce*** refers to the selling of goods or services with the expectation of making a reasonable profit. ***Electronic commerce*** or e-commerce is the use of networks or the Internet to carry out business of any type. Many ***e-tailers***—Web-based retailers—hope that while you are surfing the Web, you will stop and make a purchase.

E-commerce supports many types of traditional business transactions, including buying, selling, renting, borrowing, and lending. E-commerce is not new; companies have used networks to conduct business with suppliers for years. What is new is that, thanks to the Internet and

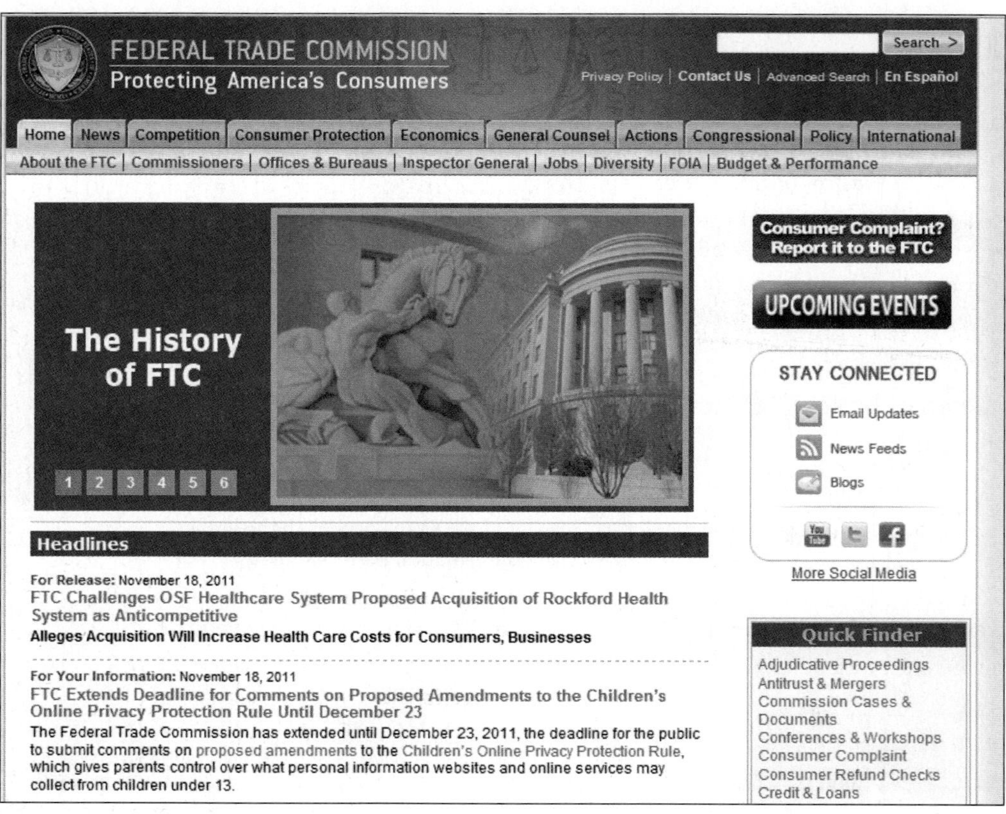

SOURCE: http://www.ftc.gov/index.shtml

FIGURE 12.33 The Federal Trade Commission Web site at http://www.ftc.gov even has a link for filing a consumer complaint.

inexpensive PCs, e-commerce has become accessible to anyone with an Internet connection and a Web browser.

Concept 12.26 | Identifying Types of E-Commerce

There are three types of e-commerce:

- When a business uses the Internet to provide another business with the materials, services, and/or supplies it needs to conduct its operations, they are engaging in ***business-to-business (B2B) e-commerce***. For instance, the popular office supplies chain Staples has a B2B division that operates the Web site **www.staplesadvantage.com** for mid-size and Fortune 1000 companies.
- The online exchange or trade of goods, services, or information between individual consumers is ***consumer-to-consumer (C2C) e-commerce***. Often C2C e-commerce involves the use of an intermediate site, such as the popular online auction destination eBay. Other C2C sites include craigslist and Amazon Marketplace.
- When a business uses the Internet to supply consumers with services, information, or products, they are engaging in ***business-to-consumer (B2C) e-commerce***. B2C is essentially the same as shopping at a physical store—you have a need or want, and the online marketplace offers products and solutions. The primary difference is that B2C e-commerce is not place- or time-specific.

The FTC pursues vigorous and effective law enforcement for consumers and businesses (Figure 12.33).

Concept 12.27 | Avoiding E-Commerce Hazards

Although there are many benefits to engaging in e-commerce, it also entails risks. These risks include identity theft, personal information exposure, money loss, and being taken advantage of by unscrupulous retailers. To protect yourself, be sure to create user names and passwords carefully, avoid doing e-commerce with little-known companies, and use caution when giving out your credit card information—do so only on secure sites.

Objective 7 | Practice Appropriate Internet Behavior

In your job as Library Assistant at a college, you have been asked to speak to student groups regarding proper etiquette in electronic communications and social network postings. Where do you start?

Concept 12.28 | Practicing Netiquette

Courtesy is not required when using Internet services but, as in the real world, it can create a difference in the impression you make and contacts you keep.

Netiquette, short for *Internet etiquette*, is the code for acceptable behavior and manners while on the Internet. The basic rule is this: talk to others the same way you would want them to talk to you. Some more specific, useful rules of netiquette for e-mail, chat rooms, instant messaging, and message boards include the following:

- Keep the message short.
- Avoid sarcasm or the use of phrases or words that could offend the reader.
- Read the message before sending or posting it, correcting spelling and grammar mistakes.
- Do not type in all capital letters because that is interpreted as yelling.
- Do not assume that everyone knows what IM acronyms such as BRB (be right back) and LOL (laughing out loud) mean.
- Avoid sending a ***flame***—a message that expresses an opinion without holding back any emotion and that may be seen as being confrontational and argumentative.

When you follow the rules of netiquette, you make a good impression.

Concept 12.29 | Insisting on Safe Surfing

There are just as many hazards online as there are in the real world. The added online element is that individuals are difficult to recognize due to the anonymity the Internet provides.

By taking some simple precautions, you can make your Internet experience an enjoyable and safe activity. Follow these precautions:

- Never give out identifying information.
- Never respond to suggestive messages.
- Never open e-mail from an unknown source.
- Never allow a child to make arrangements for a face-to-face meeting alone, for any reason, without being accompanied by an adult.
- Remember individuals online may not be who they seem.
- Set reasonable rules and guidelines for computer use by children.
- Make using the computer a family activity.

Additional online hazards to avoid include malware, identity theft, threats to you and your family, and unscrupulous vendors.

Concept 12.30 | Avoiding Malware

Malware refers to software programs designed to damage a computer system. Examples of malware events include deleting files on a hard drive, removing directory information, gathering data from your system such as Web sites you visited and account numbers or passwords that you typed. Unfortunately, there are individuals out there with malicious intent—and you must be prepared. You can keep your system free of malware by installing antivirus and antispyware utilities on your computer. These utility programs will seek and destroy the malware programs they find on your computer.

Concept 12.31 | Protecting Your Identity

More than half a million people find themselves victims of identity theft each year. Nothing is more frustrating than having to spend the time and energy to clean up the mess created by a loss of identification. There are steps you can take to greatly reduce the risk of having your identity stolen. Try to avoid shoulder surfers—individuals who stand close enough to see

PIN numbers you key in at ATMs. When shopping with an e-merchant for the first time, look for the secure Web site features before entering any personal or credit card information. These features usually include one or more of the following:

- *https://* in the address of the site instead of the usual *http://*. The added *s* stands for *secure site* and means that the data is encrypted all the way from your computer to the computer that receives it. No other computer will be able to read your input as it passes along the Internet.
- A site seal provided by a security vendor, such as VeriSign, GeoTrust, or SSL.com.
- A locked padlock symbol somewhere on the Web site that, when double-clicked, displays details of the site's security. Be sure the logo is not just an image and a fake.
- The logo from other site security entities, such as *Verified by Visa.*
- A message box that notifies you when you are leaving or entering a secure site.

In addition to these visible identifiers, investigate feedback provided by previous purchasers or any comments by the Better Business Bureau. You should shop only on Web sites that enable you to view their privacy policy.

Concept 12.32 | Protecting Children in Cyberspace

Statistics support the growing use of social networks, chat rooms, and other forms of anonymous communication by minors. There are creative protections to insulate youth from cyberstalkers, cyberbullies, and other online predators. A couple in Fanwood, New Jersey, contacted CyberAngels at **www.cyberangels.org**, which is a volunteer organization of thousands of Internet users worldwide, after their computer-addicted 13-year-old daughter ran away from home. The group's purpose is to protect children in cyberspace, and they used their network to identify the child's online contact and eventually located the child.

The Internet can be dangerous for children of all ages. Cyberbullying and cyberstalkers can target anyone. To learn more about how to protect yourself or the children in your household, visit Stop Cyberbullying at **www.stopcyberbullying.org**, SocialSafety.org at **www.socialsafety.org**, and the Family Online Safety Institute at **http://fosi.org/icra/**.

Speaking with children about Internet safety practices, being aware of where and when they surf, and knowing who their cyber friends are should be a top priority. Concerned parents can implement the parental controls that are provided by their ISPs or included in safety and security software. Another level of protection can be applied by purchasing Web site blocking and content-filtering software and monitoring programs. For those interested in legislation, the Federal Trade Commission is currently soliciting comments on the revisions proposed to the Children's Online Privacy Protection Rule (Figure 12.34).

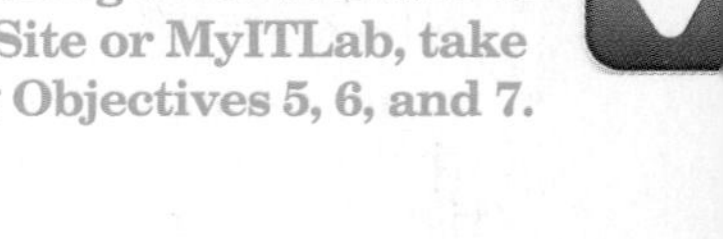

Check Your Knowledge: From either the Companion Web Site or MyITLab, take the quiz covering Objectives 5, 6, and 7.

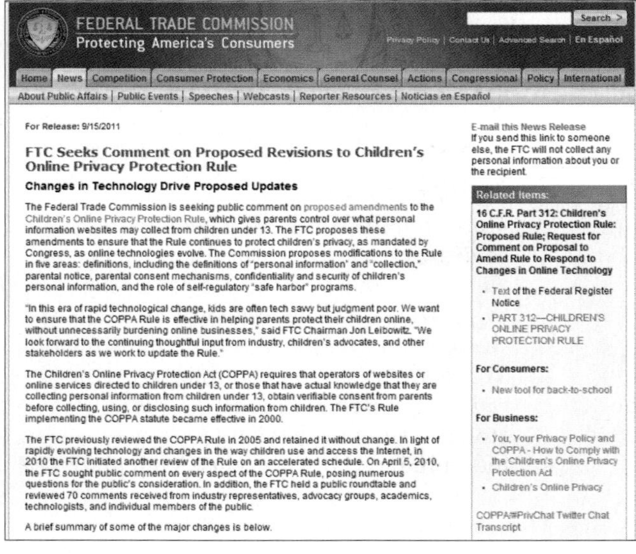

For Release: 9/15/2011

FTC Seeks Comment on Proposed Revisions to Children's Online Privacy Protection Rule

Changes in Technology Drive Proposed Updates

The Federal Trade Commission is seeking public comment on proposed amendments to the Children's Online Privacy Protection Rule, which gives parents control over what personal information websites may collect from children under 13. The FTC proposes these amendments to ensure that the Rule continues to protect children's privacy, as mandated by Congress, as online technologies evolve. The Commission proposes modifications to the Rule in five areas: definitions, including the definitions of "personal information" and "collection," parental notice, parental consent mechanisms, confidentiality and security of children's personal information, and the role of self-regulatory "safe harbor" programs.

"In this era of rapid technological change, kids are often tech savvy but judgment poor. We want to ensure that the COPPA Rule is effective in helping parents protect their children online, without unnecessarily burdening online businesses," said FTC Chairman Jon Leibowitz. "We look forward to the continuing thoughtful input from industry, children's advocates, and other stakeholders as we work to update the Rule."

The Children's Online Privacy Protection Act (COPPA) requires that operators of websites or online services directed to children under 13, or those that have actual knowledge that they are collecting personal information from children under 13, obtain verifiable consent from parents before collecting, using, or disclosing such information from children. The FTC's Rule implementing the COPPA statute became effective in 2000.

The FTC previously reviewed the COPPA Rule in 2005 and retained it without change. In light of rapidly evolving technology and changes in the way children use and access the Internet, in 2010 the FTC initiated another review of the Rule on an accelerated schedule. On April 5, 2010, the FTC sought public comment on every aspect of the COPPA Rule, posing numerous questions for the public's consideration. In addition, the FTC held a public roundtable and reviewed 70 comments received from industry representatives, advocacy groups, academics, technologists, and individual members of the public.

A brief summary of some of the major changes is below.

E-mail this News Release
If you send this link to someone else, the FTC will not collect any personal information about you or the recipient.

Related Items:

16 C.F.R. Part 312: Children's Online Privacy Protection Rule: Proposed Rule; Request for Comment on Proposal to Amend Rule to Respond to Changes in Online Technology

- Text of the Federal Register Notice
- PART 312—CHILDREN'S ONLINE PRIVACY PROTECTION RULE

For Consumers:

- New tool for back-to-school

For Business:

- You, Your Privacy Policy and COPPA - How to Comply with the Children's Online Privacy Protection Act
- Children's Online Privacy

COPPA#PrivChat Twitter Chat Transcript

SOURCE: http://www.ftc.gov/opa/2011/09/coppa.shtm

FIGURE 12.34 Visit http://www.ftc.gov/opa/2011/09/coppa.shtm to view the changes proposed in the Children's Online Privacy Protection Rule and for contact phone numbers to express concerns.

Chapter Summary

The Internet and World Wide Web

- The Internet is the network of networks that, because of its interoperability and use of TCP/IP transmission protocol, enables connected computers to exchange data regardless of model, brand, or operating system.
- You access the Internet through an Internet access provider. Access providers fall into three categories: Internet service provider (ISP), online service provider, and wireless Internet service provider.
- You connect to an access provider by using a telephone modem, a digital subscriber line (DSL), a cable modem, a satellite, or a fiber-optic cable.
- The World Wide Web is a global system of billions of hypertext documents, called Web pages. These documents connect to each other through hyperlinks, use the Internet as a transport mechanism, are written in HTML or XHTML, and are displayed by a browser.
- Information on the Web can be located by entering the URL—Web address—in the address bar of the browser, by general surfing, by using searches with search operators to get more specific results, and using sites and technology that allow the sharing of information with other Web users, such as RSS feeds, blogs, and wikis.
- Features of a reliable Web source include an author with credentials, the affiliation of the Web site with the host, the objectivity of the material presented, the overall purpose of the site, and the accuracy and currency of the information.
- Popular Internet services include e-mail and instant messaging (IM) for sending messages, Internet relay chat (IRC) for text chatting, chat rooms, social networking sites for online communities, discussion groups, newsgroups, VoIP, message boards, and File Transfer Protocol (FTP) for file exchange, and e-commerce.
- There are three types of e-commerce: business-to-business (B2B), consumer-to-consumer (C2C), and business-to-consumer (B2C).
- When using the Web, be courteous and respect the rules of netiquette.
- Follow safe surfing guidelines, avoid malware, change your passwords frequently, never enter your account number unless you are on a secure site, watch the computer usage of your children, and install software to protect your children from cyberstalkers, cyberbullies, and undesirable Web sites. When conducting online business, be aware of security indicators on Web sites conducting e-commerce, and perform transactions only with secure sites.

Key Terms and Concepts

Matching

Match each term in the second column with its correct definition in the first column by writing the letter of the term on the blank line in front of the correct definition.

_____ 1. A list of related categories such as business, news, or trends that, when selected, displays a page of more related links.

_____ 2. The .com or .edu portion of a Uniform Resource Locator (URL).

_____ 3. Computer programs that roam the World Wide Web via the Internet, visit sites and databases, and keep the search engine's database of Web pages up to date.

_____ 4. A Web page that acts as a gateway to diverse sources and presents those sources in an organized way.

_____ 5. A computer that can receive requests and reply to those requests.

_____ 6. Hyperlinks that no longer work because Web pages that have been removed or restructured.

_____ 7. The trail of Web links you follow to get to a particular site.

_____ 8. Elements in an electronic document that act as the connector to another place in the same document or to an entirely different document.

_____ 9. A specialized device that connects networks, locates the best path of transmission, and ensures that your data reaches its destination.

_____ 10. The default page that is displayed automatically when you enter a site at its top level.

_____ 11. Transferring files from your computer to another computer.

_____ 12. A free program installed on your computer that displays a Web document by interpreting the HTML or XHTML format.

_____ 13. The ability of the Internet to exchange data between computers regardless of the brand, model, or operating system the computers are running.

_____ 14. A feature provided by a Web site that permits you to connect to it and receive constant updates over the Internet.

_____ 15. Transferring files from another computer to your computer.

A Clickstream
B Domain name
C Downloading
D Home page
E Host
F Hyperlinks
G Interoperability
H Link rot
I Portal
J Router
K RSS
L Spider
M Subject guide
N Uploading
O Web browser

Multiple Choice

Circle the correct answer.

1. The main high-speed routes through which data travels is:
   A. cyberspace **C.** a portal
   B. the Internet backbone
2. A collection of related Web pages connected by hyperlinks is a:
   A. Web site **C.** subject guide
   B. browser cache
3. A section of your hard drive in which Web pages visited for the first time are stored and reused if you access that Web page again is:
   A. browser cache **C.** a subject guide
   B. a Web server
4. The second part of a complete URL, which correlates to the Web server's IP address, is referred to as the:
   A. protocol **C.** domain name
   B. host name
5. A list of previously visited Web pages is a:
   A. portal **C.** history list
   B. subject guide
6. The Internet equivalent of a journal or diary is:
   A. a wiki **C.** an RSS feed
   B. a blog
7. A simple Web page that can be public or restricted to specific members, requires no elaborate coding, and which any visitor or member can post text or images, read previous posts, change posted information, and track earlier changes is a:
   A. blog **C.** wiki
   B. portal
8. A program that uses databases of Web pages to locate information you requested is a:
   A. search engine **C.** search operator
   B. spider
9. A symbol or word used to refine a search is a:
   A. search engine **C.** browser
   B. search operator
10. A symbol such as * and ? used to search for word endings and spellings simultaneously is:
    A. an inclusion operator **C.** an exclusion operator
    B. a wildcard

Teamwork

1. **Security Vendors** As a team, research three security certificate vendors. Include a brief description of each and describe the logo by which each is identified. Then locate five Web sites that display one of the logos that you described. Present your vendor's descriptions, logos, and the 5 associated Web sites in a PowerPoint presentation. Remember to cite your references and include the full URL of your Web site examples.
2. **Evaluating Web content** As a team of two or three, locate a Web site with information on the use of social networks—or another topic approved by your instructor. Evaluate the site based on the criteria listed in this chapter. Using your word processor, create a table to display your findings. List the criteria in column 1 and your evaluation in column 2. Using the reference feature of your word processor, or an MLA or APA reference guide, create end notes and reference the Web sites you used. Present your evaluations in a one- to two-page document.

3. **Using a Search Engine** As a team, evaluate each of the search statements in the table and describe the result that each will achieve. Use **www.internettutorials.net** for help with symbols you might not understand. Then, create the search string to meet the specified change. Take a screen capture of the results from each search. Complete the table and submit the completed table and the screen capture from each one of the five searches.

   To create a screen capture, first press *PrtScrn* on the keyboard while the search result is on the screen. Open the Word file you plan to submit for this question. Click in the location where you want the capture to appear, and from the contextual menu in the Word window select *Edit*, then select *Paste*. The PrtScrn image captured earlier will display in the Word document. You can also capture the search result by using the Windows 7 Snipping tool. Save and print the Word document.

Search String	Purpose	Change to Be Made	Search String with Change
Sports + Hockey		exclude the Sabres hockey team	
"Absence makes the heart grow fonder"		include Shakespeare	
logo sports		include baseball	
clothing + LLBean + women		remove women and add men	
Go Green + US		remove US and add clothing	

On the Web

1. **Blogging for Beginners** Go to **www.blogger.com/start** and create a blog. Plan to add content every day for one week. Each day record some information about your classes and about your experience in using a blogging site, the features of the site that you like or do not like, and an evaluation of your experience. Invite some of your classmates to participate in the blog. Your blog will be your report, so make it detailed and professional. Provide your instructor with the blog address so he or she can follow the postings.
2. **Using an Aggregator** Use a search engine to locate free aggregators, and then select one to use in this exercise. Aggregator sites usually have categories like news or sports that contain several Web sites having RSS feeds. Select a category, and then view the individual subscriptions that are available. Use the *Add* option to subscribe to a feed, and include a few of your own preferred Web sites (ESPN, USA Today) with RSS feeds in the subscription list. When they appear, locate the *manage subscription* option and organize the ones you added by placing them into existing categories or by creating a new separate category. Delete a few of the ones that are in the category you chose. Investigate some of the other features of the aggregator. There is usually an option to return to a home page, some way to track your reading trends, and even a way to share your reader with others. After using the program for several days, review your experience. In a one-page, double-spaced paper, describe the aggregator site you chose and explain why you chose that site. Also discuss how easy or difficult the site was to use, the number of feeds you received, and whether or not you would use such a program. Include any other observations and bits of advice for another user. Remember to cite your references.
3. **Plug-ins: Are They Cool or Irritating?** Go to **www.coolhomepages.com/** or **www.ebizmba.com/articles/best-flash-sites** to view Web sites that make use of Flash animation. Select and view three sites. Did you have to download a plug-in, or did you already have the necessary plug-in on your system? Are the displayed graphics of high quality and does the animation enhance the site? How long was the load time? If the site had a Flash introduction, would you like the opportunity to skip the intro? Evaluate the three sites you viewed. Answer the previously listed questions and provide any other thoughts about your Flash experience in a one-page, double-spaced paper. Remember to cite the URL of each reference.

Ethics and Social Media

1. **Internet Ethics** Using a search engine, identify at least two Web sites that facilitate music downloads. Review their policy, legal statements, and agreements. Who is liable if the sharing done on their site is found to be illegal? Are there any fees to subscribe to or use the site? In what country is the site being hosted? Attempt to locate statistics on the number of music downloads and the loss of revenue to the music and related industries related to downloading music files. In a PowerPoint presentation, review your findings for these and other related issues you discover in your research. Suggest two viable solutions that you see as a compromise to this ongoing controversy. Remember to cite your references.

2. **Social Networks** With business using social networks as an inexpensive method of advertising, some promotional techniques have been very successful and some a total flop. Using the Internet and a search engine, locate at least three business Facebook sites that have successfully used this social network for advertising or to have customers successfully interact with their product. Then locate at least three business Facebook sites whose strategy failed. In a slide show of seven slides or more, state the name of the business, describe the type of campaign they developed, and point out the reasons for success or failure. Remember to cite your references.

Sources

http://books.google.com/books?id=e2ZTGynvU9kC&pg=PA173&lpg=PA173&dq=an+Internet+hosts+between+2008+and+2010.&source=bl&ots=b7laa-IMDv&sig=ezW8rQG4x3-gBiveCqPIAdO0MvU&hl=en&ei=RpawTr36BoLr0gHwpcHUAQ&sa=X&oi=book_result&ct=result&resnum=5&sqi=2&ved=0CEoQ6AEwBA#v=onepage&q=an%20Internet%20hosts%20between%202008%20and%202010.&f=false

http://www.blogpulse.com/

http://www.pewinternet.org/Press-Releases/2011/65-of-online-adults-use-social-networking-sites.aspx

Create, Query, and Sort an Access Database; Create Forms and Reports

OUTCOMES At the end of this chapter you will be able to:	OBJECTIVES Mastering these objectives will enable you to:
PROJECT 13A Create a new database.	1. Identify Good Database Design (p. 588) 2. Create a Table and Define Fields in a New Database (p. 589) 3. Change the Structure of Tables and Add a Second Table (p. 597) 4. Create and Use a Query, Form, and Report (p. 605) 5. Save and Close a Database (p. 611)
PROJECT 13B Sort and query a database.	6. Open an Existing Database (p. 613) 7. Create Table Relationships (p. 614) 8. Sort Records in a Table (p. 618) 9. Create a Query in Design View (p. 620) 10. Create a New Query from an Existing Query (p. 622) 11. Sort Query Results (p. 623) 12. Specify Criteria in a Query (p. 625)
PROJECT 13C Create complex queries.	13. Specify Numeric Criteria in a Query (p. 629) 14. Use Compound Criteria (p. 633) 15. Create a Query Based on More Than One Table (p. 635) 16. Use Wildcards in a Query (p. 636) 17. Use Calculated Fields in a Query (p. 637) 18. Calculate Statistics and Group Data in a Query (p. 639) 19. Create a Crosstab Query (p. 642)

Job Focus: Database Technician for a College

In This Chapter

In this chapter, you will learn how a Database Technician at a college uses Microsoft Access 2010 to assist students and faculty in organizing related information. Access is a powerful program that enables you to organize, search, sort, retrieve, and present information in a professional-looking manner. You will create new databases, enter data into Access tables, and create a query, form, and report—all of which are Access objects that make a database useful. You will also sort Access database tables and create and modify queries. To convert data into meaningful information, you must manipulate your data in a way that you can answer questions. One question might be: *Which students have a grade point average of 3.0 or higher?* With such information, you could send information about scholarships or internships to selected students.

At the end of this Unit, following Chapter 14, you will have an opportunity to complete a case project that focuses on the career of a Library Assistant at a college.

Project 13A Contact Information Database with Two Tables

Project Activities

In Activities 13.01 through 13.17, you will assist Dr. Justin Mitrani, Vice President of Instruction at Capital Cities Community College, in creating a new database for tracking the contact information for students and faculty members. Your completed database objects will look similar to Figure 13.1.

Project Files

For Project 13A, you will need the following files:

New blank Access database
e13A_Students (Excel workbook)
e13A_Faculty (Excel workbook)

You will save your database as:

Lastname_Firstname_13A_Contacts

Project Results

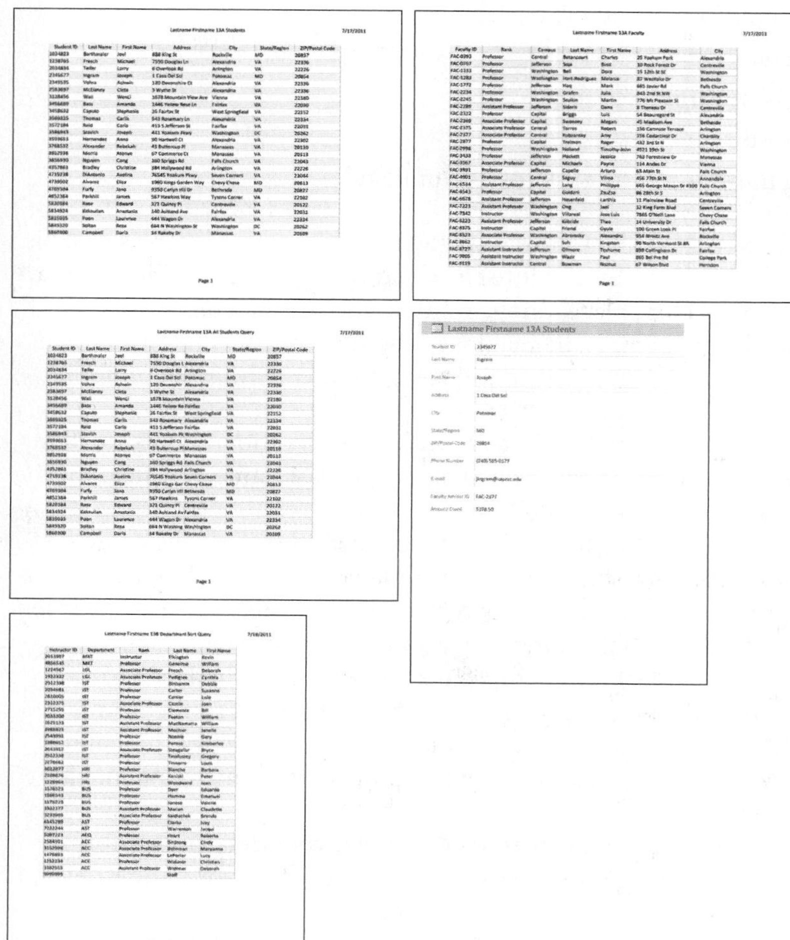

Figure 13.1
Project 13A Contacts

Objective 1 | Identify Good Database Design

View the video on the Companion Web Site or in MyITLab

A ***database*** is an organized collection of ***data***—facts about people, events, things, or ideas—related to a specific topic or purpose. ***Information*** is data that is organized in a useful manner. Your personal address book is a type of database, because it is a collection of data about one topic—the people with whom you communicate. A simple database of this type is called a ***flat database*** because it is not related or linked to any other collection of data. Another example of a simple database is a list of movie DVDs. You do not keep information about your DVDs in your address book because the data is not related to your addresses.

A more sophisticated type of database is a ***relational database***, because multiple collections of data in the database are related to one another; for example, data about the students, the courses, and the faculty members at a college. Microsoft Access 2010 is a relational ***database management system***—also referred to as a ***DBMS***—which is software that controls how related collections of data are stored, organized, retrieved, and secured.

Activity 13.01 | Using Good Design Techniques to Plan a Database

The first step in creating a new database is to determine the information you want to keep track of, and then ask yourself, *What questions should this database be able to answer for me?* The purpose of a database is to store the data in a manner that makes it easy for you to get the information you need by asking questions. For example, in the Contacts database for Capital Cities Community College, the questions to be answered might include:

How many students are enrolled at Capital Cities Community College?

How many faculty members teach in the Accounting Department?

Which and how many students live in Arlington, Virginia?

Which and how many students have a balance owed?

Which and how many students are majoring in Information Systems Technology?

Tables are the foundation of an Access database because all of the data is stored in one or more tables. A table is similar in structure to an Excel worksheet; that is, data is organized into rows and columns. Each table row is a ***record***—all of the categories of data pertaining to one person, place, thing, event, or idea. Each table column is a ***field***—a single piece of information for every record. For example, in a table storing student contact information, each row forms a record for only one student. Each column forms a field for a single piece of information for every record; for example, the student ID number for all students.

When organizing the fields of information in your database, break each piece of information into its smallest useful part. For example, create three fields for the name of a student—one field for the last name, one field for the first name, and one field for the middle name or initial.

The ***first principle of good database design*** is to organize data in the tables so that ***redundant***—duplicate—data does not occur. For example, record the contact information for students in only *one* table, because if the address for a student changes, the change can be made in just one place. This conserves space, reduces the likelihood of errors when recording the new data, and does not require remembering all of the different places where the address is stored.

The ***second principle of good database design*** is to use techniques that ensure the accuracy of data when it is entered into the table. Typically, many different people enter data into a database—think of all the people who enter data at your college. When entering a state in a contacts database, one person might enter the state as *Virginia* and another might enter the state as *VA*. Use design techniques to help those who enter data into a database do so in a consistent and accurate manner.

Normalization is the process of applying design rules and principles to ensure that your database performs as expected. Taking the time to plan and create a database that is well designed will ensure that you can retrieve meaningful information from the database.

The tables of information in a relational database are linked or joined to one another by a ***common field***—a field in one or more tables that stores the same data. For example, the Student Contacts table includes the Student ID, name, and address of every student. The Student Activities table includes the name of each club, and the Student ID—but not the name or address—of each student in each club. Because the two tables share a common field—Student ID—you can create a list of names and addresses of all the students in the Photography Club.

The names and addresses are stored in the Student Contacts table, and the Student IDs of the Photography Club members are stored in the Student Activities table.

Objective 2 | Create a Table and Define Fields in a New Database

View the video on the Companion Web Site or in MyITLab

There are two methods to create a new Access database: create a new database using a ***database template***—a preformatted database designed for a specific purpose—or create a new database from a blank database. A ***blank database*** has no data and has no database tools; you create the data and the tools as you need them. Regardless of the method you use, you must name and save the database before you can create any ***objects*** in it. Objects are the basic parts of a database; you create objects to store your data and to work with your data. The most common database objects are tables, forms, and reports. Think of an Access database as a container for the objects that you will create.

Activity 13.02 | Starting with a New Database

1 **Start** Access. Take a moment to compare your screen with Figure 13.2 and study the parts of the Microsoft Access window described in the table in Figure 13.3.

From this Access starting point in Backstage view, you can open an existing database, create a new blank database, or create a new database from a template.

Figure 13.2

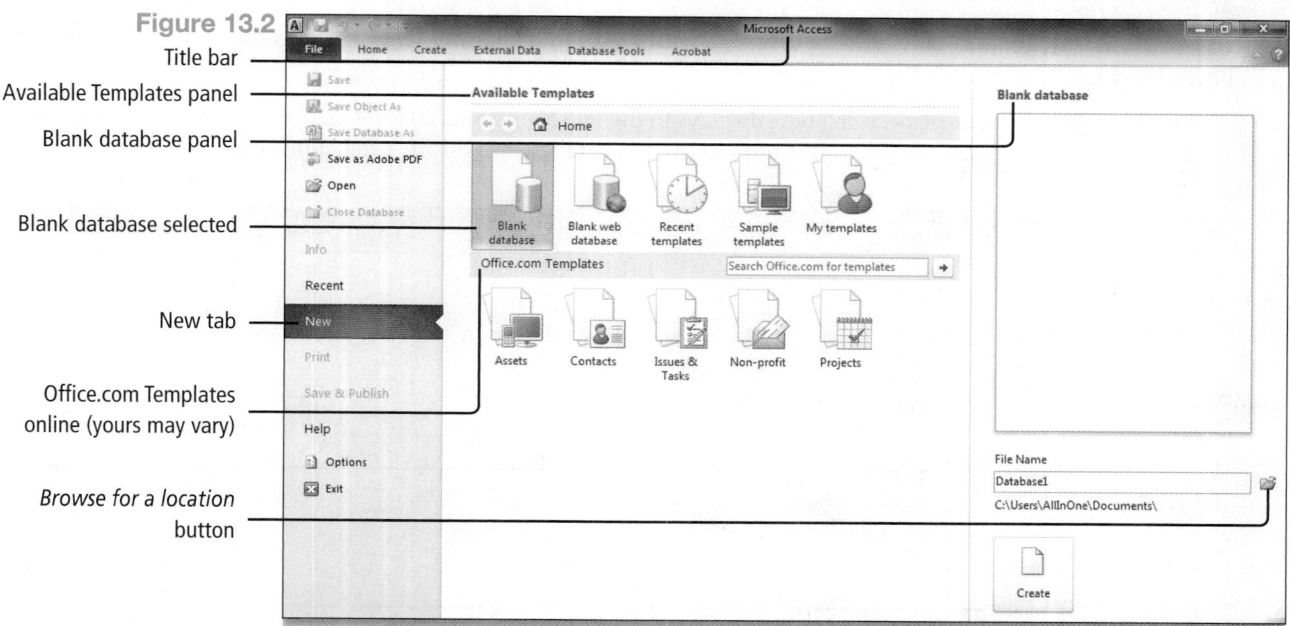

Microsoft Access Opening Window

Window Part	Description
Available Templates panel	Displays alternative methods of creating a database.
Blank database	Starts a new blank database.
Blank database panel	Displays when *Blank database* button is selected under Available Templates.
Browse for location button	Enables you to select a storage location for the database.
New tab	Displays, when active in Backstage view, the various methods by which you can create a new database.
Office.com Templates	Displays template categories available from the Office.com Web site.
Title bar	Displays the Quick Access Toolbar, program name, and program-level buttons.

Figure 13.3

2 On the right, under **Blank database**, to the right of the **File Name** box, click the **Browse** button. In the **File New Database** dialog box, navigate to the location where you are saving your databases for this chapter, create a new folder named **All In One Chapter 13** and then notice that *Database1* displays as the default file name—the number at the end of your file name might differ if you have saved a database previously with the default name. In the **File New Database** dialog box, click **Open**.

3 In the **File name** box, replace the existing text with **Lastname_Firstname_13A_Contacts** Press Enter, and then compare your screen with Figure 13.4.

On the right, the name of your database displays in the File Name box, and the drive and folder where the database is stored displays under the File Name box. An Access database has the file extension *.accdb*.

Figure 13.4

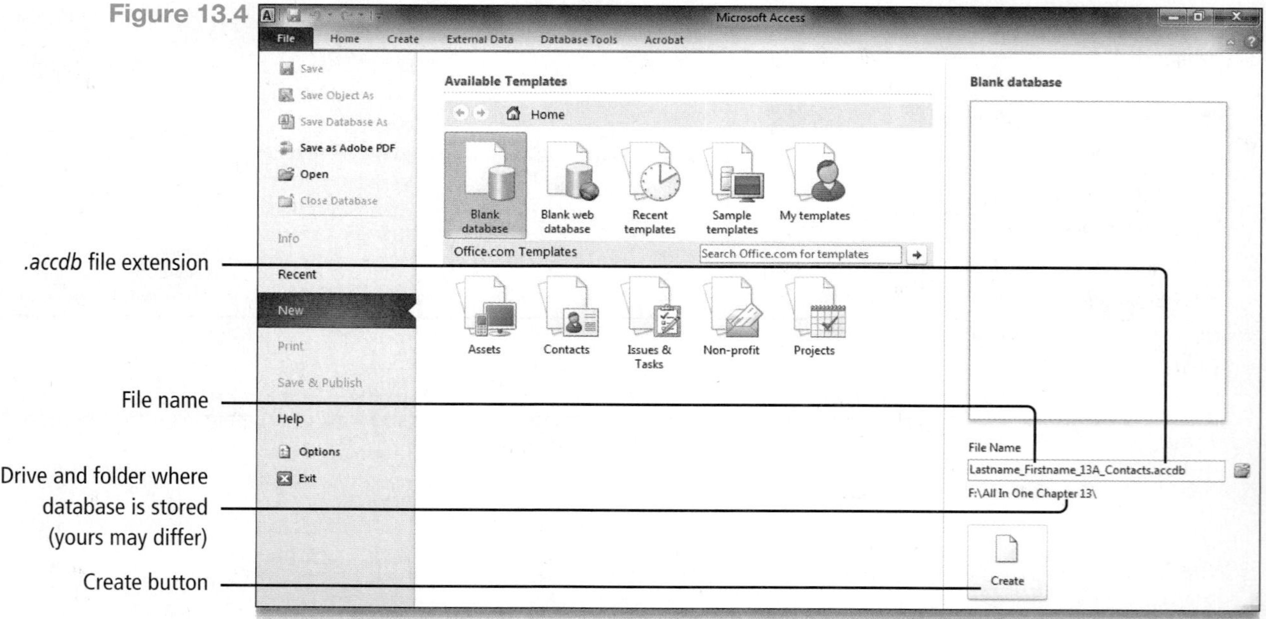

4 Under the **File Name** box, click the **Create** button, compare your screen with Figure 13.5, and then take a moment to study the screen elements described in the table in Figure 13.6.

Access creates the new database and opens *Table 1*. Recall that a *table* is an Access object that stores your data in columns and rows, similar to the format of an Excel worksheet. Table objects are the foundation of a database; they store the data.

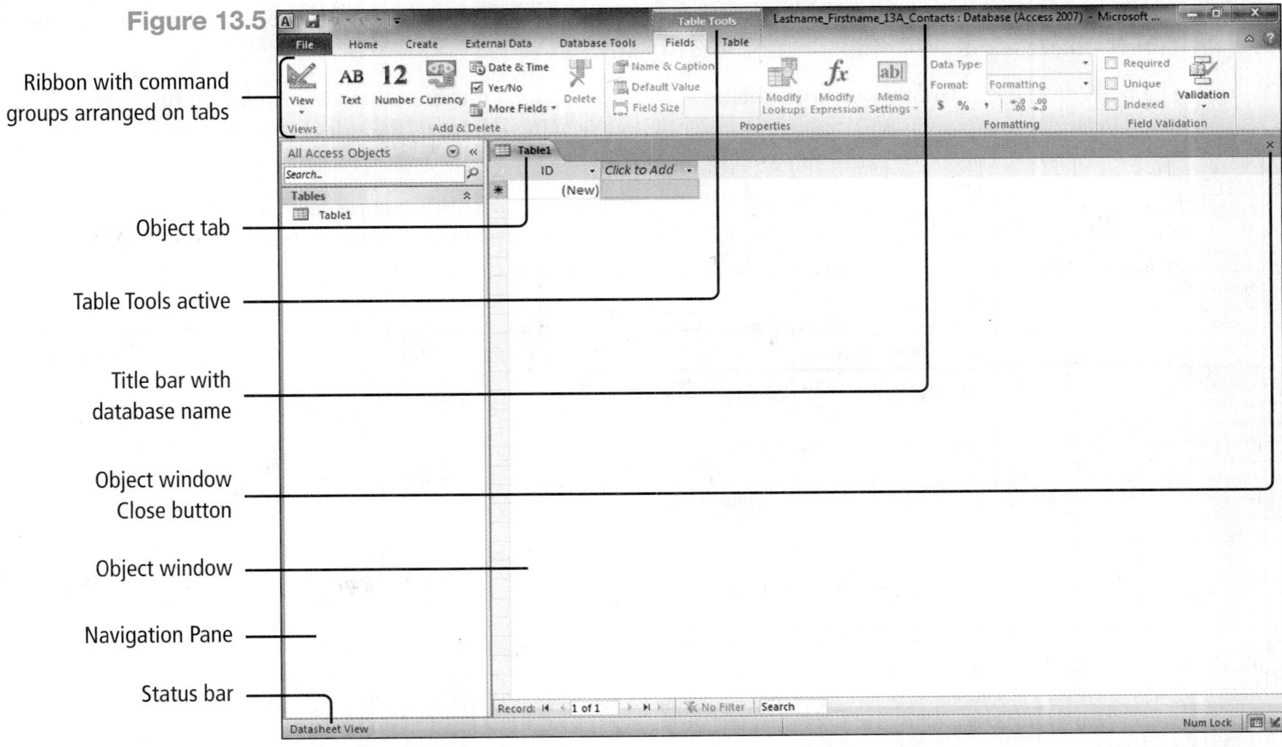

Figure 13.5

Parts of the Access Database Window

Window Part	Description
Navigation Pane	Displays the database objects; from here you open the database objects to display in the object window at the right.
Object tab	Identifies and enables you to select the open object.
Object window	Displays the active or open object (table, query, or other object).
Object window Close button	Closes the active object (table, query, or other object).
Ribbon with command groups arranged on tabs	Groups the commands for performing related database tasks on tabs.
Status bar	Indicates the active view and the status of actions occurring within the database on the left; provides buttons to switch between Datasheet view and Design view on the right.
Table Tools	Provides tools for working with a table object; Table Tools are available only when a table is displayed.
Title bar	Displays the name of your database.

Figure 13.6

Activity 13.03 | Assigning the Data Type and Name to Fields

After you have saved and named your database, the next step is to consult your database plan, and then create the tables in which to enter your data. Limit the data in each table to *one* subject. For example, in this project, your database will have two tables—one for student contact information and one for faculty contact information. Recall that each column in a table is a field and that field names display at the top of each column. Recall also that each row in a table is a record—all of the data pertaining to one person, place, thing, event, or idea. Each record is broken up into its smallest usable parts—the fields. Use meaningful names to name fields; for example, *Last Name*.

1 Notice the new blank table that displays in Datasheet view, and then take a moment to study the elements of the table's object window. Compare your screen with Figure 13.7.

The table displays in ***Datasheet view***, which displays the data as columns and rows similar to the format of an Excel worksheet. Another way to view a table is in ***Design view***, which displays the underlying design—the ***structure***—of the table's fields. The ***object window*** displays the open object—in this instance, the table object.

In a new blank database, there is only one object—a new blank table. Because you have not yet named this table, the object tab displays a default name of *Table1*. Access creates the first field and names it *ID*. In the ID field, Access assigns a unique sequential number—each number incremented by one—to each record as it is entered into the table.

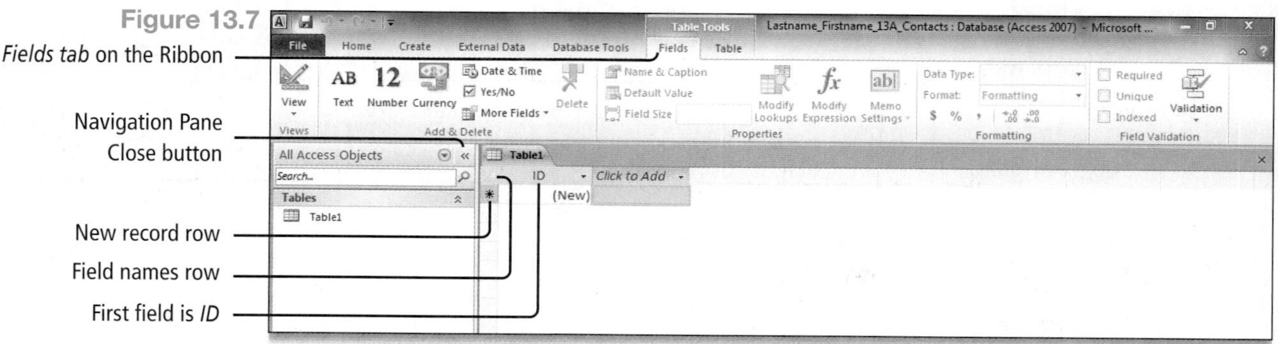

Figure 13.7

2 In the **Navigation Pane**, click the **Open/Close** button [«] to collapse the **Navigation Pane** to a narrow bar on the left and to display more of the table.

The ***Navigation Pane*** is an area of the Access window that displays and organizes the objects in a database. From the Navigation Pane, you can open objects for use.

3 In the field names row, click anywhere in the text *Click to Add* to display a list of data types. Compare your screen with Figure 13.8.

Data type is the characteristic that defines the kind of data that you can type in a field, such as numbers, text, or dates. A field in a table can have only one data type. Part of your database design should include deciding on the data type of each field. After you have selected the data type, you can name the field.

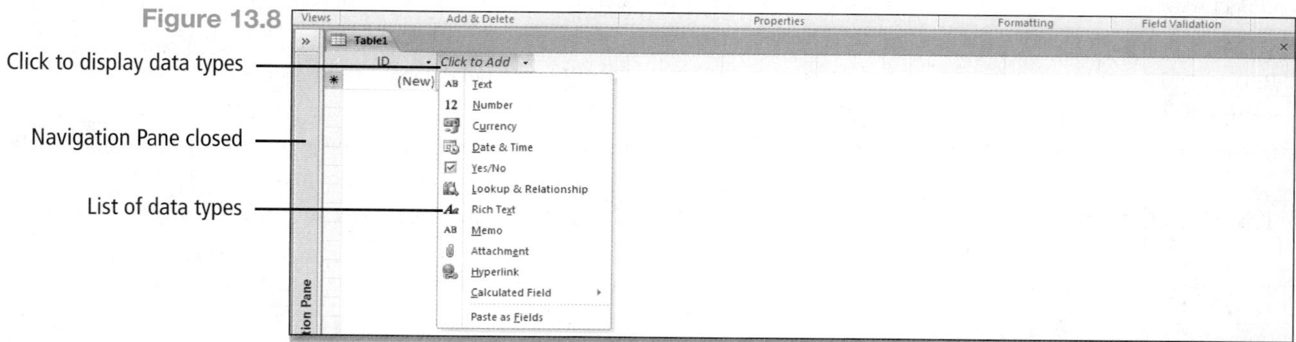

Figure 13.8

4 In the list of data types, click **Text**, and notice that in the second column, *Click to Add* changes to *Field1*, which is selected. Type **Last Name** and then press [Enter].

The second column displays *Last Name* as the field name, and the data type list displays in the third column. The ***Text data type*** describes text, a combination of text and numbers, or numbers that are not used in calculations, such as a ZIP code.

5 In the third field name box, click **Text**, type **First Name** and then press [Enter]. In the fourth field name box, click **Text**, type **Middle Initial** and then press [Enter].

6 Using the technique you just practiced, create the remaining fields as follows by first selecting the data type, then typing the field name, and then pressing Enter. The field names in the table will display on one line.

The ZIP/Postal Code field is assigned a data type of Text because the number is never used in a calculation. The Amount Owed field is assigned a data type of Currency; the ***Currency data type*** describes monetary values. Access automatically adds a U.S. dollar sign ($) and two decimal places to all of the numbers in the fields with a data type of *Currency*.

Data Type		Text	Text	Text	Text	Text	Text	Text	Text	Text	Text	Currency
Field Name	ID	Last Name	First Name	Middle Initial	**Address**	**City**	**State/ Region**	**ZIP/ Postal Code**	**Phone Number**	**E-mail**	**Faculty Advisor ID**	**Amount Owed**

7 If necessary, by using the horizontal scroll bar at the bottom of the screen, scroll to the left to bring the first column into view. Compare your screen with Figure 13.9.

Access automatically created the ID field, and you created 11 additional fields in the table. The horizontal scroll bar indicates that there are additional fields that are not displayed on the screen—your screen width may vary.

Figure 13.9

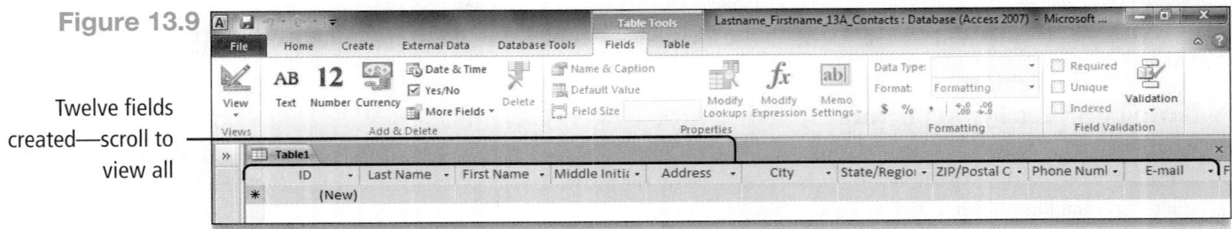

Activity 13.04 | Renaming Fields and Changing Data Types in a Table

1 Click anywhere in the text *ID*. On the **Fields tab**, in the **Properties group**, click the **Name & Caption** button. In the **Enter Field Properties** dialog box, in the **Name** box, change *ID* to **Student ID** and then click **OK**.

The field name *Student ID* is a better description of the data in this field. In the Enter Field Properties dialog box, the ***Caption*** property is used to display a name for a field other than that listed as the field name. Many database designers do not use spaces in field names; instead, they might name a field LastName—with no spaces—and then create a caption for that field so it displays with spaces in tables, forms, and reports. In the Enter Field Properties dialog box, you can also provide a description for the field.

2 In the **Formatting group**, notice that the **Data Type** for the **Student ID** field is *AutoNumber*. Click the **Data Type arrow**, click **Text**, and then compare your screen with Figure 13.10.

In the new record row, the Student ID field is selected. By default, Access creates an ID field for all new tables and sets the data type for the field to AutoNumber. The ***AutoNumber data type*** describes a unique sequential or random number assigned by Access as each record is entered. By changing the data type of this field from *AutoNumber* to *Text*, you can enter a custom student ID number. When records in a database have *no* unique value, for example the names in your address book, the AutoNumber data type is a useful way to automatically create a unique number so that you have a way to ensure that every record is different from the others.

Figure 13.10

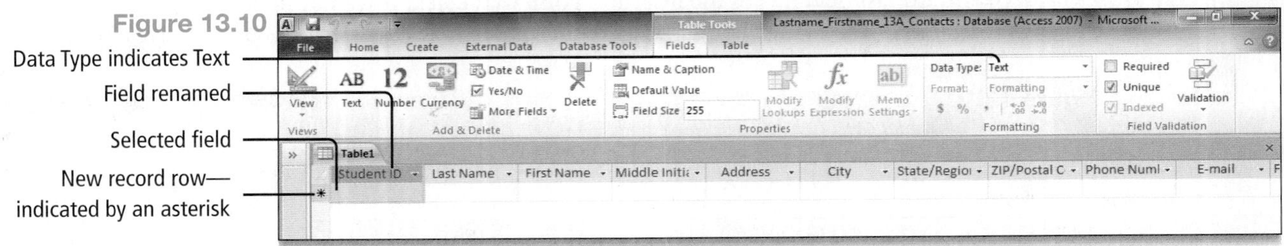

Activity 13.05 | Adding a Record to a Table

1 In the new record row, click in the **Student ID** field to display the insertion point, type **1238765** and then press Enter. Compare your screen with Figure 13.11.

The pencil icon in the ***record selector box***—the small box at the left of a record in Datasheet view that, when clicked, selects the entire record—indicates that a record is being entered or edited.

Figure 13.11

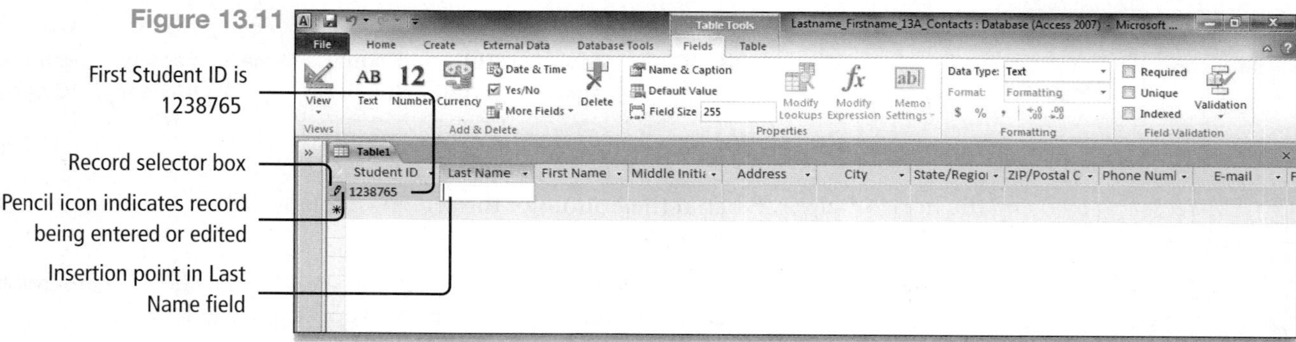

2 With the insertion point positioned in the **Last Name** field, type **Fresch** and then press Enter.

> **Note | Correct Typing Errors**
>
> Correct typing errors by using the techniques you have practiced in other Office applications. For example, use Backspace to remove characters to the left, Delete to remove characters to the right, or select the text you want to replace and type the correct information. Press Esc to exit out of a record that has not been completely entered.

3 In the **First Name** field, type **Michael** and then press Enter. In the **Middle Initial** field, type **B** and then press Enter.

4 In the **Address** field, type **7550 Douglas Ln** and then press Enter.

Do not be concerned if the data does not completely display in the column. As you progress in your study of Access, you will adjust the column widths so that you can view all of the data.

5 Continue entering data in the fields as indicated below, pressing Enter to move to the next field.

City	State/Region	ZIP/Postal Code	Phone Number	E-mail	Faculty Advisor ID
Alexandria	**VA**	**22336**	**(571) 555-0234**	**mfresch@capccc.edu**	**FAC-2289**

> **Note | Format for Typing Telephone Numbers in Access**
>
> Access does not require any specific format for typing telephone numbers in a database. The examples in this project use the format of Microsoft Outlook. Using such a format facilitates easy transfer of Outlook information to and from Access.

6 In the **Amount Owed** field, type **150** and then press Enter. Compare your screen with Figure 13.12.

Pressing Enter or Tab in the last field moves the insertion point to the next row to begin a new record. As soon as you move to the next row, Access saves the record—you do not have to take any specific action to save a record.

Figure 13.12

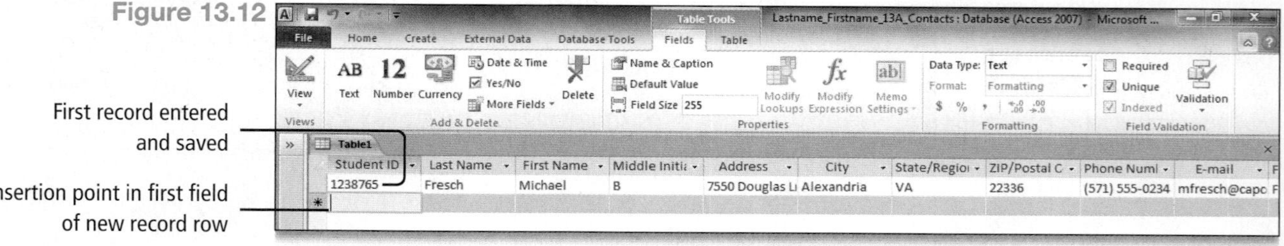

7 On the Quick Access Toolbar, click the **Save** button. In the **Save As** dialog box, in the **Table Name** box, using your own name, replace the highlighted text by typing **Lastname Firstname 13A Students**

Save each database object with a name that identifies the data that it contains. When you save objects within a database, it is not necessary to use underscores. Your name is included as part of the object name so that you and your instructor can identify your printouts or electronic files.

8 In the **Save As** dialog box, click **OK**, and then notice that the object tab displays the new table name you just typed.

> **More Knowledge | Renaming a Table**
>
> To change the name of a table, close the table, display the Navigation Pane, right-click the table name, and then on the shortcut menu, click Rename. Type the new name or edit as you would any selected text.

Activity 13.06 | Adding Additional Records to a Table

1 In the new record row, click in the **Student ID** field, and then enter the contact information for the following two additional students, pressing Enter or Tab to move from field to field. The data in each field will display on one line in the table.

Student ID	Last Name	First Name	Middle Initial	Address	City	State/ Region	ZIP/ Postal Code	Phone Number	E-mail	Faculty Advisor ID	Amount Owed
2345677	Ingram	Joseph	S	1 Casa Del Sol	Potomac	MD	20854	(240) 555-0177	jingram@capccc.edu	FAC-2377	378.5
3456689	Bass	Amanda	J	1446 Yellow Rose Ln	Fairfax	VA	22030	(703) 555-0192	abass@capccc.edu	FAC-9005	0

2 Compare your screen with Figure 13.13.

Figure 13.13

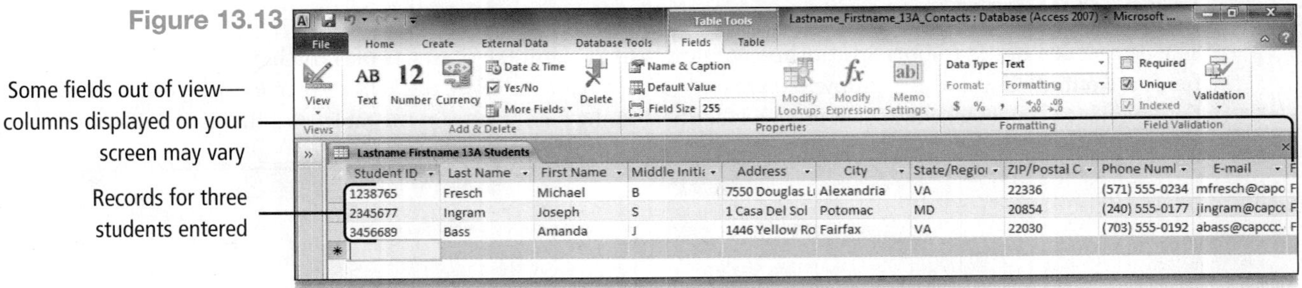

Activity 13.07 | Importing Data from an Excel Workbook into an Existing Access Table

When you create a database table, you can type the records directly into a table. You can also ***import*** data from a variety of sources. Importing is the process of copying data from one source or application to another application. For example, you can import data from a Word table or an Excel worksheet into an Access database because the data is arranged in columns and rows, similar to a table in Datasheet view. In this activity, you will ***append***—add on—data from an Excel spreadsheet to your *13A Students* table. To append data, the table must already be created, and it must be closed.

1 In the upper right corner of the table, below the Ribbon, click the **Object Close** button to close your **13A Students** table. Notice that no objects are open.

2 On the Ribbon, click the **External Data tab**. In the **Import & Link group**, click the **Excel** button. In the **Get External Data - Excel Spreadsheet** dialog box, click the **Browse** button.

3 In the **File Open** dialog box, navigate to your student files, locate and double-click the Excel file **e13A_Students**, and then compare your screen with Figure 13.14.

The path to the ***source file***—the file being imported—displays in the File name box. There are three options for importing data from an Excel workbook—import the data into a *new* table in the current database, append a copy of the records to an existing table, or link the data from Excel to a linked table. A ***link*** is a connection to data in another file. When linking, Access creates a table that maintains a link to the source data.

Figure 13.14

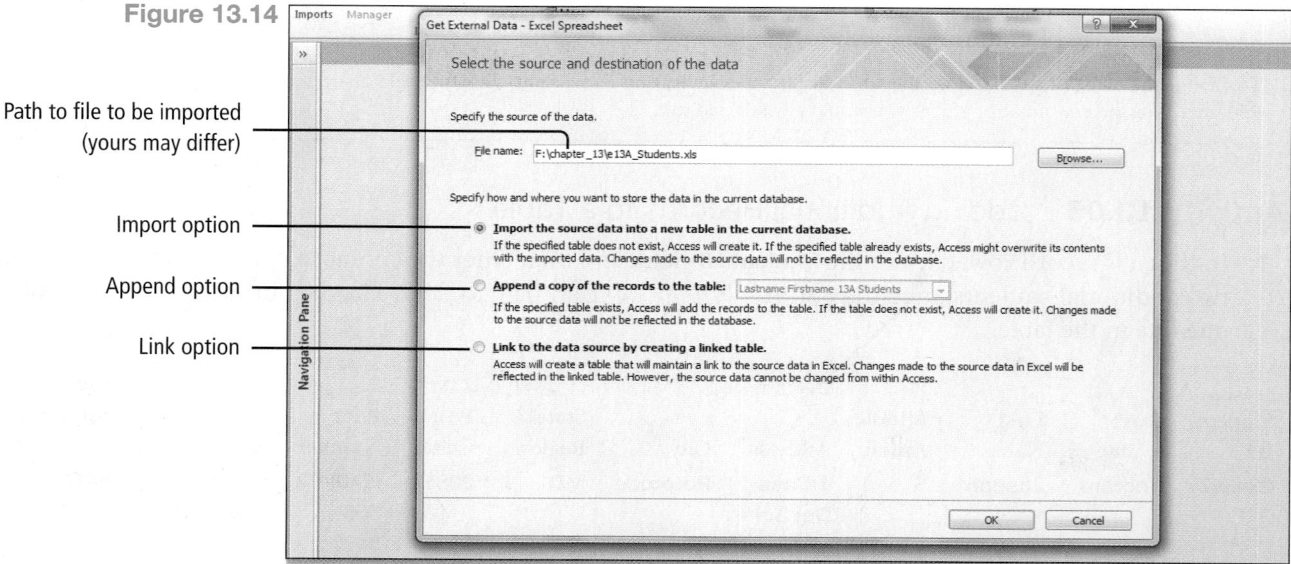

4 Click the **Append a copy of the records to the table** option button, and then in the box to its right, click the **arrow**.

Currently your database has only one table, so no other tables display on the list. However, when a database has multiple tables, here you can select the table to which you want to append records. The table into which you import or append data is referred to as the ***destination table***.

5 Press Esc to cancel the list, and then in the lower right corner of the dialog box, click **OK**. Compare your screen with Figure 13.15.

The first screen of the Import Spreadsheet Wizard displays, and the presence of scroll bars indicates that records and fields are out of view in this window. To append records from an Excel worksheet to an existing database table, the field names in the Excel worksheet must be identical to the field names in the table, and that is true in this table.

Figure 13.15

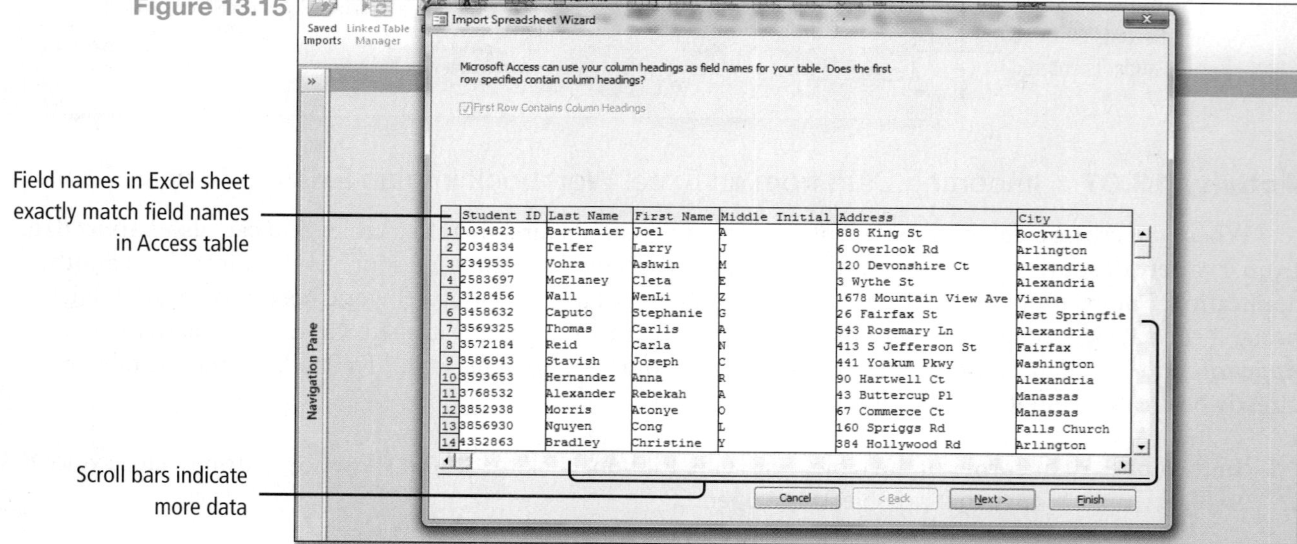

6 In the lower right corner, click **Next**. Notice that the name of your table displays under **Import to Table**. In the lower right corner, click **Finish**. In the **Get External Data - Excel Spreadsheet** dialog box, click **Close.**

7 **Open** [»] the **Navigation Pane**. Point to the right edge of the **Navigation Pane** to display the [⟺] pointer. Drag to the right to widen the pane to display the entire table name, and then compare your screen with Figure 13.16.

Figure 13.16

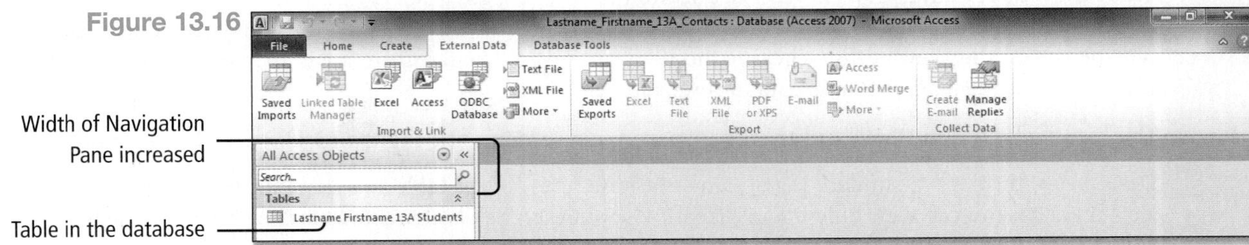

8 In the **Navigation Pane**, double-click your **13A Students** table to open the table in Datasheet view, and then **Close** [«] the **Navigation Pane**.

9 At the bottom left corner of your screen, locate the navigation area, and notice that there are a total of **26** records in the table—you created three records and imported 23 additional records. Compare your screen with Figure 13.17.

The records from the Excel worksheet display in your table, and the first record is selected. The ***navigation area*** indicates the number of records in the table and contains controls (arrows) with which you can navigate among the records.

Figure 13.17

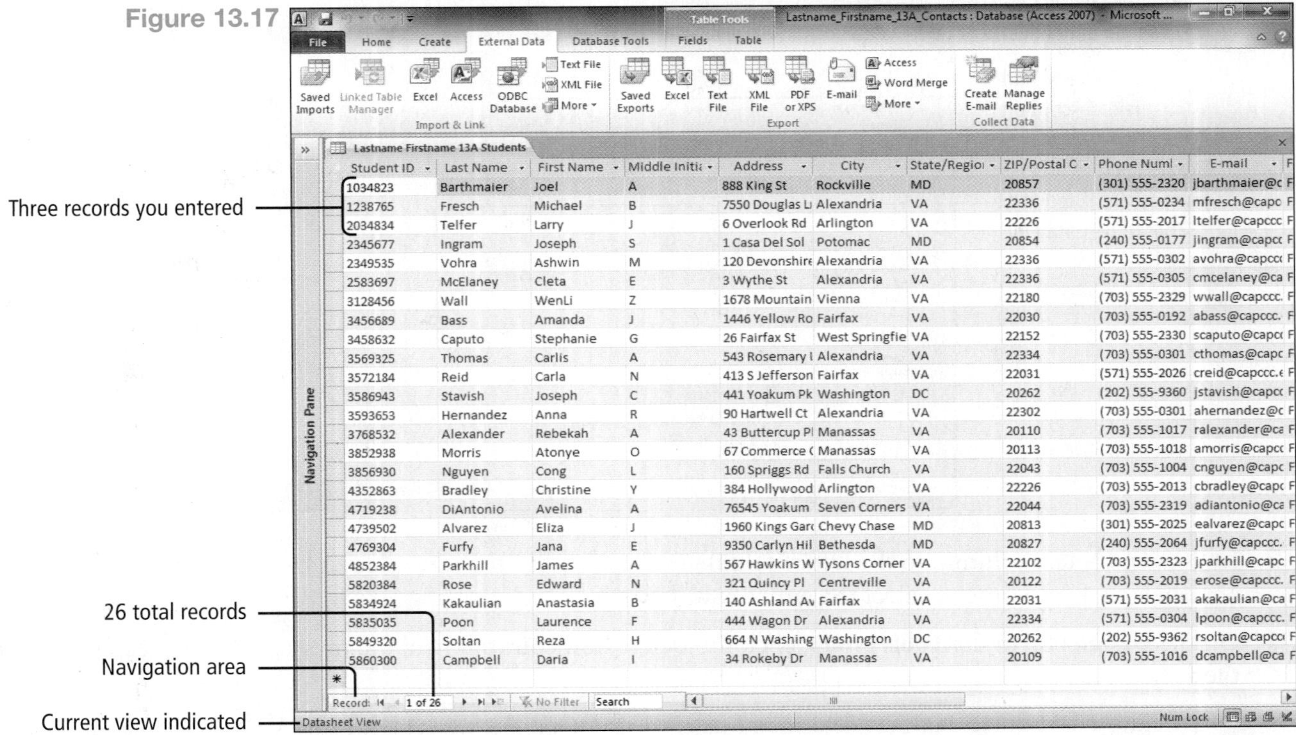

Objective 3 | Change the Structure of Tables and Add a Second Table

Recall that the structure of a table is the underlying design, including field names and data types. You can create a table or modify a table in Datasheet view. To define and modify fields, many database experts prefer to work in Design view, where you have many additional options for defining the fields in a table.

View the video on the Companion Web Site or in MyITLab

Activity 13.08 | Deleting a Table Field in Design View

In this activity, you will delete the *Middle Initial* field from the table.

1 Click the **Home tab**, and then in the **Views group**, click the **View button arrow**.

There are four common views in Access, but two that you will use often are Datasheet view and Design view. On the displayed list, Design view is represented by a picture of a pencil, a ruler, and an angle. When one of these four icons is displayed on the View button, clicking the View button will display the table in the view represented by the icon. Datasheet view displays the table data in rows and columns.

2 On the list, click **Design View**, and then compare your screen with Figure 13.18.

Design view displays the underlying design—the structure—of the table and its fields. In Design view, you cannot view the data; you can view only the information about each field's characteristics. Each field name is listed, along with its data type. A column to add a Description—information about the data in the field—is provided.

In the Field Properties area, you can make additional decisions about how each individual field looks and behaves. For example, you can set a specific field size.

Figure 13.18

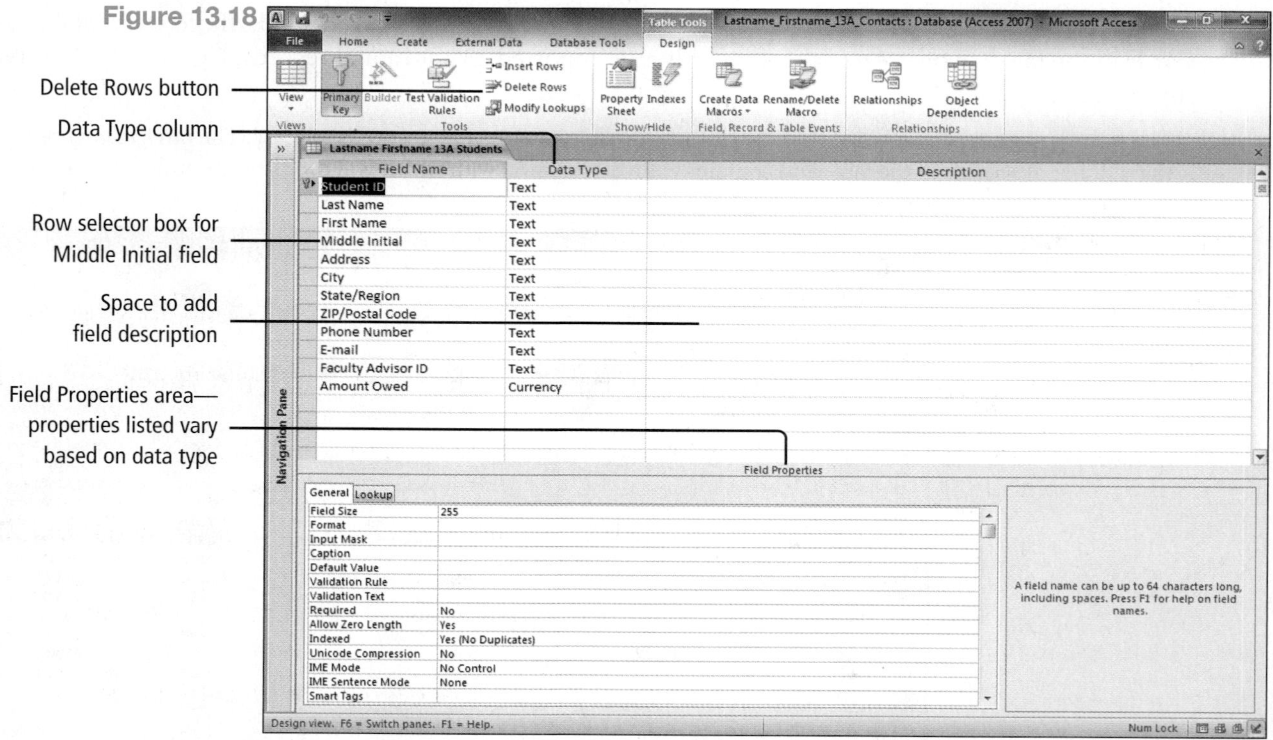

3 In the **Field Name** column, to the left of **Middle Initial**, point to the row selector box to display the [→] pointer, and then click one time to select the entire row.

4 On the **Design tab**, in the **Tools group**, click the **Delete Rows** button, read the message in the message box, and then click **Yes**.

Deleting a field deletes both the field and its data; you cannot undo this action. Thus, Access prompts you to be sure you want to proceed. If you change your mind after deleting a field, you must add the field back into the table and then re-enter the data in that field for every record.

Activity 13.09 | Modifying a Field Size and Adding a Description

Typically, many individuals enter data into a table. For example, at your college many Registration Assistants enter and modify student and course information daily. Two ways to help reduce errors are to restrict what can be typed in a field and to add descriptive information.

1 With your table still displayed in **Design** view, in the **Field Name** column, click anywhere in the **State/Region** field name.

2 In the lower portion of the screen, under **Field Properties**, click **Field Size** to select the text *255*, type **2** and then compare your screen with Figure 13.19.

Field properties control how the field displays and how data can be entered in the field. This action limits the size of the State/Region field to no more than two characters—the size of the two-letter state abbreviations provided by the United States Postal Service. However, this does not prevent someone from entering two characters that are incorrect. Setting the proper data type for the field and limiting the field size are two ways to *help* to reduce errors.

Figure 13.19

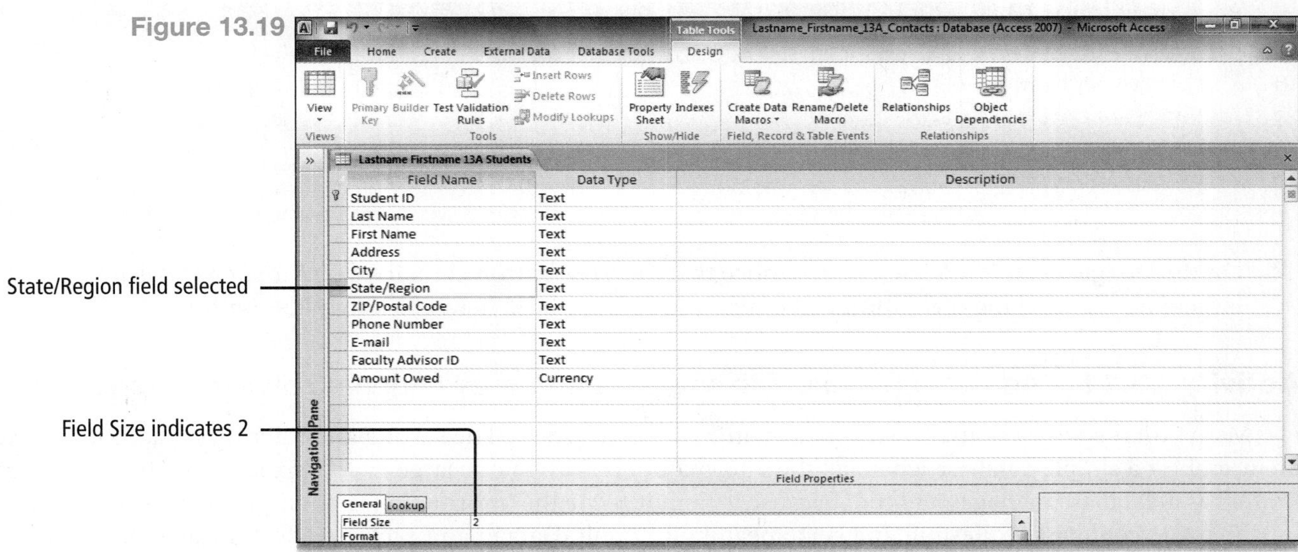

3 In the **State/Region** row, click in the **Description** box, type **Two-character state abbreviation** and then press Enter.

Descriptions for fields in a table are optional. Include a description if the field name does not provide an obvious explanation of the field. Information typed in the description area displays on the left side of the status bar in Datasheet view when the field is active, providing additional information to individuals who are entering data.

4 Click in the **Student ID** field name box. Using the technique you practiced, in the **Field Properties** area, change the **Field Size** to **7**

By limiting the field size to seven characters, which is the maximum number of characters in a Student ID, you help to ensure the accuracy of the data.

5 In the **Student ID** row, click in the **Description** box, and then type **Seven-digit Student ID number**

6 Click in the **Faculty Advisor ID** field name box. In the **Field Properties** area, change the **Field Size** to **8** In the **Description** box for this field, type **Eight-character ID of faculty member assigned as advisor** and then press Enter.

7 On the Quick Access Toolbar, click the **Save** button to save the design changes to your table, and then notice the message.

The message indicates that the field size property of one or more fields has changed to a shorter size. If more characters are currently present in the Student ID, State/Region, or Faculty Advisor ID than you have allowed, the data could be ***truncated***—cut off or shortened—because the fields were not previously restricted to a specific number of characters.

8 In the message box, click **Yes**.

Activity 13.10 | Viewing a Primary Key in Design View

Primary key refers to the field in the table that uniquely identifies a record. For example, in a college registration database, your Student ID number uniquely identifies you—no other student at the college has your exact student number. In the 13A Students table, the Student ID uniquely identifies each student.

When you create a table using the Blank database command, by default Access designates the first field as the primary key field. It is a good database design practice to establish a primary key for every table, because doing so ensures that you do not enter the same record more than once.

1 With your table still displayed in Design view, in the **Field Name** column, click in the **Student ID** box. To the left of the box, notice the small icon of a key, as shown in Figure 13.20.

Access automatically designates the first field as the primary key field, but you can set any field as the primary key by clicking in the box to the left of the field name, and then clicking the Primary Key button.

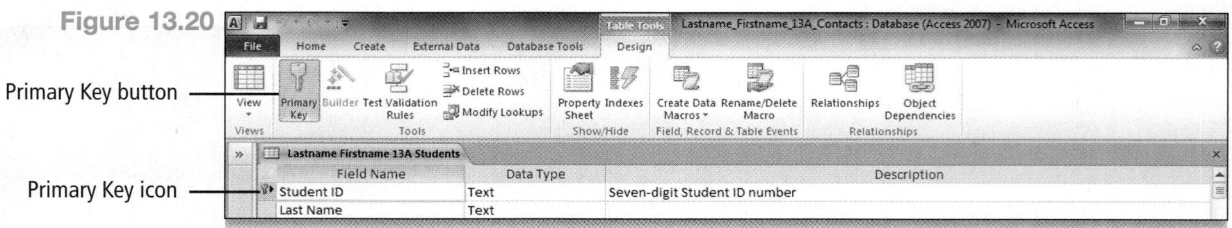

Figure 13.20

2 On the **Design tab**, in the **Views group**, notice that the **View** button contains a picture of a Datasheet, indicating that clicking the button will return you to Datasheet view. Click the **View** button.

Activity 13.11 | Adding a Second Table to a Database by Importing an Excel Spreadsheet

Many Microsoft Office users track data in an Excel spreadsheet. The sorting and filtering capabilities of Excel are useful for a simple database where all the information resides in one large Excel spreadsheet. However, Excel is limited as a database management tool because it cannot *relate* the information in multiple spreadsheets in a way in which you could ask a question and get a meaningful result. Data in an Excel spreadsheet can easily become an Access table by importing the spreadsheet, because Excel's format of columns and rows is similar to that of an Access table.

1 On the Ribbon, click the **External Data tab**, and then in the **Import & Link group**, click the **Excel** button. In the **Get External Data – Excel Spreadsheet** dialog box, to the right of the **File name** box, click **Browse**.

2 In the **File Open** dialog box, navigate to your student files, and then double-click **e13A_Faculty**. Compare your screen with Figure 13.21.

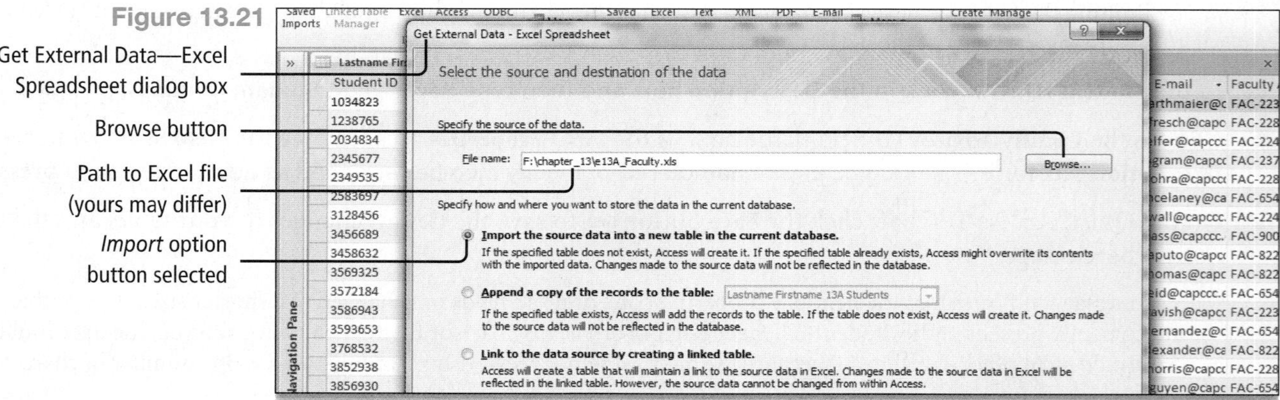

Figure 13.21

3 Be sure that the **Import the source data into a new table in the current database** option button is selected, and then click **OK**.

The Import Spreadsheet Wizard opens and displays the spreadsheet data.

4 In the upper left portion of the **Import Spreadsheet Wizard** dialog box, select the **First Row Contains Column Headings** check box.

The Excel data is framed, indicating that the first row of Excel column titles will become the Access table field names, and the remaining rows will become the individual records in the new Access table.

5 Click **Next**. Notice that the first column—*Faculty ID*—is selected, and in the upper portion of the Wizard, the **Field Name** and the **Data Type** display. Compare your screen with Figure 13.22.

Here you can review and change the field properties for each field (column). You can also identify fields in the spreadsheet that you do not want to import into the Access table by selecting the Do not import field (Skip) check box.

Figure 13.22

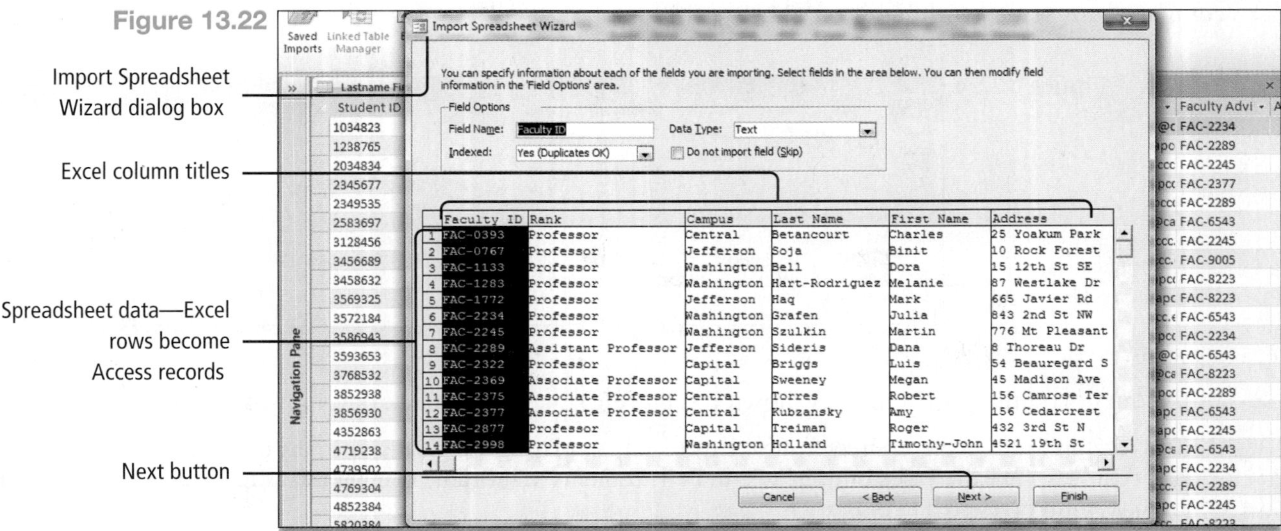

6 Click **Next**. In the upper portion of the Wizard, click the **Choose my own primary key** option button, and then be sure that **Faculty ID** displays.

In the new table, Faculty ID will be the primary key. No two faculty members have the same Faculty ID. By default, Access selects the first field as the primary key, but you can click the arrow to select a different field.

7 Click **Next**. In the **Import to Table** box, type **Lastname Firstname 13A Faculty** and then click **Finish**. In the **Get External Data – Excel Spreadsheet** dialog box, click **Close**.

8 **Open** [»] the **Navigation Pane**. Double-click your **13A Faculty** table to open it in Datasheet view, and then **Close** [«] the **Navigation Pane**.

9 Click in the **ZIP/Postal Code** field, and then on the Ribbon, click the **Fields tab**. In the **Formatting group**, change the **Data Type** to **Text**. Compare your screen with Figure 13.23.

The data from the *e13A_Faculty* worksheet displays in your *13A Faculty* table in the database. Recall that if a field contains numbers that are not used in calculations, the data type should be set to Text. When you import data from an Excel spreadsheet, check the data types of all fields to ensure they are correct.

Figure 13.23

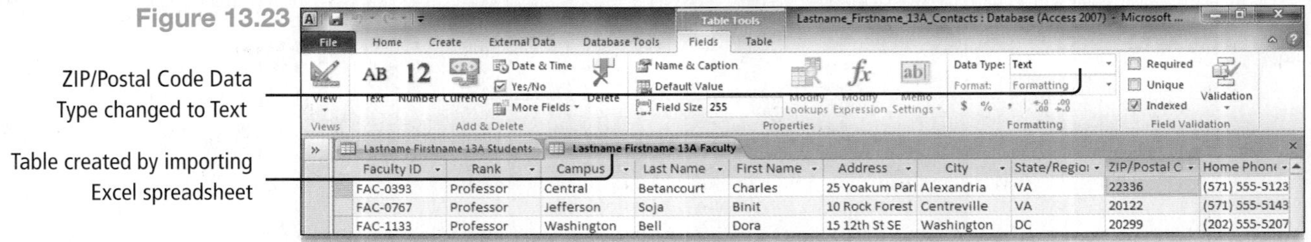

Activity 13.12 | Adjusting Column Widths

By using techniques similar to those you use for Excel worksheets, you can adjust the widths of Access fields that display in Datasheet view.

1 In the object window, click the **object tab** for your **13A Students** table.

All of the columns are the same width regardless of the amount of data in the field, the field size that was set, or the length of the field name. If you print the table as currently displayed, some of the data or field names will not fully print until you adjust the column widths.

2 In the field names row, point to the right edge of the **Address** field to display the pointer [⟺], and then compare your screen with Figure 13.24.

Figure 13.24

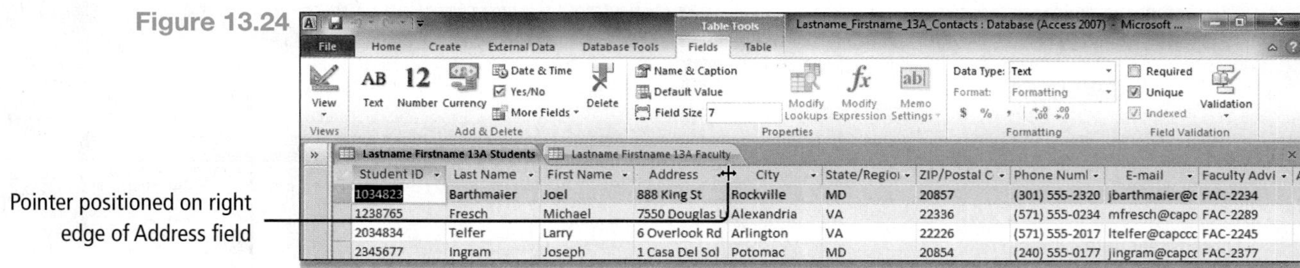

3 With your [⟺] pointer positioned as shown in Figure 13.24, double-click the right edge of the **Address** field.

The column width of the Address field widens to fully display the longest entry in the field. In this manner, the width of a column can be increased or decreased to fit its contents in the same manner as a column in an Excel worksheet. In Access this is referred to as ***Best Fit***.

4 Point to the **Phone Number** field name to display the [↓] pointer, right-click to select the entire column and display a shortcut menu, and then click **Field Width**. In the **Column Width** dialog box, click **Best Fit**.

5 Scroll to the right until the last three fields display. Point to the **E-mail** field name to display the [↓] pointer, hold down the left mouse button, and then drag to the right to select this column, the **Faculty Advisor ID** column, and the **Amount Owed** column. By double-clicking the [⟺] pointer on the right boundary of any of the selected columns, or by displaying the Field Width dialog box from the shortcut menu, apply **Best Fit** to the selected columns.

6 Scroll all the way to the left to view the **Student ID** field. To the left of the *Student ID* field name, click the **Select All** button [ ]. Click the **Home tab**, and in the **Records group**, click the **More** button. Click **Field Width**, and in the **Column Width** dialog box, click **Best Fit**. In the first record, scroll to the right as necessary, click in the **Amount Owed** field, and then compare your screen with Figure 13.25.

In this manner, you can adjust all of the column widths at one time. After applying Best Fit, be sure to click in any field to remove the selection from all of the records; otherwise, the layout changes will not be saved with the table. Adjusting the width of columns does not change the data in the table's records; it changes only the *display* of the data.

Figure 13.25

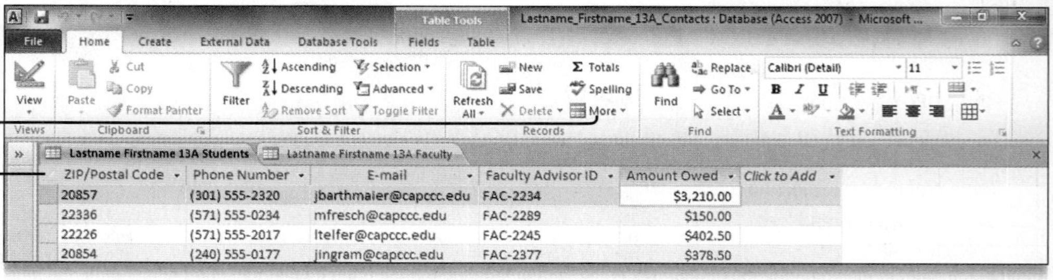

More button

Select All button

Note | Adjusting Column Widths

If you adjust column widths individually, scroll to the right and scroll down to be sure that all of the data displays in all of the fields. Access adjusts the column widths to fit the screen size based on the displayed data. If data is not displayed on the screen when you adjust a column width, the column may not be adjusted adequately to display all of the data in the field. For that reason, select all of the columns and apply Best Fit to be sure that all of the data displays when scrolling or printing. Click in any field after applying Best Fit to remove the selection, and then save the table before performing other tasks.

7 On the Quick Access Toolbar, click the **Save** button to save the table design changes—changing the column widths.

If you do not save the table after making design changes, Access will prompt you to save when you close the table.

Activity 13.13 | Printing a Table

Although a printed table does not look as professional as a printed report, there are times when you will want to print a table. For example, you may need a quick reference or want to proofread the data that has been entered.

1 On the Ribbon, click the **File tab** to display **Backstage** view, click the **Print** tab, click **Print Preview**, and then compare your screen with Figure 13.26.

Figure 13.26

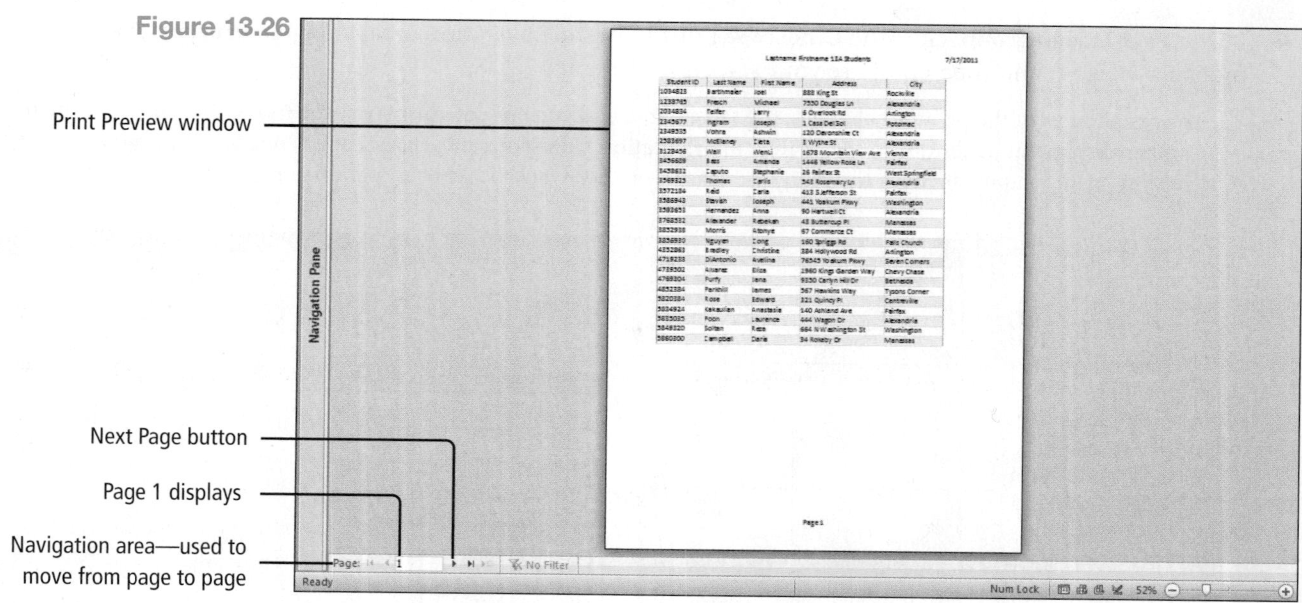

2 In the lower left corner, click the **Next Page** button two times. Point to the top of the page to display the pointer, click one time to zoom in, and then compare your screen with Figure 13.27.

The display enlarges, and the Zoom Out pointer displays. The third page of the table displays the last two field columns. The Next Page button is dimmed, indicating there are no more pages. The Previous Page button is darker, indicating that pages exist before this page.

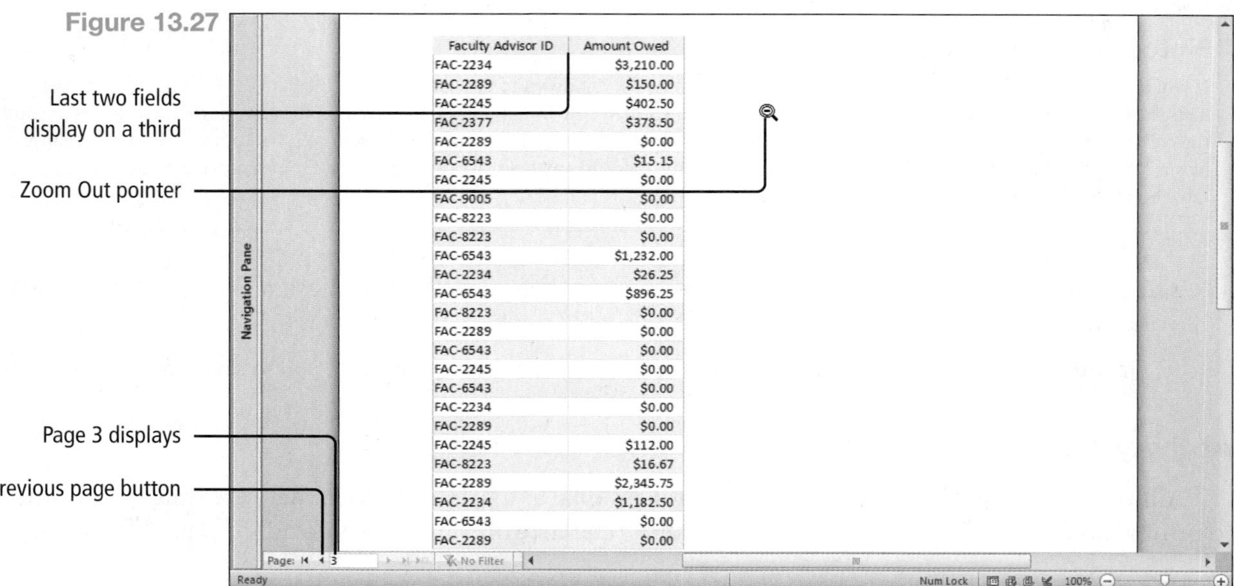

Figure 13.27

3 On the Ribbon, in the **Zoom group**, click the **Zoom** button to zoom back to Fit to Window view.

4 In the **Page Layout group**, click the **Landscape** button. In the navigation area, click the **Previous Page** button to display **Page 1**, and then compare your screen with Figure 13.28.

The orientation of the printout changes, the table name and current date display at the top of the page, and the page number displays at the bottom. The change in orientation from portrait to landscape is not saved with the table. Each time you print, you must check the margins, page orientation, and other print parameters to print as you intend.

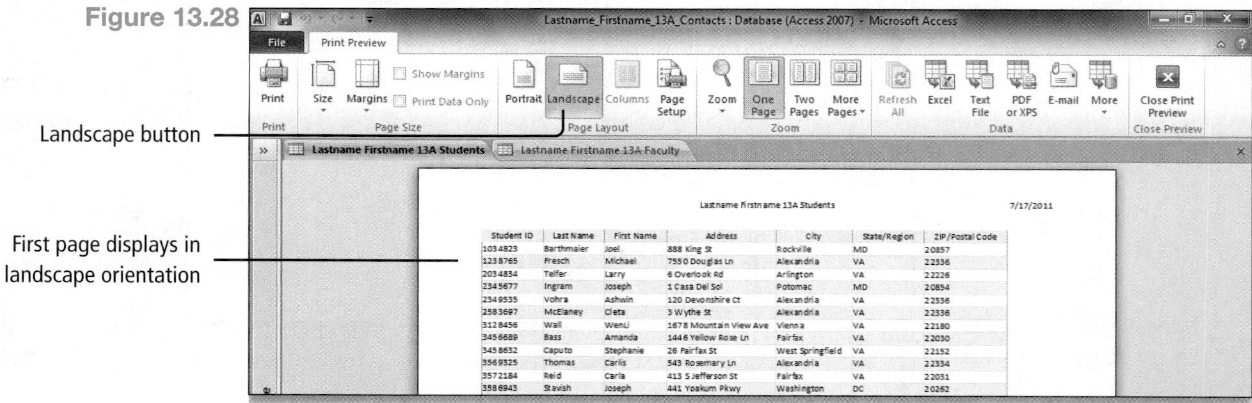

Figure 13.28

> **Note | Headers and Footers in Access Objects**
>
> The headers and footers in Access tables and queries are controlled by default settings; you cannot add additional information or edit the information. The object name displays in the center of the header area with the date on the right—that is why adding your own name to the object name is helpful to identify your paper or electronic results. The page number displays in the center of the footer area. The headers and footers in Access reports and forms, however, are more flexible; you can add to and edit the information.

5 On the **Print Preview tab**, in the **Print group**, click the **Print** button. In the **Print** dialog box, under **Print Range**, verify that the **All** option button is selected. Under **Copies**, verify that the **Number of Copies** is **1**. Compare your screen with Figure 13.29.

Figure 13.29

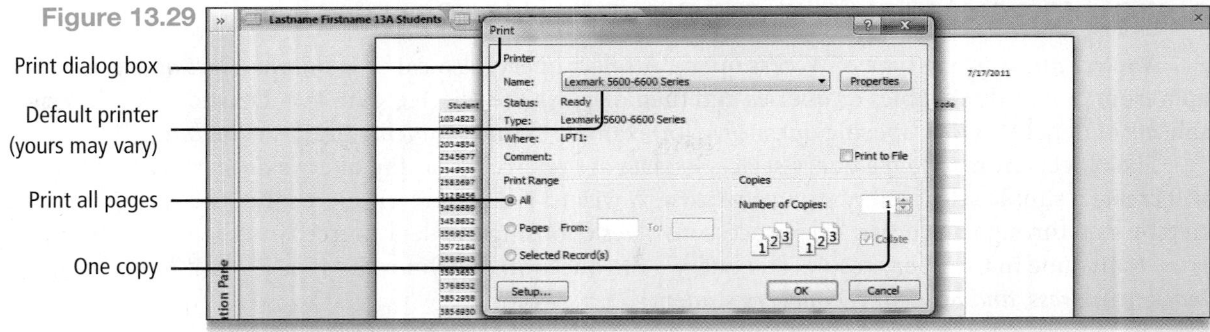

6 Determine how your instructor wants you to submit your work for this project—on paper or electronically. If submitting electronically, determine if, in addition to submitting your Access database, you are to create and submit electronic printouts of individual database objects.

7 To print on paper, in the **Print** dialog box, click **OK**, and then in the **Close Preview group**, click the **Close Print Preview** button. This printout will have two pages. To create an electronic PDF printout of this table object, in the Print dialog box, click Cancel, and then follow the steps in the following Note—or follow the specific directions provided by your instructor.

Note | To Create a PDF Electronic Printout of an Access Object

Display the object (table, report, and so on) in Print Preview and adjust margins and orientation as desired. On the Print Preview tab, in the Data group, click the PDF or XPS button. In the Publish as PDF or XPS dialog box, navigate to your chapter folder. Use the default file name, or follow your instructor's directions to name the object. In the lower right corner, click Publish—the default setting is PDF. If necessary, close the Adobe Acrobat/Reader window and the Export-PDF dialog box. Click the Close Print Preview button; your electronic printout is saved.

8 At the far right edge of the object window, click the **Close Object** button to close the **13A Students** table.

9 With your **13A Faculty** table displayed, to the left of the **Faculty ID** field name, click the **Select All** button to select all of the columns. On the **Home tab**, in the **Records group**, click the **More** button. Click **Field Width**, and in the **Column Width** dialog box, click **Best Fit**. Click in any field in the table to remove the selection, and then **Save** the table.

10 Display the table in **Print Preview**. Change the **Orientation** to **Landscape**. If directed to do so by your instructor, create a paper or electronic printout, and then **Close Print Preview**—two pages result.

11 Click the **Close Object** button.

All of your database objects—the *13A Students* table and the *13A Faculty* table—are closed; the object window is empty.

Objective 4 | Create and Use a Query, Form, and Report

View the video on the Companion Web Site or in MyITLab

A ***query*** is a database object that retrieves specific data from one or more database objects—either tables or other queries—and then, in a single datasheet, displays only the data that you specify. Because the word *query* means *to ask a question*, think of a query as a question formed in a manner that Access can answer.

A ***form*** is an Access object with which you can enter data, edit data, or display data from a table or a query. In a form, the fields are laid out in an attractive format on the screen, which makes working with the database easier for those who must enter and look up data.

A ***report*** is a database object that displays the fields and records from a table or a query in an easy-to-read format suitable for printing. Create reports to *summarize* information in a database in a professional-looking manner.

Activity 13.14 | Using the Simple Query Wizard to Create a Query

A ***select query*** is one type of Access query. A select query, also called a ***simple select query***, retrieves (selects) data from one or more tables or queries and then displays the selected data in a datasheet. A select query creates subsets of data to answer specific questions; for example, *Which students live in Arlington, VA?*

The objects from which a query selects its data are referred to as the query's ***data source***. In this activity, you will create a simple select query using a ***wizard***. A wizard is a feature in Microsoft Office programs that walks you step by step through a process. The process involves choosing the data source, and then indicating the fields you want to include in the query result. The query—the question that you want to ask—is *What is the name, complete mailing address, and Student ID of every student?*

1 Click the **Create tab**, and then in the **Queries group**, click the **Query Wizard** button. In the **New Query** dialog box, click **Simple Query Wizard**, and then click **OK**. Compare your screen with Figure 13.30.

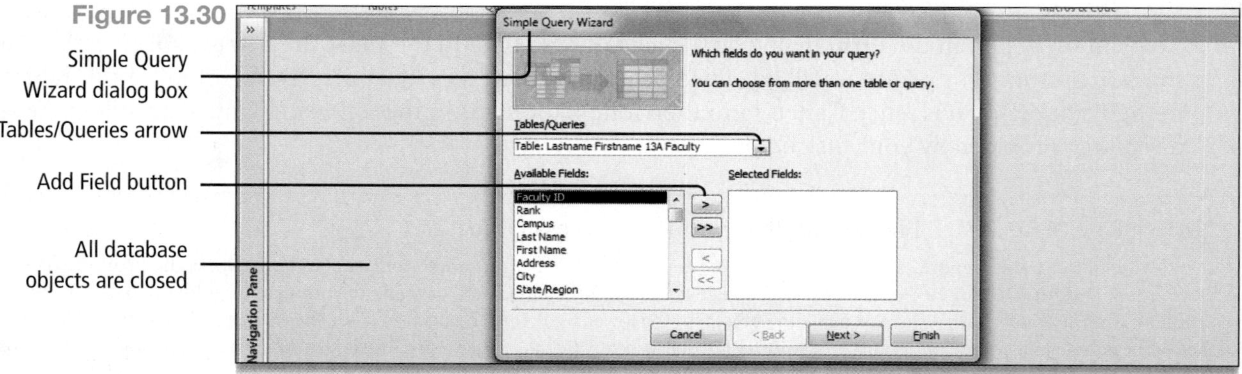

Figure 13.30

2 Click the **Tables/Queries arrow**, and then click your **Table: 13A Students**.

To create a query, first choose the data source—the object from which to select data. The name and complete mailing address of every student is stored in the 13A Students table, so this table will be your data source.

3 Under **Available Fields**, click **Student ID**, and then click the **Add Field** button [>] to move the field to the **Selected Fields** list on the right. Point to the **Last Name** field, and then double-click to add the field to the **Selected Fields** list.

Use either method to add fields to the Selected Fields list. Fields can be added in any order.

4 By using the **Add Field** button [>] or by double-clicking the field name, add the following fields to the **Selected Fields** list: **First Name**, **Address**, **City**, **State/Region**, and **ZIP/Postal Code**. Compare your screen with Figure 13.31.

Choosing these seven fields will answer the question, *What is the Student ID, name, and address of every student?*

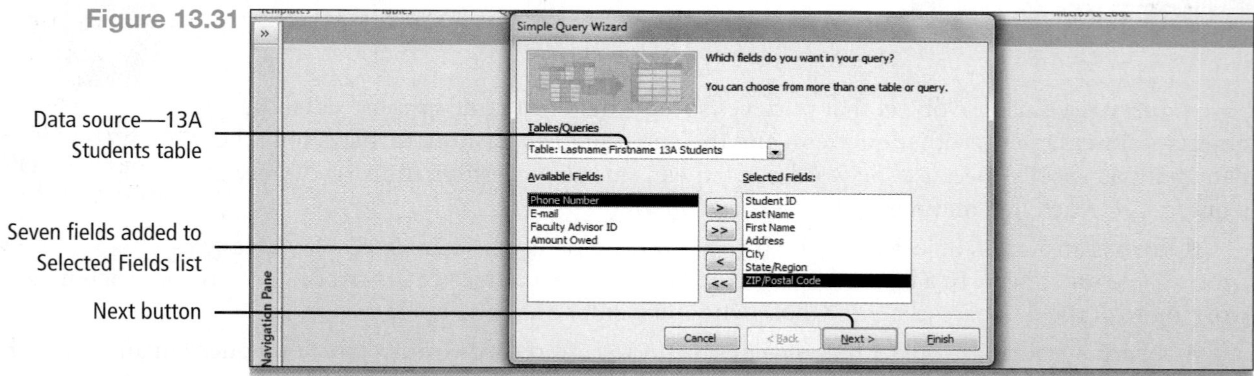

Figure 13.31

5 Click **Next**. In the **Simple Query Wizard** dialog box, click in the **What title do you want for your query?** box. Edit as necessary so that the query name, using your own last and first name, is **Lastname Firstname 13A All Students Query** and then compare your screen with Figure 13.32.

Figure 13.32

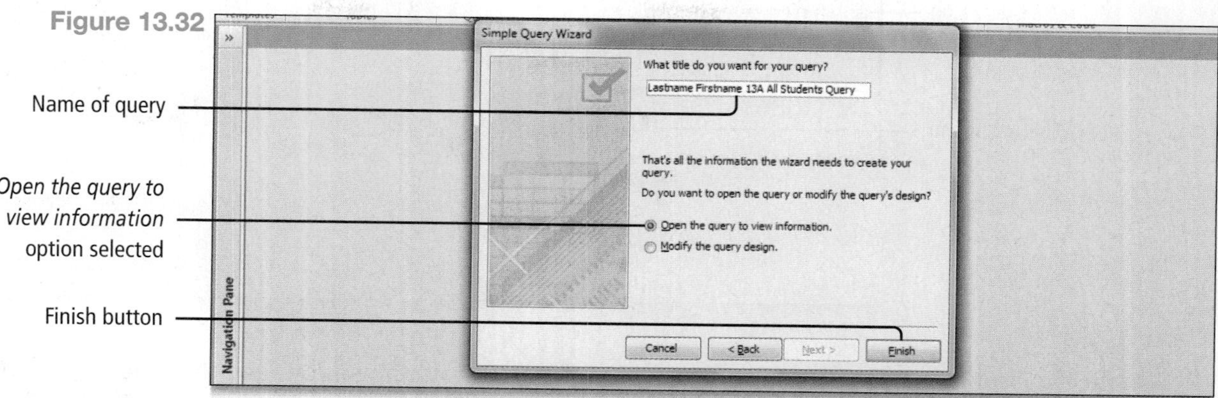

6 Click **Finish**.

Access ***runs*** the query—performs the actions indicated in your query design by searching the records in the data source you selected, and then finding the records that match specified criteria. The records that match the criteria display in a datasheet. A select query *selects*—pulls out and displays—*only* the information from the data source that you requested, including the specified fields. In the object window, Access displays every student record in Datasheet view, but displays *only* the seven fields that you moved to the Selected Fields list in the Simple Query Wizard dialog box.

7 If necessary, apply Best Fit to the columns and then Save the query. Display the query in **Print Preview**. Change the **Orientation** to **Landscape**, and then create a paper or electronic printout as instructed. **Close** the **Print Preview**.

8 In the object window, click the **Close Object** button [X] to close the query.

Activity 13.15 | Creating and Printing a Form

One type of Access form displays only one record in the database at a time. Such a form is useful not only to the individual who performs the data entry—typing in the actual records—but also to anyone who has the job of viewing information in a database. For the viewer, it is much easier to look at one record at a time, using a form, than to look at all of the student records in the database table.

The Form command on the Ribbon creates a form that displays all of the *fields* from the underlying data source (table)—one record at a time. You can use this new form immediately, or you can modify it. Records that you create or edit in a form are automatically added to or updated in the underlying table or tables.

1 **Open** [»] the **Navigation Pane**. Increase the width of the **Navigation Pane** so that all object names display fully. Notice that a table displays a datasheet icon, and a query displays an icon of two overlapping datasheets. Right-click your **13A Students** table to display a menu as shown in Figure 13.33.

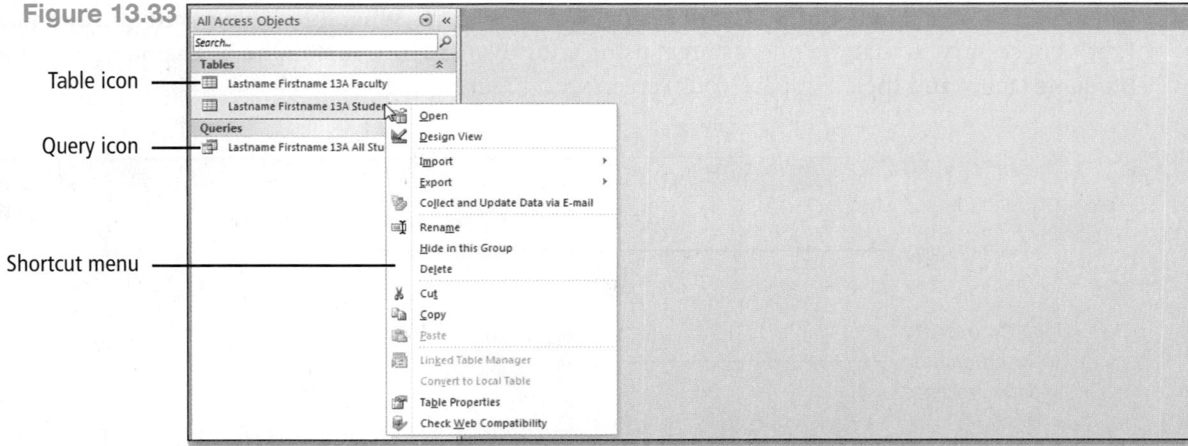

Figure 13.33

2 On the shortcut menu, click **Open** to display the table in the object window, and then **Close** « the **Navigation Pane** to maximize your object space.

3 Scroll to the right, and notice that there are 11 fields in the table. On the **Create tab**, in the **Forms group**, click the **Form** button. Compare your screen with Figure 13.34.

Access creates a form based on the currently selected object—the 13A Students table. Access creates the form in a simple top-to-bottom format, with all 11 fields in the record lined up in a single column. The form displays in ***Layout view***—the Access view in which you can make changes to a form or to a report while the object is open. Each field displays the data for the first student record in the table—*Joel Barthmaier*.

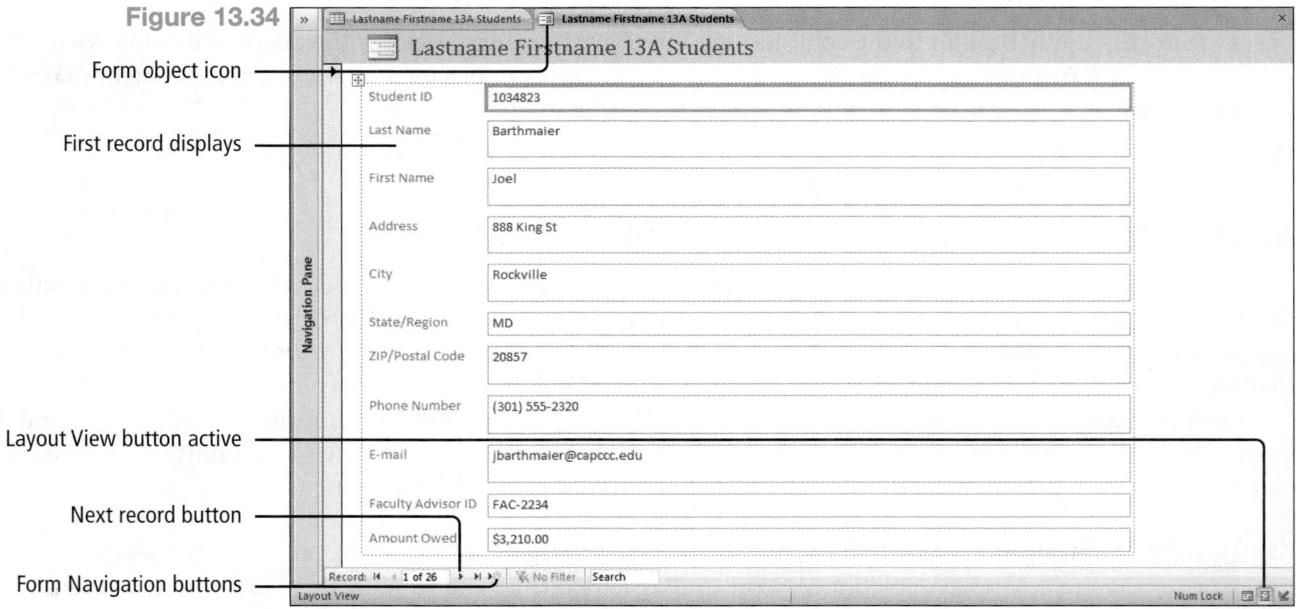

Figure 13.34

4 At the right edge of the status bar, notice that the **Layout View** button is active, indicating that the form is displayed in Layout view. At the right edge of the status bar, click the **Form View** button.

In ***Form view***, you can view the records, but you cannot change the layout or design of the form.

5 In the navigation area, click the **Next record** button three times. The fourth record—for *Joseph Ingram*—displays.

You can use the navigation buttons to scroll among the records to display any single record.

6 **Save** the form with the default name—*Lastname Firstname 13A Students*. Along the left edge of the record, above the Record navigation area, click anywhere in the narrow gray bar—the ***record selector bar***—to select only the record for *Joseph Ingram*. Notice that the bar turns black, indicating that the record is selected.

7 To print the form for *Joseph Ingram* only, click the **File tab**, and then click **Print**—do *not* display Print Preview. Instead, click **Print**. In the **Print** dialog box, in the lower left corner, click **Setup**. Click the **Columns tab**, change the **Width** to **7.5** so that the form prints on one page, and then click **OK**. The maximum column width that you can enter is dependent upon the printer that is installed on your system. In the lower left corner of the **Print** dialog box, click the **Selected Record(s)** option button, and then click **OK**.

> **Note | To Print a Single Form in PDF**
>
> To create a PDF electronic printout of a single record in a form, change the column width to 7.5 as described in step 7 above, and then in the Print dialog box, click Cancel. On the left edge of the form, click the Record Selector bar so that it is black—selected. On the Ribbon click the External Data tab. In the Export group, click the PDF or XPS button. Navigate to your chapter folder, and then in the lower left corner of the dialog box, if necessary, select the Open file after publishing check box. In the lower right corner of the dialog box, click the Options button. In the Options dialog box, under Range, click the Selected records option button, click OK, and then click Publish. Close the Adobe Reader or Acrobat window.

8 **Close** the form, saving changes if necessary. Notice that your **13A Students** table remains open.

Activity 13.16 | Creating, Modifying, and Printing a Report

1 **Open** the **Navigation Pane**, and then open your **13A Faculty** table by double-clicking the table name or by right-clicking and clicking Open from the shortcut menu. **Close** the **Navigation Pane**.

2 Click the **Create tab**, and then in the **Reports group**, click the **Report** button.

When you click the Report button, Access generates the report in Layout view and includes all of the fields and all of the records in the table, and does so in a format suitable for printing. Dotted lines indicate how the report would break across pages if you print it. In Layout view, you can make quick changes to the report layout.

3 Click the **Faculty ID** field name, and then on the Ribbon, click the **Arrange tab**. In the **Rows & Columns group**, click the **Select Column** button, and then press Delete. Using the same technique, delete the **Rank** field.

The Faculty ID and Rank fields and data are deleted, and the report readjusts the fields.

4 Click the **Address** field name, and then use the scroll bar at the bottom of the screen to scroll to the right to display the **Mobile Phone** field; be careful not to click in the report. Hold down Shift and then click the **Mobile Phone** field name to select all of the fields from *Address* through *Mobile Phone*. With all the field names selected—surrounded by a colored border—in the **Row & Columns group**, click the **Select Column** button, and then press Delete.

Use this technique to select and delete multiple columns in Layout view.

5 Scroll to the left, and notice that you can see all of the remaining fields. In any record, click in the **E-mail** field. Point to the right edge of the field box to display the pointer. Drag to the right slightly to increase the width of the field so that all E-mail addresses display on one line.

6 Click the **Last Name** field name. On the Ribbon, click the **Home tab**. In the **Sort & Filter group**, click the **Ascending** button. Compare your screen with Figure 13.35.

By default, tables are sorted in ascending order by the primary key field, which is the Faculty ID field. You can change the default and sort any field in either ascending order or descending order. The sort order does not change in the underlying table, only in the report.

Figure 13.35

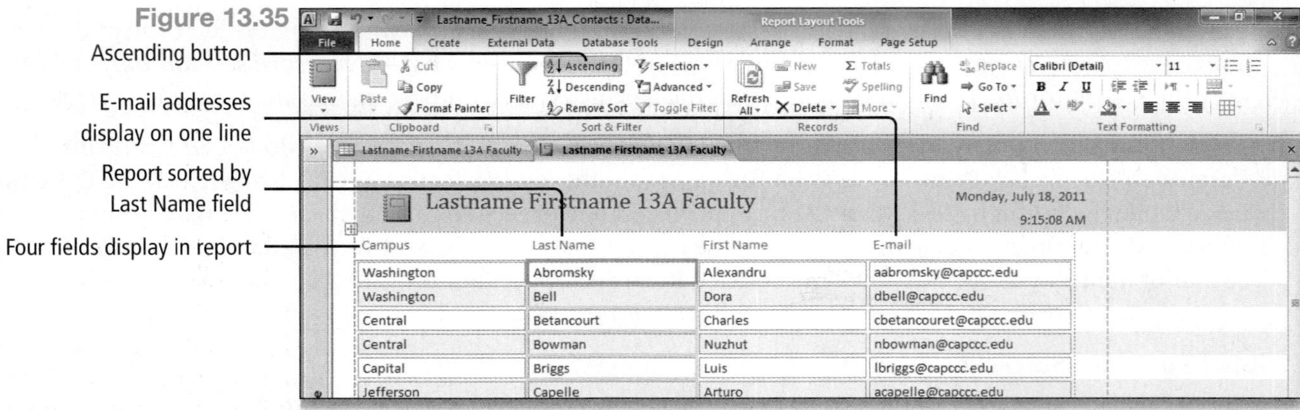

7 Click the **Save** button. In the **Report Name** box, add **Report** to the end of the suggested name, and then click **OK**.

8 Display the report in **Print Preview**. In the **Zoom group**, click the **Two Pages** button, and then compare your screen with Figure 13.36.

The report will print on two pages because the page number at the bottom of the report is located beyond the right margin of the report.

Figure 13.36

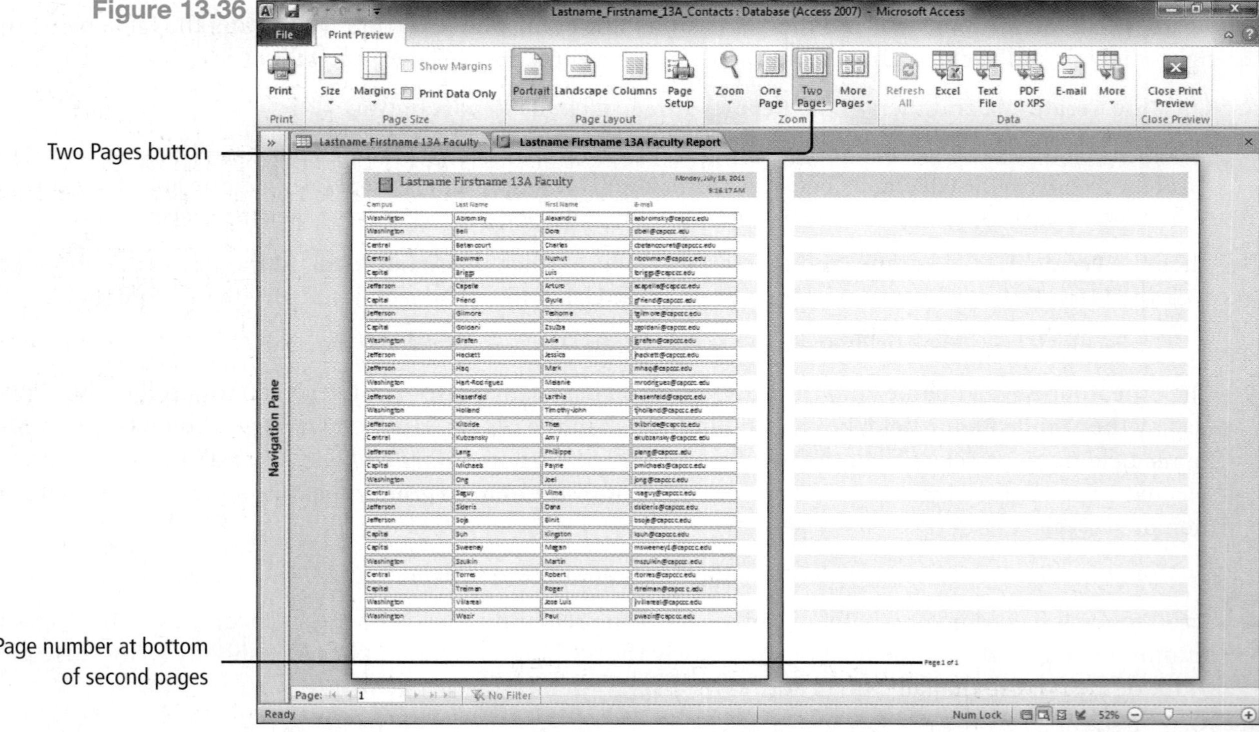

9 In the **Close Preview group**, click the **Close Print Preview button**. Scroll down to the bottom of the report, and then scroll to the right to display the page number. Click the page number—**Page 1 of 1**—and then press Delete.

10 Display the report in **Print Preview** and notice that the report will print on one page. In the **Zoom group**, click the **One Page** button. **Save** the changes to the design of the report, and then create a paper or electronic printout as instructed. At the right end of the Ribbon, click the **Close Print Preview** button.

The default margins of a report created with the Report tool are 0.25 inch. Some printers require a greater margin so your printed report may result in two pages—you will learn to adjust this later.

11 Along the top of the object window, right-click any object tab, and then click **Close All** to close all of the open objects and leave the object window empty.

Objective 5 | Save and Close a Database

When you close an Access table, any changes made to the records are saved automatically. If you change the design of the table or change the layout of the Datasheet view, such as adjusting the column widths, you will be prompted to save the design changes. At the end of your Access session, close your database and exit Access. If the Navigation Pane is open when you close Access, it will display when you reopen the database.

View the video on the Companion Web Site or in MyITLab

Activity 13.17 | Closing and Saving a Database

1 **Open** [»] the **Navigation Pane**. Notice that your report object displays with a green report icon. Compare your screen with Figure 13.37.

Figure 13.37

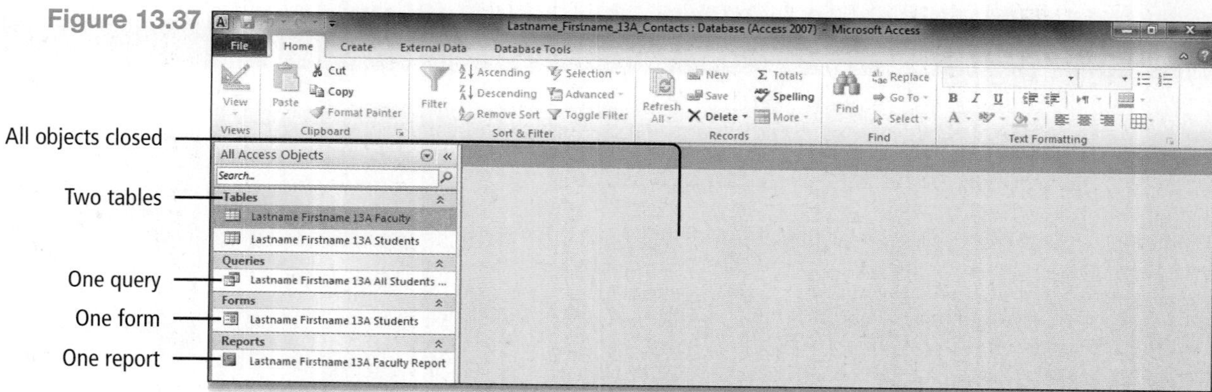

2 Display **Backstage** view, click **Close Database**, and then click **Exit**. As directed by your instructor, submit your database and the five paper or electronic printouts—two tables, one query, one form, and one report—that are the results of this project.

End **You have completed Project 13A**

Project 13B Instructors and Courses Database

Project Activities

In Activities 13.18 through 13.30, you will assist Carolyn Judkins, the Dean of the Business and Information Technology Division at the Jefferson Campus, in locating information about instructors and courses in the Division. Your results will look similar to Figure 13.38.

Project Files

For Project 13B, you will need the following file:

a13B_Instructors_Courses

You will save your database as:

Lastname_Firstname_13B_Instructors_Courses

Project Results

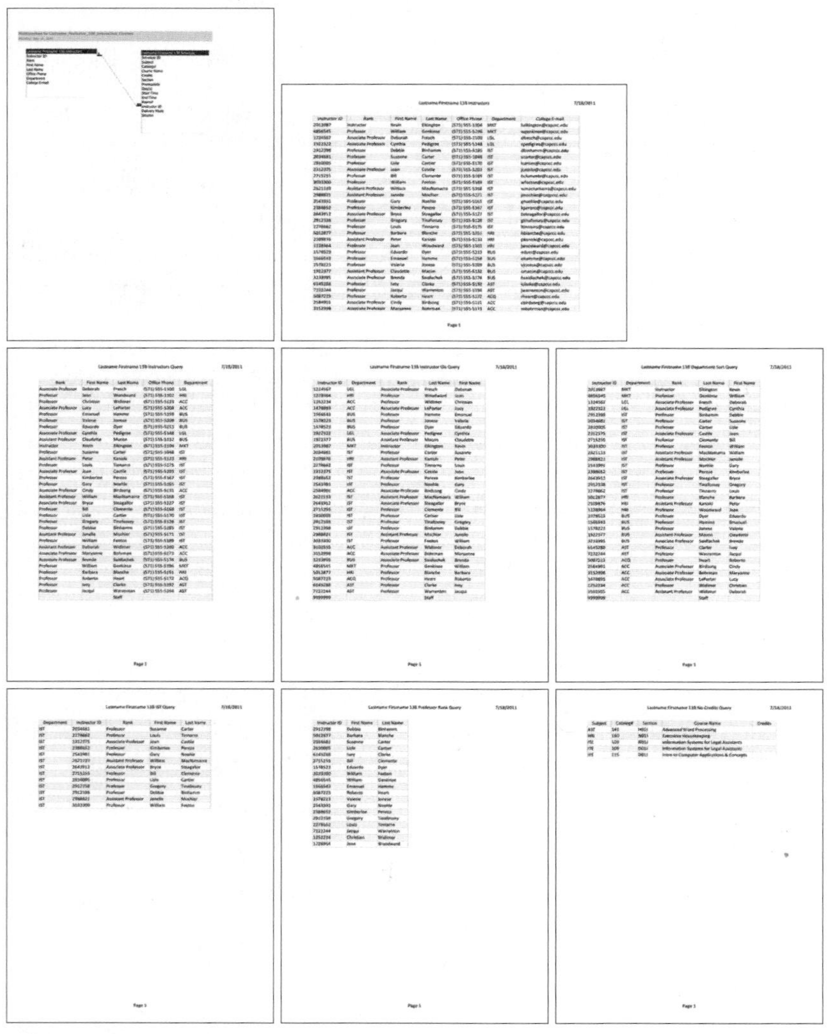

Figure 13.38
Project 13B Instructors and Courses

Objective 6 | Open an Existing Database

There will be instances in which you may want to work with a database and still keep the *original* version of the database. Like the other Microsoft Office 2010 applications, you can open a database file and save it with a new name.

View the video on the Companion Web Site or in MyITLab

Activity 13.18 | Opening and Renaming an Existing Database

1 Start **Access**. In **Backstage** view, click **Open**. Navigate to the student data files for this textbook, and then open the Access database **a13B_Instructors_Courses.**

2 Click the **File tab** to return to **Backstage** view, and then click **Save Database As**. Navigate to your **All In One Chapter 13** folder. In the **File name** box, select the file name, to which 1 has been added at the end. Edit as necessary to name the database **Lastname_Firstname_13B_Instructors_Courses** and then press Enter.

Use this technique when you want to keep a copy of the original database file.

3 On the **Message Bar**, notice the **Security Warning**. In the **Navigation Pane**, notice that this database contains two table objects. Compare your screen with Figure 13.39.

Figure 13.39

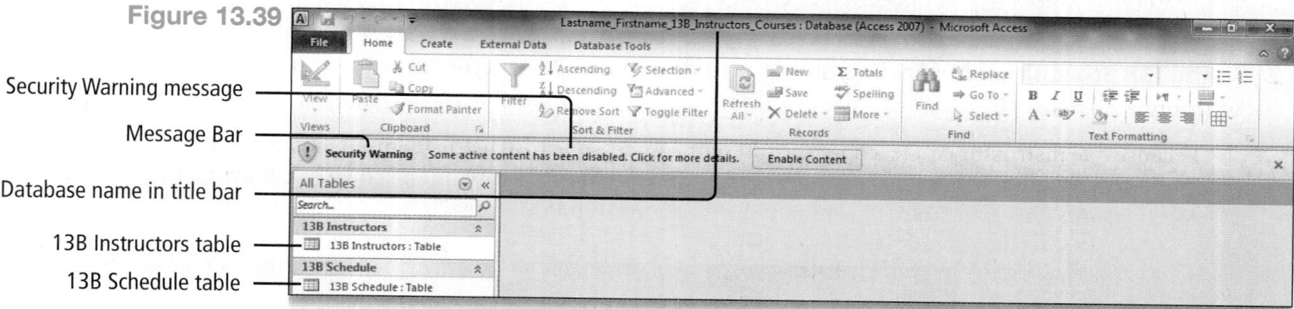

Activity 13.19 | Resolving Security Alerts and Renaming Tables

The ***Message Bar*** is the area below the Ribbon that displays information such as security alerts when there is potentially unsafe, active content in an Office document that you open. Settings that determine the alerts that display on your Message Bar are set in the Access ***Trust Center***, which is an area of Access where you can view the security and privacy settings for your Access installation. You may or may not be able to change the settings in the Trust Center, depending upon decisions made within your organization's computing environment.

1 On the **Message Bar**, click the **Enable Content** button.

When working with the student files that accompany this textbook, repeat these actions each time you see this security warning. Databases for this textbook are safe to use on your computer.

2 In the **Navigation Pane**, right-click the **13B Instructors** table, and then click **Rename**. With the table name selected and using your own name, type **Lastname Firstname 13B Instructors** and then press Enter to rename the table. Using the same technique, **Rename** the **13B Schedule** table to **Lastname Firstname 13B Schedule**

Including your name in the table enables you and your instructor to easily identify your work, because Access includes the table name in the header of printed and PDF pages.

3 Point to the right edge of the **Navigation Pane** to display the ⟺ pointer. Drag to the right to widen the pane until both table names display fully.

Objective 7 | Create Table Relationships

Access databases are relational databases because the tables in the database can relate—actually connect—to other tables through common fields. After you have a table for each subject in your database, you must provide a way to connect the data in the tables when you need meaningful information. To do this, create common fields in related tables, and then define table relationships. A ***relationship*** is an association that you establish between two tables based on common fields. After the relationship is established, you can create a query, a form, or a report that displays information from more than one table.

Activity 13.20 | Creating Table Relationships and Enforcing Referential Integrity

In this activity, you will create a relationship between two tables in the database.

1 Double-click your **13B Instructors** table to open it in the object window and examine its contents. Then open your **13B Schedule** table and examine its contents.

In the 13B Instructors table, no two instructors have the same Instructor ID since *Instructor ID* is the primary key field. In the 13B Schedule table, *Schedule ID* is the primary key field. Every scheduled course section during an academic term has a unique Schedule ID. The 13B Schedule table includes the *Instructor ID* field, which is the common field between the two tables.

2 In the **13B Schedule** table, scroll to the right to display the Instructor ID field, and then compare your screen with Figure 13.40.

Because *one* instructor can teach *many* different courses, *one* Instructor ID number can be present *many* times in the 13B Schedule table. This relationship between each instructor and the courses is known as a ***one-to-many relationship***. This is the most common type of relationship in Access.

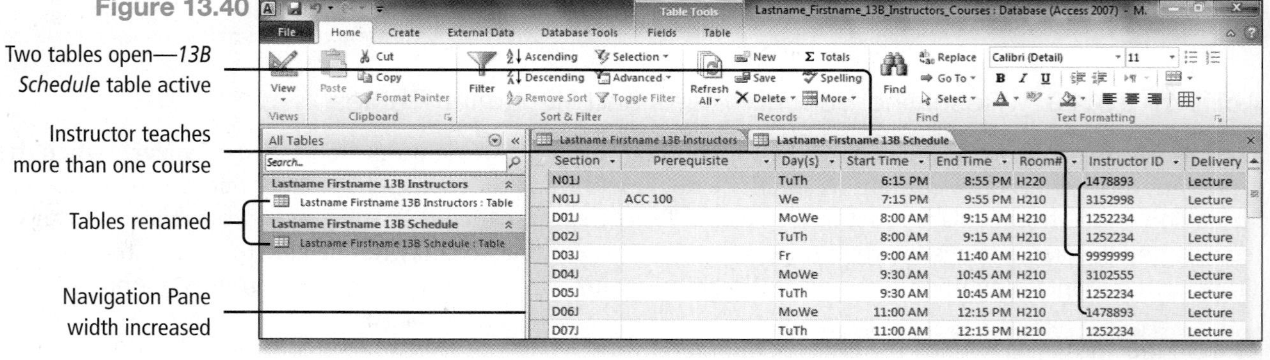

Figure 13.40

3 In the upper right corner of the object window, click **Close** [X] two times to close each table. Click the **Database Tools tab**, and then in the **Relationships group**, click the **Relationships** button. Compare your screen with Figure 13.41.

The Show Table dialog box displays in the Relationships window. In the Show Table dialog box, the Tables tab displays all of the table objects in the database. Your two tables are listed.

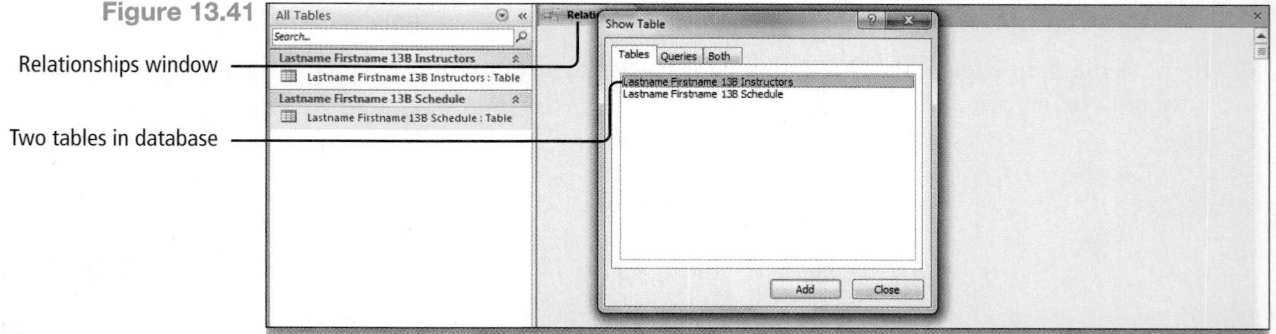

Figure 13.41

4 Point to the title bar of the **Show Table** dialog box, and then drag down and to the right slightly to move the **Show Table** dialog box away from the top of the **Relationships** window.

Moving the Show Table dialog box enables you to see the tables as they are added to the Relationships window.

5 In the **Show Table** dialog box, click your **13B Instructors** table, and then at the bottom of the dialog box, click **Add**. In the **Show Table** dialog box, double-click your **13B Schedule** table to add the table to the **Relationships** window. In the **Show Table** dialog box, click **Close**, and then compare your screen with Figure 13.42.

You can use either technique to add a table to the Relationships window. A ***field list***—a list of the field names in a table—for each of the two table objects displays, and each table's primary key is identified. Although this database currently has only two tables, larger databases can have many tables. Scroll bars in a field list indicate that there are fields that are not currently in view.

Figure 13.42

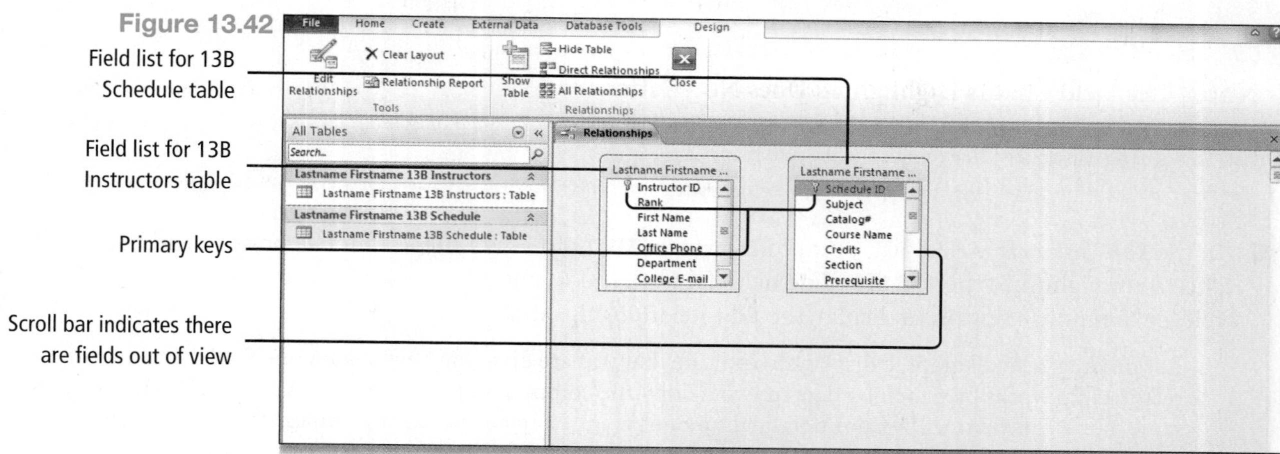

> **Alert! | Are There More Than Two Field Lists in the Relationships Window?**
>
> If you double-click a table more than one time, a duplicate field list displays in the Relationships window. To remove a field list from the Relationships window, right-click the title bar of the field list, and then click Hide Table. Alternatively, click anywhere in the field list, and then on the Design tab, in the Relationships group, click the Hide Table button.

6 In the **13B Schedule** field list—the field list on the right—point to the title bar to display the [pointer] pointer. Drag the field list to the right until there is about 2 inches between the field lists.

7 In the **13B Instructors** field list—the field list on the left—point to the lower right corner of the field list to display the [pointer] pointer, and then drag down and to the right to increase the height and width of the field list until the entire name of the table in the title bar displays and all of the field names display.

This action enables you to see all of the available fields and removes the vertical scroll bar.

8 By using the same technique and the [pointer] pointer, resize the **13B Schedule** field list so that all of the field names and the table name display as shown in Figure 13.43.

Recall that *one* instructor can teach *many* scheduled courses. This arrangement of the tables on your screen displays the *one table* on the left side and the *many table* on the right side.

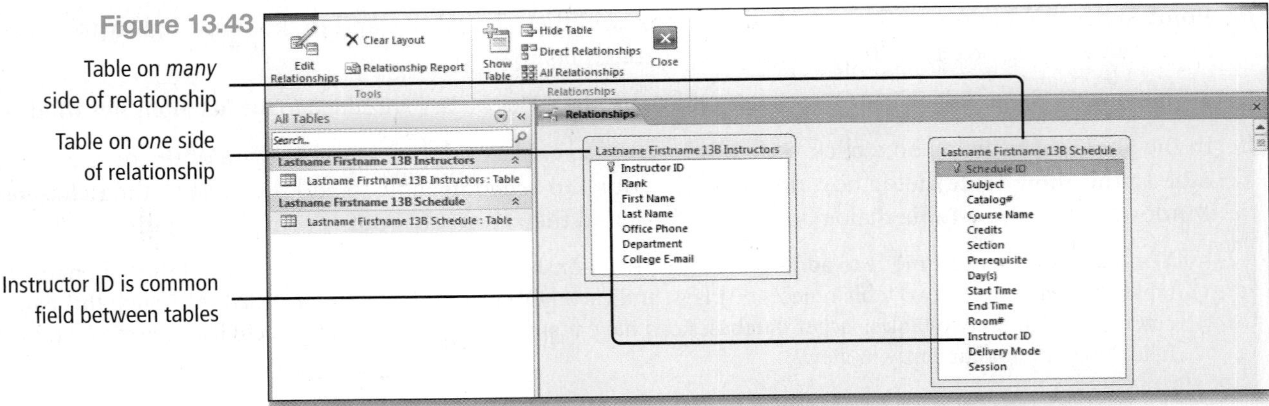

Figure 13.43

Note | The Field That Is Highlighted Does Not Matter

After you rearrange the two field lists in the Relationships window, the highlighted field indicates the active field list, which is the list you moved last. This is of no consequence for completing the activity.

9 In the **13B Instructors** field list, point to **Instructor ID**, hold down the left mouse button, and then drag down and to the right into the **13B Schedule** field list until the pointer's arrow is on top of **Instructor ID**. Then release the mouse button to display the **Edit Relationships** dialog box.

As you drag, a small graphic displays to indicate that you are dragging a field from one field list to another. A table relationship works by matching data in two fields—the common field. In these two tables, the common field has the same name—*Instructor ID*. Common fields are not required to have the same names; however, they must have the same data type and field size.

10 Point to the title bar of the **Edit Relationships** dialog box, and then drag the dialog box below the two field lists as shown in Figure 13.44.

Both tables include the Instructor ID field—the common field between the two tables. By dragging, you create the *one-to-many* relationship. In the 13B Instructors table, Instructor ID is the primary key. In the 13B Schedule table, Instructor ID is referred to as the ***foreign key*** field. The foreign key is the field in the related table used to connect to the primary key in another table. The field on the *one* side of the relationship is typically the primary key.

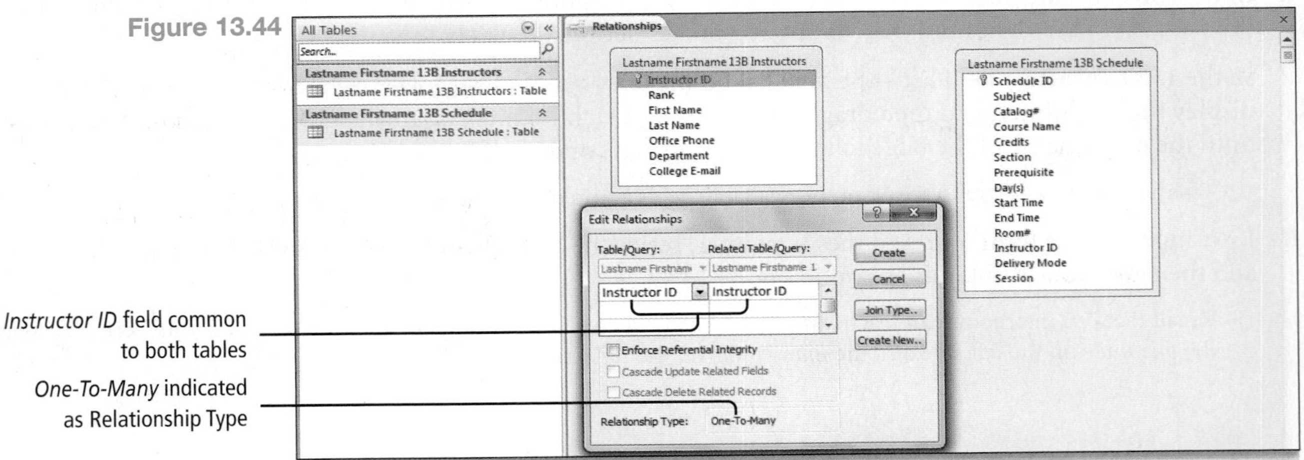

Figure 13.44

11 In the **Edit Relationships** dialog box, click to select the **Enforce Referential Integrity** check box.

Referential integrity is a set of rules that Access uses to ensure that the data between related tables is valid. Enforcing referential integrity ensures that an instructor cannot be added to the 13B Schedules table if the Instructor ID is *not* included in the 13B Instructors table. Similarly, enforcing referential integrity ensures that you cannot delete an instructor from the 13B Instructors table if there is a course listed in the 13B Schedule table for that instructor.

12 In the **Edit Relationships** dialog box, click the **Create** button, and then compare your screen with Figure 13.45.

A ***join line***—the line joining two tables—displays between the two tables. On the join line, *1* indicates the *one* side of the relationship, and the infinity symbol (∞) indicates the *many* side of the relationship. These symbols display when referential integrity is enforced.

Figure 13.45

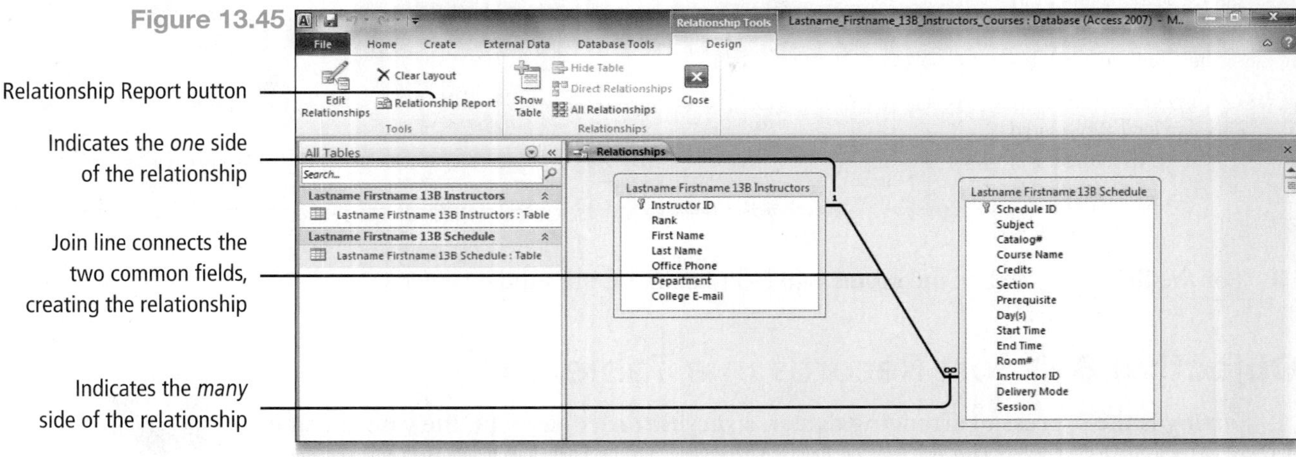

Activity 13.21 | Printing a Relationship Report and Displaying Subdatasheet Records

The Relationships window provides a map of how your database tables are related, and you can print this information as a report.

1 With the **Relationships** window open, on the **Design tab**, in the **Tools group**, click the **Relationship Report** button to create the report and display it in Print Preview.

2 On the **Print Preview tab**, in the **Page Size group**, click the **Margins** button, and then click **Normal**. If instructed to do so, create a paper or electronic printout of this relationship report.

3 On the **Quick Access Toolbar**, click the **Save** button to save the report. In the **Save As** dialog box, click **OK** to accept the default name.

The report name displays in the Navigation Pane under *Unrelated Objects*. Because the report is just a map of the relationships, and not a report containing actual records, it is not associated with any of the tables.

4 In the object window, **Close** the report, and then **Close** the **Relationships** window.

5 From the **Navigation Pane**, open your **13B Instructors** table, and then **Close** the **Navigation Pane**. For the first record—*Instructor ID 1224567*—on the left side of the record, click the **plus sign** (+), and then compare your screen with Figure 13.46.

Plus signs to the left of a record in a table indicate that *related* records exist in another table. Clicking the plus sign displays the related records in a ***subdatasheet***. In the first record, for *Deborah Fresch*, you can see that related records exist in the 13B Schedule table—she is teaching five LGL courses that are listed in the schedule. The plus sign displays because you created a relationship between the two tables using the Instructor ID field—the common field.

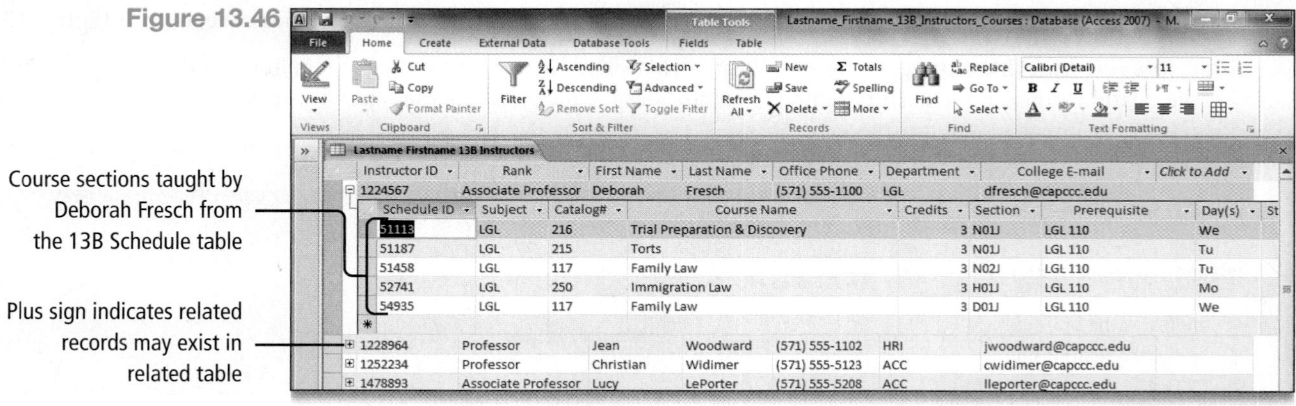

Figure 13.46

6 For the first record, click the **minus sign** (–) to collapse the subdatasheet.

Objective 8 | Sort Records in a Table

View the video on the Companion Web Site or in MyITLab

Sorting is the process of arranging data in a specific order based on the value in a field. For example, you can sort the names in your address book alphabetically by each person's last name, or you can sort your DVD collection by the date of purchase. Initially, records in an Access table display in the order they are entered into the table. When a primary key is established, the records display in order based on the primary key field.

Activity 13.22 | Sorting Records in a Table in Ascending or Descending Order

In the following activity, you will determine the departments of the faculty in the Business and Information Technology Division by sorting the data. You can sort data in either ***ascending order*** or ***descending order***. Ascending order sorts text alphabetically (A to Z) and sorts numbers from the lowest number to the highest number. Descending order sorts text in reverse alphabetical order (Z to A) and sorts numbers from the highest number to the lowest number.

1 Notice that the records in the **13B Instructors** table are sorted in ascending order by **Instructor ID**, which is the primary key field.

2 In the field names row, click the **Department arrow**, click **Sort A to Z**, and then compare your screen with Figure 13.47.

To sort records in a table, click the arrow to the right of the field name in the column on which you want to sort, and then choose the sort order. After a field is sorted, a small arrow in the field name box indicates its sort order. The small arrow in the field name points up, indicating an ascending sort; and in the Ribbon, on the Home tab, the Ascending button is selected.

The records display in alphabetical order by Department. Because the department names are now grouped together, you can quickly scroll the length of the table to see the instructors in each department. The first record in the table has no data in the Department field because the Instructor ID number *9999999* is reserved for Staff, a designation that is used until a scheduled course has been assigned to a specific instructor.

Figure 13.47

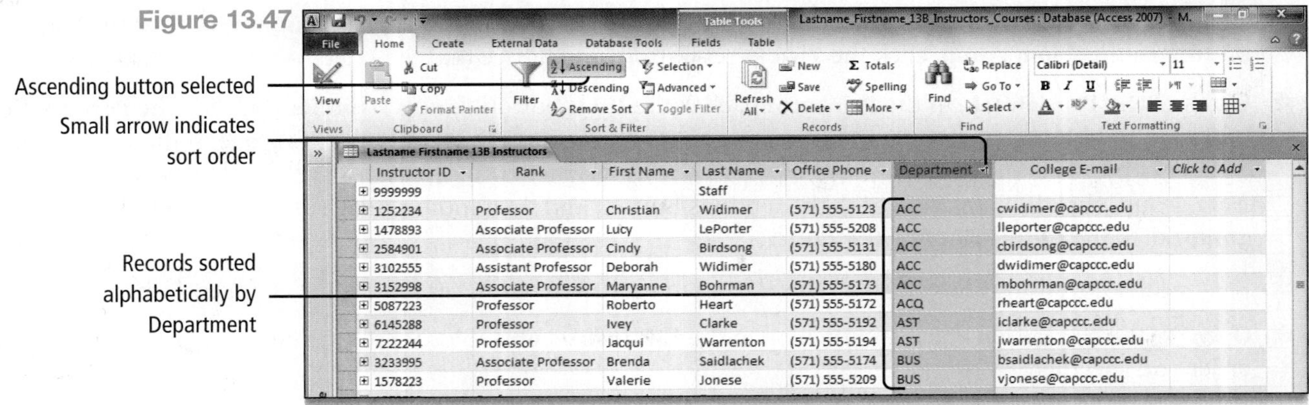

3 On the **Home tab**, in the **Sort & Filter group**, click the **Remove Sort** button to clear the sort and return the records to the default sort order, which is by the primary key field—*Instructor ID*.

Activity 13.23 | Sorting Records in a Table on Multiple Fields

To sort a table on two or more fields, first identify the fields that will act as the ***outermost sort field*** and the ***innermost sort field***. The outermost sort field is the first level of sorting, and the innermost sort field is the second level of sorting. For example, you might want to sort first by the Last Name field, which would be the outermost sort field, and then by the First Name field, which would be the innermost sort field. After you identify your outermost and innermost sort fields, sort the innermost field first, and then sort the outermost field.

In this activity, you will sort the records in descending order by the department name. Within each department name, you will sort the records in ascending order by last name.

1 In the **Last Name** field, click any record. In the **Sort & Filter group**, click the **Ascending** button.

The records are sorted in ascending alphabetical order by Last Name—the innermost sort field.

2 Point anywhere in the **Department** field, and then right-click. From the shortcut menu, click **Sort Z to A**. Compare your screen with Figure 13.48.

The records are sorted in descending alphabetical order first by Department—the *outermost* sort field—and then within a specific Department grouping, the sort continues in ascending alphabetical order by Last Name—the *innermost* sort field. The records are sorted on multiple fields using both ascending and descending order.

Figure 13.48

Small arrow indicates sort order

Small arrow indicates sort order

Within *Department*, *Last Name sorted in ascending order*

Records sorted in descending order by Department

Lastname Firstname 13B Instructors

Instructor ID	Rank	First Name	Last Name	Office Phone	Department	College E-mail	Click to Add
2013987	Instructor	Kevin	Elkington	(571) 555-1104	MKT	kelkington@capccc.edu	
4856545	Professor	William	Genkinse	(571) 555-5196	MKT	wgenkinse@capccc.edu	
1224567	Associate Professor	Deborah	Fresch	(571) 555-1100	LGL	dfresch@capccc.edu	
1922322	Associate Professor	Cynthia	Pedigree	(571) 555-5148	LGL	cpedigree@capccc.edu	
2912398	Professor	Debbie	Binhamm	(571) 555-5185	IST	dbinhamm@capccc.edu	
2034681	Professor	Susanne	Carter	(571) 555-1048	IST	scarter@capccc.edu	
2810005	Professor	Lisle	Cartier	(571) 555-5170	IST	lcartier@capccc.edu	
2312375	Associate Professor	Joan	Castile	(571) 555-5203	IST	jcastile@capccc.edu	
2715255	Professor	Bill	Clemente	(571) 555-5169	IST	bclemente@capccc.edu	
3033300	Professor	William	Feeton	(571) 555-5189	IST	wfeeton@capccc.edu	
2621133	Assistant Professor	William	MacNamarra	(571) 555-5168	IST	wmacnamarra@capccc.edu	
2988821	Assistant Professor	Janelle	Mochier	(571) 555-5171	IST	jmochier@caqpccc.edu	
2543991	Professor	Gary	Noehle	(571) 555-5165	IST	gnoehle@capccc.edu	
2388652	Professor	Kimberlee	Perezo	(571) 555-5167	IST	kperezo@capccc.edu	
2643912	Associate Professor	Bryce	Steagallor	(571) 555-5127	IST	bsteagallor@capccc.edu	
2912338	Professor	Gregory	Tinafossey	(571) 555-5128	IST	gtinafossey@capccc.edu	
2278662	Professor	Louis	Tinnarro	(571) 555-5175	IST	ltinnarro@capccc.edu	
5012877	Professor	Barbara	Blanche	(571) 555-5151	HRI	bblanche@capccc.edu	
2109876	Assistant Professor	Peter	Kaniski	(571) 555-5133	HRI	pkaniski@capccc.edu	
1228964	Professor	Jean	Woodward	(571) 555-1102	HRI	jwoodward@capccc.edu	
1578523	Professor	Eduardo	Dyer	(571) 555-5213	BUS	edyer@capccc.edu	

3 Display **Backstage** view, click **Print**, and then click **Print Preview**. In the **Page Layout** group, click the **Landscape** button. In the **Zoom group**, click the **Two Pages** button, and notice that the table will print on two pages.

4 On the **Print Preview tab**, in the **Print group**, click the **Print** button. Under **Print Range**, click the **Pages** option button. In the **From** box, type **1** and then in the **To** box, type **1** to print only the first page. If directed to submit a paper copy, click OK or create an electronic copy as instructed. To create a PDF of only the first page, in the Data group, click PDF or XPS, click the Options button, and then indicate Page 1 to 1. In the **Close Preview group**, click the **Close Print Preview** button.

5 In the object window, **Close** [X] the table. In the message box, click **Yes** to save the changes to the sort order.

6 **Open** [»] the **Navigation Pane**, and then open the **13B Instructors** table. Notice the table was saved with the sort order you specified.

7 In the **Sort & Filter group**, click the **Remove Sort** button. **Close** [X] the table, and in the message box, click **Yes** to save the table with the sort removed. **Close** [«] the **Navigation Pane**.

Generally, tables are not stored with the data sorted. Instead, queries are created that sort the data; and then reports are created to display the sorted data.

Objective 9 | Create a Query in Design View

View the video on the Companion Web Site or in MyITLab

Recall that a select query is a database object that retrieves (selects) specific data from one or more tables and then displays the specified data in Datasheet view. A query answers a question such as *Which instructors teach courses in the IST department?* Unless a query has already been set up to ask this question, you must create a new query. A query is useful because it creates a ***subset*** of records—a portion of the total records—according to your specifications and then displays only those records.

Activity 13.24 | Creating a New Select Query in Design View

Previously, you created a query using the Query Wizard. To create complex queries, use Query Design view. Recall that the table or tables from which a query selects its data is referred to as the data source.

1 On the Ribbon, click the **Create tab**, and then in the **Queries group**, click the **Query Design** button. Compare your screen with Figure 13.49.

A new query opens in Design view and the Show Table dialog box displays, which lists both tables in the database.

Figure 13.49

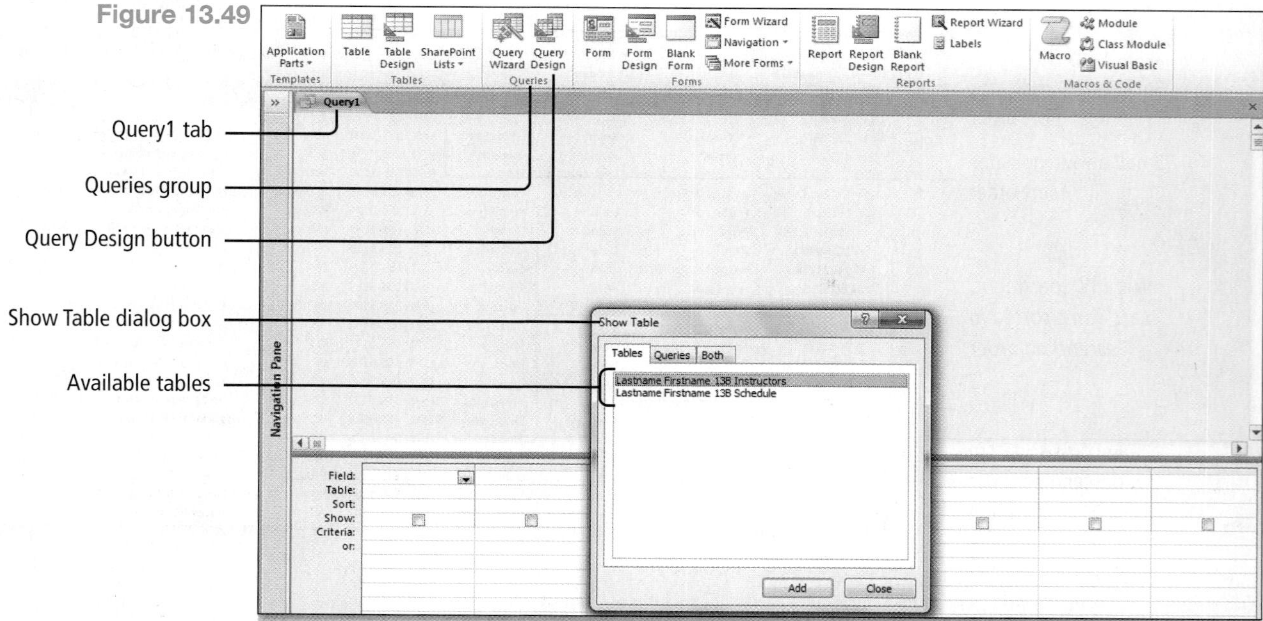

2 In the **Show Table** dialog box, double-click **13B Instructors**, and then **Close** the **Show Table** dialog box.

A field list for the 13B Instructors table displays in the upper area of the Query window. The Instructor ID field is the primary key field in this table. The Query window has two parts: the ***table area*** (upper area), which displays the field lists for tables that are used in the query, and the ***design grid*** (lower area), which displays the design of the query.

> **Alert! | Is There More Than One Field List in the Query Window?**
>
> If you double-click a table more than one time, a duplicate field list displays in the Query window. To remove a field list from the Query window, right-click the title bar of the field list, and then click Remove Table.

3 Point to the lower right corner of the field list to display the pointer, and then drag down and to the right to expand the field list, displaying all of the field names and the table name. In the **13B Instructors** field list, double-click **Rank**, and then look at the design grid.

The Rank field name displays in the design grid in the Field row. You limit the fields that display when the query is run by placing only the desired field names in the design grid.

4 In the **13B Instructors** field list, point to **First Name**, hold down the left mouse button, and then drag down into the design grid until the pointer displays in the **Field** row in the second column. Compare your screen with Figure 13.50.

This is a second way to add field names to the design grid.

Figure 13.50

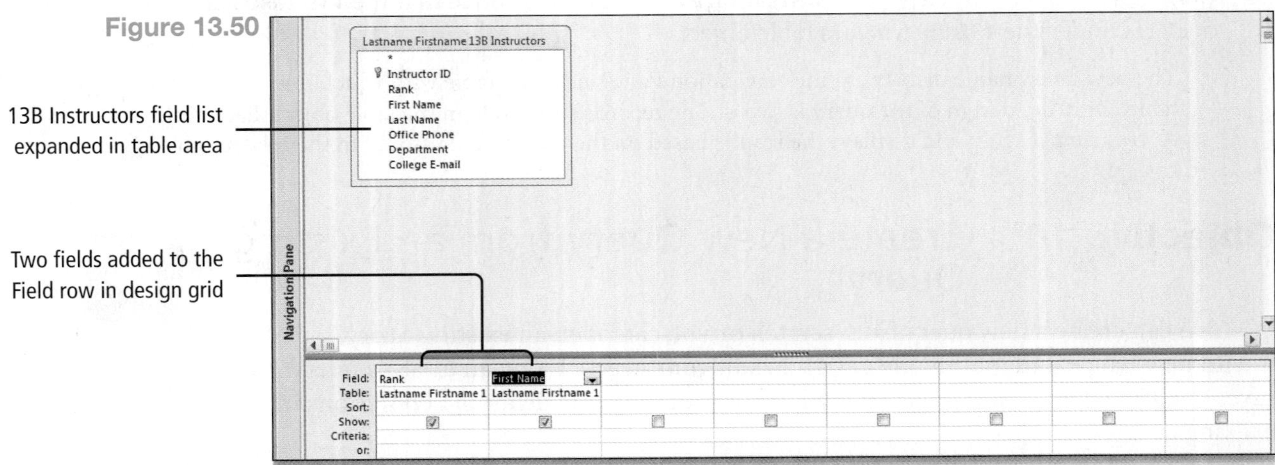

5 In design grid, in the **Field** row, click in the third column, and then click the **arrow** that displays. From the list, click **Last Name** to add the field to the design grid, which is a third way to add a field to the design grid.

6 Using one of the techniques you just practiced, add the **Office Phone** field to the fourth column and the **Department** field to the fifth column in the design grid.

Activity 13.25 | Running, Saving, Printing, and Closing a Query

Recall that after you create a query, you run it to display the results. When you run a query, Access looks at the records in the table (or tables) you have included in the query, finds the records that match the specified conditions (if any), and displays only those records in a datasheet. Only the fields that you have added to the design grid display in the query results. The query always runs using the current table or tables, presenting the most up-to-date information.

1 On the **Design tab**, in the **Results group**, click the **Run** button, and then compare your screen with Figure 13.51.

This query answers the question, *What is the Rank, First Name, Last Name, Office Phone number, and Department of all of the instructors in the 13B Instructors table?* The five fields that you specified in the design grid display in columns, and the records from the 13B Instructors table display in rows.

Figure 13.51

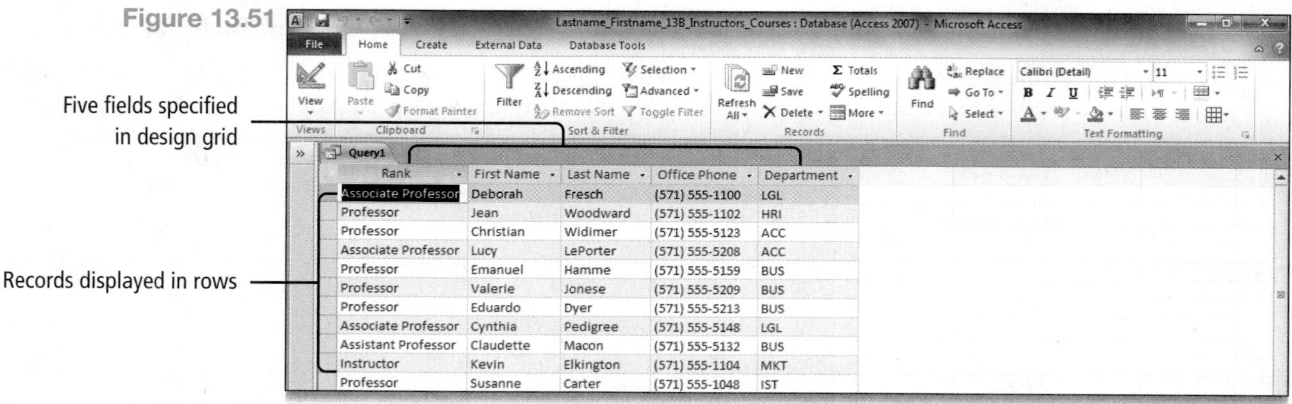

2 On the **Quick Access Toolbar**, click the **Save** button [Save]. In the **Save As** dialog box, type **Lastname Firstname 13B Instructors Query** and then click **OK**.

Save your queries if you are likely to ask the same question again; doing so will save you the effort of creating the query again to answer the same question.

3 Display **Backstage** view, click **Print**, and then click **Print Preview**. Create a paper or electronic printout if instructed to do so, and then **Close Print Preview**.

4 **Close** [×] the query. **Open** [»] the **Navigation Pane**, and then notice that the **13B Instructors Query** object displays under the **13B Instructors** table object.

The new query name displays in the Navigation Pane under the table with which it is related—the 13B Instructors table. Only the design of the query is saved. The records still reside in the table object. Each time you open the query, Access runs it again and displays the results based on the current data stored in the related table(s).

Objective 10 | Create a New Query from an Existing Query

View the video on the Companion Web Site or in MyITLab

You can create a new query from scratch or you can open an existing query, save it with new name, and modify the design to suit your needs. Using an existing query saves you time if your new query uses all or some of the same fields and conditions in an existing query.

Activity 13.26 | Creating a New Query from an Existing Query

1 From the **Navigation Pane**, open your **13B Instructors Query** by either double-clicking the name or by right-clicking and clicking Open.

The query runs, opens in Datasheet view, and displays the records from the 13B Instructors table as specified in the query design grid.

2 Display **Backstage** view, and then click **Save Object As**. In the **Save As** dialog box, type **Lastname Firstname 13B Instructor IDs Query** and then click **OK**. Click the **Home tab**, and then in the **Views group**, click the **View** button to switch to **Design** view.

A new query, based on a copy of the 13B Instructors Query, is created and displays in the object window and in the Navigation Pane under its data source—the 13B Instructors table.

3 **Close** [«] the **Navigation Pane**. In the design grid, point to the thin gray selection bar above the **Office Phone** field name until the [↓] pointer displays. Click to select the **Office Phone** column, and then press [Delete].

This action deletes the field from the query design only—it has no effect on the field in the underlying 13B Instructors table. The Department field moves to the left. Similarly, you can select multiple fields and delete them at one time.

4 From the gray selection bar, select the **First Name** column. In the selected column, point to the selection bar to display the [pointer icon] pointer, and then drag to the right until a dark vertical line displays on the right side of the **Last Name** column. Release the mouse button to position the **First Name** field in the third column.

To rearrange fields in the query design, select the field to move, and then drag it to a new position in the design grid.

5 Using the technique you just practiced, move the **Department** field to the left of the **Rank** field.

6 From the field list, drag the **Instructor ID** field down to the first column in the design grid until the [pointer icon] pointer displays, and then release the mouse button. Compare your screen with Figure 13.52.

The Instructor ID field displays in the first column, and the remaining four fields move to the right. Use this method to insert a field to the left of a field already displayed in the design grid.

Figure 13.52

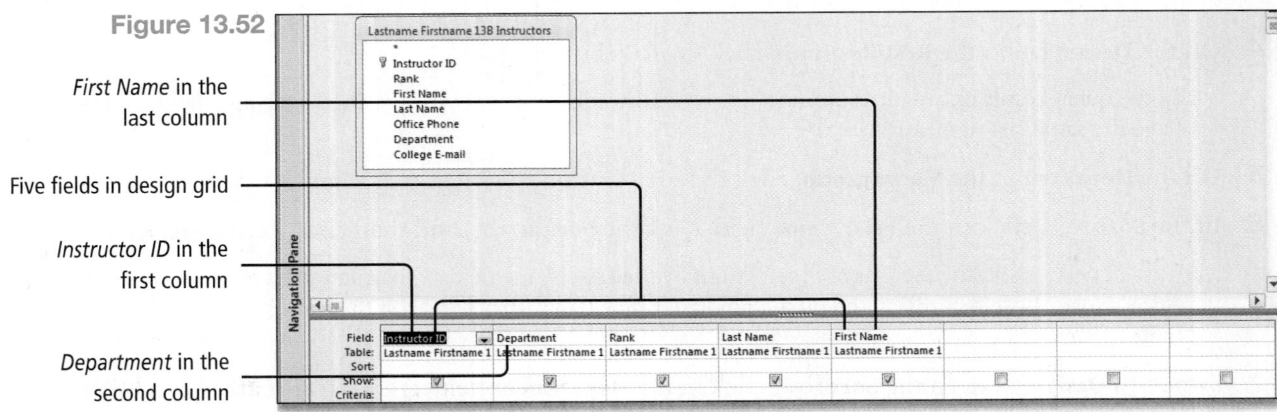

7 On the **Design tab**, in the **Results group**, click the **Run** button.

This query answers the question, *What is the Instructor ID, Department, Rank, Last Name, and First Name for every instructor in the 13B Instructors table?* The results of the query are a subset of the records contained in the 13B Instructors table. The records are sorted by the primary key field—Instructor ID.

8 From **Backstage** view, display the query in **Print Preview**. Create a paper or electronic printout if instructed to do so, and then **Close Print Preview**.

9 **Close** [X] the query, and in the message box, click **Yes** to save the changes to the design. **Open** [»] the **Navigation Pane**.

The new query name displays in the Navigation Pane under the related table.

Objective 11 | Sort Query Results

You can sort the results of a query in ascending or descending order in either Datasheet view or Design view. Use Design view if your query results should display in a specified sort order, or if you intend to use the sorted results in a report.

View the video on the Companion Web Site or in MyITLab

Activity 13.27 | Sorting Query Results

In this activity, you will save an existing query with a new name, and then sort the query results by using the Sort row in Design view.

1 On the **Navigation Pane**, click your **13B Instructor IDs Query**. Display **Backstage** view, and then click **Save Object As**. In the **Save As** dialog box, type **Lastname Firstname 13B Department Sort Query** and then click **OK**. Click the **Home tab**, and then drag the right edge of the **Navigation Pane** to the right to increase its width so that the names of the new query and the relationship report display fully.

2 In the **Navigation Pane**, right-click your **13B Department Sort Query**, and then click **Design View**. **Close** [«] the **Navigation Pane**.

3 In the design grid, in the **Sort** row, click in the **Last Name** field to display the insertion point and an arrow. Click the **Sort arrow**, and then in the list, click **Ascending**. Compare your screen with Figure 13.53.

Figure 13.53

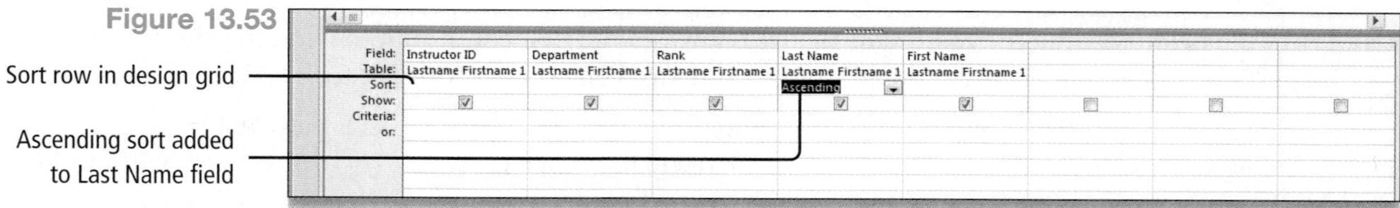

4 On the **Design tab** in the **Results group**, click the **Run** button.

In the query result, the records are sorted in ascending alphabetical order by the Last Name field, and two instructors have the same last name of *Widimer*.

5 On the **Home tab** in the **Views group**, click the **View** button to switch to **Design** view.

6 In the **Sort** row, click in the **First Name** field, click the **Sort** arrow, and then click **Ascending**. **Run** the query.

In the query result, the records are sorted first by the Last Name field. If instructors have the same last name, then Access sorts those records by the First Name field. The two instructors with the last name of *Widimer* are sorted by their first names.

7 Switch to **Design** view. In the **Sort** row, click in the **Department** field, click the **Sort** arrow, and then click **Descending**. **Run** the query; if necessary, scroll down to display the last records, and then compare your screen with Figure 13.54.

In Design view, fields with a Sort designation are sorted from left to right. That is, the sorted field on the left becomes the outermost sort field, and the sorted field on the right becomes the innermost sort field. Thus, the records are sorted first in descending alphabetical order by the Department field—the leftmost sort field. Then, within each same department name field, the last names are sorted in ascending alphabetical order. And, finally, within each same last name field, the first names are sorted in ascending alphabetical order.

Figure 13.54

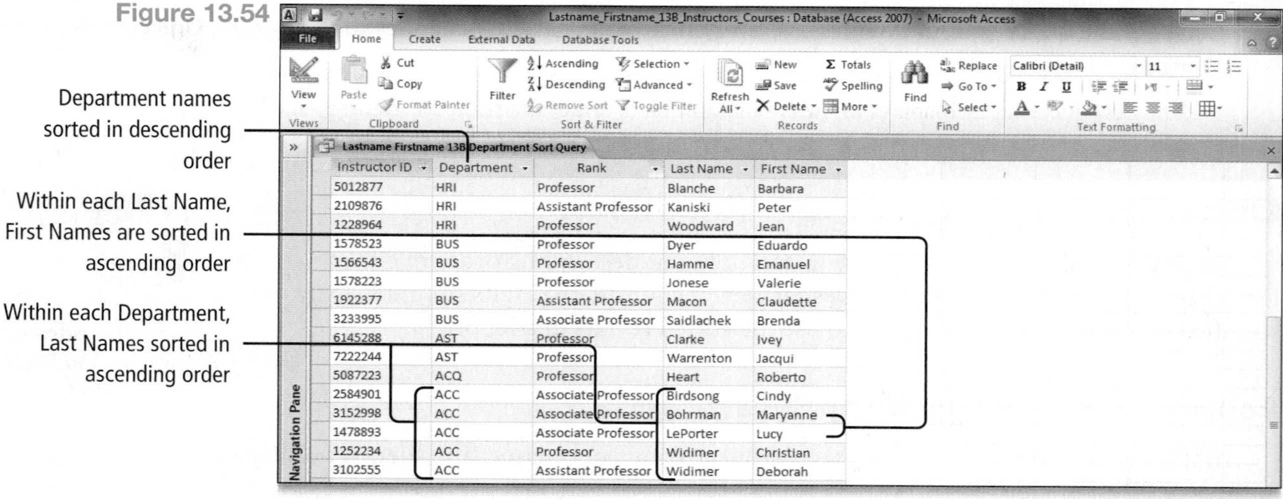

8 Display the query in **Print Preview**. Create a paper or electronic printout if instructed to do so, and then **Close Print Preview**. **Close** [×] the query. In the message box, click **Yes** to save the changes to the query design.

Objective 12 | Specify Criteria in a Query

Queries locate information in a database based on ***criteria*** that you specify as part of the query. Criteria—the conditions that identify the specific records for which you are looking—enable you to ask a more specific question. Therefore, you will get a more specific result. For example, if you want to find out how many instructors are in the IST department, limit the results to that specific department, and then only the records that match the specified department will display.

View the video on the Companion Web Site or in MyITLab

Activity 13.28 | Specifying Text Criteria in a Query

In this activity, you will create a query to answer the question *How many instructors are in the IST Department?*

1. Be sure that all objects are closed and that the **Navigation Pane** is closed. Click the **Create tab**, and then in the **Queries group**, click the **Query Design** button.
2. In the **Show Table** dialog box, **Add** the **13B Instructors** table to the table area, and then **Close** the **Show Table** dialog box.
3. Expand the field list to display all of the fields and the table name. Add the following fields to the design grid in the order given: **Department**, **Instructor ID**, **Rank**, **First Name**, and **Last Name**.
4. In the **Criteria** row of the design grid, click in the **Department** field, type **IST** and then press Enter. Compare your screen with Figure 13.55.

   Access places quotation marks around the criteria to indicate that this is a ***text string***—a sequence of characters. Use the Criteria row to specify the criteria that will limit the results of the query to your exact specifications. The criteria is not case sensitive, so you can type *ist* instead of IST.

Figure 13.55

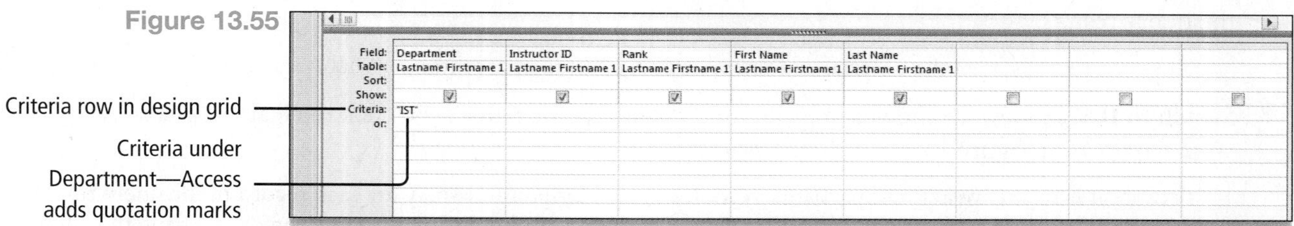

5. **Run** the query, and then compare your screen with Figure 13.56.

   Thirteen records display that meet the specified criteria—records that have *IST* in the Department field.

Figure 13.56

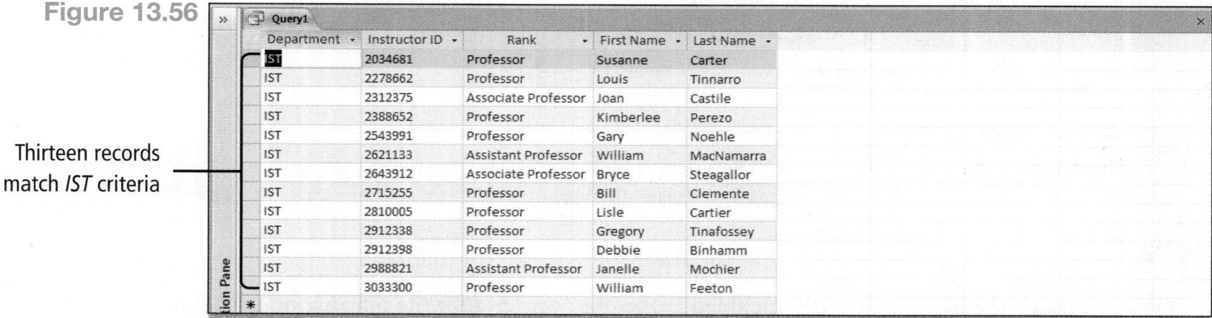

Department	Instructor ID	Rank	First Name	Last Name
IST	2034681	Professor	Susanne	Carter
IST	2278662	Professor	Louis	Tinnarro
IST	2312375	Associate Professor	Joan	Castile
IST	2388652	Professor	Kimberlee	Perezo
IST	2543991	Professor	Gary	Noehle
IST	2621133	Assistant Professor	William	MacNamarra
IST	2643912	Associate Professor	Bryce	Steagallor
IST	2715255	Professor	Bill	Clemente
IST	2810005	Professor	Lisle	Cartier
IST	2912338	Professor	Gregory	Tinafossey
IST	2912398	Professor	Debbie	Binhamm
IST	2988821	Assistant Professor	Janelle	Mochier
IST	3033300	Professor	William	Feeton

Alert! | Do Your Query Results Differ?

If you mistype the criteria, or enter it under the wrong field, or make some other error, the result will display no records. This indicates that there are no records in the table that match the criteria as you entered it. If this occurs, return to Design view and reexamine the query design. Verify that the criteria is typed in the Criteria row, under the correct field, and without typing errors. Then run the query again.

6 **Save** the query as **Lastname Firstname 13B IST Query** and then display the query in **Print Preview**. Create a paper or electronic printout if instructed to do so, and then **Close Print Preview**.

7 **Close** the query, and **Open** the **Navigation Pane**.

Activity 13.29 | Specifying Criteria Using a Field Not Displayed in the Query Results

So far, all of the fields that you included in the query design have also been included in the query results. It is not required to have every field in the query display in the results. In this activity, you will create a query to answer the question, *Which instructors have a rank of Professor?*

1 **Close** the **Navigation Pane**. Click the **Create tab**, and then in the **Queries group**, click the **Query Design** button.

2 From the **Show Table** dialog box, **Add** the **13B Instructors** table to the table area, and then **Close** the dialog box. Expand the field list.

3 Add the following fields, in the order given, to the design grid: **Instructor ID**, **First Name**, **Last Name**, and **Rank**.

4 In the **Sort** row, in the **Last Name** field, click the **Sort** arrow; click **Ascending**.

5 In the **Criteria** row, click in the **Rank** field, type **professor** and then press Enter.

Recall that criteria is not case sensitive. As you start typing *professor*, a list of functions displays, from which you can select if including a function in your criteria. When you press Enter, the insertion point moves to the next criteria box and quotation marks are added around the text string that you entered.

6 In the design grid, in the **Show** row, notice that the check box is selected for every field. **Run** the query to view the query results.

Nineteen records meet the criteria, and the records are sorted in ascending alphabetical order by the Last Name field.

7 Switch to **Design** view. In the design grid, under **Rank**, in the **Show** row, click to clear the check box. Compare your screen with Figure 13.57.

Because it is repetitive and not particularly useful to have *Professor* display for each record in the query results, clear this check box so that the field does not display. However, you should run the query before clearing the Show check box to be sure that the correct records display.

Figure 13.57

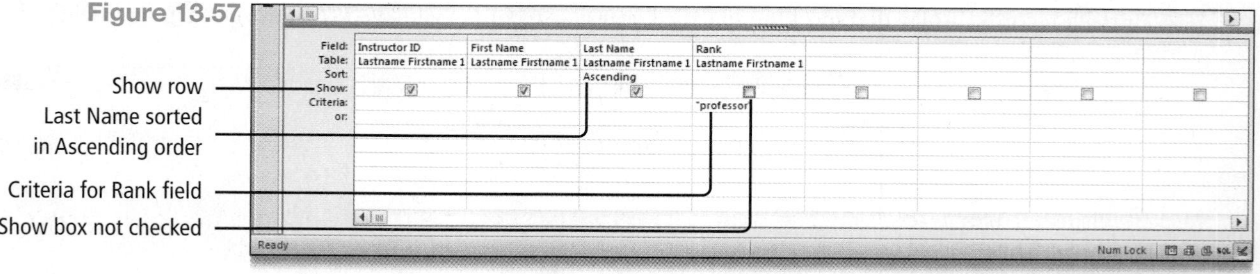

8 **Run** the query, and then notice that the Rank field does not display.

Although the Rank field is still included in the query criteria for the purpose of identifying specific records, it is not necessary to display the field in the results.

9 **Save** the query as **Lastname Firstname 13B Professor Rank Query** and then display the query in **Print Preview**. Create a paper or electronic printout if instructed to do so, and then **Close Print Preview**. **Close** the query.

Activity 13.30 | Using Is Null Criteria to Find Empty Fields

Sometimes you must locate records where data is *missing*. You can locate such records by using ***Is Null***—empty—as the criteria in a field. Additionally, you can display only the records where a value *has* been entered in a field by using ***Is Not Null*** as the criteria, which will exclude records where the specified field is empty. In this activity, you will design a query to find out *Which scheduled courses have no credits listed?*

1. Click the **Create tab**. In the **Queries group**, click the **Query Design** button. Add the **13B Schedule** table to the table area, **Close** the **Show Table** dialog box, and then expand the field list.
2. Add the following fields to the design grid in the order given: **Subject**, **Catalog#**, **Section**, **Course Name**, and **Credits**.
3. In the **Criteria** row, click in the **Credits** field, type **is null** and then press Enter.

   Access capitalizes *is null*. The criteria *Is Null* examines the field and looks for records that do *not* have any values entered in the Credits field.
4. In the **Sort** row, click in the **Subject** field, click the **Sort arrow**, and then click **Ascending**. **Sort** the **Catalog#** field in **Ascending** order. Compare your screen with Figure 13.58.

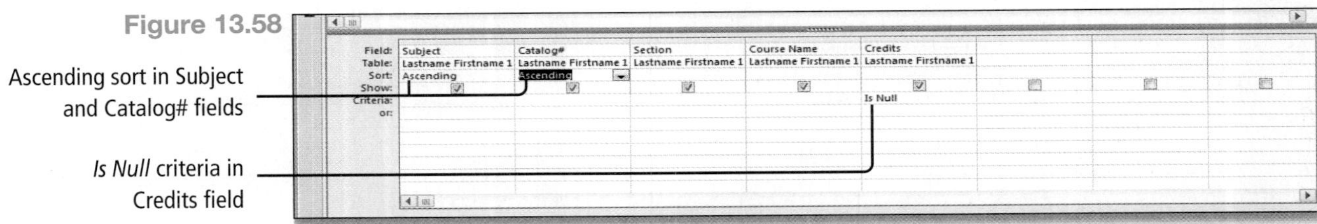

Figure 13.58

5. **Run** the query, and then compare your screen with Figure 13.59.

   Five scheduled courses do not have credits listed—the Credits field is empty. The records are sorted in ascending order first by the Subject field, then by the Catalog # field. Using the information displayed in the query results, a course scheduler can more easily locate the records in the table to enter the credits.

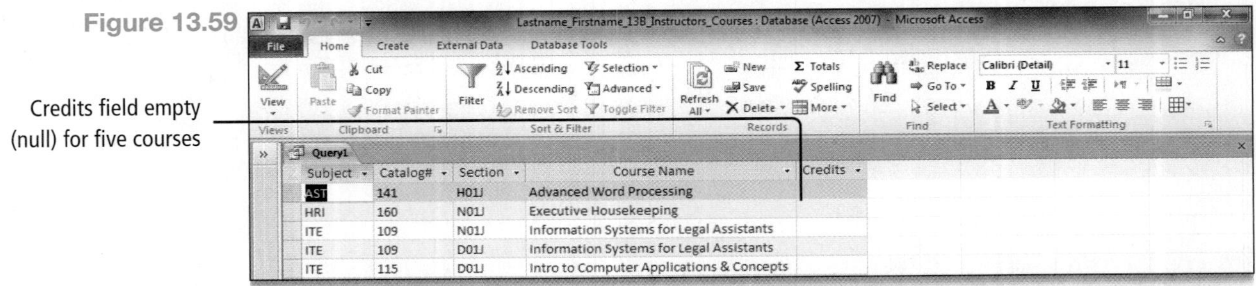

Figure 13.59

6. **Save** the query as **Lastname Firstname 13B No Credits Query** and then display the query in **Print Preview**. Create a paper or electronic printout if instructed to do so, and then **Close Print Preview**.
7. **Close** the query. **Open** the **Navigation Pane**.
8. From **Backstage** view, click **Close Database**, and then click **Exit** to close the Access program. As directed by your instructor, submit your database and the eight paper or electronic printouts—relationship report, sorted table, and six queries—that are the results of this project.

You have completed Project 13B

Project 13C Athletic Scholarships Database

Project Activities

In Activities 13.31 through 13.43, you will assist Randy Shavrain, Athletic Director for Capital Cities Community College, in developing and querying the Athletic Scholarships database. Your results will look similar to Figure 13.60.

Project Files

For Project 13C, you will need the following files:

a13C_Athletes_Scholarships
e13C_Athletes (Excel file)

You will save your database as:

Lastname_Firstname_13C_Athletes_Scholarships

Project Results

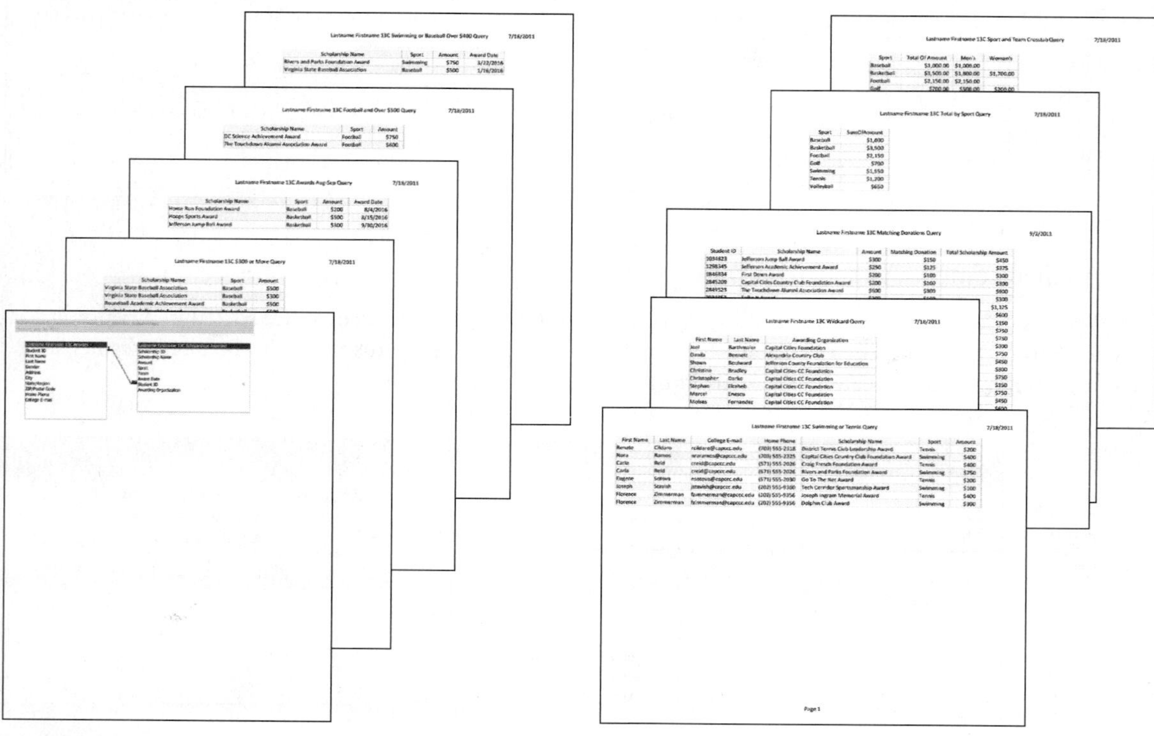

Figure 13.60
Project 13C Athletes Scholarships

Objective 13 | Specify Numeric Criteria in a Query

View the video on the Companion Web Site or in MyITLab

Criteria can be set for fields containing numeric data. When you design your table, set the appropriate data type for fields that will contain numbers, currency, or dates so that mathematical calculations can be performed.

Activity 13.31 | Opening an Existing Database and Importing a Spreadsheet

In this activity, you will open, rename, and save an existing database, and then import an Excel spreadsheet into Access as a new table.

1. **Start** Access. In **Backstage** view, click **Open**. From your student files, open **a13C_Athletes_Scholarships.**

2. From **Backstage** view, click **Save Database As**. In the **Save As** dialog box, navigate to your **All In One Chapter 13** folder, and save the database as **Lastname_Firstname_13C_Athletes_Scholarships**

3. On the **Message Bar**, click the **Enable Content** button. In the **Navigation Pane**, **Rename 13C Scholarships Awarded** to **Lastname Firstname 13C Scholarships Awarded** and then double-click to open the table. **Close** « the **Navigation Pane**, and then examine the data in the table. Compare your screen with Figure 13.61.

   In this table, Mr. Shavrain tracks the names and amounts of scholarships awarded to student athletes. Students are identified only by their Student ID numbers, and the primary key is the Scholarship ID field.

Figure 13.61

4. **Close** ✕ the table. On the Ribbon, click the **External Data tab**, and then in the **Import & Link group**, click the **Excel** button. In the **Get External Data – Excel Spreadsheet** dialog box, to the right of the **File name** box, click **Browse**.

5. In the **File Open** dialog box, navigate to your student data files, and then double-click **e13C_Athletes**. Be sure that the **Import the source data into a new table in the current database** option button is selected, and then click **OK**.

   The Import Spreadsheet Wizard opens and displays the spreadsheet data.

6. Click **Next**. In the upper left portion of the **Import Spreadsheet Wizard** dialog box, select the **First Row Contains Column Headings** check box. Click **Next**, and then click **Next** again.

7. In the upper portion of the Wizard, click the **Choose my own primary key** option button, and then be sure that **Student ID** displays.

   In the new table, Student ID will be the primary key. No two students have the same Student ID.

8. Click **Next**. In the **Import to Table** box, type **Lastname Firstname 13C Athletes** and then click **Finish**. In the **Get External Data – Excel Spreadsheet** dialog box, click **Close**, and then **Open** » the **Navigation Pane**. Widen the **Navigation Pane** so that the table names display fully.

9. Open the new **13C Athletes** table, and then on the **Home** tab, switch to **Design** View.

10 For the **Student ID** field, click in the **Data Type** box, click the **arrow**, and then click **Text**. For the **ZIP/Postal Code** field, change the **Data Type** to **Text**, and then set the **Field Size** to **5** Click in the **State/Region** field, set the **Field Size** to **2** and then switch back to **Datasheet View**, saving the changes.

Recall that numeric data that will not be used in any calculations, such as the Student ID, should have a Data Type of Text.

11 In the message box, click **Yes**—no data will be lost. **Close** the **Navigation Pane**. Take a moment to review the imported data. Using the **Select All** button, apply **Best Fit** to all of the fields. Click in any field to cancel the selection, **Save** the table, and then **Close** the table.

Activity 13.32 | Creating Table Relationships

In this activity, you will create a one-to-many relationship between the 13C Athletes table and the 13C Scholarships Awarded table by using the common field—*Student ID*.

1 Click the **Database Tools tab**, and then in the **Relationships group**, click the **Relationships** button.

2 In the **Show Table** dialog box, **Add** the **13C Athletes** table, and then **Add** the **13C Scholarships Awarded** table to the table area. Close the **Show Table** dialog box.

3 Move and resize the two field lists to display all of the fields and the entire table name, and then position the field lists so that there is approximately one inch of space between the two field lists.

4 In the **13C Athletes** field list, point to the **Student ID** field. Hold down the left mouse button, drag into the **13C Scholarships Awarded** field list on top of the **Student ID** field, and then release the mouse button to display the **Edit Relationships** dialog box.

5 Point to the title bar of the **Edit Relationships** dialog box, and then drag it below the two field lists. In the **Edit Relationships** dialog box, be sure that **Student ID** is displayed as the common field for both tables.

The two tables relate in a one-to-many relationship—one athlete can have many scholarships. In the 13C Athletes table, Student ID is the primary key. In the 13C Scholarships Awarded table, Student ID is the foreign key.

6 In the **Edit Relationships** dialog box, select the **Enforce Referential Integrity** check box. Click **Create**, and then compare your screen with Figure 13.62.

The one-to-many relationship is established. The *1* and ∞ indicate that referential integrity is enforced, which ensures that a scholarship cannot be awarded to a student whose Student ID is not in the 13C Athletes table. Similarly, you cannot delete a student athlete from the 13C Athletes table if there is a scholarship listed for that student in the 13C Scholarships Awarded table.

Figure 13.62

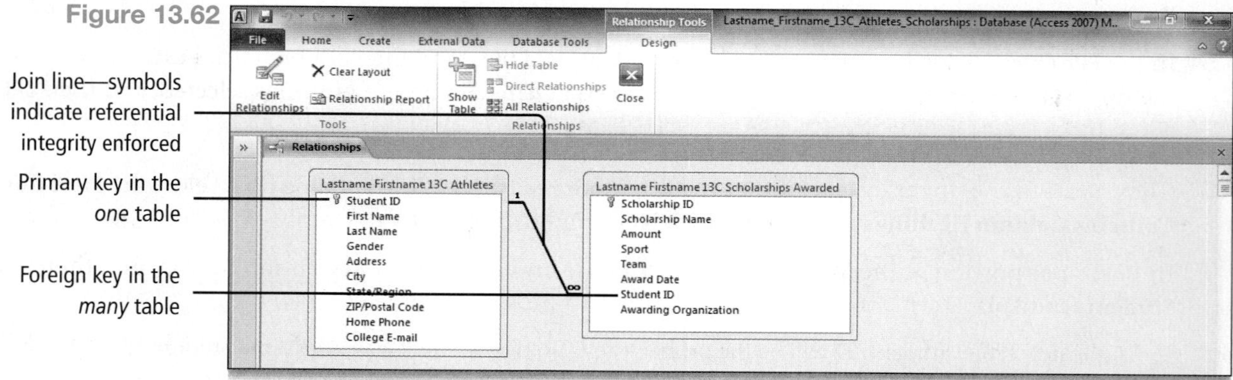

7 On the **Design tab**, in the **Tools group**, click the **Relationship Report** button. Create a paper or electronic printout if instructed to do so.

8 **Save** the report as **Lastname Firstname 13C Relationships** and then click **OK**. **Close** the report, and then **Close** the **Relationships** window.

9 **Open** [»] the **Navigation Pane**, open the **13C Athletes** table, and then **Close** [«] the **Navigation Pane**. On the left side of the table, in the first record, click the **plus sign** (+) to display the subdatasheet for the record.

In the first record, for Joel Barthmaier, one related record exists in the 13C Scholarships Awarded table. The related record displays because you created a relationship between the two tables using Student ID as the common field.

10 **Close** [X] the **13C Athletes** table.

Activity 13.33 | Specifying Numeric Criteria in a Query

In this activity, you will specify criteria in the query to answer the question, *Which scholarships are in the amount of $300, and for which sports?*

1 Click the **Create tab**. In the **Queries group**, click the **Query Design** button.

2 In the **Show Table** dialog box, **Add** the **13C Scholarships Awarded** table to the table area, and then **Close** the **Show Table** dialog box. Expand the field list to display all of the fields and the entire table name.

3 Add the following fields to the design grid in the order given: **Scholarship Name**, **Sport**, and **Amount**.

4 In the **Sort** row, click in the **Sport** field. Click the **Sort arrow**, and then click **Ascending**.

5 In the **Criteria** row, click in the **Amount** field, type **300** and then press [Enter]. Compare your screen with Figure 13.63.

When entering currency values as criteria, do not type the dollar sign. Include a decimal point only if you are looking for a specific amount that includes cents—for example 300.49. Access does not insert quotation marks around the criteria because the field's data type is Number.

Figure 13.63

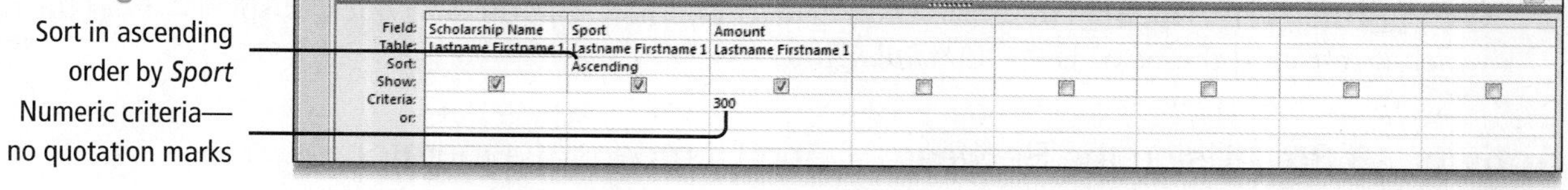

Sort in ascending order by *Sport*

Numeric criteria—no quotation marks

Field:	Scholarship Name	Sport	Amount
Table:	Lastname Firstname 1	Lastname Firstname 1	Lastname Firstname 1
Sort:		Ascending	
Show:	☑	☑	☑
Criteria:			300
or:			

6 On the **Design tab**, in the **Results group**, click the **Run** button to view the results.

Five scholarships were awarded in the exact amount of $300. In the navigation area, 1 of 5 displays to indicate the number of records that match the criteria.

7 On the **Home tab**, in the **Views group**, click the **View** button to switch to **Design** view.

Activity 13.34 | Using Comparison Operators

Comparison operators are symbols that evaluate each field value to determine if it is the same (=), greater than (>), less than (<), or in between a range of values as specified by the criteria. If no comparison operator is specified, equal (=) is assumed.

1 Be sure your query is displayed in **Design** view. In the **Criteria** row, click in the **Amount** field, delete the existing criteria, type **>300** and then press [Enter].

2 On the **Design tab**, in the **Results group**, click the **Run** button.

Fourteen records have an Amount that is greater than $300. The results show the records for which the Amount is greater than $300, but do not display amounts that are equal to $300.

3 Switch to **Design** view. In the **Criteria** row, under **Amount**, delete the existing criteria. Type **<300** and then press [Enter]. **Run** the query.

Eleven records display and each has an Amount less than $300. The results show the records for which the Amount is less than $300, but does not include amounts that are equal to $300.

4 Switch to **Design** view. In the **Criteria** row, click in the **Amount** field, delete the existing criteria, type **>=300** and then press Enter.

5 **Run** the query, and then compare your screen with Figure 13.64.

Nineteen records display, including the records for scholarships in the exact amount of $300. The records include scholarships greater than or equal to $300. In this manner, comparison operators can be combined. This query answers the question, *Which scholarships have been awarded in the amount of $300 or more, and for which sports, with the Sport names in alphabetical order?*

Figure 13.64

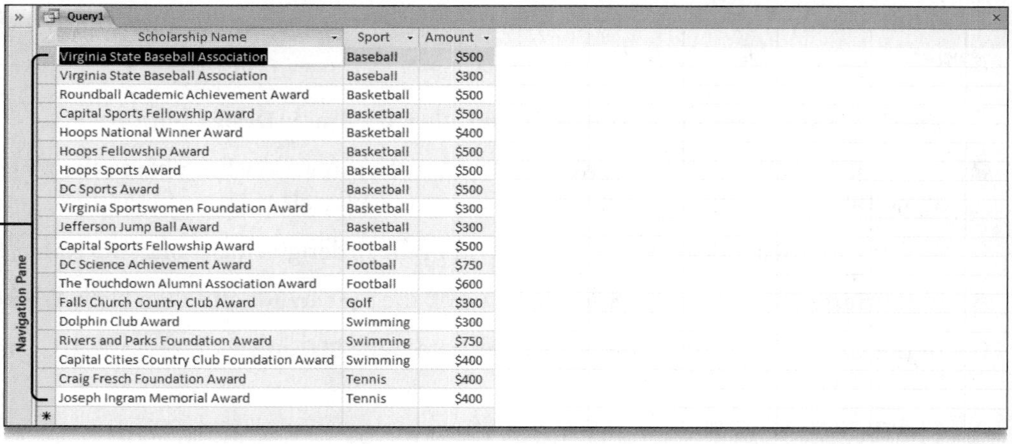

Nineteen records with a scholarship of $300 or more

Scholarship Name	Sport	Amount
Virginia State Baseball Association	Baseball	$500
Virginia State Baseball Association	Baseball	$300
Roundball Academic Achievement Award	Basketball	$500
Capital Sports Fellowship Award	Basketball	$500
Hoops National Winner Award	Basketball	$400
Hoops Fellowship Award	Basketball	$500
Hoops Sports Award	Basketball	$500
DC Sports Award	Basketball	$500
Virginia Sportswomen Foundation Award	Basketball	$300
Jefferson Jump Ball Award	Basketball	$300
Capital Sports Fellowship Award	Football	$500
DC Science Achievement Award	Football	$750
The Touchdown Alumni Association Award	Football	$600
Falls Church Country Club Award	Golf	$300
Dolphin Club Award	Swimming	$300
Rivers and Parks Foundation Award	Swimming	$750
Capital Cities Country Club Foundation Award	Swimming	$400
Craig Fresch Foundation Award	Tennis	$400
Joseph Ingram Memorial Award	Tennis	$400

6 **Save** the query as **Lastname Firstname 13C $300 or More Query** and then display the query in **Print Preview**. Create a paper or electronic printout if instructed to do so, and then **Close Print Preview**.

7 **Close** the query. **Open** the **Navigation Pane**, and notice that the new query displays under the table from which it retrieved the records—*13C Scholarships Awarded*.

Activity 13.35 | Using the Between … And Comparison Operator

The ***Between … And operator*** is a comparison operator that looks for values within a range. It is useful when you need to locate records that are within a range of dates; for example, scholarships awarded between August 1 and September 30. In this activity, you will create a new query from an existing query, and then add criteria to look for values within a range of dates. The query will answer the question, *Which scholarships were awarded between August 1 and September 30?*

1 On the **Navigation Pane**, click the **13C $300 or More Query** object to select it. Display **Backstage** view and click **Save Object As**. In the **Save As** dialog box, type **Lastname Firstname 13C Awards Aug-Sep Query** and then click **OK**.

2 Click the **Home tab**. Open the **13C Awards Aug-Sep Query** object, **Close** the **Navigation Pane**, and then switch to **Design** view. From the **13C Scholarships Awarded** field list, add the **Award Date** as the fourth field in the design grid.

3 In the **Criteria** row, click in the **Amount** field, and then delete the existing criteria so that the query is not restricted by amount. In the **Criteria** row, click in the **Award Date** field, type **between 8/1/16 and 9/30/16** and then press Enter.

4 In the selection bar of the design grid, point to the right edge of the **Award Date** column to display the pointer, and then double-click. Compare your screen with Figure 13.65.

The width of the Award Date column is increased to fit the longest entry, enabling you to see all of the criteria. Access places pound signs (#) around dates and capitalizes *between* and *and*. This criteria instructs Access to look for values in the Award Date field that begin with 8/1/16 and end with 9/30/16. Both the beginning and ending dates will be included in the query results.

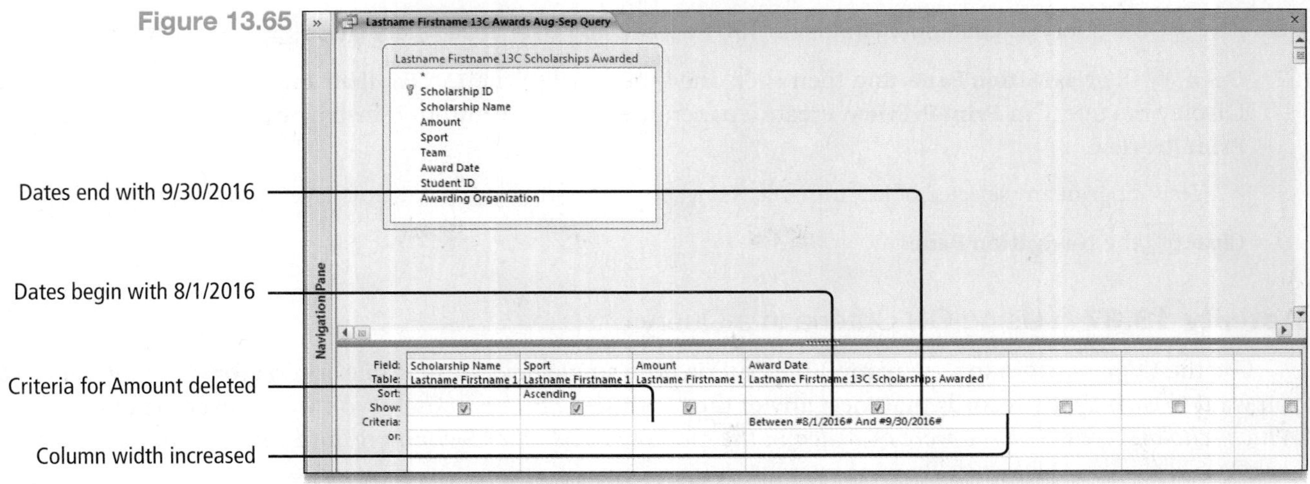

Figure 13.65

5 **Run** the query, and notice that three scholarships were awarded between 08/1/16 and 9/30/16.

6 Display the query in **Print Preview**, create a paper or electronic printout if instructed to do so, and then **Close Print Preview**.

7 **Close** [X] the query. In the message box, click **Yes** to save the changes to the query design.

Objective 14 | Use Compound Criteria

View the video on the Companion Web Site or in MyITLab

You can specify more than one condition—criteria—in a query; this is called ***compound criteria***. Compound criteria use AND and OR ***logical operators***. Logical operators enable you to enter criteria for the same field or different fields.

Activity 13.36 | Using AND Criteria in a Query

Compound criteria use an ***AND condition*** to display records in the query results that meet all parts of the specified criteria. In this activity, you will answer the question, *Which scholarships over $500 were awarded for Football?*

1 On the Ribbon, click the **Create tab**. In the **Queries group**, click the **Query Design** button. Add the **13C Scholarships Awarded** table to the table area. **Close** the **Show Table** dialog box, and then expand the field list.

2 Add the following fields to the design grid in the order given: **Scholarship Name**, **Sport**, and **Amount**.

3 In the **Criteria** row, click in the **Sport** field, type **football** and then press Enter.

4 In the **Criteria** row, in the **Amount** field, type **>500** and then press Enter. Compare your screen with Figure 13.66.

You create the AND condition by placing the criteria for both fields on the same line in the Criteria row. The results will display only records that contain Football AND an amount greater than $500.

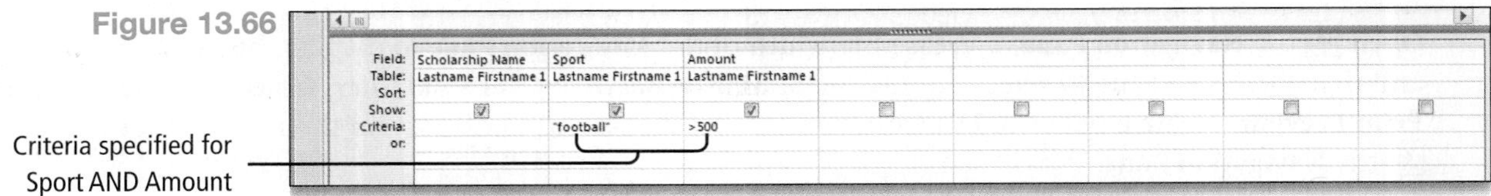

Figure 13.66

5 On the **Design tab**, in the **Results group**, click the **Run** button.

Two records display that match both conditions—Football in the Sport field *and* greater than $500 in the Amount field.

6 **Save** the query as **Lastname Firstname 13C Football and Over $500 Query Close** the query.

7 **Open** the **Navigation Pane**, and then click one time to select the **13C Football and Over $500 Query** object. Display the query in **Print Preview**, create a paper or electronic printout if instructed to do so, and then **Close Print Preview**.

You can print any selected object from the Navigation Pane—the object does not have to be open to print.

8 **Close** the **Navigation Pane**.

Activity 13.37 | Using OR Criteria in a Query

Use the ***OR condition*** to specify multiple criteria for a single field, or multiple criteria for different fields when you want to display the records that meet any of the conditions. In this activity, you will answer the question, *Which scholarships over $400 were awarded in the sports of Baseball or Swimming, and what is the award date of each?*

1 Click the **Create tab**. In the **Queries group**, click the **Query Design** button. Add the **13C Scholarships Awarded** table. **Close** the dialog box, and expand the field list.

2 Add the following four fields to the design grid in the order given: **Scholarship Name**, **Sport**, **Amount**, and **Award Date**.

3 In the **Criteria** row, click in the **Sport** field, and then type **baseball** On the **or** row, click in the **Sport** field, type **swimming** and then press Enter. **Run** the query.

The query results display seven scholarship records where the Sport is either Baseball or Swimming. Use the OR condition to specify multiple criteria for a single field.

4 Switch to **Design** view. In the **or** row, under **Sport**, delete *swimming*. In the **Criteria** row, under **Sport**, delete *baseball*. Type **swimming or baseball** and then in the **Criteria** row, click in the **Amount** field. Type **>400** and then press Enter. Increase the width of the **Sport** column. Compare your screen with Figure 13.67.

This is an alternative way to use the OR compound operator in the Sport field. Because criteria is entered for two different fields, Access selects the records that are Baseball or Swimming and that have a scholarship awarded in an amount greater than $400. If you enter swimming on the Criteria row and baseball on the or row, then you must enter >400 on both the Criteria row and the or row so that the correct records display when the query runs.

Figure 13.67

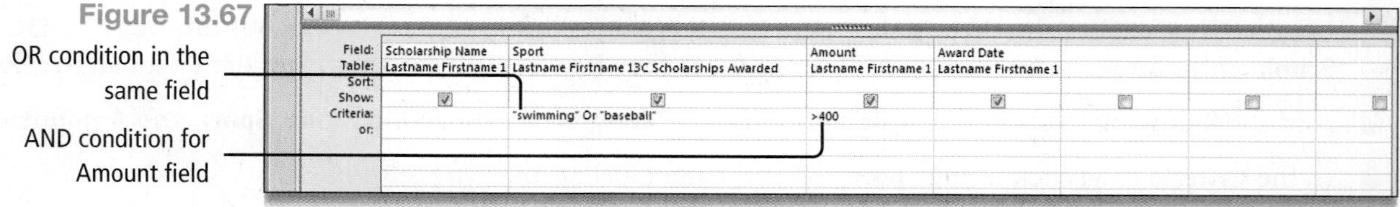

5 **Run** the query to display the two records that match the conditions.

6 **Close** the query. In the message box, click **Yes** to save changes to the query. **Save** the query as **Lastname Firstname 13C Swimming or Baseball Over $400 Query**

7 **Open** the **Navigation Pane**, increase the width of the **Navigation Pane** to display the full name of all objects, and then click one time to select the **13C Swimming or Baseball Over $400 Query** object. Display the query in **Print Preview**, create a paper or electronic printout if instructed to do so, and then **Close Print Preview**. **Close** the **Navigation Pane**.

3 To select the row headings, under **Available Fields**, double-click **Sport** to sort the scholarship amounts by the different sports. Click **Next**, and then compare your screen with Figure 13.80.

The sports are displayed as row headings; here you are prompted to select column headings.

Figure 13.80

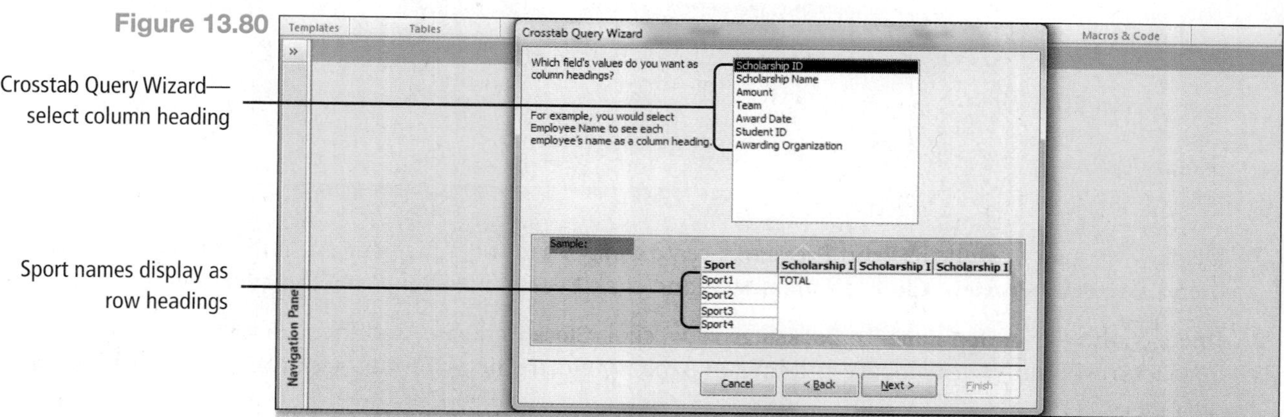

4 To select the column headings, in the field list, click **Team**. Click **Next**, and then compare your screen with Figure 13.81.

The teams will be listed as column headings; here you are prompted to select a field to summarize.

Figure 13.81

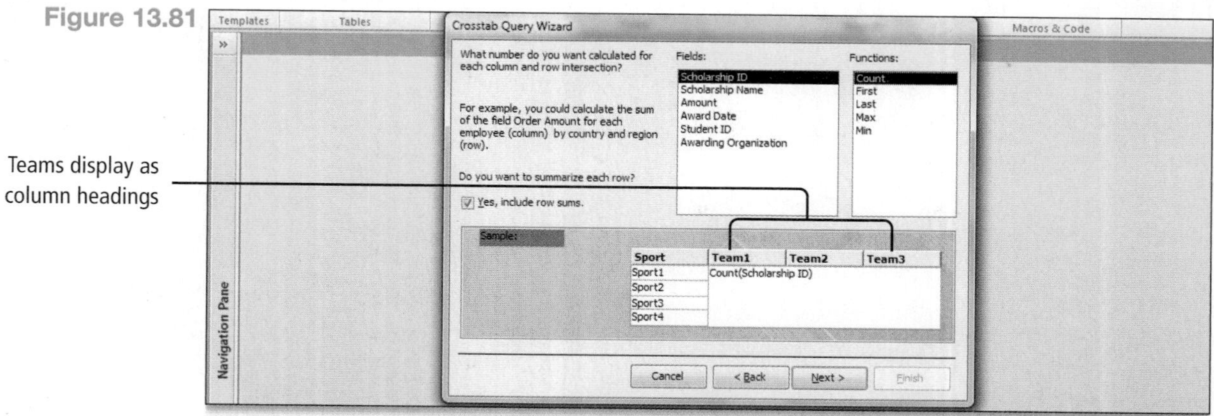

5 Under **Fields**, click **Amount**. Under **Functions**, click **Sum**, and then click **Next**.

The crosstab query will sum the Amount field for each sport and team.

6 In the **What do you want to name your query?** box, type **Lastname Firstname 13C Sport and Team Crosstab Query** and then click **Finish**. Apply **Best Fit** to the columns, click in any field to cancel the selection, and then compare your screen with Figure 13.82.

The crosstab query displays the total amount of scholarships awarded by sport and also by men's or women's teams. For example, for the sport of Golf, a total of $700 was awarded in scholarship money; $500 to men's teams and $200 to women's teams. A crosstab query is useful to display a summary of data based on two different fields—in this case, by sport and by teams.

Figure 13.82

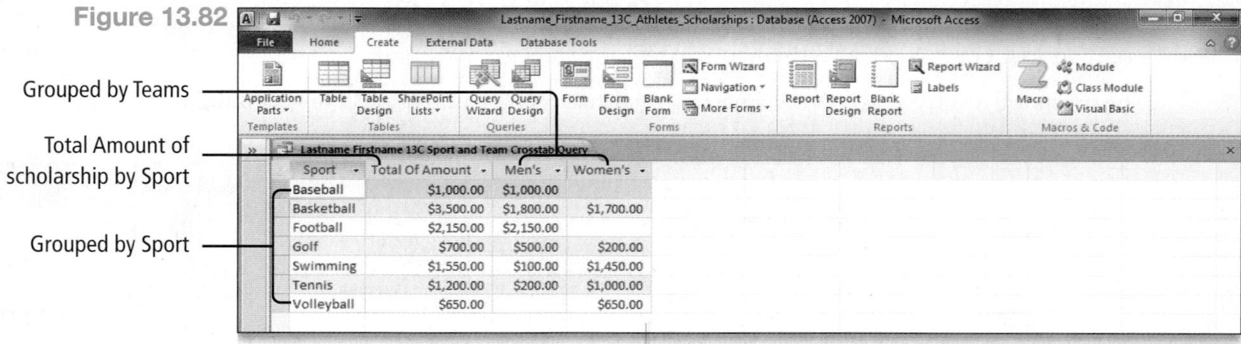

Sport	Total Of Amount	Men's	Women's
Baseball	$1,000.00	$1,000.00	
Basketball	$3,500.00	$1,800.00	$1,700.00
Football	$2,150.00	$2,150.00	
Golf	$700.00	$500.00	$200.00
Swimming	$1,550.00	$100.00	$1,450.00
Tennis	$1,200.00	$200.00	$1,000.00
Volleyball	$650.00		$650.00

7 Display the query results in **Print Preview**. Create a paper or electronic printout if instructed to do so, and then **Close Print Preview**. **Close** [×] the query, and click **Yes** to save changes to the query layout.

8 **Open** [»] the **Navigation Pane**. In **Backstage** view, click **Close Database**, and then click **Exit**. As directed by your instructor, submit your database and the ten paper or electronic printouts—relationship report and nine queries—that are the results of this project.

End **You have completed Project 13C**

Content-Based Assessments

Summary

Microsoft Access 2010 is a database management system that uses various objects—tables, forms, queries, reports—to organize information. Data is stored in tables in which you establish fields, set the data type and field size, and create a primary key. Data from a database can be reported and printed. Sorting data in a table reorders the records based on one or more fields.

Use queries to ask complex questions about the data in a database in a manner that Access can interpret. Save queries so they can be run as needed against current records. Use queries to limit the fields that display, add criteria to restrict the number of records in the query results, create calculated values, include data from more than one table, and to display data grouped by two types of information.

Chapter 13 | GO! All In One

Key Terms

Check Your Knowledge

Matching and Multiple Choice items are available in MyITLab and on the Companion Web Site.

Content-Based Assessments

Apply 13A skills from these Objectives:

1. Identify Good Database Design
2. Create a Table and Define Fields in a New Database
3. Change the Structure of Tables and Add a Second Table
4. Create and Use a Query, Form, and Report
5. Save and Close a Database

Mastering Access | Project 13D Kiosk Inventory

In the following Mastering Access project, you will create a database to track information about the inventory of items for sale in the kiosk located on the quad at the Central Campus of Capital Cities Community College. Your completed database objects will look similar to Figure 13.83.

Project Files

For Project 13D, you will need the following files:

New blank Access database
e13D_Inventory (Excel workbook)
e13D_Inventory_Storage (Excel workbook)

You will save your database as:

Lastname_Firstname_13D_Inventory

Project Results

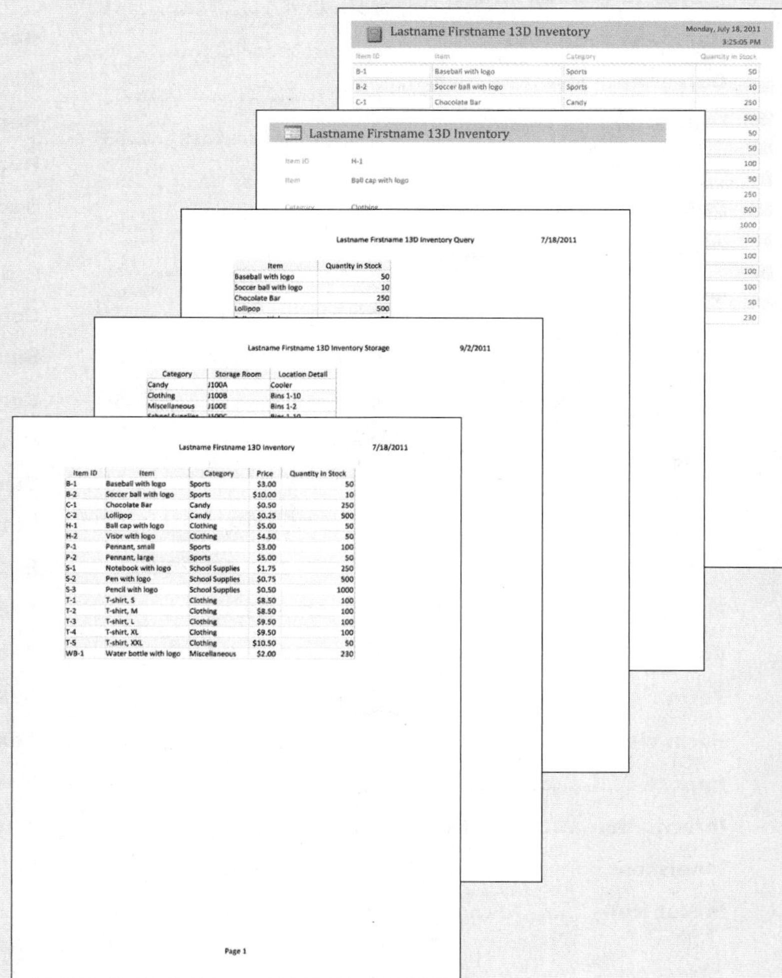

Lastname Firstname 13D Inventory Storage

Category	Storage Room	Location Detail
Candy	J100A	Cooler
Clothing	J100B	Bins 1-10
Miscellaneous	J100E	Bins 1-2

Lastname Firstname 13D Inventory 7/18/2011

Item ID	Item	Category	Price	Quantity in Stock
B-1	Baseball with logo	Sports	$3.00	50
B-2	Soccer ball with logo	Sports	$10.00	10
C-1	Chocolate Bar	Candy	$0.50	250
C-2	Lollipop	Candy	$0.25	500
H-1	Ball cap with logo	Clothing	$5.00	50
H-2	Visor with logo	Clothing	$4.50	50
P-1	Pennant, small	Sports	$3.00	100
P-2	Pennant, large	Sports	$5.00	50
S-1	Notebook with logo	School Supplies	$1.75	250
S-2	Pen with logo	School Supplies	$0.75	500
S-3	Pencil with logo	School Supplies	$0.50	1000
T-1	T-shirt, S	Clothing	$8.50	100
T-2	T-shirt, M	Clothing	$8.50	100
T-3	T-shirt, L	Clothing	$9.50	100
T-4	T-shirt, XL	Clothing	$9.50	100
T-5	T-shirt, XXL	Clothing	$10.50	50
WB-1	Water bottle with logo	Miscellaneous	$2.00	230

Page 1

Figure 13.83

(Project 13D Kiosk Inventory continues on the next page)

Mastering Access | Project 13D Kiosk Inventory (continued)

1 **Start** Access. Create a new **Blank database** in your **All In One Chapter 13** folder. Name the database **Lastname_Firstname_13D_Inventory** and then **Close** the **Navigation Pane**. Create additional fields as shown in **Table 1**.

2 Change the **Data Type** of the **ID** field to **Text**, rename the field to **Item ID** and then enter the records as shown in **Table 2**.

3 **Save** the table as **Lastname Firstname 13D Inventory** and then **Close** the table. From your student data files, **Import** and then **Append** the **e13D_Inventory** Excel file to the **13D Inventory** table. Then, from the **Navigation Pane**, open your **13D Inventory** table—17 records display. Widen and then **Close** the **Navigation Pane**.

4 In **Design** view, delete the **Storage Location** field. Click in the **Category** field, change the **Field Size** to **25** and in the **Description** box, type **Enter the category of the Item** Click in the **Item ID** field, and then change the **Field Size** to **10** **Save** the changes to the design of your table, click **Yes**, and then switch to **Datasheet** view. Apply **Best Fit** to all of the fields in the table, **Save** the table, and then display the table in **Print Preview**—one page results. Create a paper or electronic printout as directed by your instructor. **Close** the table.

5 From your student data files, **Import** the **e13D_Inventory_Storage** Excel file into the database as a new table; use the first row as the column headings and the **Category** field as the primary key. As the last step in the Wizard, name the table **Lastname Firstname 13D Inventory Storage** and then **Open** the **Navigation Pane**. **Open** your **13D Inventory Storage** table, and then **Close** the **Navigation Pane**. Display the new table in **Design** view, click in the **Location Detail** field, change the **Field Size** to **30** and then as the **Description**, type **Enter room and bin numbers or alternate location of inventory item.** In **Datasheet** view, apply **Best Fit** to all of the fields, **Save** the table, and then display the table in **Print Preview**. Create a paper or electronic printout as directed—one page results. **Close** the table.

6 **Create**, by using the **Query Wizard**, a **Simple Query** based on your **13D Inventory** table. Include only the fields that will answer the question, *For all Items, what is the Quantity in Stock?* **Save** the query with the default name. Create a paper or electronic printout as directed and then **Close** the query.

7 Display the **13D Inventory** table, and then **Create** a **Form** for this table. **Save** the form as **Lastname Firstname 13D Inventory Form** Display and then select the fifth record. By using the instructions in Activity 13.15, print or create an electronic printout of only this record as directed. **Close** the form object.

8 With the **13D Inventory** table open, **Create** a **Report**. **Delete** the **Price** field, and then sort the records in **Ascending** order by the **Item ID** field. Scroll down to the bottom of the report and delete the page number—**Page 1 of 1**. **Save** the report as **Lastname Firstname 13D Inventory Report** and then create a paper or electronic printout as directed.

9 **Close All** open objects. **Open** the **Navigation Pane**. If necessary, widen the pane so that all of the object names display fully. In **Backstage** view, click **Close Database** and then click **Exit**. As directed by your instructor, submit your database and the five paper or electronic printouts—two tables, one query, one form, and one report—that are the results of this project.

Table 1

Data Type		Text	Text	Text	Currency	Number
Field Name	ID	Item	Category	Storage Location	Price	Quantity in Stock

Return to Step 2

Table 2

Item ID	Item	Category	Storage Location	Price	Quantity in Stock
C-1	Chocolate Bar	Candy	J100A	.5	250
C-2	Lollipop	Candy	J100A	.25	500
T-1	T-shirt, S	Clothing	J100B	8.5	100

Return to Step 3

End You have completed Project 13D

Apply **13B** skills from these Objectives:

6 Open an Existing Database
7 Create Table Relationships
8 Sort Records in a Table
9 Create a Query in Design View
10 Create a New Query from an Existing Query
11 Sort Query Results
12 Specify Criteria in a Query

Mastering Access | Project **13E** Grants and Organizations

In the following Mastering Access project, you will assist Susan Elkington, Director of Grants for the college, in using her database to answer questions about public and private grants awarded to the college departments. Your results will look similar to Figure 13.84.

Project Files

For Project 13E, you will need the following file:

a13E_Grants_Organizations

You will save your database as:

Lastname_Firstname_13E_Grants_Organizations

Project Results

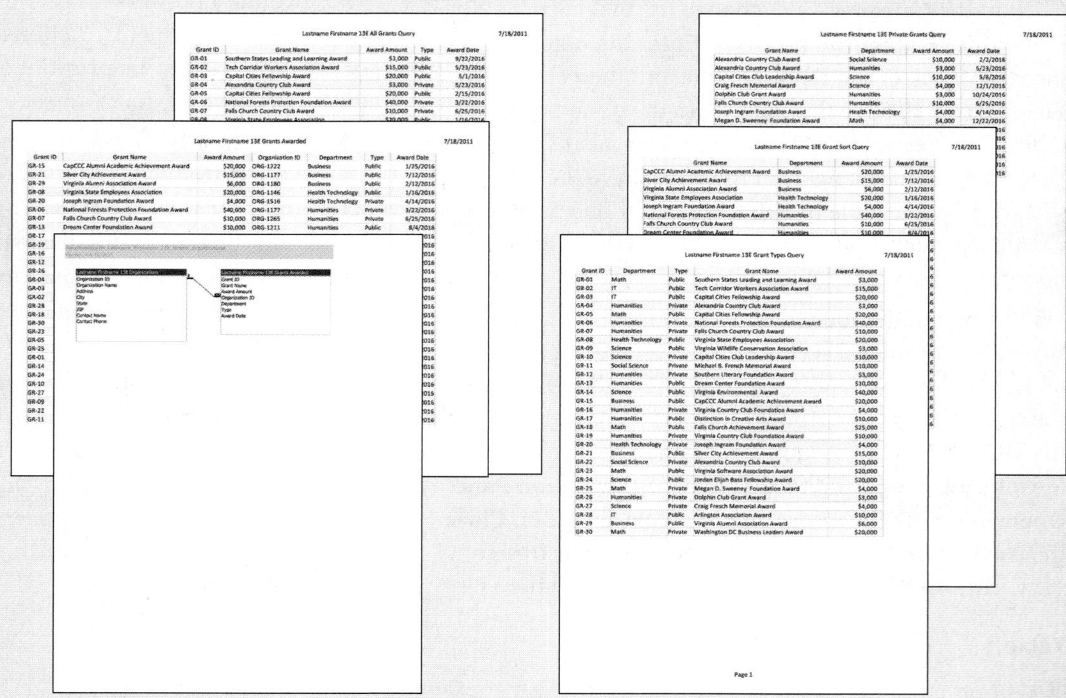

Figure 13.84

(Project 13E Grants and Organizations continues on the next page)

Mastering Access | Project 13E Grants and Organizations (continued)

1 **Start** Access. From your student files, open the **a13E_Grants_Organizations** database. Save the database in your **All In One Chapter 13** folder as **Lastname_ Firstname_13E_Grants_Organizations** and then enable the content. In the **Navigation Pane**, **Rename** the tables by adding **Lastname Firstname** to the beginning of each table name, and then widen the **Navigation Pane** to display fully both table names. **Open** both tables and examine their contents to become familiar with the data. **Close** both tables, and leave the **Navigation Pane** open.

2 Create a *one-to-many* relationship between the **13E Organizations** table and the **13E Grants Awarded** table based on the **Organization ID** field, and then **Enforce Referential Integrity**. *One* organization can award *many* grants. Create a **Relationship Report**, saving it with the default name. Create a paper or electronic printout as directed, and then **Close** all open objects, saving changes if prompted.

3 **Open** the **13E Grants Awarded** table, and then **Close** the **Navigation Pane**. Sort so that the records in the table are in alphabetical order by the **Department** and then in descending order by **Award Amount**. Create a paper or electronic printout as directed, being sure that the table prints on only one page by using **Landscape**, with **Normal** margins. **Close** the table, and do not save changes to the table.

4 **Create** a query in **Query Design** view, using the **13E Grants Awarded** table to answer the question, *What is the Grant ID, Grant Name, Award Amount, Type, and Award Date for all of the grants?* Display the fields in the order listed in the question. **Save** the query as **Lastname Firstname 13E All Grants Query** and then, with **Normal** margins, create a paper or electronic printout as directed. **Close Print Preview**, and leave the query open.

5 Use **13E All Grants Query** to create a new query. **Save** the object as **Lastname Firstname 13E Grant Types Query** and then redesign the query to answer the question, *What is the Grant ID, Department, Type, Grant Name, and Award Amount for all grants?* Display the only the fields necessary to answer the question and in the order listed in the question. With **Normal** margins, create a paper or electronic printout as directed. **Close** the query, saving the design changes.

6 From the **Navigation Pane**, open the **13E All Grants Query**, and then **Close** the **Navigation Pane**. **Save** the query as **Lastname Firstname 13E Grant Sort Query** and then switch to **Design** view. Redesign the query to answer the question, *What is the Grant Name, Department, Award Amount, and Award Date for grants sorted first in alphabetical order by Department and then in descending order by Amount?* Display only the fields necessary to answer the question and in the order listed in the question. With **Normal** margins, create a paper or electronic printout as directed. **Close** the query, saving changes to the query design.

7 **Open** the **Navigation Pane**, open **13E Grant Sort Query**, and then **Close** the **Navigation Pane**. **Save** the query as **Lastname Firstname 13E Private Grants Query** and then switch to **Design** view. Redesign the query to answer the question, *What is the Grant Name, Department, Award Amount, and Award Date for grants that have a Type of Private, sorted in alphabetical order by Grant Name?* Do not display the Type field in the query results; display the fields in the order listed in the question. With **Normal** margins, create a paper or electronic printout as directed. **Close** the query, saving changes to the query design.

8 **Create** a query in **Query Design** view, using the **13E Organizations** table to answer the question, *What is the Organization Name, Contact Name, and Contact Phone where the Contact Phone number is missing from the table, sorted in alphabetical order by the Organization Name?* Two records meet the criteria. **Save** the query as **Lastname Firstname 13E Missing Phone# Query** and then create a paper or electronic printout as directed. **Close** the query.

9 **Open** the **Navigation Pane** and widen it so that all object names display fully. In **Backstage** view, click **Close Database**, and then click **Exit**. As directed by your instructor, submit your database and the seven paper or electronic printouts—relationship report, sorted table, and five queries—that are the results of this project.

End **You have completed Project 13E**

Content-Based Assessments

Apply 13C skills from these Objectives:

13 Specify Numeric Criteria in a Query

14 Use Compound Criteria

15 Create a Query Based on More Than One Table

16 Use Wildcards in a Query

17 Use Calculated Fields in a Query

18 Calculate Statistics and Group Data in a Query

19 Create a Crosstab Query

Mastering Access | Project 13F Events and Clients

In the following Mastering Access project, you will assist Hank Schwan, the Capital Cities Community College Facilities Manager, in using his database to answer questions about facilities that the college rents to community and private organizations at times when the facilities are not in use for college activities. Your results will look similar to Figure 13.85.

Project Files

For Project 13F, you will need the following files:

a13F_Events_Clients
e13F_Rental_Clients (Excel file)

You will save your database as:

Lastname_Firstname_13F_Events_Clients

Project Results

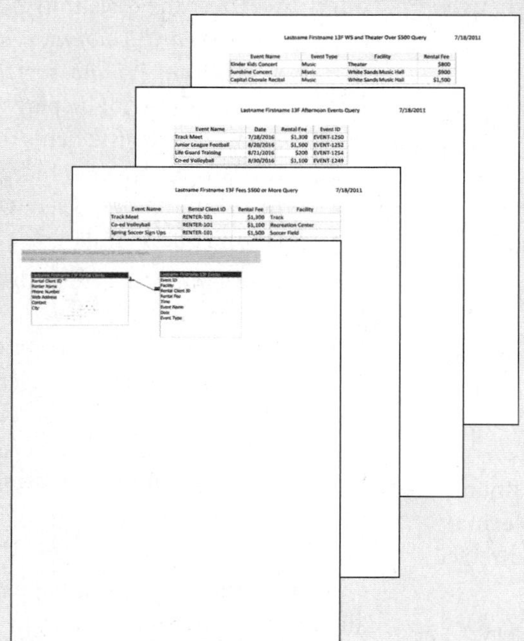

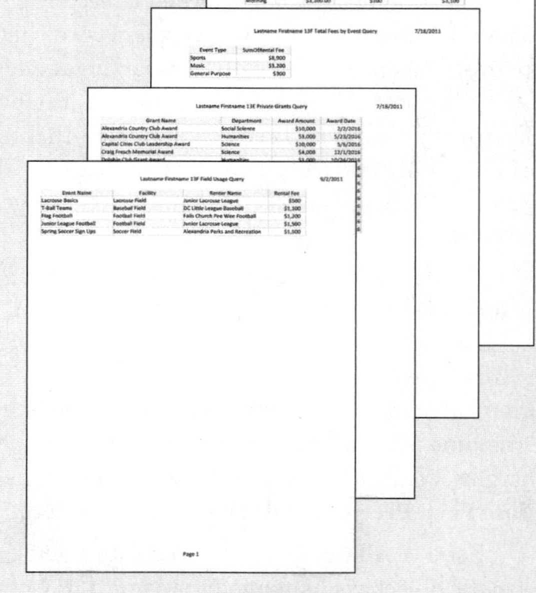

Figure 13.85

(Project 13F Events and Clients continues on the next page)

Mastering Access | Project 13F Events and Clients (continued)

1 **Start** Access. From your student files, open the **a13F_Events_Clients** database. Save the database in your **All In One Chapter 13** folder as **Lastname_Firstname_13F_Events_Clients** and then enable the content. In the **Navigation Pane**, **Rename** the table by adding **Lastname Firstname** to the beginning of the table name.

2 **Import** the **e13F_Rental_Clients** Excel spreadsheet from the student data files that accompany this textbook into the current database as a new table. Designate the first row of the spreadsheet as column headings. Select the **Rental Client ID** field as the primary key. Name the table **Lastname Firstname 13F Rental Clients** and then widen the **Navigation Pane** to display fully the two table names. **Open** both tables and examine their contents to become familiar with the data. In the **13F Rental Clients** table, apply **Best Fit** to all of the columns. **Close** both tables, saving changes, and then **Close** the **Navigation Pane**.

3 Create a *one-to-many* relationship between the **13F Rental Clients** table and the **13F Events** table based on the **Rental Client ID** field, and then **Enforce Referential Integrity**. *One* rental client can have many events. Create a **Relationship Report**, saving it with the default name. Create a paper or electronic printout as directed, and then **Close** all open objects, saving changes if prompted.

4 **Create** a query in **Query Design** view using the **13F Events** table to answer the question, *What is the Event Name, Rental Client ID, and Rental Fee for events with fees greater than or equal to $500, and in which Facility was the event held displayed in ascending order by Rental Client ID?* Display the fields in the order listed in the question. Eleven records meet the criteria. **Save** the query as **Lastname Firstname 13F Fees $500 or More Query** Create a paper or electronic printout as directed. Leave the query open.

5 Using the **13F Fees $500 or More Query** object, create a new query, and save it as **Lastname Firstname 13F Afternoon Events Query** Redesign the query to answer the questions, *Which Events were held in the Afternoon between 7/1/16 and 8/31/16, in chronological order by date, what was the Rental Fee, and what was the Event ID?* (Hint: Open the 13F Events table to see how the Time field data is stored.) Do not display the **Time** field in the results, and do not restrict the results by **Rental Fee**. Four records meet the criteria. Create a paper or electronic printout as directed, **Close** the query, and **Save** changes to the design.

6 **Create** a query in **Query Design** view using the **13F Events** table to answer the question, *Which Events and Event Types were held in either the White Sands Music Hall or the Theater that had Rental Fees greater than $500?* Display the fields in the order listed in the question. Three records meet the criteria. **Save** the query as **Lastname Firstname 13F WS and Theater Over $500 Query** and then create a paper or electronic printout as directed. **Close** the query.

7 **Create** a query in **Query Design** view using both tables to answer the question, *Which Events were held on one of the sports fields, for which Renter Name, and what was the Rental Fee in order of lowest fee to highest fee?* (Hint: Use a wildcard with the word *Field*.) Display the fields in the order listed in the question. Five records meet the criteria. **Save** the query as **Lastname Firstname 13F Field Usage Query** and then with **Normal** margins, create a paper or electronic printout as directed. **Close** the query.

8 The college Alumni Association will donate money to the Building Fund in an amount based on 10 percent of total facility rental fees. **Create** a query in **Query Design** view using the **13F Events** table to answer the question, *In ascending order by Event ID, what will be the total of each Rental Fee if the Alumni Association donates an additional 10% of each fee?* (Hint: First compute the amount of the donation, name the new field **Donation Amount** and run the query to view the results. Then calculate the new rental fee and name the new field **Rental Fee with Donation**) **Run** the query.

Switch back to **Design** view, change the properties of the new fields to display in **Currency** format with **0** decimal places, and then **Run** the query again. For *EVENT-1244, the Donation Amount is $150 and the Rental Fee with Donation is $1,650*. Apply **Best Fit** to the columns in the query results. **Save** the query as **Lastname Firstname 13F Alumni Donation Query** and then create a paper or electronic printout as directed. **Close** the query.

(Project 13F Events and Clients continues on the next page)

Mastering Access | Project 13F Events and Clients (continued)

9 **Create** a query in **Query Design** view using the **13F Events** table and the **Sum** aggregate function to answer the question, *In descending order by Rental Fee, what are the total Rental Fees for each Event Type?* Change the properties of the appropriate field to display **Currency** format with **0** decimal places, and then **Run** the query. For a *Sports* Event Type, Rental Fees total *$8,900*. Apply **Best Fit** to the columns in the query results. Save the query as **Lastname Firstname 13F Total Fees by Event Query** and then create a paper or electronic printout as directed. **Close** the query.

10 By using the **Query Wizard**, create a **Crosstab Query** based on the **13F Events** table. Select **Time** as the **row headings** and **Event Type** as the **column headings**. **Sum** the **Rental Fee** field. Name the query **Lastname Firstname 13F Time and Type Crosstab Query** Change the design to display **Currency** format with **0** decimal places in the **Rental Fee** column, and then apply **Best Fit** to all of the columns. This query answers the question, *What are the total Rental Fees for each time of the day and for each Event Type?* Create a paper or electronic printout as directed. **Close** the query, saving changes to the design.

11 **Open** the **Navigation Pane** and widen it so that all object names display fully. In **Backstage** view, click **Close Database**, and then click **Exit**. As directed by your instructor, submit your database and the eight paper or electronic printouts—relationship report and seven queries—that are the results of this project.

End **You have completed Project 13F**

Apply **13B** and **13C** skills from these Objectives:

6 Open an Existing Database
7 Create Table Relationships
8 Sort Records in a Table
9 Create a Query in Design View
10 Create a New Query from an Existing Query
11 Sort Query Results
12 Specify Criteria in a Query
13 Specify Numeric Criteria in a Query
14 Use Compound Criteria
15 Create a Query Based on More Than One Table
16 Use Wildcards in a Query
17 Use Calculated Fields in a Query
18 Calculate Statistics and Group Data in a Query
19 Create a Crosstab Query

Mastering Access | Project 13G Academic Scholarships

In the following Mastering Access project, you will assist Thao Nguyen, Director of Academic Scholarships, in using her database to answer questions about scholarships awarded to students. Your results will look similar to Figure 13.86.

Project Files

For Project 13G, you will need the following file:

a13G_Academic_Scholarships

You will save your database as:

Lastname_Firstname_13G_Academic_Scholarships

Project Results

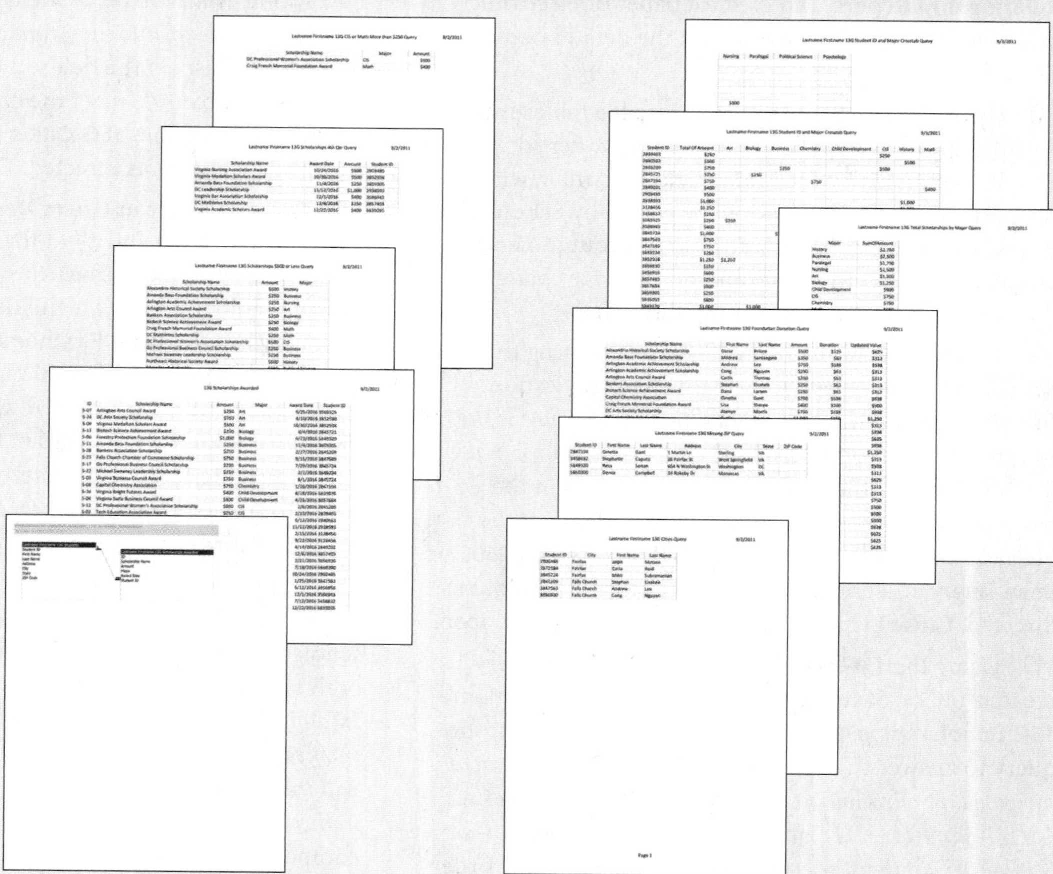

Figure 13.86

(Project 13G Academic Scholarships continues on the next page)

Mastering Access | Project 13G Academic Scholarships (continued)

1 **Start** Access. From your student files, open the **a13G_Academic_Scholarships** database. Save the database in your **All In One Chapter 13** folder as **Lastname_Firstname_13G_Academic_Scholarships** and then enable the content. **Rename** both tables by adding **Lastname Firstname** to the beginning of the table name, and then widen the **Navigation Pane** to display fully the object names.

2 **Open** the two database tables to become familiar with the data. **Close** the tables, and then create a *one-to-many* relationship between the **13G Students** table and the **13G Scholarships Awarded** table based on the **Student ID** field, and then **Enforce Referential Integrity**; *one* student can have *many* scholarships. Create the **Relationship Report**, and create a paper or electronic printout as directed, saving it with the default name. **Close** all open objects.

3 **Open** the **13G Scholarships Awarded** table, and then Sort the appropriate fields in **Ascending** order so that the records are sorted by the **Major** field, and then, within each **Major**, the records should be sorted by **Scholarship Name**. Create a paper or electronic printout in **Landscape** orientation. **Close** the table, and do not save changes to the table design. **Close** the **Navigation Pane**.

4 **Create** a query in **Query Design** view using the **13G Scholarships Awarded** table to answer the question, *In alphabetical order by Scholarship Name, what is the Amount and Major for scholarships less than or equal to $500?* Display the fields in the order listed in the question. Twenty records meet the criteria. **Save** the query as **Lastname Firstname 13G Scholarships $500 or Less Query** and create a paper or electronic printout as directed. **Close Print Preview**, and leave the query open.

5 Using the **13G Scholarships $500 or Less Query**, create a query. **Save** the Object As **Lastname Firstname 13G Scholarships 4th Qtr Query** and then redesign the query to answer the question, *Which scholarships were awarded, in chronological order by Award Date, between 10/1/16 and 12/31/16, for what amount, and what was Student ID of the student?* Display the fields in the order listed in the question, display only the fields listed in the question, do not restrict the amount, and sort only by date. Seven records meet the criteria. Create a paper or electronic printout as directed. **Close** the query, saving changes.

6 **Create** a query in **Query Design** view using the **13G Scholarships Awarded** table to answer the question, *Which scholarships were awarded for either CIS or Math majors for amounts of more than $250, listed in descending order by amount?* Display the fields in the order listed in the question. Two records meet the criteria. (Hint: If three records display, switch to **Design** view and combine the majors on one criteria line using OR.) **Save** the query as **Lastname Firstname 13G CIS or Math More Than $250 Query** and then create a paper or electronic printout as directed. **Close** the query.

7 **Create** a query in **Query Design** view. Use the **13G Students** table and a wildcard to answer the question, *In alphabetical order by City and in alphabetical order by Last Name, what are the Student ID, City, First Name, and Last Name of students from cities that begin with the letter F?* Display the fields in the order listed in the question. Six records meet the criteria. **Save** the query as **Lastname Firstname 13G Cities Query** Create a paper or electronic printout as directed. **Close** the query.

8 **Create** a query in **Query Design** view using the **13G Students** table and all of the table's fields to answer the question *For which students is the ZIP Code missing?* Four students are missing ZIP Codes. Save the query as **Lastname Firstname 13G Missing ZIP Query** and then, with **Normal** margins, create a paper or electronic printout as directed. **Close** the query. Using the information that displays in the query results, an enrollment clerk can use a reference to look up the ZIP codes for the students and then enter the ZIP codes in the student records in the underlying table.

9 For each scholarship, the college Foundation Board will donate an amount equal to 25 percent of each scholarship. **Create** a query in **Query Design** view. Use both tables and calculated fields to answer the question, *In alphabetical order by scholarship name, and including the first and last name of the scholarship recipient, what will the value of each scholarship be if the Foundation makes a matching 25 percent donation?* (Hint: First compute the amount of the donation, naming the new field **Donation** and then calculate the new scholarship value, naming the new field **Updated Value**)

Run the query, switch back to **Design** view, and as necessary, change the properties of all the numeric fields to display in **Currency** format with **0** decimal places, and

(Project 13G Academic Scholarships continues on the next page)

Mastering Access | Project 13G Academic Scholarships (continued)

then **Run** the query. For the *Alexandria Historical Society Scholarship*, the *Donation* is *$120* and the *New Value* is *$625.* Apply **Best Fit** to the columns in the query results. **Save** the query as **Lastname Firstname 13G Foundation Donation Query** and then create a paper or electronic printout in **Landscape** orientation as directed. **Close** the query.

10 **Create** a new query in **Query Design** view. Use the **13G Scholarships Awarded** table and the **Sum** aggregate function to answer the question, *For each major, in descending order by amount, what are the total scholarship amounts?* Display the fields in the order listed in the question. Use the **Property Sheet** to display the sums in the **Currency** format with **0** decimal places. *History* majors received *$2,750* in scholarships. Apply **Best Fit** to the columns in the query results. **Save** the query as **Lastname Firstname 13G Total Scholarships by Major Query** and then create a paper or electronic printout as directed. **Close** the query.

11 **Create** a **Crosstab Query** using the **13G Scholarships Awarded** table. Use the **Student ID** field as row headings and the **Major** field as column headings to answer the question, *For each student or major, what is the total scholarship Amount awarded?* Name the query **Lastname Firstname 13G Student ID and Major Crosstab Query** In **Design** view, apply **0** decimal places to the **Amount** and **Total Amount** fields. Apply **Best Fit** to the columns in the query results. **Save** the query, and then as directed, create a paper or electronic printout in **Landscape** orientation—the query results will print on two pages. **Close** the query.

12 **Open** the **Navigation Pane** and widen it to display all of the object names. In **Backstage** view, click **Close Database**, and then click **Exit**. As directed by your instructor, submit your database and the ten paper or electronic printouts—relationship report, sorted table, and eight queries—that are the results of this project.

End **You have completed Project 13G**

Explore Cloud Computing Using Windows Live and Microsoft Office Web Apps

OUTCOMES At the end of this chapter you will be able to:	**OBJECTIVES** Mastering these objectives will enable you to:
PROJECT 14A Use Windows Live Email, Calendar, and Messenger to communicate online.	1. Create a Windows Live Account (p. 657) 2. Send and Receive Email (p. 662) 3. Manage and Share Your Windows Live Calendar (p. 668) 4. Use Windows Live Messenger to Communicate (p. 673)
PROJECT 14B Use Office Web Apps to create, edit, manage, and collaborate on documents.	5. Use Windows Live SkyDrive (p. 678) 6. Use Office Web Apps to Create and Edit a Word Document (p. 680) 7. Use Office Web Apps to Create and Edit an Excel Workbook (p. 685) 8. Use Office Web Apps to Create and Edit a PowerPoint Presentation (p. 689) 9. Share and Collaborate on Office Documents in Windows Live (p. 690)

© Poznyakov/Shutterstock

Job Focus: College Library Assistant

In This Chapter

With a Windows Live ID, you can store and share files online by using Windows Live SkyDrive, create and store Office Web Apps documents, and communicate by using email and instant messaging. As a Windows Vista or Windows 7 user with an Internet connection, you have access to Windows Live Essentials, a set of free programs available for download.

In this chapter, you will learn how a College Library Assistant creates a free Windows Live account and uses its SkyDrive to store Microsoft Office documents on the Web. You will also see how a College Library Assistant uses Microsoft Office Web Apps to create, edit, store, and collaborate on documents in a cloud computing environment. Additionally, you will learn how a College Library Assistant creates a OneNote notebook and stores it on the Web. Because the daily operations of organizations increasingly rely on real time collaboration by sharing information on the Web, it will be valuable for you to practice using these tools and applications. You might already be familiar and comfortable with cloud-based applications in the area of games and entertainment.

Project 14A Windows Live Email, Calendar, and Messenger

Project Activities

In Activities 14.01 through 14.08, you will create a Windows Live account with a secure password and profile. The CapCCC Library Book Club members use their Windows Live accounts to communicate using email, manage their calendars, and communicate instantly. You will create snip files that look similar to Figure 14.1.

Project Files

For Project 14A, you will not need any files.

You will save your files as:

Lastname_Firstname_14A_Profile_Details.jpg
Lastname_Firstname_14A_Email_Reply.jpg
Lastname_Firstname_14A_Deleted_Folder.jpg
Lastname_Firstname_14A_To-do.jpg
Lastname_Firstname_14A_Calendar.jpg
Lastname_Firstname_14A_Instant_Messenger.jpg

Project Results

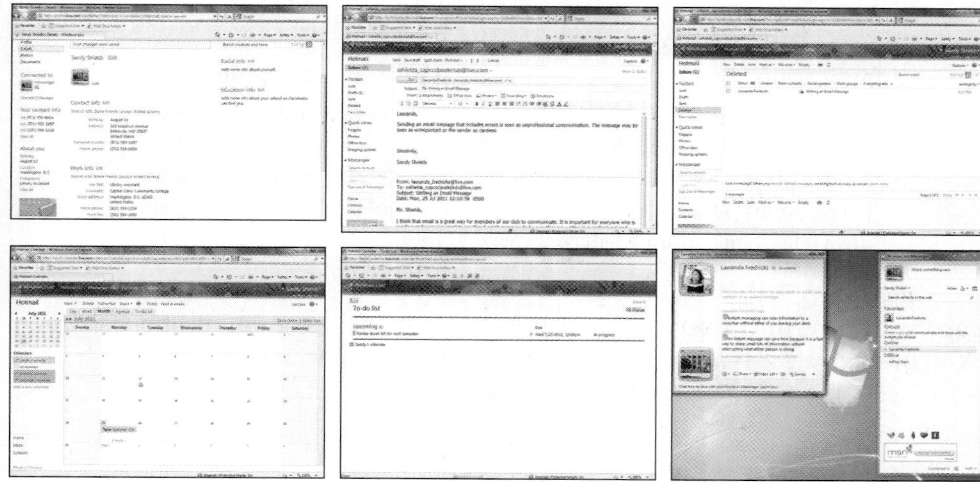

Figure 14.1
Project 14A Windows Live Email, Calendar, and Messenger

Objective 1 | Create a Windows Live Account

Alert! | When you reach Activity 14.03 of this project, identify a classmate with whom you can partner to complete the project, and then set a time and place to work together.

In Objectives 3 through 5 of this project, which includes Activities 14.03 through 14.08, you will benefit from working together with a classmate to exchange emails, share calendars, and use instant messaging. Identify a partner now, and then with him or her, agree on a convenient time and place to work through Activities 14.03 through 14.08. You will need approximately 30 minutes.

Windows Live is a collection of programs and services for individuals that work together, and which includes Hotmail email, SkyDrive, ***Office Web Apps***, Windows Live Messenger ***instant messaging (IM)***, applications such as Photo Gallery and Movie Maker, and mobile phone applications. Office Web Apps are the online companions to Microsoft Office Word, Excel, PowerPoint, and OneNote. You can use Office Web Apps to create, access, share, and perform light editing on Microsoft Office documents from any computer connected to the Internet and using a supported ***Web browser***—software that displays Web pages, for example, Internet Explorer, Firefox, Safari, and Chrome.

One way to think about all of the Windows Live technologies is to consider the ***platform***—the underlying hardware or software for a system—on which you might use them, for example on the Web, on your PC, or on your smartphone.

Windows Live Programs and Services

On the Web as an online service	On your PC (desktop, laptop, netbook, tablet) as a Windows application	On your smartphone
Windows Live Home view, Profile, Hotmail, People, Calendar, Photos, Events, SkyDrive, Groups, and Office Web Apps.	The suite of programs referred to as ***Windows Live Essentials***, which includes Messenger, Mail, Mesh, Writer, Photo Gallery, Movie Maker, Bing Toolbar, and Family Safety.	The mobile programs and services that enable you to access Hotmail, Messenger, music, and games, as well as photos from your smartphone.

Windows Live provides free access to these online services and applications to make communication, sharing, and storage easy and accessible. You must create a ***Windows Live ID***—an account with which you can sign in to the Windows Live technologies—to access and use these features from any of the three platforms.

Activity 14.01 | Creating a Windows Live Account

In this activity, you will create a Windows Live account if you do not already have one.

Alert! | Do you already have a Windows Live ID?

If you already have a Windows Live account and ID, you can skip this activity and begin with Activity 14.02.

1 Start your Web browser, navigate to http://explore.live.com and then compare your screen with Figure 14.2.

Information about the various services within Windows Live is constantly being updated by Microsoft, so your screen may not match exactly the one shown in Figure 14.2.

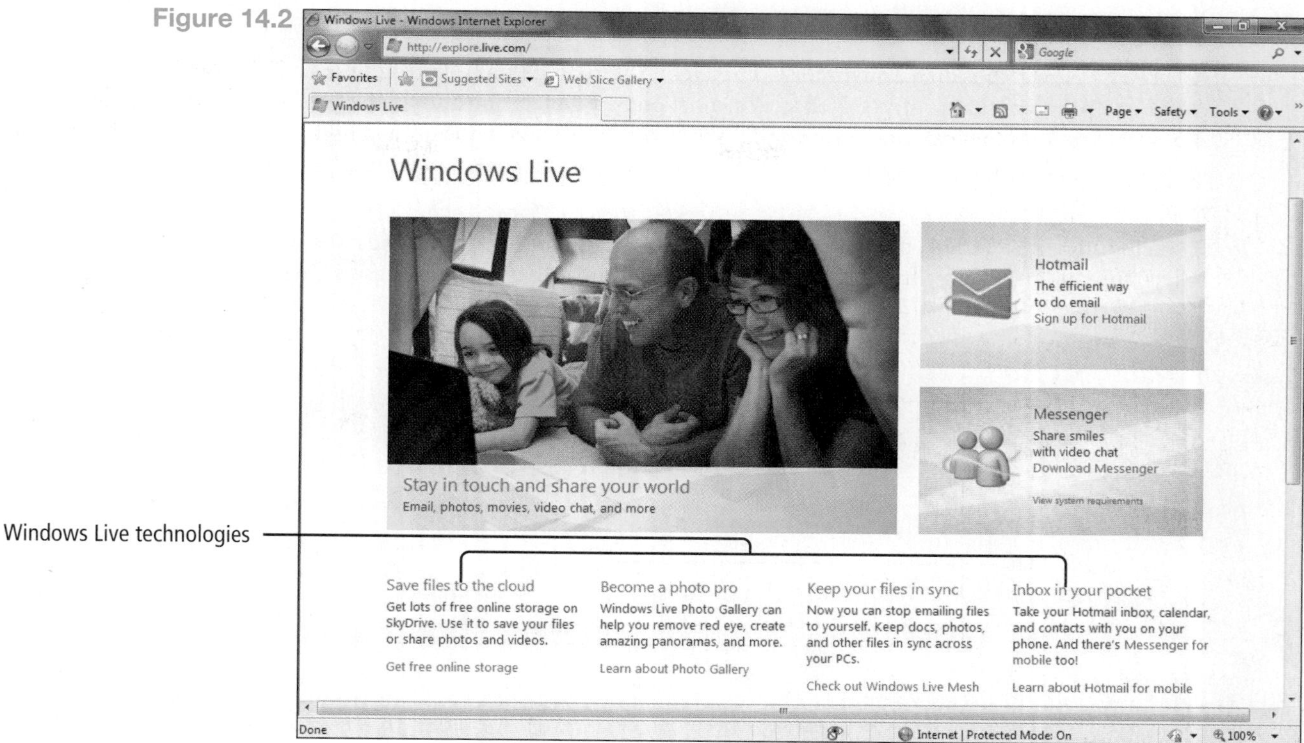

Figure 14.2

2 Locate and click **Sign up for Hotmail**, click in the **Windows Live ID** box, and then type the name you want to use as your Windows Live ID, for example *Firstname_Lastname* using the underscore instead of spaces. In the second box, click the arrow, and then click **live.com**.

The live.com designation is considered to be more modern than the hotmail.com designation, although you can use either. The system will check the availability of your selected address. If the first address is not available, try variations using your middle initial, last name first, and so on, until you have a logical address that includes your name.

Note | Be Sure You Have an Email Address for Professional Messages

It is a good idea to create an email address to use professionally, for example, when contacting potential employers. If you have an email address with a cute or descriptive name, for example, luv2dance@capccc.edu, use it only to communicate with friends and family.

3 Create a password. Type an alternate email address or choose a security question for password reset in a manner similar to Figure 14.3.

A ***strong password*** uses a combination of uppercase letters, lowercase letters, numbers, and special characters in a character string so it will be hard to guess and therefore will keep your account secure. A ***weak password***—one that is short and consists of only letters in a single case—can compromise the security of your data because it is easy to guess.

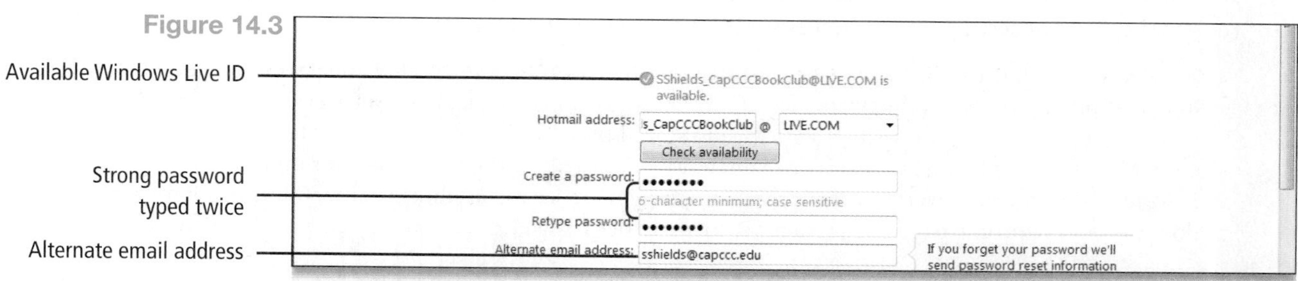

Figure 14.3

4 Fill in the remainder of the form and the CAPTCHA in a manner similar to Figure 14.4.

A ***CAPTCHA***, which is an acronym for Completely Automated Public Turing Test To Tell Computers and Humans Apart, is a program that protects Web sites against ***bots*** by generating and grading tests that only humans can pass. A bot is a program that can run automated tasks over the Internet, typically at a higher rate than would be possible for a human alone. Humans can read distorted text, like the text shown in Figure 14.4, but current computers cannot.

By including a CAPTCHA, the site prevents bots from signing up for thousands of email accounts every minute—only a human can obtain a free account. You can find many other reasons to use a CAPTCHA at *www.captcha.net*

Figure 14.4

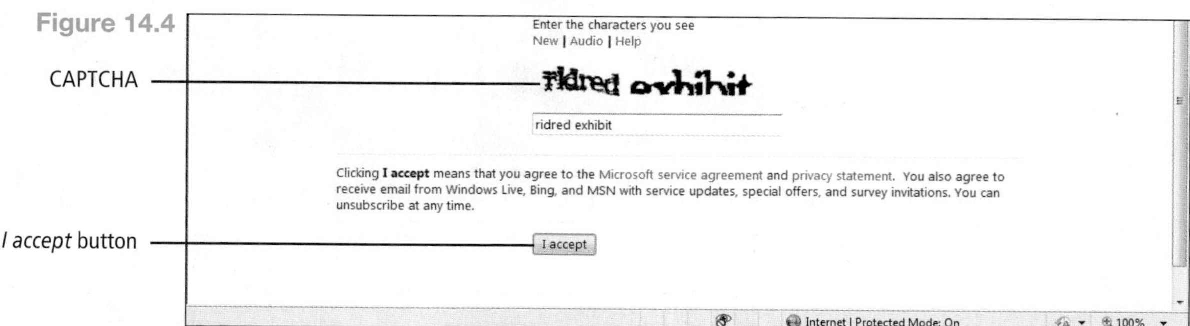

5 At the bottom of the screen, click **I accept**. Remain signed in to your account for the next activity, and then compare your screen with Figure 14.5.

Your new Windows Live site displays with your name in the upper right corner. Because this is a free set of applications, some advertising may display.

Figure 14.5

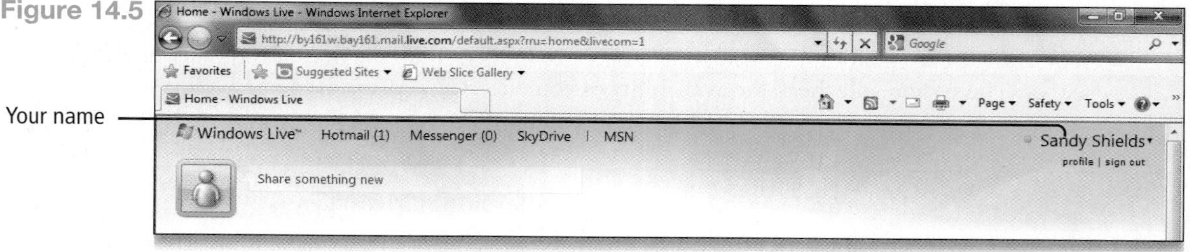

Activity 14.02 | Creating Your Windows Live Profile

Because you will use Windows Live to communicate and share information with others online, you should create a ***profile*** to identify yourself in a manner appropriate for the particular account. You might have a profile on other social networking sites such as Facebook, Twitter, or LinkedIn. Those profiles, however, are for different purposes and include different types of information. Consider the level of detail you want to provide in a profile. In Windows Live, and in most other profiles, you can modify the profile settings and details.

1 If necessary, sign in to your Windows Live account. In the upper right corner of your window, click **profile**, review the privacy settings, and then compare your screen with Figure 14.6.

The profile window displays so you can secure your Windows Live account at an appropriate level before entering information. The *Public* setting provides unlimited access to everyone; it allows everyone to search for you, see your profile, and see your Windows Live activity and stored files. The *Limited* setting protects your online activity and content. It allows everyone to search for you, but you must allow them to view your online activity and content. The *Private* setting restricts everyone from searching for you or seeing anything online unless you have allowed them to do so. From the profile page, the privacy settings can be changed at any time by clicking the Privacy settings menu.

Figure 14.6

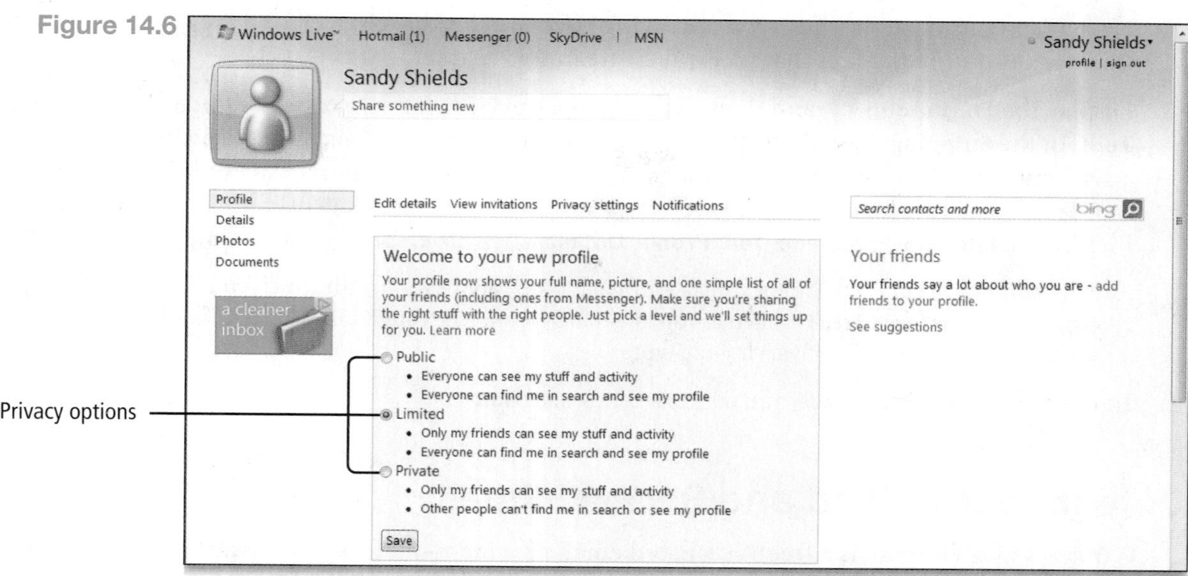

2 Click **Save** to accept the default setting providing *Limited* access to your account. If necessary, **Close** the summary box.

3 Review the way your name will appear in Windows Live applications. Make changes, if necessary, and then click **Save**.

4 Click the **Add a photo** button to add a picture to identify yourself. Browse to the location where the picture is stored, and double-click the file. Drag or resize the preview box to capture the area that you like, and then click **Save**.

Adding a photo to your account will provide you with an icon that displays when you access your account. The image can be changed by returning to the profile at any time.

5 Click **Edit details** to edit your contact, work, and general information. Click **Save** on each page before clicking on another. When you are finished, your screen will look similar to Figure 14.7.

Additional sections are also available for you to add information; be cautious about the details you provide if you chose a Public privacy setting.

Figure 14.7

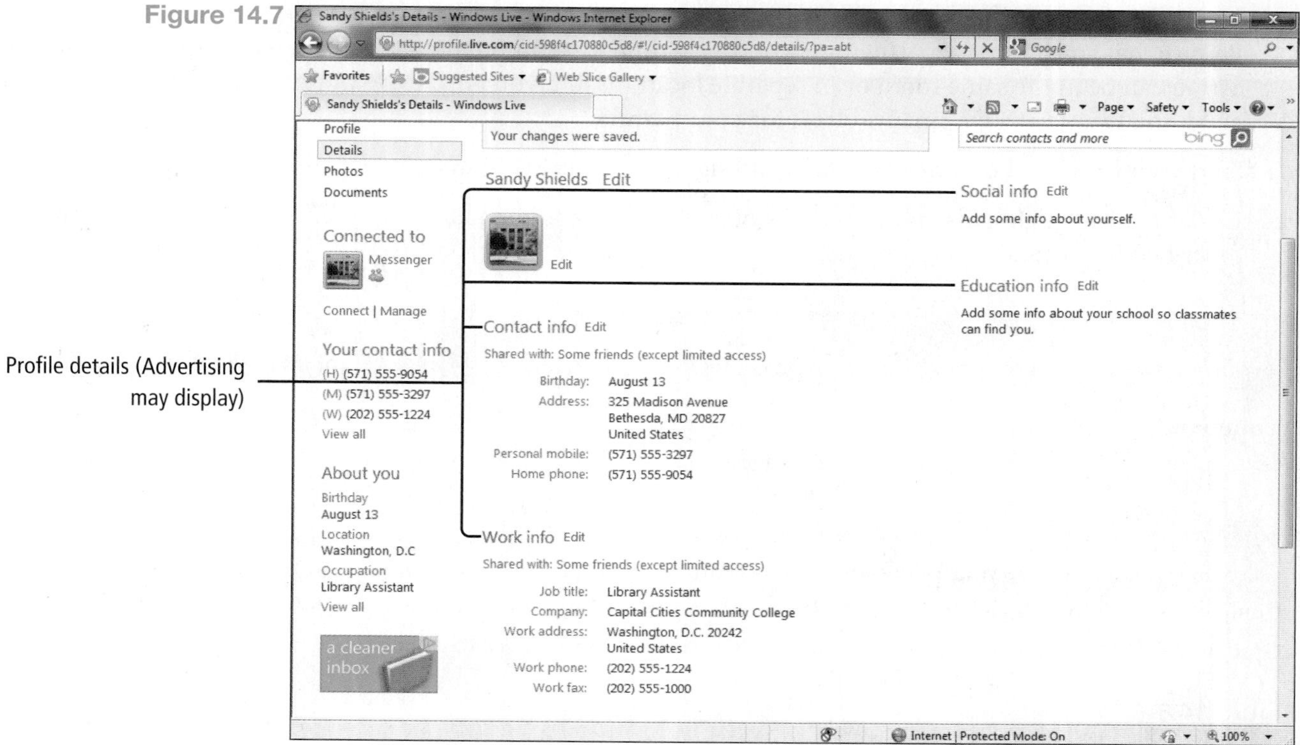

6 Navigate to the location where you are saving your files for this chapter, and create a folder named **All In One Chapter 14** to store the files that you will create in this chapter.

7 Display the **Start** menu, and then click **All Programs**. Click the **Accessories** folder, and then click **Snipping Tool**. In the **Snipping Tool** dialog box, click the **New arrow**. On the displayed list, click **Window Snip**. Click anywhere in the window to capture the window, and then click the **Save Snip** button. Navigate to your **All In One Chapter 14** folder, click the **Save as type arrow**, and then click **JPEG** file. Click in the **File name** box, and then type **Lastname_Firstname_14A_Profile_Details** Click **Save**. **Close** the **Snipping Tool** window.

The ***Snipping Tool*** is a Windows Vista and Windows 7 application with which you can capture all or part of a screen. The captured area is called a ***snip***; it can be annotated using tools provided, copied to a document or email, or saved as an image file of varying file types.

8 In the upper right corner of your window, click **sign out**.

Objective 2 | Send and Receive Email

Windows Live Hotmail is a free Web-based email provider—there is no software to download or install on your computer. ***Email*** is a method of exchanging messages via the Internet where the message resides in the recipient's mail box until he or she signs in to read it. Windows Live refers to the Microsoft email service called ***Hotmail***, whether you are using an @live.com or @hotmail.com Windows Live ID. Accessing Hotmail enables you to create a customized environment for handling, sending, and receiving email messages.

Activity 14.03 | Using Hotmail

In this activity, you will customize your email window.

Alert! | Identify a classmate with whom you can partner to complete Activities 14.03 through 14.08 of this project, and then set a time and place to work together.

In Objectives 2 through 4 of this project, which includes Activities 14.03 through 14.08, you will benefit from working together with a classmate to exchange emails, share calendars, and use instant messaging. With the partner you have identified, agree on a convenient time and place to work through Activities 14.03 through 14.08 together. Allow approximately 30 minutes.

1 Be sure that you and your partner are working at different computers and can access the Internet—the two of you can be in the same room or in separate locations, but you need to be working at the same time. Write down the Windows Live email address for your partner.

2 Start your browser, go to **www.live.com** and sign in to your Windows Live account.

3 Under **Hotmail highlights**, notice the row of commands, and then take a moment to study these commands as described in the table in Figure 14.8.

Hotmail Commands

Command	Description
Go to inbox	Directs you to a list of the messages you have received; a number in parentheses refers to the number of new, unread messages currently in your Inbox.
Send email	Opens a new, blank message window to compose an email.
Calendar	Displays your Windows Live Calendar.
Contacts	Includes options for editing your contact list, sending email, and managing friends.
Options	Includes options for customizing the way you send and receive email.

Figure 14.8

4 Under **Hotmail highlights**, in the row of commands, click **Options** to choose which page to display when you sign in to Hotmail. Compare your screen with Figure 14.9.

The default setting displays the Windows Live Home screen—the window you viewed when you signed in. Alternatively, you can display the Hotmail Inbox first.

Figure 14.9

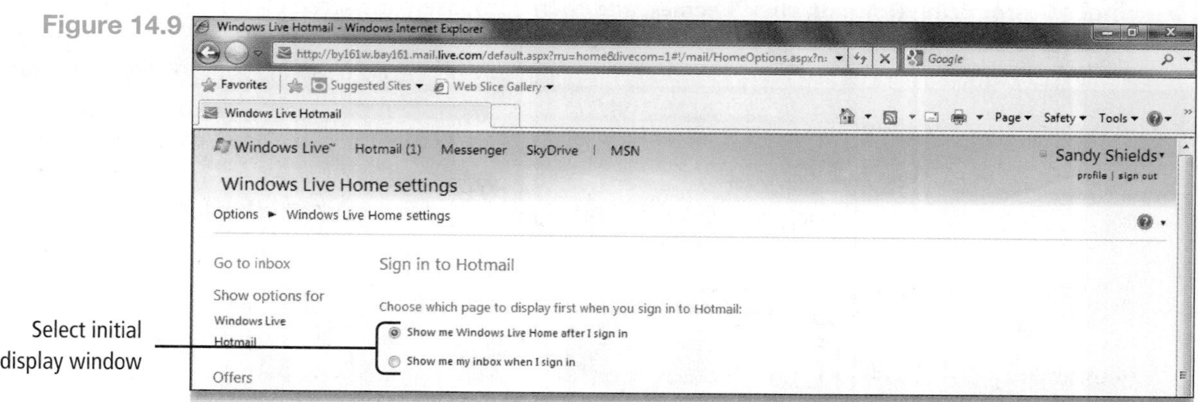

5 On the left, under **Show options for**, click **Hotmail** to view options related to managing your account, writing email, reading email, preventing junk email, customizing Hotmail, and customizing your contacts. Under **Writing email**, click **Message font and signature**, and then compare your screen with Figure 14.10.

You can select a font to start with when you write a new message and create a personal signature to display at the end of all of your email messages.

Figure 14.10

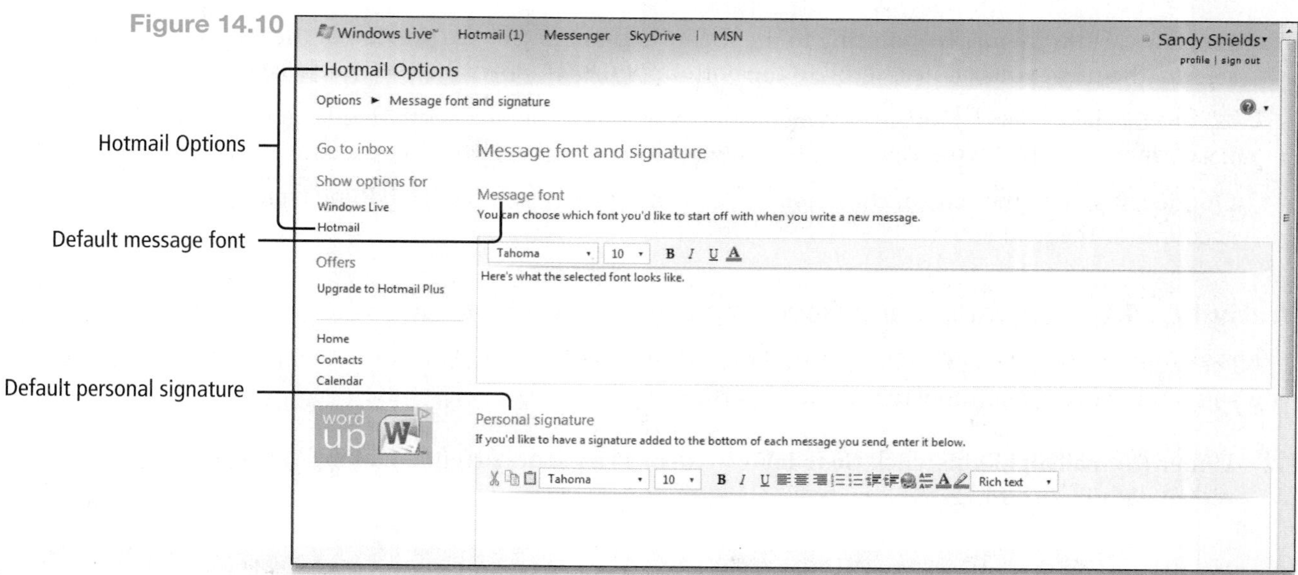

6 Under **Message font**, click **the Font size arrow** [11 ▾], and then click **12**.

The default font size is 10 points, so the new font size will be a little larger and easier to read on a computer monitor.

7 Under **Personal signature**, click the **Font size arrow** [11 ▾], and then click **12**. Click in the area below the toolbar, type **Sincerely,** press Enter two times, and then type your first and last name. Scroll down to view the Save button, if necessary, and then click **Save** to apply the default font size and signature to your account.

A polite signature demonstrates professionalism; be sure there are no typographical errors. By setting a default signature with the same font settings as your email message, you save time and present a consistent professional image. When necessary, you can replace your default signature by typing a different one.

8 Under **Writing email**, click **Saving sent messages**. Be sure the **Save all sent messages in the Sent items folder** option button is selected, and then click **Save**.

Saving the email messages that you send confirms a message was sent to the recipient on a particular date and time. This can be a good reference for later communication.

9 Under **Customizing Hotmail**, click **Themes**, and then compare your screen with Figure 14.11.

Figure 14.11

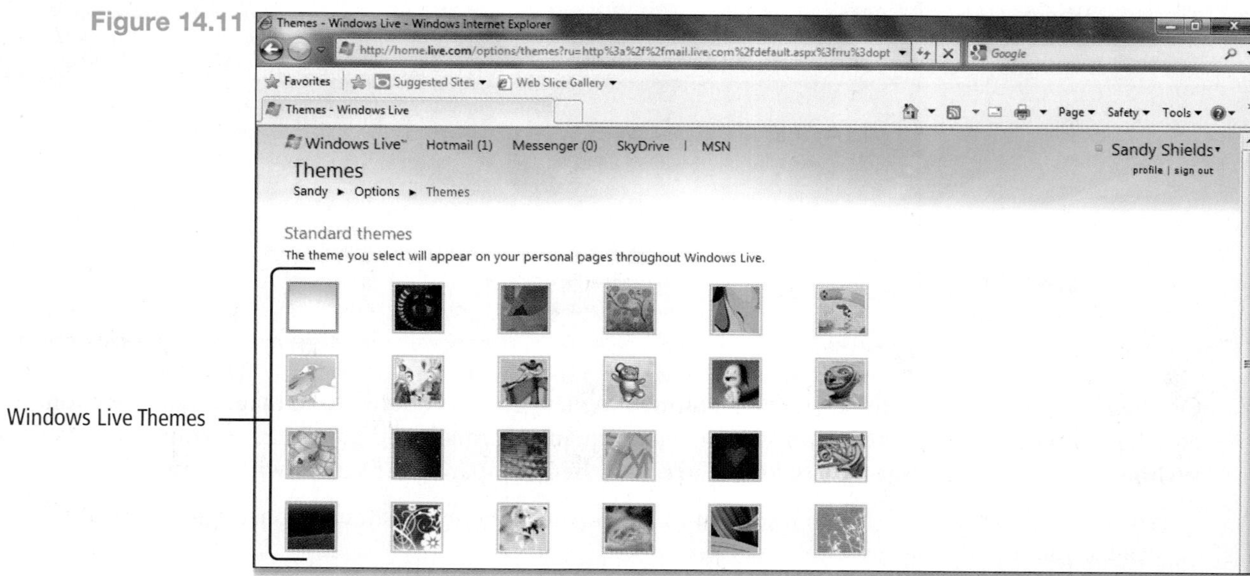

10 Preview various themes by pointing to the theme and looking at the preview at the top of the screen. Click to select a theme of your choice, scroll to the bottom of the window, and then click **Save**.

The theme is applied throughout Windows Live applications; it modifies the header graphics and the color scheme of your Hotmail window. Here the Chrysanthemums theme is applied.

11 On the left side of the screen, click **Home** to return to the Windows Live Home page. Stay signed in to your account for the next activity.

Activity 14.04 | Sending and Receiving Email Using Hotmail

The members of the CapCCC Book Club use email to stay in contact regarding club activities. In this activity, you will send, receive, and reply to an email by using Hotmail.

1 Under **Hotmail highlights**, click **Go to inbox** to display a list of current email messages, and then compare your screen with Figure 14.12.

Figure 14.12

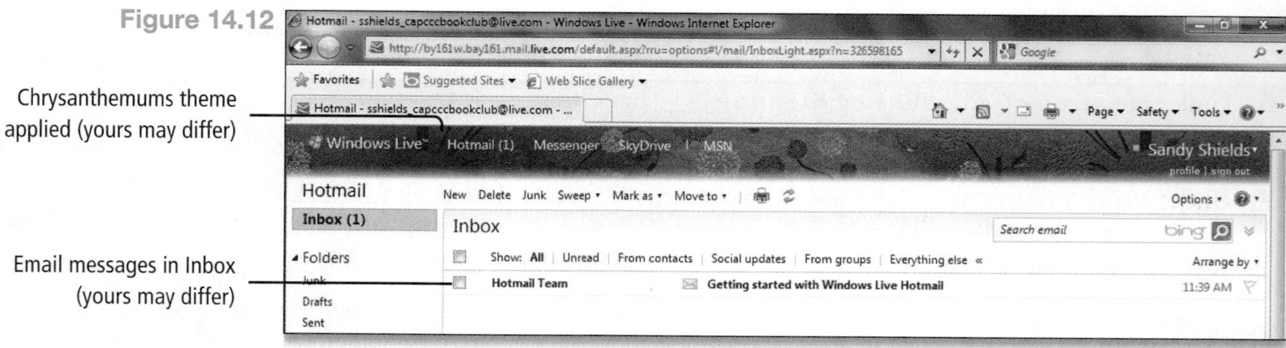

2 At the top of the window, in the row of commands, click **New** to prepare an email to your partner. Click in the **To:** box and type the email address or Windows Live ID for your classmate.

If you have corresponded with your classmate in the past, his or her email address may appear in the box after you have typed the first few characters, at which point you can click his or her name.

3 In the **Subject** box, type **Writing an Email Message** Notice that your default signature displays in the message window.

4 Click above your signature inside the message box. Type your partner's name followed by a comma, and then press Enter two times. Type a short message to your partner identifying a good practice for writing professional emails.

Always include a subject for email messages; it identifies to the recipient the reason for the email. Always begin with a greeting, and type the message using correct grammar, capitalization, and complete sentences. Proofread all messages before sending them.

5 Click **Send**. If necessary, click in the yellow bar, type the CAPTCHA, and verify your account. Then click **Send** again.

Occasionally you may be asked to verify your account with a CAPTCHA, as a security measure. A message indicates that your message was sent.

6 If your message was sent to someone to whom you have never sent email, fill in the **First name** and **Last name** and then click **Add to contacts**. If you have sent email to this person before, he or she is already a contact.

By adding someone to your contacts, in future emails you will be prompted with his or her email address after typing just a few characters.

Note | Receiving an Error Message

If a message cannot be sent, an error message will display identifying a reason and instructions to continue. If you receive an email indicating the email was undeliverable, the message will state the reason, and then you can try again.

7 If necessary, click **Inbox** to redisplay your Inbox. Notice that messages you have received display in bold. Compare your screen with Figure 14.13.

All unread emails appear in bold. If you read and close an email without moving or deleting it, the message will remain in your Inbox, but the bold formatting is removed.

Figure 14.13

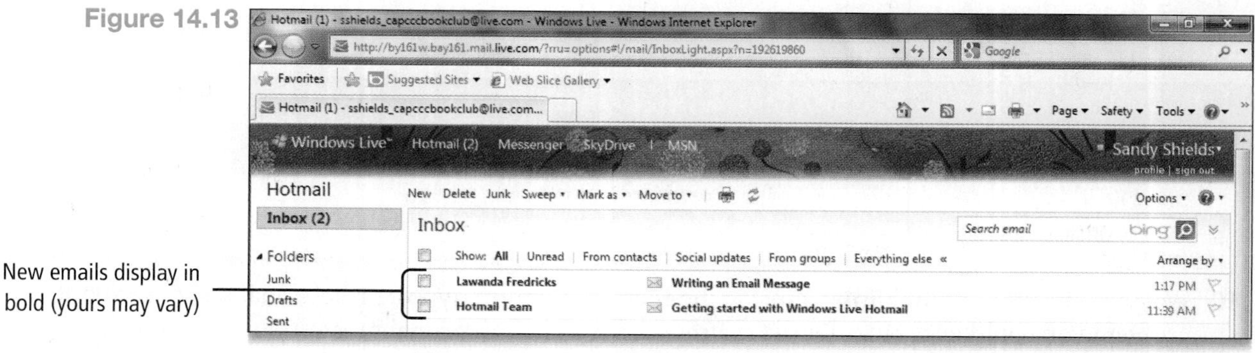

8 Point to the email sent by your partner, and then click to open it. Take a moment to study the commands you have available in email, which display along both the top and the bottom of the message area, as described in the table in Figure 14.14.

Email Commands

Email Command	Description
New	Opens a new email window for you to enter the recipient's email address, a subject, a message, and any attachments.
Reply	Opens a new email window with the original sender's email address in the *To:* box and the original subject with a *RE:* notation to imply the reply is *in reference to* or *in regard to* the previous email subject.
Reply all	Opens a new email window exactly like the one above, except the sender and all other recipients of the previous message are included on the *To:* text box. Use this option cautiously, only when it is necessary for everyone who received the message to see your reply.
Forward	Opens a new email window that includes the message from the previous email and original subject with a *FW:* notation to indicate that the message is being forwarded. Here you can add the email address of the person to whom you are forwarding along with any additional information in the message window.
Delete	Removes the email from your Inbox by sending it to your Deleted folder; your Inbox will display.
Junk	Identifies the email as spam or junk mail and moves it to the Junk folder.
Sweep	Enables you to choose to Move or Delete all messages from the active contact at one time.
Mark as	Displays options to identify the email for later use. Mark an email as *Unread* if you want it to display in bold the next time you open your Inbox—as if it was just received.
Move to	Displays options to select folders in the Inbox for storing emails that you may need to refer to later.

Figure 14.14

9 In the open email message, click **Reply**. Notice that the sender becomes the recipient and that the **Subject** indicates *RE: Writing an Email Message*—the subject of your original message. Compare your screen with Figure 14.15.

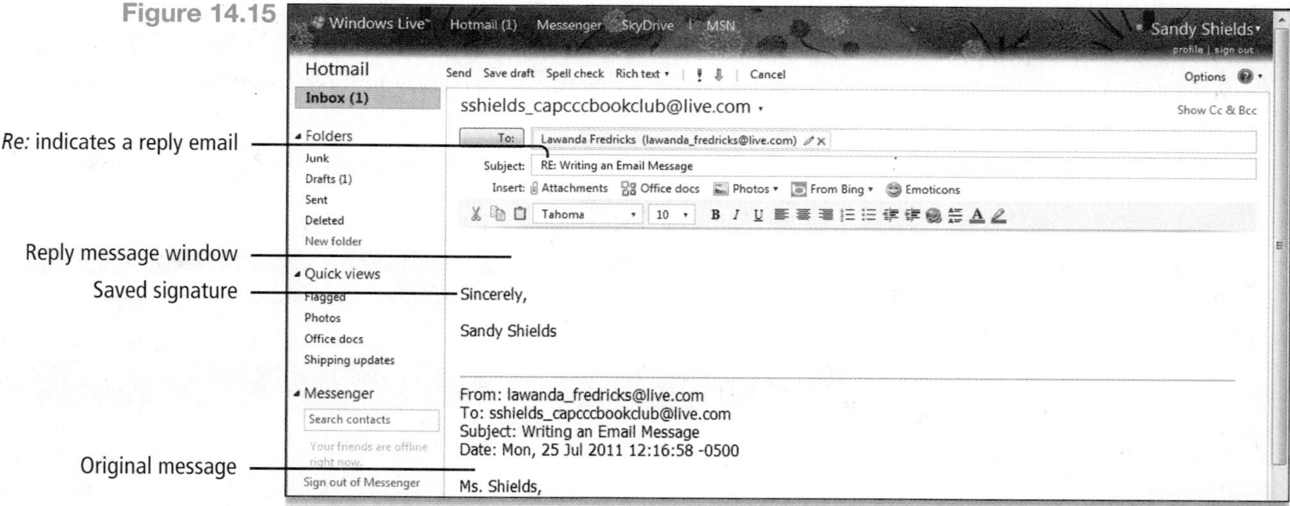

Figure 14.15

10 With the insertion point blinking inside the Message window, type a professional response about a potential problem you could encounter by *not* writing emails in a professional manner. Be sure to include a greeting.

Your default signature is also applied to replies. The original message displays below the reply. This enables the recipient to review the text of the original message if necessary.

11 Start the **Snipping Tool**, and then create a **Window Snip** of your current window. In your **All In One Chapter 14** folder, save the **JPEG** image as **Lastname_Firstname_14A_Email_Reply** Close [X] the **Snipping Tool**.

12 Click **Send** to send the reply email. Click **Return to inbox** to view the original email message you received, and then compare your screen with Figure 14.16.

The window displays the subject line above the header identifying the sender and recipient. Only the original email is displayed in this view, not the reply that you just sent.

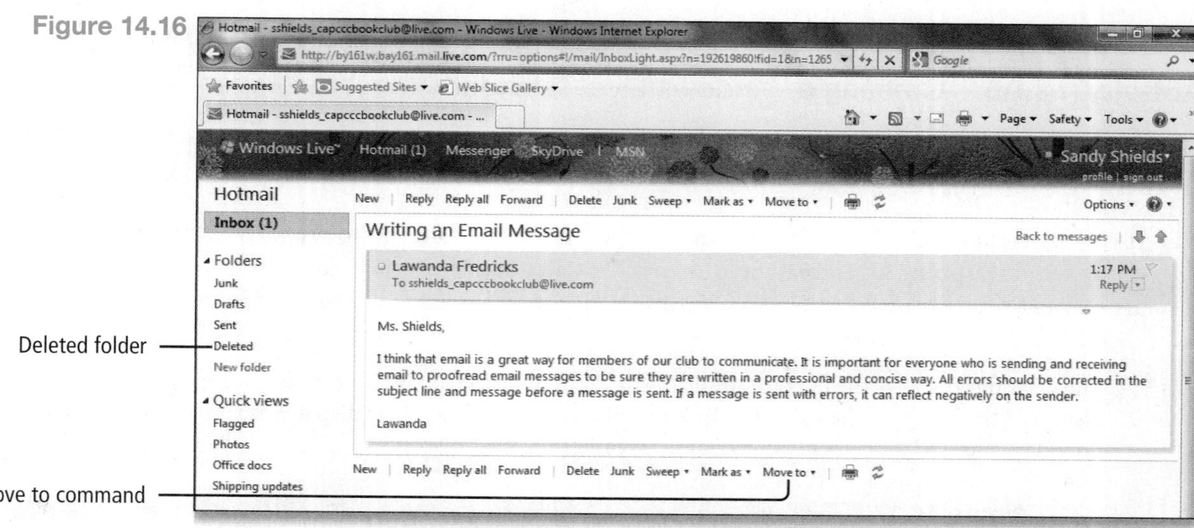

Figure 14.16

13 On the row of commands above the email, click **Move to**, and then click **Deleted**. Then, on the left side of your window, under **Folders**, click **Deleted** to display the contents of the **Deleted** folder.

The Deleted folder stores emails that you want to remove from your Inbox; however, they are not actually removed from your account until you select the emails in the Deleted folder and click Empty. This allows you to separate emails you do not think you need, and then empty the folder when you are certain you will not need them again.

Note | Create Folders to Organize Your Emails

To organize your emails efficiently, create as many folders as you want. From the Folders list on the left side of the Hotmail window, click New folder to name the new folder and add it to your list. All folders on the list will display in the Move to list.

14 Start the **Snipping Tool**, and then create a **Window Snip** of your current window. In your **All In One Chapter 14** folder, save the **JPEG** image as **Lastname_Firstname_14A_Deleted_Folder Close** the **Snipping Tool**.

15 Remain signed in to your account for the next activity.

More Knowledge | What Are Some Good Email Practices?

- **Subject lines that indicate the content of the email**—Help your email recipient know what the content of your email is by typing a clear and concise subject line.
- **Revising the subject line if the topic changes**—If you want to reply to a message but your reply is on a different topic, change the subject line accordingly.
- **Single-topic content**—Your email message should be about the topic in the subject line *and nothing else*. If you need to communicate about another topic, send another email with a clear subject line.
- **A conversational tone that is informal, but not too informal**—Write your message in a friendly tone, but avoid being as casual as you would be with your friends or family members. Within an organization, email messages are considered business communications.
- **Concise writing**—Write your message concisely. Get to the point without wordy phrases.
- **Including only a few short paragraphs**—If you cannot convey your message in a few short paragraphs of no more than two or three sentences each, you should probably call the person or meet with him or her.
- **Proofreading**—Re-read your message to make sure you have not made typing errors or omitted words that would change the context of your message entirely.
- **Never using all capital letters**—Writing in all capital letters is considered to be shouting. Additionally, it is very difficult to read messages in all capital letters.
- **Attaching indicated attachments**—An embarrassing yet common error is to indicate that you are attaching something and then forgetting to attach it. Then you must send another email with the attachment.
- **Never clicking the Send button without a final check**—Before clicking the Send button, re-read your message for clarity and appropriateness, take out any unnecessary text, attach any attachments, and be sure you have used the correct email addresses.

Objective 3 | Manage and Share Your Windows Live Calendar

Activity 14.05 | Creating a Windows Live Calendar

The CapCCC Book Club wants to use Windows Live calendar to track upcoming activities. In this activity, you will enter new events and To-do items on your calendar.

1 If you are not already signed in to your own Windows Live site, go to www.live.com and sign in. At the top of the window, point to **Hotmail**, and then click **Calendar**. If this is your first time using Calendar, click the arrow next to the time zone, click your time zone, and then click Go to your calendar. Compare your screen with Figure 14.17.

The calendar displays the current month. Any content displayed is color-coded according to the Calendar list displayed to the left of the calendar. In Figure 14.17, Sandy's calendar displays, but so do the US Holidays and Birthday calendar. For the next few days, a weather forecast displays.

Figure 14.17

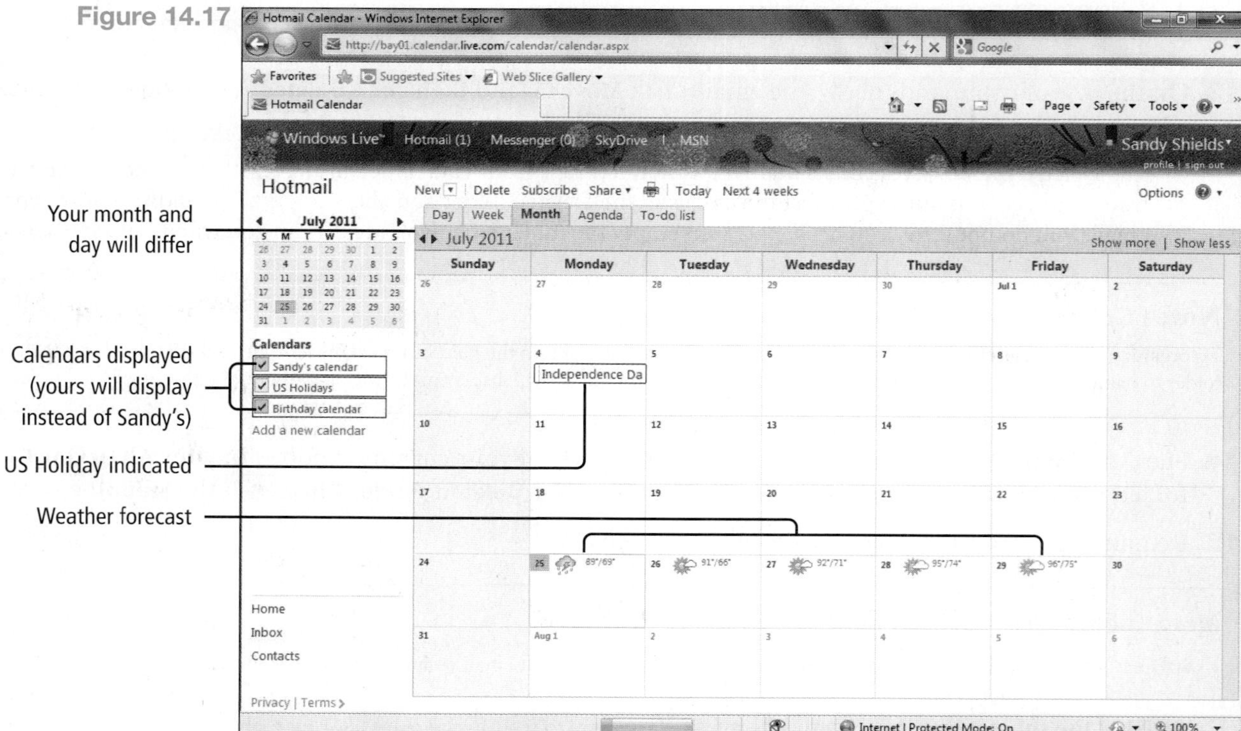

2 On the left, under **Calendars**, click to deselect—remove the check mark—next to **US Holidays**. Then, take a moment to study the commands that display in the row above the calendar as described in the table in Figure 14.18.

Calendar Commands

Command	Description
New	Displays a list of items that you can add to the calendar: Event, To-do, Birthday, Calendar.
Delete	Deletes an event after it has been selected.
Subscribe	Displays a dialog box in which you can subscribe to a public calendar or import from other calendars using the ***.ics file format***. This is a computer file format known as ***iCalendar*** that enables Internet users to send meeting requests and tasks to other Internet users via email.
Share	Displays a list of calendars currently available to share with others.
Print (Printer icon)	Displays the current calendar view in Print Preview; enables you to click a link to print the calendar.
Today	Displays the calendar so the current date is visible.
Next 4 weeks	Displays the calendar with today as the beginning point and showing the next four weeks.

Figure 14.18

3 Click the **New arrow**, and then click **Event** to display the **Add an event** dialog box. Compare your screen with Figure 14.19.

Here you enter the details of the event and the calendar in which it should be placed. You could also add a birthday to this calendar to serve as a reminder or a To-do item to keep track of the progress on a project.

Figure 14.19

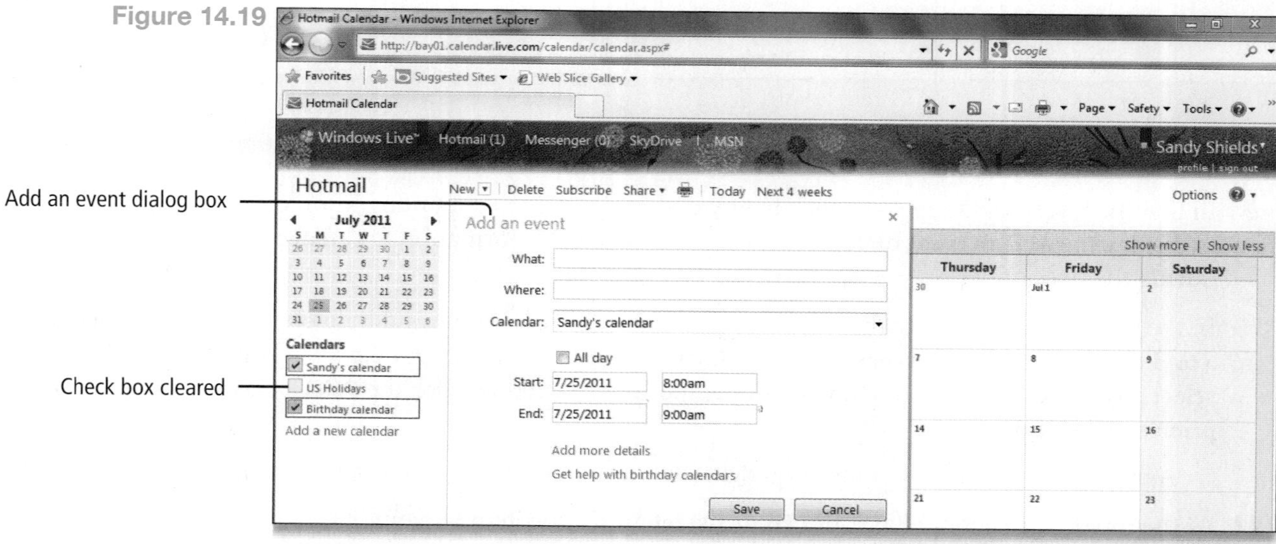

4 In the **What** box, type **Summer Orientation** Click in the **Where** box and type **3B Library Annex** Verify that today's date displays as the **Start** date. To the right of **Start**, click in the time box, and then click **7:00pm**. Set the **End** time to **8:30pm**. Click **Save** to add the event to your calendar.

5 Point to the event on your calendar, and notice that all of the information regarding the event displays.

Here, you can click *Edit event* to make any changes to the date or reminders, or click *Delete event* to remove it from the calendar.

6 At the top of the calendar, click the **Day tab** to display a schedule for today, and then click the **Week tab** to display a schedule for the week. Click the **Month tab** to display the full month's calendar.

In the *Day* and *Week* views, you can see the entire event name and the time scheduled for each activity on the calendar. When you return to the *Month* view, you see limited information.

7 Click the **New arrow**, and then click **Birthday** to display the **Add a birthday** dialog box. In the appropriate boxes, type your **First Name** and **Last Name**. Select any day during the second week of the month for your birthday along with any year. Click **Save**. On the date of the birthday, point to the charm—the small icon that represents the birthday—and then click **Edit birthday details**. Click the **Reminders arrow** for your Email, and then click **2 days**. Notice that you can also set reminders to display on your various clients—your instant messaging or your mobile phone. Click **Save**.

An email reminder is generated based on your reminder selection. Sandy will receive one reminder about the birthday two days prior to the date.

8 Click **Save** and compare your screen with Figure 14.20.

Briefly, a window displays in the lower right corner indicating that a birthday was added to the calendar. When you add a birthday, a small birthday cake charm displays on the date, unless you have selected a different charm.

Figure 14.20

Birthday added

Event added

9 In the third week of the month, click in any day, and notice that an **Add** button displays. Click the **Add** button to display the **Add an event** dialog box. Enter and save the information for an event that you have scheduled during that week.

10 In the command row above the Calendar tabs, click the **New arrow**, and then click **To-do** to display the **Add a to-do** dialog box. In the **What** box, type **Review book list for next semester**. Click in the **Due date** boxes, and select any day during the fourth week of the month at **12:00pm**. Click the **Priority arrow**, and then click **Low priority**. Click **Save**.

A message displays briefly in the lower right corner, but the To-do list item does not display on the Calendar.

11 At the top of the calendar, click the **To-do list tab** to see the item on your To-do list. To the right of the item, click the **Not started arrow**, and then click **In progress**. Compare your screen with Figure 14.21.

Figure 14.21

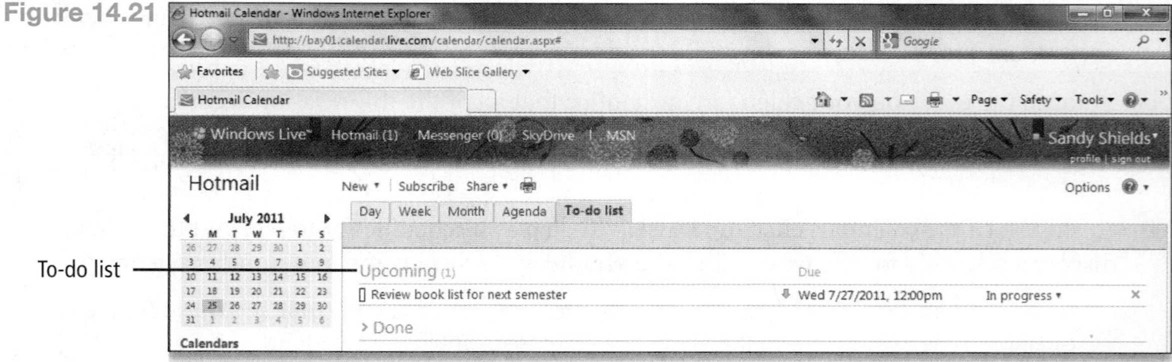

12 At the top of the calendar, in the row of commands, click the **Print** button to display a Print Preview of the **To-do list**. Start the **Snipping Tool**, create a **Window Snip**, and then in your **All In One Chapter 14** folder, save the **JPEG** image as **Lastname_Firstname_14A_To-do Close** the **Snipping Tool**. **Close** Print Preview.

13 Click the **Month tab** in the Calendar window, and leave the Calendar open for the next activity.

> **More Knowledge | Outlook Hotmail Connector**
>
> With the Outlook Hotmail Connector, you can view your Windows Live Hotmail and Calendar in Microsoft Outlook, including calendars that have been shared with you. You can also view Hotmail and Messenger contacts.

Activity 14.06 | Sharing a Windows Live Calendar

Sharing calendars is useful if one of the book club members needs to add events to the calendar; for example, a special meeting. In this activity, you will share your calendar with your partner.

1 At the top of the screen, point to **Hotmail**, and then click **Contacts**. On the left, click **Add people**, use the default privacy settings, and then click **Save**. Type the email address of your partner and click **Next**. Click **Invite**.

Your partner will receive an email message, but he or she need not respond. The contact will still display in your list.

2 In the command row, click **Share**. In the displayed list, click your calendar, and then compare your screen with Figure 14.22.

The default Sharing settings are currently set to keep your calendar private.

Figure 14.22

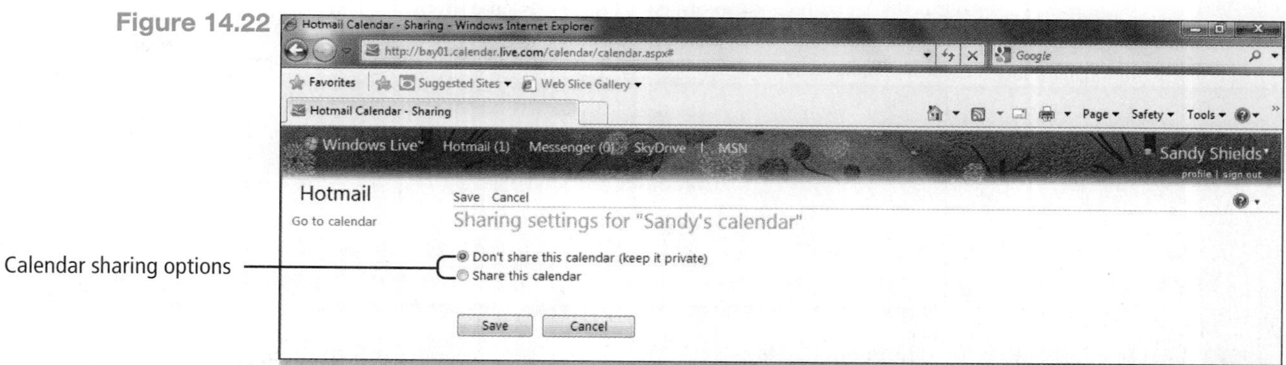

3 Click the **Share this calendar** option button to display sharing options.

The default option for sharing is to share your calendar privately with friends and family by adding people with specific rights. Other options include sending a link to contacts so they can view your calendar without a Windows Live ID and making your calendar public for anyone to see on a Web site or through a search engine.

4 Click the **Add people** button to see a list of your contacts, and then select your partner's email address. At the bottom of the window, click the **View details arrow**. Compare your screen with Figure 14.23.

Be cautious with the information you share. If you allow friends to have any editing rights, they can add, change, or delete items in your calendar. You must monitor your calendar carefully to meet deadlines. If you share only viewing rights, you can choose what others can view—details about the events, free/busy times along with titles and locations, or only the free/busy times. Each of these options restricts a little more of what you are sharing.

Figure 14.23

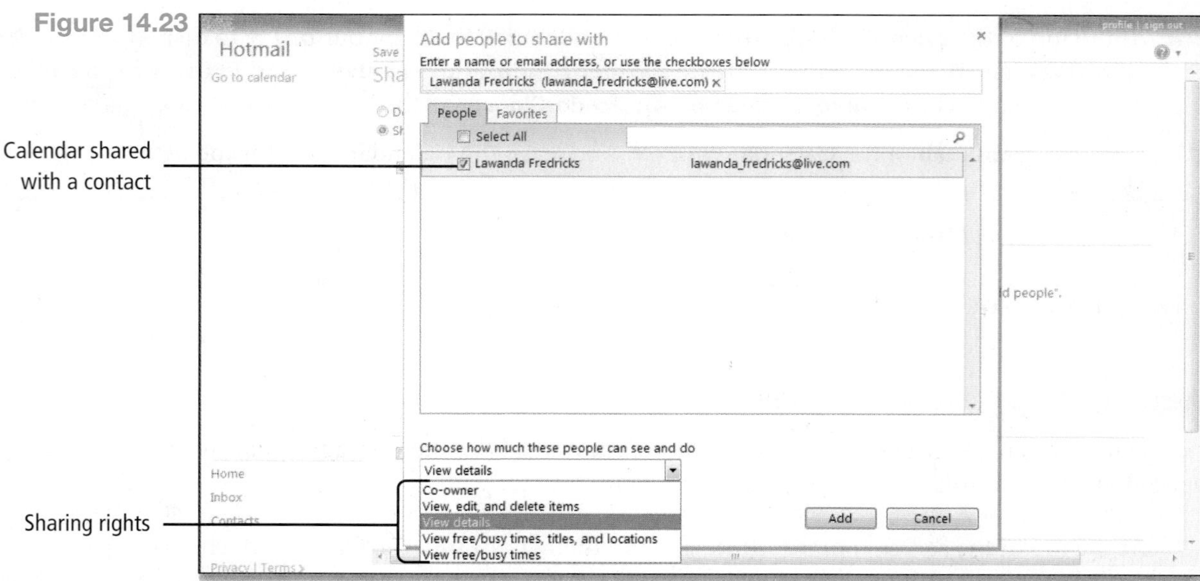

5 On the list, click **View, edit, and delete items**, and then click the **Add** button. Compare your screen with Figure 14.24.

The sharing summary displays for you to verify the sharing rights given to each person.

Figure 14.24

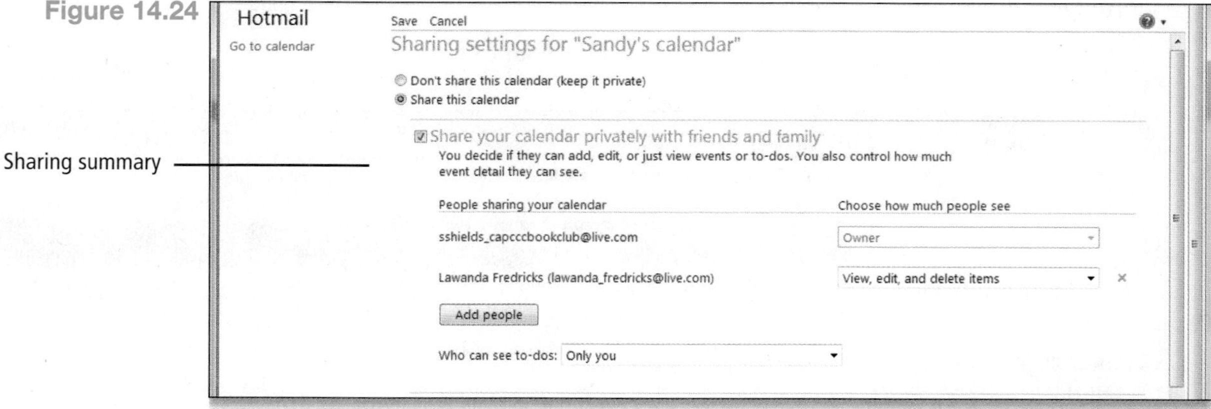

6 If necessary, scroll to view the bottom of the window, click **Save** to save the sharing options, and then click **OK** to send the email invitation to your partner.

7 On the lower left side of your screen, click **Inbox**. Click the email from your partner, and compare your screen with Figure 14.25.

Figure 14.25

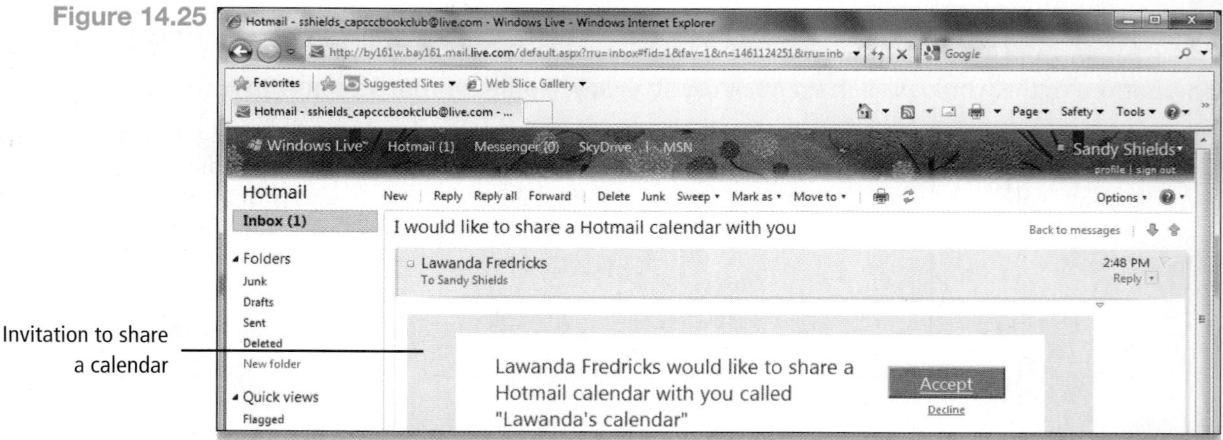

8 Click **Accept** to be able to view your partner's calendar.

A *Calendar* window displays with a new color identifying your partner's calendar on your calendar. Birthdays are not shared because they are part of a separate calendar called *Birthdays*.

9 **Maximize** the Calendar window, and scroll to be sure all events are visible. Start the **Snipping Tool**, create a **Window Snip**, and then save the **JPEG** image in your **All In One Chapter 14** folder as **Lastname_Firstname_14A_Calendar Close** the **Snipping Tool**.

10 In the upper left corner of the screen, point to **Windows Live**, and then click **Home**.

Objective 4 | Use Windows Live Messenger to Communicate

Instant messaging is the real-time communication between two or more participants over the Internet. ***Windows Live Messenger*** is the Windows Live application that you can download and use to communicate with friends that are online.

Activity 14.07 | Adding Friends in Windows Live Messenger

In this activity, you will sign in to Windows Messenger and add a friend.

1 If you are not already signed in to your own Windows Live site, go to www.live.com and sign in.

2 At the top of the screen, point to **Messenger**, and if necessary, click Sign in to Messenger. Compare your screen with Figure 14.26.

Any friends you had previously added will appear at the top of the list, *if* they are online. ***Contacts*** include the people you have added to your Hotmail account for email, instant messaging, sharing calendars, and sharing documents. ***Friends*** are people that must be added before you can share information and chat using Windows Live Messenger. Both groups of people are accessed using their Windows Live ID.

Figure 14.26

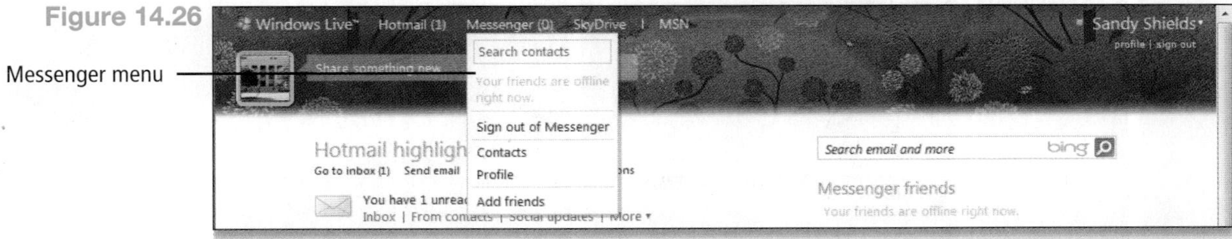

3 Click **Add friends**. If a box with privacy settings displays, click the Limited option button, and then click Save.

4 If you have not previously added your partner as a contact, in the displayed box, type your partner's Windows Live ID, and then compare your screen with Figure 14.27.

Figure 14.27

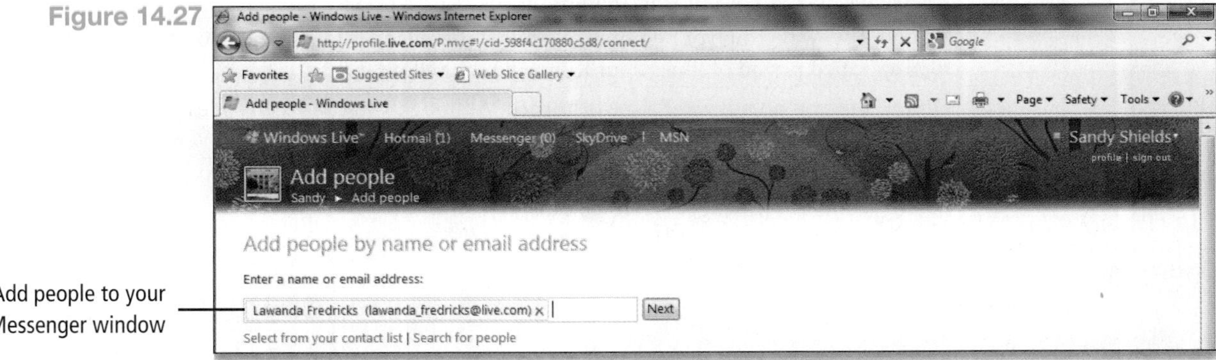

5 Click **Next**, select the check box to **Make this person a favorite**, and then click **Invite**.

6 In the upper right corner, to the right of your name, click the small arrow, and then click **Sign out of Messenger** to remain in Windows Live, but not in Messenger. Then under your name, click **sign out** to exit Windows Live.

Activity 14.08 | Communicating with Windows Live Messenger

In this activity, you will send and receive instant messages using Windows Live Messenger.

1 Display the **Start** menu. With your insertion point blinking in the **Search** box, type **Windows Live Messenger** and then on the menu above, click **Windows Live Messenger**.

This is a convenient method to find programs that you have not pinned to your taskbar or Start menu. The Sign in screen for Windows Live Messenger displays.

2 Type your Windows Live ID and password in the appropriate boxes, and then click the **Sign in as arrow**. Compare your screen with Figure 14.28, and then review the options described in the table in Figure 14.29.

The Sign in as options identify how you will appear to your contacts. You can change status any time you are online by clicking the arrow next to your name and clicking another option.

Figure 14.28

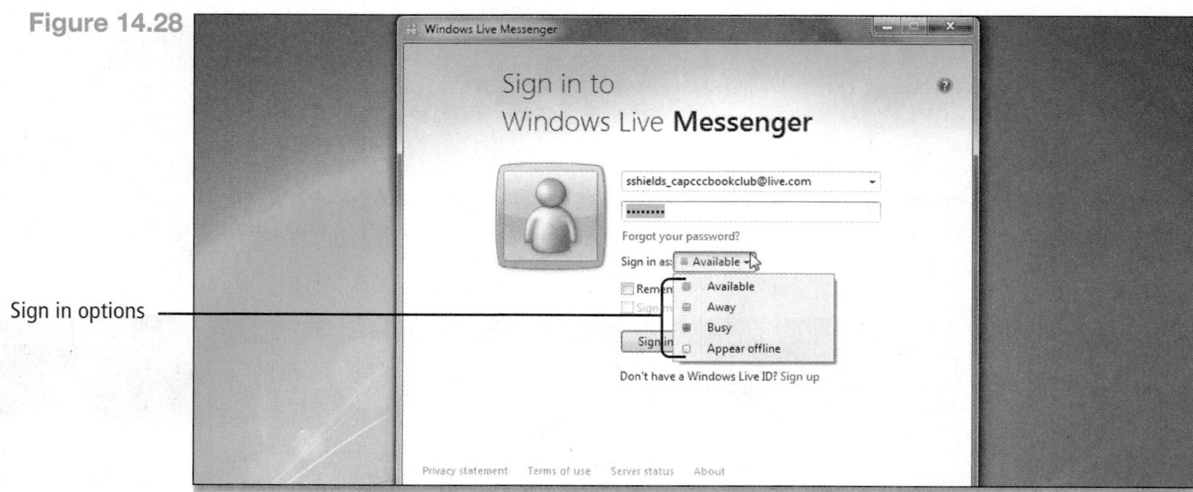

Messenger Sign in Options

Sign in as option	If you select this option, you are:
Available	Online to all of your contacts along with your display picture or a green icon. You can send and receive messages to any of your online contacts.
Away	Online, but away from your computer. Your status changes to Away if you are inactive in Messenger for a specified period of time. Your icon will turn yellow.
Busy	Online, but you do not want to be disturbed. Although you can receive messages, there is no sound associated with the receipt of a message. Your icon will display in red.
Appear Offline	Online and able to view your contacts; however, you appear offline to your contacts. It is as if you are not logged in to Messenger. Your icon displays in white.

Figure 14.29

3 Click **Available** and then click **Sign in**. If a welcome screen displays, click **MSN**.

Check boxes might display to enable you to make logging in faster in the future. You can click the *Remember my ID and password* option if you want your ID and password already entered in the appropriate boxes the next time you sign in. You can click the *Sign me in automatically* option if you want to sign in automatically when you log in to the computer. Choosing any of these options makes your account vulnerable to outsiders, so choose them carefully.

4 In the upper right corner, click the **Switch to compact view** icon to minimize your **Messenger** pane, and then compare your screen with Figure 14.30.

Minimizing the Messenger pane removes any other MSN content from your window while displaying your contacts and their status. You can continue working on other tasks on your computer by opening those applications while Messenger is open.

Figure 14.30

5 Notice the green frame around your profile icon indicating you are **Available**. Click the arrow next to your name and click **Away**. Compare your screen with Figure 14.31.

Change your status to *Away* before you step away from your computer. This will tell your online friends that you are not available to answer messages you receive.

Figure 14.31

6 Click the arrow next to your name and click **Available**.

7 Under **Online**, double-click your partner's name—your screen will look similar to Figure 14.32.

Any friends that are online and available at the same time as you are will display with a green icon to the left of their display name. After you double-click their name, the message window displays with the picture of the sender and receiver.

Figure 14.32

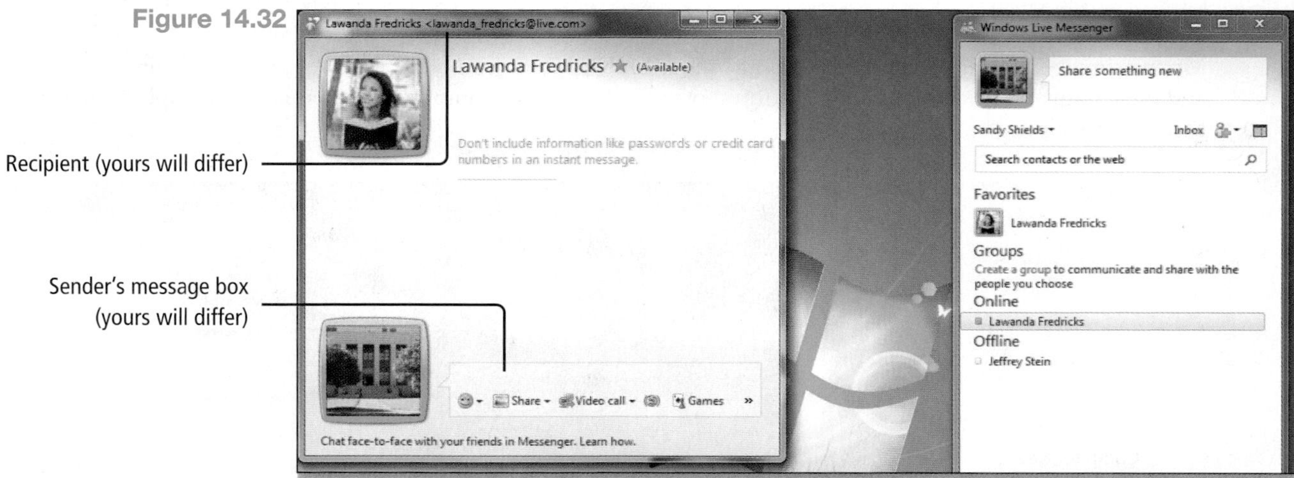

Note | Send a Message to an Offline Contact

When a contact displays in the Offline list in your Messenger pane, click his or her name to see options for sending a message. Send an offline IM to a contact so he or she can see it when signing back into Messenger, or send an email so the message will be sent to the contact's Hotmail Inbox.

8 In the message window, click the first icon below the text box, and select an emoticon that shows how you are feeling today.

An ***emoticon*** is an image that represents facial expressions; they should be used only in informal electronic communication to convey feelings. Additional options are available as you use Messenger: you can share a photo with your message, start a video call if you are using a webcam, nudge or shake the message window, or play a game with your online friend.

9 In the text box, type a short message to tell your partner about a benefit of instant messaging in the workplace. Press Enter to send the message to your partner.

In the message window, you can see both the message you sent and the one you received identified by each person's display name and photo. You can continue the conversation by typing a new message in the Message text box and pressing Enter.

10 Start the **Snipping Tool**, create a **Window Snip** of your current window, and then save the **JPEG** image in your **All In One Chapter 14** folder as **Lastname_Firstname_14A_Instant_Messenger Close** the **Snipping Tool**.

11 In the **Messenger** window, click the arrow next to your name, and then click **Sign out from everywhere** to be sure you are signed out of Windows Live completely. If necessary click **No, do not save my messages on this computer (recommended for shared computers)** and click **OK**.

If you want to remain signed in to Windows Live and exit Messenger only, you can choose that option from the menu. For security of your account, do not save your messages and be sure to be completely signed out of Messenger and Windows Live before leaving your computer.

12 **Close** the Messenger window, if necessary.

End **You have completed Project 14A**

Project 14B Using SkyDrive and Office Web Apps to Create, Edit, and Share Office Files

Project Activities

In Activities 14.09 through 14.18, you will create and edit Word, Excel, and PowerPoint files using Office Web Apps. You will also share files. You will create snip files that look similar to Figure 14.33.

Project Files

For Project 14B, you will need the following files:

w14B_Campus_Center
pdf14B_CapCCC_Book_Club_Constitution (PDF)
w14B_Meeting_Announcement

You will save your snip files as:

Lastname_Firstname_14B_Book_Suggestions.jpg
Lastname_Firstname_14B_Membership_Stats.jpg
Lastname_Firstname_14B_CapCCC_Folder.jpg
Lastname_Firstname_14B_Shared_Folder.jpg

Project Results

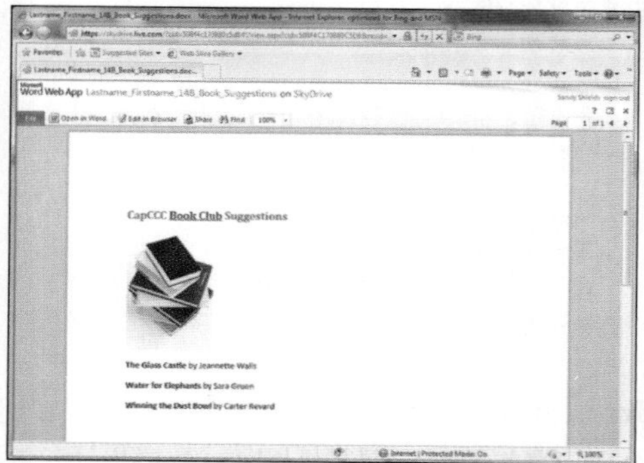

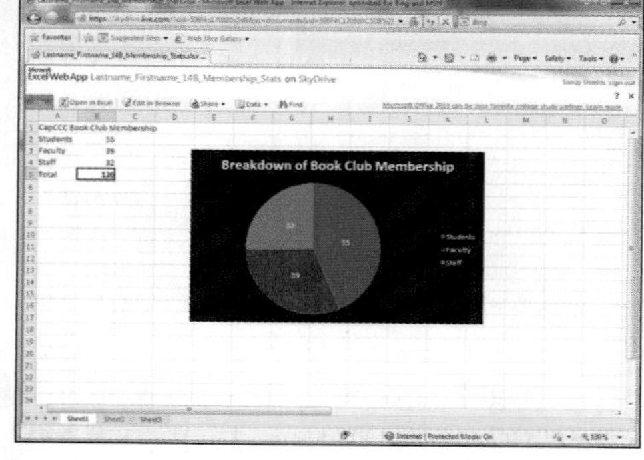

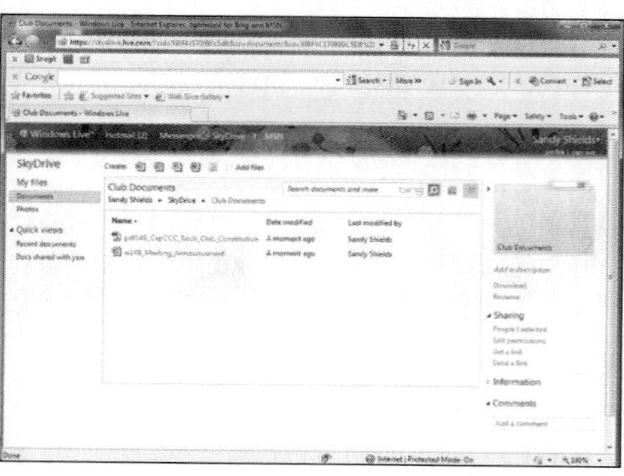

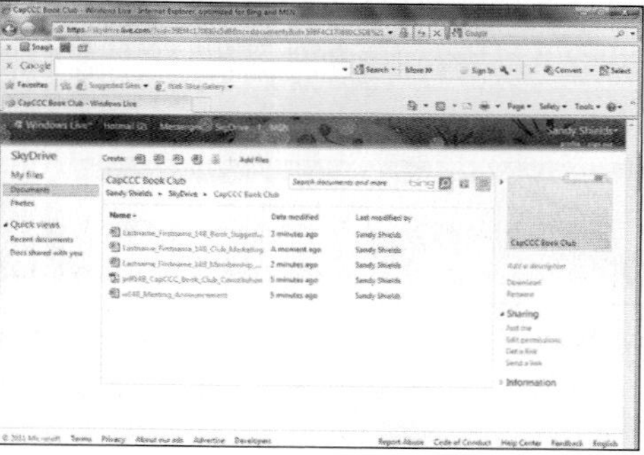

Figure 14.33
Project 14B Windows Live Web Apps

Objective 5 | Use Windows Live SkyDrive

When you create your Windows Live ID, you get a ***Windows Live SkyDrive***, which is a free file storage and file sharing service. You also have access to Office Web Apps. To use Office Web Apps, you must store your document in a compatible shared location.

In an organization, the compatible storage location for your Office Web Apps documents could be in a ***SharePoint*** library. SharePoint is a related group of technologies from Microsoft for collaboration, file sharing, and Web publishing within organizations. As an individual, your compatible storage location is a Windows Live SkyDrive.

Using Web servers on the Internet—for example, SkyDrive or a SharePoint library—to store files and run applications is referred to as ***cloud computing***. By using SkyDrive or a SharePoint library, your documents are easy to access from anywhere and easy to share with others—regardless of whether you have a PC or a Mac, and regardless of whether you have a version of Microsoft Office on your computer.

Activity 14.09 | Creating Folders and Storing Documents on SkyDrive

By storing files on your SkyDrive, you can access them from anywhere that you have Internet access and a supported browser. In this activity, you will create a new folder in your SkyDrive and upload two documents.

1 Start your Web browser, navigate to www.live.com and sign in to Windows Live. At the top of the window, click **SkyDrive**. Compare your screen with Figure 14.34.

Figure 14.34

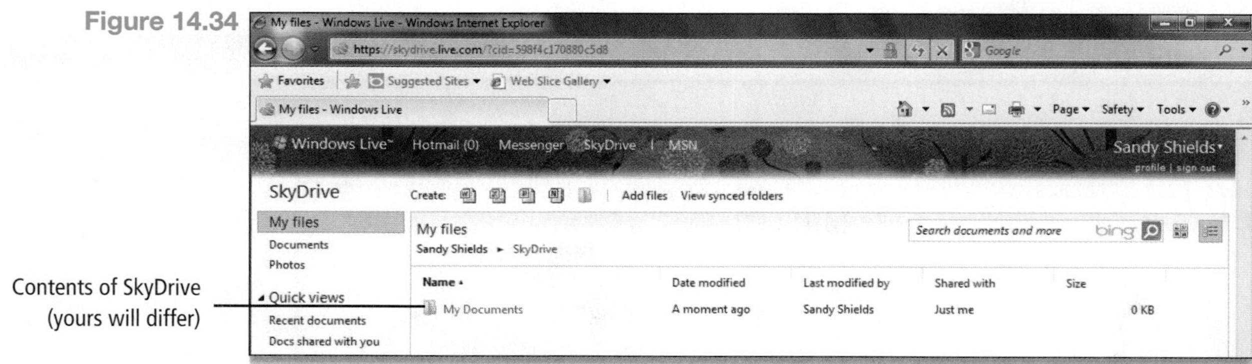

2 Near the top of the window, to the right of **Create**, click the **Create folder** button. In the **Name** box, with the text *New folder* selected, type **CapCCC Book Club** and then click **Next**. Compare your screen with Figure 14.35.

This action creates a new folder on your SkyDrive that is available only to you. The new folder is open to enable you to add files. Under *Add documents to CapCCC Book Club*, you can click locations in the displayed path to navigate within SkyDrive.

Figure 14.35

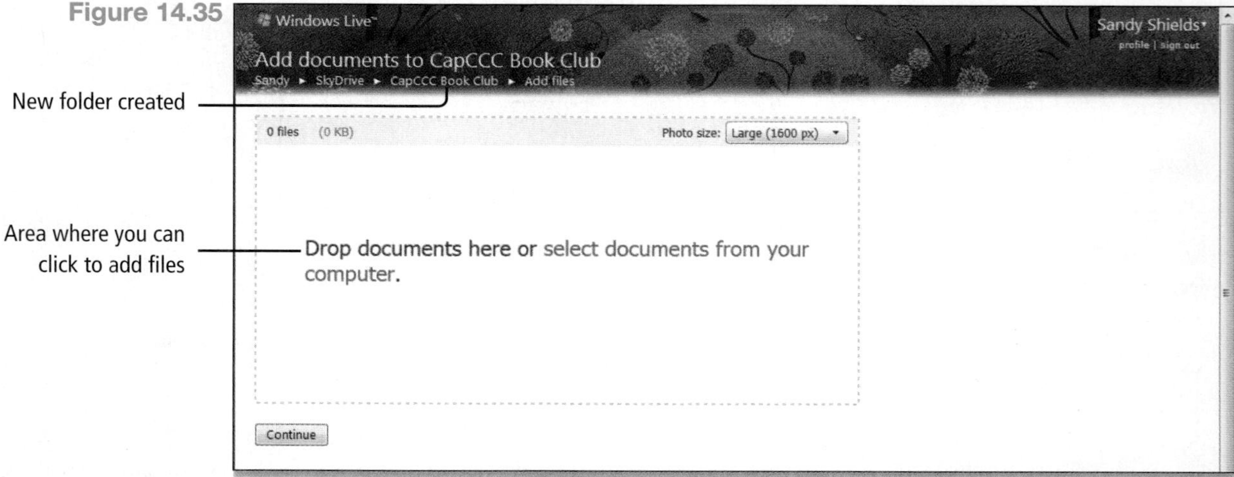

3 With the **CapCCC Book Club** folder open, click **select documents from your computer** to display the **Open** dialog box, from which you can navigate to files you want to add to this folder on your SkyDrive.

4 In the **Open** dialog box, navigate to the location where your student data files are stored, hold down Ctrl so that you can select multiple files, and then while holding down Ctrl, select the files **pdf14B_CapCCC_Book_Club_Constitution** and **w14B_Meeting_Announcement**. With the two files selected, in the lower right corner of the dialog box, click **Open**. Wait a moment for both files to upload, and then compare your screen with Figure 14.36.

The two files, a Word document and a PDF document, upload to your SkyDrive and display ***thumbnails***—a reduced-size image of a graphic.

Figure 14.36

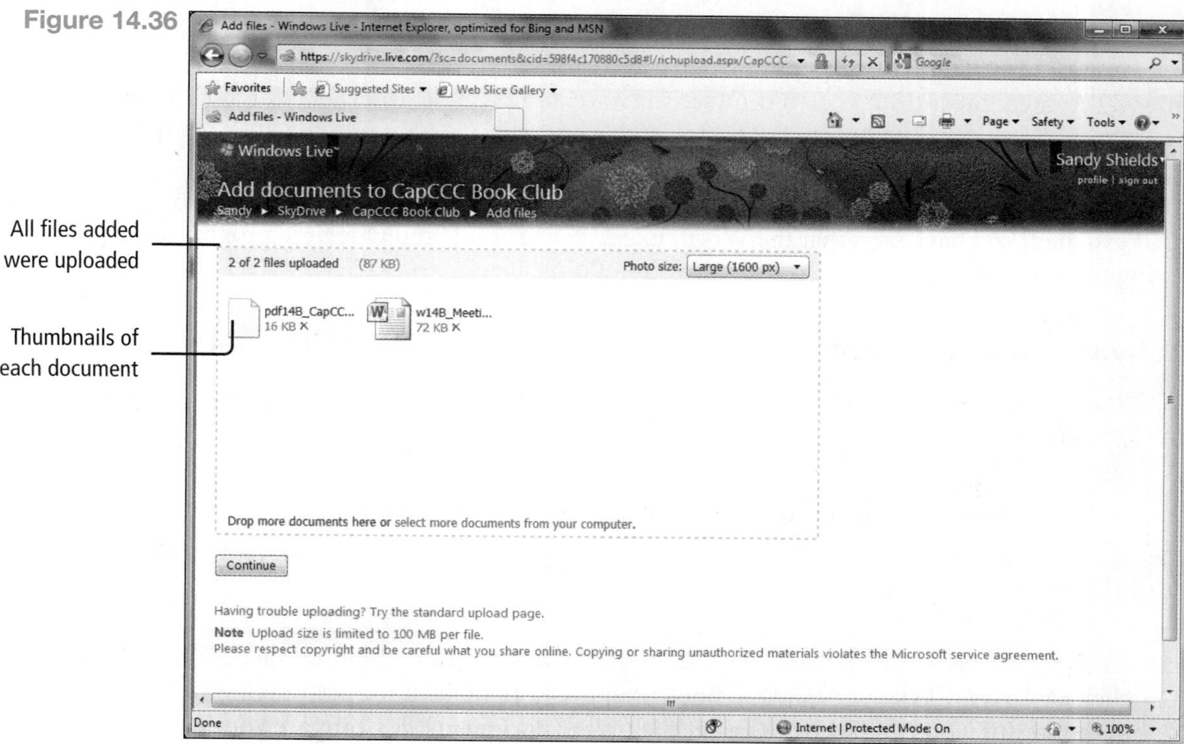

5 Click **Continue**, and notice that the files are added with an icon that represents the file type, the amount of time that has elapsed since the upload, the last person who modified the document, document sharing information, and the file size. Compare your screen with Figure 14.37.

Figure 14.37

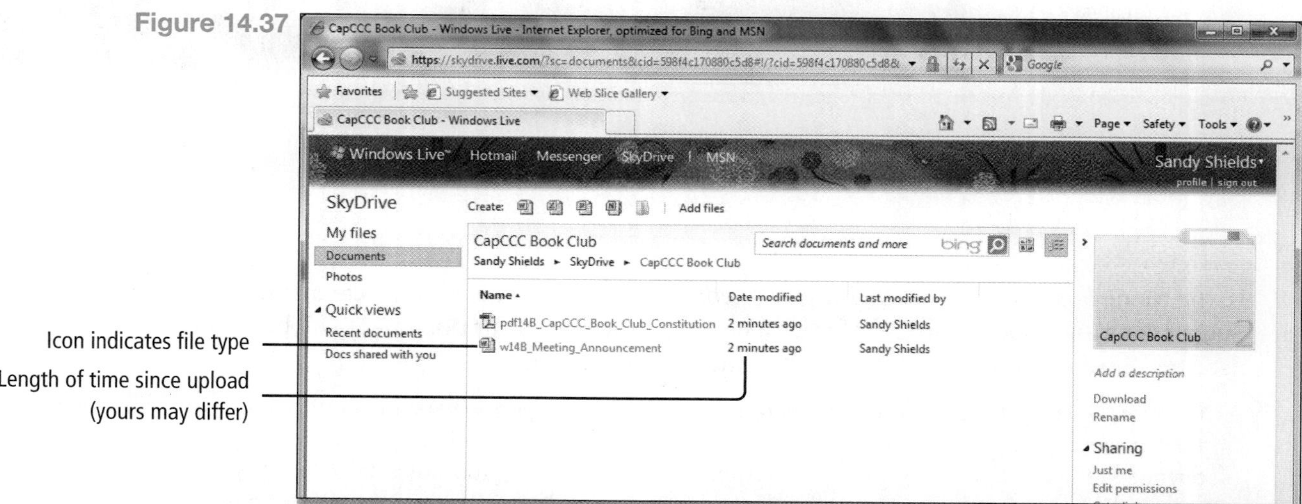

6 Sign out of Windows Live. **Close** your browser.

Objective 6 | Use Office Web Apps to Create and Edit a Word Document

Office Web Apps are the online companions to Microsoft Office Word, Excel, PowerPoint, and OneNote that enable you to create, access, share, and perform light editing on Microsoft Office documents from any device that connects to the Internet and uses a supported Web browser; for example from a laptop, a netbook, a tablet, a MAC, or a smartphone. Office Web Apps are available in two ways—either in Windows Live by signing in with your personal Windows Live ID or on a SharePoint site for individuals in organizations that have installed and configured Office Web Apps on a SharePoint site.

Personal use of Office Web Apps is free, and requires only a Windows Live ID and a computer with an Internet connection and supported browser software; for example, Internet Explorer 7 or later, Safari 4 or later, or Firefox 3.5 or later. ***Business use of Office Web Apps*** requires a SharePoint site with appropriate software and a SharePoint user ID provided by the organization.

You do not need to have Office 2010 installed on your computer to use Office Web Apps. If you have Office 2010 installed, you have seen that the Word, Excel, PowerPoint, and OneNote programs include commands for saving files directly to your SkyDrive or to a SharePoint site.

Activity 14.10 | Creating a New Word Document in Office Web Apps

You can navigate to a SkyDrive folder and create a new document in that folder. The New menu is available in any SkyDrive folder.

> Alert! | **To complete this project, you must complete Project 14A.**
>
> Because you will use the same Windows Live ID and the folders you created in Project 14A, be sure you have completed Project 14A before you begin this project.

1 Open your browser, go to **live.com** and then sign in with your Windows Live ID. At the top of the window, click **SkyDrive**. Click your **CapCCC Book Club** folder to make it the active folder. Near the top of the window, in the row of icons to the right **Create**, click **Word document**. Compare your screen with Figure 14.38.

Figure 14.38

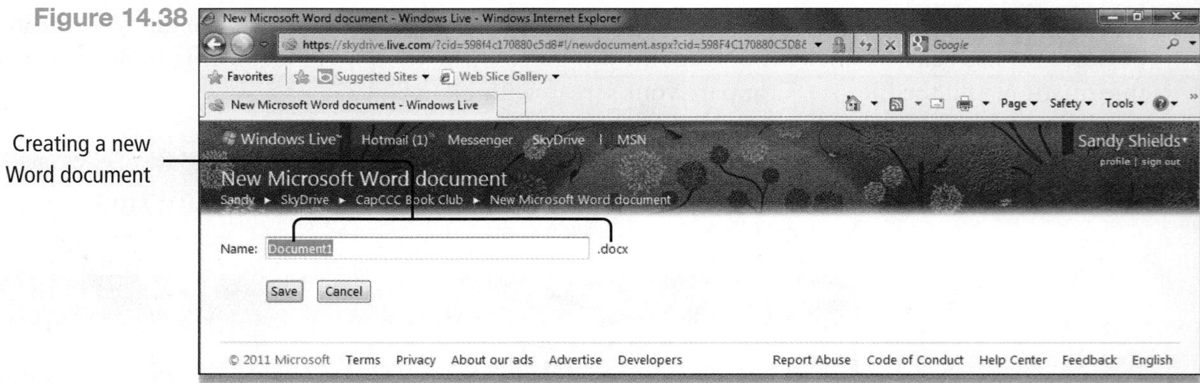

2 In the **Name** box, with *Document1* highlighted, using your own name, type **Lastname_Firstname_14B_Book_Suggestions** and then at the end of the **Name** box, notice that your document will be created in the file format used by Word documents in Office 2010—the *.docx* file format.

Because Office Web Apps use the standard file formats of the desktop version of Office 2010, you will have ***high-fidelity viewing*** of documents. That is, in documents created in the full desktop version of Office 2010 and then opened in the corresponding Office Web App, you will see images, footnotes, table borders, text effects, and so on, even though some of these more sophisticated features are not available in Office Web Apps.

3 Click the **Save** button, and then compare your screen with Figure 14.39.

The Word Web App displays and looks similar to the Office 2010 Word application. Three Ribbon tabs display, and you can see familiar tools that you will recognize from Word, such as Spelling and font and paragraph formatting.

Figure 14.39

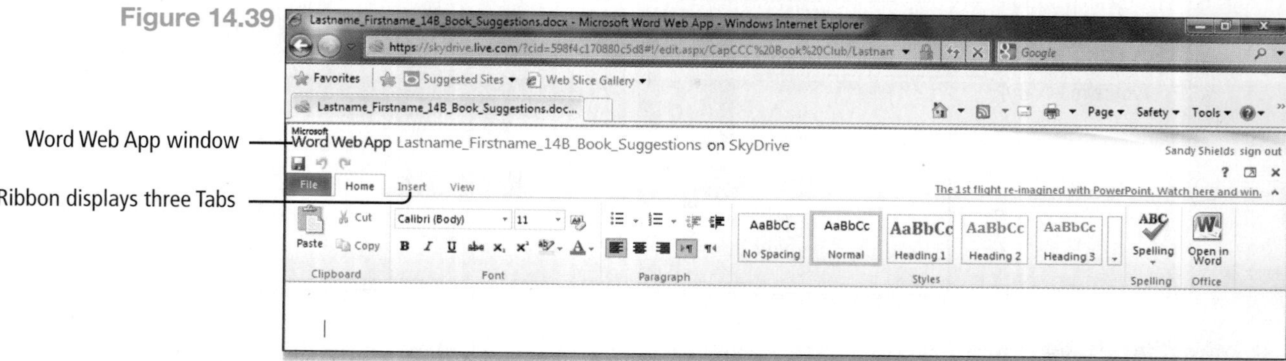

4 With the insertion point blinking, type **CapCCC Book Club Suggestions** and then press Enter. Type **The Glass Castle by Jeannette Walls** and then press Enter.

5 Type **Water for Elephants by Sara Gruen** press Enter, and then type **Winning the Dust Bowl by Carter Revard**

6 Select the first line of text—*CapCCC Book Club Suggestions*—and then on the **Home tab**, in the **Styles group**, click the **Heading 1** button. Click anywhere outside of the selected text, and then compare your screen with Figure 14.40.

The Home tab has commands for formatting text. Here you can apply direct formatting like Bold, Italic, and Underline, or you can apply styles, which give a professional look to your document.

Figure 14.40

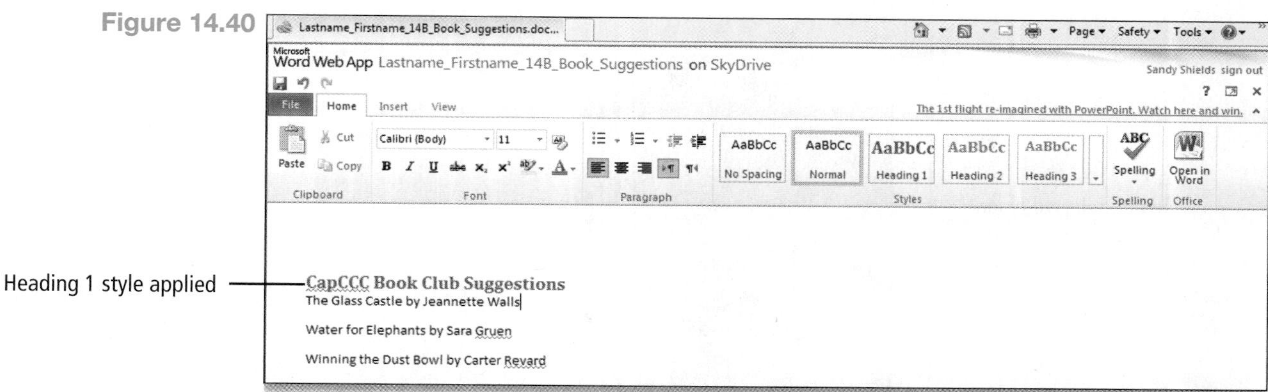

7 Select the text *The Glass Castle*, and then on the **Home tab**, in the **Font group**, click the **Bold** button B. Using the technique you practiced, apply bold formatting to the other two titles: *Water for Elephants* and *Winning the Dust Bowl*.

8 In the upper left corner, just above the Ribbon, click the **Save** button to save the changes to your document. Leave your document displayed for the next activity.

Activity 14.11 | Inserting a Clip Art in Office Web Apps

1 In the line of text that begins *The Glass Castle*, click to position the insertion point to the left of the *T* in *The*.

2 On the Ribbon, click the **Insert tab**, and then in the **Pictures group**, click the **Clip Art** button. In the **Insert Clip Art** dialog box, type **Books** and then to the right, click the **Search** button. Compare your screen with Figure 14.41.

From the Insert tab, you can insert tables, pictures, or clip art.

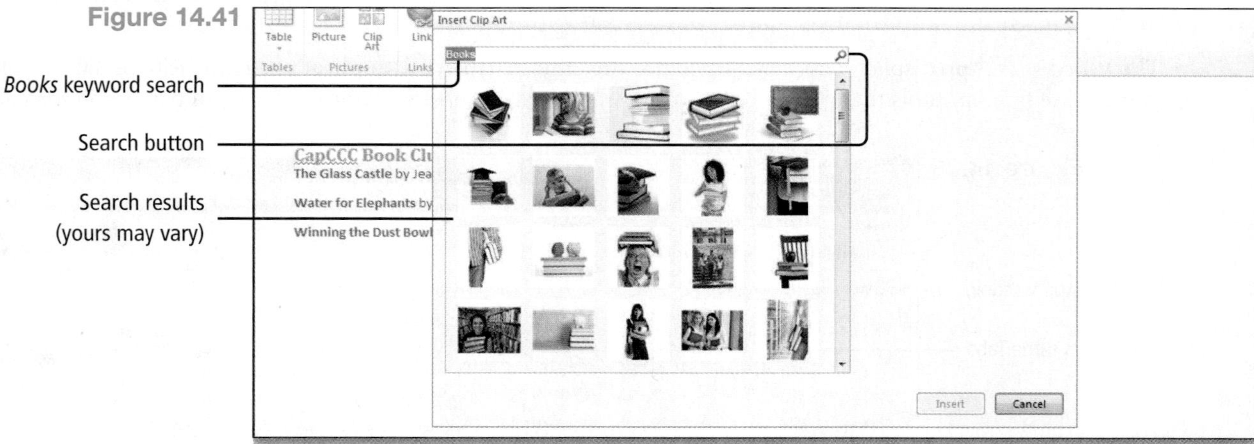

Figure 14.41

3 In the displayed Clip Art results, click the image for the fanned stack of books displayed in Figure 14.42—or a similar image, and then in the lower right corner of the dialog box, click **Insert**.

4 Click on the inserted image to select it. Notice that on the Ribbon, the **Format tab** for **Picture Tools** displays. Click the **Picture Tools Format tab**, and then compare your screen with Figure 14.42.

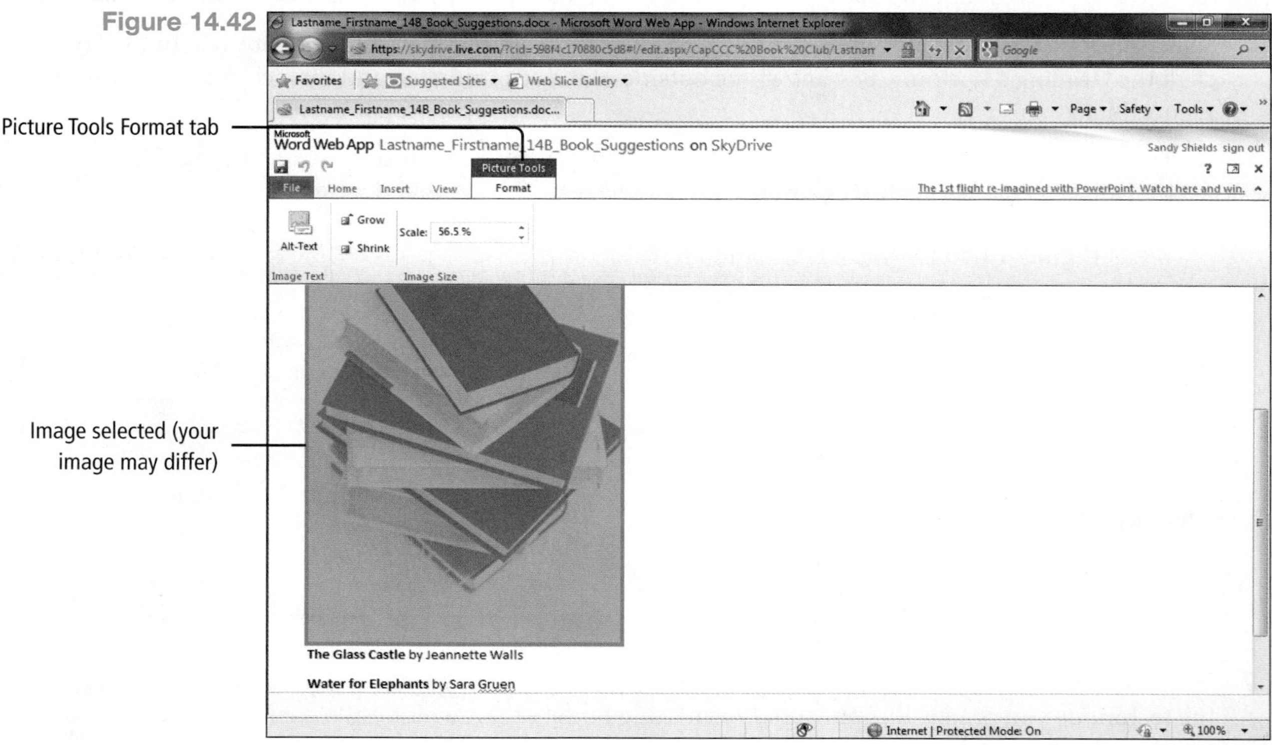

Figure 14.42

5 In the **Image Size group**, click in the **Scale** box, type **25** and then press Enter. Click anywhere in the text to deselect the picture, and then compare your screen with Figure 14.43.

Figure 14.43

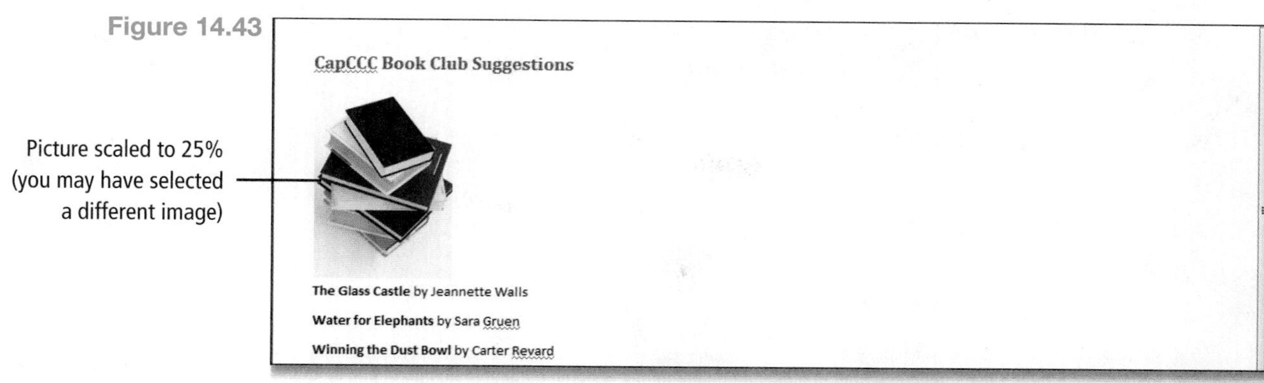

6 In the upper left corner, just above the Ribbon, click the **Save** button to save the changes to your document. Leave your document displayed for the next activity.

Activity 14.12 | Inserting a Hyperlink in Office Web Apps

In this activity, you will insert a ***hyperlink***—text, buttons, pictures, or other objects that when clicked, access other Web pages, other sections of the active page, or another file—so that the individuals working with this document can jump quickly to information about the book club. By providing the hyperlink, anyone viewing this document can go quickly to information about book clubs.

1 In the line of text that begins *CapCCC Book Club Suggestions*, select the words *Book Club*.

2 On the **Insert tab**, in the **Links group**, click the **Link** button. In the **Link** dialog box, in the **Address** box, type **http://www.book-clubs-resource.com** and then click the **Insert** button. Notice that the text is formatted as a hyperlink. Compare your screen with Figure 14.44.

Individuals who use this document will be able to learn about book clubs and reading groups by visiting the link.

Figure 14.44

3 In the upper left corner, just above the Ribbon, click the **Save** button to save the changes to your document. Leave your document displayed for the next activity.

Activity 14.13 | Using the Reading View and the Find Command

1 On the Ribbon, click the **View tab**, and then in the **Document Views** group, click **Reading View**. Compare your screen with Figure 14.45.

In ***Reading View***, you can see how the document will look on a page. This view is useful to see the effect of changes you make in your document. Here you can also navigate, by page, in a multipage document.

Figure 14.45

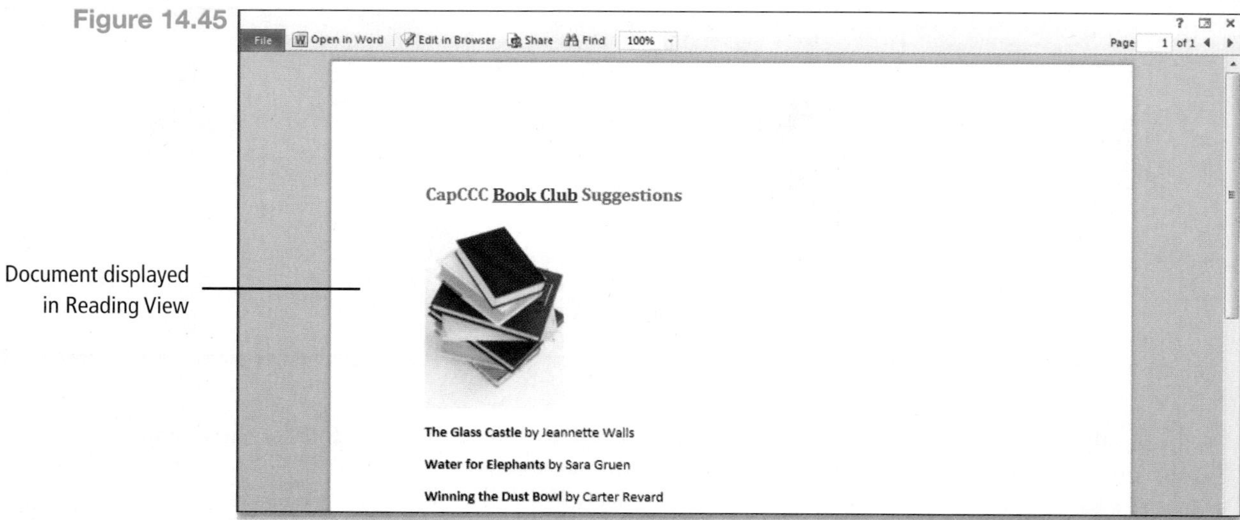

2 At the top of the document, click the **Find** button. On the left side of your screen, in the **Find in Document** pane, type **Elephants** and then click the **Search** button. Compare your screen with Figure 14.46.

Use the Find command to find text quickly within a document.

Figure 14.46

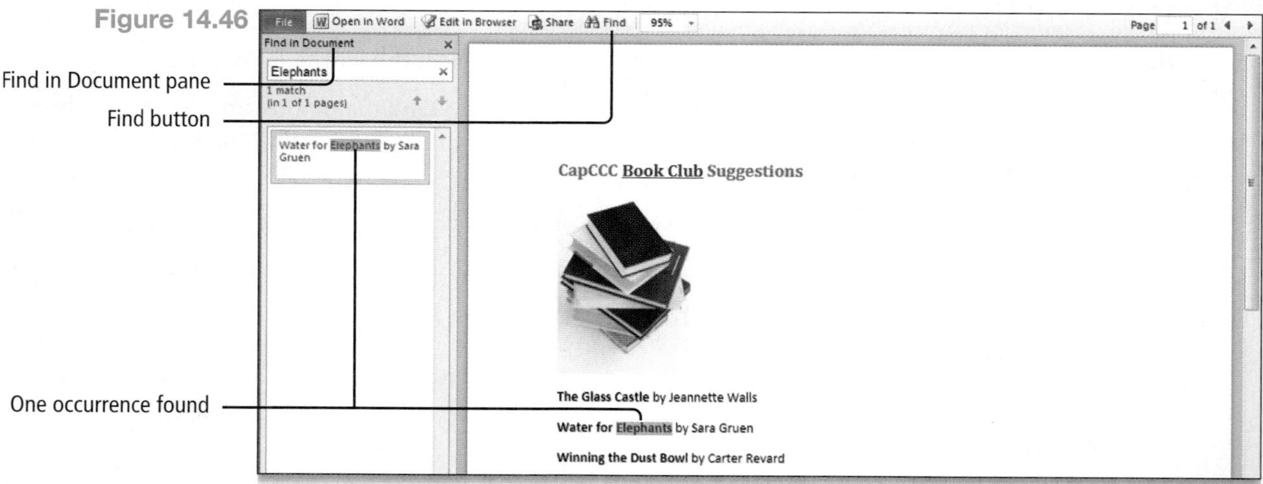

3 **Close** the **Find in Document** pane. Start the **Snipping Tool**, and then create a **Window Snip** of your current window. In your **All In One Chapter 14** folder, save the **JPEG** image as **Lastname_Firstname_14B_Book_Suggestions Close** the **Snipping Tool**.

4 At the top of the document, click the **Edit in Browser** button to return to Editing view.

5 On the Ribbon, click the **File tab**, and then at the bottom of the displayed menu, click **Close**. If necessary, click Save.

More Knowledge | Use the Pop-Out Button to Make the Browser Go Away

The ***Pop-Out button*** which is in the upper right corner of the document window, displays the current document in its own window with the viewing and editing menus from the Web App, but without the toolbars and tabs from the browser. When you maximize the Pop-Out window, you have additional space to view and edit.

Objective 7 | Use Office Web Apps to Create and Edit an Excel Workbook

In Excel Web App, you can navigate through the worksheets in a workbook and sort, filter, and recalculate worksheet data. You can also expand and collapse ***PivotTables***—interactive, cross-tabulated Excel reports that summarize and analyze large amounts of data—that were created in the Office 2010 Excel program.

Activity 14.14 | Creating a New Excel Workbook in Office Web Apps

In this activity, you will enter data and formulas, and then create a chart.

1 If necessary, click your **CapCCC Book Club** folder to open it. Then, near the top of the window, to the right of **Create**, click the **Excel workbook** icon.

Before creating a new Web Apps file, be sure you are in the folder in which you want to create the file.

2 As the **Name**, using your own name type **Lastname_Firstname_14B_Membership_Stats** Click the **Save** button, and then compare your screen with Figure 14.47.

In Excel Web App, three tabs display on the Ribbon. The Home tab has commands for formatting text and cells, for adding rows and columns, and for recalculating data. The Insert tab has commands to add tables, charts, and hyperlinks. The View tab has commands to display the workbook in different views.

Figure 14.47

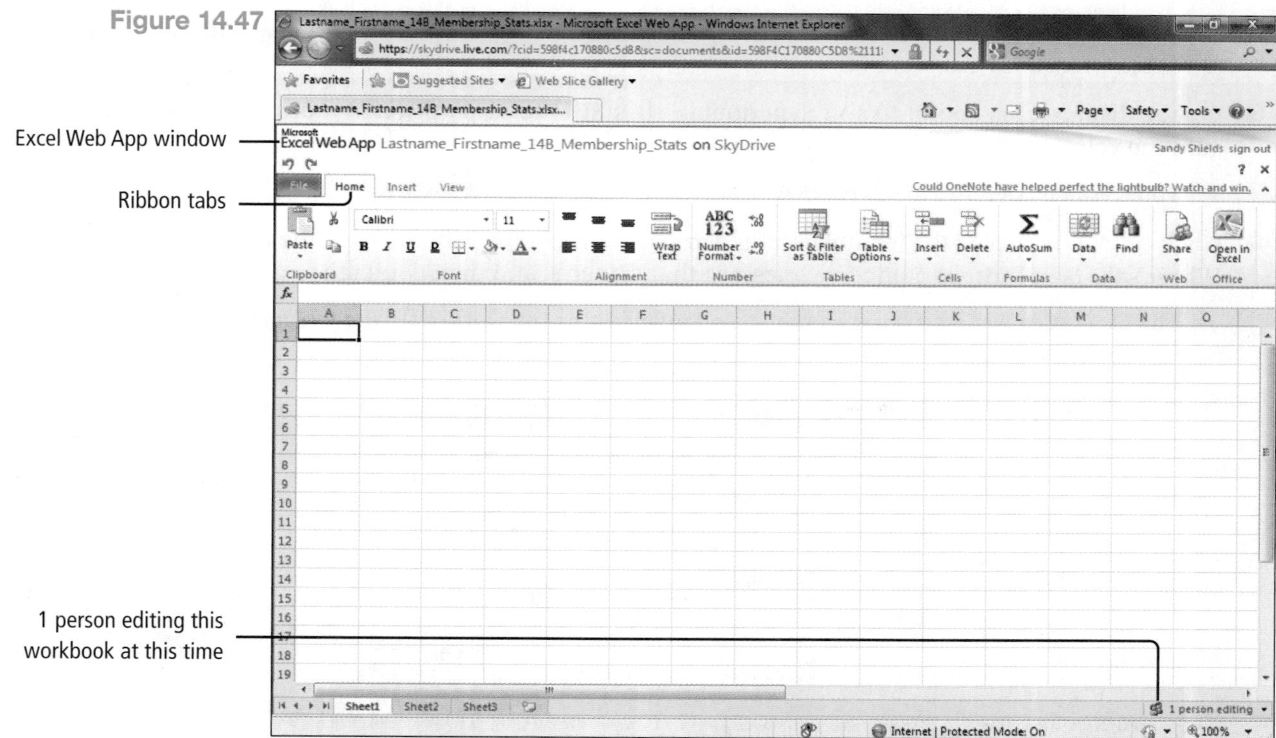

3 In the lower right corner of the screen, notice the text *1 person editing.*

If you share an Excel file stored on a Windows Live SkyDrive, two or more individuals can edit the file at the same time. This is known as ***simultaneous editing***. You will be able to see the changes others make in real time. No special command is necessary—you simply edit the file at the same time others are doing so.

4 With cell **A1** as the active cell, type **CapCCC Book Club Membership** and then press Enter.

5 In cell **A2** type **Students** and then press Tab. In cell **B2** type **55** and then press Enter.

6 Under *Students*, click cell **A3** and type **Faculty** Press Tab and type **39** Click cell **A4** and type **Staff** Press Tab and type **32** Press Enter and compare your screen with Figure 14.48.

If you have any errors, click the cell and type the correct data.

Figure 14.48

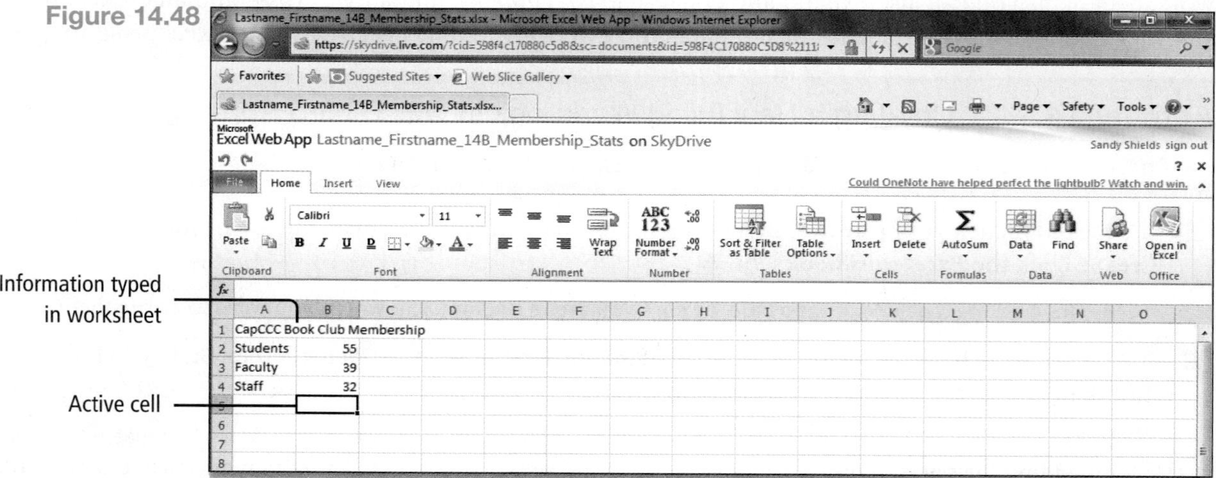

7 Be sure that cell **B5** is the active cell, and then type **=su**

To enter formulas in the Excel Web App, type the equal sign (=), and then the formula or function name. Here, a list displays functions that begin with *su*.

8 On the displayed list, point to and then double-click **SUM** to display *=SUM(* and then type **b2:b4)** Press Enter to sum the values in the range.

Your result is *126*.

9 Click cell **B5** to display the formula on the **Formula Bar**. On the Ribbon, click the **File tab**, and then click **Where's the Save Button?** Notice the message that displays, and then compare your screen with Figure 14.49.

The Excel Web App saves your workbook automatically as you work. Use Undo to get rid of any changes you do not want to keep.

Figure 14.49

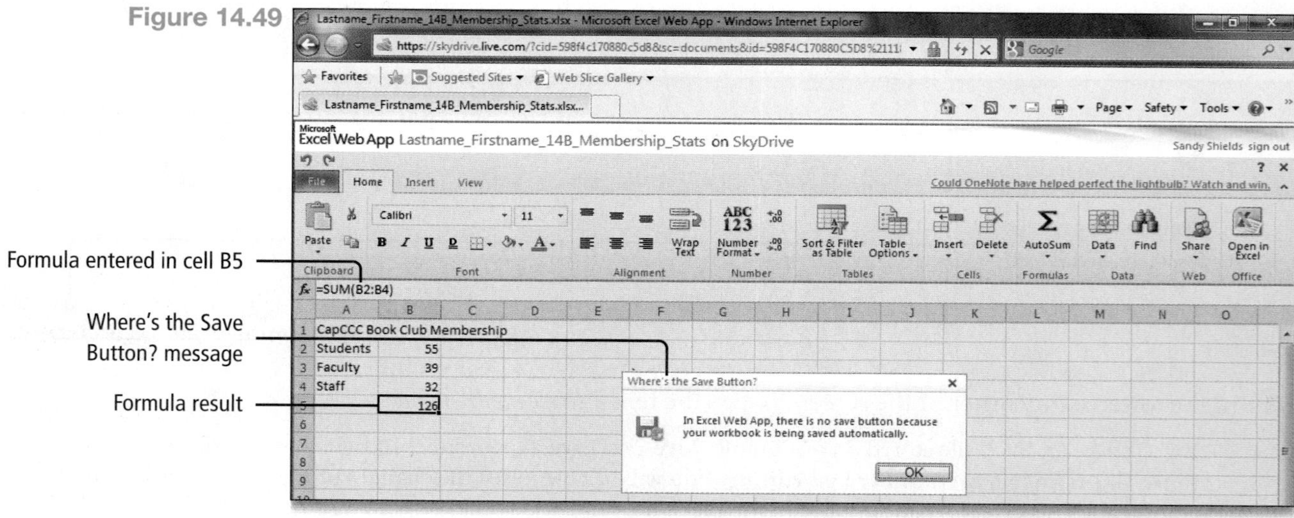

10 Click **OK** to close the message. On the Ribbon, click the **Insert tab**, and then select the range **A2:B4**, as shown in Figure 14.50.

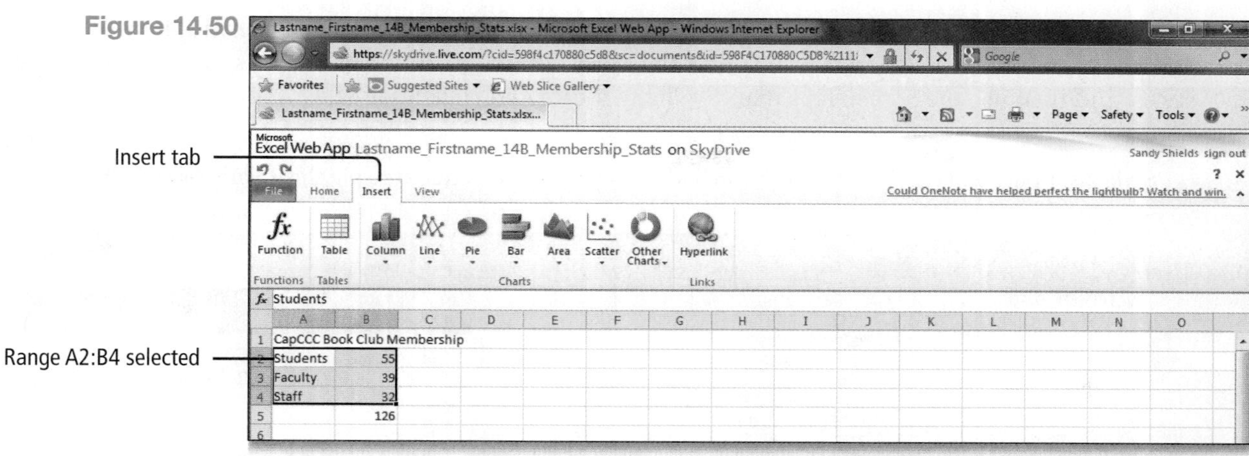

Figure 14.50

11 With the range selected, in the **Charts group**, click the **Pie** button, and then click the first chart type—**Pie**.

12 In the **Labels group**, click **Chart Title**, click **Above Chart**, and then as the **Title text** type **Breakdown of Book Club Membership** Click **OK**.

13 In the **Labels group**, click **Data Labels**, and then click **Center**. Compare your screen with Figure 14.51.

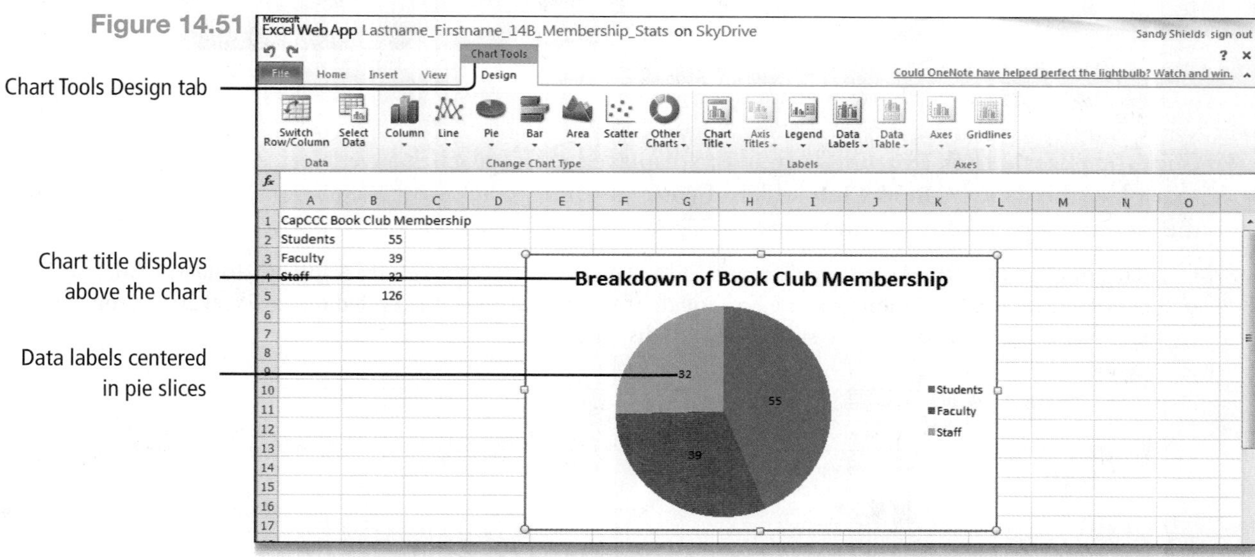

Figure 14.51

14 Leave your workbook displayed for the next activity.

Activity 14.15 | Editing a Web App Workbook in the Excel 2010 Program

Each Office Web App has a subset of the features and commands in the corresponding Office 2010 program. In Excel Web App, you can perform basic editing; for example, you can change fonts, font sizes, and text styles. You can also insert and delete rows and columns. To use more advanced formatting, you must use the Excel 2010 program.

1 On the Ribbon, click the **Home tab**, and then in the **Office group**, click the **Open in Excel** button. If a message displays regarding harmful files, read the message, and then click OK. If necessary, enter your Windows Live ID email address and password and click OK. When the workbook opens in Excel, if necessary, at the top of the Window, click Enable Editing.

2 Click cell **A5** and type **Total** Click cell **B5**, and then in the **Styles group**, click the **Cell Styles** button. Under **Titles and Headings** click **Total**.

3 Click the edge of the chart to select it, and notice that the **Chart Tools** display on the Ribbon. Click the **Design tab**, and then in the **Chart Styles group**, click the **More** button. In the gallery of styles, point to various styles, and then use the ScreenTips that display to locate and click **Style 42**. Compare your screen with Figure 14.52.

Style 42 applies a black background, formats text in white, and defines the pie slices with 3-D effects and shading.

Figure 14.52

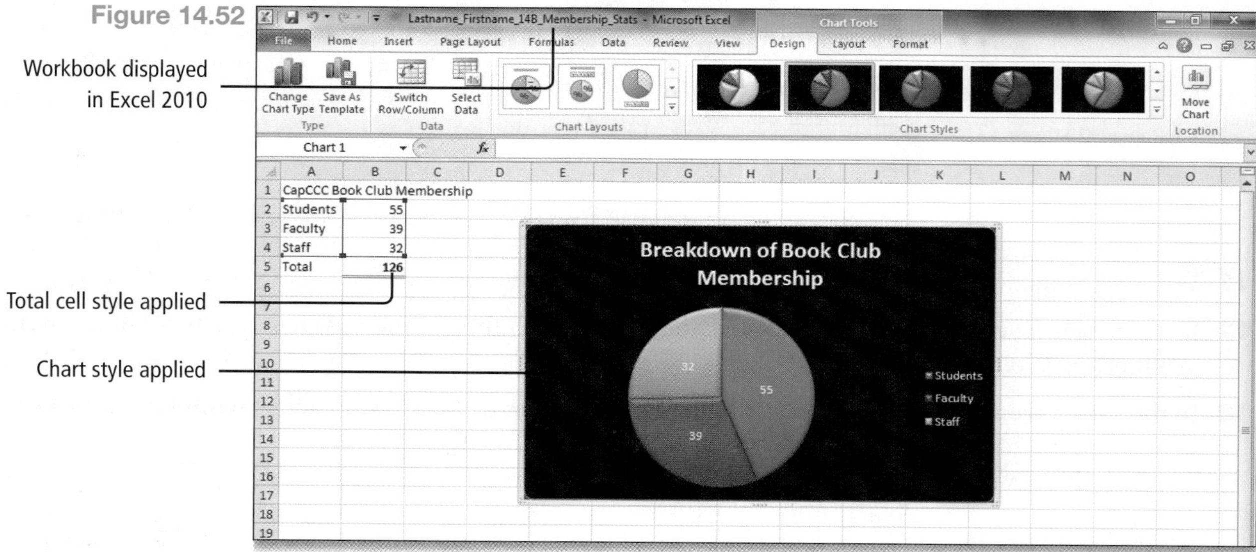

4 Click the **File tab**, click **Exit**, and then in the displayed message, click **Save**. Notice that your Windows Live site redisplays the **CapCCC Book Club** folder of your SkyDrive. Click your **Membership_Stats** file to open it, and then compare your screen with Figure 14.53.

You can see that Office Web Apps ***render***—add realism to graphics with three-dimensional qualities such as shadows and color variations—some but not all of the formatting you applied in the Excel 2010 program. For example, the shading on the pie slices does not display.

Figure 14.53

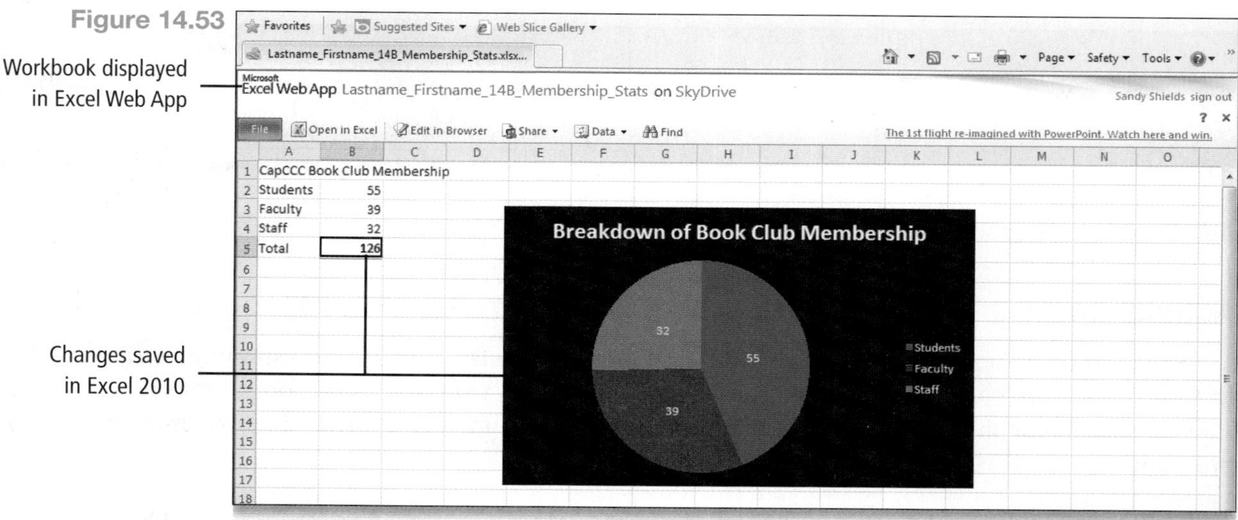

5 Start the **Snipping Tool**, and then create a **Window Snip** of your current window. In your **All In One Chapter 14** folder, save the **JPEG** image as **Lastname_Firstname_14B_Membership_Stats Close** the **Snipping Tool**.

6 Click the **File tab**, and then click **Close** to redisplay your **CapCCC Book Club** folder.

More Knowledge | Silverlight Can Improve the Performance of Office Web Apps

While using one of the Office Web Apps, you might be prompted to install ***Silverlight***, which is a free ***plug-in*** that improves the appearance of some applications in your browser. A plug-in is a software module that adds a specific feature or service to a larger system—it simply *plugs in* to the existing software. If you are using the Word or PowerPoint Web App, installing Silverlight will assist in faster page loading and smoother animations. It also enables PowerPoint slides to scale with the browser. The plug-in has no effect on OneNote or Excel.

Objective 8 | Use Office Web Apps to Create and Edit a PowerPoint Presentation

If you use PowerPoint for presentations away from your desktop PC, the PowerPoint Web App is especially useful, because whether you are traveling or just away from your PC, you can run your slide presentation with high fidelity. You can also make last minute changes to your presentation by using PowerPoint Web App.

Activity 14.16 | Creating and Editing a New PowerPoint Presentation in Office Web Apps

1 Be sure that your **CapCCC Book Club** folder is still active. From the row of commands, create a new **PowerPoint presentation** .

2 As the **Name**, using your own name type **Lastname_Firstname_14B_Club_Marketing** and then click **Save**.

The PowerPoint Web App opens and prompts you to select a Theme. Three tabs display. From the Insert tab, you can insert pictures, SmartArt, and hyperlinks. You can use the View tab to switch back to view mode or to run the slide show.

3 In the **Select Theme** gallery, click the **Pushpin** theme, and then click **Apply**.

4 Click the text *Click to add title* and then type **GET INVOLVED!** Click the text *Click to add subtitle* two times to place the insertion point in the placeholder, and then type **Join CapCCC Book Club**

5 On the **Home tab**, in the **Slides group**, click **New Slide**. In the **New Slide** gallery, click **Title and Content**, and then click **Add Slide**.

The Home tab has commands for formatting text, and for adding, deleting, duplicating, and hiding slides.

6 As the slide title, type **WHY Join?** and then double-click the text *Click to add text.*

PowerPoint Web App saves your work automatically.

7 As the first bullet type **Meet people that share an interest in reading** and press Enter. As the second bullet, type **Read a wide variety of books** Compare your screen with Figure 14.54.

Figure 14.54

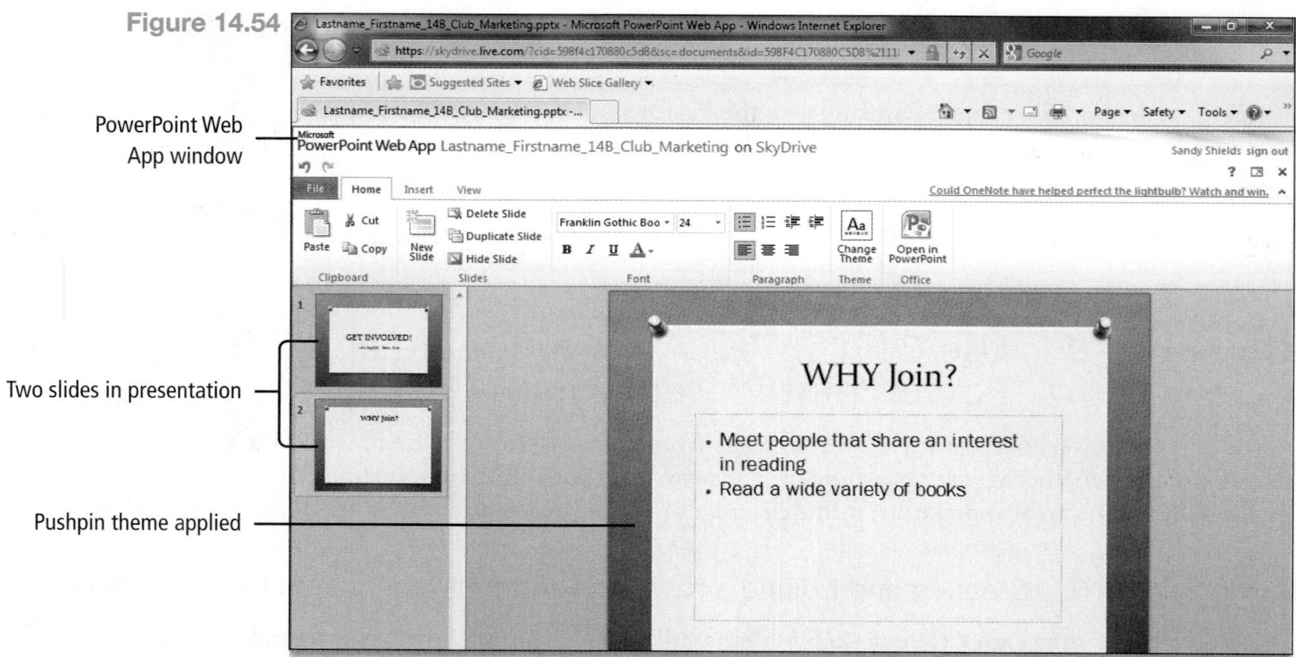

8 On the **Home tab**, in the **Office** group, click **Open in PowerPoint**. If necessary, click OK, enter your Windows Live ID email address and password, and click Enable Editing.

9 On the left, click **Slide 2** to display it. Click the **Animations tab**, and then click the first bullet to select the bulleted item—the bullet and its text. In the **Animation group**, click **Fly In**. Select the second bulleted item, and then click **Float in**.

10 Click the **File tab**, click **Exit**, and then click **Save**.

11 With your **CapCCC Book Club** folder displayed, click the name—**Club_Marketing** presentation. Above the first slide, click **Start Slide Show**. A window opens from which you can run the slide show; if necessary, temporarily enable pop-ups.

12 Click your left mouse button one time to move to the second slide. Click again to display the first bulleted item, and then click again to display the second bulleted item. Notice that the animations you applied display.

You must use the PowerPoint Office 2010 program to apply animations and other advanced formatting, but as you can see, you can still use PowerPoint Web App to run the slide show and see all the effects.

13 Click your left mouse button one time to display the black end slide, and then click again to close the slide show window. Then, click the **File tab** and click **Close**.

Objective 9 | Share and Collaborate on Office Documents in Windows Live

One advantage to using Office Web Apps is that you can share and work with others on the Web. Those with whom you share and collaborate need not have Office installed, can work on a PC or a Mac, or can be using an earlier version of Office.

You can maintain a single copy of a document and share it with others by sending a link to it. Those with whom you share can access the document in their Web browser and also in their desktop versions of Word, Excel, PowerPoint, or OneNote.

Activity 14.17 | Sharing Documents by Using Email

When you attach a Word document, an Excel workbook, or a PowerPoint presentation to an email message in Hotmail, you have the opportunity to save the file to your SkyDrive. Then, when the recipient clicks the link in the message, the document opens in his or her Web browser.

> **Alert! | If you have not installed the free Silverlight application, these activities may not work as described.**
>
> You can install Silverlight from www.microsoft.com/silverlight.

1 If necessary, sign in to your Windows Live account. At the top of the screen, point to **Hotmail**, and then click **Send email**. In the **To:** box, type your partner's email address. In the **Subject:** box, type **Campus Center**

2 Click in the message area and type a greeting and press Enter two times. Type **Here is the information you requested about the Campus Center.**

3 To the right of **Insert**, click **Office docs**. In the **Open** dialog box, navigate to the student files that accompany this textbook, in the lower right above the **Open** button, be sure that *All Files* is indicated—if necessary click the down arrow and select All Files—and then click **w14B_Campus_Center**. In the lower right corner of the dialog box, click **Open**. Compare your screen with Figure 14.55.

If you decide you do not want to send the file, or you selected the wrong file, click the Remove icon to delete the file from your SkyDrive. To set an expiration date for the file, or to give the recipient read-only permission, click Edit details and change the settings.

Figure 14.55

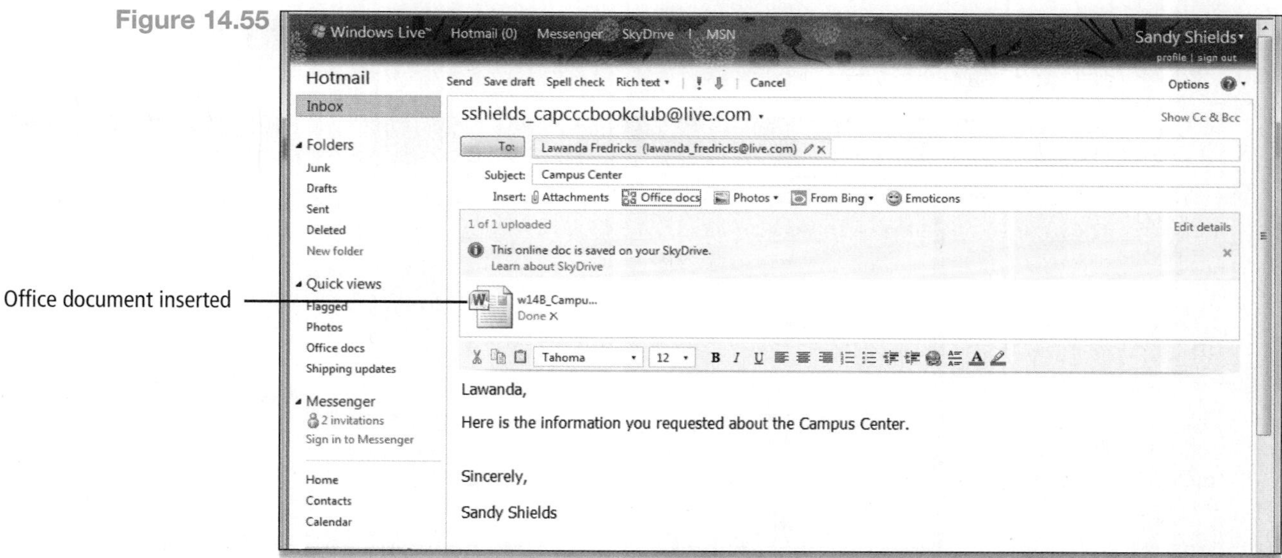

4 Click the **Send** button. If a yellow bar displays at the top of the message regarding spammers, click *enter characters before sending your message*, fill in the CAPTCHA and click **Continue**, click **Close**, and click **Send** again. Compare your screen with Figure 14.56.

A message is displayed to indicate the message was sent, and a link is displayed to allow you to edit the document on your SkyDrive.

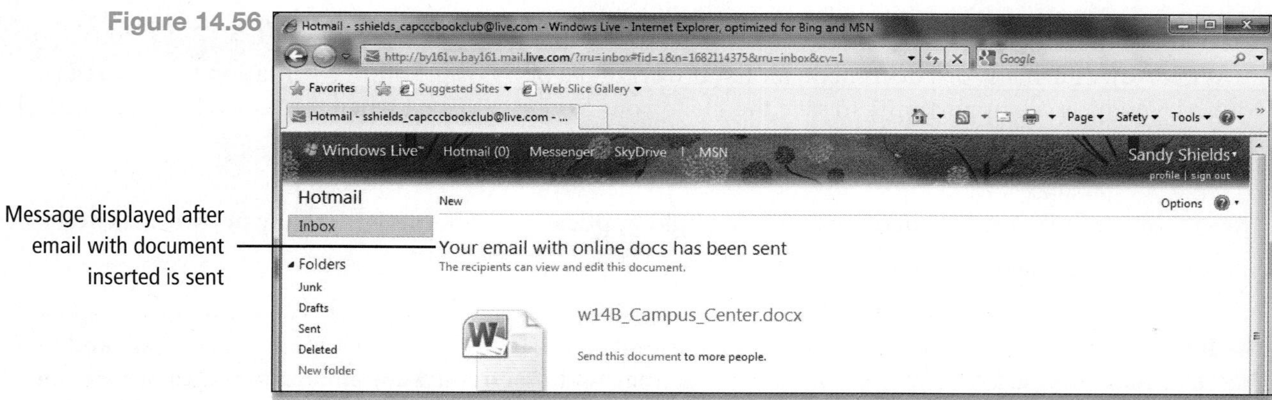

Figure 14.56

Activity 14.18 | Creating a Folder for Sharing Multiple Documents

To share a collection of documents with the same people, create a folder for the documents on your SkyDrive. Anyone to whom you give permission to access the folder will have access to all of the documents in the folder. Within the folder, you can specify permissions; for example, some people can only view the documents, while others can both view and edit documents.

1 At the top of the window, click **SkyDrive** to return to your SkyDrive. Next to **Create**, click **Create folder**. Name the new folder **Club Documents** and then under the folder name, to the right of *Share with: Just me*, click **Change**.

2 In the **Enter a name or an email address** box, type your partner's email address. Compare your screen with Figure 14.57.

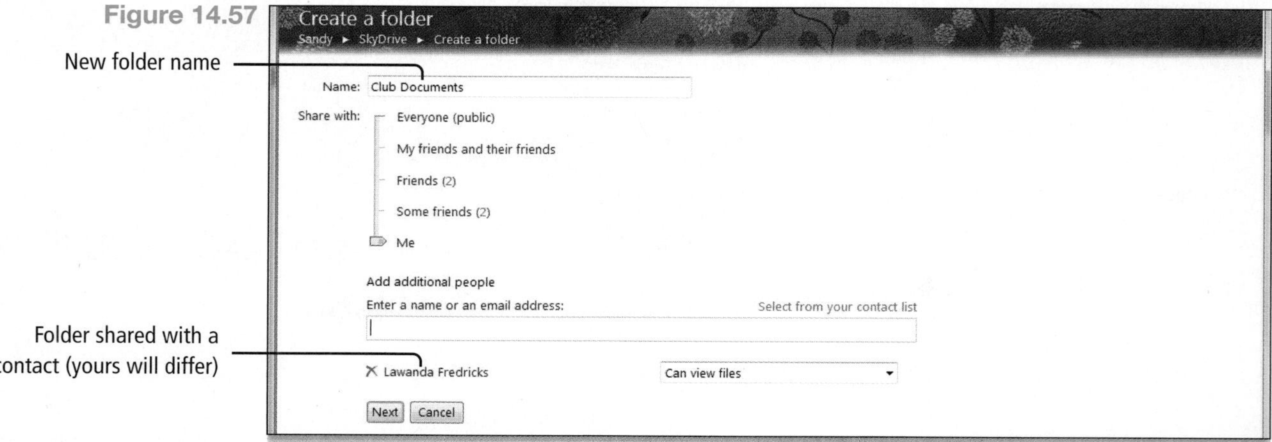

Figure 14.57

3 Click **Next**, click **select documents from your computer**, and then from your student files, add the **pdf14B_CapCCC_Book_Club_Constitution** and the **w14B_Meeting_Announcement** to the folder. Compare your screen with Figure 14.58.

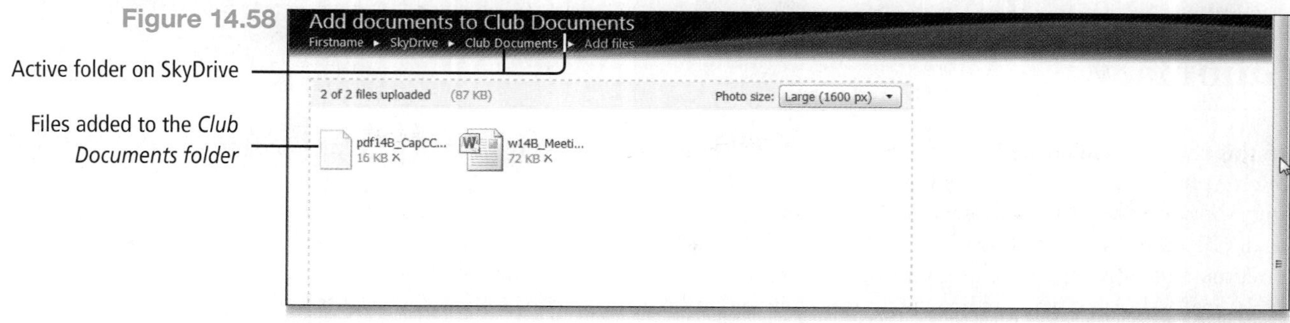

Figure 14.58

4 Click **Continue**. With the two files displayed in your **Club Documents** folder, create a **Window Snip**, and then save the snip as a **JPEG** file in your chapter folder, using your own name, as **Lastname_Firstname_14B_Shared_Folder**

5 Return to your SkyDrive, display your **CapCCC Book Club** folder, and then create a **Window Snip**. Save the snip as a **JPEG** file in your chapter folder, using your own name, as **Lastname_Firstname_14B_CapCCC_Folder**

6 Submit your three snip files to your instructor as directed, and then sign out of your Windows Live account.

End **You have completed Project 14B**

Content-Based Assessments

Summary

In this chapter, you created a Windows Live ID and profile to use with Windows Live and Office Web Apps. With your Windows Live ID, you were able to communicate with others via email using Hotmail, send instant messages using Messenger, and manage and share calendars with a Hotmail Calendar. Your account also includes access to Windows Live SkyDrive, where you can store documents of any type—including those you create using Office Web Apps. By using the features of Office Web Apps, you get browser-based viewing and editing of your Office documents from anywhere that you have a Web connection. If you have Microsoft Office 2010, you can save your Word, Excel, and PowerPoint documents directly from your Microsoft Office programs to SkyDrive, which is the free online storage service you get when you create a Windows Live ID. If you have an earlier version of Office, you can upload Office documents to SkyDrive, and if you have no Office, for example if you are using a Mac, you can use your Web browser to create new Office documents in SkyDrive.

Key Terms

Bot 660
Business use of Office Web Apps 680
CAPTCHA 660
Cloud computing 678
Contacts 673
Email 662
Emoticon 676
Friends 673
High-fidelity viewing 680
Hotmail 662
Hyperlink 683
iCalendar 669
.ics file format 669
IM 658
Instant messaging 658
Office Web Apps 658
Personal use of Office Web Apps 680
PivotTables 685
Platform 658
Plug-in 689
Pop-Out button 684
Profile 660
Reading View 683
Render 688
SharePoint 678
Silverlight 689
Simultaneous editing 685
Snip 662
Snipping Tool 662
Strong password 659
Thumbnail 679
Weak password 659
Web browser 658
Windows Live 658
Windows Live Essentials 658
Windows Live ID 658
Windows Live Messenger 673
Windows Live SkyDrive 678

Check Your Knowledge

Matching and Multiple Choice items are available in MyITLab and on the Companion Web Site.

Apply 14A skills from these Objectives:

1 Create a Windows Live Account
2 Send and Receive Email
3 Manage and Share Your Windows Live Calendar
4 Use Windows Live Messenger to Communicate

Mastering Windows Live | Project 14C Membership Drive

In the following Mastering Windows Live project, you will send an email, add items to your calendar, and use Messenger to communicate instantly. Your screen snips will look similar to Figure 14.59.

Project Files

For Project 14C, you will not need any files.

You will save your files as:

Lastname_Firstname_14C_Email.jpg
Lastname_Firstname_14C_Calendar.jpg
Lastname_Firstname_14C_Messenger.jpg

Project Results

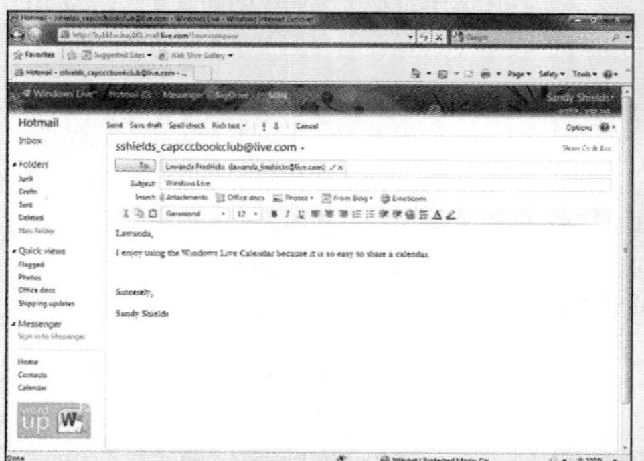

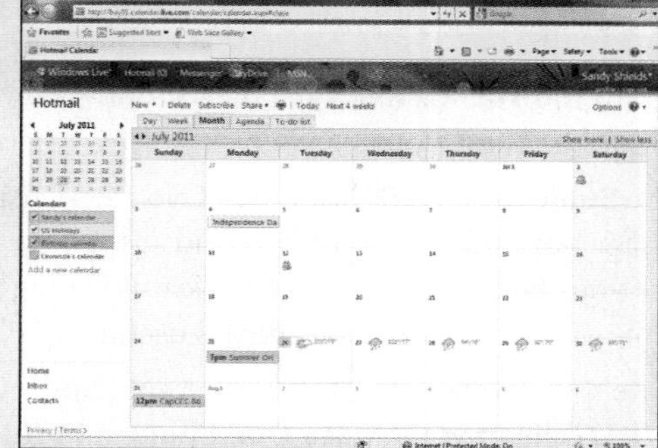

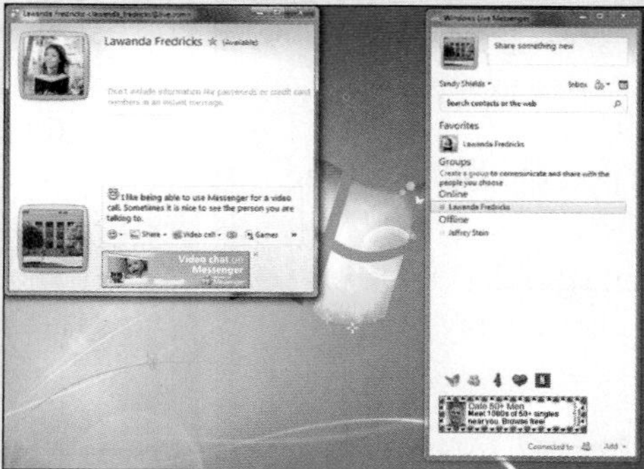

Figure 14.59

(Project 14C Membership Drive continues on the next page)

Mastering Windows Live | Project 14C Membership Drive (continued)

Alert! | To complete this project, you will need to partner with a classmate in the same manner you did in Activities 14.03 through 14.08.

1 From your browser, navigate to **www.live.com** and sign in using your Windows Live ID and password.

2 Under **Hotmail highlights**, click **Options**, and then, under *Show options for*, click **Hotmail**.

a. Under **Writing email**, click **Message font and signature**.

b. Under **Message font**, change the font to **Garamond**. Under **Personal signature**, select your signature lines, and then change the font to **Garamond**.

c. **Save** the changes.

3 At the top of the screen, point to **Hotmail**, and then click **Send email**.

a. Click in the **To:** box and type the Windows Live email address for your partner.

b. In the **Subject** box, type **Windows Live** Click inside the message box and type a greeting and short message to share your favorite Windows Live feature along with a reason why you think the feature is useful.

c. Create a **Window Snip** of your current window. Save the **JPEG** file in your **All In One Chapter 14** folder as **Lastname_Firstname_14C_Email Close** the **Snipping Tool**.

d. Click **Send**.

4 At the top of the window, point to **Hotmail**, and then click **Calendar**.

a. On the left side of the calendar, select the **US Holidays** check box to display holidays on your calendar. If necessary, select your partner's calendar check box to clear his or her events from your calendar.

b. Click the **New arrow**, and then click **Event** to display the **Add an event** dialog box. Enter and save the information for an event that you have scheduled for next week. Enter a birthday on the second of the month using your own name.

c. Create a **Window Snip** of your current window. Save the **JPEG** file in your **All In One Chapter 14** folder as **Lastname_Firstname_14C_Calendar Close** the **Snipping Tool**.

d. **Sign out** of Windows Live. **Close** your browser.

5 Start **Windows Live Messenger** and sign in using your Windows Live ID and password. Find your partner in the **online** group, and display the message window.

a. Below the message window, click the first icon, and then select an emoticon showing happiness. Then type a short message telling your friend about a feature in Windows Live Messenger you like and why you think the feature is useful.

b. Create a **Window Snip** of your current window. Save the **JPEG** file in your **All In Chapter 14** folder as **Lastname_Firstname_14C_Messenger Close** the **Snipping Tool**.

c. **Send** the message. **Close** the message window. In the upper right corner, click your name, and then click **Sign out from everywhere**. **Close** the Messenger window without saving the messages.

6 Submit you three screen snips as directed by your instructor.

End You have completed Project 14C

Apply **14B** skills from these Objectives:

5 Use Windows Live SkyDrive
6 Use Office Web Apps to Create and Edit a Word Document
7 Use Office Web Apps to Create and Edit an Excel Workbook
8 Use Office Web Apps to Create and Edit a PowerPoint Presentation
9 Share and Collaborate on Office Documents in Windows Live

Mastering Office Web Apps | Project 14D Read Now!

In the following project, you will create folders and files on your Windows Live SkyDrive related to the Read Now! event that the book club is planning. You will create four snip files that will look similar to Figure 14.60.

Project Files

For Project 14D, you will need the following files:

w14_Read_Now
w14D_Membership_Breakfast

You will save your snip files as:

Lastname_Firstname_14D_Read_Now_Folder
Lastname_Firstname_14D_Email_Link
Lastname_Firstname_14D_New_Members
Lastname_Firstname_14D_Membership_Folder

Project Results

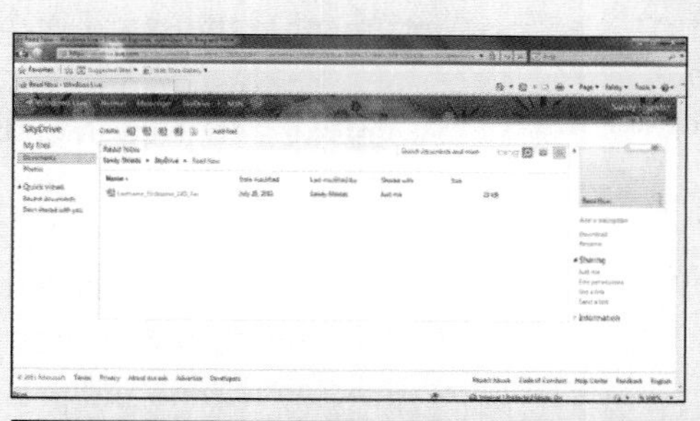

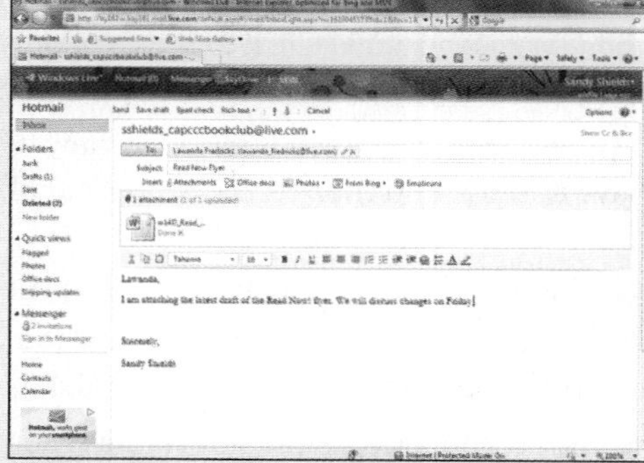

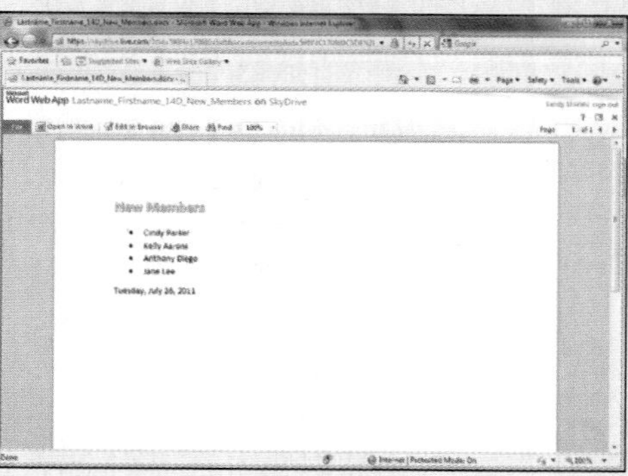

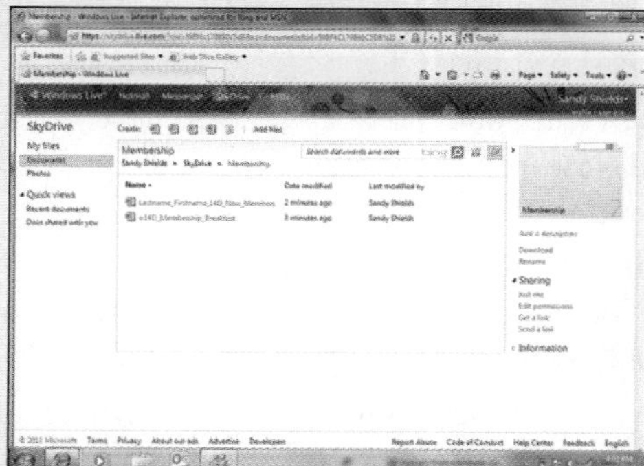

Figure 14.60

(Project 14D Read Now! continues on the next page)

Content-Based Assessments

Mastering Office Web Apps | Project 14D Read Now! (continued)

> **Alert! | To complete this project, you will need to partner with a classmate in the same manner you did in Activities 14.03 through 14.08.**

1 Sign on to your Windows Live account. At the top of the window, click **SkyDrive**, and then create a new folder named **Read Now**

- **a.** On your computer, start **Word**, and then From **Backstage** view, then on the left, click **New**.
- **b.** Under **Office.com Templates**, click **Faxes**, and then click the **Fax cover sheet (Clipboard design)**. In the lower right portion of the screen, click **Download**.
- **c.** Click to the right of *For:*, press Spacebar one time, and then type **Sandy Shields** Click to the right of *Fax number:*, press Spacebar one time, and then type **(202) 555-3159**
- **d.** Click to the right of *Regarding:*, press Spacebar one time, and then type **Read Now!** Click to the right of *Number of pages:*, press Spacebar one time, and then type **3**

2 Click the **File tab** to display **Backstage** view. On the left click **Save & Send**, and then in the center panel, under **Save & Send**, click **Save to Web**.

- **a.** If necessary, in the right panel, sign in to your Windows Live site, and then open your **Read Now** folder. At the bottom of the folder list, click **Save As**.
- **b.** Using your own name, as the **File name** type **Lastname_Firstname_14D_Fax** and then click **Save**. If necessary, click OK.
- **c.** **Close** Word, and then in your SkyDrive, open the **Read Now** folder and verify that your new document is saved there.
- **d.** Create a **Window snip**. Save it as **JPEG**, using your own name, as **Lastname_Firstname_14D_Read_Now_Folder**

3 At the top of the window, point to **Hotmail**, and then click **Send email**. Send the email to your partner, and as the **Subject** type **Read Now! Flyer**

- **a.** In the message area, type a greeting followed by this message: **I am attaching the latest draft of the Read Now! flyer. We will discuss changes on Friday.**
- **b.** Below the Subject box, to the right of **Insert**, click **Office docs**, and then navigate to your student files. In the lower right, if necessary click the arrow and click **All Files**. Click the Word document **w14D_Read_Now** and then click **Open**.
- **c.** Create a **Window Snip** of this **email** message with the link to the SkyDrive document, save it as a **JPEG**, using your own name, as **Lastname_Firstname_14D_Email_Link**
- **d.** Send the email.

4 At the top of the window, click **SkyDrive**, and then in the upper portion of the screen, to the right of **Create**, click the **Create folder** button. Name the folder **Membership**

- **a.** Click **Next**, click **select documents from your computer**, and then navigate to the location where you can access the student files that accompany this textbook. Click the **w14D_Membership_Breakfast**, and then click **Open**.
- **b.** Click **Continue**.

5 With your **Membership** folder open, in the upper portion of the screen, click the **Word** icon to create a new document in the Word Web App.

- **a.** Using your own name, type **Lastname_Firstname_14D_New_Members** and then click **Save** to open Word Web App.
- **b.** Type **New Members** and then press Enter one time. On the **Home tab**, in the **Paragraph group**, click the **Bullets** button, and then type **Cindy Parker** Press Enter.
- **c.** Type **Kelly Aarons** and press Enter. Type **Anthony Diego** and press Enter. Type **Jane Lee** and press Enter. Press Backspace two times.
- **d.** Click the **File tab**, and then click **Open in Word**. Click **Save**; if necessary click OK and enter your Windows Live ID credentials. When Word starts, click **Enable Editing**.
- **e.** Select the title *New Members*. On the **Home tab**, in the **Font group**, click the **Font Size arrow**, and then click **18**.
- **f.** While the text is selected, on the **Home tab**, in the **Font group**, click the **Text Effects** button. In the gallery, click the first text effect.
- **g.** Click the blank line at the bottom of the document to move the insertion point. On the **Insert tab**, in the **Text group**, click the **Date & Time** button. Click the second format on the list (Day, Date), and then click **OK**.

(Project 14D Read Now! continues on the next page)

Mastering Office Web Apps | Project 14D Read Now! (continued)

h. Display **Backstage** view, and then click **Exit**. Click **Save**.

6 In the list of files in your **Membership** folder, click the name of the file you were just editing—**New_Members**. Notice that the document opens in the Reading View of Word Web App.

a. Create a **Window snip** of your document displayed in Reading View, and then save it as a **JPEG**, using your own name, as **Lastname_Firstname_14D_New_Members**

b. Click the **File tab**, and then click **Close**.

7 Create a **Window snip** of your **Membership** folder, and then save it as a **JPEG**, using your own name, as **Lastname_Firstname_14D_Membership_Folder**

8 **Sign out** of Windows Live, and submit your snip files to your instructor as directed.

End **You have completed Project 14D**

Apply 14A and 14B skills from these Objectives:

1. Create a Windows Live Account
2. Send and Receive Email
3. Manage and Share Your Windows Live Calendar
4. Use Windows Live Messenger to Communicate
5. Use Windows Live SkyDrive
6. Use Office Web Apps to Create and Edit a Word Document
7. Use Office Web Apps to Create and Edit an Excel Workbook
8. Use Office Web Apps to Create and Edit a PowerPoint Presentation
9. Share and Collaborate on Office Documents in Windows Live

Mastering Windows Live and Office Web Apps | Project 14E Food Drive

In the following project, you will use Windows Live to plan and manage the CapCCC Book Club's annual food drive. Your screen snips will look similar to Figure 14.61.

Project Files

For Project 14E, you will need the following files:

pdf14E_Food_Drive_Flyer (PDF)
w14E_Food_Pantry
jpg14E_Food_Photo (jpg)

You will save your files as:

Lastname_Firstname_14E_Email_Request.jpg
Lastname_Firstname_14E_Next_Week.jpg
Lastname_Firstname_14E_Delivery_Plan.jpg
Lastname_Firstname_14E_Food_Drive_Folder.jpg

Project Results

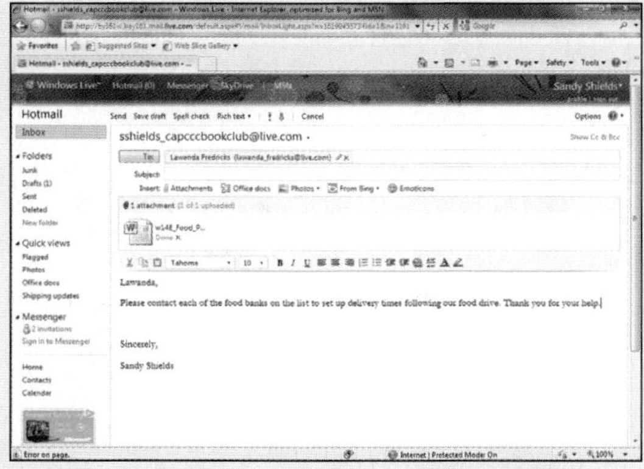

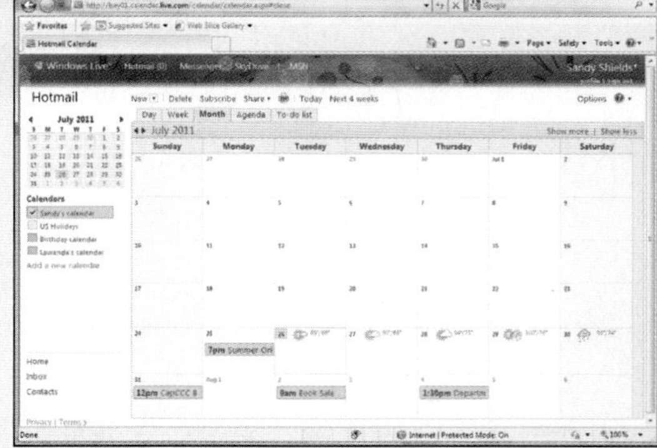

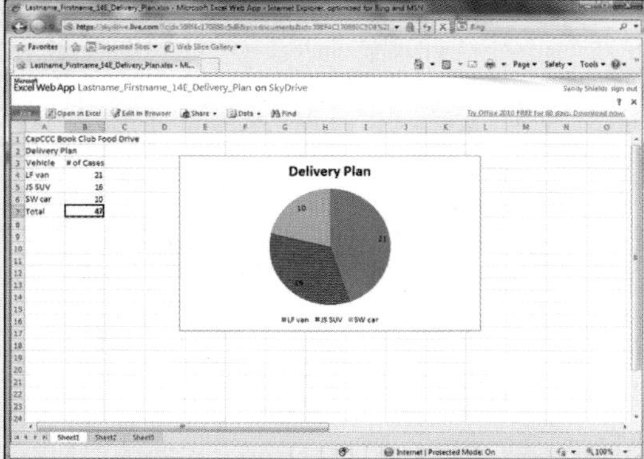

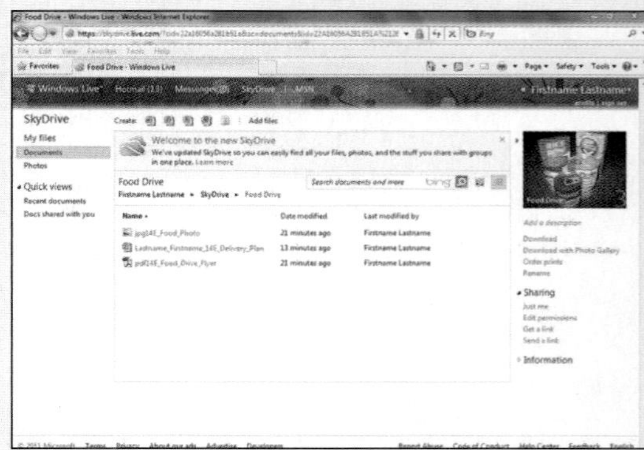

Figure 14.61

(Project 14E Food Drive continues on the next page)

Mastering Windows Live and Office Web Apps | Project 14E Food Drive (continued)

> Alert! | **To complete this project, you will need to partner with a classmate in the same manner you did in Activities 14.03 through 14.08.**

1 From your browser, navigate to **www.live.com** and sign in using your Windows Live ID and password.

2 Using **Hotmail**, send an email to your partner.

a. In the **Subject** box, type **Food Drive** Click inside the message box, type a greeting, and then type **Please contact each of the food banks on the list to set up delivery times following our food drive. Thank you for your help**.

b. Below the **Subject** box, on the **Insert** row, click **Office docs**, and then from your student files, insert the Word document **w14E_Food_Pantry**.

c. Create a **Window Snip** of this **email** message with the link to the document on the SkyDrive. Save it as a **JPEG** file in your **All In One Chapter 14** folder, using your own name, as **Lastname_Firstname_14E_Email_Request** and then **Send** the email.

3 Using **Calendar**, create an event that you have scheduled two different days next week. Do not display the **US Holidays** or **Birthday calendar** on your calendar. Create a **Window Snip** of your Calendar window. Save the **JPEG** file in your **All In One Chapter 14** folder, using your own first and last name, as **Lastname_Firstname_14E_Next_Week**

4 Display your SkyDrive. Create a new folder named **Food Drive** Share the folder with your partner who can add, edit details, and delete files.

a. From your student data files, add **pdf14E_Food_Drive_Flyer** and **jpg14E_Food_Photo** to your **Food Drive** folder. Display the folder list with the two files.

b. Using Excel Web App, in your **Food Drive** folder, create an Excel workbook named **Lastname_Firstname_14E_Delivery_Plan**

c. In cell **A1**, type **CapCCC Book Club Food Drive** and press Enter. In cell **A2**, type **Delivery Plan** and press Enter.

d. In the cell range **A3:B6**, type the following data:

Vehicle	# of Cases
LF van	21
JS SUV	16
SW car	10

e. Click in cell **A7**, type **Total** and then press Tab. Insert a function to total the **# of Cases** column. Press Enter.

f. Insert a pie chart to display the data in the range **A4:B6**.

5 Open the workbook in Excel 2010. If necessary click OK, enter your Windows Live ID credentials, and then Enable Editing.

a. Apply the **Total** cell style to cell **B7**.

b. Click the chart to select it. On the **Layout tab**, in the **Labels group**, click the **Legend** button, and then click **Show Legend at bottom**. On the **Layout tab**, in the **Labels group**, click the **Chart Title** button, and then click **Above Chart**. Select **Chart Title** and type **Delivery Plan** On the **Layout tab**, in the **Labels group**, click the **Data Labels** button, and then click **Inside End**.

c. Click the **File tab**, and then click **Exit**. Click **Save**.

d. In your **Food Drive** folder, click the name of the file you were just editing—**Delivery Plan** to display it. Create a **Full-screen snip** of your document, and then save it as a **JPEG**, using your own name, as **Lastname_Firstname_14E_Delivery_Plan Close** the workbook.

e. Click the **File tab**, and then click **Close**.

6 Create a **Window snip** of your **Food Drive** folder, and then save it as a **JPEG**, using your own name, as **Lastname_Firstname_14E_Food_Drive_Folder**

7 **Sign out** of Windows Live, and submit your four snip files to your instructor as directed.

End **You have completed Project 14E**

Unit 5 Case Project

© Dmitry Yashkin/ Shutterstock

Databases Created by a Library Assistant at a College; Windows Live and Excel Web App

In this Unit Case Project, you will create a new Work Study Students table in the Career Resources database and append data from Excel into it. You will use the table to create a form and a report. You will also use the database to answer questions about the career resources by creating, editing, and formatting queries. Additionally, you will use Office Web Apps to create and store documents. Your completed objects will look similar to the ones shown in Figure 5.1.

Project Files

For Unit 5 Case Project, you will need the following files:

aU5_Career_Resources
eU5_WorkStudy_Students

You will save your files as:

Lastname_Firstname_U5_Career_Resources
Lastname_Firstname_U5_Work_Schedule
Lastname_Firstname_U5_SkyDrive_Folder

Project Results

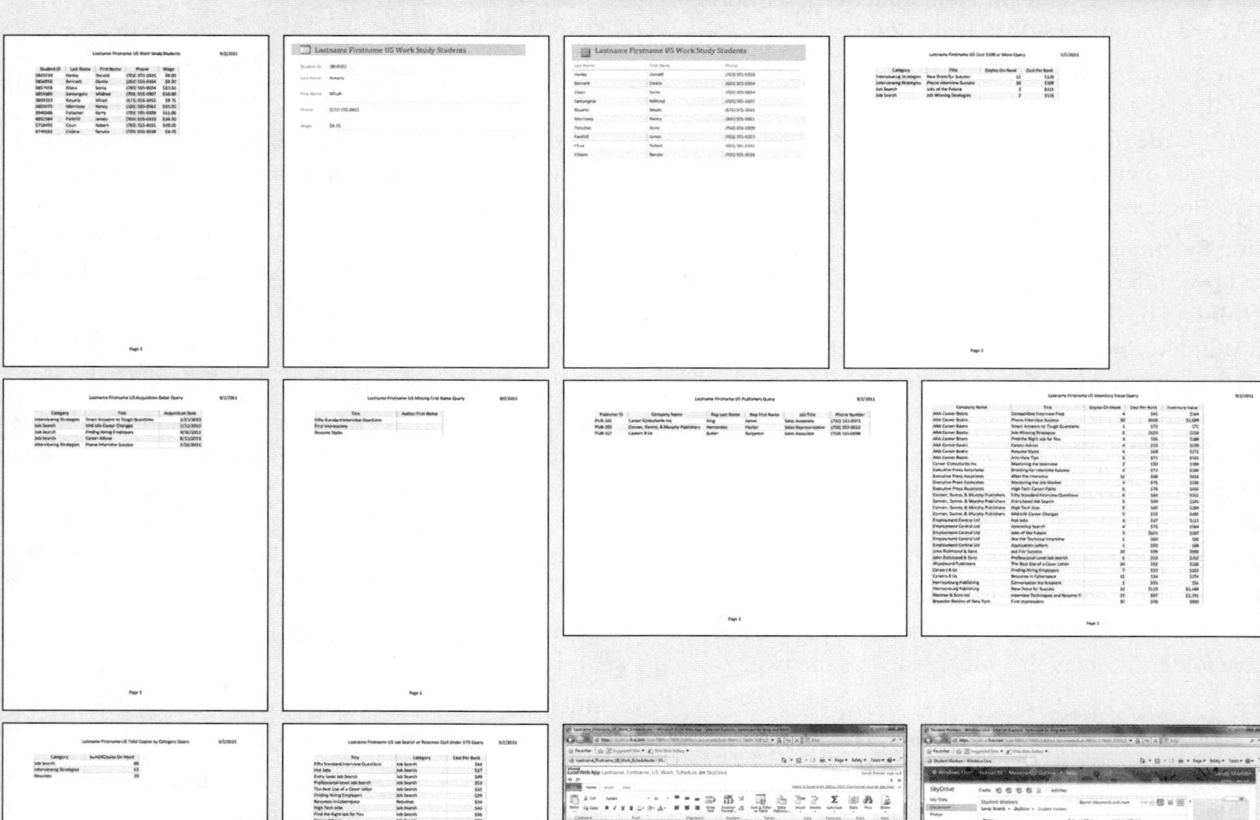

Figure 5.1

Databases Created by a Library Assistant at a College; Windows Live and Excel Web App (continued)

1 Start **Access**. From your student files, open the **aU5_Career_Resources** database; if necessary, enable the content. On your storage device, create a new folder named **All In One Unit 5** and then save the database as **Lastname_Firstname_U5_Career Resources** Enable the content if necessary.

2 Open the two tables to become familiar with the data, view the relationship between the two tables, and then close all the database objects. One book publisher can have many book titles in the Career field.

3 **Create** a new table in **Datasheet** view. Change the field name of the **ID** field to **Student ID** Using the **Text** data type, name the next three fields as **Last Name** and **First Name** and **Phone** Name the fifth field **Wage** and use the **Currency** data type.

4 Switch to **Design** view; name the table **Lastname Firstname U5 Work Study Students** In **Design** view, click in the **Student ID** field, and then change the **Data Type** of the field to **Text**. Change the **Field Size** to **7** Be sure that **Student ID** field is set as the **Primary Key**. Close the table and save the design changes.

5 From the **External Data tab**, import an **Excel** spreadsheet. **Browse** to the location of your student files, and then select the Excel file **eU5_WorkStudy_Students**. Click the **Open** button, and then **Append** a copy of the records to your **U5 Work Study Students** table. If necessary, click Open in response to the security message, and then complete the steps in the wizard by clicking **Next** and then **Finish** and then **Close**. Open your **U5 Work Study Students** table to display the data that was imported from Excel. Select all the fields and apply **Best Fit**. **Save** the table. Create a paper or electronic printout as directed, and then hold this file until you complete the project.

6 With the **U5 Work Study Students** table open, **Create** a **Form**. **Save** the form as **Lastname Firstname U5 Work Study Students Form** Using **Form** view, display the fifth record, and then click the **Record Selector bar** on the left to select only this record. Display the **Print** dialog box, and in the lower left corner, click **Setup**. Click the **Columns tab**, change the **Width** to **7.5** so that the form prints on one page, and then click **OK**. Print or create an electronic printout of this record and hold the file until you complete this project. **Close** the form.

7 With the **U5 Work Study Students** table open, **Create** a **Report**. Delete the **Student ID** and **Wage** fields from the report. At the bottom of the report, select and then delete the page number control. At the top of the form in the blue title, click the current date, and then with the date selected—bordered in orange—press Delete. Delete the current time in the same manner. Click the title of the report, and then drag the right orange border to the right as necessary to display the title on one line. **Save** the report as **Lastname Firstname U5 Phone List** Display the **Print** dialog box and change the column width to 7.5. Create a paper or electronic printout as directed. Hold this file until you complete this project. **Close** the report and the table. **Close** the **Navigation Pane**.

8 **Create** a query in **Query Design** view using the **Career Titles** table to answer the question, *In alphabetical order by Category, what are the Titles, the number of Copies On Hand, and the Cost Per Book for titles that cost $100 or more?* Display the fields in the order listed in the question. Four records meet the criteria. Apply **Best Fit** to the columns in the query results. **Save** the query as **Lastname Firstname U5 Cost $100 or More Query** and create a paper or electronic printout as directed. Close the query.

9 Display the **Navigation Pane**, open the **Acquisition Dates** query, and then display the query in **Query Design** view. Save a copy of the query object as **Lastname Firstname U5 Acquisition Dates Query** Modify the query to answer the question *By category, which titles were acquired—shown in reverse chronological order by Acquisition Date—between 1/15/2011 and 6/15/2013?* Display the fields in the order listed in the question. Five records meet the criteria. Apply **Best Fit** to the columns in the query results. Create a paper or electronic printout as directed. Hold this file until you complete the project. **Close** the query, saving changes.

10 Create a query in **Query Design** view using **Career Titles** table to answer the question, *For which titles is the author's first name missing?* Three records meet the criteria. **Save** the query as **Lastname Firstname U5 Missing First Name Query** and then create a paper or electronic copy as directed. Hold the file until you complete the project. **Close** the query.

(Unit 5 Case Project continues on the next page)

Unit 5 Case Project

Databases Created by a Library Assistant at a College; Windows Live and Excel Web App (continued)

11 **Create** a query in **Query Design** view using the **Publishers** table and all of the table's fields to answer the question *Which company names begin with the letter C?* Three records meet the criteria. **Save** the query as **Lastname Firstname U5 Publishers Query** Display the Print Preview dialog box and set the **Page Layout** to **Landscape**. **Close** the query and hold the file.

12 **Create** a query in **Query Design** view using the **Career Titles** and **Publishers** tables and a calculated field to answer the question, *For each Company Name and Title, what is the inventory value (copies on hand x cost per book)?* **Save** the query as **Lastname Firstname U5 Inventory Value Query Run** the query, switch back to **Design** view, and format the **Inventory Value** field to display in **Currency** format with **0** decimal places. **Run** the query again. Apply **Best Fit** to the columns in the query results. Display **Print Preview** and set the **Page Layout** to **Landscape** and set the margins to **Normal**. Create a paper or electronic printout, hold the file, and then **Close** the query, saving changes.

13 **Create** a query in **Query Design** view. Use the **Career Titles** table and the **Sum** aggregate function to answer the question, *For each category, how many copies are on hand displayed in descending sort order?* Apply **Best Fit** to the columns in the query results. **Save** the query as **Lastname Firstname U5 Total Copies by Category Query** and then create a paper or electronic copy as directed. **Close** the query and hold the file.

14 **Create** a query in **Query Design** view. Use the **Career Titles** table to answer the question, *Which titles in the category of Job Search or Resumes cost less than $75 per book?* **Save** the query as **Lastname Firstname U5 Job Search or Resumes Cost Under $75 Query** and then create a paper or electronic copy as directed. Hold the file and **Close** the query.

15 **Close** any open database objects. **Close** the database and then **Exit** Access. Submit your database and the ten paper or electronic printouts—table, single record form, report, and seven queries—that are the results of this project.

Windows Live and Excel Web App

1 From your browser, navigate to **www.live.com** and sign in using your Windows Live ID and password.

2 Display your **SkyDrive**. Create a new folder named **Student Workers** From your student data files, add the Excel file **eU5_WorkStudy_Students** to this folder.

3 Using Excel Web App, open a new workbook, and then save it in your **Student Workers** folder as **Lastname_Firstname_U5_Work_Schedule**

4 In cell **A1**, type **Hours Worked** and press Enter. In cell **A2**, type **May 1-30** and press Enter.

5 Widen **column A** to approximately 2 inches, and then in the range **A3:B7**, type the following data:

Robert Chun	21
Donald Hanby	19
Nancy Morrissey	30
James Parkhill	23
Mildred Santangelo	33

6 Click in cell **A8**, and type **Total** Press Tab, and then on the Ribbon, in the **Formulas group**, click the **AutoSum** button to total the *Hours Worked*. Press Enter. Your result is 126.

7 Select the range **A1:A2** and apply **Bold** and **Italic** formatting. Select the range **A3:B7**, and then insert a **Clustered Column** chart. Remove the **Legend**.

8 Click cell **B8**, create a **Window Snip** of your worksheet, and then save it as a **JPEG**, using your own name, as **Lastname_Firstname_U5_Work_Schedule** From the **File tab**, **Close** the workbook to display the contents of your **Student Workers** folder.

9 Create a **Window Snip** of your Student Workers folder, and then using your own name, save the snip as a **JPEG** as **Lastname_Firstname_U5_SkyDrive_Folder**

10 **Sign out** of Windows live, and submit your snip files to your instructor as directed.

Networks, Communication, and Cloud Computing Applications

Chapters in Unit 6:

© Netfalls/Shutterstock

Job Focus: Director of Sales for a Hotel

View Unit 6 Video to meet a Director of Sales for a hotel

At the end of this unit, you will have the opportunity to complete a case project that focuses on the job of a Director of Sales at a hotel. If you had a position like this, some of the things you might do are: make sure that guest rooms are equipped with the types of Internet and wireless communications that business travelers expect in a hotel; present the benefits of the hotel to local companies for their employees who visit on business; track sales information; and collaborate with local businesses to set up business meetings and events at the hotel.

Computer Networks and Communication

OUTCOMES

At the end of this chapter you will be able to:

Recognize the components, importance, advantages, and disadvantages of networking computers.

Identify types of networks, wired transmission media, wireless transmission media, related applications, and their influence on convergence.

OBJECTIVES

Mastering these objectives will enable you to:

1. Examine Network Fundamentals (p. 707)
2. Assess the Structure and Value of Networks (p. 712)
3. Implement Local Area Networks (p. 712)
4. Analyze Wide Area Networks (p. 721)
5. Set Up a Home Network (p. 724)
6. Understand Data Transmission (p. 726)
7. Evaluate Wired and Wireless Transmission Media (p. 728)
8. Assess Wired and Wireless Applications (p. 736)
9. Recognize Convergence (p. 740)

© olly/Shutterstock

Job Focus:
Director of Sales for a Hotel

In This Chapter

As a Director of Sales for a hotel that is part of a global chain, your success depends on your ability to sell rooms and meeting space. This will require you to work with your Marketing Department and to connect with perspective customers quickly. Your connection will most likely be in digital form—an e-mail, Facebook reply, or a response to an entry in the hotel's blog. You will need to be knowledgeable of these methods of communication and know how to access them and create replies.

In this chapter, you will learn the fundamentals of networking, which is the feature of computers that enables connectivity and communication. By using computer networking, you will be able to maximize technology to successfully perform your job.

Objective 1 | Examine Network Fundamentals

As the Director of Sales for a hotel that is part of a global hotel chain, you communicate with clients who are planning large events such as weddings, business meetings, and conferences. You conduct your communications with clients by using e-mail and wireless technologies. Sometimes you must redirect clients to a member hotel that is larger, has more appropriate space or amenities, or that has enough available rooms. Communication with clients that is fast and secure is critical to what you do. You need to understand network and communication terminology so that you can explain the value and importance of these communications to your staff. Where do you start?

Computer networking is essential to both business and home users. As an informed and literate computer user and employee, you must know enough about networking to understand the benefits and potential problems of connecting computers. Organizations spend billions of dollars on networking equipment each year to create centralized pools of information and connect international offices with the goal of increasing service and profit. These organizations are looking to employ individuals who understand basic networking concepts, know how to utilize this technology, and are able to discuss problems and suggest improvements.

Concept 15.01 | Overviewing Networks

A ***network*** is a group of two or more computer systems linked together to exchange data and share an Internet connection and resources, including expensive peripherals such as high-performance laser printers. Just a few years ago, computer networks for business and organizations had only two classifications—local area networks and wide area networks—that were based on the size of the geographical region that a network spans. Now, additional categories have evolved:

- A ***local area network (LAN)*** uses cables, radio waves, or infrared signals to link computers or peripherals, such as printers, within a small geographic area, for example, in a building or a group of buildings. LANs are typically owned and managed by a single person or organization.
- A ***wide area network (WAN)*** uses long-distance transmission media, like satellites and leased lines, to link computers separated by a few miles or even thousands of miles. A WAN is a geographically dispersed collection of LANs (Figure 15.1). The Internet is the largest WAN; it connects millions of LANs all over the globe. Unlike the Internet, which is not owned by any individual or organization, some WANs are privately owned.
- A ***metropolitan area network (MAN)*** links a city or town, and is usually larger than a LAN but smaller than a WAN. Typically, a MAN is owned by a single government or organization, for example, a network to connect Fire Stations across a region or county, or a network that supports a site like 511NY (**www.511ny.org/traffic.aspx**), which informs travelers of statewide traffic conditions.
- A ***campus area network (CAN)*** links a college campus or business park. A CAN is smaller than a WAN and is created by connecting several LANs (Figure 15.2).
- A ***personal area network (PAN)*** connects an individual's own personal communication devices, like a notebook, cell phone, personal digital assistant, and portable printer. A PAN is typically arranged within a range of 30 feet or less and usually involves wireless technology.

Concept 15.02 | Clarifying Communication Devices

Any type of network requires communications devices to convert data into signals that can travel over a physical wired or wireless medium. ***Communication devices*** include computers, modems, routers, switches, hubs, wireless access points, and network interface cards. These devices transform data from analog to digital signals and back again, determine efficient data-transfer pathways, boost signal strength, and facilitate digital communication (Figure 15.3).

Any device connected to a network is referred to as a ***node***, and can be any computer, peripheral, or communication device. Each device on the network

GO! All In One | Chapter 15

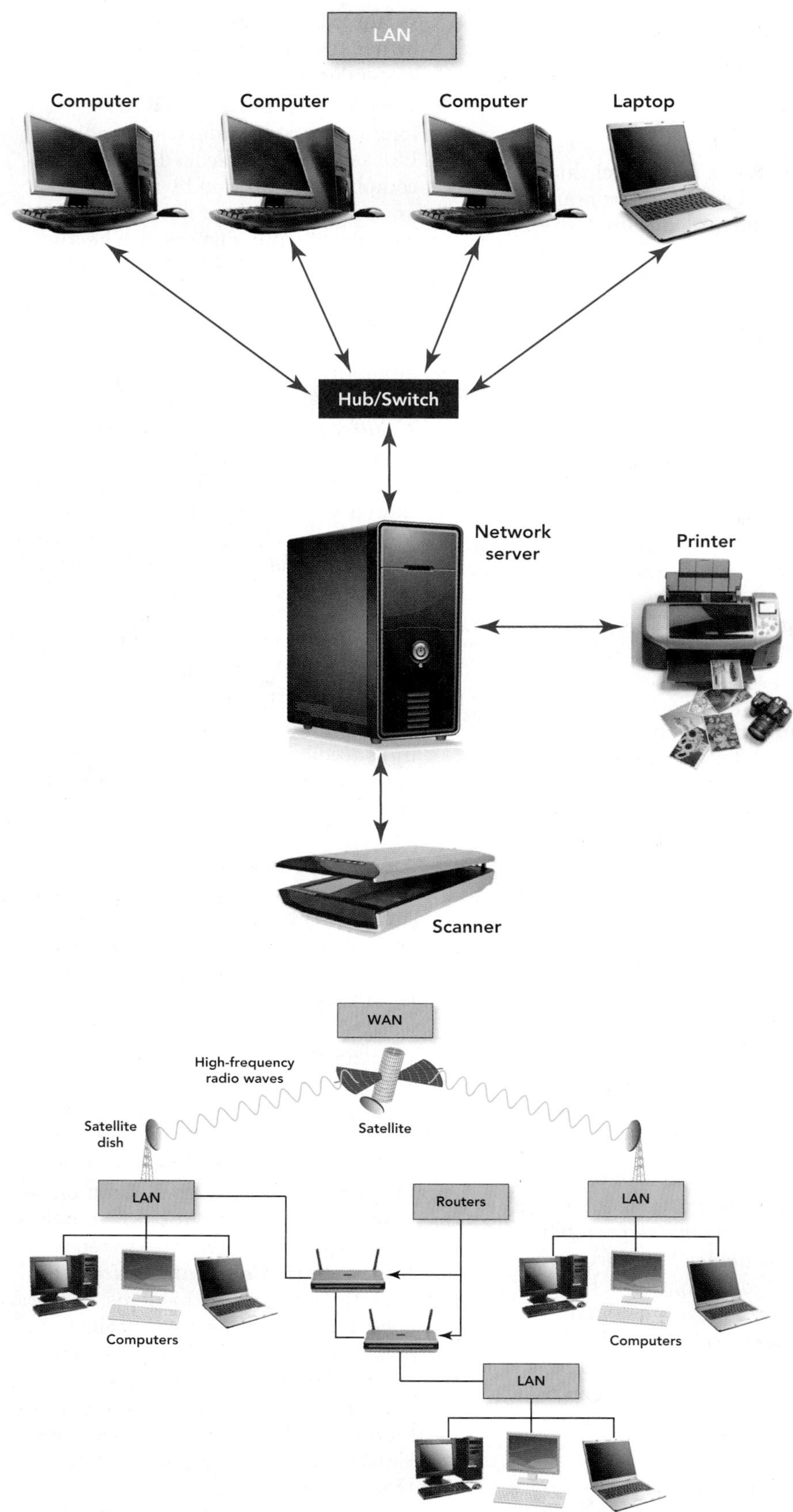

FIGURE 15.1 LANs appear simpler due to the lack of leased lines and satellites, which are essential in a WAN because of the geographical distance it spans.

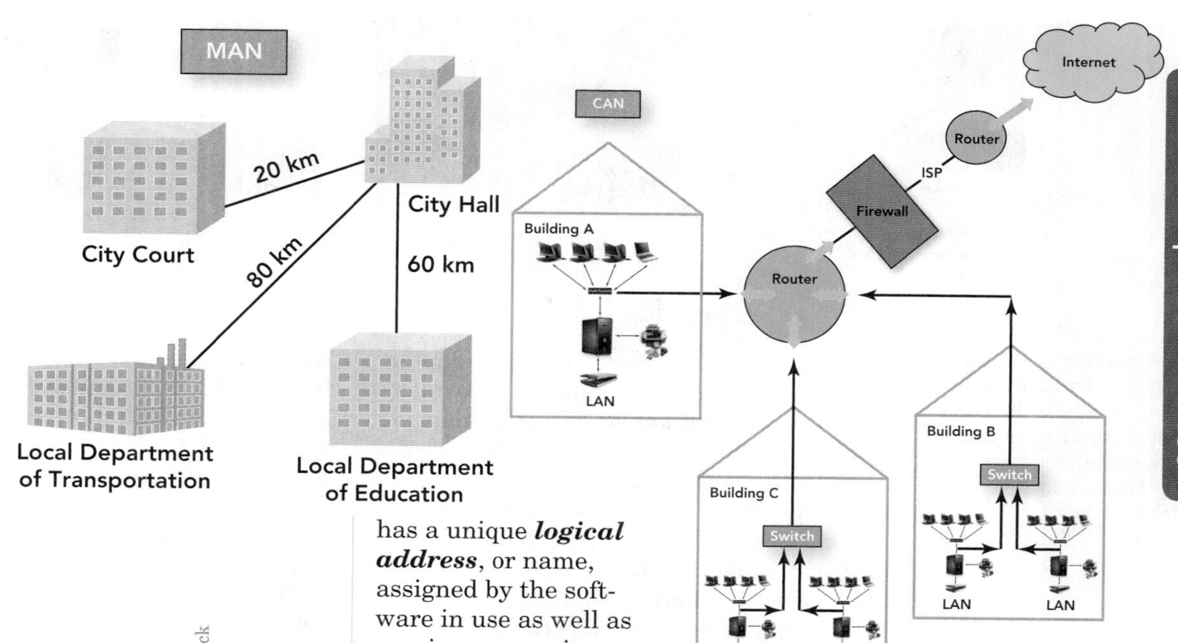

FIGURE 15.2 A MAN and a CAN each use several network devices and methods of transmission to connect devices across their geographical region.

has a unique ***logical address***, or name, assigned by the software in use as well as a unique numeric or ***physical address*** built into the hardware. This physical address is also referred to as the *data link control address*, *data link control/connection identifier* (DLCI), or *media access control* (MAC) *address*. Depending on the format of the network, the physical address or logical address can be used to identify a device.

A computer must have the electronic components to physically connect to a network. These components can either be built into the motherboard or located on a ***network interface card (NIC)***. A NIC is an expansion board that fits into an expansion slot, or adapter, that is built into the computer's motherboard. Current computing and communication devices most likely will come with some means of wireless connectivity. The three common means for a device to connect wirelessly to a network include a USB wireless network adapter, a wireless PC card adapter, or wireless capability built into the motherboard's chipset (Figure 15.4).

A ***USB wireless network adapter*** is a communication device that plugs into a USB port and usually provides an intuitive graphical user interface (GUI) for easy configuration. This device is the same size as a USB flash drive or thumb drive. It is ideal for the traveler and notebook user.

A ***wireless PC card adapter***, approximately the size of a credit card, is inserted into a slot on the side of most notebooks that do not have wireless capability

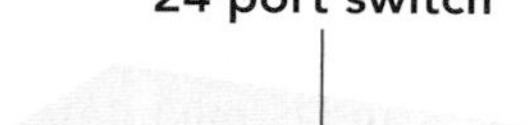

© Norman Chan/Shutterstock

24 port switch

© Jiri Pavlik/Shutterstock

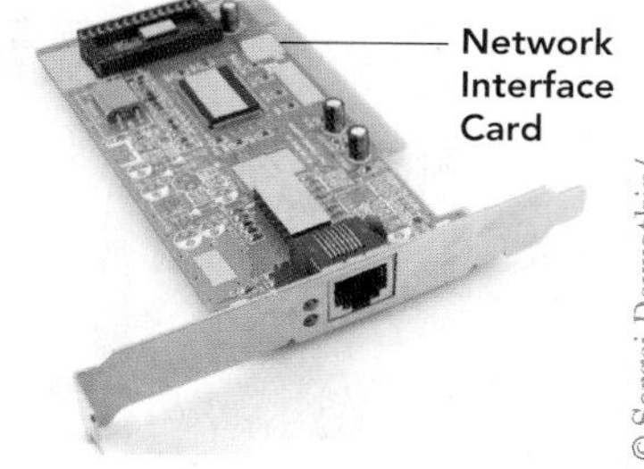

© asharkyu/Shutterstock

© Sergei Devyatkin/Shutterstock

FIGURE 15.3 Devices used to facilitate communication include computers, modems, routers, switches, hubs, and network interface cards.

© Charles B. Ming Onn/Shutterstock

© andres balcazar/ iStockphoto

© ene/Shutterstock

FIGURE 15.4 Mobile devices can connect to a network through a USB wireless adapter, through a wireless PC card, or through the wireless capability embedded within the portable device.

embedded on its chipset. The card adapter has a built-in WiFi antenna that provides wireless capability and LED lights that indicate whether the computer is connected.

If you are purchasing a new notebook, you might want to look for one in which the wireless technology is built into the ***chipset***, providing fast wireless connectivity without the hassle of having to insert an external peripheral. The chipset is a group of integrated circuits located on the motherboard, developed for a specific microprocessor (CPU), and that cannot be removed or upgraded. A chipset's primary function is to connect the microprocessor to all other components of the computer. For more detailed information on the chipset, visit **http://computer.howstuffworks.com/motherboard3.htm**.

In addition to your data passing through a NIC card or wireless adapter to get to and from a network, your data has probably also passed through such devices as modems, routers, switches, hubs, and wireless access points on its network journey from source to destination.

A ***modem*** is a communication device that sends and receives data from one transmission system to another. On the sending end, a modem uses a process called modulation to transform the computer's digital signals into signals appropriate for the transmission system being used. On the receiving end, the process used is demodulation, whereby the receiving modem transforms the signal from the transmission system back into a digital form that a computer can understand. The term modem comes from combining the words modulate and demodulate. In its early stages, a computer sending digital data would pass it through a modem that would modulate the digital data into analog form, permitting it to travel over telephone lines. On the computer receiving the data, a modem would demodulate the analog signal into the digital form enabling it to be understood by the receiving computer (Figure 15.5). Today your modem connects your computer to an Internet service provider (ISP) that in turn connects you to the Internet. Your modem still modulates a signal when sending and demodulates the signal when receiving. In the case of a fiber-optic transmission, a modem modulates the digital signal into light signals and demodulates light signals to digital signals.

The ***data transfer rate***, the rate at which two modems can exchange data, is measured in bits per second and is referred to as the ***bps rate***. Often, a single message travels over several different wired and wireless transmission media, including telephone lines, coaxial cable, fiber-optic cable, radio waves, microwaves, and satellite, before it arrives at its destination.

A ***hub*** is a simple, inexpensive device that joins multiple computers together

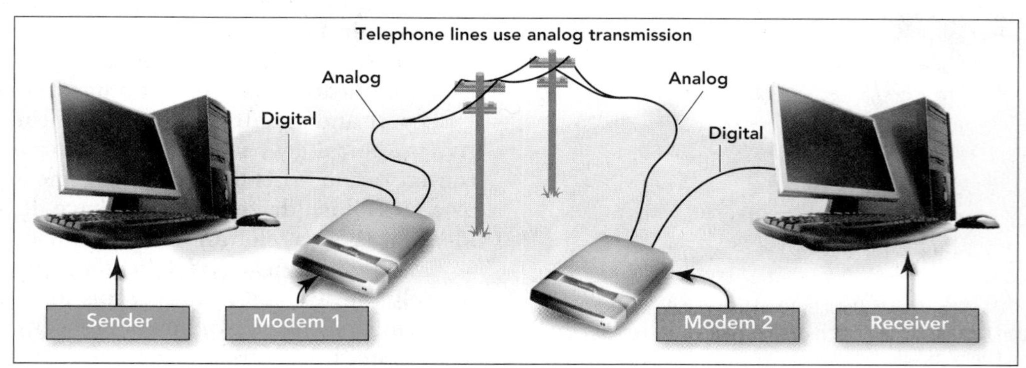

FIGURE 15.5 Early modems transformed the computer's digital signals into telephone analog signals and transmitted them through the telephone system. On the receiving computer, a modem would demodulate the analog signal back to a digital signal.

FIGURE 15.6 A wireless broadband router saves the time, hassle, and expense of running cable to connect devices in a hard-to-wire home or office.

in a single network but does not manage the traffic between the connections, which usually results in frequent collisions. ***Switches*** are more intelligent than hubs. Instead of just passing data packets along the network, a switch contains software that inspects the source and target of a data package and attempts to deliver it to that destination. By doing this, a switch condenses bandwidth and has better performance than a hub. Switches and hubs move data only between devices within a single network. A ***router*** is a more complex network device that provides intelligent network management; it has the capability to inspect the source and target of a data package and determine the best path to route data. A ***wireless access point***, also known as an ***AP*** or ***WAP***, connects wireless devices to a wired network. Usually this technology is embedded within wireless broadband routers that also include a switch to connect your wired Ethernet devices and a router to permit all devices to share a cable, DSL, or FiOS Internet connection (Figure 15.6).

Concept 15.03 | Utilizing a Network Operating System

Each computer on a network must include software that enables the computer to connect to the network and exchange data with other computers. This capability to configure a system to connect to a network is built in to modern operating systems.

On business networks, you can expect to see one or more dedicated ***servers***, a computer or device with software that manages network resources like files, e-mails, printers, and databases. The most common type of server is the ***file server***, a high-capacity, high-speed computer with a large hard disk. A file server is dedicated to make program files and data files available to those users on a network that have been granted access permission. The file server is where the ***network operating system (NOS)*** is installed. A network operating system differs from the operating system you use on your PC or notebook, because a network operating system contains instructions enabling data transfer and application sharing among computers and other devices connected in the network. A network operating system requires installation by a skilled technician. Network operating systems like SUSE Linux Enterprise Server, Microsoft Windows Server 2008 R2, and Mac OS X Lion Server provide the following:

- File directories that make it easy to locate files and resources on the LAN
- Automated distribution of software updates to the desktop computers on the LAN
- Support for Internet services such as access to the World Wide Web and e-mail
- Protection of services and data located on the network
- Access to connected hardware by authorized network users

In addition to a network's special hardware and software, people are also necessary for the proper functioning of a network. ***Network administrators***, sometimes called ***network engineers***, install, maintain, and support computer networks (Figure 15.7). They interact with users, handle security, and troubleshoot problems.

A network administrator's most important task is granting access to the network. This includes setting permissions for which files, folders, and network devices each network user has the right to access, based on such items as the division of the organization where the user is employed, the level of security clearance the user holds, and the confidentiality of the data itself.

FIGURE 15.7 Network administrators must understand both the hardware and software to manage a network efficiently.

Objective 2 | Assess the Structure and Value of Networks

As the Director of Sales for a hotel that is part of a global hotel chain, you recently participated in a regional sales meeting. A topic that was discussed in depth was the creation of a single networked regional calendar that displays all conference reservations at all of the chain's hotels within a region. The Regional Director of Sales thinks this will speed up the process of directing customers to available accommodations in the hotel chain that are available and match the clients requested services. Your experience indicates that this would involve constantly updating the calendar on the corporate network in order to avoid embarrassment caused by incorrect or omitted entries. You want to point out the pros and cons of this new plan. Where do you start?

Concept 15.04 | Reviewing the Pros and Cons of Networking

When you connect two or more computers, you see gains—especially with regard to efficiency and costs. For example, you can expect to see:

- Reduced hardware costs: The sharing of equipment like high-capacity printers and storage devices in a network reduces the cost of purchasing duplicate devices.
- Reduced software costs: Network versions of applications installed on a file server can be accessed by the number of users that the purchased network license specifies. Purchasing software this way is usually less expensive than purchasing individual copies.
- Reduced, secured, and centralized data management: With data stored on a central file server and access secured by restricting accessibility and editing features on a user by user basis, an organization can enforce strong passwords, maintain a backup schedule, and permit a single data file to be accessed and edited by multiple users.
- More extensive collaboration: Networks enable colleagues to communicate and work as a team without time and location constraints.

There are also some risks when implementing a network, for example:

- Loss of independence: Network users must follow the restrictions imposed by the network administrator.
- Loss of privacy: This risk applies to the use of any employer-owned equipment, not just the use of a network. If the employer owns the equipment, the employer owns the data on the equipment.
- Increased socialization resulting in a decrease in productivity: If e-mail and instant messaging are permitted on a network, the social communication between employees usually increases. The result is a decrease in productivity. Often an employer will limit social networking features and even block Internet access.

Objective 3 | Implement Local Area Networks

As the Director of Sales for a hotel that is part of a global hotel chain, you want to expand your hotel's conference facilities and Internet hot spots. You must make a presentation to the corporate Vice President of Sales to support your proposal to expand and upgrade the hotel's network. Where do you start?

Recall that a LAN is a network of two or more computers, in a close geographical setting, connected together to facilitate communication with each other and with peripheral devices such as a printer or cable modem (Figure 15.8).

LANs transform individual hardware devices into what appears to be one gigantic computer system. From any computer on the LAN, you can access any data, software, or peripherals such as fax machines, printers, or scanners that are on the network.

With a ***wireless LAN***, users access and connect to other devices on the network through radio waves instead of wires. Wireless LANs are useful when you need to move around in or near a building. In hotels, for example, wirelesses LANs notify housekeeping staff about room checkouts and bookings.

FIGURE 15.8 Setting up a LAN in a hotel enables anyone in any room to access the connected devices located anywhere in the hotel.

Many wireless LANs ensure security with a radio transmission technique that spreads signals over a seemingly random series of frequencies. Only the receiving device knows the series, so it is not easy to eavesdrop on the signals. A conscientious user should still use encryption software to guarantee a higher level of protection. Wireless LAN signals have an effective inside range of between 125 and 300 feet but can be shorter if the building construction interferes with the signal.

Whether wired or wireless, LANs can be differentiated by the networking model they use: peer-to-peer or client/server.

Concept 15.05 | Joining a Peer-to-Peer Network

In a ***peer-to-peer network (P2P)***, all of the computers on the network are equals, or peers—that is where the term *peer-to-peer* comes from. They are generally used in small offices or home networks, do not require a NOS (network operating system), and can be set up through options available in current standalone operating systems.

On a P2P network, there is no central controlling unit; each computer user decides which files, directories, storage devices, printers, and scanners they want to share with other network users (Figure 15.9).

P2P networking gained notoriety when Napster, a peer-to-peer music file-sharing site, was sued for copyright infringement. Since then, other sites, like Kazaa and LimeWire, which claim their P2P network is just like sharing a music or movie CD with a friend, have also lost similar battles with the entertainment industry. Current proposed legislation is seeking to hold colleges and universities responsible for monitoring students' download activity. Additionally, ISPs are in contention with Web sites like BitTorrent, a P2P site that consumes large amounts of bandwidth by sharing videos and thus causing other users to experience excessive delays.

However, not everybody wants to stop P2P music swapping. Some artists offer free downloads hoping that fans will share the files with friends and buy more songs. Some companies are even sponsoring music downloads that link their products with promising new groups and build goodwill as the music of the new group moves from computer to computer. The P2P network model is the foundation of legitimate companies like Skype (**www.skype.com**) that uses P2P technology to provide voice over Internet Protocol (VoIP) phone service to their users (Figure 15.10).

If you decide to join a P2P network, give some thought to privacy and security. If you are a Skype user and you are not behind a firewall, there is a good chance that your computer will be utilized as a supernode without your knowledge. You might have to disable some security features on your system in order to make use of some offered features. Read all of the information before signing up to a P2P network

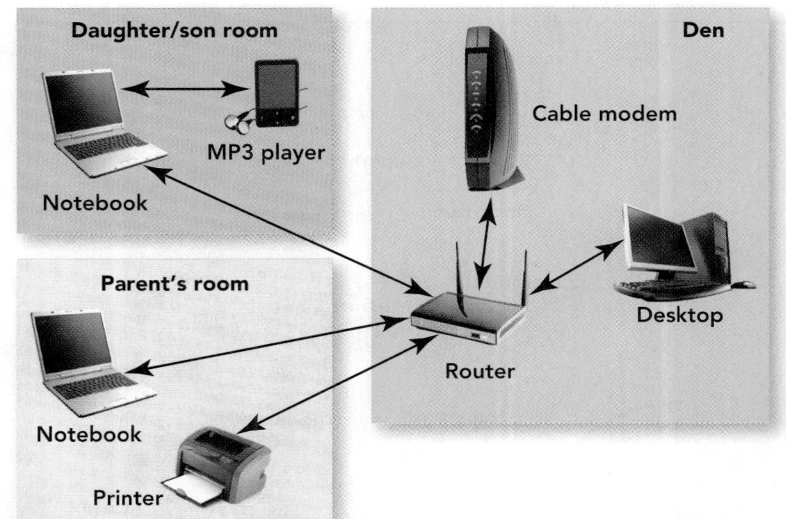

FIGURE 15.9 A peer-to-peer home network

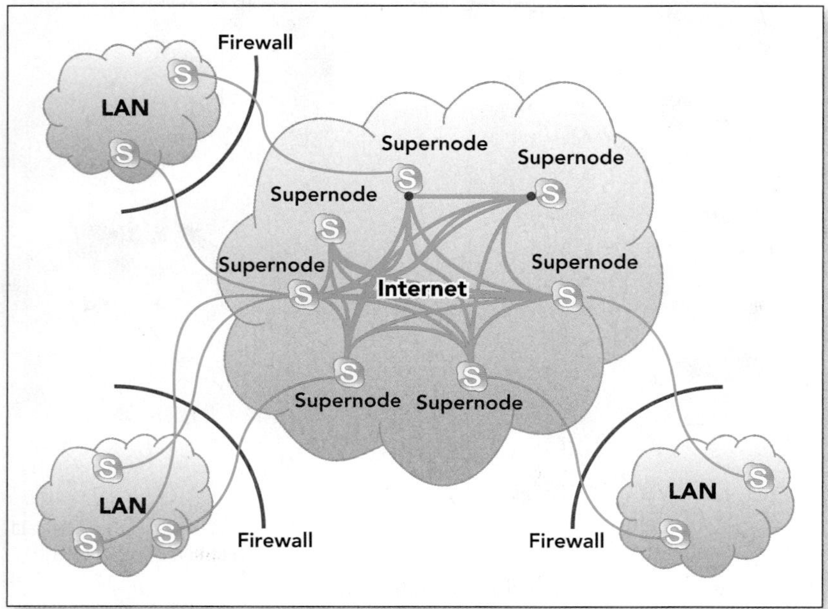

FIGURE 15.10
Because Skype users are on the public Internet, not behind a firewall, the P2P model used by Skype relies on a large number of supernodes to mediate the communication between two Skype clients.

From either the Companion Web Site or MyITLab, watch Chapter 15 Video 1

and keep your antivirus software up to date to avoid receiving infected files from other P2P network users.

Concept 15.06 | Connecting to a Client/Server Network

The typical corporate or university LAN is a ***client/server network***, which includes one or more servers as well as clients (Figure 15.11). Some common servers on a client/server network include those that provide e-mail, file storage, database storage, and facilitate communication with other networks, including the Internet. A ***client*** can be any type of computer—PC, Mac, desktop, notebook, or even a handheld device—that is connected to a network and contains the software that enables it to send requests to a server. It can connect via modem, a physical Ethernet connection, or a wireless connection. The client/server model works with any size or physical layout of LAN and does not tend to slow down with heavy use.

Concept 15.07 | Recognizing a Virtual Private Network

Many businesses have extended their network structure from an ***intranet***, a password-protected network controlled by the company and accessed by employees, clients, or vendors, to a ***virtual private network (VPN)***. A VPN operates as a private network over a public network, usually the Internet, making data accessible to authorized users in remote locations through the use of secure, encrypted connections and special software (Figure 15.12).

Concept 15.08 | Examining LAN Topologies

Network topology is the physical arrangement of computers in a local area network (LAN) and methods by which the arrangement manages the problem of ***contention***—the conflict that occurs when two computers try to access the LAN at the same time. Contention sometimes results in ***collisions***, the corruption of network data caused when two computers transmit simultaneously.

In a ***bus topology***, every device is attached to a common cable or pathway referred to as the *bus* (Figure 15.13). At the end of the bus, a special connector called a ***terminator*** signifies the end of the circuit. In a bus topology, only one device can transmit at a time. If more than one device tries to send data at the same time, each device waits a small random amount of time and then attempts to retransmit the data. Other limitations of a bus topology include length restrictions because of the loss of signal strength and limits as to the number of attached devices because of increases in contention caused by each added device. To resolve contention problems, networks use some type of ***contention management***—a plan of action to follow when a collision occurs. On the plus side, bus networks are simple, reliable, and easy to expand. The bus topology is practical in a relatively small environment such as a home or small office.

A ***star topology*** solves the expansion problems of the bus topology with a central wiring device, which can be a hub, a switch, or a computer (Figure 15.14). Adding users is simple; you run a cable to the hub or switch and plug the new device into an available connector. Star networks also use a contention management plan to deal with collisions. The star topology is ideal for office buildings, computer labs, and WANs. The downside of a star topology is that the loss of the hub, switch, or central

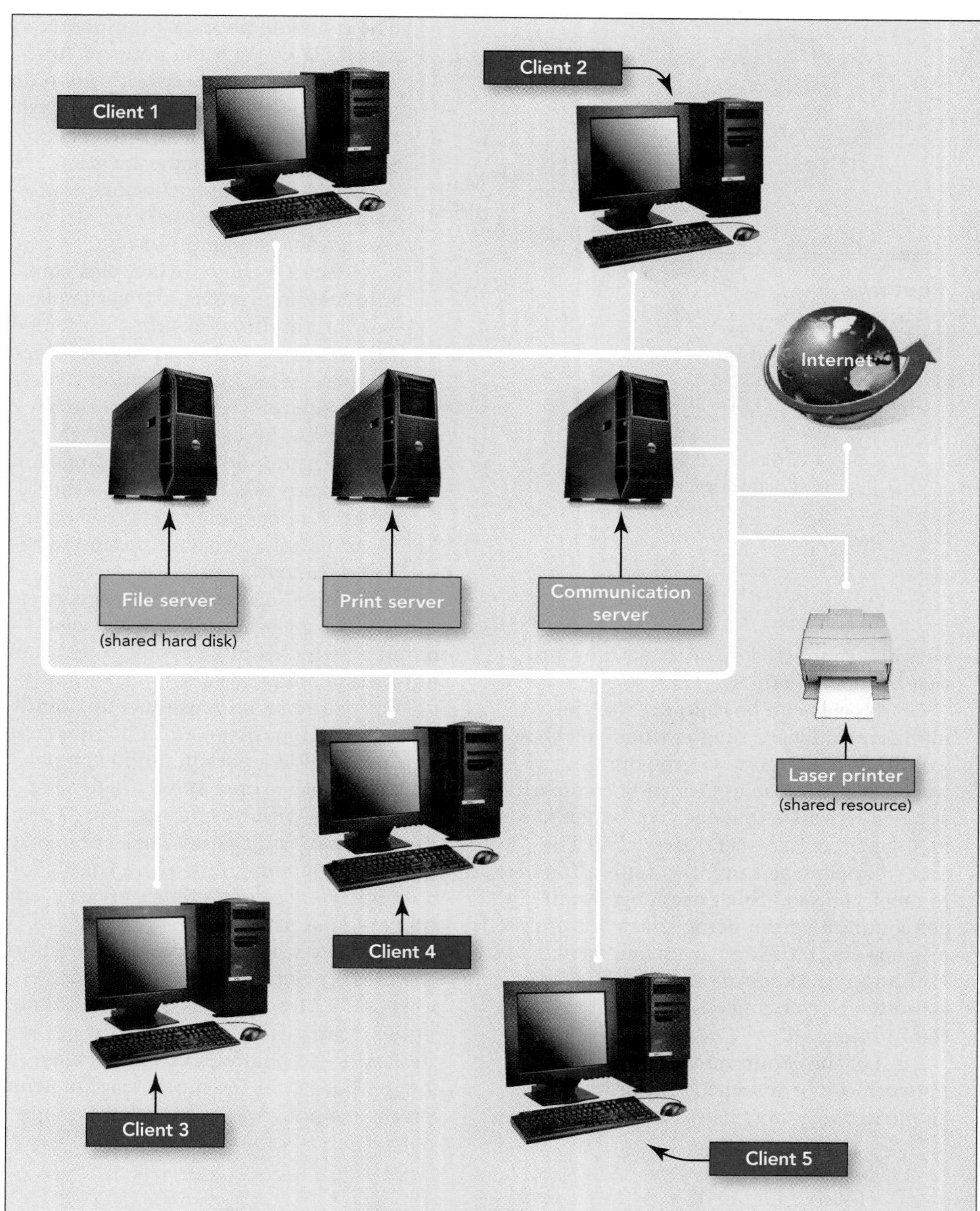

FIGURE 15.11 A client/server network includes one or more servers as well as other devices.

computer caused by a power outage or virus invasion can bring down the entire network.

With a ***ring topology***, all of the devices are attached in a circular wiring arrangement. This topology is not in common use today. It provides a unique way to prevent collisions (Figure 15.15). A special unit of data called a ***token*** travels around the ring. A device can transmit only when it possesses the token. The ring topology is well-suited for use within a division of a company or on one floor of a multi-floor office building.

Concept 15.09 | Examining LAN Protocols

In addition to the physical or wireless transmission media that carry the network's signals, a network also uses ***protocols***. Protocols are a set of standards or rules implemented by hardware, software, or a combination of the two, which enable

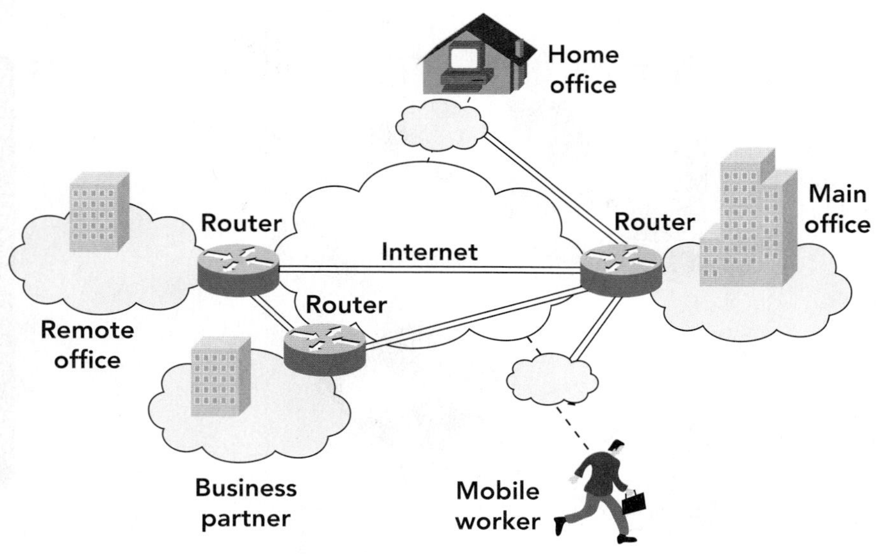

FIGURE 15.12 In a virtual private network, the Internet is used to transmit data between authorized locations and remote mobile employees.

network-connected devices to communicate with each other.

Protocols can be compared to the manners you were taught when you were a child. When you were growing up, you were taught to use appropriate comments, such as "It's nice to meet you," when you met someone in a social situation. The other person was taught to reply, "It's nice to meet you too." Such exchanges serve to get communication going. Network protocols are similar. They are fixed, formalized exchanges that specify how two dissimilar network components can establish a communication.

All of the communication devices in a network conform to different protocols. A single network may use dozens of protocols. The complete package of protocols that specify how a specific network functions is called the network's ***protocol suite***. The protocol suite is a component of the ***network architecture***—the design of the communication system including the backbones, routers, switches, wireless access points, access methods, and protocols.

Because they are complex communication systems, networks use a network architecture that is divided into separate ***network layers***. Each network layer has a function that can be isolated and treated separately from other layers. Because each layer's protocol precisely defines how each layer passes data to another layer, it is possible to make changes within a layer without having to rebuild the entire network.

To understand the layer concept, remember that protocols are like good manners, which enable people to get communication going.

For example, suppose you are sending an e-mail message and imagine that each protocol is a person, and each person has an office on a separate floor of a multi-story office building. You are on the top floor, and the network connection is in the basement. When you send your message, your e-mail client software calls the person on the next floor down: "Excuse me, but would you please translate this message into a form the server can process?" The person on the floor below replies, "Sure, no problem." That person then calls the person on the next floor down: "If it is not too much trouble, would you please put this translated message

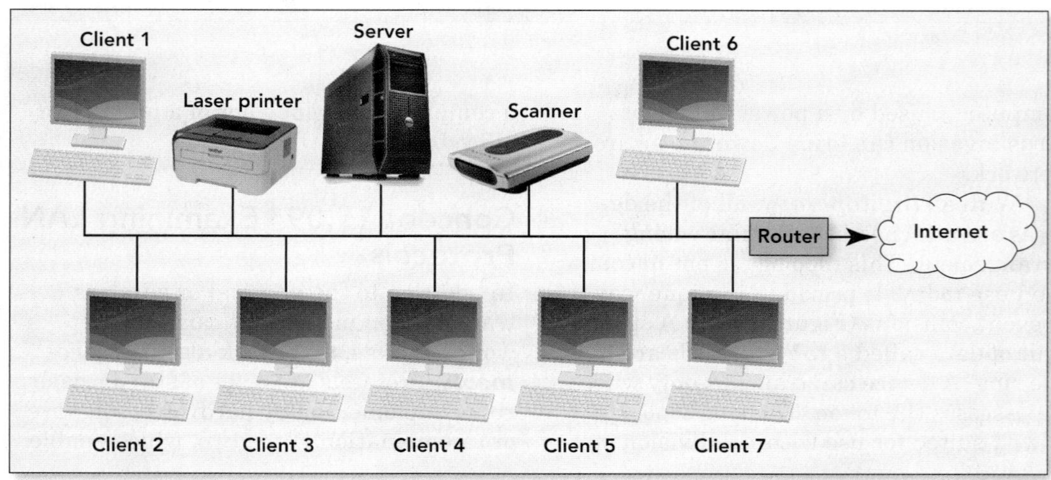

FIGURE 15.13 In a bus topology, the network cable forms a common pathway to which every computer or peripheral device is attached.

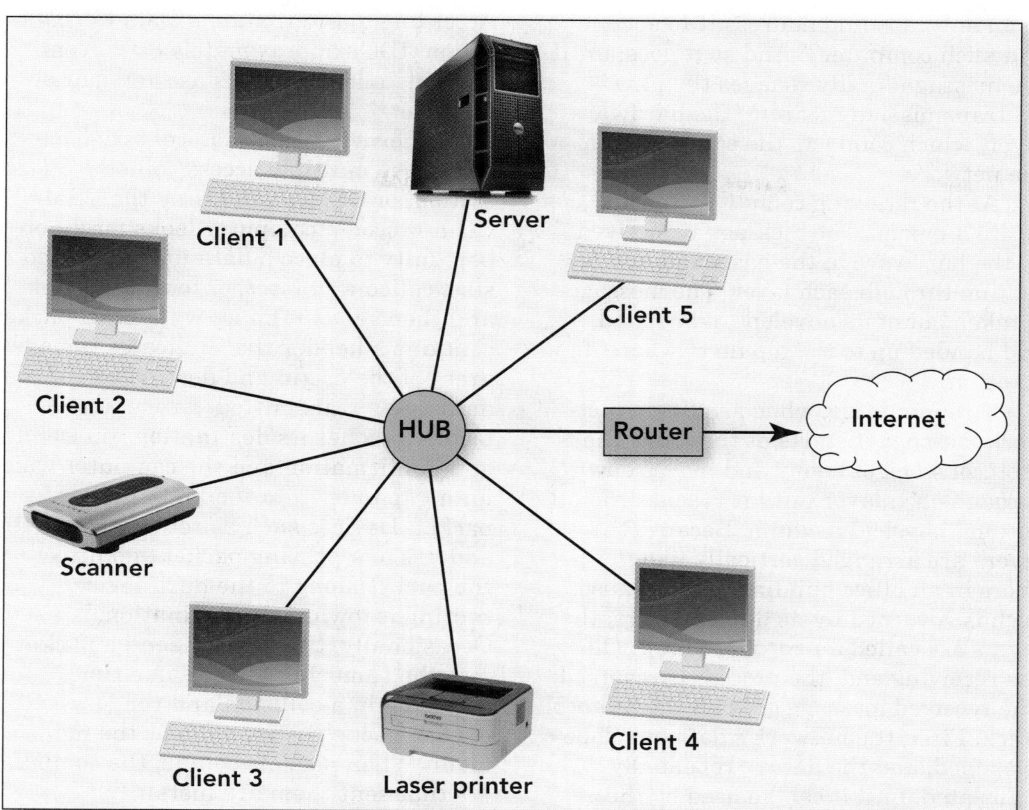

FIGURE 15.14 A star topology uses a central wiring layout, making it easier to connect new devices.

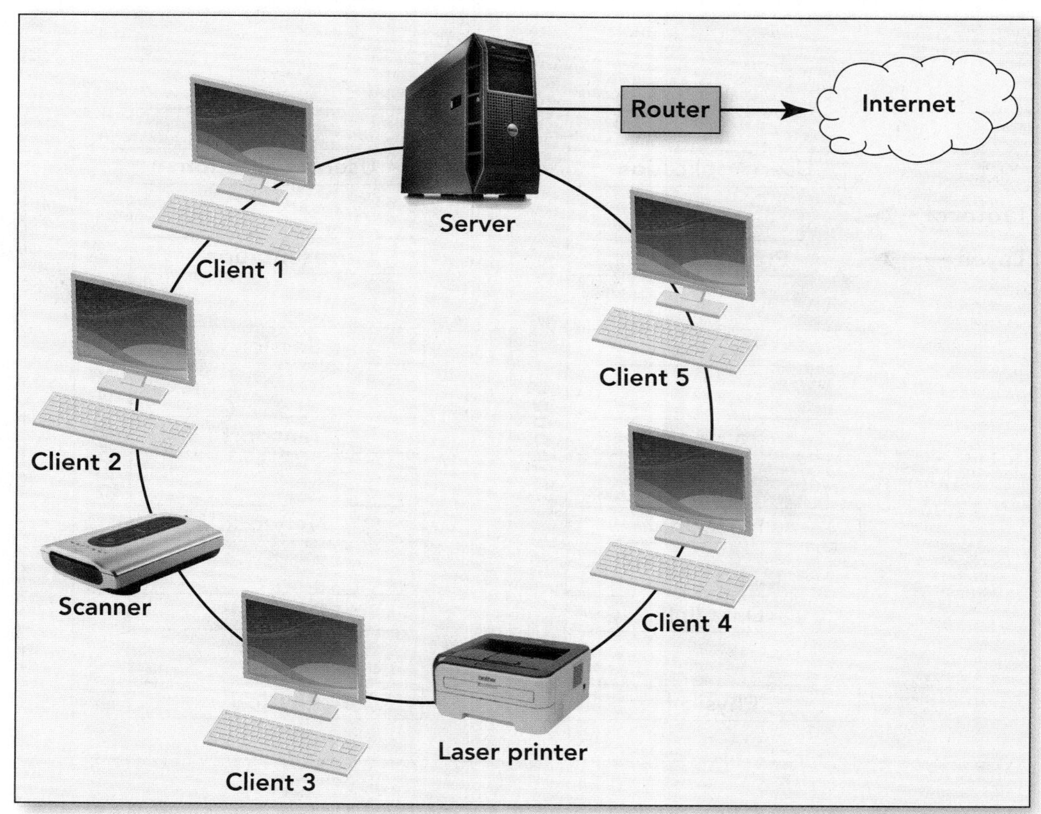

FIGURE 15.15 Ring topologies connect devices in a circular wiring arrangement.

in an envelope and address it to such-and-such computer?" And so it goes, until the message finally reaches the physical transmission medium, the hardware layer, which connects the computers in the network.

At the receiving computer, the opposite happens. The message is received by the hardware in the basement and is sent up through each layer. The message is taken out of its envelope, translated, and handed up to the top floor, where it is acted on.

To summarize, when sending a network message it starts at the top of the protocol stack of layers and moves down through each layer until it reaches the bottom, physical medium. Because the layers are arranged vertically like the floors in an office building, and because each is governed by its own software, the layers are called a ***protocol stack***. On the receiving end, the process is reversed: The received message goes up the protocol stack. First, the network's data envelope is opened, and the data is repeatedly translated until it can be used by the receiving application. Figure 15.16 illustrates this concept.

By far the most popular LAN standard for large and small businesses is ***Ethernet***. According to International Data Corporation (IDC), approximately 85 percent of all installed networks use versions of Ethernet.

Ethernet uses a protocol called carrier sense multiple access/collision detection, or CSMA/CD. Using the CSMA/CD protocol, a computer looks for an opportunity to place a data unit of a fixed size, called a ***packet***, onto the network and then sends it on its way. Each packet contains a header that indicates the address of the origin and destination of the data being transmitted. Every time a packet reaches its destination, the sender gets confirmation and the computer waits for a gap to open to send off another packet. Devices such as routers read the address of a passing packet and direct the packet along to the next device, routing it toward its destination. Occasionally, two devices send a packet into the same gap at the same time, resulting in a collision and the loss of both packets—but only for the moment. When packets collide, the computers that sent them are instantly notified, and each chooses a random interval to wait before it resends the packet. This approach helps prevent network gridlock.

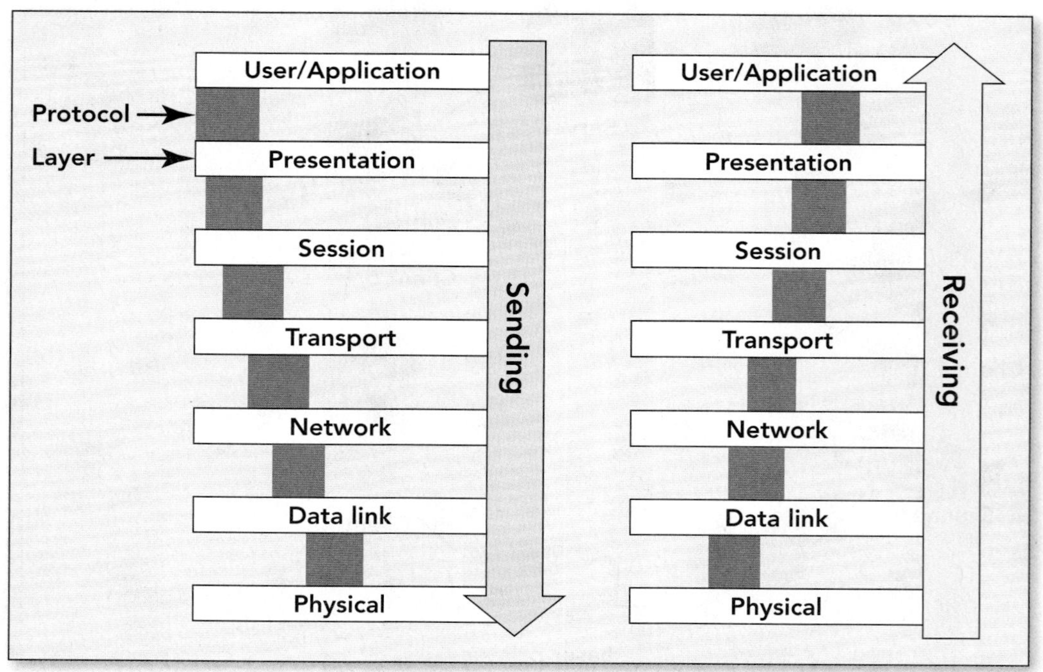

FIGURE 15.16 Open system interconnection (OSI) model defines a networking framework for implementing protocols in seven layers.

A SMART, GREEN HOUSE

Chicago's Museum of Science and Industry has on display a modular urban home that is both smart and green. This house is networked to monitor gas, electric, and water to minimize usage and maximize comfort. In addition to being smart, the house is environmentally friendly, and it is manufactured and decorated from recycled and reusable resources. In homes like this, the electrical monitoring system will turn up the thermostat a few degrees or turn off the water heater to conserve energy. View a slide show of the Smart Home: Green + Wired at **www.msichicago.org/whats-here/exhibits/smart-home/**. Houses like this are also being tested in Toronto and may be extended to Baltimore and Boulder in the future.

Although early versions of Ethernet (called 10Base2 and 10Base5) used coaxial cable in bus networks, the most popular versions today are Ethernet star networks that use switches and twisted-pair wire. Currently, three versions of Ethernet are in use: 10Base-T (10 Mbps), Fast Ethernet (100 Mbps, also called 100Base-TX), and Gigabit Ethernet. The newest version, 10 Gigabit Ethernet, is making possible next-generation applications such as cloud computing, server virtualization, network convergence, and multicasting.

These superfast connections are often used to create large metropolitan and regional networks because they prevent data bottlenecks. To learn more about Ethernet, check out Charles Spurgeon's Ethernet Web site at **http://www.ethermanage.com/ethernet/ethernet.html**. The site covers all of the Ethernet technologies in use today and includes a practical guide for do-it-yourselfers. Figure 15.17 provides a comparison of several popular LAN protocols.

WiFi is a wireless LAN standard that offers Ethernet speeds through the use of radio waves instead of wires. Devices with WiFi technology need a wireless access point or a wireless router to communicate in general or access the Internet. Wireless routers sold for home use contain a wireless access point inside the router. The router also has an omnidirectional antenna to receive the data transmitted by wireless transceivers. External WiFi transceivers connect to desktop computers through USB wireless adapters or PC adapter cards; however, today most laptops are equipped with built-in wireless network adapters or with wireless capability on their chipset.

WiFi uses the IEEE 802.11 wireless networking standard (Figure 15.18) and transmits on the 2.4-GHz or 5-GHz radio frequency band. There are currently three popular IEEE 802.11 standards. The 802.11g standard is the most common, with 802.11n and 802.11r being the newest standards. IEEE 802.16e and IEEE 802.16 are becoming two promising technologies for broadband wireless access systems. Figure 15.19 displays the standards and the network for which each is best suited to serve.

Although WiFi is convenient, there are some security risks.

Popular LAN Protocols

Protocol Name	Data Transfer Rate	Physical Media
Ethernet (10Base-T)	10 Mbps	Twisted-pair cable
Fast Ethernet (100Base-TX)	100 Mbps	Twisted-pair or fiber-optic cable
Gigabit Ethernet	1,000 Mbps	Fiber-optic cable
10 Gigabyte Ethernet	6.375 Gbps	Fiber-optic cable
IBM Token Ring Network	4–16 Mbps	Twisted-pair cable

Figure 15.17

Global Wireless Networking Standards

Standard	Frequency	Transmission Speed	Description
802.11g	2.4 GHz	Up to 54 Mbps	The most commonly used standard, 802.11g is fast and backward compatible with 802.11b.
802.11n	2.4 GHz and/or 5 GHz	Up to 540 Mbps	This recently approved standard improves speed and range and operates on both frequencies, as well as being backward compatible with 802.11a/b/g standards.
802.11r	2.4 GHz and/or 5 GHz	Up to 540 Mbps	An amendment to the 802.11 standard that governs the way roaming mobile clients communicate with access points; this standard will speed up the hand-off of data between access points or cells in a wireless LAN to less than 50 ms (milliseconds), greatly improving VoIP or Internet-based telephony.
802.15	2.4 GHz	Up to 50 Mbps	Used for Bluetooth technology; this standard has a very short range (up to 32 feet).
802.16	2–11 GHz	Up to 70 Mbps	Mobile WiMax provides high-speed wireless Internet access over long distances (more than 30 miles).
802.20	3.5 GHz	Up to 80 Mbps	A multi-megabyte mobile data and voice system, this standard can be used in vehicles moving at up to 250 km/hr.

Figure 15.18

Wired networks require a computer or other device to be physically connected, but wireless networks broadcast radio waves that can be picked up by anyone using the correct configuration. These signals can extend beyond the walls of your home or office, so it is important to properly secure your network and

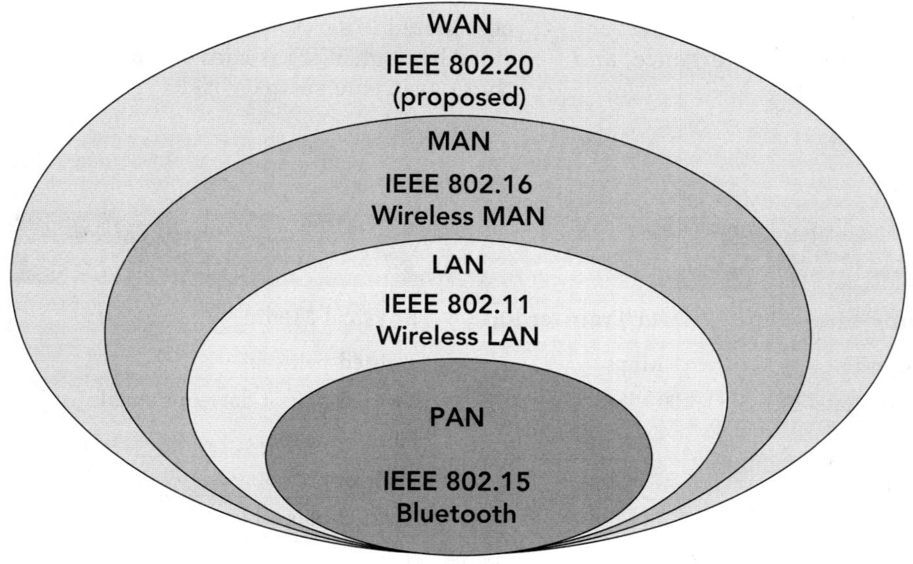

FIGURE 15.19 Transmission standards are constantly being upgraded and new standards proposed by the IEEE to stay in step with current technology.

data. To safeguard your network, do the following:

- Always use firewall software and updated antivirus and antispyware software.
- Change the router's default network name, also known as an SSID, and the default password.
- If possible, turn off SSID broadcasting to avoid detection by hackers.
- Ensure your router's software has been upgraded to the most recent version.
- Turn on WPA (WiFi Protected Access) to enable encryption.
- Turn on MAC (media access control) address filtering so only authorized devices can gain access.

Similarly, when using a public wireless Internet access location, known as a ***hot spot***, you should take the following precautions:

- Be aware of your surroundings—ensure no one is watching over your shoulder for log-on and password information.
- Be sure to log on to the correct wireless network, not a look-alike or so-called evil twin network.
- Disable file and printer sharing.
- Do not transmit confidential data, but if you must do so, be sure to use encryption.
- Turn off your wireless access when it is not in use.

Whether wired or wireless, LANs enable an organization to share computing resources in a single building or across a group of buildings. However, a LAN's geographic limitations pose a problem. Many organizations need to share computing resources with distant branch offices, with employees who are traveling, and with people outside the organization, including suppliers and customers. This is what wide area networks (WANs) are used for—to link computers separated by thousands of miles.

Objective 4 | Analyze Wide Area Networks

As the Director of Sales for a hotel that is part of a global hotel chain, corporate management liked your plan for a networked regional calendar and wants to expand that idea into a weekly report on all business and conference bookings across the entire hotel chain worldwide. You have been asked to assist in the implementation of the plan across the entire global chain of hotels. You must study the differences between WANs and LANs and wired and wireless network security. Where do you start?

Like LANs, WANs have all of the basic network components—cabling, protocols, and devices—for routing information to the correct destination. WANs are like long-distance telephone systems. In fact, much WAN traffic is carried by long-distance voice communication providers and cable companies. So you can picture a WAN as a LAN that has long-distance communication needs among its servers, computers, and peripherals. Special components of WANs differentiate them from LANs—point of presence and backbones.

Concept 15.10 | Defining a Point of Presence

To carry computer data over the long haul, a WAN must be locally accessible. Like long-distance phone carriers or Internet access providers, WANs have what amounts to a local access number, called a point of presence. A ***point of presence (POP)*** is a wired or wireless WAN network connection point that enables users to access the WAN. To provide availability to it users, WANs have a POP in as many towns and cities as needed. However, in many rural areas, POPs may still not be available, reducing a potential subscriber's choices and ability to connect.

Concept 15.11 | Transmitting via Backbones

The LANs and WANs that make up the Internet are connected to the Internet ***backbone***, which refers to the collection of high-capacity transmission lines that carry Internet traffic. A variety of physical media are used for backbone services, including microwave relays, satellites, and dedicated telephone lines. Some backbones are regional, connecting towns and cities in a region such as Southern California or New England. Others are continental, or even transcontinental, in scope (Figure 15.20).

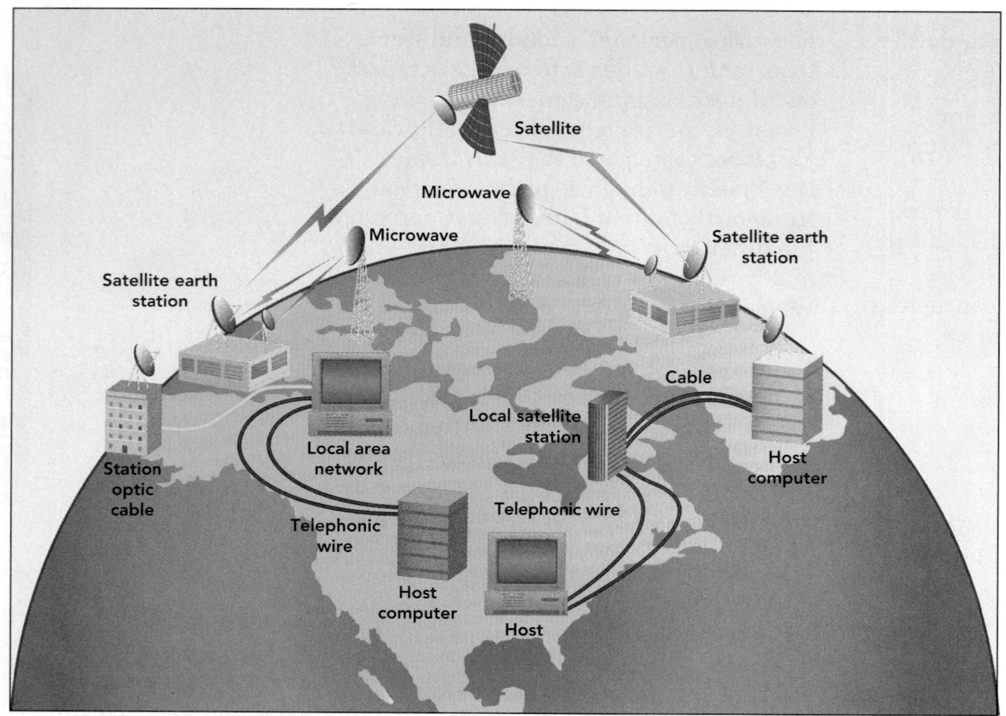

FIGURE 15.20 Backbone media, like microwave relays, satellites, and dedicated phone lines, connect local users as well as those in transcontinental destinations.

Concept 15.12 | Examining WAN Protocols

Like any computer network, WANs use protocols. The Internet, the most popular WAN, uses more than 100 protocols that specify every aspect of Internet usage, such as how to retrieve documents through the Web or send e-mail to a distant computer. Internet data can travel over any type of WAN because of Internet protocols. Collectively the Internet protocols are called ***TCP/IP***, an abbreviation for Transmission Control Protocol (TCP)/Internet Protocol (IP).

The ***Internet Protocol (IP)*** is the lower and most fundamental layer of the TCP/IP suite of protocols. It handles the addressing scheme embedded within each packet transmitted over the Internet enabling each packet to reach the correct destination. IP is a connectionless protocol; that is, two computers do not have to be online at the same time to exchange data. The sending computer just keeps trying until the message gets through.

Because IP enables direct and immediate contact with any other computer on the network, the Internet bears some similarity to the telephone system, although the Internet works on different principles. Every computer on the Internet has a unique ***Internet address***, or ***IP address***, similar to a phone number. A computer can exchange data with any other Internet-connected computer by "dialing" its IP address. Currently an IP address, in Internet Protocol version 4 (IPv4), is 32 bits long, written in decimal, and has four parts that are separated by periods such as 128.254.108.7. The

FAST FORWARD

FCC's Broadband Access Target

Networking and using the Internet for communication, education, and commerce will continue to increase. In a bid to ensure broadband access to all people in the United States within a decade, the Federal Communications Commission (FCC) has set a 4 Mbps download target for universal broadband. This project will cost $23.5 billion. Although nearly 200 million Americans had broadband access in 2009, there were still approximately 100 million that did not. The FCC plan is to plug the gaps in the current infrastructure and establish DSL, 4G wireless, or satellite coverage—depending on the location—in underserviced areas.

Download speed of 4 Mbps is not fast by current standards, but for those with no access or poor access, this will be an improvement. Additionally, this plan seeks to provide improved service over the next decade to 100 million homes in the United States by increasing download speeds to 100 Mbps and upload speeds to 50 Mbps. The FCC project is just a goal and is not mandated. However, the plan should get a boost toward its goal, because Google plans to release its own 1Gbps fiber-to-the-home (FTTH) network in locations across the United States.

successor to IPv4 is IPv6 and is 128 bits long, written in hexadecimal, and has 8 parts separated by colons such as 3ffe:1900:4545:3:200:f8ff:fe21:67cf.

The ***Transmission Control Protocol (TCP)*** is the higher layer of the TCP/IP layer of protocols that defines how one Internet-connected computer can contact another to exchange control and confirmation messages. You can see TCP in action when you use the Web; just watch your browser's status bar. You will see messages such as "Contacting server," "Receiving data," and "Closing connection."

WAN protocols are based on either circuit- or packet-switching network technology, but most use packet switching. The Internet uses packet switching, whereas the public switched telephone network (PSTN) uses circuit switching. Still, the Internet does for computers what the telephone system does for phones—it enables any Internet-connected computer to connect almost instantly and effortlessly with any other Internet-connected computer anywhere in the world.

In ***circuit switching***, the method used in the public switched telephone system, there is a direct connection between the communicating devices. Data is sent over a physical end-to-end circuit between the sending and receiving computers. Circuit switching works best when avoiding delivery delays is essential. In a circuit-switching network, high-speed electronic switches handle the job of establishing and maintaining the connection.

In ***packet switching***, the method used for computer communication, no effort is made to create a single direct connection between the two communicating devices. The sending computer's outgoing message is divided into packets (Figure 15.21). Each packet is numbered and addressed to the destination computer. The packets then travel to a router, which examines each packet it detects. After reading the packet's address, the router consults a table of possible pathways that the packet can take to get to its destination. If more than one path exists, the router sends the packet along the path with the least congestion.

The packets may not all take the same path or arrive in the order they were sent, but that is not a problem. On the receiving computer, protocols put the packets in the correct order and decode the message they contain. If any packets are missing, the receiving computer sends a message requesting retransmission of the missing packet.

So which type of switching is best? Compared with circuit switching, packet

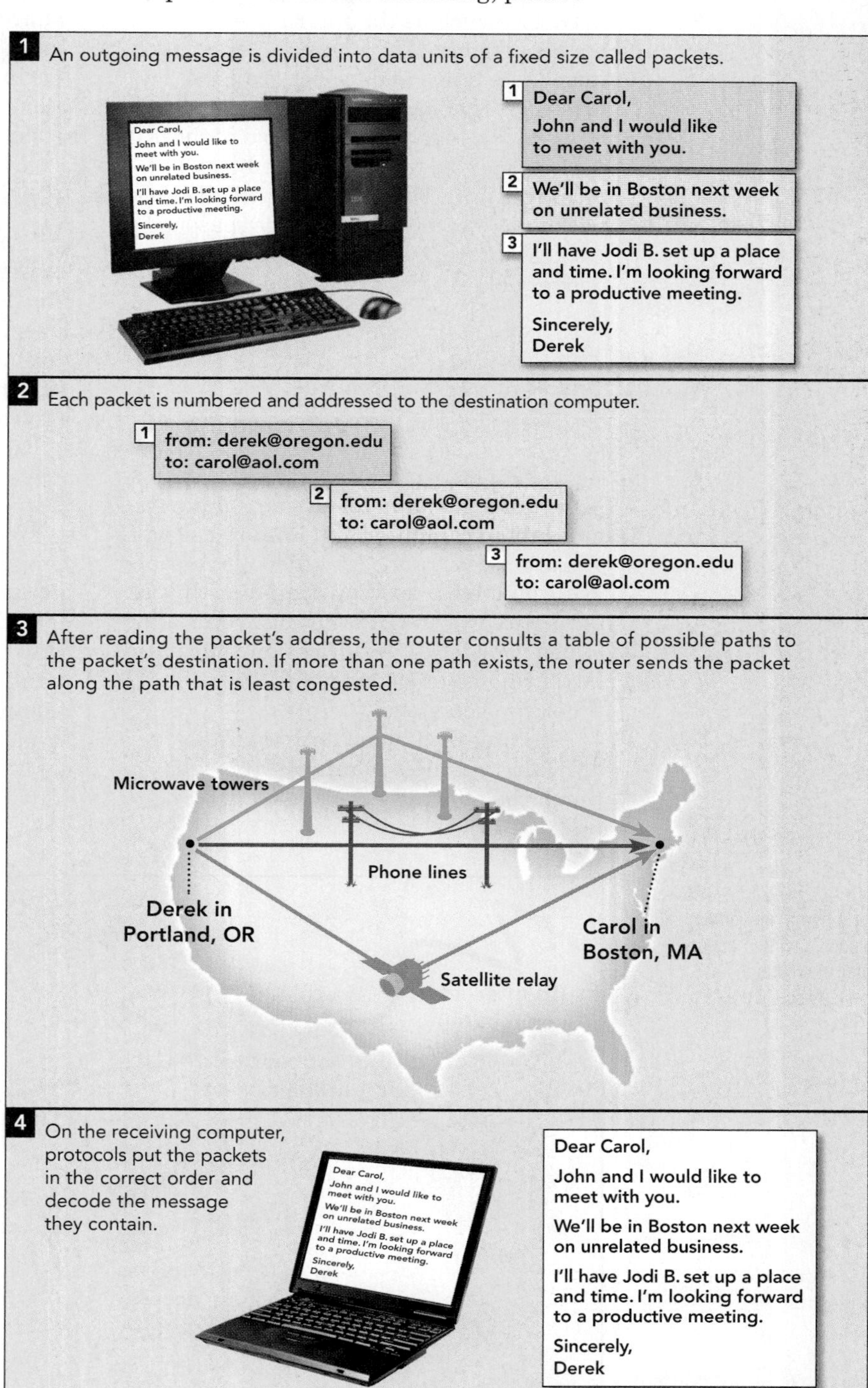

FIGURE 15.21 A sample of the use of packet switching on a message as it is sent from its source to its destination.

switching has many advantages. It is more efficient and less expensive than circuit switching. Additionally, packet-switching networks are more reliable. A packet-switching network can function even if portions of the network are not working.

Packet switching has some drawbacks. When a router examines a packet, it delays the packet's progress by a tiny fraction of a second. In a huge packet-switching network—such as the Internet—a packet may be examined by many routers, which introduces a noticeable delay called ***latency***. If the network experiences ***congestion*** (overloading), some of the packets may be further delayed, and the message cannot be decoded until all of its packets are received. For these reasons, packet switching is not well suited to the delivery of real-time voice and video.

Objective 5 | Set Up a Home Network

As the Director of Sales for a hotel that is part of a global hotel chain, you have a new laptop computer and iPad to use when you are away from your office. In your office, you have a desktop computer that is hard-wired to the Internet but you want to use your portable devices on your patio, in your home office, and while traveling. Where do you start?

Setting up a home network is not difficult, and the advantages are well worth the effort. By the end of 2012, it is estimated that there will be more than 160 million home networks in place worldwide, and as many as 70 percent of them will be using wireless technology. A ***home network***, also referred to as a ***home area network*** or ***HAN***, is a personal and specific use of network technology that provides connectivity between you and devices located in or near your residence. It enables you to quickly and conveniently share files and resources by using network connections between computers and peripheral devices. In a HAN, the connections between devices can be wired, wireless, or a combination of the two.

Concept 15.13 | Clarifying Wired Home Networks

A wired network is the network of choice for those that transfer large files where speed is a priority. Wired home networks are not as popular due to the inconvenience of physically pulling wire to each device on the network and the low cost of a wireless network setup. Still, learning to set up a network and understanding how it works can be helpful, because most home networks are a ***hybrid network***—a combination of both wired and wireless technology (Figure 15.22).

Ethernet, the communication standard for home networks, uses packets to send data between physically connected computers in a network. The most popular type of Ethernet wiring is twisted-pair wire. Home networks use either the Cat-5 or Cat-6 version of twisted-pair wire.

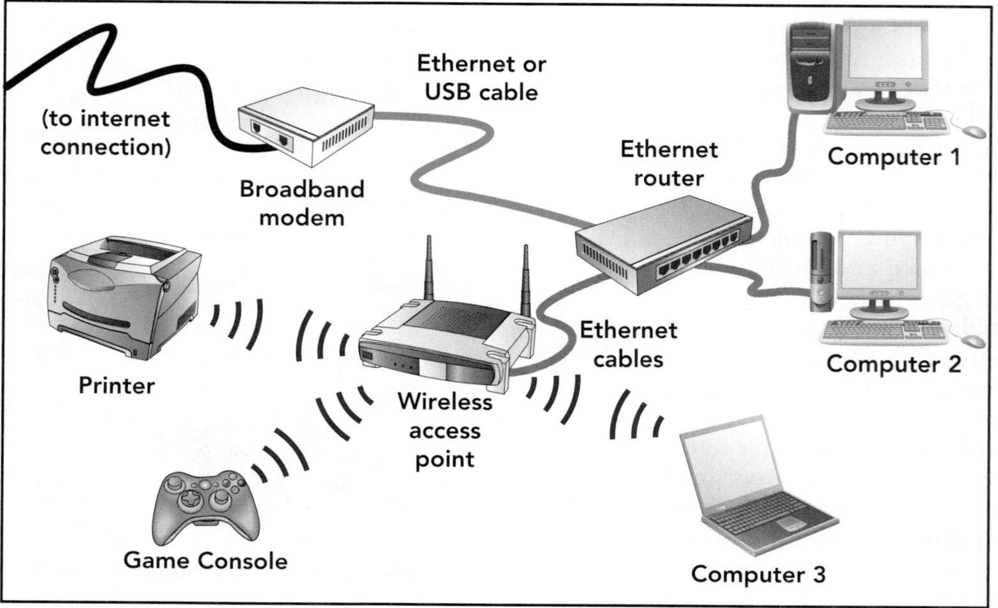

FIGURE 15.22 The hybrid home network usually includes a wired network router that contains a wireless access point.

These wires are connected by RJ-45 connectors, which look like large telephone jacks. Cat-5 wire transfers data at speeds of up to 100 Mbps; Cat-6 transfers data at speeds of up to 1,000 Mbps (1 Gbps).

The simplest form of Ethernet network links different computers with a connecting switch or router. See Figure 15.23 for an example of a simple Ethernet network. In this example, the computer can send a message to the notebook or the printer by way of the router. Routers and switches are available in many configurations. Most have 4 to 12 ports. The majority of home networks use a 100Base-TX router that is capable of a transfer rate of 100 Mbps (100 million bits per second). A more expensive option is to upgrade to a 1000Base-T router with a transfer rate of 1 Gbps. Also known as gigabit Ethernet, 1000Base-T is useful when transferring large amounts of data, such as digital multimedia.

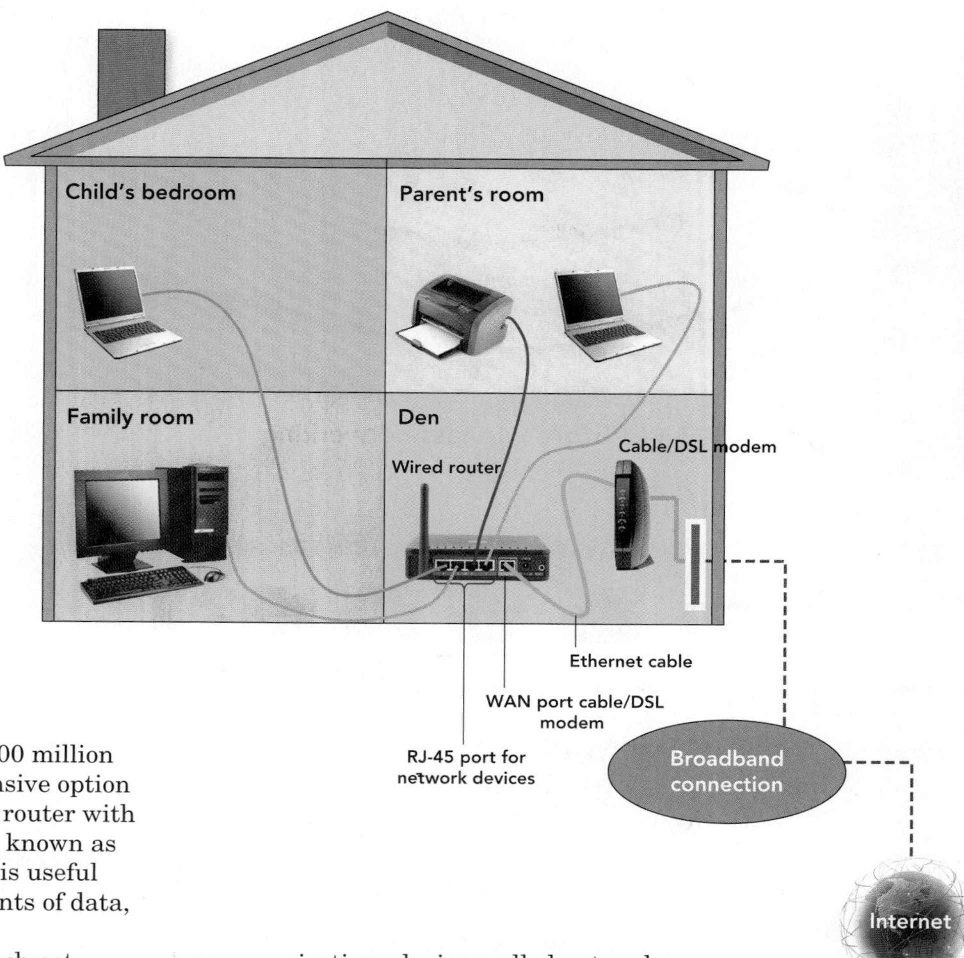

FIGURE 15.23 A typical Ethernet network setup using a router.

In an Ethernet network, each networked computer must have an Ethernet network adapter, also called a network interface card (NIC). Most newer computers already include a NIC, but a NIC can also be installed as an expansion card on an older system.

Concept 15.14 | Simplifying Wireless Home Networks

Although several wireless network standards are currently available, WiFi is the wireless standard used for home networking. Established wireless network standards ensure that companies that build wireless connecting devices do so in compliance with strict definitions and rules. Ultimately, three factors determine which standard best suits your needs—the cost of the hardware or software, the speed at which data can travel over the network, and the range within which you can reliably transmit between devices.

Home WiFi networks are wireless networks in which each computer on the network broadcasts its information to another using radio signals. WiFi networks use communications devices called network access points, also referred to as wireless access points (Figure 15.24), built into home wireless routers, to send and receive data between computers that have wireless adapters. Network access points enable you to move a laptop with a wireless adapter from room to room or to place computers in different locations throughout a house.

A peer-to-peer relationship exists among all of the computers in most wireless home networks. This means that all the computers are equals, or peers, with no particular computer acting as the server. However, some home wireless networks can also be of the client/server type. In a client/server home network, each computer communicates with the server, and the server then communicates with other computers or peripherals. All peripherals in a wireless network must be within the router's range, which is usually 100 to 300 feet, depending on the building's construction and thickness of the walls, floors, and ceilings.

WiFi networks use the 802.11 wireless transmission specifications. Although some older systems may still use the

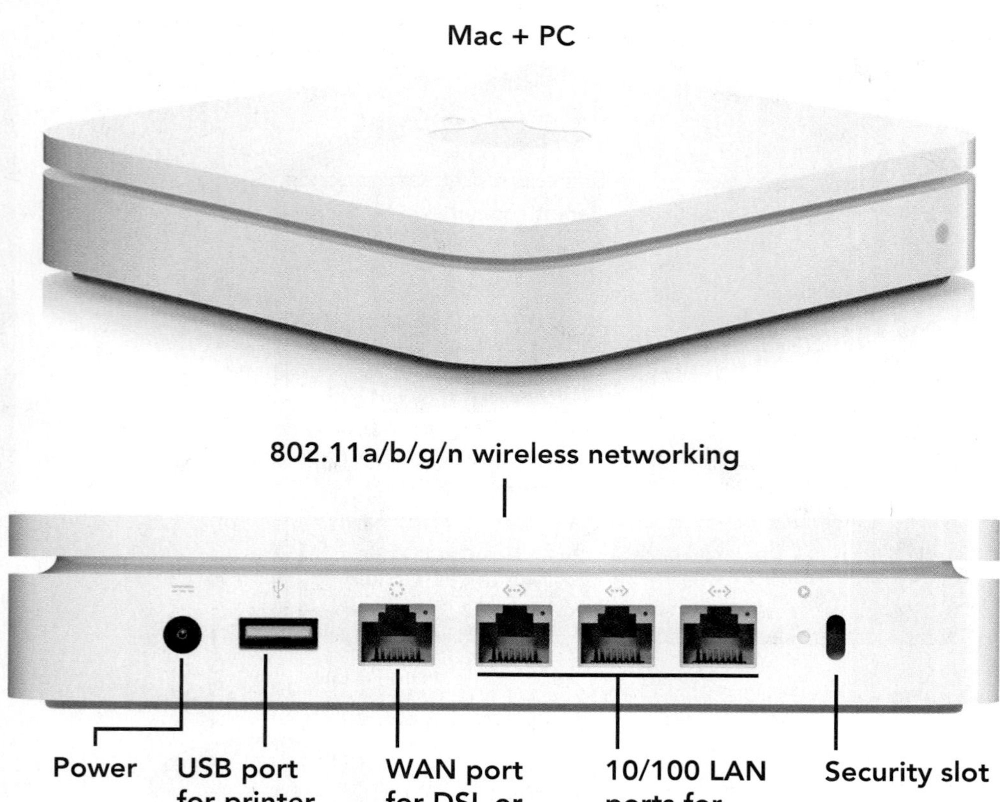

FIGURE 15.24 A wireless access point removes the distance and location restriction associated with a wired network.

802.11a or 802.11b standards, the most prevalent standards are 802.11g and 802.11n. The 802.11g specification operates in the 2.4 GHz radio band and is capable of data transfer rates of up to 54 Mbps. The 802.11n can operate in both the 2.4 GHz and 5 GHz radio band, and the average data transfer rate is about 300 Mbps.

Wireless networks are gaining in popularity because of their ease of setup and convenience. There are no unsightly wires to run through the home, and you are no longer limited to working in just one location. However, there are some disadvantages to wireless networks:

- Newer laptop computers are usually equipped for wireless access, but older notebooks may require the addition of a wireless adapter card.
- Wireless networks may be affected by interference from other devices such as microwave ovens and cordless phones. Additionally you might find that reception can be a problem if the radio waves are unable to pass through interior walls.
- Conversely, because radio waves are able to pass through walls, it is important to take appropriate measures to safeguard your privacy from someone passing by outside your home.

In the future, home network systems will almost certainly be wireless and have the capability to adapt to new technologies as they develop. Currently, knowledge of both wired and wireless technology is essential to seamlessly integrate convenience, simplicity, and long-term cost savings.

Check Your Knowledge: From either the Companion Web Site or MyITLab, take the quiz covering Objectives 1, 2, 3, 4, and 5.

Objective 6 | Understand Data Transmission

As the Director of Sales for a hotel that is part of a global hotel chain, you are updating your sales presentation for business and corporate clients to include an overview of the network capabilities of your conference center. Your understanding of such technical terms like bandwidth and throughput must be refined and phrased in such a way that clients of all technology levels are comfortable with this portion of your sales presentation. Where do you start?

Communication is the process of electronically sending and receiving messages between two or more computers or devices regardless of the distance between those devices. The ***sending device*** initiates the transmission, while the ***receiving device*** accepts the transmission and responds. Communications can be split into two parts: the message—also referred to as data, information, or an instruction—and the ***communications channel*** also referred to as the ***link***. The communications channel is the transmission media over which the message is sent from one location to another.

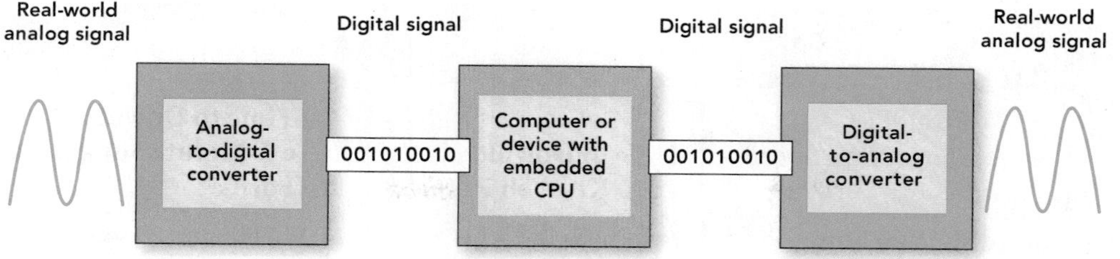

FIGURE 15.25 The transmission of real-world sounds through digital communication devices requires the conversion of analog signals to digital signals for transmission and then back to analog in order to be heard by the receiving party.

Signals in the real world, like sound and light, are ***analog signals***—continuous waves that vary in strength and quality. Before these real-world signals can be used by digital equipment, like a computer, the signal must pass through an analog-to-digital converter. An ***analog-to-digital converter (ADC)*** is simply a microchip that contains the circuitry to convert an analog signal into a digital signal. A ***digital signal*** is one that includes discontinuous pulses in which the presence or absence of electronic pulses is represented by 1s and 0s. In reverse, when a computer signal must be sent out to the real world, for example as sound, the digital signal must pass through a digital-to-analog converter. A ***digital-to-analog converter (DAC)*** is a microchip that contains the circuitry to convert a digital signal to analog (Figure 15.25).

In communications, both analog and digital signals move data over communications channels. The conversion from analog to digital or digital to analog is normally not something you can detect or must be concerned with. However, if you have ever scanned an image, recorded your voice, used VoIP on your computer, or talked on a phone, you used an analog-to-digital converter. Likewise, if you have ever listened on the phone or played a CD, you made use of a digital-to-analog converter.

A codec, short for code-decode algorithm, is responsible for the conversion between analog and digital signals. Codecs accomplish the conversion by sampling the analog signal several thousand times per second. A common audio codec, the G.711 codec, samples the audio 64,000 times a second. It then converts each sample into digitized data and compresses it for transmission. When the samples are reassembled, the missing pieces between the samples go undetected by the human ear. The most common codec for VoIP samples the analog signal 8,000 times a second. Because a digital signal is discrete, composed of 0s and 1s that are sampled from an analog signal, the data arrives in a much clearer format. The receiving end knows exactly how to reconstruct the data back into its original form (Figure 15.26). Digital signals also transfer much more data than analog and at much greater speeds. For instance, digital TV systems can now deliver more than 500 stations across digital cable.

From either the Companion Web Site or MyITLab, watch Chapter 15 Video 2

Concept 15.15 | Assessing Bandwidth

Bandwidth refers to the theoretical maximum amount of data that can be transmitted through a given communications channel at one time—usually per second.

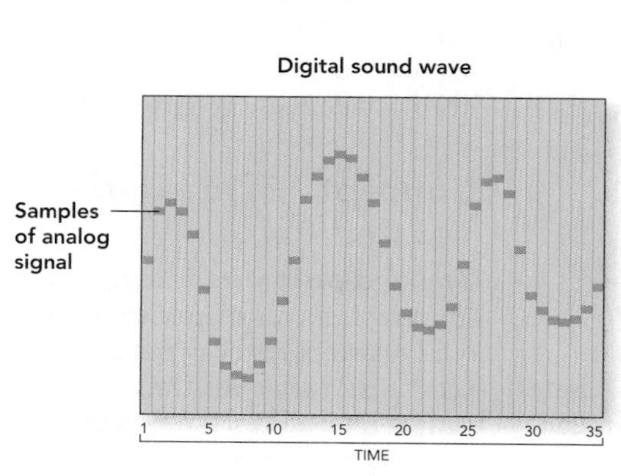

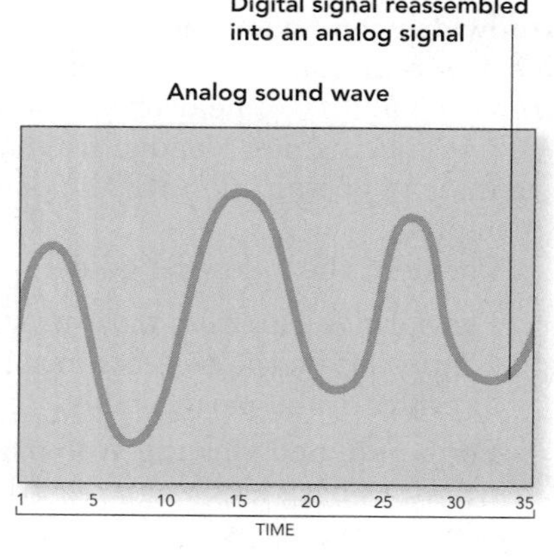

FIGURE 15.26 Digital signals are composed by sampling an analog wave at discrete points in time. The analog wave is then approximated by these discrete measurements.

Basic Wired Internet Speeds

Internet Connection Speed	Time to Download a 100 KB Web Page	Time to Download a 5-Minute Song in MP3 Format
56 Kbps dial-up modem	14 seconds	12 minutes 30 seconds
256 Kbps broadband	3 seconds	3 minutes
512 Kbps broadband	1.6 seconds	1 minute 30 seconds
1 Mbps broadband	0.8 seconds	41 seconds
2 Mbps broadband	0.4 seconds	20 seconds
4 Mbps broadband	0.1 seconds	5 seconds
6 Mbps broadband	instantaneous	3.5 seconds
8 Mbps broadband or higher	instantaneous	2.5 seconds

Figure 15.27

Two factors affect bandwidth: the physical characteristics of the transmission medium and the method used to represent and transmit the data. For analog signals, bandwidth is expressed in cycles per second, or hertz (Hz). For digital signals, bandwidth is expressed in bits per second (bps). ***Throughput***, often used incorrectly as a synonym for bandwidth, is the actual amount of data that is transmitted. It is almost always lower than bandwidth, especially with wireless communications.

Broadband is a communication transmission that uses a wide band of frequencies to transport high volumes of data at high speeds, typically greater than 1 Mbps megabits per second (Mbps). Cable TV uses broadband transmission. So how much bandwidth do you need? Conventional dial-up connections to the Internet use a relatively low bandwidth of 56 Kbps or less. Although cheaper, most users find this painfully slow when searching the Web. Through the practical comparisons provided in Figure 15.27, you should get an idea of what increased bandwidth can do for such Internet activities as streaming music or video. ***Streaming*** is the ability to hear or see content while it is being downloaded from a Web site instead of waiting until the download is complete.

Consider the following guide:

- For normal use, from most providers, 1 Mbps offers the best balance between cost and performance.
- For e-mail and viewing Web pages but not streaming audio or video, then 256 Kbps to 512 Kbps is adequate.
- For gaming, a 2 Mbps connection or faster is necessary.
- To share a connection between two or more computers, a minimum of a 4 Mbps connection is necessary to take advantage of music or video on demand or digital broadband Internet TV.

Broadband digital connections are widely available in the United States. A study in June 2010 indicated that 62 percent of broadband subscribers in the United States subscribe to a wireless broadband plan.

Objective 7 | Evaluate Wired and Wireless Transmission Media

As the Director of Sales for a hotel that is part of a global hotel chain, you know that renovation of the conference facilities and the addition of hot spots on the hotel grounds and attached restaurants has been approved. The general manager has asked you for more input on the network connectivity required by hotel guests and event attendees. Where do you start?

Concept 15.16 | Understanding Twisted Pair

Twisted-pair wire is a copper cable used for telephone and data communications in which two pairs of wires are interwoven together, a practice that provides a shield that reduces interference from electrical fields generated by other devices like

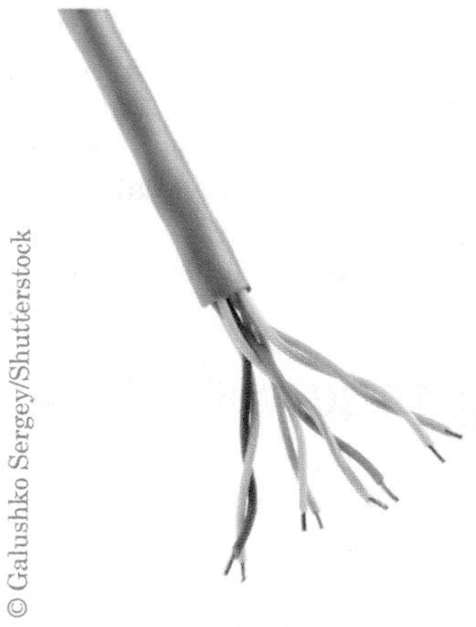
© Galushko Sergey/Shutterstock

FIGURE 15.28 Cat-5e cable uses four pairs of twisted wire and transmits data at 1,000 Mbps (1 Gbps).

electric motors and power lines. Twisted-pair is an inexpensive medium with bandwidth too low to simultaneously carry video, voice, and data. Twisted-pair wiring carries data at transfer rates of less than 1 Kbps.

Concept 15.17 | Reviewing Variations of Twisted-Pair

Cat-5 cable, short for ***Category 5***, is the fifth generation of twisted-pair data communication cable. Cat-5 cable contains four pairs of twisted-copper wire and supports speeds up to 100 Mbps over a maximum distance of 100 m (328 feet). However, only two of the four pairs of wires are actually used for most network communications. A newer variation of the Cat-5 cable, ***Cat-5e***, short for ***Category 5 enhanced***, uses all four wire pairs, enabling speeds up to 1,000 Mbps (1 Gbps) over a short distance. This enhanced medium is backward compatible with ordinary Cat-5 (Figure 15.28).

Cat-6, short for ***Category 6***, is the sixth generation of twisted-pair cable and is backward compatible with Cat-5 and Cat-5e. It contains four pairs of copper wire like the previous generation, utilizes all four pairs, supports speeds up to 1 gigabit per second (Gbps), expands available bandwidth from 100 MHz for Cat-5e to 200 MHz, and has superior immunity from external noise.

Concept 15.18 | Advancing to Coaxial Cable

Coaxial cable, familiar to cable TV users (Figure 15.29), consists of a center

© zwola fasola/Shutterstock

FIGURE 15.29 In coaxial cable, data travels through the center copper wire core. The cable is connected to a coaxial wall jack.

copper wire surrounded by insulation, which is then surrounded by a layer of braided wire. Data travels through the center wire, and the braided wire provides a shield against electrical interference (Figure 15.30). Coaxial cable carries data at transfer rates of up to 52 Mbps to an Internet service provider but no more than 10 Mbps to individual computers. In contrast to twisted-pair, coaxial cable allows for broadband data communications. Your home is probably already wired with coaxial cable if you subscribe to a cable TV service.

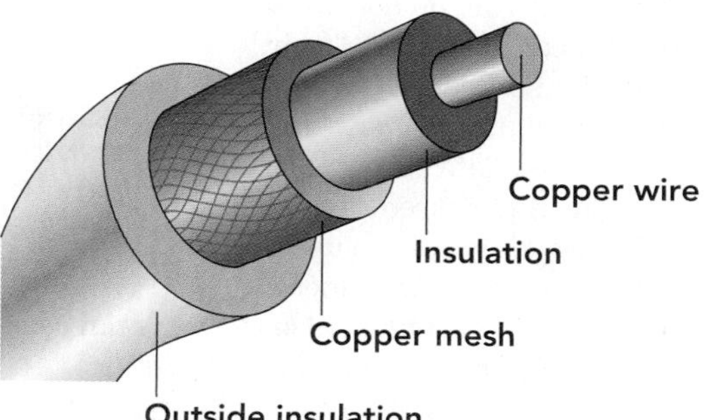

FIGURE 15.30 The copper core of a coaxial cable is shielded from interference by a braided wire shield and an external layer of rubber that provides additional insulation.

Concept 15.19 | Considering Fiber-optic Cable

Fiber-optic cable, another broadband transmission medium, consists of thin strands of glass or plastic about the diameter of a human hair. You might recognize the acronym ***FiOS***, which stands for ***fiber-optic service***. This medium is arranged in bundles called *optical cables* that carry

FIGURE 15.31 Fiber-optic cable consists of a bundle of fiber-optic strands.

data by means of pulses of light. Fiber-optic cable (Figure 15.31) provides transfer rates of 10 Gbps (gigabits per second) or more. A single fiber-optic strand is composed of three parts: the core, the cladding, and the buffer coat (Figure 15.32). The core is a thin glass or plastic center through which the light travels. The cladding is the optical material surrounding the core that reflects the light back into the core. The plastic coating that protects the fiber from moisture and damage is the buffer coat. Besides increased speed, additional benefits of fiber-optic cable include:

- Light pulses are not affected by random radiation in the environment.
- Fiber-optic lines have a significantly lower error rate.
- Fiber-optics can span longer distances before needing expensive repeaters to boost the signal.
- Security breaches in a fiber-optic line can be easily detected.
- As compared to coaxial cable, installation is simplified due to the reduced weight and size of fiber-optic cable.

Wireless media do not use solid substances like twisted-pair, coaxial, and fiber-optic cables to transmit data. Rather, wireless media send data through air or space using infrared, radio, or microwave signals. To use these wireless transmission media, a computer system must also use a special communications device called a wireless access point, which sends and receives data between computers that contain wireless adapters. Access points are usually built into wireless routers. Wireless media is essential in situations where installing cables is impossible, the costs of wired media are prohibitive, or the popularity of portable computing devices mandates a wireless environment.

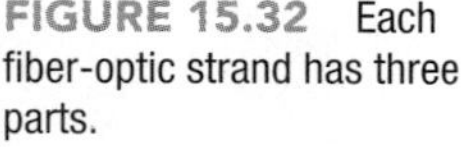
FIGURE 15.32 Each fiber-optic strand has three parts.

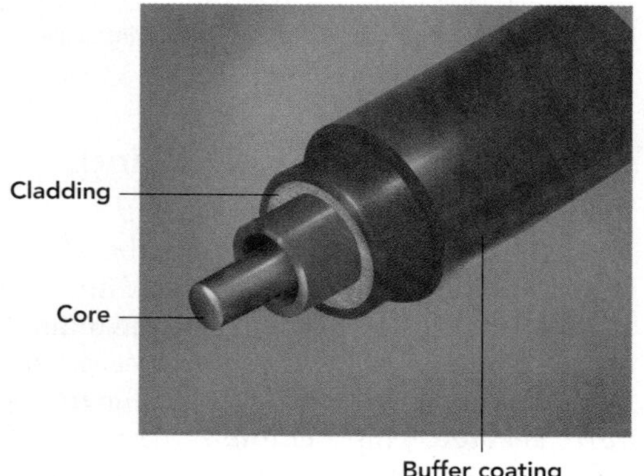

Concept 15.20 | Understanding Infrared

If you use a remote control to change television channels, you are already familiar with infrared signaling. ***Infrared*** is a wireless transmission medium that carries data via beams of light through the air. No wires are required, but the transmitting and receiving devices must be in line of sight or the signal is lost. When the path between the transmitting and the receiving devices is not obstructed by trees, hills, mountains, buildings, or other structures, infrared signals can work within a maximum of about 100 feet.

To use infrared technology with your computer system, you need an ***IrDA (infrared data association) port*** (Figure 15.33). You may have encountered an IrDA port on a mobile computing device or wireless peripheral such as a PDA, digital camera, laptop, mouse, printer, or keyboard. Wireless technology, and to some degree Bluetooth, has replaced this technology.

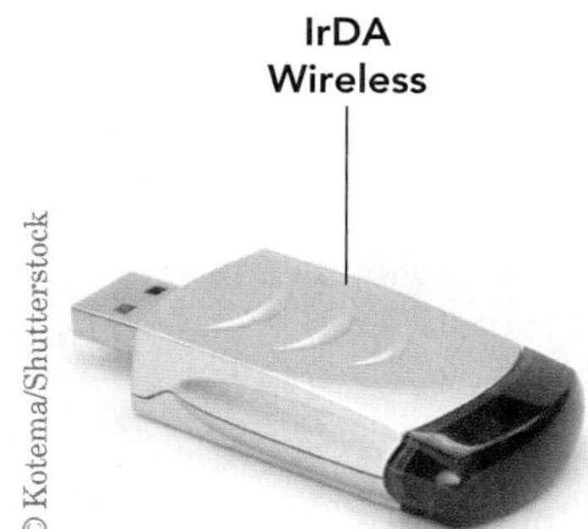

FIGURE 15.33 An IrDA port allows for wireless management of external devices such as a mouse, keyboard, phone, or PDA.

Concept 15.21 | Reviewing Radio Transmissions

Radio transmissions offer an alternative to infrared transmissions. You probably have experienced one type of radio transmission by listening to your favorite radio station. But you may not realize the impact that radio waves have on your daily life or on society in general. All kinds of gadgets—from cell and cordless phones to baby monitors—communicate via radio waves. Although humans cannot see or otherwise detect them, radio waves are everywhere.

With ***radio transmission***, data in a variety of forms like music, voice conversations, and photos travels through the air as radio frequency (RF) signals or radio waves via a transmitting device and a receiving device. Instead of separate transmitting and receiving devices, radio transmissions can also use a wireless transceiver, which is a combination transmitting–receiving device equipped with an antenna. Data transfer rates for wireless devices have the potential to reach up to 3 Mbps for cell phones and up to 250 Mbps for wireless networks.

A major disadvantage of radio transmission is susceptibility to noise and interference. One of radio's advantages is that radio signals are effective at both long range between cities, regions, and countries and short range within a home or office.

WiFi is a popular wireless network technology that uses radio waves to provide high-speed Internet and network connections for home systems, laptops, video game consoles, and other enabled wireless devices. WiFi can be based on any of the IEEE 802.11 standards and communicates through radio frequency technology, with ranges reaching 300 to 500 feet. The cornerstone of a WiFi system, like other wireless systems, is the access point that broadcasts a signal that devices equipped with wireless network adapters detect.

Bluetooth is a short-range radio transmission technology that does not require direct line of sight and has become very popular in recent years (Figure 15.34). Bluetooth technology relies on a network called a piconet or a PAN (personal area network) that enables all kinds of devices—desktop computers, mobile phones, printers, pagers, PDAs, and more—within 30 feet of each other to communicate automatically and wirelessly.

Concept 15.22 | Managing Microwaves

Microwaves are the upper part of the radio frequency spectrum and are electromagnetic radio waves with short frequencies that travel at speeds of 1 to 10 Mbps. Microwaves are used to transmit data from a source to a receiving site in wireless PANs like Bluetooth, wireless LANs like WiFi, wireless MANs, and wireless WANs. Using relay stations similar to satellite dishes, including an antenna and transceiver, microwave signals are sent from one relay station to the next. Microwaves get weaker as they get farther away from their source, must travel in a straight line, and cannot be obstructed by buildings, hills, and mountains. Thus, relay stations are positioned approximately every 30 miles—the line-of-sight distance to the horizon—or closer if the terrain blocks transmission. To avoid obstacles, microwave relay stations are often situated on the tops of buildings or mountains (Figure 15.35). Microwaves are used in weather monitoring, air traffic control, speed limit enforcement, and missile guidance systems.

The advantages of microwave transmission include the elimination of a wired infrastructure, enabling cellular telephone networks and connectivity in areas where the use of physical wires is impractical or impossible, and providing security through encrypting data as it is transmitted.

FIGURE 15.34 Bluetooth-enabled devices make tasks like synchronizing your phone calendar with your computer calendar easier.

FIGURE 15.35 Any information that can travel over a telephone or coaxial cable can be transmitted via microwave.

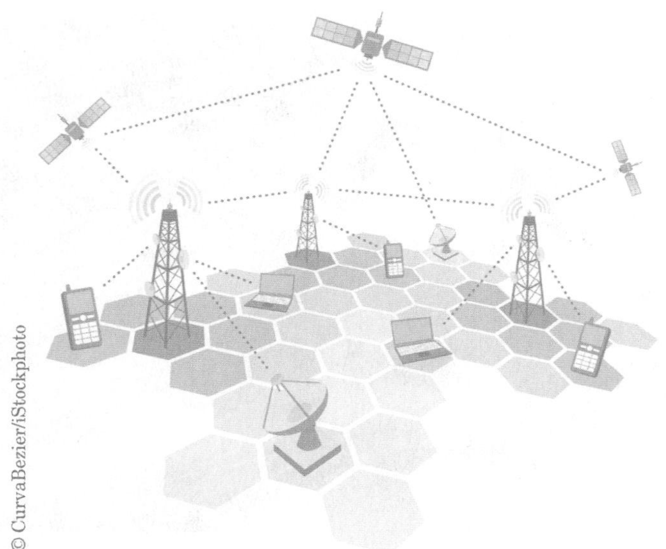
© CurvaBezier/iStockphoto

FIGURE 15.36
Communication satellites in space work by receiving information from one microwave station and sending it back to another at a different location on Earth.

Disadvantages include the 30-mile line-of-sight restriction, sensitivity to electrical or magnetic interference, and costs of maintaining the multitude of relay stations it takes to transfer messages across long distances.

Concept 15.23 | Investigating the Use of Satellites

Satellites are essentially microwave relay stations in space positioned in a geosynchronous orbit that matches the satellite's speed to that of the Earth's rotation. Thus, satellites are permanently positioned with respect to the ground below. Data is transmitted by sending and receiving microwave signals to and from Earth-based stations (Figure 15.36).

Direct broadcast satellite (DBS) is a consumer satellite technology that uses a reception dish to receive digital signals at microwave frequencies directly from geostationary satellites broadcast at a bandwidth of 12 Mbps. Increasingly, DBS operators offer Internet access as well as digital TV service. The delay caused by the distances that data must travel in a satellite Internet connection is called *latency*.

A good overview of a DBS can be found at **www.groundcontrol.com/How_Does_Satellite_Internet_Work.htm**. Broadband access is still not available in many rural or other low-population areas, so many of these areas are prime candidates for DBS.

What is it about wireless connectivity that is so interesting? Well, one answer is that wireless technology removes place-specific restrictions—the need to be in a certain place to receive a service. Some forms of wireless technology allow you to be wherever you choose and still have the ability to be connected.

Concept 15.24 | Communicating Via the Public Switched Telephone Network

Although many components of the conventional phone system have been enhanced, until all devices have been replaced with digital equivalents, limitations still exist.

The ***public switched telephone network (PSTN)*** is the global telephone system, a massive network used for data as well as voice communications, comprising transmission media ranging from twisted-pair wire to fiber-optic cable. Some computer users derisively (and somewhat unfairly) refer to the PSTN as plain old telephone service (POTS). The derision comes from most analog telephone lines being based on standards that date back more than a century. Although a few parts of the PSTN remain based on analog communications, many sections of the system have been switched over to digital communications.

Those still using analog devices today include many homes and small businesses. These telephones are linked to subscriber loop carriers by means of twisted-pair wires. *A* ***subscriber loop carrier (SLC)*** is a small, waist-high curbside installation that connects as many as 96 subscribers; you have probably seen one in your neighborhood. The area served by an SLC is called the ***local loop***. When the analog signal reaches the SLC, it is converted to digital form and remains that way throughout the PSTN network.

From the SLC, the digital signals are routed via high-capacity fiber-optic cables to the ***local exchange switch***, a digital device capable of handling thousands of calls located in the local telephone company's central office (CO). From the local phone company's CO, the call can go anywhere in the world. It can continue on the digital portion of the PSTN's fiber-optic cables or be converted to radio waves and sent out over cellular networks (Figure 15.37).

Although analog connections still exist, ***digital telephony***, a system in which the telephones and transmissions are digital, is the trend. Compared with analog devices, which are prone to noise and

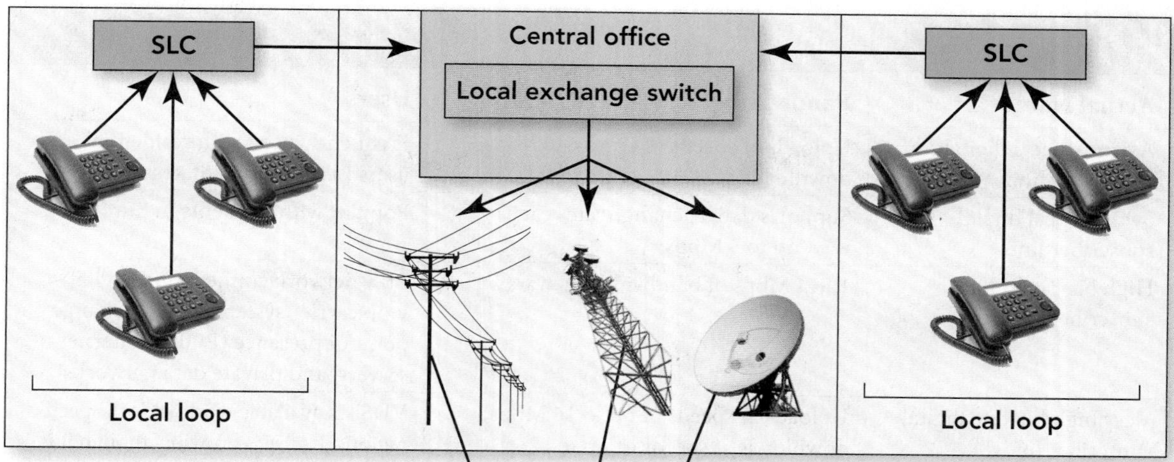

interference, digital phones offer noise-free transmission and high-quality audio.

Because long-distance lines must handle thousands of calls simultaneously (32 calls per second, 24 hours a day, 7 days a week in the United States), a technique called ***multiplexing*** is used to send more than one call over a single line. The electrical and physical characteristics of copper wire impose a limit of 24 multiplexed calls per line, whereas fiber-optic cables can carry as many as 48,384 digital voice channels simultaneously. In contrast to the analog local loop, most long-distance carriers use digital signals so that they can pack the greatest number of calls into a single circuit.

The ***last-mile problem*** is the term that refers to the inability of homes or businesses to access the PSTN's high-speed fiber-optic cables and the bottleneck of data on the last mile of twisted-pair phone lines that connect homes and businesses.

However, with telephone companies replacing analog local loop technology with digital technology such as FiOS, the last-mile problem might soon be solved in your neighborhood!

Concept 15.25 | Reviewing Last-Mile Technologies

Local loops are being upgraded, but until the upgrade is complete, phone companies and other providers offer a number of interim digital telephony technologies to bridge the gap from the Internet to a residence. This last section of the circuit is referred to as the *last mile*. Technologies that help bridge that gap, known as ***last-mile technologies***, include digital telephone standards such as DSL that use twisted-pair wiring, as well as high-speed wired services such as coaxial cable and FiOS (Figure 15.38).

FIGURE 15.37 Pathways on the PSTN. For the signal to reach its final destination, it may travel across several different transmission media, including a cellular network.

Digital subscriber line (DSL), another method of Internet access available in the United States, is also called ***xDSL***. This term refers to a group of related technologies, including ADSL (asymmetric digital subscriber line), SDSL (symmetrical digital subscriber line), HDSL (high bit-rate digital subscriber line), and VDSL (very high bit-rate digital subscriber line)—all forms of Internet access. DSL technologies, in general, can deliver data transfer rates of 1.54 Mbps or higher. An overview of the technology

© Ivaschenko Roman/ Shutterstock

© Vangelis Thomaidis / Alamy

© Piotr Malczyk / Alamy

FIGURE 15.38 Various types of modems facilitate the connection between your computer and last-mile technologies.

The Details Behind DSL Technologies

Name	Actual Name	Bandwidth	Users
ADSL	Asymmetrical digital subscriber line	Uploads at speeds of up to 640 Kbps, downloads at speeds of up to 8.1 Mbps	Frequently used with residential users in the United States
SDSL	Symmetrical digital subscriber line	Supports data exchange rates each way, up to 3 Mbps	Popular with residents in Europe
HDSL	High bit-rate digital subscriber line	1.544 Mbps of bandwidth each way	PBX network connections, digital loop carrier systems, interexchange point of presence (POPs), Internet servers, and private data networks
VDSL	Very high bit-rate digital subscriber line	Uploads at speeds of up to 16 Mbps, downloads at speeds of up to 52 Mbps	VDSL is available worldwide in specific regions. Its use is growing, though it is not easily found in the United States

Figure 15.39

features of each type of DSL presented in Figure 15.39 provides clarification.

To use DSL, you must have a DSL phone line and a DSL service subscription. Unlike conventional telephone service, which is available to almost any home, DSL service is limited by the distance from the CO, or telephone switching station, to your home. You also need a ***DSL modem***, which is similar to a traditional telephone modem in that it modulates and demodulates analog and digital signals for transmission over communications channels. However, DSL modems use signaling methods based on broadband technology for much higher transfer speeds. DSL service is now standardized so that almost any DSL modem should work with the wiring your telephone provider uses. However, it is best to buy a DSL modem that your provider recommends. Although DSL service is more expensive than dial-up, it is usually cheaper than other broadband access options, such as cable or fiber-optics (Figure 15.40)

Internet access via cable-based broadband is usually provided by your local cable TV company. This type of Internet access reached approximately 41 million subscribers in the United States in 2009.

When cable and cabling equipment for TV were originally installed in homes, signals ran in only one direction—to the home. When the Internet became popular, the cable companies invested tremendous amounts of money in equipment and cable to enable two-way communication to capture the Internet market.

For computer users, these services offer data transfer rates that exceed the speed of DSL. ***Cable modems***, devices that enable computers to access the Internet by means of a cable TV connection, now deliver data at bandwidths of 1.5 to 6 Mbps or more, depending on how many subscribers are connected to a local cable segment. Bandwidth across a cable connection is shared among subscribers who are connected to the cable company in local groups. If you are lucky enough to have subscribers in your group who do not use much bandwidth, you can experience impressive speed—up to 20 Mbps—while using the Internet.

Gaining in popularity as a last-mile technology is fiber-optic cable. Fiber-optic service, or FiOS, is not currently available in many rural areas but in suburbs and outlying areas of cities where the installation of fiber-optic cable is less difficult to install, this option is becoming more popular.

A ***leased line***, sometimes called a dedicated line, is a connection set up by a telecommunication carrier and is usually a permanent fiber-optic or telephone connection that enables continuous, end-to-end communication between two points. Larger organizations, such as ISPs, corporations, and universities, connect using leased ***T1 lines***, which are fiber-optic or specially conditioned copper cables that can handle 24 digitized voice channels or carry computer data at a rate of up to 1.544 Mbps. If the T1 line is used for telephone conversations, it plugs into your phone system. If it is carrying data, it plugs into the network's router. The price of T1 lines ranges from $1,000 to $1,500 a

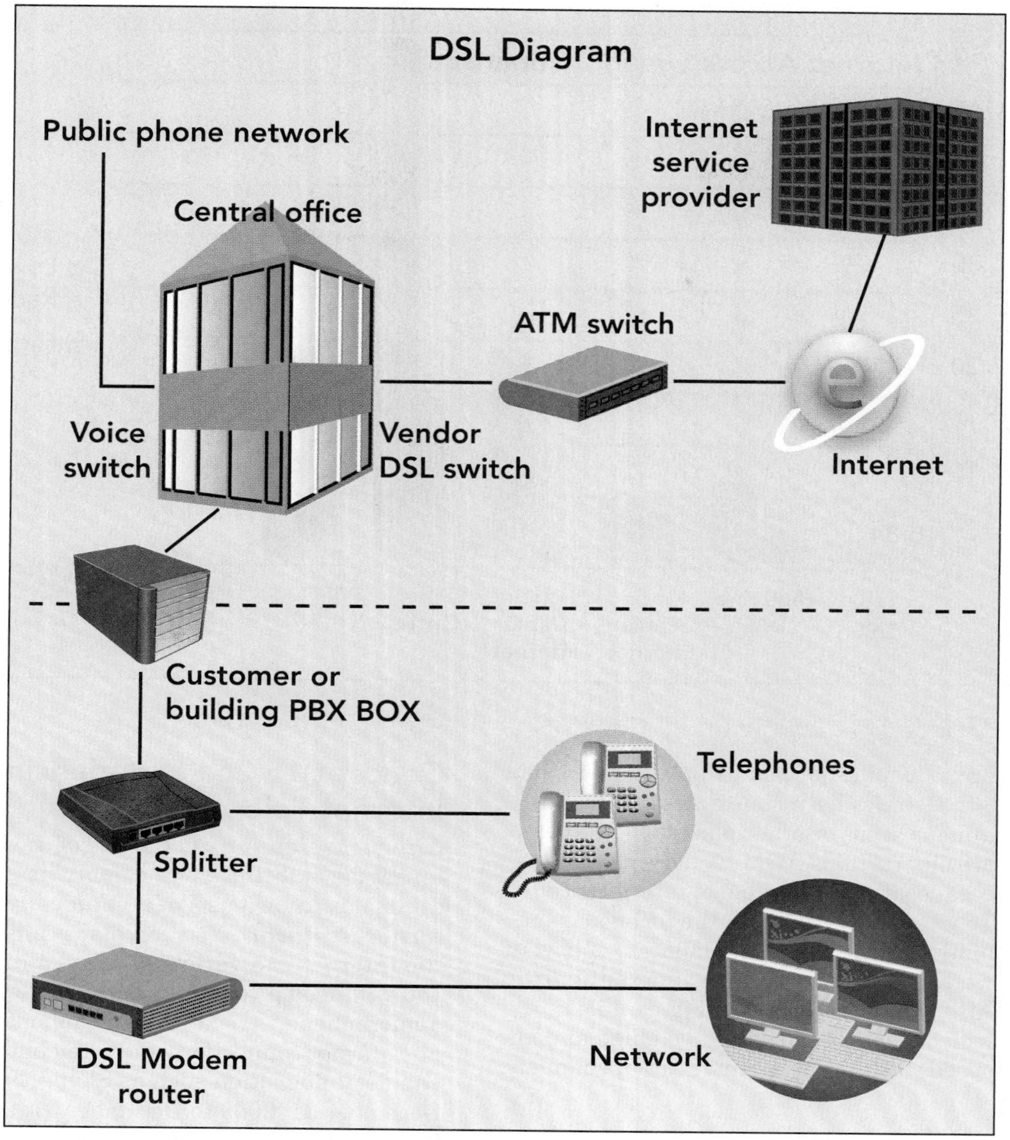

FIGURE 15.40 The Path of Data from an Internet Service Provider to a DSL Subscriber's Residence.

month, depending on the provider, the location, and the use. Leased lines may use modems, cable modems, or other communications devices to manage the transfer of data.

There are also interim technologies that make better use of existing fiber-optic cables. Fiber-optic ***T2 lines*** and ***T3 lines*** can handle up to 44.7 Mbps of computer data. Although T3 lines can cost approximately $3,000 per month, Internet service providers, financial institutions, and large corporations that move a large amount of data find these lines critical to their operations. One T3 line is equivalent to having 28 T1 lines. Another technology, ***SONET (synchronous optical network)***, is a physical layer of network technology that uses fiber-optic cable and carries large volumes of data over long distances. It is the standard for high-performance networks. The slowest SONET standard calls for data transfer rates of 52 Mbps; some higher levels enable rates of 20 Gbps or faster. SONET is widely used in North America, and a similar standard, synchronous digital hierarchy (SDH), is used in the rest of the world.

In addition to adapting twisted-pair wiring, broadband coaxial cable, and fiber-optic cable, wireless technologies are helping to solve the last-mile problem as well.

WiMAX (worldwide interoperability for microwave access) is a wireless up-and-coming digital communication system that delivers high-speed access over long distances, either point-to-point where both sender and receiver are stationary or through mobile access where sender or receiver is moving. WiMAX is effective for

From either the Companion Web Site or MyITLab, try the Chapter 15 Networks Simulation

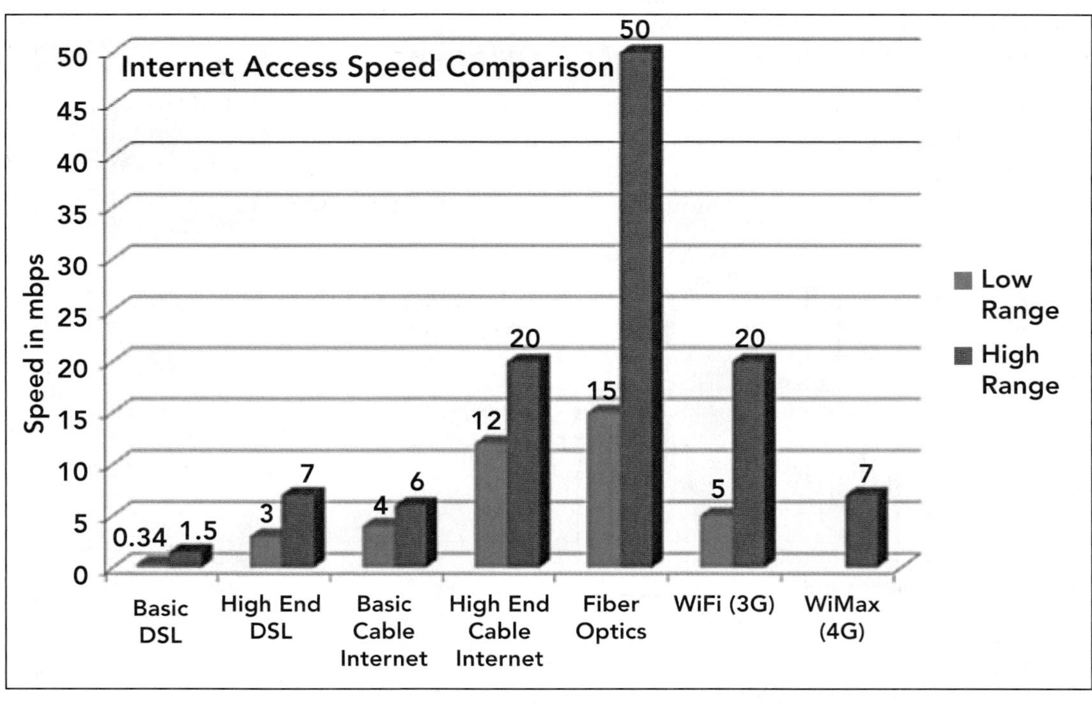

SOURCE: Data compiled from www.high-speed-internet-access-guide.com/overview.html (and other links from this site)

FIGURE 15.41 In addition to speed, price and availability can determine which method of Internet connection a user selects.

up to 30 miles for point-to-point access and 3 to 10 miles for mobile access. In mountainous areas or other places where there are obstructions, WiMAX faces challenges because it is susceptible to interference. To view a brief video on the technology behind WiMAX and an explanation of how it works, visit **www.wimax.com/education**. Also, review the chart in Figure 15.41, which displays the advertised high and low speeds of various communication channels.

Objective 8 | Assess Wired and Wireless Applications

As the Director of Sales for a hotel that is part of a global hotel chain, you have been asked for additional input regarding the plans to enhance electronic communications in the hotel's guest rooms and conference facilities. You want to stay ahead of your competition, so you want to review current requests and also include new technologies and incorporate the capability to connect future devices into the expansion design. Where do you start?

The world of wired and wireless applications is receiving more attention every day. You cannot open a magazine, surf the Web, or watch TV without seeing ads for the latest wireless solutions.

Concept 15.26 | Experiencing Internet Telephony

Internet telephony is the use of the Internet for real-time voice communication, commonly known as ***VoIP (Voice over Internet Protocol)***. You can place calls via the Internet in a variety of ways, but first you will need a computer equipped with a microphone, speakers or headphones, an Internet connection, and a telephony-enabled application such as Skype. From December 31, 2009 to December 31, 2010, Skype has increased registered users from 474 million to 663 million and had net revenues increase from $719 million in 2009 to $860 million in 2010. Visit **www.skype.com** for the latest information and charges for this service.

The basic idea of Internet telephony has an enormous advantage—the Internet does not rely on switches to route messages like the PSTN does, and it is cheaper to operate. Providers can route dozens, hundreds, or even thousands of calls over the same circuit. Many conventional phone companies already send voice calls over the Internet. You may have actually experienced VoIP without even knowing it.

If you and the person you are calling have a digital video camera or a ***webcam***, you can converse through real-time videoconferencing. A webcam is an inexpensive, low-resolution digital video camera that is integrated into a notebook computer or sits on top of a computer monitor. ***Videoconferencing***, also called ***Web conferencing***, is the use of this digital video technology to transmit sound and video images to facilitate online, virtual meetings through which two or more people can have a face-to-face meeting even though they are geographically separated (Figure 15.42). To learn more about telephone technology from wiring a system to video conferencing and VoIP visit **http://telecom.hellodirect.com/docs/Tutorials/default.asp**.

Streaming video was not practical for home viewing before broadband and cheap, powerful computers became available for the home market. Now, streaming video sites such as YouTube are some of the most visited sites on the Internet. As popular as YouTube is for viewing videos, it has a file size limit of 2GB. An alternative to viewing clips of your favorite television programs on YouTube is ***Internet TV***—the ability to view television shows, videos, and movies over the Internet, for no additional cost, via download or streaming video. The benefit of this type of viewing over YouTube is that the content is provided by the original source, so copyright is not an issue; there is no limit on length; you have a variety of selections from which to choose; and there is no time restriction on when you must watch the video. The only problem you might encounter with streaming is the download or bandwidth limitations set by your Internet service provider (ISP).

FIGURE 15.42 A videoconference or Web conference eliminates the frustration, time, and cost of travel.

Concept 15.27 | Exchanging Documents via Faxing

Facsimile transmission—or ***fax*** as it is popularly known—traditionally enabled you to use a fax machine to send an image of a document over a telephone line to another fax machine. With the use of an Internet fax service, it is possible to send and receive digital documents directly from your computer or portable devices. All you need is an Internet connection, an e-mail account, and a subscription to an Internet fax service. If the receiving fax machine is a conventional machine attached to a phone line, the fax is forwarded to the public switched telephone network for delivery. See Figure 15.43 for the sequence

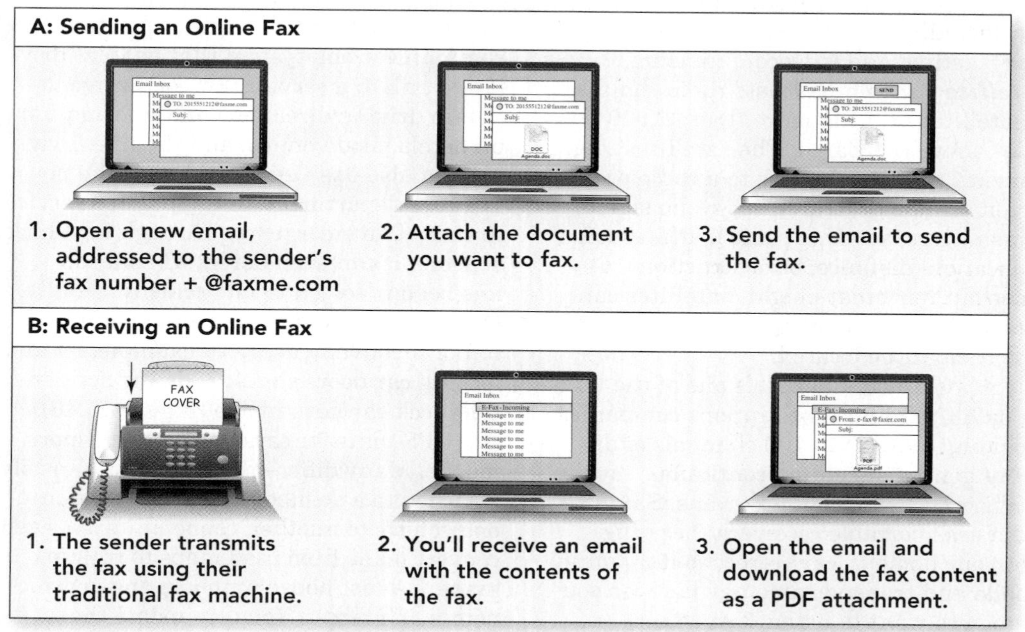

A: Sending an Online Fax
1. Open a new email, addressed to the sender's fax number + @faxme.com
2. Attach the document you want to fax.
3. Send the email to send the fax.
B: Receiving an Online Fax
FAX COVER
1. The sender transmits the fax using their traditional fax machine.
2. You'll receive an email with the contents of the fax.
3. Open the email and download the fax content as a PDF attachment.

FIGURE 15.43 Facsimile transmissions sent via a computer or portable device require a subscription to an Internet fax service.

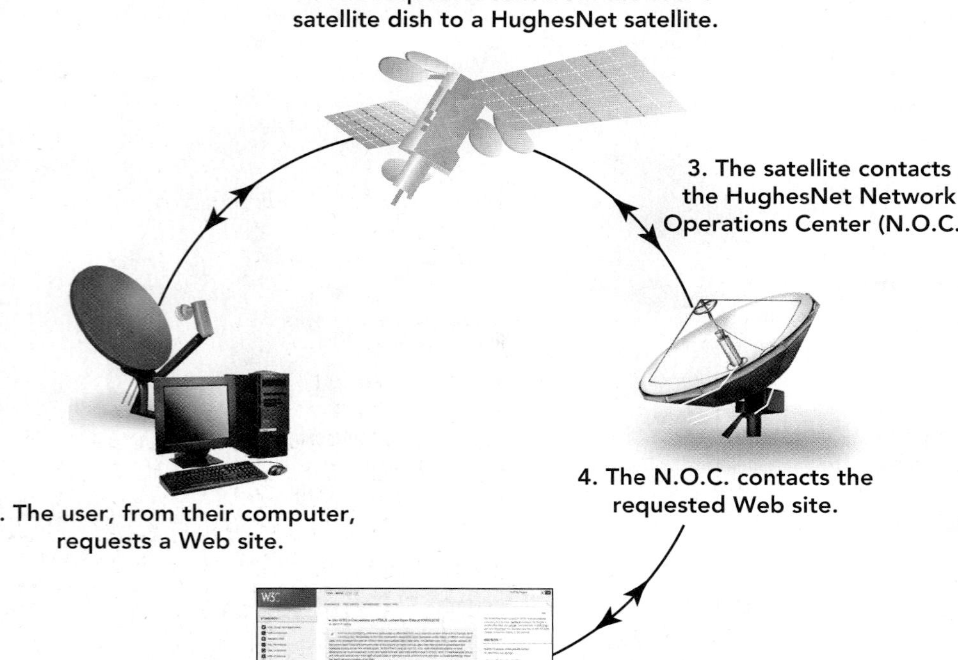
2. The request is sent from the user's satellite dish to a HughesNet satellite.
3. The satellite contacts the HughesNet Network Operations Center (N.O.C.).
1. The user, from their computer, requests a Web site.
4. The N.O.C. contacts the requested Web site.
5. The Web site forwards the information back to the user through the same path.

FIGURE 15.44 Hughes has over 2.5 million systems in over 100 countries.

of steps for this activity. If you need more information on how Internet faxing works, go to **http://home.howstuffworks.com/how-internet-faxing-works.htm**.

Concept 15.28 | Considering Satellite Radio, GPS, and More

Many applications use satellite technology, including air navigation, TV and radio broadcasting, and videoconferencing. ***Satellite radio*** broadcasts radio signals to satellites orbiting more than 22,000 miles above the Earth. The satellites then transmit the signals back to a radio receiver. Unlike ground-based radio signal transmitters, satellite radio is not affected by location, distance, or obstructions. Because of their great height, satellites can transmit signals to a radio receiver wherever it might be located.

Sirius XM Radio Inc. is one of the largest satellite radio subscriptions companies providing more than 100 channels of different genres, including continuous music, sports, news, and talk programs. Satellite radio uses portable receivers that plug into your home or car stereo, so it is totally mobile and transportable to wherever you happen to want to listen. Sirius now offers Backseat TV, which streams live TV broadcasts to subscribers who have video receivers in their vehicles.

HughesNet is a nationwide provider of high-speed Internet by satellite. After your satellite dish is installed, you can send and receive secure Internet access through your satellite modem (Figure 15.44).

GPS (Global Positioning System) is another example of satellite technology. It functions through a cluster of 27 Earth-orbiting satellites (24 in operation and 3 extras in case one fails). Each of these 3,000- to 4,000-pound solar-powered satellites circles the globe at an altitude of 12,000 miles, making two complete rotations every day. The orbits are arranged so that at anytime, anywhere on Earth, at least four satellites are "visible" in the sky. A GPS receiver's job is to locate four or more of these satellites, figure out the distance to each, and use this information to deduce its own location. Most systems are accurate to within 109 yards; some systems boast a 164-yard range (Figure 15.45).

A GPS receiver can be either handheld or installed in a vehicle. Navigation systems in rental cars are a typical application of GPS. OnStar is a multifaceted GPS communications system that enables drivers to talk to a service representative to obtain driving directions and information on hotels, food venues, and the like. Drivers can also use OnStar to notify the police, fire department, or ambulance service in case of an emergency. Through in-vehicle sensors, it can even detect when a car has been involved in an accident. Finally, OnStar can also aid a driver experiencing minor inconveniences, for example, by unlocking car doors should a driver accidentally lock car keys inside (Figure 15.46).

GPS units for cars have become more mobile. Many different models can be easily attached to a dashboard and moved from one vehicle to another. Some units can even convert maps from road maps to walking maps that list house numbers and specific points of interest. You can update the

4 of 24 possible satellites

Locking into three satellites determines location in latitude and longitude.

Locking into a fourth satellite provides altitude and 3D positioning.

GPS receivers

FIGURE 15.45 GPS units lock in the signal from four satellites and use a mathematical principle called *triangulation* to determine the position of the receiving device in three dimensions.

1. A GPS receiver in the vehicle connects to a satellite, establishes the location of the vehicle, and stores that location.
2. When an emergency feature of OnStar is activated, the unit places a call to the OnStar center and transmits the vehicle ID and GPS location.
3. The cellular call is routed to the landline phone system.
4. The call is picked up by a trained OnStar advisor.

FIGURE 15.46 OnStar makes use of a built-in GPS and cell phone system to provide assistance to drivers.

GPS Devices: Benefits Versus Drawbacks

GPS devices can be extremely useful to individuals who are lost, trying to navigate through an unfamiliar neighborhood, or looking to avoid a traffic jam. But this same technology can also be viewed as an invasion of privacy. Taxi cab drivers in New York City are protesting against the installation of GPS units in all cabs citing the fear of constant surveillance. Large trucking firms are using units to keep track of drivers and inform them of alternate shorter routes or possible delays while in route. Some see the use of GPS units as a technological advance in providing knowledge and safety while reducing time and energy. Others view their use as an invasion of privacy. Do the benefits of GPS units outweigh the risk of reducing privacy?

TECHNOLOGY ON THE JOB

As a Sales Director for a global hotel chain, your customers will have a diverse set of technology skills and a varied ability to express their technology needs. Your success will depend on your ability to make a technology-uncomfortable customer at ease when discussing the wired and wireless capabilities of your conference center and demonstrating the enhanced videoconferencing abilities you have installed. Your ease in discussing and demonstrating a technology feature that seems complex to some customers will make them feel comfortable with the technology, their ability to use it for their meeting, and will establish their confidence in the ability of your organization to assist when needed.

So do not isolate your sales skills and technology skills. Blending them will help you relate better to customers and other employees, create stronger customer relationships, give you a competitive edge over other sales managers in the region, and help you to reach your projected sales goal.

maps on many GPS units via the Internet. Higher-priced units allow you to swap media cards to provide foreign travel maps or convert your unit into a marine GPS unit.

One cell phone application that is more popular with parents than kids is ***location awareness***, which is also called ***position awareness***. This technology uses a GPS enabled chip to pinpoint the location of the cell phone. Teens might find this a downside to owning a cellphone.

Objective 9 | Recognize Convergence

As the Director of Sales for a hotel that is part of a global hotel chain, you understand that business customers use multiple devices that require wireless connectivity—smartphones, laptops, and tablet computers. Thus, within your hotel's facilities, the number and quality of hot spots must be increased. You would like to propose hiring a technology consultant that can help customers sync their devices with the hotel's network and facilitate in the location of apps, like a navigation or location awareness app, that might make their stay more enjoyable. When making your pitch for this position, you need more information; where do you start?

You have learned about technologies that carry computer data over voice lines as well as through the air. At the core of this process is ***digitization***, the transformation of data such as voice, text, graphics, audio, and video into digital form. Digitization enables ***convergence***, a term that refers to the merging of disparate objects or ideas and even people into new combinations and efficiencies. Within the IT industry, convergence means two things: (1) the combination of industries like computers, consumer electronics, and telecommunications and (2) the coming together of products such as PCs and telephones. This trend could be signaling the end of the traditional public switched telephone network.

Cellular telephones are computing devices. Although cell phones started out as analog devices (1G, for first generation), the current generation of wireless cell phones (4G, for fourth generation) are all digital systems that provide high-speed access to transmit voice, text, images, and video data. They are now referred to as ***smartphones*** and integrate mobile phone capability, computing power, and Web access. For more information, dates, and features of each cell phone technology generation, refer to Figure 15.47.

In 1971, AT&T built a network of transmitters that automatically repeat signals. This network of transmitters, which are called ***cell sites***, broadcasts signals throughout specific, but limited, geographic areas called ***cells***. When callers move from cell to cell, each new cell site automatically takes over the signal to maintain signal strength. But who or what monitors your cell phone's signal strength so that you have the best reception? That's the job of the ***mobile switching center (MSC)***, and each cellular network contains several MSCs that handle communications within a group of cells (Figure 15.48). Each cell tower reports signal strength to the MSC, which then switches your signal to whatever cell tower will provide the clearest connection for your conversation.

Cell Phone Generations

Wireless Technologies	Year	Feature
1G	1981	Analog mobile phone service allowed callers to make their own calls without operator assistance and move seamlessly from cell to cell.
2G	1991	Digital signaling decreased interference, improved reception, and provided better protection from eavesdropping. This generation also increased security features to discourage cell phone fraud.
3G	2001	These technologies enabled faster data transmission, greater network capacity, more advanced network services, and allowed transmission of voice, text, images, and video data.
4G	2010–2015	This generation provides even higher data rates as well as real-time (streamed) formatting for voice, data, and high-quality multimedia.

Figure 15.47

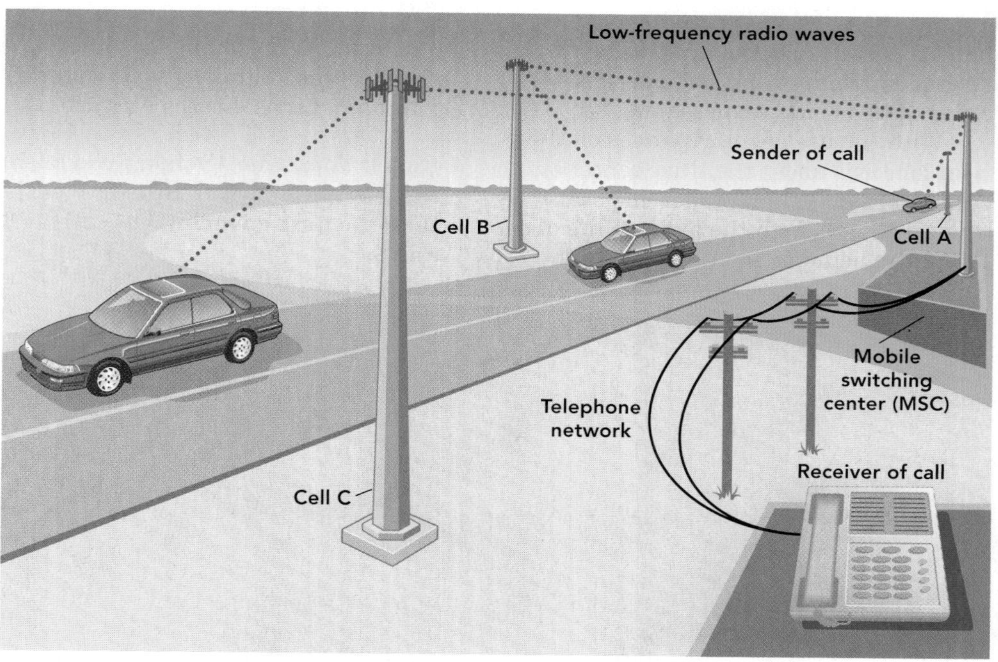

FIGURE 15.48 When callers move from cell to cell, the mobile switching center locates the cell with the strongest signal strength and that cell automatically takes over transmission.

MSCs route calls to the gateway mobile switching center (GMSC), which in turn sends calls to their final destination. If the call is headed for a land-based phone, the GMSC sends the call to the PSTN. Otherwise, it forwards the call directly to another cellular network.

Terrain, weather, antenna position, and battery strength can all interfere and affect signal strength. However, there may be times when you have recharged your battery, have clear weather, and are standing at the top of a hill—and still cannot achieve a good signal. Cell coverage is not perfect, and cellular networks have holes—areas in which you can't send or receive calls.

MSCs are also key players in a widely used cellular service called SMS—*short messaging service*—which you probably

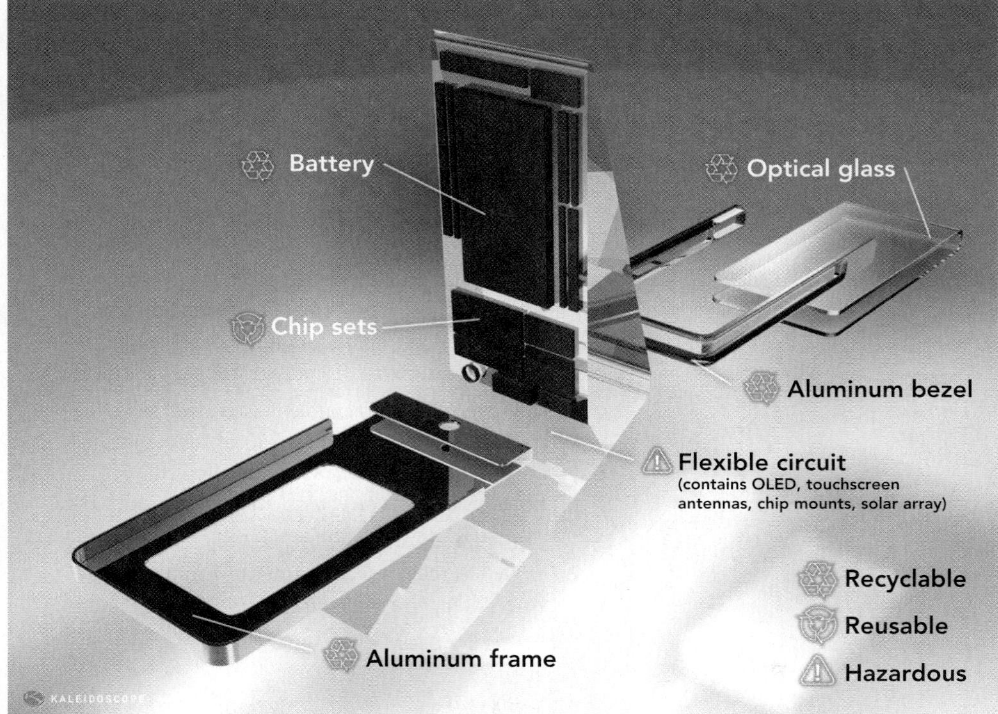

FIGURE 15.49 Over 130 million cell phones are disposed of annually in the United States, with only 10 percent of that number being recycled.

know as *text messaging* and MMS—multimedia messaging service—also referred to as picture messaging.

With the use of smartphones on the rise, concerns about their use center on etiquette, safety, and proper disposal (Figure 15.49). With the average life of a cell phone being 18 months, and only 3 percent of all cell phones globally being recycled, the volume of toxic water from improper disposal poses a problem.

Check Your Knowledge: From either the Companion Web Site or MyITLab, take the quiz covering Objectives 6, 7, 8, and 9.

Chapter Summary

Computer Networks and Communication

- Computer networks link two or more computers so they can exchange data and share resources.
- Local area networks (LANs) serve a building or an equivalent region. Wide area networks (WANs) span multiple buildings, states, and nations. A WAN can be viewed as a geographically dispersed collection of LANs. Additional network designations include the metropolitan area network (MAN), the campus area network (CAN), the home area network (HAN), and the personal area network (PAN).
- A peer-to-peer LAN does not use a central control unit. It is most appropriate for small networks of fewer than 10 computers. Client/server networks include one or more file servers as well as clients such as desktops, notebooks, and handheld devices. A virtual private network operates as a private network over a public network, usually the Internet, making data accessible to authorized users in remote locations through the use of secure, encrypted connections and special software.
- The physical layout of a LAN is called its network topology. The three different LAN topologies are bus (single connections to a central line), star (all connections to a central switch), and ring (tokens carry messages around a ring).
- Protocols are the rules that define how network devices can communicate with each other. The most widely used LAN protocol for wired networks is Ethernet. The most commonly used wireless protocol is 802.11g.
- WANs and LANs have all the same basic components—cabling, protocols, and routing devices. But a WAN is different in that it has a backbone, high-capacity transmission lines, and points of presence—connection points that enable users to access the network.
- WAN protocols include circuit switching and packet switching. Circuit switching creates a permanent end-to-end circuit that is optimal for voice and real-time data. Packet switching does not require a permanent switched circuit and can funnel more data through a medium with a given data transfer capacity.
- Home area networks can be wired, wireless, or a hybrid and have a peer-to-peer or client/server relation.
- Bandwidth refers to the maximum data transfer capacity of a communications channel and is measured in Hertz (Hz) and bits per second (bps).
- To transmit digital data over dial-up phone lines, it is necessary to use a modem. On the sending end, the modem modulates the signal (transforms it into analog form). On the receiving end, the modem demodulates the signal (transforms it back into digital form).
- Communications require physical media, like twisted-pair wire, coaxial cable, and fiber-optic cable, or wireless media like infrared, radio, microwaves, and satellite. Additionally, WiMAX and MMDS are wireless technologies used to transmit signals over large geographic areas.
- The public switched telephone network (PSTN) is the global telephone system used for both data and voice. This system usually sends transmissions across media ranging from twisted-pair to fiber-optic cable and makes use of a modem to convert between analog and digital signals.
- Last-mile technologies refer to the technologies, like DSL, cable, leased lines, SONET, FIOS, and WiMAX, that bring data into your home or business.
- Wired and wireless applications like VoIP, GPS systems, videoconferencing, fax transmissions, and satellite radio help communicate, collaborate, entertain, and share text, graphics, audio, and video.
- Convergence refers to the use of technology to facilitate the coming together of products such as PCs and telephones.

Key Terms and Concepts

Analog signals 727
Analog-to-digital converter (ADC) 727
Backbone 721
Bandwidth 727
Bluetooth 731
Bps rate 710
Broadband 728
Bus topology 714
Cable modems 734
Campus area network (CAN) 707
Category 5 (Cat 5) 729
Category 5 enhanced (Cat 5e) 729
Category 6 (Cat 6) 729
Cells 740
Cell sites 740
Cellular telephones 740
Chipset 710

Matching

Match each term in the second column with its correct definition in the first column by writing the letter of the term on the blank line in front of the correct definition.

_____ 1. A communication device used to send and receive data from one transmission system to another.

_____ 2. The actual amount of data that is transmitted through a given communication channel.

_____ 3. The physical layout of a network where devices are attached in a circular wiring arrangement.

_____ 4. In a packet switching network, a performance interruption that occurs when a segment of the network experiences an overload.

_____ 5. A high-capacity transmission line that carries Internet traffic.

_____ 6. The physical layout of a network that uses a central wiring device to which all devices are connected.

_____ 7. A device that assists in passing data packets along in a single network, condenses bandwidth, and contains software that inspects the source and target of a data package and attempts to deliver it to that destination.

_____ 8. The physical layout of a network where every device is attached to a common cable or pathway.

_____ 9. A more complex network device that intellectually manages a network and has the ability to determine the best path to route data.

_____ 10. The problem that occurs when two computers try to access the LAN at the same time.

_____ 11. A simple, inexpensive device that joins multiple computers together in a single network but does not manage the traffic between the connections.

_____ 12. The theoretical maximum amount of data that can be transmitted through a given communications channel at one time.

_____ 13. A technique used to send more than one call over a single line.

_____ 14. The ability to hear or see content while it is being downloaded from a Web site instead of waiting for the download is complete.

_____ 15. The merging of disparate objects or ideas and even people into new combinations and efficiencies.

A Backbone
B Bandwidth
C Bus
D Congestion
E Contention
F Convergence
G Hub
H Modem
I Multiplexing
J Ring
K Router
L Star
M Streaming
N Switch
O Throughput

Multiple Choice

Circle the correct answer.

1. A network created among an individual's own personal devices, usually within a range of 32 feet and that involves wireless technology, is a:
   a. HAN b. CAN c. PAN

2. The unique numeric identifier built into the hardware of each device on a network is its:
   a. logical address c. chipset
   b. physical address

3. Skype is an example of a:
   a. P2P network c. virtual private network
   b. client/server network

4. A password-protected network controlled by an organization and accessed only by employees is:
   a. an intranet c. a TCP/IP network
   b. a PSTN

5. A broadband data transmission medium that carries data at transfer rates of 10 Mbps and consists of a center copper wire surrounded by insulation, which is then surrounded by a layer of braided wire, is:
   a. twisted pair
   b. fiber-optics
   c. coaxial cable
6. A popular short-range wireless radio transmission technology that does not require direct line of sight and enables devices like computers, mobile phones, and printers, within 30 feet of each other to communicate automatically and wirelessly is:
   a. WiFi
   b. Bluetooth
   c. infrared
7. A high-bandwidth fiber-optic or specially conditioned copper cable trunk line that can handle 24 digitized voice channels or carry computer data at a rate of up to 1.544 Mbps is a:
   a. digital subscriber line
   b. T1 line
   c. public switched telephone network (PSTN)
8. Making use of the Internet for real-time voice communication is referred to as:
   a. Internet telephony
   b. multiplexing
   c. videoconferencing
9. The ability to view television shows, videos, and movies over the Internet, for no additional cost, via download or streaming video is:
   a. videoconferencing
   b. digitization
   c. Internet TV
10. A satellite-based system consisting of a cluster of 27 Earth-orbiting satellites that enable portable receivers to determine their location with an accuracy of 109 yards or less is a:
    a. mobile switching center
    b. Global Positioning System
    c. satellite radio

Teamwork

1. **Your Campus Area Network** As a team, or in subgroups, interview the IT staff at your college and inquire about the physical layout of your campus network (CAN). How many local area networks (LANs) are connected? What is the topology of each LAN? Are all LANs wired, or are some wireless? How many routers/switches/hubs compose the CAN? What network operating system is running the CAN? Ask these and any additional questions that help you understand the configuration of your school's network. Using Microsoft's Visio or any other drawing program, create a diagram of the CAN. Submit the diagram and a one-page, double-spaced paper that combines the questions asked and the answers received that led to your network diagram.
2. **Toys to Tools** As a team, investigate the use of cell phones in the area of education. Use your own school as an example. Inquire about courses and instructors that use cell phones or other digital technology in their classrooms like blogs, wikis, and tweets. Investigate how they incorporate it into the subject matter. Use online references for additional examples and ideas. As a group, come up with a list of five ways in which cell phones (including text and picture messaging) or other digital technology can be helpful in learning. Present your best five in a PowerPoint presentation and indicate whether the team felt the idea was workable and how it would help or hinder learning. Remember to cite your references.
3. **Creating Your Own Business** Assume the members of your team are going to create a small business selling items on e-Bay for individuals that are not computer confident. Come up with a company name, statement of policy, services that you will provide, and fees that you will charge. Initially, there will be three individuals in this small business: a secretary, an e-Bay expert, and a photographer that will take images of the products and post them on e-Bay. As a team, decide whether a wired, wireless, or hybrid network would best suit this company and its three employees. Use any drawing program that the team members are familiar with to create a diagram of your dream office suite. Include the number of rooms needed, the computer equipment needed by each individual, and a schematic of the ideal network. Make sure the diagram is detailed and clearly labeled. Using a word processor, organize all of this information into a one-page, double-spaced report. Submit both your diagram and report.

On the Web

1. **Green Cell Phones** Investigate the movement to control damage to the environment by reducing the toxic waste from the disposal of cell phones through the development of portable devices that are more environmentally friendly. Using your favorite browser, search the Internet for companies that are creating green cell phones and research the methods they are using to create them. List the companies that are leading the way, and explain exactly how they are making this change. Present your findings in one-page, double-spaced report. Remember to cite your references.

2. **Network Administrators** Especially essential to the efficient management of a network is the network administrator. Interview the network administrator at your school and use job postings on the Web to obtain the education and/or certifications required, the level or years of experience needed, and a range of possible salaries for this type of position. Compile your information in a word processing document and create an advertisement for a network administrator. Remember to cite your references.

3. **Technology and Your Responsibility** GPS units were instrumental in locating and leading to the rescue of an experienced hiker lost in the Australian desert in January 2009. On the flip side, a female lost in Death Valley National Park in California in August 2009 is blaming a GPS unit for providing her with faulty directions that led her and her son to a desolate and extremely remote region of the park. After several days, she and her son depleted their water supply. Her 11-year-old son died. She places blame on the GPS provider. Using the Internet and other reliable forms of information, research cases in which technology helped people and cases in which it has been used inappropriately or relied on when common sense should have prevailed. When is an incident the fault of the provider and when is it the fault of the human operator? What are the limits of technology and whose responsibility is it to know those limits? What can the technology provider do to disclaim responsibility? What can the user do to validate reliability of, in the case of the Death Valley episode, navigational instructions? Present your findings and opinions in a one-page, double-spaced report. Remember to cite your references.

Ethics and Social Media

1. **Hiring a Hacker** Although the practice has been going on for some time, the ethics of hiring a former hacker as a security consultant always seems to be a touchy issue. There are strong opinions on both sides. Using the Internet and any other reliable sources of research, locate two hackers that have turned into consultant and investigate both sides of this debate. Present the pros and cons in a one-page, double-spaced paper; include your references.
2. **The Network Behind Social Media** This chapter explains the workings of Skype as a P2P network. Investigate a social media site. Determine the type of network, P2P or client/server, running the network. Try to locate the current number of users with accounts on the network; if there has been any noticeable occurrences of congestion that caused either network to slow down or shut down in the last two years; and if the site had user data compromised or a security breach occur within the last two years. Present your findings in a slide show of at least six slides. Remember to cite your references.

Sources

http://www.jaec.info/Home%20Automation/Communication-house/communication-house.php

http://www.broadband.gov/plan/

http://www.websiteoptimization.com/bw/1012/

http://www.internetworldstats.com/am/us.htm

http://techie-buzz.com/tech-news/with-663-million-registered-users-skype-earned-860-million-last-year.html

Cloud Computing with Google Docs and Microsoft OneNote

OUTCOMES

At the end of this chapter you will be able to:

OBJECTIVES

Mastering these objectives will enable you to:

PROJECT 16A
Create a notebook in OneNote, integrate your Office and Internet files in a OneNote notebook, and find information by searching a OneNote notebook.

1. Create a OneNote Notebook (p. 750)
2. Create Sections and Pages in a Notebook (p. 752)
3. Insert and Format Notes (p. 757)
4. Integrate Office and Internet Files with OneNote (p. 763)
5. Search Notebooks (p. 768)

PROJECT 16B
Use Google Docs to create, edit, manage, and collaborate on documents in the cloud.

6. Store Files Online in Google Docs (p. 772)
7. Use Google Docs to Create and Edit a Word Processing Document (p. 776)
8. Share Documents Using Google Docs (p. 779)

© Leah-Anne Thompson/Shutterstock

Job Focus: Sales Director for a Hotel

In This Chapter

In this chapter, you will experience how a Sales Director for a hotel uses Microsoft OneNote to provide a single place to gather all the notes and information associated with hotel events. For example, weddings are an important revenue stream for the hotel, and OneNote has a wedding planner template to organize all the information related to wedding events. You will also learn how this Sales Director uses Google Docs to collaborate with colleagues and customers.

Following this chapter, you will have an opportunity to complete a case project that focuses on the career of a Sales Director for a hotel.

Project 16A Event Planning Notebook

Project Activities

In Activities 16.01 through 16.15, you will create a notebook that Gwen Moreau will use to store information related to her college courses and her major in Hospitality Management. You will insert text, tables, pictures, video, and file printouts into the notebook. The pages in your completed notebook will look similar to Figure 16.1. (Note: Not all pages are shown in the figure.)

Project Files

For Project 16A, you will need the following files:

w16A_Job_Descriptions
jpg16A_HMA_Logo
p16A_Food_Safety
e16A_Budget_Worksheet

You will save your OneNote folder as:

Lastname_Firstname_16A_School_Notebook

Project Results

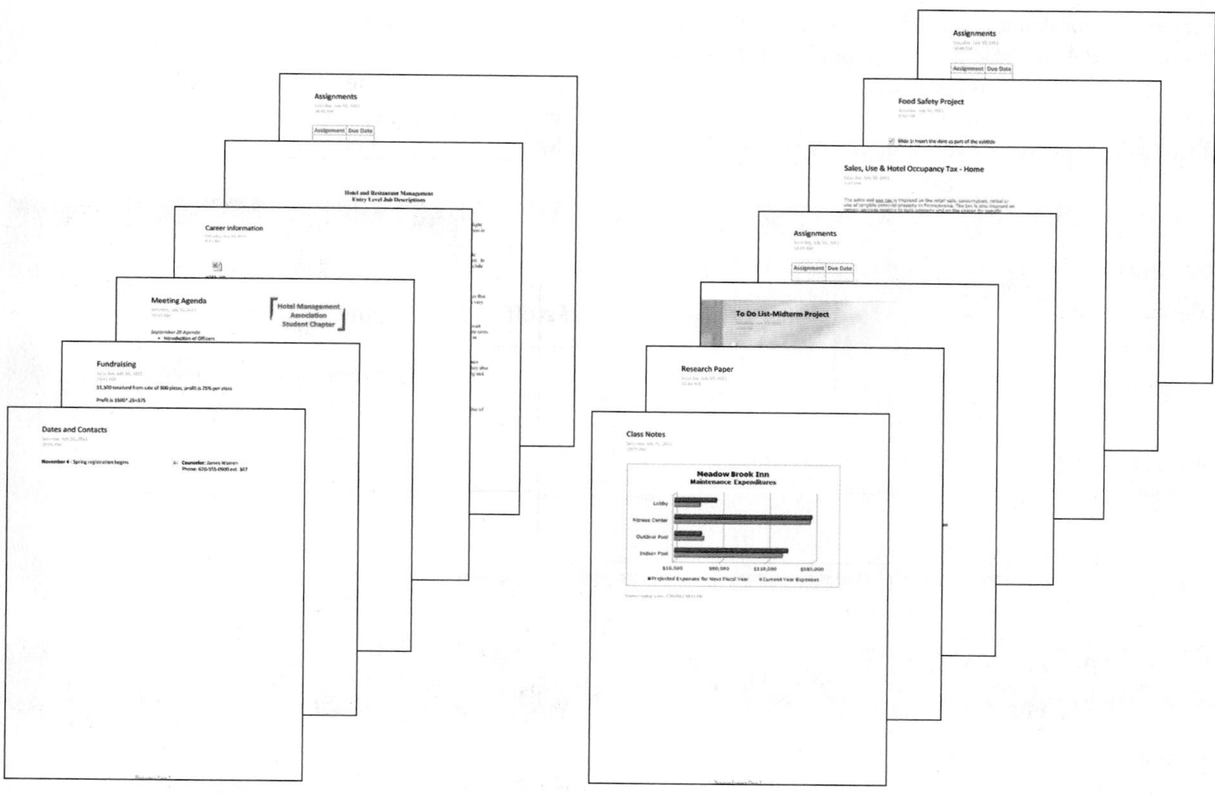

Figure 16.1
Project 16A School Notes

Objective 1 | Create a OneNote Notebook

OneNote is a Microsoft application with which you can create a digital notebook that gives you a single location where you can gather and organize information in the form of ***notes***. A note can include typed text, handwritten text if you have a tablet PC, pictures and graphics—including images and text that you capture from Web pages—audio and video recordings, and documents from other applications such as Word or Excel.

The advantage to using OneNote—instead of paper notes and notebooks—for all of your information is that you can use powerful search capabilities to find information in your notebook quickly. You can also share a OneNote notebook with others, or store your notebook on the Web so that you can view and edit your notes from any computer with an Internet connection.

Activity 16.01 | Exploring OneNote

OneNote is an integrated part of Microsoft Office 2010, so if you are familiar with the Microsoft Office system, you will recognize the Ribbon and tab layout as being similar to what you have used in Word, Excel, and so on. You will also see that many of the formatting commands you use in these applications perform similarly in OneNote. In this activity, you will examine the elements of the OneNote window.

1 On the Windows taskbar, click the **Start** button, and then locate and open **Microsoft OneNote 2010**.

2 Compare your screen with Figure 16.2, and then take a moment to study the OneNote window elements described in the table in Figure 16.3.

In OneNote, a ***notebook*** is a collection of files organized by major divisions and stored in a common folder. OneNote includes one pre-made notebook named *Personal*, which contains one ***section***—the *General* section. A section is the primary division of a notebook, identifying a main topic and containing related ***pages*** of notes. A page is a subdivision of a section where notes are inserted. Think of a section just like the tabbed sections you would have in a three-ring notebook, and think of a page just like the paper pages you have in a notebook.

Figure 16.2

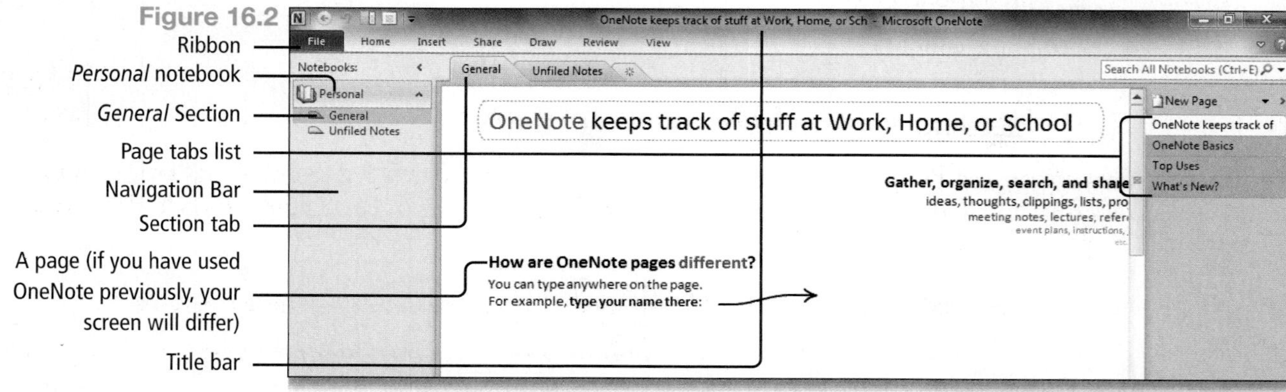

OneNote Window Elements	
Window Element	**Description**
Title bar	Displays the program icon, the title of the active page, and the name of the program.
Ribbon	Groups, on tabs, the commands for performing related tasks.
Navigation Bar	Displays the names of available notebooks and also enables you to navigate within an open notebook.
Section tab	Identifies a primary division of the active notebook.
Page tabs list	Displays the name of each page in the active section.
Page	Displays the content of the active page.

Figure 16.3

> **Alert! | What if the Personal notebook does not display?**
>
> When you open OneNote, the window displays as it was the last time OneNote was open at the computer at which you are working, so your screen may differ from Figure 16.2. The window elements, however, are the same. If another notebook displays, read the steps in this activity, and then begin with Activity 16.02.

3 In the **Navigation Bar**, to the right of *Notebooks*, click the **Collapse Navigation Bar** button.

This action reduces the width of the Navigation Bar and displays the name of the notebook—*Personal*—vertically.

4 With the **General** section tab active, on the right side of your screen, in the **page tabs list**, locate the **OneNote keeps track of** page tab. If necessary, click the page tab so it displays in white. Compare your screen with Figure 16.4.

The General section contains four pages of notes, created by Microsoft, that explain features of OneNote. The page tab of the active page is white; other page tabs display in the same color as the section tab.

Figure 16.4

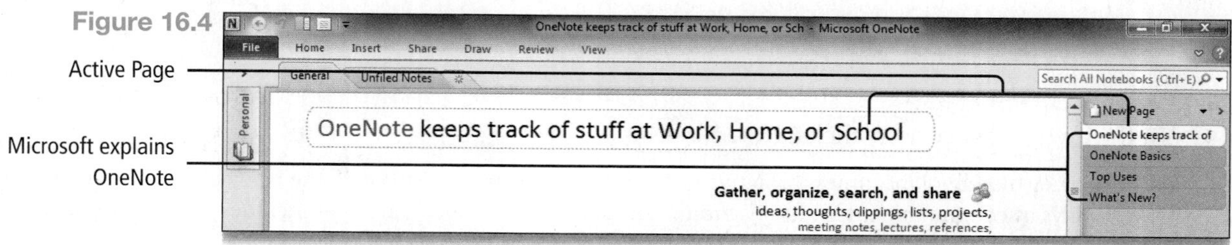

5 On the right edge of the active page, drag the scroll box down to the bottom of the page. Locate and then click the link **Click here to play**. In the displayed window—your browser—maximize the window, click the **Play** button and watch this short video. If you cannot see the link, go to **www.onenotehelp.com/2010/04/06/how-to-organize-stuff-in-onenote/**

6 **Close** the browser window.

Activity 16.02 | Creating a Notebook

In addition to the default Personal notebook, you can create new notebooks for specific purposes. In this activity, you will create a notebook to store notes related to Gwen's courses in her major, which is Hotel and Restaurant Management.

1 With the default notebook still open, on the Ribbon, click the **File tab** to display **Backstage** view.

In OneNote, the Ribbon is minimized by default to provide more space on the screen for inserting notes in the pages of your notebook.

2 On the left, in the **Backstage tabs**, click the **New tab**, and then in the **1. Store Notebook On:** section, click **My Computer**. In the **2. Name:** section, using your own name, type **Lastname_Firstname_16A_School_Notebook** In the **3. Location:** section, click **Browse**, navigate to the location where you are saving your files for this chapter. In the **Select Folder** dialog box, click **New folder**, and then, with *New folder* selected, type **All In One Chapter 16** Press Enter to rename the folder, and then, in the **Select Folder** dialog box, click **Select**. Compare your screen with Figure 16.5.

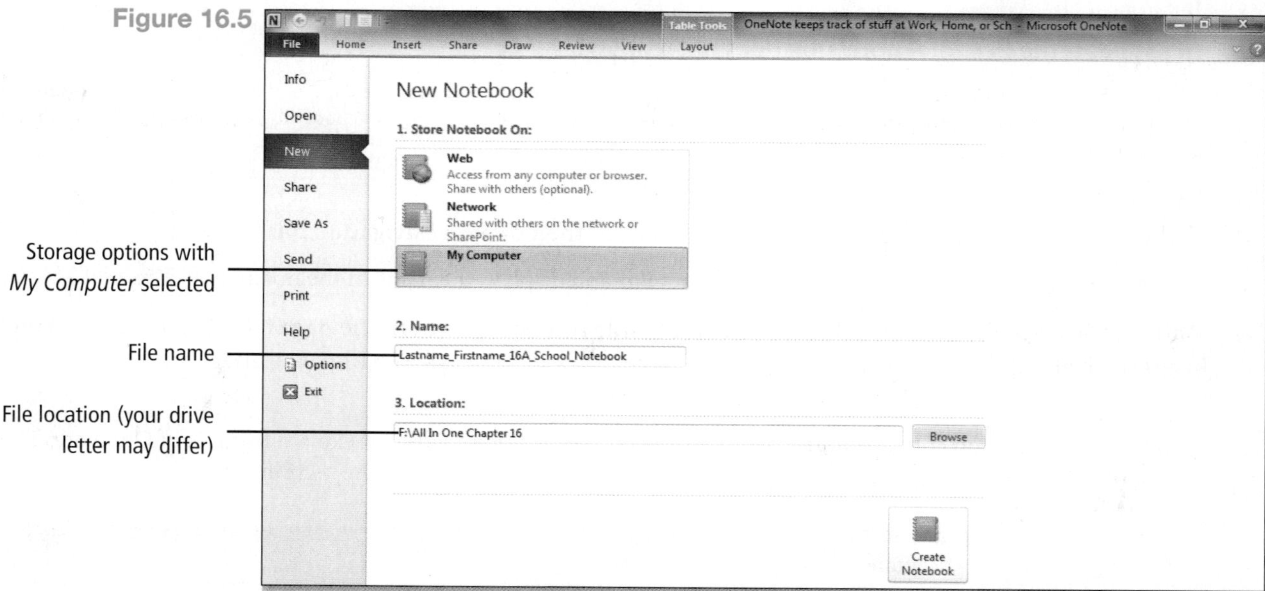

Figure 16.5

3 In the lower right corner, click **Create Notebook**.

Your new notebook becomes the active notebook, and its name displays in the Navigation Bar. The new notebook displays a section tab named *New Section 1* containing an *Untitled* page that includes the current date.

4 In the **Navigation Bar**, right-click your **Lastname_Firstname_16A_School_Notebook**, and then on the shortcut menu, if it displays, click **Move Up**. If necessary, repeat this action so that your new notebook displays at the top of the **Navigation Bar**. Compare your screen with Figure 16.6.

This action changes the order in which notebooks display on the Navigation Bar.

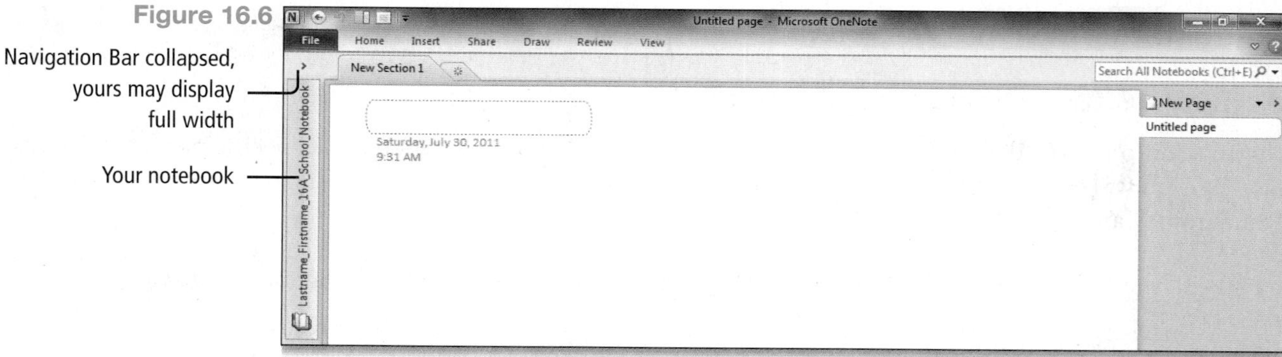

Figure 16.6

5 If necessary, at the top of the **Navigation Bar**, to the left of the *New Section 1* tab, click the **Expand Navigation Bar** button [›].

Objective 2 | Create Sections and Pages in a Notebook

In a OneNote notebook, you can create as many sections as you need to organize your notes.

Activity 16.03 | Creating Sections in a Notebook

By creating a section for each of her courses and a section for the Hospitality Management Association (HMA), Gwen will be able to organize her notes.

1 Below the Ribbon, right-click the section tab **New Section 1**, and then on the shortcut menu, click **Rename**.

2 With the text selected, type **HMA** and then press Enter.

The new section name displays on the section tab and in the expanded Navigation Bar.

3 To the right of the **HMA tab**, point to the small tab to display the ScreenTip *Create a New Section*, and then compare your screen with Figure 16.7.

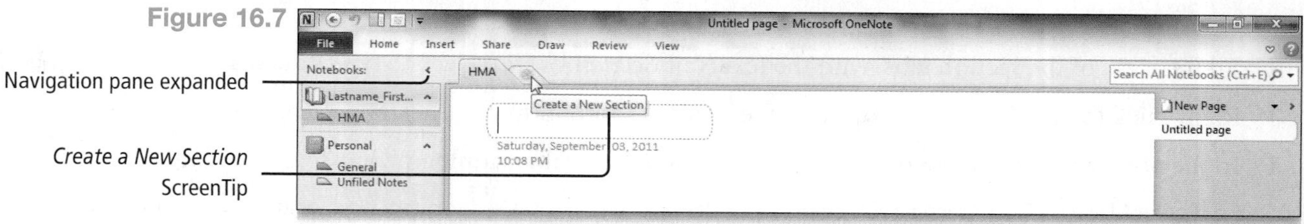

Figure 16.7

4 Click one time, and then with *New Section 1* selected, type **Reminders** Press Enter.

You can create as many sections as you need in a notebook. The Create a New Section tab will always display to the right of existing section tabs.

5 Using the technique you just practiced, create two additional sections named **Hospitality Law** and **Business Finance**

> **Alert! | What if all my section tabs do not display?**
>
> Depending upon the number of sections, section names, and your screen resolution, some of the tabs may be collapsed. All section names display in the expanded Navigation Bar, or you can click the arrow to the right of the last displayed tab to view a list of any tabs that are hidden from view.

6 Right-click the **HMA tab**. On the shortcut menu, point to **Section Color**, and then near the bottom of the list, click **Red Chalk**.

The section tab color for an active tab displays around the edges of the active page. When adding notes to pages, the section color reminds you of the section in which you are working. Here, the Red Chalk color displays in the page tabs list and around the page border.

7 Point to the **Reminders tab**, hold down the left mouse button, and then drag the **Reminders tab** to the left of the **HMA tab**. When a small black triangle displays at the top left of the **HMA tab**, release the mouse button, and then compare your screen with Figure 16.8.

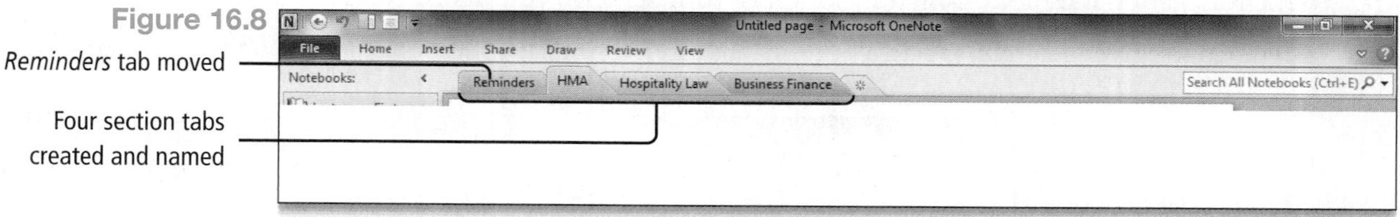

Figure 16.8

Activity 16.04 | Creating a Section Group

Gwen has an individual section for each of her courses. In this activity, you will designate these related sections as a ***section group***—related sections that are identified by a single name and stored as a subfolder with the same name within the notebook folder. For example, in a notebook for your leisure activities, sections named *Favorite Campgrounds*, *Camping Trips*, and *Camping Equipment* could be grouped as the *Camping* section group.

1 In the **Navigation Bar**, right-click your notebook named **Lastname_Firstname_16A_School_Notebook**, and then on the shortcut menu, click **New Section Group**. Compare your screen with Figure 16.9.

New Section Group displays below the Business Finance section in the Navigation Bar and to the right of the section tabs with the text selected. You can distinguish a section group from a section by the different icon. A section group tab displays as a small group of tab shapes followed by the section group name.

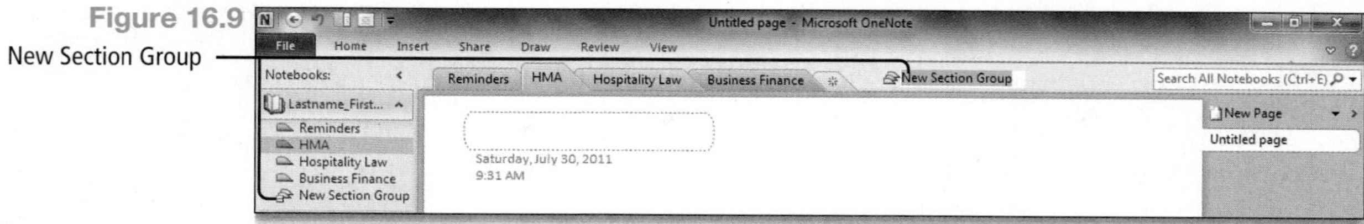

Figure 16.9

2 To the right of the section tabs, with the text *New Section Group* selected, type **Courses** and then press Enter.

3 Right-click the **Hospitality Law tab**, and then on the shortcut menu, click **Move or Copy**.

4 In the **Move or Copy Section** dialog box, click **Courses**, and then compare your screen with Figure 16.10.

In the Move or Copy Section dialog box, you can move or copy a section to a new location in any open notebook.

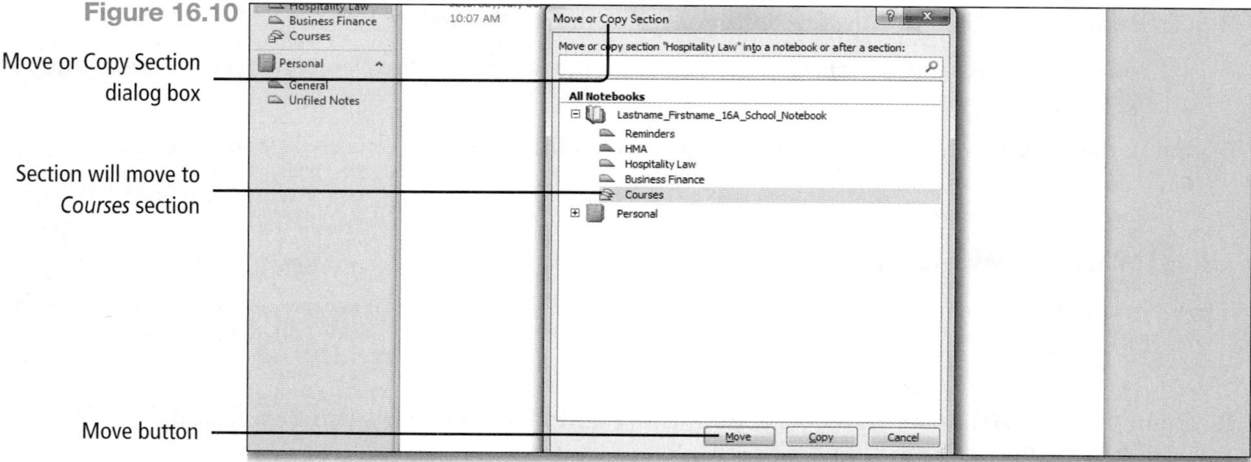

Figure 16.10

5 At the bottom of the **Move or Copy Section** dialog box, click **Move**.

In the Navigation Bar, the Hospitality Law section displays below *Courses*. Because it is a subdivision of the Courses section group, the section is indented below *Courses*, and no longer displays as a section tab.

6 In the **Navigation Bar**, point to the **Business Finance** section, hold down the left mouse button, and then drag it below *Hospitality Law*.

7 In the **Navigation Bar**, click **Courses**. Compare your screen with Figure 16.11.

The Courses section group is active. Section tabs display for the two sections that are in the section group.

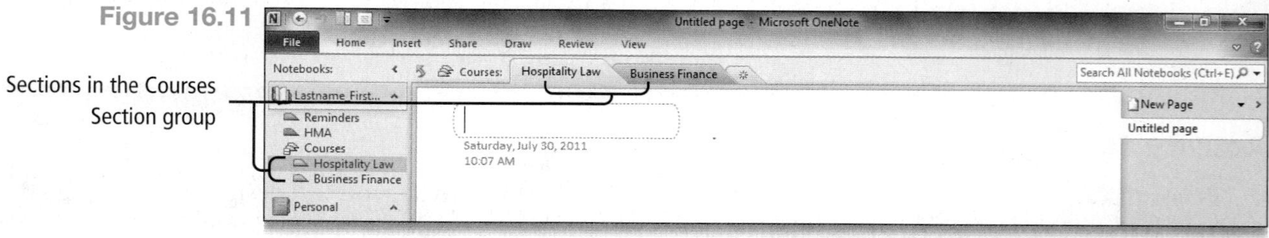

Figure 16.11

8 Click the **Create a New Section tab**, type **English Composition** and press Enter.

9 In the **Navigation Bar**, point to **Hospitality Law**, hold down the left mouse button, and then drag down until a heavy black line displays below **English Composition**. Release the mouse button, and then compare your screen with Figure 16.12.

When you have several sections in a group, it is useful to arrange them in alphabetical order.

Figure 16.12

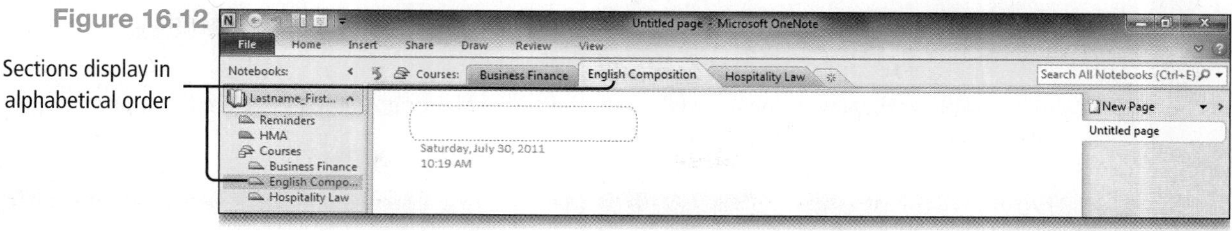

10 On the Ribbon, click the **File tab**, and then click **Exit** to close OneNote.

11 To the right of the **Start** button, click the **Windows Explorer** button. Navigate to your **All In One Chapter 16** folder, and then locate and open your folder **Lastname_Firstname_16A_School_Notebook**. Compare your screen with Figure 16.13.

Each section of your notebook displays as a file. *HMA* and *Reminders* are sections that you created. *Open Notebook* is a default section—it contains the Table of Contents for your notebook and is created whenever you create a new notebook or section group. Opening this file will open OneNote and display the last active section and page in the notebook or section group. Sections that are subdivisions of a section group are stored in the section group folder, in this instance *Courses*.

Figure 16.13

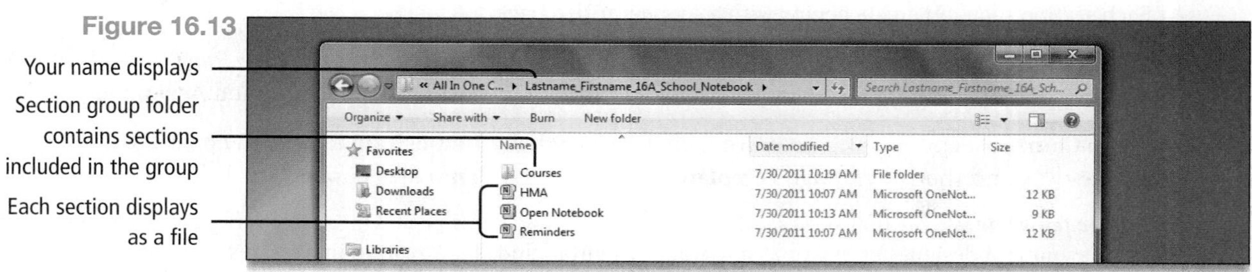

12 Double-click the folder **Courses**.

The three section files you created and the default Open Notebook file display in the folder.

13 In the **Courses** folder, double-click the **Open Notebook** file.

OneNote opens and the Courses section group is active, because it was active when you closed OneNote.

14 On the taskbar, to the right of the **Start** button, right-click the **Windows Explorer** button, and then on the shortcut menu, click **Close window**.

Activity 16.05 | Creating Pages

Sections in your OneNote notebook can contain one or more pages. In this activity, you will add pages to the sections of Gwen's notebook.

1 In the **Navigation Bar**, click **HMA** to make the section active. On the title bar, notice that this is an *Untitled page*.

2 In the upper left corner of the *Untitled page*, above the date and time, with the insertion point blinking in the **Page Title** box, type **Career Information** to title the page. Notice that the title also displays on the right in the **page tabs list**.

When you create a new page, the date and time display below the page title.

3 On the right, in the **page tabs list**, click the **New Page** button to display a new untitled page.

4 In the **Page Title** box, type **Fundraising**

5 Using the technique you just practiced, create another new page titled **Meeting Agenda** and then compare your screen with Figure 16.14.

Your three new pages display in the page tabs list. The active Meeting Agenda page tab is white; the other two page tabs display in a darker shade of the section color.

Figure 16.14

6 In the **page tabs list**, point to **Career Information**, hold down the left mouse button, and then drag down until a heavy black line displays below **Meeting Agenda**. Release the mouse button.

7 At the top of the page, to the right of the section tabs, click the **Courses** section group tab, and then click the **Hospitality Law** section tab.

Each section that you create begins with a single untitled page.

8 In the **Page Title** box, type **Class Notes** and then, in the **page tabs list**, click the **New Page** button. In the **Page Title** box, type **Research Paper** Using the same technique, insert a third page named **Assignments**

9 With the **Courses** section group displayed, click the **English Composition** tab. In the **page tab list**, click the **New Page arrow** [▾], and then click **Page Templates** to display the **Templates** pane.

A ***page template*** is a file that serves as a pattern for creating a new page. Use a page template to ensure a uniform page layout and design. For example, a template might include background images, text formatting, and consistent use of color that you want for your note pages.

10 In the **Templates** pane, click **Planners**, and then compare your screen with Figure 16.15.

Page templates are arranged by categories. You can download additional templates from Microsoft or create your own.

Figure 16.15

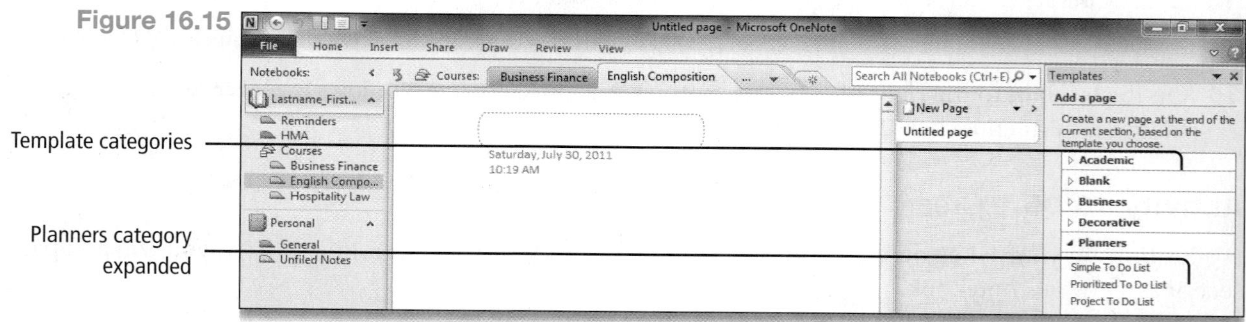

11 In the **Templates** pane, under **Planners**, click the first template—**Simple To Do List**. **Close** [×] the **Templates** pane, and then take a moment to study the page components.

12 In the **Page Title** box, click to the right of the text *To Do List* to place your insertion point, and then type **-Midterm Project**

Gwen wants to plan her project carefully to be sure she completes it on time.

Activity 16.06 | Copying Pages to Other Sections

In this activity, you will copy existing pages to other sections in the notebook.

1 Click the **Hospitality Law section tab**.

2 On the right, in the **page tabs list**, click the **Class Notes** page, hold down Shift, and then click the **Assignments** page tab to select all three pages. Release the Shift key, and then without clicking, move your mouse pointer below the **Assignments** page tab. Compare your screen with Figure 16.16.

All page tabs display in blue, and the current page, *Assignments*, is surrounded by a blue border. This indicates that a group of pages is selected. You can select all adjacent items in a list—in this case the page tabs—by clicking the first item, holding down Shift, and then clicking the last item. You can use Ctrl to select nonadjacent items.

Figure 16.16

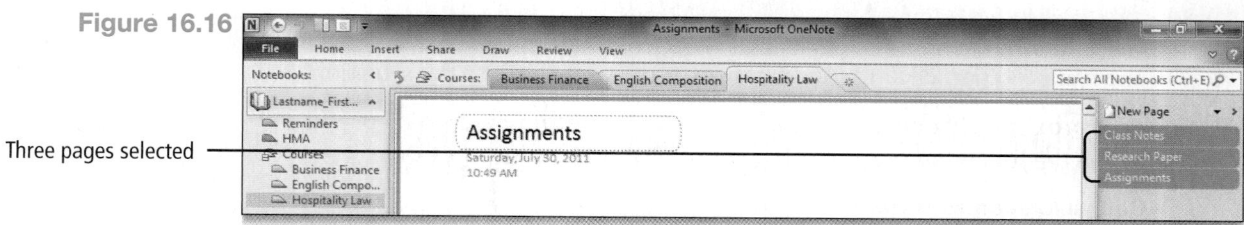

3 Right-click anywhere on the selected page tabs, and then on the shortcut menu, click **Move or Copy** to place a copy of the selection on the Office Clipboard.

4 In the **Move or Copy Pages** dialog box, under **All Notebooks**, click **Business Finance**, and then click **Copy**.

5 Click the **Business Finance** section tab, and then compare your screen with Figure 16.17.

All pages have been copied to the *Business Finance* section.

Figure 16.17

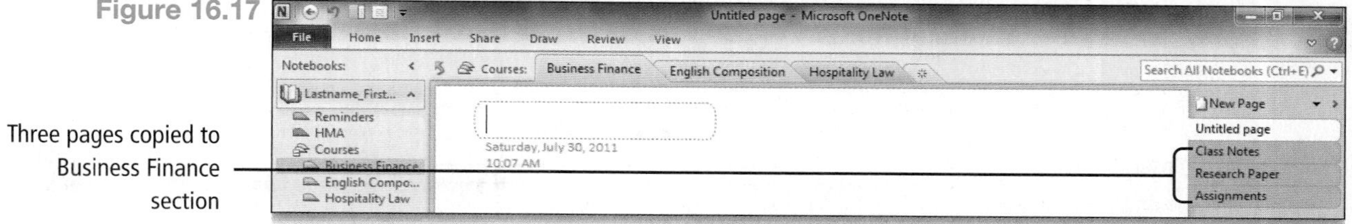

6 Repeat the process for the English Composition section.

Objective 3 | Insert and Format Notes

To insert a typed note, you can click anywhere on a page and begin typing; or you can insert a picture, video, or other object. You can also record a lecture or draw a diagram. Because you can keep so many types of information, you will find it easy to brainstorm and organize your thoughts in OneNote.

Activity 16.07 | Inserting and Formatting Text

1 In the **Navigation Bar**, click **Reminders**. With the **Untitled page** displayed and the insertion point in the **Page Title** box, type **Dates and Contacts**

2 On the left side of the page, point approximately one inch below the date and time and click one time to insert a note container. Type **November 4: Spring registration begins**

When you click on a page, a ***note container***—a box that can contain text, pictures, video clips, and other types of notes—displays.

3 Select the text *November 4*, and then move your pointer up and slightly to the right. Compare your screen with Figure 16.18.

When text is selected, the Mini toolbar displays.

Figure 16.18

4 On the Mini toolbar, click the **Bold** button [B] to apply bold to the selection.

5 Point approximately one inch to the right of the note container to display the [I] pointer, click one time, and then type the following text, pressing [Enter] after the first line.

Counselor: James Warren

Phone: 610-555-0900 ext. 367

Only one note container—the active container—displays at a time.

6 Select the text *Counselor*, and then from the Mini toolbar, apply **Bold** [B]. Click to the right of *Warren*, and then compare your screen with Figure 16.19.

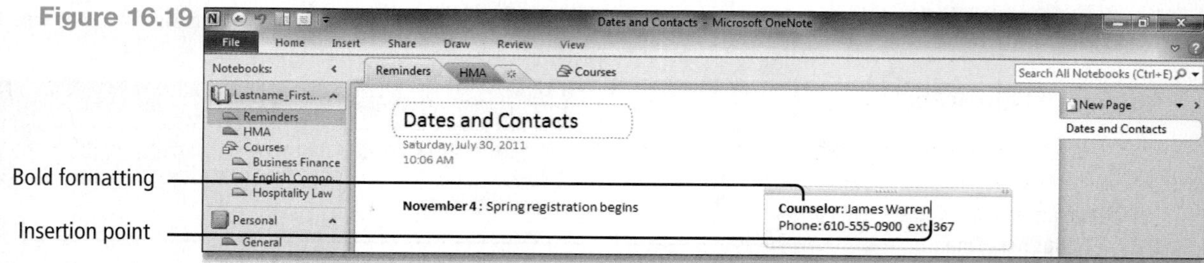

Figure 16.19

7 Display the **HMA** section, and then click the **Meeting Agenda** page tab.

8 Click below the date and time to open a new note container, and then type the following text, pressing [Enter] after each line.

September 20 Agenda

Introduction of Officers

Approval of Minutes

New Members

Career Fair Update

9 Select the text *September 20 Agenda*, and then on the Mini toolbar, click the **Quick Styles** button [A]. Compare your screen with Figure 16.20.

Quick Styles are combinations of formatting options that look attractive together. On the Mini toolbar, the Quick Styles are available without having to display any Ribbon tabs.

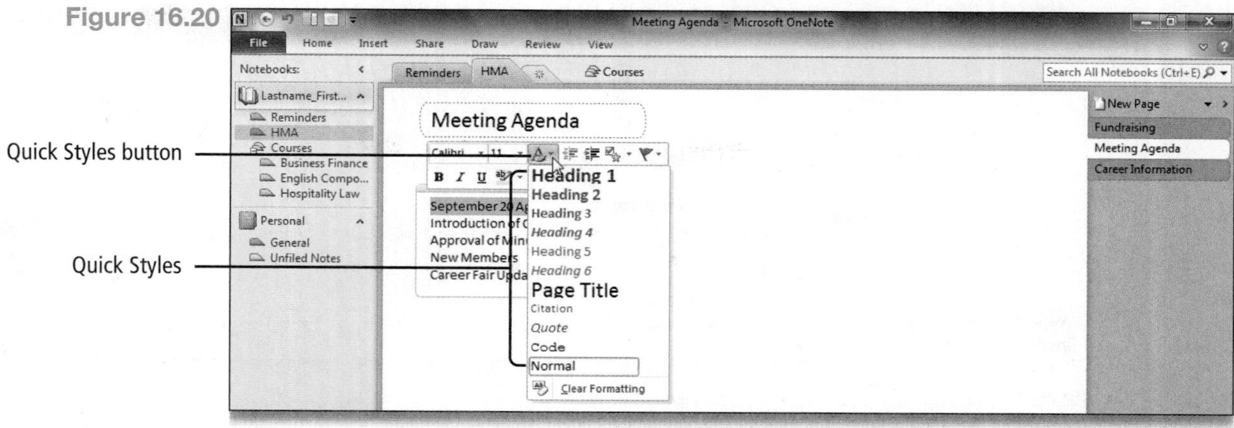

Figure 16.20

10 On the displayed list, click **Heading 4**. Select the remaining four lines of text, and then on the Mini toolbar, click the **Bullets** button. Press Esc to deselect the text.

Bullets display to the left of the selected lines of text.

11 On the Ribbon, point to the **Insert tab** and right-click. On the displayed list, notice that a check mark displays to the left of **Minimize the Ribbon**.

The check mark indicates that the Minimize the Ribbon command is turned on. Recall that in OneNote, the Ribbon is minimized by default.

12 Click **Minimize the Ribbon**, and then compare your screen with Figure 16.21.

The Ribbon is expanded and all commands on the Insert tab display. The commands are arranged in groups—the group names display below the commands. It will be useful to leave the Ribbon expanded throughout the remainder of this project.

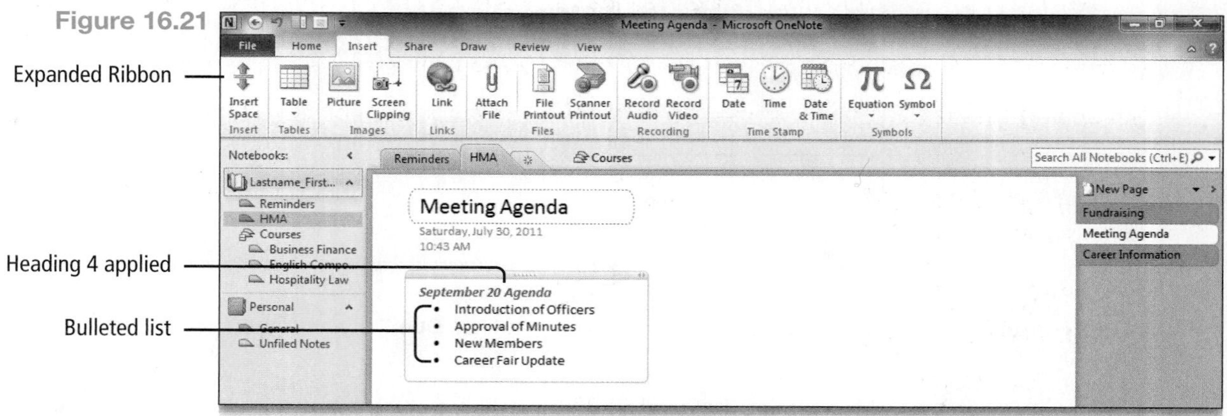

Figure 16.21

13 On the right, on the **page tabs list**, click the **Fundraising** page tab. Click below the date and time to open a new note container, and then type **$1,500 received from sale of 300 pizzas, profit is 25% per pizza** Press Enter two times.

14 Type **Profit is 1500*.25=** and then press Spacebar. Notice the result *375* displays to the right of the equal sign. Compare your screen with Figure 16.22.

OneNote includes a calculator feature that supports simple arithmetic operations, mathematical functions such as square root, and trigonometric functions. Type the mathematical expression with no spaces, and then type an equal sign followed by a space to display the result.

Figure 16.22

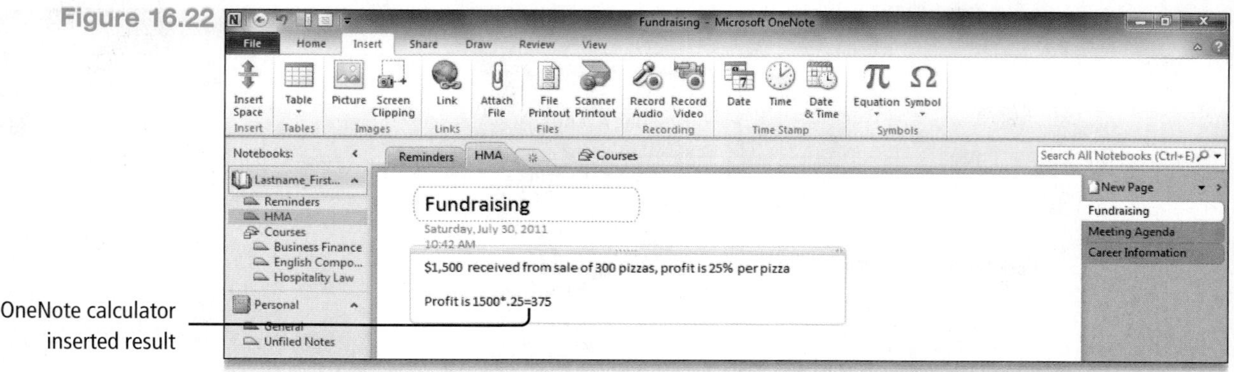

Activity 16.08 | Inserting a Table

To help Gwen keep track of her assignments in each course, you will insert a table—a format for organization that displays data in columns and rows.

1. On the **Navigation Bar**, click **Hospitality Law**, and then in the **page tabs list**, click the **Assignments** page tab.

2. Click below the date and time to display a note container. Type **Assignment** and then press Tab. Compare your screen with Figure 16.23.

   Pressing Tab while typing text in a note container will begin a new table that you can expand as necessary. The commands for *Table Tools* display on the Ribbon, and on the Layout tab, you can select table-specific formatting and selection tools and control the display of the table borders.

Figure 16.23

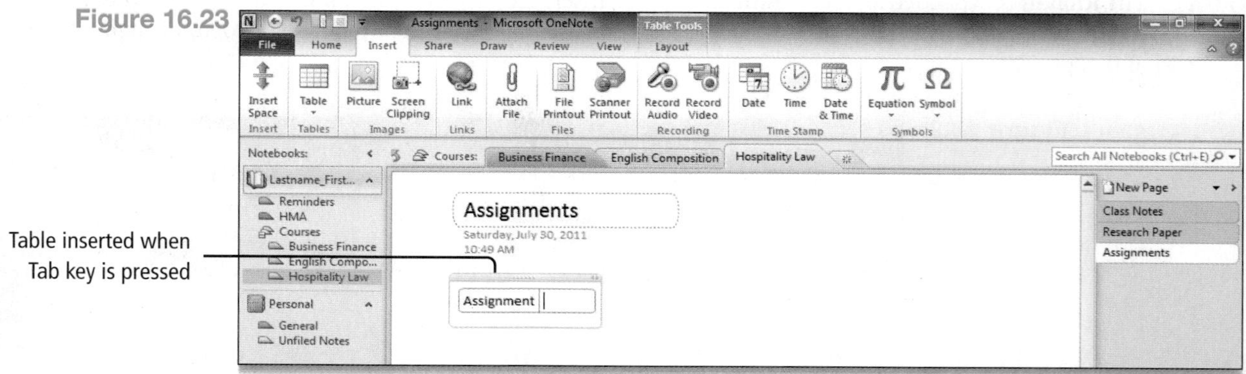

3. With the insertion point blinking in the second column, type **Due Date** and then press Enter. Compare your screen with Figure 16.24.

   After you start a new table, pressing Tab creates additional columns, and pressing Enter creates new rows. To stop expanding the table, click outside of it or press Enter two times.

Figure 16.24

4. In the table, position the insertion point to the left of *Assignment*, and then drag to the right to select all the text in the first row. On the Mini toolbar, click the **Quick Styles** button, and then click **Heading 2**. Deselect the text.

5 At the top of the note container, point to and then right-click the gray border, and then compare your screen with Figure 16.25.

The entire table is selected and a shortcut menu displays.

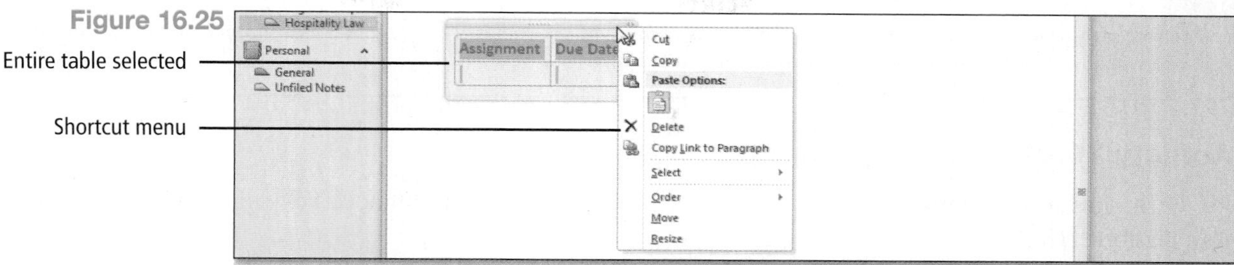

Figure 16.25

6 On the shortcut menu, click **Copy**. Click the **English Composition** section tab, and then click the **Assignments** page tab.

7 Right-click below the date and time, and then on the shortcut menu, under **Paste Options**, point to each of the four icons and read the ScreenTips. Compare your screen with Figure 16.26.

OneNote lets you determine how information is pasted in the displayed note container. Paste Options will vary depending on the type of content you are pasting.

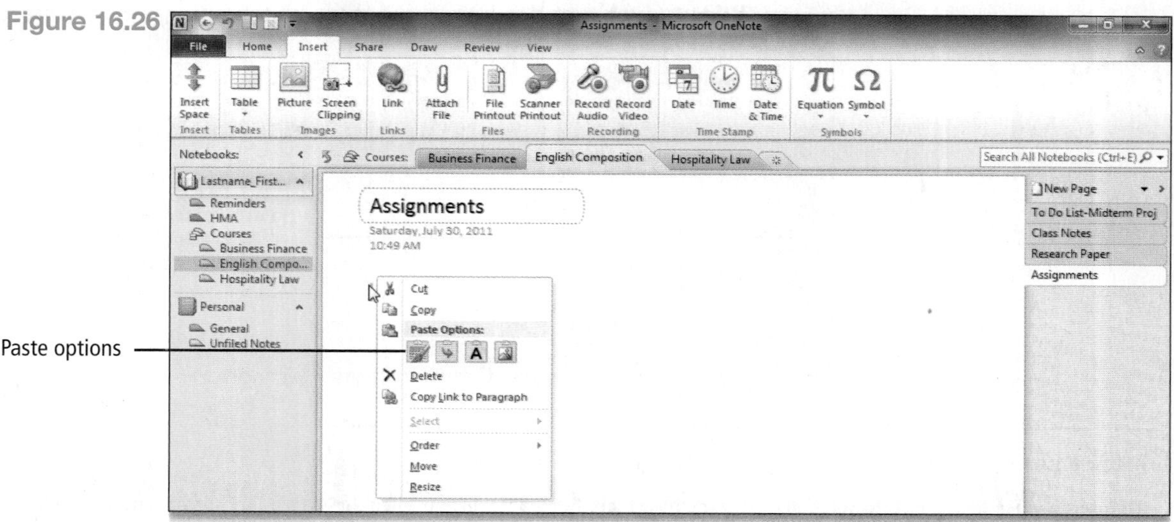

Figure 16.26

8 On the shortcut menu, under **Paste Options**, click the first option—**Keep Source Formatting**. Compare your screen with Figure 16.27.

A copy of the table displays. The *Keep Source Formatting* paste option retains the formatting of the original text—in this case the formatted text in the first row of the table.

A Paste Options button displays at the bottom right of the note container. Clicking the button will allow you to change how the text is pasted on the page. If you want to cancel the display of the button, press Esc or click anywhere outside of the note container.

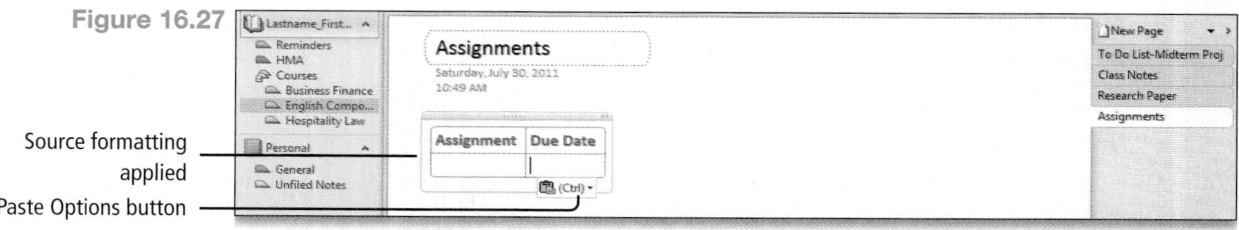

Figure 16.27

GO! All In One | Chapter 16

9 Using the technique you just practiced, paste the table, which is still on the Office Clipboard, into the **Assignments** page of the **Business Finance** section.

> **More Knowledge | OneNote Saves Automatically and Continuously**
>
> OneNote saves your work automatically and continuously while you take notes, when you switch to another page or section, and when you close a section or a notebook. You need not save any notes manually.

Activity 16.09 | Inserting Objects

Gwen has several items she wants to keep track of in her School notebook related to the Hotel Management Association (HMA).

1 In the **Navigation Bar**, click **HMA**. Display the **Meeting Agenda** page.

2 Click to the right of the *Meeting Agenda* title. Click the **Insert tab**, and then in the **Images group**, click the **Picture** button. In the **Insert Picture** dialog box, navigate to the location where the student files for this chapter are stored. Click the file **jpg16A_HMA_Logo**.

The Insert Picture command displays only files that are image file types.

3 In the **Insert Picture** dialog box, click **Insert** and then compare your screen with Figure 16.28.

Figure 16.28

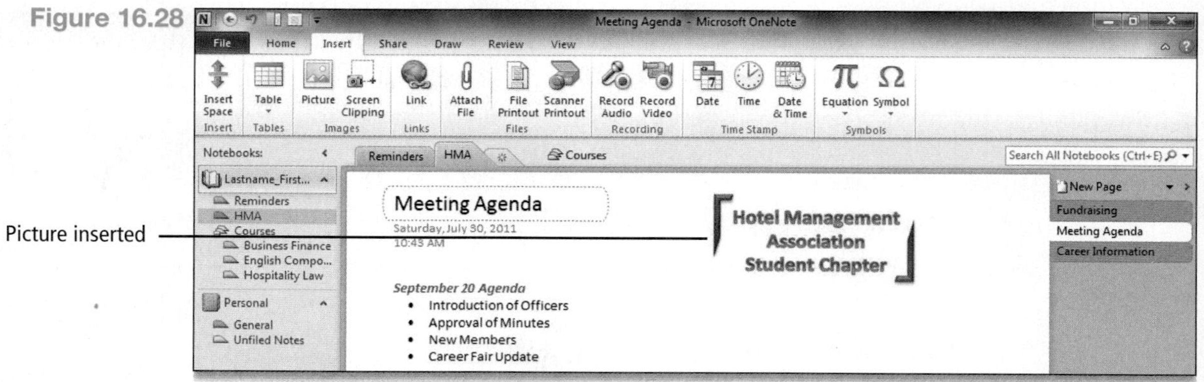

> **More Knowledge | Insert a Video in a OneNote Notebook**
>
> To insert a video in a OneNote notebook, click the Insert tab. In the Files group, click the Attach File button, and then select the video file you want to insert. After the video is inserted, you can double-click the icon to play the video.

4 In the **HMA section**, click the **Career Information** page.

5 Click below the date and time to insert a new note container. Click the **Insert tab**, and then in the **Files group**, click the **File Printout** button.

File Printout is a feature that inserts information from a file as a printed copy in the page. This feature is useful because text in the printout can be searched just like any other content in OneNote.

6 In the **Choose Document to Insert** dialog box, from your student files, select **w16A_Job_Descriptions**, and then click **Insert**. Wait for the Inserting Documents indicator to complete, and then compare your screen with Figure 16.29.

The text from the selected file displays in the page as an image—it cannot be edited. A link to the actual file also displays.

Figure 16.29

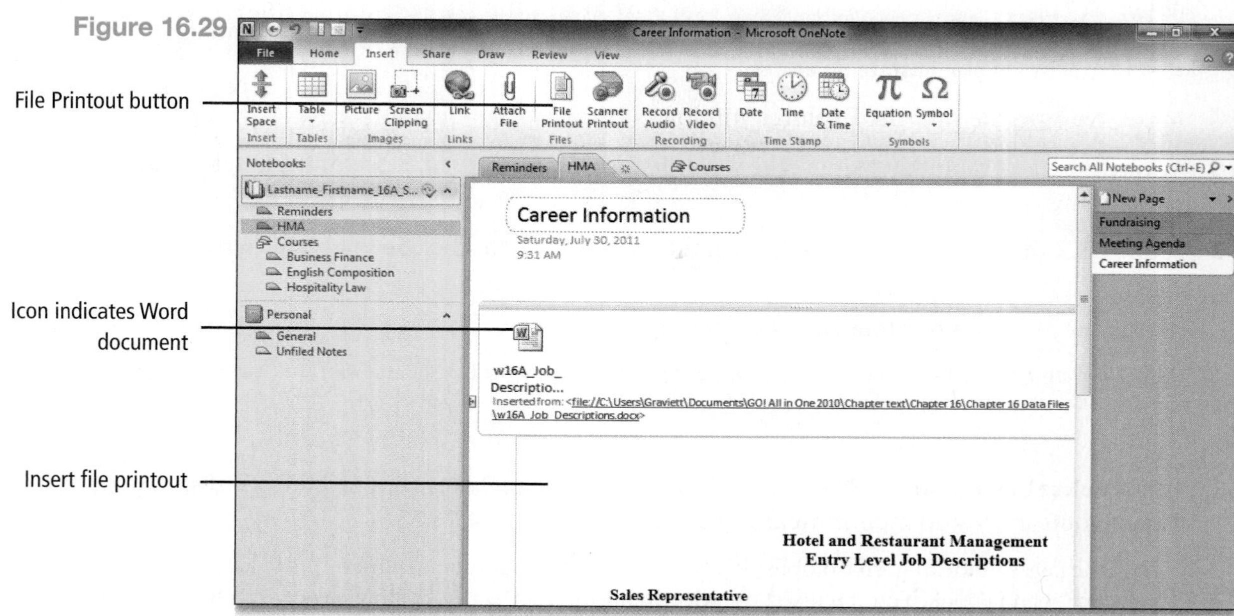

Objective 4 | Integrate Office and Internet Files with OneNote

Microsoft Office 2010 is an integrated suite of applications. This integration enables you to use each application for its specified purpose, and then combine components for a final result. For example, you can create notes that are linked to a Microsoft Word document.

Activity 16.10 | Using the Send to OneNote Feature

1 In the **Navigation Bar**, click **Hospitality Law**. Notice that there are three pages in this section.

2 On the Ribbon, click the **Review tab**, and then in the **Spelling group**, click the **Research** button.

3 In the **Research** task pane, in the **Search for** box, type **sales use hotel tax pa** In the second box, if necessary, click the arrow, and be sure that **Bing** is indicated, and then press Enter. Compare your screen with Figure 16.30.

Bing is Microsoft's search engine. The results of the search display in the task pane.

Figure 16.30

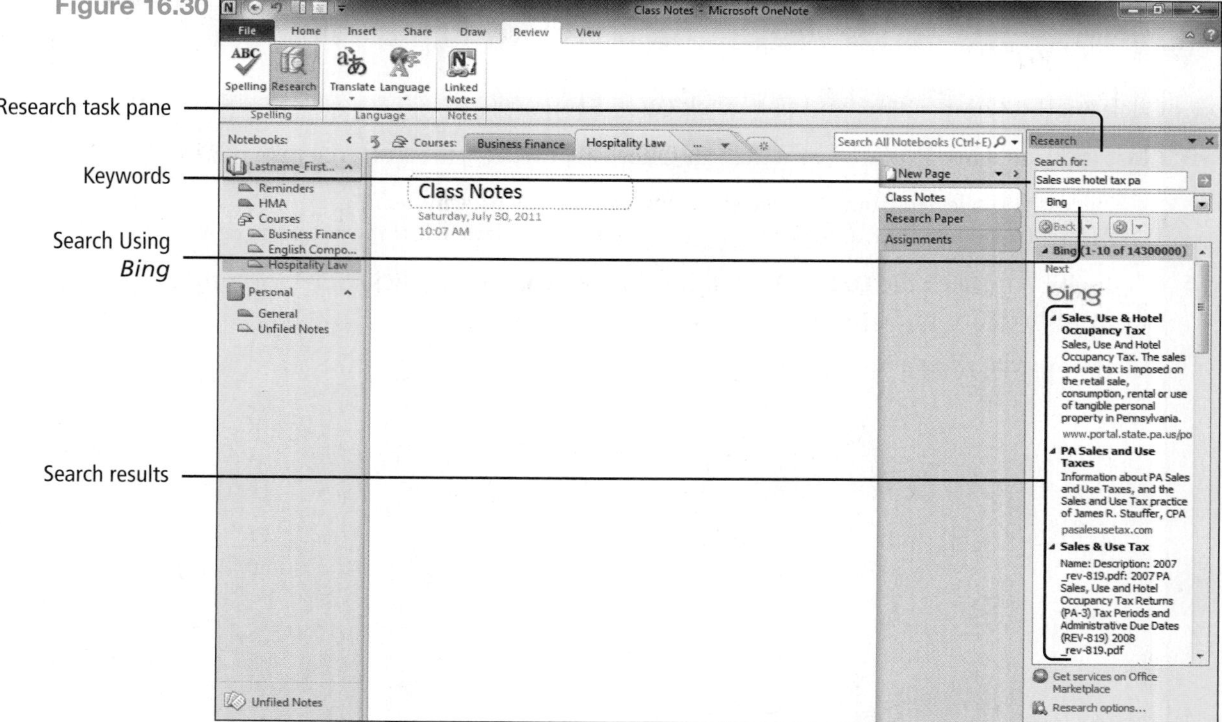

4 Locate the first result **Sales, Use & Hotel Occupancy Tax**. Below the last line of explanatory text, click the link that begins **www.portal.state.pa.us**.

5 **Maximize** the Internet Explorer window.

6 Locate the paragraph that begins *The sales and use tax is imposed*. Select this paragraph and the following paragraph.

7 Right-click the selected text, and then on the shortcut menu, click **Send to OneNote**.

> **Alert! | Is the Send to OneNote Option Missing?**
>
> If *Send to OneNote* does not display on the shortcut menu, it may not be supported by your browser. To ensure it displays, use Internet Explorer as your default browser in this exercise.

8 In the **Select Location in OneNote** dialog box, under **All Notebooks**, to the left of **English Composition**, click the **Expand** button, and then compare your screen with Figure 16.31.

All the pages in the English Composition section display in addition to all sections in any open notebook—in this case the School notebook. You can insert the selected information on an existing page or create a new page within a section.

Figure 16.31

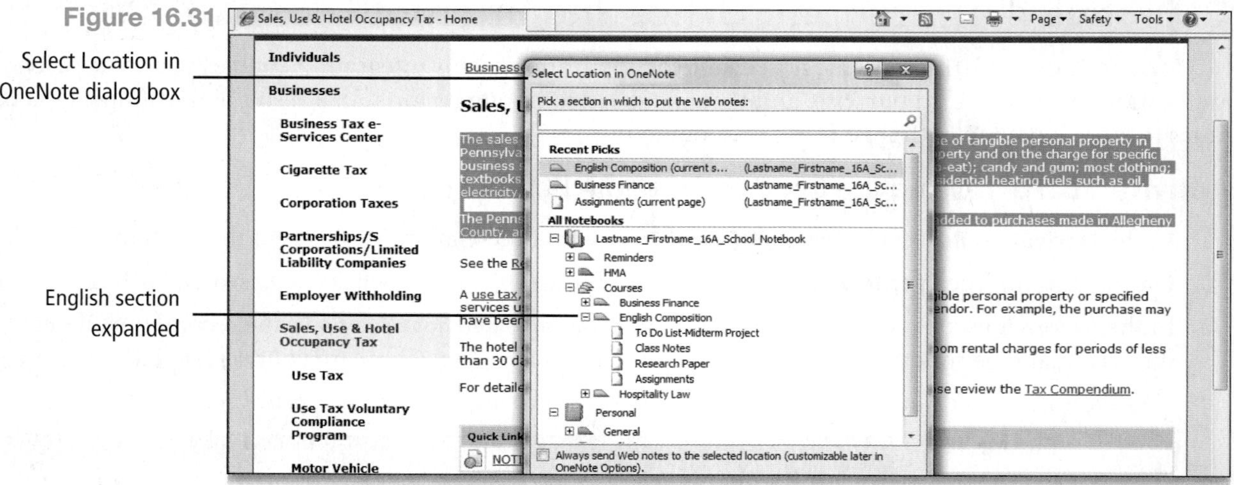

9 Click **English Composition**, and then click **OK**.

10 **Close** Internet Explorer, and then in OneNote, **Close** the **Research** task pane.

The text you selected from the Web site displays on a new page in the English Composition section titled *Sales, Use & Hotel Occupancy Tax*. A hyperlink to the Web page displays below the last paragraph.

11 On the Ribbon, click the **Draw tab**, and then in the **Tools group**, click the **More** button. Compare your screen with Figure 16.32.

Here you can select a pen style or create your own style.

Figure 16.32

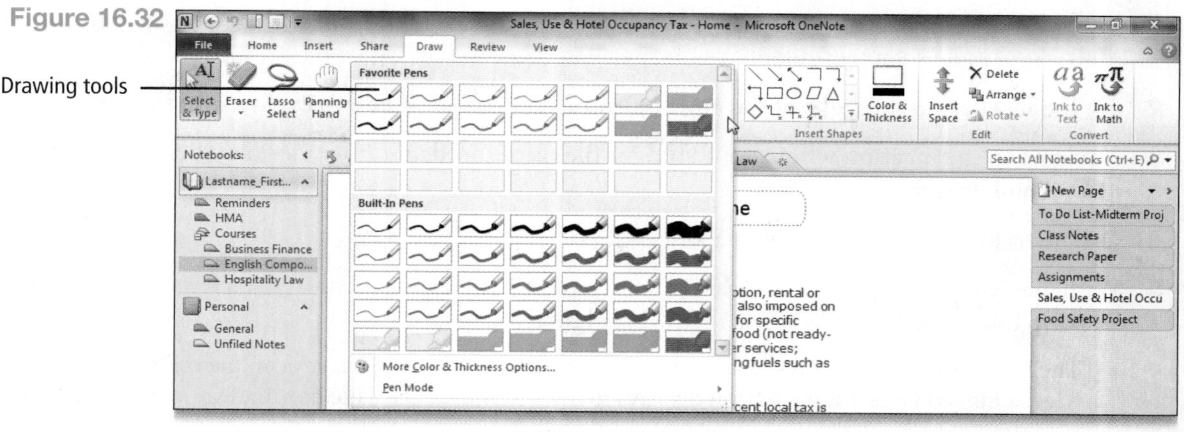

12 Under **Built-In Pens**, in the fifth row, click the third style—**Aqua Highlighter (4.0 mm)**.

The pointer changes to an aqua bar.

13 Position your pointer to the left of the text *6 percent* in the second paragraph, press and hold the left mouse button, and then drag to the right to select *6 percent*. Release the mouse button. Using the technique you just practiced, highlight *1 percent* and *2 percent* in the same paragraph. Compare your screen with Figure 16.33. If you are not satisfied with your result, for example, if the line is too jagged, on the **Quick Access Toolbar**, click **Undo**, and then begin again.

Use the pen feature in OneNote to highlight or underline by simply dragging the mouse pointer on the page.

Figure 16.33

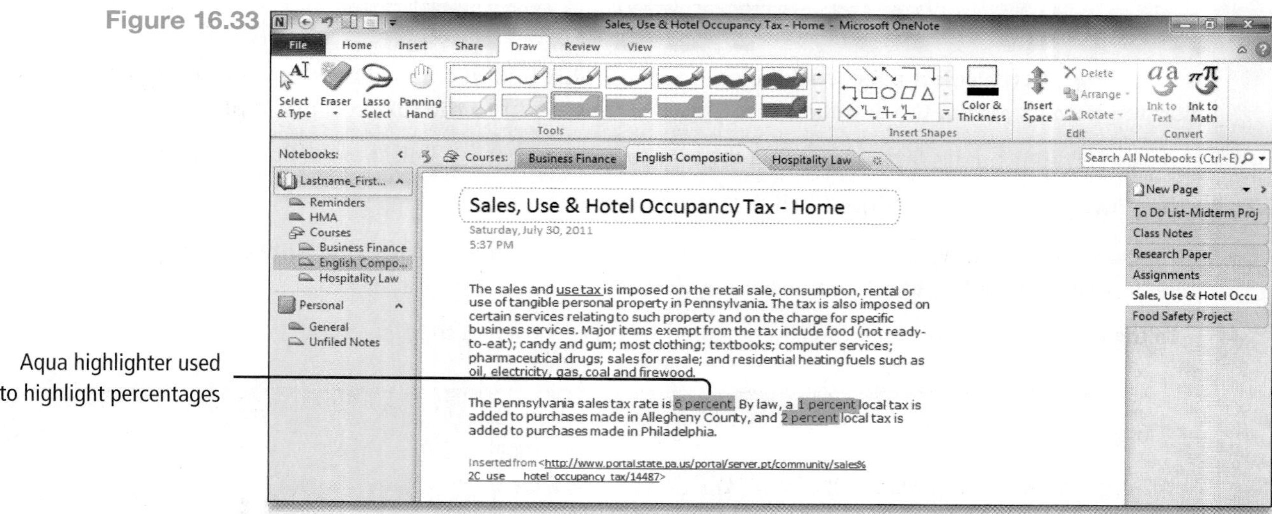

14 On the **Draw tab**, in the **Tools group**, click the **Select & Type** button to turn off the pen feature.

The insertion point redisplays as a blinking line and the default mouse pointer—an I-beam—displays.

15 In the note container, point to one of the the aqua lines and double-click. Notice that sizing handles display around the line.

The pen feature inserts lines as images on a page. The images can be resized, moved, modified, or deleted.

Activity 16.11 | Linking Files and Docking a OneNote Window to the Desktop

Gwen has a PowerPoint presentation that she going to modify for an assignment in her English Composition course. In this activity, you will insert notes about updates and improvements to the presentation.

1 In the **Navigation Bar**, click **English Composition** to open that section, and then in the **page tabs list**, add a new page named **Food Safety Project**

2 On the taskbar, to the right of the **Start** button, click the **Windows Explorer** button.

3 Navigate to the location where your student files are stored, and then double-click to open the file **p16A_Food_Safety**.

4 On the taskbar, click the **OneNote** icon.

5 With **OneNote** displayed, on the Ribbon, click the **View tab**, and then in the **Views group**, click the **Dock to Desktop** button. Compare your screen with Figure 16.34.

The PowerPoint file displays in a window on the left and OneNote displays on the right. On the Food Safety Project page, a Linked Note Taking button displays to the left of the Page Title box, indicating that this feature is enabled.

Figure 16.34

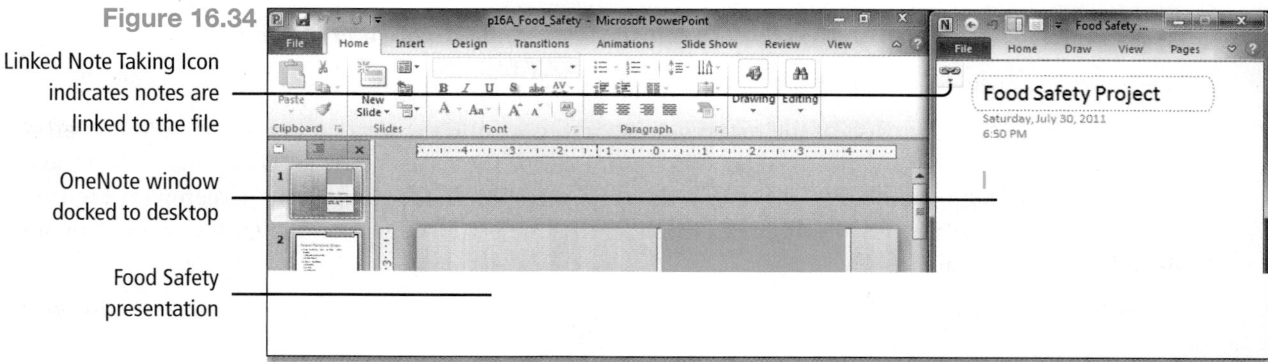

6 On the **Food Safety Project** page, click below the **Page Title** box to create a new note, and then type **Slide 1: Insert the date as part of the subtitle** Press Enter, and then point to the text you just typed.

A PowerPoint icon displays to the left of the note to indicate that it is linked to the PowerPoint file.

7 In the **PowerPoint** window, double-click the thumbnail for **Slide 3**.

8 In the **OneNote** window, click below the text you typed, and then in the same note container, type **Slide 3: Move bulleted text below title** Compare your screen with Figure 16.35.

In the OneNote window, the PowerPoint icon displays to the left of the *Slide 3* text.

Figure 16.35

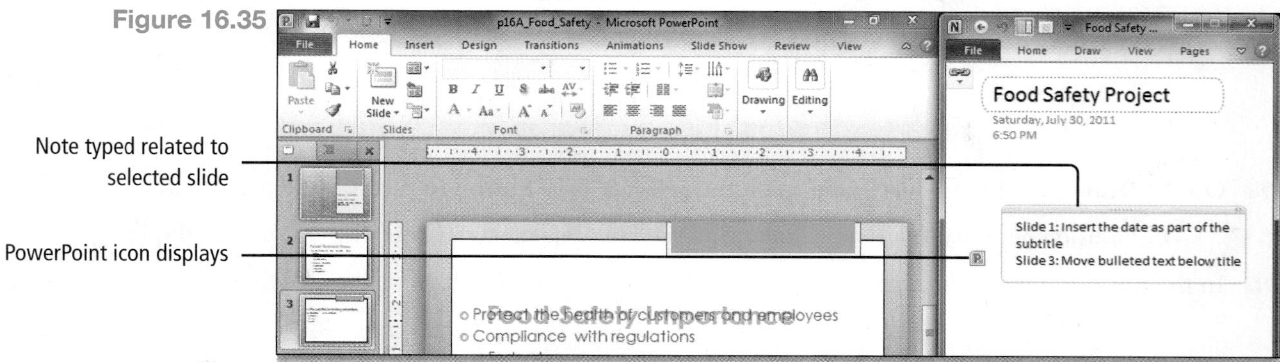

9 In the **OneNote** window, click the **View tab**, and then in the **Views group**, click the **Dock to Desktop** button to turn off the feature. To the left of the note container, point to the **PowerPoint** icon, and then compare your screen with Figure 16.36.

The OneNote window is maximized. The Linked Note Taking button indicates that this feature is currently disabled. The PowerPoint icon ScreenTip displays the linked file name and a thumbnail of the most recently selected slide—in this instance, Slide 3.

Figure 16.36

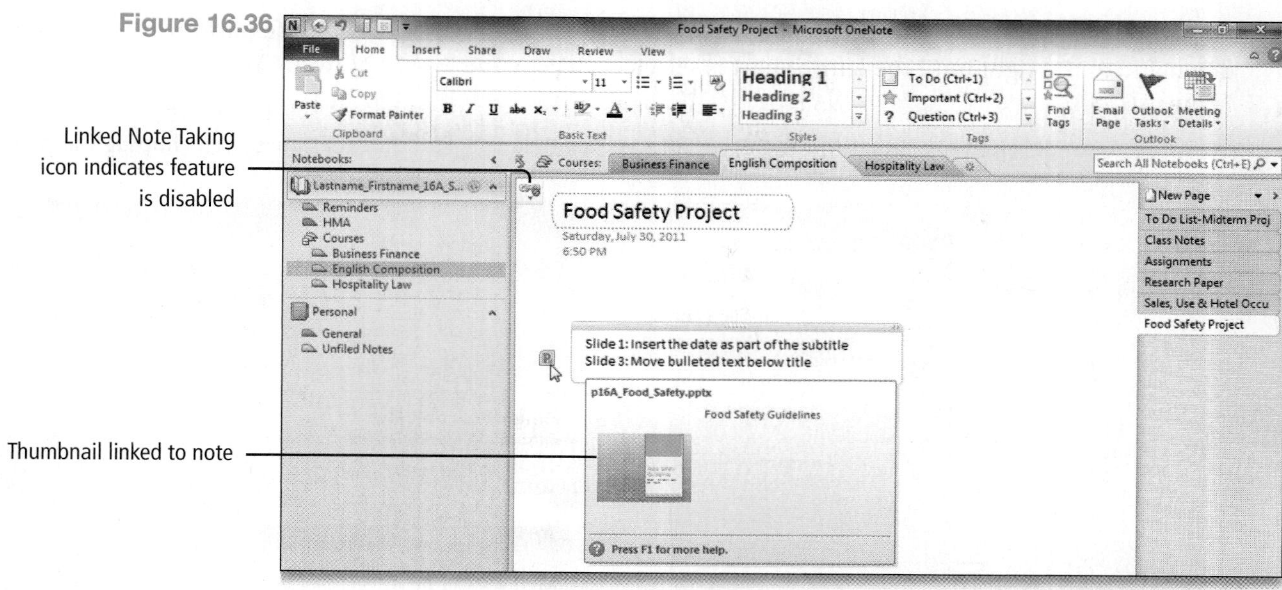

10 On the taskbar, right-click the **PowerPoint** icon, and then click **Close window**.

Activity 16.12 | Using Screen Clippings

OneNote's Screen Clipping tool enables you to insert additional information in your notebook. A ***screen clipping*** is an image copied from part of the computer screen, a Web page, or a document.

1. On the taskbar, to the right of the **Start** button, click the **Windows Explorer** button.
2. Navigate to the location where your student files are stored, and then double-click the file **e16A_Budget_ Worksheet**.

   This Excel file contains data comparing budget data and a related chart.

3. Scroll down if necessary so that the entire bar chart displays on your screen. Then, on the taskbar, click the **OneNote** icon. In the **Navigation Bar**, click **Business Finance** to open that section.
4. In the **page tabs list**, click the **Class Notes** page tab. On the Ribbon, click the **Insert tab**, and then in the **Images group**, click the **Screen Clipping** button. Compare your screen with Figure 16.37.

   The screen dims, and the pointer changes to +.

Figure 16.37

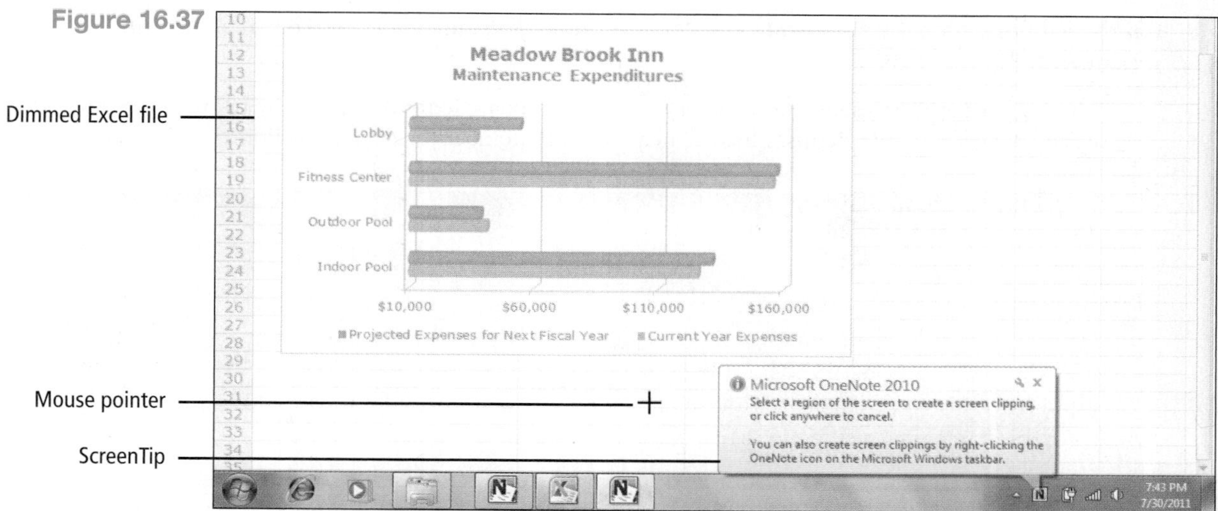

5 Position the [+] pointer at the top left corner of the chart, hold down the left mouse button, and then drag down and to the right until the entire chart is selected. Release the mouse button. Compare your screen with Figure 16.38.

An image of the chart displays below the Page Title box with the date and time that the screen clipping was taken.

Figure 16.38

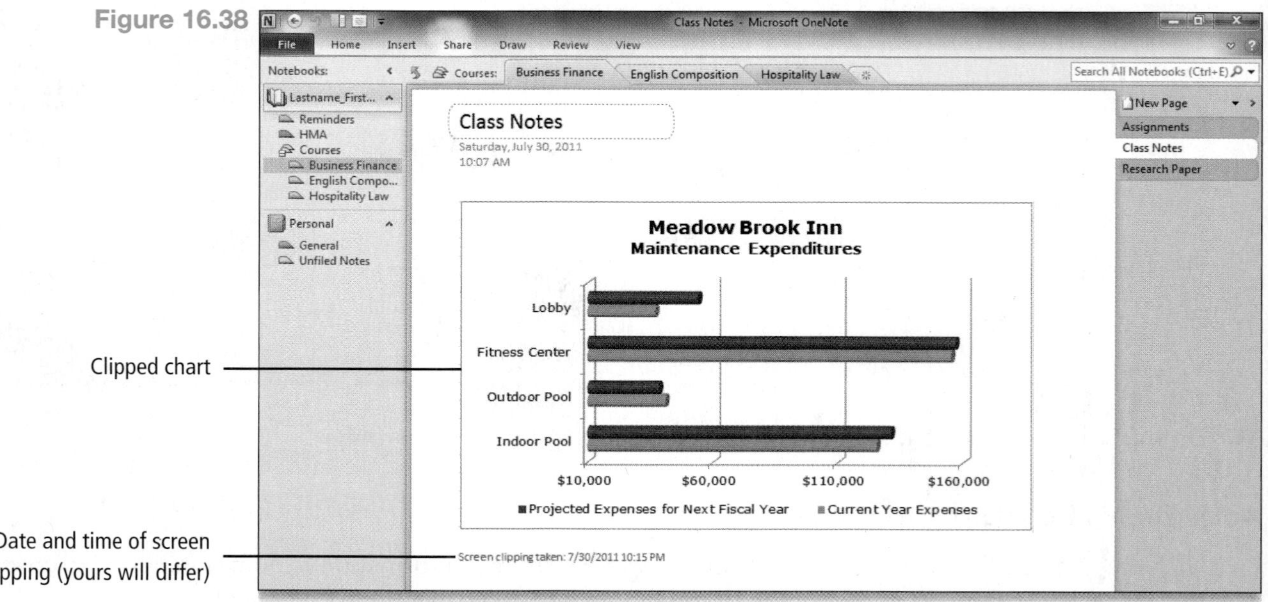

Objective 5 | Search Notebooks

It can be difficult to find the exact notes you want when you have a lot of information stored in notebooks. ***Note tags*** can help you locate specific information quickly. A note tag is both a descriptive term representing a category, such as *Important* or *To Do*, and a related icon that can be associated with a specific note.

Activity 16.13 | Assigning Note Tags

1 If necessary, in the **Navigation Bar**, click **English Composition** to open the section, and then in the **page tabs list**, click the **Food Safety Project** page tab.

2 Click to position the insertion point to the left of the text *Slide 1*, and then select all the text in the note container.

3 On the Ribbon, click the **Home tab**, and then in the **Tags group**, click the **To Do** tag button. Compare your screen with Figure 16.39.

A blue square icon represents the To Do tag. Two blue square icons display to the left of *Slide 1* and *Slide 3*. These notes are tagged as *To Do* items. This will help Gwen remember that the PowerPoint presentation needs to be edited.

Figure 16.39

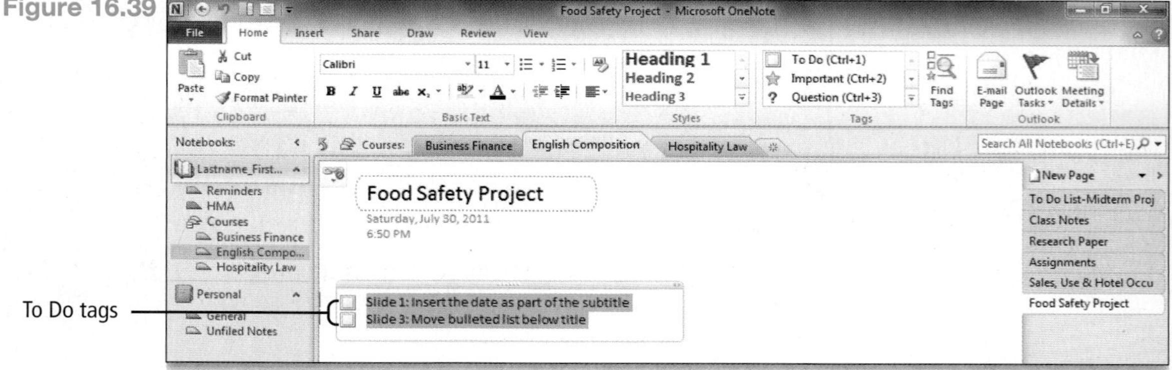

4 From the **Navigation Bar**, open the **Reminders** section.

5 On the **Dates and Contacts** page, click to position the insertion point to the left of the text *Counselor*. On the **Home tab**, in the **Tags group**, click the **More** button.

All the built-in tags in OneNote display.

6 In the **Tags** list, click **Contact**.

Activity 16.14 | Searching for Content

1 On the **Home tab**, in the **Tags group**, click the **Find Tags** button. Compare your screen with Figure 16.40.

The Tags Summary task pane displays at the right of your screen. The note tag categories you assigned—To Do and Contact—display in alphabetical order and include links to each of the respective notes.

Figure 16.40

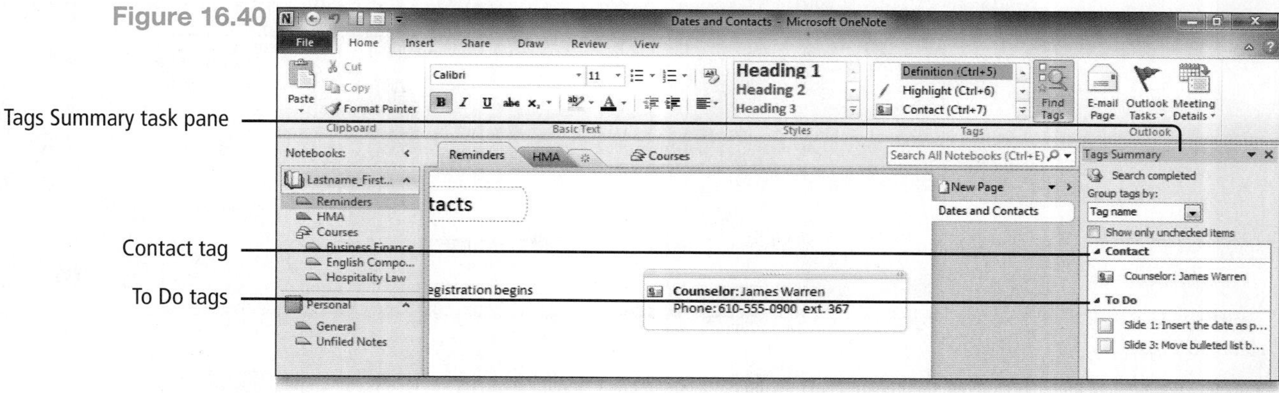

2 In the **Tags Summary** task pane, under **To Do**, click the text that begins *Slide 1*.

The Food Safety page displays with the first line of notes selected.

3 Click the blue square icon to the left of **Slide 1**, and then click the blue square icon to the left of **Slide 3**.

Red check marks display in the squares to indicate that a *To Do* item has been completed. For purposes of this instruction, you will assume that Gwen has made the necessary changes to the PowerPoint presentation.

4 **Close** the **Tags Summary** task pane.

Activity 16.15 | Editing and Printing a Notebook

In your notebook, you can modify or delete notes, pages, and sections as necessary. For example, you might want to correct spelling errors or insert or delete information to create accurate notes. You can also print pages of your notebook.

1 In the **Navigation Bar**, click **HMA**, and then click the **Meeting Agenda** page tab.

2 In the note container, click to place the insertion point to the right of the text *Approval of Minutes*, press Enter, and then type **Treasurer's Report**

3 In the **Navigation Bar**, click **English Composition**. Click the **Research Paper** page tab, hold down Ctrl and then click the **Class Notes** page tab. Right-click the selected pages, and then on the shortcut menu, click **Delete**. By using the same technique, delete the **Research Paper** and **Class Notes** pages in the **Hospitality Law** section.

The pages are deleted and no longer display in the page tabs list. You can right-click a tab, and then use the shortcut menu to delete any component of the notebook—a page, section, or section group.

4 On the Ribbon, right-click any tab, and then click **Minimize the Ribbon** to restore the default view of the Ribbon.

5 In the **Navigation Bar**, click **Reminders**, and then click the **File tab** to display **Backstage** view.

6 In **Backstage** view, in the tabs list, click the **Print tab**, and then click **Print Preview**. Near the top right of the **Print Preview and Settings** dialog box, click the **Print range** arrow, and then compare your screen with Figure 16.41.

The Print range options enable you to designate the components of a notebook that you want to print—the current page, a page group (determined by the current page), or the current section. You can also choose the page orientation and the type of footer to display. The current page, *Dates and Contacts*, displays in the Print Preview box.

Figure 16.41

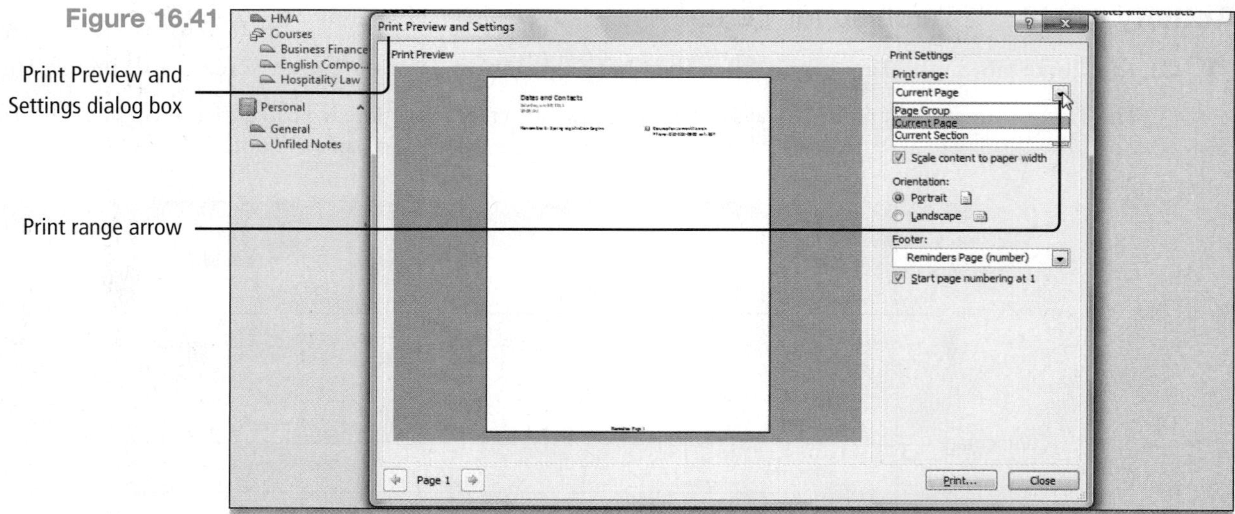

7 In the **Print Preview and Settings** dialog box, click the **Close** button, and then **Close** OneNote without printing.

8 In Windows Explorer, navigate to the location where you are saving your files for this chapter. Open your folder **Lastname_Firstname_16A_School_Notebook**.

The folder OneNote_RecycleBin is automatically created whenever you delete a page or section from a notebook. The folder contains pages and sections that were deleted—in this case, the Untitled page and Research Paper page.

9 In the **Windows Explorer** window, to the left of the **Address Bar**, click the **Back** button.

10 Print your notebook or submit electronically as directed by your instructor. If submitting electronically, you can either use Windows Explorer to compress the folder and submit your work as a *.zip* file or submit a PDF of your notebook, as described in the following Note.

Note | **Saving Your Notebook as a PDF File**

You can save your entire notebook as a single PDF file. From Backstage view, click Save As. Under Save Current, click Notebook. Under Select Format, click PDF, and then click the Save As button. In the Save As dialog box, navigate to the location where you want to save the file, and then click Save.

11 **Close** the Windows Explorer window and then **Close** OneNote. Close any other open windows.

More Knowledge | **Deleting a Notebook**

You can delete an entire notebook that is no longer needed. In Windows Explorer, select the folder, press Delete, and then in the Delete Folder dialog box, click Yes to confirm the deletion.

End **You have completed Project 16A**

Project 16B Google Docs

Project Activities

In Activities 16.16 through 16.19, you will assist Petra Young, Catering Manager for the Rockport Inn, in uploading, editing, and creating a document using Google Docs and sharing files online. You will create snip files that will look similar to Figure 16.42.

Project Files

For Project 16B, you will need the following file:

e16B_Advertising_Expenses

You will save your files as:

Lastname_Firstname_16B_Google_Spreadsheet
Lastname_Firstname_16B_Sandwich_Options
Lastname_Firstname_16B_Sharing
Lastname_Firstname_16B_Email_Copy

Project Results

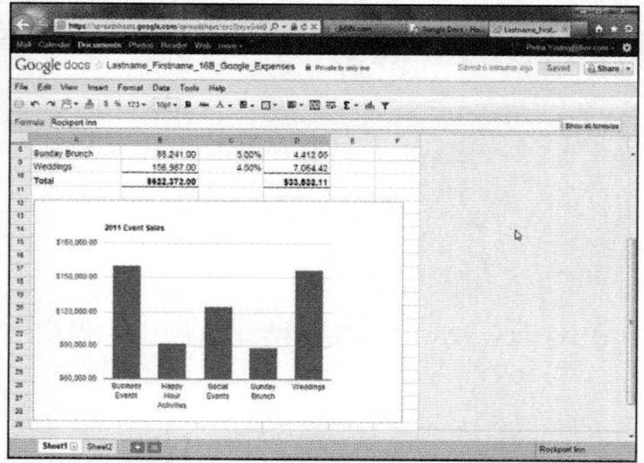
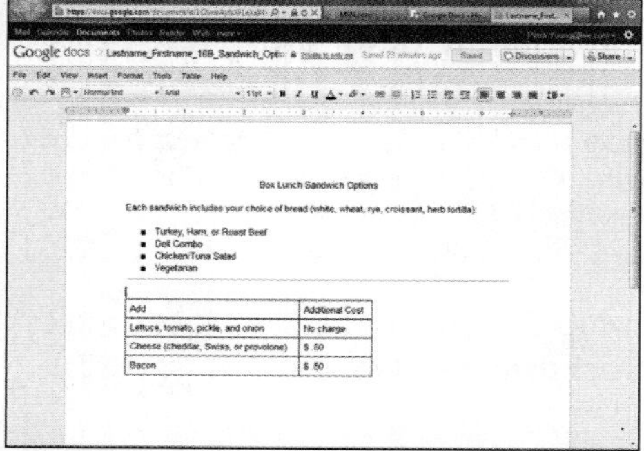

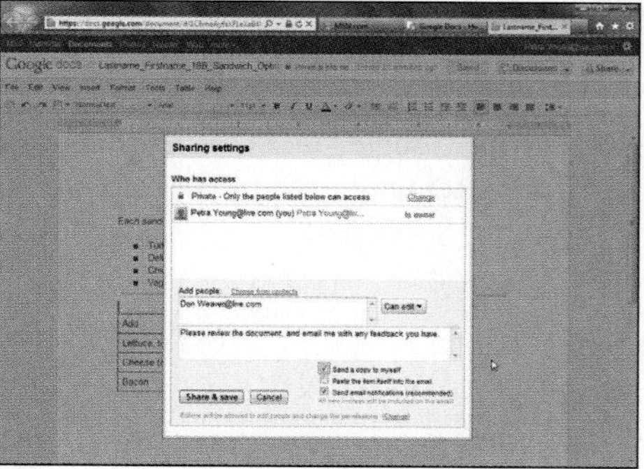

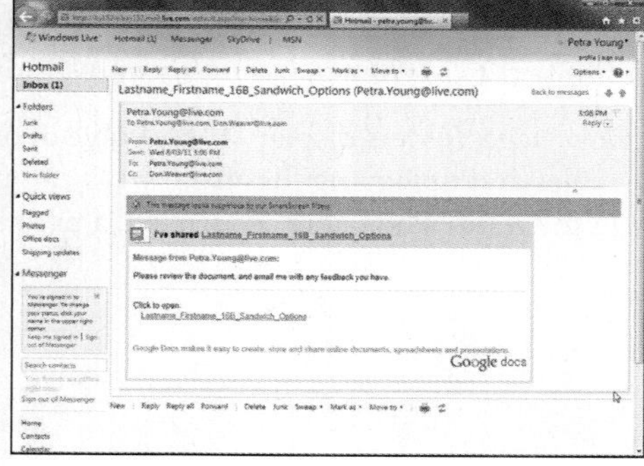

Figure 16.42
Project 16B Google Docs

Objective 6 | Store Files Online in Google Docs

Alert! | When you reach Activity 16.19 of this project, identify a classmate with whom you can partner to complete the project.

In Objective 8 of this project, which includes Activity 16.19, you will benefit from working together with a classmate to share files created in Google Docs. You do not need to be working at the same time or the same place.

Google Docs is a free application from Google you can use to store, create, edit, and share documents online using a free Google account. The application operates completely online, so no downloads are required. Google Docs enables you to access files and folders from any computer, so long as you have an Internet connection. You can also share files with others in real time for collaboration.

Alert! | Working with Web-Based Applications and Services

Computer programs and services on the Web receive continuous updates and improvements. Thus, the steps to complete this Web-based Activity may differ from the ones shown. You can often look at the screens and the information presented to determine how to complete the activity.

Activity 16.16 | Converting an Excel Worksheet to a Google Docs Spreadsheet

Alert! | If you do not have a Google account, follow these steps to set up your account now.

Start your Web browser and go to *http://docs.google.com*. On the right side of the window, under *Don't Have a Google Account?*, click Create an account now. On the Google accounts Sign up page, under Use an email address you already have, click Windows Live Hotmail. On the Windows Live page, sign in to your account. In the Allow Access page, click *Yes*. Under Email address, click the Save and continue button to create the account and display the Google docs page.

You can upload existing files and folders, including file types such as documents, images, and videos. In this activity, you will convert an Excel worksheet to a Google Docs spreadsheet.

1 Start your Web browser and navigate to **http://docs.google.com** On the right side of the window, sign in to your Google account to display the Google docs page. If asked to provide your mobile phone number, you can skip this step—near the bottom click the text *Click here to skip this step*. Compare your screen with Figure 16.43.

On the left side of the Google Docs page, folders display where you can organize your Google Docs files. Buttons display options for creating new files and uploading files from your computer. In the center pane, any files stored in the selected folder display. On the right, when a file is selected, a preview and other document information will display.

Figure 16.43

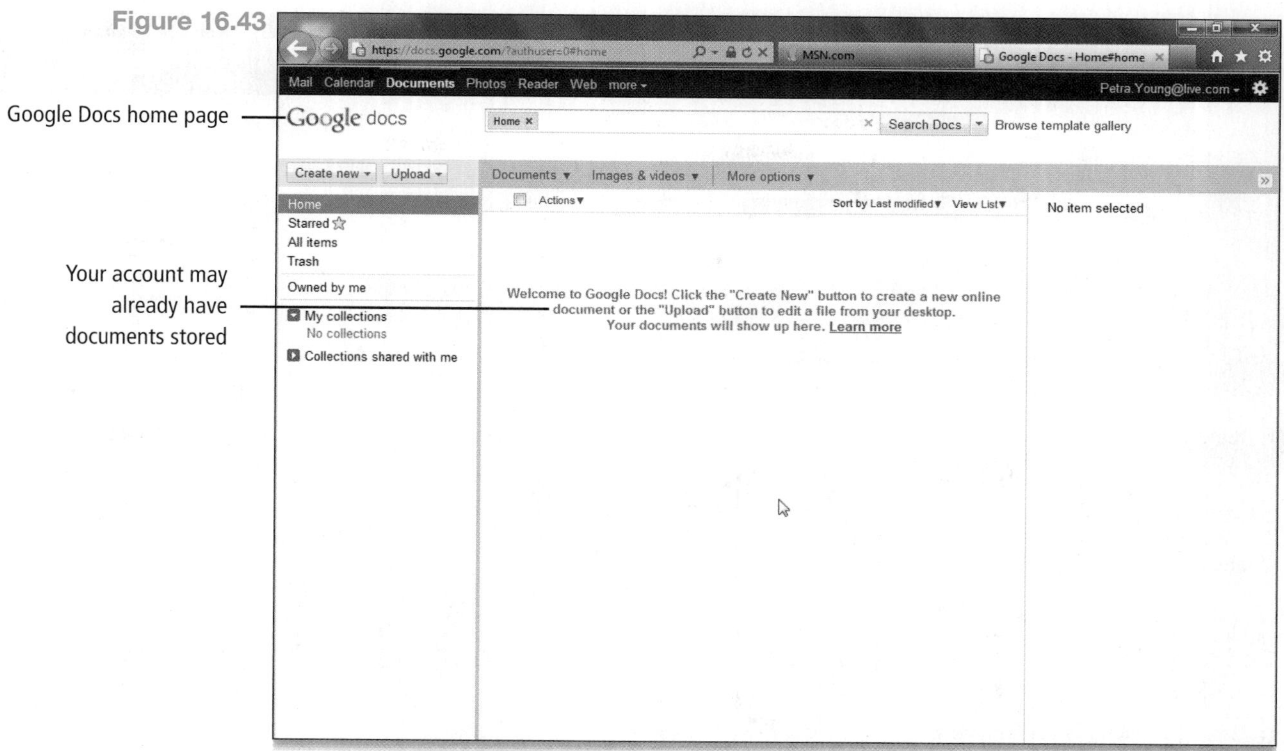

2 On the left side of your screen, click the **Upload** button, and then click **Files**. Navigate to the location where your student data files are stored, and then select **e16B_Advertising_Expenses**. Click **Open**. If the Upload settings message box displays, if necessary, select the first check box, and then click Start upload to display a message box that indicates the upload progress of your file.

The file was created using Microsoft Excel, but uploading will convert the Excel file to a Google Docs spreadsheet.

3 When the title bar of the message box indicates *Upload complete*, **Close** the message box.

At the top of the window, a yellow bar indicates that the upload is complete and in the center of your screen, under MODIFIED TODAY, your file name displays.

4 Right-click the **e16B_Advertising_Expenses** file, and on the shortcut menu, click **Rename**. In the box, type **Lastname_Firstname_16B_Google_Expenses** Click **OK**, and then compare your screen with Figure 16.44.

Figure 16.44

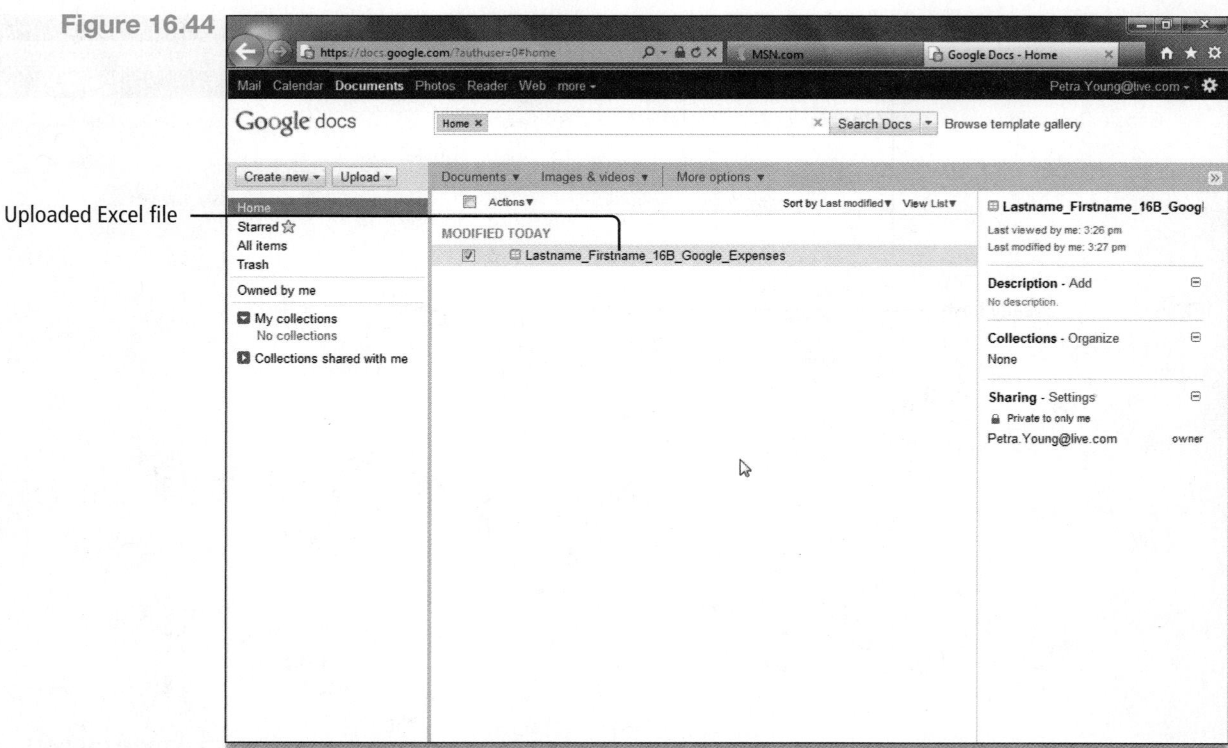

5 Click your **Lastname_Firstname_16B_Google_Expenses** file to open the file in Google Docs.

The worksheet displays column letters and row numbers, data, and a chart. If necessary, Maximize your window.

6 Click the edge of the chart to select it, and notice that in the upper left corner, the word **Chart** displays. Click **Chart** to display a menu, and then click **Delete chart**.

7 On the row numbers, click **6** to select the entire row. At the top of the screen, click **Insert**, and then on the displayed menu, click **Row above**.

A new row 6 is added to the worksheet and the remaining rows move down one row.

8 In cell **A6**, type **Happy Hour Activities** and press Tab. In cell **B6** type **91720** and press Tab. In cell **C6** type **6.25%** and press Enter.

Google Docs updates the total in cell B10 to reflect the data that you inserted.

9 Click cell **B6**, and then at the top of the window, display the **Format** menu. Point to **Number**, and then click **1,000.12 2 Decimals**—the third item on the menu.

10 Click cell **D6**, and then type **=b6*c6** Press Enter. Using the technique you practiced, format **D6** as **2 Decimals**. Compare your screen with Figure 16.45.

In a manner similar to Excel, typing a formula in a cell also displays on the Formula bar and uses color to refer to the cells in the formula.

Figure 16.45

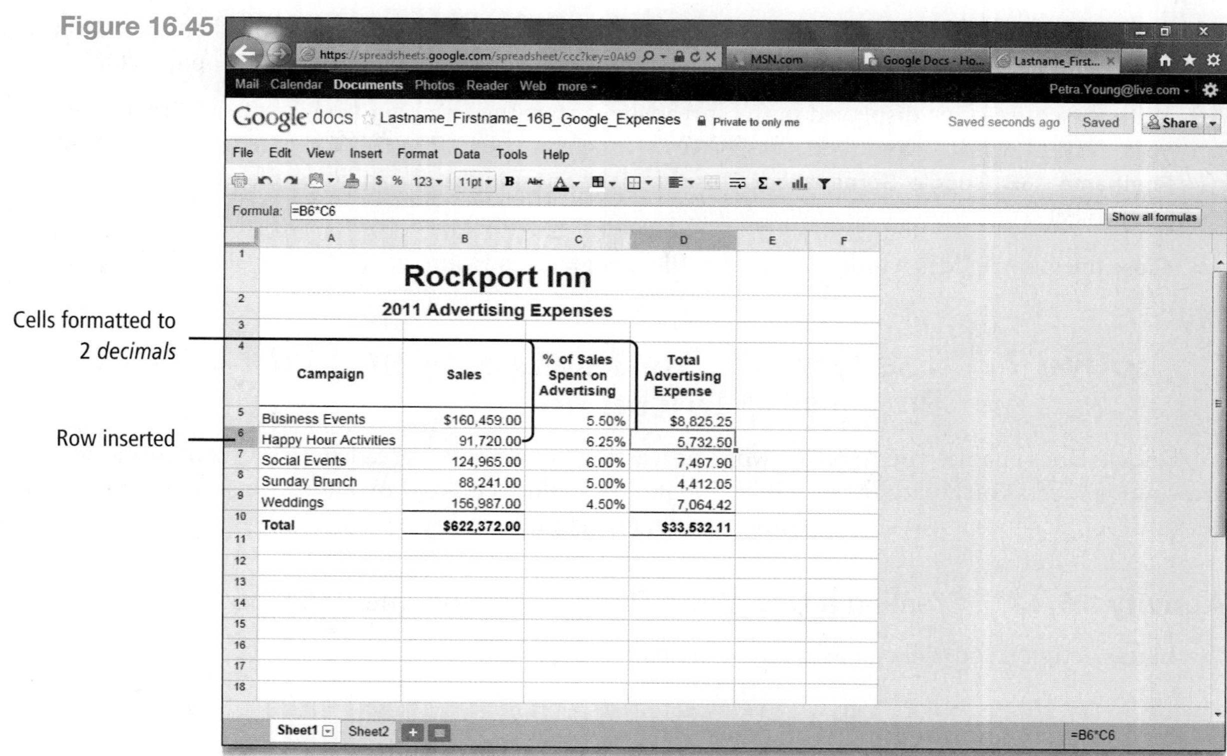

11 Scroll down to view the lower portion of the spreadsheet. Below the spreadsheet, in the **Add** box, type **10** and then click **Add** to add 10 additional rows to the spreadsheet.

12 Select the range **A5:B9**. Display the **Insert** menu, and then click **Chart**. In the **Chart Editor** dialog box, under **Recommended charts**, point to each chart to display a ScreenTip of the column type, and then locate and click **column chart**. Near the top of the dialog box, click the **Customize tab**. In the **Chart title** box, type **2011 Event Sales** Under **Layout: Legend** click the **None** option button. Compare your screen with Figure 16.46.

Figure 16.46

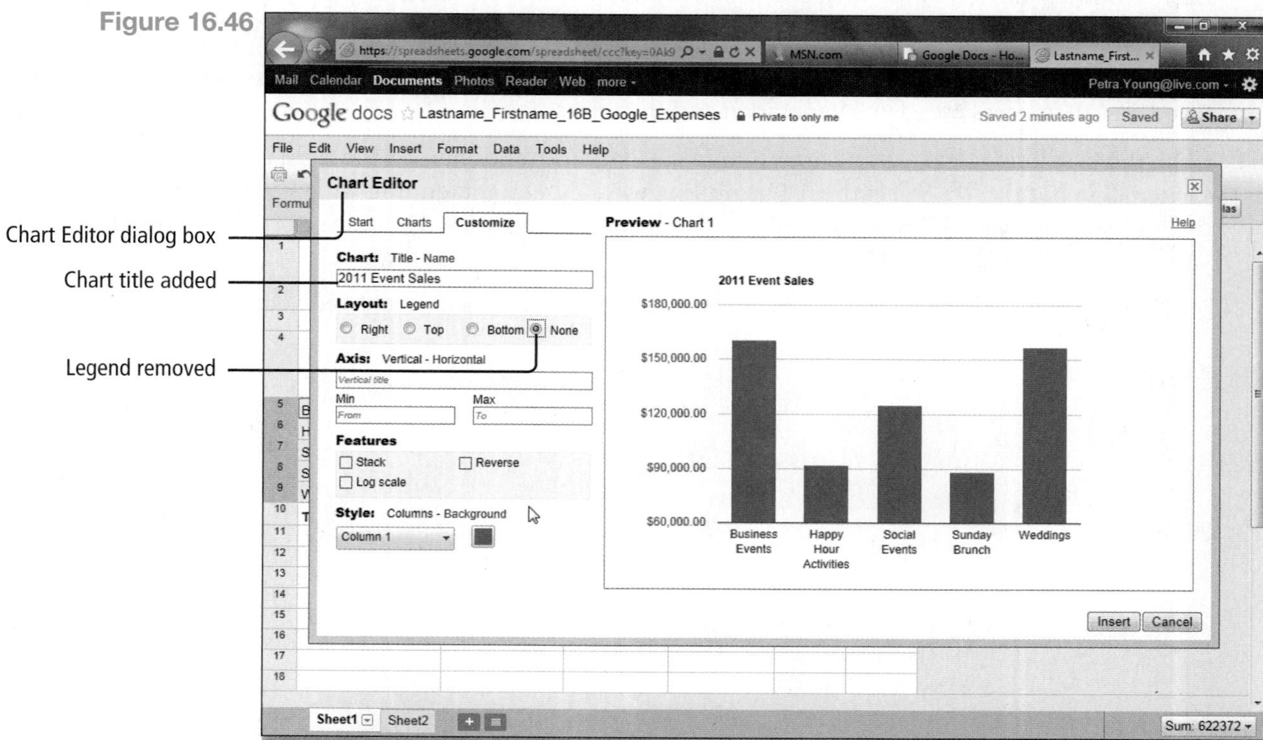

13 In the lower right corner of the **Chart Editor**, click the **Insert** button to insert the chart. Select the chart, and then point to its gray title bar so that the pointer displays. Drag down to position the chart in row 12.

14 With the entire chart displayed in the spreadsheet, start the **Snipping Tool**, create a **Window Snip** of your current window, and then save the **JPEG** image in your **All In One Chapter 16** folder as **Lastname_Firstname_16B_Google_Spreadsheet Close** the **Snipping Tool**. Hold this file until you complete the project.

15 **Close** the Google docs window to display the Google docs Home page. Remain signed in for the next activity.

Objective 7 | Use Google Docs to Create and Edit a Word Processing Document

Google Docs enables you to create word processing documents, spreadsheets, presentations, forms, and drawings. Objects you create are stored in Google Docs folders unless you choose to save them somewhere else. Because Google Docs is a Web-based application, the window and application options can change often.

Activity 16.17 | Creating a New Word Processing Document in Google Docs

In this activity, you will create an event menu using Google Docs.

> Alert! | **To complete this project, you must have a Google Account.**
>
> If you have not created your Google account, see Activity 16.16.

1 If necessary, sign in to your Google Docs account. On the left side of your screen, click the **Create new** button, and then click **Document** to display a new document window. If necessary, **Maximize** the window.

The new document window is added to your open pages. Click the text *Google docs* to return to the home page.

2 With the insertion point blinking, type **Box Lunch Sandwich Options** and then press Enter two times. Type **Each sandwich includes your choice of bread (white, wheat, rye, croissant, herb tortilla):** and then press Enter two times.

3 Type **Turkey, Ham, or Roast Beef** and then press Enter. Type **Deli Combo** and then press Enter. Type **Chicken/Tuna Salad** and then press Enter. Type **Vegetarian** and then press Enter.

4 Click the first line of text—*Box Lunch Sandwich Options*—and then on the right side of the toolbar, click the **Center align** button. Select the list beginning with *Turkey* and ending with *Vegetarian*. On the right side of the toolbar, click the **Bulleted list** button. Click anywhere outside of the selected text, and then compare your screen with Figure 16.47.

Notice the document has been saved automatically; however, it is still an untitled document.

Figure 16.47

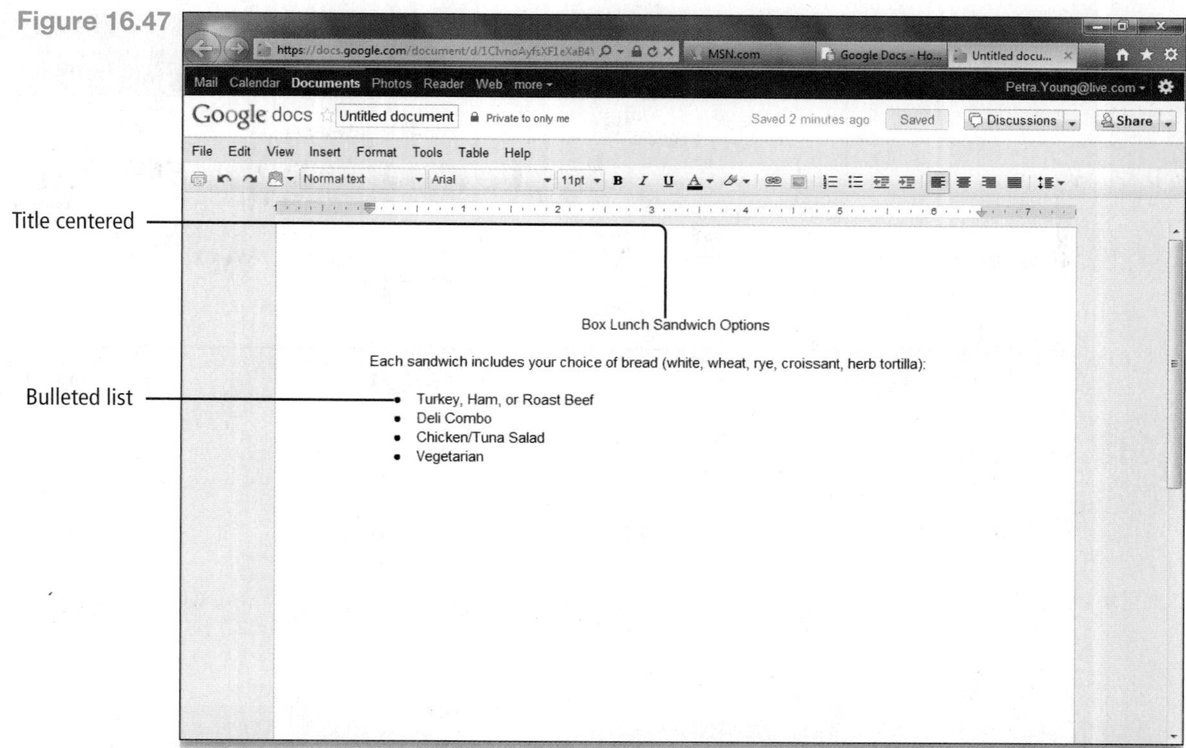

5 Next to the **Google docs** logo, click in the **Untitled document** box to display a **Rename Document** dialog box. With the insertion point blinking in the blank box, type **Lastname_Firstname_16B_Sandwich_Options** Click **OK**.

6 Close the document window to return to Google Docs Home page.

Activity 16.18 | Editing a Google Docs Document

In this activity, you will create an event menu using Google Docs.

1 If necessary, sign in to Google Docs. In the file list, click the check box to the left of the **16B_Sandwich_Options** file name, and then compare your screen with Figure 16.48.

The files you have added to Google Docs appear in the center pane. Information about the selected file appears in the right pane. A preview of the document and viewing/editing information appears at the top and additional tools display at the bottom.

Figure 16.48

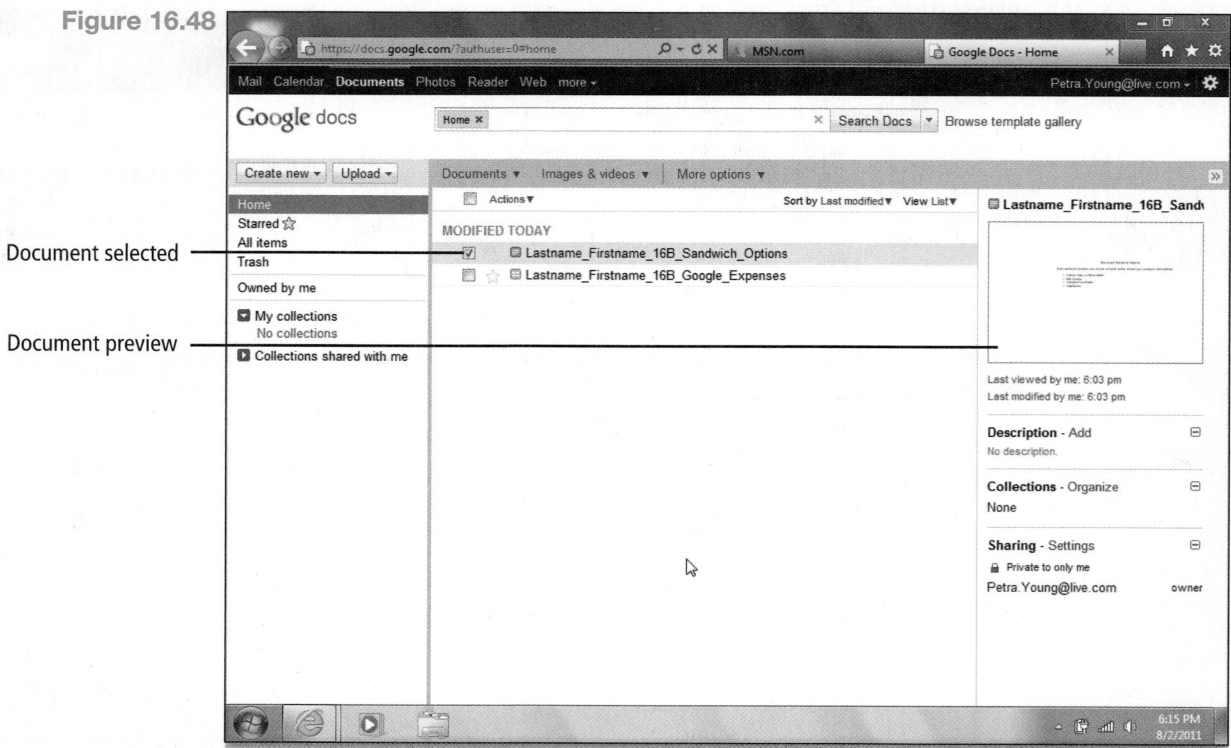

2 At the top of the right pane, click the **16B_Sandwich_Options** link to open the document.

3 In the document window, click in the blank line below *Vegetarian*. Click the **Insert** menu, and then click **Horizontal line** to insert a line in the document. Press Enter.

4 Click the **Table** menu, click **Insert table**, and then drag your mouse arrow across to the second column and down to the fourth row. Compare your screen with Figure 16.49 and then release the mouse button.

The selected area of the grid displays the number of rows and columns in the table that is inserted in the document. Once the table is inserted, the insertion point is blinking in the first cell in the table.

Figure 16.49

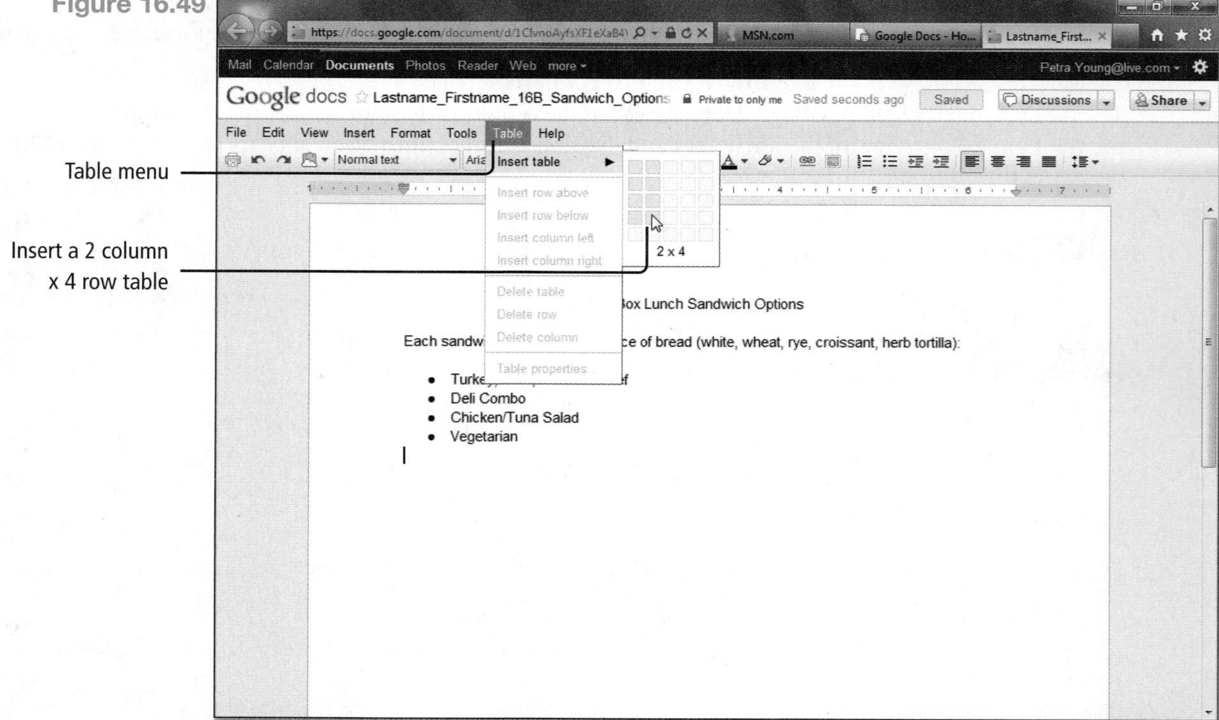

5 Type **Add** and then press [Tab]. Type **Additional Cost** and then press [Tab].

6 Type the following, pressing [Tab] to move from cell to cell.

Lettuce, tomato, pickle, and onion

No charge

Cheese (cheddar, Swiss, or provolone)

$ .50

Bacon

$ .50

7 Point to the right boundary of the first column to display the [+||+] pointer, and drag to the left to resize the column so it is just wide enough to display the text. Using the same technique, resize the second column to avoid excess blank space in the column.

8 Select the bulleted list. Click the **Format** menu, and then click **List style**. Compare your screen with Figure 16.50.

Figure 16.50

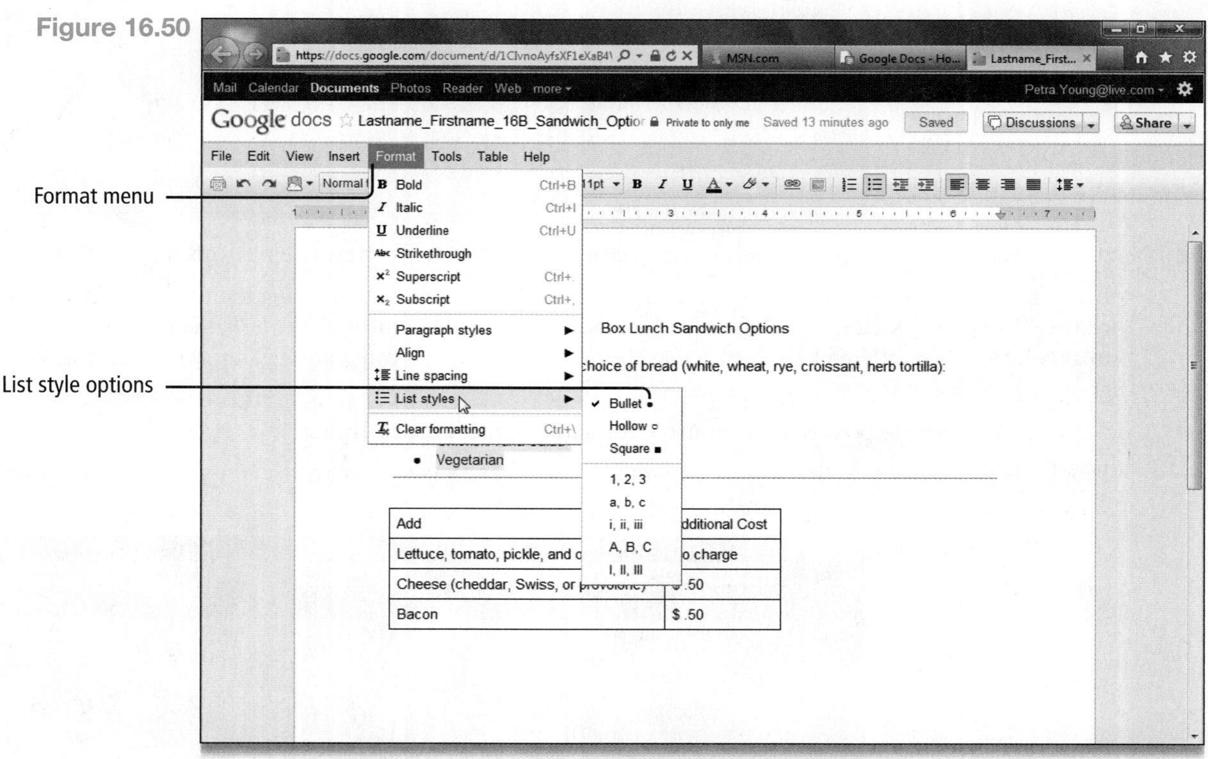

9 From the *List styles*, click **Square** ▪ Click in a blank area of your document to deselect the list.

10 With the entire document displayed on your screen, start the **Snipping Tool**, create a **Window Snip** of your current window, and then save the **JPEG** image in your **All In One Chapter 16** folder as **Lastname_Firstname_16B_Sandwich_Options Close** [X] the Snipping Tool. Hold this file until you complete the project.

Objective 8 | Share Documents Using Google Docs

Activity 16.19 | Sharing a Document

1 If necessary, sign in to your Google Docs account and display the **16B_Sandwich_Options** document. At the top of the window, click the **Share** button, and then compare your screen with Figure 16.51.

The Sharing settings dialog box displays the level of access a document has as well as a list of individuals who have access.

Figure 16.51

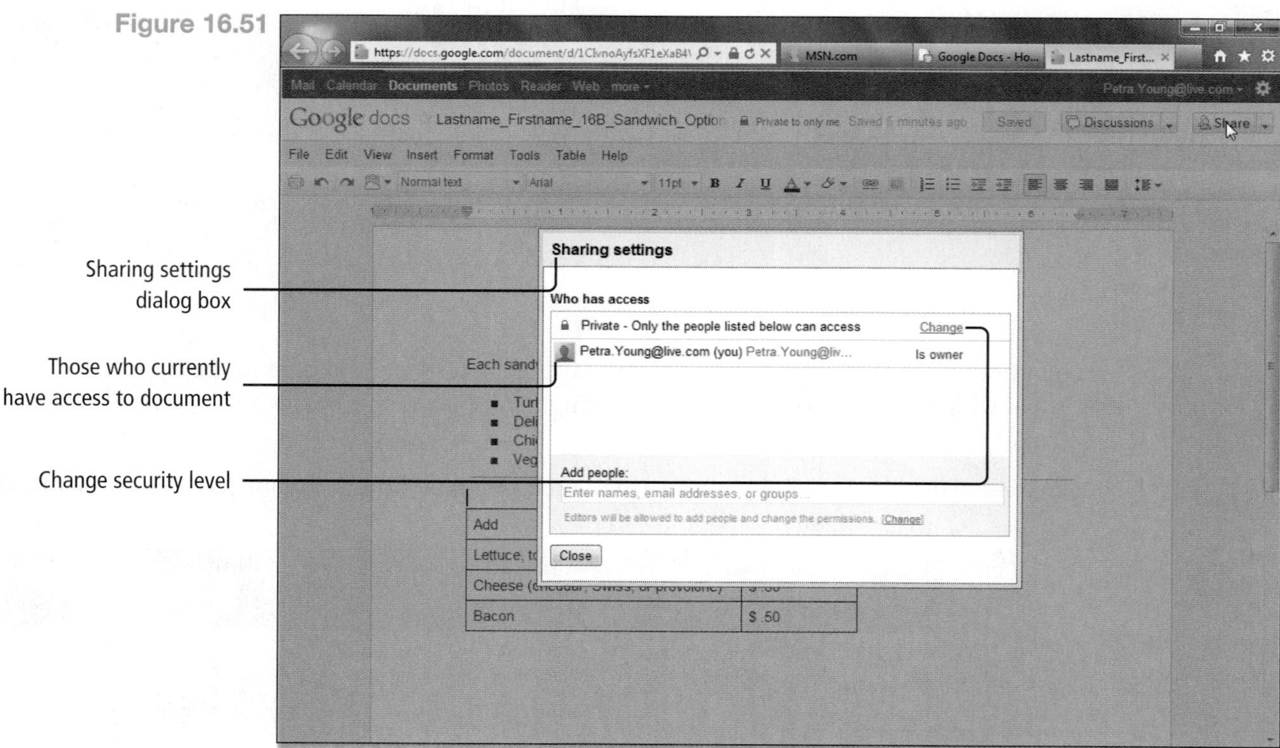

2 Next to **Private – Only the people below can access**, click **Change**. Review the options, and then click **Cancel**.

If a document is made *Public on the web*, anyone can access the document using the Internet. This is the least restrictive visibility setting. If a document is made available to *Anyone with the link*, then the link can be forwarded to anyone who would then be able to access the document. The *Private* setting is the default setting; anyone who is granted permission to view the document must sign in to access it.

3 Click in the **Add people** box, and compare your screen with Figure 16.52.

People are given access to the document with their email address. Notice that sending email notifications is the default (and recommended) setting.

Figure 16.52

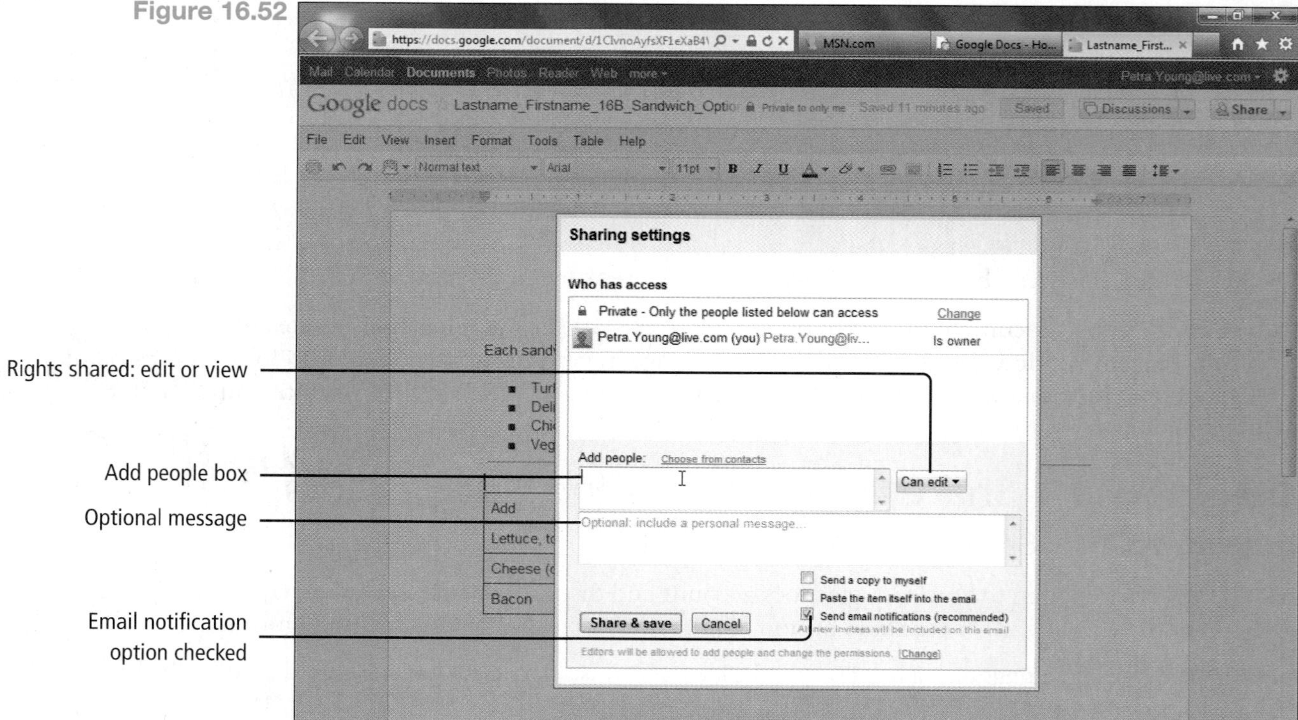

4 In the **Add people** box, type your partner's Google account email. Click the **Can edit** arrow and click **Can view**. In the personal message box, type a short message asking your partner to review the document for you and provide feedback via email.

Access to documents can be given at two levels. Anyone who can edit the document can make changes to it. If viewing rights are given, then only the owner can make changes.

5 Click the **Send a copy to myself** checkbox so you receive a copy of the invitation.

6 Start the **Snipping Tool**, create a **Window Snip** of your current window, and then save the **JPEG** image in your **All In One Chapter 16** folder as **Lastname_Firstname_16B_Sharing Close** the Snipping Tool.

7 At the bottom of the **Sharing settings** dialog box, click **Share & save**. Close the dialog box. Close the document window.

8 In the top right corner of the Google Docs home page, click the arrow next to your Google account name, and then click **Sign out**.

9 Navigate to **http://live.com** and sign in to your Windows Live account. Under **Hotmail highlights**, click **Go to Inbox**.

10 Notice an email from yourself and one from your partner, both with file names as the subject line. Open the message from your Google account. If a safety message displays, click Show content. Compare your screen with Figure 16.53.

The email message displays the message you typed along with a link for your partner to open the document. Because of the privacy settings, your partner will have to sign in to access the document.

Figure 16.53

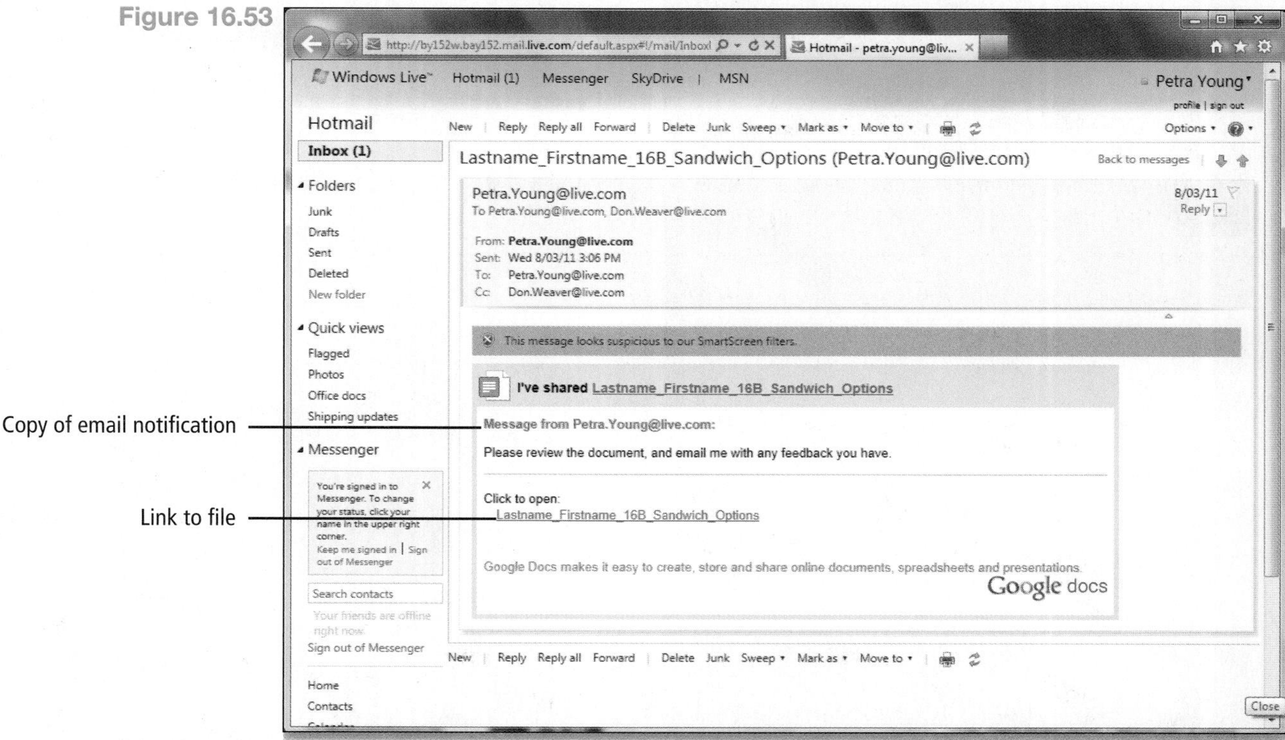

11 Start the **Snipping Tool**, create a **Window Snip** of your current window, and then save the **JPEG** image in your **All In One Chapter 16** folder as **Lastname_Firstname_16B_Email_Copy Close** the Snipping Tool.

12 **Sign out** of Windows Live. **Close** your browser. Submit your four snip files to your instructor as directed.

End You have completed Project 16B

Content-Based Assessments

Summary

You can create notebooks in OneNote to organize information within each notebook by creating sections and pages within each section. Notes can include typed text, pictures and videos, links to other files such as Word, Excel or PowerPoint, or screen clippings. You can assign note tags to enable you to quickly find specific information.

You can use Google Docs to store, create, edit, and share documents using the Google account. Documents can maintain various levels of security set by the document owner.

Key Terms

Check Your Knowledge

Matching and Multiple Choice items are available in MyITLab and on the Companion Web Site.

Apply 16A and 16B skills from these Objectives:

1. Create a OneNote Notebook
2. Create Sections and Pages in a Notebook
3. Insert and Format Notes
4. Integrate Office and Internet Files with OneNote
5. Search Notebooks
6. Store Files Online in Google Docs
7. Use Google Docs to Create and Edit a Word Processing Document
8. Share Documents Using Google Docs

Mastering OneNote | Project 16C Senior Center

In the following project, you will create a notebook for Gwen Moreau to store information related to her volunteer work at the Harrison Senior Center. Your completed notebook will look similar to Figure 16.54.

Project Files

For Project 16C, you will need the following files:

w16C_Volunteer_Eligibility
jpg16C_Photo_Frame
p16C_Nutrition

You will save your files as:

Lastname_Firstname_16C_Senior_Center
Lastname_Firstname_16C_Volunteers

Project Results

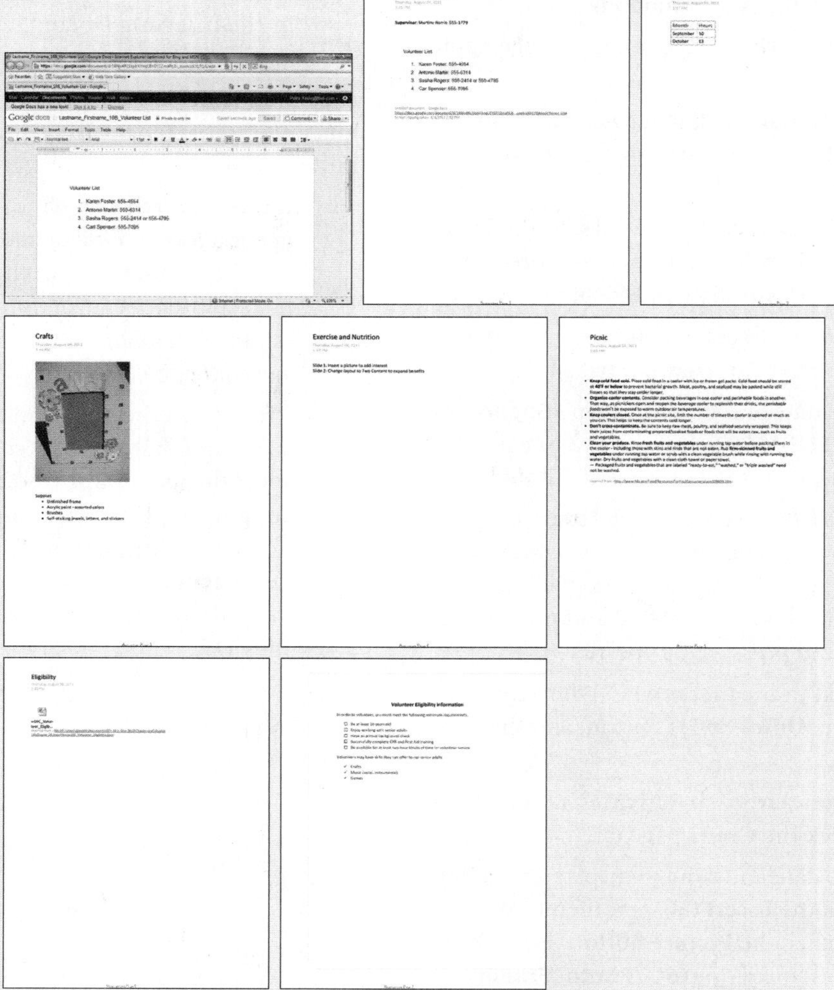

Figure 16.54

(Project 16C Senior Center continues on the next page)

Mastering OneNote | Project 16C Senior Center (continued)

1 Open **Microsoft OneNote 2010**. If any open notebooks display, in the Navigation Bar, right-click the notebook name, and then on the shortcut menu, click **Close This Notebook**. Create a new notebook stored in your **All In One Chapter 16** folder. Using your name, save it as **Lastname_Firstname_16C_Senior_Center**

2 Rename **New Section 1** as **Schedules**

a. In the **Navigation Bar**, create a **New Section Group**, named **Programs**

b. In the **Programs** section group, add two new sections named **Regulations** and **Activities**

c. In the **Navigation Bar**, drag the **Activities** section above **Regulations**.

3 In the **Navigation Bar**, click **Schedules** to make the section active. With the insertion point blinking in the **Page Title** box, type **Contact Information**

a. In the **Schedules** section, create another page named **Work Hours**

b. In the **Navigation Bar**, click **Regulations**. In the **Page Title** box, type **Eligibility** to title the first page of this section.

c. In the **Navigation Bar**, click **Activities**. In the **Page Title** box, type **Crafts** and create a two more pages titled **Exercise and Nutrition** and **Picnic**

4 Display the **Schedules** section, and then in the **page tabs list**, click the **Contact Information** page tab.

a. Click below the date and time, and type **Supervisor: Martina Norris 555-1779** Select the text *Supervisor*, and then, on the Mini toolbar, click the **Bold** button.

b. In the **page tabs list**, click the **Work Hours** page tab. Click below the date and time. Type **Month** and press Tab. Type **Hours** and press Enter. Type **September** and press Tab. Type **10** and press Enter. Type **October** and press Tab. Type **13**

c. Select all the text in the first row. On the Mini toolbar, click the **Quick Styles** button, and then click **Heading 2**.

5 In the **Navigation Bar**, click **Activities**, and then on the **page tabs list**, click the **Crafts** page tab.

a. Click below the date and time to display a note container. Click the **Insert tab**, and then in the **Images group**, click the **Picture** button. From your student data files, insert **jpg16C_Photo_Frame**.

b. With the insertion point below the picture, press Enter two times. Type the following lines, pressing Enter after each line:

Supplies

Unfinished frame

Acrylic paint – assorted colors

Brushes

Self-sticking jewels, letters, and stickers

c. Select the last four lines you typed, and then on the Mini toolbar, click the **Bullets** button.

d. In the **Navigation Bar**, click **Regulations**. With the **Eligibility** page displayed, click below the date and time. Click the **Insert tab**, and then in the **Files group**, click **File Printout**. From your student files, insert **w16C_Volunteer_Eligibility**. Be sure to wait for the Inserting Documents indicator to complete.

6 Display the **Activities** section. In the **page tabs list**, click the **Picnic** page tab. On the Ribbon, click the **Review tab**, and then in the **Spelling group**, click the **Research** button.

a. In the **Research** task pane, in the **Search for** box, type **fda food handling** and then in the next box, be sure *Bing* is indicated as the search location. Locate the result that begins *Eating Outdoors*. Below the last line of explanatory text, click the link that begins *www.fda.gov/Food*.

b. Scroll down the page and locate the bulleted paragraph that begins *Keep cold food cold*. Select this paragraph and the next four bulleted paragraphs. Right-click the selected text, and then on the shortcut menu, click **Send to OneNote**. In the **Select Location in OneNote** dialog box, expand the **Activities** section, and select the **Picnic** page. Click **OK**.

c. **Close** your browser window. **Close** the **Research** task pane.

(Project 16C Senior Center continues on the next page)

Mastering OneNote | Project 16C Senior Center (continued)

7 Display the **Exercise and Nutrition** page. Open **Windows Explorer**, navigate to the location where your student files are stored, and then open the file **p16C_Nutrition**.

a. On the taskbar, click the **OneNote** icon. On the **View tab**, in the **Views group**, click the **Dock to Desktop** button.

b. On the **Exercise and Nutrition** page, click below the **Page Title** box, and then type **Slide 1: Insert a picture to add interest**

c. In the **PowerPoint** window, double-click the thumbnail for **Slide 2**. In the **OneNote** window, click below the text you typed, and then type **Slide 2: Change layout to Two Content to expand benefits**

d. In the **OneNote** window, click the **View tab**, and then in the **Views group**, click the **Dock to Desktop** button to turn off the feature.

e. On the taskbar, close the PowerPoint window. **Minimize** OneNote.

8 Start your Web browser, and navigate to **http://docs.google.com**. Sign in to your account. Create a new Document.

a. Type **Volunteer List** and press Enter two times. Type the following lines, pressing Enter after each line:

Karen Foster: 555-4654

Antonio Martin: 555-6314

Sasha Rogers: 555-2414 or 555-4795

Carl Spenser: 555-7095

b. Select the last four lines of text. On the toolbar, click the **Numbered List** button. With the text selected, click the **Format** menu, and then click **Line spacing**. On the displayed list, click **1.5**.

c. Click the **File** menu, and then click **Rename**. In the **Rename Document** dialog box, type **Lastname_Firstname_16C_Volunteer_List** Click **OK**.

d. Start the **Snipping Tool**, create a **Window Snip** of your current window, and then save the **JPEG** image in your **All In One Chapter 16** folder as **Lastname_Firstname_16C_Volunteers Close** the Snipping Tool. Submit as directed by your instructor.

9 On the taskbar, click the **OneNote** icon. Display the **Schedules** section, and then display the **Contact Information** page. Click below the note container.

a. On the Ribbon, click the **Insert tab**, and then in the **Images group**, click the **Screen Clipping** button. In Google Docs, position the pointer to the left of **Volunteer List**, hold down the left mouse button, and then drag down and to the right until the entire list is selected. Release the mouse button

b. **Close** OneNote. **Sign out** of Google Docs and **Close** your browser.

c. Print your notebook or submit electronically as directed by your instructor. If submitting electronically, you can either use Windows Explorer to compress the folder and submit your work as a *.zip* file or submit a PDF of your notebook.

End **You have completed Project 16C**

Unit 6 Case Project

A OneNote Notebook and Google Doc Created by a Director of Sales for a Hotel; Your Own College Notebook

In this Unit Case Project, you will create a notebook to store information related to the upcoming Bridal Show that will be held at the hotel. This is an important event for the hotel, because brides attending the show will also be looking for venues to hold their weddings and receptions. Your completed notebook will look similar to Figure 6.1.

Project Files

For Unit Project 6, you will need the following files:

wU6_Saturday_Schedule
pU6_Cake_Flyer

You will save your file as:

Lastname_Firstname_U6_Bridal_Show

Project Results

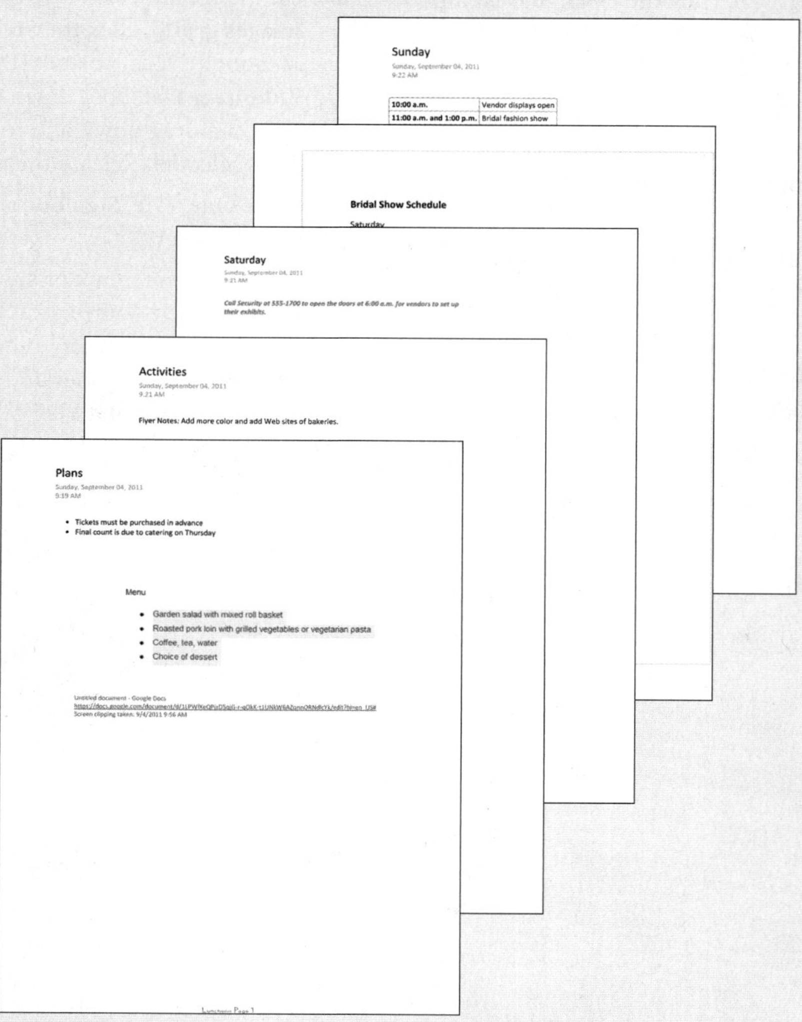

Figure 6.1

A OneNote Notebook and Google Doc Created by a Director of Sales for a Hotel; Your Own College Notebook (continued)

1 On your storage device, create a new folder named **All In One Unit 6** Open **OneNote**. If any open notebooks display, in the Navigation Bar, right-click the notebook name, and then on the shortcut menu, click **Close This Notebook**. Create a new notebook stored on your computer. Using your own name, as the notebook **Name,** type **Lastname_Firstname_U6_Bridal_Show** Click the **Browse** button, navigate to your **All In One Unit 6** folder, and then click **Select**. Click **Create Notebook**.

2 Rename *New Section 1* as **Luncheon** In the **Navigation Bar**, right-click and create a **New Section Group** named **Program** In the **Program** section group, add two new sections named **Schedule** and **Special Events**

3 In the **Navigation Bar**, click **Schedule** to make the section active. Create two pages in the section, and name them **Saturday** and **Sunday**

4 In the **page tabs list**, click the **Saturday** page tab. Click below the date and time, and type **Call Security at 555-1700 to open the doors at 6:00 a.m. for vendors to set up their exhibits.** Select the text in the container, and then, on the Mini toolbar, click the **Quick Styles** button and click **Heading 4**.

5 On the **Saturday** page, click below the note related to security and time. On the Ribbon, click the **Insert tab**, and then in the **Files group**, click the **File Printout** button. From your student files, insert **wU6_Saturday_Schedule**, and then wait a few moments for the Inserting Documents indicator to complete.

6 In the **page tabs list**, click the **Sunday** page tab. Click below the date and time, and then type **10:00 a.m.** press Tab, type **Vendor displays open** and then press Enter. Type **11:00 a.m. and 1:00 p.m.** press Tab, type **Bridal fashion show** and then press Enter. Type **2:00 p.m.** press Tab, type **Workshops begin** and then press Enter. Type **4:00 p.m.** press Tab, and then type **Show closes** Select all the text in the first column, and then on the Mini toolbar, click **Bold**.

7 In the **Navigation Bar**, click **Luncheon**. In the **Page Title** box, type **Plans** to title the first page of this section. Click below the date and time to display a note container. Type **Tickets must be purchased in advance** and press Enter Type **Final count is due to catering on Thursday** Select the two lines you typed, and then on the Mini toolbar, click the **Bullets** button.

8 Display the **Special Events** section. In the **Page Title** box, type **Activities** to title the first page of this section. Open **Windows Explorer**, navigate to the location where your student files are stored, and then double-click the file **pU6_Cake_Flyer** to open it in PowerPoint. On the taskbar, click the **OneNote** icon to redisplay the OneNote window. On the Ribbon, click the **View tab**, and then in the **Views group**, click **Dock to Desktop**.

9 On the **Activities** page, click below the date and time, and then type **Flyer Notes:** Press Spacebar and then type two formatting suggestions for making this flyer more effective—for example, *Add more color and add Web sites of bakeries*. In the OneNote window, on the **View tab**, click **Dock to Desktop** to turn off the feature. On the taskbar, click the **OneNote** icon to minimize the window but leave OneNote open. **Close** the PowerPoint window.

10 Start your Web browser and navigate to **http://docs.google.com**. Sign in to your Google account. Click the **Create new** button, and then click **Document**.

11 Type **Menu** and press Enter two times. Type the following lines, pressing Enter after each line:

Garden salad with mixed roll basket

Roasted pork loin with grilled vegetables or vegetarian pasta

Coffee, tea, water

Choice of dessert

12 Select the last four lines of text. On the toolbar, click the **Bulleted list** button. With the text selected, click **Format**, click **Line spacing**, and then click **1.5**. On the taskbar, click the **OneNote** icon to maximize the window. In the **Luncheon section**, display the **Plans page**. On the Ribbon, click the **Insert tab**, in the **Images group** click **Screen Clipping**, and then capture the menu text from Google Docs.

13 In the **Navigation Bar**, rearrange your notebook so the **Special Events** section is before the **Schedule** section.

14 **Print** your notebook or submit electronically as directed by your instructor. If submitting electronically, you can either use Windows Explorer to compress the folder and submit your work as a .zip file or submit a PDF of your notebook. **Close** OneNote, **Sign out** of Google Docs, and then **Close** your browser.

(Unit 6 Case Project continues on the next page)

Unit 6 Case Project

A OneNote Notebook and Google Doc Created by a Director of Sales for a Hotel; Your Own College Notebook (continued)

Your Personal College Notebook

Set up a OneNote notebook for your college classes. Create a section for each course, and if appropriate for you, add sections for any extracurricular activities in which you participate. For example, you could have a section for *Volleyball* or *Student Government* or *Jazz Band*. If you have a job, you could create a section for your job with notes about your work schedule, phone numbers for your boss and fellow workers, and so on. Within each section, add pages for assignments or for class notes. For class notes, it is useful to have a page for each date you are in class. You could also create a section for a specific project, such as a term paper, and then use it to store links to Web sites and other references that you plan to use for the paper. Save your notebook as **Lastname_Firstname_U6_College_Notebook** and submit to your instructor as directed.

Glossary

.ics file format A computer file format known as iCalendar that enables Internet users to send meeting requests and tasks to other Internet users via email.

3-D The shortened term for *three-dimensional*, which refers to an image that appears to have all three spatial dimensions—length, width, and depth.

Absolute cell reference In Excel, a cell reference that refers to cells by their fixed position in a worksheet; an absolute cell reference remains the same when the formula is copied.

Access time The amount of time it takes a device from the request for the information to the delivery of that information.

Account The reference to your user name, password, and allotted storage space.

Accounting Number Format The Excel number format that applies a thousand comma separator where appropriate, inserts a fixed U.S. dollar sign aligned at the left edge of the cell, applies two decimal places, and leaves a small amount of space at the right edge of the cell to accommodate a parenthesis for negative numbers.

Active badge A small device you wear that transmits a unique infrared signal every 5 to 10 seconds used to establish your location.

Active cell The cell, surrounded by a black border, ready to receive data or be affected by the next Excel command.

Address bar (Internet Explorer) The area at the top of the Internet Explorer window where you can type a URL.

Address bar (Windows Explorer) The area at the top of a folder window that displays your current location in the folder structure as a series of links separated by arrows.

Adware Spyware that generates pop-up ads and targeted banner ads.

Aero Flip 3D In Windows, a feature that arranges your open windows in a three-dimensional stack that you can flip through quickly without having to click buttons on the taskbar.

Aero Peek In Windows, a technology that assists you when you have multiple windows open by allowing you to *peek* at either the desktop that is behind open windows or at a window that is hidden from view by other windows; then, you can move the mouse back into the taskbar to close the peek.

Aero Shake In Windows, a feature in which you can shake an active window by moving the mouse vigorously back and forth on the title bar to have all other open windows minimize; you can then restore all the windows by shaking the open window again.

Aggregate functions Calculations such as MIN, MAX, AVG, and SUM that are performed on a group of records.

Aggregator A program that remembers your RSS subscription list, checks each site on a regular basis, alerts you if new information has been published, and organizes the results for you.

Air mouse A motion-sensing device that does not need to rest on a surface to function. It works as it moves through the air recognizing the typical forward, back, left, and right motions made by a mouse.

Algorithm A series of steps that describe what a computer program must do to solve a logical or mathematical problem or to perform a task.

Alignment The placement of paragraph text relative to the left and right margins.

All Programs An area of the Start menu that displays all the available programs on your computer system.

All-in-one computer A compact version of a desktop computer for individual use and that combines the system unit and monitor into one.

American Psychological Association (APA) One of two commonly used style guides for formatting research papers.

Analog signals Real-world signals, like light and sound, sent via continuous waves that vary in strength and quality; the signal sent over a wired telephone.

Analog-to-digital converter (ADC) A microchip that contains the circuitry to convert an analog signal into a digital signal.

Anchor The symbol that indicates to which paragraph an object is attached.

AND Condition A condition in which only records where all of the values are present in the selected fields.

Android 2.2 Google's operating system for mobile devices.

Anonymity The ability to convey a message without disclosing your name or identity.

Antivirus software Software developed to protect a computer from computer viruses.

Append To add on to the end of an object; for example, in a database, to add records to the end of an existing table.

Application Another term for a *program*.

Application software Programs that direct your system's hardware to carry out specific tasks; for example, doing word processing, playing a game, or computing numbers on a worksheet.

Appointment An Outlook calendar activity occurring at a specific time and day that does not require inviting people or reservations.

Appointment area The area on the right side of the screen in Outlook that displays a one-day view of the current day's calendar entries.

Appointment form The area in which you enter detailed information about an appointment in Outlook.

Archive A single file that contains two or more files stored in a compressed format along with additional information about each file—like the name and file lengths—so that proper reconstruction is possible.

Arguments The values that an Excel function uses to perform calculations or operations.

Arithmetic logic unit (ALU) The portion of the central processing unit (CPU) that performs arithmetic operations, which return numeric values, and logical operations, which return a value of true or false.

Arithmetic operations One of two groups of operations performed by the arithmetic logic unit (ALU).

Arithmetic operators The symbols +, -, *, /, %, and ^ used to denote addition, subtraction (or negation), multiplication, division, percentage, and exponentiation in an Excel formula.

Arrow keys A set of four keys, on a keyboard, located to the left of the number pad that move the cursor up, down, left, or right. Also referred to as the cursor-movement keys.

Artistic effects Formats applied to images that make pictures resemble sketches or paintings.

Ascending order A sorting order that arranges text in alphabetical order (A to Z) or numbers from the lowest to highest number.

ASCII (American Standard Code for Information Interchange) A character coding format that uses seven bits and can represent 128 different characters. It is used in notebooks, personal computers, and computers that make information available on the Internet.

Asymmetric key encryption A computer security process in which two different keys are used. Also referred to as public key encryption.

At sign (@) The symbol that separates the two parts of an e-mail address.

Authentication The request for a user name and password to verify that you are the person authorized to use the computer. Also called login.

Auto Fill An Excel feature that generates and extends values into adjacent cells based on the values of selected cells.

AutoComplete (Excel) A feature that speeds your typing and lessens the likelihood of errors; if the first few characters you type in a cell match an existing entry in the column, Excel fills in the remaining characters for you.

AutoCorrect A feature that corrects common typing and spelling errors as you type, for example changing *teh* to *the*.

AutoFit An Excel feature that adjusts the width of a column to fit the cell content of the widest cell in the column.

Automation The replacement of human workers by machines and computer-guided robots.

AutoNumber data type A data type that describes a unique sequential or random number assigned by Access as each record is entered and that is useful for data that has no distinct field that can be considered unique.

AutoPlay A Windows 7 feature that lets you choose which program to use to start different kinds of media, such as music CDs, or CDs and DVDs containing photos; it displays when you plug in or insert media or storage devices.

AutoSum Another name for the SUM function.

Auxiliary storage The action of keeping software and data so it can be accessed in the future. Also referred to as mass storage, storage, or secondary storage.

AVERAGE function An Excel function that adds a group of values, and then divides the result by the number of values in the group.

Axis A line that serves as a frame of reference for measurement and that borders the chart plot area.

Back and Forward buttons Buttons at the top of a folder window that work in conjunction with the address bar to change folders by going backward or forward one folder at a time.

Backbone A high-capacity transmission lines that carry WAN traffic.

Background application The term that refers to an application that is open and loaded into random access memory but not currently active.

Background Removal A command that removes unwanted portions of a picture so that the picture does not appear as a self-contained rectangle.

Backstage tabs The area along the left side of Backstage view with tabs to display various pages of commands.

Backstage view A centralized space for file management tasks; for example, opening, saving, printing, publishing, or sharing a file. A navigation pane displays along the left side with tabs that group file-related tasks together.

Backup The process of duplicating programs, data, and information saved on one secondary storage medium to another.

Backup software Copies data from the computer's hard disk to backup devices such as flash drives, CDs, DVDs, an external hard drive, or an online storage location.

Bad sector A portion of the disk that is unable to store data reliably.

Bandwidth The theoretical maximum amount of data that can be transmitted through a given communications channel at one time, usually per second.

Banner ad An ad that is not actually part of the Web page but is supplied separately by an ad network.

Bar code reader A device that scans an item's Universal Product Code (UPC) to update inventory, ensure correct pricing, and track packages.

Bar tab stop A vertical bar that displays at a tab stop.

Base The starting point when you divide the amount of increase by it to calculate the rate of increase.

Best Fit An Access command that adjusts the width of a column to accommodate the column's longest entry.

Beta versions Versions of forthcoming programs that are in the final phases of testing and are sometimes available for free.

Between ... And operator A comparison operator that looks for values within a range.

Bevel A shape effect that uses shading and shadows to make the edges of a shape appear to be curved or angled.

Bibliography A list of cited works in a report or research paper also referred to as *Works Cited*, *Sources*, or *References*, depending upon the report style.

Binary digit The digits 0 and 1, which are used to visualize current flowing or not flowing through a circuit, bit. In the Off state, represented by the digit 0, current is not flowing through the circuit. In the On state, represented by the digit 1, current is flowing through the circuit.

Binary number representation A unique pattern of 0s and 1s that represent a keyboard character.

Bing Microsoft's search engine.

Biometric authentication The use of a physical trait or behavioral characteristic to identify an individual.

Biometric input device A device that uses physical or chemical features of an individual's body to provide a unique method of identification.

BIOS (basic input/output system) A set of start-up instructions permanently encoded in the computer's read-only memory (ROM) that checks and initializes such devices as your keyboard, display screen, and disk drives.

Bit A single circuit, or path, that either contains a current or does not. It is the smallest piece of data a computer can process.

Bitmap An image format that can display millions of colors and can be used to share images with others who may be using different graphic programs.

Bitmapped graphics (raster graphics) An image formed by a pattern of tiny dots, each corresponding to one pixel on the computer's display. Also called raster graphics.

Bitmapped image A representation of an image as a matrix of dots called picture elements (pixels).

Black hat Another term for cracker.

Black slide A slide that displays at the end of an electronic slide show indicating that the presentation is over.

Blank database A database that has no data and has no database tools—you must create the data and the tools as you need them.

Blog The Internet equivalent of a journal or diary.

Blu-ray Disc (BD) An optical storage format developed to enable recording, rewriting, and playing back of high-definition video (HD), as well as storing large amounts of data. The format offers more than five times the storage capacity of traditional DVD.

Bluetooth A popular short-range wireless radio transmission technology that does not require direct line of site and enables all kinds of devices—desktop computers, mobile phones, printers, pagers, PDAs, and more—within 30 feet of each other to communicate automatically and wirelessly.

Body The text of a letter.

Boolean search Searches that use logical operators (AND, OR, and NOT) to link the words you are searching for and gain more precise control over your search results.

Boot disk A storage device, like a USB drive, CD, DVD, or network device, which in case of an emergency or boot failure, can load a reduced version of the operating system for troubleshooting purposes. Also called emergency disk.

Boot sector virus A virus that installs itself on the beginning tracks of your hard drive where code is stored that automatically executes every time you start your computer.

Booting The process of loading the operating system into memory.

Bootstrap loader A startup program permanently encoded in the computer's read-only memory (ROM) that locates the operating system on your hard drive and loads it into RAM.

Bot Also known as an Internet bot or a Web robot, a program that can run automated tasks over the Internet typically at a higher rate than would be possible for a human alone A bot can connect the commandeered computers (zombies) in a denial of service attack to the controller.

Botnet A group of unprotected commandeered computers, under the control of a hacker's program (zombies), used to create a denial of service (DoS) attack on a network.

Bps rate Stands for bits per second, it is the unit of measurement for data exchange between two modems.

Broadband A communication transmission that uses a wide band of frequencies to transports high volumes of data at high speeds, typically greater than 1 Mbps megabits per second (Mbps).

Browser cache A section of your hard drive in which copies of Web pages visited for the first time are stored.

Browsing The term used to describe the process of using your computer to view Web pages.

Browsing history The information stored by Internet Explorer about the sites you have visited and the information you have typed into a site.

Buffer An area of random access memory assigned to running programs and some devices to keep them from interfering with each other's use of memory.

Bug An error in a program.

Bulleted list A list of items with each item introduced by a symbol such as a small circle or check mark, and which is useful when the items in the list can be displayed in any order.

Bullets Text symbols such as small circles or check marks that precede each item in a bulleted list.

Bus topology The physical layout of a network where every node, whether it is a computer or peripheral device, is attached to a common cable or pathway referred to as the bus.

Business use of Office Web Apps For business use, Office Web Apps requires a SharePoint site with appropriate software and a SharePoint user ID provided by the organization.

Business-to-business e-commerce (B2B) The use of the Internet by one business to provide another business with the materials, services, and/or supplies it needs to conduct its operations.

Business-to-consumer e-commerce (B2C) The use of the Internet by a business to supply consumers with services, information, or products.

Busy The default setting for Outlook appointments you set and used when you are in the building but are unavailable.

Byte A group of eight bits used to represent one character of data, such as the essential numbers (0–9), the basic letters of the alphabet like the character Z (uppercase and lowercase), and the most common punctuation symbols.

Cable access A type of broadband Internet connection that uses a television's cable service provider to connect to the Internet.

Cable modems Devices that enable computers to access the Internet by means of a cable TV connection and deliver data at bandwidths of 1.5 to 6 Mbps.

Cache memory A small unit of ultrafast memory built into or near the processor that stores frequently or recently accessed program instructions and data, increasing the computer's overall performance.

Calculated field A field that stores the value of a mathematical operation.

Calendar A component of Outlook that stores your schedule and calendar-related information.

Calendar folder The default location for Outlook's calendar information.

Campus area network (CAN) A network that is usually smaller than a WAN and includes several LANs that are housed in various locations on a college campus or business park.

CAPTCHA An acronym for *Completely Automated Public Turing Test To Tell Computers and Humans Apart*, which is a program that protects Web sites against bots by generating and grading tests that humans can pass but current computer programs cannot.

Caption A property setting that displays a name for a field in a table, query, form, or report other than that listed as the field name.

Carbon copy The term, rarely used now, that refers to an old-fashioned copy made with carbon paper.

Cascade An arrangement of open windows on your screen that display in a single stack fanned out so that each title bar is visible.

Case sensitive In a password, a program's ability to distinguish between uppercase letters and lowercase letters.

Category 5 (Cat-5) The fifth generation of twisted-pair data communication cable that contains four pairs of twisted-copper wire but only uses two of the four and supports speeds up to 100 Mbps over a maximum distance of 328 feet.

Category 5 enhanced (Cat-5e) Uses all four pairs of twisted-copper cable, enabling speeds up to 1,000 Mbps over a short distance and is backward compatible with ordinary Cat-5.

Category 6 (Cat-6) The sixth generation of twisted-pair cable that utilizes all four pairs of twisted-copper cable, supports speeds up to 1 gigabit per second, expands available bandwidth from 100 MHz for Cat-5e to 200 MHz, has superior immunity from external noise, and is backward compatible with Cat-5 and Cat-5e.

Category axis The area along the bottom of a chart that identifies the categories of data; also referred to as the *x-axis*.

Category labels The labels that display along the bottom of a chart to identify the categories of data; Excel uses the row titles as the category names.

CD drives One type of optical storage that holds up to 700 MB of data.

CD-R Optical storage media to which you "write-once" but read many times. This means that after data has been written to the disc, you cannot erase or write over it but you can read it as many times as needed. CD-R is short for compact disc–recordable.

CD-ROM Optical storage media from which data can be read many times; it cannot be changed or erased. CD-ROM is short for compact disc read-only memory.

CD-RW Optical storage media that allows data that has been saved to be erased and rewritten, thus providing full read/write capabilities. CD-RW is short for compact disc–rewritable.

Cell In a cellular telephone network, a limited geographical area in which a signal can be broadcast.

Cell (Excel) The intersection of a column and a row.

Cell (Word) The box at the intersection of a row and column in a Word table.

Cell address Another name for a cell reference.

Cell content Anything typed into a cell.

Cell reference The identification of a specific cell by its intersecting column letter and row number.

Cell sites In a cellular telephone network, an area in which a transmitting station repeats the system's broadcast signals so that the signal stays strong.

Cell style A defined set of formatting characteristics, such as font, font size, font color, cell borders, and cell shading.

Cellular telephones Computing devices that started out as analog devices but are now all digital systems that provide high-speed access to transmit voice, text, images, and video data.

Center alignment An arrangement of text in which the text is centered between the left and right margins.

Center tab stop A tab stop in which the text centers around the tab stop location.

Central processing unit (CPU) A chip that contains processing circuitry that enables it to behave as the brain of the computer, control all the functions performed by the other components, and processes all the commands it receives from software. The CPU is also called the microprocessor or just processor.

Character code An established procedure used to create bit patterns for the letters, numbers, and symbols on your keyboard.

Characters The letters, numbers, and symbols on your keyboard.

Chart (Excel) The graphic representation of data in a worksheet; data presented as a chart is usually easier to understand than a table of numbers.

Chart area The entire chart and all of its elements.

Chart Elements box The box in the Chart Tools tabs from which you can select a chart element so that you can format it.

Chart layout The combination of chart elements that can be displayed in a chart such as a title, legend, labels for the columns, and the table of charted cells.

Chart Layouts gallery A group of predesigned chart layouts that you can apply to an Excel chart.

Chart sheet A workbook sheet that contains only a chart.

Chart style The overall visual look of a chart in terms of its graphic effects, colors, and backgrounds; for example, you can have flat or beveled columns, colors that solid or transparent, and backgrounds that are dark or light.

Chart Styles gallery A group of predesigned chart styles that you can apply to an Excel chart.

Chart types Various chart formats used in a way that is meaningful to the reader; common examples are column charts, pie charts, and line charts.

Chipset A collection of chips that work together to provide the switching circuitry needed by the microprocessor to move data throughout the computer by linking the microprocessor's system bus with the computer's input/output buses.

Ciphertext The result of encryption performed on plaintext.

Circuit switching The method used in the public switched telephone system that requires a direct connection between the communicating devices.

Citation A note inserted into the text of a research paper that refers the reader to a source in the bibliography.

Click The action of pressing the left mouse button.

Click wheel A pad that looks like a circle and uses a circular motion to move through song lists, movie lists, or photos. The click wheel is the method of navigation on the iPod and the iTouch.

Clickstream The trail of Web links you have followed to get to a particular site.

Client Any type of computer—PC, Mac, desktop, notebook, or even a handheld device—that is connected to a network and contains the software that enables it to send requests to a server.

Client/server network A network designation in which connection to one or more servers is accomplished through one or more clients that can be a desktop PC, notebook, workstation, or terminal.

Clip A single media file, for example art, sound, animation, or a movie.

Clip Art Predefined graphics included with Microsoft Office or downloaded from the Web.

Clipboard A temporary storage area for information that you have copied or moved from one place and plan to use somewhere else.

Cloud computing The use of Web servers on the Internet—for example a SkyDrive or SharePoint library—to store files and run applications.

Clusters A storage unit, on a hard disk or platter, that consists of two or more sectors.

CMOS (complementary metal-oxide semiconductor) A startup program permanently encoded in the computer's read-only memory (ROM) that controls a variety of actions including starting the power-on self-test and verifying that other components of the system are functioning correctly.

Coaxial cable A broadband data transmission media that carries data at transfer rates of 10 Mbps and consists of a center copper wire surrounded by insulation, which is then surrounded by a layer of braided wire; data travels through the center wire, and the braided wire provides a shield against electrical interference.

Codecs The technical name for compression/decompression or code/decode algorithms that reduce file size.

Cold boot Starting a computer that has not yet been turned on.

Collaboration software Software that helps people work together to complete a shared task or achieve a shared goal. Also referred to as groupware or workgroup support systems.

Collisions The corruption of network data caused when two computers transmit simultaneously.

Column A vertical group of cells in a worksheet.

Column break indicator A single dotted line with the text *Column Break* that indicates where a manual column break was inserted.

Column chart A chart in which the data is arranged in columns and is useful for showing data changes over a period of time or for illustrating comparisons among items.

Column heading The letter that displays at the top of a vertical group of cells in a worksheet; beginning with the first letter of the alphabet, a unique letter or combination of letters identifies each column.

Comma Style The Excel number format that inserts thousand comma separators where appropriate and applies two decimal places; Comma Style also leaves space at the right to accommodate a parenthesis when negative numbers are present.

Command An instruction to a computer program that causes an action to be carried out.

Command line user interface A user interface that requires you to type in a command, one line at a time, in a strict syntax using reserved keywords.

Comments area In an Outlook appointment form, the area in the lower half in which you can enter information about the appointment not otherwise specified in the form.

Commerce The selling of goods or services with the expectation of making a reasonable profit.

Commercial software Software that must be purchased.

Common dialog boxes The dialog boxes, such as Save and Save As, provided by the Windows programming interface that enable programs to have a consistent appearance and behavior.

Common field A field in one or more tables that stores the same data.

Communication devices Devices that determine efficient data-transfer pathways, boost signal strength, and facilitate digital communication; for example modems, cables, ports, and devices like smartphones, tablets, and notebooks.

Communications The high-speed exchange of information within and between computers or other communication devices like modems, cables, ports, smartphones, tablets, and notebooks.

Communications channel (link) The transmission media on which the message is sent from one location to another.

Comparison operators Symbols used to evaluate each field to determine if it is the same (=), greater than (>), less than (<), or in between a range of values as specified by the criteria.

Complimentary closing A parting farewell in a business letter.

Compound criteria Multiple conditions in a query or filter.

Compress To reduce the size of a file; compressed files take up less storage space and can be transferred to other computers, for example in an e-mail message, more quickly than uncompressed files.

Compressed file A file that has been reduced in size and thus takes up less storage space and can be transferred to other computers quickly.

Computer An electronic device that performs the four basic operations that comprise the information processing cycle—input, processing, output, and storage.

Computer crime Computer-based activities that violate state, federal, or international laws.

Computer ethics A branch of philosophy that deals with computer-related moral dilemmas to guide your decisions.

Computer forensics A complex branch of forensic science that pertains to legal evidence found in computers and digital storage media.

Computer security risk Any event, action, or situation—intentional or not—that could lead to the loss or destruction of your computer system or the data it contains.

Computer system A collection of related components—including both hardware and software—that work together to accomplish a task. Also just called system.

Computer virus Hidden code that attaches itself to your program, files, or e-mail messages.

Conditional format A format that changes the appearance of a cell—for example, by adding cell shading or font color—based on a condition; if the condition is true, the cell is formatted based on that condition, and if the condition is false, the cell is *not* formatted.

Congestion In a packet switching network, a performance interruption that occurs when a segment of the network experiences an overloaded.

Connections In LinkedIn, the people with which you have some level of online relationship.

Connector A physical receptacle that is visibly located on the outside system unit or extending from an expansion card. Plugs for various devices are inserted into the connectors.

Constant value Numbers, text, dates, or times of day that you type into a cell.

Consumer-to-consumer e-commerce (C2C) The online exchange or trade of goods, services, or information between individual consumers.

Contact A person or organization about whom you can save information such as street and e-mail addresses, telephone and fax numbers, birthdays, and pictures.

Contacts In Outlook, a component that serves as your e-mail address book for storing information about people, organizations, and businesses with whom you communicate.

Contacts In Windows Live, the people you have added to your Hotmail account for email, instant messaging, sharing calendars, and sharing documents.

Contacts folder The default location for Outlook's Contacts information.

Content control In a template, an area indicated by placeholder text that can be used to add text, pictures, dates, or lists.

Contention The problem that occurs when two computers try to access the LAN at the same time.

Contention management The plan of action a network follows when a collision occurs.

Context sensitive A command associated with activities in which you are engaged; often activated by right-clicking a screen item.

Context sensitive command A command associated with activities in which you are engaged.

Contextual tabs Tabs that are added to the Ribbon automatically when a specific object, such as a picture, is selected, and that contain commands relevant to the selected object.

Control unit The portion of the central processing unit that, under the direction of an embedded program, switches from one stage to the next and performs the action of that stage.

Convergence The merging of disparate objects or ideas and even people into new combinations and efficiencies.

Cookie A small text file stored on your computer's hard disk by Web sites that you visit.

Cooling fan A fan within the system unit, often part of the power supply that keeps the system cool.

Copy A command that duplicates a selection and places it on the Clipboard.

Copy-protected software Programs that include some mechanism to ensure that you do not make or run unauthorized copies.

COUNTIF function A statistical function that counts the number of cells within a range that meet the given condition; this function has two arguments—the range of cells to check and the criteria.

Courtesy copy Represented by the letters *Cc*, a copy of an e-mail message that is sent to a recipient who needs to view the message.

Cracker Hackers who become obsessed with gaining entry to highly secure computer systems.

Criteria (Access) Conditions in a query that identify the specific records for which you are looking.

Criteria (Excel) Conditions that you specify in a logical function.

Crop A command that reduces the size of a picture by removing vertical or horizontal edges.

Crosshair pointer A pointer that indicates that you can draw a shape.

Crosstab query A query that uses an aggregate function for data that can be grouped by two types of information and displays the data in a compact spreadsheet-like format.

Currency data type An Access data type that describes monetary values and numeric data that can be used in mathematical calculations involving data with one to four decimal places.

Cursor-movement keys A set of four keys, on a keyboard, located to the left of the number pad that move the cursor up, down, left, or right. Also referred to as the arrow keys.

Custom software Software designed for specialized fields or businesses and is tailor-made to suit their exact needs.

Cut A command that removes a selection and places it on the Clipboard.

Cyberbullying Situations in which one or more individuals harass or threaten another individual less capable of defending himself or herself, using the Internet or other forms of digital technology.

Cybercrime Crimes carried out by means of the Internet.

Cybergangs Groups of hackers working together to coordinate attacks, post online graffiti, or engage in other malicious conduct.

Cyberlaw A legal field dealing with tracking and combating computer-related crime.

Cyberspace The intangible, nonphysical territory that the Internet encompasses.

Cyberstalking Using the Internet, social networking sites, e-mail, or other electronic communications to repeatedly harass or threaten a person and disrupt his or her life.

Data Facts about people, events, things, or ideas.

Data (Excel) Text or numbers in a cell.

Data bar A cell format consisting of a shaded bar that provides a visual cue to the reader about the value of a cell relative to other cells; the length of the bar represents the value in the cell—a longer bar represents a higher value and a shorter bar represents a lower value.

Data diddling The modification of data by altering accounts or database records so that it is difficult or impossible to tell that they have stolen funds or equipment.

Data marker A column, bar, area, dot, pie slice, or other symbol in a chart that represents a single data point; related data points form a data series.

Data point A value that originates in a worksheet cell and that is represented in a chart by a data marker.

Data projector An output device that projects your computer's video output on a screen for an audience to view.

Data series Related data points represented by data markers; each data series has a unique color or pattern represented in the chart legend.

Data source In Access, table or tables from which a form, query, or report retrieves its data.

Data source In Word, a list of variable information, such as names and addresses, that is merged with a main document to create customized form letters or labels.

Data transfer rate The rate at which two modems can exchange data; it is measured in bits per second and is referred to as the bps rate.

Data type The characteristic that defines the kind of data that can be entered into a field, such as numbers, text, or dates.

Database An organized collection of facts about people, events, things, or ideas related to a specific topic or purpose.

Database management system Database software that controls how related collections of data are stored, organized, retrieved, and secured; also known as a *DBMS*.

Database template A preformatted database designed for a specific purpose.

Datasheet view The Access view that displays data organized in columns and rows similar to an Excel worksheet.

Date line The first line in a business letter that contains the current date; the line is positioned just below the letterhead if a letterhead is used.

Date Navigator A one-month, or multiple-month, view of the calendar in Outlook that you can use to display specific days in the month.

DBMS An acronym for *database management system.*

Dead link (broken link) A link to a document or feature that has disappeared and is no longer accessible on the Web.

Decimal tab stop A tab stop in which the text aligns with the decimal point at the tab stop location.

Dedicated devices A device that focuses on a specific activity, for example, the Kindle DX.

Default The term that refers to the current selection or setting that is automatically used by a computer program unless you specify otherwise.

Denial of service (DoS) attack A form of network vandalism in which an attacker attempts to make network services unavailable to legitimate users of the service by bombarding the services with meaningless data.

Descending order A sorting order that arranges text in reverse alphabetical order (Z to A) or numbers from the highest to lowest number.

Deselect The action of canceling the selection of an object or block of text by clicking outside of the selection.

Design grid The lower area of the Query window that displays the design of the query.

Design view The Access view that displays the underlying structure or design of an object—the data is not displayed.

Desktop The opening screen that displays after the operating system loads and simulates your work area.

Desktop computer A computer that consists of a system unit, an independent monitor, for individual use in a fixed location such as a home or office.

Destination table (Access) The table to which you import or append data.

Detail sheets The worksheets that contain the details of the information summarized on a summary sheet.

Device drivers Programs containing specific instructions to allow a particular brand and model of input or output device to communicate and function properly with the operating system.

Dial-up access A connection to the Internet using a standard telephone line.

Dialog box A small window that contains options for completing a task.

Dialog Box Launcher A small icon that displays to the right of some group names on the Ribbon, and which opens a related dialog box or task pane providing additional options and commands related to that group.

Digital camera An input device that can transfer images into your system directly through a USB or FireWire port.

Digital certificates A method of validating a user, server, or Web site.

Digital divide The disparity in computer ownership and Internet access caused by education, race, age, and geographical location.

Digital piracy The unauthorized reproduction and distribution of computer-based media.

Digital signal A signal used by digital equipment, like a computer, sent via discontinuous pulses in which the presence or absence of electronic pulses is represented by 1s and 0s.

Digital signatures A technique that guarantees a message has not been tampered with.

Digital subscriber line (DSL or xDSL) A method of Internet access available in the United States that can deliver data transfer rates of 1.54 Mbps or higher.

Digital telephony A telephone system in which the telephones and transmissions are digital offering noise-free transmission and high-quality audio.

Digital-to-analog converter (DAC) A microchip that contains the circuitry to convert a digital signal to an analog signal.

Digital video camera An input device that can transfer videos into your system directly through a USB or FireWire port.

Digitization The transformation of data such as voice, text, graphics, audio, and video into digital form.

Direct broadcast satellite (DBS) A consumer satellite technology that uses a reception dish to receive digital signals at microwave frequencies directly from geostationary satellites broadcast at a bandwidth of 12 Mbps.

Directory A file folder on a disk in which you store files.

Disk cleanup utility A utility program that improves system performance and increases storage space by removing files that you no longer need.

Disk defragmentation programs Utility programs that reorganize data on the disk so that file pieces are reassembled as one chunk of disk space, which decreases disk search time.

Disk scanning program A program that detects and resolves physical and logical problems on a disk. Also known as an error checking program.

Displayed value The data that displays in a cell.

Distributed denial of service (DDoS) attack An attack where multiple networked systems are involved in a denial of service (DoS) attack.

Document properties Details about a file that describe or identify it, including the title, author name, subject, and keywords that identify the document's topic or contents; also known as *metadata*.

Documentation A collection of printed or online material that provides instructions and brief tutorials.

Domain name An organization's unique name on the Internet, which consists of a chosen name combined with a top level domain such as *.com* or *.org* or *.gov*.

Domain name registration A process by which individuals and organizations register a *unique* domain name with a service organization, such as InterNIC, and are assigned a *unique* Internet address (IP address) that will be associated with that domain name.

Domain Name System (DNS) A system used by the Internet to link domain names with their corresponding numerical IP addresses, functioning like a phone book for the Internet.

Dot leader A series of dots preceding a tab.

Double-click The action of pressing the left mouse button twice in rapid succession while holding the mouse still.

Downloading Transferring files from another computer to your computer, as in downloading music from iTunes.

Drag The action of holding down the left mouse button while moving your mouse.

Drag and drop A technique by which you can move, by dragging, selected text from one location in a document to another.

Drawing object A graphic object, such as a shape, diagram, line, or circle.

Drive An area of storage that is formatted with a file system compatible with your operating system and is identified by a drive letter.

Drive activity light The light on the front of some computers that lights up when the hard disk is being read from or written to.

Drive bays Slots within the system unit that accommodate your computer's storage devices, such as the hard disk drive, CD, or DVD drive.

Drive imaging software Creates a mirror image of the entire hard disk.

Driver A program containing instructions that make a peripheral device, like an external hard drive, printer, or DVD player, usable by an operating system.

DSL modem A device similar to a traditional telephone modem in that it modulates and demodulates analog and digital signals for transmission over communications channels however DSL modems use signaling methods based on broadband technology providing higher transfer speeds.

Dual inline memory modules (DIMM) A RAM module that fits into special slots on the motherboard and has a168-pin connector and a 64-bit data transfer rate.

Dumpster dive The act of going through the garbage of an individual or enterprise to obtain personal or sensitive data.

DVD drives One type of optical storage that holds up to 17 GB of data.

DVD-R Optical storage media that operates the same way as CD-R; you can write to the disc once and read from it many times.

DVD-ROM Optical storage media from which data can only be read; it cannot be changed or erased. DVD-ROM stands for digital video or versatile disc read-only memory.

DVD-RW Optical storage media that allows data that has been saved to be erased and rewritten, thus providing full read/write capabilities.

DVD+R Optical storage media that operates the same way as CD-R; you can write to the disc once and read from it many times.

DVD+RW Optical storage media that allows data that has been saved to be erased and rewritten, thus providing full read/write capabilities.

DVI (digital visual interface) port An interface used with LCD monitors.

E-book reader An electronic reader that receives books in electronic form as downloads from an electronic bookstore accessed via the Internet.

E-commerce (electronic commerce) The use of networks or the Internet to carry out business of any type.

E-discovery The process in which documents that exist in electronic form are searched for, located, and obtained for the purpose of being used in a civil or criminal case. Also referred to as electronic discovery.

E-learning The use of computers and computer programs to replace traditional classrooms and the time-place specificity of learning.

E-mail (electronic mail) A system that enables you to send and receive messages over a network.

E-mail address A unique cyberspace identity for a particular recipient that follows the form myname@somedomain.com.

E-mail attachment Any type of computer file—document, photo, audio, or video—that is included with an e-mail message.

E-tailer Web-based retailers.

E-waste Obsolete, discarded computer equipment.

EBCDIC (extended binary coded decimal interchange code) An eight-bit character code format used in IBM mainframe computers and some midrange systems.

Edit The actions of making changes to text or graphics in an Office file.

Editing The process of modifying a presentation by adding and deleting slides or by changing the contents of individual slides.

Electronic mailing list A system that automatically broadcasts messages to all individuals on a mailing list.

Ellipsis A set of three dots indicating incompleteness; when following a command name, indicates that a dialog box will display.

Email A method of exchanging messages via the Internet where the message resides in the recipient's mailbox until he or she signs in to read it.

Embedded operating system A specialized operating system designed for specific applications.

Embedded processors Processors designed and programmed to perform only the tasks intended to be done by a specific device.

Emoticon In instant messaging, an image that represents facial expressions.

Employee monitoring The practice of an employer observing employees' phone calls, e-mails, Web browsing habits, and computer files.

Enclosures Additional documents included with a business letter.

Encryption A coding or scrambling process that renders a message unreadable by anyone except the intended recipient.

Encryption key A formula that makes a plaintext message unreadable.

Endnote In a research paper, a note placed at the end of a document or chapter.

Enhanced keyboards A keyboard containing additional keys, such as media control buttons that adjust speaker volume and access the optical disc drive, and Internet controls that open e-mail, a browser, or a search window with a single keystroke.

Enhanced ScreenTip A ScreenTip that displays more descriptive text than a normal ScreenTip.

Enterprise A unit of economic organization or activity that provides goods, services, or both to individuals and to other enterprises.

Ergonomics The field of study concerned with matching your posture and body design to your equipment and your work environment.

Ethernet The only local area network standard for large and small businesses.

Ethical hacker Hackers or crackers who have turned professional, offering their services to companies hoping to use their expertise to improve their computer systems' defenses.

Evil twin A phony WiFi hot spot.

Exabyte (EB) A unit of measurement for computer memory and disk capacity approximately equal to one quintillion bytes.

Excel table A series of rows and columns that contains related data that is managed independently from the data in other rows and columns in the worksheet.

Exclusion operator A symbol in a Web search string, usually a minus sign (-), used to instruct the search software to omit displaying results that contain the word or phrase following the exclusion.

Execution cycle In the processing cycle, the phase consisting of the execute and store operations.

Expand Formula Bar button An Excel window element with which you can increase the height of the Formula Bar to display lengthy cell content.

Expand horizontal scroll bar button An Excel window element with which you can increase the width of the horizontal scroll bar.

Expansion cards Additional circuit boards that contain the circuitry for peripheral devices, like enhanced sound cards and network interface cards, which are not normally included as standard equipment. Also referred to as expansion boards, adapter cards, or adapters.

Expansion slots Receptacles, located within the system unit, which accept additional circuit boards or expansion cards.

Explode The action of pulling out one or more pie slices from a pie chart for emphasis.

ExpressCard Credit card–sized devices that fits into a designated slot to provide expanded capabilities such as wireless communication, additional memory, multimedia, or security features.

Expression A formula.

Extended ASCII A character coding format that uses eight bits and can represent 256 different characters.

Extensible Hypertext Markup Language (XHTML) A language used to create Web pages by combining the flexibility of HTML with Extensible Markup Language (XML).

Extensible Markup Language (XML) A language that allows Web page developers to create their own set of rules to define how data is to be represented on the Web.

Extract The action of decompressing—pulling out—files from a compressed form.

Facebook The largest of the social networking sites used to keep in touch, post photos, share links, and distribute information with friends or by business to promote themselves and their products.

Facsimile transmission (fax) The process of sending an image of a document over a telephone line.

Fat client A client that accesses the server for data, but does its own processing independently.

Favorites bar A toolbar in Internet Explorer 8 that displays directly below the Address bar and to which you can add or drag Web addresses you use frequently.

Fax modem A computerized version of a standalone fax machine.

Fiber-optic cable A broadband transmission medium that provides transfer rates of 10 Gbps and consists of thin strands of glass or plastic about the diameter of a human hair arranged in bundles, called optical cables that carry data by means of pulses of light.

Fiber-optic service An Internet connection that uses fiber-optic cable.

Field A single piece of information that is stored in every record and formatted as a column in a database table.

Field (Word) A placeholder that displays preset content, such as the current date, the file name, a page number, or other stored information.

Field list A list of the field names in a table.

Field properties Characteristics of a field that control how the field displays and how data can be entered in the field.

Fields In a mail merge, the column headings in the data source.

File A collection of information that is stored on a computer under a single name, for example a text document, a picture, or a program.

File compression utility A utility program that enables the exchange of programs and data efficiently by reducing the size of a file by as much as 80 percent without harming the data.

File infector Viruses that are attached to program files like documents created in Word or spreadsheets created in Excel.

File manager A program that helps you organize and manage the data stored on your disk.

File Printout A OneNote feature that inserts information from a file as a printed copy in the page; this feature is useful because text in the printout can be searched in the same manner as other content in OneNote.

File properties Information about a file such as its author, the date the file was last changed, and any descriptive tags.

File server A high-capacity, high-speed computer with a large hard disk dedicated to make program and data files available to users on a network who have been granted access permission.

File tab In Microsoft Office, the first tab on the Ribbon that displays everything one can do *with* a file; for example, print, save, send, and so on.

File Transfer Protocol (FTP) A way that files can be transferred over the Internet that is especially useful when the files are too large to send by e-mail.

Fill The inside color of an object.

Fill Color The inside color of text or of an object.

Fill handle The small black square in the lower right corner of a selected cell.

Filter The process of displaying only a portion of the data based on matching a specific value to show only the data that meets the criteria that you specify.

Find and Replace (Excel) A command that searches the cells in a worksheet—or in a selected range—for matches and then replaces each match with a replacement value of your choice.

FiOS An acronym for fiber-optic service.

Firewall A program or device to access the Internet but strictly limits the ability of outside users to access local, corporate, or personal data.

Firewire (1394 Port) An interface created by Apple that offers high-speed connections for peripherals, especially ones that need greater throughput like video cameras and audio transmissions.

First principle of good database design A principle of good database design stating that data is organized in tables so that there is no redundant data.

Flame An Internet message that expresses an opinion without holding back any emotion and are frequently seen as being confrontational and argumentative.

Flash drive A portable storage device that uses solid-state circuitry and has no moving parts. Also referred to as solid-state drives or SSDs.

Flash memory Nonvolatile, electronic memory that stores data electronically on a chip in sections known as blocks.

Flash memory cards Portable, solid-state, nonvolatile, flash memory storage systems that are wafer-thin, and capable of storing as much as 64 GB of data. They are used with smartphones, MP3 players, digital video cameras, and other portable digital devices.

Flash memory reader A slot or compartment into which the flash memory card is inserted so its content can be read and transferred to RAM.

Flat database A simple database file that is not related or linked to any other collection of data.

Flexible OLED displays (FOLED) An extremely thin, flexible, and lightweight output display that can be paper-thin and appear as posters on walls or be made so small and flexible that they can be worn on your wrist and used to watch a movie or surf the Web.

Floating object A graphic that can be moved independently of the surrounding text characters.

Floating point standard A method set by the Institute of Electrical and Electronics Engineers (IEEE), that has no fixed number of digits before or after the decimal point making it suitable to represent very small or very large numbers.

Folder A container in which you store files.

Folder structure The hierarchy of folders in Windows 7.

Folder window Displays the contents of the current folder, library, or device, and contains helpful parts so that you can navigate—explore within the organizing structure of Windows.

Font A set of characters with the same design and shape.

Font styles Formatting emphasis such as bold, italic, and underline.

Footer (PowerPoint) Text that displays at the bottom of every slide or that prints at the bottom of a sheet of slide handouts or notes pages.

Footer (Word) A reserved area for text or graphics that displays at the bottom of each page in a document.

Footnote In a research paper, a note placed at the bottom of the page.

Foreground application The term that refers to the application that is open, loaded into random access memory, and is active and visible on the monitor.

Foreign key The field that is included in the related table so the field can be joined with the primary key in another table for the purpose of creating a relationship.

Forgery Alteration of Internet data to make it appear as if it came from one place when it really came from another.

Form A database object used to enter data, edit data, or display data from a table or query.

Form factor The layout of components mounted within the system unit.

Form view The Access view in which you can view the records, but you cannot change the layout or design of the form.

Format (Excel) Changing the appearance of cells and worksheet elements to make a worksheet attractive and easy to read.

Format as you type The Excel feature by which a cell takes on the formatting of the number typed into the cell.

Format Painter An Office feature that copies formatting from one selection of text to another.

Formatting The process of establishing the overall appearance of text, graphics, and pages in an Office file—for example, in a Word document.

Formatting (PowerPoint) The process of changing the appearance of the text, layout, and design of a slide.

Formatting marks Characters that display on the screen, but do not print, indicating where the Enter key, the Spacebar, and the Tab key were pressed; also called nonprinting characters.

Formula An equation that performs mathematical calculations on values in a worksheet.

Formula AutoComplete An Excel feature that, after typing an = (equal sign) and the beginning letter or letters of a function name, displays a list of function names that match the typed letter(s), and from which you can insert the function by pointing to its name and pressing the Tab key or double-clicking.

Formula Bar An element in the Excel window that displays the value or formula contained in the active cell; here you can also enter or edit values or formulas.

Fragmented A term used to refer to a disk with scattered data.

Free An indicator displayed by Outlook indicating you are available for appointments.

Free-form snip When using Snipping Tool, the type of snip that lets you draw an irregular line, such as a circle, around an area of the screen.

Freeware Software given away for no charge but with the restriction that you cannot turn around and sell it for profit.

Freeze Panes A command that enables you to select one or more rows or columns and freeze (lock) them into place; the locked rows and columns become separate panes.

Friends In Windows Live Messenger, the people that you approve, using an invitation-acceptance process, before you can share information and chat.

Full backup Copies all files and data on the entire hard disk.

Full-screen snip When using Snipping Tool, the type of snip that captures the entire screen.

Full-Screen Window Preview In the Aero Peek technology, the ability to *peek* at a window that is hidden from view by other windows.

Function A predefined formula—a formula that Excel has already built for you—that performs calculations by using specific values in a particular order or structure.

Function keys A row of keys, on a keyboard, labeled F1 through F12 or F15 located above the letters and numbers on your keyboard.

Fund A sum of money set aside for a specific purpose.

Gallery An Office feature that displays a list of potential results instead of just the command name.

General format The default format that Excel applies to numbers; this format has no specific characteristics—whatever you type in the cell will display, with the exception that trailing zeros to the right of a decimal point will not display.

General fund The term used to describe money set aside for the normal operating activities of a government entity such as a city.

General-purpose applications Programs to accomplish frequently performed tasks.

Gigabits per second (Gbps) A data transfer rate of approximately 1 billion bits per second.

Gigabyte (GB) A unit of measurement for computer memory and disk capacity approximately equal to one billion bytes.

Global Positioning System (GPS) A satellite based system consisting of a cluster of 27 Earth-orbiting satellites that enable portable GPS receivers to determine their location with an accuracy of 109 yards or less.

Goal Seek A what-if analysis tool that finds the input needed in one cell to arrive at the desired result in another cell.

Google docs A free application from Google with which you can store, create, edit, and share documents online using your Google account.

Google Groups A free service provided by Google that permits group members interested in discussing a common topic to collaborate on shared Web pages.

Graphic A picture, clip art image, chart, or drawing object.

Graphical user interface (GUI) A user interface that uses graphics and the point-and-click technology of the mouse to give commands to the operating system and your application programs.

Graphics Interchange Format (GIF) A 256-color graphic file format that uses lossless compression and is best for simple images with large areas of solid color.

Group names In Microsoft Office, the name assigned to related commands on a Ribbon tab.

Groups On the Office Ribbon, the sets of related commands that you might need for a specific type of task.

Hacker ethic Unwritten code of conduct of hackers, which forbids the destruction of data.

Hackers Computer hobbyists who enjoy pushing computer systems to their limits.

Handheld computer A computer that fits in the palm of your hand or in a pocket and allows you to use a stylus or virtual keyboard. Also referred to as a personal digital assistant or PDA.

Hanging indent An indent style in which the first line of a paragraph extends to the left of the remaining lines, and that is commonly used for bibliographic entries.

Hard copy Output viewed in printed form.

Hard disk controller An electronic circuit board that provides an interface between the CPU and the hard disk's electronics.

Hard disk drive A high-capacity, high-speed, random access, magnetic storage device, usually housed in the system unit, that consists of several rapidly rotating disks called platters on which your programs, data, and processed results are stored. Also referred to as a hard disk.

Hardware All the physical components of the computer and its related devices.

Header (PowerPoint) Text that prints at the top of each sheet of slide handouts or notes pages.

Header (Word) A reserved area for text or graphics that displays at the top of each page in a document.

Heat sink A heat-dissipating component, located on some central processing units that drain heat from the chip.

Hibernate state A power state to conserve battery power on a laptop; saves your open documents and programs on your hard disk and then turns off your computer.

Hierarchy An arrangement where items are ranked and where each level is lower in rank than the item above it.

High-fidelity viewing The viewing quality when documents created in the full desktop version of Office 2010 and then opened in the corresponding Office Web App display all elements and formatting, even though some more sophisticated features are not available in Office Web Apps.

History list A list of previously visited Web pages.

Holographic storage A storage device that uses two laser beams to create a pattern on photosensitive media, resulting in a three-dimensional image similar to the holograms you can buy in a novelty shop.

Home and educational programs General-purpose software that is used for less complex or more personal activities like personal finance and tax preparation software.

Home area network (HAN) A personal and specific use of network technology that provides connectivity between users and devices located in or near one residence.

Home page On your own computer, the Web page you have selected—or that is set by default—to display on your computer when you start Internet Explorer; when visiting a Web site, the starting point for the remainder of the pages on that site.

Home page (index page) The default page that is displayed automatically when you enter a site at its top level.

Honeypots Computers baited with fake data and purposely left vulnerable to study how intruders operate in order to prepare stronger defenses.

Horizontal window split box (Excel) An Excel window element with which you can split the worksheet into two horizontal views of the same worksheet.

Host A computer that can receive requests and reply to those requests.

Host name The name of the group or institution hosting the site.

Hotspots Locations like a coffee shop or restaurant that provides Internet access for devices fitted with wireless technology.

Hot swapping Refers to the ability to connect and disconnect devices without shutting down your computer.

Hotmail Free Web-based email from Microsoft.

HTML See Hypertext Markup Language (HTML).

http The protocol prefix for HyperText Transfer Protocol.

Hub A simple, inexpensive device that joins multiple computers together in a single network but does not manage the traffic between the connections, which usually results in frequent collisions.

Hybrid network A network created from the combination of both wired and wireless technology.

Hybrid sleep state An option that combines the sleep and hibernate power state and places open documents and programs in both RAM and on your hard disk.

Hyperlink (Link) Elements in an electronic document that act as the connector to another place in the same document or to an entirely different document.

Hypertext A markup language feature that enables objects like text, pictures, music, and programs to be linked to each other.

Hypertext Markup Language (HTML) The language used to format documents that can be opened using any Web browser.

Hypertext Transfer Protocol (Http) The Internet standard that supports the exchange of information on the Web.

iCalendar A computer file format that enables Internet users to send meeting requests and tasks to other Internet users via email with the extension of .ics.

Icons Small images that represent computer resources such as programs, data files, and network connections.

Identity theft Obtaining an individual's personal information, without their permission, in order to impersonate them.

IF function A function that uses a logical test to check whether a condition is met, and then returns one value if true, and another value if false.

IM The abbreviation for instant messaging.

Image editors Sophisticated versions of graphic programs used to edit and create images and save them in a variety of file formats.

Import The process of copying data from another file, such as a Word table or an Excel workbook, into a separate file, such as an Access database.

Inclusion operator A symbol in a Web search string, usually a plus sign, used to instruct the search software to only display results that contain the word or phrase following the inclusion operator.

Incremental backup Copies only those files that have been created or changed since the last backup.

Info tab The tab in Backstage view that displays information about the current file.

Information Data that is organized in a useful manner.

Information overload A feeling of anxiety and incapacity when you are presented with more information than you can handle.

Information processing (IPOS) cycle The four basic computing operations consisting of input, processing, output, and storage.

Information warfare The use of information technologies to corrupt or destroy an enemy's information and industrial infrastructure.

Infrared A wireless transmission medium that carries data via beams of light through the air, no wires are required, but the transmitting and receiving devices must be in line of sight or the signal is lost.

Infrared data association (IrDA) A wireless communication device that uses infrared technology to transfer data at rates of 4 Mbps from your PDA to your notebook or other PDA; the transmitting device must be in the line of site.

Inkjet printers Relatively inexpensive nonimpact printers that are popular choices for home users, and produce excellent color output by spraying ionized ink from a series of small jets onto a sheet of paper.

Inline object An object or graphic inserted in a document that acts like a character in a sentence.

Innermost sort field When sorting on multiple fields in Datasheet view, the field that will be used for the second level of sorting.

Input The entering of data and instructions into your computer for processing.

Input devices Devices, connected to the system unit, which enable you to enter data into the computer for processing.

Input/output (I/O) bus The electrical pathway that extends beyond your microprocessor to communicate with your input and output devices usually through expansion slots.

Insert Worksheet button Located on the row of sheet tabs, a sheet tab that, when clicked, inserts an additional worksheet into the workbook.

Insertion point A blinking vertical line that indicates where text or graphics will be inserted.

Inside address The name and address of the person receiving the letter; positioned below the date line.

Instant messaging The real-time communication between two or more participants over the Internet.

Instruction cycle In the processing cycle, the phase consisting of the fetch and decode operations.

Instruction set A unique list of instructions associated with a specific processor.

Integrated circuit (IC) A circuit that carries an electrical current and contain millions of transistors. Also referred to as a chip.

Integrated peripherals Devices embedded within the system unit case and that generally include the power supply, cooling fans, memory, CD drive, DVD drive, and internal hard drive.

Integrated program A single program that manages an entire business or set of related tasks.

Intelligent keyboard An on-screen keyboard to which software has been added to provide the user with such features as suggestions for misspelled words, corrections for grammar mistakes, magnification on the screen of text, visual confirmation of keystrokes by displaying an enlarged image of the key hit on the screen, and permitting editing features such as cut, copy, and paste with a simple touch of the screen.

Interactive white boards Devices popular in educational settings that when connected with a computer and some sort of large video display enable the video display to become touch sensitive allowing it to be used to control the computer.

Internal speaker A speaker located within the system unit, useful only for the beeps you hear when the computer starts up or encounters an error.

Internet (Net) A global computer network made up of thousands of privately and publicly owned computers and networks that grew and interlinked, over time, into one giant network; the Internet is a network of networks.

Internet access provider Companies or businesses that provide access to the Internet for free, for a fixed monthly charge, or for an itemized per use fee.

Internet address (IP address) A unique address assigned to every computer connected to the Internet; it consists of four parts such as 128.254.108.7.

Internet backbone The main high-speed routes through which data travels.

Internet Protocol (IP) The lower layer of the TCP/IP suite of protocols that handles the addressing scheme used by the Internet and embedded within each packet enabling the packets to reach their destination.

Internet Protocol address (IP Address) A numerical identification and logical address assigned to devices participating in a computer network.

Internet service A set of standards (protocols) that define how two types of programs—a client, such as a Web browser that runs on the user's computer, and a server—can communicate with each other through the Internet.

Internet service provider (ISP) A company that provides Internet access along with other features.

Internet telephony (VoIP or Voice over Internet Protocol) Making use of the Internet for real-time voice communication.

Internet TV The ability to view television shows, videos, and movies over the Internet, for no additional cost, via download or streaming video.

Interoperability The ability of the Internet to exchange data between computers regardless of the brand, model, or operating system the computers are running.

Intranet A password-protected network controlled by the company and accessed only by employees, clients, or vendors.

iOS The operating system used on Apple's iPhone.

IPOS cycle The four basic computing operations consisting of input, processing, output, and storage.

IP spoofing Sending a message with an IP address disguised as an incoming message from a trusted source.

Is Not Null A criteria that searches for fields that are not empty.

Is Null A criteria that searches for fields that are empty.

Join line In the Relationships window, the line joining two tables that visually indicates the related field and the type of relationship.

Joint Photographic Experts Group (JPEG) A graphic format that can store up to 16.7 million colors and are best for complex images such as photographs.

Joystick A pointing device used to navigate the on-screen cursor or object through the movement of a vertical rod mounted on a base with one or two buttons.

JPEG An acronym for Joint Photographic Experts Group, that is a common file type used by digital cameras and computers to store digital pictures; JPEG is popular because it can store a high-quality picture in a relatively small file.

Jump List A list that displays when you right-click a button on the taskbar, and displays locations (in the upper portion) and tasks (in the lower portion) from a program's taskbar button; functions as a mini start menu for a program.

Justified alignment An arrangement of text in which the text aligns evenly on both the left and right margins.

Kernel The central part of the operating system that manages memory, files, and devices; launches applications; and allocates system resources.

Key interception The stealing of a symmetric key encryption.

Keyboard An input device that uses switches and circuits to translate keystrokes into a signal a computer understands.

Keyboard shortcut A combination of two or more keyboard keys, used to perform a task that would otherwise require a mouse.

Keyloggers Spyware that records all the keystrokes you type—such as passwords, account numbers, or conversations—and then relays them to others.

Keypad A smaller and more compact keyboard found on smartphones. On this device, each key represents multiple letters so you need to strike a key one to four times to get the desired character entered as input.

KeyTip The letter that displays on a command in the Ribbon and that indicates the key you can press to activate the command when keyboard control of the Ribbon is activated.

Kilobits per second (Kbps) A data transfer rate of approximately 1 thousand bits per second.

Kilobyte (KB) A unit of measurement for computer memory and disk capacity equal to 1,024 bytes or characters.

Labels Another name for a text value; it usually provides information about number values.

Lands Flat reflective areas on optical storage media that bounce the light back to a light-sensing device, and correspond to the binary digit 1.

Landscape orientation A page orientation in which the paper is wider than it is tall.

Laser printer A high-resolution nonimpact printer that uses an electrostatic reproductive technology similar to that used by copiers.

Last-mile problem The problems caused by the inability of homes or businesses to access the PSTN's high-speed fiber-optic cables, along with the bottleneck of data on the last mile of twisted-pair phone lines connecting homes and businesses.

Last-mile technologies Technologies like digital telephone standards as DSL that use twisted-pair wiring and high-speed wired services such as coaxial cable and FIOS that bridge the gap from the Internet to a residence.

Latency In a packet switching network, the delay caused in by the examination of a given packet by many routers.

Layout The arrangement of elements, such as title and subtitle text, lists, pictures, tables, charts, shapes, and movies, on a PowerPoint slide.

Layout view The Access view in which you can make changes to a form or to a report while the object is open.

Leader characters Characters that form a solid, dotted, or dashed line that fills the space preceding a tab stop.

Leased line Usually a permanent fiber-optic or telephone connection set up by a telecommunication carrier that enables continuous, end-to-end communication between two points.

Left alignment (Excel) The cell format in which characters align at the left edge of the cell; this is the default for text entries and is an example of formatting information stored in a cell.

Left alignment (Word) An arrangement of text in which the text aligns at the left margin, leaving the right margin uneven.

Left tab stop A tab stop in which the text is left aligned at the tab stop and extends to the right.

Legacy technology A term used to refer to technology, devices, or applications that are being phased out for suitable replacements.

Legend A chart element that identifies the patterns or colors that are assigned to the categories in the chart.

Lettered column headings The area along the top edge of a worksheet that identifies each column with a unique letter or combination of letters.

Letterhead The personal or company information that displays at the top of a letter.

Level 1 (L1) cache A unit of 4 KB to 16 KB of ultrafast memory included in the microprocessor chip that runs at approximately 10 nanoseconds. It is the fastest memory. Also referred to as primary cache.

Level 2 (L2) cache A unit of up to 512 KB of ultrafast memory that can be located within the microprocessor, but further from the registers than Level 1 cache.

Level 3 (L3) cache A unit of ultrafast memory that is located outside of the processor on a separate cache chip on the motherboard but in close proximity to the microprocessor. It is usually found in servers and workstations.

Library A collection of items, such as files and folders, assembled from various locations.

Line break indicator A small nonprinting bent arrow that displays where a manual line break was inserted.

Line chart A chart type that displays trends over time; time displays along the bottom axis and the data point values are connected with a line.

Line spacing The distance between lines of text in a paragraph.

Link A connection to data in another file.

Link rot Results from hyperlinks that no longer work and Web pages that have been removed or restructured.

LinkedIn A professional social networking site that enables you to maintain relationships and communicate with classmates and colleagues, past and present.

Linux A freeware operating system for personal computers.

Liquid crystal displays (lcds) A flat screen display that uses electric current to move crystals and either block light or let it through, creating the images and colors viewable on the display. Also referred to as flat-panel displays.

List level An outline level in a presentation represented by a bullet symbol and identified in a slide by the indentation and the size of the text.

Live Preview A technology that shows the result of applying an editing or formatting change as you point to possible results—*before* you actually apply it.

Local area network (LAN) A type of network that uses cables, radio waves, or infrared signals to link computers or peripherals, such as printers, within a small geographic area, such as a building or a group of buildings.

Local exchange switch A digital device in the public switch telephone network, located in the local telephone company's central office, capable of handling thousands of calls.

Local loop The area served by the subscriber loop carrier in the public switched telephone network.

Location Any disk drive, folder, or other place in which you can store files and folders.

Location awareness (position awareness) A feature of some cell phones that make use of a GPS enabled chip to pinpoint the location of the cell phone

Logic bomb Hidden computer code that sits dormant on your system until a certain event or set of circumstances triggers it into action.

Logical address A unique name, assigned by the software in use to each node on the network.

Logical functions A group of functions that test for specific conditions and that typically use conditional tests to determine whether specified conditions are true or false.

Logical operations One of two groups of operations performed by the arithmetic logic unit (ALU).

Logical operators Operators that combine criteria using AND and OR; with two criteria, AND requires that both conditions be met and OR requires that either condition be met.

Logical test Any value or expression that can be evaluated as being true or false.

Lossless compression In data compression, a method used to reduce a file size so that it can be completely restored, without flaw, when it is decompressed.

Lossy compression In data compression, a method used to reduce a file size that permanently eliminates information that is not perceived by human beings.

Mac OS The original Macintosh operating system that popularized the use of the graphical user interface.

Mac OS X Lion Apple's operating system released in 2011; touts over 250 new features.

Mac OS X Snow Leopard The version of Mac OS X released in 2009; occupies up to 50 percent less RAM than the previous version.

Machine cycle A four-step process performed in the central processing unit (CPU) that involves the fetch, decode, execute, and store operations. Also referred to as the processing cycle.

Magnetic storage devices Disks or platters that are coated with magnetically sensitive material and used to record information by transforming electrical impulses into a varying magnetic field.

Magnetic stripe card reader A device that can detect and read information stored on magnetic strips that are usually located on the back of credit cards, gift cards, and other cards of similar use.

Mail merge A Microsoft Word feature that joins a main document and a data source to create customized letters or labels.

Main document In a mail merge, the document that contains the text or formatting that remains constant.

Mainframes Powerful servers that execute many computer instructions concurrently. Also referred to as enterprise servers.

Maintenance release The decimal portion of a version number.

Major unit The value in a chart's value axis that determines the spacing between tick marks and between the gridlines in the plot area.

Malware Software designed to damage or infiltrate a computer system without the owner's consent or knowledge.

Manual column break An artificial end to a column to balance columns or to provide space for the insertion of other objects.

Manual line break The action of ending a line, before the normal end of the line, without creating a new paragraph.

Manual page break In Word, the command that forces a page to end at the insertion point location, and then places any subsequent text at the top of the next page.

Margin The space between the text and the top, bottom, left, and right edges of the paper.

Mass storage The action of keeping software and data so it can be accessed in the future. Also referred to as storage, auxiliary storage, or secondary storage.

Massively multiplayer online role-playing games (MMORGs) An extension of multiplayer online gaming in which the participants assume the characteristics of a predesigned character or a self-designed character and play the game as that character.

MAX function An Excel function that determines the largest value in a selected range of values.

Media The technology that encompasses pictures, sound, and video.

Media center PC An all-in-one entertainment that provides easy access to photos, TV, movies, and the latest in online media; all from the comfort of your couch.

MEDIAN function An Excel function that finds the middle value that has as many values above it in the group as are below it; it differs from AVERAGE in that the result is not affected as much by a single value that is greatly different from the others.

Megabits per second (Mbps) A data transfer rate of approximately 1 million bits per second.

Megabyte (MB) A unit of measurement for computer memory and disk capacity approximately equal to one million bytes.

Memo style The default print style in Outlook that prints the text of selected items one at a time, for example the contents of an e-mail message.

Memory Chips, located on your motherboard or within your CPU, that retain instructions and data to be accessed by the CPU.

Memory cards Small circuit boards that holds several RAM chips and lock into special slots on the motherboard. Also referred to as memory modules.

Memory chip An integrated circuit devoted to memory storage.

Memory modules Small circuit boards that hold several RAM chips and lock into special slots on the motherboard. Also referred to as memory cards.

Memory resident Refers to programs that stay in random access memory (RAM) during the time the system is powered on.

Menu A list of commands within a category.

Menu bar A group of menus at the top of a program window.

Menu-driven user interface A user interface that displays on-screen options for the user to select.

Merge & Center A command that joins selected cells in an Excel worksheet into one larger cell and centers the contents in the new cell.

Message Bar The area directly below the Ribbon that displays information such as security alerts when there is potentially unsafe, active content in an Office 2010 document that you open.

Message board Similar to a newsgroup, but easier to use and does not require a newsreader.

Message header The basic information about an e-mail message, such as the sender's name, the date sent, and the subject.

Metadata Details about a file that describe or identify it, including the title, author name, subject, and keywords that identify the document's topic or contents; also known as *document properties*.

Metropolitan area network (MAN) A network developed for a city or town, usually larger than a LAN but smaller than a WAN and owned by a single government or organization.

MICR reader A device that scans and automatically inputs characters printed with special magnetic ink.

Microblogging The practice of posting small pieces of digital content like text, pictures, links, or short videos on the Internet.

Microprocessor An incredibly complex integrated circuit chip that performs many different functions depending on the instructions sent to it by the program you are running. Also referred to as central processing unit (CPU) or processor.

Microsoft Office 2010 A Microsoft suite of products that includes programs, servers, and services for individuals, small organizations, and large enterprises to perform specific tasks.

Microsoft SharePoint Collaboration software for an enterprise that makes use of Web sites so individuals can share information, manage documents, and publish reports.

Microsoft Windows The most popular standalone operating system.

Microsoft Windows 7 A standalone operating system released in 2009; more efficient than its predecessor, Windows Vista.

Microsoft Windows Mobile A mobile operating system designed for smartphones and PDAs.

Microsoft Windows Server 2008 An upgrade to Microsoft Windows Server 2003; supports client/server computing systems in an environment that manages multiple users and systems.

Microwaves Electromagnetic radio waves with short frequencies that travel at speeds of 1 to 10 Mbps and are used to transmit data from a source to a receiving site; microwaves get weaker as they get farther away from their source, and must travel in a straight line.

MIN function An Excel function that determines the smallest value in a selected range of values.

Minicomputer Computers that fall between workstations and mainframes in processing power. Also referred to as midrange servers.

Mini-keyboard A keyboard option available on smartphones and portable devices that has a key for each letter of the alphabet.

Mini toolbar A small toolbar containing frequently used formatting commands that displays as a result of selecting text or objects.

Minitower case A smaller version of the tower system unit case that has less internal room for components.

Mobile switching center (MSC) The part of a cellular telephone network that handles communications within a group of cells; each cell tower reports its signal strength, relative to the cellular device, to the MSC, which then switches the signal to the cell tower that provides the clearest connection for that cellular device.

Modeling (what-if analysis) The use of current information to predict things that might happen in the future.

Modem A communication device used to send and receive data from one transmission system to another; short for modulator/demodulator.

Modern Language Association (MLA) One of two commonly used style guides for formatting research papers.

Modifier keys Keys like Shift, Alt, and Ctrl that have no effect unless you hold them down and press a second key.

Modules The functions offered by an integrated program that share the same interface, enable the user to switch among them quickly, and are not available as standalone programs.

Monitors Screens that show your data and processed information.

Motherboard The circuit board that connects the central processing unit, which is anchored to the board, along with other system components.

Mouse A palm-sized input device designed to move about on a clean, flat surface.

Mouse pointer Any symbol that displays on your screen in response to moving your mouse.

Multi-core processors A processor that attempts to correct the slowdown that occurs in the processing cycle when the CPU is held up by waiting for instructions and data from slower running RAM or a hard disk.

Multifunction devices Output devices that combine inkjet or laser printers with a scanner, a fax machine, and a copier, enabling home office users to obtain all of these devices without spending a great deal of money.

Multimedia An application that involves two or more media, such as audio, graphics, or video.

Multiplayer online gaming (MMO or MMOG) A technology that, through the Internet, connects hundreds of thousands of players, located anywhere in the world, simultaneously in a virtual world that continues to exist even after the player has signed off.

Multiplexing A technique used to send more than one call over a single line.

Multitasking A process by which the CPU gives the user the illusion of performing instructions from multiple programs at once when in reality the CPU is rapidly switching between the programs and instructions.

Multitasking operating systems An operating system that enables more than one application to run at the same time.

MySpace A social network that promotes itself as a fan-powered social entertainment destination with a major focus on music.

Name Box An element of the Excel window that displays the name of the selected cell, table, chart, or object.

Nameplate The banner on the front page of a newsletter that identifies the publication; also referred to as a *banner*, *flag*, or *masthead*.

Nanoseconds A unit of time equal to one-billionth of a second.

Navigate To explore within the folder structure of Windows for the purpose of finding files and folders.

Navigate (Excel) The process of moving within a worksheet or workbook.

Navigation area An area at the bottom of the Access window that indicates the number of records in the table and contains controls (arrows) with which you can navigate among the records.

Navigation bar In a Web page, groups of links arranged vertically or horizontally on the screen from which you can navigate to other pages in the site.

Navigation Pane In Access, an area of the Access window that displays and organizes the names of the objects in a database; from here, you open objects for use.

Navigation Pane In Outlook, a column on the left side of the screen that contains panes, shortcuts, and buttons for quick access to Outlook's components and folders.

Navigation pane In Windows Explorer, the area on the left side of a folder window; it displays favorites, libraries, and an expandable list of drives and folders.

Nesting The use of parentheses to place one search string inside of another.

Netbook A computer primarily for Web browsing, e-mail, and using online services and is small in design.

Netiquette Short for Internet etiquette, the code for acceptable behavior and manners on the Internet.

Network A group of two or more computer systems linked together to exchange data and share resources, including peripherals like laser printers.

Network access point (NAP) The location at which equipment for one network service provider connects with equipment from another provider.

Network administrators Individuals who install, maintain, and support computer networks as well as interact with users, handle security, and troubleshoot problems.

Network architecture How a network functions based on its set of protocols used within the network.

Network attached storage (NAS) Storage comprised primarily of hard drives or other media used for data storage and are attached directly to a network.

Network interface card (NIC) An expansion board, necessary to make a physical connection to a network, that fits into an expansion slot built into a computer's motherboard.

Network layers Separate divisions within the protocol architecture; each division has its own function and protocol.

Network operating system (NOS) An operating system containing instructions that enable data transfer and application usage among computers and other devices connected to a local area network.

Network service provider (NSP) A company or organization that maintains the Internet backbone.

Network topology The physical layout of a LAN and the solution that the layout provides for the problem of contention.

New from existing The Word command that opens an existing document as a new unnamed document, so that you can use it as a starting point for a new document.

Newsgroup An online discussion group devoted to a single topic.

No Spacing style The Word style that inserts *no* extra space following a paragraph and uses single spacing.

Node Any device connected to a network.

Nonprinting characters Characters that display on the screen, but do not print, indicating where the Enter key, the Spacebar, and the Tab key were pressed; also called *formatting marks.*

Nonresident Refers to programs that do not stay in random access memory (RAM) the entire time the system is powered on.

Normal template The template that serves as a basis for all Word documents.

Normal view (Excel) A screen view that maximizes the number of cells visible on your screen and keeps the column letters and row numbers close to the columns and rows.

Normal view (PowerPoint) The primary editing view in PowerPoint in which you write and design your presentations; consists of the Notes pane, Slide pane, and the Slides/Outline pane.

Normalization The process of applying design rules and principles to ensure that your database performs as expected.

Note In a research paper, information that expands on the topic, but that does not fit well in the document text.

Note container In OneNote, a box on a page that can contain text, pictures, video clips, and other types of notes.

Note tag In OneNote, a descriptive term representing a category, such as *Important* or *To Do*, and a related icon that can be associated with a specific note.

Notebook A collection of files organized by major divisions and stored in a common folder in OneNote.

Notebook computer A small computer designed for portability, and popular with students and individuals who travel for business. Also referred to as a laptop.

Notes Typed text, handwritten text if you have a Tablet PC, pictures and graphics—including images and text that you capture from Web pages—audio and video recordings, and documents from other applications such as Word or Excel that you can store in OneNote.

Notes page A printout that contains the slide image on the top half of the page and notes that you have created on the Notes pane in the lower half of the page.

Notes pane The PowerPoint screen element that displays below the Slide pane with space to type notes regarding the active slide.

NOW function An Excel function that retrieves the date and time from your computer's calendar and clock and inserts the information into the selected cell.

NTFS (new technology file system) A file allocation table that contains the name of each file and the file's exact location on the disk for Windows NT, 2000, XP, Vista, and Windows 7. It provides improved security and encryption.

Nudge The action of moving an object on the page in small precise increments.

Number format A specific way in which Excel displays numbers in a cell.

Number values Constant values consisting of only numbers.

Numbered list A list of items in which each item is introduced by a consecutive number to indicate definite steps, a sequence of actions, or chronological order.

Numbered row headings The area along the left edge of a worksheet that identifies each row with a unique number.

Object window An area of the Access window that displays open objects, such as tables, forms, queries, or reports; by default, each object displays on its own tab.

Objects The basic parts of a database that you create to store your data and to work with your data; for example, tables, forms, queries, and reports.

Office Clipboard A temporary storage area that holds text or graphics that you select and then cut or copy.

Office Web Apps The online companions to Microsoft Office Word, Excel, PowerPoint, and OneNote that enable you to create, access, share, and perform light editing on Microsoft Office documents from any device that connects to the Internet and uses a supported Web browser.

Offline A computer connection status in which you are not connected to a network or to the public Internet.

OLED (organic light emitting diode) displays Emissive output devices that display images by emitting light rather than modulating transmitted or reflected light.

Onboard video Video circuitry built into the motherboard with a connector that extends out the back of the system unit case.

One-to-many relationship A relationship between two tables where one record in the first table corresponds to many records in the second table—the most common type of relationship in Access.

OneNote A Microsoft program with which you can create a digital notebook that gives you a single location where you can gather and organize information in the form of notes.

Online A computer connection status in which you are connected to a network or to the public Internet.

Online service provider (OSP) A for-profit firm that provides a proprietary network and offers special services that are available only to subscribers.

Open dialog box A dialog box from which you can navigate to, and then open on your screen, an existing file that was created in that same program.

Open source software Software whose source code—the code of the program itself—is available for you to see and use.

Operating system A computer program that manages all the other programs on your computer, stores files in an organized manner, and coordinates the use of computer hardware such as the keyboard and mouse.

Operators The symbols with which you can specify the type of calculation you want to perform in an Excel formula.

Optical character recognition (OCR) Software to automatically convert scanned text into a text file instead of a bitmapped image. Most scanners come with OCR software.

Optical mark reader (OMR) A device that scans markings made by a no. 2 pencil, or other device that produces such marks, and compares those marks against a key containing the correct answers.

Optical mouse A mouse that makes use of an LED (light-emitting diode) light on the underside of the mouse and a small camera that takes continuous images of the changes in the surface under the mouse as it is moved.

Optical storage devices Portable storage devices that make use of laser beams to read minute patterns of data encoded on the surface of plastic discs.

Option button A round button that allows you to make one choice among two or more options.

Options dialog box A dialog box within each Office application where you can select program settings and other options and preferences.

OR condition A condition in which records that match at least one of the specified values are displayed.

Order of operations The mathematical rules for performing multiple calculations within a formula.

Out of Office In Outlook, a free/busy setting that indicates that you are away from your office and not available for other meetings or appointments.

Outermost sort field When sorting on multiple fields in Datasheet view, the field that will be used for the first level of sorting.

Outlook Microsoft's application included with Microsoft Office to manage e-mail and organizational activities.

Output The display of processed data.

Output devices Devices connected to the system unit, like monitors, printers, and speakers, that enable you to view, see, and hear the results of processing operations.

Outsourcing The subcontracting of portions of a job to a third party to reduce cost, time, and energy.

Packaged software Software purchased off the shelf that is aimed at fulfilling the needs of the general public including the basic home and business user.

Packet A unit of fixed size data in a packet switching network that contains a header that indicates its origin and destination.

Packet header A portion of an Internet protocol packet that precedes its body and contains addressing and other data that is required for it to reach its intended destination.

Packet switching The method used for computer communication that does not require a single direct connection between the two communicating devices.

Pad A portable device that is larger than a smartphone but smaller than a notebook, and that uses a touchscreen for input and access to the Web and downloadable apps.

Page In OneNote, a subdivision of a section where notes are inserted.

Page break indicator A dotted line with the text *Page Break* that indicates where a manual page break was inserted.

Page group In OneNote, a group of pages that contains a page and its related subpages.

Page Layout view A screen view in which you can use the rulers to measure the width and height of data, set margins for printing, hide or display the numbered row headings and the lettered column headings, and change the page orientation; this view is useful for preparing your worksheet for printing.

Page tabs list A list on the right side of a OneNote notebook that displays the name of each page in the active section.

Page template In OneNote, a file that serves as a pattern for creating a new page; ensures a uniform page layout and design.

Pages Fixed size units used to transfer programs and data between random access memory and virtual memory.

Paging The process of transferring files from the section of hard disk identified as virtual memory to RAM and back.

Paint A program that comes with Windows 7 with which you can create and edit drawings and display and edit stored photos.

Palm OS A mobile operating system initially developed by Palm Inc. for personal digital assistants (PDAs) in 1996.

Pane (Excel) A portion of a worksheet window bounded by and separated from other portions by vertical and horizontal bars.

Paragraph symbol The symbol ¶ that represents a paragraph.

Parallel processing A technique that uses more than one processor to run two or more portions of a program at the same time.

Parenthetical citation In the MLA style, a citation that refers to items on the *Works Cited* page, and that is placed in parentheses; the citation includes the last name of the author or authors, and the page number in the referenced source.

Paste The action of placing text or objects that have been copied or moved from one location to another location.

Paste Area The target destination for data that has been cut or copied using the Office Clipboard.

Paste Options Icons that provide a Live Preview of the various options for changing the format of a pasted item with a single click.

Paste Options gallery (Excel) A gallery of buttons that provides a Live Preview of all the Paste options available in the current context.

Path A sequence of folders (directories) that leads to a specific file or folder; also, the third part of a complete URL that specifies the location of the document on the server.

Payload The dangerous actions the virus performs.

PCI (peripheral component interconnect) bus A slower bus that connects devices like hard drives and sound cards to the faster microprocessor system bus.

PDF (Portable Document Format) file A file format that creates an image that preserves the look of your file, but that cannot be easily changed; a popular format for sending documents electronically, because the document will display on most computers.

Peer-to-peer network (P2P) A network with no central control unit, all of the computers on the network are equal or peers and each decides which, if any, files will be accessible to other users on the network.

Percent for new value = base percent + percent of increase The formula for calculating a percentage by which a value increases by adding the base percentage—usually 100%—to the percent increase.

Percentage rate of increase The percent by which one number increases over another number.

Peripheral devices Components outside the system unit that are connected physically or wirelessly to the system unit and motherboard.

Personal area network (PAN) A network that connects an individual's own personal communication devices, like a notebook, cell phone, personal digital assistant, and a portable printer, arranged within a range of 30 feet or less and generally involves wireless technology.

Personal computer (PC) A computer for individual computing needs or, when connected to a network, to contribute to collaborative projects. Also referred to as a microcomputer.

Personal digital assistant (PDA) A computer for individual use and portability, that fits in the palm of your hand, and that interfaces with software to schedule appoints and open e-mail.

Personal information manager An application that enables you to store information about your contacts, your daily schedule, tasks to complete, and other information in electronic form.

Personal use of Office Web Apps For personal use, Office Web Apps is free, and requires only a Windows Live ID and a computer with an Internet connection and supported browser software; for example, Internet Explorer 7 or later, Safari 4 or later, or Firefox 3.5 or later.

Petabyte (PB) A unit of measurement for computer memory and disk capacity approximately equal to one quadrillion bytes.

Petaflop A unit of measure for evaluating computing and processing performance of supercomputers; equivalent to one quadrillion calculations per second.

Phishing An e-mail or a Web site that poses as a legitimate company, like a bank or credit agency, in an attempt to obtain personal information such as your Social Security number, user name, password, and account number.

Photo printers Inkjet or laser printers and use special inks and good-quality photo paper to produce pictures that are as good as those generated by commercial photo developers.

Phrase searching A search in which you type a phrase within quotation marks to search for only those documents that contain the exact phrase rather than some or all of the words anywhere in the document.

Physical address A unique numeric address built into the hardware; also called the data link control address, data link control/connection identifier (DLCI), or media access control (MAC) address.

Picture element A point of light measured in dots per square inch on a screen; 64 pixels equals 8.43 characters, which is the average number of digits that will fit in a cell in an Excel worksheet using the default font.

Picture styles Frames, shapes, shadows, borders, and other special effects that can be added to an image to create an overall visual style for the image.

Pie chart A chart that shows the relationship of each part to a whole.

Pinned Placing programs on the Start menu in a manner that remains until you remove them.

Pipelining A processing technique used in CPUs built with superscalar architecture.

Pits Microscopic indentations on optical storage media that do not reflect light back to the light-sensing device and correspond to the binary digit 0.

PivotTables Interactive, cross-tabulated Excel reports that summarize and analyze large amounts of data.

Pixel The smallest addressable element of a display device; abbreviated name for a *picture element*.

Placeholder A box on a slide with dotted or dashed borders that holds title and body text or other content such as charts, tables, and pictures.

Placeholder text Text in a content control that indicates the type of information to be entered in a specific location.

Plaintext A readable message with no encryption.

Platform The underlying hardware or software for a system; for example, the Web, your PC, or a smartphone.

Platters Rapidly rotating, high-capacity disks coated with magnetically sensitive material. Hard disk drives usually have two or more platters.

Plot area The area bounded by the axes of a chart, including all the data series.

Plotter A printer that produces high-quality output by physically moving ink pens over the surface of the paper.

Plug-and-Play (PnP) The capability of some operating systems to automatically detect new peripheral devices when connected to the computer, install the necessary drivers, and check for conflicts with other devices

Plug-in A software module that adds a specific feature or service to a larger system—it simply *plugs in* to the existing software.

Pod slurp USB drives, iPods, or other removable storage media used to create an unauthorized copy of confidential data.

Podcast A digital file that contains audio, images, and video and is available as a download from the Internet or released periodically by means of Web syndication.

Podcatcher An application that can automatically identify and retrieve new podcast files in a given series and make them available through a centrally maintained Web site.

Point The action of moving the mouse pointer over something on the screen.

Point and click method The technique of constructing a formula by pointing to and then clicking cells; this method is convenient when the referenced cells are not adjacent to one another.

Point of presence (POP) A wired or wireless WAN network connection point that enables users to access the WAN.

Pointer A symbol (usually an arrow) that shows the current location of on-the-screen activity.

Pointing device An input device that allows you to control the movements of your on-screen pointer.

Pointing stick A pointing device that looks like a pencil eraser usually positioned between the G, H, and B keys on notebook computers. It is pressure sensitive and is pressed and moved in various directions with the forefinger.

Points A measurement of the size of a font; there are 72 points in an inch, with 10-12 points being the most commonly used font size.

Pop-Out button A small button in the upper right corner of an Office Web Apps window that, when clicked, displays the current document in its own window with the viewing and editing menus from the Web App, but without the toolbars and tabs from the browser; allows additional space to view and edit.

Port The electronic pathway or interface for getting information into and out of the computer.

Portable Network Graphics (PNG) A patent-free graphic format alternative to GIF, PNG produces images that use lossless compression and is best suited to Web use only.

Portable storage A storage device that can be removed from one computer and inserted into another or re-inserted into the same machine with little effort. Also referred to as removable storage.

Portal A Web page that acts as a gateway to diverse sources and presents those sources in an organized way.

Portrait orientation A page orientation in which the paper is taller than it is wide.

Position awareness A feature of some cell phones that make use of a GPS enabled chip to pinpoint the location of the cell phone

Positioning performance The time that elapses from the initiation of drive activity until the hard disk has positioned the read/write head so that it can begin transferring data.

POST (power-on self-test) A startup program permanently encoded in the computer's read-only memory (ROM) activated by CMOS, that checks the circuitry and RAM, marking any locations that are defective so that they do not get used.

PostScript An automated page-description language (PDL) that describes image elements as geometric objects such as lines and arcs and consist of commands given by the program and carried out by the printer to precisely re-create the computer image on a printed page.

Power-on self-test (POST) A series of tests conducted during system startup to make sure that the computer and associated peripherals are operating correctly.

Power supply A component within the system unit that transforms the alternating current (AC) from standard wall outlets into the direct current (DC) needed for the computer's operation. It also steps the voltage down to the low level required by the motherboard.

Preemptive multitasking An environment in which programs do not run from start to finish but are interrupted or suspended in order to start or continue to run another task.

Preview Desktop In the Aero Peek technology, the ability to *peek* at the desktop that is behind open windows.

Preview pane An additional pane on the right side of the file list to display a preview of a file (not a folder) that you select in the file list.

Primary cache A unit of 4 KB to 16 KB of ultrafast memory included in the microprocessor chip that runs at approximately 10 nanoseconds. It is the fastest memory. Also referred to as Level 1 (L1) Cache.

Primary key The field that uniquely identifies a record in a table; for example, a Student ID number at a college.

Print Preview A view of a document as it will appear when you print it.

Print style In Outlook, a combination of paper and page settings applied to printed Outlook items.

Print Titles An Excel command that enables you to specify rows and columns to repeat on each printed page.

Printers An output device that produces a permanent version, or hard copy, of the contents on a computer's display screen.

Private key The decryption key used to decode an encrypted message.

Processing The manipulation of input by a program.

Processing cycle A four-step process performed in the central processing unit (CPU) that involves the fetch, decode, execute, and store operations. Also referred to as the machine cycle.

Processor An incredibly complex integrated circuit chip that performs many different functions depending on the instructions sent to it by the program you are running. Also referred to as microprocessor or central processing unit (CPU).

Productivity programs General-purpose applications that help individuals work more efficiently and effectively on both personal and business-related documents.

Professional workstation High-end desktop computers with powerful processing and output capabilities typically used by engineers, architects, circuit designers, financial analysts, and game developers.

Profile In Outlook, the feature that identifies which e-mail account you use and where related data is stored.

Profile In social networking sites, the details about yourself that you post to public Web sites; you might have a profile on social networking sites such as Windows Live, Facebook, Twitter, or LinkedIn.

Profile In Windows, a record of a specific user's preferences for the desktop theme, icons, and menu styles.

Program A set of instructions that a computer uses to accomplish a task, such as word processing, accounting, or data management; also referred to as an *application*.

Program-level control buttons In an Office program, the buttons on the right edge of the title bar that minimize, restore, or close the program.

Progress bar In a dialog box or taskbar button, a bar that indicates visually the progress of a task such as a download or file transfer.

Property Sheet A list of characteristics—properties—for fields or controls on a form or report in which you can make precise changes to each property associated with the field or control.

Proprietary file A file whose format is patented or copyright protected and controlled by a single company.

Protected View A security feature in Office 2010 that protects your computer from malicious files by opening them in a restricted environment until you enable them; you might encounter this feature if you open a file from an e-mail or download files from the Internet.

Protocol The first part of a complete URL.

Protocol prefix The letters that represent a set of communication rules used by a computer to connect to another computer.

Protocol stack A means of conceptualizing network architecture as vertical layers connected by protocols that move the data from the transmission level to the physical hardware.

Protocol suite The complete package of protocols that specify how a specific network functions.

Protocols A set of standards or rules, implemented by hardware, software, or a combination of the two, which enable network-connected devices to communicate with each other.

Pt. The abbreviation for *point*; for example when referring to a font size.

Public domain software Software that is expressly free from copyright. You can do anything you want with it, including modify it or sell it to others.

Public key The encryption key used to encrypt a message and make it unreadable except for the intended receiver.

Public key encryption A computer security process in which two different keys are used. Also referred to as *asymmetric key encryption*.

Public switched telephone network (PSTN) The global telephone system, a massive network used for data as well as voice communications, comprising various transmission media ranging from twisted-pair wire to fiber-optic cable.

Query A database object that retrieves specific data from one or more database objects—either tables or other queries—and then, in a single datasheet, displays only the data you specify.

Quick Access Toolbar In an Office program, the small row of buttons in the upper left corner of the screen from which you can perform frequently used commands.

Quick Commands The commands Save, Save As, Open, and Close that display at the top of the navigation pane in Backstage view.

Quick Styles In OneNote, combinations of formatting options that look attractive together.

Racetrack memory Memory currently under development that uses the spin of electrons to store information. This allows the memory to operate at much higher speeds than current storage media.

Radio frequency identification (RFID) An object that can be tracked by radio waves via a chip or tag somewhere in or on an object.

Radio transmissions A wireless transmission media that moves data, in a variety of forms like music, voice conversations, and photos through the air as radio frequency signals or radio waves via a transmitting device and a receiving device.

Random access memory (RAM) Nonpermanent memory, located on the motherboard, whose contents are erased when the computer's power is switched off either on purpose or accidentally.

Random access storage device A storage device that can directly get to the requested data without having to go through a sequential order.

Range Two or more selected cells on a worksheet that are adjacent or nonadjacent; because the range is treated as a single unit, you can make the same changes or combination of changes to more than one cell at a time.

Range finder An Excel feature that outlines cells in color to indicate which cells are used in a formula; useful for verifying which cells are referenced in a formula.

Range of recurrence In Outlook, the date of the final occurrence of the appointment based on its end date or the number of times an appointment occurs.

Rate = amount of increase/base The mathematical formula to calculate a rate of increase.

Ray tracing An image rendering technique that adds amazing realism to a simulated three-dimensional object by manipulating variations in color intensity that would be produced by light falling on the object from multiple directions, which is the norm in the real world.

RE: A prefix added to a reply to an e-mail message; commonly used to mean *in regard to.*

Read-only memory (ROM) A type of nonvolatile memory, located on the motherboard, in which essential start-up instructions are prerecorded by the manufacturer of your system and not erased when the system is shut down.

Read/write head A device used with magnetic storage media that writes information by transforming electrical impulses into a varying magnetic field and reads by sensing the recorded magnetic pattern and transforms it into electrical impulses that are decoded into text characters.

Reading Pane An Outlook window in which you can preview a message without opening it.

Reading view In PowerPoint, the view that displays a presentation in a manner similar to a slide show but in which the taskbar, title bar, and status bar remain available in the presentation window.

Reading View In Word, the view in which you can see how the document will look on a page; this view is useful to see the effect of changes you make in your document.

Really Simple Syndication (RSS) A feature provided by a Web site that permits a user to connect to it and receive constant updates over the Internet from that site without any further involvement.

Receiving device The component of communication that receives the transmission.

Recent Pages A button on the address bar that displays a list of recently accessed locations; the current location is indicated by a check mark.

Record In Access, all of the categories of data pertaining to one person, place, thing, event, or idea, and which is formatted as a row in a database table.

Record In a Word mail merge, a row of information that contains data for one person.

Record selector bar The bar at the left edge of a record when it is displayed in a form, and which is used to select an entire record.

Record selector box The small box at the left of a record in Datasheet view that, when clicked, selects the entire record.

Rectangular snip When using Snipping Tool, the type of snip that lets you draw a precise box by dragging the mouse pointer around an area of the screen to form a rectangle.

Recurrence pattern The frequency of an appointment, which may be daily, weekly, monthly, or yearly.

Redundant In a database, information that is repeated in a manner that indicates poor database design.

Referential integrity A set of rules that Access uses to ensure that the data between related tables is valid.

Registers Fast temporary storage areas located within a microprocessor. Some registers accept, hold, and transfer instructions or data while others perform arithmetic or logical comparisons at high speed.

Registry A database stored in read-only memory (ROM) that contains configuration information about installed peripheral devices and software.

Relational database A sophisticated type of database that has multiple collections of data within the file that are related to one another.

Relationship An association that you establish between two tables based on common fields.

Relative cell reference In a formula, the address of a cell based on the relative position of the cell that contains the formula and the cell referred to.

Remote storage Storage space on a server that is accessible from the Internet. In most cases, a computer user subscribes to the storage service and agrees to rent a block of storage space for a specific period of time. Also referred to as an Internet hard drive.

Removable storage device A portable device on which you can store files, such as a USB flash drive, a flash memory card, or an external hard drive, commonly used to transfer information from one computer to another.

Render The ability to add realism to computer graphics with three-dimensional qualities such as shadows and color variations.

Report A database object that displays the fields and records from a table or query in an easy-to-read format suitable for printing.

Resource (filename) The fourth part of a complete URL that specifies name of the file or resource to access.

Resources A term used to refer collectively to the parts of your computer such as the central processing unit (CPU), memory, and any attached devices such as a printer.

RFID reader A device used to detect radio signals being emitted from a radio frequency identification tag placed on an item.

Ribbon The user interface in Office 2010 that groups the commands for performing related tasks on tabs across the upper portion of the program window.

Ribbon tabs The tabs on the Office Ribbon that display the names of the task-oriented groups of commands.

Right alignment An arrangement of text in which the text aligns at the right margin, leaving the left margin uneven.

Right-click The action of clicking the right mouse button one time.

Right tab stop A tab stop in which the text is right aligned at the tab stop and extends to the left.

Ring topology The physical layout of a network where nodes are attached in a circular wiring arrangement.

Rogue program Programs that use a false advertisement or bogus malware scan results to scare you into purchasing fake anti-malware programs to remove the made-up security threats it claims to have found on your system.

Rootkit A malicious program disguised as a useful program.

Rotation handle A green circle that provides a way to rotate a selected image.

Rounding A procedure in which you determine which digit at the right of the number will be the last digit displayed and then increase it by one if the next digit to its right is 5, 6, 7, 8, or 9.

Router A more complex network device that provides intelligent management for a network; it has the ability to inspect the source and target of a data package and determine the best path to route data.

Row A horizontal group of cells in a worksheet.

Row heading The numbers along the left side of an Excel worksheet that designate the row numbers.

RSS An acronym for *Really Simple Syndication*, which is a syndication format popular for aggregating—gathering together—updates to blogs and news sites.

RSS feed Frequently updated content published by a Web site and delivered to a feed reader.

RSS viewer A program that displays RSS feeds to which you have subscribed.

Ruler guides Dotted vertical and horizontal lines that display in the rulers indicating the pointer's position.

Run The process in which Access searches the records in the data source included in the query design, finds the records that match the specified criteria, and then displays the records in a datasheet; only the fields that have been included in the query design display.

Safe mode An operating mode in which Windows loads a minimal set of drivers that are known to function correctly.

Salami shaving Occurs when a programmer alters a program to subtract a very small amount of money from an account for example, two cents, and diverts the funds to an embezzler's account.

Salutation The greeting line of a business letter.

Sans serif A font design with no lines or extensions on the ends of characters.

Satellite access Internet access by using a small satellite dish, which is placed outside the home and is connected to a computer with a coaxial cable.

Satellite radio A type of communications technology that broadcasts radio signals back and forth between satellites orbiting around the Earth.

Satellites Microwave relay stations in space positioned in geosynchronous orbit, which match the satellite's speed to that of the Earth's rotation, and are, therefore, permanently positioned with respect to the ground below; data is transmitted by sending and receiving microwave signals to and from Earth-based stations.

Scale to Fit Excel commands that enable you to stretch or shrink the width, height, or both, of printed output to fit a maximum number of pages.

Scaling (Excel) The process of shrinking the width and/or height of printed output to fit a maximum number of pages.

Scanner An automated form of input that copies anything you enter on a sheet of paper, including artwork, handwriting, and typed or printed text, and converts the content into a graphics image for input into a computer.

Screen capture An image file that contains the contents of a computer screen.

Screen clipping In OneNote, an image copied from part of the computer screen, a Web page, or a document.

Screenshot An image of an active window on your computer that you can paste into a document.

ScreenTip A small box that displays useful information when you perform various mouse actions such as pointing to screen elements or dragging.

Scroll arrow Arrows at the top and bottom, or left and right, of a scroll bar that when clicked, move the window in small increments.

Scroll bar A bar that displays on the bottom or right side of a window when the contents of a window are not completely visible; used to move the window up, down, left, or right to bring the contents into view.

Scroll box The box in the vertical and horizontal scroll bars that can be dragged to reposition the contents of a window or pane on the screen.

Search engine Programs that make use of databases of the Web pages they have indexed to locate information you requested in a search bar on their Web site.

Search operator Symbols or words used to fine tune a search.

Search provider A Web site that provides search capabilities on the Web.

Search term A word or phrase that describes the topic about which you want to find information.

Search utility A utility program used to search an entire hard disk or any indexed network storage device for a file.

Second principle of good database design A principle stating that appropriate database techniques are used to ensure the accuracy of data entered into a table.

Secondary storage or fixed storage Hardware that retains data even when the power is disrupted or turned off. Examples include hard disks, USB flash drives, CDs, and DVDs.

Section In OneNote, the primary division of a notebook identifying a main topic and containing related pages of notes.

Section In Word, a portion of a document that can be formatted differently from the rest of the document.

Section break A double dotted line that indicates the end of one section and the beginning of another section.

Section group In OneNote, related sections that are identified by a single name and stored as a subfolder with the same name within the notebook folder.

Section tab A tab that identifies a primary division of the active OneNote notebook.

Sectors A pie-shaped wedge unit of storage consisting of concentric tracks on a hard disk or platter. Two or more sectors form a cluster.

Secure electronic transaction (SET) Shopping security standard for merchants and customers.

Seek time The time it takes the read/write head to locate the data before reading begins.

Select To highlight, by dragging with your mouse, areas of text or data or graphics, so that the selection can be edited, formatted, copied, or moved.

Select All box A box in the upper left corner of the worksheet grid that, when clicked, selects all the cells in a worksheet.

Select query A type of Access query that retrieves (selects) data from one or more tables or queries, displaying the selected data in a datasheet; also known as a *simple select query*.

Semiconductor The material that transistors are made of that either conducts electrical current or blocks its passage through the circuit.

Sending device The component of communication that initiates the transmission.

Series A group of things that come one after another in succession; for example, January, February, March, and so on.

Serif font A font design that includes small line extensions on the ends of the letters to guide the eye in reading from left to right.

Server Computers equipped with the hardware and software that store programs and data and that make the programs and data available to you if you are connected via a network.

Server operating system An operating system installed on the server computer of a network with specific instructions for delivering programs and data over the network.

Servers A computer or device with software that manages network resources like files, e-mails, printers, and databases.

Shape (Word) A drawing object—including lines, arrows, stars, banners, ovals, and rectangles—that conveys a message by showing process or by containing and emphasizing text.

Shapes (PowerPoint) Lines, arrows, stars, banners, ovals, rectangles, and other basic shapes with which you can illustrate an idea, a process, or a workflow.

SharePoint A Microsoft technology that enables employees in an organization to access information across organizational and geographic boundaries.

Shareware More of a marketing method than a type of software. It permits a user to have a set period of time in which to "try before buying" the program.

Sheet tabs The labels along the lower border of the Excel window that identify each worksheet.

Sheet tab scrolling buttons Buttons to the left of the sheet tabs used to display Excel sheet tabs that are not in view; used when there are more sheet tabs than will display in the space provided.

Shift Click A technique in which the SHIFT key is held down to select all the items in a consecutive group; you need only click the first item, hold down SHIFT, and then click the last item in the group.

Shilling The use of a secret operative, on Internet auction sites, who bids on another seller's item to drive up the price.

Shortcut menu A context-sensitive menu that displays commands and options relevant to the selected object.

Shoulder surfing The attempt by an individual to obtain information by watching your monitor and keyboard strokes usually by looking over your shoulder.

Side by side An arrangement of open windows on your screen that appear side by side.

Side note A quick note that is written in a miniature OneNote window while working in other applications.

Silverlight A free plug-in that improves the appearance of some applications in your browser.

Simple select query Another name for a select query.

Simultaneous editing The ability for two or more individuals to edit the same file at the same time, and see the changes others make in real time.

Single File Web Page A document saved using HTML; the page opens using a Web browser.

Single inline memory modules (SIMM) A RAM module that fits into special slots on the motherboard and has a 72-pin connector and a 32-bit data transfer rate.

Site licenses Contracts between the software publisher and an organization that enable the organization to install copies of a program on a specified number of computers.

Sizing handles Small circles and squares that indicate that a picture is selected.

Skype A software application with which you can make phone calls over the Internet and participate in Web conferencing from any location in the world.

Sleep Turning off your computer in a manner that automatically saves your work, stops the fan, and uses a small amount of electrical power to maintain your work in memory; the next time you turn the computer on, you need only to enter your password (if required) and your screen will display exactly like it did when you turned off.

Sleep state An option on your computer system that places your system in a low power setting, turns off all unneeded functions, and transfers a copy of the current state of your computer to RAM.

Slide A presentation page that can contain text, pictures, tables, charts, and other multimedia or graphic objects.

Slide handouts Printed images of slides on a sheet of paper.

Slide pane A PowerPoint screen element that displays a large image of the active slide.

Slide Sorter view A presentation view that displays thumbnails of all of the slides in a presentation.

Slide transitions The motion effects that occur in Slide Show view when you move from one slide to the next during a presentation.

Slides/Outline pane A PowerPoint screen element that displays the presentation either in the form of thumbnails (Slides tab) or in outline format (Outline tab).

Small caps A font effect, usually used in titles, that changes lowercase text into capital (uppercase) letters using a reduced font size.

Smart card A credit card–sized device that combines flash memory with a tiny microprocessor, enabling the card to process as well as store information. Also referred to as a chip card, integrated circuit card or ICC.

SmartArt A designer-quality visual representation of your information that you can create by choosing from among many different layouts to effectively communicate your message or ideas.

SmartArt graphic A visual representation of information that you can create by choosing from among many different layouts to communicate your message or ideas effectively.

SmartArt Styles Combinations of formatting effects that you can apply to SmartArt graphics.

Smartphones Cellular phones that integrate mobile phone capability, computing power, and Web access.

Snap A Windows 7 feature that automatically resizes windows when you move—*snap*—them to the edge of the screen.

Snip The image captured using the Snipping Tool.

Snipping Tool A program included with Windows 7 with which you can capture an image of all or part of a computer screen, and then annotate, save, copy, or share the image via email.

Social networking site Online services that initially were created to foster relationships among people but since have extended their usage to promote business, events, bands, and other such events.

Soft copy Output that is not a permanent record, such as information displayed on a monitor or played through speakers.

Soft keyboard A keyboard that appears on a touch-sensitive screen. Also referred to as a virtual or on-screen keyboard.

Software A set of instructions that tells the computer hardware how to perform. Also referred to as a program.

Software license A contract distributed with a program that typically gives you the right to install and use the program on one computer.

Software piracy The unauthorized copying and distribution of copyrighted and licensed software.

Software suite (office suite) A collection of individual, full-featured, standalone programs, possessing a similar interface and a common command structure, which are bundled and sold together.

Software upgrading The process of keeping your version of an application current with the marketplace.

Solid-state storage device Any portable storage option that consists of nonvolatile memory chips, which retain the data stored in them even if the chips are disconnected from a computer or power source. The term *solid state* indicates that these devices have no moving parts; they consist only of semiconductors.

SONET (synchronous optical network) A physical layer of network technology that uses fiber-optic cable and carries large volumes of data over long distances; it is the standard for high-performance networks.

Sort The process of arranging data in a specific order based on the value in each field.

Sorting The process of arranging data in a specific order based on the value in a field.

Sound files Files that contain digitized data in the form of recorded live sounds or music, which are saved in one of several standardized sound formats.

Source file When importing a file, refers to the file being imported.

Spam Unsolicited messages sent in bulk over electronic mailing systems.

Sparkline A tiny chart in the background of a cell that gives a visual trend summary alongside your data; makes a pattern more obvious.

Specialized search engines Search engines that index specialized information such as names and addresses, job advertisements, quotations, or newspaper articles.

Speech recognition The conversion of spoken words into computer text.

Spider Computer programs that roam the World Wide Web via the Internet, visit sites and databases, and keep a search engine's database of Web pages up to date.

Spim A spam text message sent on a cell phone or an instant messaging service.

Spimming Spam that targets users of instant messaging.

Spin box A small box with an upward- and downward-pointing arrow that lets you move rapidly through a set of values by clicking.

Split button A button that has two parts—a button and an arrow; clicking the main part of the button performs a command and clicking the arrow opens a menu with choices.

Sponsored links Paid advertisements shown as a link, typically for products and services related to your search term; sponsored links are the way that search sites like Bing, Google, and others earn revenue.

Spooling program A program that monitors the print requests in the buffer and the busy state of the printer.

Spreadsheet Another name for a worksheet.

Spyware Software that can collect your personal information or monitor your Web surfing habits, and then distribute this information to a third party.

Squarespace A Web publishing company that provides an easy way to create and maintain an online presence with a Web site and blog.

Stack An arrangement of open windows on your screen that displays each window across the width of the screen in a vertical stack.

Standalone operating system An operating system that works on a desktop computer, laptop, notebook, or any portable computing device.

Standalone program A program that can be purchased and installed separately, function independently, and is fully self-contained.

Standard user account A user account that lets you use most of the capabilities of the computer, but requires permission from an administrator to make changes that affect other users or the security of the computer.

Star topology The physical layout of a network that uses a central wiring device, which can be a hub, switch, or computer to which all nodes are connected.

Start menu A list of choices that provides access to your computer's programs, folders, and settings when you press the Start button.

Statistical functions Excel functions, including the AVERAGE, MEDIAN, MIN, and MAX functions, which are useful to analyze a group of measurements.

Status bar The area along the lower edge of an Office program window that displays file information on the left and buttons to control how the window looks on the right.

Status bar (Excel) The area along the lower edge of the Excel window that displays, on the left side, the current cell mode, page number, and worksheet information; on the right side, when numerical data is selected, common calculations such as Sum and Average display.

Storage The action of keeping software and data so it can be accessed in the future. Also referred to as mass storage, auxiliary storage, or secondary storage.

Storage device Hardware components, such as hard disks, flash memory, USB drives, CDs, and DVDs, on which data is held for future use.

Streaming The ability to hear or see content while it is being downloaded from a Web site instead of waiting till the download is complete.

Streaming audio Accessing sounds that play almost immediately after you click an audio link on a Web page, without waiting for the entire file to download.

Streaming video Accessing video that plays almost immediately after you click a video link on a Web page, without waiting for the entire file to download.

Strong password A password that uses a combination of uppercase letters, lowercase letters, numbers, and special characters in a character string so it will be hard to guess and therefore will keep your account secure.

Structural unemployment Unemployment created when technology makes an entire job category obsolete.

Structure In Access, the underlying design of a table, including field names, data types, descriptions, and field properties.

Style A group of formatting commands, such as font, font size, font color, paragraph alignment, and line spacing, that can be applied to a paragraph with one command.

Style (PowerPoint) A collection of formatting options that can be applied to a picture, text, or an object.

Style guide A manual that contains standards for the design and writing of documents.

Stylus An input device, which looks like an ordinary pen except that the tip is dry and semi-blunt, that is commonly used as an alternative to fingers on touch-screen devices such as smartphones.

Subdatasheet A format for displaying related records when you click the plus sign (+) next to a record in a table on the *one* side of a relationship.

Subfolder A folder within a folder.

Subject guide A list of related categories such as business, news, or trends that, when selected, displays a page of more related links.

Subject line The optional line following the inside address in a business letter that states the purpose of the letter.

Subnotebook A small computer that is suited for people who like full application features but not all the peripheral devices such as a DVD player.

Subpoints Secondary-level information in a SmartArt graphic.

Subscriber loop carrier (SLC) A small, waist-high curbside installation used in the public switched telephone network that connects as many as 96 subscribers.

Subset A portion of the total records available.

SUM function A predefined formula that adds all the numbers in a selected range of cells.

Summary sheet A worksheet where totals from other worksheets are displayed and summarized.

Supercomputer A single computer or a series of computers working in parallel to process large amounts of data focusing on executing a few sets of instruction as fast as possible.

Surfing The process of navigating the Internet either for a particular item or for anything that is of interest, and quickly moving from one item to another.

Swap file A unit of pages stored on a section of a hard disk identified as virtual memory.

Switches A device that assists in passing data packets along in a single network, condenses bandwidth, and has better performance than a hub; it contains software that inspects the source and target of a data package and attempts to deliver it to that destination.

Symmetric key encryption A type of encryption where the same key is used for encryption and decryption.

Syn flooding A form of denial of service attack in which a hostile client repeatedly sends SYN (synchronization) packets to every port on the server.

Synchronized Multimedia Integration Language (SMIL) A language designed to standardize the display of Web pages without the use of plug-ins.

Synchronous optical network (SONET) A physical layer of network technology that uses fiber-optic cable and carries large volumes of data over long distances; it is the standard for high-performance networks.

Synonyms Words with the same or similar meaning.

Syntax In an e-mail message, the way in which the parts of an e-mail message are put together.

Syntax In computer programming, a set of rules for entering commands.

System requirements The minimal level of equipment that a program needs in order to run.

System software Programs that enable the computer's hardware to work with and run the application software and that is a combination of the operating system and system utilities.

System tray Another name for the notification area on the taskbar.

System unit The base unit of the computer made up of the plastic or metal enclosure, the motherboard, and the integrated peripherals.

System utilities System software that works in tandem with the operating system and aids in the maintenance of your system, your individual devices, or your installed programs. Also called utility programs.

T1 line A high-bandwidth fiber-optic or specially conditioned copper cable trunk line that can handle 24 digitized voice channels or carry computer data at a rate of up to 1.544 Mbps.

T2 line A high-bandwidth trunk line made of fiber-optic cable that can handle 44.7 Mbps of computer data.

T3 line A high-bandwidth trunk line made of fiber-optic cable that can handle 44.7 Mbps of computer data and cost $3,000 a month; one T3 line is equivalent to having 28 T1 lines.

Tabbed browsing A feature provided by most browsers that open new Web pages as tabs within one window instead of opening a new window for each site.

Table The database object that stores data organized in an arrangement of columns and rows, and is the foundation of an Access database.

Table (Word) An arrangement of information organized into rows and columns.

Table area The upper area of the Query window that displays field lists for the tables that are used in the query.

Tablet PC A computer with a screen that swivels and lies flat over the keyboard allowing input with a stylus.

Tab stop Specific locations on a line of text, marked on the Word ruler, to which you can move the insertion point by pressing the Tab key, and which is used to align and indent text.

Tabs On the Office Ribbon, the name of each activity area in the Office Ribbon.

Tag A custom file property that you create to help find and organize your files.

Tag Image File Format (TIFF or TIF) A lossless graphic format, used in publishing because it allows specific instructions to be embedded within the file to retain image quality.

Tailgate The entering of a secure physical or digital area on someone else's authorization instead of entering your own authorized access code.

Task pane A window within a Microsoft Office application in which you can enter options for completing a command.

Taskbar The area that contains the Start button, optional program buttons, and buttons for all open programs.

TCP/IP (Transmission Control Protocol/Internet Protocol) A standard suite of methods used to package and transmit information transported over the Internet.

Template An existing document that you use as a starting point for a new document; it opens a copy of itself, unnamed, and then you use the structure—and possibly some content, such as headings—as the starting point for new document.

Tentative In Outlook, a free/busy setting that indicates that you have scheduled an appointment but that it is not confirmed; also a meeting response in which the meeting organizer is notified that you might attend the meeting.

Terabyte (TB) A unit of measurement for computer memory and disk capacity approximately equal to one trillion bytes.

Terminal An inexpensive input/output device consisting of a keyboard and video display but that has little processing capability.

Terminator A special connector located at the end of a bus topology that signifies the end of the circuit.

Text alignment (PowerPoint) The horizontal placement of text within a placeholder.

Text box A movable resizable container for text or graphics.

Text box In PowerPoint, an object within which you can position text anywhere on a slide.

Text control A content control that accepts only a text entry.

Text data type An Access data type that describes text, a combination of text and numbers, or numbers that are not used in calculations, such as a number that is an identifier like a Student ID.

Text effect Decorative format, such as shadowed or mirrored text, text glow, 3-D effects, and colors that makes text stand out.

Text string A sequence of characters.

Text values Constant values consisting of only text and usually provides information about number values; also referred to as labels.

Text wrapping The manner in which text displays around an object.

Theme (PowerPoint) A set of unified design elements that provides a look for your presentation by applying colors, fonts, and effects.

Theme (Word) A predesigned set of colors, fonts, lines, and fill effects that look good together and that can be applied to your entire document or to specific items.

Thermal-transfer printers A printer that uses a heat process to burn images or adhere a wax-based ink to a paper's surface.

Thesaurus A research tool that provides a list of synonyms.

Thin client A client that relies on the server for processing ability.

Thrashing Excessive paging.

Thread A series of articles that offer a continuing commentary on the same specific subject.

Throughput The actual amount of data that is transmitted through a given communication channel; it is almost always lower than bandwidth, especially with wireless communications.

Thumbnail A reduced size image of a graphic.

Thumbnails (PowerPoint) Miniature images of presentation slides.

Thumbscrews Small screws that are usually attached to the plug and secure the plug to the system unit or expansion card.

Tick marks The short lines that display on an axis at regular intervals.

Time Bar The times next to the appointment area of the calendar, displayed in one-hour intervals.

Time bomb Hidden piece of computer code set to go off on some date and time in the future usually causing a malicious act to occur to your system.

Title bar The bar across the top of the window that indicates the name of the current file and displays the program name.

Title slide The first slide in a presentation the purpose of which is to provide an introduction to the presentation topic.

Toggle button A button that can be turned on by clicking it once, and then turned off by clicking it again.

Toggle keys A key on a keyboard that has only two positions: on and off. The Caps Lock and Num Lock keys are toggle keys.

Token The special unit of data that travel around a token ring topology allowing only the node that possesses it to transmit.

Toolbar A row, column, or block of buttons or icons, usually displayed across the top of a window, which contains commands for tasks you can perform with a single click.

Top-level domain (TLD) name The extension such as .com or .edu that follows the host name and indicates the type of group or institution to which the site belongs.

Top-level points The main text points in a SmartArt graphic.

Touch screen A display screen that is sensitive to the touch of a finger or stylus.

Touchpad A small, stationary, pressure-sensitive, flat surface located on a notebook with an area set aside along the right and bottom edges of the pad to accommodate vertical or horizontal scroll operations created when you slide you finger in these reserved sections. Also referred to as a trackpad.

Tower case A vertically designed system unit case that sits on the floor next to a desk.

Trackball A stationary pointing device that contains a movable ball held in a cradle.

Tracks Concentric circular bands on a hard disk, or platter, where data is recorded. Tracks are divided into sectors.

Transfer performance The time it takes the read/write head to transfer data from the disk to random access memory.

Transistor An electronic switch that controls the flow of electrical signals through a circuit.

Transmission control protocol (TCP) The higher layer of the TCP/IP layer of protocols that defines how one Internet-connected computer can contact another to exchange control and confirmation messages.

Transmission Control Protocol/Internet Protocol (TCP/IP) A standard suite of methods used to package and transmit information transported over the Internet.

Trap door Security holes through which an employee can reenter a system, without authentication, after leaving the firm.

Travel mouse A pointing device half the size of a normal mouse, but with all the same capabilities.

Triple-click The action of clicking the left mouse button three times in rapid succession.

Trojan horse A program disguised as useful, but actually contains hidden instructions to perform a malicious action.

Truncated Refers to data that is cut off or shortened.

Trust Center An area of the Access program where you can view the security and privacy settings for your Access installation.

Trusted Documents An Office 2010 security feature that remembers which files you have already enabled; you might encounter this feature if you open a file from an e-mail or download files from the Internet.

Tweets Messages posted by a user on Twitter.

Twisted-pair A copper cable used for telephone and data communications in which two pairs of wires interwoven together.

Twitter A free, real-time microblogging—smaller posts—system in which you send and read short messages of up to 140 characters.

Ubiquitous computing A trend in which you no longer interact with one computer at a time but rather with multiple devices connected through an omnipresent network, enabling technology to become virtually embedded and enabling you to interact seamlessly with devices you use.

Underlying formula The formula entered in a cell and visible only on the Formula Bar.

Underlying value The data that displays in the Formula Bar.

Unicode A 16-bit character coding format that can represent over 65,000 characters, and thus the entire world's written languages. The first 128 codes in the Unicode system represent the same characters as the first 128 in the ASCII and Extended ASCII systems.

Uniform Resource Locator (URL) An address that uniquely identifies a location on the Internet.

Uninterruptible power supply (UPS) A battery-powered device that provides power to your computer for a limited time when it detects an outage or critical voltage drop.

Universal Serial Bus (USB) A standard for data transfer when connecting peripherals to a computer. USB is an acronym for universal serial bus.

UNIX A pioneering operating system developed at AT&T's Bell Laboratories in 1969; continues to define what an operating system should do and how it should work.

Uploading Transferring files from your computer to another computer, as you do when you upload a video you created to YouTube.

URL (Uniform Resource Locator) A string of characters that precisely identifies an Internet resource's type and location.

USB flash drive A small, portable, secondary storage device that plugs into a computer's universal serial bus (USB) port.

USB hub A device that plugs into an existing USB port and contains four or more additional ports.

USB ports A port that was designed to replace older parallel and serial ports and connect a variety of devices including keyboards, mice, printers, and digital cameras.

USB wireless network adapter A communication device that plugs into a USB port and supports data encryption for secure wireless communication.

Usenet A worldwide computer-based discussion system accessible through the Internet.

User account A collection of information that tells Windows 7 what files and folders the account holder can access, what changes the account holder can make to the computer system, and what the account holder's personal preferences are.

User interface The part of the operating system that enables you to interact with the computer and the programs.

Validate With respect to software, verifying that you own a legal copy by providing a special code or product key before you can use it.

Value Another name for a *constant value.*

Value after increase = base × percent for new value The formula for calculating the value after an increase by multiplying the original value—the base—by the percent for new value (see the *Percent for new value* formula).

Value axis A numerical scale on the left side of a chart that shows the range of numbers for the data points; also referred to as the *y-axis*.

Vector graphics Images created by using a vector program that requires you to define points to draw line segments—paths—and are stored as mathematical equations by the graphic program.

Version history A list that the application software keeps of each iteration of a file; viewing the version history is useful when several individuals work together to create a file or when a file goes through several stages of development and review.

Vertical window split box (Excel) A small box on the vertical scroll bar with which you can split the window into two vertical views of the same worksheet.

VGA (video graphics array) connector An interface used with cathode ray tube (CRT) monitors.

Video adapter An expansion board, in your computer, that provides display capabilities. These adapters have hardware that decodes videos at high speed.

Video editors Programs that enable you to modify digitized videos.

Videoconferencing (Web conferencing) The use of this digital video technology to transmit sound and video images to facilitate online, virtual meetings through which two or more people can have a face-to-face meeting even though they are geographically separated.

Virtual laser keyboard A keyboard the size of a small cellular phone and was designed to work with portable devices like PDAs and smartphones.

Virtual memory A portion of a hard disk that the operating system, treats like RAM when RAM is full.

Virtual private network (VPN) A network that operates as a private network over a public network, usually the Internet, making data accessible to authorized users in remote locations through the use of secure, encrypted connections and special software.

Voice recognition Software that translates spoken words into typed text.

VoIP (Voice over Internet Protocol) Allows a user to speak to others over a broadband Internet connection instead of traditional analog phone line.

Volatile A term used to describe an Excel function that is subject to change each time the workbook is reopened; for example the NOW function updates itself to the current date and time each time the workbook is opened.

Volatile memory Fast storage, located on the motherboard, which is erased when power goes off.

Wallpaper Another term for the desktop background.

Warm boot Restarting a computer that is already on. Also called a restart.

Weak password A password that is short and consists of only letters in a single case; such a password can compromise the security of your data because it is easy to guess.

Web-based applications Applications that reside on a remote server and are accessed through the Internet.

Web browser Software, such as Internet Explorer, Firefox, Safari, or Chrome, that displays Web pages.

Web feeds The distribution of syndicated news and other Web content for subscribers.

Web pages The documents that make up the World Wide Web and are transported over the Internet.

Web server A computer running special software that enables it to respond to requests for information or accept inputted information.

Web site A collection of related Web pages connected by hyperlinks.

Webcam An inexpensive camera attached or embedded within your computer. It can be used to hold live chat sessions and make video phone calls.

Week view In Outlook, the calendar arrangement in which only a full seven-day week displays.

What-if analysis The process of changing the values in cells to see how those changes affect the outcome of formulas in a worksheet.

Wheel mouse A mouse developed by Microsoft that includes a rotating wheel used to scroll text vertically within a document or on a Web page.

White hat Another term for an ethical hacker.

Wide area network (WAN) A geographically dispersed collection of LANs that uses long-distance transmission media to link computers separated by a few miles or even thousands of miles.

WiFi A wireless LAN standard that offers Ethernet speeds through the use of radio waves instead of wires.

Wiki A simple Web page, which can be public or restricted to specific members, on which any visitor or member can post text or images, read previous posts, change posted information, and track earlier changes.

Wildcard (truncation symbol) Symbols such as * and ? that take the place of zero or more characters in the position in which they are used to search for various word endings and spellings simultaneously.

Wildcard character In a query, a character that serves as a placeholder for one or more unknown characters in your criteria; an asterisk (*) represents one or more unknown characters, and a question mark (?) represents a single unknown character.

WiMAX (worldwide interoperability for microwave access) A wireless up-and-coming digital communication system that delivers high-speed access over long distances, either point to point where both sender and receiver are stationary or through mobile access where sender or receiver is moving.

Window A rectangular area on your screen that displays programs and content, and can be moved, resized, minimized, or closed; the content of every window is different, but all windows display on the desktop.

Window snip When using Snipping Tool, the type of snip that captures the entire displayed window.

Windows 7 An operating system developed by Microsoft Corporation.

Windows bitmap (BMP) This standard graphic format was developed for Microsoft Windows. Compression is optional, so BMP files tend to be very large.

Windows Defender A spyware scanning and removal tool included with Windows 7.

Windows Embedded Compact An embedded operating system introduced in 1996 as Windows CE with a significant upgrade in 1997.

Windows Explorer The program within Windows 7 that displays the contents of libraries, folders, and files on your computer, and also enables you to perform tasks related to your files and folders such as copying, moving, and renaming. Windows Explorer is at work anytime you are viewing the contents of a library, a folder, or a file.

Windows Live A collection of programs and services for individuals that work together, and which includes Hotmail e-mail, Live Messenger instant messaging, applications such as Photo Gallery and Movie Maker, the Office Web Apps, and mobile phone applications.

Windows Live Essentials The free suite of Microsoft programs that you can download and run on your PC, and which includes Messenger, Mail, Writer, Photo Gallery, and Movie Maker.

Windows Live ID An account with which you can sign in to Windows Live to access and use its features.

Windows Live Messenger The Windows Live instant messaging application that you can download and use to communicate with friends who are online.

Windows Live SkyDrive A free file storage and file sharing service provided by Windows Live.

Windows Phone 7 A mobile operating system for both the consumer and business market.

Windows Update An operating system update service that keeps your operating system up to date with fixes—also called service patches—and protections against external environment changes.

Wireless access point (AP or WAP) A device that connects wireless devices to a wired network.

Wireless Internet service provider A local or national company that provides wireless Internet access to computers and other mobile devices, such as notebooks and smartphones.

Wireless keyboards A keyboard that connects to your computer through infrared (IR), radio frequency (RF), or Bluetooth connections instead of physical cables.

Wireless LAN A network in which users access and connect to other devices on the network through radio waves instead of wires.

Wireless memory card A flash memory card that adds wireless circuitry so it can connect with your PC via a wireless network or send pictures directly from your digital camera to your favorite online photo site.

Wireless mouse A mouse that eliminates the cord and transmits infrared or radio signals (RF) to a base station receiver on the computer.

Wireless PC card adapter A device, approximately the size of a credit card, with a built-in WiFi antenna that enables wireless capability on notebooks that do not have the capability embedded on its chipset.

Wizard A tool that walks you through a process in a step-by-step manner.

WordArt A gallery of text styles with which you can create decorative effects, such as shadowed or mirrored text.

Wordwrap (Outlook) In Outlook, the feature in which text typed in the Message form is moved automatically from the end of one line to the beginning of the next line to fit within the established margins.

Wordwrap (Word) The feature that moves text from the right edge of a paragraph to the beginning of the next line as necessary to fit within margins.

Workbook An Excel file that contains one or more worksheets.

Workbook-level buttons Buttons at the far right of the Ribbon tabs that minimize or restore a displayed workbook.

Work Week view The Outlook calendar arrangement in which only Monday through Friday displays.

Works Cited In the MLA style, a list of cited works placed at the end of a research paper or report.

Worksheet The primary document that you use in Excel to work with and store data; it is formatted as a pattern of uniformly spaced horizontal and vertical lines.

World Wide Web (Web or WWW) The portion of the Internet that contains billions of documents; the Web uses the Internet as its transportation mechanism for documents and resources but is a separate entity.

Worm Program that takes control of affected computers and uses their resources to attack other network-connected systems.

Writer's identification The name and title of the author of a letter, placed near the bottom of the letter under the complimentary closing—also referred to as the *writer's signature block.*

Writer's signature block The name and title of the author of a letter, placed near the bottom of the letter, under the complimentary closing—also referred to as the *writer's identification.*

WYSIWYG An acronym for *what you see is what you get* (pronounced WIZ-zee-wig).

x-axis Another name for the horizontal, or *category axis.*

XML feed Another name for an RSS feed.

y-axis Another name for the vertical, or *value axis.*

Yottabyte (TB) A unit of measurement for computer memory and disk capacity approximately equal to one septillion bytes.

Zettabyte (ZB) A unit of measurement for computer memory and disk capacity approximately equal to one sextillion bytes.

ZIP file A folder that contains one or more files that have been compressed to reduce file size. When downloading files from the Internet, a zipped file will download a group of files at one time, and it will be faster than downloading each file individually.

Zombie An unprotected commandeered computer, under the control of a hacker's program, used to create a denial of service (DoS) attack on a network.

Zoom The action of increasing or decreasing the viewing area on the screen.

Index

C

D

E

F

G

H

I

N

X

Y

Z